THE WESTERN PERSPECTIVE

A History of Civilization in the West

Volume II: The Renaissance to the Present

SECOND EDITION

PHILIP V. CANNISTRARO

Queens College, The City University of New York

JOHN J. REICH

Syracuse University in Florence, Italy

THE WESTERN
PERSPECTIVE

A History of Civilization in the West

Volume II: The Renaissance to the Present

SECOND EDITION

THOMSON

WADSWORTH

Australia • Canada • Mexico • Singapore • Spain
United Kingdom • United States

THOMSON

WADSWORTH

Publisher: Clark Baxter
Senior Development Editor: Sue Gleason
Assistant Editor: Stephanie Sandoval
Editorial Assistant: Eno Sarris
Technology Project Manager: Jennifer Ellis
Executive Marketing Manager: Caroline Croley
Marketing Assistant: Mary Ho
Advertising Project Manager: Tami Strang
Project Manager, Editorial Production: Jennie Redwitz
Print/Media Buyer: Barbara Britton
Permissions Editor: Sue Howard
Production Service: Carol O'Connell, Graphic World
   Publishing Services

Text Designer: Garry Harman
Photo Researcher: Sue Howard
Cover Designer: Lisa Devenish
Cover Image: Bella, Gabriele (fl. 1700–1750). "Orphan
   Girls Singing for the Dukes of the North in the
   Philharmonic Hall." Galleria Querini Stampalia, Venice,
   Italy. Copyright Scala/Art Resource, NY.
Compositor: Graphic World, Inc.
Text and Cover Printer: Transcontinental Printing/
   Interglobe

For more information about our products, contact us at:
Thomson Learning Academic Resource Center
1-800-423-0563
For permission to use material from this text, contact us by:
Phone: 1-800-730-2214
Fax: 1-800-730-2215
Web: http://www.thomsonrights.com

Library of Congress Control Number: 2003107114

ISBN 0-534-61067-6

Wadsworth/Thomson Learning
10 Davis Drive
Belmont, CA 94002-3098
USA

Asia
Thomson Learning
5 Shenton Way #01-01
UIC Building
Singapore 068808

Australia/New Zealand
Thomson Learning
102 Dodds Street
Southbank, Victoria 3006
Australia

Canada
Nelson
1120 Birchmount Road
Toronto, Ontario M1K 5G4
Canada

Europe/Middle East/Africa
Thomson Learning
High Holborn House
50/51 Bedford Row
London WC1R 4LR
United Kingdom

Latin America
Thomson Learning
Seneca, 53
Colonia Polanco
11560 Mexico D.F.
Mexico

Spain/Portugal
Paraninfo
Calle/Magallanes, 25
28015 Madrid, Spain

DEDICATED TO

Our Students

About the Authors

PHILIP V. CANNISTRARO

Born in New York City, Philip V. Cannistraro is an authority on modern Italian history and the Italian-American experience. He studied in both the undergraduate and graduate programs at New York University and is now Distinguished Professor at Queens College and at the Graduate School, the City University of New York. Professor Cannistraro serves on the boards of several journals and is editor of *The Italian American Review*. He has written or edited a number of books, including *Civilization of the World* (with R. Greaves, R. Murphey, and R. Zaller, Third Edition, 1997), *La Fabbrica del Consenso: Fascismo e Mass Media* (1975), *Fascismo, Chiesa e Emigrazione* (with G. Rosoli, 1979), *Historical Dictionary of Fascist Italy* (1981), and *Il Duce's Other Woman*, a biography of Margherita Sarfatti (with B. Sullivan, 1993).

JOHN J. REICH

A native of England, John J. Reich was trained as a classical archaeologist and did both his undergraduate and graduate work at the University of Manchester. He is an authority on Minoan civilization, pre-Roman Italy, and music. Professor Reich is associated with the Syracuse University study program in Florence, Italy. Reich lectures frequently in Europe and the United States on history, art, and the humanities and is the author of many scholarly articles and several books, including *Italy Before Rome* (1979) and the widely acclaimed *Culture and Values* (with Lawrence S. Cunningham, Wadsworth, Fifth Edition, 2002). He lives in a medieval castle in the hilltop town of Panzano in Chianti, in Italy.

BRIEF CONTENTS

Contents

**Historical
Perspectives**
The First Africans
in Europe   422

PART V   THE EARLY MODERN WORLD   426

**Historical
Perspectives**
The Social Life of
European Jewry   434

**Public Figures
and Private Lives**
Marie de' Medici
and Henry IV
of France   458

PART VII THE MODERN AGE 606

**Historical
Perspectives**
How Enlightened
Were the Enlightened
Despots? 616

**Historical
Perspectives**
The Historians'
French Revolution
642

**Perspectives
from the Past**
The Rights
of Women 678

**Public Figures
and Private Lives**
Mary Wollstonecraft
and Percy Bysshe
Shelley   688

**Perspectives
from the Past**
The *Risorgimento*
724

**Public Figures
and Private Lives**
Vita Sackville-West
and Harold
Nicolson 932

**Perspectives
from the Past**
The Destruction
of the European
Jews 960

**Public Figures
and Private Lives**
Simone de Beauvoir
and Jean-Paul Sartre
1010

**Historical
Perspectives**
Sovereignty, Law,
and Unity   **1032**

Across Cultures
Martha Gellhorn
in Cuba   **1043**

**Perspectives
from the Past**
Analyzing Terrorism
1050

PERSPECTIVES FROM THE PAST

HISTORICAL PERSPECTIVES

PUBLIC FIGURES AND PRIVATE LIVES

ACROSS CULTURES

MAPS

TABLES AND GRAPHS

PREFACE

To vary a cliché, each generation rewrites the history textbooks. As a result, there are today well over a dozen books on the market that are suitable for use as texts in college-level Western civilization courses.

Why, then, still another one?

We have each taught Western civilization or similar courses at large universities for more than 30 years and, like countless colleagues, have wished for a book that we felt met the needs of our students as well as our own requirements as teachers. Existing books run the full range, from traditional works that emphasize political, diplomatic, and military history and look at developments largely from the point of view of leaders and elites, to more recent books that emphasize one approach, particularly social history, and try to present historical change as experienced by ordinary people. Traditional treatments reinforce the views of earlier generations but do not stress the trends in more recent scholarship. Another characteristic in recent textbook writing has been the tendency to underrate students and to "unclutter" the picture by omitting the kind of detail that is the guts of history. Such texts can leave students confused about how history changes and civilizations evolve. Conversely, stress on analysis and pattern, rather than on facts, of necessity emphasizes broad economic and social forces to the exclusion of human agency and, yes, even of historical accident.

We believe the best approach is one that conveys the full range of human experience and that considers both the material processes and the spiritual values of historical development. We have sought to achieve a genuine balance between narrative and analysis. The writing of history at its best has always been the ability to tell a story—by which we mean a narrative of the record of human struggle and achievement, of conflict and community, of cultural diversity and social change. It is not always a pleasant or easy story to relate, but it should be told as much as possible as it unfolded rather than as we would have wanted it to. Moreover, history without detail may leave students bored and deprive them of the kind of vivid images that give life and breath to the story. Abstract analysis, while important to critical thinking, is not a substitute for factual knowledge. Both are necessary to our understanding of history and vital to navigating the ever more complex world in which we live.

In this edition, we have updated events on which new light has been shed since the publication of the first edition. We have in general enriched the connections between Western history and developments beyond the West, such as the Roman Empire's contact with Han China. Recent developments, including those in Iraq, the European Union, and, of course, September 11 and terrorism, have been included.

OUR STRUCTURAL DESIGN

A textbook is a learning and teaching tool and should reflect the realities of the classroom. It occurred to us early on that our text should correspond to the needs and interests of today's teachers. A major case in point is the fact that the 30 to 35 chapters into which most books are divided do not conform to the number of class sessions usually available to the instructor. As teachers we must constantly think about how to break up and present material in topics that can be handled in one class period and that students can digest. This means, inevitably, dividing the conventional large textbook chapters into smaller units.

To correct this longstanding pedagogical problem, we have given our book a unique—although not a startlingly different—structure by arranging the story of Western civilization in 95 smaller "topics," corresponding to the approximate number of class sessions in an academic year. Most of our topics are appropriate for a single class period.

In addition, we have renumbered the topics in this edition to run sequentially from 1 through 95, which will allow instructors to refer to them more easily in their syllabi. A correlation guide between the previous part and topic numbers and the new topic numbers is provided in the *Instructor's Manual*.

At first glance, instructors might assume that this structural design artificially separates material that should be presented in an "integrated" manner. But a closer look will reveal that we have simply divided the overly large chapters of conventional texts into logical, teachable units. The result provides the instructor with a great deal more flexibility in terms of assigning student reading, syllabus design, and in-class analysis.

We have also taken pains to provide students with ways to connect these smaller topics to the larger stream of historical narrative, as well as with methods to focus on important themes. Furthermore, we grouped the 95 topics into eight broad chronological parts, corresponding to the traditional divisions of Western history.

Our approach has been to provide full coverage of all major aspects of historical experience. In addition to the political, diplomatic, and military events of the more traditional texts, each part contains topics that deal individually with social, economic, cultural, and intellectual history. Our treatment of cultural history in particular is unusually rich, including a full discussion of art and music. We have also written topics that deal fully with regions that are generally neglected or given only brief mention, such as eastern and southern Europe, and we have included topics that examine economic and technological developments in depth. Our discussion of social trends seeks to offer students an understanding of daily life and the broad patterns of social change, as well as of the status of slaves, Jews, and other ethnic, religious, or sexual minorities. We have, of course, tried to incorporate the most recent findings from the burgeoning world of women's history into our narrative.

It is no accident that the title of our book, *The Western Perspective*, reflects the fact that, while our focus is on the Western experience, we believe it is important to place that experience in the wider context of world history. We therefore discuss developments in Africa, Asia, the Americas, and the Pacific when they had an impact on or were affected by Western history. Indeed, "perspective" has become a stronger theme in this edition, appearing in part openers, chapter overviews, boxed features, and the conclusion to each chapter, now entitled "Putting [Topic] in Perspective."

SPECIAL FEATURES

In addition to the overall structure of our book, we have designed a number of innovative special features that we believe lend both deeper insight and immediacy to the narrative.

Each part is introduced by an essay that puts the broad trends and patterns characterizing the period in perspective. For a further sense of perspective, each part now includes a **new** culturally and topically comparative timeline, which allows students to see at a glance parallel political, social, economic, and cultural developments in different cultures or countries.

Within topics are a number of boxed features.

- **New** *Across Cultures* features explore interactions of individuals with cultures of different times or places. Some depict contemporaries observing the differences of other cultures (such as Bishop Liutprand in Constantinople and Catherine Wilmot in Russia); others deal with those from later times providing their views on older cultures (such as Herodotus visiting the land of ancient Egypt or Lord Byron visiting Athens).

- Many texts print short quotations from primary sources to add flavor to the narrative. Our *Perspectives from the Past* sections are designed with a specific pedagogical purpose in mind. Each of these document sections consists of a variety of readings from primary sources on a selected issue, such as "The Black Death." In this way, students are able to gain a serious, in-depth insight into historical method, analyze conflicting accounts, and engage in genuine class discussion.

- *Historical Perspectives* essays have been written especially for this book by leading experts in the field. These essays furnish students with a sense of the clash of scholarly opinion about particular subjects, such as the French Revolution or Fascism, or shed special light on a particularly interesting or unusual aspect of historical experience, such as the status of women in ancient Mesopotamia or the earliest Africans in Europe.

- Each part also contains boxes entitled *Public Figures and Private Lives*. These are portraits of the private and public lives of couples in which one or both partners played an influential part in culture, politics, or society. Such sketches serve a number of useful purposes: By relating larger trends to individuals, they give students immediate and easily understandable insight into an important era or development; they provide specific examples of the different roles of and the interaction between men and women in various historical periods; and they suggest the impact of gender on social and private lives.

In addition, each of our 95 topics begins with an overview, which provides perspective on the major themes and subjects to be discussed. Where appropriate, the topics contain a box of *Significant Dates* for principal events, as well as boldface key terms, which also appear in a **new** end-of-book Glossary. Each topic ends with a *Putting in Perspective* conclusion, set off from the text; a series of questions for further study; an up-to-date bibliography; and **new** *InfoTrac College Edition*® search terms, which allow students to do further exploration and research on selected topics in the powerful InfoTrac College Edition database made available with this textbook.

Further, all illustrations are now accompanied by expanded captions that point out details of significance to the place and era, which students may not notice on their own. Newly expanded map captions point out much more detail about the movements and places shown on the maps. Web icons next to the captions indicate that similar maps can be found on the book-specific Web site in an interactive format.

FORMATS

To accommodate teachers at institutions with different versions of Western Civilization courses, this book has been produced in seven different formats:

A complete, one-volume edition containing the entire text

An alternate volume, Since the Middle Ages (Parts III–VIII): ISBN 0-534-61068-4

Volume I: Prehistory to the Enlightenment (Parts I–VI): ISBN 0-534-61066-8

Volume II: The Renaissance to the Present (Parts IV–VIII): ISBN 0-534-61067-6

Volume A: Prehistory to the Renaissance (Parts I–IV): ISBN 0-534-61069-2

Volume B: The Middle Ages to World War I (Parts III–VII): ISBN 0-534-61070-6

Volume C: The Old Regime to the Present (Parts VI–VIII): ISBN 0-534-61071-4

ANCILLARY PACKAGE

A wide variety of ancillary materials are available for instructors and students using this textbook.

For Students

Study Guide, Volumes I and II Prepared by Gerald Anderson of North Dakota State University, the *Study Guide* includes a brief overview of each topic, as well as identifications, geographical identifications, map exercises, timeline questions, short-answer exercises, and essay questions.

Map Exercise Workbooks Prepared by Cynthia Kosso of Northern Arizona University, these two volumes include 20 maps and exercises that ask students to identify important cities and countries.

MapTutor This interactive map tutorial helps students learn geography by having them locate geographical features, regions, cities, and sociopolitical movements. Each map exercise is accompanied by questions that test knowledge and promote critical thinking.

Document Exercise Workbook, Volumes I and II Prepared by Donna Van Raaphorst of Cuyahoga Community College, this is a collection of exercises based around primary sources.

Exploring the European Past: Text and Images A new custom reader for Western civilization. Written by leading educators and historians, this fully customizable reader of primary and secondary sources is enhanced with an online module of visual sources, including maps, animations, and interactive exercises. Each reading also comes with an introduction and a series of questions. To learn more, visit http://etep. thomsonlearning.com or call Thomson Learning Custom Publishing at (800) 355–9983.

History: Hits on the Web Hits on the Web (HOW) is an exciting, class-tested product specially designed to help history students utilize the Internet for studying, conducting research, and completing assignments. HOW consists of approximately 80 pages of valuable teaching tools that can be bundled with any Wadsworth textbook at a very affordable price. Available through Thomson Custom Publishing.

The Journey of Civilization CD-ROM This CD-ROM takes the student on 18 interactive journeys through history. Enhanced with QuickTime movies, animations, sound clips, maps, and more, the journeys allow students to engage in history as active participants rather than as readers of past events.

Magellan Atlas of Western Civilization Available with any Western civilization text, this atlas contains 44 four-color historical maps, including "The Conflict in Afghanistan, 2001," and "States of the World, 2001."

Documents of Western Civilization, Volumes I and II This reader, containing a broad selection of carefully chosen documents, can accompany any Western civilization text.

InfoTrac College Edition A Wadsworth exclusive. Students receive 4 months of real-time access to InfoTrac College Edition's online database of continuously updated, full-length articles from more than 900 journals and periodicals. By doing a simple keyword search, users can quickly generate a powerful list of related articles from thousands of possibilities, then select relevant articles to explore or print out for reference or further study. For professors, InfoTrac College Edition articles offer opportunities to ignite discussions or augment their lectures with the latest developments in the discipline. For students, InfoTrac College Edition's virtual library allows Internet access to sources that extend their learning far beyond the pages of a text.

The Western Perspective Web Site The Web site specifically accompanying this text may be found at *http://wadsworth.com/history*. Both instructors and students will enjoy the Wadsworth History Resource Center, which includes access to topic-by-topic resources for *The Western Perspective*, Second Edition. Text-specific content for students includes tutorial quizzes, glossary, Web links, InfoTrac College Edition exercises, Internet activities, interactive maps, and interactive timelines. Instructors also have access to the *Instructor's Manual*, lesson plans, and PowerPoint slides (access code required). From the History home page, instructors and students can access many selections, such as an Internet Guide for History, a career center, the World History image bank, and links to history-related Web sites.

For Instructors
Available to qualified adopters. Please consult your local sales representative for details.

Instructor's Manual Prepared by James T. Baker of Western Kentucky University, this manual includes a summary of each topic, lecture notes, suggested readings, and discussion questions to spark debate among students. The *Instructor's Manual* also includes a correlation guide for topics of the First and Second Editions, as well as a Resource Integration Guide (RIG) featuring grids that link each topic of the text to instructional ideas and corresponding supplemental resources. At a glance, you can see which selections from the text's teaching and learning ancillaries are appropriate for each key topic theme.

Test Bank This test bank, prepared by Marlette Rebhorn of Austin Community College, provides a variety of question styles. In addition to multiple-choice questions, there are identification questions, essay questions, illustration questions, and book report questions.

ExamView® You can create, deliver, and customize tests and study guides (both print and online) in min-

utes with this easy-to-use assessment and tutorial system. ExamView offers both a Quick Test Wizard and an Online Test Wizard, which guide you step by step through the process of creating tests, while its unique WYSIWYG capability allows users to see tests on-screen exactly as they will print or display online. You can build tests of up to 250 questions using up to 12 question types. Using ExamView's complete word-processing capabilities, you can enter an unlimited number of new questions or edit existing questions.

Transparency Acetates for Western Civilization Includes over 100 four-color map images from this and other texts.

Multimedia Manager for Western Civilization: A Microsoft® PowerPoint® Link Tool An advanced PowerPoint presentation tool containing text-specific lecture outlines, figures, and images that allows you to quickly deliver dynamic lectures. In addition, it provides the flexibility to customize each presentation by editing what is provided or by adding a personal collection of slides, videos, and animations. All of the map acetates and selected photos have been incorporated into each of the lectures. In addition, the extensive Map Commentaries for each map slide are available through the Comments feature of PowerPoint.

Lecture Enrichment Slides Prepared by George Strong and Dale Hoak of The College of William and Mary, these 100 slides contain images of famous paintings, statues, architectural achievements, and interest photos. The authors provide commentary for each individual slide.

Listening to Music CD-ROM Set Available to instructors upon request, this CD-ROM includes musical selections to enrich lectures, from Purcell through Ravi Shankar.

ArtStudy Version 1.0 This comprehensive set of fine art images is made up of full images as well as alternate and detail/closeup views, and includes caption information on artists and embedded audio files to assist students with pronunciation.

History Video Library A selection of videos from *Films for the Humanities and Sciences* and other sources, including "Colonialism, Nationalism, and Migration"; "From Workshops to Factory"; "Revolution, Progress: Politics, Technology, and Science"; and many more. Contact your Thomson/Wadsworth representative for additional information on requesting videos. Available to qualified adopters.

CNN Today Video: Western Civilization You can launch lectures with riveting footage from CNN, the world's leading 24-hour global news television network. This video allows you to integrate the news-gathering and programming power of CNN into the classroom to show students the relevance of course topics to their everyday lives. Organized by topics covered in a typical course, these videos are divided into short segments perfect for introducing key concepts. A Thomson/Wadsworth exclusive.

Sights and Sounds of History Video Short, focused video clips, photos, artwork, animations, music, and dramatic readings are used to bring life to historical topics and events that are most difficult for students to appreciate from a textbook alone. For example, students will experience the grandeur of Versailles and the defeat felt by a German soldier at Stalingrad. The video segments average 4 minutes in length and make excellent lecture launchers.

ACKNOWLEDGMENTS

A number of friends and colleagues have contributed to this book over the years in many important ways, and we wish especially to thank the following individuals: Berit Bredahl-Nielsen, Eric D. Brose, Robert S. Browning, H. James Burgwyn, Elisheva Carlebach, Peter Carravetta, Jennifer Cook, Patricia A. Cooper, Alexander DeGrand, Spencer DiScala, Karen Dubno, Monte Finkelstein, Elisabeth Giansiracusa, Charles L. Killinger, Julie Mostov, David Nasaw, Nunzio Pernicone, Alma Reich, Cecil O. Smith, Donald F. Stevens, David Syrett, Elena Frangakis-Syrett, Frank Warren, and M. Hratch Zadoian.

In addition, we are indebted to our colleagues who generously shared with us their wealth of experience and knowledge. Our sincere thanks to the following instructors who advised us on the First Edition: Phillip Adler, East Carolina State University; Gerald Anderson, North Dakota State University; Jay P. Anglin, University of Southern Mississippi; Martin Arbagi, Wright State University; Patrick Armstrong, Jefferson State Community College; Frank Baglione, Tallahassee Community College; Carol Bargeron, Louisiana State University; Ed Beemon, Middle Tennessee State University; Alan Beyerden, Ohio State University; Lawrence Blacklund, Montgomery County Community College; Stephen Blumm, Montgomery County Community College; Melissa Bokovoy, University of New Mexico; Paul Bookbinder, University of Massachusetts at Boston; Darwin Bostick, Old Dominion University; James Brink, Texas Tech University; Daniel P. Brown, Moorpark College; Tom Bryan, Alvin Community College; Gary Burbridge, Grand Rapids Community College; Thomas Burns, Emory University; Elizabeth Carney, Clemson University; Lamar Cecil, University of North Carolina at Chapel Hill; Thomas Christofferson, California State University at Northridge; Orazio Ciccarelli, University of Southern Mississippi; Franz Coetzee, Yale University; Fred Colvin, Middle Tennessee State University; William Connell, Rutgers University; John Contreni, Purdue University; Jessica Coope, University of Nebraska; Marc Cooper, Southwest Missouri State University; Frederick M. Crawford, Middle Tennessee State University; Gary Cross, Pennsylvania State University; Paige Cubbison, Miami Dade Community College; Nancy Curtin, Fordham University; Maribel Dietz, Louisiana State University; Spencer M. Di Scala, University of Massachusetts at Boston; Michael Doyle, Ocean Community College; Charles Endress, Angelo State University; Thomas Fabiano, Monroe Community College; Gery Ferngren, Oregon State University; Monte Finkelstein, Tallahassee Community College; Edward W. Fox, Cornell University; Carl Frasure, University of Alaska; Elizabeth Furdell, University of North Florida; Alan Galpern, University of Pittsburgh; Richard Golden, Clemson University; Seella Gomezdelcampo, Roane State Community College; Karen Gould; David Gross, University of Colorado at Boulder; Alan Grubb, Clemson University; James D. Hardy, Louisiana State University; Jeanne Harrie, California State University at Bakersfield; Stephen Hauser, Marquette University; Peter Hayes, Northwestern University; Neil Hayman, San Diego State University; Susan Holt, Houston Community College; Robert Houston, University of the South; Bill Hughes, Essex Community College; Laura Hunt, University of Dayton; Frances Kelleher, Grand Valley State University; Charles Killinger III, Valencia Community College; Lloyd Kramer, University of North Carolina at Chapel Hill; Thomas Kselman, University of Notre Dame; David Large, Montana State University; Frederick Lauritsen, Eastern Washington University; Ron Lesko, Suffolk Community College; Mary Ann Lizondo, Northern Virginia Community College; Paul Lockhart, Wright State University; Gary Long, Methodist College; Leo Loubere, State University of New York at Buffalo; Gladys Luster, John C. Calhoun College; David MacDonald, Illinois State University; Paul Maier,

Western Michigan University; James Martin, Campbell University; William Matthews, Ohio State University; John Matzko, Bob Jones University; John McFarland, Sierra College; James Mini, Montgomery County Community College; Thomas Mockaitis, DePaul University; Marjorie Morgan, Southern Illinois University; Rex Morrow, Trident Technical College; Pierce Mullens, Missouri State University; Francis J. Murphy, Boston College; Martha Newman, University of Texas at Austin; Bill Olsen, Marist College; Fred Olsen, Northern Virginia Community College; Thomas Ott, University of North Alabama; Neil Pease, University of Wisconsin at Milwaukee; John Pesda, Camden County Community College; Donald Pryce, University of South Dakota; Herman Rebel, University of Arizona; Marlette Rebhorn, Austin Community College—Rio Grand Campus; Larry Rotge, Slippery Rock University; John Rothney, Ohio State University; Jose Sanches, St. Louis University; Lura Scales, Hinds Community College; Robert G. Schafer, University of Michigan at Flint; Ezel Kural Shaw, California State University at Northridge; Susan Shoemaker, University of Delaware; Ronald Smith, Arizona State University; Eileen Soldwedel, Edmonds Community College; William Stiebing, University of New Orleans; David Tait, Oklahoma State University; Maxine Taylor, Northwestern State University; Janet TeBrake, University of Maine; David Tengwall, Anne Arundel Community College; Jack Thacker, Western Kentucky University; Richard Todd, Wichita State University; Spenser Tucker, Texas Christian University; Thomas Turley, Santa Clara University; Jeffry von Arx, Georgetown University; and L. J. Worley, University of Washington.

And for the Second Edition:

Bruce F. Adams, University of Louisville

Lynn Brink, North Lake College

Spencer M. Di Scala, University of Masschusetts at Boston

Lorettann Gascard, Franklin Pierce College

Joanne Klein, Boise State University

William Percy, University of Massachusetts at Boston

Dan Ringrose, Minot State University

Claire A. Sanders, Texas Christian University

Phyllis L. Soybel, College of Lake County

Melanie H. Vansell, Riverside Community College

And a special thanks to Charles L. Killinger of Valencia Community College for all of his contributions to the text and the text's Web site.

Finally, the authors would like to thank each other: Their long friendship over many years has not only survived but actually strengthened since working together on this project. All collaboration should be this good.

THE WESTERN PERSPECTIVE

A History of Civilization in the West

Volume II: The Renaissance to the Present

SECOND EDITION

PART IV

THE RENAISSANCE AND REFORMATION

The Renaissance and Reformation represent a turning point in history—that is, a series of developments that together produce fundamental change in the human experience.

In its most immediate sense, the Renaissance was a rebirth of interest in Classical civilization and its underlying values that began some time in the 14th and 15th centuries. In a broader sense, however, it represented a revolution in how human beings thought about themselves and their place in the universe. Renaissance ideas, which first appeared in the sophisticated urban environment of the Italian city-states but soon spread northward, placed people at the center of human concerns, emphasizing both the importance of the human condition and a more secular, worldly approach to culture and society.

In politics, the growth of royal government at the expense of feudal nobility and the church accelerated. Increasingly efficient, centralized states evolved under the leadership of several so-called new monarchs in places like England, France, and Spain. The really innovative political development, however, came in Italy, where divisive conditions led to the invention of new methods through which states dealt with each other, methods known collectively as "diplomacy."

Closely related to the intellectual and cultural innovations of the Renaissance was the religious upheaval produced by the Protestant and Catholic reformations. The Protestant revolt against the Roman Church and the papacy provided people with new attitudes toward their relationship to God and questions of sin and salvation. In addition, for millions of people, religious

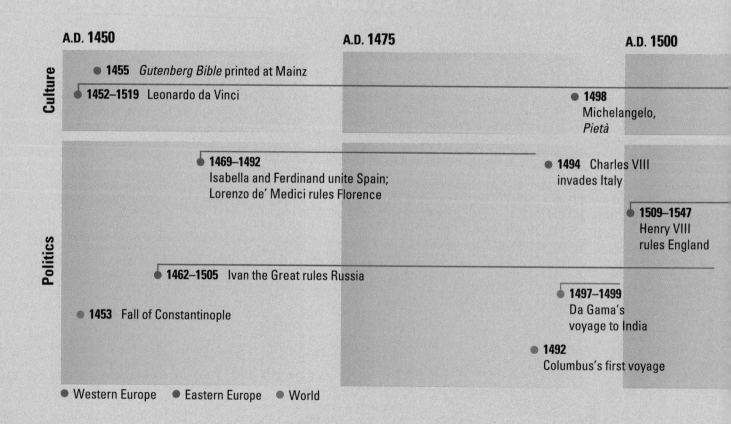

A.D. **1450** A.D. **1475** A.D. **1500**

Culture

● **1455** *Gutenberg Bible* printed at Mainz
● **1452–1519** Leonardo da Vinci
● **1498** Michelangelo, *Pietà*

Politics

● **1469–1492** Isabella and Ferdinand unite Spain; Lorenzo de' Medici rules Florence
● **1494** Charles VIII invades Italy
● **1509–1547** Henry VIII rules England
● **1462–1505** Ivan the Great rules Russia
● **1453** Fall of Constantinople
● **1497–1499** Da Gama's voyage to India
● **1492** Columbus's first voyage

● Western Europe   ● Eastern Europe   ● World

reformers like Luther, Calvin, and Knox helped establish regional and "national" religious identities. The Reformation, then, shattered a millennium of religious unity in the West, while producing a far-reaching impact on the political and social life of Europe. For a variety of reasons that often had little to do with matters of faith, monarchs took sides in the religious struggles of the age, further dividing the Christian commonwealth by making new demands for popular allegiance and state control. At the same time, the Protestant Reformation was an important step in releasing the Western mind from the constraints of religious and political authority that had been so pervasive in the Middle Ages.

The Renaissance and the Reformation both contributed significantly to the intellectual and technical preparation that lay behind the great

A.D. 1525

A.D. 1550

● **1513** Macchiavelli, *The Prince*

● **1517** Luther's 95 Theses begin Reformation

● **1519** Charles V becomes Holy Roman Emperor

● **1527** Sack of Rome

● **1545–1563** Council of Trent

● **1514** Peasant uprising in Hungary

● **1533–1584** Ivan the Terrible rules Russia

● **1520–1566** Suleiman the Magnificent rules Ottoman Empire

● **1532–1536** Spanish conquer Peru

● **1517** Egypt becomes Ottoman province

● **1519** Spanish conquer Mexico; Magellan begins voyage

epoch of exploration and conquest known as the European Reconnaissance. In less than a century, between roughly 1450 and 1550, Europeans broke their geographic boundaries and sailed literally around the globe. They claimed dominance over the lands and peoples they encountered, establishing overseas territorial and economic empires while embracing a world of rich cultural diversity, with far-reaching consequences.

Out of the vast upheavals wrought by the Renaissance and Reformation came profound, long-range changes that reshaped Europe and the rest of the globe. The long centuries of transition from the Middle Ages established the foundations for the early modern world.

THE AGE OF THE NEW MONARCHS

The great political transformation of the 14th and 15th centuries was the emergence of modern states in Western Europe. At the same time that distinctive national cultures were being consolidated there in the late 15th century, a group of rulers known as the "new monarchs" forged powerful, centralized states that controlled large national territories in England, France, and Spain.

In the case of France and Spain, the new monarchs completed the territorial unity of their nation-states. All of them, however, were determined to reinforce their power over the nobility and extend their control over the church within their borders. They also demanded complete loyalty from their subjects and engaged in deliberate efforts to forge a national spirit designed to create popular consensus. To the degree that these monarchs used all of the techniques available to increase their power, they were typical princes of the Renaissance.

In France, the Valois dynasty fought a long and devastating war with England for mastery of France, and in the aftermath shaped an increasingly powerful national monarchy. The English experienced not only the war with France but also a divisive civil war between two competing noble families, the Yorks and the Lancasters. By the time the domestic conflict was over, Henry Tudor had seized power and became the first of England's new monarchs, laying the foundation for a powerful new dynasty. In Spain, centralization began to take place in Castile and in Aragon, the two kingdoms ruled jointly by Ferdinand and Isabella in the latter part of the 15th century. The process of royal centralization was completed in the next century under the reign of their grandson, Charles V. By then, Spain had become merely one part of a much wider Hapsburg empire.

THE HUNDRED YEARS' WAR AND ITS AFTERMATH

In England and especially in France, the new monarchies emerged against the background of the greatest military conflict of the 14th century, the so-called Hundred Years' War. Rather than a single continuous war, however, the Hundred Years' War was really a series of conflicts between the two states interrupted by periods of peace.

THE ORIGINS OF THE WAR

A complicated series of factors lay behind the conflict. The emergence of France as a centralized monarchy was difficult because its territory had long been divided by strong regional differences in culture, language, and history. Complicating the situation was the fact that the English kings were vassals of the French monarch and controlled significant parts of French territory. Henry II (ruled 1154–1189), founder of the Plantagenet, or Angevin, dynasty, had inherited the French provinces of Anjou and Normandy. Moreover, through his marriage to Eleanor of Aquitaine (1122?–1204), Henry also acquired Aquitaine, a territory that stretched through southwestern France to the Pyrenees (see Topics 26 and 29).

In addition to the territorial problem, economic conflicts disturbed relations between the two monarchies. Flanders, to the northeast of France, was the major market for English wool, but serious conflicts between the artisans

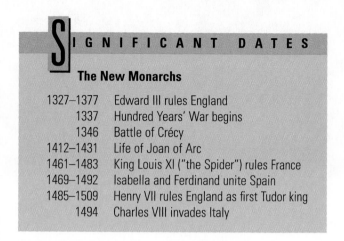

SIGNIFICANT DATES

The New Monarchs

1327–1377	Edward III rules England
1337	Hundred Years' War begins
1346	Battle of Crécy
1412–1431	Life of Joan of Arc
1461–1483	King Louis XI ("the Spider") rules France
1469–1492	Isabella and Ferdinand unite Spain
1485–1509	Henry VII rules England as first Tudor king
1494	Charles VIII invades Italy

and the wealthy merchants there threatened to disrupt a lucrative source of revenue for the English kings. Accordingly, when the French monarchy began supporting the merchants, the English gave their support to the artisans.

English and French relations reached another crisis point in 1328, when the Capetian dynasty came to an end with the death of the French king, who had no sons. Because the Salic Law recognized royal inheritance only through the male line, a Capetian cousin, Philip of Valois, claimed the throne as Philip VI (ruled 1328–1350). But Edward III (ruled 1327–1377) of England, the son of the dead king's sister, challenged the Valois by claiming the throne for himself. When Philip VI invaded Gascony in 1337, Edward declared war.

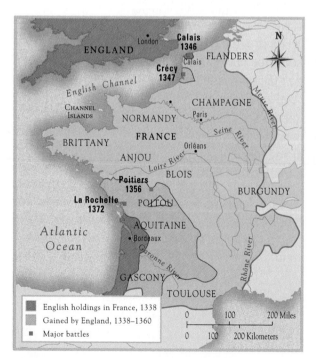

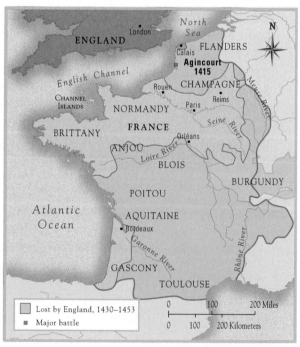

 Map 33.1 The Hundred Years' War. The two maps illustrate the extent of English gains and losses in France between 1338 and 1453. After that the English held only Calais, until 1558, and the Channel Islands. (This group of islands has been a dependency of the British Crown since 1066. They are still under British sovereignty, but each island is locally governed, under its own constitution.) Go to http://info.wadsworth.com/053461065X for an interactive version of this map.

THE EARLY PHASE OF THE CONFLICT

The war changed the nature of warfare and undermined the old feudal system that was based on knightly combat. Both sides still relied on heavily armed aristocratic cavalry to do most of the fighting, and the French knights dismissed the importance of the peasant infantry and crossbow soldiers. The English, on the other hand, already employed large numbers of paid infantry, many of whom carried the much superior longbow, which had greater firing speed and range than the crossbow. This difference would determine the outcome of the early fighting.

In an effort to break the pattern of costly failures that marked the first English campaigns in France, Edward III invaded Normandy in 1346. Here, too, he encountered setbacks. When the French forces cut off the English while they were attempting to retreat into Flanders, a major battle took place at Crécy. There the English longbows decimated the larger French army. Edward then pressed his advantage by seizing the port of Calais, which the English held for 200 years and used for later landings. Despite the victory at Crécy, the war dragged on indecisively because the English, with less than half the population of France, were unable to muster sufficient troops or resources to achieve total victory. Under the leadership of Edward, the prince of Wales—known as the Black Prince—the English wreaked havoc and destruction on the French countryside. Rather than risking all on head-to-head battles, the Black Prince attacked unfortified towns, burned crops, and spread terror among the peasantry. Finally, at the Battle of Poitiers in 1356, the French forces were again defeated and their king captured. A peace treaty was signed three years later at Brétigny, but the peace of Brétigny never went into effect because the war began again under the leadership of a new French king. Using mercenary soldiers to strengthen their position, the French eventually recovered the territory lost to the English. This time, a truce negotiated in 1396 lasted 20 years.

JOAN OF ARC AND THE END OF THE WAR

The war erupted again in 1415, when the English invaded France. After a smashing victory at Agincourt in which some 1,500 French knights were killed, the English conquered Normandy and persuaded the duke of Burgundy to join forces with them. The French monarchy, now led by the weak and indecisive *dauphin* (or royal heir), Charles (ruled 1422–1461 as Charles VII), controlled only the southern two-thirds of the country. When the English pushed south toward the Loire Valley and the heart of France, the moment was unexpectedly saved by a young French peasant girl, Joan of Arc (c. 1412–1431).

The daughter of a comfortable peasant family from the Champagne region, Joan was a devout Catholic who claimed to have experienced divinely inspired visions. In 1429, believing that she was charged by saints to save France from the English, she convinced Charles to allow her to accompany the French army. Inspired by Joan's sincerity and bravery, the French fought with renewed energy and routed the English, driving them from the Loire Valley. Joan's purpose was realized later that year, when the dauphin was crowned as King

Miniature painting of the Battle of Crécy, 1347. **14th century.** Note the English soldiers, on the right, armed with their superior longbows; the first French casualty has already fallen. The English troops fight in armor decorated with the red Cross of St. George. The battle proved an important turning point in the first phase of the Hundred Years' War.

Manuscript illumination showing a portrait of Joan of Arc, bareheaded and wearing a full suit of armor. **15th century.** The scroll behind her head refers to the divine visions that inspired her to rally the French forces against the English.

Charles VII at Reims, thereby confirming the legitimacy of the Valois line. In 1430, however, the Burgundian allies of the English captured Joan. In a calculated effort to destroy a powerful symbol of a new French patriotism, the English accused her of witchcraft and turned her over to the Inquisition. Although the trial was not conducted by normal Inquisitorial procedures, Joan was condemned as a heretic and burned at the stake in 1431—five centuries later, the Catholic Church made her a saint.

Despite Joan's lamentable end, the French people rallied around Charles as the war continued for another 20 years. Both sides were exhausted, and after a series of English defeats that drove them from Normandy and Aquitaine, the fighting finally stopped in 1453, although no peace treaty was ever signed. England, left only with Calais on the French coast, withdrew from the continent. A devastated France began the slow and difficult process of recovering and solidifying its newly found national unity.

THE VALOIS KINGS AND THE REVIVAL OF FRANCE

The destruction that the Hundred Years' War had caused in France made it difficult for the monarchy to reimpose its authority on the country. Yet the war had enabled Charles VII to strengthen royal power, a trend that continued into the following century.

The three principal "estates" of French society—the clergy, the nobles, and the bourgeoisie—composed the institution known as the Estates General (see Topic 29), a body that endorsed the king's decisions and approved new taxes. During the war crisis, the Estates General had given Charles permission to raise a professional royal army and to pay for it by levying an annual property tax, the *taille*. During the last years of the war, Charles drew strength from the advice of his powerful mistress, Agnes Sorel (c. 1422–1450), whose influence so angered the nobility that they are said to have poisoned her to death.

LOUIS THE SPIDER

The power of the French state was advanced by Charles's successor, King Louis XI (ruled 1461–1483), whose devious and crafty personality earned him the nickname of Louis the Spider. To restore the prosperity of France in the wake of the economic impact of the war, Louis developed new industries, including the manufacture of silk in Lyons, and stimulated trade. Although the *taille* was designed as a temporary war measure, Louis continued to impose it as a regular source of royal income.

Louis strengthened the state by keeping in place the standing army of professional soldiers that the *taille* tax had enabled his father to create. Military expenditures absorbed half of all royal revenues because modern armies were increasingly more expensive and only the royal government

Portrait of Louis XI, king of France, known as the "Spider." 15th century. The chain around his shoulders is a string of cockle-shells, symbol of the Order of St. James of Compostela. Louis was responsible for creating a firm basis for absolute monarchy in France.

could afford them. Once gunpowder was introduced, new weapons required even more revenue. The invention of the cannon required costly manufacturing and logistical supplies, while a kind of handgun known as the *arquebus* called for large numbers of additional soldiers carrying pikes to protect those armed with guns. Although it was expensive to maintain, the importance of an army that was loyal to the monarchy could not be overlooked.

The royal courts increased their power, and the king's use of Roman law gave him the authority to issue edicts and decrees. Nevertheless, the judicial system reflected the fact that the provinces remained important centers of local privilege: while the crown appointed judges of a central court known as the Parlement of Paris, it also granted important provinces their own parlements. Moreover, the Parlement was expected to register all edicts issued by the king. Louis never succeeded in completely destroying the power of the local nobility, but his reign established the monarchy on a solid footing.

THE CONSOLIDATION OF THE MONARCHY

Charles VIII (ruled 1483–1498), like his father Louis, proved to be an ambitious ruler. His marriage to the heiress of Brittany brought him control of that important province, the last independent region in France. Charles

PUBLIC FIGURES AND PRIVATE LIVES

MARGARET OF ANJOU AND HENRY VI OF ENGLAND

By Courtesy of the National Portrait Gallery, London

Hulton Getty Collection

In 1445, a temporary truce in the Hundred Years' War was sealed by Henry's marriage to Margaret of Anjou (1430–1482), the 15-year-old daughter of the count of Anjou. The women in Margaret's family provided her with important role models because both her grandmother and mother ruled their own lands and had frequently acted for the men in the family.

For many years, Henry and Margaret did not have children. Furthermore, by the time the war ended, Henry had begun to exhibit clear signs of mental instability. His hold on the crown was further weakened by economic unrest that beset England in the aftermath of the war. The discontent coalesced around the figure of Richard, duke of York, who had gained recognition as Henry's heir; Margaret played a central role in the Lancastrian circle opposed to Richard. In 1453, the situation became suddenly unsettled when Margaret produced a son, who now replaced Richard as heir to the throne. Richard took up arms against Henry, and

the conflict raged for several years, until in 1460 the Yorkists captured Henry and a compromise was reached by which Henry remained on the throne but Richard was declared his legal heir.

Furious that her son had been disinherited, Margaret formed an army and fought for 16 years in defense of his claim to the throne. She raised money and organized support in her husband's name, acting with courage and determination. The queen's followers defeated the Yorkists and killed Richard on the battlefield. In 1461, Margaret rescued her husband from captivity and together they fled to Scotland, while Richard's son Edward seized the throne, taking the name Edward IV (ruled 1461–1470, 1471–1483). In 1465, Henry was captured a second time by the Yorkists and held in the Tower of London.

With help from King Louis XI of France, Margaret invaded England and restored Henry to the throne in 1470, although the Yorkists quickly recovered and captured the entire royal family. Margaret and Henry's son died, and Henry was murdered in the Tower of London, most likely on Edward's orders. In 1476, Louis XI secured Margaret's release by paying Edward a ransom, although on condition that Margaret gave up all claims to French territory. The former queen of England returned to France, where she spent her last years in obscurity and poverty.

---

invaded Italy in 1494 at the invitation of Lodovico Sforza of Milan. The Italian campaign eventually went against Charles, who struggled for decades against the Hapsburg rulers of the Holy Roman Empire for hegemony over the Italian peninsula.

The Italian wars further expanded the size and powers of the royal government in France. The cost of the campaigns forced the monarchy to increase its revenues, but the wealthiest groups—the nobles, the clergy, and the royal towns—were traditionally exempt from taxes. In a desperate effort to raise money, Charles and his successors began the practice of selling government offices in the bureau-

cracy and the courts to buyers interested in the tax exemptions and titles that generally went with such positions.

King Francis I (ruled 1515–1547) continued the policy of expanding the bureaucracy by selling positions. He also focused on the Catholic Church, which was a major landowner and a source of revenue for the papacy. In 1516, following military successes in Italy, he secured from the papacy the right to appoint all French bishops and abbots, and this new power gave him access to a tremendous patronage system. Francis increased royal authority in a variety of other administrative ways and embarked on a program of overseas exploration (see Topic 38). By the death of Francis in the mid-16th century, the power that had been accumulated by the French monarchy was considerable, although the subsequent outbreak of religious unrest was to undermine the royal achievement.

ENGLAND AND THE RISE OF THE TUDORS

Even while England was engaged in the costly and draining experience of the Hundred Years' War, the kingdom was thrown into social and political turmoil. Two branches of the royal family, the House of York, which sported a white rose as its symbol, and the House of Lancaster, whose symbol was a red rose, began a struggle for power. Known as the War of the Roses, this conflict eventually pulled other families and England itself into a 30-year civil war. When it was over, a new dynasty, the House of Tudor, ascended to the throne.

THE WAR OF THE ROSES

Although the constant state of warfare between England and France had been the result of intermarriage and disputed inheritances, family links between the two monarchies continued to be forged. In 1420, Henry V of England, head of the House of Lancaster, married Catherine of Valois, the daughter of the French king. The following year, Catherine gave birth to a son, who came to the throne as Henry VI (ruled 1422–1471) when he was still an infant. For some years, an uncle ran the affairs of state for Henry. This hapless monarch was the pawn in the bitter War of the Roses that engulfed his realm.

THE FIRST TUDOR KING

At Edward IV's death in 1483, his eldest son ruled for only three months before the boy's uncle, Richard, duke of Gloucester, sent him and his younger brother to the Tower of London, where they died mysteriously. Richard then assumed the throne as Richard III (ruled 1483–1485). Two

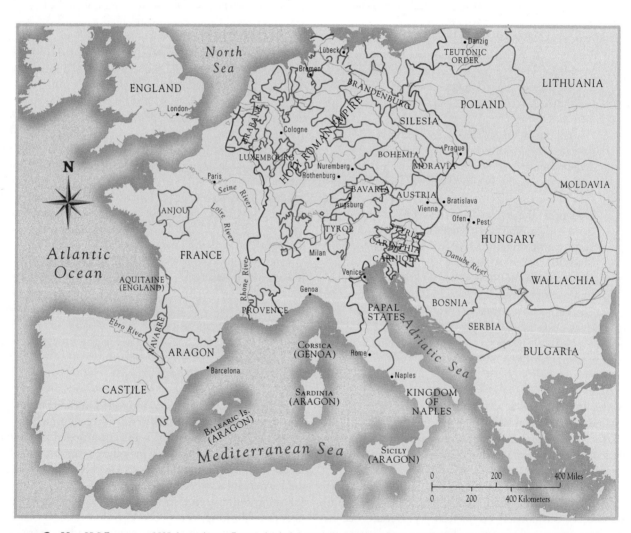

Map 33.2 Europe, c. 1400. In southwest France, Aquitaine was taken from the English in 1453, at the end of the Hundred Years' War. Navarre caused a century of conflict between France and Spain. During the 16th century, the southern part became conquered by Spain while the king of Navarre became king of France, and the two thus became joined. Anjou remained a powerful independent Duchy until 1480, when it was incorporated into France. Go to http://info.wadsworth.com/053461065X for an interactive version of this map.

years later, Henry Tudor defeated Richard at Bosworth Field and founded the Tudor dynasty.

Henry VII (ruled 1485–1509) was an energetic king who wanted to build an autocratic monarchy that could put an end to domestic discord and govern effectively. To accomplish this purpose, Henry prohibited nobles from maintaining private armies, a practice that had been common because the crown did not yet have a standing army. When recalcitrant nobles refused to comply with the king's demand for internal peace, he had them hauled before a new tribunal, the Court of the Star Chamber, which was presided over by royal judges.

These methods were balanced, however, by the fact that Henry did not arouse noble resistance by seeking to extract special taxes from them. Instead, he increased revenues from royal estates and made the collection of traditional taxes more efficient. Henry not only paid off the royal debt but also accumulated a vast private fortune. To overcome the economic distress that the disruptions of war had produced, Henry refused to engage in costly military adventures and tried instead to promote trade and manufacturing. He relied increasingly on the landed gentry to staff the administrative offices of his government. After almost 25 years on the throne, Henry—England's first new monarch—left a stable and increasingly prosperous kingdom in which the monarchy had once again become a respected institution with much popular support.

SPAIN: FROM ARAGON AND CASTILE TO HAPSBURG MONARCHY

At the time that the new monarchs were forging single nation-states in other parts of Europe, the Iberian peninsula was still divided into separate units. On the western coast, Portugal was a small kingdom with an ambitious monarchy that was leading the way in overseas exploration. On the southern Mediterranean coast lay Granada, the last real stronghold of Muslim power (see Topic 26). The vast central portion of the peninsula consisted of the kingdom of Castile, whose unruly nobles controlled much of the countryside and still waged the war against the Muslims that had begun centuries earlier. The eastern part of the peninsula was dominated by the kingdom of Aragon, which contained three distinct areas: Valencia, a fishing and farming region on the Mediterranean; Aragon, an interior region of unproductive land; and Catalonia, the commercial center of the kingdom containing the important port of Barcelona.

THE KINGDOM OF SPAIN

Although Portugal remained an independent state, the kingdom of Spain was formed in the late 15th century as a result of the union of Castile and Aragon. In 1469, Isabella (ruled 1474–1504), the heir to the throne of Castile, married Ferdinand (ruled 1479–1516), future ruler of Aragon.

Ferdinand was already king of Sicily, and his marriage to Isabella promised to create a kingdom of great influence and wealth. After a decade-long civil war against the nobles of Castile, who feared the power of a centralized monarchy, Ferdinand and Isabella were at last able to create the Kingdom of Spain.

Ferdinand and Isabella continued to recognize the deep-rooted local traditions that had long characterized Aragon. The region remained a collection of autonomous provinces, each with a viceroy and a parliamentary assembly known as the *Cortes*. Separate coinage systems, customs, and dialects continued to prevail even after unification. In Castile, however, the unstable conditions produced by the civil war had caused the spread of banditry in the countryside.

In response, the monarchs began to build a more highly centralized administration. Using the Cortes of Castile as a special tribunal to bring criminals to justice, Ferdinand and Isabella pacified the region. They reduced the power of the nobility in the royal government and relied increasingly on the lesser aristocrats known as *hidalgos*, who were more loyal to the crown.

The monarchs of Spain used religious policy as a force for cohesion. After the end of the civil war, Ferdinand and Isabella launched a renewed crusade against the Muslims in southern Spain, making themselves the symbols of Catholic unity and popular fervor. In 1478, they obtained permission from the pope to create a Spanish Inquisition, an institution that was used to uncover *Marranos*—Jews who pretended to convert to Christianity—and *Moriscos*—converted Muslims. Headed by the infamous Tomas de Torquemada, the Spanish Inquisitors often abused their authority and were fanatical in their efforts to uncover heretics and other nonconformists, including homosexuals and practitioners of magic. When Granada fell in 1492, Ferdinand and Isabella redirected their attack against the Jews, some 150,000 being expelled that same year. Religious policy, with its emphasis on uniformity and loyalty, became an important weapon in the growing arsenal of royal power.

Unlike the case of England, where Parliament restricted the power of the monarchy, royal authority in Spain was not seriously challenged by the Cortes. The rulers could raise taxes without approval of the Cortes and presided directly over the administration of justice. A royal compendium of law codes made the legal system uniform for the entire realm. In addition, Ferdinand and Isabella strengthened the state by replacing the old feudal armies, which relied so heavily on the loyalty of nobles, with a professional royal army. The collection of taxes became more efficient, and as royal revenues increased, so did the strength of the central government.

SPAIN AND THE HAPSBURGS

Ferdinand took an active role in foreign affairs, conquest, and overseas exploration (see Topic 38). With both Granada in the south and Navarre in the north now annexed to Spain, Ferdinand began to look beyond the peninsula.

Portrait of Maximilian I, by Albrecht Dürer. 16th century. Maximilian was a member of the Hapsburg family, Holy Roman Emperors after 1438. The family symbol of the double eagle is visible in the top left-hand corner, while Maximilian holds a pomegranate, whose many seeds represent abundance.

Kunsthistorisches Museum, Wien oder KHM, Wien

In 1495, he sent an army into Italy to prevent Charles VIII of France from bringing all of the Italian city-states under his control, and some nine years later he succeeded in conquering Naples. Spain had become a significant power, and by the end of the era of Ferdinand and Isabella, they had arranged marriages for their five children into prominent European dynasties. It was through one such marriage alliance with the Hapsburgs of Austria that the fate of Spain became enmeshed with that of the Holy Roman Empire.

Over the centuries, the Hapsburg family had gained control of Austria, a series of possessions along the Danube River in central Europe, and ruled a growing empire from their capital at Vienna. In 1438, the Hapsburgs secured the imperial crown of the Holy Roman Empire, and when Maximilian (ruled 1493–1519) married the daughter of the ruler of Burgundy, he expanded Hapsburg rule over the Low Countries, Luxembourg, and into eastern France. Maximilian continued the Hapsburg policy of carefully arranging marriages to further the family's dynastic interests. The link with Spain came in 1496, when Maximilian's son,

Philip of Burgundy, married Joanna, the daughter of Ferdinand and Isabella.

Twenty years later, when Ferdinand died, Aragon and Castile finally came together under the rule of one sovereign, Charles I (ruled 1516–1556), the grandson of both the Hapsburg emperor and the Spanish monarchs. Because Charles had been raised in Flanders, the Spanish nobility resented him. His election as Holy Roman Emperor in 1519 (he took the imperial title as Charles V) aroused even further hostility from his Spanish subjects, who felt that Charles's imperial interests had little to do with them. When he left Spain in 1520, a vague sense of Spanish nationalism was already beginning to stir.

Although Charles returned to Spain periodically, his attention was now focused on the immense possessions that he ruled—an empire that, with the exception of France, encompassed virtually all of continental Europe west of Poland and Hungary. Charles V was to be at the center of most of the major political and religious events of the first half of the 16th century (see Topic 39).

Putting the Age of the New Monarchs in Perspective

The development of the modern European nation-state was the work of the new monarchs, ambitious rulers who shaped powerful central governments controlling large national territories. The new Tudor dynasty in England, the Valois kings in France, and the joint reigns of Ferdinand and Isabella in Spain all began the process. The monarchs eliminated or at least reduced the power of the old nobility and extended their control over the church. They also created a bureaucratic structure designed to make the workings of royal government more effective and used several instruments of royal power to advance their program, including the extension of royal justice and the efficient collection of taxes.

In the process, they insisted on complete loyalty from their subjects and encouraged a national spirit designed to create popular support for their centralizing policies. The power and influence of the new monarchs and their centralizing states proved to be irresistible. The trends begun in the 15th century accelerated with time, and the centralized nation-state provided a model for rulers in other parts of Europe.

Questions for Further Study

1. What were the causes of the Hundred Years' War?
2. What was "new" about the new monarchs?
3. What issues led to the War of the Roses? Why were the Tudors successful in establishing their dynasty?
4. How did Ferdinand and Isabella unite Spain?

Suggestions for Further Reading

Allmand, C. *The Hundred Years' War: England and France, c. 1300–c. 1450*. Cambridge, MA, 1988.

Faur, Jose. *In the Shadow of History: Jews and Conversos at the Dawn of Modernity*. Albany, NY, 1992.

Gillingham, John. *The War of the Roses: Peace and Conflict in Fifteenth Century England*. London, 1981.

Hay, Denys. *Europe in the Fourteenth and Fifteenth Centuries*, 2nd ed. New York, 1989.

Hicks, M.A. *Richard III*. Stroude, 2000.

Hillgarth, J.N. *The Spanish Kingdoms, 1250–1516*, vol. II, *Castilian Hegemony*. New York, 1978.

Kadourie, Elie, ed. *Spain and the Jews: The Sephardi Experience 1492 and After*. New York, 1992.

Pernoud, Regine, and Marie-Veronique Clin. Jeremy du Quesnay Adams, trans. Bonnie Wheeler, ed. *Joan of Arc: Her Story*. London, 2000.

Potter, David. *A History of France, 1460-1560*. New York, 1995.

Wood, Charles T. *Joan of Arc and Richard III: Sex, Saints, and Government in the Middle Ages*. New York, 1988.

Wright, Nicholas. *Knights and Peasants: The Hundred Years War in the French Countryside*. Rochester, NY, 1998.

InfoTrac College Edition

Enter the search term *Hundred Years' War* using Key Terms.

Enter the search term *Joan of Arc* using Key Terms.

Enter the search term *Edward III* using Key Terms.

POWER AND CULTURE IN RENAISSANCE ITALY

The period in Western history known as the **Renaissance** (1300–1550) saw a remarkable flowering of artistic and literary genius. It was accompanied by the rise of a new world view that placed a concern for the human condition at the center of intellectual life. The Renaissance began in Italy, the product of its unique social and economic development. Renaissance culture, urban and increasingly secular, flourished in a land that had largely escaped feudalism. Moreover, the rebirth of Classical values was tied closely both to the long tradition of secular learning in Italy and to the memory of ancient Roman civilization, the physical remains of which were scattered throughout the peninsula.

Born in the Italian cities of the 14th century, humanism was a literary movement that stressed the study of Classical texts, new philosophical approaches inspired by Platonic ideas, and the historical sciences. These humanist values gave rise to a new kind of intellectual who participated actively in a political culture inspired by ancient ideals. Humanists regarded themselves as active citizens of their city-states and immersed themselves in the material affairs of their urban settings; they were not ivory tower intellectuals removed from the everyday world. Precisely because they were an educated elite, they believed they had responsibilities to their fellow citizens. This spirit of civic humanism was one of the outstanding characteristics of the Renaissance.

The visual arts played a central role in the public life of the city-states of Renaissance Italy, where political power and culture were inextricably linked. The princes of Florence and Milan, the aristocratic families of Venice, and the popes of Rome all were active and enthusiastic patrons of painting, sculpture, and architecture. Political leaders recognized the powerful role that the arts could have in forging popular consensus behind authority and instilling civic pride in citizens.

Although Renaissance culture represented a community of shared values, standards, and ideals, the political experience of Italy was far less unified. Because the peninsula was divided among several highly competitive and often warring states, it fell prey to more powerful foreign states. In response to their political divisiveness, Italians developed the concept of balance-of-power politics and the new art of diplomacy. By the 16th century, the Florentine writer Machiavelli drew on his Classical training as well as on the bitter political events of his times to fashion a new vision of power removed from the moral codes of Christianity and rooted directly in the gritty realities of everyday experience.

POLITICS, CLASS, AND CIVIC IDENTITY: THE ITALIAN CITY-STATES

The political and social development of Italian Renaissance cities followed a similar pattern. The remarkable economic expansion that had occurred in Medieval Italy had caused the rise of northern and central Italian cities such as Venice, Genoa, Milan, and Florence. The merchants and bankers who controlled this commercial revival accumulated great wealth. By the 11th century, they allied themselves with the local nobles in the countryside in order to secure independence from the bishops who ruled their cities. The communes came into being as a result of the oaths that the burghers and the nobles took to fight for their common rights. Once independence from the bishops was achieved, the communes took over the municipal governments, often creating new institutions, and soon came to control the hinterland around the cities. On this basis the city-states of the Renaissance eventually emerged.

FROM COMMUNES TO THE SIGNORIE

Political institutions in the cities reflected evolving social arrangements. Many of the rural nobles, attracted to the possibilities of wealth to be gained in trade or by marriage to rich burghers, moved into the cities, forming a new kind of urban nobility connected to the merchants through economic and family ties. This ruling elite strictly limited power and the rights of citizenship in the communes to people like themselves, who owned property and enjoyed high social status. Most of the inhabitants, including males of the middle and lower classes and all women, were excluded from holding office.

The members of the middle class, the *popolo*, particularly resented their second-class status. In the 13th century these alienated groups organized violent seizures of power and replaced communes with republican governments in such important cities as Florence, Siena, and Genoa.

Republican institutions were popular both because of their connection to Roman tradition and because they allowed for access to power by new elites. Once in power the *popolo* sought to exclude the working classes below them—the *popolo minuto*, or little people—from power. As a result, the republican governments never achieved popular consensus and found it difficult to maintain public order. In the early 1300s, republican governments collapsed and were replaced by one of two kinds of new regimes: either group rule by wealthy merchants (oligarchies) or individual despotisms (*signorie*).

THE STATES OF RENAISSANCE ITALY

By the opening of the 15th century, five major states had so expanded their territorial base that they exercised virtual hegemony over the Italian peninsula: Venice and Milan in the north, Florence in north-central Italy, the Papal States in the center, and the Kingdom of Naples in the south. Venice, at the head of the Adriatic Sea, had dominated the commercial revival of the High Middle Ages. Tremendous wealth poured into the city from its galleys and its overseas outposts. The Venetians had also conquered a mainland empire in Italy in order to have steady access to food and to protect themselves from the ambitious Milanese. Behind its long-established republican institutions, some 200 of Venice's merchant nobles ruled one of the most powerful states in Europe.

In Milan, the principal city of the region known as Lombardy, the Visconti family had ruled as tyrants since 1311. In 1395 Gian Galeazzo Visconti (ruled 1395–1402) transformed his rule into a hereditary duchy. By the time of his death, his armies had overrun all of Lombardy and were at the gates of Florence. In 1447, when the last of the Visconti died, Francesco Sforza (ruled 1450–1466), a soldier of fortune in the pay of the Milanese, turned against his masters and conquered the city. The Sforza family governed Milan with a strong hand and dominated the lesser cities of northern Italy.

The republic of Florence had long been controlled by representatives of the trade guilds, and from 1434 to 1494 the Medici, one of the most powerful and wealthy of the guild families, controlled the city. The Medici, who first made their money in banking, ruled behind the city's republican façade for more than half a century, turning Florence into a center of international power and cultural brilliance. Cosimo de' Medici (ruled 1434–1464), the great patron of civic humanists and artists, was a cultivated man of letters. On Cosimo's death, his son Piero (ruled 1464–1469) assumed the position of de facto ruler of Florence. Piero's era was marked by continuing artistic achievement and much political turmoil. He died after only five years in power and was succeeded in turn by his son Lorenzo de' Medici (ruled 1469–1492). Known as Lorenzo the Magnificent, he was the most distinguished of the Medici rulers of Florence. In his youth he was tutored by the humanist scholar Marsilio Ficino, who instilled in him a great love for learning and poetry. He continued the family's

Painting of Venice. 18th century. The main building, center-right, is the Doges' Palace, built 1345–1438, during the city's first great commercial expansion. The open arches on the lower level and the pink stone used for the upper half give the huge building a sense of lightness. To the left is visible the Basilica of St. Mark's, with its tall bell-tower, and to the right the Palace is connected to the Prison of Venice by the "Bridge of Sighs."

Painting of Florence, c. 1490. The city is divided into two unequal parts by the river Arno and surrounded by a wall with watchtowers, most of which was demolished in the 19th century. In the center of the left-hand section are the *Duomo* (Cathedral) and towered Palazzo Vecchio (Old Palace), which is still the center of city government. The main building across the river is the Pitti Palace, residence of the Medici.

tradition of patronage for the scholars and artists who worked in Florence during Cosimo's day.

Lorenzo's reign was challenged in 1478 when the so-called Pazzi Conspiracy erupted. This complicated plot was fomented by the prominent Pazzi family, who resented Medici rule. Lorenzo succeeded in foiling the conspiracy and imposing an even more firm control on the city. The last years of Lorenzo's life were again marked by turmoil, this time surrounding the career of the Dominican preacher Fra Girolamo Savonarola (1452–1498). Savonarola in-

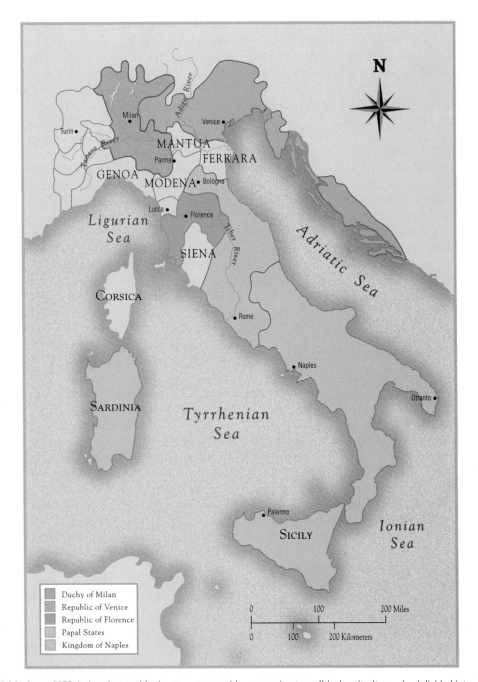

 Map 34.1 Italy, c. 1450. Italy refers at this time to a geographic area and not a political entity. It remained divided into separate states until the 19th century. The leading economic centers were Milan, Venice, and Florence; Siena, soon to pass under Florentine control, had lost its commercial supremacy at the time of the Black Death (1348). Rome had recently regained the prestige of housing the papacy but had little in the way of commerce. Go to http://info.wadsworth.com/053461065X for an interactive version of this map.

veighed against what he saw as the degeneration of life and culture in Florence and gathered a large and enthusiastic following, including some of the most talented artists of the city. He wanted a restoration of the Florentine republic based on Christian morality. In 1496 he staged a huge bonfire in the city in which gambling paraphernalia, cosmetics, and other symbols of decadence were burned. Savonarola eventually came into conflict with the papacy, which had him executed for heresy.

The Papal States, stretching across the peninsula from the Adriatic to the Tyrrhenian seas, were ruled by the popes from Rome. During the papal residency at Avignon, however, several noble families had grown influential in Rome. Moreover, in the course of the 14th century, secular lords had achieved independence in Ferrara, Urbino, and other cities of the Papal States. With the return of the pope to Rome in 1417, the papacy became increasingly more secular and involved in Italian politics. Some of the most famous Renaissance popes illustrated the temporal attitudes of the papacy: Pope Sixtus IV (ruled 1471–1484) became embroiled in the Pazzi Conspiracy; Alexander VI (ruled 1492–1503) and his sinister son Cesare Borgia schemed in the diplomatic intrigues of the day; and Julius II (ruled 1503–1513), the "warrior pope," personally led his armies in battle.

South of the Papal States lay the Kingdom of Naples, including the island of Sicily. After the death of Frederick of Hohenstaufen in the 13th century, the kingdom had fallen prey to the competing ambitions of the rulers of Aragon and France. In 1435, Naples and Sicily came under Aragonese domination and in 1504 were annexed to the Spanish crown.

The Italian cities were able to develop into sovereign territorial states primarily because Italy, like Germany, possessed no powerful central monarchy such as those that emerged in France and England. In this world of small Italian Renaissance states, ruled by despots and oligarchies, the elite learned to derive significant power from the sponsorship of culture. Out of this age of Renaissance humanism, when one neighbor was pitted against another in endless cycles of wars and alliances, a new conception of power politics was born.

THE INTELLECTUAL WORLD OF THE EARLY RENAISSANCE

In the 14th century, Petrarch introduced the notion of the self-conscious artist in search of personal fame (see Topic 32). The following generation of scholars advanced the notion of humanism further, with the arrival of Byzantine intellectuals who fled westward after the fall of Constantinople in 1453. Under constant external danger from other city-states, especially Milan, Florentine intellectuals turned to the Classical past to find inspiration. Among their models was Marcus Tullius Cicero, the ancient Roman statesman and writer, whose orations, letters, and essays stressed that the educated upper classes should provide leadership for society (see Topic 14). In 15th-century Florence, the civic humanist Leonardo Bruni (1370–1444) wrote a biography of Cicero that portrayed him as the model of the Renaissance ideal of the scholar-activist. Bruni was part of a circle of scholars around Coluccio Salutati who collected and studied ancient manuscripts; the greatest collector of ancient manuscripts was Poggio Bracciolini (1380–1459), a longtime papal secretary. These and other scholars perceived civic activism not only as a duty but also as a stimulant to intellectual creativity.

HUMANISTS AND NEOPLATONISTS
Lorenzo Valla (1407–1457) was the epitome of the civic humanist. Raised and educated in Rome, Valla studied both the Latin and the Greek classics, as Bruni had done. Humanists admired virtually all Latin writers before the 7th century, but Valla's studies—especially his *Elegances of the Latin Language*—revealed distinct periods in the development of Latin. He most admired the style of the late Republic and early Empire (1st century B.C.–1st century A.D.). Valla devoted much of his energy to close textual

analysis of ancient manuscripts. His discovery that the document known as the Donation of Constantine was a fake, actually written in the 8th century, brought him much attention; the Donation, which claimed that the Emperor Constantine had actually given political authority over the West to the church in 313, had long been used by popes to assert their temporal rule.

By the middle of the 15th century, humanism had become widely diffused; its basic tenets and methods were accepted; and many of the key Classical texts were known. Humanists now shifted their attention to philosophy, especially as it was influenced by the Greek philosophers, chief among them Plato. The Florentine humanists flourished under the patronage of the city's de facto ruler, the highly cultivated banker Cosimo de' Medici. Cosimo invested much of his wealth in the search for and copying of Classical manuscripts and in supporting the discussion group that came to be known as the Platonic Academy. Marsilio Ficino (1433–1499), one of the circle's most gifted intellectuals, was taken under Cosimo's protection as a child. Ficino received a regular income and access to the library at the Medici villa, and the Neoplatonists gathered here for their discussions.

Ficino's numerous translations from Greek into Latin included the *Corpus Hermeticum*, a series of Hermetic essays prepared at Cosimo's request. Among the subjects covered in the *Corpus* were the supposed secrets of the pagan world, including alchemy, astrology, and magic. The Hermeticists held that although human beings had been created as divine creatures, they had elected to be part of the material world. According to this view, humans could reattain their divine state by becoming sages. These magi, as they were known in the Renaissance, were endowed with knowledge of God and of the powers of nature, which they could use to help humans.

KNOWLEDGE AND EDUCATION
Among the best-known of those regarded as magi in the 15th century was Pico della Mirandola (1463–1494), a churchman who had studied with Ficino and was perhaps the most brilliant of the Florentine humanists—he once boasted that he had read every book in Italy. Believing that it was possible to organize human learning to reveal basic truth, Pico set out to master all knowledge. He learned Latin, Greek, Hebrew, Aramaic, and Arabic, as well as philosophy. When he was 20 years old he claimed to have summed up knowledge in 900 theses, which he described in a treatise called *Oration on the Dignity of Man*.

To the Renaissance mind, education was crucial to the intelligent and proper conduct of public affairs because humanism placed humans at the center of historical development. The authors of medieval chronicles had attributed events in human affairs to divine inspiration or direct intervention by God. The humanists, so taken with the search for texts and the analysis of sources, looked to documents rather than miracles for explanations of historical

PUBLIC FIGURES AND PRIVATE LIVES

ISABELLA D'ESTE AND FRANCESCO GONZAGA

Along with the Medici in Florence and the Sforza in Milan, Italy's smaller city-states were also centers of art and learning. Among the most brilliant of these smaller Renaissance courts was that of Francesco Gonzaga (ruled 1484–1519) of Mantua and his wife, Isabella d'Este (1474–1539).

Like many of his contemporaries, Francesco Gonzaga was first and foremost a warrior-prince. A short, ugly man without serious education, he seems not to have inherited the cultural interests that had long been a tradition at Mantua; while courting his future wife, he sent her poems that he had commissioned but pretended were his own. In 1490, he married Isabella, the 16-year-old daughter of Ercole d'Este, ruler of Ferrara, and Eleonora of Aragon. From that moment, Isabella overshadowed her husband in virtually all matters of domestic state policy and made Mantua a major center of Renaissance culture.

Isabella and her sister, Beatrice, two of the most remarkable women of the Renaissance, grew up in the rarified atmosphere of the Este court at Ferrara. The sisters were both competitive and different, for while Beatrice enjoyed a luxurious lifestyle, Isabella was more serious and mastered both Greek and Latin. Their arranged marriages resulted in major political alliances: While Isabella went to Mantua, Beatrice married Ludovico Sforza of Milan.

Because Francesco spent much time away from Mantua, the self-assured Isabella, who exhibited considerable skill at diplomacy and matters of state, often assumed the reins of government. Isabella's fame, however, rests on her role as an astute and sophisticated patron of arts and letters. Her cultural tastes were broad, ranging from painting, music, and architecture to philosophy, literature, and astrology. She competed for the talents of some of the greatest artists and writers of the era. Titian and Leonardo da Vinci painted portraits of her; Mantegna decorated her private rooms in the ducal palace; and Correggio called her "the first lady of the world."

Francesco Gonzaga's fame rests on his victory at the Battle of Fornovo in 1495, where he led the military forces of the Italian League (including Venice, Milan, and the Papal States) against the invading army of Charles VIII of France. Later, however, he continuously switched sides, and in 1509 he was captured and held prisoner for a year by the Venetians. During that time, Isabella not only made important military decisions and directed the defenses of Mantua but also founded the city's lucrative cloth industry. When he was finally liberated, a humiliated Francesco felt resentful of his talented consort's achievements. "We are ashamed," he wrote to her, "that it is our fate to have as a wife a woman who is always ruled by her head." Increasingly estranged from Francesco because of his repeated infidelities, she spent many of her last years at the papal court in Rome. After her husband died in 1519, Isabella acted as regent and adviser to her son Federigo II and was able to have her younger son, Ercole, made a cardinal. She died a much revered and respected figure, and very much a woman of the Renaissance.

events. Similarly, they saw individual motives behind political developments. The most accomplished of the new secular historians of the Renaissance was Francesco Guicciardini (1483–1540), who had considerable experience as a diplomat and government official. His *History of Italy*, the first work of history since antiquity based on original documents, provided detailed comparative analysis of political affairs in the city-states and decried the lack of unity in Italy. Most of all, Guicciardini saw the need for wise rulers endowed with learning and experience. These and other humanist values remained the core of upper-class education in the West for centuries.

PATRONAGE AND STATECRAFT IN RENAISSANCE ITALY

It was no accident that the cities of the Italian Renaissance were centers of both political power and culture because art served as a medium of education and as propaganda. The church, of course, had always been a great patron of the arts, using architecture, painting, and sculpture to promote worship and respect for religious institutions. In the Renaissance, just as artistic themes became increasingly secular, so laymen emerged as active and generous patrons of the arts.

THE NATURE OF RENAISSANCE PATRONAGE

Following in the tradition of the Middle Ages, guilds and religious organizations commissioned artists to create works of sculpture and paintings that reflected their wealth and influence. In Florence, the cloth merchants hired Filippo Brunelleschi to design and erect the stunning dome of the city's *duomo* (cathedral).

Individual rulers and nobles also came to recognize the power of culture and patronized art and scholarship to show off their wealth and status. Many tried to trace their ancestry back to Roman times and deliberately imitated the lifestyles of the ancient patricians. In their zeal to identify with Classical civilization, princes poured money into excavating archaeological sites and locating lost manuscripts. Wealthy families spent lavishly to build and decorate tombs and chapels in the principal churches of their cities.

Princes used the creative talents they supported to strengthen and legitimize their rule. They brought poets and essayists to their palaces, and hired architects and artists to plan and decorate their public rooms and erect statues and monuments to their achievements. As the social status of the artists grew during the Renaissance, patrons competed to hire the best-known painters and sculptors because the fame of the artist enhanced the prestige of the patron.

ITALY AND EUROPE: POWER POLITICS AND THE ART OF DIPLOMACY

In 1454, the Italian states established a precarious balance of power through the Peace of Lodi. The agreement between Venice and Milan, which conceded Milan to Francesco Sforza and restored Venetian holdings in northern Italy, brought peace to Italy for many years. The Italian states were exhausted by the continuous warfare and agreed to observe the terms of the peace and to join an Italian League for mutual defense.

The Peace of Lodi collapsed in 1494, when Lodovico Sforza of Milan asked for the military support of Charles VIII of France in the midst of rising tensions with Florence and Naples. The French invasion of Italy began a long series of disastrous wars that revealed the inability of relatively weak city-states to withstand the power of centralized nation-states. Italy became a battleground of larger European dynastic interests as the houses of Hapsburg, Valois, and Aragon jockeyed for hegemony. Charles pushed the Medici out of Florence (they returned in 1512), the Hapsburg Emperor Charles V seized Milan, and Ferdinand of Aragon took Naples. When the wars finally ended in 1559, the Hapsburgs were masters of the peninsula, with only Venice and the Papal States remaining independent. Although the memory of Italy's great cultural legacy lingered, its political subservience to foreign powers would not end for three centuries.

DIPLOMACY AND POWER POLITICS

As political life in Europe grew more complex, states began to develop new and more formal ways of relating to each other. The advantages of economic and cultural cooperation, as well as of finding alternatives to war, became increasingly evident to the great powers. Nowhere was the need for organized international relations greater than in Italy, where in the process of creating a balance of power the Italians had invented the art of diplomacy. During the Italian wars that erupted at the end of the 15th century, the Italian style of managing foreign policy was copied by other European states.

The most important novelty devised by Italian diplomats was the use of resident ambassadors. In the place of roving envoys who traveled to accomplish specific missions, states now maintained permanent ambassadors in foreign capitals. The advantages were obvious: Resident ambassadors could not only collect intelligence about conditions and attitudes in their host country, but they also developed personal relationships that could be used to represent the interests of their sovereign more quickly and efficiently. Resident ambassadors gave rise to elaborate embassies staffed by military and commercial experts and using sophisticated reporting procedures. Diplomatic staffs lived in foreign countries with immunity from local laws and adopted both fixed procedures and formal styles of protocol to govern diplomatic relations. These procedures evolved under the impact of the Italian wars because rulers throughout Europe were drawn into the intricate dynastic struggles that marked the struggles for power there. It gradually became clear that the general interests of all states required a balance in which no one power dominated the others.

The collapse of the independence of the Italian city-states, together with the emergence of centralized monarchies elsewhere in Europe, attracted the attention of political analysts, who now began to study diplomacy, politics, and the nature of power from a more practical and secular point of view. The Italians, anxious to understand why their independence had disappeared so completely, were in the

The Departure of the Ambassadors, painting by Carpaccio, c. 1496–1498. 9 feet 2 inches by 8 feet 8 inches (2.80 by 2.53 m). The painting comes from a cycle depicting the Legend of St. Ursula and shows the king of Brittany receiving ambassadors from England. In fact, however, it represents Italian diplomatic practice of the Early Renaissance, and the interior walls decorated with colored stone are typical of Venetian architecture.

Scala/Art Resource

forefront of this new approach to the study of political power. The historian Guicciardini, for example, had examined the histories of the Italian states comparatively and concluded that the lack of unity in the peninsula had enabled foreign powers to crush them. It was, however, the Florentine Niccolò Machiavelli (1469–1527) who epitomized the new politics of the age (see Topic 36).

Many contemporaries were shocked by Machiavelli's advocacy of the amoral manipulation of power, and the term "Machiavellian" became a label for unscrupulousness and evil. The 16th century was perhaps not yet ready to accept this new approach to the use of state power, but the realities of the day pointed to a different direction in political affairs.

Putting Renaissance Italy in Perspective

The Renaissance was the product of Europe's cultural and social vitality, and it set the tone for the modern age. The humanist concerns with Classical virtues and learning, the strength and beauty of Michelangelo's *David,* the raw pragmatism of Machiavelli's advice to the prince, all bespoke a new viewpoint freed from superstition and focused on the human condition. The secular and urban values of Renaissance culture emerged first in Italy, where a combination of history, social development, and economic factors encouraged its flowering. Conditions there first stimulated the growth of humanism,

Continued next page

which in turn nurtured the sense of civic virtue and responsibility that marked the public life of the Renaissance city-states.

As in earlier epochs, rulers of the Renaissance period appreciated and used painting, sculpture, and architecture to enhance their prestige and legitimize their power. Political leaders recognized the powerful role that the arts could have in forging popular consensus behind authority and instilling civic pride in citizens. The experience of numerous city-states vying with each other to control the peninsula had resulted in the invention of important political techniques, although Machiavelli, the most jarringly objective observer of his times, recognized in that lesson that the realities of power were working against the Italians. For all their wisdom and skill in developing effective political systems, Italian rulers were unable to forge unity or to maintain the integrity of their own states against the military power of the newly emerging national monarchies. The Italians, it seemed, had chosen culture over power.

Questions for Further Study

1. What forms did "civic identity" take in Renaissance Italy?
2. With what issues were early Renaissance intellectuals concerned?
3. Why did Italian Renaissance rulers and merchants act as patrons of the arts?
4. What conditions in Italy led to the invention of "diplomacy" in the modern sense?

Suggestions for Further Reading

Brucker, Gene A. *Renaissance Florence*, rev. ed. New York, 1983.
Burke, Peter. *The Italian Renaissance: Culture and Society in Italy*, rev ed. Princeton, NJ, 1999.
D'Amico, John F. *Renaissance Humanism in Papal Rome*. Baltimore, 1983.
Godman, Peter. *From Poliziano to Machiavelli: Florentine Humanism in the High Renaissance*. Princeton, NJ, 1998.
Hale, J.R. *The Civilization of Europe in the Renaissance*. New York, 1995.

Hay, Denys, and J. Law. *Italy in the Age of the Renaissance*. London, 1989.
Holmes, George. *Florence, Rome and the Origins of the Renaissance*. Oxford, 1986.
Johnson, P. *The Renaissance*. New York, 2000.
King, Margaret L. *Venetian Humanism in an Age of Patrician Dominance*. Princeton, NJ, 1986.
Rubinstein, Nicolai. *The Government of Florence under the Medici (1434-1494)*. New York, 1997.
Stephens, J. *The Italian Renaissance: The Origins of Intellectual and Artistic Change Before the Reformation*. New York, 1990.
Trinkaus, Charles E. *The Scope of Renaissance Humanism*. Ann Arbor, MI, 1983.

InfoTrac College Edition

Enter the search term *Renaissance* using the Subject Guide.

Enter the search term *Machiavelli* using Key Terms.

THE VISUAL ARTS OF THE ITALIAN RENAISSANCE

The rise of the Medici in Florence, together with the city's increasing prosperity, culminated in an artistic explosion there. Painters, sculptors, and architects vied to produce works in the "modern style," commissioned by their patrons, which influenced the arts throughout Europe.

Although the Renaissance style was a natural development of the late medieval interest in the expression of powerful feelings, Renaissance artists felt that in turning back to ancient models they were making a decisive break with their immediate past. The greatest sculptor of the Early Renaissance, Donatello, combined a rediscovery of Classical forms with a strong sense of drama.

Brunelleschi, the leading architect of the period, used techniques learned from his study of ancient Roman buildings to create structures dominated by logic and order. Many of his buildings are centrally planned, and the design of details expresses the Renaissance belief in reason. The paintings of Masaccio show a similar concern with order and proportion, combining them with physical realism. Botticelli, one of the leading painters at the Medici court, reflected his patrons' interest in Neoplatonic humanism, while in northern Italy the frescoes of Mantegna continued to experiment with perspective.

The three towering figures of the High Renaissance were Leonardo da Vinci, Raphael, and Michelangelo. Leonardo is known as much for the incredible breadth of his ideas and interests as for his few surviving works. Raphael's paintings express the High Renaissance love of ideal beauty based on Classical standards. Michelangelo's vision was more complex. Recognized in his own day as the greatest artist of the Renaissance, he has been regarded ever since as the archetype of the supreme creative genius.

The masterpieces produced in Florence in the Early Renaissance and at Rome in the High Renaissance emphasized order, form, and line. Venetian painters were more interested in color and light, and their works are often mellower and more relaxed than those produced elsewhere in Italy. Bellini and Titian both used Classical themes. Titian was also a master of portraiture, while his reclining female nudes are among the most sensual in Western art.

The artistic movement of the late *Cinquecento* (16th century), Mannerism, took the main features of Renaissance style to extremes, with the drama becoming artificial, and technical virtuosity an end in itself. By the end of the 16th century, artists and critics were already looking back with awe at the "old masters" of the High Renaissance.

THE "MODERN STYLE": DONATELLO, BRUNELLESCHI, AND MASACCIO

With the rediscovery of Classical Antiquity, artists began to develop new styles based on ancient models. Turning to Roman sculptures, the remains of ancient Roman buildings, and Classical texts on art, they aimed for a "modern style" that would express Classical ideals of order and balance for their own times. Behind their use of perspective and realism to achieve dramatic effect lay the late medieval emotionalism seen in the works of Giovanni Pisano (see Topic 30), but the powerful directness of Early Renaissance art represents a revolutionary break with the past.

SCULPTURE IN THE EARLY RENAISSANCE: DONATELLO

One of the most profoundly original of all Renaissance artists, the sculptor Donatello (1386?–1466) used Classical principles to achieve startling dramatic effects. His statues of *St. Mark* and *St. George*, carved between 1413 and 1417 to decorate the façade of the Florentine church of Orsanmichele, show a sense of the shifting weight of the bodies. This depiction of movement, which was characteristic of ancient Greek sculpture, disappeared with the end of Classical Antiquity, to be reborn in the Early Renaissance. At the same time, Donatello avoids the generalized idealism of Greek art. The two saints emerge as distinct individuals: the venerable St. Mark brooding and intense, St. George youthfully proud and determined.

In his small bronze relief panel of *The Feast of Herod* (c. 1425), which decorates the baptismal font of Siena Cathedral, Donatello's sense of the theatrical makes powerful use of the newly discovered technique of linear perspective. To create the illusion of depth on a flat surface, Early Renaissance artists devised a mathematical system whereby all lines met at a single point on the horizon—an example of the important new relationship in the Early Renaissance between the arts and scholarly learning.

Donatello's panel combines several separate incidents in the story of Salome's dance and the execution of John the Baptist. Herod recoils in terror as the executioner presents the saint's head to him on a dish, and a variety of other figures in the three interconnected rooms express their horror with violent gestures, while Salome continues the sinuous movements of her dance. The remarkable sense of depth represents a break with the generally flat backgrounds of most medieval sculpture. Like ancient Roman artists, Donatello aimed to create the illusion of space, but for the first time in Western art he used the scientific principle of linear perspective to do so.

BRUNELLESCHI AND THE CLASSICAL TRADITION OF ARCHITECTURE

The inventor of linear perspective was the architect and sculptor Filippo Brunelleschi (1377–1446). One of his earliest works was a bronze panel of *The Sacrifice of Isaac*

Donatello, statue of *St. George*. 1415–1417. Height c. 6 feet 10 inches (2.08 m). The work was originally made to stand in a niche on the façade of the Florentine Church of Orsanmichele, and thus only visible from the front. The figure is one of Donatello's earlier statues, with its Classical severity, taut pose, and tense expression.

Summerfield Press, Ltd.

(1401–1402), made as an entry into the competition organized in Florence to choose an artist for the north doors of the baptistery there. The winner was the sculptor and goldsmith Lorenzo Ghiberti (c. 1378–1455), whose style blended naturalism and classicism to create realistic figures. In disappointment, Brunelleschi devoted most of his remaining career to architecture and went on to become the greatest architect of the Early Renaissance.

One of the key events in the formation of Brunelleschi's style was his journey to Rome in 1402, perhaps in the company of his friend Donatello. After several more visits to study the construction principles used by ancient Roman builders there, he returned to Florence, where he managed to solve an engineering problem that baffled his contemporaries: how to construct a dome for the city's huge unfinished cathedral. The vast octagonal-shaped structure, with its inner and outer shells, still dominates the Florence skyline.

Masaccio, *Expulsion of Adam and Eve from Eden,* c. 1425. 7 feet by 2 feet 11 inches (2.14 by .90 m). The scene combines poignant emotion with a realistic portrayal of human anatomy. A fig leaf added to cover Adam's genitals in the late 15th century was only removed—amid considerable controversy—in the 1980s.

THE REVOLUTIONARY PAINTING OF MASACCIO

The first painter to adopt Brunelleschi's linear perspective was the young Masaccio (1401–1428), whose brief career—he died at the age of 27, probably of the plague—catapulted painting forward into the "modern style." Breaking completely with the elaborate and crowded style of International Gothic artists (see Topic 30), Masaccio used principles of mathematical organization to produce startling effects of realism.

In the frescoes he painted for the Brancacci Chapel in the Church of Santa Maria del Carmine, Florence, at the very end of his short life, Masaccio added an unforgettable emotional impact to his ability to create the illusion of volume. The figures of Adam and Eve, in *The Expulsion from the Garden of Eden,* stumble out of Eden into an inexorably harsh light—Adam unable to face the future and Eve crying piercingly aloud. The weight of their limbs and their leaden footsteps combine with the hazy background to present one of the most poignant images in Western art.

TRADITION AND EXPERIMENT: THE LATER QUATTROCENTO

The most important of Brunelleschi's successors was the architect and art theorist Leone Battista Alberti (1404–1472), whose writings on architecture and painting profoundly influenced later Renaissance artists. In accordance with the humanist ideas of the period, Alberti believed that beauty—whether of a figure or a building—depended on an ideal balance and order, creating a perfect harmony.

PAINTING IN THE LATER QUATTROCENTO

Toward the end of the Quattrocento, some painters continued to work within the mainstream of earlier developments, whereas others broke new ground. Among the traditionalists was Domenico Ghirlandaio (1449–1494), who placed his depictions of scenes drawn from the Bible within the rich Florentine palaces and aristocratic life of his day.

The art of Piero della Francesca (c. 1420–1492) is far more intellectual. Like Alberti, with whom he worked at Rimini, Piero continued to experiment with mathematical and geometrical structures. Many of his paintings use light as one of the elements of composition. *The Resurrection* is based on a triangular arrangement, with the sleeping soldiers forming the base and the head of the risen Christ, set on its strong, column-like body, the apex. The cold light of dawn in the background emphasizes Christ's triumphant stance.

If Piero was inspired by the clarity of mathematical proportion, his younger contemporary Sandro Botticelli (1445–1510) began his career under the influence of the Neoplatonist ideas circulating at the Medici court. The Neoplatonists combined elements of Classical mythology and Christianity in elaborate allegories. Thus the Christian

ACROSS CULTURES

CHARLES DICKENS ON RENAISSANCE ITALY

In July 1844, the eminent Victorian novelist, Charles Dickens (1812–1870), set off with his family to spend a year in Italy. As many earlier travelers had done, he intended to turn his experiences into a book. First published as a series of letters to a newspaper, the *Daily News*, his account of the year appeared in the form of a book, *Pictures From Italy*, in 1846.

Many of the events he narrates offer an incomparably vivid impression of life in 19th century Italy—he includes, for example, a characteristically sensitive description of a public execution—but, like most visitors to Italy, then and now, he made a point of visiting as many of the most important works of art as he could see. His comments unwittingly provide an impression of the tastes of the mid-19th century.

In Florence, Dickens admired the architecture: "Magnificently stern and sombre are the streets of beautiful Florence; and the strong old piles of building make such heaps of shadow, on the ground and in the river, that there is another and a different city of rich forms and fancies, always lying at our feet." Among the artists whose work he saw in "these rugged Palaces of Florence," he especially picks out "Michael Angelo, Canova, Titian, Rembrandt, Raphael." Few art historians today would place the sculptor Canova in such exalted company. Meditating on the transience of life and the permanence of art, he cites a painting so well known to his readers that he needed to name neither title or artist: "The nameless Florentine Lady, preserved from oblivion by a Painter's hand, yet lives on, in enduring grace and youth." (Leonardo's *Mona Lisa* is now in Paris, in the Louvre.)

Visiting the Vatican while in Rome, Dickens was struck once again by "the exquisite grace and beauty of Canova's statues," and works by Titian and Tintoretto, but was less impressed by Michelangelo's achievement: "I cannot imagine how the man who is truly sensible of the beauty of Tintoretto's great pictures can discern in Michael Angelo's Last Judgement, in the Sistine chapel, any general idea, or one pervading thought, in harmony with the stupendous subject." Similarly, the interior of St. Peter's did not appeal to his Anglican tastes: "It is not religiously impressive or affecting. It is an immense edifice, with no one point for the mind to rest on; and it tires itself with wandering round and round. A large space behind the altar was fitted up with boxes, shaped like those at the Italian Opera in England, but in their decoration much more gaudy."

The one city to win unqualified approval is described in a chapter called "An Italian Dream."

> We advanced into this ghostly city, continuing to hold our course through narrow streets and lanes, all filled and flowing with water. . . . Going down upon the margin of the green sea, rolling on before the door, and filling all the streets, I came upon a place of such surpassing beauty, and such grandeur, that all the rest was poor and faded in comparison with its absorbing loveliness.
>
> It was a great Piazza, as I thought; anchored like all the rest in the deep ocean. On its broad bosom was a Palace, more majestic and magnificent in its old age than all the buildings of the earth, in the high prime and fullness of their youth. Cloisters and galleries: so light they might have been the work of fairy hands: so strong that centuries had battered them in vain: wound round and round this palace, and enfolded it with a Cathedral, gorgeous in the wild luxuriant fancies of the East.

The author remains spellbound, "until I awoke in the old market place at Verona. I have many and many a time, thought since of this strange Dream upon the water; half wondering if it lies there yet, and if its name be Venice."

Piero della Francesca, *The Resurrection,*
c. 1463. 7 feet 5 inches by 6 feet 6 inches (2.26
by 2 m). The upturned faces of the two soldiers
flanking the figure of the risen Christ lead the
viewer's eye toward Christ, and the contrast between his light flesh and the dark costumes of
all the sleeping figures emphasizes the triangular composition.

INDEX/Tosi

Summerfield Press, Ltd.

Botticelli, *The Birth of Venus,* c. 1482. 5 feet 8 inches by 9 feet 1 inch (1.72 by 2.77 m). The Venus figure, based on statues from
Classical Antiquity, represents a synthesis of Classical naturalism and Christian mysticism. At the same time, Botticelli aims to express
the Platonic ideal of feminine beauty, rather than the literal appearance of a particular woman.

teaching that "God is love" becomes personified in the form of the Roman Venus, goddess of love.

At first sight, Botticelli's *Birth of Venus* seems a purely pagan image, with the nude goddess—one of the earliest female nudes since Classical Antiquity—borne forward by the winds. Yet not only is the beauty of Venus symbolic of Christian love, but the idea of the birth of Venus corresponds also to Christ's baptism, itself a form of rebirth.

By the end of the 15th century, the overthrow of the Medici and the preaching of Savonarola (see Topic 34) reduced the dominant role of Florentine artists, but the main features of Florentine Renaissance art had already spread to other parts of Italy.

HARMONY AND DESIGN IN THE HIGH RENAISSANCE

For a few brief years, from the French invasion of Italy in 1494 to the death of Raphael in 1520, the Renaissance reached a new peak. Lavish papal patronage made Rome the center of High Renaissance art, although Leonardo da Vinci, one of the three leading figures of the age—the others were Raphael and Michelangelo—worked mainly in Milan and died in France.

RENAISSANCE MAN: LEONARDO DA VINCI
No figure of the Renaissance has evoked greater admiration for the breadth of his mind than Leonardo (1452–1519), the illegitimate son of a notary at Vinci, a small town to the west of Florence. He studied painting in Florence and worked at the court of the Sforza family, rulers of Milan, as architect, military engineer, inventor, scientist, musician, and painter. He set down many of his ideas in thousands of pages of notes and sketches, exploring the human and natural worlds.

Leonardo's fresco of *The Last Supper*, painted for the Milanese Church of Santa Maria delle Grazie, is the first great work of the High Renaissance. Despite severe damage caused by flaking paint, the work remains a powerful illustration of Renaissance ideals of clarity and harmony. The central figure of Jesus, his head outlined against the open window behind, is flanked by six apostles to each side. Jesus remains still, while shockwaves pass through the others in response to his words to them: "One of you will betray me." The dramatic range of emotions the apostles convey, the careful balance of the composition, and the absence of irrelevant details all combine to produce one of the high points of Western art.

If *The Last Supper* is the most famous of Renaissance religious scenes, Leonardo's portrait of *Mona Lisa*, wife of the merchant Giocondo (the painting is often known as *La Gioconda*—a pun on her husband's name that refers to her smile), is no less celebrated. The sitter's ambiguous smile and the hazy background are made possible by the artist's use of a technique called *sfumato* or "smoky."

THE CLASSICAL HARMONY OF RAPHAEL
Born in Urbino, the painter Raphael (1483–1520) studied in Florence before moving to Rome in 1508, where he received important papal commissions. His Classical balance and order are visible in the series of frescoes with which he decorated a suite of rooms in the Vatican palace, known as

Leonardo da Vinci, *The Last Supper*. 1495–1498. 14 feet 5 inches by 28 feet (4.4 by 7.9 m). The careful, mathematical precision behind the composition of this famous fresco does not detract from its emotional impact on the viewer. The doorway visible below the figure of Christ was cut by soldiers using the monastery where Leonardo painted the fresco as a military headquarters, and the room was also hit by a bomb in World War II.

Scala/Art Resource

Raphael, *The School of Athens*. 1509-1511. 26 feet by 18 feet (7.92 by 5.48 m). The Vatican fresco sets the great philosophers of antiquity in a vast illusionistic architectural framework inspired by the ruins of Roman baths and basilicas, and perhaps also by construction on the new Basilica of St. Peter's, which was then in progress.

the *Vatican Stanze*. The most famous, *The School of Athens*, depicts the most renowned ancient Greek and Roman philosophers engaged in earnest discussion.

Like Leonardo's *Last Supper*, the scene shows the figures arranged in groups. The two greatest minds of antiquity, Plato and Aristotle, stand at the center under the receding arches. Plato points upward, to indicate abstract thought, while Aristotle gestures to the ground, symbol of practical and down-to-earth experiment. The round arches and coffered ceilings of the background provide a Classical setting.

For his contemporaries, Raphael's most popular works were his many depictions of the Madonna and Child. Among the best-known is the *Madonna of the Meadows*, which provides another Renaissance example of pyramidal composition. Unlike Leonardo, with his love of mysterious haze, Raphael bathed his figures in a glowing clarity, which emphasizes their High Renaissance blend of Christian devotion and pagan beauty. In the background, the details of the feathery trees are all rendered with loving precision.

THE SUBLIME MICHELANGELO

Even in an age of giants, Michelangelo Buonarroti (1475–1564) inspired awe mixed with fear in his contemporaries, who spoke of his *terribilità*—a combination of the terrible and the sublime. For posterity he has become the

symbol of creative genius, fighting with his patrons and rivals in the pursuit of his titanic visions.

Architect, painter, poet, and engineer, Michelangelo always regarded himself as first and foremost a sculptor because sculptors possessed the almost divine power to "make man." Wrestling with the stone, he strove to release the image, the Idea, locked within it. The basis for Michelangelo's artistic philosophy was Plato's theory of Forms, or Ideas (see Topic 10), and he held that by imitating Nature an artist could reveal the highest eternal truths. Unlike other Renaissance artists, he rejected Classical notions of balance and proportion, claiming that only the inspired judgment of the individual artist could create the rules for his art. His stubborn independence, coupled with his irascible and impulsive manner, won him few friends—the popular and worldly Raphael described him as "lonely as the hangman."

One of the early works to win him fame was the *Pietà*, which shows Mary holding the body of the dead Christ. The contrast between the youthful grace of the grieving mother and the leaden weight of the body, legs dangling, already looks forward to the emotional extremes of later versions of the same subject.

Another figure from the same period, the *David*, has become one of the icons of the Florentine Renaissance. After finishing the *Pietà*, Michelangelo returned from

Raphael, *Madonna of the Meadows.* 1508. 44½ inches by 34 inches (113 by 87 cm). This is one of a series of scenes showing the Virgin with the Christ Child and the infant St. John the Baptist (identified by the cross he carries) for which Raphael used a pyramidal composition.

Erich Lessing/Art Resource, New York

Rome to Florence, drawn by the chance to "release" from a gigantic block of stone—on which other sculptors had worked in vain—the "Idea" within it. The result was the stern, tense image of David, a young man poised between thought and action.

The climax of the first part of Michelangelo's career was the colossal decoration of the ceiling of the Sistine Chapel in the Vatican. Michelangelo painted the entire ceiling, some 5,800 square feet in area, in the four years between 1508 and 1512. In glowing, luminous colors (revealed by their recent cleaning), the paintings depict no less a theme than the Creation, Fall, and Redemption of Man. On the sides, Classical and Hebrew figures foretell the coming of Christ, while in the very center Michelangelo shows *The Creation of Adam* (see p. 370). The hand of God reaches out to awaken the first man by endowing him with the divine spark of life. Adam's body represents not only natural beauty but also the manifestation of the soul itself.

Toward the end of his long artistic odyssey, Michelangelo's style became increasingly complex and tormented. The terrifying scene of *The Last Judgment*, painted on the end wall of the Sistine Chapel 25 years after the ceiling frescoes, echoes to the blaring of trumpets. All creation seems to cower before the gigantic figure of Christ, as the dead arise and the damned hurtle down to eternal torment. Gone is the idealizing Neoplatonic beauty and calm order of the earlier works. The swirling forms and distorted proportions foreshadow the Baroque art of the 17th century, which they directly inspired.

HARMONY AND COLOR: THE PAINTING OF THE VENETIAN REPUBLIC

While many of the leading Renaissance artists and their styles moved between Florence, Rome, and the cities of northern Italy, the Republic of Venice maintained its cultural independence. Venetian artists used ideas developed elsewhere in Italy, but in distinct ways. The main interest of Florentine Renaissance artists was design, and drawing was regarded as crucial in achieving a sense of intellectual order. For the Venetians, color was the primary means of expression. The light of the lagoon that surrounds the city, soft and warm in summer, pearly grey with mist in winter, glows in the paintings of the painters of the *Serenissima*—most serene of cities.

Venice's detachment from the mainstream of Renaissance cultural movements in part reflected the strength of earlier Byzantine influence there, but a more important cause was the city's geographic position and economic ties. As gateway to the East, the Venetian Republic found itself increasingly involved in a protracted struggle with the Ottoman

Erich Lessing/Art Resource

Michelangelo, *David.* 1501–1504. Height 18 feet (5.49 m). As the figure leans back, most of the weight is borne by the right leg (supported by a tree trunk), in a position called in Italian *contraposto*. The statue was intended to be seen from below—hence the slightly elongated neck.

PERSPECTIVES FROM THE PAST

ART AND ARTISTS IN THE RENAISSANCE

Our knowledge of art, artists, and patrons in Renaissance Italy owes much to the *The Lives of the Artists* of Giorgio Vasari (1511–1574), himself a painter and architect. *The Lives* first appeared in 1550, and Vasari published an enlarged version in 1568. His account includes descriptions of more than 100 artists working over a period of some three centuries and combines comments on their works with information about their patrons and the world around them—in the case of the most recent artists, including Michelangelo, based on Vasari's personal observations and inquiries.

Another artist who also wrote was the sculptor Benvenuto Cellini (1500–1571), although his *Autobiography* is devoted to recording, in suitably embroidered form, his own glories rather than the achievements of others. His account of the casting of the *Perseus* describes the artist's triumph in the face of the technical problems of casting a lifesize bronze statue, as well as over the knaves, fools, and doubters who surrounded him.

The production of art objects was, of course, a matter of business in Renaissance Italy. The portion from Cellini's *Autobiography* is followed by a rather more prosaic document, a contract drawn up by the Venetian painter Cima da Conegliano (c. 1459–1518) for the payment for one of his altarpieces.

Vasari on Michelangelo

Behind Vasari's Lives of the Artists, *there is a not-so-hidden agenda: After the empty years under Byzantine influence, Italian art was brought back to life by Giotto, and proceeded to develop until it reached its highest point in the work of the divinely inspired Michelangelo. The fact that this thesis may seem familiar is a tribute to the enormous influence of Vasari on subsequent art historians.*

Michelangelo: Cosmic Genius

While the artists who came after Giotto were doing their best to imitate and to understand nature, bending every faculty to increase that high comprehension sometimes called intelligence, the Almighty took pity on their often fruitless labor. He resolved to send to earth a spirit capable of supreme expression in all the arts, one able to give form to painting, perfection to sculpture, and grandeur to architecture. The Almighty Creator also graciously endowed this chosen one with an understanding of philosophy and with the grace of poetry. And because he had observed that in Tuscany men were more zealous in study and more diligent in labor than in the rest of Italy, He decreed that Florence should be the birthplace of this divinely endowed spirit.

In the Casentino, therefore, in 1475, a son was born to Signor Lodovico di Leonardo di Buonarotti Simoni. . . .

[The painting of the Sistine Chapel.] Michelangelo returned to Rome and was asked by Pope Julius II to paint the ceiling of the [Sistine] chapel, a great and difficult labor. Our artist, aware of his own inexperience, excused himself from the undertaking. He proposed that the work be given to Raphael. The more he refused, the more the impetuous Pope insisted. A quarrel threatened. Michelangelo saw that the Pope was determined, so he resolved to accept the task. His Holiness ordered Bramante to prepare the scaffolding. This he did by suspending the ropes through perforations in the ceiling. Michelangelo asked how the holes were going to be filled in when the painting was done. Bramante replied that they could think about it when the time came.

Michelangelo saw that the architect was either incapable or unfriendly, and he went straight to the Pope to say that the scaffolding would not do and that Bramante did not know how to construct one. Julius, in the presence of Bramante, replied that Michelangelo might make it his own way. This he did by the use of a method that did not injure the walls, and which has since been pursued by Bramante and others. Michelangelo gave the ropes that were taken from Bramante's scaffolding to a poor carpenter, who sold them for a sum that made up his daughter's dowry.

For this work Michelangelo was paid three thousand crowns by the Pope. He may have spent twenty-five for colors. He worked under great personal inconvenience, constantly looking upward, so that he seriously injured his eyes. For months afterward he could read a letter only when he held it above his head. I can vouch for the pain of this kind of labor. When I painted the ceiling of the palace of Duke Cosimo [Palazzo Vecchio in Florence], I never could have finished the work without a special support for my head. As it is, I still feel the effects of it, and I wonder that Michelangelo endured it so well. But, as the work progressed, his zeal for his art increased daily, and he grudged no labor and was insensible to all fatigue.

Down the center of the ceiling is the History of the World, from the Creation to the Deluge. The Prophets and the Sibyls, five on each side and one at each end, are painted on the corbels. The lunettes portray the genealogy of Christ. Michelangelo used no perspective, nor any one fixed point of sight, but was satisfied to paint each division with perfection of design. Truly this chapel has been, and is, the very light of our art. Everyone capable of judging stands amazed at the excellence of his work, at the grace and flexibility, the beautiful truth of proportion of the exquisite nude forms. These are varied in every way in expression and form. Some of the figures are seated, some are in motion, while others hold up festoons of oak leaves and acorns, the device of Pope Julius. . . .

Michelangelo's powers were so great that his sublime ideas were often inexpressible. He spoiled many works because of this. Shortly before his death he burned a large number of designs, sketches, and cartoons so that none might see the labors he endured in his resolution to achieve perfection. None will marvel that Michelangelo was a lover of solitude, devoted as he was to art, and, therefore, never alone or without food for contemplation. . . . Those who say he would not teach others are wrong. I have been present many times when he assisted his intimates or any who asked his counsels . . . he was an ardent admirer of beauty for art, and knew how to select the most beautiful, but he was not liable to the undue influence of beauty. This his whole life has proved. In all things he was most moderate. He ate frugally at the close of the day's work. Though rich, he lived like a poor man and rarely had a guest at his table. He would accept no gifts for fear of being under an obligation.

This master, as I said at the beginning, was certainly sent by God as an example of what an artist could be. I, who can thank God for unusual happiness, count it among the greatest of my blessings that I was born while Michelangelo still lived, was found worthy to have him for my master, and was accepted as his trusted friend.

From Vasari, G., trans. A. B. Hinds. *Lives of the Painters, Sculptors and Architects.* Copyright © 1900.

Cellini on the Casting of the Perseus

By contrast to the unworldly and reclusive Michelangelo, the Florentine goldsmith and sculptor Benvenuto Cellini led a violent and adventurous life. He fought for the pope in Rome and for Francis I in Paris, and spent time in prison on a charge of theft brought by the bastard son of Pope Paul III. Toward the end of his life, he dictated to an apprentice in his workshop his autobiography, from which the following passage comes.

Continued

All his stories feature himself as the hero, generally triumphing against the plots of his enemies and overcoming the most insuperable difficulties. The casting of the lifesize bronze statue of Perseus with the Head of Medusa, a work still standing in Florence's Piazza Signoria, presented him with his greatest artistic challenge, and his account of it is justly famous.

As his workshop prepares the mold and lights the furnace, Cellini himself is overcome with a fever—probably brought on by nervous strain—and takes to his bed in despair: "I feel more ill than I ever did in all my life and verily believe that it will kill me before a few hours are over." When one of his assistants, however, brings him the news that the statue is ruined, he rushes back to take charge.

Casting the Perseus: The Final Stages

When I had got my clothes on, I strode with soul bent on mischief toward the workshop; there I beheld the men, whom I had left erewhile in such high spirits, standing stupefied and downcast. I began at once and spoke: "Up with you! Attend to me! Since you have not been able or willing to obey the directions I gave you, obey me now that I am with you to conduct my work in person. Let no one contradict me, for in cases like this we need the aid of hand and hearing, not advice." When I had uttered these words, a certain Maestro Alessandro Lastricati broke silence and said: "Look you, Benvenuto, you are going to attempt an enterprise which the laws of art do not sanction, and which cannot succeed." I turned on him with such fury and so full of mischief, that he and all the rest of them exclaimed with one voice: "On then! Give orders! We will obey your least commands, so long as life is left

in us." I believe they spoke thus feelingly because they thought I must fall shortly dead on the ground. I went immediately to inspect the furnace, and found that the metal was all curdled; an accident which we call "being caked." I told two of the hands to cross the road, and fetch from the house of the butcher Capretta a load of young oak-wood, which had lain dry for above a year; this wood had previously been offered me by Madama Ginevra, wife of the said Capretta. So soon as the first armfuls arrived, I began to fill the grate beneath the furnace. Now oak-wood of that kind heats more powerfully than any other sort of tree; and for this reason, where a slow fire is wanted, as in the case of gun-foundry, alder or pine is preferred. Accordingly, when the logs took fire, oh! how the cake began to stir beneath that awful heat, to glow and sparkle in a blaze! At the same time I kept stirring up the channels, and sent men upon the roof to stop the conflagration, which had gathered force from the increased combustion in the furnace; also, I caused boards, carpets, and other hangings to be set up against the garden, in order to protect us from the violence of the rain of sparks.

All of a sudden an explosion took place, attended by a tremendous flash of flame, as though a thunderbolt had formed and been discharged amongst us. Unwonted and appalling terror astonished every one, and me more even than the rest. When the din was over and the dazzling light extinguished, we began to look each other in the face. Then I discovered that the cap of the furnace had blown up, and the bronze was bubbling up from its source beneath. So I had the mouths of my mold immediately opened, and at the same time drove in the two

Turks in the century following the Turkish conquest of Constantinople (Istanbul) in 1453. The French and Spanish invasions that shook Florence and Rome in the years of the High Renaissance (see Topic 34) had no significant effect on Venetian politics. On the only important occasion when the other Italian and European powers did intervene in Venetian affairs, it was to fight at the Battle of Lepanto, in 1571, on the side of the Venetians against the Turks.

One of the factors that helped Venetian painters to develop their love of color was the arrival in Venice in 1475 of Antonello da Messina (c. 1430–1479), the only major artist of the Quattrocento born south of Rome. Either in Flanders, or, more probably, through contact with a Flemish artist working in northern Italy, Antonello had learned to work with oil paint, and he introduced the new technique to the Venetians. Oil paint permitted a far greater range of colors than the tempera (egg-based paint) or fresco used by artists elsewhere in Italy, and Venetian artists quickly took advantage of its possibilities. As for style, there is little in Venetian art of the intellectual rigor of Leonardo, let alone the *terribilità* of Michelangelo. Instead, Venetian painters concentrated on more gentle, poetic themes.

plugs which kept back the molten metal. But I noticed that it did not flow as rapidly as usual, the reason being probably that the fierce heat of the fire we kindled had consumed its base alloy. Accordingly I sent for all my pewter platters, bowls, and dishes, to the number of some two hundred pieces, and had a portion of them cast one by one into the channels, the rest into the furnace. This expedient succeeded, and every one could now perceive that my bronze was in most perfect liquefaction, and my mold was filling; whereupon they all with heartiness and happy cheer assisted and obeyed my bidding, while I, now here, now there, gave orders, helped with my own hands, and cried aloud: "O God! Thou that by Thy immeasurable power didst rise from the dead, and in Thy glory didst ascend to heaven!" . . . even thus in a moment my mold was filled; and seeing my work finished, I fell upon my knees, and with all my heart gave thanks to God.

From Cellini, B., trans. J. A. Symonds. *The Life of Benvenuto Cellini Written by Himself.* Copyright © 1906.

A Venetian Painter Contracts to Produce an Altarpiece

Many of the most important Renaissance works of art were made on commission for churches or monasteries. The following document was written in his own hand by the Venetian painter Cima da Conegliano for a work he painted in 1513.

Contract Between Cima da Conegliano and the Fathers of St. Anna

In the name of Jesus Christ and Mary. 18 April 1513, in Venice. Memorandum of agreement between me, Giovanni Battista da Conegliano, painter, living in the parish of San Luca in Venice, and Messer Alvise Grisoni, citizen of Capodistria, and procurator of the reverend fathers of S. Anna, Observants of the order of St. Francis. That I shall make for the said church a painted altarpiece and gild its frame, using good quality colors, all at my own expense, and with the figures represented as they appear in the drawing made by the frame-carver. All this shall be for a fee of seventy ducats, on the condition that when the work is complete, the said Messer Alvise, acting in the name of the aforementioned fathers, shall be at liberty to seek professional advice from experts chosen by him and by myself, Giovanni Battista, regarding the value of the work. And I promise to have the work ready for him by next Christmas. I acknowledge receipt of a first payment of ten ducats now, and I understand that I will receive thirty ducats when the work is complete, and the final thirty when it is delivered. As a sign of my good faith, this agreement is written in my own hand, and it is witnessed by master Vettor da Feltre, woodcarver, and my pupil Marco Luciani, both of whose signatures are appended below.

From Humfrey, Peter, *The Altarpiece in Renaissance Venice.* Yale University Press. Copyright © 1993.

THE HIGH RENAISSANCE IN VENICE: TITIAN

Titian (c. 1490–1576) was the dominating figure in Venetian art for more than 50 years and one of the supreme masters of Western painting. He was the first to use oil paint on canvas, rather than on wooden panels, the technique followed by most painters ever since. His ability to use color to depict texture—rich satin, glossy skin, thick rich hair—seems limitless. His subjects ranged from frankly sensual nudes to psychologically acute portraits to the deep spirituality of his later religious paintings.

One of his most influential works was *The Venus of Urbino* (see p. 370), painted when Titian was at the height of his powers for the duke of that city. The nude goddess reclines diagonally on crumpled sheets, in a pose imitated countless times by later artists. In the background two servants search in a chest, perhaps for a gown. The warm flesh, the fluffy little dog dozing at the foot of the couch, the deep red tones in the skirt of the standing servant behind—all play their part in building the composition by means of color.

No other Venetian artist after Titian equaled his breadth of vision. In the works of Tintoretto (1518–1594),

Michelangelo, *The Creation of Adam*. 1508–1512. 8 feet by 9 feet 2 inches (2.44 by 2.8 m). The scene forms part of a complex symbolic meaning behind the ceiling frescoes of the Sistine Chapel. Behind God's left arm, Michelangelo has placed a woman and child, representing both Eve with her children and the "New Eve," the Virgin and Child of the New Testament. Michelangelo signed the fresco—perhaps the summit of Renaissance painting—as "Michelangelo, sculptor."

Titian, *The Venus of Urbino*. 1536. 3 feet 11 inches by 5 feet 5 inches (1.19 by 1.62 m). Titian here shows a characteristic Venetian interest in richness of color and texture, rather than the Florentine preoccupation with mathematical precision of line and composition. Note the emphasis on luxury: the rich brocade, the bouquet of flowers, and the small, fluffy pet dog.

Titian's mystery becomes theatrical, with twisting figures combined in dynamic compositions. Tintoretto's emphatic style had much in common with similar developments elsewhere in Italy in the latter part of the Cinquecento. Following the extremes of Michelangelo's *Last Judgment,* artists developed a style called **Mannerism,** in which the figures were deliberately distorted and exaggerated. Mannerists such as the Florentine Bronzino (1503–1572) replaced the calm, Classical balance of Renaissance art with sophisticated elegance and intricate fantasy. The artificiality of the Mannerist conventions soon proved stilted and repetitive, and by the end of the century Mannerism was a spent force.

Putting the Visual Arts of the Italian Renaissance in Perspective

The Renaissance in Italy represented the rebirth of Classical culture, and, like the artists of Periclean Athens, the artists of the Renaissance knew that theirs was a unique moment in Western civilization. Like the builders of the Parthenon, Michelangelo intended his work in the Sistine Chapel as a "monument for all time."

In the past, sculptors and painters built on the achievements of their immediate predecessors to create new styles. The artists of the Renaissance, beginning with Brunelleschi and Donatello, deliberately and decisively broke with their traditions, to rediscover truth and beauty by following the aesthetic and philosophical ideals of antiquity. They invented more than they rediscovered, and by looking back they thrust art forward. The rapid speed with which Renaissance artists found new ways of describing human life and the world of nature gives their work a special excitement.

At the same time, Renaissance art represented just one aspect of a more general change of outlook in Western society. The career of a Michelangelo exemplified the growing development of civic identity, coupled with a new awareness of individual possibilities. The new learning, the birth of science, and the art of diplomacy are all other ways in which Renaissance culture and society reflected the sense of a fresh beginning.

The Early Renaissance in Florence was the product of several historical forces: the rise of the city-state and the economic developments that made possible the accumulation of personal fortunes such as that of the Medici. Other events also played their part: The precipitous decline of the Byzantine Empire and the fall of Constantinople in 1453 drove Byzantine scholars and intellectuals to take refuge in the West, bringing with them precious manuscripts of Classical works.

The remarkable achievement of Renaissance artists was to forge from these varied historical conditions a "modern style," which changed the way we look at the world. Their works remain relevant still and central to the Western intellectual tradition.

Questions for Further Study

1. How did Renaissance artists break with traditions? To what extent did they return to Classical styles?
2. What were the main developments in Renaissance architecture?
3. What role did private patronage play in the artistic life of the Renaissance? In what ways did it change the status of the artist?
4. Which characteristics of Michelangelo's art led his contemporaries to regard him as exceptional even by Renaissance standards? How far have later generations echoed their judgment?

Suggestions for Further Reading

Adams, Laurie Schneider. *Key Monuments of the Italian Renaissance*. Denver, CO, 1999.

Brown, Patricia. *Art and Life in Renaissance Venice*. New York, 1997.

Carmen, Charles H. *Images of Humanist Ideals in Italian Rennaissance Art*. Lewiston, NY, 2000.

Cole, Alison. *Virtue and Magnificence: Art of the Italian Renaissance Courts*. New York, 1995.

Gilbert, Creighton, ed. *Italian Art 1400-1500. Sources and Documents*. Evanston, IL, 1992.

Hollingsworth, Mary. *Patronage in Renaissance Italy: From 1400 to the Early Sixteenth Century*. Baltimore, 1994.

Humfrey, Peter. *Painting in Renaissance Venice*. New Haven, CT, 1995.

Kemp, Martin. *Behind the Picture: Art and Evidence in the Italian Renaissance*. New Haven, CT, 1997.

Nuland, Sherwin B. *Leonardo da Vinci*. New York, 2000.

Partridge, Loren. *The Art of Renaissance Rome*. New York, 1996.

Turner, A. Richard. *Renaissance Florence: The Invention of a New Art*. New York, 1997.

Welch, Evelyn. *Art and Society in Italy, 1350-1500*. Oxford, 1997.

InfoTrac College Edition

Enter the search term *Renaissance* using the Subject Guide.

Enter the search term *humanism* using the Subject Guide.

Enter the search term *Leonardo da Vinci* using Key Terms.

Enter the search term *Michelangelo* using Key Terms.

ARTS AND LETTERS IN RENAISSANCE EUROPE

As the effects of the Italian Renaissance began to diffuse throughout the rest of Europe, they produced vast and rapid cultural changes. The most powerful new force was printing, which was first invented in the mid-15th century. By 1500, books and pamphlets were circulating in increasing numbers, spreading ideas as the rate of literacy rose. One of the most important long-term consequences was the rise of vernacular literature.

In northern Europe, the humanistic learning developed in Italy took on new forms, as Christian humanists like the Dutch Erasmus combined Classical ideas with traditional Christian attitudes. Both Erasmus and his English friend Thomas More wrote books attacking the religious and social attitudes of their times, in an attempt to define the nature of a truly Christian society. Erasmus's attacks on corruption in the church foreshadowed many of the criticisms of Martin Luther.

In Italy, the leading humanists of the High Renaissance continued to develop themes taken from Classical literature and learning. Castiglione's book, *The Courtier,* discussed the nature of virtue and the ideals of Platonic love. Machiavelli drew on the history of Republican Rome as background for his book, *The Prince,* a study of political power.

As the artistic advances made in Italy began to cross the Alps, Northern artists adapted their styles accordingly. Van Eyck and his Flemish school, working in oils, soon established a market throughout Europe—including Italy—for their finely detailed panel paintings. The Flemish painters retained stylistic links with their Late Medieval past. The great German painter Albrecht Dürer, by contrast, drew on the High Renaissance to forge his own personal style.

The art of Renaissance music often transcended national boundaries. The musical traditions of northern Europe influenced composers in both Rome and Venice, where two musicians from the Low Countries, Josquin des Pres and Adrian Willaert, held important posts.

Toward the middle of the 16th century, the Reformation began to exert a growing influence on the arts in northern Europe. Protestant denunciations of the use of paintings and statues in churches caused a rapid decline in the production of sacred visual art. Literature and music, however, met with the reformers' approval. The results laid the foundations for the flourishing of sacred music and secular painting in 17th-century northern Europe.

THE PRINTING REVOLUTION

The invention of printing with movable type revolutionized Western civilization. The earliest known manufacture of individual characters that could be combined and reused occurred in China as early as the 11th century, but a similar technique developed in Europe only in the mid-15th century. Its introduction is generally credited to the German Johann Gutenberg (c. 1397–1468). The first printed Bible, the so-called Gutenberg Bible, appeared in 1455. Twenty years later, William Caxton (c. 1422–1491) published the first book printed in English, and in 1501 Aldus Manutius (1450–1515) began to sell inexpensive editions of the classics, printed by his Aldine Press in Venice.

THE IMPLICATIONS OF PRINTING

Probably no technological development before the 19th century created such profound changes in Western culture as the invention of printing. The implications of the communications revolution it inaugurated are still with us at the dawn of the 21st century. Among its consequences were the standardization of texts, the acceleration of science, the spread of education—including, increasingly, that of women—and the rapid diffusion of new ideas. Martin Luther's Protestant Reformation was one of the first movements to benefit from the circulation of books and pamphlets (see Topic 39).

Before the mid-15th century, books were extremely expensive, and the supply never equalled the demand. Handwritten copies were produced by stationers—so-called because they worked in a settled, or stationary, place of business—and sold or rented out by booksellers. Most dealers in books worked for the universities. University officials kept a stringent control on the trade and fixed the prices for the benefit of their students, who often hired a book for use during a university session and then returned it to the bookshop. The only people who received no financial benefit from the circulation of books were the authors.

With the introduction of printing technology, the publishers took over the production and distribution of books. The figures attest to the astonishing growth in the publishing industry. By 1500, European presses had distributed between 6 and 9 million books in 13,000 different editions. One of the most popular works of Erasmus, *In Praise of Folly*, went through 27 editions in his own lifetime. Many of these were pirated, generally from the printers to whom authors customarily sold their rights. Unless authors published their own works, they continued to make little profit from their "intellectual property." The first international copyright agreement was signed only in 1886, and the United States did not subscribe until 1929.

PRINTING AND THE VERNACULAR

Most educated Europeans before the Renaissance used two languages: their own native tongue—the vernacular—and Latin. Some popular literature in the vernacular appeared in France, Germany, and England (see Topic 28), but in many countries the first literary works in their own languages were printed ones, often translations of the Bible into the vernacular. In Finland, the Finnish language appeared in written form for the first time as late as the 16th century, in the first printed Bible in Finnish.

In preparing their translations, scholars did not restrict themselves to the standard Latin version of the Bible. Erasmus used three separate Greek manuscripts to compile an edition of the New Testament in Latin. Martin Luther used Erasmus's work in making his great translation of the Bible into German, while for the Psalms he turned to the original Hebrew edition, which had been published in 1516.

When, a century later, the so-called King James Version of the Bible appeared in England, its translators claimed to have consulted editions and commentaries in Hebrew, Chaldean, Syriac, Greek, and Latin, as well as modern versions in Spanish, French, Italian, and Dutch. The consequences for the development of literary culture were profound. In England, the wide diffusion of both the King James Bible and the Anglican *Book of Common Prayer* shaped the future history of the language.

By no means were all printed works in the vernacular of a religious nature. Scholars continued to use Latin for learned communications, but authors who wanted to reach the wider, less academic audience made possible by printing increasingly wrote in their own languages. Castiglione and Machiavelli both published in Italian, and Sir Thomas More in English. Montaigne wrote his essays, inspired by a study of the Classics, in French.

Portion of a page from the Gutenberg Bible. 1455. The Latin text of the Lord's Prayer (Matthew 6, 9-13) begins on the fourth line with "Pater noster." The first edition of this Bible, printed at Mainz, probably consisted of no more than 150 copies.

The printing revolution was not limited to literary texts. The publication of music led to the wide circulation of Lutheran hymns and secular Italian madrigals. Dürer and other contemporary artists were quick to exploit the possibilities of the print, first in the form of relatively easily produced woodcuts and then in the more difficult medium of line engravings on copper plates. Book publishers began to include visual material in the form of illustrations or diagrams in their printed volumes. No less important in an era of exploration was the printing and circulation of maps and charts (see Topic 38).

The long-term consequence of all these innovations was to undermine the authority of the established institutions of medieval culture and society. People who could read for themselves had independent access to the ideas of others and had less need to turn to the church, the monasteries, or the universities for guidance and instruction. The invention of printing was a key factor in the evolution of the secular state.

Albrecht Dürer, *Portrait of Erasmus of Rotterdam.* 1526. 9¼ inches by 7½ inches (25 by 19 cm). The inscribed panel in the upper left corner is, in characteristic Renaissance style, written in both Latin and Greek. The Latin lines tell us that Erasmus posed for Dürer's portrait, while the Greek refers to the power of the written word. The artist's monogram below appears on almost all of his work.

THE NORTHERN HUMANISTS: EDUCATION FOR A CHRISTIAN SOCIETY

As humanism began to spread in northern Europe, thinkers there tried to reconcile humanist principles with Christianity. These northern Christian humanists accepted many of the values of Classical Antiquity—idealism, the power of reason, the importance of ancient texts—but used them as a basis for reforming the Christianity of their day, rather than as an end in themselves.

In part, Christian humanism in northern Europe drew its strength from resentment at the corruption of the church in Rome. In Germany, in particular, hostility toward Italian religious leaders combined with nationalism to create a wish to throw off Roman domination and return Christianity to its simple origins. Elsewhere, northern humanists directed their fire against social inequities as well as religious abuses. The English statesman and writer Sir Thomas More (1478–1535) published a satire called *Utopia* (1516–1517). It describes an ideal state, Utopia (his invented name means "no place" in Greek), on an island in the New World. The citizens of Utopia live in a social and political paradise, and when one of them visits England, he contrasts his own society with the social injustices he finds there. The title of More's book added a new word to the English language.

ERASMUS, PRINCE OF HUMANISTS

One of More's closest friends was the man recognized by his contemporaries as the "Prince of Humanists," the Dutch priest and intellectual Desiderius Erasmus (1466–1536). A truly international figure, Erasmus studied and taught in Italy, at Oxford and Cambridge, and at Paris.

The writings of Erasmus were the most comprehensive humanist attempt to reconcile Classical learning and simple Christianity. He revered the Classical emphasis on the personal dignity of the individual and on the importance of education. He steeped himself in the works of ancient literature available to him. At the same time, as a Christian, he tried to return to the original "philosophy of Christ," as it was expressed in the Sermon on the Mount, claiming that pure faith was more important than formal religious ceremony. He also attacked the complexity of Medieval Catholic theology, claiming that some issues could never be known: He felt that Christians needed to believe only such basic aspects of their faith as the Creed.

Erasmus wrote his most successful book in 1509 while staying in England as a house guest of Sir Thomas More. The original Latin form of its title, *In Praise of Folly*, was a pun in honor of his distinguished host: The Latin words *Encomium Moriae* can mean "praise of folly" or "praise of More." The tone is lighthearted, but Erasmus is unsparing in his denunciations of social and religious corruption. Among his targets are hypocritical priests and cardinals, fraudulent scholars, and venal lawyers.

For all the force of his criticism, Erasmus was a true moderate. Unlike Martin Luther, he believed that it was possible to reform the church from within. When Luther's

Reformation split the Christian world, Erasmus remained a Catholic. Both sides denounced him: the Catholics for his criticisms of the church and the Protestants because he would not throw his considerable weight behind the Reform movement. The final break between Erasmus and Luther came in 1524, when Erasmus published a pamphlet asserting that humans had free will. Luther's reply came in a tract published the following year. Human will, he claimed, was fatally flawed, and only the grace of God could rescue an individual from the fires of hell. The two men never spoke again.

THE COURTIER AND THE PRINCE: HANDBOOKS OF RENAISSANCE STRATEGY

While Christian humanists in northern Europe hotly debated the best way to achieve religious reform, humanist writers in Italy occupied themselves with more worldly affairs.

CASTIGLIONE THE COURTIER

Baldassare Castiglione (1478–1529), born into an ancient aristocratic family, received a thorough humanistic educa-

Raphael, *Portrait of Baldassare Castiglione*, c. 1514. 2 feet 6 inches by 2 feet 2 inches (76 by 66 cm). The expert on good manners turns gravely toward us, dressed in rich but not ostentatious clothes. The neutral background and sober gaze reflect Castiglione's views on how the ideal courtier should behave.

tion before serving in the diplomatic corps of Milan, Mantua, and eventually Urbino, where he settled for several years. The duke of Urbino was one of the leading artistic patrons of the day, and his court was a center for writers and intellectuals.

Early in his stay at Urbino, Castiglione conceived the idea of writing a book about life at an ideal court. The result, *The Courtier*, appeared in an edition published by the Aldine Press in 1528, the year before its author's death. Castiglione's work takes the form of a series of imaginary discussions between members of the court on the qualities of the ideal courtier. Drawing on the works of a host of ancient authors, from Plato to Cicero, Castiglione's characters discuss a wide range of topics: Classical views of virtue, the notion of chivalry, Platonic (that is, ideal) love, and above all the nature of the true courtier.

The most important quality in an ideal courtier—and human being—is versatility. Humanistic learning is important, as is a knowledge of Greek and Latin, but so are horsemanship and skills with a sword. The ideal courtier should write both prose and verse, appreciate music and painting, and also hunt, wrestle, and play tennis. Impeccable morals must be combined with exquisite manners and the ability to make fascinating conversation. In love, the true gentleman should worship his beloved's beauty of mind as much as that of her body.

None of these attributes should be so marked that it dominates the others—Castiglione's ideal is the *uomo universale*, the well-rounded person. Equally important is the cultivation of *sprezzatura*, an almost untranslatable Italian word, which suggests an air of casual ease. None of the courtier's accomplishments must seem an effort or draw attention to itself.

The imaginary participants in Castiglione's dialogues also discuss the ideal court lady. With the exception of athletics and warfare, she should cultivate the same skills as men, adding to them charm, grace, and physical attractiveness. She should wear little makeup and avoid calling attention to herself in dress, conduct, or reputation. Above all, she should be feminine, for women exert a civilizing influence on the rough male world. Castiglione argues that women should be the educated equals of men because they make an equally important contribution to society. The emphasis on education and the worth of the individual, whether male or female, is the product of Castiglione's humanistic training, and in strong contrast with the medieval tradition whereby women were excluded from universities.

It is easy to criticize Castiglione for his excessive concern with refinement and the details of courtly decorum, but his description of the ideals of Italian Renaissance court society at the moment of its greatest splendor is deeply felt and elegantly expressed.

MACHIAVELLI THE REALIST

Castiglione's essentially optimistic view of human nature is certainly in the strongest contrast with the opinions of Niccolò Machiavelli (1469–1527), whose writings on political theory drew on his practical experience as statesman. In

1498, when the Florentines drove out their Medici rulers and set up a republic, Machiavelli served his city as diplomat. In the course of his missions, he met many of the leading figures of the day. Among those to make a mark on the observant ambassador were the ruthless Cesare Borgia (1476–1507) and his notorious sister Lucrezia Borgia (1480–1519).

In 1512, with the fall of the Republic and the return of the Medici, the new rulers dismissed Machiavelli from his post, imprisoned and tortured him, and eventually banished him to his family's country estate just outside Florence. Living in exile there, within a year he had completed his most influential work, *The Prince,* a practical guide to the use of political power. It circulated in manuscript during Machiavelli's lifetime, but was published only in 1532, after his death.

Reactions to its apparently cynical endorsement of tyranny and treachery were predictably mixed. The Catholic Church denounced it and listed it on the *Index of Prohibited Books.* The very word *Machiavellian* soon came to mean scheming and unscrupulous, and in England "Old Nick" became synonymous with the devil. On the other hand, many rulers turned to *The Prince* for practical guidance in running a state. Among Machiavelli's later readers and admirers were Catherine the Great of Russia and Napoleon.

Machiavelli's attitude toward political power grew out of the specific historical context of his times. He saw the Italian states of the 16th century as helpless and at the mercy of the rivalries of France and Spain. Italy was "without head, without order, beaten, despoiled, lacerated." When the republic that the Florentines had set up to regain control over their own destiny ended in abject failure, Machiavelli believed that only the creation of a powerful and stable Florentine state could protect Italy against constant foreign intervention. The Medici seemed to offer the promise of strong government, and the Medici pope then ruling in Rome, Leo X, could provide support.

For Florence's new rulers to be effective, however, they needed to set aside moral scruples and take firm charge. Machiavelli's ideal of good government was that of the ancient Roman Republic (509–31 B.C.): He saw its citizens as virtuous and considered the volunteer citizen legions of ancient Rome infinitely preferable to the mercenary armies of his own day. The first crucial step for a modern ruler, he believed, was to reduce the political power of the church. Christianity's role in government had proved disastrous, and the church should limit itself to purely spiritual matters.

The head of state, the Prince of the book's title, should rule by using power wisely and ruthlessly. No moral consideration should deter the Prince from performing this task. Thus cruelty, sensibly used, consolidates power and discourages revolution. Nor was honesty a factor: "A prince must not keep faith when by doing so it would be against his self-interest." In short, because his subjects lack virtue, the Prince must do whatever is necessary to keep the state intact. Nor should he overestimate his subjects: "They are ungrateful, changeable, runaways in danger, eager for gain; while you do well by them, they are all yours; when you are in need, they turn away."

THE CONQUEST OF REALITY: RENAISSANCE ART IN THE NORTH

As in the other arts, developments in Italian Renaissance painting took a while to circulate north of the Alps. When, in the mid-15th century, Florentine merchants began to expand their trade with Flanders, they found a brilliant school of painters already flourishing there.

JAN VAN EYCK AND THE FLEMISH SCHOOL

The greatest of all Flemish painters was Jan van Eyck (before 1395–1441), whose art, according to the father of Raphael, "challenges nature itself." His fame was based on his remarkable use of color, his extraordinary ability to render details realistically, and his technical innovations in the use of oil paint. When Antonello da Messina introduced the use of oil paint into Italy in 1475 (see Topic 35), he was using methods developed earlier in the century by Jan van Eyck.

One of Van Eyck's most celebrated works is a further illustration of the growing links between Italy and northern Europe. Another of the Medici agents in Flanders, Giovanni Arnolfini, who came from Lucca in Tuscany, was a counselor of the ruler of Flanders, the duke of Burgundy.

Jan van Eyck, *Giovanni Arnolfini and His Bride.* 1434. 32 by 23 inches (81 by 59.7 cm). One of the figures reflected in the mirror is perhaps the artist, as he stands in the doorway. The Latin words on the wall read: "Jan van Eyck was here."

The duke was patron of Van Eyck, and it was probably through this connection that Arnolfini commissioned Van Eyck to paint *The Marriage of Giovanni Arnolfini and Giovanna Cenami*. The artist signed the work and dated it, 1434, on the back wall visible in the painting.

Van Eyck's mastery is apparent in his naturalistic depictions of the various textures: fur, wood, metal, cloth. The sense of space is realistically conveyed, with the cool light coming in from the window illuminating bride and groom in the foreground, while the inner recesses of the room are in shadow. On the back wall, below the artist's signature, there hangs a mirror in which two figures (perhaps witnesses to the marriage) are reflected.

The literal, almost photographic, quality of the scene is the equivalent in three dimensions of the pages from the *Très Riches Heures* (see Topic 30), and typical of the finest Flemish art of the period. So is the abundant use of symbolism. The dog at the couple's feet perhaps represents fidelity. The apples by the window symbolize Adam and Eve, and thereby original sin, and the broom leaning on the wall outside stands for domestic care. Giovanna's hand is over her womb, and the tiny carved statue atop the chair in the background is of Margaret, patron saint of child-bearing.

BOSCH AND BRUEGHEL

If many of Van Eyck's contemporaries and immediate successors imitated his style, although without his superlative technique, two other Flemish artists of the period fit into no general category.

The first of them, Hieronymus Bosch (c. 1450–1516), is one of the great originals in the history of painting. His bizarre scenes depict a fantasy world of demons and monsters, in which the human activities seem as inexplicable as the creatures surrounding them. His most elaborate work, *The Garden of Earthly Delights*, illustrates Bosch's belief that the pleasures of the flesh lead to damnation. The journey from the Creation of Adam and Eve in the left-hand panel to the horrors of hell in the right-hand panel involves frantic scenes of erotic activity. Bosch's message seems to be that even if sinners have the possibility of seeking redemption through Christ, most people are too foolish and depraved to do so.

The other great Flemish painter of the 16th century, Pieter Brueghel (1525–1569), shared Bosch's pessimism, and many of his scenes show the violent consequences of human folly. For Brueghel, however, the transcendent power and beauty of Nature compensate for human sin. In paintings such as *Hunters in the Snow*, the figures shrink to mere specks, dwarfed by the majesty of the mountain landscape—perhaps a memory of the Alps, brought back from a trip the artist made to Italy.

DÜRER AND THE RENAISSANCE IN GERMANY

No northern painter was more influenced by Italian Renaissance ideas than the great German artist Albrecht Dürer (1471–1528). He visited Italy in 1494 and again in 1505–1507, when he spent most of his time in Venice, discussing art with Bellini and other Venetian painters. The

Hieronymus Bosch, *The Garden of Earthly Delights*, c. 1505–1510. 7 feet 2 inches by 6 feet 5 inches (2.2 by .97 m). Perhaps surprisingly, this catalog of the sins of the flesh was one of the favorite works of the gloomy Spanish king, Philip II. Its three panels represent a journey from Eden, where God nervously contemplates his new creations, Adam and Eve, to the diabolical scenes on the right-hand panel.

Derechos Reservaados © Museo Nacional del Prado, Madrid

Albrecht Dürer, *The Fall of Man (Adam and Eve)*. 1504. 10 by 7½ inches (25 by 19 cm). The animals symbolize the sins and diseases resulting from Adam and Eve's eating the apple from the Tree of Knowledge: The cat stands for pride and cruelty, the ox gluttony and sloth. The detailed anatomy of the human figures is an attempt to return to Classical models.

splendor of the Venetians' use of color made a deep impression on Dürer, and many of his works at this time imitate Venetian color techniques.

A true student of the Renaissance interest in Classical art, Dürer worked out a careful system of proportion based on his readings of Classical authors. In his engraving of *Adam and Eve*, the anatomy and proportions of the figures are based on Classical sculptures—an example of Christian humanism in visible form.

Toward the end of his life, Dürer abandoned painting and devoted himself to engraving and the writing of theoretical works on art. At the time of his death he was preparing *Four Books on Human Proportions*, a work that combined two of the basic concerns of the Renaissance: a return to Classical ideals of beauty, and the quest for scientific precision.

MUSIC IN THE HIGH RENAISSANCE

With the invention of printing and the circulation of printed music, the barriers between musical life in northern and southern Europe became less severe, and by the end of the 15th century, musicians were beginning to travel from one region to the other. The main musical centers in the High Renaissance were Rome and Venice in Italy; and France, Flanders, and England in the North.

MUSIC AT THE PAPAL COURT

The leading choir in Italy, that of the Sistine Chapel, was founded by Pope Sixtus IV in 1473. Its members were all male, with adolescent boys, their voices still unbroken, singing the soprano parts. Between 1486 and 1494, the director of music in the Sistine Chapel was the Flemish composer Josquin des Pres (c. 1440–1521), the greatest musician of his day. His works, many of them written especially for the Sistine choir, have a strong sense of formal structure and balance, and show careful attention to the word-setting—all characteristics likely to appeal to the Italian humanists.

Toward the mid-16th century, the dominant musical figure at Rome was Giovanni Pierluigi da Palestrina (1525–1594). After working his way up directing the choirs of various Roman basilicas, in 1571 he took charge of all music at the Vatican. Palestrina's period at the Vatican coincided with the reforms introduced at the Council of Trent, in response to the Protestant Reformation (see Topic 41). His music is generally traditional in style and preserves the roots of church music in Gregorian chant.

VENICE: MUSIC AT ST. MARK'S

By contrast with the essentially traditional style favored at Rome, Venetian composers were more experimental. In 1527 a Dutchman, Adrian Willaert (c. 1490–1562), became director of music at St. Mark's. Among his pupils were Andrea Gabrieli (c. 1520–1586) and Gabrieli's nephew Giovanni (c. 1556–1612). The latter became the most important Venetian composer of the day, and one of the most remarkable in Europe.

Many of the works written for performance in St. Mark's took advantage of the building's design, with two galleries, one on each side of the church. Giovanni Gabrieli frequently stationed a choir on either side, often reinforced with instruments, generally organ, but sometimes trumpets and even drums. The effect of the sounds coming from left and right—a kind of Renaissance stereophony—is often thrilling, as the massed voices and brass instruments echo and overlap in the interior of the church, which glittered with mosaics. If Roman composers such as Palestrina sought to find the equivalent of Raphael's ideal Classical beauty, the music of Gabrieli glows with the rich colors of Titian.

MUSIC IN NORTHERN EUROPE

Just as northern composers carried their styles south to Italy, so Italian musical forms worked their way to the North. The Italian madrigal, a setting of secular verse for three or more voices, became especially popular with northern composers.

One of the leading French composers of *chansons*, as madrigals were called in France, was Clément Janequin

(c. 1485–c. 1560). Janequin was famous for writing songs that told a story by imitating specific sounds—a form of early "program music." One of his best-known pieces was "La Guerre"—"The War"—in which the voices reproduce the noises of rattling guns, fanfares, and the shouts of soldiers. These French *chansons* lack the calm beauty and rich harmonies of the best Italian madrigals, but they have a striking rhythmic vitality and sense of fun to compensate.

In England the leading composer of the 16th century was Thomas Tallis (c. 1505–1585). A master of counterpoint, Tallis developed the art of combining different vocal lines to new heights of complexity. In his great setting of the text *Spem in Alium* ("Hope in Another"), he used no less than 40 separate individual voices, each winding independently around the others. The effect is of extraordinary emotional complexity coupled with the highest intellectual control.

Putting Arts and Letters in Renaissance Europe in Perspective

While writers and artists in Italy continued in the 16th century to work through many of the implications of the 15th-century Renaissance developments, those in northern Europe had a more complex task. In the first place, the break in the North between medieval culture and the new Renaissance ideas was less abrupt than in Italy. Painters like Bosch and composers like Tallis retained their links with the long medieval religious and cultural tradition of their art.

Then, too, Italians had the material remains of ancient culture around them. Raphael could study actual Roman sculptures as they emerged from the excavations he supervised in Rome, while Dürer had to develop his theories of ideal proportion from reading ancient texts.

The greatest difference of all was the religious split caused by the Reformation. There is scarcely a northern creative figure of note whose work was not influenced in one way or another by the upheavals of faith that marked the 16th century. Even Erasmus, who rejected Luther's break with the Catholic Church, reflected the uncertainty of the times in his writings.

Protestant attitudes toward the arts had long-term consequences for future cultural developments in northern Europe. Their rejection of the use of painting and sculpture in sacred buildings meant that, by the end of the 16th century, religious art had virtually died out there, to be replaced by secular themes such as the portrait and still life. Luther's encouragement of music, on the other hand, stimulated a wave of creative energy, which was to reach its highest point a century later in the works of Johann Sebastian Bach.

Questions for Further Study

1. How did Renaissance cultural developments differ in Italy and northern Europe? Were the differences consistent in all of the arts?
2. What was the effect of printing on Renaissance culture?
3. In what ways did Castiglione and Machiavelli, for all their differences, both express the spirit of their times?

Suggestions for Further Reading

Brown, Howard Mayer, and Louise K. Stein. *Music in the Renaissance.* Upper Saddle River, NJ, 1999.

Campbell, Lorne. *The Fifteenth Century Netherlandish Schools.* London, 1998.

Eisenstein, E. *The Printing Revolution in Early Modern Europe.* Cambridge, MA, 1983.

Harbison, Craig. *The Mirror of the Artist: Northern Renaissance Art in its Historical Context.* New York, 1995.

Landau, David, and Peter Parshall. *The Renaissance Print:* New Haven, CT, 1994.

Marius, R. *Thomas More.* New York, 1984.

McGrath, A.E. *The Intellectual Origins of the European Reformation.* Oxford, 1987.

Rabil, A., ed. *Renaissance Humanism.* Philadelphia, 1988.

Skinner, Q. *Machiavelli.* Oxford, 1981.

Snyder, J. *Northern Renaissance Art.* Englewood Cliffs, NJ, 1985.

Viroli, Maurizio. Antony Shugaar, trans. *Niccolo's Smile: A Biography of Machiavelli.* New York, 2000.

InfoTrac College Edition

Enter the search term *Renaissance* using the Subject Guide.

Enter the search term *humanism* using the Subject Guide.

Enter the search term *Machiavelli* using Key Terms.

UPHEAVAL AND TRANSFORMATION IN EASTERN EUROPE

During the 15th and 16th centuries, Western Europe underwent important political changes as centralized states emerged in the place of feudal localism. In the East, the same period saw a similar transformation, although often in quite different circumstances. The venerable Byzantine Empire, which had held sway over the eastern half of the Mediterranean world since the 4th century, experienced a severe decline under the impact of the Western crusading armies and the Mongol invasions. The Paleologus restoration in the 13th century tried to halt the decline, but two centuries later the Empire finally collapsed in the face of the rising power of the Ottoman Turks. The Ottomans built their own state on the foundations of Byzantium, extending the rule of Islam throughout the Balkans, Asia Minor, the Middle East, and North Africa.

The process of state formation in eastern Europe was complicated by the fact that portions of the Slavic peoples who inhabited the Balkan region had come under the influence of Eastern Orthodox Christianity, while other Slavs living in areas of central Europe had been converted to Roman Christianity. Despite this religious division, however, centralized monarchies developed in Hungary, Bohemia, and Poland, along with distinctive national cultures. Further east, in Russia, which the Mongols dominated for two centuries, a centralized state also emerged, first at Kiev, and then at Moscow.

THE COLLAPSE OF BYZANTIUM

Ever since the 11th century, when the Seljuk Turks began to overrun Asia Minor, the Byzantine Empire had suffered one crippling disaster after another. The Western crusaders who moved east in response to the appeal of the Emperor Alexius Comnenus in 1095 had sacked Constantinople in 1204 and divided the empire into feudal states. When Michael VIII Paleologus managed to retake the throne in 1261, (see Topic 27), the reestablished Empire was a remnant of its former greatness. Nevertheless, it persisted for almost another two centuries until its final collapse in 1453.

THE PALEOLOGUS RESTORATION

The Paleologus dynasty was the last of the Byzantine families to rule the Eastern Empire. Michael and his descendants, under whom the Greeks took back control of the state apparatus as well as of the church, tried to restore the earlier glory of Constantinople. But with their power and wealth reduced, they were increasingly subject to domestic challenges and to the political and military ambitions of their neighbors.

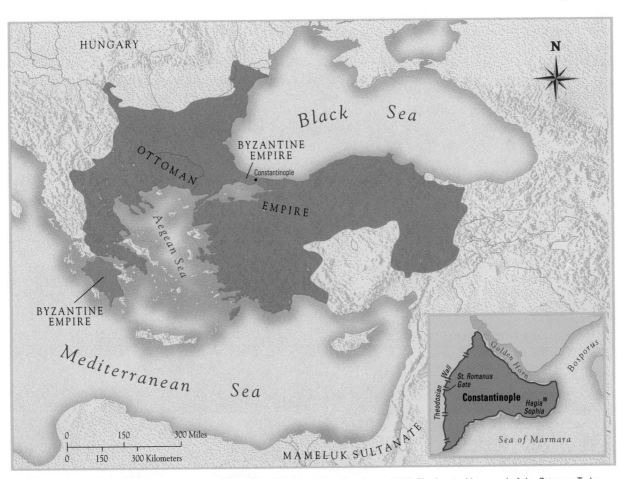

Map 37.1 The Ottoman Empire and Collapse of the Byzantine Empire, c. 1450. The inexorable spread of the Ottoman Turks, and the fratricidal feuding of the Crusaders, had reduced the Byzantine Empire to the land within the walls of Constantinople and a few fiefdoms in southern Greece. All that protected the city were the Theodosian Walls, built a millennium earlier. The final Turkish assault came in the early hours of Tuesday, May 29, 1453 (see p. 385). In the late afternoon, Mehmed II (afterwards known as Mehmed the Conqueror) entered Justinian's Church of Hagia Sophia (Holy Wisdom) and ordered it converted into a mosque. He was 21 years old. Go to http://info.wadsworth.com/053461065X for an interactive version of this map.

The Byzantine nobles successfully ignored imperial authority and ruled their own estates as independent feudal lords, pressing the peasantry on their lands into archaic forms of serfdom. With the dominance of Venice, Genoa, and other Italian trading empires in the Mediterranean, the Byzantine economy steadily declined, and even its once solid coinage began to be debased as inflation spread. The Eastern Orthodox Church, which had provided the emperors with divine blessing and had played an important role in maintaining imperial authority, was mired in doctrinal disagreements that weakened its hold over the people.

BYZANTIUM AND THE MONGOLS

Added to these difficulties was the fact that within its own borders Byzantium experienced growing unrest and resistance from its Slavic populations (see Topic 22), while from the outside came a sudden and shocking danger from the Mongols.

The Mongols were nomadic Asiatic tribes from the area of north-central China where Mongolia is located today. Although they were wild and unruly, one of their chieftains, Genghis Khan (c. 1162–1227) succeeded in uniting them and forging a powerful army. From his capital at Karakorum, Genghis Khan's army, known as the Golden Horde, quickly overran large tracts of China before moving westward through Russia and into Persia. The Mongols killed and conquered with great ferocity and struck terror in their enemies.

Under the successors of Genghis Khan, one Mongol force captured Baghdad and destroyed the 500-year-old Abbasid caliphate in 1258. Meanwhile, another group moved north into Europe, conquering Russia, invading Poland and Hungary, and subduing the Bulgarians and other Slavic peoples of the region. In 1242, however, as they stood on the plains of Hungary, the Mongols suddenly stopped their westward expansion and began to withdraw, racked by divisions over the question of succession. Although they established their dominance over a vast region that stretched from Russia to the Pacific, the Mongols bequeathed no significant cultural legacy. They did, however, leave the Byzantine Empire seriously weakened and unable to resist the last great external threat that arrived in the form of the Ottoman Turks.

THE OTTOMANS AND THE EUROPEAN RESPONSE

The Ottoman (or Osmanli) Turks had settled in northwestern Asia Minor in the 13th century, where they became vassals of the Seljuks. They began to emerge as an autonomous state as the Seljuk empire disintegrated and subsequently expanded into the Balkans, where they overran the Bulgarians and the Serbs. Like the Bulgarians, the Serbs had converted to Orthodox Christianity and founded their own state under King Stephen Dushan (ruled 1331–1355). The Serbs copied the legal structures and courtly practices of the Byzantines, and Stephen laid claim to rule over other peoples in the area, including the Bulgarians, Albanians, and Greeks. The Ottomans crossed the Straits into the

Map 37.2 Expansion of the Slavs. Note the three main divisions into East, West, and South Slavs. These labels describe their eventual destinations, not their origins: Yugoslavia, created in 1919 out of parts of the fallen Austrian and Ottoman Empires, means literally "Land of the South Slavs." All of the Slavs spoke (and still speak) related languages. The language of Romania, which was never settled by Slavs, belongs to the Romance family (i.e., like French and Italian, it derives from Latin). Go to http://info.wadsworth.com/053461065X for an interactive version of this map.

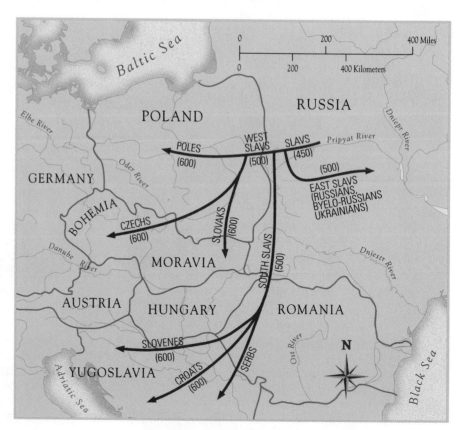

Balkans in 1354, defeating the Serbs at the Battle of Kosovo in 1389 and establishing their capital at Adrianople.

THE FALL OF CONSTANTINOPLE

When the Ottomans proceeded to lay siege to Constantinople, the West gathered a crusade to turn them back. The crusade was poorly organized, and at Nicopolis in 1396 the Turks defeated the knights and killed or captured some 10,000 Europeans. Six years later Tamerlane (c. 1336–1405), a Mongol tribal leader who claimed descent from Genghis Khan, defeated the Turks and relieved the siege of Constantinople. But Tamerlane's victory only delayed the inevitable.

In May 1453, some 160,000 Turkish soldiers under Sultan Mehmed (or Muhammad) II (ruled 1451–1481) smashed a tiny force of 9,000 Byzantines and Genoese troops led by Constantine XI (ruled 1449–1453). Mehmed personally commanded the attack on the walls of the city, which were breached with specially designed cannons of immense size, and Constantine, the last Byzantine emperor, died defending one of the city's gates. The fall of Constantinople—renamed Istanbul by its conquerors—after only 50 days of fighting came as a great demoralizing shock to the rest of Europe.

Portrait of Mehmed II, who personally led the Ottoman forces that took Constantinople—thereafter Istanbul—in 1453. The Sultan, known as "the Conquerer," is shown sniffing a flower. The Ottoman Turks were enthusiastic cultivators of plants and gardens, and many of the designs that appear on Turkish painted tiles show flowers; the most popular was the tulip.

Ara Guler, Istanbul

Mehmed, known as the Conqueror, must be considered the true founder of the Ottoman Empire, and his policies set the pattern for centuries to come. Moving his capital from Adrianople to Istanbul, he began to restore the city to its former glory, repopulating it with Muslim, Christian, and Jewish immigrants. Mehmed personally embraced the Sunni version of Islam (see Topic 23), and although he permitted his Christian and Jewish subjects to practice their religion freely, he converted the Church of Hagia Sophia to a mosque. A patron of learning and the arts, he brought skilled craftsmen and the most talented artists to work on his new capital.

THE OTTOMAN EMPIRE

The Ottomans became famous for their excellent military and political organization. Their empire, which reached its peak in the 16th century, extended deep into Persia and Arabia. Selim I "the Grim" (ruled 1512–1520) defeated the Mamelukes of Egypt and Syria, seizing Cairo in 1517. Under the Turks, Egypt became a province ruled by a *pasha*, or viceroy, appointed from Istanbul. The next year, when the Ottomans took Algiers, they created an empire that stretched across North Africa into the Middle East and up into Asia Minor and the Balkans.

In the hinterland of North Africa, known as the Maghreb, the Ottomans ruled several separate provinces through the same kind of local administrations as they had established in Egypt. Tripoli, Algiers, and Tunis were quasi-independent of Istanbul and controlled by governors and the famous slave corps of troops known as the Janissaries, originally Christians from the Balkans who were converted to Islam. These cities, especially Algiers, were the headquarters for the Turkish *corsairs*, or pirates, who raided European shipping off the coast.

Morocco held a unique place in the Ottoman Empire. In the mid-16th century, an Arab family, the Sa'dids—who claimed descent from Muhammad—united Morocco and ruled the region until 1659. The Sa'dids extended their control south, beyond the Sahara, where they conquered the kingdom of Songhay in 1591 and sacked Timbuktu. In the hinterland and the Atlas Mountains, the nomads were sometimes forced to pay tribute but otherwise remained independent.

Ottoman achievements reached their zenith under Selim's son, Suleiman I, "the Magnificent" (ruled 1520–1566). The golden age of Ottoman culture began after the conquest of Istanbul. Poets began writing in original forms rather than copying from the Persians, as they had done in the past, and court writers produced magnificent plays and short stories. Turkish literature, architecture, and art also flourished. Mehmed built a great Seraglio Palace, whose formidable walls surrounded courtyards and fountains, while Suleiman achieved even more splendid results in the Suleimanye, a complex containing a mosque and his own mausoleum.

TURKS AND EUROPEANS

The Ottoman conquest unleashed a struggle between the Turks and the Christian monarchs of Europe. Suleiman's

Painting of the Battle of Lepanto, which took place in 1571. Early 17th century. The painting, with its bird's-eye view, is an idealized impression of the event, rather than a literal piece of reporting. In the foreground, the artist has placed one of the large European ships, the superiority of which helped defeat the Turks.

military campaigns won him Rhodes and other Mediterranean islands and the city of Belgrade. In 1526, he won a major victory at Mohacs and took Buda in 1541, absorbing most of Hungary. His armies reached as far west as Vienna, the Hapsburg capital, which he besieged, but logistical problems eventually forced him to withdraw. A shrewd diplomat as well as a warrior, Suleiman forged an alliance with the Valois dynasty of France against the Hapsburgs.

The Ottoman Empire had begun to decline by the time of Suleiman's death. The Ottomans had long vied with European rulers for control of the sea lanes of the western Mediterranean. The important port cities, such as Tangier, Algiers, and Tripoli, changed hands several times as first Christians and then Muslims seized them. In the end, however, the Christians gained mastery of the sea lanes following the seizure of Malta in 1565 and the naval battle of Lepanto, off western Greece, in 1571. The Europeans also reconquered lost territory. The Hapsburgs retook Hungary, and by the early 18th century the sultans were forced to surrender Serbia and Dalmatia to the Christians. Moreover, in Istanbul, court intrigue and bribery had become rampant and the Janissaries, once the sultan's loyal soldiers, now began to manipulate their former overlords. Over the course of the next two centuries, the once great Turkish empire gradually shrank.

HUNGARY, BOHEMIA, AND POLAND

Although Serbs, Bulgarians, and Bosnians followed Orthodox Christianity, much of Eastern Europe lay in the cultural and religious sphere of the Roman Catholic Church. The Catholic populations, including Hungarians, Czechs, and Poles, achieved a vibrant cultural life during the 13th century through prestigious universities in Prague, Cracow, and elsewhere. Scholars from the region took part in the great humanist revival of the Renaissance.

THE KINGDOM OF HUNGARY

The Hungarians were a group of nomadic tribes from Asia who spoke a language distantly related to Finnish. Under Arpad (d. 907), the Magyars—the largest of the tribes—crossed the Carpathian Mountains into the plains of Hungary along the middle Danube and expanded steadily until 955, when the Holy Roman Emperor Otto the Great defeated them at Augsburg. By then they had established the basis of a state ruled by the king with the help of a royal council consisting of nobles and clergymen. Under King Stephen (ruled 977–1038), Hungary adopted Western Christianity. Stephen acknowledged the supremacy of the papacy in Rome when he received a royal crown sent by Pope Sylvester II for his coronation in the year 1000. Stephen became a zealous Catholic who bestowed land and abbeys on the church and tried to stamp out both Eastern Christianity and heresy in his kingdom. After his death, Stephen was made a saint.

Stephen's reign proved to be the early high point of Hungarian achievement because over the following century the kingdom was overrun by Germans and Poles and divided by internal strife. In 1046, an uprising of tribal chieftains, who still professed to follow paganism, resulted in the massacre of Christians and the destruction of many churches. The powerful feudal nobles of the realm, known as magnates, ruled their private lands as virtual sovereign lords, a condition reflected in the autonomy of the provinces and the elective nature of the Hungarian monarchy. The kings relied, instead, on the lesser nobility, who filled positions in the royal administration.

Despite the centrifugal force of feudalism, the state founded by Stephen endured. King Ladislas I (ruled 1077–1095) began to restore royal authority and supported the papacy in its struggles against the Holy Roman Empire. In the 12th century, King Bela III (ruled 1173–1196), who had been educated at Constantinople, brought great prestige to the Hungarian crown by marrying the sister of Philip Augustus of France. In 1222, the

Map 37.3 Eastern Europe, c. 1450–1500. By 1500, the Ottomans had conquered not only the former Byzantine territory of Greece and the islands, but also a large part of southern Europe, known as the Balkans. Turkish rule finally ended there with the Balkan Wars of 1912–1913. The Ottomans, however, were to find themselves under pressure from the Mongols, whose power increased around 1500 under the rule of Babur.

lesser nobility forced the king to accept a charter of feudal privilege, similar to the Magna Carta, known as the Golden Bull. Unlike the Magna Carta, this document did exempt the clergy and the nobility from taxation, guaranteed them against arbitrary arrest and imprisonment, and established an annual assembly, or diet, in which they could present grievances to the king. The Golden Bull also prohibited foreigners and Jews from receiving offices or land in the realm.

The Mongols invaded Hungary in 1241 and defeated the king's armies. Although the Mongols soon retreated, they left the country in a state of great devastation, of which the nobles took advantage to strengthen their own position. In the 14th century, various foreign princes vied with each other for control of the crown, and Hungary came under the rule of Charles Robert of Anjou (ruled 1308–1342). Charles established a vibrant dynasty that strengthened royal authority and brought Hungary into closer contact with the West.

The new dynasty expanded Hungarian power south into the northern Balkans and defeated the Ottomans in 1365. Nevertheless, the magnates took back much of their power, and the crown eventually came into the hands of a great frontier nobleman, John Hunyadi, whose son Matthias Corvinus (ruled 1458–1490) succeeded him. Matthias was a skilled ruler and soldier who also brought to his court in the city of Buda famous scholars from France and Italy and who was a great patron of Magyar literature and art. With a powerful standing army of mercenaries, Hungary had become the strongest kingdom in eastern Europe at the time of Matthias's death.

Matthias's successors surrendered his conquests in exchange for recognition from the Hapsburgs and gave up royal power to the magnates. More troubles soon struck the country. In 1514, a great peasant uprising erupted against the exploitation of the magnates, who crushed the revolt with much bloodshed. That same year, the diet passed a constitution, known as the *Tripartitum*, which imposed a permanent system of serfdom on the peasantry. A few years later, the Turks began their invasion of Hungary, which culminated in Suleiman's great victory at Mohacs in 1526 and the occupation of Buda in 1541. The Ottomans occupied the great plain of Hungary and divided it into administrative districts, while the western portion of the country was seized by the Hapsburgs, and Transylvania remained a vassal state of the Turks.

JAN HUS AND THE CZECHS

Sandwiched between southeastern Germany, northern Austria, and western Hungary lay the land of the Czechs, the name used for the Moravians and the Bohemians. When the Magyars invaded central Europe in the early 10th century, they destroyed the empire known as Great Moravia, a Bohemian state with its capital at Prague on the Danube. Given their location, the Czechs maintained close economic ties with the Germans and developed a thriving merchant class. Although they had been first converted to Eastern Christianity, the Czechs eventually became Catholics. A native dynasty known as the Přemyslide attempted to restore an effective Czech state and established royal authority over the nobles. In the 12th century, Frederick Barbarossa awarded the Přemyslide a hereditary crown. Under Ottokar II (ruled 1253–1278) the Bohemian state reached the furthest limits of its power in the region. Ottokar was defeated and killed in 1278 by Rudolf of Hapsburg. Early in the next century John of Luxembourg (ruled 1310–1346), son of Emperor Henry VII, who had married the last Přemyslide's daughter, came to the throne. It was John's son, Charles IV (ruled 1347–1378), who made Prague a great European capital with its own university and a rich cultural life. By the Golden Bull of 1356, the king of Bohemia became the principal member of the seven electors of the Holy Roman Empire.

At the University of Prague in the 15th century, a professor of philosophy named Jan Hus (1374–1415) unleashed a powerful movement of religious reform that soon swept across Bohemia. Hus was greatly influenced by the works of an English scholar of theology, John Wycliffe (c. 1330–1384), who attacked papal authority and the institutions of the church and looked to the Bible as the only source of doctrine. Hus began to preach sermons in the Czech language, calling for church reforms and a simpler religion based on reading the Bible. In 1415, Hus was called under safe conduct before a church council at Constance, which condemned his doctrines and burned him at the stake.

Hus was also the center of a growing nativist movement of Czech patriots who opposed German influence in the kingdom. The condemnation of Hus at Constance led to the outbreak of a revolt in Bohemia, where nobles and burghers joined with peasants in fighting the Hussite Wars against the Germans.

THE POLISH STATE

In their migrations across central Europe, the Slavs settled in the region of the Vistula basin in the 7th century. There in the 10th century the Polish state emerged as a result of the unification of six tribes under the Piast dynasty, whose first ruler was Mieszko I (ruled 960–992). The early Poles found themselves constantly at war, whether against the Germans to the east, the Prussians to the north, or the Bohemians and the Hungarians to the south.

Mieszko was converted to Latin Christianity by Bohemian missionaries. Thereafter, Poland became an outpost of crusading Christianity on the northeastern frontiers of Europe. For centuries the church maintained an alliance with the Polish nobles that worked to undermine royal authority. As in Hungary, the Polish nobility remained a powerful and autonomous force in the country.

An early exception to the rule of weak kings, however, was Boleslav I (ruled 992–1025), generally considered the real founder of the Polish state. An ambitious and unscrupulous king, he created an administrative system, endowed the church, and seems to have aimed at bringing all Slavs under his rule. Nevertheless, when the Piast dynasty ended and the Jagiellonian family came to power in 1386, noble power increased even more.

In the 14th century, the history of Poland consisted largely of the struggle by the new dynasty to reestablish royal authority, while the nobility managed to extract numerous privileges and maintain considerable control over the state. Under the reign of Casimir III the Great (ruled 1333–1370), Poland thrived as the king sought to create an efficient administration, encourage trade, and stimulate cultural developments. In 1364, Casimir established a school at Cracow that soon became a full-fledged university. As early as 1474, a printing press operated in Cracow.

Despite his success in domestic and foreign policy, Casimir left a considerably weakened monarchy at his death. Because he had no direct heir, he promised that on his death the crown would pass to Louis of Hungary, but on condition that he respect the rights of the nobles. This declaration gave rise to the practice of electing the king, who generally felt the need to buy off the magnates with concessions. In 1367, the magnates formed the first diet, and under Louis they extracted further privileges.

In 1384, Princess Jadwiga (ruled 1384–1399) was elected queen after making significant concessions to the magnates, and this was followed two years later by the granting of still further rights to the nobles. In return, they permitted Jadwiga to marry Jagiello, grand duke of Lithuania. Jagiello, a pagan, converted to Christianity and joined his territory, which was three times the size of Poland, to the Polish state.

In 1466, after a war against the Teutonic Knights, the Polish monarchy realized the goal of extending its reach to the Baltic Sea by securing a corridor through Prussian territory to the port of Danzig. Members of the Jagiellonian family also ruled in Bohemia and in Hungary. In Poland, however, the power of the nobility had grown so extensive that the monarchy was unable to put together sufficient force to stop the Ottoman invasion of central Europe in the 16th century. Effective centralized government in Poland ceased in fact with the end of the Jagiellonian dynasty.

THE GROWTH OF THE PRINCIPALITY OF MOSCOW

The Russian Empire that straddled the great Eurasian plain in modern times had its origins in two earlier states, the principalities of Kiev and Moscow. The East Slavs who settled this huge region in the early Middle Ages had ex-

Map 37.4 Growth of the Principality of Moscow. Like the Ottomans (see previous map), the rulers of the growing territory of Moscow had to deal with the Mongols. Successive Grand Princes drove the Mongol forces eastward, tripling the size of their holdings. By making Moscow the center of Russian Orthodox Christianity, Ivan I gave the city great symbolic prestige and turned the wars with the Mongols into a struggle between Christians and "heathens." Go to http://info.wadsworth.com/053461065X for an interactive version of this map.

panded as far as the Volga River, while other Slavic tribes went north almost as far as the Baltic Sea. During the 9th century, Vikings from Scandinavia had pushed into the lands of the East Slavs, where they laid the foundations of the principality of Kiev.

THE GREATNESS AND DECLINE OF KIEV

In the late 10th century, Vladimir (ruled 980–1015), who ruled a kingdom that stretched from the Baltic to the Ukraine, converted to Orthodox Christianity (on the early history of Kiev, see Topic 22). The Principality of Kiev experienced its greatest period during the reign of Vladimir's son, Yaroslav the Wise (ruled 1015–1054).

Yaroslav was both a ruthless military commander and a skilled administrator. After extending his realm to the border of Finland and clearing the area south of Kiev of nomads known as the Pechenegs, he secured religious autonomy for the principality from the patriarch of Constantinople in 1037, establishing an independent "metropolitan" as the head of the East Slavic Church. Yaroslav encouraged cultural development and contact with the West. Known as a great builder, he imported Byzantine architects and artists to construct and decorate important churches, including the great St. Sophia Cathedral in Kiev, inspired by Hagia Sophia in Constantinople. Following Justinian's example in Byzantium, Yaroslav ordered the codification of East Slavic law.

After Yaroslav's death, Kiev was racked by incessant feuds and struggles to secure the succession to the throne. These internal troubles rendered the principality unable to resist the constant incursions of nomadic peoples from the steppes. In the 11th century, the Cumans blocked Kiev from the Black Sea, thus breaking a longstanding and profitable trade connection with the Byzantine Empire. Eventually the nomads pushed the southern frontier of Kiev farther and farther north, isolating the Rus, or Russians, around the forests and the city of Moscow. Kiev fell to attack from the north in 1169.

The Mongol invasions of the 13th century completed the destruction of Kievan civilization. Because the Mongols were relatively few in number, they could do little more than control southern Russia along the Caspian and Black seas as tributary rulers and asserted even less direct authority over northern regions. In the 1240s, a prince of Novgorod, Alexander Nevsky (c. 1220–1263), began cooperating with the Mongols and defeated invading German forces.

Novgorod was a prosperous commercial city that traded with the Hanseatic League of northern German cities. Unlike their treatment of most of the other Russian cities, the Mongols left Novgorod untouched, and for his cooperation the Mongol Khan bestowed on Nevsky the title of Grand Prince. From that basis, Nevsky's descendants built a dynasty that would eventually rule most of Russia.

Manuscript illustration showing Ivan III the Great. 16th century. The stylized treatment of the hair and beard suggests that this is an "icon" of the Russian ruler rather than a realistic portrait. Note the fur collar on his robe; the export of furs was one of the chief economic resources of Ivan's state.

THE ORIGINS OF MOSCOW

By the 15th century, the centuries-old traditions of autonomy that the citizens of Novgorod had enjoyed came to an end. Weakened by strife among the citizens of different classes, and with its economy devastated by the decline of Baltic trade, in 1478 Novgorod fell under the aegis of Moscow.

Moscow had been little more than a frontier fortress on the Moskva River protected by surrounding marshes and forests. Its name first appeared in the chronicles only in 1147. Moscow had been established by a son of Nevsky, who skillfully expanded his powers in the service of the Mongols. The princes of Moscow adopted the policy of primogeniture, whereby the lands and possessions of the ruler passed to the oldest son; this ensured the continuation of power from one generation to another.

The city's rulers pursued a policy of steady expansion as they brought more and more Russian cities into its orbit. In 1328 the Mongols gave Ivan I (ruled 1328–1341), like Nevsky, the title of Grand Prince, with the right to collect all Russian tribute for the Khan—a function that brought him the contemporary nickname "money bags." Ivan also made Moscow the center of the Russian Orthodox Church. In 1380, Dmitri (ruled 1359–1389) greatly enhanced the prestige of his family when he won a victory over the Mongols at Kulikovo, on the Don, in 1380, earning him the title "Donskoi."

The greatest of the early princes of Moscow was Ivan III the Great (ruled 1462–1505). In 1478 Ivan the Great acquired control of Novgorod by incorporating its lands into the state of Moscow. Several years later, at the Oka River, he faced down the Mongol armies, who finally withdrew from Russia. Under Ivan and his successors, the Muscovite principality continued to expand, almost tripling the size of its territory by the mid-16th century. In a deliberate move to enhance his status so as to realize his great ambitions, Ivan married Sophia Paleologus, daughter of the last emperor of Byzantium. Ivan transformed Moscow into the core of a powerful empire and himself into the first tsar of all Russia (see Topic 53).

Putting Upheaval and Transformation in Eastern Europe in Perspective

The formation of national monarchies in Hungary, Bohemia, Poland, and Russia, together with the conquests and expansion of the Ottoman Turks, established the pattern of development for the eastern Mediterranean world for the next four centuries. This process was accompanied by equally fundamental social transformations as the system of serfdom that had developed in earlier periods in Western societies now was imposed by deliberate decision in eastern lands. Although separated from the Western European experience by ethnic, cultural, and religious differences, the entire region gradually established links with the dominant states of the West. As a result, as major political and religious upheavals unfolded in the West in the 16th century, Eastern Europe could not remain isolated from their impact.

Questions for Further Study

1. What effect did Ottoman expansion have on Europe?
2. What common social and economic conditions prevailed throughout eastern and central Europe?
3. How would you describe the Mongols and their impact on Russia?
4. What obstacles stood in the way of building a centralized state in Russia?

Suggestions for Further Reading

Allsen, Thomas T. *Mongol Imperialism*. Berkeley, CA, 1987.

Atil, Esin. *The Age of Sultan Suleyman the Magnificent*. Washington, DC, 1987.

Crummey, Robert O. *The Formation of Muscovy, 1304–1613*. New York, 1987.

Engel, Pal. Tamas Palosfalvi, trans. *The Realm of St Stephen: A History of Medieval Hungary, 895-1526*. New York, 2001.

Franklin, S., and J. Shepard. *The Emergence of Rus*. London, 1996.

Goodwin, Jason. *Lords of the Horizons: A History of the Ottoman Empire*. London, 1998.

Halperin, Charles J. *Russia and the Golden Horde*. Bloomington, IN, 1985.

Kazhdan, A.P., and others, eds. *The Oxford Dictionary of Byzantium*. New York, 1991.

Manz, Beatrice Forbes. *The Rise and Rule of Tamerlane*. Cambridge, 1989.

Morgan, D.O. *The Mongols*. Oxford, 1986.

Norwich, John Julius. *Byzantium: The Decline and Fall*. New York, 1995.

Taylor, J. *Imperial Istanbul*. London, 1989.

Wheatcroft, Andrew. *The Ottomans, Dissolving Images*. New York, 1993.

InfoTrac College Edition

Enter the search term *Ottoman Turks* using the Subject Guide.

Enter the search term *Jan Hus* using Key Terms.

THE ERA OF RECONNAISSANCE

Although the 16th and 17th centuries were a time of great religious upheaval in Europe, the period also saw serious economic and political crisis compounded by war and revolution. Yet, despite these difficulties, European civilization embarked on an unprecedented era of energetic and often ruthless overseas expansion. This age of "reconnaissance" dramatically changed Europe's relationship with the rest of the world, ushering in another fundamental revolution in modern history. The remarkable experience altered the nature of Europe's economy, had important social and cultural repercussions, and broadened the European imagination.

The age of exploration and expansion actually began in the 15th century with the first forays and technical discoveries of the Portuguese sailors. By the end of the 15th century, several Portuguese sailors, especially Bartholomeu Dias and Vasco da Gama, had rounded the Cape of Good Hope and explored the eastern coast of Africa along the Indian Ocean, opening great trade routes to India. These early Portuguese adventurers were followed by the Spanish. In 1492, Christopher Columbus reached the Americas, and within less than a generation Ferdinand Magellan circumnavigated the entire globe.

The immediate result of these early voyages was the establishment of vast overseas empires ruled by the Portuguese and the Spanish. This early experience in political and economic imperialism had tremendous, and often devastating, consequences for the native populations of the Western Hemisphere. For Europe, it laid the basis for the future commercial—and, eventually, for the industrial—development of the modern age.

EUROPEANS AND THE WORLD: THE EARLY TRAVELERS

The great explorations of the 16th century did not, of course, represent the first expansion beyond Europe's borders. In the 9th and 10th centuries, the Vikings may have crossed the Atlantic and had penetrated into Russia from the north. The waves of successive crusades that invaded the Muslim-controlled Middle East starting in the 11th century revealed aggressive tendencies in the European psyche that presaged later movements beyond the frontiers of Christian society, and conditioned relations between Europeans and non-Europeans for centuries.

EUROPE AND THE LUXURY TRADE

Europeans had long been fascinated by Africa, India, and East Asia. In the Middle Ages, examples of the fabulous products to be found in these regions had trickled back to Europe. Europe's elite grew thirsty for leopard and zebra skins, ivories, rare silks, and precious gems, to say nothing of the wonderful spices that could transform the bland and boring European diet—indeed, nothing was so coveted by those who could afford it as plain, ordinary black pepper, a product that came principally from India and Indonesia.

Since Roman times, a lucrative trade had supplied Europe with the luxurious products of Africa and Asia. Many silks, spices, and other exotic products had flowed through Constantinople and the Byzantine Empire. After the 7th century, however, when the Arabs began to conquer North Africa and the Middle East, Europeans had to buy such goods mainly from the Muslims, who positioned themselves as middlemen between the European market and the source of most of these items. Muslim traders plied the waters of the Indian Ocean between India and Africa as well as up the Red Sea, and caravans snaked their way into the African and Asian interiors.

The Mongol conquests that began in the 13th century established a broad area of stability in the Asian heartland and opened a line of communication between Europe and central Asia. This situation prompted the Polo family of Venetian merchants to make the long and hazardous journey to the Mongol court of Kublai Khan (ruled 1259–1294), a grandson of the fierce Genghis Khan. Kublai controlled most of China, which he ruled from his capital at Tatu, the site of present-day Beijing. A man of broad, sophisticated tastes

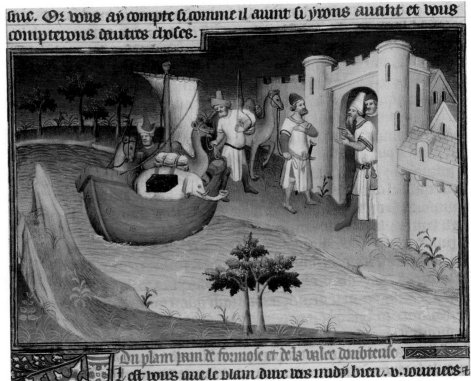

Manuscript illumination showing Marco Polo arriving at the port of Hormuz, on the Persian Gulf. 14th–15th century. The picture, which shows Marco Polo's arrival from India with exotic animals, is based on his account dictated while in prison. The original written version was probably—like the text above and below this illustration—in French.

who patronized artists and scholars, Kublai also encouraged contact with outsiders. In the 13th century, Pope Innocent IV sent monks to visit the Mongol court, but the Polos were Kublai's most famous Western visitors.

Between 1253 and 1260, Niccolò Polo and his brother Maffeo made several trading expeditions to Constantinople. From there, they went eastward into Kublai's kingdom, returning to Venice in 1269. Two years later, the brothers set out once again for Kublai's court, this time with Niccolò's son, Marco (c. 1254–c. 1324), and two Catholic missionaries. The group reached the capital in 1275, and the young Marco soon became a favorite of the khan, who sent him on trading missions throughout China, as far south as India and as far west as Japan. He apparently even ruled one Chinese city, Hangchow, for three years in the khan's name, describing his own city of Venice as a poor provincial village when compared with what he called the greatest city in the world.

Marco Polo is remembered today mainly for his famous account of his travels, which he wrote while he was a prisoner of the Genoese. His book tells of the customs and peoples he encountered, including those in the Arab world, Persia, East Africa, and Asia; he also described strange products such as paper currency, coal, and other things unknown in the West. He is said to have brought back to Venice a kind of wheat noodle that later became popular throughout Italy as pasta.

Most of all, Marco's account gave Europeans a sense of how he was awestruck by the fabulous splendors and wealth he had seen. These tales made his readers somewhat incredulous, especially because he repeated several mythical stories about things he had been told by others. Nevertheless, Marco Polo's account of his experiences did keep alive the appetites of Europeans for knowledge about Asia, as well as for its rare and exotic products.

The invasions of the Ottoman Turks and the collapse of the Mongol Empire eventually cut off the routes to Asia for Europeans. Nevertheless, an occasional brave traveler from the West, fed by stories such as Marco's or by religious missionary zeal, continued to penetrate beyond Europe's now relatively closed borders. The legend of a Christian

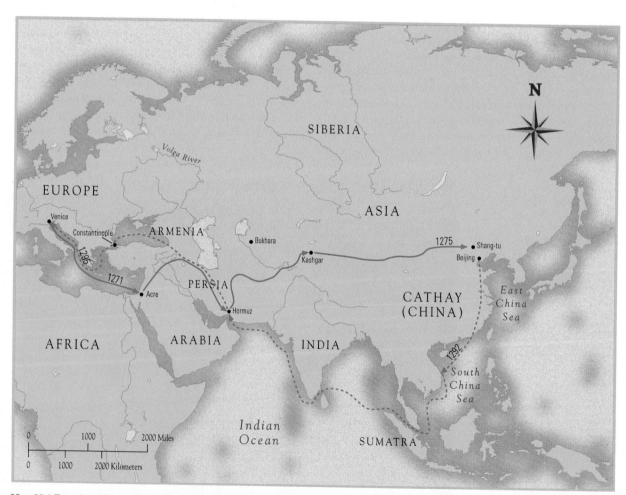

Map 38.1 Travels of Marco Polo. The exact route Marco Polo followed is by no means certain, and his account is unclear in places; some modern experts have cast doubt on the truth of his tales, which were in any case dictated and written down many years later. Whatever the facts, the wide circulation of his stories throughout Europe greatly stimulated European curiosity about the rest of the world. Christopher Columbus's journeys were originally undertaken in search of a sea passage to the East, which Polo described.

king known as Prester John beyond the Muslim world prompted the Portuguese to sail along the western African coast as late as the 15th century.

A THIRST FOR DISCOVERY

The motives that lay behind the growing European interest in the world beyond their borders were complex. Certainly the opportunities for profit in the luxury trade were tremendous, so that the lure of wealth was important. On the other hand, the crusading zeal that European Christians had demonstrated over the centuries also prompted much of the early efforts to reach foreign lands. Nor should we overlook the genuine interest that some of the early explorers and their sponsors had in expanding their knowledge of the world—the first voyages of discovery, it should not be forgotten, took place while Europe was at the height of the Renaissance, when interest in worldly matters was paramount.

The economic motives must surely have been the most powerful and pressing. Some merchants and rulers speculated about the possibility of finding vast deposits of gold and other precious metals. At the time, the Europeans had to pay for most of the luxury goods they imported from Asia with bullion, so that a supply of precious metals was the only real way for the new monarchs of Europe to bring the trade imbalance under control.

Most Europeans, however, thought of the incredible riches that could be made if only they could discover direct sea routes to India and East Asia. In this way, they would be able to bypass both the Muslim middlemen and the Venetians, who dominated the trade of the eastern Mediterranean. Moreover, the price of spices was incredibly inflated, not only because of their scarcity but also as a result of the Muslims' marking them up even higher. Spices dominated the trade with Asia and still captured most of the traders' attention. They served to enhance the flavor of foods and preserve them, as well as for a variety of other purposes, from the manufacture of perfumes and incense to medicinal potions. In addition to pepper, the principal items of the luxury trade were cinnamon, nutmeg, and cloves. Although the risks of the long-distance spice route were great, the return was enormous.

In the case of Portugal and Spain, the two countries that took the early lead in overseas exploration, the religious factor was also a strong motivation. The popes had sent missionary expeditions to Asia in the Middle Ages. It was, after all, on the Iberian peninsula where the Christians had fought the Muslims for centuries, finally conquering them or driving them out. The Spanish conquerors who overran Mexico and Central America were accompanied by missionaries and spoke constantly of the goal of converting the inhabitants of the New World to Christianity. This was especially true after the Reformation and the launching by Rome of the Counter-Reformation, which the church undertook with a renewed zeal.

One final reason explains why Europeans seemed so taken with the spirit of adventure and the desire to explore new regions of the world. The Muslims and the Chinese had been plying the waters of the Indian Ocean and southeast Asia for centuries, but neither had sailed much beyond the regions with which they were familiar. European society had matured to the point where its people simply could no longer remain prisoners of such restricted regions of the globe; perhaps, too, the development of the nation-states of the era had aroused a spirit of competition that drove the explorers to strike out in new directions.

GEOGRAPHY AND TECHNOLOGY

The Europeans had been limited by geopolitical factors to fairly well-defined sea basins—the Baltic and North Seas, and the Mediterranean—since the fall of the Roman Empire. As a result, in 1450 their knowledge of the world's geography was still essentially what it had been at the time of the ancient Romans. European travelers acquired the information necessary to make possible the "age of reconnaissance" only in the latter half of the 15th century, but within 100 years they had circled the entire globe. In addition to geographic knowledge, Westerners had to make certain technological advances, especially in ship design and navigational instruments, before they could set out to explore distant seas.

MAPS AND GEOGRAPHY

Most geographers of the Renaissance were still wedded to the notion put forth by Ptolemy (c. 90–c. 168) that the globe was a large mass of connected land made up of the continents of Europe, Africa, and Asia. Ptolemy also thought the circumference of the globe to be much smaller than it actually is, so that some explorers—like Columbus—thought they could reach Asia easily by sailing westward.

The most up-to-date geographic information available to Europeans came from the *portolani*, which were marine charts drawn on the basis of personal observation by sailors. The *portolani* mainly showed coastlines along the Mediterranean, the Atlantic coast, and eventually the coast of western Africa. Often drawn by sailors working with mathematicians, they contained detailed practical information needed for sailing, including distances, compass directions, and the depth of channels and ports. Mapmakers of the 14th century also prepared charts based on the information contained in the journals of Marco Polo, and Arab and Indian sailors who came to western ports on European ships provided specific knowledge of distant waterways.

Around 1500, mapmakers began to make important advances. The rediscovery of Ptolemy's *Geographia* at about this time, together with the invention of printing and engraving, made great strides possible. In 1538, by which time the information gathered by the early Portuguese and Spanish sailors was available, Gerardus Mercator (1512–1594), a Flemish cartographer, published his earliest map of the world. In 1568, Mercator made his first projection maps, which became widely used for navigational charts.

SHIPBUILDING AND NAVIGATION

Two developments were necessary in order to establish the practical basis for the age of discovery: a new kind of ship capable of traversing the open seas or the oceans, and new navigational instruments to guide the ships in uncharted regions. In the Mediterranean Sea, ships operated mainly along the coast, which navigators had mapped in great detail over the centuries. These ships were galleys rowed by teams of 50 or more slaves or sailors pressed into service from prisons. Because the oar-propelled ships were difficult to operate in rough, open waters, they traveled away from the coast only when the distance to the next island or land mass was relatively short.

Ships that hoped to sail in larger bodies of water, such as the Indian and Atlantic Oceans, had to use sails rather than oars to move them. In addition, instead of the long, narrow shapes of the galleys, which were designed for slicing through calmer waters with the least amount of resistance, oceangoing vessels needed wider hulls that could carry enough provisions to feed crews on long ocean voyages and hold the precious cargoes carried on return trips.

The first ships capable of making the months-long ocean voyages were known as *caravels* and were the work of Portuguese shipbuilders. In the 15th century, the Portuguese, whose ports lay on the Atlantic coast, were pushing carefully along the North African coastal waters. The caravel design innovation drew from both European and Muslim sailing experience. Two of its masts carried large square sails, which used strong winds to move the ship. A third mast supported a more narrow triangular-shaped sail; these were used to give the ship more maneuverability. The large hulls solved the problem of carrying provisions and cargo.

The navigational instruments that medieval European sailors had at their disposal were of limited value. The astrolabe, which may have been available as far back as Roman times, was widely used by the 11th century to determine the height of the sun and stars in order to calculate latitude (measured along imaginary lines around the earth in the form of circles running parallel to the equator). As early as the 13th century, Europeans had developed the compass, which sailors could use to determine direction, especially in bad weather that obscured the stars and the sun. Not until the 18th century, however, were sailors able to calculate longitude (imaginary lines in the form of circles running from pole to pole) with any degree of precision.

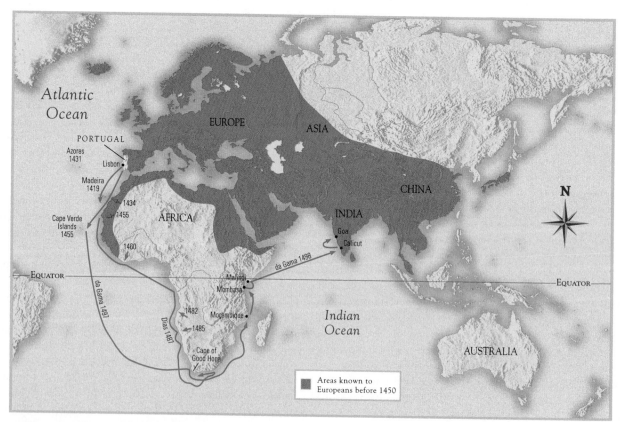

 Map 38.2 The Portuguese Voyages. Dias's circumnavigation of Africa in 1487 was the first great exploit of the Era of Reconnaissance, opening up India and China to commercial exploitation. The Portuguese retained the colony Goa in India until 1961, and their territory of Macao, in southeast China, only passed under Chinese rule in 1999. Mozambique, one of the stops on the east coast of Africa, became a center for the slave trade. The Portuguese colony there became independent in 1975. Go to http://info.wadsworth.com/053461065X for an interactive version of this map.

THE PORTUGUESE INITIATIVE

Once the Portuguese had pioneered the new caravel ship design, they set out on their first voyages of discovery. These early explorations were the work of the remarkable Prince Henry, who sponsored a navigational school and supplied the funds for the trips. After his death, the voyages continued to ever-greater distances around the globe.

PRINCE HENRY THE NAVIGATOR

Henry (1394–1460) was the younger son of King John I of Portugal (ruled 1385–1433). With little prospect of inheriting the throne, Henry devoted himself to geography and navigation. He built a school and observatory at Sagres, situated on the Atlantic at the southwesternmost point of Portugal. He brought sailors, captains, scientists, and mapmakers there and sent out annual expeditions to explore the northwestern coast of Africa.

A stimulus to this interest in Africa came in Henry's youth when the Portuguese captured the Muslim city of Ceuta on the coast of Morocco. Consumed with a passion for knowledge, as well as with the practical ambition of discovering a source of gold that would enrich the kingdom, he eventually sent a fleet as far as Guinea and the Gold Coast (in the vicinity of modern-day Ghana). The hope was that the sea route would circumvent the trans-Saharan caravan routes that the Arabs had used to control the gold supply to the Mediterranean.

THE BIRTH OF PORTUGUESE IMPERIALISM

In the years following Henry's death in 1460, the Portuguese expeditions declined for a time, although they did discover the Azores and the Madeiras, two small island groups hundreds of miles out in the Atlantic that would later serve as stopping places for transoceanic voyages. King John II (ruled 1481–1495) eventually organized new expeditions, this time with the specific goal of tracing a sea route to reach the spices of India. John established trading posts on the Guinea coast and was able to send a Portuguese group inland as far as Timbuktu.

In 1487, Bartholomeu Dias discovered and rounded the Cape of Good Hope on the southern tip of Africa, although bad weather, combined with the threat of a mutiny, made him turn back to Portugal. A decade later, Vasco da Gama retraced the Dias trip and actually crossed the Indian Ocean to the port of Calicut on the coast of India. When da Gama returned to Portugal with a cargo of goods from India, the king sent out a fleet of 13 ships under Pedro Alvares Cabral, who sighted Brazil in April 1500 and claimed it for the king.

From there, Cabral crossed the southern Atlantic, rounded Africa, and arrived in India. Once there, Cabral, assisted by da Gama, set up Portuguese trading posts. Although half his fleet sank before he arrived back in Lisbon, the profit from his cargo of spices was huge. Soon the Portuguese had established regular fleets that sailed to India each year, giving Lisbon a virtual monopoly on the Asian trade with Europe.

To secure their control of that trade, the Portuguese attempted to clear the Indian Ocean of Muslim presence. Under the command of Alfonso de Albuquerque, the Portuguese forces had already taken many of the most strategic ports on the east African coast. Albuquerque, who served as governor of India from 1509 to 1515, now bombarded and seized the Muslim forts along the Indian coast—including Goa and Calicut—and converted them to military and trading facilities.

These assaults on the Indian ports gave Portugal control over the spice trade and established Portuguese imperialism in Asia. They reached as far as Macao, situated at the mouth of the Pearl River in China. Despite the early successes of Portugal, however, the country simply did not have the economic or military strength needed to establish a truly global empire or to colonize the regions under their control. Spain eventually took Portugal's place as Europe's leading colonial power.

A *portolan* map showing Central America and the West Indies. Late 16th century. The *portolani* were based on information supplied by sailors and enabled early explorers to plan their voyages. Note the use of Spanish and the naming of the region now called the Gulf of Mexico as "New Spain."

PERSPECTIVES FROM THE PAST

THE PORTUGUESE IN THE WIDER WORLD

Portugal, a small country that hugged the southernmost corner of Europe's Atlantic coast, had not played a major role in European or in global affairs. Beginning in the 15th century, however, the sailors, explorers, and traders of the kingdom suddenly pushed Portugal to the forefront of overseas expansion. A century later, the Portuguese had circled the globe and brought back to Europe the first accounts of the world beyond the West.

The spirit of enterprise and courage that drove Portugal's global expansion was matched, however, by a cultural arrogance and a thirst for conquest that made them the spearhead of a more general Western colonialism. These conflicting attitudes and values are revealed in the documents that follow.

An Early Account of Slavery in Africa

In 1455 and 1456, Alvise da Ca' da Mosto, a Venetian merchant, made two separate voyages to West Africa under a license granted to him by Prince Henry. A hardheaded businessman with a good eye for detail, Cadamosto provides one of the earliest European descriptions of the Guinea coast and the slave trade that had developed there. Along this region of the coast of western Sudan lay Arguim, a small island in the gulf where the Portuguese built a fort in 1448 for the protection of merchants. Arguim was a principal trade site where the Portuguese met caravans coming north from Timbuktu and west from the Sahara.

These Arabs [of the western Sudan] also have many Berber horses, which they trade, and take to the Land of the Blacks, exchanging them with the rulers for slaves. Ten or fifteen slaves are given for one of these horses, according to their quality. The Arabs likewise take articles of Moorish silk, made in Granada and in Tunis for Barbary, silver, and other goods, obtaining in exchange any number of these slaves, and some gold. These slaves are brought to the market and town of Hoden [Wadan, a desert market some 350 miles east of Arguim]; there they are divided: some go to the mountains of Barcha [in Libya], and thence to Sicily, [others to the said town of Tunis and to all the coasts of Barbary], and others again are taken to this place, Argin, and sold to the Portuguese leaseholders. As a result every year

the Portuguese carry away from Argin a thousand slaves. Note that before this traffic was organized, the Portuguese caravels, sometimes four, sometimes more, were wont to come armed to the Golfo d'Argin, and descending on the land by night, would assail the fisher villages, and so ravage the land. Thus they took of these Arabs both men and women, and carried them to Portugal for sale; behaving in a like manner along all the rest of the coast, which stretches from Cauo Bianco to the Rio di Senega and even beyond. This is a great river, dividing a race which is called Azanaghi from the first Kingdom of the Blacks. These Azanaghi are brownish, rather dark brown than light, and live in places along this coast beyond Cauo Bianco, and many of them are spread over this desert inland. They are neighbors of the above mentioned Arabs of Hoden.

They live on dates, barley, and camel's milk: but as they are very near the first land of the Blacks, they trade with them, obtaining from this land of the Blacks millet and certain vegetables, such as beans, upon which they support themselves. They are men who require little food and can withstand hunger, so that they sustain themselves throughout the day upon a mess of barley porridge. They are obliged to do this because of the want of victuals they experience. These, as I have said, are taken by the Portuguese as before mentioned and are the best slaves of all the Blacks. But, however, for some time all have been at peace and engaged in trade. The said Lord Infante will not permit further hurt to be done to any, because he hopes that, mixing with Christians, they may without difficulty be converted to our faith, not yet being firmly attached to the tenets of Muhammad, save from what they know by hearsay.

From *The Voyages of Cadamosto,* trans. and ed. G. R. Crone (London: The Hakluyt Society. Copyright © 1937). Reprinted with permission.

The Portuguese in India

In May 1498, after crossing the Indian Ocean, da Gama sailed into the harbor of Calicut Road on the western coast of India. Other Portuguese sailors followed da Gama's path and explored the cities of the Malabar coast, including Goa and Cochin. In 1510 Alfonso de Albuquerque, who served as governor of India, seized Goa from its Muslim ruler. In Cochin, which Duarte Barbosa described in the following account, the Portuguese found great storehouses of valuable spices.

Further in advance along the coast is the Kingdom of *Cochin,* in which there is much pepper which grows throughout the land on trees like unto ivy, and it climbs on other trees and on palms, also on trellises to a great extent. The pepper grows on these trees in bunches. . . . This Kingdom possesses a very large and excellent river, which here comes forth to the sea by which come in great ships of Moors and Christians, who trade with this Kingdom. On the banks of this river is a city of the Moors natives of the land, wherein also dwell Heathen Chatims, and great merchants. They have many ships and trade with Charamandel, the great Kingdom of Cambaia, Dabul, and Chaul, in areca, cocos, pepper, jagara, and palm sugar. At the mouth of the river the King our Lord possesses a very fine fortress, which is a large settlement of Portuguese and Christians, natives of the land, who became Christians after the establishment of our fortress. And every day also other Christian Indians who have remained from the teaching of the Blessed Saint Thomas come there also from Coilam and other places. In this fort and settlement of Cochin the King our Lord carries out the repairs of his ships, and other new ships are built, both galleys and caravels in as great perfection as on the Lisbon

strand. Great store of pepper is here taken on board, also many other kinds of spices, and drugs which come from Malacca, and are taken hence every year to Portugal. The King of Cochin has a very small country and was not a King before the Portuguese discovered India, for all the Kings who had of late reigned in Calicut had held it for their practice and rule to invade Cochin and drive the King out of his estate, . . . thereafter, according as their pleasure was, they would give it back to him or not. The king of Cochin gave him every year a certain number of elephants, but he might not strike coins, nor roof his palace with tiles under pain of losing his land. Now that the King our Lord has discovered India he has made the King independent and powerful in his own land, so that none can interfere with it, and he strikes whatsoever money he will.

From *The Book of Duarte Barbosa,* trans. and ed. Mansel Longworth Dames, 2 vols. (The Hakluyt Society. Copyright © 1921). Reprinted with permission.

The First Impressions of China

Since the 1430s, China had been essentially closed to the outside world. The so-called Ming Code had forbidden subjects to travel outside the country, and despite the interest of local merchants in south China in expanding trade, foreign travelers had been discouraged from visiting China. The first Portuguese traders arrived in China in 1514, and three years later Tomé Pires set out as official Portuguese envoy to China. After having been kept in Canton for three years on orders of the emperor, Pires was allowed to proceed to Beijing but never saw the emperor. Instead, in 1521 an imperial decree prohibited trade with foreigners and Pires and his followers were imprisoned in Canton. The letter that follows, written by Cristavao Vieira and smuggled back to Portugal, was the first account of conditions in China to arrive in Europe.

The country of China is divided into fifteen provinces. . . . All these fifteen provinces are under one king. The advantage of this country lies in its rivers all of which descend to the sea. No one sails the sea from north to south; it is prohibited by the king, in order that the coun-

Continued

try may not become known. Where we went was all rivers. They have boats and ships broad below without number. . . . I must have seen thirty thousand including great and small. . . .

No province in China has trade with strangers except this of Cantao: that which others may have on the borders is a small affair, because foreign folk do not enter the country of

China, nor do any go out of China. The sea trade has made this province of great importance, and without trade it would remain dependent on the agriculturalists like the others. . . .

The custom of this country of China is, that every man who administers justice cannot belong to that province; for instance, a person of Cantao cannot hold an office of justice in

SPAIN, THE AMERICAS, AND THE EUROPEAN ECONOMY

The Kingdom of Spain, once it had been united under the joint rule of Ferdinand and Isabella, and the Muslims had been driven out, proved capable of mustering the resources to build a world empire. Moreover, whereas the Portuguese had required a century in order to extend their reach around Africa and across the Indian Ocean, the Spanish sponsored a single expedition that suddenly discovered a vast new continent.

The Metropolitan Museum of Art, Gift of J. Pierpont Morgan, 1900. (00.18.2) Photograph ©1979 The Metropolitan Museum of Art

Sebastiano del Piombo, *Portrait of a Man Called Christopher Columbus*. 1519. The identity of the subject is not certain. Columbus, whose voyages to the Western Hemisphere opened the way for colonization of the Americas, has become the object of controversy for those who see him as the symbol of European imperialism.

COLUMBUS AND THE NEW WORLD

In 1484, even before Dias had rounded the tip of Southern Africa, Christopher Columbus (Cristoforo Colombo, 1451–1506), an Italian sailor from Genoa, attempted to convince the Portuguese to fund a voyage westward across the Atlantic. From studying the geography of Ptolemy and the findings of earlier Portuguese expeditions, Columbus was certain that he could reach Japan and China in a much shorter time by sailing due west. When King John II of Portugal turned down his request, Columbus went to Spain, where Queen Isabella agreed to back his voyage. With three ships under his command, Columbus actually reached landfall in the Bahamas in October 1492. Thinking he had reached Asia, Columbus explored Cuba and Haiti before returning to Spain with news of his discovery. Despite three later expeditions between 1493 and 1502, during which he sailed the Caribbean as far north as Honduras, Columbus would not abandon his conviction that he had reached Asia; therefore, he called the people inhabiting the islands "Indians."

The explorers who came after Columbus were the first to understand that he had in fact discovered an entirely "New World," a term coined by another Italian, Amerigo Vespucci. A banker who was obsessed by exploration fever, Vespucci sailed on several voyages to the Americas—the name that cartographers gave to the two continents after Vespucci described the regions that he explored. Still a third Italian sailor, John Cabot (Giovanni Caboto), was the first European to reach the North American mainland. Commissioned by the English monarch to find a western route to Asia, Cabot sailed along the coast of Nova Scotia and Newfoundland. His son, Sebastian Cabot, sailed to South America on behalf of the Spanish.

The early Spanish and Portuguese explorers were in open competition with each other, and the two states appealed to Pope Alexander VI to divide the world into respective spheres of exploration. In 1493, Alexander, a Spaniard, allocated the New World to Spain and granted Africa and India to Portugal. The Portuguese were not, however, very pleased by this distribution because it removed Brazil, which they had discovered and claimed, from their jurisdiction. In order to avoid war, Spain and Portugal settled

Cantao . . . This is vested in the literates; and every literate when he obtains a degree begins in petty posts, and thence goes on rising to higher ones, without their knowing when they are to be moved; . . . These changes are made in Pequim. . . . Hence it comes that no judge in China does equity, because he does not think of the good of the district. . . . they do nothing but rob, kill, whip and put to torture the people. The people are worse treated by these mandarins than is the devil in hell: hence it comes that the people have no love for the king and for the mandarins, and every day they go on rising and becoming robbers. . . .

From "Letters from Portuguese Captives in Canton," trans. and ed. by D. Ferguson, *The Indian Antiquary*, XXXI (January 1902).

the dispute by the Treaty of Tordesillas (1494), which moved the line westward to include Brazil in the Portuguese zone.

By proving that it was possible to sail westward without incident, Columbus had enticed a generation of explorers to try to find the elusive passage to Asia. In 1513, the Spanish explorer Vasco de Balboa crossed Central America, where he became the first European to look on the Pacific Ocean. During the early 16th century, when voyages to the Western Hemisphere became almost commonplace, a Portuguese navigator named Ferdinand Magellan became the first European to circle the globe. Magellan had served in India before joining the service of the Emperor Charles V. In September 1519, he sailed from Spain with five ships, and a year later he discovered the strait now named for him at the southern end of South America. With three of his ships, he sailed north along the coast and then headed west across the Pacific, reaching Guam in March 1521. Magellan was killed in a clash with the local inhabitants in the Philippines, but eventually one of his ships made it back to Spain. Magellan's expedition finally put to rest the question about whether the earth was round, and it demonstrated that Ptolemy had indeed underestimated the size of Earth.

SPANISH EMPIRE IN THE NEW WORLD

The region that Columbus explored on his four voyages embraced the major islands of the Caribbean. These so-called West Indies islands included Cuba, Jamaica, Puerto Rico, Trinidad, San Salvador, and the island the Spanish called Hispaniola (Haiti). For the Spanish, the chief aims of their travels lay in converting the Indians to Christianity and searching for gold and silver. In a short time, the population of the region, which is estimated to have been about as high

Drawing of Amerindians as cannibals. Around 1500. The illustration appeared in an early account of travels in the Americas and was intended as propaganda to justify the forcible conquest of the indigenous population, here portrayed as breaking the taboo against cannibalism and living without government or shame.

The Granger Collection

as 100,000, had been decimated by the oppressive conditions under which the Indians were forced to work and the impact of European diseases, such as smallpox, to which the Indians had never been exposed.

The thirst for gold and silver led the Spanish to transfer their attentions from the Caribbean islands to the mainland. Although the American cultures were advanced, their weapons were no match for European military power. In 1519, a *conquistador* named Hernán Cortés (1485–1547) invaded Mexico with an army of 600 heavily armed soldiers. Cortés captured the Aztec emperor Montezuma and conquered his wealthy empire. Mexico yielded large quantities of precious metals and provided missionaries with another large population to convert.

In the 1530s, Francisco Pizarro (1470–1541) invaded northern South America and destroyed the Inca empire, on

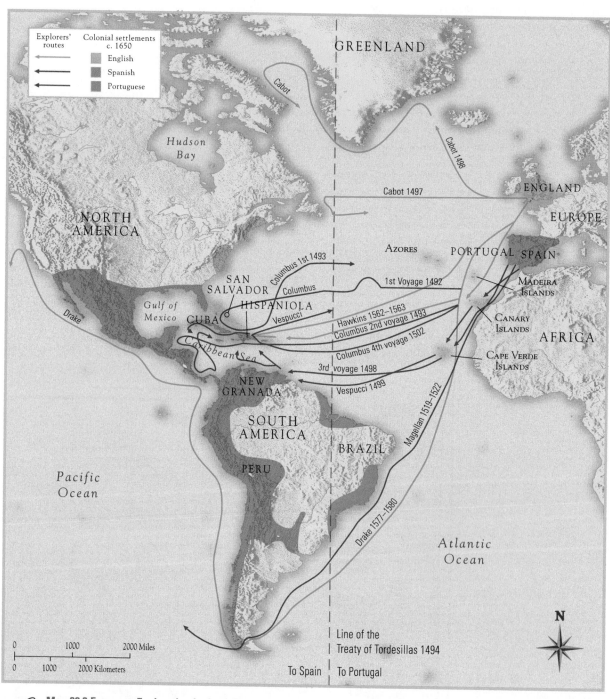

 Map 38.3 European Exploration in the Americas. Although Columbus's original mission had been to find a sea passage to the East, the early Spanish and Portuguese explorers soon realized that the Americas' natural resources could bring rich rewards, and transferred the struggle between Spain and Portugal to distant shores. Go to http://info.wadsworth.com/053461065X for an interactive version of this map.

whose territory he created the viceroyalty of Peru. Rich silver mines were later discovered in both Mexico and Peru. In the second half of the 16th century, up to 60 ships per year sailed for Spain laden with silver bullion.

Gold and silver were only part of the return that the Europeans got from their explorations in the New World. Settlers who migrated from Spain to the New World established huge landed estates that they ran with forced labor. When it was found that the Indian population had high mortality rates from working the sugar fields, the settlers began to import African slaves to take their place. Smallpox, typhus, and other diseases ravaged those whom forced labor failed to kill.

The European diet, as well as that of much of the rest of the world, was dramatically changed as vegetables and plants indigenous to the region were introduced to other cultures: Tomatoes, chili peppers, potatoes, and corn—and especially tobacco—were some of the important products brought to Europe and Asia. On the other hand, the Spanish introduced goats, sheep, and cattle to the New World, with major ecological results, because as they roamed the ranges they destroyed the roots of plants as well as ate the leaves. The impact of the European invasion was as devastating to South and Central America as it was in the Caribbean. By 1650, the Indian population of Mexico was reduced to about 5 percent of its original size of 25 million. A few Europeans, like the Spanish Dominican friar Bartolomé de Las Casas, tried to secure better treatment for the Indians. Las Casas argued that, once they were converted, the Indians should be thought of as fellow Christians. Spanish scholars and clergy debated the question of whether the Indians were fully human and deserved to be treated as such. As the Spanish administrators applied confused policies wavering between paternal dominance and ruthless enslavement, the toll on both sides was heavy: Vast loss of life among the Indian population was accompanied by the moral corruption of the conquerors.

A WIDENING WORLD ECONOMY

One crucial result of the age of discovery was that Europe placed itself at the center of an ever-widening global economy. On the commercial level, European powers, which before 1500 had traded almost entirely along the northern and southern shores of the continent and within Europe, now began to establish trade routes that reached around the world. The implications of this change were felt both in Europe and elsewhere. The first major impact was to be seen in the shifting fortunes of the Italian trading states that had dominated Mediterranean commerce and Europe's supply of spices and other Asian luxury goods for centuries. By 1600, Venice and Genoa were in sharp decline as the nations facing the Atlantic, principally Spain and Portugal, became the new trading powers of Europe. Gradually, the dominant position of the Iberian states was replaced by the Dutch Republic, England, and France.

As in the case of the indigenous American cultures, the spread of Europe's trading network around the globe had equally important consequences for non-European civilizations. In the Indian Ocean, Arab commerce was largely swept away as the Portuguese established their primacy along the East African and Indian coasts. The same was true, although perhaps to a lesser degree, in the trading waters of the Spice Islands and southeast Asia. Profits that had once remained in the hands of Muslim or Chinese merchants now began to flow to Europe, with important results for the decline of prosperity in the regional economy.

The establishment of Portugal's and Spain's overseas empires brought with it both problems and opportunities. The problems of communication and supply made close control from Europe extremely difficult. The principal purpose of these empires had, of course, been to produce revenues for the monarchs, who claimed them as personal property of the crown. At first, the Portuguese kings had allowed for a rather decentralized, almost feudal system of administration. By 1548, however, this cumbersome system was replaced with a more direct royal control over Brazil and the other colonies, and in 1580 the king established municipal councils that governed in his name. To help readminister the Spanish colonies and ensure the steady supply of bullion, Spain's

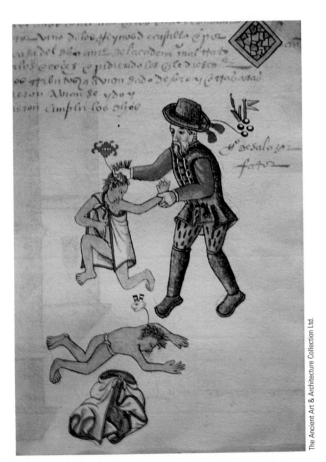

Manuscript page showing a European mistreating indigenous Amerindians. 16th century. The European is wearing typical Spanish dress—broad-brimmed hat, leather jerkin, high boots—as he strips the clothes from his two victims.

The Ancient Art & Architecture Collection Ltd.

kings established a system of viceroys, who ruled the colonies with the assistance of local governors as well as through advisory councils known as *audiencias*. Because of their obsession with supplying the home country in Europe with revenues, Spain and Portugal strictly limited the commercial opportunities of their colonies. Local trade within the Americas, or between them and other parts of the world, was discouraged.

Despite such problems, by 1600 the basis for a truly global economy had been established. The effects of this widening system of trade and production would have important implications for Europe (see Topic 46).

Putting the Era of Reconnaissance in Perspective

The long-range results of the European "discovery" of the Western Hemisphere were incalculable. The flow of gold and silver bullion to Europe not only enriched the coffers of the national states but also seriously affected the economy by impacting prices. Moreover, the increase in trade had a major impact on the development of commercial capitalism and a global economy. The fact, too, that the Europeans assumed an attitude of moral and cultural superiority over the indigenous populations they encountered, and simply claimed these vast regions as their own by right of discovery, reflected an attitude of dominance that was to characterize Europe's relationship with the rest of the globe for centuries to come.

Questions for Further Study

1. What conditions in Europe led to the increase in geographic knowledge and overseas discovery?
2. What technical advances were necessary before the age of discovery could take place?
3. What policies characterized Spanish rule in the Americas?

Suggestions for Further Reading

Braudel, Fernand. S. Reynolds, trans. *Civilization and Capitalism*, 3 vols. New York, 1979–1984.

Curtain, Philip D. *Cross-cultural Trade in World History.* Cambridge, MA, 1984.

Kriedte, Peter. *Peasants, Landlords and Merchant Capitalists: Europe and the World Economy, 1500–1800.* Leamington, Great Britain, 1983.

McAlister, Lyle N. *Spain and Portugal in the New World, 1492–1700.* Minneapolis, MN, 1984.

Tracy, James E., ed. *The Rise of Merchant Empires.* Cambridge, MA, 1990.

Waldman, Carl, and Alan Wexler. *Who Was Who in World Exploration.* New York, 1992.

Whitfield, Peter. *New Found Lands: Maps in the History of Exploration.* New York, 1998.

Wilford, J.N. *The Mysterious History of Columbus: An Exploration of the Man, the Myth, the Legacy.* New York, 1991.

Wood, Frances. *Did Marco Polo Go to China?* Boulder, CO, 1996.

InfoTrac College Edition

Enter the search term *Vasco da Gama* using Key Terms.

Enter the search term *Ferdinand Magellan* using Key Terms.

Enter the search term *Christopher Columbus* using the Subject Guide.

der his protection, and the outcast monk took up residence in Wartburg Castle. Luther eventually returned to Wittenberg, where he translated the Bible into German and began teaching at the university, spreading his ideas about the Scriptures to thousands of students. In 1525, he married Katherine von Bora, who remained his lifelong companion and aid.

Luther laid the foundations of a reformed church, which was independent from Rome and based on his teachings but which nevertheless kept many Catholic practices. Stressing the fundamental importance of faith rather than rituals and good works, Luther preserved only baptism and the Eucharist among the sacraments. He replaced the traditional Mass with a communion ceremony in which priests were not necessary to achieve the miracle of transubstantiation, whereby the wine and wafer were transformed into the blood and body of Christ. Instead, Luther spoke of all believers functioning as a new kind of communal priesthood and maintained that Christians were responsible for their own salvation. He also abandoned Latin in favor of German in services and emphasized the importance of music in teaching the Gospel.

THE LUTHERAN MOVEMENT: PEASANT REBELLION AND ARISTOCRATIC STRIFE

Lutheranism spread rapidly throughout the states of northern and central Germany and became especially popular among the middle classes of the free cities. Among Luther's earliest disciples was Philip Melanchthon (1497–1560), a Christian humanist who wrote some of the first rigorous theological statements on the new faith. Erasmus and other humanists, however, eventually rejected Lutheranism both on theological grounds and because they were dismayed at the prospect of a divided Christendom.

Other problems of a political nature also affected the early Lutheran movement in Germany. As a former Augustinian, Luther believed in the notion of two spheres of existence: the kingdom of God and the kingdom of the material world. Unlike the popes, who had argued for their supremacy over secular rulers, Luther's ideas gave support and strength to the growing power of secular government, which he saw as the protectors of his church. Luther, whose political and social views were generally quite conservative, supported the position of rulers and state power.

THE PEASANT REBELLIONS

If he lent his prestige and that of his new church to the princes of Germany, Luther was, on the other hand, fearful that his appeal for Christian freedom would be used to justify challenges to established authority. This attitude was fully revealed in 1522, when a rebellion broke out among lesser knights who sought to make common cause with the emperor against the more powerful princes, the free cities,

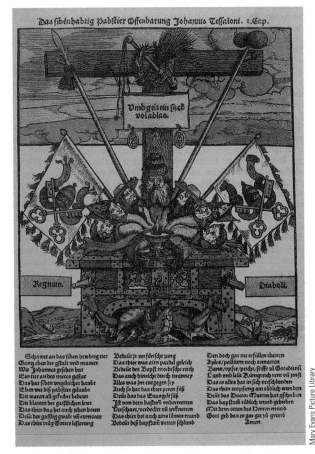

Satirical German print. 16th century. Part of the propaganda war against the Catholic Church, this print compares the "Papist" (i.e., Catholic) sellers of indulgences to the seven-headed beast of the Book of Revelations. One of the chief features of the Reformation movement was its use of the vernacular, in this case German, to reach the widest possible readership.

and the Catholic Church. Although they declared themselves Lutherans, Luther, who was scandalized by their breach of discipline, gave the rebellious knights no support, and the uprising was put down.

More revealing of Luther's conservative social views was the so-called Peasant War that erupted a few years later. The event actually began as a series of revolts among discontented peasants who protested the oppressive treatment that many landowners still meted out to their peasants. Supported by burghers in many cities, and under the leadership of a former follower of Luther, Thomas Muntzer, the peasants presented petitions demanding an end to serfdom and onerous taxes, and claiming religious autonomy.

When violence erupted in 1524, Luther immediately reacted by condemning the peasants in a vicious pamphlet called *Against the Thieving and Murderous Gangs of Peasants*, in which he called on the princes to wipe out the rebels without mercy. Luther believed it was the responsibility of subjects to obey their rulers, who were divinely chosen, and identified social revolution as a great evil. Luther applauded the massacre of peasants in 1525 by the princes, whom he had identified as the mainstay of his church. His reaction to the rebellions cost him support among the lower classes.

THE HAPSBURG-VALOIS WARS

One reason Lutheranism spread with relative ease throughout Germany was because the Emperor Charles V was so preoccupied with holding together his far-flung Hapsburg possessions that he could not focus his attention on stamping out Lutheranism in Germany. The emperor felt that his political aspirations were endangered by the policies of his chief enemy, Francis I (ruled 1515–1547), the Valois king of France. At home, Francis was a vigorous ruler who suppressed the nobles and struck against Protestantism. In the international arena, Francis, whose kingdom was encircled by Hapsburg lands, fought a long and costly series of military engagements—known as the Hapsburg-Valois Wars—against Charles throughout the Continent.

Besides having to contend with Francis, Charles frequently disagreed with the papacy. Pope Clement VII (ruled 1523–1534), who saw Hapsburg dominance in Italy as a danger to the Papal States, sided with Francis. In retaliation, in 1527, Charles's army sacked Rome, an event that shocked Catholic opinion in Europe but that strengthened the emperor's position in Italy. It was perhaps a measure of the times that, instead of joining forces with Charles in the struggle against Lutheranism, the papacy had opted to fight its most powerful ally.

Only after the emperor had repelled the Ottoman Turks from the walls of Vienna in 1529 did he try to deal with the German crisis. The next year, Charles convened the Diet of Augsburg, where he presented the Lutherans with an ultimatum that they return to the church by April 1531. Before the deadline, however, a group of Lutheran princes and free cities formed the Schmalkaldic League to protect themselves from the emperor. Renewal of war with the Turks and then with Francis diverted Charles's attention once again, and only in 1546, after finally having made peace with both enemies, did he act. That year, with a huge army drawn from his various possessions, Charles launched a war against the Schmalkaldic League. By then, Luther was dead and military victory seemed to presage the end of the Lutheran heresy. In 1552, the League joined forces with Henry II (ruled 1547–1559), the new king of France, and forced Charles to make peace. Dispirited by his efforts and broken in health, Charles abdicated in 1556 and retired to Spain, where he died two years later.

With Charles removed from the scene, in 1555 the religious conflict in Germany ended with the Peace of Augsburg. According to the agreement, Lutheranism was legally recognized and the rulers of the German states were free to choose between Lutheranism and Catholicism, although prince-bishops had to either remain Catholic or resign. The existence of the hundreds of independent territorial states in Germany was thereby accepted as an established principle, while the permanent religious division of Europe had become an unavoidable fact.

THE ADVANCE OF PROTESTANTISM IN CONTINENTAL EUROPE

By the time of the Peace of Augsburg, Scandinavia and part of northern Germany had separated from Roman Catholicism and joined the Protestant Reformation. Not only had Luther shattered more than a millennium of religious unity, but in each area of Europe a different variety of Protestantism evolved. In the countries of Scandinavia—Denmark, Norway, and Sweden—official Lutheran churches were established by the monarchies.

JOHN CALVIN AND THE SWISS REFORMATION

It was in Switzerland rather than in Scandinavia that some of the most important reform developments took place. A former part of the Holy Roman Empire until it won independence in 1499, Switzerland was a prosperous region of hard-working merchants and craftsmen. When the stirrings of reform came, many Swiss reacted favorably to another opportunity of distancing the country from papal Rome.

The first reformer in Switzerland was Huldrych Zwingli (1484–1531), a priest and humanist scholar who lived in Zurich. Zwingli always claimed that he arrived at his ideas about the superiority of biblical over papal authority and about justification by faith alone independently of Luther.

Woodcut of John Calvin. 1574. The upper inscription describes Calvin as resident in Geneva, and the lower one links him to Luther and Huss, other leading reformers. As in the previous illustration, the text is in German rather than Latin, a sign of the growing importance of literacy in the battle for Reform.

He and Luther differed on several doctrinal issues, including the meaning of baptism and the Eucharist, which Zwingli thought had only symbolic importance. A practical man with a keen sense of political realities, Zwingli convinced the Zurich town council to authorize an assembly of magistrates and clergymen to oversee religious and secular life in the city. As more cities were influenced by Protestantism, a brief but intense civil war erupted, during which Zwingli was killed. A settlement based on freedom of religious choice for each canton restored peace to Switzerland.

John Calvin (1509–1564) represented a later generation of Reformation leadership and spearheaded a more radical form of Protestantism. Born in France, he studied law until, in 1533, he underwent a religious awakening that led him to convert to Protestantism. Accused of heresy by the church, he fled to Basel, where he published a treatise entitled *Institutes of the Christian Religion*, in which he tried to make Lutheran principles into a systematic system of belief.

Calvin, like Zwingli, agreed with Luther's insistence on the importance of faith rather than good works. He also shared with his German predecessor the notion that Christians were constantly engaged in a struggle between good and evil. Humans, they both believed, were depraved sinners, but Calvin was convinced that God's purpose was beyond any human understanding. Before an omnipotent and supreme God, Calvin believed, humans were weak and lacked the necessary free will to bring about their own salvation. Instead, Calvin—like Luther and Zwingli, who were more circumspect in professing the belief—taught the doctrine of predestination, according to which God had decided before the Creation who would be saved and who would be damned. Because humans cannot know who has been chosen and who rejected, good Christians should focus on doing good works—which Calvin thought were a sign of having been selected for salvation—and leading a moral life. Above all, humans should devote themselves to the worship of God.

GENEVA AND THE SOCIAL VISION OF CALVINISM

A man of strong views and determination, Calvin is often thought of as the organizer of Protestantism. When in 1541 he was invited to come to Geneva, he built a Christian society to which reformers of the 16th century looked with pride and where religious refugees found sanctuary. Calvin's most powerful popular attraction was his sermons, and through them he preached his faith and set the tone for the life of morality and seriousness to which he wanted all citizens to aspire.

Calvin hoped to organize Geneva along religious lines, although a civilian magistracy continued to run the city government. On the other hand, Calvin presided over a Consistory made up of laymen and pastors, which established detailed rules by which citizens were to live. Personal conduct, including the manner of dress and the hours during which people could be outside their homes, was strictly controlled. Drunkenness, gambling, and frivolity were prohibited, and religious dissent was harshly punished.

Calvinism represented the most activist and compelling Protestant faith of the period, and his church provided an example that inspired reformers in other countries, from France and Scotland to North America.

THE ANABAPTISTS

As we have seen, Zwingli believed that baptism had symbolic rather than real meaning for Christians. Other reformers, known as **Anabaptists** ("baptized again"), made concern over the idea of baptism a central aspect of their doctrine. Rejecting the idea of predestination, the Anabaptists based their doctrine on the belief that adults alone, not children, were able to choose to enter a religious faith. Although opposed to baptizing children, they insisted that adults should be baptized.

The Anabaptists were considered radicals who thought that Luther had not gone far enough in his reforms. Although the Anabaptists accepted Luther's teachings, they insisted on a literal interpretation of the Scriptures and engaged in only those practices they believed were followed in the early church. Moreover, they saw the true church as

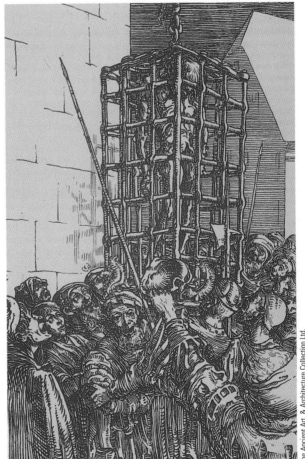

Illustration of an Anabaptist leader being tortured in a cage. 16th century. Popular prints such as this circulated widely as weapons in the Reformers' campaigns, and were intended to stimulate popular resentment against the authorities. The Anabaptists believed in adult baptism and rejected government control.

The Ancient Art & Architecture Collection Ltd.

a voluntary community of equal believers, much like the early Christian church as described in the New Testament. This spirit of democracy may have reflected the fact that most of their members were peasants, artisans, and other laborers linked by social and economic dissatisfaction. Their advocacy of communal property and their prohibition of interest reflected the class base of the movement and partly explains the ferocity of persecution against them. Their radicalism extended to politics as well. Anabaptists, contrary to most other Christians, wanted a total separation of church and state, refusing to serve in government positions or fight in the army.

Anabaptists established groups in Switzerland, Germany, and Austria, and later still in eastern Europe. In Zurich, Zwingli exiled them, and in Germany they were viciously persecuted because their ideas challenged both religious and secular power. In Münster, Germany, the Anabaptists at first were officially recognized in the early 1530s, and the city became a refuge for fellow believers from elsewhere. Here they instituted the practice of polygamy, and women were permitted to become priests.

A less radical Anabaptist group under the leadership of Menno Simons (1496–1561) established a movement that came to be known as the Mennonites, who wanted to withdraw from the world to live a pure Christian existence. Yet Simons too introduced severe discipline among his followers.

THE BREAK WITH ROME: HENRY VIII AND THE ENGLISH CHURCH

In England, where the monarchy and the papacy had often struggled for supremacy, Protestantism was established for reasons that often had little to do with the desire for religious reform. Here, the Reformation was led—unlike the experiences in Germany or Switzerland—by a monarch rather than a priest: King Henry VIII dominated the religious controversies of his age and lent his weight to the drive to separate the English church from Rome.

THE TUDOR SUCCESSION

The Tudor dynasty had been founded in the 15th century by Henry VII, England's first "new monarch" (see Topic 33). His son, Henry VIII (ruled 1509–1547), solidified the Tudor monarchy and proved to be one of the most important kings in English history.

An ambitious, ruthless man of strong appetites, Henry's concern for the future of the dynasty accounted for his decision to break with Rome. A long marriage to Catherine of Aragon (1485–1536) failed to produce a male heir to ensure the Tudor succession, and in 1527 he appealed to the pope for an annulment so that he could take a new queen. Henry had already gone on record in opposition to Luther, and under ordinary circumstances his request would no doubt have been approved in Rome. But two factors worked against

him. First, Catherine had originally been married to Henry's brother, and only a special papal dispensation had allowed him to marry his dead brother's wife. Henry was now convinced that God's punishment had prevented him from having a son, but an annulment now would have suggested that the first papal dispensation had been a mistake. Perhaps more important, Catherine, who refused to accept an annulment, was the aunt of the Emperor Charles V, whose soldiers had already sacked Rome and who had an obvious influence on the pope's decision.

Henry, who had contemplated divorce from Catherine, had already begun an affair with Anne Boleyn (c. 1507–1536), a lady in waiting at the court, who was now pregnant with the king's child. In January 1533, Henry and Anne secretly married. Thomas Cranmer (1489–1556), whom Henry had made archbishop of Canterbury, annulled the marriage to Catherine without waiting for the pope to act and then approved the marriage to Anne. When Anne did give birth, it was to a daughter, whom they named Elizabeth. When the pope finally moved, it was to excommunicate Henry.

THE FOUNDATIONS OF THE ANGLICAN CHURCH

These actions were taken only after a special act of Parliament had prohibited English ecclesiastical courts from appealing cases to Rome. Moreover, in 1534 Parliament passed the Act of Supremacy, which made Henry the supreme head of the English—or Anglican—church. Thomas Cromwell (1485–1540), the king's secretary, then devised plans that ended payments to the papacy and closed hundreds of monasteries, whose confiscated lands were sold to pay off Henry's debts. Sir Thomas More, the humanist scholar who had served as the king's chancellor, was beheaded when he refused to accept Henry's triumph over the church.

Henry's confrontation with the papacy received wide support in England, where Protestantism was spreading, both from Parliament and from the public. But Henry moved cautiously in matters of doctrine, securing passage in 1539 of the Six Articles Act that endorsed important aspects of Catholic doctrine, including celibacy for priests and the miracle of transubstantiation, and rejected only the idea of papal supremacy. Henry's refusal to make substantial changes in religious doctrine or practice was part of a shrewd policy for gaining popular consensus behind the break with Rome.

THE ENGLISH REFORMATION

Despite these major transformations made to secure Henry's marriage to Anne Boleyn, the irony was that Henry eventually had four other wives, two of whom, Anne Boleyn and Catherine Howard, were accused of adultery and beheaded. The successor he so desperately wanted was produced by his third wife, Jane Seymour, whose son eventually took the throne as Edward VI (ruled 1547–1553). During the minority of Edward's reign, religious reformers such as Cranmer were free to establish Protestantism more firmly in England. Through further acts of Parliament, the clergy were eventually permitted to marry, and a new liturgy, contained in the *Book of Common Prayer,* was adopted in 1549.

After Edward's early death, the throne passed to Mary (ruled 1553–1558), Henry's daughter with Catherine. Mary tried to restore Catholicism, a policy that produced widespread hostility and resistance, and the burning of some 300 Protestants earned her the nickname "Bloody Mary." The queen then made herself even more unpopular by marrying Philip II of Spain, the son of Charles V. By the time of her death in 1558, Protestantism had been even more firmly established in England.

In Ireland, which was dominated by the English landlords, the parliament passed measures endorsing the separation from Rome and establishing the Church of Ireland modeled on the Anglican Church, with the king as its head. When the majority of Irish people remained Catholic, no doubt partly to express their opposition to the English, the Catholic monasteries and the churches were ordered closed.

In Scotland, where King James V (ruled 1528–1542) and his daughter, Mary, Queen of Scots (ruled 1542–1567), were both strong supporters of the Catholic Church, the state fought the reform movement. The Scottish Reformation was led by John Knox (c. 1505–1572). Knox, a former priest and a fiery preacher, had studied with John Calvin in Geneva. In 1560, he encouraged the parliament in Scotland to pass laws abolishing the Catholic Mass and paving the way for Knox to establish the Presbyterian Church, which took its name from the *presbyters,* or ministers, who controlled it. In 1564, Knox wrote *The Book of Common Order,* which determined the liturgy for the Church of Scotland.

Putting the Reformation in Perspective

The movement for reform within the Catholic Church started by Martin Luther in the early 16th century destroyed the religious unity that western Europe had enjoyed since the late Roman Empire. The establishment of the Protestant churches and the rapid spread of their doctrines revealed deep popular discontent in spiritual affairs. Its reverberations, however, spilled over from religious issues into the secular realm.

The Reformation profoundly influenced the political and social realities of the day. The broad appeal of many reform doctrines especially touched the lower classes, sometimes unleashing popular unrest. The upper classes responded to the Reformation in different ways. In some regions of Europe, rulers and nobles supported reform as a means of undermining papal authority within their own borders, while others remained attached to Roman Catholicism. In defense, the Church of Rome would soon embark on a vigorous program of internal change and counter-reformation that would aim at pushing back the tide of Protestantism. The religious controversies kept Europe in turmoil for centuries to come.

Questions for Further Study

1. What were the origins of the Protestant Reformation?
2. What were Luther's principal ideas, and how did they differ from conventional Christianity?
3. In what ways did religious reformation reflect and affect social and political conditions in Germany?
4. How did the ideas of the other major reformers differ from those of Luther?

Suggestions for Further Reading

Ackroyd, Peter. *The Life of Thomas More.* New York, 1998.

Bouwsma, William J. *John Calvin: A Sixteenth Century Portrait.* New York, 1987.

Edwards, Mark. *Luther's Last Battles.* Ithaca, NY, 1983.

Galer, U.R. Gritsch, trans. *Huldrych Zwingli: His Life and Work.* Philadelphia, 1986.

Haigh, Christopher. *English Reformations: Religion, Politics and Society under the Tudors.* Oxford, 1993.

Jensen, De Lamar. *Reformation Europe: Age of Reform and Revolution.* Lexington, KY, 1981.

Marius, Richard. *Martin Luther: The Christian Between God and Death.* Cambridge, MA, 1999.

McGrath, Alister E. *The Intellectual Origins of the European Reformation.* Oxford, 1987.

Oberman, Heiko. E. Walliser-Schwarzbart, trans. *Luther: Man Between God and the Devil*. New Haven, CT, 1989.

Pettegree, Andrew, ed. *The Reformation World*. New York, 2000.

Scarisbrick, J.J. *The Reformation and the English People*. Oxford, 1984.

Spitz, Lewis W. *The Protestant Reformation, 1517–1559*. New York, 1985.

Tracy, James D. *Europe's Reformations, 1450-1650*. Lanham, MA, 1999.

InfoTrac College Edition

Enter the search term *Reformation* using the Subject Guide.

Enter the search term *Martin and Luther not King* using the Subject Guide.

Enter the search term *John Calvin* using the Subject Guide.

THE SOCIAL WORLDS OF THE RENAISSANCE AND REFORMATION

The sweeping changes that the Renaissance and Reformation produced in cultural and political life in Europe also profoundly affected social patterns. Despite their long-term significance, however, the immediate repercussions of these developments did not have a consistent impact on all sectors of society, although the rate of change was more intense than at any time since the early Middle Ages.

European society was becoming increasingly urbanized, and a new and more complex class structure began to develop in the growing cities. Although rural life remained comparatively static, the urban setting allowed for significantly more social mobility. Foremost among the new social groups of the cities to emerge in this period was a rapidly expanding middle class. This category included the wealthier merchants who arose as a result of the commercial revolution, as well as the less affluent burghers who operated shops and small businesses. Other factors in stimulating social change included the spread of education among urban dwellers and the growing tendency of urban women of the poorer classes to work. This change, in turn, affected patterns of marriage and family life.

The broad changes in society had both positive and negative effects on women, depending on their status. Aristocratic women lost some of the authority and equality they had enjoyed during the High Middle Ages as the values attached to the concept of chivalry were replaced by the more rigid and confining notions associated with formal court life. One of the consequences of the new code of conduct for these women was a double standard of sexual behavior for men and women. For women of the non-noble classes, on the other hand, new employment opportunities, especially in commerce, arose in the walled cities, allowing them the possibility of greater social mobility than ever before.

While Western society remained overwhelmingly Christian and white, urban life contained small but significant minorities, including Jews and Muslims. With the expansion of Europe overseas as a result of the era of reconnaissance, the growth of the slave trade produced a new minority in ever-greater numbers: black slaves, some of whom eventually won their freedom.

The net result of all these developments was to speed up the transformation of European life from its medieval patterns to a society on the eve of the modern world.

CLASS, MOBILITY, AND CHANGING VALUES

During the 16th century, the three most important long-term forces determining social patterns were demographic change, status, and wealth.

POPULATION TRENDS

During the 16th century, Europe began to recover fully from the destructive effects of the Black Death. Before the 19th century, when governments began to collect the first accurate statistics, all calculations of population can be at best very rough estimates. It seems clear, however, that in the course of the 16th century, population increased significantly, perhaps by as much as one-third. By 1600, Europe may have had more than 100 million inhabitants. The growth pattern was neither constant in time nor geographically even throughout the continent, and a sometimes wildly fluctuating death rate—determined largely by famine, disease, and war—helped keep growth in check.

The repercussions of population growth were varied. For one thing, the supply of labor increased significantly. At first, a larger agrarian workforce resulted in an increase in the amount of food available, while rising wages created a demand for manufactured products.

This expansion in turn stimulated economic activity in the towns, which began to attract ever larger numbers of people. By today's standards, towns in the 16th century were quite small. In 1500, Cologne, situated on the Rhine River, was the largest urban center in Germany with a mere 20,000 inhabitants. In that same year, few European cities had populations of more than 100,000. A century later, however, Paris counted a half-million people, Naples 300,000, and London 250,000.

As the urban population of Europe increased, a surplus labor force was created. This drove down real wages, a setback accompanied by a startling rise in prices in the later 16th century known as the "price revolution" (see Topic 46). The inflation in commodity prices, especially for basic necessities such as bread and wheat, was immense—by 1600, prices had risen to four times their level of a century earlier. Wages did not, however, keep up with prices, and the standard of living for the poorer classes declined.

By the 17th century, therefore, population and economic growth began to slow down and in some cases to reverse themselves. Yet if the rise and decline in population was a volatile aspect of social reality, status remained constant as a determining feature of life for every member of European society. A person's status was fixed in a social hierarchy that determined not only how specific groups related to each other, but also how each class lived. The element in 16th-century society that began to undermine social position was wealth.

OLD NOBLES AND NEW MERCHANTS

The 16th century was a time of great expansion and prosperity for the middle classes, and it also saw crisis and read-

Contemporary painting of *Market Place at Antwerp*. 16th century. The painting conveys something of the bustle of the scene. Note the distinction in dress between the middle classes, wearing sober black, and the more colorful costumes of the peasants who are selling their goods. The high, narrow buildings are characteristic of architecture in the Low Countries.

justment for the traditional noble landowning class. Despite their declining financial status, they continued to occupy the most important political posts and government offices. With the strengthening of the monarchy's power, the nobility retained their prestige while losing their old feudal authority over the peasant class.

In France and elsewhere, kings used their ability both to create new categories of nobles and to enlarge the existing ranks of aristocrats in order to enhance royal authority. The French monarchs, for example, limited the power of the old feudal families ("nobles of the sword") by elevating members of the middle class to the status of "nobles of the robe" to serve as bureaucrats in the state system (see Topic 44).

The rise in population and the growth of towns sharply affected the income of those who made their living by manufacturing, creating an ever-rising demand for their products. Moreover, the price revolution redistributed significant wealth to the manufacturing class of the towns by increasing profits. The commercial revolution made possible an equally rapid accumulation of wealth in the hands of a new middle class of merchants and traders. As a result, the definition of status relaxed, and position in the social hierarchy became more fluid.

The leading middle-class citizens were those involved in international trade, banking, and industry, who dominated civic affairs. These powerful families established social customs and patronized the arts. Beneath them were the urban shopkeepers and craftsmen, whose prosperity depended on local rather than international markets. Their economic and social status derived from their membership in guilds, the trade and craft organizations that controlled business and professional standards in the cities.

THE POOR IN TOWN AND COUNTRY

For all the increase in prosperity for the upper classes of society, most of the urban and rural population remained poor and often lived at the edge of subsistence. In the towns, the bulk of the population consisted of manual laborers who earned their daily wages by working on building sites, at ports, and as carters and carriers. Much of this work was seasonal, and in winter the laborers who crowded the towns in good weather often found themselves unemployed. Workers with some degree of specialized skill were employed in the small factories that produced textiles, metal and glass goods, and food products such as beer and bread.

Another principal source of employment in the towns was domestic labor. With the rise of middle-class prosperity, the demand for assistance in the home—maids, cooks, and personal servants—continued to grow. Domestic employment sometimes provided greater job security than casual

Marinus van Reymerswaele, *Bankers.* 15th century. The two men are engaged in counting the coins piled on the table and recording the transaction. The system of double-entry bookkeeping was invented earlier in the century by Florentine bankers and soon spread throughout Europe.

Sketch showing an episode from the Peasants' Revolt of 1524–1526. The scene depicts the destruction of a monastery. The main church is on the left, its doors about to be battered down, while other rebels are climbing steps to a large room on the upper floor of the main building, the monks' refectory, or dining-room.

labor, although family servants depended on the goodwill of their employers. Whatever their occupation, workers in the towns played no part in the political affairs of their community and benefited only marginally from the better standard of living and enlarged horizons of the urban environment.

In the countryside, conditions were little better for the peasantry. Nature and the seasons determined the tempo of rural life, where almost all activities focused on farming and the raising of animals. Throughout much of Europe the most widespread and important agricultural product was grain (wheat, rye, barley, and oats), which was baked into bread, the principal item in the peasant diet. In the Mediterranean region, more specialized crops such as grapes and olives provided a more varied source of nutrition while also offering additional products and occupations. In England, the Netherlands, and Germany, the staple drink was beer, while in Italy, France, and Spain farmers used grapes to make wine.

Living conditions for the working classes in both town and country were grim. Urban laborers lived in crowded and unsanitary tenements in slum districts, while peasant housing generally consisted of small and unheated huts in which people dwelled alongside animals. For both groups, fire and disease were constant hazards and starvation a perpetual preoccupation.

EDUCATION, MARRIAGE, AND THE FAMILY

One of the effects of the Renaissance and Reformation was an increase in the importance of education for the nobility and middle classes. The poor and working classes of Europe, who comprised the overwhelming majority of the population, remained excluded from the rise in educational standards until the 19th century. In all classes of society, the family remained the basic social unit, although the period saw a transition from the traditional extended family to the more modern nuclear family.

EDUCATION IN RENAISSANCE AND REFORMATION

The humanists of the Renaissance believed that education should prepare citizens to assume their responsibilities to society as well as to shape individual character. Humanist education combined Classical precepts with Christian teaching to create a fully rounded personality.

In the 15th century, Vittorino da Feltre (1378–1446) translated these ideas into an actual curriculum, which he applied to the students who attended his famous secondary school at Mantua. Vittorino provided a core program of Latin, Greek, philosophy, mathematics, and music, as well as physical training. Vittorino's school attracted students from throughout Italy, and his model curriculum was widely adopted.

Many of the leading Protestant reformers adapted humanist principles to their religious concerns. Whereas Renaissance schools were designed principally to serve the needs of the upper classes, Reformation educators aimed at reaching a broader range of society. Some leaders, like Martin Luther, even encouraged the state to provide free public education for children of all classes. German Protestants introduced secondary school education, which added religious instruction to the traditional humanist curriculum of the liberal arts. Similarly, the newly founded Jesuit order established colleges whose students were taught the classics along with Catholic doctrine. For women, the Ursuline order, founded by St. Angela Merici, provided girls with training in religion and morals (see Topic 41).

MARRIAGE AND THE FAMILY

In all family arrangements, women were subservient to men. Although mothers were responsible for raising children, fathers had ultimate authority over them and arranged their marriages. Husbands also decided matters of family finances and managed their property. Once married, wives generally gave up their independence, including the right to own property in their own name.

Traditionally, European families had consisted of several generations and degrees of kinship living in the same household. A typical family unit might therefore contain father, mother, and children together with grandparents, uncles and aunts, and cousins. With the emphasis on the individual at the heart of both Renaissance and Reformation, this extended family arrangement tended to break up into smaller nuclear units made up of parents and their children. This pattern, typical of Western Europe, foreshadowed the family structure of the 19th and 20th centuries; in eastern Europe, the extended family remained the prevailing model. Despite the changing living arrangements, extended families continued to function as a unit in financial and political matters. This was as true for the old ruling families of the Italian city-states—the Medici and the Visconti, for example—as it was for the newer commercial dynasties of northern Europe.

Given the importance of family connections in business and politics, upper-class parents generally arranged their children's marriages. Such alliances involved the payment of large dowries by the parents of the bride to the husband. Even poor families were expected to provide a dowry for their daughters, making the raising of girls more of an economic strain. In some communities, private charities financed by the wealthy provided subsidies for the payment of dowries among needy families.

Protestants developed new attitudes toward the family. In theory, with the abolition of a celibate clergy, the relationship between husband and wife became the focus of family life, and marriage partners placed new emphasis on mutual love and respect. In practice, however, husbands continued to be the dominant force in most marriages. Martin Luther's example demonstrated the contradictions that often characterized Protestant views of marriage. Luther, a conservative in most social matters, encouraged his followers to maintain the authority of the husband: "The wife," he wrote, "is compelled to obey him by God's command." His own private life, however, seemed to reflect a different, more loving relationship. In 1525, Luther, who had been an Augustinian monk, married a former Cistercian nun, Katharine von Bora (1499–1552). For the 21 years of their marriage, she remained a constant companion and assistant to Luther, who wrote toward the end of his life, "Next to God's Word there is no more precious treasure than holy matrimony."

THE BURDENS OF GENDER: WOMEN IN A CHANGED WORLD

In the Renaissance period, women generally married while still in their teens, whereas men usually postponed marriage until their late thirties. This discrepancy in age was deter-

mined by the need for men to achieve financial independence; while the extended family had offered economic support for young families, nuclear families required that fathers had sufficient financial means to maintain their own wives and children. By the 17th century, as women increasingly entered the workplace, they too tended to marry at a later age.

In both courtship and marriage, women of all classes were expected to conform to different standards from men. Young women were kept under constant supervision in order to preserve their virginity before marriage. Newly wed husbands who found that their wives were not virgins had the right to break the marriage without being obliged to return the dowry. Men, on the other hand, were expected to be sexually experienced. For many single men in their twenties and thirties, professional prostitutes provided their services, often under state regulation. In reality, of course, both men and women engaged in sexual activity before marriage, and by the 18th century illegitimate births were commonplace.

EDUCATION, CULTURE, AND THE ECONOMY

The double standard was particularly striking among the aristocracy, who cultivated the courtly way of life. In the Renaissance, children of noble families received a higher level of education than their counterparts in the medieval period. Whereas the training of boys prepared them to participate in business and public affairs, the education of girls was mostly confined to the classics, painting, music, and the other fine arts. University students were almost entirely males, whereas women were educated at home by family or private tutors. As a result, women were unable to train for the professions, although printing made it easier for women to study.

Despite these obstacles, we know of several dozen women Renaissance humanists and a few prominent artists. Vittoria Colonna (1492–1547), for example, wrote love poems and religious sonnets that were widely admired and corresponded with Michelangelo. Generally, however, women found it extremely difficult to pursue intellectual careers, both because they were expected to marry and bear children and because men regarded intellectual pursuits as unwomanly. Among the well-known artists of the day was Sofonisba Anguissola of Cremona (c. 1535–1625), one of six sisters who painted. Anguissola, whose work was admired by Michelangelo, was court painter for Philip II of Spain and received the patronage of rulers and popes.

The medieval tradition of chivalry had required men to pay homage to and respect women. By contrast, Renaissance experts in life at court, such as Castiglione, expected women to serve primarily a purely decorative function in what was essentially a man's world of power and politics (see Topic 36). It was not uncommon for noblewomen in the feudal age to take charge of governments and manage estates in the absence of their husbands. In the leading families of the Renaissance period, however, aristocratic

Collection The Right Honorable Earl Spencer, Althorp House

Sofonisba Anguissola, *Self-Portrait*. 1561. Born in the northern Italian city of Cremona, Anguissola was influenced by Florence Mannerist artists such as Bronzino. Vasari wrote that she handled "design with greater study and better grace than any other woman of our times." By the time of this self-portrait, she had moved to Spain, to work for the Spanish court.

women were limited to performing traditional roles as wives, mothers, and daughters.

Women from the families of wealthy merchants had a greater range of responsibilities. While merchants traveled abroad, their wives ran the family business and were trained to keep records and balance the books. Contessina de' Medici, the wife of the Florentine banker Cosimo, employed a secretary to assist her with her correspondence, while the English diarist Samuel Pepys (1633–1703) taught his wife mathematics so that she could maintain the household accounts.

After the death of her husband, a widow was able to inherit his property and business. Many women used the capital thus acquired to enlarge existing businesses or start their own firms. In the 16th century, women in northern Europe engaged in international commerce and became members of overseas trading companies. In Ravensberg, Germany, in the same period, more than 10 percent of the members of the Merchant's Society were women.

For women of lower economic status, opportunities for social mobility and employment were also available in the towns. Most guilds restricted membership to men, but some allowed a widow to inherit her husband's membership, and a few even permitted women to become members in their

own right. One of the fields open to women was publishing. In Strasbourg in the 16th century and London in the 17th, widows ran publishing houses that they had inherited from their husbands. In the century following 1550, some 10 percent of all publishers in London were women.

In rural areas, women led equally complex but dependent lives. In farming households, wives and daughters were expected to perform multiple roles, including traditional domestic activities, feeding and caring for farm animals, and helping with labor in the fields. The wives of men who worked away from home often ran the farms on their own, including the heavy manual labor of plowing and harvesting. In many cases, women also engaged in cottage industries such as spinning, weaving, and basket making. If she became a widow, a country woman would generally seek to remarry in order to have a man to take charge of work on the farm.

Once they came of age, the daughters of rural families often migrated to the cities. There they looked for employment, generally in domestic work, which remained the chief form of urban women's work until modern times. Domestic labor involved long working hours and low pay, and young girls were often subjected to sexual violence by their employers. Women also found jobs in other fields, including manual labor in construction, mining, and retailing. In market towns, women ran most businesses involving the preparation, buying, and selling of food. In all occupations that they shared with men, women were paid significantly less. The overwhelming majority of townswomen were poor, and some of those who did not find employment or a husband supported themselves by prostitution.

The vast transformations that unfolded in the era of the Renaissance and Reformation brought widespread and generally beneficial changes to Europe. For women, however, they had mixed consequences. The overall pattern of European women's lives did not improve substantially until the 18th century, when the Industrial Revolution wrought a massive restructuring of European society.

FEAR OF WITCHES: SUPERSTITION AND PERSECUTION

Women were also seriously affected by one of the most striking aspects of the fanatical atmosphere that accompanied the religious upheavals of the 16th century—the growing fear of witches that seemed to grip society. When the papacy instituted the Inquisition against the Albigensians in the 13th century (see Topic 27), it also began to persecute witches as part of that same campaign. On the eve of the Reformation, the church renewed its interest in stamping out witchcraft. The campaign against witchcraft was not, however, limited to Catholic states, and the hysteria over witches appears to have swept Europe, affecting Germany, Switzerland, England and Scotland, and the English colonies in North America.

Witchcraft was an ancient form of worship that had long been widespread in Europe's villages and rural areas. In the Middle Ages, the church identified witches with worship of the devil and made witchcraft a heresy. The

Woodcut showing a witch being abducted by the Devil. 1555. The devil, painted in green, has horns and three-toed feet. The scale of the horse, rider, and captive contrasts with the peasants on the right, working in the fields outside the town nearby.

AKG London

Inquisition made witches a target of its activities, and during periods of social and economic crisis, witches often became targets of popular wrath. In 1484, the papacy condemned witches as having become instruments of Satan and the cause of a variety of evils. Two Dominican friars investigated witchcraft in Germany on behalf of the papacy and authored a handbook about the practices of witches and methods by which to identify them. Witches were said not only to have participated in nighttime ceremonies and sexual orgies but also to have cast spells on others.

At the time of the Reformation, the belief in witches seems to have become the source of popular hysteria, with people accusing each other indiscriminately and tens of thousands being prosecuted for witchcraft. The fear of witches in the 16th and early 17th centuries multiplied, and trials of accused persons were a daily occurrence in many parts of Europe. The victims of the witchcraft craze came from all walks of life, although people from the lower classes seem more likely to have been accused.

The frenzy over witchcraft had serious implications for the position of women; three out of four people charged with witchcraft were women, most of whom were widows. Most were from the lower classes, including peasants and domestic servants. The identification of women with witches further marginalized them in society, creating identifications in the popular mind with devil worship and sin. Some witch hunters thought women were evil by nature, an attitude supported both by the biblical tale of Eve's corruption of Adam and by medieval folk tales.

Certainly part of the cause of the witchcraft craze was the aroused passion of religious controversy during a time of heightened sensitivity to charges of heresy. The social turmoil of the period also seems to have contributed to the fear of unrest among the poorer classes. The great witchcraft fear declined in the second half of the 17th century, when the religious conflicts and the wars that accompanied them ended. As conditions began to settle down, the tensions and divisiveness that inspired the trials diminished, and by the early 18th century the superstitions that had fed the fear began to be dispelled.

The great contradiction of the witchcraft craze was, of course, that it occurred at the very time that reformers were seeking spiritual regeneration. Luther, Calvin, and other Protestant leaders condemned witches as savagely as they did the Catholic clergy, and its victims were burned at the stake by both churches.

OUTSIDERS IN CHRISTIAN EUROPE: JEWS, MUSLIMS, AND BLACKS

The 16th and 17th centuries saw much of European life dominated by religious conflict between Catholics and Protestants. On the fringes of European society, several non-Christian religious minorities had maintained a precarious existence for centuries. Jews and Muslims lived side by side in Spain and in Spanish possessions in Italy until 1492. Yet there were differences in the status of Muslims and Jews in Christian society. Muslims were tolerated partly because strong Muslim states with large Christian populations provided them with some degree of protection. In the Middle Ages, Jews were the only group to whom Christians granted the right of dissent. On the other hand, nowhere were Jews accorded the full rights of active citizenship.

The consolidation of the kingdom of Spain under Ferdinand and Isabella, together with the religious upheavals of the Reformation and Counter-Reformation, had a dramatic effect on the lives of the Jewish minority there. In the early 15th century, the largest concentrations of Jews in Europe were in Iberia, where perhaps 80,000 lived, as well as in Sicily, which had some 35,000. Another 35,000 Jews lived in Italy, while southern France and the German areas of the Holy Roman Empire had smaller numbers. As Jews were forced out of Spain, many moved to eastern Europe and others to the Ottoman Empire. In the 16th century, Jews were expelled from some Italian states, and by the end of that century, there were more than 100,000 Polish Jews (on Jewish life in Europe, see Topic 41).

As far back as the age of Classical Greece, artists portrayed black people on painted vases and in small figurines. The earliest Africans to live in ancient Europe were the slaves who were brought by traders toward the end of the Roman Republic at the time of the Punic Wars.

HISTORICAL PERSPECTIVES

THE FIRST AFRICANS IN EUROPE

TREVOR P. HALL   Bethune-Cookman College

The first Africans in Europe fell into three ca-tegories: (1) élite noblemen, clerics, and ambassadors; (2) freemen/women vendors, translators, sailors, artisans, and laborers; and (3) slaves. The major questions are, how many Africans lived in ancient Europe, what were they doing in Europe, where did they live, and when did they arrive?

Black Africans have lived in "Europe" since ancient times when North Africa and the Sahara Desert formed the southern frontier of the Roman Empire. Beginning in the 4th century A.D., German invaders sacked Rome and began settling in the Empire, and in the process disrupted long-distance trade with Africa and began the rapid political disintegration of the Empire in the West. Portugal and Spain were removed from Germanic control when Muslims from North Africa conquered the Iberian peninsula in A.D. 711 and linked it to Muslim states in Africa. From A.D. 711 to 1492, a few black Africans who were Muslims lived in Europe's southwest frontiers in Portugal and Spain. During this period, some Africans also lived in Genoa and Venice as Italian ships traded with North Africans from Morocco to Egypt.[1]

From time to time, African clerics from the Coptic Church of Christian Ethiopia visited Rome when benevolent Muslim leaders in Egypt permitted pilgrims to cross Islamic territories. One Portuguese tale has Prince Henry the Navigator of Portugal meeting an Ethiopian cleric in Portugal. The African convinced Prince Henry that the powerful Christian Kingdom of Ethiopia lay south of Muslim Egypt. According to the 15th-century Portuguese royal chronicler, Gomes Eannes de Azurara, one of the five reasons Prince Henry first sent ships to West Africa was to find the Christian king of Ethiopia whom the Portuguese called Prester John.[2] Prince Henry envisioned a military alliance with black Christians of Ethiopia that would destroy Islam by attacking its southern underbelly.

Searching for Ethiopia, Prince Henry the Navigator sent Portuguese mariners past Morocco to West Africa where in 1441, they kidnapped four black Muslim fishermen from the mouth of the Senegal River and brought them back to Europe. The Portuguese became the first to sail from Europe to West Africa. By the 1470s Spain sent ships to West Africa. Over the next four centuries, European ships would transport hundreds of thousands of West Africans to Europe.

The earliest European mariners in 15th-century West Africa were traders, not conquerors. These Portuguese established peaceful diplomatic relationships with several African kingdoms, especially states that had strategic Atlantic harbors. In 1488, four years before Christopher Columbus sailed to the Americas, a Muslim nobleman and Portuguese ally named Bemoim visited Portugal from his Wolof kingdom in modern-day Senegal. He sought Portuguese military assistance to regain his lost throne. The mission ended with Bemoim's death at the hands of his Portuguese patrons, but his visit marked the first of a long line of African nobles in Europe.[3]

From the 1480s through the 1700s, African nobles visited Portugal, Spain, and France. Most African nobles in early modern Europe lived in Portugal and came from the Congo. As early as the 1480s, a Congolese ambassador sailed to Portugal where he represented his nation.[4] In the 1490s, Congolese noble children lived in the Portuguese king's castle in Évora, Portugal. According to the modern historian Basil

[1] Jacques Heers, *Escravos E Servidão Doméstica Na Idade Média No Mundo Mediterranico* (Lisbon: Publicações, 1983).

[2] Gomes Eannes de Azurara, *The Chronicle of the Discovery and Conquest of Guinea,* trans. and eds., Charles Raymond Beazley and Edgar Prestage (London: The Hakluyt Society, 1st wer., no. 100; reprint New York: Burt Franklin, 1899).

[3] José Goncalves and Paul Teyssier, "Textes Portugais sur les Wolofs au XV siècle—Batême du prince Bemoi (1488)" *Bulletin de'IFAN,* t. xxx, ser., B. no. 3 (Paris, 1968), 822–846.

[4] Antonio Brásio, *Hortórica Do Reino Do Congo* [Ms. 8080 da Biblioteca Nacional de Lisboa] (Lisboa: Centro De Estudos Historicos Ultramarinos, 1969).

Davidson, 20 young Congolese students were sent to Europe in 1516. A few years later, the son of the Congolese king visited the pope in Rome. One Congolese prince became a bishop in the Catholic Church and was then called Dom Henrique.[5] Other African ambassadors in early modern Portugal included representatives from Benin, Angola, and Ethiopia, as well as Serers from Senegal.

After Portuguese ships established direct maritime links with West Africans in 1441, other Africans migrated to Europe, where many retained their freedom. A few enslaved Africans in Europe regained their liberty and formed free African communities. In the centuries after 1441, most free Africans in Europe lived in the Portuguese capital Lisbon, or in the Spanish cities Seville and Valencia. After the 1520s, however, small groups of free blacks were found in England, France, and Holland after these nations started trading directly with West Africa.

European historians record isolated cases of Africans who were set free when they arrived in Europe aboard European ships. For example, in 1571 France, "a shipowner placed some blacks on sale in Bordeaux, but they were ordered released by the Parlement."[6] Holland had a similar case, in 1596, when 130 Africans whom Captain Pieter van der Haagen had brought to Middleburg were set free by the town council and ordered to find jobs as free workers.[7] The English romanticize about Africans who regained their freedom upon setting foot on English soil.[8]

Some free Africans discovered innovative ways to maintain their freedom. As early as March 17, 1490, the black man Pedro Alvares secured a letter from the king of England certifying him to be a free man before he migrated to Portugal.[9] One enslaved African regained his freedom from his Portuguese master, Joao de Coimbra, on March 23, 1498, when he jumped ship in East Africa during Vasco da Gama's maiden voyage to India. These cases were the exception; as a rule most free blacks in Europe worked, saved money, and purchased their freedom, or that of their families.

Some free blacks in Portugal worked as mariners and translators aboard European merchant ships that traded in West Africa and the Americas. Portuguese archival records indicate that some blacks who were granted their freedom in a deceased master's will were still kept in bondage. On March 20, 1518, King Manuel of Portugal acted on the request from a black fraternity in Lisbon to ensure that wills were honored.[10] Free blacks in Seville, Spain, also had a fraternity to protect their interests in the 16th century.[11] Once additional European nations joined Portugal and Spain in trading with Africa, free African communities appeared all over western Europe.

Most black Africans in early modern Europe lived in bondage. Most enslaved Africans lived in Lisbon, Portugal's capital city where the 9950 captives formed almost 10 percent of the population in 1551–1553.[12] Thousands of other enslaved Africans lived throughout Portugal, especially in the southern port towns in Algarve province. After Portugal, the greatest number of enslaved blacks lived in the Spanish cities of Seville and Valencia. From 1482 to 1516 some 5000 enslaved Africans arrived in Valencia from Portugal and its colonies.[13]

After the 1530s, France, England, and Holland sent ships to West Africa, and these European merchants transported captive Africans to Europe. By the early 1600s, England and France joined Spain and Portugal in establishing colonies in the West Indies and North America. Once European planters began exploiting enslaved African laborers in the Americas, plantation owners who returned to Europe transported captive Africans to Europe. Despite maritime trade from Africa to Europe, and planters bringing enslaved Africans from their Caribbean plantations, Europe never had more Africans than the 10 percent of 1551–1553 Lisbon.

[5] D. Charles-Martail De Witte, *Henri de Congo, Eveque titulaire d 'Utique* (Roma, 1968).

[6] William B. Cohen, *The French Encounter with Africans, White Response to Blacks, 1530–1880* (Bloomington: Indiana University Press, 1980), 5.

[7] Johannes Menne Posta, *The Dutch in the Atlantic Slave Trade, 1500–1815* (Cambridge: Cambridge University Press, 1990), 10.

[8] Folarin Shyllon, *Black People in Great Britain* (London: Oxford University Press, 1977).

[9] Arquivo Nacional da Torre do Tombo, "Chancelaria De. D. Joao II," livro 16, fol. 61. Printed in Azevedo "Os Escravos" *Archivo Historico Portuquez 1*, no. 9 (1903), 300.

[10] Arquivo Nacional da Torre de Tombo, "Chancelaria de D. Joao III," Liv. 22, fols. 100–100v, and Liv. 17, fol. 44v. Printed in Antonio Brásio, *Monumenta Missionaria Africana, Africa Ocidental*, 2d. ser. (1500–1569) (Lisboa: 1963), vol. 2, 151–152.

[11] Ruth Pike, *Aristocrats and Traders, Sevillian Society in the Sixteenth Century* (Ithaca: Cornell University Press, 1972).

[12] A. Saunders, *A Social History of Black Slaves and Freedmen in Portugal 1441–1555* (London: Cambridge University Press, 1982), 55.

[13] P. E. H. Hair, "Black African Slaves at Valencia, 1482–1516: An Onomastic Inquiry," *History in Africa* 7 (1980).

Detail of Benozzo Gozzoli, *The Journey of the Magi.* 1459. Length (entire work) 12 feet 4½ inches (3.77 m.). Although in theory the scene represents an episode from the Biblical story of the Nativity, in practice the riders and their attendants are recognizable as personalities from Early Renaissance Italy. The two seen here in front are Galeazzo Sforza of Milan and Sigismondo Malatesta of Rimini. Note the African attendant in the center.

During the Roman Empire, slave traders imported Africans as both domestic and farm laborers. After the fall of the Empire, Muslim and Christian traders continued to bring black African slaves into the Byzantine Empire and North Africa. Although medieval artists sometimes portrayed blacks in their works, the number of blacks in Europe remained small.

Blacks began to appear in Europe in larger numbers in the early 16th century, as a result of the Portuguese voyages of exploration. The increasing knowledge about remote regions of the world and their exotic inhabitants stimulated European curiosity about Africans. In addition to serving as domestic servants and manual laborers, blacks were prized as court entertainers and personal attendants for the ruling class. The early interest in Africa and its people would be replaced in later centuries by the horrors of the massive transatlantic slave trade.

Putting the Social Worlds of the Renaissance and Reformation in Perspective

Although European society during the Renaissance and Reformation underwent profound change, its effects were uneven. Among the most significant developments of the period were the growth of urban life and the rise of the merchant classes, which introduced an element of unprecedented social mobility. Other features of social change included the new importance attributed to education among urban dwellers, and the growing number of women of the poorer classes who found work and new lives in the towns. These changes greatly modified existing patterns of marriage and family arrangements. Rural life, on the other hand, retained its essentially medieval character of isolation and poverty as millions of peasants lived according to the cycle of nature.

Women were affected by the sweeping social changes in both favorable and unfavorable ways, depending on their status. The Renaissance, for example, saw the introduction of a double standard of sexual behavior for men and women. By contrast, poorer women who in earlier times had little opportunity to work outside the home now found new kinds of employment in the towns.

Still another new factor in society was the presence of a largely unknown minority—blacks from Africa—who, together with the Jews and Muslims, formed the only significant non-Christian elements in the population of Europe.

For all the inconsistency of these developments, the general impact was to intensify the slow but irrevocable breakdown of medieval patterns of European life. The broad structural forces that were transforming Europe—urbanization, the emergence of a global economy, and the development of new modes of production—led in the 18th century to revolutionary change.

Questions for Further Study

1. What were the principal barriers to class mobility? Was movement between classes at all possible?
2. What social and cultural constraints limited the role of women in European society? Does the witchcraft craze reveal anything about attitudes toward women?
3. How did Christian society treat "outsiders"?

Suggestions for Further Reading

Barstow, Anne L. *Witchcraze: A New History of European Witch Hunts.* San Francisco, 1994.

Bornstein, Daniel, and Roberto Rusconi, eds. *Women and Religion in Medieval and Renaissance Italy.* Chicago, 1996.

Clark, Stuart. *Thinking with Demons: The Idea of Witchcraft in Early Modern Europe.* New York, 1997.

Cohen, Elizabeth S., and Thomas V. Cohen. *Daily Life in Renaissance Italy.* Westport, CT, 2001.

Faur, Jose. *In the Shadow of History: Jews and Conversos at the Dawn of Modernity.* Albany, NY, 1992.

Hale, John. *The Civilization of Europe in the Renaissance.* New York, 1994.

Jardine, Lisa. *Worldly Goods: A New History of the Renaissance.* New York, 1996.

Kedar, Benjamin Z. *Crusade and Mission: European Approaches Towards the Muslim.* Princeton, NJ, 1984.

Levack, Brian P. *The Witch-Hunt in Early Modern Europe.* New York, 1987.

Ozment, Steven. *When Fathers Ruled: Family Life in Reformation Europe.* Cambridge, MA, 1983.

Rocke, Michael. *Forbidden Friendships: Homosexuality and Male Culture in Renaissance Florence.* New York, 1996.

Ruggiero, Guido. *The Boundaries of Eros: Sex, Crime and Sexuality in Renaissance Venice.* Oxford, 1985.

Stone, Lawrence. *The Family, Sex and Marriage in England, 1500–1800.* New York, 1979.

InfoTrac College Edition

Enter the search term *Renaissance* using the Subject Guide.

Enter the search term *Reformation* using the Subject Guide.

PART V

THE EARLY MODERN WORLD

The hundred and fifty years following the Reformation, with its conflicts and divisions, were marked by the intensification and culmination of many earlier trends. Europe began a period of consolidation, growth and expansion, and cultural innovation that established its global primacy.

In politics, the early modern period saw the successful concentration of power in the hands of absolutist monarchs in their long struggle with the nobles. In England, Henry VIII defied the papacy and established Protestantism in his realm, disciplined the nobility, and bent Parliament to his will. His daughter Elizabeth, avoiding direct confrontation, achieved an uneasy balance in her relationship with Parliament, but her successors,

James I and Charles I, again took up the struggle. The result was a far-reaching civil war that led to the triumph of Parliament and the temporary end of the monarchy. There followed a period of military dictatorship under Oliver Cromwell.

Elsewhere in Europe, royal power increased. In Spain, Philip II micromanaged not only his kingdom but also a vast overseas empire. In France in the 16th and 17th centuries, monarchs laid the foundations of absolutism, building up the royal administration, taming the nobility, and securing state authority over the appointment of bishops and other ecclesiastical officials.

The age was further marked by bitter religious conflicts that were in part the legacy of the Reformation and in part the result of politics.

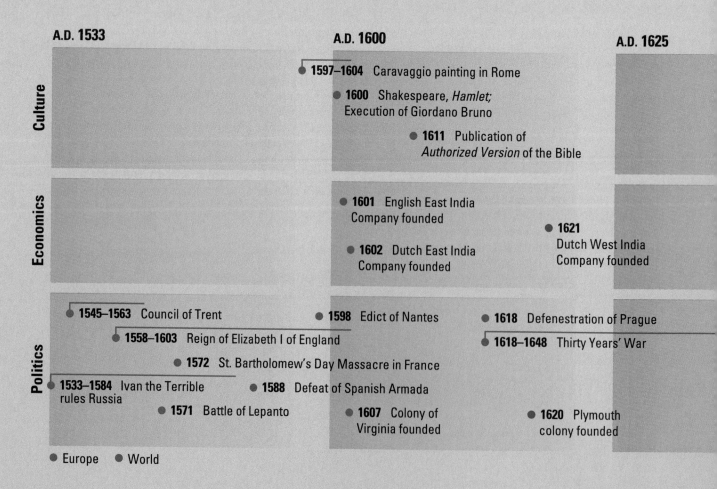

A.D. 1533 **A.D. 1600** **A.D. 1625**

Culture

- 1597–1604 Caravaggio painting in Rome
- 1600 Shakespeare, *Hamlet;* Execution of Giordano Bruno
- 1611 Publication of *Authorized Version* of the Bible

Economics

- 1601 English East India Company founded
- 1602 Dutch East India Company founded
- 1621 Dutch West India Company founded

Politics

- 1545–1563 Council of Trent
- 1558–1603 Reign of Elizabeth I of England
- 1533–1584 Ivan the Terrible rules Russia
- 1572 St. Bartholomew's Day Massacre in France
- 1571 Battle of Lepanto
- 1598 Edict of Nantes
- 1588 Defeat of Spanish Armada
- 1607 Colony of Virginia founded
- 1618 Defenestration of Prague
- 1618–1648 Thirty Years' War
- 1620 Plymouth colony founded

● Europe ● World

Protestantism gave new urgency to Catholic pressure for spiritual and institutional reform. The Council of Trent produced a huge body of revised doctrine and settled several important disputes raging within the church. New religious orders such as the Jesuits were founded, and old institutions such as the Inquisition were revived.

Religion continued to dominate European politics. In the 16th and 17th centuries, religious wars devastated Germany, shaped much of the domestic history of France, and greatly influenced events in Spain and England. In eastern Europe the Catholic offensive against

A.D. **1650**   A.D. **1700**

● **1633**   Galileo tried and condemned

　　　　　　　　　　　　　　　　● **1663**   Bernini completes piazza
　　　　　　　　　　　　　　　　and colonnades for St. Peter's, Rome

● **1642–1648**   English Civil Wars

● **1643–1715**   Reign of Louis XIV of France

● **1648**   Peace of Westphalia

　　　　　　　　● **1660**   English monarchy restored

Protestantism ensured that the region remained largely immune to Protestantism. From 1618 to 1648, most of Europe's great powers were drawn into a terrible religious and secular conflict, the Thirty Years' War.

Despite the rapid pace of political change, the social patterns of daily life evolved more slowly, gradually influencing the basic aspects of living, including the health and well-being of Europeans, diet and housing, and clothes. The period was one of economic growth, although not without its difficulties. The principal change after 1500 was the shift in trade patterns from the Mediterranean to the Atlantic and northern European coasts. The resulting commercial revolution was dominated at first by Spain and Portugal, but later by the English and the emergence of the Dutch Republic.

The cultural life of Europe in the early modern period was characterized by the emergence of a new style known as Baroque. In the Renaissance, artists sought ideal principles of beauty and harmony to express eternal values. Baroque artists, by contrast, tried to express the emotional states of individuals, whether in words, music, or painting. In doing so, they laid the ground for the arts in the modern era with their search for self-expression and the answers to personal questions.

CATHOLIC REFORM AND THE COUNTER-REFORMATION

The age of the Reformation was also a time of renewal and change within the Catholic Church. This Catholic reform movement resulted partly because the call for change inspired many devout Catholics to renew their religious faith and restore the purity of their church. After all, there had been Catholic reformers long before Luther and Calvin. On the other hand, the startling spread of Protestantism and the victories scored by the reformers and monarchs alike in breaking with Rome drove the papacy and the Catholic hierarchy to clean out their own house. As the Catholic Church began to be energized by its own reforms, the papacy struck back at the Protestants, declaring war against them everywhere and creating new institutions to combat the heresies of the day.

The Council of Trent that first met in 1545 began the process of both reaffirming the theological principles of the church and of launching the Counter-Reformation. Moreover, new religious orders dedicated to Catholic revival were founded by Angela Merici and Ignatius Loyola, while the papacy established the Inquisition to stamp out heretics. By the late 16th century, the offensive of the Catholic Church had not destroyed Protestantism but had at least halted its spread. Yet in international relations, the religious controversies of the age would continue to be fought out for almost another century.

SIGNIFICANT DATES

Catholic Reform and Counter-Reform

1425	Thomas à Kempis writes *The Imitation of Christ*
1478	Spanish Inquisition established
1492	Jews expelled from Spain
1452–1498	Life of Savonarola
1542	Papal Inquisition revived
1534–1549	Paul III reigns as pope
1545–1563	Council of Trent
1491–1556	Life of Ignatius Loyola
1515–1582	Life of Teresa of Avila
1600	Giordano Bruno burned at the stake

THE CATHOLIC CHURCH AND THE SPIRIT OF RENEWAL

Spiritual renewal and institutional reform were not new to the Catholic Church. Throughout the Middle Ages, movements had arisen within the faith to end corruption and rekindle popular belief, and some of these efforts were responses to broader problems in European society.

THE ROOTS OF CATHOLIC REFORM

The resulting growth in popular devotion was expressed by turning away from the formal religious practices of the church to mysticism and new forms of piety. Popular religious practices, like the payment of indulgences to escape the consequences of sin, were designed to generate divine grace and achieve salvation; they included pilgrimages, processions, and special masses for the dead. Many devout Christians joined special lay branches of the mendicant orders founded by St. Dominic and St. Francis.

The most significant expression of the new piety was mysticism. Mystics were convinced that believers experienced God not through theological discourse or institutional rituals but rather through love and emotional availability. Mystics sought to establish a sense of union with God through contemplation and spiritual meditation.

The focus of popular mysticism in the 14th century was the Rhine Valley of western Germany, where Meister Eckhart (1260–1327) developed a large following through his impassioned preaching. Eckhart denied the importance of traditional dogma, stressing instead the cultivation of a "divine spark" that would achieve oneness with God. Lay followers of the Dutch mystic Gerhard Groote (1340–1384) founded the Brethren of the Common Life for men and a similar organization known as the Sisters of the Common Life for women. Groote maintained that communion with God could best be achieved by imitating Christ and devoting oneself to good works. His followers founded schools and lived according to self-imposed rules of simplicity and humility.

Several localized efforts at church reform had been attempted in the late 15th and early 16th centuries. The Dominican friar Girolamo Savonarola (1452–1498) had tried to bring discipline and moral leadership to the people of Florence, where he held sway for two years before the church ordered his execution for heresy. Working within the church had been Cardinal Francisco Ximines (c. 1437–1517), confessor to Queen Isabella of Spain. He imposed stricter controls over the clergy and infused the Spanish Church with a spirit of discipline and fervor. New religious orders, such as the Capuchins, reached out to the common people in an ef-

Painting of *The Council of Trent*. 1586. The Council, which met sporadically from 1545 to 1563, redefined Catholic teachings and reaffirmed the dogmas of transubstantiation, the apostolic succession, and celibacy for the clergy—all of which had been challenged by Luther and his followers. The solemn grandeur of the scene was to be one of the effects sought for by Baroque artists.

fort to help improve the lives of the poor and the sick. But leadership from Rome seemed to be needed if the church was to transform in a significant way.

POPE PAUL III

Soon after Luther launched the Protestant revolution against Rome, the Catholic Church had at its head a zealous and learned pope, Paul III (ruled 1534–1549). Paul had been a cardinal from the powerful Roman Farnese family and stood out among his fellow cardinals as an astute diplomat and genuine reformer. Paul's election to the papacy came at a crucial time because many people believed the church was on the edge of collapse. Paul gave vigorous leadership to the reforming party within the hierarchy, favoring the calling of a new council that would try to reconcile Protestants and Catholics and reform the church. Attacking the worldliness of the clergy, Paul appointed a special commission of ardent reformers to advise him. The commission recommended curbing the abuses in the sale of indulgences and reported to the pope on the corruption of high officials and cardinals. Paul appointed many new, reform-minded members of the College of Cardinals and approved the establishment of the Jesuit order.

THE COUNCIL OF TRENT

Paul's commission also aided in the detailed preparations for the Council of Trent, the great meeting of church reformers that he had proposed for 10 years. The more reactionary-minded clergy had steadily and bitterly opposed the idea of a council, which held its first session in the northern Italian city of Trento in 1545. Just as it began to get down to serious work, however, Paul died, so that the reform initiative was deprived of his leadership.

The council, which met on and off until 1563, devoted its energies to settling theological questions, reinforcing traditions within the church, and organizing a counterattack against the Protestants. Its sessions were often stormy and rife with dissension and division. Yet in the end, some important decisions were reached. The council condemned the selling of church offices and fake indulgences, limited the secular activities of the clergy, and demanded greater supervision of the clergy by bishops and cardinals. Bishops were now required to live in their dioceses, and priests and monks were exhorted to go among the people to preach and act as personal examples of spiritual uprightness. The council emphasized the importance of church tradition that went back centuries, an approach the Protestants countered with the argument that the church was a human institution.

In the theological sphere, the Council of Trent reaffirmed the basic doctrines that Luther and the Protestants had challenged. These included the seven sacraments, the idea of salvation both by good works and by faith, and the doctrine of transubstantiation that held that the bread and wine of the communion became by miracle the body and blood of Christ. The Latin translation of the Bible known as the Vulgate was proclaimed the official version of the Scriptures, the veneration of saints and relics was reasserted, and clergy were forbidden to marry.

EDUCATION AND CONVERSION: THE JESUITS AND THE URSULINES

The reforming spirit that Paul had inaugurated resulted in the creation of several new religious orders. The Capuchins, a Franciscan brotherhood, devoted themselves to preaching and working among the poor, while the Theatines focused on inspiring faith among the clergy. The most famous and important of the new organizations, however, was the Society of Jesus.

IGNATIUS LOYOLA AND THE JESUITS

The Jesuit order, as it is more commonly known, was founded by a Spanish soldier, later priest, named Ignatius Loyola (1491–1556). Loyola, descended from a noble family of the Basque country, had been a soldier in the army of Charles V. While convalescing from wounds he had received in 1521, Loyola began reading the lives of religious figures, including biographies of St. Francis and St. Dominic. As a result, he underwent a conversion and dedicated his life to doing God's work. Loyola engaged in meditation exercises and studied at universities in Spain and France, and in the process developed a small but dedicated following.

Loyola founded his society in 1524 at the University of Paris. His *Spiritual Exercises,* a work of powerful Christian

Engraving showing Ignatius Loyola. 16th century. Images such as this one, based on a portrait from life, were printed in large numbers and circulated widely. Both the Reformation and the Counter-Reformation movements used the new medium of printing to further their causes. Devotional images of popular saints, like this one, were intended to inspire the faithful.

inspiration and spiritual discipline, claimed that through critical self-study and the surrender of individual will, each person can achieve union with God. His teachings insisted on the importance of obedience and self-discipline rather than free choice. Ironically, Loyola came under suspicion by the Inquisition several times.

En route to Palestine to convert the Muslims, Loyola and his disciples, chief among them Francis Xavier, found themselves in Italy when they learned that unsettled conditions in the Holy Land made it impossible for them to continue their journey. They decided to remain in Italy and preach their message of devotion there. In 1537, he and his followers were ordained in Rome, and two years later he sent a draft of a constitution for a new order to the papacy for approval. In 1540 Pope Paul III endorsed it. The plan called for a centralized order governed along military lines by a "general" who reported directly to the pope. The Jesuits took the same kind of vows of poverty and chastity as members of other orders but were devoted to a militant spirit of defending and advancing the faith.

The Jesuits were trained to push back Protestantism by working among the Catholic masses as well as among their leaders. To the common people they preached the need for confession. They restructured secondary education so as to instill Catholic devotion in the young. In this spirit they launched a program to found a series of schools, later known as colleges, to provide Catholic education and discipline for tens of thousands of boys from among the poor as well as the upper classes. The Jesuit curriculum linked humanist education with Catholic religious teachings. Their schools became the training ground for generations of religious and secular leaders, many of whom found employment in the burgeoning state bureaucracies. In this way, the Jesuit order was able to influence government policies indirectly, while many Jesuits became private confessors to important nobles and rulers.

In the spirit of their new militancy, the Jesuits embarked on a worldwide program of missionary work aimed at converting "heathens" in Asia, Africa, and the Americas to the Catholic faith. By the end of the 16th century, Jesuit missions had been established in China, Japan, the Congo, Brazil, Mexico, and many other distant outposts of Catholic activity. Some of their missionaries, such as Francis Xavier, achieved widespread fame as zealous bearers of God's word to non-Christian civilizations around the world. Others spread knowledge of secular aspects of Western culture, particularly in China.

THE JESUITS IN CHINA

Not long after the Counter-Reformation, China fell under the rule of a new dynasty, the Qing, which lasted until 1911. The Qing invaded China from Manchuria to the south in 1644, at the collapse of the Ming dynasty, and were considered as foreigners by most Chinese. Unlike virtually all of their predecessors, they made serious efforts to establish contact with other peoples. One of the first Qing em-

Painting of St. Teresa of Avila, a devoted visionary, who founded the Carmelite order of nuns. 16th century. The dove of the Holy Spirit descends from the top left, as the words of the saint's prayer are legible in the ribbon above her head: "I shall sing for eternity of the mercies of the Lord."

perors, Kang Hsi (1654–1722), signed a treaty with Peter the Great of Russia in 1689, in an attempt to establish recognized borders between the two empires.

Kang Hsi also encouraged the introduction, under careful control, of Western education and arts. Jesuit missionaries had already reached China; one of the first, Matteo Ricci (1552–1610), studied Chinese in order to teach Western astronomy, geography, and mathematics to Chinese scholars. Kang Hsi used other Jesuits as mapmakers and took Jesuit physicians with him on his travels. In some cases he appointed Jesuits to official positions at court. The Flemish missionary and astronomer Ferdinand Verbiest (1623–1688) became the director of the Imperial Astronomical Bureau in 1669 and played a part in negotiations to fix the Chinese–Russian border.

Encouraged by the Jesuit successes—and perhaps to keep an eye on future developments—the pope sent an ambassador to see if a permanent papal legation could be opened in Beijing. The emperor refused permission and required all Jesuits then resident in China to sign a statement declaring that they understood and accepted the imperial definition of Confucianism and ancestral rituals.

Thus the Jesuit order was to achieve significant influence in secular as well as religious affairs, especially through their educational programs and their private influence on individual monarchs. Yet the Jesuit experience was originally conceived as a weapon in the war for religious conviction that had been launched by the Protestant revolt. Loyola's "soldiers of Christ" were sometimes viewed too literally as religious warriors, but certainly Loyola was consumed with the passion for discipline and proselytizing. In 1622, the church made Loyola a saint.

THE URSULINES AND CATHOLIC WOMEN

Societies devoted to religious work by and among women had been founded before Luther's time. The Sisters of the Common Life, for example, had been inspired by the movement for popular religious devotion. St. Teresa of Avila (1515–1582) founded the Carmelite order of nuns, who devoted themselves to works of charity.

Most similar to the Jesuits, however, was the Ursuline order, founded by St. Angela Merici (1473–1540). The Ursulines were essentially an order of teaching nuns designed to educate girls in religious and moral affairs. Of Venetian background, the young Merici had been inspired by the good works of local nuns and religious orders and volunteered to work with the Franciscan monks. In 1516, she founded a girl's school for scriptural instruction. Although she never took official church vows, Merici devoted herself to helping the sick and the poor. In 1535, she founded the Company of St. Ursula, which was modeled on the Franciscan order. Because her followers—that is, women—chose to work among the people rather than remain in secluded cloisters, it was only some 30 years later that the papacy finally extended formal approval to the company.

THE WAR AGAINST THE HERETICS: THE SACRED CONGREGATION OF THE HOLY OFFICE

The reforms instituted from above by Pope Paul III were complemented by the devotion, discipline, and fervor of countless reformers such as Loyola and Merici. It was through the Inquisition, however, that the church fought its unremitting war against those who had left the Catholic fold. Its harsh and often brutal techniques, far from advancing the cause, often sparked the opposite effect, giving the Counter-Reformation a negative reputation.

THE INQUISITION

The movement known as the **Inquisition** had been suggested by Loyola with the support of Cardinal Giampietro Caraffa (ruled as Pope Paul IV 1555–1559), who became its head. Nevertheless, there had been precedents, including the formal papal Inquisition established in 1233 by Gregory IX, who had placed the war against the Albigensian heretics in the hands of the Dominicans.

The Inquisition, like its medieval predecessor, was a traveling tribunal that conducted inquiries in various locations. Persons accused of heresy were not given the names of their accusers, although they were often permitted to list their enemies as a way of checking against false accusations. Those who refused to confess were tried, often with the use of torture to extract confessions—and without confession, there could be no conviction. Because heresy was considered a civil as well as a religious crime, those found guilty were punished by the local rulers rather than by the church. Penance, fine, and imprisonment were the usual penalties, although burning at the stake was also used. The most notorious manifestation of the Inquisition was the so-called Spanish Inquisition, established in 1478 and headed by the infamous Tomas de Torquemada. Those responsible for the Inquisition in Spain often abused their authority and were fanatical in their efforts to uncover heretics and other nonconformists, including homosexuals and practitioners of magic.

In 1542, Pope Paul III revived the Inquisition and assigned it to the Sacred Congregation of the Holy Office under Cardinal Caraffa and six fellow cardinals. Known as the Roman Inquisition, its purpose was to combat Protestantism, but its effects were more widespread. It did succeed in eliminating most vestiges of Protestantism in the Italian states, although pockets of the older Waldensians still remained (see Topic 27).

The Inquisition demanded religious and intellectual conformity and terrorized university professors as well as students. The Roman Inquisition burned the Dominican philosopher Giordano Bruno (1548–1600) at the stake for his ideas about the nature of the physical universe, just as it tried Galileo, the Italian astronomer and mathematician, in 1633 for similar ideas. To prevent the spread of dangerous

THE SOCIAL LIFE OF EUROPEAN JEWRY

ELISHEVA CARLEBACH   Queens College, City University of New York

"It passes belief, all the strange things that can happen to us . . . " So wrote Glikl Hameln, a 17th-century Jewish woman, in her remarkable memoir. In it she promised to tell "everything that has happened to me from my youth upward," as a family remembrance and ethical guide for her 12 children. From her colorful descriptions we can glean some of the most important aspects of 17th-century western European Jewish life. Glikl belonged to a class of Jews who were able to prosper during times of turmoil as the medieval anti-Jewish barriers in western and central Europe began to break down. Her writing provides a marvelous look at the inner rhythms of Jewish life as well as the external forces that shaped it.

Glikl lived in Hamburg, a north German port city which contained two small but separate Jewish communities. The Ashkenazi community consisted of Jews of eastern and central European background; their language of daily discourse was Yiddish. One of Glikl's earliest memories was caring for Jewish refugees who fled westward from Poland's Cossack Rebellion of 1648. The Sephardi community, wealthier and more urbane, boasted a splendid synagogue. Its members were descendants of the Jews who had been expelled from Spain and Portugal at the end of the 15th century. Tens of thousands of exiles were left to seek new domiciles; many began to settle in western Europe in the 17th century. Many members of the Sephardi community had lived as marranos, secret Jews who passed down their Jewish identity for generations until they could escape the coercive pressures of the post-1492 Iberian world.

The Reformation shattered the absolute authority of the Roman Church throughout Europe and paved the way for Jews and members of other religious minorities to be viewed in a more just and realistic way. Although some founders of Protestantism held to malevolent medieval images of Jews, the prolonged struggle over religious beliefs ultimately led to greater tolerance of different faiths. The chaos caused by the religious wars provided some Jews in central Europe entry into nascent economies. Glikl's family seems to have prospered as a result of the Thirty Years' War (1618–1648) when both sides of the conflict turned to Jewish financiers and suppliers. The new class of European Jews that emerged used their influence to become advocates for Jewish causes, founders of new communities, and patrons of Jewish scholarship.

Events such as the advance of the Ottoman Empire, the rupture in the church, and constant warfare appeared fearful and momentous to Europeans. These upheavals caused many Europeans, Christian and Jewish, to hope that the end of history was near. Several aspiring redeemers were announced; one 16th-century hopeful, David Reubeni, was greeted by the pope and the emperor. Glikl recalled the excitement of the appearance of Sabbatai Zevi in 1665, leader of a very widespread Jewish messianic movement.

While some kings and princes banned Jews from their territories, others pursued more lenient, or sometimes inconsistent policies. The reason for toleration of Jewish communities usually had less to do with the religious or cultural life of Jews than with the economic self-interest of the ruler. Because Jews had been excluded for centuries from land ownership as well as from crafts guilds, they developed acumen in the areas that were less restricted for them, finance and commerce. The exiled Spanish and Portuguese Jews and the marranos who followed them into Europe acquired a reputation for developing commerce on a grand scale. Retaining or readmitting Jews in western Europe came about as a result of a desire to develop national economies. When an Italian Jew, Simone Luzzatto, presented a plea for toleration to the Venetian authorities in the 17th century, or Menasseh ben Israel petitioned Oliver Cromwell to permit Jews to return to England, their arguments centered on the idea that a flourishing Jewish community aided the commercial and economic development of the cities and nations in which they lived. England and the Netherlands permitted Jews to settle for the purpose of developing their economies. The Jewish resettlement in western Europe reversed a centuries-long Medieval process of expulsion of Jews that had emptied the region of its Jewish communities.

Despite new economic and social opportunities, most European Jews in the 16th through 18th centuries still lived under great restrictions. In many cities, Jews were legally restricted to residing in quarters known as ghettos. The word *ghetto* may have orignated from the Italian word for *foundry*, the area of Venice that became the compulsory quarter for Jews in 1516. Jewish quarters existed throughout Europe, in Frankfurt, in Prague, in Rome, in some cases through the 19th century. Surrounded by walls, gates bolted at night, their purpose was to separate Jews from others in every socially significant way. The walled ghetto meant that Jews could not expand their quarters horizontally as their population grew by nature and immigration. Instead, they were forced to extend their living space by building vertically, erecting structures that were higher and closer together than in other areas of European cities. These conditions made the ghettos seem darker, more crowded, and with poorer sanitation than anywhere else in Europe. Ghetto populations were also more vulnerable to plagues and fires than other urban districts. When Christian masses were aroused by anti-Jewish agitation, the same conditions of the ghetto made it more dangerous. When Christian clerics wanted to use coercive measures, from compulsory sermons to burnings of Jewish books, as for example the Talmud in 1553, they knew just where to locate their targets.

Yet a closer look at life inside the ghetto walls, and the many ways these walls were breached, shows a more complex picture. During the Renaissance period, Jews and Christians mingled rather freely during the day. Jews left the ghetto to conduct every sort of business, including serving as physicians and teachers of Hebrew to Christians. Christians found many reasons, curiosity among them, to visit the crowded ghetto.

Jewish communities maintained a strong and distinctive social organization. Jews educated their own young, cared for their sick and poor, and buried their dead within the framework of an autonomous judicial and cultural structure, known as the *Kehillah*. In addition to serving the traditional functions of worship and study, synagogues also functioned as social centers where news and information circulated together with official announcements.

In addition to the formal communal structures, and essential to the fabric of daily life, were the overlapping networks of voluntary associations. Their goals were religious, educational, or social, such as study of holy texts, dowering poor brides, or occupational association. Rich and poor lived in proximity, creating a sense of mutual responsibility that expressed itself in every conceivable form of charitable endeavor.

These configurations of Jewish life, which combined medieval elements with recent European developments, endured through the late 18th century. The ideals of the Enlightenment began to change European thought, so that segregation on the basis of religion no longer remained acceptable policy for European states. When the French Revolution implemented the changes, Jews were granted legal and civic equality.

Map 41.1 The Two Major Divisions of European Jewry. Jews whose ancestors lived in medieval Germany are known as Ashkenazim; up to the beginning of the 20th century they spoke Yiddish. The Sephardic Jews of Spain fled the Inquisition of the late 15th century for North Africa, Holland (in particular Amsterdam), the Ottoman Empire (Istanbul and Salonika), and the Near East. Most American Jews are Ashkenazim.

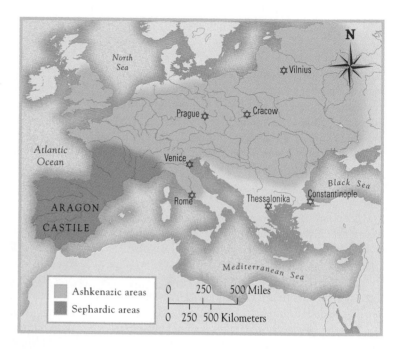

Engraving of an attack on Jews in the German city of Frankfurt. 1614. The religious fervor created by the campaigns for Reform and Counter-Reform created a general climate of intolerance, which often fastened on Europe's Jewish communities as victims. Scenes like this of mass beatings and the destruction of Jewish property were especially common in countries affected by the Reformation.

ideas, the Sacred Congregation instituted an *Index of Prohibited Books*, which established a master list of works that Catholics should not read.

THE JEWS IN THE AGE OF THE COUNTER-REFORMATION

The era of the Reformation and the Counter-Reformation created an atmosphere of repression and intolerance that also extended to non-Christians throughout society. The Spanish Inquisition had targeted those Jews who had converted to Christianity, known as the *conversos*. Many of these converted Jews continued to practice their own religion in secret. Over the next half century, more than 100,000 Jews emigrated, among them some of the most important merchants, physicians, and bankers.

The Jews were further victimized by the climate of religious zeal in the countries most affected by the Reformation. The German princes who followed Luther's teachings grew increasingly concerned about their Jewish populations when Luther found himself unable to convert them to his doctrines. As a result, many were expelled and their synagogues closed. In Italy, the formerly tolerant policies of the papacy were abandoned under the influence of the Inquisition. In the mid-16th century, the first *ghettos*—defined districts within which local Jews were forced to live behind walls and locked gates—were established in Venice and Rome. Nonetheless, Jewish communities throughout Europe managed to maintain a rich and vibrant social and cultural life.

Putting Catholic Reform and the Counter-Reformation in Perspective

Whether the movement for religious and spiritual renewal is called the Catholic Reformation, as Catholics describe it, or the Counter-Reformation, as Protestants refer to it, there is no doubt that significant change and renewal took place among Catholic believers as well as among leaders of the church. It is also clear that by the end of the 16th century the influence and power of the Roman Catholic Church had been greatly reduced in places where Protestants took over. Almost everywhere secular rulers had taken advantage of the church's weakness to assert their control over the religious lives of their subjects and the ecclesiastical institutions in their realms.

Although rulers everywhere assumed greater authority over the church, in countries that remained Catholic, such as Spain, the monarchs sometimes assisted the church in stamping out Protestantism. The centuries-long tradition of alliance between altar and throne had proven a useful tool of governance and was not easily or lightly broken. But despite the vigorous leadership provided to the church by Pope Paul III and the powerful reforming impulse generated by Loyola and others, few Catholic leaders of the late 16th century expected Protestantism to disappear. Moreover, the deep and often bitter religious disputes of the age would continue to affect secular affairs in profound ways. The century and a half following the start of Luther's movement was an age of religious wars. In Europe as a whole, the cultural and spiritual unity that had marked the Middle Ages had been irretrievably shattered.

Questions for Further Study

1. To what extent was the movement for change within the church a Catholic reform or a Catholic counter-reformation?
2. What methods did the Inquisition use against heretics? How did it justify such practices?
3. In the generally hostile environment that was Christian Europe, what forms did Jewish social and cultural life take and under what constraints did it thrive?

Suggestions for Further Reading

Birely, Robert. *The Refashioning of Catholicism, 1450-1700: A Reassessment of the Counter Reformation.* Washington, DC, 1999.

Cameron, E. *The European Reformation.* Oxford, 1991.

Caraman, Philip. *Ignatius Loyola.* San Francisco, 1990.

Jedin, Hubert. E. Graf, trans. *History of the Council of Trent*, 2 vols. London, 1957–1961.

Jensen, D. Lamar. *Reformation Europe: Age of Reform and Revolution.* Lexington, KY, 1981.

Jones, Martin D.W. *The Counter Reformation: Religion and Society in Early Modern Europe.* New York, 1995.

Lindberg, Carl. *The European Reformations.* New York, 1996.

Luebke, David Martin. *The Counter Reformation: The Essential Readings.* New York, 1999.

Meissner, William. *Ignatius Loyola: Psychology of a Saint.* New Haven, CT, 1994.

Mullett, Michael A. *The Catholic Reformation.* New York, 1999.

Po-Chia Hsia, R. *The World of Catholic Renewal, 1540-1770.* New York, 1998.

InfoTrac College Edition

Enter the search term *Counter-Reformation* using the Subject Guide.

CATHOLIC SPAIN AND THE STRUGGLE FOR SUPREMACY

For many decades following the beginning of the Protestant Reformation, religion continued to dominate European politics. Nowhere was the primacy of religion stronger than in the Spain of Philip II. A controversial figure whose historical image has been shaped largely by the religious question, Philip saw himself as the champion of Catholicism. Following in the tradition of his father, the Emperor Charles V, Philip undertook to free Spain of religious differences and remove all traces of dissent, moving in ruthless fashion against the Jews and Muslims of the kingdom. He very much acted the role of the "new monarch," building a highly centralized administration in the tradition of absolutism. He tried, too, to strengthen Spain's hold on its huge colonial possessions in the Americas and to extract from them the maximum profit.

Even under the "most Catholic monarch," the influence of religion on public policy was limited. Moreover, religious controversies prevented Philip from focusing on building and improving the government administration. In the Spanish Netherlands, where first the Anabaptists and then Lutheranism and Calvinism took hold, a bitter religious struggle for power led to a revolt of far-reaching consequences. Nor did Spain's foreign affairs escape the pernicious influence of religious struggle. After the diplomatic settlement with France in 1559, which recognized Spain's predominance in the Netherlands and in Italy, Philip became trapped in a monumental struggle for supremacy with Protestant England that ended in the ignominious defeat of the Spanish Armada.

SIGNIFICANT DATES

The Spanish Empire

1566	Revolt in the Netherlands erupts
1571	Ottomans defeated at Battle of Lepanto
1576	Pacification of Ghent
1579	Union of Arras
1588	Defeat of the Armada
1556–1598	Philip II reigns as king of Spain
1618	Thirty Years' War breaks out
1640	Portugal achieves independence
1648	United Provinces achieve independence

RELIGION AND MONARCHY: THE REIGN OF PHILIP II

Philip II (ruled 1556–1598) inherited the crown and the burdens of a far-flung empire from his father, the Emperor Charles V, who retired to a monastery in 1556 (see Topic 33). Philip's uncle Ferdinand, who became the new Holy Roman Emperor, received control of Austria, Bohemia, and Hungary. Philip became ruler of the Hapsburg domains in Italy—Milan, Naples, and Sicily—as well as of the Netherlands and Spain, and Spanish colonies outside of Europe.

At the time, Spain possessed the greatest military force and was one of the wealthiest states in the West, thanks largely to the silver and gold bullion supplied by the American colonies. Although a relatively large country, it was thinly populated and lacked significant resources of its own. When the king of Portugal died in 1580 without an heir, Philip occupied the country, laying claim to it because his mother was Isabella of Portugal and he had married Maria of Portugal (Portugal remained a Spanish possession until a revolt in 1640 secured its independence).

The legacy Philip inherited when he became king also included a fierce Catholicism, for the *reconquista* and the Spanish Inquisition had given Spain a reputation as the bastion of the Roman Catholic Church.

POLITICS AND RELIGION IN HAPSBURG SPAIN

Philip assumed the throne of Spain along with serious burdens, including the task of combating Protestantism in Europe and the Ottoman Turks in the Mediterranean. Moreover, the question of how to keep his widely spread possessions together concerned him deeply. Philip was an intensely serious and deeply religious man who seldom revealed his emotions. He married four times, but always for diplomatic reasons rather than for love, and he seldom spent time with his family. His father had imbued him with a deep distrust of official advisers, and especially of women, so that he tried to keep his own counsel as much as possible.

Painting of Philip II, king of Spain and Mary Tudor, daughter of Henry VIII who succeeded her father as queen of England. 16th century. After the Catholic couple married in 1554, Mary attempted to reconvert England to Catholicism. The two little dogs in the foreground of the painting symbolize fidelity.

Mary Evans Picture Library

Map 42.1 The European Empire of Philip II. The three chief regions are the Iberian peninsula (Spain, Navarre, and Portugal), the Kingdom of Naples and the Two Sicilys (Sicily and Sardinia), and parts of the Holy Roman Empire, notably the Netherlands. Because the Empire was regarded as a bastion of Catholicism, the Netherlands, where Protestantism was strong, threatened to be at risk.

Despite his religious faith, Philip was a shrewd and calculating ruler who used the church to further his domestic and foreign policies. He was not above employing the Inquisition to destroy resistance to his authority among the nobles and middle class, although, like other new monarchs, he worked to undermine the power of the church in his country. He insisted on his right to appoint clerical officials in Spain and objected to the pope's control over ecclesiastical courts in his realm. When the influence of the Jesuits grew too powerful, he resisted their policies and acted in defiance of several popes when they challenged his authority. Philip aided the church when it did not undermine his absolutism but insisted in return that it be a loyal ally of the government. The deep faith of his subjects enabled the king to use religion to arouse popular consensus behind the monarchy.

As a ruler, Philip was a micromanager who refused to allow his bureaucrats to make most of their decisions without his direct involvement. He spent much of his time in the seclusion of his private office in the Escorial palace outside of Madrid, working on official papers. Heeding his father's advice too well, he was unable to delegate any significant power. Nor did he broach any limitations on his authority. In each of the former kingdoms that constituted the Spanish crown, such as Castile, Aragon, and León, a *Cortes*, or medieval assembly representing the clergy, nobles, and commoners, often gave Philip considerable trouble. Only in Castile, where he concentrated his attention, was he able to use the *Cortes* to rubber stamp his decisions and legislated personally through the royal decrees. The rest of the kingdom was less effectively managed. In his other European possessions, as well as in the American empire, he used viceroys to represent and implement his will, but he constantly fought the obstructionism of the powerful nobility. Moreover, the slowness of communications in the 16th century made colonial administration all the more difficult.

The administration of Philip's vast empire required tremendous resources, especially because he was almost constantly at war somewhere in the world. Nevertheless, only the more prosperous Castile and the American colonies provided much-needed revenue, whereas the bankers and nobles of the Low Countries felt that Spain was a drain on local resources. In Spain, the church owned half of the landed estates and the nobles owned most of the rest, yet both were essentially tax exempt. The old feudal nobility so ruthlessly impoverished the peasants, and their use of the most productive land for sheep grazing so depleted agricultural productivity, that Spain could not raise enough food for its own needs. Yet despite their poverty, the Spanish people were the most heavily taxed in Europe. To operate the government, Philip regularly resorted to borrowing and then just as regularly defaulted on the loans he had contracted.

Religious policies in Spain often hurt economic development, as with the campaigns against the Jews and Muslims. The Spanish Inquisition had been used initially against the *conversos*, the Jews who had converted to Christianity but who continued secretly to practice their own religion. Jews and *conversos* were among the most important merchants, physicians, and bankers, and many had achieved significant status in Spanish society. Large numbers of these economic leaders had left Spain to escape the repression and, in 1492, following the conquest of Granada, more than 100,000 Jews emigrated when the crown insisted that all Jews had either to convert or leave.

Similar policies affected the Muslims, who in 1502 were given the same choice as the Jews. Because most Muslims were modest farmers rather than merchants or professionals, and lacked the resources to emigrate, they opted to become Christians. Yet these *Moriscos,* like many of the *conversos,* were Christian in name only. Between 1568 and 1571, Philip brutally suppressed an uprising among the *Moriscos,* and in 1609 they were expelled from Spain. These policies seriously hurt the middle class, on whom most of the tax burden fell, and undermined a valuable source of economic prosperity.

SPAIN AND ITS OVERSEAS EMPIRE

The importance of the empire as a source of much-needed revenue explains why the Spanish crown held the colonies so tightly to the authority of Madrid. One result of this policy, however, was that when the supply of bullion from the Americas began to run dry, and other nations competed for a share of colonial trade, Spain began to suffer economic depression.

ECONOMIC POLICY AND THE COLONIES

After the brutal plundering of the ancient civilizations of the Americas had exhausted the easy supply of wealth, the Spanish introduced European mining techniques to the fabulously rich silver mines of Peru and Mexico. By the end of the 16th century, bullion still made up most of the value of imports from the Spanish possessions in the Americas. Even then, however, although the government directly secured almost half of all the bullion brought to Spain, it made up no more than 25 percent of all revenues. As the mines were gradually exhausted, other products from Asia and the New World began to take their place in Spain's overseas trade. By the end of the 17th century, new kinds of goods—particularly coffee, tea, cocoa, cotton, dyes, and tobacco—began to dominate imports to Europe.

Unlike the Portuguese, the Spanish began from the outset to settle their colonies and develop a local economy that mirrored the techniques and institutions found at home. They introduced European agricultural products into the Americas, including wheat and other grains, a wide variety of vegetables, and citrus fruit, while importing into Europe foodstuffs unknown there, such as the potato, the tomato, and corn.

The cultivation of sugar cane in the Western Hemisphere had a great impact on the economic and demographic patterns of the colonies, especially on the islands of the West Indies, where African slaves were brought in large numbers to work the plantations. Control of labor in the colonies was also managed under the *encomienda* system; this was similar to European manorialism, in which a grant of land gave the landholder the right to use the inhabitants of the land as forced workers. Local landholders and their overseers so widely abused the system, however, that it was eventually abandoned in the second half of the 16th century.

To control all trade, the government had established an agency known as the *Casa de Contratacìon,* which sought to make commerce a royal monopoly. Because the New World had been "discovered" by navigators in the employ of Queen Isabella of Castile, Castilian merchants were given a trade monopoly there. Trade with foreigners, including other Spanish merchants, was forbidden. This encouraged smuggling and the subterfuge of foreign merchants hiring Spanish ships to trade with the colonies. Direct commerce between the Americas and the Philippines, Spain's Pacific possession, was virtually prohibited.

A crucial shortcoming of Philip's reign was that such a potentially lucrative and important source of wealth as the American colonies was so thoroughly mismanaged. Several times in the course of the 16th century, Spain went into bankruptcy. Instead of making Spain a part of a developing and expanding overseas agricultural economy, Philip was content to allow the draining of its resources and the inhuman exploitation of its people. In doing so, he basked in the glow of the Hapsburg empire, little realizing that his policies had planted the seed of future crisis.

REBELLION IN THE NETHERLANDS: RELIGIOUS FREEDOM AND POLITICAL INDEPENDENCE

The Netherlands (sometimes called the Low Countries; their low elevation made them susceptible to flooding) had long been one of the most prosperous and strategically important areas of the Hapsburg domains, supplying Spain with large revenues. Throughout the Middle Ages, the Netherlands was the center of commerce and banking as well as a leading manufacturer of textiles. Amsterdam and Antwerp were important North Sea ports, and the country was densely populated and highly urbanized.

On the other hand, the 17 provinces that constituted the Netherlands had old traditions of self-government and feudal autonomy, and its inhabitants were deeply suspicious of Charles V when he inherited them, although he had been raised there. To complicate matters further, the southern provinces were primarily French- and Flemish-speaking, while the northern provinces were populated by people of German origin, whose language was Dutch. Charles annexed the provinces in 1548 and added them to the Hapsburg empire.

PHILIP II AND THE NETHERLANDS

To bring the two areas together, Charles had placed them under the regency of Philip, who lived there until he became king in 1556. Thereafter, Philip left the administration of the Netherlands in the hands of his sister, Margaret of Parma (1522–1586), who ruled with a group of Spanish advisers. Estrangement from Philip's absentee overlordship was made worse by the king's Catholic program. By the mid-16th century, Calvinism was spreading rapidly in the Netherlands and, like his father before him,

Philip encouraged local officials to use the Inquisition to stamp it and other heresies out. He also instructed his sister to enforce regulations against heresy. These policies enraged the local nobles, many of whom had become Calvinists and were already smarting under Philip's desire to centralize his control at the expense of their privileges. In 1566 Calvinists erupted in a fury that desecrated Catholic churches. Philip responded by sending 10,000 Spanish troops to the area under the command of the duke of Alva (1507–1582), who imposed an authoritarian military rule on the inhabitants.

Alva could not have alienated the people more if he had set out to do so deliberately. Not only did he levy new taxes, but he also established a special tribunal—popularly known as the Council of Blood—to root out heresy and crush the revolt. Alva was a brutal regent, responsible for thousands of deaths, including the execution of prominent Protestant nobles, and the expropriation of property. Tens of thousands of Protestants emigrated in the face of the terror that Alva unleashed. Outraged by his brutality, Margaret of Parma resigned the regency.

Alva's policies provoked full-scale rebellion as merchants and common people joined with the Protestant nobles against Spanish repression. Opposition to Philip centered on William of Nassau, Prince of Orange (ruled 1579–1584), who organized armed resistance in the north in 1568. Five years later Philip recalled Alva in a futile attempt to calm the population. William was an ideal leader of the rebellion. Born a Lutheran, he was raised as a Catholic. An experienced military leader, William raised a privateer army popularly called the "Sea Beggars." Although he had been an imperial official under Charles V and was not enthusiastic about leading a rebellion against Philip, under the pressures and heat of battle, he eventually became devoted to the Protestant cause.

THE REBELLION

For the first six years of the revolt, William and the rebel forces suffered one setback after another. William, who had used his own private wealth to help finance his army, was almost bankrupt, and his early military defeats spoiled his reputation. In 1572, however, the tide suddenly

Anthony Moro, *Portrait of William of Orange*, c. 1570. The painter was Dutch; he went to Spain to work for Charles V, who sent him to England to paint a portrait of Mary Tudor for her future husband, Philip II. Remaining there, he was knighted by Elizabeth, Mary's successor, as Sir Anthony More, and returned to his native land to paint this portrait of the leader of the Protestant revolt against Spanish rule.

changed when his soldiers captured the port of Brill, which inspired a series of uprisings throughout the northern provinces. To stop the advance of the imperial troops, William then opened the dikes and flooded the plains, a tactic that succeeded in cornering Philip's army and prompting the recall of Alva.

The war dragged on, and terrible atrocities and brutalities took place on both sides as religious passions inflamed the mutual hatreds. To terrorize the population, Alva had authorized his soldiers to pillage town after town and murder their inhabitants. In 1576, Antwerp was destroyed and thousands massacred. Three years later Spanish troops raped the women of Maestricht, who had helped defend the town against them, and then slaughtered much of the population.

The same year that Maestricht fell, Protestant and Catholic leaders of all 17 provinces joined together against Philip to form an alliance. The Catholic provinces of the South had been goaded into rebellion because of a special tax that Philip had imposed on them in order to fight the Protestants. The alliance suggested the possibility that national and political interests could be used in the Netherlands as the basis for forging a new state.

The united citizens of the Netherlands demanded that Philip withdraw his army and allow the provinces to be governed by their traditional assembly, the States General. But the unity that was achieved in adversity soon gave way to religious divisions between the Calvinist nobles of the North and the Catholic nobles of the South.

Philip's new military commander, Alexander Farnese, duke of Parma, skillfully manipulated these divisions by luring the Catholic aristocrats back into the Spanish fold after restoring their confiscated lands. After a series of victories, in 1579 Parma persuaded the southern provinces (which formed a Catholic alliance known as the Union of Arras) to make a separate peace with Philip. In the face of this abandonment, William brought together the Dutch leaders of the northern provinces into the Protestant Union of Utrecht, which announced that they would continue to resist the king.

In 1581, after trying unsuccessfully to become subjects first of the king of France and then of Queen Elizabeth of England, the northern provinces proclaimed their independence. After William was assassinated in 1584, the Dutch continued their struggle for self-government under his 17-

HAERLEM.

Print showing Spanish atrocities committed against the Dutch rebellion. 1573. As the print indicates, the scene shown is outside the city of Haarlem (modern spelling), some 20 miles from Amsterdam. The inscriptions below describe the hangings and executions depicted in the engraving, which did much to reinforce Dutch resistance to Spanish rule.

year-old son Maurice. Philip never lived to see the end of the revolt of the Netherlands. In 1609, eleven years after his death, a truce was arranged at long last, but not before the Spanish had inflicted much additional brutality and terror on the Protestant population of the region. Spain recognized the Protestant Dutch Republic of the northern provinces in the treaty of Westphalia in 1648, while maintaining control of the southern Catholic provinces.

SPAIN VERSUS ENGLAND: THE ARMADA DISASTER

As if the Netherlands were not sufficient provocation to Philip's Catholic policies, another source of conflict lay in England, where Henry VIII had created and assumed control of the Anglican Church and severed ties with Rome. In 1554, before he assumed the throne, Philip had married the daughter of Henry and Catherine of Aragon, Mary Tudor. Although the marriage was extremely unpopular in England, Mary was hopelessly in love with Philip, who encouraged her efforts to restore Catholicism there (see Topic 39).

THE SPANISH-ENGLISH RIVALRY
Several factors operated to exacerbate English-Spanish hostility. When Mary died, Philip offered his hand to her sister, Elizabeth (ruled 1558–1603), the new English queen, but Elizabeth spurned the offer. However, the underlying reason for the longstanding hostility between Spain and England was economic rivalry. Elizabeth's ships and English pirates attacked Spanish galleons laden with bullion from the Americas. Moreover, the English, who were anxious to break into the Spanish monopoly imposed on their colonies, tried to force their way into the lucrative trade. Sir John Hawkins, an ambitious English merchant, violated Spanish policy and sold goods directly to the Spanish colonies. In the late 1570s, Hawkins' cousin Francis Drake seized a fortune in booty from Spanish ships along the Pacific coast of South America.

English and Spanish policy also clashed during the revolt in the Netherlands. Since the Middle Ages, England had close commercial contact with the Flemish cloth manufacturers, who purchased large quantities of English wool.

Then, too, the English supported the aspirations of the Dutch Protestants, and English privateers continued to harass Spanish shipping along the coast. For their part, Spanish envoys in England had even been implicated in plots to assassinate Elizabeth.

THE ARMADA AND THE ECLIPSE OF SPAIN
In 1587, Francis Drake, who was knighted by Elizabeth, destroyed a large Spanish fleet anchored in the harbor of Cadiz. In reaction to what he regarded as English perfidy and the wounding of his pride, Philip decided to attack England's power directly. He devoted significant resources and energy to building a huge fleet, known as the Invincible Armada, which was designed to seize control of the English Channel and permit a Spanish invasion of England. The invasion forces were to be commanded by the duke of Parma. It was an imaginative plan but one filled with danger because much of Philip's war against England rested on this effort.

The Armada consisted of 130 ships carrying some 27,000 men. Arrayed against it was a much weaker flotilla of English ships, which nevertheless were smaller and faster than the cumbersome Spanish vessels. Moreover, some of England's best naval officers, including Hawkins and Drake, were in command of the operations. When running battles between the two fleets drove the Spanish ships to take refuge off Calais, Hawkins sent fire ships into the harbor and caused the Spanish to panic. As the Armada moved north to try to return to Cadiz, the English attacked again, and ferocious storms destroyed more Spanish ships than did the enemy. When the battle was over, less than half of Philip's ships had survived, although most of Spain's firepower made it back home.

The outcome of the struggle between England and Spain had immediate significance for Spain and long-range meaning for Europe. Philip's prestige was damaged, and Spain's once-supreme military power had been compromised. Moreover, the English victory gave encouragement to the Protestant forces struggling against the Counter-Reformation. Had Philip's reign ended with the Battle of Lepanto in 1571, in which his forces defeated the Ottoman Turks, he would no doubt have been regarded as the greatest ruler of his age. Instead, it culminated in the Armada disaster. The moment of Spain's greatness had passed.

Putting Catholic Spain in Perspective

The abdication of Charles V in 1556 signaled the fact that even such an ambitious monarch realized the insurmountable challenges and difficulties of ruling the vast Hapsburg empire. The division of his empire confirmed that the day of universal empires was over. The ascension of Philip II to the throne of Spain, on the other hand, suggested that greatness might have still been possible on a more limited scale. But Philip was not up to the task, and circumstances seem to have conspired against him.

Philip was an intensely Catholic monarch in an age of religious divisiveness that had shattered a millennium of Catholic unity. Although his inheritance included a huge overseas empire stretching from the Atlantic to the Pacific, shortsighted administrative and economic policies rendered it less useful to Spain than it might have been. Even in Europe, however, Philip's empire was too diverse. Against the centralizing and heavy-handed absolutism of the Hapsburgs, local patriotism and religious faith joined forces to wrest the all-important Dutch provinces from Philip's orbit. The longstanding Hapsburg-Valois conflict had ended with the withdrawal of France, and in the end Spain's nemesis came unexpectedly from England. The Armada symbolized a new era in European history, one that marked the decline of Spain and ushered in the ascendancy of England.

Questions for Further Study

1. What were the chief concerns of Philip's domestic program?
2. What was the nature of the relationship between Spain and its colonies? How did Spain view its American possessions?
3. What were the major aims of Spanish foreign policy under Philip II?

Suggestions for Further Reading

Braudel, Fernand. S. Reynolds, trans. *The Mediterranean and the Mediterranean World in the Age of Philip II*, 2 vols, 2nd ed. Berkeley, CA, 1996.

Dunn, Richard S. *The Age of Religious Wars, 1559–1715*, 2nd ed. New York, 1979.

Elliott, John H. *The Revolt of the Catalans: A Study in the Decline of Spain, 1598–1640*. Cambridge, MA, 1963.

Kamen, Henry. *Philip of Spain*. New Haven, CT, 1997.

Maltby, William S. *Alba*. Berkeley, CA, 1983.

Martin, Colin, and Geoffrey Parker. *The Spanish Armada*. New York, 1999.

Parker, G. *The Grand Strategy of Philip II*. New Haven, CT, 1998.

Rodriguez-Salgado, Mia. *The Changing Face of Empire: Charles V, Philip II, and Habsburg Authority*. Cambridge, MA, 1988.

Stradling, Robert A. *Europe and the Decline of Spain: A Study of the Spanish System, 1580–1720*. London, 1981.

InfoTrac College Edition

Enter the search term *Philip II of Spain* using Key Terms.

CROWN AND PARLIAMENT IN TUDOR-STUART ENGLAND

The death of Henry VIII in the mid-16th century ended a tumultuous era in English history during which that ambitious monarch had established a powerful royal autocracy. Henry successfully defied the papacy and established Protestantism in his realm, disciplined the nobility, and bent Parliament to his will. The unanswered question was whether Henry's reign had set a precedent for further royal power at the expense of the social and economic elites represented in Parliament. Moreover, the religious controversy he stirred up continued to disturb English life for many years.

Contrary to his own expectations, Henry's daughter, Elizabeth I, proved to be one of the most important monarchs of English history. Brilliant and determined, she fought back the efforts at mastery of Philip II of Spain and strengthened England's hegemony on the seas, while presiding over an era of significant economic and cultural achievement. Moreover, shrewd tactician that she was, Elizabeth avoided direct confrontation and achieved an uneasy balance in her relationship with Parliament.

It was left to her successors, James I and Charles I, to take up the struggle between monarch and Parliament again. The result was a far-reaching civil war that ended with the triumph of Parliament and the temporary end of the monarchy, with the added complication of renewed religious struggle under the Puritans. In place of the monarchy there followed a difficult period of military dictatorship under Oliver Cromwell. Only then, after the English had experimented with alternative forms of government, did they return to the monarchy, but in a form that would share power increasingly with Parliament.

Portrait of Elizabeth I of England. 16th century. The queen is shown treading on the enemies of England. Her white dress and the figure of an ermine, which is shown on her ruffle to her left, both symbolize virginity. The painting is an official court portrait, intended to convey the queen's majesty rather than provide a literal description of her appearance.

By Courtesy of the National Portrait Gallery, London

ELIZABETH I AND THE POLITICS OF COMPROMISE

Following the brief reigns of Edward VI and Mary Tudor, Elizabeth I (ruled 1558–1603) became queen. The daughter of Henry VIII and Anne Boleyn, the young Elizabeth ascended the English throne at a crucial moment in history, when both domestic and foreign affairs were at a crossroads. The Elizabethan era achieved an extraordinary level of power and prosperity, which was rarely matched in English history. Furthermore, during her reign, English culture reached a peak that culminated in the creative genius of William Shakespeare (see Topic 47).

ELIZABETH THE QUEEN

Despite this aspect of real accomplishment, however, Elizabeth was a complex ruler. She believed genuinely in the advantages and legitimacy of absolute monarchy, yet she often compromised these principles for the sake of political expediency. Her personal sympathies in religion were, like those of her father, not predisposed toward Protestantism, although she restored the Protestant Church. Throughout her life she carefully cultivated suitors but never married, suppressing her personal inclinations for the sake of policy. She projected a strong, willful character in public, although in private she was often indecisive. In the end, it can be said that she embraced her country and its people as the inspiration for her life and work.

One of the first serious challenges she faced came from the north, in Scotland, where the Catholic Mary Stuart (ruled 1542–1567) ruled. After the death in 1560 of her husband, Francis II of France, Mary returned to Scotland. When her subjects, converted to Protestantism by John Knox, forced Mary into exile in 1568, she fled to England. Elizabeth treated her coolly and kept her under tight surveillance because as a direct descendant of Henry VII, Mary stood in the line of royal succession. Mary became the focus of several plots against Elizabeth hatched by Catholic dissidents. Finally, after Parliament demanded Mary's death and further plots were revealed, in 1587 Elizabeth had Mary executed.

THE RETURN TO PROTESTANTISM

From the religious point of view, the years from 1547 to 1558 were difficult ones for the average English citizen. Henry's break with the Roman Church had disconcerted many of his subjects, and the support of Edward VI for Protestantism had created further uncertainty. Mary Tudor had then added to the confusion of her subjects by attempting to bring England back into the Catholic faith, at first with moderation and then with brutality and bloodshed. Elizabeth, who had been brought up a Protestant, enjoyed a long reign in which she was able to bring a measure of clarity back to religious life: The secret of her success was pragmatism rather than religious fervor.

Mary Tudor's death heartened English Protestants, many of whom had left the country for exile abroad and now returned home, relishing the prospect of more radical reform. Elizabeth repealed Mary's Catholic legislation and restored the major laws setting up the Anglican Church passed by Henry VIII. Under Elizabeth, the Church of England simplified its structure and actually embraced the notion of predestination preached by the Calvinists, whose doctrines the exiles had absorbed abroad.

In 1563, the Thirty-Nine Articles adopted a position of compromise on many doctrinal issues but kept a good many long-established Catholic liturgical practices, although now translated into English. The kingdom continued to be home to many dissenters who wanted a purer church, as well as to Jesuits who worked secretly to reestablish Catholicism. The so-called nonconformists, who included Puritans and Presbyterians, kept the religious question unsettled for years to come. The **Puritans** spearheaded a religious reform movement that wanted to "purify" the Church of England of all remnants of Catholicism. They became noted for their spirit of moral and religious earnestness that drove them to want to reform the entire kingdom.

Elizabeth's reign also saw steady economic progress based on England's widening involvement in overseas trade and the reduction of the debt. Joint stock companies such as the East India Company competed with its Dutch and French counterparts for primacy in global trade (see Topic 46). Elizabeth positioned England against the expansionist policies of her would-be suitor, Philip II of Spain. In 1588, her sea captains, including Sir Francis Drake, destroyed the Spanish Armada, although Spain continued to be a major power for some time. Lasting peace between Spain and England came only after the death of Philip in 1598 and Elizabeth's death five years later.

TOWARD CONFRONTATION: JAMES I AND PARLIAMENT

During the last years of Elizabeth's reign, tensions with Parliament had risen as a result of the queen's demands for special financial grants to pay for her struggle with Spain. In response, Parliament had raised constitutional issues designed to further weaken the crown. The Stuart kings who followed her turned the relationship of the monarchy with Parliament into a major crisis.

COMPROMISE AND CONFRONTATION
Elizabeth was succeeded by James VI of Scotland, the son of Mary Stuart. He ascended the English throne as James I (ruled 1603–1625). Well educated and a fervent believer in the divine right of kings, James disliked the pretensions of Parliament. Before the authority of a monarch, he argued, no other authority could or should prevail. Having been raised in Scotland, he had little direct experience of issues involving English tradition and constitutional history.

Along with the crown, James inherited debt and hard times from the last years of Elizabeth's wars against Spain.

He made matters worse by spending lavishly on his court. In addition, the Puritans began pressing James, who had accepted Presbyterianism as the dominant form of Protestantism in Scotland, to move the Reformation forward. In this the radicals were disappointed. James was cautious in matters of faith, and his best-remembered contribution to religious life was the English translation of the Bible he commissioned, known as the King James Version, which appeared in 1611.

In politics James was as practical as Elizabeth in his thinking. Only a year after becoming king, he participated in a Protestant conference at Hampton Court, where radicals insisted that the episcopal system be abolished. James turned down their demands and took a hard line against the Calvinists, warning them that they would be banished if they continued waging religious war. On the other hand, after James issued an edict banishing Catholic priests, Protestant sympathies for him increased, especially when the so-called Gunpowder Plot was uncovered in 1605: A Catholic named Guy Fawkes (1578–1606) was caught placing 36 barrels of gunpowder under the houses of Parliament one day before the king was to appear before the assembly. Under torture, Fawkes revealed the names of fellow conspirators, who were tried and executed. November 5—when the explosion was to have occurred—is still celebrated in England as Guy Fawkes Day.

In the years following the plot against him, James experienced growing difficulties with Parliament. Twice—in 1611 and 1614—the king dissolved Parliament after it had turned down his proposed budgets and ruled by decree for several years. In 1621, when Parliament threatened to remove some of the king's powers, he went personally to the House of Commons to oppose the challenge. As his popularity began to suffer, James compounded his problems by arranging the marriage of his son Charles to a French princess, whose Catholic faith aroused resentment in England.

Although James angered members of Parliament with his high-handed behavior and his arguments in favor of divine right monarchy, about which he had written a treatise, the skillful monarch ended his reign with restored popularity when he went to war with Spain in 1624.

SOCIAL AND RELIGIOUS TRANSFORMATIONS
James's confrontations with Parliament had far-reaching implications, especially because membership in that body had begun to undergo important social change since the mid-16th century. In general, by the early 17th century England had a much larger group of entrepreneurs—virtually all of whom were not nobles—who had made money in trade, manufacturing, and in capitalist farming and sheep raising. The most significant development was the increase in the size of the gentry class—that is, either the younger, landless brothers of nobles or landowners who used their newfound wealth to purchase estates and country residences in order to achieve a higher social status. The rise of the

gentry was accompanied by a decline in the importance of the old feudal nobility, whose role as military leaders had all but disappeared as the feudal armies were replaced by a royal army.

Although never a united group, the gentry were forming a majority in the House of Commons, the branch of Parliament that controlled government finances, and were beginning to insist on a larger share of political influence. By the time of the death of James I, the gentry formed perhaps three-quarters of the membership of the Commons. Finances were at the heart of the tension between the gentry and the monarchy. The monarchy required ever-larger income, and while the gentry bore an increasingly larger share of the tax burden, they demanded a voice in policy making and in how their tax money was to be spent. James I and his successors, however, correctly saw such pursuit of power as undermining royal absolutism.

Compounding these problems was the fact that the period of religious strife was by no means over in England, and religious issues were linked to the country's social transformation. The Calvinists and Puritans, both of which were gaining followers, continued to demand a more strenuous program of reform for the Church of England, which they wanted to see shorn of its remaining Catholic influences. The Puritan emphasis on the work ethic and high moral standards in everyday life reflected the values of some of the gentry and the merchant class that had come to dominate the House of Commons. The early settlements in the American colonies in Virginia, Massachusetts, Pennsylvania, and Rhode Island were organized by Puritans seeking communities of their own.

CHARLES I AND THE CIVIL WAR

The mounting political and religious trouble between Parliament and the monarchy reached the crisis point under Charles I (ruled 1625–1649). His marriage to Henrietta Maria, the sister of King Louis XIII of France, made him unpopular from the start. Matters worsened when Charles's requests for money were met with demands from Parliament for political reforms. He dismissed two Parliaments, but in 1628, he was forced to accept the Petition of Right, a constitutional document that asserted the legal rights and protections of the English people as they had evolved since Magna Carta—no taxation without Parliamentary consent, no billeting of troops in civilian homes, freedom from arbitrary arrest and imprisonment, and no martial law in peacetime.

THE CIVIL WAR

As soon as Charles had his money, however, he dissolved Parliament and refused to call another for more than 10 years. The gentry and Puritans of the Commons seethed with revolt, especially as Charles ran the government by imposing special levies that in the eyes of Parliament were improper and represented taxation without consent. The Puritans turned to Parliament for support, finding increasing common cause with sectors of the gentry.

The religious question provoked a crisis that forced Charles to call Parliament back into session. William Laud (1573–1645), archbishop of Canterbury, was a man of moderate persuasion but obstinate mind. Laud tried to bully the Puritans, prosecuting his Puritan critics in royal law courts, and in 1639 attempted to introduce a uniform *Anglican Book of*

Color engraving of the English king Charles I with his French wife, Henrietta Maria, c. 1630. The image is based on a painting by the Flemish artist Anthony van Dyck, who was knighted by the king in 1632 and became official court painter. Many of his works, like this one, are official portraits; he produced more than five hundred.

Alinari/Art Resource

Mary Evans Picture Library

Print of Quaker woman preaching. Mid-17th century. The Quakers were one of several radical Protestant groups to emerge during the English Civil Wars, several of which encouraged women to preach. This contemporary engraving makes fun of the practice. The preacher's audience is held gripped by her words, but at the window above the onlookers express astonishment and scorn.

Map 43.1 England in the Civil War. Note the site of Naseby, where King Charles I was captured at the battle fought there in 1645. The two major universities, the centers of intellectual life, split over the political division of the age: Cambridge sided with Parliament, while Oxford remained loyal to the king. The "bloodless revolution" had little military effect outside England.

Common Prayer in England as well as in Scotland. Riots against Laud's policies erupted in Scotland, where Presbyterianism was dominant, and Charles had to ask Parliament for the money to raise an army to put down the rebellion.

The so-called Long Parliament, which met from 1640 to 1660, had as its leader a Puritan opponent of the monarchy named John Pym. Under his guidance, the Commons passed a series of measures designed to limit the power of the king, including the abolition of royal courts such as the Star Chamber, which the king had used to try nobles, and an act requiring the king to call Parliament at least every three years. One member of the Commons, Oliver Cromwell (1599–1658), urged Parliament to abolish the *Book of Common Prayer* and bitterly attacked the institution of bishops in the Anglican Church. Archbishop Laud was impeached, and the following year the House of Commons issued the Grand Remonstrance: a restatement of Parliament's position and the measures it had passed.

All the while, Parliament had refused to grant Charles the money he needed for the army, preferring to deal directly with the Scots in the hope of forcing the king to give in to their wishes. Instead, Charles tried unsuccessfully to have the leaders of the Commons arrested. In June 1642, when the Commons put forward its last set of demands, including control of the church and the army and the right to appoint ministers, Charles fled London for the north of

England. There he condemned the Parliamentary leaders as traitors and took to the battlefields to reassert royal authority. Civil war had come.

The English Civil War, which lasted from 1642 to 1646, was a struggle in which both sides fought reluctantly. Neither Charles nor the leaders of Parliament had wanted matters to result in violence, but the issues were of great importance and fraught with decades of tension. Conflict between the freedoms and laws of England and the power of kings was exacerbated by religious passions that had been brewing since the time of Henry VIII.

Yet the underlying causes of the struggle, long debated by historians, do not appear to be quite so simple. The momentous decision to take up arms against the crown so divided the country, including the Puritans, that half of the members of the House of Commons sided with Charles. Marxist historians have argued that the more prosperous segments of the gentry, anxious to consolidate their power, led the fight for Parliament and the Puritans. On the other hand, another school of thought insists that the most prosperous group supported the king and that the less prosperous gentry, living off declining agricultural incomes, backed the Puritans and Parliament. Moreover, the southern and eastern areas of England, where merchants and businessmen were concentrated, opposed the king, whereas the more rural northern and western regions supported him. In the end, the Civil War is perhaps best seen as a complicated struggle that was fueled by religious conflict.

While Pym gave the rebels political direction, Cromwell provided military leadership. Cromwell designed what he called the New Model Army, whose soldiers were indoctrinated and impassioned by sermons and religious worship. In June 1645, after almost three years of fighting, the Civil War reached a turning point when the antiroyalists won a major victory at Naseby and took the king.

THE END OF THE MONARCHY

During the course of the Civil War, two broad factions emerged in the opposition to Charles: The Independents, whose leader in the Commons was Cromwell, wanted to replace the Anglican Church with a decentralized church in which each congregation chose the kind of worship it wanted; the Presbyterians, on the other hand, wanted a Calvinist church similar to the system in Scotland, where a central authority presided over local congregations. On the religious issue, Cromwell gave in to the majority, who were Presbyterians, and the victors proceeded to abolish the bishops and establish a Presbyterian church. To Cromwell, however, this was only a temporary compromise, and his determination to break the king's power only widened the divisions wrenching apart English society.

Charles's surrender made the struggle even more complicated because the question of what to do with the king revealed how deeply divided his foes were. When the Independents and the Presbyterians failed to agree on the fate of the king, the Civil War broke out again in 1647. This time, however, the Independents were pitted against the Presbyterians, while the Scots now supported the king. The Parliament's army added to the instability because it had gone unpaid for so long that it was threatening to rebel.

In fact, in June 1647 the army kidnapped Charles and demanded payment in return for his release. When the Presbyterians in London tried to stop the military, the soldiers occupied the capital, gaining the backing of the Independents and other radicals. The next year, Cromwell crushed the royalists completely, and his soldiers now insisted on the king's execution. In the House of Commons, the Presbyterian majority refused to support the army's demands, but their defiance prompted the army to purge the Parliament of all those who resisted.

The resulting Rump Parliament, consisting of fewer than 100 members, voted to try the king for crimes against his subjects. Charles was founded guilty and beheaded on January 30, 1649—he went to the block with great dignity, and his execution was by no means universally applauded. Cromwell declared England a republican "commonwealth" without a monarch and without a House of Lords.

THE PROTECTORATE: THE DICTATORSHIP OF OLIVER CROMWELL

The years from 1649 to 1660 are known in English history as the Interregnum, or the period between kings. For the first several years of that period, a council of state exercised executive authority, while the Rump Parliament served as

the legislature. Unable to decide on a new constitutional system for the country, and increasingly frustrated by the hostility between religious factions, in 1653 Cromwell used the army to close down the Rump institution and replaced it with a new body of his own loyal supporters.

For the next five years, Cromwell ruled England as a military dictator, confusing even further the already debated question of sovereignty, or the source of political power. Under the monarchy, sovereignty had been explained as the divine right of kings; now, in times of upheaval, some claimed that sovereignty rested with the people. But what form of sovereignty did Cromwell exercise?

THE PROTECTORATE

Cromwell's hand-picked Parliament proved so destabilizing that a group of army officers took matters into their own hands. They drafted a constitutional document known as the Instrument of Government, which gave Cromwell the title of Lord Protector.

The new ruler of England was a man of the gentry class, a Puritan of the Independent persuasion who believed in parliamentary government. He said repeatedly that he wanted to bring genuine constitutional government and religious freedom to the country, but both goals eluded him. During his rule, he called three different Parliaments into session, but none was able to arrange a long-term constitutional settlement. Cromwell seemed to be inspired by high-minded ideals, but he was inflexible and unwilling to make the kind of realistic concessions required by the political process. In 1657, one Parliament offered him the crown, but he declined it. In the end, he believed the dictatorship to be the only way to bring peace to England.

Cromwell's tenure as Lord Protector of England was made difficult by the bitter factionalism within the Puritan ranks. The most radical group was known as the Diggers, who wanted to abolish private property, while the Levellers made quasi-democratic demands for parliamentary elections based on nearly universal male suffrage. Neither of these views found support among the landed gentry, from whose ranks Cromwell had come. A host of other ideologies surfaced during these years, and conspiracies against the Protectorate came from the defeated royalists as well as from the ranks of the Puritans.

The former king's son, the future Charles II, lived in France, where exiled nobles hatched countless plots to restore the monarchy. Caught between opposition to the monarchy and resistance to the Protectorate, Cromwell became reinforced in his conviction that only he had the objective interests of the country at heart.

Cromwell reorganized the country into 11 military and administrative districts, each in the hands of a major general who reported directly to him. The man who claimed to detest power could not, however, abide dissent. To control the opposition and those who would criticize the dictatorship, Cromwell created a system of domestic surveillance and prohibited all newspapers. He crushed a rebellion in Ireland with great brutality, convinced that the Catholicism of the Irish was a form of treason against the state. In religious

Print showing the royal court of Charles II. Late 17th century. The moment depicted is the entry of the king and his courtiers. The Restoration saw a return to the splendor and luxury that had disappeared under Oliver Cromwell; note the rich costumes of both men and women—the latter wearing full, heavy skirts.

affairs, Cromwell's record was mixed. Among his Christian subjects, he allowed freedom of worship only for non-Anglican Protestants; on the other hand, he welcomed the return of Jews to England. In social matters, Cromwell tried to influence the tone of public life by banning plays, sports, and popular music, but these policies were never well received.

Cromwell's last days were spent in disillusionment and concern for the future of England. Before his death, he arranged for the Lord Protectorate to be given to his son,

Richard (1626–1712), but his unseasoned successor lacked his father's energy and skill and could not maintain control. In truth, the English people were tired of military rule as well as of the drab tenor of life that Cromwell had imposed. In May 1660, General George Monck, who commanded the New Model Army in Scotland, seized control of the government and asked Charles II to return to England. After years of civil war and the execution of a king, of religious strife and a harsh dictatorship, the Stuart monarchy was restored.

Putting Tudor-Stuart England in Perspective

Despite the painful experiences of the mid-17th century, England did derive some positive long-term lessons about the balance of power between Parliament and the crown. The notion that there would be no taxation without the consent of Parliament was now a permanent part of the constitutional arrangement, as was the writ of habeas corpus and the prohibition against quartering soldiers among civilians.

The social transformation of the country that had produced the gentry class also reflected a permanent reality that guided domestic politics for the next two centuries. When, a generation after the restoration of the monarchy, Stuart rule proved unworkable, it was brought to an end peacefully, in what came to be called England's "bloodless revolution."

Questions for Further Study

1. How can Tudor religious policies best be characterized?
2. What were the origins of the civil wars in England?
3. Why was the monarchy restored after the end of the Protectorate?

Suggestions for Further Reading

Ashton, Robert. *The English Civil War: Conservatism and Revolution, 1603–1649.* London, 1978.

Aylmer, Gerald E. *Rebellion or Revolution? England, 1640–1660.* New York, 1986.

Brimacombe, Peter. *All the Queen's Men: The World of Elizabeth I.* New York, 2000.

Elton, Geoffrey R. *The Parliament of England, 1559–1581.* Cambridge, MA, 1986.

Guy, John. *The Tudors.* Oxford, 2000.

Kennedy, D.E. *The English Revolution, 1642-1649.* New York, 2000.

MacCaffrey, W.T. *Queen Elizabeth and the Making of Policy, 1572–1588.* Princeton, NJ, 1981.

Palliser, David M. *The Age of Elizabeth.* London, 1983.

Plowden, Alison. *Elizabeth Regina: The Age of Triumph, 1588-1603.* Stroud, 2000.

Russell, Conrad. *The Causes of the English Civil War.* New York, 1990.

Zagorin, Perez. *Rebels and Rulers, 1500–1660,* 2 vols. Cambridge, MA, 1982.

InfoTrac College Edition

Enter the search term *Elizabeth I* using Key Terms.

Enter the search term *Oliver Cromwell* using Key Terms.

RELIGIOUS WAR AND THE ASCENDANCY OF THE FRENCH MONARCHY

If in England the 16th and 17th centuries saw the conflict between constitutionalism and monarchy resolve itself in favor of Parliament, in France the same period witnessed the growing power of royal government and the foundations of French absolutism. After the conclusion of the Hundred Years' War in 1453, a succession of kings built up the royal administration, tamed the nobility, and secured state authority over the appointment of bishops and other ecclesiastical officials.

As in other states, the Reformation caused deep religious conflicts in France. These conflicts erupted into a series of wars of religion that took on the character of civil strife. The religious struggles, primarily those of the monarchy against the **Huguenots,** or French Calvinists, dominated events in the 16th century, temporarily ending the consolidation of the royal state. Nevertheless, the fact that the end of the strife came as a result of an edict of religious toleration by the king suggested the value that a strong monarchy could have in the country.

In the aftermath of the religious wars, the process of building the nation around the monarchy resumed. With the skillful and energetic leadership of two cardinals, Richelieu and Mazarin, who served as royal ministers, the French monarchs imposed ever-greater royal authority over the realm. The government these kings controlled reached into the lives of more subjects than ever before.

Religious strife was not, of course, confined to France. In the second decade of the 17th century, while Richelieu still presided as the king's chief minister, most of the great powers of Europe were plunged into a terrible religious and secular conflict known as the Thirty Years' War. The antagonism between Catholics and Protestants was certainly an important factor in bringing about the war, but not the only one: The conflict also involved a broader struggle for mastery between the Bourbon dynasty of France and the imperial aspirations of the Hapsburgs.

RELIGIOUS CONFLICT: FROM THE ST. BARTHOLOMEW'S DAY MASSACRE TO THE EDICT OF NANTES

Nowhere did the spread of Protestantism, and especially of the militant Calvinist variety, inflame religious passions more than in France, where the bitter and bloody French Wars of Religion destroyed social tranquility and exasperated already existing economic and political tensions.

CATHERINE DE' MEDICI AND THE WARS OF RELIGION

The religious turmoil in France endured for a generation, from 1562 to 1598, but its roots went back further, to the reign of Henry II (ruled 1547–1559). Despite his energetic and robust appearance, Henry was a weak and pliable ruler who was influenced by his mistresses and his ambitious advisers. He continued the Valois-Hapsburg War against Emperor Charles V and then against Philip II, siding with the German Protestants in their struggles against the Hapsburg emperor, despite his own Catholic faith.

When peace came in 1559, Henry reversed himself, instituting severe restrictions against the Protestants in his own country. Later that year, when Henry was accidentally killed in a tournament, his Italian wife, Catherine de' Medici (1519–1589), daughter of Duke Lorenzo de' Medici of Urbino, became regent. Acting for her three sons, who succeeded each other as king over the following years, Catherine's religious policies ranged from toleration to persecution. During her regency, the religious question came to a head.

Calvinism had continued to spread despite persecutions by Henry II. During his reign, there were Huguenots among all social classes, from artisans to merchants, and half of the nobility had become Protestant. Because the

aristocracy had always challenged the king's efforts to create centralized government, the existence of so large a proportion of Huguenot nobles posed a special danger to the monarchy.

Beyond the nobility, the Huguenots formed a distinct minority of the French population, but they were zealous in their faith and determined to fight for their freedom to worship as they chose. The Huguenot Church was well organized, with a centralized administration that reached down to the provincial and congregational levels. By the time the Wars of Religion began, more than 2,000 Huguenot congregations existed throughout the country.

Catherine de' Medici tried unsuccessfully to diffuse the growing tensions by brokering religious compromise and fostering reforms in the French Church. The Catholic extremists, headed by the influential Guise family, demanded unremitting opposition to the Huguenots. The anti-Protestant campaign received support from the papacy and the Jesuits, as well as from Philip II of Spain.

The war broke out in 1562 when the private armies of the Guise slaughtered an entire congregation of Huguenots at the town of Vassy. The fighting spread, but both sides found themselves unable to win a clear victory. Catherine, who was concerned that the crusade against the Protestants might undermine the Valois monarchy, joined forces with the Catholic party led by the Guise family.

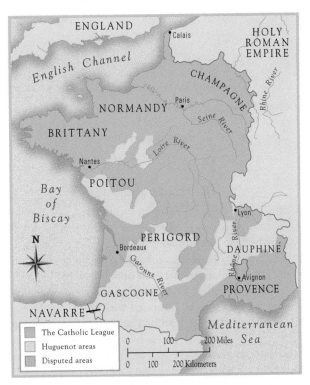

Map 44.1 Religious Conflict in France. The bitterness of France's religious wars was complicated by the extent of the geographical divisions. The Catholics were divided between the northern regions and Provence in the south, while central France was the scene of constant battles. The Edict of Nantes was proclaimed in a city that lay in the vicinity of disputed territory.

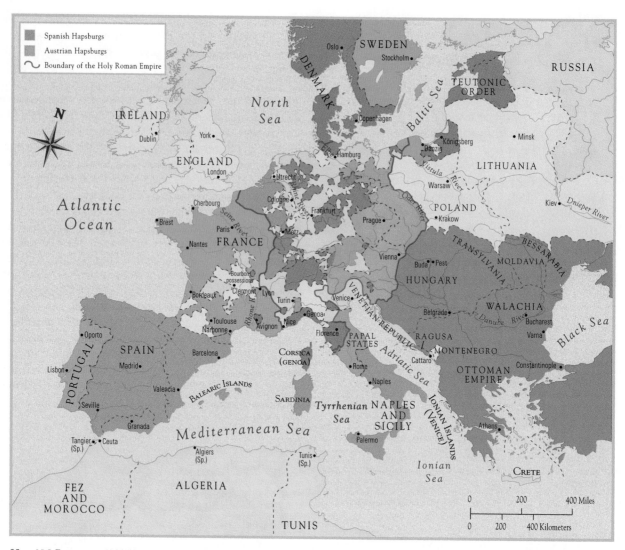

Map 44.2 Europe, c. 1560. While France and Spain have begun to resemble their modern forms, Italy and Germany remain divided into a series of smaller states. The Ottoman Empire is at its strongest, extending almost to the gates of Vienna. In Eastern Europe, only the island of Crete remained a Western possession, governed by Venice; it was taken by the Turks a century later.

In 1570, after the Huguenot military leader Gaspard de Coligny (1519–1572) defeated a royal army, Catherine decided to make peace. Reconciled with Catherine, de Coligny became an intimate adviser to her son, Charles IX (ruled 1560–1574), and urged him to support the Dutch Protestant rebellion against their Spanish rulers.

Fearing de Coligny's growing influence over her weak-minded son, Catherine conspired with the Guise to have de Coligny assassinated, but he escaped, although severely wounded. Coligny's survival led Catherine and the Guise to organize an even wider plot to eliminate the Huguenot leadership. Huguenot nobles had gathered in Paris for the marriage of Catherine's daughter Margaret to the Bourbon leader Henry of Navarre (the future Henry IV, he had wavered between Catholicism and Protestantism, but was now Huguenot). Catherine persuaded Charles to authorize what is known as the St. Bartholomew's Day Massacre (August 24, 1572). As the slaughter spread from Paris to

the countryside, thousands of Huguenots, including de Coligny, were killed.

HENRY IV AND THE EDICT OF NANTES

The brutal massacre, which destroyed much popular support for the Valois family, broke the tenuous truce, and the religious wars erupted again. In 1576, the Catholic party created the Holy League to wipe out the Protestants and to make Henry of Guise king of France in place of Catherine's son, Henry III (ruled 1574–1589), who had succeeded his brother Charles.

The subsequent War of the Three Henries (1588–1589) first saw Henry of Guise pitted against Henry III. The Catholic king, after having Guise murdered, now joined forces with the Protestant Henry of Navarre in defeating the Holy League. Following the defeat of the extreme Catholics, however, Henry III was assassinated, and Henry of Navarre now claimed the throne. As King Henry IV (ruled

Painting of the St. Bartholomew's Day Massacre of 1572. Late 16th century. As the scene shows, the killing of French Protestants involved residents of both town and countryside. Note that most of the attackers are wearing the dress of official government troops, while the victims are civilians.

1589–1610), he became the first Bourbon ruler of France. This action immediately drove the extreme Catholics into bitter opposition and provoked the intervention of Philip II of Spain. Henry IV countered this action by securing English support and converted again to Catholicism, thus undermining many of his critics.

Henry was determined to bring the devastating Wars of Religion to an end. With this goal in mind, in 1598 he issued the Edict of Nantes, a document that made Catholicism the official religion of the country but gave the Huguenots some guaranteed protections. Awarding them the right to control more than 100 fortified towns throughout France, the edict also granted them the right to free worship in certain localities and full political privileges. Henry's willingness to accept religious toleration was a pragmatic political decision based on his recognition that France was exhausted by the destructive wars and required strong, effective government. Henceforth, matters of state became paramount as France's rulers set about rebuilding both country and monarchy.

ROYAL GOVERNMENT AND ECONOMIC REVIVAL

The Wars of Religion had been deeply divisive of French society and had ruined the economy. The most pressing problem facing Henry IV was financial because the wars had drained the treasury, heaping enormous debt on the government. Only after putting the economy back on a firm footing could the king turn to rebuilding the power of the monarchy.

Henry and his Bourbon successors had the good fortune of being served by a succession of skillful and dedicated ministers. In reconstructing the economy, Henry had the assistance of a brilliant finance minister, Maximilien, duke of Sully (1560–1641). Like the king, Sully was earlier a Protestant but converted as a matter of policy. Beginning as a member of the king's finance commission, in 1598 he was made superintendent of finances.

Sully set out to increase royal revenues and reduce the debt. He established a new direct tax that was more easily calculated and collected. He raised the *gabelle*, a tax on salt, which virtually all citizens had to use as a preservative for keeping food. He reformed the tax-collecting mechanisms: Under earlier kings, the revenue agents took a portion of the revenues they collected for themselves, and Sully now forced them to accept a lower percentage. Sully also raised money by increasing the number of royal offices and, as previous kings had done, continued to sell them for cash to nobles of the robe, a new class of aristocrat created by the monarchy to hold the key bureaucratic positions. Sully induced the older, landowning nobility of feudal origins, the nobles of the sword, to retire to their rural estates with government pensions. At the same time, he required the payment of an annual fee from all those nobles of the robe who occupied government offices.

PUBLIC FIGURES AND PRIVATE LIVES

Marie De' Medici and Henry IV of France

© Réunion des Musées Nationaux/Art Resource, NY

SuperStock

In 1600, Henry IV married Marie de' Medici (1573–1642), daughter of the grand duke of Tuscany, an alliance that solidified Henry's conversion to Catholicism. Marie was a strong-willed, self-possessed woman from one of Italy's most distinguished families. She thought of the French as culturally inferior and set about bringing some of the sophisticated tastes of her own background to the court at Paris. Henry, on the other hand, proved to be a popular sovereign who demonstrated a real concern for the welfare of even his most lowly subjects.

When Henry was assassinated in 1610, Marie became regent for their son, Louis XIII (ruled 1610–1643). She completely dominated her son, and when the nobles began to raise objections to her rule, she summoned the Estates General of the Realm in 1614 and declared Louis of age—the Estates General, which was without real power, was not called again for 175 years, on the eve of the French Revolution.

Although in theory the regency was now dissolved, Marie continued to exclude Louis from the affairs of state. Instead, she dismissed Sully and relied on the advice of the Florentine adventurer Concino Concini (d. 1617) and the French cleric, Cardinal Armand du Plessis de Richelieu (1585–1642). Concini set up an elaborate spy system among the nobility and became universally despised for his greed and duplicity. In 1617, the young Louis arranged to have Concini assassinated and forced his mother into exile. She returned, however, five years later and was reconciled with Louis, whom she persuaded to appoint Richelieu secretary of state.

After her husband's death, Marie had the Luxembourg Palace in Paris, a large and elaborate residence modeled in part on the Pitti Palace in Florence, built for herself. When Marie returned from exile in 1622, she commissioned the artist Peter Paul Rubens to paint a cycle of huge paintings dedicated to her and her marriage with Henry IV.

Marie's influence on French policy was considerable. She managed to keep the great nobles in check and established close relations with the Hapsburg Catholic powers, Spain and Austria. Her ambitions finally overstepped her talents when she tried to undermine Richelieu, whose growing influence over the king she began to resent. In 1631, Louis banished her again. She fled to the Netherlands, never returning to France.

While royal revenues were being increased, Sully had Henry cancel a portion of the public debt, so that he eventually was able to accumulate a surplus of funds. Sully negotiated trade treaties with the other powers and adopted the mercantilist policies that guided their trade programs. He used the new state income to invest in long-range economic development by building and improving roads, canals, and other infrastructure, a program that also had the immediate effect of putting people to work. Both Sully and the king were interested in increasing the general prosperity of all classes of French subjects, and Henry is reputed to have said, "There should be a chicken in every peasant's pot every Sunday."

The Cardinals and the State: The Administrations of Richelieu and Mazarin

Between 1624 and 1661, the government of France was in the hands of two extraordinary ministers, Armand du Richelieu and Giulio Mazarin. Both were cardinals of the Catholic Church and proved to be two of the greatest statesmen in French history. The brilliant and crafty cardinals dedicated all of their energies toward making the French monarchy as absolute as possible and keeping themselves in power. They balanced and held in check the various forces working against royal authority: the nobility, the bureaucracy, and the Huguenots.

TOWARD ROYAL ABSOLUTISM

In light of the destructive force of the Wars of Religion, religious policy was perhaps the most sensitive issue confronting Richelieu. Under Marie de' Medici and her Italian advisers, the Huguenots had worried about renewed persecution. Incidents of local conflict with royal troops did erupt from time to time. In the 1620s, after one Huguenot stronghold had allied with the English against the monarchy, the government began to seize the fortified towns the Huguenots had been granted under the terms of the Edict of Nantes. Richelieu then secured the revocation of the edict and replaced it with the Peace of Alais, which granted the Huguenots only religious and political rights.

For years, the constant wars that disturbed French public life had required royal governments to raise monies for their armies, and this had proved to be a major impetus in the drive toward absolutism. Richelieu, needing revenues to finance his foreign and domestic policies, was no exception. He encouraged the sale of government offices, which continued to grow in number. By the 1630s, almost half of all government income came from this source. As a result, the efficient collection of taxes and control over local affairs assumed increasing importance.

Richelieu was never able to bring royal finances under control and had to resort to increasing taxes on ordinary citizens in order to meet the mounting national debt. The tax burden and the ever-growing power of the royal government sometimes sparked protests and uprisings in the countryside, especially among the peasantry and the nobility. Richelieu was able, however, to put them down with the royal troops.

CARDINAL MAZARIN AND THE FRONDE

Louis XIII died in 1643. Because his son, Louis XIV (ruled 1643–1715), was only five years old at the time, once again France came under the regency of the queen mother, this time Anne of Austria (1601–1666). Anne turned the gov-

The National Gallery, London

Philippe de Champagne, *Triple Portrait of Cardinal Richelieu*, c. 1630. The painter, a Belgian, went to Paris in 1621 to help in the decoration of the Luxembourg Palace and remained as court painter to Louis XIII. This image conveys the many aspects of the cardinal's sharp intelligence and authority.

ernment over to Giulio Mazarin (1602–1661), to whom she may have been secretly married (this suspicion has never been confirmed). Mazarin was an Italian-born soldier who had served in the papal diplomatic corps. Although never ordained as a priest, he was Richelieu's protégé, and Louis XIII had recommended that he be made a cardinal.

Mazarin continued the two policies of his predecessor: the centralization of power in the hands of the king, and increasing taxation to pay for the costs of royal government. These programs incurred the wrath of both the nobles and the members of the law court known as the Parlement of Paris, who in any case disliked Mazarin on principle because he was a foreigner. Mazarin further weakened his position by involvement in personal financial corruption. The nobles and the members of the Parlement joined forces against the monarchy when Mazarin tried to squeeze money out of them to meet the mounting costs of the French involvement in the Thirty Years' War (see following section). The result was an organized conspiracy against the government, known as the *Fronde*—a word that has come to mean violent political opposition from within the ruling class.

In 1648, the Parlement and nobles of the robe, who held many of the important bureaucratic offices, demanded that the king agree to levy no new taxes without consent. When Mazarin arrested the leaders of the Parlement, a popular revolt in Paris forced him and the royal family to flee the capital. The disturbances spread to other cities, and in several locations the protestors took over local governments and random acts of violence erupted. This first episode of the Fronde ended only after Mazarin pledged to concede the demands of the Parlement.

A second Fronde developed in 1650 around two nobles of the sword who held important military positions. This time, the ringleaders insisted that Mazarin be dismissed and that many of the traditional local powers of the old nobility be restored. The Spanish, with whom the French had continued to fight even after the end of the Thirty Years' War, sent aid to the Fronde. The effort failed, however, when the nobles began fighting among themselves. Mazarin shrewdly played one group off another and was able to use army elements loyal to the monarchy to crush the conspiracy. In 1652, Mazarin strengthened royal authority by having the minority of Louis XIV declared at an end. Never again would the monarchy be seriously threatened by rebellious nobles. The failure of the Fronde had the opposite effect, strengthening the power of the state. After Mazarin's death in 1661, Louis XIV excluded his mother Anne from all participation in the affairs of state and assumed full powers over one of the most powerful forms of absolute monarchy in Western Europe.

A SCANDAL IN BOHEMIA: THE PROTESTANT REVOLT AND THE THIRTY YEARS' WAR

The last of the great wars of religion that shook Europe is known as the Thirty Years' War, a complex struggle that unfolded in four distinct phases between 1618 and 1648: the Bohemian Phase (1618–1625), the Danish Phase (1625–1629), the Swedish Phase (1630–1635), and the French-Swedish Phase (1635–1648). Much of the fighting took place in Germany, but the struggle dragged in most of the great states of Europe and many of the lesser powers as well. Three principal participants, Spain, Austria, and France, were at the center of the conflict.

The vast Hapsburg empire had been established when Charles V inherited the throne of Spain and three years later became Holy Roman Emperor. Eventually, he ruled over Austria, Bohemia, Hungary, and the Netherlands as well as Spain, the German lands of the Holy Roman Empire, and portions of Italy. When Charles retired in 1556, his holdings were divided. His son Philip II received Spain and its overseas colonies, the Netherlands, and Italy, while his brother Ferdinand took the imperial title along with Austria, Bohemia, and Hungary. From the time of Charles V, the French had felt encircled by the lands and ambitions of the Hapsburgs, and an ongoing struggle between first the Valois and then the Bourbon rulers of France and the Hapsburgs marked European politics for more than a century.

The religious wars engulfing the German states ended with the Peace of Augsburg in 1555. The two sides, however, continued to fight sporadically, eventually forming opposing military alliances: the Protestant Union, supported by France, England, and the Netherlands; and the Catholic League, supported by Spain and the Holy Roman Empire. Clearly, the war involved political and dynastic issues that had little to do with religion.

The war began in Bohemia, however, over religious issues. In 1609, the Holy Roman Emperor had pledged himself to a policy of religious toleration for Catholics and Protestants alike. He intended his promise to mollify the Calvinist nobles in Bohemia. When, however, Ferdinand II of Hapsburg (ruled as king of Bohemia 1617–1637, and as Holy Roman Emperor 1619–1637) became king of Bohemia in 1617, he began an effort to impose Catholicism and a rigid centralizing policy on the country.

SIGNIFICANT DATES

The Thirty Years' War

1608	Protestant Union formed
1609	Catholic League formed
1618	Defenestration of Prague
1618–1625	Bohemian Phase of war
1625–1629	Danish Phase of war
1630–1635	Swedish Phase of war
1635–1648	French-Swedish Phase of war
1648	Peace of Westphalia
1659	Peace of Pyrenees

Jacques Callot, etching from *The Miseries of War* series. 1632–1633. Callot, a French painter and engraver who worked for the Medici court in Florence, is best known for being the first artist to have made etching an independent art. This horrific image is one of a series showing the death and destruction visited on Germany by the Thirty Years' War.

THE CATHOLIC TRIUMPH

The result was a rebellion in 1618, begun when the nobles threw three imperial officials out of the window of the castle in Prague—the so-called defenestration of Prague. The Bohemians declared Ferdinand deposed and replaced him with Frederick II of the Palatinate, the leader of the Protestant Union and the most prominent Calvinist prince in the Holy Roman Empire. The war had begun.

The hostilities brought an invading army into Bohemia under Ferdinand, now Holy Roman Emperor, and his German ally, Duke Maximilian of Bavaria. In 1620, Catholic forces under the Flemish general Johann von Tilly won a crushing victory against the Calvinists at the Battle of the White Mountain. Ferdinand proceeded to end the autonomy of Bohemia and to declare Catholicism the official religion. The emperor also deprived the Calvinist nobles of their landed estates and forced tens of thousands of Protestants to leave the country.

Moreover, while Frederick was fighting in Bohemia, the Spanish intervened by invading and occupying the Palatinate, which was then divided between them and the Bavarians. The first phase of the Thirty Years' War ended triumphantly, with the Catholic forces in possession of Bohemia and the Palatinate and Spanish troops marching once again into the United Provinces in an effort to recapture the northern territories that Spain had lost in the Dutch revolt of the previous century.

In 1625, the Thirty Years' War was widened by intervention from an unexpected source. Christian IV (ruled 1588–1648), king of Denmark and Norway, invaded northern Germany. Ostensibly joining the struggle in order to assist the Protestant forces, Christian was really motivated by his own expansionist drives; he had already fought against Sweden for control of Lapland and now seemed bent on securing hegemony over the Baltic region around Denmark and Germany.

Christian's ambitions exceeded his abilities. Tilly defeated the Danish army in 1626, and the next year the commander of the imperial forces, Albrecht von Wallenstein, defeated Christian again. Wallenstein, a Bohemian nobleman who had raised an army on behalf of the emperor, had enriched himself on the lands taken from the Protestants.

 Map 44.3 The Expansion of Sweden. Sweden's growth was created by its participation in the religious wars of the 17th century. Gustavus Adolphus used the assistance of the French to counter Hapsburg influence by pushing southward. The results, which were underwritten by the Treaty of Westphalia in 1648, saw the French victorious, with little permanent benefit for Sweden. Go to http://info.wadsworth.com/053461065X for an interactive version of this map.

His troops lived off the lands through which they moved, pillaging and destroying peasant villages and large estates with equal ferocity.

From the Swedish Victory to the French Intervention

By 1629, Christian was forced to withdraw from the war, and the Catholics occupied Denmark and the chief ports of northern Germany. Following these victories, the Emperor Ferdinand announced the Edict of Restitution, which gave back to the Catholic Church all lands taken from it since 1552. The edict also outlawed Calvinism, which had not been protected by the Peace of Augsburg in 1555, in all imperial territories. Yet the very extent of the Catholic victory proved its undoing. The German princes grew worried by the startling increase in imperial power and began to rebel against Ferdinand. At a meeting of the imperial diet in 1630, they demanded that he relieve Wallenstein of his command or see the end of Hapsburg control of the imperial crown.

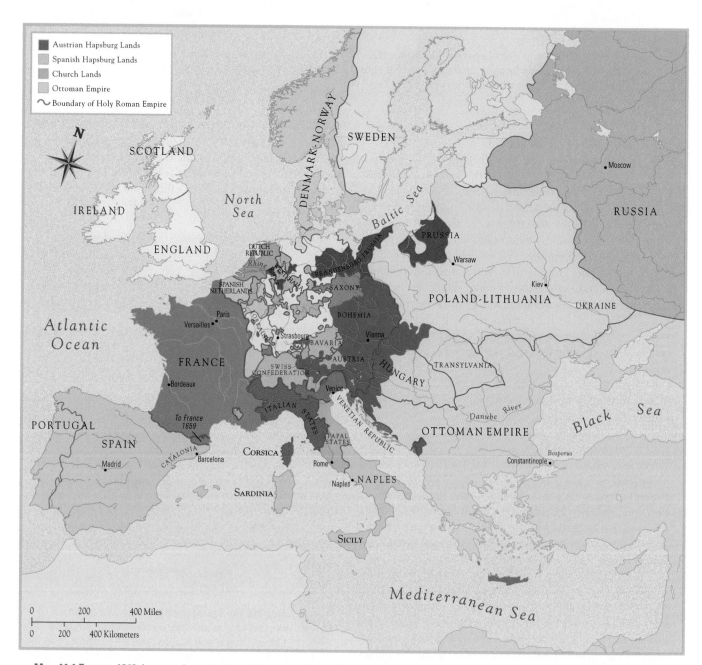

Map 44.4 Europe, 1648. In comparison with Map 44.2, note the loss of Ottoman territory south of Vienna and the huge size of Poland-Lithuania. The Holy Roman Empire continues to fragment, while France has consolidated its regions. A century or so before the founding of St. Petersburg, Moscow remains the only major city in Russia.

GUSTAVUS ADOLPHUS

Ferdinand gave in, and the price was high, because he was deprived of Wallenstein's military talents just as a major new phase of the war began. In 1630, King Gustavus Adolphus of Sweden (ruled 1611–1632) joined the Protestant cause. Gustavus Adolphus had proven to be a vigorous monarch who restructured the Swedish state, disciplined its nobles, and won major victories against the Russians and Poles in the Baltic. Yet he, too, was motivated by political as well as religious questions. Gustavus Adolphus aimed to make Sweden the predominant power in the Baltic and feared the spread of Hapsburg power along the coast of Germany.

Assisted financially by the French, the Swedish king organized a strong military force and moved rapidly and deeply into Germany, pushing the imperial armies before him. Gustavus Adolphus, who was a brilliant field commander, defeated Tilly at Breitenfeld in 1631 and Lech the next year. Recoiling from these blows, Ferdinand recalled Wallenstein to head the imperial forces. At Lutzen in 1632, the Swedes defeated Wallenstein's soldiers, but Gustavus Adolphus was mortally wounded and died shortly afterward.

The tide of battle soon turned against the Swedish army, which was still in Germany. In 1634, the imperial armies—although deprived once again of Wallenstein's command when the general was assassinated—won the Battle of Nordlingen and cleared southern Germany of Swedish troops. The following year, Ferdinand signed the Treaty of Prague with the German princes, bringing a settlement of the tensions between them and the Hapsburgs.

Although the war appeared to be over, in 1635 Cardinal Richelieu decided to involve Catholic France in the conflict, but on the side of the Lutheran Swedes against the Catholic Hapsburgs. Thus began the final phase of the war, in which political and dynastic issues were paramount.

For more than a decade, some of the most bitter and destructive fighting took place in Germany and the Netherlands. The international situation had become chaotic, and both sides realized that it was in the general interest to stop the carnage. Tentative peace talks started in 1641 but dragged on for seven more years.

THE PEACE OF WESTPHALIA

The French victories over the Spanish in 1643, followed by further victories in southern Germany, reactivated the negotiations. By 1648 all sides were ready to end the fighting (the struggle between Spain and France continued until peace was signed between them in 1659). The Peace of Westphalia was arranged as a result of a large meeting of representatives from all of the participants, including France, Spain, Denmark, Sweden, the United Provinces, and the Holy Roman Empire.

France, which dominated the fighting in the last years of the war, gained territories along its northeastern border, notably Alsace and Lorraine. Sweden, France's principal ally, secured control over lands in Germany. In a broad sense, the French finally won their longstanding struggle to tame the Hapsburg empire. The representatives agreed to the independence of the United Provinces and Switzerland, two areas that the Hapsburgs had claimed; at the same time, the German princes of the Holy Roman Empire pledged not to take up arms again against the emperor, who in turn acknowledged their autonomy.

Westphalia represented a major victory for Protestantism. The religious autonomy of the German princes was confirmed, both for Calvinists and Lutherans, and all Catholic properties seized before 1624 now became possessions of the Protestant states. Most far-reaching was the fact that the treaty finally ended the idea that the split between Catholic and Protestant could be healed.

Putting Religious War and the Ascendancy of the French Monarchy in Perspective

The end of the war signaled the final eclipse of Spain and the rise of France as the dominant power on the Continent. In addition, the religious passions that had been the cause of so much destruction and killing for a century began to subside. Henceforth, economic and political ambitions rather than dynastic and religious issues would determine relations among the states of Europe.

The Westphalia agreements established a peace that remained effective for more than a century. The Thirty Years' War had caused terrible destruction, including widespread economic havoc and millions of deaths; estimates suggest that the fighting had wiped out almost one-third of the people of Germany. Even though these figures may be exaggerated, European leaders recognized the extent of the carnage and concluded that diplomacy was a better solution than armed conflict.

Questions for Further Study

1. What was the relationship between politics and religion in France?
2. How did Richelieu and Mazarin strengthen the authority of the king?
3. What were the major issues involved in the Thirty Years' War?

Suggestions for Further Reading

Bergin, Joseph. *Cardinal Richelieu: Power and the Pursuit of Wealth*. New Haven, CT, 1985.

Diefendorf, Barbara. *Beneath the Cross: Catholics and Huguenots in Sixteenth-Century Paris*. New York, 1991.

Levi, Anthony H.T. *Cardinal Richelieu and the Making of France*. London, 2000.

Maltby, William S. *Alba*. Berkeley, CA, 1983.

Parker, Geoffrey, ed. *The Thirty Years War*. New York, 1997.

Parrot, David. *Richlieu's Army: War, Government and Society in France, 1624-1642*. New York, 2001.

Pennington, Donald H. *Seventeenth-Century Europe*, 2nd ed. London, 1989.

Salmon, John H.M. *French Government and Society in the Wars of Religion*. St. Louis, MO, 1976.

Sutherland, Nicola M. *The Massacre of St. Bartholomew and the European Conflict, 1559–1572*. New York, 1973.

InfoTrac College Edition

Enter the search term *Thirty Years' War* using Key Terms.

PATTERNS OF LIFE IN A TIME OF UPHEAVAL

The decades following the Reformation saw tumultuous political events and rapid cultural innovation. The social patterns of everyday life, however, changed slowly. This gradual evolution influenced the basic aspects of daily experience, including the health and well-being of all classes of Europeans, their diet and housing, and the way in which they dressed.

The two factors that affected health most acutely were the food supply and infectious disease, both of which remained largely beyond the control of humans until the Industrial Revolution of the 18th century. Life expectancy was low, and repeated cycles of disease continued to take their toll.

The rich and poor led vastly different lives in terms of diet and housing. For 200 years following the Black Death, food and nutrition improved for most Europeans. With the religious and political upheavals of the 16th and 17th centuries, however, general standards declined.

The same disparity marked the kind of housing available to rich and poor. More durable building materials, such as brick and stone, began to replace wood in public buildings and in the private residences of the wealthy. The houses of the nobility and the rich merchants of the cities used elaborate decorations and furnishings, reflecting a new level of domestic comfort and a growing concern for privacy. The urban poor, on the other hand, were increasingly crammed into densely populated and unsanitary tenement buildings, while the rural poor continued to live under much the same conditions as their ancestors had done.

One of the most visible manifestations of the social hierarchy was dress. For the poor and the peasantry, clothing style remained relatively unchanged for hundreds of years after the 14th century. For the rich, however, dress reflected the availability of new raw materials, including cotton and silk, and the development of new manufacturing processes.

Material aspects of life such as clothing and housing provide a way of understanding broad social and economic transformations. At the same time, they offer insight into the lives of average Europeans, who played no active part in the great political events of their times but who bring us into contact with the daily realities of human existence.

HEALTH AND MEDICINE

In the two centuries before the French Revolution, Europeans had achieved a rough balance between the rate of births and the rate of deaths. Infant mortality was high, with perhaps as many as one-third of all children in the 17th century dying before their first birthday. Among the chief factors keeping the death rate high were disease and starvation, and people lived to an average age of only 25. The wealthy tended to live somewhat longer than the poor, and childbirth made women especially vulnerable to illness and death.

THE CYCLE OF DISEASE

The great plague of the 14th century, the Black Death, was by no means unique. Throughout European history all segments of society, but especially the poor, were highly susceptible to disease. This was generally because of low resistance to illness caused either by diets lacking in nutritional value or by the famines that periodically struck the population—almost always, in fact, epidemics followed incidences of famine.

The plague recurred time and again from the 15th to the 17th centuries. In a 200-year period, the French town of Besançon experienced it 40 times, while Seville in southern Spain saw outbreaks during 11 of the years from 1507 to 1649. In Western Europe, the plague appeared for the last time in 1720 when it killed perhaps half the inhabitants of the French port city of Marseilles. In Eastern Europe, however, where health and sanitary conditions were even worse, the plague continued to ravage cities into the 19th century—thousands fell victim to it in Moscow in 1770 and in the Balkans as late as 1841.

Plague was merely one among a host of prevalent diseases, and often adverse conditions caused the spread of several different maladies at the same time: Smallpox, typhus, cholera, tuberculosis, influenza, grippe, whooping cough, diphtheria, and scarlet fever were some of the diseases that were an ever-present fear. At the time, diseases were often diagnosed incorrectly or confused with the plague, and contemporary descriptions of many illnesses make it difficult to identify them today.

Epidemics spread from one population group to another, usually following the movement of people along trade routes and other heavily traveled itineraries. The Black Death reached Europe on ships from the Crimea, and in the early 18th century cholera came to the Continent from India. Perhaps the best-known example of the movement of disease from one culture to another was the result of the so-called Columbian Exchange. Spanish explorers and soldiers brought diseases like smallpox to the Amerindians of the New World, where no resistance had been developed to these unknown illnesses. The result was the devastation of huge numbers of people.

The process also worked in the other direction. Syphilis, which had been rare in Europe, appears to have become widespread after 1492. One theory holds that members of Columbus's crew contracted it on their arrival in America following the first voyage. Syphilis became a real epidemic that spread rapidly around Europe, and by the end of the 16th century it had affected all classes of society, including many members of royal families.

MEDICAL CARE

The measures taken to deal with the plague in the 17th century were the same as those in the 14th. The rich fled the cities for more isolated homes in the country, while the poor remained in the crowded cities, often locked behind the town gates with the roads to and from the cities blocked. The sick were quarantined, dead bodies burned, and neighborhoods sometimes disinfected, although city officials often abandoned their duties until the danger was over. Medical treatment remained generally primitive until modern times. In the 16th century, some physicians believed they could treat syphilis by cauterizing sores with red-hot irons.

Madeleine de Boulogne, *Nuns Giving Care to Female Patients,* c. 1700. The (female) artist distinguishes clearly between the costumes of the nuns and the middle-class dresses of their patients. On the right-hand wall there hangs a painting of the crucified Christ; such images were commonly displayed in hospitals as a sign of divine suffering.

The Granger Collection, New York

Improved personal hygiene, the replacement of wood with stone or brick as building material for homes, and the elimination of animals from households all reduced fleas and help explain why the plague eventually disappeared. In the 18th century, however, smallpox, which replaced the plague as the most devastating disease, killed perhaps 60 million people. For many years, smallpox had been treated successfully by Muslim physicians, who developed the technique of inoculation. The practice was slowly adopted in the West during the 18th century. Moreover, some scholars suggest that the eventual elimination of particular diseases may be explained not only by such preventive measures, but also by the mutation of the bacteria or virus causing the disease.

Several important medical techniques—systematic observation and deductive reasoning, the use of dissection to study anatomy, and the discovery of the circulation of blood—led to a better understanding of the human body. Moreover, the number of doctors and their training increased greatly. Yet well into the 18th century, faith healing and peasant folk remedies based largely on superstition continued to be practiced widely. Sometimes herbs and drugs prescribed by apothecaries actually worked to cure a patient. Bloodletting and purging remained common and often harmful treatments. Surgery was performed without the use of anesthetic and under extremely unsanitary conditions, especially on battlefields and in hospital wards for the poor. Until the 19th century saw improved treatment of patients, medical knowledge had little practical impact on the health of most Europeans.

Despite the terrible toll on human life taken by the plague and other diseases, the cycle of European marriages and births generally compensated for the demographic losses. In 1451, for example, 21,000 inhabitants of Cologne died of plague, but within a few years 4,000 marriages had taken place in the same city. Similarly, after the plague had decimated the inhabitants of Verona, Italy, in 1637, many of the French soldiers occupying the town married the widows. In Germany as a whole, the devastating impact of the Thirty Years' War, which had claimed perhaps one-third of the population, soon eased as the population began to increase again. The overall demographic pattern in the West changed significantly in the course of the 18th century, when births finally began to gain over deaths, with the result that Europe experienced a far-reaching population explosion.

CHANGING TASTES: FOOD AND DIET

Ever since ancient times, the fundamental food source for Europeans was grain, supplemented by vegetables and only very occasionally by other kinds of food. Wealthier people ate meat, fish, and cheese, and were able to improve the taste and variety of their food with spices and sauces. Europe's diet changed significantly as a result of overseas exploration and the discovery of the Americas, and eventually the potato replaced grain as the staple ingredient for many poor people.

FARMING AND SCARCITY

In the Roman Empire and the Middle Ages, Europe's poor—the overwhelming majority of people—consumed the same monotonous, uninspiring diet, consisting largely of grains: The major crop was wheat. The problem with grain, and especially wheat, was that it required large amounts of land to produce relatively low yields. Wheat could not be grown two years in a row on the same land because the soil became rapidly depleted. Farmers therefore resorted to the two-field system, and later the three-field system, whereby some portion of the land was allowed to be restored by letting it lie fallow. Although effective, this method of growing made it impossible to use all the land at once. In addition, wheat cultivation also required the use of manure for fertilizer, which in turn meant that some of the land had to be reserved for the grazing of animals that produced the manure.

The supply of basic foods like grain was always precarious. Crop yields did increase slowly over time, especially between the 16th and 18th centuries, when the yield was almost twice that in the late Middle Ages. Nevertheless, most of Europe suffered from a condition of chronic scarcity.

THE EUROPEAN DIET

From wheat and other grains, peasants made two kinds of food: bread and gruel. Bread was the staple food item, and it has been estimated that in good times an adult peasant ate more than four pounds of bread per day. Peasant bread was generally made from wheat or rye, and often a combination of the two. Because the grain was ground into flour by rough stone wheels, the wheat germ and outer husk of bran remained as part of the flour. This flour produced a dark, rough-textured bread that was the principal—and often the only—food that peasants consumed. Gruel was a kind of thick porridge, like oatmeal, made by boiling grains in water. It was seldom if ever flavored with spices and rarely contained other ingredients.

Vegetables were also available except in winter and early spring. These most often included peas, beans, lentils, carrots, onions, and cabbages, and less fortunate rural dwellers cooked wild grasses and roots. Vegetables were boiled or mixed with grains to make soups. Only rarely, several times per year, did peasants eat meat or fish, which were usually the preserve of the nobles who owned the land and rivers. More prosperous peasants had a few animals from which they made cheese and butter, but these were eaten sparingly, and milk was reserved almost exclusively for the very young and the old.

An old European proverb, "Tell me what you eat and I will tell you who you are," reflects the social reality of how the diet of the poor differed significantly from that of the rich. The upper classes developed a passion for eating meat, whether it was beef, lamb, venison, or pork. For dinner parties, the nobility would often serve several courses of these

Jean Michelin, *The Baker's Cart.* 1656. The baking of bread, which involved both space and potentially dangerous hot ovens, generally took place on the outskirts of a town. The baker—or his employees—would then bring the bread into town by cart and travel around selling it. Note the heavy clothes and architecture of Northern Europe.

meats, interspersed with fish and fowl of various kinds. They seldom ate vegetables, which they considered the loathsome diet of the poor. Not only would they prohibit peasants on their lands from hunting and fishing, but they devoted themselves to hunting as a favorite social pastime.

The meals of the ruling class were far more interesting and varied than those of the peasantry. Only they could afford the rare and costly spices that came from Asia, and their cooks used these and the juices of meats and fish to make sauces to flavor their food. They also could buy fruit, sugar, and honey, for making sweets and pastries. Moreover, the rich avoided the coarse dark bread eaten by the peasants, preferring finer grades of white bread made from sifted flour. Specialty breads contained brewer's yeast, milk, and sometimes eggs and sugar.

It is not surprising that the European diet was determined first and foremost by wealth and social status. The irony, however, is that the poorer classes seem to have consumed a more nutritious diet. Today we know that the common dark bread eaten by peasants was nutritiously bal-

anced, containing a mixture of carbohydrates, proteins, and minerals; when supplemented with vegetables, the vitamin and mineral content was even higher. During the winter and spring, however, the diet of the peasantry suffered because they did not have access to fresh vegetables, with the result that they often suffered from scurvy, brought on by a lack of vitamin C.

The rich, on the other hand, ate a much less healthy diet, heavy in protein but low in vitamins and minerals. This deficiency was compounded by the white bread they preferred, which lacked the minerals and vitamins of the peasant bread. Those with the most balanced, and therefore the healthiest, diets were probably the middle classes, who ate some meat and cheese but also consumed vegetables and often could not afford white bread.

NEW FOODS AND CONSUMPTION PATTERNS

The original purpose of the great European explorations that began in the 15th century had been to find a direct sea route to Asia in order to obtain prized spices and luxury products directly from their source. In the process, the explorers accomplished much more than this goal because the discovery of the Americas resulted in the importation of a host of new foods to Europe. Among these were the potato, tomatoes, squash, and Indian corn (maize). These new products changed the kinds of foods eaten in different cultures of the world, including several European countries. The chili pepper, which originally developed on the slopes of the Andes in Peru, is not related botanically to the pepper at all. Its piquant flavor led the early explorers to misname it, however, and it soon acquired worldwide popularity, transforming the cuisine of China and much of Asia as well as of Africa. In a similar fashion, the tomato became the rage in much of southern Italy, where it was first introduced into Naples by the Spanish in the 16th century. From there, its use spread to southern France, where Provençal cooking still uses it in great quantity. Sugar, which probably was native to India, was known in the West since ancient times and was as costly as any of the spices. In the 16th century, a Spanish merchant transported cane to Hispaniola, where it began to grow profusely and became the crop of many plantations.

The potato, which was native to South America, had a major impact on the European diet. Although it could not be used like wheat to make bread, it was rich in vitamins as well as in carbohydrates. It provided a solution to the lack of vitamins and minerals for the peasant diet during those months when vegetables were not available.

At first, most Europeans ridiculed the potato and felt it was unworthy of being consumed, but famines in the 18th century proved its importance. Soon, potatoes were being grown extensively in Ireland, Germany, and Eastern Europe, where they joined, and eventually replaced, wheat as the staple item in the peasant diet.

In the 15th and 16th centuries, the growing availability of once extremely rare foodstuffs enabled the wealthy of Europe to develop increasingly more sophisticated and luxurious eating habits. Elaborate formal dinners for the royal courts and official state occasions called for the training of expert chefs. Sauces, creams, and jellies were invented, and special dishes were named after monarchs. In Italy and France, multicourse meals were accompanied by rich table decorations, fanciful pastries, and elaborate eating rituals. Moreover, from Italy there spread to France and other countries the use of differently shaped plates, the fork, and serving utensils, often made from the gold and silver pouring into Europe from the Americas.

Once the price of pepper and chilies fell as their quantity grew, they ceased to be prestige items for the very wealthy. In their place, coffee, chocolate (or cocoa), tea, sugar, and tobacco rose in popularity among the privileged. In 1664 the British writer Samuel Pepys records in his diary that he went to a coffeehouse, still a novel establishment, "to drink jocolatte"; by the 18th century the use of habit-forming stimulants like coffee and tobacco became a virtual mania, and the popularity of coffeehouses among the middle classes had mushroomed.

Print showing the interior of a coffeehouse. Late 17th century. As the paintings on the wall show, the newly introduced coffeehouses were often luxuriously decorated. The scene captures the way in which they served as places for social encounters as much as for drinking the new beverage.

Perspectives from the Past

Food and the Columbian Exchange

When Columbus set foot on the island of Hispaniola in October 1492, he began a complex process of interaction between the Old World and the New known as the Columbian Exchange. This process had a profound impact—both positive and negative—on both civilizations.

Among the many aspects of European and Amerindian life that each encountered was food. The Spanish introduced such vegetation as wheat, bananas, oranges and lemons, grapes, and sugar cane to the Western Hemisphere. The early European visitors also brought goats, sheep, horses, pigs, chickens, and cattle to the New World, with adverse ecological results, for as these animals roamed the ranges they destroyed the roots of plants and ate the leaves. On the other hand, as we have seen, the diet of much of the rest of the world was dramatically changed as vegetables and plants indigenous to the Americas were introduced to Europe, Africa, and Asia.

Food of the Amerindians

As the Spanish conquistadors ravaged Mexican and South American cultures, they were generally forced to live off the land and to become accustomed to eating local foods.

Hernán Cortés

The food they [the inhabitants of islands off the Yucatan] eat is maize and some chili peppers, as on the other islands, and *patata yuca,* just the same as is eaten in Cuba, and they eat it roast, for they do not make bread of it; and they both hunt and fish and breed many chickens [probably turkeys] such as those found on Tierra Firme, which are as big as peacocks.

From Hernán Cortés, *Letters from Mexico,* trans. and ed. A. R. Pagden Yale University Press, Copyright © 1971.

Bernal Díaz del Castillo

When we got on shore we found three Caciques, one of them the governor appointed by Montezuma, who had many of the Indians of his household with him. They brought many of the fowls of the country and maize bread such as they always eat, and fruits such as pineapples and zapotes, which in other parts are called mameies, and they were seated under the shade of the trees, and had spread mats on the ground, and they invited us to be seated, all by signs, for Julianillo the man from Cape Catoche, did not

understand their language, which is Mexican. Then they brought pottery braziers with live coals, and fumigated us with a sort of resin.

From Bernal Díaz del Castillo, *The Discovery and Conquest of Mexico, 1517–1521,* ed. Genaro Garcia and trans. A. P. Maudslay Farrar, Straus and Giroux, Copyright © 1956.

Food at the Royal Palace

The Amerindians ate several foods that the Europeans found strange and sometimes disquieting, including dogs and worms from the maguey plant. Columbus records that on first landing in the Americas he encountered "a serpent" about six feet long, no doubt an iguana, which his men killed—"The people here eat them and the meat is white and tastes like chicken." Díaz del Castillo tells that when his party met the Caciques, "they wished to kill us and eat our flesh, and had already prepared the pots with salt and peppers and tomatoes."

Montezuma's Banquet

Díaz del Castillo gives a detailed description of a great banquet.

For each meal, over thirty different dishes were prepared by his cooks according to their ways and usage, and they placed small pottery braziers beneath the dishes so that they should not get cold. They prepared more than three hundred plates of the food that Montezuma was going to eat, and more than a thousand for the guard. When he was going to eat, Montezuma would sometimes go out with his chiefs and stewards, and they would point out to him which dish was best, and of what birds and other things it was composed, and as they advised him, so he would eat, but it was not often that he would go out to see the food, and then merely as a pastime.

I have heard it said that they were wont to cook for him the flesh of young boys, but as he had such a variety of dishes, made of so many things, we could not succeed in seeing if they were of human flesh or of other things, for they daily cooked fowls, turkeys, pheasants, native partridges, quail, tame and wild ducks, venison, wild boar, reed birds, pigeons, hares and rabbits, and many sorts of birds and other things which are bred in this country, and they are so numerous that I cannot finish naming them in a hurry; so we had no insight into it, but I know for certan that after our Captain censured the sacrifice of human beings, and the eating of their flesh, he ordered that such food should not be prepared for him thenceforth.

Let us cease speaking of this and return to the way things were served to him at meal times. It was in this way: if it was cold they made up a large fire of live coals of a firewood made from the bark of trees which did not give off any smoke, and the scent of the bark from which the fire was made was very fragrant, and so that it should not give off more heat than he required, they placed in front of it a sort of screen adorned with figures of idols worked in gold. He was seated on a low stool, soft and richly worked, and the table, which was also low, was made in the same style as the seats, and on it they placed the table cloths of white cloth and some rather long napkins of the same material. Four very beautiful cleanly women brought water for his hands in a sort of deep basin which they call xicales [gourds], and they held others like plates below to catch the water, and they brought him towels. And two other women brought him tortilla bread, and as soon as he began to eat they placed before him a sort of wooden screen painted over with gold, so that no one should watch him

eating. Then the four women stood aside, and four great chieftains who were old men came and stood beside them, and with these Montezuma now and then conversed, and asked them questions, and as a great favor he would give to each of these elders a dish of what to him tasted best. . . .

They brought him fruit of all the different kinds that the land produced, but he ate very little of it. From time to time they brought him, in cup-shaped vessels of pure gold, a certain drink made from cacao, and the women served this drink to him with great reverence . . . .

Montezuma was fond of pleasure and song, and to these he ordered to be given what was left of the food and the jugs of cacao. . . .

As soon as the Great Montezuma had dined, all the men of the Guard had their meal and as many more of the other house servants, and it seems to me that they brought out over a thousand dishes of the food of which I have spoken, and then over two thousand jugs of cacao all frothed up, as they make it in Mexico, and a limitless quantity of fruit, so that with his women and female servants and break makers and cacao makers his expenses must have been very great. . . .

[W]hile Montezuma was at table eating, as I have described, there were waiting on him two other graceful women to bring him tortillas, kneaded with eggs and other sustaining ingredients, and these tortillas were very white, and they were brought on plates covered with clean napkins, and they also brought him another kind of bread, like long balls kneaded with other kinds of sustaining food, and pan pachol, for so they call it in this country, which is a sort of wafer. There were also placed on the table three tubes much painted and gilded, which held liquidambar mixed with certain herbs which they call tabaco, and when he had finished eating, after they had danced before him and sung and the table was removed, he inhaled the smoke from one of those tubes, but he took very little of it and with that he fell asleep.

From Bernal Díaz del Castillo, *The Discovery and Conquest of Mexico, 1517–1521*, ed. Genaro Garcia and trans. A. P. Maudslay Farrar, Straus and Giroux, Copyright © 1956.

Continued

Aztec Markets

The Aztecs had a highly sophisticated system of trade and barter, much of which was conducted in the central markets of large towns. Díaz del Castillo was much impressed by the market in Mexico at the Tlaltelolco square.

When we arrived at the great market place, called Tlaltelolco, we were astounded at the number of people and the quantity of merchandise that it contained, and at the good order and control that was maintained, for we had never seen such a thing before. The chieftains who accompanied us acted as guides. Each kind of merchandise was kept by itself and had its fixed place marked out. Let us begin with the dealers in gold, silver, and precious stones, feathers, mantles, and embroidered goods. Then there were other wares consisting of Indian slaves both men and women; and I say that they bring as many of them to that great market for sale as the Portuguese bring negroes from Guinea; and they brought them along tied to

THE SOCIAL PATTERN OF HOUSING

In the centuries before 1500, the housing of both the rich and the poor in Europe changed little and continued to use traditional materials, including straw thatching for roofs and wood. By the 16th century, however, urban housing began to use stone and brick. Moreover, the increasingly crowded cities made space a premium and building sites became smaller, so that houses took on a more vertical design.

BUILDING THE CITIES

Over time, the ever-present risk of fire, a constant preoccupation for medieval city dwellers, lessened because of the new construction materials. In Paris, large numbers of stone masons, plasterers, and tool makers began to transform public buildings and private houses by setting them on stone foundations. During the same period, builders in London abandoned wood and straw. After the great fire of London in 1666, which destroyed three of every four buildings, most of the new housing was made of brick. This transformation was visible as far east as Moscow, where a Western traveler observed the same change in the mid-17th century. On the Continent, municipal authorities now often prohibited the use of straw roofing and sometimes provided subsidies to encourage builders to make their roofs of tile or slate.

The wealthy nobility and merchants of the cities lived in massive and elaborately decorated palaces, generally designed by major architects. Many of the residences of the wealthy built after 1500 still stand today, most now used for public purposes. In Paris, for example, the National Archives of France was once the private house of the Guise family, while the Parisian site of the National Library is now located in a palace where Cardinal Mazarin lived. The palace of the Strozzi family in Florence today contains a library and is used for public exhibitions.

Middle-class housing was much less grand than the palaces of the nobility. Plans for several houses of the middle class in 16th-century Paris have survived. A typical residence was on three floors, with the rooms arranged around an open courtyard. A spiral staircase connected the levels. On the ground floor was the main reception room, together with the kitchen and larder, while the bedrooms were on the upper floors. Starting in Italy during the 17th century, ceilings—once only the underside of the flooring of the room above—began to be plastered, encased in wood, and painted. Wallpaper was first used in the 18th century.

Today we know much about housing through the painting of the period. In Amsterdam, the most common form of housing for the lower middle class was made up of two rooms, one at the front and one at the back. These houses, with their narrow façades, were later enlarged by the addition of rooms above and below, connected by a series of dangerously steep staircases or ladders. Even today, the house fronts along the canals of the city of Delft preserve the original appearance of the buildings in Vermeer's famous paintings of the period, which also illustrate the new vogue for glass window panes.

Poor city dwellers generally lived in rented lodgings in the least desirable quarters of the city. The cheapest and most wretched apartments were either in basements or attics. The poor lived alongside prostitutes and criminals in flea-ridden and unsanitary squalor, often subject to unannounced police searches. In the absence of running water and toilet facilities, chamber pots—emptied out of the window—were often kept side by side with cooking utensils.

COUNTRY LIVING

Peasant housing in Europe is much more difficult to document because of the perishability of the materials used in the countryside. Most houses were small huts built of wood,

long poles, with collars round their necks so that they could not escape, and others they left free. Next there were other traders who sold great pieces of cloth and cotton, and articles of twisted thread, and there were *cacahuateros* who sold cacao. In this way one could see every sort of merchandise that is to be found in the whole of New Spain. There were those who sold cloths of henequen and ropes and the sandals with which they are shod, which are made from the same plant, and sweet cooked roots, and other tubers which they get from this plant, all were kept in one part of the market in the place assigned to them. In another part there were skins of tigers and lions, of otters and jackals, deer and other animals and badgers and mountain cats, some tanned and others untanned, and other classes of merchandise.

From Bernal Díaz del Castillo, *The Discovery and Conquest of Mexico, 1517–1521*, ed. Genaro Garcia and trans. A. P. Maudslay Farrar, Straus and Giroux, Copyright © 1956.

Piet de Hooch, *The Linen Cupboard.* 1663. Painted by one of the most famous artists of the Delft school, the scene is of a quiet domestic interior in the house of a prosperous Dutch merchant. Note the inlaid furniture, the paneled wooden walls, and the rich costumes of the mistress and her maid. On the wall hang paintings, presumably by Piet's contemporaries.

Rijksmuseum, Amsterdam

straw, and mud. Farming people generally lived under the same roof as their animals, often sharing a single primitive room. These dwellings were generally unheated except for a small cooking stove, in front of which the inhabitants slept in cold weather.

Recent archeological excavations provide further data about how peasants lived. The sites of deserted villages throughout Europe reveal both the kinds of houses and other facilities—churches, cemeteries, wells, and streets—and the changing layout of the community. Nor were conditions always uniform. Some villages were more prosperous than others. In Burgundy, France, for example, one typical village consisted of around 25 dwellings on stone foundations, in which the living rooms had beaten earth floors and small slanting windows.

Many wealthy landowners lived in old and uncomfortable family manor houses dating back to the late medieval period. By the 16th century, it became fashionable for the new urban rich to invest their money in country residences. They commissioned elaborate stone villas containing works of art, surrounded by formal gardens. Most of the famous and elegant chateaux that dot the French countryside date from the period after 1600, when the French monarchy had created stable political and social conditions.

CLOTHING, FASHION, AND CLASS

Social distinctions were nowhere more striking than in the kind of clothing people wore. Among the peasants and the urban poor, the form of dress changed little over the centuries from about 1350 to 1600. The wealthy, on the other hand, were quick to adopt new styles and new materials for their clothing.

DRESS AND STYLE

As in the case of housing, paintings and engravings are also important sources of information about clothing. Even at a quick glance, the viewer can distinguish between peasants and the middle classes from their costumes. Some occupations involved their own uniforms or typical forms of dress. Soldiers, fishermen, shepherds, and blacksmiths each wore specific garments. Sometimes the color and design of clothing indicate a particular condition of life—widows, for example, traditionally dressed in plain black clothes, while butchers often wore red smocks.

Jean-Baptiste Chardin, *The Food Supplier.* 1739. Note the contrast between the costume of the peasant girl delivering food and the more elaborate one of the domestic servant in *The Linen Cupboard.* Chardin was famous for his scenes of daily life, filled with sharply observed detail.

Peasants owned simple garments of coarse, homespun fabric made of a mixture of hemp and wool and generally dyed black or some other dark color. The paintings of the 16th-century Flemish artist Pieter Bruegel the Elder and his sons Pieter the Younger and Jan record numerous scenes of peasants and tradesmen in villages and market towns, showing the details of their clothing. Until the Industrial Revolution of the 18th century, cotton was too expensive for all but the wealthiest people. Much of the cotton available in Europe was brought by Venetian galleys from Syria, sometimes in the form of raw cotton and sometimes already worked into cloth.

Poor peasants spent relatively little of their resources on clothing, which had to be practical, both for durability and for protection against the cold. When peasants acquired wealth, however, they generally spent lavishly on dress in order to demonstrate their new status and distance themselves from their origins. The standard form of dress for peasants was a loose shirt and tight-fitting pants that hugged the body. Most went barefoot, and wearing underwear became common only after 1300. The absence of undergarments caused the spread of ringworm, scabies, and other skin diseases. Both rich and poor generally did not wear nightclothes to bed.

For the nobility and the wealthy merchant class, clothing was an essential symbol of social status. At the beginning of the 17th century, the Venetian ambassador to the court of France observed that a man was considered rich only if he possessed some 30 suits of different kinds and styles, and changed them daily.

As style developed into fashion, clothing became associated with national origin. In the 15th century, the most common forms of dress were French, Italian, and English. At royal courts, the ladies of the nobility wore expensive dresses of cotton, silk, and velvet, embroidered and decorated with gold thread and jewels. By the 16th century, with the spread of the Hapsburg empire, the ruling classes of Europe adopted Spanish court dress, which was generally dark and severe, with padded stockings, high collars, and short capes. With the decline of Spain in the 17th century, however, the bright colors of French clothing became fashionable again.

Unlike today's world, in which styles change every season, in early modern Europe fashions remained in vogue for a century or so. The idea of constantly changing styles was introduced to the upper and middle classes of Europe only in the 18th century. The Industrial Revolution made inexpensive cotton readily available to most of the middle class, while the elaborate court etiquette of France established among the nobility a fetish for the new designs and the latest styles.

Along with the variations in clothing style, hygiene and other aspects of personal appearance also evolved. The ancient Romans had used soap for washing, and bathing was an important social activity for them. In pre–Black Death Europe, public bathhouses were common. As late as the 18th century, however, hardly anyone in Paris or London bathed, and those who did took only one or two baths per year. Instead, both men and women used perfumes to cover their body odor. While men grew facial hair, women deco-rated their faces with makeup. By the early 1600s, both sexes began to wear artificial hairpieces as a form of social distinction.

Putting Life in a Time of Upheaval in Perspective

The aspects of everyday life discussed in this topic—health, food, housing, and dress—are vital indicators of the condition of a society at a given moment in history. Differences in these factors among the various levels of European society underscore one constant point—the vast gulf separating the lifestyles of most ordinary people from those of the comfortable middle class and the wealthy nobility. Moreover, the fact that for hundreds of years the lifespan of Europeans remained short while the infant mortality rate stayed high, suggests a great deal about how people might have viewed issues of life, death, and faith. Similarly, the monotonous diet of most Europeans explains much about the sense of excitement and the hunger for the strange and exotic generated by the overseas explorations of the 15th and 16th centuries.

How people dressed and the kind of homes they lived in are important indices of social, and even psychological, attitudes. Fashion, as opposed to practical, everyday costume, is not only a sign of social distinction but also of the desire of wealthier classes to distance themselves from those below them and to ape those above. Standards of personal hygiene prevalent as late as the 18th century differed significantly from the generally accepted habits of the early 21st century in the West. That fact underscores the degree to which society has become more sophisticated, but it also tells us a great deal about the abysmally low level of material comfort to which millions of Europeans were accustomed.

The history of wars, religion, economics, and politics is of course fundamental to our ability to understand the past. It is often difficult, however, for us to grasp in an immediate sense how these events affected human lives. Social history, understood as the way in which real people lived, allows us to identify with people of earlier historical eras because we can compare our immediate daily experiences with theirs.

Social behavior and custom also provide considerable insight about the workings of historical change. The relatively stable nature of these ordinary but fundamental aspects of life for centuries at a time reveals just how powerful the weight of tradition was and how gradually the lives of most people were altered. Daily life as well as politics moved at a far slower pace, and popular attitudes toward change were much more cautious.

Questions for Further Study

1. What factors affected the health of Europeans? How would you judge the medical practices of the period?
2. In what ways were food and diet affected by the age of discovery?
3. How did class and social position affect such practices as housing and clothing?
4. Based on what you know about the lifespan of Europeans and infant mortality rates, what would you conclude were people's attitudes toward life, death, and faith?

Suggestions for Further Reading

Braudel, Fernand. *The Structures of Everyday Life*. London, 1981.

Fraser, Antonia. *The Weaker Vessel: Woman's Lot in Seventeenth-Century England*. London, 1984.

Goubert, Pierre. I. Patterson, trans. *The French Peasantry in the Seventeenth Century*. Cambridge, MA, 1986.

Grassby, Richard. *Kinship and Capitalism: Marriage, Family and Business in the English-Speaking World, 1580-1720*. New York, 2001.

Hanawalt, Barbara A., ed. *Women and Work in Preindustrial Europe*. Bloomington, IN, 1986.

Hardwick, Julie. *The Practice of Patriarchy: Gender and the Politics of Household Authority in Early Modern France*. University Park, PA, 1998.

Houston, Robert A. *Literacy in Early Modern Europe: Culture and Education, 1500–1800*. New York, 1988.

Kamen, Henry. *Early Modern European Society*. New York, 2000.

Ladurie, Le Roy. *The French Peasantry, 1450–1660*. Berkeley, CA, 1986.

Macfarlane, Alan. *Marriage and Love in England: Modes of Reproduction, 1300–1840*. New York, 1986.

Maynes, Mary J. *Schooling in Western Europe: A Social History*. New York, 1985.

Ozment, Steven. *Flesh and Spirit: Private Life in Early Modern Germany*. New York, 1999.

Schama, Simon. *An Embarrassment of Riches: An Interpretation of Dutch Culture in the Golden Age*. New York, 1987.

InfoTrac College Edition

Enter the search term *Black Death* using Key Terms.

THE EUROPEAN ECONOMY AND OVERSEAS EMPIRE

From 1300 to 1650, while Europe underwent the cultural changes associated with the Renaissance as well as the religious upheavals of the Reformation, the Western economy was also transformed. The principal change after 1500 was the shift in trade patterns from the Mediterranean to the Atlantic and northern European coasts. The commercial revolution was dominated at first by Spain and Portugal, but the decline of their empires was accompanied by the emergence of new economic powers, especially the Dutch Republic.

Several other new features appeared in the economic expansion of the 16th and 17th centuries. For one thing, a new era emerged in banking and international finance as Italian banking firms like the Medici were overshadowed by the new international firm of the Fuggers of Germany. These bankers created networks of credit across the borders of the European states and engaged in high-level loans to monarchs and popes as well as to private business owners.

The new banking firms were overshadowed by the appearance of stock companies, which attracted investors in growing numbers. Besides the expansion of international finance, new industries and technologies evolved in this period, including growth in the printing business, luxury industries, and mining.

By the late 17th century, even the thriving Dutch commercial empire was beginning to decline as the English and French monarchies expanded their colonial holdings around the globe. Britain and France followed a rigidly conceived and highly centralized economic policy known as mercantilism, and the two powers increasingly competed for control of overseas markets and products. By the 18th century, the system of merchant capitalism that drove the commercial revolution was poised to provide the investment necessary to begin the new, industrial phase of capitalism.

TRADE, FINANCE, AND PRICES

The three centuries following the discovery of the New World saw the development of an important economic phenomenon called commercial capitalism, in which merchants sought profits through buying, selling, and shipping goods. The profits derived from commerce were tremendous, and the unfolding of global trade patterns made life in Europe infinitely more interesting and colorful. Agriculture, however, remained the primary economic activity of most Europeans. In Eastern Europe, where the commercial revolution was less important, perhaps as much as 95 percent of the population lived off the land; even in Western Europe, where commerce was most intense, 60 or 70 percent of the inhabitants still farmed.

THE ATLANTIC AND NORTHERN COMMERCE

In the early 15th century, control of trade in the North Sea and the Baltic had moved into the hands of German cities, with the formation of the Hanseatic League. The league eventually included more than 80 cities and controlled a large fleet and impressive resources, giving it a virtual monopoly over trade in northern Europe. Although the league continued to exist for some 300 years, it began to decline by the end of the 15th century in the face of the growing commercial power of the Dutch.

Throughout the first half of the 16th century, Venice managed to control the trade in spices that came through Muslim hands from the eastern Mediterranean. Yet signs of change were clear as the Venetian galleys, which linked Italian ports with northern Europe, sailed at an alarmingly decreasing rate. As the Atlantic powers like Spain and Portugal developed direct sea routes around Africa to Asia and across the Atlantic to their new colonies in the Americas, the Italian commercial empires fell into serious decline.

By 1600, even the Iberian trading powers were being bypassed by the spectacular rise of Dutch, English, and French traders as commercial patterns shifted once again. The new and exotic products from overseas were flooding Europe's markets in ever-greater quantity and creating business opportunities that bypassed the rigid Spanish economic system. Moreover, in the waters off Newfoundland, a seemingly inexhaustible supply of codfish had been discovered that became the basis for a salted cod industry of major proportions, and the French and English eventually seized most of this business. Joint stock companies were formed to pool resources in order to take advantage of the increasing volume of trade.

Etching showing a European sugar mill worked by slave labor in the West Indies. 18th century. The vegetation is typical of the Caribbean Islands. Sugar cane, which is still the source of more than half the world's sugar, was originally native to East Asia. In the 18th century, colonists transplanted it to the warm, humid Caribbean region and cultivated large plantations.

THE GROWTH OF MANUFACTURING

The rising commercial activities were accompanied by the growth of manufacturing as new industries developed that became increasingly important in Europe's economy. Shipbuilding became a major and highly profitable industry. Metalworking, especially armor and cannon making, also grew enormously, while mining expanded as new technology allowed mine shafts to be sunk hundreds of feet below the surface. The new digging and draining methods opened up rich new mines in central Europe. The discovery of a way to extract silver from lead alloy led to a plentiful supply of silver for making coins, which in turn increased the money supply and economic growth.

One result of the rise in commerce was that merchants involved in the textile business turned increasingly to the domestic, or "putting out" system. Instead of supplying raw wool exclusively to the guild artisans, whose costs were relatively high, the merchants began to deliver the wool to individual workers in the villages. There they spun, wove, and dyed the cloth in their own homes, where they operated as family units and at a lower cost. The domestic system increased merchant profits and remained the basic method of finishing wool until the Industrial Revolution shifted production to factories.

FROM THE MEDICI TO THE FUGGERS

The depressed economic climate of the 14th century drove businesses to become more efficient. The invention of double-entry bookkeeping in mid-14th century Italy was accompanied by the introduction of insurance and book transfer procedures, and all of these procedures made business practices more sophisticated. Merchants from other regions of Europe learned most of the Italian techniques in business organization and began to establish their own firms. The most successful of these were the Fuggers, whose business centered in Augsburg in southern Germany. The earliest Fugger merchants had been weavers and small manufacturers of woolen textiles. Expanding the range of their commercial activity, they opened a branch in Venice, where they ran a wholesale warehouse in spices and silks, and by the 15th century were engaging in banking.

The Fugger dynasty achieved its first major success when it began lending money to the Holy Roman emperors. Jacob Fugger II (1459–1525) was the dominant figure in the rise of the dynasty. Jacob oversaw branches in major European cities such as Antwerp, Lisbon, and London. In addition to continuing operations in the spice trade, the Fuggers began to engage in a variety of banking operations, such as issuing credit, bills of exchange, and paying interest on deposits. They became major bankers to the kings of Spain and Portugal as well as to the popes. As a result of extending major loans to Emperor Charles V, Jacob eventually came to control the silver and copper mines of Austria and Hungary, enterprises that gave him a tremendous return on his investment. The house of Fugger collapsed in the late 16th century as the result of the Hapsburgs defaulting on their loans.

Illustration showing Jacob Fugger (right)—the greatest banker of his age—dictating to a secretary. 16th century. The file drawers behind the clerk's head, labeled with the names of the cities where the Fuggers did business, indicate the international scope of their affairs: The two lowest ones are for the Polish city of Cracow and Lisbon, the capital of Portugal.

Eventually, the private family banking firms that had dominated European finance for centuries gave way to large, stock-based banking companies regulated by the state. In the 17th century, England, France, and the Netherlands granted monopolies to companies engaged in overseas trade or for settling colonial areas. These establishments were better suited to the new era of commercial capitalism that was unfolding.

THE PRICE REVOLUTION

Throughout the 16th century, as Europe recovered from the devastating impact of the Black Death, population increased, perhaps by as much as one-third. By 1600, Europe may have had more than 100 million inhabitants, although the growth pattern was unevenly spread throughout the continent. The larger workforce meant an increase in the amount of food and in the demand for manufactured products; this expansion in turn stimulated economic activity in the towns as well as in the countryside.

One result of these demographic changes was that as the urban population of Europe increased significantly, a surplus labor force was created, driving down real wages. This setback was accompanied by a startling rise in prices in the later 16th century that had widespread repercussions. The causes and impact of this so-called price revolution have been seriously debated by historians, but a few factors seem obvious. The flow of gold and silver into Spain and Portugal in the early 16th century seems to have been the major cause of the inflationary cycle. The supply of bullion in Europe more than tripled, with some 16,000 tons of American silver flowing through the Spanish port of Seville alone by 1650.

Although Spain tried to regulate the bullion it collected by prohibiting its export, the wars it fought and the administrative costs of operating its far-flung government inevitably meant the circulation of silver throughout Europe. Other factors contributed to the inflation besides American bullion. The productivity of European silver mines increased as a result of the application of new mining techniques, and some monarchs sparked price increases by debasing their coinage. The increase in population may also have driven prices up. In any case, the inflation in commodity prices was immense—by the close of the 16th century, prices had risen to four times their level at the start of the century. Prices went up higher and faster in Western Europe than elsewhere on the continent, and the greatest impact was seen in basic necessities such as grains and bread.

Overall, the inflationary pattern increased prices no more than 3 percent per year, which by modern standards is not a significant jump. In the 16th century, however, the price revolution had the effect of redistributing income among social groups. Wages did not, however, rise accordingly, so that the standard of living for the poorer classes declined. Those living on fixed incomes, especially pensioners, were also hurt by the inflation. Similarly, people who rented out property at long-term rates suffered. On the other hand, merchants, farmers, and manufacturers benefited from the rise in prices, especially because the costs of production did not rise as quickly as prices.

The inflationary cycle, which was irregular but of long duration, had a negative impact on governments, whose expenses and deficits rose along with the prices. Cities felt the impact severely because they depended on the purchase of food, the cost of which rose steadily. The dislocation and social tensions created by the price revolution were felt for decades to come.

Merchant Capitalists and the State

The changes that were transforming the commercial revolution in the 16th and 17th centuries created a form of economic organization and activity known as *merchant capitalism*. Under this system, merchants with investment resources—venture capital—invested in overseas trade or in necessary support operations such as banking, insurance, and stock companies. The private ownership of shipping firms and banks entailed huge profits. Risks in commercial activity were high, but the general rise in prices made the profit potential even greater.

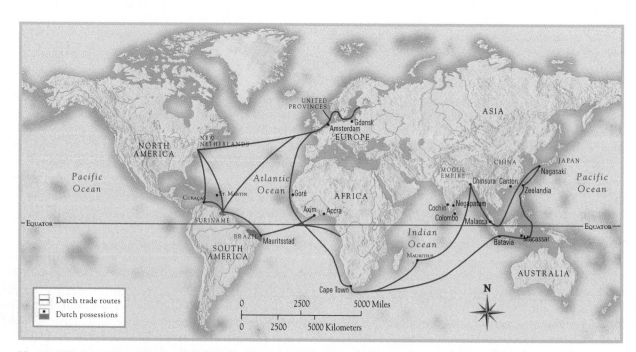

Map 46.1 The Dutch Sea Trade, c. 1650. Note the closeness of Dutch sea-routes to Australia; the continent was first discovered by Dutch sailors in the early 1600s but only claimed and occupied by the British almost two centuries later. The Dutch East India Company founded the city of Batavia in 1619 as the capital of their holdings in Indochina. It remained a Dutch colony until 1949, when, with the new name of Jakarta, it became the capital of the State of Indonesia.

Other developments encouraged commercial capitalism. Not all successful merchants had the cash to invest in risky ventures, but once the church had abandoned its prohibition against *usury*—charging interest on loans—credit was more readily available. The state was a major stimulus to capitalist development. In the increasingly competitive arena of a global economy, governments used their military power to protect national trade, while military contracts provided an incentive for investment in manufacturing.

THE MERCANTILIST SYSTEM

From the onset of the age of exploration, the state had undertaken to regulate the economic activity of its citizens through policies known as **mercantilism.** These policies were designed to increase national revenue and economic power at the expense of other states, as well as to enhance private business. Hence, at the very time that merchant capitalism was evolving, economic affairs were subjected to increasing state regulation. Mercantilism denied the right of businessmen to operate in a free market in order to ensure the primacy of the state's interests. Under the mercantilist system, the government imposed rigid controls on trade and manufacturing, including import tariffs and monopolies.

International trade was a particular object of mercantilist regulation because governments believed that a favorable trade balance was the only way to keep a sufficient quantity of bullion at home. Spain was the most vigorous advocate of this theory because precious metals were necessary to pay its massive military expenditures. On the other hand, the Dutch, whose wealth came from the fees its ships charged to carry the goods of other countries, sought to increase the overall volume of trade in which they were involved.

Tariffs were designed to protect domestic industries, whereas monopolies gave to a particular individual or company the sole right to trade, manufacture, or sell certain kinds of goods. Sometimes, as in the case of the Spanish empire, the purpose of controls was to block foreign competition or to prevent the all-important precious metals from going anywhere except to the home country.

In the later 18th century, the Scottish economist and philosopher Adam Smith (1723–1790), who advocated an unfettered free market system, attacked mercantilism because it obstructed the natural operation of economic laws. Smith insisted that the only real source of the "wealth of nations" was the flowering of rational self-interest. Depending on the circumstances, mercantilist policies helped or hurt national economies. In the Spanish case, controls hindered the development of domestic industries and retarded the economic welfare of the American colonies, while the monarchy's profligate spending made it impossible for the government to maintain bullion supplies at home. On the other hand, in the 17th century, French mercantilist controls under Louis XIV enabled the state to develop manufacturing, attract foreign artisans, and establish a solid economic base.

In all these ways, mercantilist regulations were part of the broader strategy through which the state attempted to centralize and impose its authority on all aspects of national—and in this case, international—life.

THE HEYDAY OF THE DUTCH REPUBLIC

Perhaps the European state with the most intelligent economic policy was the United Provinces of the Netherlands, which was ruled not by a king but by a class of wealthy urban merchants. The rise of the Dutch commercial empire is one of the most spectacular success stories of the age of the commercial revolution. More than any other nation, the Dutch Republic depended on international trade for its economic livelihood.

THE RISE OF THE NETHERLANDS

The foreign affairs of the seven northern provinces that constituted the Dutch Republic were governed by the legislative body known as the States General. Domestic issues, including economic policy, were determined by the provincial town councils, composed of oligarchies of merchants and landlords known as "regents."

The Dutch economy had several important strengths. Even during the long and bitter war of independence against Spain, the Dutch prospered on the seas, especially by attacking Spanish bullion ships. In addition, they wisely welcomed the Protestant immigrants who flocked to the northern provinces, a migration that included skilled artisans, bankers, and merchants. The regents managed to maintain a degree of religious freedom in the Netherlands that was unmatched anywhere, and this despite the Calvinist extremists who sometimes tried to work against the Catholics and Jews who lived there.

Because of excellent drainage and irrigation techniques and intensive farming methods, Dutch agriculture was the most productive in Europe. The herring fisheries were also important to the Dutch, who dried, salted, and smoked the catch and sold it throughout Europe. Finally, as their prosperity grew to depend more and more on commerce, the Dutch became master shipbuilders who designed and constructed the best ships of the day, many of which they sold to foreign merchants.

Like the Venetians, the Dutch were skilled at living and working on the water and at carrying their own products and those of other nations in their fleets. Their two chief cities, Antwerp (now in the modern state of Belgium) and Amsterdam, were at the trading crossroads of Europe and became two of the world's greatest commercial and business centers. These efficient and crowded cities were well positioned to take advantage of trade from the Mediterranean and the North Atlantic as well as from the Baltic and the North Sea. Antwerp, with 100,000 inhabitants in 1650, ranked second in size to Amsterdam but was a vital commercial hub: English wool and the spice trade of the 15th century both came through its port.

When the Spanish seized Antwerp during the revolt of the Netherlands, Amsterdam easily took its place as the principal Dutch port. Between 1600 and 1650, Amsterdam's population had grown from about 65,000 to 175,000, and its intricate network of docks and warehouses made it one of the most important *entrepôts* (trade intermediaries) in Europe. By building a series of canals, the Dutch were able to enlarge the size of the city to accommodate its growing population. Moreover, the Exchange Bank of Amsterdam, founded in 1609, soon became one of the principal banking institutions in Europe.

The Dutch ensured their economic prosperity by enlightened policies that deviated from the mercantilist norms of most other states. For example, they erected no tariffs either on imports or exports, and all their chief cities observed free trade policies. Because the trade in bullion was also free in the Netherlands—in contrast to policies in Spain and other states—Amsterdam became the chief center of the gold and silver trade.

The essence of Dutch prosperity was the "carrying trade." In 1600, Spanish and Portuguese ships carried a major portion of overseas trade, but by the mid-17th century, half of Europe's merchant ships were Dutch. Their chief strength lay in European commerce, where Dutch shipping made up perhaps three-quarters of all trade in the region. The Dutch Republic was the most prosperous example of merchant capitalism to emerge from the commercial revolution.

GLOBAL COMPETITION: THE INDIA COMPANIES

If the Dutch dominated the carrying trade in Europe, elsewhere in the world the English and French competed with them more effectively. In contrast to their policies of European free trade, the Dutch followed a more conventional mercantilist agenda outside of Europe. The overseas trade soon became a battleground of competing national companies struggling for dominance.

PRIVATE TRADING COMPANIES

In 1601, the English government of Queen Elizabeth I granted a charter to establish the English East India Company, which monopolized trade with India and operated until 1858. The English also attempted to develop a colonial enterprise along the Atlantic coast of North America, and in 1606 the crown extended charters to the Virginia Company, which tried unsuccessfully to establish a permanent settlement there. Farther north, the Plymouth Company was given the right to colonize anywhere from Virginia to Maine. In 1620, it founded the Plymouth Colony, which later merged with the Massachusetts Bay Colony. Nevertheless, these early experiments with permanent settlements did not generate large profits.

The States General of the Netherlands empowered private joint stock companies with almost complete economic and administrative authority to control its trade beyond Europe. In 1602, private merchants and investors of the Netherlands joined forces with the city government of Amsterdam to found the Dutch East India Company. The aim of the new company was to establish commercial primacy in the Indian Ocean and the Southeast Asia seas.

Unlike the Spanish and Portuguese, who made trade a state monopoly, the Dutch East India Company, controlled by the same class of wealthy business interests that dominated the town councils, was given extraordinary power to govern the entire Asian region. Company officials could conduct war on foreign shipping, appoint administrators for the colonies, and operate trading bases.

H.V. Schulylenberg, *Head Offices of the Dutch East India Company of Hugly in Bengal.* 1665. The Dutch flag flies in the lower left-hand corner. Note the attempt to impose European architectural order in an alien environment. The long, low building, with a central block and two side wings, houses the chief administrative offices.

Rijksmuseum, Amsterdam

Victoria & Albert Museum, London/Art Resource

Printed cloth from the Muslim city of Golconda, Hyderabad state, India. 17th century. The design provides a local view of the foreign (in this case, Dutch) traders in India. The two merchants seated at the table are notable for their costume and facial hair (and their pet dog); the servants waiting on them are natives, wearing local dress.

Although these and other firms assumed differing legal forms, most were joint stock companies in which individual investors pooled resources. This approach was especially useful in long-distance commerce, where the risks were considerable and required large investments. Although originally each voyage was considered a separate undertaking, later the companies established a permanent form of organization in which investors bought shares. In order to leave the company, investors had to sell their shares.

COMMERCIAL RIVALRY ON THE SEAS

The English and the Dutch were rivals in Asia, but both regarded the Portuguese as their principal enemy there. The Dutch East India Company succeeded in pushing the Portuguese out of East Asia and established direct commercial links with Japan and China. In the 18th century, the English company exercised administrative control of most of India, keeping that power until the English government took it from them.

The Dutch West India Company, set up in 1621, was given similar authority along the African coast and in the Americas. In North America, the company actually founded the Dutch settlement of New Netherlands along the Hudson River valley of the future New York. Regardless of how aggressive the Dutch traders were, however, they ultimately proved unable to seize and hold control of the Caribbean and the Atlantic seaboard, where the French and the English were operating. In the second half of the 17th century, the English took the New Netherlands from them, renaming it New York. Before long, the Dutch West India Company closed down. The French, who established their own East India companies in Asia, were less successful than the English and Dutch in the region. In North America, where they had greater success, they turned to a different system, governing Canada directly as a possession of the crown, rather than through a private company.

Most countries in the 17th century passed navigation laws designed to give their merchant marines monopolies over their international trade. In 1651, the English Parliament passed the Navigation Acts, which were designed to end the Dutch control over shipping and fishing in English waters. In response, the Netherlands declared war against England. In 1660, another law required that all commodities imported into England had to be carried on English ships (or on ships from the country of origin); moreover, in order to circumvent Amsterdam's primacy, the English government required all foreign goods to be brought

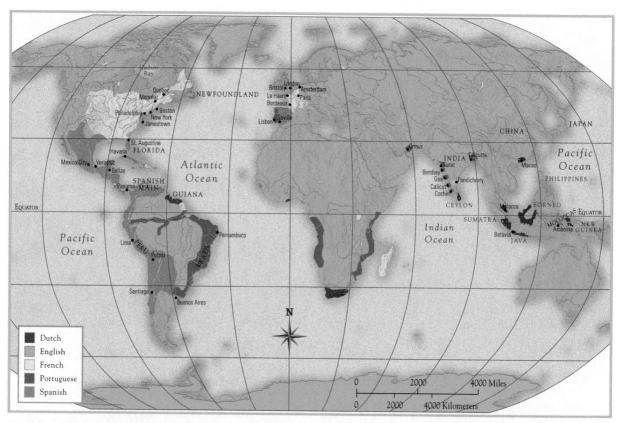

Map 46.2 European Possessions Overseas at the End of the 17th Century. Note the presence of the Dutch in the Far East and in the southern tip of Africa. Both Dutch and Portuguese colonies were to fall to the British over the following century. While North America is already the site of conflict between British and French, the scramble for Africa has not yet begun.

directly from the country of origin. Trade along Britain's coast and from its colonies in North America could be carried only on British ships.

These techniques of economic nationalism were applied in the spirit of mercantilism, but they had the effect of stimulating smuggling and were an important factor in driving the American colonies to break with England. In the 18th century, the competition among the commercial powers of Europe unfolded on a global scale and resulted in a continuing series of costly wars for dominance (see Topic 56).

Putting the European Economy and Overseas Empire in Perspective

By 1500, Europe had achieved a remarkable recovery from the disasters of the previous century. New products and better production techniques, combined with rationalized and diversified business organization, all contributed to building a reinvigorated and more prosperous economy. Finance and credit operations were already becoming international in scope when the age of exploration opened. The truly new aspect of the European economy was the commercial revolution that accompanied the encounter with the Western Hemisphere. The voyages of the Portuguese and Spanish seamen opened up an entirely new, unimagined world for the Europeans and set in motion economic forces that transformed the Old World. Moreover, out of the commercial concerns that developed among the great powers in the 17th and 18th centuries, there emerged a global economy and imperial interests that were to provide the basis for the Western dominance of the globe in the modern era.

Questions for Further Study

1. What was the price revolution and what were its causes?
2. In what ways did the state compete with merchants, and how did it support their interests?
3. What explains the economic prosperity of the Netherlands?

Suggestions for Further Reading

Braudel, Fernand. S. Reynolds, trans. *Civilization and Capitalism*, 3 vols. New York, 1979–1984.

Cameron, Rondo. *A Concise Economic History of the World*. New York, 1989.

Day, John. *Money and Finance in the Age of Merchant Capitalism*. Malden, MA, 1999.

Gauci, Perry. *The Politics of Trade: The Overseas Merchant in State and Society, 1660-1720*. Oxford, 2001.

Israel, Jonathan I., ed. *Dutch Primacy in World Trade, 1585–1740*. Oxford, 1989.

Kriedte, Peter. *Peasants, Landlords and Merchant Capitalists: Europe and the World Economy, 1500–1800*. Leamington, England, 1983.

McAlister, Lyle N. *Spain and Portugal in the New World, 1492–1700*. Minneapolis, 1984.

Musgrave, Peter. *The Early Modern European Economy*. New York, 1999.

Schama, Simon. *The Embarrassment of Riches: An Interpretation of Dutch Culture in the Golden Age*. New York, 1987.

Tracy, James E., ed. *The Rise of Merchant Empires*. Cambridge, MA, 1990.

InfoTrac College Edition

Enter the search term *mercantilism* using the Subject Guide.

THE BAROQUE ERA

By the early 17th century, in response to the enormous political and economic changes occurring throughout Europe, a new artistic style had developed: the **Baroque.** One of its features was the appearance of new forms and subjects, ranging from still life painting to the design of private townhouses to opera.

Despite the enormous range of the arts in the Baroque period, they shared certain characteristics in common. The expression of strong emotions, an interest in psychological states of mind, and the invention of elaborate technical display are all typical of 17th-century art.

In the fields of painting, sculpture, and architecture, the first major developments occurred in Rome. Caravaggio's dark, emotional style influenced countless painters in Italy and northern Europe. Bernini's contribution was a double one: As sculptor, he brought his extraordinary technique to subjects as different as religious ecstasy and portraits of his contemporaries. As architect and town planner, he left his mark on the most grandiose project of the times: St. Peter's, Rome.

In the North, many of the leading painters worked on secular themes: landscape, portraits, scenes from life. The only major northern religious painter was Rembrandt. Although Italy remained the center of religious painting, the years around 1600 saw the birth there of opera, a frankly popular form of entertainment aimed at a broad general public. In the North the situation was reversed. Few painters devoted their careers to sacred subjects, but in Germany, Bach composed some of the greatest religious music of all time.

The roots of the supreme writer in the English language, Shakespeare, were in the Renaissance. He wrote many of his masterpieces, however, in the first decade of the 17th century, and their extraordinary richness owes much to the new spirit of the age. The same is true of the greatest novel of the century, Cervantes' *Don Quixote.* In poetry, the works of Donne and others of the Metaphysical poets illustrate the Baroque interest in virtuosity and heightened states of emotion, with their special blend of the spiritual and the erotic.

EMOTION AND ILLUSIONISM: THE AFFIRMATION OF BAROQUE ART

By 1600, Italy was no longer at the center of European culture, and the chief powers in the North—England, France, and the Netherlands—began to develop their own independent schools of art. One factor in this shift was the Reformation, and the challenge to a single Universal Church. Another was the rise in northern Europe of the merchant class, which created a new public for the arts. A third factor was the spread of European culture in other parts of the world, as earlier exploration by the European powers became transformed into colonization, and England, France, the Netherlands, Spain, and Portugal established overseas territories in Africa, Asia, and the Americas.

One of the consequences of this diversification was the growth of new subjects for art. Instead of continuing to paint the same repertory of religious subjects, artists turned to genres like the portrait or scenes from daily life. Architects designed private houses or urban complexes as well as churches. New musical forms developed, including opera and purely instrumental works such as the *concerto grosso*. Writers aimed for a deeper sense of psychological understanding of human behavior.

Scala/Art Resource

Caravaggio, *The Calling of St. Matthew*, c. 1597–1601. 11 feet 1 inch by 11 feet 5 inches (3.38 by 3.48 m). The painter dramatizes the scene by directing a brilliant beam of light from the darkened figure of Jesus, half-hidden on the right. The glare illuminates the card-players around the tavern table and spotlights the future apostle, who points doubtfully at himself.

THE BAROQUE SPIRIT

Yet behind these different manifestations, certain common principles were in operation. The most striking was the expression of strong emotions. Far from seeking ideal statements of universal truth, as Renaissance artists had done, Baroque artists aimed to portray individual states of mind. The paintings of Rembrandt or the dramas of Shakespeare create specific characters with their own personal dramas. In doing so, the artists turned inward rather than outward to explore the depths of human feeling and not the calm heights of Classical perfection.

In order to express their new insights, artists forged a whole range of fresh techniques. Both painters and sculptors invented ways to convey complex illusions of light and shade. Musicians devised styles of increased virtuosity, which led to the growth of instrumental music, while the birth of opera added new dramatic possibilities. In literature, elaborate imagery and complicated grammatical structure made possible heightened emotional effects—the supreme example of the mid-17th century was Milton's *Paradise Lost*.

The subject of Milton's masterpiece is a reminder that attitudes toward religion continued to dominate European culture. Most artists working in northern Europe chose to work under the influence of Reformation ideas, while the leading figures in Italy dedicated themselves to the

Bernini, *St. Theresa in Ecstasy.* 1645–1652. Height of group 11 feet 6 inches (3.5 m). This famous work uses stone, gilded bronze, and natural light to bring the scene alive. Hidden from the viewer, a window above the saint sends sunlight to illuminate the gilded beams, as St. Theresa awaits the blow of the angel, about to pierce her to the heart with ecstatic love.

Counter-Reformation mission to restore the Catholic Church to its triumphant preeminence. At the same time, the 17th century saw the continued rise of science, which challenged both religious camps and laid the basis for the skepticism of the 18th-century Age of Reason.

THE MAKING OF BAROQUE ROME: CARAVAGGIO AND BERNINI

The spirit of the Counter-Reformation dominating Italian art in the 17th century aimed for effects of power and splendor to exalt the Catholic Church's triumphant resurgence. The most influential painter working there, however, Michelangelo Merisi (1573–1610), better known as Caravaggio, developed a personal style that had little to do with official propaganda.

THE CHIAROSCURO OF CARAVAGGIO

The dark drama of many of Caravaggio's paintings echoes the violence of his own life. Notorious for his stormy temper, the rebellious artist spent his last years in exile, after killing an opponent in a tennis match. His love of strong contrasts between light and dark—the Italian term is *chiaroscuro*—often dramatizes his scenes. In *The Calling of*

St. Matthew, Caravaggio's first important Roman commission, a beam of light follows the gesture of Jesus, who stands in the shadows and calls the future apostle. Matthew leans back into the darkness, as if trying to avoid the summons. The church disapproved of Caravaggio's directness, but both the public and his fellow artists fell under the spell of his dramatic realism and psychological perception.

THE PSYCHOLOGICAL REALISM OF BERNINI

The most important of all Italian artists of the Baroque was Gian Lorenzo Bernini (1598–1680). Throughout his long career he produced a bewilderingly varied range of sculptures, while his buildings and urban planning changed the face of Rome.

Bernini's marble and gilt bronze *St. Teresa in Ecstasy* is a masterpiece of dramatic expression. The saint, in the midst of her ecstatic vision, awaits the blow to the heart, which a smiling angel is poised to deliver. St. Teresa's billowing dress, the cloud on which she floats, and the golden beams of light pouring down on the scene are all brought to life with theatrical realism—an effect heightened by the figures to the sides of the chapel, who seem to be watching the action from stage boxes. The combination of heightened emotion, religious passion, and the sense of drama make for one of the supreme monuments of the Baroque style.

Aerial view of St. Peter's Basilica, Vatican City. The nave and façade were finished by Carlo Maderna between 1606 and 1612, and the colonnades around the piazza were built between 1656 and 1663 to the design of Bernini. The completion of the whole complex was one of the first great achievements of Baroque architecture.

Alinari/Art Resource, New York

Bernini poured his seemingly inexhaustible powers of invention into designing palaces, churches, and fountains. His most ambitious project was the *piazza* (square) in front of St. Peter's Basilica, where he created a huge space surrounded by an oval colonnade, with fountains and a central obelisk, which continues to provide the majestic setting for hundreds of thousands of pilgrims to the Vatican.

REMBRANDT AND HIS CONTEMPORARIES IN NORTHERN EUROPE

If the main architectural achievement of the Roman Baroque was religious in inspiration, the largest construction in northern Europe was Louis XIV's Royal Palace at Versailles (see Topic 50). The king intended the building to symbolize his secular power as Grand Monarch, the self-styled Sun King. On rising each morning, Louis made his way through the Hall of Mirrors, surrounded by his courtiers, and entered the main path of the garden, which ran on an east-west axis, following the path of the sun.

PAINTING IN FRANCE AND FLANDERS

For all the conscious splendor of Versailles, in general French and Flemish artists avoided the lavishness of the Italian Baroque. Nicholas Poussin (c. 1593–1665) claimed to detest the work of Caravaggio and intended his own lucid, restrained paintings as a deliberate criticism of the Italian painter's emotionalism. His famous *Et in Arcadia Ego* (*I Too Am in Arcadia*; the words of Death, present even in

the tranquil countryside) conveys a still hush, its figures rapt in solemn thought.

Much of the art produced in northern Europe was specifically aimed at the new middle-class public. The most prolific of all northern artists, however, Peter Paul Rubens (1577–1640), produced works of just about every conceivable kind: portraits, landscapes, religious subjects, and mythological tales. In addition to his art, Rubens traveled widely as a diplomat, speaking six modern languages and reading Latin fluently.

Something of the restless energy of the man emerges in many of his vast paintings. Yet Rubens could also touch quieter, more intimate feelings. At the age of 53, after the death of his first wife, he married the 16-year-old Helene Fourment. His painting of Helene with two of their young children is a rare depiction of the quiet joys of married love, in contrast to the intensity of most Baroque art.

PAINTING IN THE NETHERLANDS: REMBRANDT

Unlike their colleagues elsewhere in Europe, artists in the Netherlands lacked the two chief sources of patronage: the church and the aristocracy. The Dutch Calvinist Church forbade the use of religious images, and the Netherlands never had the kind of wealthy and powerful nobility that existed in France or England. Dutch painters needed therefore to find middle-class customers to commission works.

One handy source of income was the portrait. The greatest painter of the age, Rembrandt van Rijn (1606–1669), began his career as a successful painter of middle-class patrons. One of his early masterpieces is a

Poussin, *Et Ego in Arcadia.* 1638–1639. 33½ inches by 47⅝ inches (85 by 121 cm). In an idealized landscape, four country dwellers decipher with difficulty the inscription on a gravestone, which reads: "I, too, am in Arcadia." The words are spoken by the spirit of Death, present even in this peaceful scene. The artist uses the calmly posed figures to recapture the lofty spirit of Classical Antiquity.

Rubens, *Helene Fourment and her Children.*
1636–1637. 44½ inches by 32¼ inches (118 by 85 cm). After the death of his first wife, at the age of 53 Rubens married Helene Fourment, a girl of 16. The happiness of this marriage produced some of the great artist's most intimate and tender works. Here we see Helene with two of their children.

group portrait, generally known as *The Night Watch,* although recent cleaning has revealed that the chief figures were originally bathed in light.

The complexity of the composition of *The Night Watch* illustrates the subtlety of Rembrandt's genius. As he began to produce more introspective and somber works, his clients gradually stopped commissioning him. They wanted cheerful portraits and colorful still lifes to decorate their houses, not deep spiritual meditations. By the end of his career, Rembrandt was producing religious paintings inspired by his lifelong meditation on the Scriptures. *Jacob Blessing the Sons of Joseph* conveys all the painful tenderness of the family's three generations, united lovingly at the old man's deathbed. The strong contrasts of light and darkness show the continuing influence of Caravaggio, but the sense of spiritual concentration is a far cry from the drama of Caravaggio and his followers.

MUSIC FOR A NEW PUBLIC: THE BIRTH OF OPERA AND THE WORKS OF BACH

As in the case of the visual arts, musical developments in Italy and northern Europe differed in their attitude toward religion. Italy saw the birth of musical forms that could satisfy the demand for popular secular entertainment, whereas in the North, Bach, Handel, and other composers produced some of the greatest sacred music ever written.

THE BIRTH OF OPERA

The inventors of opera, a group of Florentine intellectuals known as the "Camerata," intended it as a revival of ancient Greek tragedy. The first play set to music, *Dafne,* by Jacopo Peri (1561–1633), was staged in Florence in 1594. Within a

Rembrandt, *Jacob Blessing the Sons of Joseph*. 1656. 5 feet 8¼ inches by 6 feet 9 inches (1.75 by 2.1 m). Painted toward the end of his life, in the year of his financial collapse, the scene—like that of Caravaggio's *Calling of St. Matthew*—uses light and shadow to deepen the emotions, as the old man, on the point of death, bids farewell to his family.

few years the new entertainment had spread throughout Europe. Opera houses sprang up in Austria and Germany and then in England, where by the late 17th century Italian singers could command astronomical fees. Under the encouragement of Louis XIV, French composers developed their own kind of operas, involving long sections of ballet.

Opera made a special appeal to Baroque tastes for three reasons. First, the combination of words and music could explore psychological states of mind more vividly and dramatically than either on its own. Even in later times, many operas contained a "mad scene" for one of the protagonists. Second, an operatic performance was a chance for virtuosity, both in the brilliance and flexibility of the singing and in the sumptuous stage settings and effects. Audiences loved to see magical transformation scenes or blazing fires that seemed to engulf the stage. Third, the design of the opera house, with its tiers of boxes and upper gallery, made it possible for all social classes to attend performances while maintaining them physically separate.

Claudio Monteverdi (1567–1643), the first great genius in the history of opera, proved the dramatic power of the medium as early as his first stage work, *Orfeo*. By skillful use of instrumentation and a vocal line that mirrored the character's emotions, Monteverdi breathed dramatic life into the familiar story. The composer spent the last 30 years of

his life at Venice, where 16 opera houses were built in the second half of the 17th century—an astonishing demonstration of the breadth of appeal of the new entertainment.

MUSIC IN GERMANY: BACH

Baroque composers in northern Europe generally did not write operas. The only important exception was Georg Frideric Handel (1685–1759), who composed a string of operatic masterpieces when he moved to England and became a naturalized citizen. London was one of the operatic centers of Europe, and Handel's operas written for performance there depict a wide range of characters and states of mind.

The greatest figure in Baroque music, Johann Sebastian Bach (1685–1750), wrote no operas and spent his life far from the glamour of London or the other musical capitals of Europe. His music was little known during his lifetime and virtually forgotten after his death. Rediscovered in the 19th century, Bach's music is now regarded as one of the supreme achievements of Western culture.

A devout Lutheran, Bach used music to glorify God and explore the deeper mysteries of the Christian faith. He composed masses, organ works, cantatas, and settings of sections of the Bible. His *Saint Matthew Passion* is a setting of the trial and Crucifixion of Jesus as recorded in the Gospel of St. Matthew. Bach proclaimed his Lutheranism by setting

PUBLIC FIGURES AND PRIVATE LIVES

ANNA MAGDALENA AND JOHANN SEBASTIAN BACH

Bach came from a large family of musicians, and family life was important to him. His first wife died in 1720, after having given birth to seven children, of whom four died in infancy. Within a year the composer remarried a young singer, Anna Magdalena Wülken (1701–1760). He was 36 at the time, she 20. The prince of Cöthen, for whom Bach was then working, allowed the couple to save money by marrying in Bach's lodgings, and the composer used the money to buy Rhine wine at the city cellars.

Early in their marriage, Bach gave his wife a book of blank music paper, on which she wrote the title "*Clavier-Büchlein*" (Little Keyboard Book). He copied into it a series of short keyboard pieces, intended to help Anna Magdalena improve her playing. In 1725, he gave her a new book, in which he continued to write pieces. One of them is a song (perhaps by Bach, perhaps by G.H. Stölzel, a contemporary), "*Bist du bei mir.*" The words are: "As long as you are with me, I could face my death and

eternal rest with joy. How peaceful would my end be if your beautiful hands could close my faithful eyes." The illustration at left shows an excerpt from one of her notebooks—no portrait survives.

Throughout their life together, Anna Magdalena took part in performances of her husband's works and helped him to copy them out, as well as bearing him 13 children. Bach suffered from deteriorating eyesight, and in 1749 he underwent two disastrous operations that left him totally blind. A few months later he was dead. His modest estate was divided between his nine surviving children and his widow. His sons and daughters sold their share of his manuscripts, but Anna Magdalena kept hers, leaving them to the Music School of the Church of St. Thomas, Leipzig. She died in abject poverty 10 years after her husband.

The lives of both Johann Sebastian and Anna Magdalena were spent far from the tumultuous events of their times. The sheer amount of music Bach wrote and the couple copied out suggests that most of their time was dedicated to music and its performance. The products of their years together can now be seen as one of the summits of the Western musical tradition, and countless beginning pianists have learned to play with the aid of the pieces Bach wrote in the "Little Keyboard Book for Anna Magdalena."

---

the text in a German translation, rather than Latin, and he included several Lutheran *chorales*—a kind of hymn that Luther had popularized.

THE GOLDEN AGE OF LITERATURE: SHAKESPEARE AND CERVANTES

The leading writers of the early 17th century owe their formation to the Renaissance. The works of both Shakespeare and Cervantes represent the culmination of a tradition—in

drama and the picaresque novel—that goes back to their predecessors of the preceding century. Yet both figures drew on the greater range of expressivity typical of Baroque art to create works that combined profundity with popular appeal. In the case of Shakespeare, moreover, the judgment of his contemporary and rival Ben Jonson (1572–1637) still holds true: "He was not of an age, but for all time!"

DRAMA IN ENGLAND: WILLIAM SHAKESPEARE

William Shakespeare (1564–1616) is universally acknowledged as the greatest writer in the English language, but

ACROSS CULTURES

SHAKESPEARE AND POSTERITY

Few figures in the history of Western culture have had Shakespeare's broad and lasting appeal. Many of his plays, and even individual lines in them, have entered the Western imagination—and beyond: The great Japanese film director Akira Kurosawa (1910–1998) based his films *Throne of Blood* (1958) and *Ran* (1985) on

Courtesy of William Duiker

Macbeth and *King Lear*, respectively. Many people quote Shakespeare without realizing that they are doing so: "frailty, thy name is woman"; "to thine own self be true"; "not a mouse stirred"; and, from the same play as all the preceding—*Hamlet*—the most famous of all, "To be or not to be, that is the question."

Thus it comes as a surprise to discover that such universal admiration is, in fact, not so universal. The earliest reference to Shakespeare's London career comes in a tract by Robert Greene, a contemporary, published in 1592: "There is an upstart Crow, beautiful with our feathers, that with his 'Tyger's hart wrapt in a

little definite information is known of his life. Born at Stratford-upon-Avon, by 1592 he was active as an actor and playwright in London. His early plays, including *The Comedy of Errors*, imitated ancient Roman comedies with their complicated plots involving mistaken identities.

By 1595, with *Romeo and Juliet*, Shakespeare was deepening and enriching both the language and psychological understanding of his characters. In the four tragedies he wrote between 1600 and 1605 (the years in which Caravaggio was at work in Rome)—*Hamlet* (1600), *Othello* (1604), *King Lear* (1604), and *Macbeth* (1605)—he explored the great questions of human existence with a profundity and power of expression that have few if any

equals. In emotional depth and virtuosity of language, the plays remain among the peaks of Western culture and a constant challenge to performers and directors.

Toward the end of his career, Shakespeare explored the frontiers between tragedy and comedy in works written for the court of King James I. *The Tempest* (1611), his last play, creates a world of fantasy in which romantic love and low comedy combine to magical effect.

THE NOVEL: CERVANTES

Something of the same blend of farce and pathos characterizes the greatest novel of the 17th century, *Don Quixote* (1605–1615). Its author, Miguel de Cervantes (1547–1616), received a humanist education and served as a soldier at the

player's hyde' (a parody of a line in Henry VI, Part 3) supposes he is well able to bombast oute a blank verse as the best of you."

Several later writers also remained unimpressed. The 17th-century diarist Samuel Pepys thought *A Midsummer Night's Dream* "the most insipid, ridiculous play that I ever saw in my life." The great French Enlightenment figure Voltaire (see Topic 58) wrote "Shakespeare is a drunken savage with some imagination whose plays can please only in London and Canada."

Perhaps the most bizarre critic of the Bard, however, was a man whose name has entered the English language as a result of his attitude toward Shakespeare's plays: Thomas Bowdler (1754–1825). Bowdler trained as a doctor, but his inability to stand the sight of blood drove him to abandon his medical practice. After traveling widely in Europe, he retired to the Isle of Wight to prepare his ten-volume *Family Shakespeare*, which appeared in 1818. As he explains on the title page, "Nothing is added to the text; but those expressions are omitted which cannot with propriety be read aloud in a family," since he had cut out "whatever is unfit to be read by a gentleman in a company of ladies."

The *Family Shakespeare* became a best-seller, and encouraged by its success Bowdler turned his attention to another of the indisputably great works of English literature, Edward Gibbon's *History of the Decline and Fall of the Roman Empire*, from which he removed "all passages of an irreligious or immoral tendency." Ten years after his death, the verb "to bowdlerize" had already come to mean "to expurgate by omitting or modifying words or passages considered offensive or indelicate," and over time it acquired the sense of absurd and ridiculous censorship.

Meanwhile, the plays have continued to be edited, read, performed, and viewed on the widest of scales, with constant attempts to update or find modern equivalents for *Othello*, or *Hamlet*, or *Richard III*. Bowdler's attempt to "improve" the originals remains a fascinating example of an inability to communicate across cultures.

Battle of Lepanto. His most famous work was intended to poke fun at medieval tales of romance and chivalry. The book's principal character, Don Quixote, is an elderly and rather unworldly gentleman searching for the gallant world of the past in his own troubled times.

The conflict between Don Quixote's idealism and the brutal realities of the world forms Cervantes' main theme, as the novel wanders through an apparently random series of events. The hero is accompanied in his travels by his faithful squire Sancho Panza, who provides a measure of practical common sense to leaven his master's dreams. By the end of his journey, Don Quixote realizes that he cannot reconcile his ideal visions with the real world, and he dies with his illusions finally shattered.

Cervantes' hero has achieved the same archetypal fame in Western culture as Shakespeare's Hamlet or Lear. With its constant exploration of the interplay between illusion and reality, *Don Quixote* touches on many of the chief concerns of 17th-century art, while the Don himself has a depth of character and psychological truth worthy of the brush of a Rembrandt.

POETRY AND RELIGION
The English writers known as the Metaphysical poets combine religion and the erotic in a way typical of the age—Bernini's *St. Teresa in Ecstasy* is a counterpart in the visual arts to the poems of Richard Crashaw (1613–1649), with their blend of pain and religious fervor.

Title page of the First Folio (first collected edition) of the works of Shakespeare, showing a portrait of the author. 1623. The edition was prepared by two of Shakespeare's fellow actors. So little is known of Shakespeare's life or appearance that it is difficult to judge the accuracy of this image. Certainly the text of the edition is badly flawed in places.

The leading poet of the group was John Donne (1572–1631), whose range and force of expression come close to rivaling those of Shakespeare. Donne's search to understand and expose the conflicting nature of human experience leads him to range from an analysis of sexual love to meditations on human mortality and the soul. The two chief themes of his writing are physical and religious passion, and the counterpoint he weaves between them leads to daring and memorable results.

The greatest of all 17th-century English poets was John Milton (1608–1674), whose artistic life became embroiled with the events of the English Civil War (see Topic 43). His active support for Cromwell and the Puritans brought him disgrace at the Restoration of Charles II in 1660. He spent the years of his enforced retirement in the composition of his major work, *Paradise Lost* (1667), the only successful epic poem in the English language.

The aim of *Paradise Lost* was to "justify the ways of God to men" by describing the fall of Adam and Eve. The poem's 12 books, written in blank verse, use imagery from the two great streams of Western culture—Classical Antiquity and Christianity—to reconcile humanist philosophical ideas with Christian doctrine. With the sure sense of drama of Bernini, Bach's spiritual convictions, and Rembrandt's understanding of the human heart, Milton's epic epitomizes the Age of the Baroque.

Putting the Baroque Era in Perspective

The arts served in the 17th century as weapons in the battle between Reformation and Counter-Reformation. In the process, they acquired new powers of expression and explored fresh areas of human experience. For all the apparent moral conflict between the Catholic Bernini and Puritan Milton, both drew on the advances of the Renaissance to produce works of dazzling insight.

There were times when the Baroque love of display and virtuosity crossed the line between extravagance and tastelessness, and for many at the beginning of the 21st century, Baroque art is less accessible than the more austere products of the Renaissance—the very word *Baroque* has come to mean "grotesque" or "exaggerated." The typical Baroque quest for illusionism can seem artificial and forced.

Yet many of the works created in the Baroque style retain much of the passion that their makers poured into them. Furthermore, in their struggle to represent the emotions and mental states of individuals, the greatest figures of the age—Bach, Rembrandt, and Shakespeare—created statements of universal truth.

Questions for Further Study

1. What common characteristics do all the arts share in the Baroque period? How do they vary in different parts of Europe?
2. How did Baroque artists deal with religious subjects? Did their approach differ from that of Renaissance artists?
3. What qualities have made Shakespeare's plays so widely admired and performed? Do the works still seem relevant, and, if so, why?

Suggestions for Further Reading

Adams, Laurie Schneider. *Key Monuments of the Baroque*. Denver, CO, 1999.

Boyd, M., ed. *Oxford Composer Companions: J. S. Bach*. Oxford, 1999.

Brown, Jonathan. *Kings and Connoisseurs: Collecting Art in Seventeenth-Century Europe*. Princeton, NJ, 1994.

Franits, Wayne. *Looking at Seventeenth-Century Dutch Art: Realism Reconsidered*. Cambridge, 1997.

Krautheimer, R. *The Rome of Alexander VII, 1655–1667*. Princeton, NJ, 1985.

Lagerlof, Margaretha R. *Ideal Landscape: Annibale Carracci, Nicholas Poussin and Claude Lorrain*. New Haven, CT, 1990.

Lavin, I. *Bernini and the Unity of the Visual Arts*. New York, 1980.

Levey, Michael. *Painting and Sculpture in France, 1700-1789*. New Haven, CT, 1993.

Millon, Henry A., ed. *The Triumph of the Baroque: Architecture in Europe, 1600-1750*. New York, 1999.

Muller, Sheila D., ed. *Dutch Art: An Encyclopedia*. New York, 1997.

North, Michael. *Art and Commerce in the Dutch Golden Age*. New Haven, CT, 1997.

Robb, Peter. *M: The Man Who Became Caravaggio*. New York, 2000.

Schama, Simon. *Rembrandt's Eyes*. New York, 1999.

Paliska, C.V. *Baroque Music*. Englewood Cliffs, NJ, 1981.

InfoTrac College Edition

Enter the search term *William Shakespeare* using Key Terms.

PART VI

THE OLD REGIME

The term *Old Regime* describes the political and social conditions that prevailed in Europe from about 1600 to the French Revolution in 1789. On the surface, life in Europe continued to follow patterns set in the Middle Ages. Most Europeans lived in farming communities. Although peasants in Western Europe were free, many still owed feudal obligations to landowners; in Eastern Europe most were still serfs.

Power remained in the hands of a hereditary aristocracy, and, to a lesser extent, of the reli-gious authorities. Whether in the Dutch republic, in England—a constitutional monarchy—or ab-solute monarchies such as France or Prussia, participation in government was limited to a tiny section of the population, who used their influ-ence to protect their own interests. Moreover, in France as well as in Central and Eastern Europe, government evolved in the direction of royal absolutism.

Throughout Europe a legally recognized so-cial hierarchy concentrated privilege and status

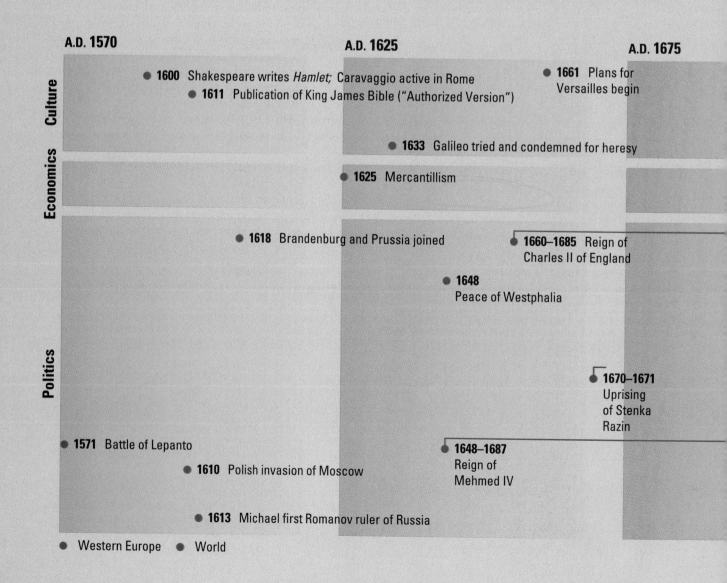

A.D. **1570**　　　　　A.D. **1625**　　　　　A.D. **1675**

Culture

● **1600**　Shakespeare writes *Hamlet;* Caravaggio active in Rome
● **1611**　Publication of King James Bible ("Authorized Version")

● **1661**　Plans for Versailles begin

● **1633**　Galileo tried and condemned for heresy

Economics

● **1625**　Mercantillism

Politics

● **1618**　Brandenburg and Prussia joined

● **1660–1685**　Reign of Charles II of England

● **1648**　Peace of Westphalia

● **1670–1671**　Uprising of Stenka Razin

● **1571**　Battle of Lepanto

● **1610**　Polish invasion of Moscow

● **1648–1687**　Reign of Mehmed IV

● **1613**　Michael first Romanov ruler of Russia

● Western Europe　● World

among traditional elites. The bulk of society—the peasantry, urban workers, and the middle classes—although excluded from government, bore the brunt of taxation. The trade in African slaves, and the institution of slavery itself, continued to be condoned and advanced by European states.

Yet behind the apparently permanent façade, there were signs of instability. The scientific revolution of the 17th century and the intellectual movement known as the Enlightenment of the

A.D. 1700

A.D. 1775

1748 Excavations begin at Pompeii

1751–1772 Diderot and others edit *Encyclopédie*

1685 Johann Sebastian Bach born

1759 Voltaire publishes *Candide*

c. 1715 Rococo style in art emerges in France

1720 South Sea Bubble

1776 Adam Smith's *Wealth of Nations*

1685 Edict of Nantes revoked

1734–1759 Charles III first Bourbon king of Naples

1683 Ottoman Turks besiege Vienna

1740–1786 Reign of Prussia's Friedrich the Great

1688 "Glorious Revolution" in England

1741–1764 Maria Theresa rules Austrian possessions

1689–1697 War of the League of Augsburg

1763 Treaty of Paris

1701–1714 War of Spanish Succession; Friedrich I king of Prussia

1707 Act of Union between England and Scotland

1713 Treaty of Utrecht

1714–1727 Reign of George I of England

1738–1746 War of Jenkins' Ear

1703 Hungarian uprising under Rákóczy

1756–1763 Seven Years' War

1700–1721 Great Northern War

1757 Battle of Plassey

1689–1725 Reign of Peter the Great in Russia

1759–1760 British take Quebec

18th century led slowly but inevitably to dissatisfaction with old ways and beliefs. Out of the English political experiment of the 17th century and the ideas of the Enlightenment there emerged theories of political sovereignty that recognized the right of ordinary citizens to resist oppression and overthrow despots. With the growth of cities, an increasing proportion of the population was within reach of education, and ideas began to spread far more rapidly. One of the major factors in the development of urban life was the Industrial Revolution, which began in the late 18th century.

In international affairs, the traditional rivalry between the two great powers of Europe, England and France, continued to dominate politics, while in the 18th century two new continental contenders began to emerge: the German state of Brandenburg-Prussia and Russia. Furthermore, with Europeans busily colonizing in Asia and the Americas, competition among the great powers resulted in military clashes on a global scale.

The buildup of a century and a half of pressure for change exploded in 1789 in the French Revolution. It was a sign of the new world that the revolutionary leaders hoped to create that they took inspiration from a revolution halfway across the globe: that of the Americans against their British colonial rulers.

THE SCIENTIFIC REVOLUTION AND WESTERN THOUGHT

During the Renaissance, as ancient scientific theories resurfaced, scholars throughout Europe began to speculate about issues that had been taken for granted in the medieval period: the nature of the physical universe, the relationship of Earth to the sun, the laws of mathematics. In order to put to the test beliefs based on tradition and Christian dogma, they started to try out theoretical ideas by means of practical experiments. In the 17th century, growing use of this **scientific method** produced a revolution in European intellectual attitudes, as scientists and thinkers such as Galileo, Descartes, and Newton laid the foundations of modern science. From then on, theologians and philosophers alike were faced with a new authority—scientific truth, objectively demonstrated.

Official church teaching, supported by the Bible, held that Earth formed the center of the universe, around which the sun, moon, and planets moved. The first to question this belief was the Polish astronomer Nicolaus Copernicus, who published his description of a universe centered around the sun in 1543. The German Johannes Kepler followed up the mathematical implications of Copernicus's revolutionary model and formulated three laws, describing the motions of the planets, which paved the way for Isaac Newton, the most prestigious mathematician and natural philosopher of early modern times, who produced a wide range of achievements. Among the most important were the theory of universal gravitation and his theories of light and motion. The astronomical observations of the Italian Galileo Galilei, using the newly invented telescope, further undermined official teaching.

The great Swiss physician Paracelsus also emphasized the importance of practical experiment. He based many of his theories on medieval alchemy, but his insistence on careful clinical observation and his use of a wide range of drugs helped lay the foundations of modern medicine. Other medical advances included the discovery of the circulation of the blood by the Englishman William Harvey.

The leading philosophical representative of the "new scientists" was the Englishman Francis Bacon, who urged the superiority of objective evidence over untested belief. Two French philosophers, René Descartes and Blaise Pascal, examined the implications of the rational method for theology and mathematics.

Thus, by the beginning of the 18th century there existed a scientific world view that challenged—implicitly, at least—centuries of accepted belief. The emphasis that scientists placed on reason, and their faith in the ability of the human mind to penetrate the mysteries of the universe, led in turn to the chief intellectual movement of the 18th century: the Enlightenment.

THE WEIGHT OF TRADITION: GOD, NATURE, AND THE WORLD

Throughout the thousand or so years that separated the fall of the Roman Empire from the Renaissance, scholars and theologians in Europe accepted a standard explanation of the nature of the physical universe. It was mainly derived from the writings of three ancient Greeks: Aristotle (384–322 B.C.) for physics, Galen (130–c. A.D. 200) for medicine, and Ptolemy (2nd century A.D.) for astronomy.

According to traditional Christian teaching, based on these authorities, the universe was finite. Earth, the most corrupt and degenerate—and therefore heaviest—part of the cosmos, was located at its center and was stationary. It was heavy, material, and subject to constant change. Around it there circled the planets, sun, stars, and heavens, moving outward from Earth in a widening series of spheres. The heavenly bodies were light, luminous disks, and in their superlunar realm, nothing ever changed. In the Renaissance, most scholars continued to accept these assumptions and tried to find complicated explanations for apparent inconsistencies rather than question the traditional explanations. When Galileo demonstrated that this distinction between Earth and the heavenly bodies was false, he created a storm of protest and bewilderment.

THE DAWN OF THE SCIENTIFIC REVOLUTION

Yet at the same time, the 15th and 16th centuries saw the first serious doubts about the accepted view of the nature of the universe. The Renaissance humanists discovered other Classical writers whose theories differed from those of Aristotle and Ptolemy. Among the most important was the physicist Archimedes (c. 287–212 B.C.), whose writings on dynamics proved highly influential.

Another reason for rethinking traditional views was a growing interest in various forms of magic, many of which were based on ancient precedents. Students of alchemy (a kind of medieval chemistry whose chief aim was to turn base metals into gold) believed that they could understand the nature of matter by using secret formulae to combine various ingredients. Others turned to the heavens and used astrology to interpret the movements of the planets. They hoped to read in them the meaning of the universe.

Various mystical schools of philosophy also flourished in the 16th century. The Hermetics were philosophers who believed that humans already possessed the key to an understanding of nature, locked up somewhere in existing texts (the term *hermetic,* taken from alchemy, refers to an airtight seal). They searched obscure writings, looking for hidden clues that would reveal the structure of the universe. Other thinkers turned to the Jewish mystical teachings of the *Kabbalah,* a Hebrew word, used to describe a body of esoteric Jewish mystical doctrines, which literally means "tradition."

More firmly based on Classical tradition were the Neoplatonists. The original school of **Neoplatonist** philos-

ophy flourished from the 3rd to the 6th century A.D. It derived from the teachings of the 4th-century B.C. Greek philosopher Plato and described the universe as consisting of a systematized order, containing all levels and states of existence. Renaissance Neoplatonists revived the idea of seeking to escape from the bonds of earthly existence in order to rise upward toward union with God, or the One, from whose Divine Mind the World Soul proceeds.

Most of these scholars may now seem unlikely forerunners of the **scientific revolution,** but by rejecting traditional solutions to age-old problems, and by using chemical experiments and mathematical formulae, they created an increasingly open spirit of intellectual inquiry.

With the surge of technological expertise that developed in the Renaissance, practical engineers, navigators, and doctors began to apply the experimental approach to their own fields. The result was to create a new way of looking at the world. When writing of motion—and with an eye on Aristotle—the great medieval thinker St. Thomas Aquinas (1225–1274) provided the baffling explanation that "motion exists because things which are in a state of potentiality seek to actualize themselves." Aquinas seems to have theorized about how things move, rather than actually watching them in motion. At the end of the 16th century, Galileo watched workmen in the Arsenal at Venice moving great weights; he went on to form a theory of motion that disproved Aristotle, and demonstrated it by dropping weights from the top of the Leaning Tower of Pisa. The age of objective scientific proof had dawned.

REDEFINING THE UNIVERSE: FROM COPERNICUS TO GALILEO

In the early 17th century, Galileo's astronomical experiments produced a revolutionary break with church teaching. Half a century earlier, however, the cleric Nicolaus Copernicus (1473–1543) had already challenged traditional opinion.

THE COPERNICAN REVOLUTION

Born in Poland of a wealthy German family, Copernicus studied in Italy, at the University of Padua. He learned there of recently rediscovered Greek scientific texts and pursued his mathematical interests. Under the influence of Platonic thought, he sought to replace the highly complex astronomical system of Ptolemy with a simpler formulation. Convinced that the sun, and not Earth, lay at the center of the universe, he devised a system whereby Earth and the planets orbit the sun in a series of perfect divine circles.

Unlike his successor Galileo, Copernicus never really tested his ideas by practical experiment. He remained a theoretical philosopher. Nor did his work, based as it was on ancient teachings, represent a real break with the past. He did not even publish his ideas until 1543, the year of his death. Yet in two crucial ways Copernicus foreshadowed the

Nicolaus Copernicus

"new science." In the first place his challenge to astronomical teachings based on the Bible was so serious that it drew the condemnation of first Protestant and then Catholic theologians.

Second, Copernicus's work revealed a new attitude. Before his time, scholars had always assumed that appearances were to be trusted. If the sun appeared to revolve around Earth, then it must be doing so. Questioning this assumption, Copernicus claimed that a system whereby Earth revolved around the sun was equally plausible. Scientific truth alone could be the basis of intellectual advance, even if it ran contrary to superficial observation. Indeed, the secrets of nature were often well concealed; in order to discover them it was often necessary to "twist the lion's tail," as Francis Bacon later observed.

The leading astronomer of the late 16th century, the Danish Tycho Brahe (1546–1601), collected important information about the planets and stars. In 1572 he discovered a new star, and three years later a comet, both of which disproved Aristotle's notions of fixed, unmoving heavenly bodies. Brahe refused to abandon his belief in the Ptolemaic system, but his remarkably accurate observations helped his successors to demonstrate that Earth revolved around the sun.

KEPLER AND HIS LAWS

Among Brahe's most brilliant pupils was the German astronomer Johannes Kepler (1571–1630). Kepler was convinced by Brahe's observations that the sun was the center of the universe. In trying to demonstrate this point, he formulated three laws, published in 1609 and 1619, to describe the motions of the planets in the solar system. According to the first law, each planet, including Earth, orbits the sun in an ellipse, of which the sun is at one focus. The second law claims that planets move faster when they are closer to the sun than when farther away. The third law describes the mathematical relationships between the planets' movements.

GALILEO GALILEI

The career of the Italian astronomer and physicist Galileo Galilei (1564–1642) demonstrated both the triumphs and the dangers of the scientific method. His experiments laid the foundations of modern physics, and he used his telescope to disprove Aristotle once and for all. He insisted that the Bible and the Aristotelian world it apparently supported should give way to modern science. As a result, he was tried and condemned by the Inquisition.

Galileo was born in Pisa in Italy to a talented aristocratic family. After beginning to study medicine at the University of Padua, Galileo changed to mathematics, and stayed on in Padua to teach there. The northern Italian city was already famous throughout Europe for its university, founded in 1222—the central building of the University of Padua today was begun in 1493, and is still in use. Research conducted by scholars at the university in the 16th century played a central role in the development of early modern

science. In addition to the Italians, foreign students such as William Harvey (see later section) studied there.

The telescope, a new astronomical tool, had been produced in Holland (its invention is generally credited to Hans Lippershey, a spectacle maker), and was used mainly for sighting ships. Driven by the curiosity that helped inspire the scientific revolution, Galileo designed and built his own model. Then he turned it toward the heavens to show a new vision: the mountains and craters of the moon, the phases of Venus, and sunspots. These observations proved that the universe is in a constant state of change. As early as 1597 he was convinced that Earth was in motion, and in 1610 he published his discovery of the satellites of Jupiter.

Galileo's attacks on traditional ideas, and his claims that he could demonstrate beyond doubt the essential truth of Copernicus's theories, created widespread controversy. One of his outraged colleagues, a Jesuit professor of philosophy at Padua, refused to look through a telescope for fear his traditional views might be shaken. More ominously, Galileo's Jesuit and Dominican opponents drew the attention of the Inquisition to his "heretical" ideas.

In 1616, after Galileo had defended his position in the presence of the pope, Paul V, the Inquisition censured him

Photograph of one of Galileo's telescopes. Date of telescope 1609. After Galileo's death in 1642, many of his instruments, including this one, were collected and preserved. They can now be seen in Florence's Museum of Science, one of the earliest examples in history of a museum dedicated to scientific rather than artistic works.

Scale/Art Resource

and prohibited him from spreading the doctrine that Earth moves, either by teaching or publication; the harsh reaction was in part because of the aggressive spirit of the Counter-Reformation, which sought to combat all traces of opposition to official views. After a period of tactful silence, Galileo returned to the attack when a former friend was elected pope as Urban VIII. In 1632 he published a *Dialogue Concerning the Two Chief World Systems*, in which he used imaginary characters to express his theories. The strategy failed to protect him. The Inquisition summoned him to Rome, imprisoned him, and in 1633 tried him for heresy. Despite his poor health and powerful friends, the tribunal forced him to undergo the humiliation of a public recantation, and sentenced him to house arrest for the remainder of his life. The case against him was reopened only in 1980, when Pope John Paul II—like Copernicus, a Pole—ordered that belated justice be done: In 1992, the church formally proclaimed its error.

Galileo spent the rest of his life under house arrest at his villa outside Florence, working on problems in physics. His last work, *Dialogues Concerning Two New Sciences* (1638), used observation and experiment to study a variety of phenomena, including motion. In trying to understand the practical character of natural events, rather than seeking to probe their cosmic purpose, he laid the foundation of modern physics.

MEDICINE AND THE HUMAN BODY

Throughout medieval Europe doctors remained largely dependent on more or less corrupted versions of the works of the Greek physician Galen of Pergamum (c. 130–c. 200). Galen catalogued illnesses, distinguished between anatomy and physiology, and described the course of various diseases. By contrast with the West, in the medieval Muslim world, significant medical and scientific research led to important medical discoveries, some of which gradually circulated in Europe.

PARACELSUS

The Renaissance, with its revival of interest in ancient texts, and its growing spirit of practical research, brought a wave of new interest. The figure who did most to change and improve methods of medical treatment was a Swiss alchemist and doctor called Theophrastus Bombast von Hohenheim; he proclaimed his superiority to ancient doctors by adopting the name by which he is best known, Paracelsus (1493–1541)—the name means "better than Celsus," who was an eminent Roman surgeon of the 1st century A.D.

Rejecting the authority of Aristotle and Galen, Paracelsus turned to his own careful observation in treating disease. After studying medicine at Ferrara in northern Italy, he taught at the University of Basle, Switzerland. He

was one of the earliest university teachers anywhere to lecture in German, his own language, rather than in Latin, and this in itself was a challenge to tradition. His unconventional approach, coupled with a legendary short temper, brought him into constant conflict with his colleagues, and he spent the last years of his life as a traveling physician. Constantly recording the various symptoms of illnesses, and their reaction to different drugs, Paracelsus was the first physician to emphasize the close relationship between chemistry and medicine.

THE CIRCULATION OF THE BLOOD

The first to make a breakthrough in understanding the system whereby blood circulates in the body was the Spanish theologian and physician Michael Servetus (1511–1553). In a theological treatise, *Christianity Restored* (1553), written while he was teaching in France, he described how blood is carried from the heart to the lungs to be purified, and then returns to the heart to be passed from there to the other parts of the body.

For all the importance of his work, Servetus failed to realize that the blood returns to the heart, circulating endlessly by means of the veins. This discovery was made by the English doctor William Harvey (1578–1657). As a young man, Harvey studied under Galileo at Padua and subsequently became personal physician to James I and Charles I. In a publication of 1628, Harvey described the blood circulation system and explained the function of heart valves and arterial pulse.

The increasing use of dissection improved knowledge of the human body and its organs. Surgeons thus became able to operate more effectively. More than half a century earlier, in 1543—the year in which Copernicus's revolutionary theory appeared—the Flemish biologist Andreas Vesalius (1514–1564) had published *On the Structure of the Human Body*. Vesalius based his anatomical treatise on his dissections of corpses. Church leaders who believed in the physical resurrection of the body on the Day of Judgment protested at his use of cadavers, however, and Vesalius abandoned his scientific studies to practice medicine at the Spanish court. By the following century, however, the wave of scientific progress had swept away such objections to the use of human cadavers.

THE ROYAL SOCIETY OF LONDON

The spectacular discoveries in anatomy, like those in astronomy and physics, inevitably aroused widespread interest. This led in turn to the establishment of organizations of scientists, to share research discoveries and promote their spread. The first such institution, the Lincean Academy, was founded in Rome in 1602. By far the most important, however, was the Royal Society of London for Improving Knowledge. The group began to meet informally at Oxford in the 1640s, during the Civil War. In 1660, 12 members formed an official organization, which received a royal charter two years later.

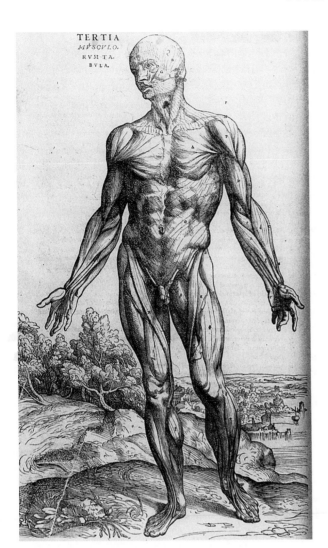

TERTIA
MVSCVLO.
RVM TA-
BVLA.

Andreas Vesalius, *Third Musculature Table,* from *De humani corporis fabrica.* 1543. The highly realistic drawing of the human muscular structure comes from a set of seven volumes dealing with human anatomy. The figure is set somewhat incongruously in a typical 16th-century landscape scene, which could almost come from an etching by Dürer (see Topic 36).

The declared aim of the Royal Society was to gather all knowledge about nature and encourage its use for the public good. The sheer quantity of information with which it was deluged soon forced the Society to function as a central clearinghouse for the circulation of ideas. In 1665 it began to publish on a regular basis *Philosophical Transactions,* the earliest scientific journal.

Similar organizations appeared in other parts of Europe. In France, Louis XIV encouraged the foundation of the Royal Academy of Sciences in 1666, and by the end of the century other academies existed in Berlin and Naples. The "new science," which had aroused so much official hostility a hundred years earlier, was now patronized by royalty and followed enthusiastically by an ever-widening group of nobles and educated middle-class men and women.

THE SCIENTIFIC METHOD: BACON, DESCARTES, AND PASCAL

Many founding members of the Royal Society believed in acquiring and evaluating information by the scientific method. They acknowledged Francis Bacon (1561–1626) as their inspiration. Bacon was a philosopher rather than a scientist, but his writings on the importance of science for human development led the way in stimulating scientific research.

A gifted and precocious young man, Bacon was a student at Cambridge by the age of 16. He distinguished himself there by attacking the works of Aristotle, which were regarded as the basis of all philosophical instruction. The character of Bacon's philosophy emerged as early as 1605, in *The Advancement of Learning.* He believed that the myths and fables of primitive peoples expressed true wisdom; Plato, Aristotle, and the other ancient philosophers had strayed from the truth by the arrogance that led them to invent their own intellectual systems. To find truth, it was necessary to study the world around us. Experiment was far more important than theorizing.

He returned to this conviction throughout his life. In *New Atlantis* he described an ideal society in which scientists would work for the state in gathering knowledge. In due course this would lead to establishing universal laws creating continuous improvements in human existence. Toward the end of his life, he tried to replace Aristotelianism with a new system of philosophy, described in *Novum Organum.* This appeared in Latin in 1620, but two years later Bacon broke with tradition and published an edition in English, the *New Organon.* This meant that a far wider audience read and thought about his challenge to Aristotle's views. In his last works, he poured his energies into what he believed to be his great mission: the exaltation of science as the savior of humanity. In the *New Atlantis* (1626), he even foreshadowed the formation of associations such as the Royal Society.

THE METHODOLOGY OF DESCARTES

If Bacon provided the philosophical underpinning to scientific research, the Frenchman René Descartes (1596–1650) set out the importance of the power of reasoning. After a period of travel, Descartes settled in Holland, where he created the branch of mathematics known as analytic geometry. His interest in mathematics led in turn to his most widely read book, *Discourse on Method* (1637).

In this work he aimed to unify all knowledge as the product of clear reasoning from verifiable evidence. The ideal of objective certitude that could be reached in mathematics should also exist, he claimed, in scientific and philosophical thought. To discover what kind of evidence could have such complete certitude, he adopted the method of universal doubt. Everything was open to question, even his own existence. In the famous phrase "*cogito, ergo sum*" ("I think, therefore I am"), he established his first certitude,

Frans Hals, *René Descartes* (1596–1650), Statens Museum for Kunst, Copenhagen. Photography by Hans Peterson

Frans Hals, *René Descartes*, c. 1640. Descartes lived in Holland from 1628 to 1649, and the great Dutch portraitist painted him there. Hals used his typically broad, dynamic brushstrokes to capture the wry, curious gaze of a man often called "the father of modern philosophy."

his existence, and following from there worked out his philosophical system.

Although the system, which became known as Cartesianism, is firmly based on reason, Descartes included in it a supreme being. His God, not necessarily to be identified with the God of the Old and New Testaments, created a world imbued with perfect mathematical principles.

As a practical scientist and physicist, Descartes produced mixed results. In his theoretical writings on physics, he was the first to make the important distinction between mass and weight. On the other hand, his attempt to locate that part of the human anatomy that contains the soul was a predictable failure. Descartes' profound influence on his contemporaries came less from the details of his theories than from his general intellectual stance. In particular, he taught the immense importance of never accepting a belief without thoroughly questioning it. After Descartes, it was never again safe to argue from tradition.

PASCAL AND FAITH

For all their temperamental differences, Bacon and Descartes shared an essential belief in the positive power of science. The all-too-brief career of the French mathematician and philosopher Blaise Pascal (1623–1662) shows a far more complex attitude toward scientific discovery. As a

child, Pascal was a mathematical prodigy. At the age of 16 he completed an original treatise on conic sections, which helped lay the basis for integral calculus. He also made pioneering discoveries in fluid mechanics and hydrodynamics, and along with his countryman Pierre Fermat (1601–1665), originated the mathematical theory of probabilities.

Pascal's sister was a nun, and through her he came into contact with a new Catholic movement, Jansenism; the name was taken from that of a Dutch theologian, Cornelius Jansen (1585–1638). In opposition to the Jesuits' belief in free will, the Jansenists claimed that human destiny was in the hands of God, so that salvation could come only from unquestioning faith. The ultimate source of these teachings was St. Augustine. The hostility between Jansenists and Jesuits led in the 17th century to Louis XIV's persecution of the French Jansenists (on Louis XIV's efforts to stamp out Jansen's beliefs in France, see Topic 50).

The asceticism and piety of the Jansenists he met profoundly shook Pascal's confidence in the value of his scientific work. Late in 1654, at the age of 30, he underwent a mystical experience that led him to abandon science in favor of seeking salvation. In the *Reflections* (1670), the writings of his few remaining years, collected and published after his early death, Pascal urged the importance of spiritual values over dry logic and intellect. He claimed that "the heart has its reasons that the mind cannot know." A lone voice in the growing enthusiasm for scientific progress, he lamented the gulf between the material and the spiritual. The passion of his protests is an indication of the degree to which science had come to dominate 17th-century European intellectual life.

NEWTON AND THE LAWS OF THE NATURAL UNIVERSE

Kepler's astronomy, Galileo's physics, and Descartes' idea of universal science reached a majestic synthesis in the work of the Englishman Isaac Newton (1642–1726), the most eminent mathematician and natural philosopher of early modern times. After attending Cambridge as a student, Newton later taught there. He became a fellow of the Royal Society and served as president from 1703 until his death. His whole life was devoted to ceaseless research—alchemy, optics, mathematics, chronology, chemistry, mechanics, theology, and the secrets of the Bible were only some of the fields to which he made significant contributions.

At the heart of Newton's work lay his belief that logic and reason were unsatisfactory tools for a scientist. It was necessary, he maintained, to prove everything by experiment or mathematics. Thus, his most widely read book, *The Mathematical Principles of Natural Philosophy* (1687), deliberately set out to refute Descartes' exaltation of rationalism. One of the last major scholarly works to be written in Latin, the book is generally referred to as the *Principia*, the first word of its Latin title.

By courtesy of the National Portrait Gallery, London

Portrait of the English physicist and mathematician, Sir Isaac Newton. 17th century. Newton's long hair (probably a wig) is characteristic of male dress after the Restoration in 1660. The great scientist served in several public positions, including as a Member of Parliament and as Master of the Royal Mint.

The most influential of his discoveries related to the problem of motion, which he defined in three laws. In formulating these laws, he arrived at concepts of mass, inertia, and force (a term in physics referring to the measurable influence that produces motion) in relation to velocity and acceleration, which dominated science down to the early 20th century and are still valid today. He extended his system to the entire universe, applying the same principles to the movements of the moon and planets. In order to explain the consistent nature of motion, he conceived the idea of the law of gravitation, whereby there exists a reciprocal force of attraction between every body in the universe.

THE NEWTONIAN UNIVERSE

Even if the lay public could not always follow the details of Newton's reasoning, the implications of his discoveries had a growing effect on how people thought about the universe. If all motion, random though it might seem, was really the result of precise and unchanging forces, then the world was like a huge machine that functioned according to laws that could be mathematically expressed. God was like a watch-maker who put the machinery in motion. For Newton, in fact, the creation of the force of gravity was an act of God because he believed that bodies do not necessarily possess that quality. Like most of his fellow scientists in the 17th century, Newton remained profoundly religious and devoted much time in his later years to theology.

Yet many people increasingly saw the mechanistic view of the universe proposed by Newton as a welcome replacement for traditional theological disputes. After more than a century of bitter religious wars, the sheer levelheadedness and impartiality of scientific debate seemed a happy relief. Science was peaceful, verifiable, and, above all, useful. This is one reason why Newton received honors never before awarded to a scholar. He became a member of Parliament, served as director of the Royal Mint, and was the first scientist to be knighted for his work.

For a few thinkers, the Newtonian universe replaced the personal God of traditional belief with a natural order. The Dutch Jewish philosopher Baruch Spinoza (1632–1677) held that nature is a fixed and unchangeable order, which serves no particular purpose. God is neither Creator nor Redeemer, but simply natural law. Humans, as part of the universe, conform to the same laws. In his book, *Ethics* (1677), Spinoza writes: "I shall consider human activities and desires in exactly the same manner as if I were concerned with lines, planes, and solids." Few of his contemporaries, however, were as willing as Spinoza to break with tradition, and he was expelled from the Amsterdam Jewish community for his radical views.

For most thinkers in the 18th century, Isaac Newton's contribution stripped away the ignorance of the past and presented a new view of science and the universe. The newly optimistic spirit was neatly caught in Alexander Pope's ironic couplet, written in the early 1700s:

> Nature and nature's law lay hid in night.
> God said, "Let Newton be!" and all was light.

Putting the Scientific Revolution in Perspective

During the 17th century, Western thought underwent wrenching change, and the foundations of the modern intellectual world were laid. The Aristotelian and medieval views of the world ended their 1,000-year-old monopoly, to be replaced by the Newtonian universe. Modern science had a generally accepted methodology, and physics, chemistry, mathematics, anatomy, and astronomy were already producing startling results.

Continued next page

Early researchers had been persecuted, imprisoned, and even executed, but by the early 18th century, scientists were honored members of society, supported by governments. The Counter-Reformation Catholic Church remained hostile to much of the new science, but its power was on the wane, at least in western Europe. Because leading figures such as Descartes and Newton saw no difficulty in reconciling their conclusions with a continuing religious faith, most Protestant communities accepted their work. During the Civil War in England, the Puritans had actually encouraged scientific research.

The scientific revolution did more than illuminate problems of astronomy or anatomy. By challenging centuries of tradition and ignorance, and by revealing the importance of questioning received wisdom, it paved the way for a vast rethinking of many of the basic assumptions underlying Western culture. The discovery of universal laws in nature led to a new belief in a "verifiable universe," in which it was possible to know and discover everything through the application of human logic. From the 17th-century scientific revolution was born the chief intellectual movement of the 18th century, the Enlightenment (see Topic 58). Furthermore, the demonstrated existence of "natural laws" in the universe inspired 18th-century thinkers and politicians to search for similar universal principles in government and devise new political constitutions. The eventual consequence at the end of the century was revolutionary social and political upheaval.

Questions for Further Study

1. What are the chief features of the scientific method? What new light did it shed on astronomy and medicine?
2. How did Descartes and Newton differ in their research methods? How did this affect their conclusions?
3. What were the long-term political consequences of the 17th-century scientific revolution?

Suggestions for Further Reading

Berlinski, David. *Newton's Gift: How Sir Isaac Newton Unlocked the System of the World.* New York, 2000.

Biagioli, Mario. *Galileo, Courtier.* Chicago, 1993.

Gingerich, Owen. *The Eye of Heaven: Ptolemy, Copernicus, Kepler.* New York, 1993.

Hall, A. Rupert. *The Revolution in Science 1500–1750.* London, 1983.

Jacob, Margaret C. *The Cultural Meaning of the Scientific Revolution.* New York, 1988.

Machamer, Peter, ed. *The Cambridge Companion to Galileo.* New York, 1998.

Rodis-Lewis, Genevieve. Jane Marie Todd, trans. *Descartes: His Life and Thought.* Ithaca, NY, 1998.

Sobel, Dava. *Galileo's Daughter.* New York, 1999.

Westfall, R.S. *Never at Rest: A Biography of Isaac Newton.* Cambridge, MA, 1980.

Willey, B. *The Seventeenth Century Background.* New York, 1982.

InfoTrac College Edition

Enter the search term *Copernicus* using Key Terms.

Enter the search term *Galileo* using Key Terms.

Enter the search term *Isaac Newton* using Key Terms.

Enter the search term *René Descartes* using Key Terms.

SOUTHERN EUROPE: SPAIN, ITALY, AND THE MEDITERRANEAN

For thousands of years the Mediterranean Sea had played a unique and vital role in the growth of civilization. The Mediterranean served as the meeting place of diverse and often hostile cultures and religions, and as the most important trade route of the entire region. Yet the 16th century saw the beginning of economic decline for the region, as the newly discovered sailing routes across the Atlantic and around Africa shifted the focus of trade from the Mediterranean to the Atlantic states.

What the Mediterranean lost in economic importance, Spain gained. In the mid-16th century, the resources of the vast Spanish empire enabled its monarchs to extend their political hegemony throughout Europe. Philip II ruled an empire that included not only Spain and huge tracts of the Americas, but also Milan, Naples, Sicily, Sardinia, and the Netherlands.

Within little more than a century after Philip's death, Spain—seething with domestic unrest and its economy devastated by a combination of virtually continuous warfare, agricultural deterioration, unchecked royal spending, and overtaxation—had lost most of its European possessions. In the diplomatic balance of power, Spain's predominance was overtaken by France.

By the 15th century, the Italian city-states had become centers of a vibrant economic revival and a brilliant cultural Renaissance. Despite Italy's achievements as the center of Western artistic and intellectual revival, however, the invasion of the peninsula by the French king Charles VIII in 1494 began a long period of foreign domination. In 1559, the destinies of Spain and Italy met when Philip II confirmed his hold over his Italian lands and ended a protracted struggle for mastery in Italy between Spain and France. Thereafter, Spain influenced Italian affairs until the early 18th century, when the Austrians became the predominant power in Italy.

Spain

1492	Columbus's first voyage; beginning of shift in sea trade from Mediterranean to Atlantic
1532	Last Flanders galley
1453–1571	Mediterranean wars with the Turks
1571	First Holy League; Battle of Lepanto
1598–1621	Philip III rules as king of Spain
1621–1665	Philip IV rules as king of Spain
1683	Second Holy League
1700–1746	Philip V rules as first Bourbon king of Spain
1738–1746	War of Jenkins' Ear

THE ECLIPSE OF THE MEDITERRANEAN↓

In the 200 years between 1500 and 1700, the economic and political importance of the Mediterranean Sea diminished as the focus of power shifted to the Atlantic and north-western Europe. One of the major reasons for this change was the new commercial sea route charted around Africa. Yet other factors, including the expansion of the Ottoman Empire, made the Mediterranean region the object of continuing European concern.

THE CHANGING DIMENSIONS OF TRADE

As the focus of European commerce, the Mediterranean had become something of an Italian lake by the 14th cen-

tury because the carrying trade that sailed its waters was almost exclusively controlled by the Italian maritime states, especially Genoa and Venice.

By the 16th century, this profitable arrangement disappeared as Dutch and English ships began to take over the carrying trade, and the Portuguese began to use the new route around southern Africa, thereby cutting out the Muslim and Venetian middlemen. In 1521, the Venetian Republic, anxious to restore its declining trade position, offered to buy all the spices brought to Europe by Portugal, but the offer was refused. The last Flanders galley sailed from Venice in 1532, that to Alexandria in 1564, and the Beirut galley in 1570.

Mediterranean commerce did not, of course, come to an abrupt end. Rather, setbacks in the luxury trade were interspersed with sudden increases as it moved along its overall downward trajectory. A variety of circumstances accounted for this up and down movement, including interruptions of Portuguese and Dutch shipping caused by war in Europe and on the seas. In 1565, for example, as much pepper from India was passing through the Red Sea as arrived by the African route in Lisbon. The spice routes of the Levant remained active until well past the end of the century. In the 1600s, British trade with Italy increased greatly, and by the end of the century, Italian goods accounted for some 10 percent of all British imports. There is, in fact, some evidence that by the 18th century the volume of trade had begun to increase.

Nevertheless, the pattern and nature of the sea trade changed, and the Mediterranean became the location for a series of smaller, regional commercial economies, such as the Adriatic area, the eastern Mediterranean, and the Spanish-French coast. Locally produced items, such as finished woolens made in Florence, blown glass in Venice, and steel armor in Milan, were still sold throughout Europe, al-

Map 49.1 Southern Europe, c. 1700. Spanish rule in Central Europe and Northern and Southern Italy was to end the following century. Ottoman control of North Africa extended to Egypt (not visible on the map). Note the independent kingdom of Piedmont, in (modern) northwest Italy, which was to become the seed-bed of Italian unification in the next century.

though by the 17th century the French were offering serious competition in the manufacture of luxury goods.

THE MEDITERRANEAN WAR

In addition to the overseas discoveries of the great age of exploration, the Mediterranean economy experienced another change in the 15th century as a result of the capture of Constantinople by the Ottoman Turks in 1453. In 1565, the Turks unsuccessfully besieged the island fortress of Malta, ruled by the Knights of Saint John. By 1570, however, the Ottomans controlled some three-quarters of the Mediterranean coastline, a zone stretching east from the Istrian peninsula in the northern Adriatic, around Greece and the Balkans, across to Asia Minor and the Middle East, and thence westward across North Africa almost as far as Gibraltar. The Turkish expansion, coming on top of the new trade routes, seriously affected the economic well-being of the trading states, especially Venice.

In response to the Turkish threat, Venice, Spain, and the papacy joined forces in forming the Holy League in 1571, which marshaled a vast fleet of some 300 ships and 80,000 men. In October, this fleet met an equally strong Turkish force off the coast of Greece at Lepanto, an engagement that resulted in a major victory for the League. The Battle of Lepanto did not, however, profoundly alter the course of events. After Lepanto, in the western Mediterranean the Turks confined themselves mainly to the North African coast, although in the east they continued to secure strategic islands, including Crete in 1669.

Despite the frequent state of war between the Turks and the European powers, the economic unity of the Mediterranean did not end. The Ottomans were deeply interested in international trade. Muslim traders maintained representatives and branch offices in Venice and other western cities, while Turkish tax policy favored foreign merchants. The entire range of western commercial products, from coin, cloth, glass, and other manufactures to furs, lumber, and raw materials, found their way to the East, while Eastern commodities, including pepper, spices, oils, dyes, ivory, and slaves, continued to be supplied to Europeans. In this commercial sense, the Mediterranean Sea remained neutral in the European-Turkish wars.

On the other hand, if the Turkish military challenge did not stop Mediterranean commerce, merchants faced constant danger from the many pirates who roamed its waters, especially along the western shores of North Africa, where a series of "Barbary" states—named after the Berber tribes who inhabited the regions—had been established under Turkish rule. The Spanish and the Venetians led the struggle against these Muslim corsairs during the 17th century. After the Treaty of Utrecht in 1713–1714 (see below), the British controlled Gibraltar and Minorca and became the predominant naval force in the Mediterranean. Nevertheless, piracy persisted, and in the late 18th century the United States even had to pay tribute to protect its shipping. In 1801, however, the United States declared war against the pasha of Tripoli, and in 1815 against Algiers, thereby curtailing piracy.

FROM HAPSBURG TO BOURBON SPAIN

THE TWILIGHT OF SPANISH POWER

Philip III (ruled 1598–1621), the successor to his father Philip II (see Topic 42), took little interest in government. Devoting himself to religious ceremonies and the social life of the court, he left the direction of royal affairs to his favorite, the corrupt duke of Lerma (1552–1625). At home, he encouraged a new era of extravagant spending by his personal behavior, while abroad he was continually drawn into disputes that further drained the treasury. The economic plight of the realm worsened as population declined as a result of wars and emigration, a situation aggravated in 1609 to 1610 when Lerma expelled the *Moriscos*—as the Muslims who had been forcibly converted to Christianity were called. The loss of the Moriscos, whose industry and business skills had enabled them to prosper, was a serious blow to the economy. Nor was Lerma's foreign policy any more successful, and in 1609 Spain was forced to end the revolt of the Netherlands by signing a truce that recognized the independence of the Protestant Dutch Republic, known as the United Provinces. Lerma was finally driven from power in 1618 by a conspiracy of young noblemen that included the count of Olivares (1587–1645).

Velazquez, *Portrait of the Count-Duke of Olivares*, c. 1640. The painting shows the Spanish politician and General at a critical point in his career, facing revolts in Flanders, Catalonia, and Portugal. The stormy weather and rearing horse convey a sense of tumult, as a city (Barcelona?) seems to be burning in the background to the left.

Scala/Art Resource

Philip IV (ruled 1621–1665), only 16 years old when he became king, proved an even weaker ruler than his father, but had in Olivares a tough and skillful minister. As the youngest son, Olivares had attended university and had prepared for a career in the church, but he succeeded unexpectedly to his father's title and wealth. Before Philip became king, Olivares had joined the prince's retinue and became a favorite courtier. Made a member of the highest noble rank, Olivares became Philip's chief minister in 1621. Although no less corrupt than Lerma, he quickly won the respect of the Spanish cortes by declaring an end to excessive spending at the court.

Olivares wanted to preserve Spain's status as a great power and to impose a rigidly centralized government on the nation. In foreign affairs, Olivares was determined to continue the war in Flanders, which soon became merely a minor aspect of two larger conflicts: the Thirty Years' War and the struggle between the Hapsburgs and the Bourbons.

Under Richelieu's leadership, France became the chief rival of Spain, which generally remained on the defensive both in Europe and the West Indies and steadily lost ground. The far-flung fighting required considerable money and large armies, and in order to meet both needs Olivares announced plans for a Union of Arms, according to which all parts of the empire would contribute men to a force of 140,000. The actual size of the army proved to be smaller, and some provinces refused to provide either men or money.

The crisis point was reached in 1640, when the French captured Arras and invaded Flanders, and separatist revolts broke out in Catalonia and Portugal. Catalonia represented a serious problem for Spanish unity because the fiercely independent Catalans had resisted all efforts by Olivares to undermine local privileges or to wrest increased taxes from the region. In 1640, as the war with France grew more precarious, Olivares sent troops to Catalonia, a move that sparked peasant uprisings against the soldiers and royal offi-

Derechos Reservados © Museo Nacional del Prado, Madrid

Velazquez, *Las Meninas (The Maids of Honor)*. 1656. 10 feet 5 inches by 9 feet (3.18 by 2.74 m). Velazquez has shown himself with paint palette in hand, wearing a red cross on his breast, symbol of the noble Order of St. James. He regarded this symbol as a sign of the recognition by the court that an artist was equal in social status to his patrons, even when they include Philip IV of Spain, who appears with his wife reflected in the rear mirror, watching work on a portrait of their daughter, the Infanta Margarita.

cials. Only after 12 years of savage fighting, during which Catalonia was overrun by Spanish and French armies, did Philip IV end the uprising.

Portugal, which had been seized by Philip II in 1580 but never formally incorporated into the Spanish realm, had been the object of Olivares' centralizing policies, including special taxation and a proposal to unite the cortes of Portugal and Castile. Governed by Philip's aunt, the viceroy Margaret of Savoy, Portugal seethed with discontent. After the outbreak of the Catalan revolt, the Portuguese rallied around the duke of Braganza, who led the break from Spain and was proclaimed King John IV (ruled 1640–1656) of an independent state.

In the wake of repeated setbacks, Olivares fell from power in 1643. Olivares, who objected to women "interfering" in political affairs, had alienated Philip IV's wife, Elizabeth (1602–1644), and the queen now insisted that Olivares be retired.

THE BOURBONS AND THE SPANISH SUCCESSION

[handwritten: Philip IV → Charles → Anjou Philip V]

On the death of Philip IV in 1665, Charles II (ruled 1665–1700) became king. Because he was only four years old at the time, the government was in the hands of his mother, Philip IV's second wife, Mariana of Austria (1634–1696). Moreover, Charles was not only mentally retarded but also handicapped by the famous "Hapsburg jaw," a physical deformity that afflicted family members in a more pronounced manner with each generation. The problem kept Charles from speaking or eating properly. After the end of the War of the League of Augsburg in 1697 (see Topic 50), Charles named Philip of Anjou, Louis XIV's grandson, as his heir. Less than a month later, the unfortunate Charles died.

Philip of Anjou ascended the throne of Spain as Philip V (ruled 1700–1746), the first Bourbon king of Spain. Philip's reign was thought by some to be the start of a new era of peace, but it began with the outbreak of the War of the Spanish Succession (see Topic 50) because the other powers feared the possible union of Spain and France. Philip was finally recognized as king of Spain by the Treaty of Utrecht (1713), in which he agreed that the crowns of the two nations would never be united.

From the outset, Philip had been influenced by Anne Marie, Princess Orsini (1635–1722), a handsome and intelligent woman who served as lady-in-waiting to the king's wife, Queen Maria Luisa (1688–1714), who ruled as regent while Philip was away during the war. Orsini supported French interests in Spain, and through her Louis XIV influenced Spanish policy. In 1708, however, Louis plotted with the British and Dutch to dismember the Spanish empire, and Orsini threw her support to Philip. When Maria Luisa died, Orsini's influence over Philip grew, together with that of the Italian Cardinal Giulio Alberoni (1664–1752).

For the remainder of Philip's reign, Spain was constantly embroiled in wars. In 1733, France and Spain concluded the Treaty of the Escorial, whereby the two states agreed to support each other in wars against the interests of

Sketch portrait of Charles III of Naples. 18th century. Charles ruled Naples from 1734 to 1759 and then succeeded to the Spanish throne on the death of his father, Philip V. A strongly absolutist monarch, Charles's attempts to expand Spanish holdings in South America met with defeat at the hands of the British.

Britain and Austria. In the War of the Polish Succession (1733–1735), in which each alliance supported a different claimant to the Polish throne, Spain occupied Naples and Sicily. Four years later, Spain and Britain began a prolonged trade war, known as the War of Jenkins' Ear, and this struggle was merged into the larger War of the Austrian Succession that erupted in 1740 (see Topic 56). Philip V died in 1746, before this conflict ended, leaving Spain weakened in power and reduced in status. By the time of Philip's death, the once-powerful Spanish empire had been seriously reduced in territory and prestige and overshadowed in international affairs by Britain and France.

EUROPE AND THE ITALIAN STATES

During the Renaissance and early modern period, while powerful, centralized monarchies emerged in France, England,

and Spain, Italy flourished as the land of culture but had no political identity. By the height of the Renaissance in the 15th century, the Italian peninsula consisted of about a dozen independent city-states, whose relations with each other were marked by economic competition and constant warfare. In response to the political anarchy of the period, Italy fell prey to foreign invasion and the larger struggle for power that consumed the great powers of Europe. For a century and a half, between 1559 and 1700, much of Italy came under the sway of the Spanish, whose policies greatly influenced social and economic conditions in the peninsula. After the War of the Spanish Succession, Spain's hegemony gave way to the influence of Austria, which dominated Italian affairs until national unification in the 19th century.

THE ITALIAN STATE SYSTEM

Five states dominated Italian affairs. In the north was the duchy of Milan, including the surrounding region of Lombardy. With the duchy of Savoy to its west, Venice to its east, and Genoa and Modena to the south, Milan was vulnerable to invasion. Because it lacked access to the sea, its economic life was more closely connected to Germany and Austria than to the rest of Italy. Venice, a republican oligarchy ruled by an elected doge and a hereditary senate, managed to maintain its maritime supremacy in the Mediterranean until the 16th century. Thereafter, its interest in the Venetian hinterland grew as its commercial empire shrank. South of Milan and Venice lay the city of Florence, which ruled the large region of Tuscany and had access to the Tyrrhenian Sea through the port of Leghorn (Livorno). South and east of Florence lay the Papal States, governed from Rome by the pope as an absolute monarch. Its territories spanned the peninsula from the Tyrrhenian to the Adriatic and included the virtually autonomous cities of Bologna and Ferrara. South of Rome and covering the remainder of the peninsula was the large Kingdom of Naples. The cities of Naples and Palermo were major commercial ports, while the large landed estates of

southern Italy and Sicily still provided much of the wheat for the Mediterranean world.

By the mid-16th century, a generation of war in the Italian peninsula left the independence and prosperity of these states in ruins. Peace came at last in 1559 with the Treaty of Cateau-Cambrésis, which left Milan, Naples, Sicily, and Sardinia directly in the hands of the Spanish Hapsburgs.

THE ERA OF SPANISH PREPONDERANCE

The century and a half of Spanish domination that followed Cateau-Cambrésis had an important impact on Italy. The period coincided with general economic difficulties for the peninsula, caused both by the changing sea routes and the fact that the position of the Italian bankers deteriorated as merchant and commercial capital began to develop in western and central Europe.

Spain attempted to centralize its administration in Italy, ruling its possessions through viceroys. In 1558, Philip II set up in Madrid a Council of Italy, whose members included two counselors from Milan and two from Sicily. One result of Spanish rule was that the political influence of the old aristocratic elites was seriously weakened, although they retained their legal and fiscal privileges on their huge estates. At the royal courts, however, a lavish and ornate social life developed among the aristocracy, and Spanish influence accelerated the aristocratic restructuring of Italian life. Campaigns were undertaken to counter periodic uprisings of the pro-French barons. The number of titles of nobility increased significantly, and Spanish nobles engaged in massive purchases of land. In addition, the close coordination between state and church that had marked Spanish history was now repeated in Spain's Italian possessions.

In Naples, Parliament, consisting of landowning nobles and members appointed by the crown, authorized the government to collect taxes, but after 1642 it was no longer summoned. Instead, the municipal government of the city of Naples became in effect the government for the entire realm. As Spain's need for money increased in the 17th century, the crown was forced to sell more of its land in the countryside, which was purchased by the quasi-feudal nobility. By the end of the century, some two-thirds of the kingdom's land consisted of noble estates. The middle class was small and without influence, so that the society of Spanish Italy proved to be inert and inflexible. Occasional popular outbreaks, most sparked by food shortages, plagued Spanish officials.

In Sicily, events took another course as a result of the island's different historical experience. The desire for independence remained strong in Sicily, but on the whole, Sicilians remained generally loyal to Spain. The island's society was rigidly feudal, with its agricultural land held by powerful barons in the form of massive estates that grew wheat and other cereals. In Sicily, however, the barons were pillars of the established order. The Parliament reflected a version of the hierarchical ordering of Old Regime society—three branches represented the barons, the church, and the crown.

S I G N I F I C A N T   D A T E S

Italy

1454	Peace of Lodi
1494	French invasion of Italy
1527	Sack of Rome
1559	Treaty of Cateau-Cambrésis
1559–1700	Spanish preponderance in Italy
1713	Treaty of Utrecht grants Milan, Naples, and Sardinia to Austrians
1720	Duke of Piedmont becomes king of Sardinia
1734–1759	Charles III rules as first Bourbon king of Naples
1741–1790	Joseph II rules Austrian possessions

Milan was attached to Spain in 1540. Political power there was exercised by a royal governor, who ruled with a senate. Overall directives, of course, came from Madrid. In Milan, as in Naples, the aristocracy aped Spanish fashions and customs, especially in an ostentatious pomp called *spagnolismo* ("Spanishism").

With the other states of Italy, Spain's relations fell into two categories: Some states, such as the Duchy of Savoy, Genoa, and the Duchy of Tuscany, were satellite clients of Madrid, whereas the Papal States and Venice continued to operate as independent states.

THE AUSTRIAN HEGEMONY

Spanish preponderance in Italy came to an end at the close of the 17th century. With the death of Charles II, Philip IV's son, in 1700 Italy became once again the object of European attention. When Louis XIV's grandson secured the throne of Spain as Philip V, he laid claim to all of the former Hapsburg possessions. But the peace treaties that ended the War of the Spanish Succession stripped Spain of its Italian possessions: the Treaty of Utrecht (1713) granted Milan, Naples, and Sardinia to the Austrian Hapsburgs, while Sicily was given to the dukes of Savoy, whose realm was now elevated to a kingdom.

Austrian dominance brought Italy out of the political and social backwater of the Spanish period. Rule from Vienna not only proved more beneficial to the Italians but by the middle of the 18th century also brought to the peninsula the widespread reforms of enlightened despotism (see Topic 59). Under Joseph II (1741–1790), who became Holy Roman Emperor in 1765, Lombardy and the other Austrian possessions underwent even more far-reaching improvements.

In Naples, too, changes were significant. The nobility and urban upper classes demanded greater local autonomy and were governed by several effective administrators, including Wierich Lorenz, Count von Daun, who served as viceroy from 1713 to 1719. Lorenz not only improved the economy but also countered church influence in Naples and instituted university reforms.

In 1734, Elizabeth Farnese, wife of Philip V of Spain, succeeded in recapturing Sicily and Naples for her son, Don Carlos, who took the throne as Charles III (ruled Naples 1734–1759 and Spain 1759–1788), the first of the Neapolitan Bourbons. When Charles succeeded to the Spanish throne in 1759, he left the Kingdom of Naples to

his son, Ferdinand (1751–1825), and an exceptionally able minister, Bernardo Tanucci (1698–1783), who ruled the realm until the young king came of age. Tanucci implemented reforms in the spirit of Enlightenment ideals, attempting to modernize the state administration.

Another key change in the Italian state system took place in 1737, when the last of the Medici rulers of Florence died. An international conference awarded the duchy to Francis of Lorraine (ruled 1738–1765), Maria Theresa's husband. Austrian authority in Italy was therefore extended further. Marked improvements in administration came along with a more liberal trade policy.

The one important counterpoint to Austrian hegemony in Italy was offered by the Savoyan rulers of the Kingdom of Sardinia. Savoy, the original homeland of the ambitious dynasty founded in 1026, lay at the strategically important location along the French Alps. In the 16th century, the Duchy of Savoy was occupied by the French, but the treaty of Cateau-Cambrésis restored its ruler, Emanuele Filiberto (ruled 1553–1580), to his realm. By skillful diplomacy he regained most of the territory that had been lost to the great powers and restored the capital at Turin.

Emanuele Filiberto's son, Carlo Emanuele (ruled 1580–1630), made the crucial decision to give portions of western Savoy to France in exchange for the tiny area of Saluzzo in 1601. The exchange marked the determination of the Savoyans to become an Italian power. In the years that followed, the dukes of Savoy gradually expanded their territory to include most of the northwestern region known as Piedmont, a program of expansion based on the skillful switching of sides in international disputes. The Savoyans developed a powerful military establishment to support their ambitions.

In 1713, Vittorio Amedeo II (ruled as duke 1675–1730, king of Sardinia 1713–1720, and king of Sardinia-Piedmont 1720–1730), who had played an important role in the War of the Spanish Succession along with his cousin Prince Eugene of Savoy (see Topic 50), was rewarded by his allies with the title of king of Sicily, which he then agreed to exchange for Sardinia in 1720. Thenceforth, the Kingdom of Piedmont-Sardinia was the only independent Italian state to play a vital role in international affairs. In the 19th century, its rulers would position themselves against the Austrian hegemony as they aspired to lead the movement to unite all of Italy under their rule.

Putting Southern Europe in Perspective

In 1500, the Mediterranean world was at the center of European civilization. While Italy represented the spectacular cultural achievements of the Renaissance, the empire of Charles V was the most powerful political and economic unit of the age. By the year 1600, the importance of the entire region had been eclipsed by the rise of

Continued next page

the states of northern and central Europe. A century later, Italy and Spain were minor players in the international arena. Spain, no longer the center of a transcontinental empire, had been reduced in territory and was economically depressed. Italy, occupied by foreign powers, underwent a long period of exploitation, only to reemerge again in the mid-18th century under the reforming impulse of the Austrian Hapsburgs.

Questions for Further Study

1. What changing conditions contributed to the decline of Spain and Italy?
2. Why did its American colonies not prevent the economic decline of Spain?
3. Why was Italy unable to achieve political centralization in the same way that France and England did?

Suggestions for Further Reading

Braudel, Fernand. *The Mediterranean and the Mediterranean World in the Age of Philip II,* 2 vols. New York, 1972–1973.

Carpanetto, Dino, and G. Ricuperati. C. Higgitt, trans. *Italy in the Age of Reason, 1685–1789.* New York, 1987.

Cochrane, Eric. J. Kirshner, ed. *Italy 1539–1630.* New York, 1988.

Darby, Graham. *Spain in the Seventeenth Century.* New York, 1994.

Elliott, John H. *The Count-Duke of Olivares: The Statesman in an Age of Decline.* New Haven, CT, 1986.

Frey, Linda, and M. Frey. *Societies in Upheaval: Insurrections in France, Hungary, and Spain in the Early Eighteenth Century.* New York, 1987.

Hanlon, Gregory. *Early Modern Italy, 1550-1800: Three Seasons of European History.* New York, 2000.

Kamen, Henry. *Philip V of Spain: The King Who Reigned Twice.* New Haven, CT, 2001.

Sella, Domenico. *Italy in the Seventeenth Century.* London, 1997.

InfoTrac College Edition

Enter the search term *Philip III of Spain* using Key Terms.

Enter the search term *Philip IV of Spain* using Key Terms.

ABSOLUTE MONARCHY: LOUIS XIV AND THE DIVINE RIGHT OF KINGS

In the 100 years after the mid-17th century, France stood at the center of European power. The sources of its strength included a population perhaps as large as 20 million by 1700, rich agricultural lands, and a strategic geographic location in western Europe, with its shores edging the English Channel and the North Sea, the Atlantic, and the Mediterranean. French preeminence was also the result of an efficient, centralized government, a powerful army, and a growing sense of national identity—all of which were characteristics of the new absolute monarchies then emerging. Much of the credit for these and other French achievements, both domestic and international, was the result of the policies of its ruler, King Louis XIV (ruled 1643–1715).

Louis advanced the centralization of the government and the building of a strong state bureaucracy, both of which had begun in the 16th century, by focusing supreme authority on his own person. The consolidation of royal power was achieved in part by further reducing the independence of an already weakened nobility and integrating its members into the structure of government. His long reign was also marked by prosperity in commerce and agriculture.

Louis would brook no domestic dissent and aimed to destroy any internal factors that threatened to weaken national unity, including religious differences. To a greater degree than any other king, he discovered the power of symbolism to mold opinion and create consensus among his subjects. His immense palace at Versailles was not only the most pronounced symbol of his grandeur, but also an important tool in bringing the nobility into the absolutist system. The resulting "absolute monarchy" that he forged became the model for many other European states and left a legacy of royal power that was destroyed only in the upheavals of the revolution of 1789.

Louis XIV espoused the beguiling ideology of power that identified reverence and obedience to his person with loyalty to and pride in France. With a thirst for military glory, he lavished huge sums on his army and undertook a series of foreign military campaigns that he hoped would round out the kingdom's borders and make it a powerful player in the international arena but that cost France dearly in resources and lives.

"I AM THE STATE": THE ABSOLUTIST GOVERNMENT

Contemporaries attributed to Louis XIV the phrase "I am the state." Whether he actually made this remark is unknown, but he certainly believed it. Louis did not, however, create centralized government or royal supremacy—these were the achievements of King Henry IV, and then of Louis XIII's chief minister, Cardinal Richelieu and his successor, Cardinal Mazarin (see Topic 44). Rather, Louis XIV reinforced the process and imbued **absolutism** with a theoretical framework and a brilliant practical example.

Louis was only a child of five years old when his father, Louis XIII, died in 1643. His Hapsburg mother, Anne of Austria, took up the reigns of power as regent and delegated extensive authority to Cardinal Mazarin. On the death of the Cardinal in 1661, Louis announced that he would be his own chief minister. The period from 1661 until his death in 1715 is known, therefore, as the "Age of Louis XIV," during which he ruled in his own right. His reign was the longest in European history.

Although he did not have a superior education, Louis XIV's appearance and personality were well suited to the role of king. His well-built body and heavy-featured face presented an impressive image. By today's standards he was short (about 5 feet 8 inches), but for his time he was of more than average height. Nevertheless, he wore platform shoes because he felt that the king should stand above his subjects. In public he dressed in the finest robes and furs and sported a long wig, cutting an elegant, if precious, figure. Serious by nature, he cultivated an imperious and dignified manner, yet he was always pleasant and courteous to his guests.

In 1660, Louis sought to solidify the Bourbon claim to the throne of Spain by marrying Princess Maria Theresa (1638–1683), daughter of the Spanish ruler Philip IV. Although they had six children—all of whom died before their father—Louis XIV had little romantic attachment to

Rigaud, *Louis XIV*. 1701. 9 feet by 6 feet 4 inches (2.77 by 1.94 m). Louis was 63 years old when this work was painted. The sagging face and stony gaze contrast with the gorgeous ermine-lined robes (decorated with the royal lily). The king's feet are arranged in a ballet pose, a reminder of the popularity of dancing at the French court.

© Réunion des Musées Nationaux/Art Resource, NY

his wife and kept several influential mistresses. He legitimized the six children he had with the Marquise de Montespan (1641–1707), but when he tired of her, she left the court. Her successor, Madame de Maintenon (1635–1719), actually married Louis on the death of Maria Theresa, but when Louis died, she too left Versailles.

DIVINE RIGHT MONARCHY AND THE STATE

Louis XIV sought unquestioned obedience from his subjects, regardless of their status or rank. He considered the royal will supreme over all political institutions. That he should wield such absolute authority was a claim based both on a political idea that had its roots in the Middle Ages and on a more recent concept. Medieval kings had been blessed with holy oil before assuming their thrones, thus, in effect, having been anointed by God. The concept of divine right implied that the monarch was God's earthly representative and that to oppose his will was a religious offense as well as political treason.

Although Louis XIV used such theories to justify his demand for far-reaching powers, he said that he used that

Painting of Madame de Maintenon, c. 1700. After the death of Louis XIV's wife, Maria Theresa, the king married his former mistress, who went to live with him at Versailles, part of which is visible at the back, through the window. The identity of the child is unknown; Louis had six children by his wife and six by an earlier mistress, the Marquise de Montespan.

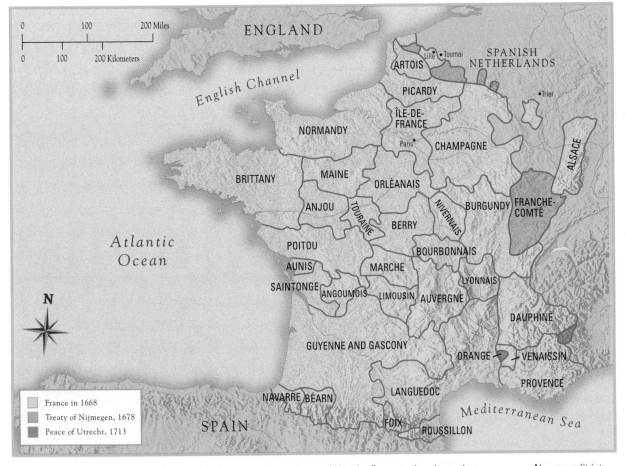

 Map 50.1 The France of Louis XIV. By 1713, with the Peace of Utrecht, France took on its modern appearance. Navarre split into two halves, the southern part going to Spain. The border with the modern state of Italy was to be modified the following century. Alsace remained contested by the new state of Germany from its creation in the 19th century, passing between France and Germany during the World Wars. In 1945, it was assigned to France. Go to http://info.wadsworth.com/053461065X for an interactive version of this map.

authority for the benefit of France. He wanted his subjects to think of the king as the embodiment of France and to see themselves as having a common destiny as subjects of a prosperous, well-ordered state. In order to generate a national consciousness, Louis tried to insert the state into more and more aspects of daily life, including the economy, religious affairs, and culture. In a kingdom in which regional loyalties were still strong and where the bulk of the inhabitants lacked a standard education or even a uniform language, the symbolism of the king was a powerful force around which to rally the masses.

Despite the theory of divine right, in actual practice age-old traditions of special rights and privileges enabled the nobility, the cities, the provinces, and the Catholic Church to limit royal authority. Louis XIV devoted considerable energy to undermining these limitations on his power, as his predecessors had done before him. His goal was for all individuals to owe loyalty to him rather than to corporations such as guilds, the church, or social class. His talents as ruler included the ability to choose intelligent and able ministers. Together with them, he reshaped the French government and its bureaucracy, reorganizing old and creating new administrative offices, and widening the powers of royal officials. As a reward for loyal service to the crown, the king sometimes gave high-ranking civil servants titles of nobility. Such bureaucratic "nobles of the pen" had little in common with the hereditary "nobles of the sword," whose estates and privileges were often of feudal origin and who worked incessantly to stave off royal encroachments on their rights.

Agents of the crown, from ministers to clerks, held office at the will of the monarch, and his ability to appoint and remove them made for a bureaucracy dependent on the king but free of other influences. The foundation of royal administration was the *intendants*, the king's chief representatives in the 30 provincial districts known as "generalities." As developed by Richelieu, the original duty of the *intendants* had been to collect taxes, but their responsibilities soon included conscripting soldiers, reporting on local economic conditions, taking part in lawsuits, and enforcing royal edicts. As the *intendants* intervened in more and more aspects of local affairs, they became the target of noble resentment, whose rights and privileges they deliberately undermined.

Two long-established administrative bodies, the estates and the parlements, continued to exercise independent authority, although their rights were also weakened. The estates were local legislative assemblies, composed of representatives of the clergy, the nobility, and the remaining population. Increasingly, however, their only purpose was to vote special sums of money to the king. The Estates General, France's national assembly, was last called in 1614 and would not meet again until 1789. The parlements, on the other hand, were provincial supreme courts of appeal that had the power to register the king's edicts. If they found just cause to do so, they could in effect veto royal action. In such instances, however, Louis XIV resorted to a royal prerogative that had been practiced by his predecessors in the 16th century: by invoking the *lit de justice*, he could appear personally before the parlement and declare his edict registered. The parlement of Paris, with jurisdiction over a vast area of central and northern France, was the only institution that presented serious resistance to Louis XIV's policies, but even here he usually had his way.

COLBERT AND THE PROSPERITY OF FRANCE

An important aspect of Louis' domestic policy was stimulation of trade and production to promote prosperity. As a result, government regulation of commerce and manufacturing increased under the policy known as mercantilism, which sought to make the kingdom as self-sufficient as possible in a government-regulated economy (on mercantilism, see Topic 46).

All economic affairs came under the direction of the Controller General Jean Colbert (1619–1683), a financial genius who had trained under Mazarin. Colbert's aims included full employment at home, a vigorous program of trade for a large French merchant marine, and lucrative overseas colonies. He negotiated favorable commercial agreements with other nations and built a powerful navy to protect the French merchant fleet. To promote colonial expansion, Colbert used government funds to found several overseas trading companies, including the East India Company and the West India Company.

Colbert did much to improve agricultural productivity and French forestry, although at first he increased the tax burden on the peasantry by raising the *taille*. Nevertheless, industry remained his major interest. He extended govern-

Portrait of Jean-Baptiste Colbert, finance minister to Louis XIV. Late 17th century. In addition to his reform of the taxation system and encouragement of industry, Colbert was also a patron of the arts. He helped organize the financing of the building program at Versailles, realizing its importance in both artistic and political terms.

The Metropolitan Museum of Art, Gift of the Wildenstein Foundation, Inc. 1951. (51.34) Photograph © 1979 The Metropolitan Museum of Art

ment loans to private manufacturers, organized companies, used tax policies to stimulate investment, and encouraged the immigration of skilled workers and artisans from abroad. Government regulations and inspectors ensured the high quality of French textiles, while Colbert fostered entirely new industries tied to colonization, such as sugar and tobacco refining. Roads were reconstructed and maintained, and a network of canals was built, including one that connected the Atlantic to the Mediterranean. Finally, Colbert restructured the French finances and reformed the tax policy to make the system more equitable: He lowered the *taille*, from which nobles were exempt, and raised taxes that were shared more equitably by all French subjects.

Colbert's policies were successful, and French industry and trade became preeminent in Europe. Nevertheless, the almost endless wars of Louis XIV set back prosperity and worsened living conditions at home for most of the population. Furthermore, while the economic programs sponsored by Colbert worked in the 17th century, by the mid-18th century France began to fall behind England, where new factory methods and machinery stimulated the Industrial Revolution.

NOBLES, JANSENISTS, AND HUGUENOTS: THE DOMESTIC OPPOSITION

In his desire to bring all elements in French society under the authority of his absolute government, Louis XIV sought to impose obedience and uniformity on the nobility and religious minorities. His methods in dealing with each group were different, but the aim was the same.

VERSAILLES: BUILDING A ROYAL COURT

Many aristocrats eventually accommodated themselves to Louis XIV's absolutism, realizing that government offices and royal favors represented a new avenue to status and influence. As the nobles were increasingly integrated into the state, they eschewed revolt and opposition in favor of cooperation and service to the king. Louis XIV intentionally made the royal court the center of social and political life for his "domesticated" nobility. The court, located originally in Paris, but eventually moved to Versailles, acted as a magnet for the entire range of nobles, from the wealthiest to the poorest. The location of the palace at Versailles kept the nobles out of Paris, where the bureaucracy was, and away from their own estates, making it difficult for them to amass regional power.

Louis XIV wanted to use the court as an instrument for molding the nobility into docile servants. In 1668, he ordered his architects to design a royal palace at Versailles, outside Paris, where his father had a hunting lodge. This 40-year project resulted in the most sumptuous royal residence in Europe, a tremendous complex consisting of an original central section designed by Louis Le Vau (1612–1670) and two later wings on each side. The northern wing was the work of the brilliant architect Jules Hardouin-Mansart (1646–1708), whose uncle François had introduced the sloping "mansard" roof. The palace was at the center of huge formal gardens, fountains, and walkways.

The great palace of Versailles, with its impressive façade and a luxurious interior resplendent with rich marbles, the golden glimmer of gilt, and mirrored hallways, proved to be an ideal stage for the court of the Sun King. To decorate the palace, Louis XIV hired a vast army of artists and craftsmen. Charles Le Brun (1619–1690), director of the famous Gobelins tapestry factories, labored for 18 years

Painting of an aerial view of the Palace of Versailles. 18th century. The painter leads the viewer's eye through the great entranceway, with its two semicircular structures back to the main palace itself, and then on to the sunlit formal garden at the rear. There are other gardens to left and right. The transformation of a simple hunting lodge into the most sumptuous royal residence in Europe took 40 years.

HISTORICAL PERSPECTIVES

LOUIS XIV: A BUREAUCRATIC KING

JOHN C. RULE   Ohio State University

Born on September 5, 1638, the infant prince Louis was dubbed "the God-given" by his delighted parents, Louis XIII and Anne of Austria, and by an ecstatic French people. The future Louis XIV's pedigree was impeccable. His mother's forebears were Hapsburgs of Spain, Burgundy, and Austria; his father sprang from a long line of Bourbon-Valois-Capetian kings of France; and his paternal grandmother descended from the Medici princes of Florence. Fortunately for France and for the Bourbon dynasty, Louis lived 77 years and ruled personally for 54.

In 1648 the kingdom was plunged into a bloody civil war, ironically named after a Parisian slingshot, the Fronde. Led by a band of prominent magistrates, great nobles, and princes of the blood, the revolt spread devastation to northern and eastern France. Ultimately the Frondeurs failed to wrest power from either Cardinal Mazarin or Queen Anne herself. Much credit for the preservation of the royal prerogative, and indeed for Louis XIV's own political and personal survival, was due to the dogged determination of his mother, the astute diplomacy of Cardinal Mazarin, and the dedicated service of a faithful group of secretaries of state and their clerks. The Fronde offered the young king practical lessons in statecraft: a fear of overmighty subjects and ambitious princes, like his cousin, the Prince of Condé; and a trust of an inner group of "new men" in politics, career diplomats and enterprising provincial magistrates.

Cardinal Mazarin, Louis' faithful guide and tutor, died early in 1661. His enemies accused the cardinal of ruling through fear, favor, and fraud. But whatever his faults, Mazarin instilled in his tutee the desire and courage to rule by himself, without a principal minister. When his courtiers asked him to whom they would now address their petitions, Louis replied: "To me." Even his mother was heard to chuckle, but the last laugh was on the king's foes from the Fronde era. Louis excluded from the High Council relatives, churchmen, great nobles, and feudal functionaries like the chancellor of France. This realignment of the High Council and subsequent growth of government departments is termed the Ministerial Revolution of the 1660s.

One of the most significant accomplishments of Louis XIV's reign, of which the Ministerial Revolution represented but a part, was the king's choice to rule his kingdom through a patrimonial bureaucratic government. That is a government of civilian ministers, who through councils and bureaus, formally governed France by executive decrees drafted in the king's name. Informally, these ministers governed through factions of cousins, clients, and "creatures" of the crown, experts and clerks in the various ministries.

Louis XIV promoted two families of Mazarin's "faithful" secretaries to lead the patrimonial bureaucratic government: the Colberts and the Le Telliers. Both families had risen from the financial-legal elite; both had recently been ennobled. These new ministers drew their support in large measure from the urban elites clustered in the provincial capitals, port cities, industrial towns, army strongholds, and from Paris itself. Both families, and their allies among the administrators, sought to influence local politics by extending to urban elites and factions at court, among other rewards, offices in the government, clerical preferment, careers in the armed forces, inexpensive leases of royal

on paintings and murals showing the glories of the king. Cabinetmakers produced the finest examples of furniture in rare woods and gilt mountings, while glassworkers made glittering chandeliers and embroiderers decorated cushions, bedspreads, and linens. Overall, the architecture of Versailles and its interiors reflect the "grand style" of the Age of Louis XIV, an elegant, Classically inspired backdrop for the daily rituals of court life.

For Louis XIV, Versailles was a system of government and social control as well as a residence. He deliberately encouraged practices in which courtiers competed with each other to carry out minor acts of service that symbolized their status, from awakening the king to lighting his way at night by bearing candles. Maintaining the kind of lifestyle required at Versailles strained the financial resources of many nobles, which in turn made them increas-

lands, long-term loans, contracts for public works, advantageous marriages for their children, noble titles, and even the "honor" of being presented at court. It was government by faction, patronage, and gesture.

The rise of royal patrimonial government witnessed the rapid centralization and increase in bureaucracy. The department of finances, headed by Controller General Colbert, quintupled in size, as did the ministries of the marine, headed by Colbert's son, and war, headed by the Le Telliers. The ministry of foreign affairs followed a similar pattern of expansion under the guidance of Colbert's brother, Croissy, and his nephew, Torcy, two of France's ablest diplomats.

Colbert and Michel-François Le Tellier vied with one another to satisfy the king's passion for the arts and architecture and, above all, for collecting. Perhaps the king felt deprived as a young man of what he considered to be a regal prerogative: the privilege of surrounding himself with objects of beauty and magnificence. Cardinal Mazarin had amassed a far greater collection of such objects than had Louis XIV. Thus Colbert and the Le Telliers dispatched agents across Europe to purchase paintings, prints, drawings, sculpture, jewels, precious plate, furniture, and rare books. These treasures were housed in the Louvre palace, rebuilt as an art gallery, a library, and home for scholars and artists. These privileged artists and men of letters trumpeted Louis as an Apollo of the Arts, a Mars in War, a New Alexander, Louis the Great.

And it was as Louis the Great that the king sought to satisfy his *gloire*, or desire for reputation, by building one of the greatest royal residences and sets of government in the West—the palace of Versailles. Versailles represented the king's vision of a new capital, a city of marble, set in a garden spot, built entirely at his orders; and though only 12 miles from Paris, it was a world apart, remote from overmighty magistrates, street mobs, and the stink of Seine River refuse.

In the mid-1660s Louis instructed Colbert to find money for the construction of his new capital at the site of his father's hunting lodge at Versailles.

Completing the work far outstretched Colbert's life and that of the marquis of Louvois. Satellite palaces at the Trianon and Marly were added, as were the extensions of the gardens. "Such wonders rival ancient Rome," exclaimed a visiting noble. "The palace," said an official, "spreads and sustains the glory of His Majesty." Other observers were not so kind. The gossipy duke of Saint-Simon thought of Versailles as a "cold, dark, damp and malodorous pile." And the English poet Matthew Prior remarked that Louis XIV's "house is . . . the foolishest in the world; he is strutting in every panel and galloping over one's head in every ceiling, and if he turns to spit he must see himself in person or his Viceregent the Sun."[1] By the end of the century Versailles had, however, become not only a shrine to kingship and the seat of government but one of the greatest tourist attractions in all Europe.

Louis was a man of enormous pride of family and dynasty. His quest for *gloire* in the field of military conquest and religious conformity has been bitterly criticized by Frenchmen and foreigners alike. But his actions at the time were popular, especially among the new urban elite, the financiers, and men of commerce, the solid Catholic middle class, patriotic churchmen, the "new men" in politics, the army and navy, and the arts. After the disturbances of the Fronde and the earlier religious wars, these groups sought a prince who would bring a measure of domestic order and external security to the kingdom. Both of these goals were to a certain extent realized: militarily, with the addition of provinces in the northeast of France and domestically with the extension of royal government, public works, town planning, and encouragement of the arts.

Louis XIV died in September 1715, fearing that he had loved war too much but certain that, though "I am dying the State lives on."

---

[1] John C. Rule, ed., *Louis XIV and the Craft of Kingship* (Columbus, Ohio: Ohio State University Press, 1970), 42.

ingly dependent on royal patronage. Perhaps as many as 10,000 people, including a vast retinue of cooks and servants, crowded into Versailles, where unheated rooms and a lack of toilet facilities created as much stench as glamour. Because anyone who served at Versailles was exempt from taxes, many of the service personnel were stand-ins for middle-class Parisians who had purchased their positions at court.

RELIGIOUS DISSENT AND ITS SUPPRESSION

Ever since the 15th century, French kings had enjoyed a high degree of control over the French Catholic Church. The Jesuits controlled education for most of the nobility and served as confessors to the 17th-century kings, including Louis XIV. Over the years, a working alliance between the crown and the French clergy evolved, and in

The Salon de la Guerre (War Chamber) at Versailles. Begun 1676. The stucco medallion showing a victorious Louis XIV on horseback is Classical in style, as are some of the decorative motifs. The whole effect, though, is one of Baroque magnificence, with plentiful use of inlaid stone and gilding.

1682, a French ecclesiastical assembly adopted the Declaration of Gallican (after Gaul, the ancient Roman name for France) Liberties, which proclaimed a degree of independence from papal authority.

Yet two religious groups—the Huguenots (Calvinists) and the Catholic Jansenists—disturbed the religious uniformity that was expressed in the formula adopted by Louis, "One king, one law, one faith." During the civil-religious wars of the 16th century, many of the old nobles of the sword had converted to Protestantism largely as an act of defiance against the monarchy, and by the reign of Louis XIV there were still some 1.5 million Huguenots.

From the start of his personal rule, Louis worked systematically to undermine the Edict of Nantes (1598) (see Topic 44), which had granted the Huguenots a measure of toleration and civil liberties and had made France an anomaly among continental monarchies. He drove them out of public office and certain professions, taxed them heavily, and quartered troops in their towns. In 1685 Louis XIV revoked the Edict entirely, leaving French Protestants little choice but conversion to Catholicism. Some went underground or did convert, but perhaps as many as 200,000 left for the Dutch Republic, Prussia, England, and the New World, depriving France of valuable skills and experience.

Although the Jansenists were smaller in number than the Huguenots, they had many prominent followers, including the philosopher Blaise Pascal (see Topic 48) and many of the magistrates in the Paris parlement. The Jansenists formed a closely knit group whose theological beliefs about predestination were close to those of Calvinism. They asserted the central importance of God's grace in achieving salvation, questioned the authority of all human beings, including kings and popes, and openly opposed the Jesuits. In 1660, Louis XIV persuaded the papacy to ban Jansenism and then destroyed its headquarters at Port-Royal.

The attacks against the Huguenots and the Jansenists earned Louis a reputation as a religious bigot and persecutor, but Louis saw both issues as a matter of religious unity and in terms of the maintenance of his authority as an absolute ruler.

WAR, DIPLOMACY, AND THE QUEST FOR FRENCH HEGEMONY

Louis XIV was a man obsessed by the quest for glory—for France, certainly, but above all for himself. He believed that his achievements would reflect on the French people, and to that end he embarked on a succession of foreign wars that some authorities believe was aimed at achieving what he called France's "natural boundaries"—the Rhine, the Pyrenees, the Alps, and the sea. In the process, Louis created the image of an aggressive, warlike France, and made himself an object of hatred throughout Europe.

MILITARY REFORM

In planning and executing his wars, as in pursuing his other policies, Louis XIV had the help of able advisers. From his vantage point as head of economic planning, Colbert had become an advocate of French sea power, having expended huge sums on building a strong navy and a merchant marine. Colbert believed that the chief obstacle to French commercial predominance was the Dutch Republic, the most prosperous trading state, in whose ships much of Europe's trade goods were carried.

In contrast to Colbert's naval strategy, the argument for a powerful land army was made by François Le Tellier, the marquis de Louvois (1641–1691). Louvois, who succeeded his father as war minister in 1666, encouraged Louis XIV in his search for military glory. He completely reorganized the army, introducing the idea of promotion on the basis of merit, providing his troops with standard uniforms, and standardizing enlistment and drafting procedures. Colonel Jean Martinet (?–1672) introduced such vigorous drill regulations that his name became a synonym for a strict disciplinarian. Gradually, Louvois increased the size of the army from about 20,000 to 400,000. He also created the first real "standing army," a permanent military force always ready for deployment, which took the place of both the mercenary private armies and the old fighting groups raised for specific purposes and commanded by feudal nobles. Such a regular army created the need for much greater government revenue. Furthermore, Louvois set up an elaborate supply system, replete with supply depots, and greatly increasing the production of munitions and gunpowder. Working alongside Louvois was Marshal Sébastien de Vauban (1633–1707), the greatest military engineer of the age. He designed and built a ring of fortresses and fortified towns to protect the frontiers, an approach to defense that the French followed for the next 300 years. He also planned brilliant siege operations against enemy installations.

THE WAR OF DEVOLUTION AND THE DUTCH CAMPAIGN

Louis' first foreign adventure was the War of Devolution (1667–1668), waged against Spain on the basis of a claim to the Spanish Netherlands through his wife, the daughter of Philip IV's first marriage. The immediate point of the claim was that Louis had never received the large dowry that Philip had promised to pay.

When the Spanish king died and left all of his property to a son by a second marriage, Louis protested and called on an old Flemish tradition whereby property devolved to the children of a first marriage. Louis launched an attack against the fortified cities of Flanders and Franche-Comté

(Burgundy). Victory seemed in his grasp, but England, Sweden, and the United Provinces joined in an alliance and forced Louis to the peace table. By the treaty of Aix-la-Chapelle (1668), Spain ceded to France strategic sections of the Belgian Netherlands, including fortified cities. The first of his wars ended, therefore, with a minor victory for Louis, intensifying his thirst for glory.

Louis blamed the Dutch for having organized the alliance against him and believed that the Dutch would make an easy target because their country was on the edge of civil war. The republican, middle-class government there, which Louis despised, was led by Jan De Witt (1625–1672), whose party was supported by middle-class town dwellers, the wealthiest business leaders, aristocrats, and religious liberals. The head of the opposition was the prince of Orange, William III (*stadholder* of the United Provinces 1672–1702, king of England 1689–1702), whose family had held the title of *stadholder* for generations and had the backing of the Calvinist clergy and nobles.

Louis declared war against the Dutch Republic in 1672, and De Witt assumed command of the Dutch forces. The French marched rapidly into Lorraine, and from there down the Rhine into the Dutch Republic. The Dutch murdered De Witt and his brother, whom they blamed for their setbacks, and William III took command. Acting boldly, William organized a determined Dutch resistance and ordered the dikes opened, thereby flooding the northern areas of the Dutch Republic and halting the French advance. But when Louis refused the generous peace terms offered by William, he aroused the fears of Prussia, the Holy Roman Empire, and Spain into joining a coalition against him. When Parliament forced Charles II of England to join the anti-French alliance, Louis agreed to make peace. The Dutch, who promised henceforth to remain neutral, lost nothing. Instead, in the treaties of Nijmegen (1678 and 1679), Spain agreed to surrender to France the province of Franche-Comté and several fortified sections of Flanders, the latter areas being contiguous to those obtained in the War of Devolution.

THE WAR OF THE LEAGUE OF AUGSBURG

The prestige of Louis XIV and the international stature of France were at a new high, although this had been achieved at a great cost. Louis had succeeded in extending French frontiers, but he nevertheless aspired to win greater glory on the battlefield. The precise extent of his ambitions remains unclear, but to his foreign contemporaries his goal appeared to be nothing less than the establishment of French hegemony over the West. Within a few years after the last Nijmegen treaty in 1679, Louis began pushing along his northern and eastern borders, where a medley of tiny estates, towns, and fiefs coexisted without clear jurisdiction. His most important gain in this process was Strasbourg, the principal city of Alsace, which he absorbed in 1681. Alarmed by this thrust into Germany, Emperor Leopold I (ruled 1658–1705) of the Holy Roman Empire formed the League of Augsburg in 1686, eventually bringing German states such as Saxony, Bavaria, and the Palatinate together with England, Spain, Sweden, and the United Provinces. It was this League against which the ever bolder Louis XIV fought his third war.

The conflict had its immediate origins in the fall of 1688, when Louis sent an army into the Palatinate, a territory located west of the Rhine. This War of the League of Augsburg assumed an international character as a result of the fighting between France and England in North America, the West Indies, and India, where it was known as "King William's War." In the two earlier wars, Louis had enjoyed the neutrality of England, but the Glorious Revolution that unseated the English monarch now put William III of Orange, Louis' staunch enemy, on the English throne (see Topic 51). William set as his goal the defeat of France. The war began in 1689 and lasted almost a decade. For the first several years, the French armies won one important victory after another in Europe, while the war at sea went in favor of the allies. The Peace of Ryswick (1697) followed a long and ruinous struggle that drained French economic strength and manpower. By its terms, Louis was forced to give back all the territories that his "chambers of reunion" had declared to be his, with the exception of Strasbourg. In addition, the borders of the Spanish Netherlands were henceforth to be protected by Dutch soldiers, and Louis promised to reduce the high import tariffs against Dutch goods that Colbert had introduced. Perhaps most humiliating of all, Louis had to recognize William III as the legitimate king of England.

THE WAR OF THE SPANISH SUCCESSION

The fourth and last war of Louis XIV brought the Sun King full circle. Louis had been induced to conclude a peace agreement in 1697 because he saw a grand opportunity to achieve Bourbon dominance over Spain. Although greatly weakened, the Spanish crown still controlled a vast empire in America as well as a portion of the Netherlands and the southern half of Italy. The hapless King Charles II (ruled 1665–1700), the son born from Philip IV's second marriage, proved to be the last Hapsburg king of Spain. Because Charles had no direct heirs, Louis hoped to gain the Spanish throne for one of his own children, since the dowry of his Spanish wife had never been paid. The major stumbling block was the fact that the Emperor Leopold I, a Hapsburg, was the nearest male relative of Charles II and therefore claimed the Spanish throne for himself.

The War of the Spanish Succession (1701–1714) brought together the Grand Alliance of England, the Holy Roman Empire, the United Provinces, Hanover, and several German princes, all determined that Louis XIV would not get his way. For his part, Louis had joined forces with Savoy and Bavaria, although England later persuaded the duke of Savoy to change sides in return for the title of king. The brilliant John Churchill, duke of Marlborough (1650–1722), drove the French from Germany at the Battle of Blenheim in 1704, while Prince Eugene of Savoy (1663–1736) pushed them out of Italy. A bloody engagement at Malplaquet in 1709 secured the Spanish Netherlands for the allies at the cost of an unprecedented 40,000 casualties. As one defeat followed another for the French, Louis XIV rallied his subjects with a patriotic appeal and called up his last recruits, melting gold ornaments from Versailles to raise the necessary funds to fight the war.

By 1712, an exhausted France and a weakened Grand Alliance agreed to a negotiated settlement. William III had died at the beginning of the war, but his successor, Queen Anne (ruled 1702–1714), pursued the conflict relentlessly in the colonies and on the seas, where it was known as "Queen Anne's War." When the Tories came to power, however, they pushed for peace. Moreover, Leopold's son became emperor as Charles VI (ruled 1711–1740), raising the specter of a Hapsburg ruling Spain, Austria, and the Holy Roman Empire. The Treaty of Utrecht (1713) recognized Louis' grandson as King Philip V (ruled 1713–1746) of Spain, with the stipulation that the thrones of Spain and France would never be united. As compensation, the Hapsburgs of Austria obtained the Spanish Netherlands, Naples, Milan, and Sardinia. Britain's reward was in the form of overseas possessions, gaining Newfoundland, Nova Scotia, and Hudson's Bay from France, and Gibraltar, along with the *Asiento* (a monopoly of the slave trade going to Spanish America) from Spain. The Dutch got back their frontier fortifications, while the Hohenzollern ruler of Brandenburg was recognized as king of Prussia.

As a result of the War of the Spanish Succession, France lost colonies but none of its European territory and had the satisfaction of seeing a Bourbon on the throne of Spain. Louis' daring bid for hegemony had failed, although it had taken the combined weight of Europe's great powers to defeat him. France was burdened with a devastated economy, marked by inflation, a huge debt, ever-higher taxes, and a serious decline in its overseas trade. Crop failures and famine made the conditions caused by war even worse.

Putting Louis XIV in Perspective

The long reign of Louis XIV was fraught with contradictions: Versailles stands not only as the timeless symbol of royal grandeur, but also as an expression of the ambition of one man. As a result of the succession of costly wars that he fought, Louis succeeded in acquiring more territory than any French monarch since the Middle Ages, but the wars also weakened the absolutist state that he had worked so tirelessly to create. He did not succeed in stamping out Protestantism in France, and the prosperity built by Colbert dissipated. Even the immense authority that he accumulated could not be passed on intact to his successors. In the end, the historical memory of glittering mirrors and elegant palaces remains as the vivid legacy of Louis XIV. Yet perhaps only a grand monarch of his stature could have acknowledged his own limitations—on his deathbed in 1715, the Sun King lectured his heir, the Dauphin Louis, to avoid the excesses of state spending and war that he had pursued so relentlessly.

Questions for Further Study

1. How would you describe the goals and methods of the absolutist state?
2. What was the nature of the relationship between Louis XIV and the French nobility? What role did Versailles play in that relationship?
3. Were Louis XIV's foreign policies a failure or a success?

Suggestions for Further Reading

Beik, William. *Absolutism and Society in Seventeenth-Century France*. New York, 1985.

Briggs, Robin. *Early Modern France, 1560–1715*. New York, 1977.

Burke, Peter. *The Fabrication of Louis XIV*. New Haven, CT, 1992.

Dunlap, Ian. *Louis XIV*. New York, 2000.

Goubert, Pierre. *Louis XIV and Twenty Million Frenchmen*. New York, 1972.

Hattan, R.M., ed. *Louis XIV and Absolutism*. Columbus, OH, 1977.

Kettering, Sharon. *French Society, 1589-1715*. Harlow, 2001.

Le Roy Ladurie, Emmanuel, with the collaboration of Jean-Francois Fitou. Arthur Goldhammer, trans. *Saint-Simon and the Court of Louis XIV*. Chicago, 2001.

Mettam, Roger. *Power and Faction in Louis XIV's France*. Oxford, 1988.

Rule, John, ed. *Louis XIV and the Craft of Kingship*. Columbus, OH, 1970.

InfoTrac College Edition

Enter the search term *Louis XIV* using Key Terms.

ENGLAND AND THE RISE OF CONSTITUTIONAL MONARCHY

The general trend toward absolute monarchy in the 17th century, exemplified by the reign of Louis XIV in France, revealed several exceptions: Poland, the United Provinces, and principally England. In the latter, despite the centralizing efforts of the Tudor rulers, especially Elizabeth I, a different tradition of government developed. A special set of religious, economic, and social conditions, combined with the peculiar personalities of Elizabeth's successors, led to the taming of royal authority.

Restrictions on royal power had been evolving in England since the Middle Ages. Feudal nobles, resisting encroachments on their rights by the kings, had enacted a series of charters that sought to protect basic liberties against royal tyranny. Parliament, consisting of the House of Lords and the House of Commons, had acquired increasing control over legislation and taxation. Finally, much of English common law, made up of legal customs and precedents compiled by judges over the centuries, had the effect of reinforcing individual rights. So strong had the force of common law become that some legal scholars argued that even the king was bound by it.

In the first half of the 17th century, the English had directly assaulted the principle of absolute monarchy. The confrontation between Parliament and the Stuart kings led to the dictatorial rule of Oliver Cromwell. Cromwell's death created a general sense of relief but left the country without an effective government. The restoration of the Stuart family to the throne in 1660 was therefore a widely popular move. Nevertheless, it seemed that the Stuarts were incapable of learning any lessons from the bloody fate of their predecessor, Charles I. In 1688, three years after the accession of James II, England experienced the "Glorious" Revolution, in which William III of the United Provinces and his wife Mary, daughter of James II, were put on the throne. In accepting the partnership of Parliament, the new monarchs eliminated any further danger of absolute monarchy in England.

Parliamentary rule continued to evolve during the course of the 18th century, as a new form of government began to develop in which day-to-day executive power was exercised by a cabinet of ministers that was responsible to the House of Commons. The members of the elected house came increasingly from two political parties: the Whigs and the Tories.

Portrait of Charles II of England. Late 17th century. Seen here in an uncharacteristically serious mood, Charles was known as the "Merry Monarch." The restoration of the monarchy in England, which he ushered in, saw a revival of the arts and scientific studies. Restoration drama, in particular comedy, marked one of the high points in the history of the theater in England.

THE STUART RESTORATION

Cromwell's experiment with republicanism convinced a majority of the English people that monarchy—albeit a chastised monarchy with severely limited powers—was a better system of government. The tumultuous experiences of the past 50 years made it clear not only that Parliament must share power with the monarch, but also that moderate Protestantism was firmly entrenched in England. Surprisingly, neither Charles II nor James II proved capable of absorbing these lessons.

CHARLES II

Known as the "Merry Monarch," Charles II (ruled 1660–1685) was a man who combined refined taste and polished manners with lustful appetites. The Puritans, scandalized by his private life, accused him of indulging in "fornication, drunkenness, and adultery." He was an avid patron of the theater, and among his numerous mistresses was the actress Nell Gwyn (1650–1687), who bore him two sons. Cromwell's rigid Calvinist policies, including the banning of plays, sports, and popular music, had never been well received, and Charles now presided over a reinvigorated court life and a new moral laxity among the nobility. Gambling was the rage, and the king led the way in hunting, dancing, and riding. Restoration drama was particularly known for bawdy scenes and dialogue that Puritans found shocking. A monarch without principles, Charles was a shrewd tactician, always willing to compromise or retreat. With the memory of his father's beheading always vivid, he trusted no one; the king, wrote one of his advisers, "lived with his ministers as he did with his mistresses; he used them but he was not in love with them."

At first, there was little evidence to suggest that a strong monarchy would be restored with the Stuarts, and the notion of "divine right" did not resurface. No effort was made to reestablish either the special law courts used against the enemies of the crown or the king's old feudal privileges. The return of the Stuarts brought with it the restoration of Anglicanism as the state church in England and Ireland. In Scotland, where it had never been established, Charles encountered serious opposition in his efforts to impose Anglicanism. Those Protestants who refused to accept the Church of England were called dissenters, groups that were especially numerous among artisans and merchants. Legal restrictions were imposed on dissenters, including the Corporation Act (1661), which excluded them from town offices. The next year, Charles issued the Declaration of Indulgence, designed to grant tolerance to Catholics and dissenters. In response, the strongly Anglican Parliament passed the Act of Uniformity (1662), which required clergymen to accept the *Anglican Book of Common Prayer* and deprived more than 1,000 Calvinist ministers of their parishes.

Charles II remained uncomfortable with the Church of England because at heart he and his brother James were Catholics—both had been influenced by their mother and the strongly Catholic atmosphere of the French court, where they had spent their exile. This problem ultimately caused the final undoing of the Stuarts. In 1670, Charles concluded the secret Treaty of Dover with Louis XIV, whereby he secured a financial subsidy in return for supporting the French war against the United Provinces and swearing to convert to Catholicism. But in view of the strong anti-Catholic sentiment in the realm, Charles was careful to keep his sentiments to himself. In 1673 he was forced to withdraw the Declaration of Indulgence in place of the Test Act, which drove Catholics from office. Anti-Catholic sentiment reached a new pitch in 1678, when rumors of a "Popish Plot," deliberately manufactured by a rogue named Titus Oates (1649–1705), caused people to believe that Catholics intended to assassinate the king, burn London, and massacre Protestants. In Oxford, a crowd surrounded the royal coach in the mistaken belief that it contained the king's Catholic mistress. Nell Gwyn, who was in fact inside, pleaded with the mob, "Pray good people, be civil; I am the *Protestant* whore." Only when near death in 1685 did Charles formally convert to Catholicism.

JAMES II AND THE CRISIS OF THE RESTORATION

Because Charles II had no legitimate children, the crown was due to pass to his brother James, the duke of York (ruled as king, 1685–1688). Less tactful than Charles, James had declared his conversion in 1672. In the aftermath of the Popish Plot, however, Parliament tried several times to enact an Exclusion Bill that would have kept James or any other Catholic from the royal succession. The issue of whether Parliament had the right to change the succession to the crown was of great importance. The bill failed to pass, but from the debates that it engendered there eventually emerged two distinct factions, or "parties." The Whig party, which supported the bill, gained the backing of a variety of people, from liberal Anglicans and landowners who wanted to strengthen Parliament against the king to dissenters and the business class. The Tory group, which opposed the Exclusion Bill, favored a strong hereditary monarchy and sought to avoid another destructive civil war. (The words *Whig* and *Tory* were originally labels used by one side to slander the other: *Whig* was the term for a Scottish horse thief, while *Tory* was the term for an Irish cattle rustler.) Because the Whigs were divided among themselves, however, Charles was able to fend off their efforts. Nor were the Whigs the only opponents of the king; a widespread radical underground had opposed royal authority since the start of the Restoration.

When James succeeded to the throne in 1685, he took the place of a king who had actually succeeded in strengthening the monarchy and in ruling for the last four years without Parliament. But James lacked his brother's political skills, and within several years dramatic changes took place in England's political order. His Catholic beliefs, together with his increasing emphasis on royal authority, aroused widespread fear and opposition. Trouble erupted from the moment James became king; uprisings in Scotland and England greeted his accession, although he put them down easily.

Like Charles, James promised to uphold the constitutional system and the Anglican Church, but he soon gave evidence to the contrary. He created a professional standing army run by Catholic officers, which he stationed near London, a move that shocked even his Tory supporters. In open violation of the Test Act of 1673, he used a Declaration of Indulgence to appoint Catholics and others to posts in local and royal government, as well as in Oxford and Cambridge Universities, arguing in self-defense that he was not subject to previous parliamentary acts. In 1688, he issued a second Declaration of Indulgence, and when seven Anglican bishops—including the archbishop of Canterbury—refused to read it from their pulpits, he had them arrested, although they were later acquitted.

James II pushed royal authority to the limits, but the event that brought his reign to the crisis point was the birth of a son. Until then, his heirs had been two daughters by a first marriage—Mary (1662–1694), who had married her cousin William III of the United Provinces (see Topic 50), and Anne (1665–1714), who married a Danish prince. These daughters and their husbands were all Protestants, so that the prospect of one of them inheriting the throne had not caused alarm among the English. But in June 1688, a son was born to James and his second wife, the Catholic Mary Beatrice (1658–1718). Because this son took precedence over his half-sisters in the royal succession, this meant that England would one day have a Catholic king, a prospect that the nobles and gentry found intolerable.

Map 51.1 England and the Netherlands, c. 1688. Note the break between the Austrian Netherlands, under Hapsburg rule, and the United Provinces of Holland. The period saw the growth of Amsterdam from a medieval fishing village to one of the leading commercial centers of Europe. Although The Hague is the seat of government in Holland, Amsterdam remains its economic heart.

THE GLORIOUS REVOLUTION

The events in England that followed the birth of James II's son in 1688 have been dubbed the "Glorious" Revolution—an upheaval that forced James from the throne and inaugurated the era of constitutional monarchy with the reign of William and Mary.

WILLIAM AND MARY

English leaders, both Whig and Tory alike, quickly joined forces to oust James. They made proposals to William III of Orange, *stadholder* of the Dutch Republic, to assume the crown with his English wife Mary, James II's daughter. Risking his fleet and the independence of his own country, William landed an invasion force of 14,000 men at Torbay on the southwest coast of England in early November. James quickly discovered that most of his soldiers had deserted him. In December, after having been once captured, he escaped and fled to France, where he joined his young son, who was known as the "Old Pretender," and recognized by Louis XIV as the legitimate English sovereign. Although the fighting in England was minor, in Ireland a popular Catholic uprising in support of James erupted. William crushed the Irish revolt only in July 1690 at the Battle of the Boyne, in which his 35,000 troops defeated some 21,000 Catholic soldiers. In the process, William executed priests and political leaders and devastated much of the land.

THE TRIUMPH OF PARLIAMENT

This unspectacular but tradition-breaking revolution was a decisive turning point in the development of representative government. Early in 1689, Parliament drafted the Declaration of Rights, the fundamental document on which the Revolutionary Settlement of 1689 rested. This Bill of Rights (as it became known once enacted into law) stipulated that all sovereigns were to be Anglican. More important, it provided that the sovereign could not suspend laws or interfere with free speech, elections, or parliamentary discussion. Furthermore, Parliament was to meet regularly, and the monarch could neither maintain an army nor levy taxes without its consent, whereas the people had the right to petition the ruler. The bill also safeguarded individual rights, making it illegal for an English citizen to be arrested without a warrant or denied just bail. In addition, Parliament approved the Toleration Act, which barred non-Anglicans from public office and imposed severe restrictions on Catholics, but which granted all Protestants full freedom of worship. The triumph of Parliament as set forth in these reforms fundamentally altered the nature of government in England.

William and Mary were asked to accept the Declaration of Rights before being offered the crown. They agreed to rule jointly because William would not tolerate serving merely as Queen Mary's consort, and Mary refused to rule by herself. Only 15 years old when they had married, Mary made herself subservient to her husband and was constantly humiliated by William's mistress, who lived in the

Engraving showing William and Mary being presented with the crown of England. Late 17th century. The representatives of the church stand to the left, while the presentation is accompanied by a proclamation of the Declaration of Rights, read by the Lord Chief Justice. William and Mary could not be crowned until they had accepted the conditions set out in this document.

PERSPECTIVES FROM THE PAST

RESISTANCE AND REVOLUTION

As the power and authority of centralized states expanded in the 15th and 16th centuries, some political philosophers and active opponents of the absolute monarchs developed theoretical arguments sustaining the right of resistance. Religious reformers like Luther and Calvin, no matter how conservative their political and social views, contributed to the theory of resistance by allowing that magistrates could oppose superior authority in order to uphold divine law. During the wars of religion in France, Huguenots claimed that royal tyrants were not ruling with God's will and that because the king's role was to defend justice, magistrates could legitimately oppose those who failed to do so. This was the theme of an influential work by Philippe Duplessis-Mornay, *A Defense of Liberty Against Tyrants* (1579). The argument was broadened significantly some years later by the Catholic philosopher Juan de Mariana, whose essay on *The King and the Education of the King* (1598) extended the right of resistance to ordinary citizens in cases where kings deliberately violated their own laws and the well-being of their subjects. During the 17th century, other writers expanded on the theory of resistance, especially under the influence of Enlightenment thought.

The English Bill of Rights

In 1689, after the Glorious Revolution, Parliament passed the Bill of Rights, which guaranteed basic civil rights and consolidated the gains of the revolution.

Whereas the said late King James II having abdicated the government, and the throne being thereby vacant, his Highness the prince of Orange (whom it hath pleased Almighty God to make the glorious instrument of delivering this kingdom from popery and arbitrary power) did (by the device of the lords spiritual and temporal, and diverse principal persons of the Commons) cause letters to be written to the lords spiritual and temporal, being Protestants, and other letters to the several counties, cities, universities, boroughs, and Cinque Ports [five port towns on the English Channel, having special privileges], for the choosing of such persons to represent them, as were of right to be sent to parliament, to meet and sit at Westminster upon the two and twentieth day of January, in this year 1689, in order to such an establishment as that their religion, laws, and liberties might not again be in danger of being subverted; upon which letters elections have been accordingly made.

And thereupon the said lords spiritual and temporal and Commons, pursuant to their respective letters and elections, being now assembled in a full and free representation of this nation, taking into their most serious consideration the best means for attaining the ends aforesaid, do in the first place (as their ancestors in like case have usually done), for the vindication and assertion of their ancient rights and liberties, declare:

1. That the pretended power of suspending laws, or the execution of laws, by regal authority, without consent of parliament is illegal.
2. That the pretended power of dispensing with the laws, or the execution of law by regal authority, as it hath been assumed and exercised of late, is illegal.
3. That the commission for erecting the late court of commissioners for ecclesiastical causes, and all other commissions and courts of like nature, are illegal and pernicious.
4. That levying money for or to the use of the crown by pretense of prerogative, without grant of parliament, for longer time or in other manner than the same is or shall be granted, is illegal.
5. That it is the right of the subjects to petition the king, and all commitments and prosecutions for such petitioning are illegal.

6. That the raising or keeping a standing army within the kingdom in time of peace, unless it be with consent of parliament, is against law.

7. That the subjects which are Protestants may have arms for their defense suitable to their conditions, and as allowed by law.

8. That election of members of parliament ought to be free.

9. That the freedom of speech, and debates or proceedings in parliament, ought not to be impeached or questioned in any court or place out of parliament.

10. That excessive bail ought not to be required, nor excessive fines imposed, nor cruel and unusual punishments inflicted.

11. That jurors ought to be duly impaneled and returned, and jurors which pass upon men in trials for high treason ought to be freeholders.

12. That all grants and promises of fines and forfeitures of particular persons before conviction are illegal and void.

13. And that for redress of all grievances, and for the amending, strengthening, and preserving of the laws, parliament ought to be held frequently.

From *The Statutes,* Eyre and Spotiswoode, Copyright © 1871.

Locke's Second Treatise on Government

John Locke, one of the most influential thinkers of the Enlightenment, wrote the Second Treatise *between 1681 and 1683, before the Glorious Revolution. The essay proposed government as the guarantor of life, liberty, and property, the three essential points of Enlightenment political ideals, and influenced colonial leaders during the American Revolution.*

When any one, or more, shall take upon them to make laws, whom the people have not appointed so to do, they make laws without authority, which the people are not therefore bound to obey; by which means they come again to be out of subjection, and may constitute to themselves a new legislative, as they think best, being in full liberty to resist the force of those, who without authority would impose any thing upon them. Every one is at the disposure of his own will, when those who had, by the delegation of the society, the declaring of the public will, are excluded from it, and others usurp the place, who have no such authority or delegation. . . .

In these and the like cases, *when the government is dissolved,* the people are at liberty to provide for themselves, by erecting a new legislative, differing from the other, by the change of persons, or form, or both, as they shall find it most for their safety and good. For the *society* can never, by the fault of another, lose the native and original right it has to preserve itself; which can only be done by a settled legislative, and a fair and impartial execution of the laws made by it. But the state of mankind is not so miserable that they are not capable of using this remedy, till it be too late to look for any. To tell *people* they *may provide for themselves,* by erecting a new legislative, when by oppression, artifice, or being delivered over to a foreign power, their old one is gone, is only to tell them, they may expect relief when it is too late, and the evil is past cure. This is in effect no more, than to bid them first be slaves, and then to take care of their liberty; and when their chains are on, tell them, they may act like freemen. This, if barely so, is rather mockery than relief; and men can never be secure from tyranny, if there be no means to escape it, till they are perfectly under it: And therefore it is, that they have not only a right to get out of it, but to prevent it. . . .

From David Wootton, ed., *Modern Political Thought: Readings from Machiavelli to Nietzsche,* Hackett Publishing Co., copyright © 1996.

Rousseau on the Social Contract

In 1771 Rousseau wrote An Inquiry into the Nature of the Social Contract *in which he added to theories of the social contract the notion of the General Will, a universal moral law through which humans recognized their interdependence and advocated the idea that the people have the right to dissolve the contract.*

What, then, is the government? An intermediate body established between the subjects

Continued

and the sovereign for their mutual correspondence, charged with the execution of the laws and with the maintenance of liberty both civil and political. [Book III, Chapter 1.]

So soon as the people are lawfully assembled as a sovereign body, the whole jurisdiction of the government ceases, the executive power is suspended, and the person of the meanest citizen is as sacred and inviolable as that of the first magistrate, because where the represented are, there is no longer any representative. [Book III, Chapter 14.]

These assemblies, which have as their object the maintenance of the social treaty, ought always to be opened with two propositions, which no one should be able to suppress, and which should pass separately by vote. The first: "Whether it pleases the sovereign to maintain the present form of government." The second: "Whether it pleases the people to leave the administration to those at present entrusted with it."

I presuppose here what I believe I have proved, viz., that there is in the State no fundamental law which cannot be revoked, not even this social compact; for if all the citizens assembled in order to break the compact by a solemn agreement, no one can doubt that it could be quite legitimately broken. [Book III, Chapter 18.]

From Lynn Hunt, Thomas R. Martin, Barbara H. Rosenwein, R. Po-chia Hsia, Bonnie G. Smith, eds., *Connecting with the Past,* Vol. I, D.C. Heath, Copyright © 1995.

The Declaration of Independence

When Thomas Jefferson drafted the Declaration of Independence in 1776, he had in mind the writings of Locke and other European philosophes.

When in the course of human events, it becomes necessary for one people to dissolve the political bands which have connected them

royal palace. Nevertheless, because William was frequently out of the country conducting military campaigns, Mary ruled alone for much of the time, a task she carried out with intelligence and vigor. Outwardly, William treated her with bad-tempered indifference, but when she died of smallpox in 1694, he grieved deeply.

The forces that controlled Parliament and had brought about these settlements were by no means democratic. The House of Lords, whose members were appointed by the monarch, was composed of landed nobility and could veto legislation passed by the Commons. The system of election for the House of Commons enabled the nobles and landed gentry to control the countryside, but the wealthy members of the middle class who exercised influence in the cities were hardly represented in the House. For a century and a half after the Glorious Revolution, England was ruled by an essentially aristocratic Parliament that chiefly represented the interests of the landlords.

After the Glorious Revolution, the temporary alliance that had bound Tories and Whigs together in common opposition to James II fell apart. Real socioeconomic differences separated the Whig and the Tory parties: the Tories, who had supported the revolution reluctantly, were landed gentry whose interests centered on rural life and who wanted England to keep aloof from continental affairs; the Whigs, by contrast, were active in commerce and overseas trade and had seen the revolution as a chance to secure the supremacy of Parliament over the king.

Taxation was now under the control of Parliament, and with state finances on a stable footing as a result of parliamentary supervision, private bankers were more willing to lend money to the government. Unable to raise taxes, William therefore borrowed more than one million pounds to fight the War of the League of Augsburg. In this way, the concept of a permanent national debt, as opposed to private royal debts, came into being. In 1694, with the approval of Parliament, he took the extraordinary step of granting a royal charter to the Bank of England, a private institution that managed the national debt by holding government deposits, sending funds abroad, and advancing credits. England also reformed its monetary system and issued new coinage in consultation with Sir Isaac Newton, master of the Mint. In addition, regular procedures were established for issuing insurance and trading stocks, thus creating an environment in which commerce and manufacturing could prosper.

THE LEGITIMACY OF REVOLUTION

Together with the mid-century Civil War, the Glorious Revolution of 1688–1689 broke the pattern of absolutist government that had entrenched itself elsewhere in Europe. The principal theorist of the Glorious Revolution was John Locke (1632–1704), whose ideas had circulated before 1688, especially among the Whigs. In *Two Treatises on Civil Government* (1690), Locke sought to justify the events of 1688 (on Locke as an Enlightenment figure, see Topic 58).

with another, and to assume among the powers of the earth, the separate and equal station to which the laws of nature and of nature's God entitle them, a decent respect to the opinions of mankind requires that they should declare the causes which impel them to the separation.— We hold these truths to be self-evident, that all men are created equal, that they are endowed by their Creator with certain unalienable rights, that among these are life, liberty, and the pursuit of happiness—That to secure these rights, governments are instituted among men, deriving their just powers from the consent of the governed,—That whenever any form of government becomes destructive of these ends, it is the right of the people to alter or to abolish it, and to institute new government, laying its foundation on such principles and organizing its powers in such form, as to them shall seem most likely to effect their safety and happiness. Prudence, indeed, will dictate that gov-

ernments long established should not be changed for light and transient causes; and accordingly all experience hath shewn, that mankind are more disposed to suffer, while evils are sufferable, than to right themselves by abolishing the forms to which they are accustomed. But when a long train of abuses and usurpations, pursuing invariably the same object evinces a design to reduce them under absolute despotism, it is their right, it is their duty, to throw off such government, and to provide new guards for their future security.—Such has been the patient sufferance of these colonies; and such is now the necessity which constrains them to alter their former systems of government. The history of the present king of Great Britain is a history of repeated injuries and usurpations, all having in direct object the establishment of an absolute tyranny over these states. To prove this, let facts be submitted to a candid world.

Portrait of John Locke, c. 1700. His writings played a major role in the Glorious Revolution, and he also became one of the founders of the European Enlightenment. He published the theoretical arguments on which the Declaration of Rights was based, *Two Treatises of Civil Government,* in 1690, the year after William and Mary's accession.

By Courtesy of the National Portrait Gallery, London

Locke believed that in order to escape the brutalities of their original "state of nature," people established government and set up rulers, whose principal role was to defend the natural rights of individuals in society. In establishing a "social contract" with their ruler, subjects gave up part of their natural rights, but they retained the fundamental rights to life, liberty, and the pursuit of property. If the sovereign interfered with these rights, or failed to protect them, then the people were free to remove him. Other revolutionaries, in America and in France, would later use Locke's "right to revolution."

THE CABINET SYSTEM AND THE HOUSE OF COMMONS

In the years following the Glorious Revolution, England not only developed the fundamental institutions of constitutional monarchy but also evolved the principles and practice of ministerial government. As a result, by the mid-18th century Parliament had extended its reach beyond its legislative functions and into the executive branch of government.

With the backing of the Whig party, William III spent much of his energy and considerable resources on war and diplomacy, for the Glorious Revolution had taken place in the midst of the wars of Louis XIV. Because of his interest in foreign affairs, William tended to leave the administration of domestic matters to his ministers. By day-to-day practice rather than by design, the king soon discovered that the government ran more smoothly, and policy matters were settled more easily, if all of his ministers were from the same party that controlled the House of Commons. Thus he began to appoint Whig ministers when the Whigs held a majority in the Commons and Tories when they were in the preponderance. In this way, the ability of a cabinet—as the body of ministers came to be called—to remain in office depended increasingly on its ability to command the confidence of a majority in Parliament. To this day, this principle of "ministerial responsibility" prevails, and government ministers must appear before the House of Commons to answer the questions of its members.

Because the Glorious Revolution was, in an immediate sense, a struggle to determine the royal succession, Parliament continued to assert its authority in this vital area. When Queen Mary died, William ruled by himself, but thereafter the succession was in doubt because William and Mary were childless. In 1701, Parliament passed the Act of Settlement, which excluded the son of James II and all other Catholics. Instead, the crown was to pass to Mary's sister, Anne. If Anne did not have children, the crown would then go at her death to Sophia (1630–1714), the granddaughter of James I and the wife of the elector of the German state of Hanover.

GOOD QUEEN ANNE

On William's death in 1702, Anne (ruled 1702–1714) became queen of England. A rather dull woman, she was fat and so crippled with gout that she had to be carried in a chair during her coronation. But she drew a deliberate contrast between William, who was Dutch by birth and sentiment, and her own "English heart," and won the sympathy of the British people, who called her "Good Queen Anne." In a less worshipful mood, a popular ballad of the day alluded to "Brandy-faced Nan," in view of the fact that she was a heavy drinker.

Unlike her predecessor, Anne's reign was marked by tensions between royal authority and Parliament. She disagreed often with Parliament and was one of the last English rulers to veto its acts and to preside regularly over cabinet meetings. Near the end of her life, she also broke with what was fast becoming established tradition when she appointed a Tory cabinet despite a Whig majority in the House of Commons. Yet Anne was careful to avoid any real crisis because she realized that her half-brother—the son of James II—still had many supporters.

In order to make sure that the thrones of both England and Scotland would pass to the Protestant descendants of Sophia of Hanover, in 1707 the parliaments of the two realms enacted the Act of Union, which created a single state known as the United Kingdom of Great Britain. The English Parliament was transformed into the Parliament of the United Kingdom, which now included Scottish lords and commoners. The union was achieved in part by force and pressure, but many Scots saw the advantages of dissolving the trade barriers between the two territories. The Scots kept their own court system but lost their own parliament and their capital. In Ireland, on the other hand, where William had returned to a harsh policy of restrictions against the Catholics, peace still proved elusive.

As a sovereign, Anne was surrounded constantly with male politicians, but in private she preferred the company and the advice of Sarah Churchill (1660–1744), the wife of the brilliant military commander John Churchill. Sarah Churchill had become Anne's trusted friend before the Glorious Revolution and had helped the princess escape during the upheaval in 1688. When Anne ascended the throne, she appointed her friend to lady of the queen's bedchamber, a position in which Sarah gained significant political influence. A Whig in politics, she dispensed patronage, controlled the cabinet, and helped herself to a large pension. Eventually, Sarah's increasingly haughty attitude alienated Anne, and she fell from royal favor.

THE BRITISH CONSTITUTION IN THE AGE OF WALPOLE

Queen Anne, who died in 1714, was the last Stuart monarch. Although she had 17 pregnancies, only five babies were born alive, and none of her children lived past the

Portrait of George I of England. Early 18th century. In 1714, George became the first Hanoverian ruler of England. Originally ruler of the German state of Hanover, he appears here in the robes of the English monarchy. He was never very popular with his subjects, perhaps because he made no serious effort to learn English.

age of eleven. She was succeeded by the first Hanoverian king, George I (ruled 1714–1727). George, a German who never learned English and had little interest in British affairs, was not terribly popular with his new subjects. He was not interested in the details of government, and at first he even tried to conduct cabinet meetings in broken Latin, but quickly gave that up and stopped attending them. Instead, the king left politics and the administration of the kingdom in the hands of his ministers.

During this period, the office of prime minister became increasingly important. By 1722, Sir Robert Walpole (1676–1745) had emerged as Great Britain's most prominent political leader. Walpole, the third son of a well-to-do member of the gentry, rose to power in Whig politics. He served for more than half his life in Parliament. A skillful administrator, Walpole was made secretary of war in 1708, during the reign of Queen Anne. In 1712, his enemies impeached him on charges of corruption and expelled him from Parliament, but he was restored to favor by George I, whose confidence he had won. Walpole was especially intent on guarding against efforts by supporters of the Stuart pretender, known as Jacobites (from the Latin for James), to unseat the Hanoverians. In 1715, "James III," the Old Pretender, supported by some Tories, actually landed in Scotland but was easily defeated and forced to flee once again.

In 1721 Walpole became chancellor of the exchequer, and he eventually emerged as the king's "prime," or chief, minister. In that position, he nominated the other ministers who served in his cabinet and wielded enormous patronage in the form of jobs, pensions, contracts, and honors, which he used to remain in power for more than 20 years. Although George II (ruled 1727–1760) did not share his father's enthusiasm for Walpole, Queen Caroline (1683–1737) helped keep him in office. Walpole kept the support of Parliament through bribery, eloquence, and political skill.

Despite Walpole's extraordinary power, his immediate successors did not imbue the position of prime minister with the authority that he had wielded. The monarch remained the head of state and the ruler of the kingdom, in whose name all laws were enacted and treaties negotiated. In addition, the British monarch still commanded enormous prestige and exercised considerable informal authority. Nevertheless, by the mid-18th century, the sovereign needed Parliament to make laws, levy taxes, control the judiciary, or maintain an army. He had delegated most of his executive functions to the prime minister and his cabinet, where the real affairs of state were conducted.

Among the great powers of Europe, Great Britain could boast a unique form of government by the mid-18th century. The country was governed by an "unwritten constitution" consisting of traditions, laws, and charters that stretched back to the Middle Ages. As it evolved between 1688 and the death of Walpole in 1745, that system was one in which the aristocracy and a landowning elite divided political power between them in cooperation with the monarchy. In this arrangement, the role of Parliament was crucial because it was the body that made laws, imposed taxes, and appropriated the revenues needed for the government to function.

Putting England and the Rise of Constitutional Monarchy in Perspective

The fact that the English revolutions took place while Louis XIV sat on the throne of France reflects the range of political systems that unfolded in 17th-century Europe: At one extreme stood the *Grand Monarque,* who perfected the instruments of absolutist power at Versailles, while at the other extreme Cromwell experimented with a republican dictatorship built on the ruins of a decapitated monarchy. The governments of most European states were closer to the French than to the English model.

The English had not been entirely spared from experience with absolute monarchy: The Tudor sovereigns came close to realizing such status in the 16th century, but the Civil War and the Puritan Revolution had stopped the growth of royal power. The restored Stuart kings tried to see how far they could go in reviving royal authority, but when they pushed too far, the forces that controlled Parliament staged the Glorious Revolution. Parliament won the struggle for power, and over the next half-century it extended its authority indirectly as a result of the evolution of the cabinet system of government. Limited, constitutional monarchy became the counterpoint to absolute monarchy based on the divine right of kings.

In retrospect, of course, the British system proved more stable and long-lived than the French form of government. England had its revolution in the 17th century, whereas France experienced a more serious turmoil 100 years later. The events that took place in England between 1640 and 1688 constituted a political rather than a social revolution, but the revolution nonetheless confirmed an important social fact, namely, that the landed gentry and merchant class had emerged as the country's uncontested ruling elite. Moreover, unlike the aristocracy on the Continent, in England nobles were not exempt from taxation, and therefore had a greater stake in the success of Parliament. If Great Britain avoided having its own Sun King, it owed its good fortune to a combination of factors, especially the existence of this elite and the strong tradition of individual rights embedded in the common law. Yet, regardless of the differences between the French and British experiences, one essential pattern remained common to both nations: the increasing centralization of power in the modern state.

Questions for Further Study

1. In what ways were the issues that led to the Glorious Revolution different from those behind the earlier civil wars?
2. What general principles of popular sovereignty emerged from the revolution?
3. What are the origins of the cabinet system of government?

Suggestions for Further Reading

Black, Jeremy, ed. *Britain in the Age of Walpole*. New York, 1984.

Earle, Peter. *The Making of the English Middle Class*. London, 1989.

Harris, Tim. *Politics Under the Later Stuarts*. London and New York, 1993.

Hill, Christopher. *The World Turned Upside Down: Radical Ideas During the English Revolution*. New York, 1972.

Hutton, Richard. *Charles the Second*. Oxford, 1990.

Jones, J.R. *The Revolution of 1688 in England*. London, 1972.

InfoTrac College Edition

Enter the search term *Stuart Restoration* using Key Terms.

Enter the search term *Charles II of England* using Key Terms.

Enter the search term *James II of England* using Key Terms.

Enter the search term *Queen Anne of England* using Key Terms.

CENTRAL EUROPE AND THE SHIFTING BALANCE OF POWER

By the 17th century, most Western European countries had a strong central government. The nobility had been tamed or incorporated into the state, the urban merchant classes were growing in prominence, and most agricultural populations had been largely freed from the restrictions of feudalism. In Central and Eastern Europe, by contrast, the growth of absolute monarchy left the nobility with considerable power and status, the middle classes were weak, and the peasants continued to live as serfs.

The chief political organization of central Europe was the Holy Roman Empire, nominally ruled by the Hapsburgs. In practice, however, the Empire consisted of a welter of separate states, each with its own ruler and political system. Many of these states used war or marriage to increase their power. In the early 17th century, Hapsburg attempts to revive the Empire led to their defeat in the Thirty Years' War. In midcentury, the Emperor Leopold I tried a different approach by seeking to unify Austria, Bohemia, and Hungary under centralized rule.

The Hohenzollerns, who had become the rulers of Brandenburg in 1415, emerged as the monarchs of a major new power during the 17th century. Early in the century, the Hohenzollerns added to their holdings by inheriting the territory of Prussia to the northeast and some scattered lands on the Rhine. Poor and undefended by natural frontiers, Brandenburg-Prussia suffered badly in the Thirty Years' War. In the midst of the destruction of many villages and a fall in population, in 1653 the young Elector Friedrich Wilhelm was able to increase his power at the expense of the regional assemblies.

Friedrich Wilhelm, later known as the Great Elector, welded together his scattered principalities into a single state. He created a powerful standing army second only to the military force of Austria. In order to pay for his army, he forcibly introduced permanent taxation over the protests of the Estates. The Prussian landowning nobles, known as Junkers, tried unsuccessfully to resist, but in return he allowed them to retain control over the serfs on their estates. By the time of the Great Elector's death in 1688, his tough programs at home and shrewd foreign policy had produced a powerful unified state with formidable military forces.

THE FICTION OF THE HOLY ROMAN EMPIRE

By contrast with the growing prosperity of Western Europe in the 16th and 17th centuries, economic conditions in Central and Eastern Europe were poor. Most of the wealth was concentrated in the hands of the landowning nobility, the middle classes remained small and politically weak, and most peasants were forced to work as unpaid serfs. The establishment of absolute monarchies in Austria, Prussia, and Russia did little to relieve these conditions (for a discussion of Russia and Poland, see Topic 53).

One of the most important factors making it possible for rulers to assert their domination was the climate of uncertainty created by decades of wars. As the states of Central and Eastern Europe fought against one another and against outside invaders, even the most independent nobles realized the necessity for a strong central authority. By seizing their opportunity, rulers such as Prussia's Friedrich Wilhelm (ruled 1640–1688) were able to control three vital sources of power: the imposition of taxes, control of a standing army, and conduct of foreign affairs. In return, they allowed their nobles to continue to maintain their estates and legal rights over their peasants.

The largest political confederation in central Europe was the Holy Roman Empire. Founded by Charlemagne, it was effectively established in 962 as an organization of some 300 German states and included the Low Countries, eastern France, northern and central Italy, and western Bohemia. According to procedures set up in 1356 (see Topic 29), its emperor, usually the dominant German sovereign, was elected by the seven "elector" princes and, until the end of the 15th century, crowned by the pope. The Hapsburg dynasty, which had ruled Austria since 1278, became rulers of the Holy Roman Empire in 1436, and they continued to serve as emperors, at least in theory, until Napoleon finally dismantled the Empire in 1806.

THE HOLY ROMAN EMPIRE AFTER THE THIRTY YEARS' WAR

The tendency for the individual member-states of the Holy Roman Empire to go their separate ways, already notable in the 15th century, increased during the Reformation, which set the Catholic Hapsburg emperor against the Protestant princes, most of whom ruled the northern states. One of the reasons the emperor Ferdinand II (ruled 1619–1637) became embroiled in the disastrous Thirty Years' War was to enforce the Counter-Reformation and impose Catholicism on Protestants in Bohemia and Hungary. Educated by Jesuits, Ferdinand fervently supported the propagation of Catholic dogma by authoritarian means (on the Thirty Years' War, see Topic 44).

Far from strengthening the Empire, the negotiations that finally brought the war to an end effectively destroyed any chance of the emperor's reestablishing central authority. The Peace of Westphalia (1648) established the separation of politics and religion and ended the emperor's attempt to turn Germany into an absolute monarchy. The treaty made it instead into a collection of absolute monarchies and confirmed the sovereignty of each member-state. In addition, it further reduced Hapsburg power over the Empire by allowing outsiders, France and Sweden, to participate in the deliberations of the Imperial Diet, the Holy Roman Empire's assembly to which the various member-states sent representatives.

By the mid-17th century the ancient organization existed in name only. The Diet continued to meet, but for all practical purposes the Empire was a political fiction. The "rulers" of its various member-states included some 2,000 imperial knights, 80 princes (50 ecclesiastical and 30 secular), more than 100 counts, around 70 prelates, and 66 city governments. Their territories ranged in size from three or four acres to the entire kingdom of Bohemia. All of the individual rulers were theoretically subordinate to the emperor, but in practice remained politically independent. The Empire had no central administration or taxation system, no common law or customs union, and not even a common calendar.

THE HAPSBURGS TURN EAST: THE TURKISH DEFEAT

Traditional Hapsburg territory in Central Europe consisted of three distinct regions: the hereditary lands of Austria, the Kingdom of Bohemia, and the Kingdom of Hungary. The Thirty Years' War put an end to Hapsburg expansion westward by legitimizing the independence of the other German states. In consequence, the emperor Leopold I (ruled 1658–1705) decided to create a larger and more powerful centralized state, the equal of those in Western Europe, by unifying these three regions and making Bohemia and Hungary subordinate to Austria.

Control over Austria was assured by the emperor's traditional ascendancy over the local feudal nobility. The Kingdom of Bohemia was still suffering the effects of the Thirty Years' War. In 1620, Ferdinand II crushed a revolt led by Bohemia's Protestant Czech nobility, killed his opponents, and confiscated their estates. He replaced them with a new upper class. For the most part, these newcomers were aristocratic mercenaries from all over Europe. Having no allegiance to Bohemia, they owed their position, and thus their loyalty, to the emperor.

With the help of this new ruling class, the Hapsburgs established direct control over Bohemia. The Bohemian peasants were required to work a minimum of three days a week without pay for their new masters, and about one-quarter of them worked every day except Sundays and religious holidays. These serfs were also responsible for paying taxes, thereby lifting the burden from the aristocracy.

HUNGARY AND THE OTTOMAN EMPIRE

The real difficulty in Leopold's scheme lay farther east, in Hungary. The Hapsburgs were the elected rulers of the kingdom. In practice, however, since the early 16th century most of Hungary was in Turkish hands, as part of the

Ottoman Empire. Many central and eastern European peasants, accustomed to exploitation at the hands of their Christian masters, found Turkish rule less oppressive than that of the Hapsburgs, especially because the Turks did not require them to become Muslims. In Hungary, moreover, the Protestant nobility tended to side with the Turks against the hated Catholic Austrians.

In the reign of Mehmed IV (ruled 1648–1687), Turkish power, which had suffered a serious setback at the Battle of Lepanto in 1571, temporarily revived—the restoration of strong central government was largely the result of energetic and effective grand viziers. The Turks once again moved westward against Austria, encouraged by Louis XIV of France, who wanted to use the Turks against his old enemies the Hapsburgs. After two unsuccessful campaigns in 1663 and 1664, an Ottoman army of more than 100,000 poured up the Danube Valley and besieged Vienna in July 1683. The Austrian forces were too weak to resist, and the emperor Leopold fled up the river to Passau, to try to put together a coalition of troops to oppose the Turks.

For the next two months, as the rest of Europe waited with horrified fascination to see if the easternmost bastion of Catholicism would fall, the Turkish encampment outside Vienna provided a vision of luxury never before seen in the West. The Turks had brought with them supplies for a long wait: oxen, camels, and mules; a flock of 10,000 sheep; corn, coffee, sugar, and honey. The quarters of the commander, Kara Mustapha, included bathrooms with perfumed waters, opulent beds, priceless carpets, and glittering chandeliers. Elsewhere were gardens with fountains and a menagerie with rare birds and animals.

After a tense summer of negotiating, Leopold succeeded in putting together an international relief force. In September, combined troops including Poles, Bavarians, and Saxons, with the blessing of Pope Innocent XI (ruled 1676–1689), came to the rescue. French troops were conspicuous by their absence from the coalition of Christians against Muslims. Louis XIV placed national political interests above religion, and in any case he was also involved in a bitter quarrel with the pope.

Among the heroes of the relief of Vienna was the Polish king, John Sobieski (ruled 1674–1696), who personally led the charge of his country's cavalry. The combined armies came crashing down on the Turks from the heights of the Kahlenberg, overlooking the city, and drove them into a hurried retreat toward Hungary. The Turkish commander stayed only long enough to prevent his two favorite possessions from falling alive into Christian hands: he decapitated a particularly beautiful wife and his ostrich.

EUGENE OF SAVOY
Over the following decade, Leopold's forces pursued the Turks down the Danube and drove them out of Hungary. Among the emperor's potent weapons was the most brilliant general of the age, Eugene, prince of Savoy (1663–1736). French by birth, Eugene had clashed with the domineering Louis XIV, and renounced his country. Renowned for his qualities of leadership and strategic insights, Eugene was also a notable

patron of the arts, and for his Viennese home he commissioned the superb palace and park known as the Belvedere.

In a series of campaigns, the Austrians conquered all of Hungary and added Transylvania (now part of Romania). The final decisive battle took place at Zenta in 1697, where forces under Eugene wiped out a Turkish army triple their size. By the Peace of Carlowitz, of January 1699, the Turks recognized Hapsburg rule over Hungary. Once in possession, Leopold was quick to impose Catholicism and clamp on Hungary the fetters of Austrian rule. The country became an Austrian colony. Many Hungarian Protestants were executed for treason. The remaining landowning nobles kept their holdings along with the serfs who worked on them, in return for their recognition of the ultimate authority of Vienna.

THE UPRISING OF RÁKÓCZY
Yet Hapsburg attempts to integrate Hungary into a single state, along with Austria and Bohemia, were immediately challenged by a series of uprisings. Hungarian resistance to Austria proved stronger than that of the Bohemians. The Hungarian nobles, although weakened, had not been completely eliminated, as had the Protestant nobility of Bohemia. In addition, both aristocracy and peasants were beginning to develop a shared sense of national identity that was to reach its fulfillment in the 19th century.

In 1703, the young Francis Rákóczy (ruled 1704–1711), a member of a noble Hungarian and Transylvanian family, led a patriotic uprising against the Hapsburg empire. Because the Austrians were at the time involved in the War of the Spanish Succession (see Topic 50), Rákóczy's forces were unexpectedly successful, and in 1704 the nobles elected him prince.

Hungarian independence lasted only a few years. The Austrians rallied to inflict a series of crushing defeats, and in 1711 Rákóczy fled into exile. Nevertheless, the Hapsburg emperor was forced to accept the traditional status of the Hungarian aristocracy, in return for their acceptance of Austrian rule. Leopold's aim of creating a single powerful state

SIGNIFICANT DATES

Central Europe in the 17th Century

1618	Brandenburg and Prussia joined
1620	Ferdinand II of Austria crushes Protestant Czech uprising
1640–1688	Reign of Friedrich Wilhelm, the Great Elector
1648	Peace of Westphalia
1660	Friedrich founds Prussian Army
1683	Ottoman siege of Vienna
1697	Eugene of Savoy defeats Ottoman forces at Zenta
1701	Friedrich I crowned king of Prussia
1703	Rákóczy leads Hungarian uprising

was thus only partly fulfilled. Austria, Bohemia, and Hungary shared a centralized administration, but the framework under which it operated was loose. The unhappy consequences of Leopold's actions would emerge a century and a half later.

THE RISE OF THE HOHENZOLLERNS

One of the chief landowning families of northeastern Germany in the 16th century was the Hohenzollerns. The decline of the traditional aristocracy had permitted wealthy landowners like the Hohenzollerns to rise to political power. The senior branch of the family became Electors of Brandenburg, a small territory around Berlin, and the junior line acquired the rule of Prussia, a province on the Baltic Sea that technically formed part of the Kingdom of Poland. The two possessions joined together in 1618, when in the absence of a direct heir Prussia passed to Brandenburg by inheritance.

The provinces had few advantages. They shared no common interests or loyalties and lacked natural frontiers. They were poor, thinly populated, and unproductive, and Brandenburg's bleak and arid lands had won it the nickname of "the sandbox of Europe." Furthermore, centralized administration of the territories was made difficult by their individual governments. The overall power of the Elector was limited by the existence of provincial assemblies known as Estates. Controlled by the great noble landowners called Junkers, these Estates passed laws, authorized, collected, and spent taxes, and raised troops. The Junker-dominated provincial administrations ran their provinces on a day-to-day basis, reserving the Elector as the court of final appeal.

The lack of defendable borders meant that Brandenburg-Prussia lay vulnerable to the ravages of the Thirty Years' War. Brandenburg, in particular, became the battleground for the rival armies of Sweden and the Hapsburgs. By 1648, the population had actually declined and, in the course of the war, Berlin lost half its inhabitants, and many villages were abandoned.

Paradoxically, by the end of the 17th century the state of Prussia (the name by which the joint territories became known) was on its way to becoming one of the leading po-

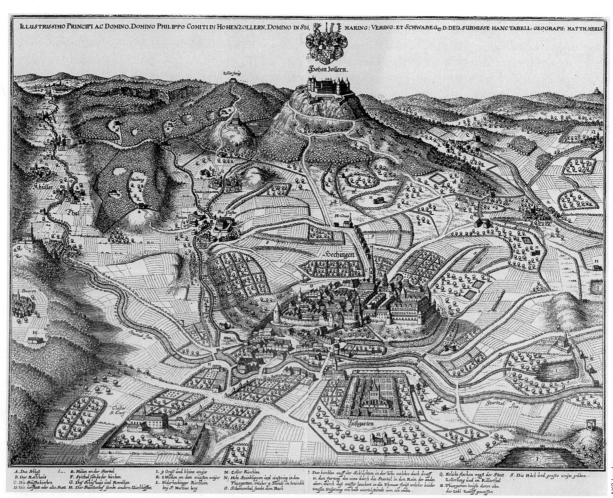

AKG London

Matthew Meria, engraving of the castle and estates of the Hohenzollern. 17th century. The inscription at the top dedicates the work to the Hohenzollern Count Philip; the family crest appears just below. In the foreground are farms and gardens forming part of the estate; the walled garden just right of center at the bottom is labeled "Garden for Walking."

litical and military powers in Europe. In part this was made possible because the state of almost total collapse underlined the need for wholesale reconstruction; however, Prussia's rise to greatness was largely the result of the policies of its remarkable ruler, Friedrich Wilhelm, whose achievements won him the title of the Great Elector.

THE GREAT ELECTOR: JUNKERS AND ARMY IN PRUSSIA

The Elector of Brandenburg for most of the Thirty Years' War was Friedrich Wilhelm's father, Georg Wilhelm (ruled 1619–1640). Weak and vacillating, Georg Wilhelm was described by one of his descendants as "utterly unfit to rule."

Famous for his piety and gluttony, he spent most of the war switching from one side to the other. By 1638, with his revenues fallen by seven-eighths, he retired to East Prussia and died there.

At the age of 14, in the middle of the war, Friedrich Wilhelm had been packed off to the Netherlands. He studied at the University of Leiden, becoming acquainted with new developments in science and technology, while in his spare time he caught up with the latest techniques of warfare and politics. He also became a dedicated Calvinist. By the time he succeeded his father in 1640, at the age of 20, his subjects were exhausted and terrorized by the horrors of a war in which they were only marginally involved.

Tall and powerfully built, with piercing blue eyes, Friedrich Wilhelm used cunning diplomacy allied with ruthless force to achieve his objectives. His first aim was to

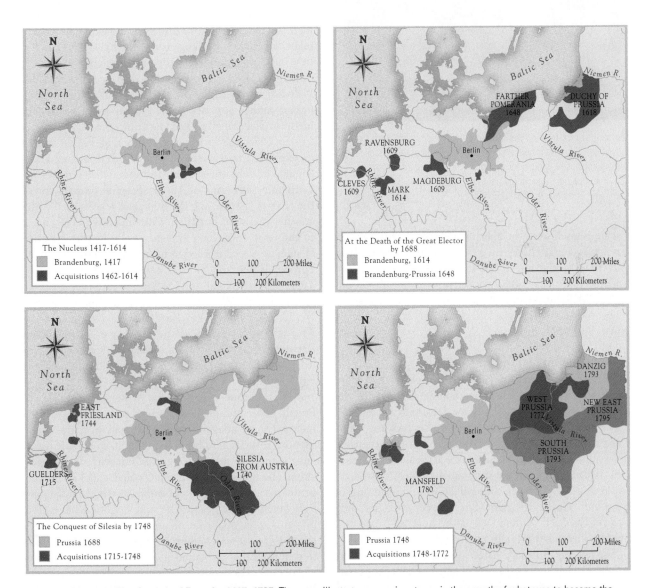

 Map 52.1 The Growth of Prussia, 1417–1795. The maps illustrate successive stages in the growth of what was to become the modern state of Germany. Note the position of Berlin, between two of the great rivers of Central Europe, the Elbe and the Oder. By the time of the latest of these maps, the southern part of modern Germany is still part of the Holy Roman Empire. Go to http://info.wadsworth.com/053461065X for an interactive version of this map.

AKG London

Portrait of Friedrich Wilhelm I, king of Prussia. Late 17th century. The king, who is best known for his reforms of the Prussian army, has chosen to pose for his portrait in military armor, rather than the robes of state. In his right hand he holds the baton of command of a Prussia Field Marshal.

extricate himself from the fighting and to clear his territory of foreign soldiers. The Peace of Westphalia in 1648, which finally brought the war to an inconclusive end, awarded Brandenburg-Prussia some new territory. More important, Friedrich Wilhelm successfully defended the Calvinists in the negotiations, winning acknowledgment as the leader of German Protestant interests.

CONFLICT WITH THE ESTATES

The bitter events of the previous generation made it clear that a state without an effective standing army was at the mercy of foreign invaders. Thus the creation of a military force became the new Elector's priority. Yet building a single army to defend all of the provinces was an expensive proposition, requiring a considerable increase in tax revenues. Because each of the provincial Estates insisted on maintaining control over the collection and spending of taxes, and refused to grant funds except for its own province, Friedrich Wilhelm spent the next few years in a series of political struggles for financial control.

The first breakthrough came in Brandenburg, where in 1653 the Elector and the Estates reached an apparent compromise. The agreement guaranteed the Junkers' social and economic privileges and allowed them to turn more peasants into serfs. Furthermore, Friedrich Wilhelm promised to consult the Estates over future policy and appointments. In

return the Junkers voted the Elector a large sum of money, to be paid over the next six years.

THE PRUSSIAN ARMY

In 1660 Friedrich Wilhelm founded his permanent standing army. Once in command of his force, he used it to collect more taxes, without the consent of the Estates. In East Prussia the Estates struggled to preserve their rights, even enlisting the support of Poland. Friedrich Wilhelm used the army to occupy the province and eliminated those Junkers who continued to defy him by imprisoning and hanging them. By the 1670s, Prussia was an absolute monarchy, in which the Elector controlled the finances and the army.

The Elector's troops not only served as a fighting force, but they also helped shape and even direct the growth of the state, thereby making Prussia unique among European nations. Soldiers functioned as tax collectors and policemen, developing thereby into a rapidly expanding state bureaucracy. Other divisions in the army also worked on public building projects, digging canals and settling underpopulated areas. As prosperity grew, Friedrich Wilhelm became increasingly successful in persuading his former Junker opponents to head his government departments and above all to become army officers.

By 1688, the Prussian army stood at 30,000 and could be expanded in wartime to 40,000. Well trained and well equipped, it was the second strongest military power in the Germanies, after that of Austria. So professional a force was the envy of Europe, and the European powers vied with one another to hire it. Friedrich Wilhelm adroitly used his army to earn ever-increasing foreign subsidies by timely changes of side, as war continued to rack both Eastern and Western Europe. When the Swedes invaded Poland in 1656 (see Topic 53), he fought first for Sweden and then for Poland. In the Dutch War of 1672–1679, he supported first the Netherlands, then France, and then the Netherlands again. This was no reflection of the indecisiveness of his father. Between 1660 and 1688 he collected handsome payments from a wide range of European powers, without having to do much fighting.

By the time of Friedrich Wilhelm's death in 1688, Prussia was a formidable centralized state, with absolute rule imposed from above. The Elector had won the grudging support of the nobles by allowing them to exploit the peasants; social reform was not part of Friedrich Wilhelm's program. The Prussian economy prospered, thanks to improved agriculture and a revival of commerce—both made possible by a generation of peace. The state became a haven for immigrants who could be of use to the state and religious refugees: Lutherans, Calvinists, Jews, and, after the revocation of the Edict of Nantes in 1685 (see Topic 50), French Huguenots. The only religious minority to whom Friedrich Wilhelm would not grant entry was the Jesuits, whom he thought too intolerant. Many of the newcomers brought skills that helped in the development of agriculture and industry. A large number of the Huguenots joined the army.

Print showing a recruiting drive for soldiers to serve in the Prussian army. 18th century. New recruits, having signed up at the table in the center, are welcomed with a drink of ale. In the foreground, some celebrate by practicing their sword-fighting technique, while to the left others seem happy to escape.

THE FIRST KINGS OF PRUSSIA

It says much for Friedrich Wilhelm's creation that Prussia survived his less dynamic immediate successor, and the eccentricity of the state's next ruler, to increase its international prestige. The Great Elector's son, Friedrich III (ruled 1688–1713 as Elector of Brandenburg and 1701–1713 as king of Prussia), was distinguished more for his ostentatious cultural programs than for his attention to the affairs of state. His principal achievement was to persuade the Hapsburg Holy Roman Emperor to grant him the title of king of Prussia. At the end of 1700, on the eve of the War of the Spanish Succession (see Topic 50), Friedrich promised the Hapsburg ruler diplomatic support and a contingent of soldiers in any eventual conflict. In return, Leopold I allowed the Elector to crown himself king; after his coronation in January 1701, Friedrich became the only German king, ruling as Friedrich I.

Friedrich's son and successor, Friedrich Wilhelm I (ruled 1713–1740), was known to his enemies, as well as to his few friends, as the Sergeant Major. Tightfisted and prudish, he was notorious for bouts of uncontrollable temper, in which he would attack generals and bureaucrats alike with his stick. Crude and violent in his tastes, he was tormented by boils, gout and colic, and religious anxieties. His obses-

sive concern for punctuality, obedience, and hard work, all of which he ruthlessly imposed on his hapless subjects, had much to do with creating the image of Prussian character.

His top priority was the army, which had doubled to 80,000 by the time of his death to become the third or fourth strongest in Europe. He formed a special battalion of grenadiers, all of gigantic height, whom his agents recruited throughout Europe. The force became known as the "Battalion of Giants." He is said to have told the French ambassador: "I am utterly indifferent to the most beautiful girl or woman on earth; tall soldiers are my weakness."

Despite his personal oddities, Prussia prospered under his rule. Rigorous state planning and centralized industrial development doubled revenues by 1740. For all Friedrich Wilhelm's obsessive militarism, his army did little actual fighting. His two reasons for avoiding military action were his belief that "God forbids unjust wars" and his reluctance to risk the lives of his precious troops. On the other hand, social rigidity increased, and the peasants and serfs continued to bear the brunt of the entire state system.

The Great Elector had inherited three small provinces, which were disunited, impoverished, and torn by war. By the time Friedrich Wilhelm I died, Prussia was on the verge of becoming one of the great powers of Europe.

Putting Central Europe and the Shifting Balance of Power in Perspective

Beginning in the mid-17th century, the states of Austria and Prussia began to dominate central Europe. The Hapsburg rulers of the combined territory of Austria, Bohemia, and Hungary were from one of the oldest of Europe's aristocratic families and titular monarchs of the Holy Roman Empire. The Hohenzollerns rose from governing insignificant provinces to presiding over an awesome military machine. Both dynasties established absolutist rule, with the monarch in complete control of financial, military, and foreign policy. The power of the local legislative assemblies was broken.

The relapse into authoritarian government was accompanied by a reinforcement of the social order. The Hungarian nobles extracted some concessions from a reluctant emperor, and the Prussian Junkers obtained a share of the growing prosperity by accepting state and military positions. In both countries, however, the middle classes never had a chance to expand: In Friedrich Wilhelm I's Prussia, private enterprise was rigorously discouraged. As for the peasants and serfs, they continued to work for the nobles, pay taxes to the state, and serve in the armies.

Of the two powers, the unity of the larger and more diverse Hapsburg empire was less secure, and the centralized administration less effective. The Great Elector started with the advantage of building his state virtually from scratch, whereas Leopold and his successors had to weld together peoples with established national and religious differences. In future struggles for power in central Europe, Prussia was victorious; it went on in the 19th century to unify the German states and create the German empire.

Questions for Further Study

1. How did the rulers of Brandenburg-Prussia create one of the most powerful European states?
2. What role did the Ottoman Turks play in European affairs in the century from the Battle of Lepanto to the siege of Vienna?
3. How did the Hapsburgs prevent the growth of Czech and Hungarian independence? What were the later consequences of their repression?
4. What were the chief differences between the lives of Central European peasant farmers and those in Western Europe?

Suggestions for Further Reading

Carsten, F.L. *The Origins of Prussia*. Westport, CT, 1982.

Dwyer, Philip G. *The Rise of Prussia, 1700-1830*. Harlow, 2000.

Ingrao, Charles W. *The Habsburg Monarchy, 1618-1815*. New York, 2000.

Macartney, Carlile A. *The Hapsburg and Hohenzollern Dynasties in the Seventeenth and Eighteenth Centuries*. New York, 1970.

McKay, Derek *The Great Elector: Frederick William of Brandenburg-Prussia*. Harlow, 2001.

Parvev, Ivan. *Hapsburgs and Ottomans between Vienna and Belgrade (1683-1739)*. New York, 1995.

Wangermann, E. *The Austrian Achievement*. New York, 1973.

Wheatcroft, Andrew. *The Hapsburgs, Embodying Empire*. New York, 1995.

InfoTrac College Edition

Enter the search term *Holy Roman Empire* using Key Terms.

THE BALTIC AND EASTERN EUROPE IN TRANSITION

By the early 16th century, virtually all the lands of the Eastern Slavs were subject to the ruler of the Principality of Moscow, the "Tsar of all the Russias." In midcentury, Ivan the Terrible (Ivan IV) drove out the few remaining Mongols from Russian territory and concentrated yet more power in his hands by purging the old Muscovite nobles. The 20 years of chaos and violence that followed his turbulent reign were justifiably named the Time of Troubles.

With the election of Michael Romanov as hereditary tsar in 1613, some degree of temporary order was restored. But while the monarch regained autocratic rule and the nobles received concessions, peasant hardships, which were already considerable, increased. The resulting popular unrest, coupled with the religious controversy of the Old Believers, produced more uprisings.

The reign of Peter the Great came as a turning point in Russian history. Following a policy of westernization, he introduced sweeping reforms in civil administration and the military. The tsar retained absolute power, but the creation of a bureaucracy along Western lines and the modernization of the army led eventually to Russia taking its place alongside the great powers of Western Europe. After victory in a long conflict with Sweden known as the Great Northern War (1700–1721), Peter founded the city of St. Petersburg on the Baltic as his new capital.

In the second half of the 17th century, Sweden had conquered most of the territory around the Baltic Sea, but rule of this new Swedish empire dangerously overextended the home country's resources. Despite the efforts of Charles XII, Sweden's king and military hero, the Great Northern War brought a series of defeats.

By contrast with the autocratic monarchies of Russia and Sweden, the nobles in Poland retained considerable power, including the right to elect their king. By the late 17th century, Poland was virtually governed by the Diet, an aristocratic national assembly. Notoriously argumentative and inefficient, the Diet could not even enforce its decisions on the rare occasions it succeeded in making them. In consequence, internal weakness combined with the scheming of Poland's neighbors to create the conditions for complete collapse: In 1794 Poland ceased to exist as an independent country and was partitioned among Austria, Prussia, and Russia.

THE EMERGENCE OF RUSSIA

The transformation of the Principality of Moscow into the capital of the territory of all the Eastern Slavs was finally accomplished in the reign of Ivan III (ruled 1462–1505), called Ivan the Great. With the Turkish capture of Constantinople, capital of the old Byzantine Empire, in 1453, Ivan claimed the title of "tsar"—the Russian equivalent of "Caesar," or "emperor"—and proclaimed himself the heir of the Roman and Byzantine empires, adopting the double-headed eagle of Byzantium as the imperial crest.

IVAN THE TERRIBLE

The Russian state became even more autocratic during the reign of Ivan IV (ruled 1533–1584)—known as Ivan the Terrible, although his nickname in Russian, Ivan Groznyi, is really better translated as Ivan the Awe Inspiring.

Ivan became grand prince of Moscow at the age of three. His youth was warped by fear and neglect and blighted by the sudden death of his mother, perhaps as the result of poisoning. After a period of bloody misrule by the *boyars* (the Russian nobles) during his early years, Ivan was crowned tsar and grand prince of all Russia in 1547; he was the first to bear this title officially. Married seven times, Ivan

Portrait of Ivan IV, Ivan the Terrible. 16th century. The style is that of Byzantine icons: Note the artificial treatment of the hair and beard. For all his justified reputation for cruelty, Ivan was the first Russian ruler to make a serious attempt to establish trading and diplomatic relations with the states of Western Europe.

The Granger Collection, New York

oscillated between states of tender affection and savage cruelty, combining drunken abandon and religious obsession.

On assuming full power, the tsar continued the policy of his predecessors in strengthening the position of the monarchy by reducing the influence of the traditionally independent princes and boyars. Under Ivan, these perpetually feuding nobles lost power to a new rising nobility, the *dvoranye*, who were granted land directly by the tsar in return for their services to him, and thus were bound in allegiance to him. Ivan revised the legal code, strengthening the hold of masters over peasants. A special army unit, the *streltsy* (shooters), was formed and garrisoned in towns throughout Russia to enforce state policy. Agriculture and industrial production improved, and the Russian economy became increasingly internationalized, as foreign exports (mainly raw materials) and imports increased.

The tsar continued the "gathering of Russia" by driving out the remaining Mongols and gaining control of most of southeastern Russia. He initiated a long and eventually unsuccessful attempt to win territory on the Baltic, losing in the end to an alliance of Poland and Lithuania. Later in Ivan's reign, Russian forces had greater success in the east, where they began the conquest of Siberia that was completed half a century later.

The last 20 years of Ivan's rule were marked by a growing reign of terror. In 1565 he assumed despotic powers, surrounding himself with a special elite guard known as the *oprichniky*. Its 6,000 members dressed in black and rode black horses. In order to provide them with estates—the land they ruled occupied half the kingdom—Ivan uprooted some 12,000 boyars and confiscated their holdings. When Philip, the saintly metropolitan archbishop of Moscow, reproached the oprichniky for their terrorist behavior, Ivan had him strangled.

The climax of his violence came in 1570. Suspicious that the city of Novgorod was planning to join his enemies the Lithuanians, Ivan razed it and had some 60,000 of its inhabitants killed. A few years later he began to disband the oprichniky, merging them by 1575 with the army. In 1581, in a sudden fit of anger with his son, Ivan struck him in the face. Within four days, his heir was dead. When Ivan died three years later, leaving no adequate successor, his country was on the brink of anarchy.

THE TIME OF TROUBLES

The years following Ivan's death are generally called the Time of Troubles (1584–1613), during which life in Russia was marked by civil war, economic crisis, and foreign invasions. The discontent of the peasants led to a series of uprisings, encouraged by the wandering armies of cossacks, who were originally bands of outlawed warrior peasants. Even the powerful boyar Boris Godunov (ruled 1598–1605), who ruled first as regent and then as tsar, failed to maintain control. Best known as the self-titled protagonist of Pushkin's drama (1831) and Mussorgsky's powerful opera (1874), Boris was overthrown by the pretender False Dimitri I, a former monk.

Only a Polish invasion in 1610, during which Polish forces briefly occupied Moscow, finally persuaded the rival boyars of the necessity of restoring some semblance of order. In 1613 they elected as tsar Michael Romanov (ruled 1613–1645), a distant relative of Ivan the Terrible's first wife. The young ruler was in poor health and thus the least threatening of the various candidates. All subsequent Russian tsars, until 1917, came from the Romanov family.

The reigns of Michael and his successor, Alexis (ruled 1645–1676), saw the restoration of imperial power and the simultaneous granting of concessions to the nobles, including the reduction of their military service. Once again the peasants paid the price because in 1649 Alexis introduced a law code that legalized serfdom.

THE OLD BELIEVERS

The peasants' resentment of their ever-worsening conditions deepened as the result of a bitter religious controversy in the latter part of the 17th century. Nikon (1605–1681), the powerful and formidable patriarch of Russia from 1652 to 1666, introduced a long list of changes to traditional services and rituals. His innovations, based on the liturgy of the Greek rather than the Russian Orthodox Church, deeply shocked the mass of old-fashioned believers. The peasants, in particular, crushed by financial and military obligations, reacted with bitterness to the loss of the traditional liturgy, their one remaining comfort.

The changes were in many cases symbolic rather than substantial (for example, three fingers were to be used instead of two for making the sign of the cross) but the result was a schism that split the Russian Church. The traditionalists, who called themselves the Old Believers, resisted the changes by political and social protests. When government forces tried to impose reform, groups of Old Believers gathered inside the wooden churches they had constructed and committed suicide by setting fire to the buildings. The religious controversy underlined the degree to which the church was really a state agency, and the resulting disillusionment of the lower classes with ecclesiastical authority lasted into the 20th century.

As chaos in Russia mounted, the cossacks once again seized their opportunity. Along with a great band of runaway serfs, religious dissidents, and other malcontents, a cossack army led by Stenka Razin (died 1671) swarmed up the Volga in 1670–1671, killing landlords and tsarist officials and proclaiming freedom. Government troops easily defeated the disorderly force. Razin, who was captured and executed in Red Square, torn limb from limb, later became one of Russian folklore's great heroes.

The revolt led to increased repression. Frightened by the violence of the rebels, the nobles redoubled the bonds of serfdom, while rallying around the autocratic rule of the tsar. Finally, with the restoration of central authority, the Romanovs began to improve the imperial administration and rebuild the economy. To achieve this goal, they encouraged contact with Western traders and manufacturers, thus preparing the way for the reforming, if autocratic, rule of Peter the Great.

Woodcut showing Cossack warrior on horseback. 17th century. These Slavic warrior peasants lived in the steppe land of modern Ukraine and were famous for their riding skills. They never accepted outside authority but served as irregular troops under their own leaders. A Cossack mounted regiment fought for the Soviet Union as late as World War II.

PETER THE GREAT AND THE ALLURE OF THE WEST

Under Peter the Great (ruled 1682–1725), Russia became transformed into a modern and aggressive European state. Without relaxing his autocratic rule, Peter improved government at both the central and provincial levels. He encouraged expansion in industry and commerce, rebuilt the army, and created a navy, using Western models for many of these reforms. Peter's chief purpose was to increase Russian military power. By raising Russia's fighting forces, he aimed to make his country the equal of the other great European nations. Many of his successors, both Russian and later Soviet, followed the same policy. By the end of his reign, Russia had replaced Sweden as the leading state in northern Europe, with a permanent place in European power politics.

Peter's early life was overshadowed by violence and marked by a series of palace coups and Moscow riots. He ascended to the throne in 1682 at the age of 10, and seven years later he overthrew the regency of his sister Sofia, making himself sole ruler. Nearly seven feet tall, he was a figure of almost demoniacal energy, ruthless and impetuous. He staggered his contemporaries by his massive consumption of food and drink, and by his incessant activity; he moved without stopping from carpentry to drilling troops to personally decapitating his opponents.

THE ARMY AND THE CHURCH

The central task in Peter's reform program was to increase Russia's military might. In place of the old amateur militias and various professional bands (such as the streltsy), he created a single standing army. From 1699 onward, all its members were recruited, dressed, trained, and armed alike. He introduced conscription of nobles and serfs for lifelong service. At the same time he built a navy whose vessels were manned by foreign officers and Russian conscripts. By the end of his reign the army contained around 130,000 men, and the fleet was made up of 48 ships and almost 800 galleys.

Building the armed forces and paying for their wars consumed some 85 percent of the royal exchequer's revenues. New taxes were necessary to pay for these extraordinary expenses, and Peter replaced the old tax on households with a "soul" tax levied on all individual males, with the important exceptions of nobles and clergy. The Old Believers had to pay double, and the neighbors of any man who fled to avoid the tax were required to pay for him. This latter provision was meant to deter peasants from escaping from their villages, and thus reinforced serfdom. Peter and his advisers also introduced indirect taxes, levied on items as varied as beehives and horse collars, and established state monopolies on tobacco, salt, dice, and rhubarb.

The church, with its vast wealth and estates, lost its independence and became subordinated to the state. When the old patriarch died in 1700 he was not replaced, and a government department took over control of church property and received monastic revenues. The state paid the monks and clergy a salary and laid down detailed regulations for their daily lives. The aim was to discipline them along military lines and to make them submit to the government.

THE INFLUENCE OF THE WEST

A further blow to ecclesiastical authority was the establishment of secular institutes of education along Western lines. As a young man, Peter had made friends in the Foreign Quarter of Moscow. Early in his reign he took a trip to Western Europe—his journey is known as the "Great Embassy" of 1697–1698—to see for himself the conditions there. On his return he set up several schools. The School of Navigation and Mathematics was founded in 1701, run initially by English and Scottish teachers. Other institutes included those for languages (1701), medicine (1707), and engineering (1712). As a further contribution to general education, Peter began Russia's first newspaper in 1703.

After his inspection of Western manufacturing methods and economic systems, the tsar tried to apply Western mercantilism to Russian agriculture and industry. The aim was to improve the Russian economy, and thus increase the taxable income of its citizens. Although the economy did begin a long period of growth, the overwhelming predominance of the state prevented the development of a middle class; private enterprise had little scope in a system dominated by government controls. Without the incentive of profits, few manufacturers introduced expensive new equipment, and agricultural methods remained generally medieval.

Not content with changing public policies, Peter also tried to Westernize the private lives and attitudes of his

Colored engraving of the Muscovite cavalry. 18th century. In contrast to the previous illustration of a Cossack horseman, these conventional Russian cavalry officers wear small leather helmets and traditional metal armor. They carry short bows, used to fire iron-tipped arrows.

Contemporary caricature showing Peter the Great cutting off the beard of a boyar (Russian noble). 18th century. Eliminating his subjects' traditional long beards was one of Peter's ways of making them more Western. Those men who insisted on retaining their beards had to pay a tax on them. Note the difference in dress between the boyar (high boots, old-fashioned tunic, and cloak) and Peter's more Westernized attire.

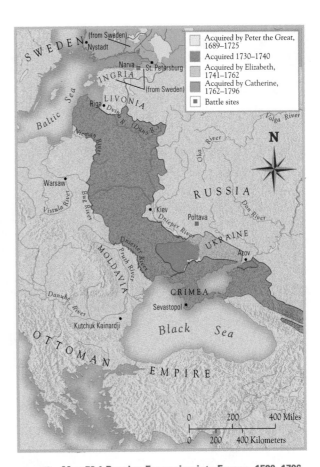

Map 53.1 Russian Expansion into Europe, 1589–1796. The crucial event in Russia's move to the West was the foundation of St. Petersburg, where work began in 1709. With the breakup of the Soviet Union in the last decade of the 20th century, some of the gains shown here became independent, notably the Ukraine. The Crimea, taken by Catherine the Great, proved to be the site of fierce fighting in the mid-19th century Crimean War, the Russian Revolution, and World War II. It was still the object of contention in the early years of the 21st century. Go to http://info.wadsworth.com/053461065X for an interactive version of this map.

subjects. He introduced decrees ordering Russian men to shave off their beards (those who refused had to pay a special tax), wear Western clothes, and bring Russian women out of seclusion. In this last respect he set an example. After a brief early marriage, he took as his mistress and drinking companion Catherine Skovorotsky (ruled 1725–1727), a tough, illiterate peasant from Lithuania. Peter married Catherine in 1712, and she ruled as empress on his death.

THE GREAT NORTHERN WAR AND THE FOUNDING OF ST. PETERSBURG

Like his predecessors, Peter devoted most of his energies to enlarging and securing Russia's territories. Among his conquests were parts of Persia, including coastal regions of the Caspian Sea, and further holdings in Siberia. In addition, he was determined to obtain easier access to Europe by sea, either through the Baltic, which was then under Swedish control, or the Black Sea, which was held by the Ottoman Turks. His campaigns against the Turks were inconclusive, and in 1700 he signed the Treaty of Constantinople with them, winning a few concessions, in order to concentrate on the struggle with Sweden.

THE GREAT NORTHERN WAR (1700–1721)

The war against Sweden occupied most of the rest of Peter's reign. His principal opponent was the Swedish king, Charles XII (see separate section), whose prowess as a military commander led to a series of early defeats for the Russian forces. As Peter's domestic reforms began to produce results, however, his troops recovered. At the decisive Battle of Poltava in 1709 he destroyed the Swedish army and advanced into Finland. By 1714, the new Russian fleet was able to defeat the Swedes and threaten the mainland of Sweden. By the Treaty of Nystad (1721), which ended the war, Russia kept Lithuania, Poland, and Estonia, all former Swedish conquests, and gave Finland back to Sweden.

THE GROWTH OF ST. PETERSBURG

Russia's new openness toward the West was symbolized by the creation of the city of St. Petersburg (Petrograd), which

ACROSS CULTURES

CATHERINE WILMOT IN RUSSIA

Travelers often keep diaries of their experiences in remote (to them) places, and these informal accounts sometimes reveal aspects of a culture that more formal writings omit. The young Irishwoman Catherine Wilmot first visited the continent of Europe in 1801, accompanying an Irish nobleman and his wife. Three years later, in 1804, she visited Russia, and her diary describing her experiences sheds interesting and unusual light on the world of the minor Russian aristocracy. It was edited for publication by the Marchioness of

Courtesy of William Duiker

Londonderry and H.M. Hyde in *The Russian Journals of Martha and Catherine Wilmot, 1803-1808* (Macmillan, 1934).

In St. Petersburg, she entertained herself on the "Mountain of Ice," an ice slide more than

SIGNIFICANT DATES

Russia from Ivan the Great to Peter the Great

1462–1505	Reign of Ivan the Great
1547–1584	Reign of Ivan the Terrible
1584–1613	Time of Troubles
1610	Polish invasion of Moscow
1649	Alexis legalizes serfdom
1671	Uprising led by Stenka Razin
1689–1725	Reign of Peter the Great
1700–1721	Great Northern War
1709	Work begins on building St. Petersburg

sessing, marshy and largely uninhabited, was nonetheless to provide the setting for Peter's new city.

Serious building began in 1709, after the Russian victory at Poltava. The city's organizers laid down a strict plan. The streets were to be broad and straight, with buildings set uniformly along them. The chief architects were Western, many of them Dutch, because Peter intended his new capital to resemble a Dutch port city. Separate parts of the city were set aside for each social class: a district for the nobility, another one for the artisans, and so on. The plan included provisions for public welfare, including street lighting, drainage canals, and parks.

To carry out this highly organized scheme, Peter made full use of his autocratic powers. He ordered the nobles and merchants to build elaborate palaces and villas and to move to the new city from Moscow when the buildings were complete. Once again, however, the peasants paid the heaviest price. Each summer, peasant workers were drafted to labor on the construction sites, while their families had to cover the costs of their upkeep. Most villages preferred to keep the

was built to replace Moscow as capital. In 1702, in the early skirmishes of the Great Northern War, Peter's forces seized a small Swedish fortress, which stood where the River Neva flows into the Baltic Sea. The land, gloomy and unprepos-

80 feet long. "It was perfectly smooth for Water had been thrown on it which froze instantly." Climbing the stairs to the top, "we sit down in an Arm Chair with one companion. The Chair has Skates instead of feet. A man who is behind you pushes you. He is provided with Skates. He directs the chair, and there you are without the least possibility of stopping till you arrive at the end of your journey. I should think the sensation must resemble the flight of a Bird."

Her picture of life on a country estate—she stayed at Troitskoe with the Princess Dashkaw—underlines the role played by servants. "It is really astonishing, but the number of servants is dreadful. Think of two, three or even four hundred to attend a small family. A Russian Lady scorns to use her own feet to go up stairs, and I do not Romance when I assure you that two powdered footmen support her lily white elbows and nearly lift her from the ground, while a couple more follow with all manner of Shawls, Pelises, etc., etc., etc. There is not a Bell in Russia except to the Churches, but if a fair one

gently calls four or five footmen are ready in an antechamber to obey her summons. We have a little theatre here, and our labourers, our Cooks, our footmen, and chamber maids turn into Princes, Princesses, Shepherds and Shepherdesses, etc., etc., and perform with a degree of spirit that is astonishing."

Other pastimes include rides through the forest on sledges drawn by three horses: "The Solitude of this Forest, which in the night is broken sometimes by the marauding of the wolves, is seldom interrupted in our course, excepting by Wood cutters who look like Satyrs rather than human beings and whose endless beards, clogged in snow and lengthened by icicles, crackle in responsive measure to their hatchets' strokes. The appearance of the Ladies of the Castle however—like magic—suspends all labour, and till the Traineau is out of sight a circle of these Shaggy Satyrs clothed in the skins of Beasts with Fur nightcaps in their paws assemble to shew their devotion and reverence by bowing repeatedly their bearheads to the ground."

stronger men at home on their farms and sent young boys or the elderly. In consequence, many workers died from the heat of summer or from accidents, and the swampy nature of the ground created a constant danger of collapse.

For all of the difficulties, the grandiose project began to take shape. At Peter's death, more than 6,000 government buildings and private residences stood on the former marshy river mouth. Less than 60 years later, in 1782, the population of St. Petersburg was almost 300,000, one of the largest in the world. During the reign of Peter's youngest daughter, Elizabeth (ruled 1741–1761), the Italian architect Bartolomeo Rastrelli (1700–1771) Europeanized Russian architecture with his Baroque and rococo palaces. One of them, the Winter Palace (Hermitage), housed the royal court and now contains the Hermitage Museum, today among the world's great art collections.

For all the undoubted achievements of Peter's reign, the price was high and the results mixed. Government remained inefficient and corrupt. Moreover, the tsar could issue orders on high, but day-to-day administration was in the hands of

local bureaucrats, who maintained their arbitrary tyranny over the helpless lower classes. The condition of the serfs became even more hopeless than under Ivan the Terrible. Religious opposition to the process of Westernization came from Old Believers and reformed Orthodox Christians alike. Many conservative nobles, who were opposed to the tsar's reforms, looked to Peter's son Alexis to restore former conditions. Peter, knowing his son to be pious and old-fashioned, had him and his followers eliminated in a purge in 1718. He claimed the right to nominate his own successor, but died before doing so, thus leaving the way open for the palace revolutions that marked 18th-century Russian political life.

Yet if Peter's reforms of government and the economy were only partially successful, his creation of a formidable military machine and aggressive foreign policy changed the course of European history. By winning the Baltic provinces, Russia replaced Sweden as the leading power in northern Europe. Newly Westernized in outlook, Russia was now ready to assume its role as a major actor on the stage of European power politics.

U
ducing
Polan
was r
by the
condit

R
Great
Russi
The d
progre
centu
Slavs
Y
Throu
to ack
the m

Quest

1. What
   affairs
   nized
2. What
   Russia
   societ
3. Which
   berme
4. How a
   velopi

Sugge

Anderson
Bain, Rob
   Swed
Bushkovi
   1671

THE ARTS IN TRANSITION

The 18th century produced a remarkably varied range of artistic styles. The elevated grandeur of Corneille's and Racine's tragedies, the charmingly erotic scenes depicted in Watteau's canvasses, the social intrigues of Mozart's operas: all of these varied forms seem to have little in common. Yet they, and the visions of other artists of the same period, share the characteristic of being addressed to an increasingly widening public.

Hitherto, most artists had served a patron, generally the church, the monarchy, or the aristocracy. Works of art, whether for the public domain or for private entertainment, conformed to the requirements of their commissioners. Ever since the 16th century, sections of the European aristocracy had cultivated the arts, playing music, patronizing artists, and engaging in amateur artistic pursuits. Toward the end of the 17th century, however, economic expansion, urbanization, and the spread of literacy produced a new public, as the middle classes began to develop an interest in the arts. Corneille's plays represent, in fact, one of the earliest attempts to address a middle-class audience.

With the change in audience came a change in the status of the artist. Although still dependent on some form of patronage—the artist as fiery, free-thinking creator did not appear until the 19th century—writers, painters, and musicians acquired a new social status. Friedrich II of Prussia entertained at his court the leading composers of the day, wrote music and played the flute, and boasted of his intimate friendship with the great French writer Voltaire. The relationship was a fiery one. When Friedrich had "squeezed all the juice from the rind," he dropped Voltaire, who in turn made sure that his own version of the break circulated as widely as possible.

When in his later years the Austrian composer Haydn traveled throughout Europe, he was feted and honored as one of the most famous figures of his times. Haydn's own career, in fact, was symbolic of the new status of the creative artist. He spent his early years as an employee at the court of one of the leading aristocratic families, the Esterhazys, as director of the prince's music; when he wanted to write music for another patron, he was obliged to ask permission. With the growth of his fame, he was able to negotiate a revised contract under which the Esterhazys no longer had exclusive rights to his work. By the time he reached his sixties, he was free to live in Vienna and travel abroad, although he still continued to compose for the Esterhazys.

The new social position that artists occupied, together with the broad changes in society that made it possible, was inevitably reflected in their works. Although the artistic styles of the 18th century were far more varied than those of the Baroque Era, many of the age's most important achievements reflect a new preoccupation: a conscious engagement with social issues. Racine and Mozart, along with Richardson and many others, used their art to explore ways of advancing and reforming society. By the mid-18th century, the intellectual movement known as the Enlightenment (see Topic 58) provided an underpinning for these concerns.

TRAGEDY AND COMEDY AT THE COURT OF LOUIS XIV

For Louis XIV, the arts served as a means of projecting his vision of himself as Grand Monarch. The court at Versailles provided an appreciative audience for the theater, and in the latter part of the 17th century three great playwrights dominated French drama. All of them concentrated on depicting universal human types and emotions, rather than reflecting the world of the court.

THE COMEDIES OF MOLIÈRE

Molière was the stage name of Jean-Baptiste Poquelin (1622–1673). He was the son of a court furnisher, but rather than follow his father's profession, at the age of 21 he joined a group of actors to form a theatrical company. The actors soon went bankrupt, and Molière spent some time in prison for debt. Undeterred, he left Paris for the provinces to learn the craft of acting and playwriting. When he returned to the capital 13 years later with his own troupe, he performed before the king. In 1665 Louis became patron of his company, and Molière wrote romances and comedies for the royal courts at Saint-Germain and Versailles. He also poured out a stream of plays for a wider public, often acting in them. He died on stage in the middle of a performance of his last play, *Le Malade imaginaire (The Hypochondriac)*—of overwork, it was said.

Ironically for one favored by Louis XIV, Molière's source of comedy was the deflation of pomposity and arrogance. Taking a human weakness or delusion, such as hypochondria, miserliness, or misanthropy, he carries it to an absurd and often explosive conclusion. Yet revelation comes through laughter, not ridicule, and the characters remain believable. Tartuffe, the oily hypocrite in the play of the same name (1664–1669), or Jourdain, the amiable social climber of *Le Bourgeois gentilhomme* (1670), are not merely symbols but living personalities.

Only in one play, *L'Avare (The Miser*; 1668), does a human foible seem cruel and deluded. The miserliness of its chief character, Harpagon, is revealed as a perverse mania, reducing its victim to a childishness that provides the comic element. On the whole the message of Molière's works is to underline the humanity of even the most absurd of his characters and to advocate reason and balance—the Classical middle way.

THE CLASSICAL TRAGEDIES OF CORNEILLE AND RACINE

The two leading tragedians of the age were Pierre Corneille (1606–1684) and Jean Racine (1639–1699). Both used as their starting point themes from Classical mythology or history, but their approaches were very different.

Corneille was already writing when Louis XIV came to the throne, creating a new kind of play—the Classical verse tragedy—for a middle-class audience. His dramas are serious in tone, often dealing with conflicts of principles that call into question established morality. They thus appealed to a middle-class public that was questioning traditional ideas. *Horace* (1640) is based on incidents recorded by the ancient Roman historian Livy, and tells of a patriot who saves the state, but at the cost of the life of his pacifist sister. *Polyeucte* (1643) presents the dilemma of a martyr, whose wish for a glorious death is tempered by duty to his faithful wife. Corneille's plays are self-consciously artificial. They make no attempt to represent literal time, place, or action. Instead, they provide abstract intellectual conflict in the cut and thrust of rhetorical debate.

Racine's first tragedy was produced by Molière's company in 1664, and he went on to write works for the leading Paris theaters. Using the Classical verse tragedy form perfected by Corneille, he brought to it a new understanding of human emotions. In plays such as *Phèdre* (1677), he explored the psychological state of mind of his characters. His dominating theme is the human tendency toward self-destruction through ambition, jealousy, passion, and other forms of what his contemporary La Rochfoucauld (1613–1680) called self-love. His characters realize the tragedy of the human condition, while their understanding of their own helplessness reinforces their suffering and our pity for them. In his last play, *Athalie* (1691), the queen whose name gives the play its title expresses this sense of abandonment in a hostile world: "Pitiless God, Thou hast willed it all!"

ACADEMIES AND SALONS IN THE REPUBLIC OF LETTERS

The growing popularity of science in the 17th century led to the formation of learned societies, or academies, for the discussion and spread of new ideas and discoveries. Among the most famous was the Royal Society of London, which received its royal charter in 1660. By the 18th century, the taste for semipublic discussion of ideas of all sorts spurred the creation of many more or less formal groups. Many of these groups sprang up in provincial cities in various parts of Europe, often in relatively small centers. As a result, knowledge of new ideas and values became more widespread than before.

In some cases these organizations sponsored the arts. London's Royal Academy of Arts was founded in 1768 by George III to encourage painting and still maintains an art school and holds open exhibitions annually. The Royal Academy's first president, Sir Joshua Reynolds (1723–1792), also sponsored the Literary Club for the discussion of literary topics. Among its members were Samuel Johnson (1709–1784), perhaps the most brilliant if idiosyncratic writer and critic of his time, the statesman and philosopher Edmund Burke (1729–1797), and the writer Oliver Goldsmith (c. 1730–1774).

Some organizations had specific goals. Catherine the Great entrusted the Imperial Russian Academy with preparing a standard Russian grammar and the first Russian dictionary, in addition to giving it the general task of providing translations of scientific and philosophical works into Russian.

By midcentury the creation of academies swelled to a flood. In Florence alone, there flourished the Accademia delle Belle Arti for painting and drawing, the Accademia della Crusca (*crusca* literally means bran; the academy was formed to preserve the purity of the Italian language by "separating the wheat from the chaff"), the Accademia dei Georgofili (literally "farming-lovers"; its members discussed scientific and economic aspects of farming), the Accademia

Painting of the young Mozart entertaining a Paris salon. 1766. Leopold Mozart, the composer's father, took the young genius on a European tour when he was seven years old, in 1763. Paris was one of the last stops, where Mozart played for the French royal court, published his compositions for the first time, and composed his first symphonies.

PUBLIC FIGURES AND PRIVATE LIVES

ELIZABETH ROBINSON MONTAGU AND EDWARD MONTAGU

Picture Library, National Portrait Gallery, London

Picture Library, National Portrait Gallery, London

The first salon may have been established by a French noblewoman, the Marquise de Rambouillet (1588–1665). Suffering from an illness that required her to remain in bed wrapped in blankets and furs, she entertained guests from a bedroom alcove in her Parisian home. The salon eventually became an established institution in Paris, where women brought the talented and the powerful into their homes. By the middle of the following century, when the influence of the salon was at its height, the practice had spread to other European cities.

In Great Britain, the salon was the creation of Elizabeth Montagu (1720–1800). Elizabeth developed a serious interest in literature at an early age and read widely. High-spirited and outgoing, she married Edward Montagu (d. 1775), grandson of the first earl of Sandwich, in 1742. Edward was a wealthy and serious-minded man who owned coal mines and estates, liked agriculture and mathematics, and served in Parliament for more than 30 years.

The couple lived in the country, where Elizabeth earned a reputation as an accomplished hostess. Their one child, a son, died after only a year, and thereafter the couple led increasingly separate lives. Soon she moved the household to London, where the social season offered more distractions, and she made the Montagu home in Mayfair a gathering place for the most important intellectuals of the city—to a friend she explained, "I never invite idiots to my house."

At first Elizabeth entertained at literary breakfasts, but she soon added more elaborate evening assemblies, which became known as "conversation parties." She refused to allow card playing, encouraging her guests instead to discuss literary subjects. On occasion, a well-known actor would recite. For 50 years, Elizabeth presided over the intellectual society of London, and writers, artists, and politicians vied with one another for invitations to the Montagu salon, where wit counted more than high birth.

The term "Bluestockings" was first applied to the women intellectuals who attended Montagu's salon. The origin of the name is disputed, but one version of the story recounts that because Elizabeth allowed her guests to dress casually, one of her poorer friends always wore blue wool stockings instead of those made of more elegant black silk. Soon the word became a collective term for the women who attended and hosted such receptions, although it later came to be used derogatively to mean a woman who was pedantic, plain, and unfeminine.

In 1775, Edward Montagu died and left Elizabeth a large income and many estates. She went to Paris the next year, where she became familiar with the works of Voltaire. She also built a large and sumptuous house in London, which became the new center for her salon. To demonstrate her social consciousness, each May she invited the chimney sweeps of London to eat roast beef and plum pudding on the lawn of her home. By 1798, when she was almost blind and very feeble, her entertaining had all but ceased. She died two years later.

The salon not only permitted women to lead and take an active part in cultural debate alongside men, but it also provided a forum that brought together aristocrats and middle-class intellectuals, helping both groups to get to know one another's ways. Furthermore, the salons of Berlin and Vienna, by their inclusion of Jews, encouraged a greater official tolerance toward Jewish minorities; many of Berlin's leading salons, in fact, were run by Jewish women. The most successful *salonières*, or hostesses, achieved considerable power behind the scenes, promoting their pet writers' work or advancing the political careers of their favorites. As one of them boasted, "It is possible to obtain through women what one wants from men."

del Cimento (Academy for Scientific Testing), and the portentously named Accademia Toscana di Scienze e Lettere "La Colombaria" (Tuscan Academy for Science and Letters "The Dovecote," so-called because of the small size of the room in which its members met).

Although some of the academies encouraged women to become members, most retained quotas. One of Italy's most admired 18th-century poets was Maria Maddalena Morelli (1727–1800), better known as Corilla. In 1776, the Roman Academy crowned her on the steps of the capitol for her abilities in declamation and improvisation. But most educated, serious women who were interested in participating in the literary and intellectual debates of the day had to do so informally. As a result of this constraint, women developed a new kind of cultural institution known as the **salon:** gatherings in private homes for the purpose of intellectual discussion (the term *salon* comes from the French word for sitting room).

THE POPULAR PRESS, NOVELS, AND THE CIRCULATION OF IDEAS

With the rapid growth of a middle-class reading public, literary culture began to spread in new ways. Just as conversation became the chief activity of the salons, so reading aloud came to occupy many middle-class families in their own homes. Because women were on their own territory in front of the family hearth, their tastes in literature became increasingly important.

THE GROWTH OF THE PRESS

The appearance of the popular press provided a potential challenge to governments, which were accustomed to controlling the spread of information. In 1662, the British Parliament passed the Licensing Act, limiting the number of licensed printers to 20, "to prevent abuses in printing seditious, treasonable, and unlicensed books and pamphlets." Yet the pressure for new sources of information was too great to resist: In 1695, Parliament decided not to renew the Licensing Act, and the next two decades saw the birth of scores of journals. The first London daily paper, the *Courant*, appeared in 1702, to be followed by a string of competitors. Even the imposition of state taxes on publications and their advertisements failed to discourage their proliferation.

Much of the contents of the dailies was practical: news of markets and shipping, prices of stocks and exchange rates, and "Names and Descriptions of Persons becoming Bankrupt." Details of births, marriages, deaths, and inquests began to appear. The largest number of pages was devoted to small commercial advertisements. The weekly magazines tended to include articles on more general topics, including politics, reviews of books and plays, and fashion.

In addition, the leading periodicals exercised a more general cultural impact. *The Spectator*, founded in 1711 by the English essayist and statesman Joseph Addison

(1672–1719), helped form the taste of the age and shaped the values and behavior of its educated middle-class subscribers. Addison's impact was acknowledged by influential London figures, such as Dr. Johnson, but it also had a wider effect as his publication reached provincial and foreign readers. Among many others, David Hume in Edinburgh and Benjamin Franklin in Philadelphia both admired Addison's style, and used it as a model.

The rise in circulation of both daily and weekly publications was rapid and consistent. The total annual sale in Great Britain rose from 2,250,000 in 1711 to 7,000,000 in 1753 and to 12,230,000 in 1776 (the figures are available because of the tax paid on each copy sold). Because many papers were bought by clubs and coffeehouses, the total readership was far larger than the number of copies in circulation. With its growth, the popular press acquired considerable power. The opponents of the British prime minister Sir Robert Walpole accused him of paying out more than £50,000 in bribes to newspapers in the last 10 years of his administration, and the freedom of the press became a major political issue.

WOMEN'S MAGAZINES

Many of the new publications were specifically addressed to women, who constituted an important and growing class of readership. In the Netherlands and Germany, women contributed many of the articles, and one of the leading Dutch papers, *The Quintessence of News*, was founded by a woman, Madame du Noyer. The most important French periodical for women, the *Journal des Dames*, first appeared in 1759, when its male publishers announced it as a "delicious nothing" for society ladies. Its women editors soon changed its character, however, publishing articles and reviews dealing with the question of women's rights and making thinly veiled attacks on the government.

By the latter part of the 18th century, middle-class families throughout Europe were exposed to a bewildering range of dailies, weeklies, and periodicals, many of which circulated outside their country of origin. One enterprising publisher even found a way to help readers who were spoiled for choice. The *Grand Magazine of Magazines, or Universal Register* contained "all that is curious, useful, or entertaining in the magazines, reviews, or chronicles, at home or abroad."

THE RISE OF THE POPULAR NOVEL

Popular novels had appeared in France as early as the reign of Louis XIV, many of them written by women. From the early 18th century on, popular writers in Europe made a deliberate appeal to middle-class ideals and values. The social background and accepted attitudes of the books reflected a world dominated by class consciousness and economic status. The rise or fall of individuals, often because of marriage, is paralleled by critical developments in fortune and character.

The first significant popular writer in English was Samuel Richardson (1689–1761). His novel *Pamela* (1740), written in the form of a series of letters, describes the triumph of a servant girl, who marries her master after successfully fighting off his attempts at seduction. Produced in only two months, *Pamela* proved a bestseller throughout Europe, especially in France. A later novel, *Clarissa* (1748), also deals with seduction, but its moral vision is more complex. Its two chief characters, the virtuous Clarissa and the cunning and immoral (and aristocratic) Lovelace, are both victims of a sexuality that is at the same time obsessive and destructive.

THE ART OF THE ROCOCO

With the death of Louis XIV in 1715, the French aristocracy abandoned the Baroque extravagance of Versailles for the elegant domestic comfort of Paris, and a new artistic style developed to provide an appropriate setting. The **rococo**—the word derives from the French *rocaille*, or grotto decoration—was intended as a contrast to the Baroque. Rarely weighty or serious, it aims for charm and lightness and replaces Baroque drama with grace and harmony. The interior decoration of buildings such as the Hotel de Soubise in Paris was appropriate for an age that put a new emphasis on civilized conversation. Rococo art, with its frank desire to please, also ap-

Fragonard, *Love Letters*. 1773. 10 feet 5 inches by 7 feet 1 inch (3.17 by 2.17 m). Both in subject—an amorous encounter—and style, this is typical of later rococo painting. The jungle of trees and bushes seems to impart a heady, humid air to what at first glance seems an innocent meeting. Rococo artists often aimed to emphasize the erotic nature of their scenes.

Germain Boffrand, Salon de la Princesse, Hotel Soubise, Paris, c. 1737–1740. Oval 33 feet by 26 feet (10.06 by 7.92 m). The architecture and decoration (painting and sculptures) all combine to create a characteristic rococo effect. The paintings flowing from ceiling to walls break down the distinction between horizontal and vertical elements, and the reflections in the large mirrors further confuse the viewer's sense of space.

pealed to middle-class clients, who were in search of works that were appropriate to an intimate domestic setting, rather than intended for grandiose palaces.

Many rococo artists explored the theme of romantic dalliance. The last great French rococo painter, Jean-Honoré Fragonard (1732–1806), achieved an erotic effect with great subtlety. His superb lightness of touch and sense of color often emerge in the scenery surrounding his figures. The sense of warmth in the air in paintings such as *Love Letters* (1773) adds a touch of danger to the apparently innocent couple in the foreground.

RELIGIOUS ART AND THE ROCOCO

The lightness of the rococo style did not lend itself naturally to religious subjects in painting but inspired some remarkable architecture. Some of the finest of all rococo buildings can be seen in southern Germany and Austria, where the bitter wars of the 17th century had discouraged the building of new churches. With the more stable conditions of the first part of the 18th century, construction started again, producing a series of rococo masterpieces.

Balthasar Neumann, Nave and High Altar of Vierzehnheiligen Pilgrim Church, near Bamberg, Germany. 1743–1772. The oval shape of the altar, typical of pilgrimage churches, is echoed in the oval ceiling paintings. The architect has rejected the soaring lines of the Gothic style and the balance of Renaissance symmetry for an intricate interweaving of surfaces, volumes, and space.

The German architect Balthasar Neumann (1687–1753), an engineer by profession, designed several churches and episcopal palaces. Perhaps his most elaborate and intricate work is the interior of the Vierzehnheiligen (Fourteen Saints) Pilgrimage Church (1743–1772) near Bamberg, in southern Germany. The decoration flows down from the ceiling, encrusting walls and columns, in a deliberate rejection of Renaissance notions of balance and symmetry. For those accustomed to the austerity of much religious architecture, the sheer lightness and exuberance of Neumann's creation may seem out of place, but it succeeds in producing a sense of joy that is not inappropriate.

THE CLASSICAL STYLE IN MUSIC: MOZART AND HAYDN

As music, like literature, began to find an ever-widening audience, composers tried to express more complex and varied emotions. By the mid-18th century, composers had developed a style to meet the requirement of unity through variety: the Classical style. Its first great master was the Austrian Franz Joseph Haydn (1732–1809), whose more

than 100 symphonies won him the name of "Father of the Symphony."

WOLFGANG AMADEUS MOZART

The life of the Austrian Wolfgang Amadeus Mozart (1756–1791) illustrates that not all artists were as fortunate as Haydn. When Haydn met the young Mozart in 1781, he observed to the young man's father, "Before God and as an honest man, your son is the greatest composer known to me either in person or by name." Posterity has seen no reason to doubt Haydn's judgment, yet Mozart's career was dogged by a constant alternation of successes and setbacks. A child prodigy, he traveled throughout Europe with his father, composing and performing to the acclaim of his aristocratic audiences.

Mozart was less fortunate in his patron than Haydn. After serving the archbishop of Salzburg, where he was born, Mozart tried to follow his great contemporary's example and obtain some measure of independence. When he asked for his freedom, the reigning archbishop, Hieronymous Colloredo, had him literally kicked out of the palace. Haydn managed to win his independence through the cooperation of his employer, and remained tied to some degree to noble patronage. Mozart's break was complete and violent.

Mozart spent the last 10 years of his life in Vienna, struggling to find a permanent position and pouring out works to earn a living—symphonies and concertos for orchestral concerts, piano sonatas and string quartets, religious music for

Joseph Lange, *Mozart at the Pianoforte*. 1789. 13½ inches by 11½ inches (35 by 30 cm). This unfinished portrait shows the composer for once without the white wig customarily worn in the 18th century. Mozart must have liked the painting, because he had a copy made and sent to his father.

church performance, even music for Masonic ceremonies (Mozart was a Freemason). The Viennese public acclaimed many of his works. With no fixed income, however, Mozart lived on the brink of financial disaster, partly because of his habit of spending money on gambling and entertainment as fast as he earned it. In 1791, he died at the age of 35 and was buried in a pauper's grave.

Mozart's music reflects little of the outward turbulence of his daily life. Perhaps more than any other musician, in his finest works he combined pure grace with profound learning to create an ideal beauty. Yet his music does not lack in drama or seriousness. Mozart's operas provide perhaps the easiest, and most enjoyable, access to his work. *The Marriage of Figaro* (1786) was based on a play of the same name by the French dramatist Pierre-Augustin Beaumarchais (1732–1799), which attacked the immorality of the aristocracy. It showed its hero, Figaro, outwitting the attempts of his noble employer to seduce Figaro's wife-to-be. Mozart's opera adds to the social protest of the original a sense of humanity, rather than personal resentment. Figaro expresses the frustration of centuries of men and women who had suffered from the injustices of class discrimination.

Putting the Culture of the Old Regime in Perspective

By the end of Mozart's life, the French Revolution had broken out and the Old Regime was swept away. Some of the art of the 18th century may have distracted its aristocratic public from the changing times and attitudes. Yet the elegant world of rococo art was to be cut short by the guillotine as the result of a revolution at least partly because of other cultural developments in the 18th century.

The social criticisms of Mozart's operas and Richardson's novels were directed at the injustice and immorality of the ruling classes. Discussion of the issues of social and political reform began to circulate increasingly widely through popular literary forms. Academies and salons made it possible for the upper and middle classes to actually meet on equal social terms and raised the question of whether high birth was really superior to inherent ability.

The lowering of social and cultural barriers was limited. Most Europeans—the lower classes—continued to live as they had for centuries. An 18th-century Italian peasant, Russian serf, or Welsh shepherd was equally deprived educationally and economically dependent. It would take the Industrial Revolution, with its cities and factories, to draw attention to the hardships of the working classes and the poor, and to give them the chance to fight to improve their lot.

Yet with the spread of culture in the 18th century, the foundation was laid for future struggles. The forerunners of artists and writers of more recent times who campaigned for political causes were those who in the 18th century used their newly gained freedom to deal with the problems of their societies.

Questions for Further Study

1. What role did social criticism play in the arts in the 18th century?
2. What are the main features of the rococo style? How do they differ from the style of Baroque art?
3. What changes, if any, were there in the status of women in middle-class 18th-century society?
4. In what ways was the public for the arts a broader one than in the Renaissance or the 17th century? What were the causes?

Suggestions for Further Reading

Conisbee, P. *Painting in Eighteenth-Century France*. Ithaca, NY, 1981.

Darnton, R. *The Literary Underground of the Old Regime*. Cambridge, MA, 1982.

Ferguson, M., ed. *First Feminists: British Women Writers 1578–1799*. Bloomington, IN, 1984.

Kalnein, W., and M. Levey. *Art and Architecture of the 18th Century in France*. Baltimore, MD, 1972.

Levey, M. *Painting and Sculpture in France, 1700-1789*. New Haven, CT, 1993.

Minor, Vernon Hyde. *Baroque and Rococo: Art and Culture*. New York, 1999.

Osborne, Charles. *The Complete Operas of Mozart*. London, 1992.

Robbins Landon, H.C. *Essays on the Viennese Classical Style*. New York, 1970.

Roston, M. *Changing Perspectives in Literature and the Visual Arts, 1650-1820*. Princeton, NJ, 1990.

Varriano, J. *Italian Baroque and Rococo Architecture*. New York, 1986.

InfoTrac College Edition

Enter the search term *Old Regime culture* using Key Terms.

Enter the search term *Louis XIV and arts* using the Subject Guide.

Enter the search term *Corneille* using Key Terms.

Enter the search term *Racine* using Key Terms.

Enter the search term *Mozart* using Key Terms.

EUROPE AND THE WORLD ECONOMY

The overseas discoveries made during the age of exploration in the 16th century had important repercussions for Europe and its economic life. The most dramatic impact came from the flow of huge amounts of gold and silver bullion to Europe from the New World, which produced an inflationary cycle that drove prices upward and created economic hardships for many millions of people. In addition, new patterns of trade emerged, particularly the shift of the center of gravity from the Mediterranean to the Atlantic, and new sources of wealth developed. The resulting "commercial revolution" saw a sharp rise in trade, both within Europe and on an international scale, and involved important new products from abroad and the increasing exportation of European-made goods. By the 18th century, a world market had come into being, with Western Europe at its center.

One feature that both reflected and affected Western values was the growth and spread of the slave trade, as well as efforts to combat it. Similarly, the allure of large and quickly made profits sparked by the prosperity often resulted in risky schemes for financial speculation that caused serious setbacks for European investors. As the profits and opportunities in commerce grew, the centralization and strict state regulation that marked the old economic doctrine of mercantilism began to give way. By the 18th century, private commercial and financial interests had become closely linked with state policy. Finally, the colonial expansion beyond Europe's borders that was a prelude to or came along with the growth in trade had adverse consequences not only on non-European peoples and their cultures, but also on the peace and prosperity of the West.

TOWARD A WORLD ECONOMY

In the aftermath of the great age of discovery, the nature of international trade, and of Europe's position in it, underwent a major transformation, as what had been essentially a series of regional economies blended and merged into an integrated world marketplace. As a byproduct of these changes, the new trade patterns had a profound impact on the material and social life of Europe.

CHANGING TRADE PATTERNS

Before the commercial revolution, a series of distinct regional trade patterns and isolated markets had characterized world commerce. Trade within Europe, consisting of long-established local complexes such as those in the eastern Mediterranean, along the southern coast of France, or between Great Britain and Flanders, represented by far the bulk of European trade. Moreover, as central governments consolidated their control over national territories in Great Britain and France, domestic markets loomed increasingly more important. Europe's commercial relations with the rest of the world were also limited largely to two distinct but crucial patterns: the shipment of bullion from colonies in the Americas to mother countries in Europe and the importation of spices from Asia.

By the 18th century, all continents were linked in an integrated, worldwide marketplace. New markets, such as that in the Baltic region, had expanded the volume of trade within Europe, while the old mercantilist monopolies that had once restricted trade between colonies and their mother country had been dissolved. Colonial items, in the form of raw materials and finished products, were increasingly being processed in Europe and then reexported to other parts of the world; the English, for example, reexported Virginia tobacco and the French sugar from the West Indies. One of the most successful innovations of the commercial revolution was the development of triangular trade. In the typical example, English manufactured goods, such as printed fabrics, were traded to Africa for slaves. The slaves were in turn exchanged in the West Indies for sugar, which was then sold and consumed in Great Britain. Triangular trade flourished in the 18th century, when the British obtained the *asiento*, or the exclusive right to trade slaves in the Spanish colonies, a right that gave them access to Spanish-American markets for illegal goods.

As the volume of domestic and international trade increased, European merchants adjusted and refined their business practices, including marine insurance, credit banking facilities, stock exchanges, and uniform weights and measures. Tremendous fortunes were made in trade among the merchant class in the 18th century, especially in Great Britain and France, which had overtaken not only Spain and Portugal but also the Dutch Republic in the carrying trade. Commercial profits, along with the rising demand for European manufactured goods, acted as a stimulus to the Industrial Revolution (see Topic 60).

One result of Europe's central role in the growth of global trade was that the West became infinitely more wealthy than any other region of the world. Europe's prosperity was, of course, the product of many factors, not the least of which were the natural resources of the Americas and the forced labor of millions of African slaves. Profits led to the accumulation of significant amounts of capital by European merchants. In addition, the general standard of living throughout western Europe increased, especially among the intermediate levels of society, although most Europeans, consisting of manual laborers and peasants, still lived close to the margin of subsistence.

NEW WORLD COMMODITIES AND OLD WORLD TASTES

In the mid-1600s, however, trade patterns began to undergo important changes. Eastern spices and Western bullion were still the most important commodities from overseas, but new products were beginning to increase in significance. The imports of bullion began to fall steadily after 1620, while the European spice market became saturated. Large amounts of New World bullion—including as much as one-third of all silver—were sent to Asia, while spices and a variety of other luxury goods came back. In the years after 1640, such products as sugar, coffee, tea, tobacco, raw cotton and cotton fabrics, dyes, and furs assumed an increasing role in world trade. These new goods had a dual impact: They accounted for the continual expansion of the volume of trade and altered patterns of consumption and diet in Europe. The 18th century saw a tremendous increase in the new kind of trade; between 1698 and 1775, Great Britain experienced a growth of some 500 percent in exports and almost as much in imports, most of the increase in colonial trade. French trade also expanded significantly in the 18th century.

Tobacco was the first new product from the Americas to be used widely by Europeans. Most of the American tobacco was grown in Virginia and Maryland and then shipped to Europe, where it was blended and sold for smoking, chewing, or to be used as snuff. As tobacco became immensely popular, governments throughout Europe imposed import duties and excise taxes on the product to raise revenues. In many nations, including France, Austria, Spain, and the Italian and German states, tobacco became a profitable state monopoly.

Of increasing importance was the importation of textiles, and especially of cotton fabrics. Cotton had been known in Europe for centuries, but had not been widely used. In the 17th century, however, imports of raw cotton from India and America began to increase substantially. Moreover, one of the most popular goods imported from abroad was the brightly colored Indian cotton of exceptionally light weight known as calico (so-called after the Indian city of Calicut). These printed fabrics were of fine quality, and the large-scale Indian textile industry produced inexpensive products because they were made by low-cost hand labor. The demand for calicoes grew rapidly because they could be used for a variety of purposes, including dresses, underclothing, stockings, and upholstery. By 1680, the

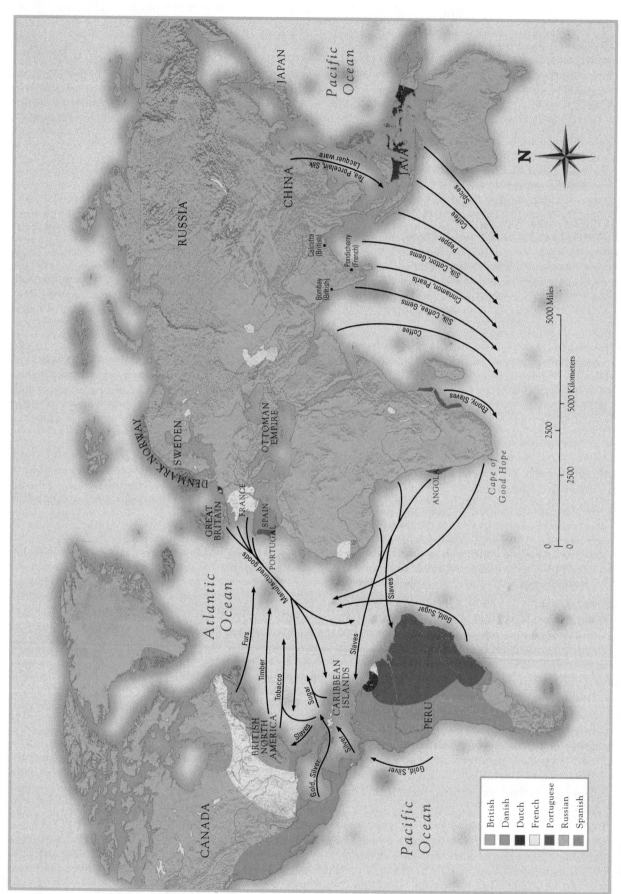

Map 55.1 European Sea Trade, c. 1750. Apart from the Americas, trade is limited to coastal regions. Africa was used as a stopping-off point on longer sails mainly for the collection of slaves, its interior yet unexplored. Australia, which was still untouched by the Europeans, was to be claimed by the British at the end of the century.

English East India Company's textile imports were more important than its spice imports.

So much in demand were calicoes by the early 18th century that Great Britain and France both imposed limitations on their importation in order to protect domestic clothing makers. In 1700, the British Parliament passed an act forbidding the importation of all printed calicoes, although it allowed white calicoes to be brought in to encourage the English dye and printer factories (printed calicoes could, however, be imported for reexport). The Calico Act of 1720 prohibited the use or wearing of calico prints in Great Britain, but such restrictions only increased the demand for the fabric and stimulated the growth of the domestic cotton industry. The act was repealed in 1774, by which time the English textile industry had so developed that it could supply the home market with enough cotton fabrics.

Three beverages—coffee, tea, and cocoa—had far-reaching effect on European tastes. The trade in coffee, which had been introduced into Europe from the Middle East and Asia in the early 17th century, was largely in the hands of the English and the Dutch, the latter eventually growing their own supply in Java. By the end of the century, coffee had become a popular drink in Great Britain, often replacing beer. Coffeehouses and cafés became meeting places for social and intellectual discourse.

Even more popular was tea, long a staple drink in China and India. In 1664, the English East India Company, which enjoyed a monopoly on the China tea trade, presented King Charles II with the rare gift of two pounds of tea; by 1790, the company was selling millions of pounds of

tea per year to the home market. Throughout the century, coffee remained the drink of the privileged classes, while tea became a staple used by all social classes in Great Britain.

Together with tea, sugar imported from the West Indies had an important effect on nutrition and worked both a commercial and a social revolution in Europe. Grown originally in southern Spain and Sicily, sugar was taken to the Canaries shortly after 1500 and then to Brazil and to the British and French West Indies, where the sugar cane thrived in the heat and humidity. By 1650, it had become another staple item in the European diet, its demand fueled by the growing use of tea, coffee, and cocoa. Sugar refineries in France numbered 18 by 1683 and processed some 18 million pounds of raw sugar each year. As the quantity of sugar produced increased steadily in the 18th century, its price fell and it ceased to be a luxury item as more people could afford it. At this point, American trade, which was based largely on sugar, became more valuable than Asian trade. Sugar also yielded two subsidiary products, molasses and rum. Molasses became a cheap and sweet addition to the European diet and was the raw material from which rum was produced.

THE SLAVE TRADE

One essential aspect of the craze for American products such as cotton, tobacco, and sugar was their relationship to the slave trade. These and other products, but principally sugar, were grown in the New World on large "plan-

Engraving showing slaves picking and processing cotton in the West Indies. 18th century. The slaves are Africans, transported to the West Indies to work, in this case, on French cotton plantations. The engraving illustrates the entire process from the picking of the cotton on the right to the loaded bales in the left foreground.

The Granger Collection

HISTORICAL PERSPECTIVES

THE SLAVE TRADE AND THE EUROPEAN ECONOMY

CHARLES L. KILLINGER   Valencia Community College

European trade in African slaves and the commercial products they produced and consumed affected the economic development of modern Europe in many important ways; however, economic historians have questioned the scale of the profits from the slave trade and the nature of their impact on European industrialization. They have also studied the influence of the slave trade on the African and American colonial economies. In the context of the European economy, the primary questions facing students of the slave trade are these: How profitable was the slave trade? In what ways did the slave trade contribute to the growth of the European economy?

Although Europeans had been trading in African slaves since the middle of the 15th century, it was not until 300 years later that the trade increased most dramatically and its profits peaked. By 1700, Portuguese and Spanish slave trade had dwindled with the decline of their imperial power, and the British had surpassed the Dutch through a series of maritime victories. In the Treaty of Utrecht of 1713 (see Topic 49), the British gained the treasured *asiento (el pacto del asiento de negros)*, the exclusive contract for supplying slaves to Spanish America; although vessels of many nations continued to participate, the British now dominated the shipping of African slaves to the New World. During the 18th century, slavers transported nearly 6 million Africans to the Americas, almost two-thirds of those imported over the entire duration of the trade.

As a result of the massive importation of free labor into the Western Hemisphere, the plantation economy expanded greatly. Plantations in the Americas produced agricultural commodities for export, including tobacco, ginger, indigo, cotton, and sugar. Because all of these products were extremely labor-intensive, the use of free labor guaranteed low production costs. The primary beneficiaries were the British and French, and the most lucrative part of that triangular trade was the importation of slave-grown sugar from Caribbean islands.

In the 18th century, primarily on the strength of sugar production, the British West Indies surpassed India, China, and North America as sources of imported British goods, and the French colony of St. Domingue (Haiti) outstripped every British possession in annual sugar production. By the end of the century, 200,000 slaves in the British colony of Jamaica were producing 50,000 tons of sugar annually; a half-million slaves on St. Domingue were producing 100,000 tons each year. By 1700, Brazil was still importing huge numbers of slaves despite the decline of the sugar industry there, while in the second half of the century Spanish imports increased as sugar production in Cuba grew.

The success of the West Indian plantations satisfied the demands of mercantilism (see Topic 46), the dominant European economic practice of the day. The major European nations competed for markets and sources of raw materials for industrial production in order to achieve a favorable balance of trade and thereby gain an advantage over their adversaries. Slave labor ensured a competitive advantage to the West Indian plantation colonies; in turn, the colonies not only enriched their owners, but also contributed to the national strength, especially of the British and French empires.

In an effort to impose mercantilist regulation of the trade, European nations competed for exclusive rights to slave markets and granted national monopolies to slave-trading companies. In 1672, for example, Britain granted such a monopoly to the Royal African Company, a joint-stock company, to compete with the Dutch for general control of international commerce. Soon it was exporting £100,000 worth of goods annually to Africa in order to meet the West Indian demand for slaves. London and Bristol merchants and shippers, envious of the trade, succeeded in breaking the company's monopoly in 1698. Thus both government and private merchants of the day clearly regarded the slave trade as profitable and potentially quite lucrative; however, Parliament dissolved the company a half-century later because of continuing financial difficulties.

The complexity of the triangular trade and the versatility of European merchants illustrate one problem in measuring slave profits with any accuracy: They are extremely difficult to isolate from general commercial profits. For example, in the early 18th century, the London financial house of Perry, Lane and Company shipped slaves to Virginia in exchange for tobacco and other commodities. Because of this overlap in its activities, its records do not clearly discriminate between profits from slaves and profits from tobacco, which were only partly grown by slave labor.

The more significant and controversial question involves broader considerations that tie together the history of the Old and New Worlds. Although there is no consensus about the specific relationship between international trade and the industrialization of Europe, strong evidence links the two in some fundamental way. In particular, the role of the Caribbean islands as both sources of raw materials and as markets has led historians to consider the slave trade a contributing factor to the development of European industry.

Controversy has focused on several issues. Some have argued that the Caribbean and African colonies provided only weak markets with a minimal capacity to consume European exports. Because the major Caribbean product, sugar, was simply consumed by Europeans and not converted into an industrial product, some scholars have argued that the impact of such imports was also insignificant. These historians contend that profits from the slave trade and related European exports made up such a small percentage of gross domestic product as to be negligible.

Other economic historians, analyzing the same statistics, have disagreed. They have shown, for example, that gross revenues of Jamaican sugar planters increased proportionally to imported slaves and that the Caribbean share of total imports into Britain rose substantially in the second half of the 18th century. Although variables other than the slave trade—such as population growth—may have contributed, gross revenues from sugar shipped to Britain increased significantly over the 18th century.

Such a debate, regardless of its outcome, tends to ignore the broader economic impact of the slave trade. It is more useful to study the slave trade not as an iso-lated issue, but as an integral part of Atlantic commercial expansion. The development of the British economy after 1750 provides a good context. English iron foundries produced tools for colonial plantations and chains for the slave trade. Manufacturers produced pottery, furniture, firearms, and ammunition for sale to the slave-worked plantations. English mills produced cotton fabrics exclusively for export to Caribbean and African markets. In fact, the expansion of the British textile industry (see Topic 60), often considered the essence of the Industrial Revolution, was intricately joined to the expansion of the slave trade. Accordingly, the cumulative impact of these new markets appears substantial.

There is another point to consider: Enormous quantities of sugar and other slave-grown commodities provided significant profits that produced a "multiplier effect" on the economy. The most convincing example is the mid-18th-century growth in British demand for colonial staples such as sugar. Increased demand for colonial imports created an opportunity for British exports to Africa and the Caribbean. British industries increased production to supply the thriving colonial markets, expanding employment and spinning off profits. These profits generally enriched the middle class, spurring consumer spending and creating great individual fortunes in the process. Profits also stimulated the related sugar-refining and shipbuilding industries, generated activity in banking and insurance, provided capital for developing factories, mines, and railroads, and led governments to expand their navies in order to protect their growing merchant fleets.

An important byproduct of the slave trade was its impact on European cities. Population and economic activity exploded in such slave ports as Liverpool and Bristol in Great Britain and Bordeaux in France. The development of Liverpool greatly increased the demand for exports, which fueled the further development of the fabric mills and factories of Manchester. Consequently it may be argued that the slave trade contributed to another modern trend, the urbanization of the continent.

Despite the inability of historians to agree either on the level of profits of the slave trade or its precise impact on Europe, the weight of evidence suggests that profits were high and that they contributed significantly to European economic development. When considered in the broadest sense, the economic consequences of the slave trade were momentous.

Watercolor of the interior of a transatlantic slave ship. 18th century. The horrendously overcrowded conditions and lack of any sanitation meant that the average shipload arrived with one in five of its "passengers" dead—which, of course, served the purposes of the slave traders. Images such as this helped arouse public opinion against the slave trade.

© National Maritime Museum, London

tation" economies by slave labor. The slave trade had flourished since ancient times, when whites and Africans had been taken into captivity by the Roman Empire and Muslim traders. The Ottoman seizure of Constantinople in 1453, however, cut off Europe's supply of white slaves, who had been taken principally from the Black Sea region and the Balkans. In the second half of the 15th century, increasingly larger numbers of African slaves were imported into Europe.

With the discovery of the New World, Europeans began to ship African slaves across the Atlantic to the sugar plantations of Brazil and the West Indies. The massive African slave trade, fueled by the wholesale deaths of Amerindians, began in 1518, when the Emperor Charles V ended Indian slavery and agreed to substitute Africans as the source of plantation labor. By the end of the 18th cen-

tury, perhaps 9 million African slaves had been brought to the Americas, half of whom went to the West Indies. Despite a 20 percent fatality rate on the transatlantic voyage, profits in slavery were high. At first, the Portuguese were the most active slavers, but by the 16th century the Dutch and French had begun to participate. In 1562, Sir John Hawkins (1532–1595) captained the first English slaving voyage, breaking the Spanish West Indies monopoly. The English eventually dominated the slave trade, both as a carrying trade and in order to supply its colonies in Jamaica and Barbados as well as the tobacco regions of Virginia and Maryland. Once in the New World, however, disease, forced labor under appalling conditions, and unspeakable living conditions continually decimated the slave population, so that new waves of slaves had to be imported regularly.

Engraving of a slave auction in the American South. Early 19th century. Taken from an antislavery tract, this image shows the cruelty whereby families were torn apart and sold to different owners. Note the evident prosperity of the purchasers and the flogging of a newly bought slave in the background.

The Granger Collection

THE SPECULATION CRAZE: STOCK BOOMS AND CRASHES

The expansion of commercial capitalism in the 17th and 18th centuries was made difficult by a persistent shortage of money, which in turn was caused by the decline in the supply of gold and silver bullion. The money shortage affected governments as well as private investors because after the costly wars of Louis XIV ended with the peace treaties of 1713–1714, France and Great Britain found themselves deeply in debt. To meet the need for capital, Western states developed modern financial institutions such as stock companies, stock exchanges, and state-run banks, all of which expanded credit.

These developments, together with the return of peace after 1714, encouraged renewed economic confidence and led to unprecedented investment in commercial undertakings. This atmosphere of unrestrained financial speculation, fueled by the fiscal plight of Britain and France, led to the first stock crashes in modern times, which people at the time called "bubbles"—schemes designed to cheat or swindle the public.

JOHN LAW AND THE MISSISSIPPI BUBBLE

Britain and France found it increasingly difficult to deal with the huge debts accumulated during the wars, and both countries faced the possibility of bankruptcy if they could not pay the annual interest on their obligations. In each case, the government believed it could solve the problem by allowing private stock companies to manage the public debt for them. The idea was that trading and financial concessions given to these companies would create profits large enough to pay off the interest owed by government and still give investors a huge return.

In France, the experiment was organized by a strange character named John Law (1671–1729), a Scottish financier with a bent for mathematics. Law had led a wild life as a youth, having been imprisoned for killing a man in a duel. Later, while traveling on the Continent, he learned much about gambling as well as the banking business. In Paris after the death of Louis XIV in 1715, Law became a friend of the regent, the duke of Orléans, and devised a plan for solving the problem of French finances. Law believed that paper money, backed by the government's wealth in trade and land, could take the place of gold and silver coin. He therefore set up a bank in 1716 as a private joint-stock company, authorized by government charter. The bank issued notes, accepted deposits, and dealt in bills of exchange and promissory notes. The idea, which was modeled after the Bank of Amsterdam, was sound and proved so successful that in 1718 the regent bought out the bank's stockholders and made it a royal institution. Branches were established in

Museum Boymans van Beuningen, Rotterdam

Painting of the Amsterdam Stock Exchange. 17th century. The painting shows the open courtyard, off which were the offices. The earliest example of a building for the purchase and sale of stocks (it was built in 1608), the Amsterdam Exchange was a center for unrestrained and reckless transactions, which were limited to its restricted opening hours: Dealing could only take place between noon and 2 P.M.

principal cities, and many of its notes, made legal tender in 1719, were used to pay off the government debt.

The problem with Law's scheme was that he was too ambitious and extended his operations to unchecked financial speculation. In 1717, he organized the Mississippi Company (officially known as the Company of the West), which received a monopoly of the trade with the French colony of Louisiana. The company took over the government debt and purchased the government's tobacco monopoly. Within another year, the company—now called the Company of the Indies—bought out the East India Company and several other trading firms, and then took over the collection of taxes. Law therefore came to control government finances through his bank as well as most of the country's overseas trade.

Each expansion that Law undertook was financed by the issuance of more and more stock, the purchase of which was made easy by the fact that the bank rapidly increased the quantity of its notes. By the spring of 1720 the face value of notes in circulation had gone from about 150 million to almost 2.7 billion livres. The result was an inflation that pushed prices up by 88 percent. In addition, Law's bank actually lent money for the purchase of company stock. This crazed specu-lation and expansion were sustained by the fact that the shares in Law's enterprise were constantly increasing in value, to the point where the price bore no relation to actual earnings. So amazing seemed the prosperity engineered by Law that in January 1720 the king made him finance minister. The next month, the bank and the company were joined together.

The bubble in Mississippi shares finally burst that spring, when the price of shares became so high that some speculators decided to sell their holdings in order to protect their investments. As the selling turned into a panic, Law's empire collapsed because the banknotes that investors received for their stocks were then turned in for gold and silver, and the bank's reserves of specie was exhausted. In December, Law fled into exile.

THE SOUTH SEA BUBBLE

The Mississippi Bubble had a serious impact. It undermined French public confidence in stock companies as well as in banks and paper money, yet the inflation had enabled the government to pay off part of the public debt. Moreover, Law's fiasco had international reverberations because at almost the same time another bubble—the South Sea Bubble—burst in London.

Engraving depicting the "bursting" of the South Sea Bubble. 1721. The Wheel of Fortune, labeled "Company of Traders," rides over a series of books with the titles "Journal," "Ledger," and "Cash Book," while the goddess of Fortune rises to the sky, scattering stock certificates as she goes. The division between the stricken investors, on the left, and those seated on the right, contemplating their misery, is reminiscent of Biblical scenes of the damned and the blessed.

The Bank of England, organized in 1694 by William of Orange, managed the public debt for the government and, like Law's bank, issued notes. In 1710, however, a charter was issued for a joint-stock company known popularly as the South Seas Company (officially the "Governor and Company of Merchants of Great Britain Trading to the South Seas and Other Parts of America and for the Encouragement of Fishing"), which took over part of the government's debt. Under the terms of a special agreement, holders of government bonds were to turn them in to the company in exchange for company stock. The interest paid by the government on its bonds would be passed on as dividends to the stockholders. In addition, the company was granted a monopoly on all British trade with Spanish America. The South Sea Company was further strengthened when England obtained the *asiento*, which permitted it to send some 4,800 slaves and one merchant ship per year to South America.

As company profits grew, speculative fever mounted, especially as news of Law's operations reached English investors in 1719. The company eventually offered to take over the entire government debt and pay the government a bonus for the privilege. By June 1720, the price for South Sea Company stock had increased 10 times to more than £1000 per share. The thirst for speculation became a craze as innumerable companies—almost 200 in a single year—were created, many of dubious legitimacy, and sold stock to the public with only a minimum downpayment. The South Sea Company, concerned over the increased competition, persuaded Parliament to pass the Bubble Act, which prevented any company from selling stock without a royal charter. With the crash in Paris already underway, prices began to tumble on the London exchange, and by December the South Sea stock had collapsed to £120.

The British crash exposed a widespread scandal of government corruption as it was discovered that ministers and parliamentary officials had taken bribes from some of the companies. In an effort to clean up this scandal, Sir Robert Walpole was appointed as the king's chief minister (see Topic 51). The South Sea Company actually survived on a much reduced scale as a holding company for government securities, and the Bank of England reemerged as the principal financial institution of the nation.

The effects of the bubbles on both sides of the channel were eventually overcome as governments and private investors learned caution from the dangers of speculation. These episodes were, however, symptomatic both of the end of the old mercantilist principle—which held that government protection and monopolies were needed to protect national economic prosperity—and the rise of the new capitalist doctrine, developed first by Adam Smith and then by the later Manchester School (see Topic 58), that accompanied the commercial expansion and the Industrial Revolution.

Putting Europe and the World Economy in Perspective

A global economy had begun to emerge in the 18th century as a result of the expansion of trade. At the center of that commercial economy was an increasingly prosperous Europe, which reaped huge profits from the growing interdependence in production and markets that characterized the world of commerce. European states took tremendous resources from the Americas, first in the form of gold and silver bullion and then in agricultural products.

This economic transformation drastically altered the lives of millions of Europeans, whose hunger for the new products—coffee, tea, sugar, tobacco, and others—resulted in important changes in diet, nutrition, and customs. As the market in such goods as sugar, tobacco, and cotton grew, Europeans began to raid the African continent to obtain the labor its New World enterprises required, creating a slave trade that persisted with unrelenting horror for three and a half centuries. The European exploitation of the rest of the world that began with the overseas discoveries came to a head as a result of the commercial revolution, to be superseded only in the next century as Western imperialism carved up the continents. As the 18th century opened, the expansion of commerce was closely tied to the evolution of banking systems and public finance, a relationship that led to a series of financial schemes that ended in crisis. By the end of the century, however, these scandals had been set behind as Europe moved into the age of industrial capitalism.

Questions for Further Study

1. What were the principal elements in the emerging world economy?
2. In what ways was the slave trade tied to the European economy? Was it profitable?
3. What were the new forms of investment that emerged? What were the principal causes of the speculation crashes?

Suggestions for Further Reading

Braudel, Fernand. S. Reynolds, trans. *Civilization and Capitalism,* 3 vols. New York, 1979–1984.

Cameron, Rondo. *A Concise Economic History of the World.* New York, 1989.

Carswell, John. *The South Sea Bubble.* New York, 2002.

Day, John. *Money and Finance in the Age of Merchant Capitalism.* Oxford, 1999.

Eltis, David. *The Rise of African Slavery in the Americas.* New York, 2000.

Epstein, S.R. *Freedom and Growth: The Rise of States and Markets in Europe, 1300-1750.* New York, 2000.

Frank, A.G. *World Accumulation, 1492–1789.* New York, 1978.

Klein, Herbert S. *The Atlantic Slave Trade.* New York, 1999.

Kriedte, Peter. *Peasants, Landlords and Merchant Capitalists: Europe and the World Economy, 1500–1800.* Leamington, England, 1983.

Northrop, David, ed. *The Atlantic Slave Trade (Problems in World History).* Lexington, MA, 2001.

Phillips, Caryl. *The Atlantic Sound.* New York, 2000.

Thomas, Hugh. *The Slave Trade: The Story of the Atlantic Slave Trade, 1440-1870.* New York, 1997.

Van Zaanden, J.L. *The Rise and Decline of Holland's Economy: Merchant Capitalism and the Labour Market.* Manchester, 1993.

InfoTrac College Edition

Enter the search term *slavery* using the Subject Guide.

THE GLOBAL CONFLICT: WARS FOR EMPIRE

With the spread of European colonization, wars among the leading European powers tended to extend to their colonial possessions. Virtually every major European conflict in the 18th century involved the colonies and ended with the redistribution of territory outside Europe.

At the end of the War of the Spanish Succession in 1713 (see Topic 50), Spain was forced to make important concessions to British traders in the Spanish-American colonies. Ill feeling between Spain and Britain continued to smolder, and the War of Jenkins' Ear broke out in 1739—the first important confrontation to involve two European countries fighting over a colonial dispute.

There followed the War of the Austrian Succession (1740–1748), a complex series of interlocking power struggles, which brought France and Spain together to contend with Britain for supremacy in America. In 1744 France declared war on Britain, and in return the British seized the French settlement of Louisbourg in Canada. Both countries, however, were too committed to European campaigns to do more than skirmish overseas. Clearly, however, a definitive struggle for control of North America was at hand. In the meantime, the French continued to build a chain of forts down the Ohio River, to block British expansion west of the Appalachians and keep them restricted to the Atlantic seaboard. The British prepared for war by dispatching two regiments to America—the first British regular soldiers to serve there.

In 1755, in fighting near the French stronghold of Fort Duquesne, the British forces were routed and their general killed. The following year saw a fresh outbreak of general hostilities in the Seven Years' War (1756–1763), which set Britain and Prussia together against France, Austria, and Russia. The British provided financial subsidies to the Prussians and attacked the French fleet and coast to reduce France's pressure on Prussia. In return, the Prussians pinned down French troops and thereby restricted French efforts in North America.

After early setbacks, Britain increased its American war effort at the insistence of the prime minister, William Pitt. Massive forces crossed the Atlantic, defeated the French at Louisbourg, and then took Quebec and Montreal. By the end of the war, Britain had acquired its first empire.

Meanwhile, in Europe, Friedrich II's Prussian forces were engaged in a tenacious but increasingly desperate attempt to keep their enemies at bay. In 1762, however, the unexpected withdrawal of Russia broke up the quadruple alliance. Prussia kept Silesia and emerged from the war firmly established as one of Europe's leading military powers.

BRITAIN VERSUS SPAIN IN THE WEST INDIES

As the leading European colonial powers continued to expand their holdings in Asia, Africa, and the Americas, rivalries hitherto fought out on European soil began to spread to the colonies abroad. In the context of the commercial expansion of the 18th century, the domestic economic benefits of overseas territories—access to raw materials, new markets for the sale of manufactured goods—encouraged the colonizers to defend and add to them.

At the same time, the three strongest colonial powers, Britain, France, and Spain, tried equally hard to prevent the growth of each other's overseas holdings. As a result, the incessant wars fought out by the major European nations throughout the 18th century almost invariably involved them in conflicts both in Europe and elsewhere. Most of the conflicts of the 18th century in Europe involved colonial powers like Britain and Spain that were also simultaneously fighting outside Europe. In addition, the peace negotiations that ended the European wars served to pursue colonial competition outside Europe because treaties generally reassigned colonial holdings, and thus inextricably linked them with European power politics.

The first major redistribution of colonies occurred at the end of the War of the Spanish Succession, from which the British emerged the principal victors. By the Treaty of Utrecht (1713), the French gave up Newfoundland, Nova Scotia, and the Hudson Bay territory to the British, retaining New France (Quebec). Spain held on to its American possessions, but was forced in return to award Britain trading privileges there.

THE WAR OF JENKINS' EAR

British expansion only exacerbated the ill feelings between the rising imperial power and a declining Spain, which was embittered by the concessions it had been forced to grant. The focus of tension was the Caribbean, where British undercover traders and Spanish coast guards—often private operators hired by the government—were in constant friction. Most of the illicit ships operated out of Jamaica, a British possession in the middle of Spanish territory. When British vessels fell into the hands of the Spanish *guardacostas*, who were patrolling in search of booty as much as enforcing the law, their crews generally received rough handling.

As reports of the Spanish ill-treatment spread back to Great Britain, public indignation over the behavior of their traditional enemies began to rise. In 1738, an English sailor, Robert Jenkins (active 1731–1738), brought to the House of Commons a jar containing his ear; he claimed it had been ripped off by a Spanish coast guard. The prime minister, Sir Robert Walpole (see Topic 51), already under pressure, was accused by his opponents of weak-kneed indifference to Spanish aggression. After trying unsuccessfully to cool tempers, Walpole gave way and declared war on Spain—the War of Jenkins' Ear—in 1739.

The immediate cause of hostilities was allegedly national honor, but deeper considerations prompted the clash. In the first place, Spain, one of the first great imperialist powers, was beginning to decline just at the moment that British fortunes were rising. Furthermore, the real issue at stake was not the theoretical right of smugglers to ply their trade in peace, but the practical ability of one colonial power to deny access to a rival. The War of Jenkins' Ear was in itself trivial enough, and in any case the hostilities between Britain and Spain soon became subsumed in the far more involved War of the Austrian Succession, but it set an important precedent. For the first time two European powers went to war over questions of trade outside Europe.

Anti-Spanish cartoon published at the time of the War of Jenkins' Ear. 1738. On the left Sir Robert Walpole, the Prime Minister, sits back, trying to decide whether to sign the Declaration of War against Spain, while Captain Robert Jenkins thrusts his ear, in his left hand, toward Walpole. The crouching dog in the bottom left-hand corner, with its features distorted in a grimace, presumably symbolizes Spain.

Corbis-Bettmann

DYNASTY AND POWER POLITICS: THE WAR OF THE AUSTRIAN SUCCESSION

In the years from 1740 to 1763, the chief European nations fought out a complex series of interrelated power struggles. The War of the Austrian Succession (1740–1748) was followed by a brief period of uneasy peace dominated by feverish diplomatic activity. In 1756 hostilities broke out again, in the form of the Seven Years' War (1756–1763). By its close, there were two main victors: Britain, which had won its first empire, and Prussia, which had confirmed its status as a great power.

The initial cause of the War of the Austrian Succession was the death of the Emperor Charles VI (ruled 1711–1740). In 1713, Charles had decided that the Hapsburg empire would be regarded as indivisible and named his young and inexperienced daughter, Maria Theresa (ruled 1740–1780), as his successor. Most of the powers of Europe, including Prussia, agreed to abide by this pronouncement. The Prussian king Friedrich II (ruled 1740–1786) subsequently contested Maria Theresa's right to inherit her father's possessions and invaded the resource-rich province of Silesia (on Friedrich's career, see Topic 59). Despite her youth and inexperience, Maria Theresa ultimately proved to be one of the most capable rulers in the long line of Hapsburg monarchs. Years later, Friedrich admiringly described the tenacious young empress as "the only man among my opponents."

Britain came to Maria Theresa's aid. The British foreign secretary, Sir John Carteret (1690–1763), was an enthusiastic player of diplomatic games who claimed that his favorite pastime was "knocking the heads of the kings of Europe together, and jumbling something out of it that may be of service to this country." In 1743, Carteret put together an alliance of Austria, Britain, and Piedmont-Sardinia, but his achievement only succeeded in driving the former rivals France and Spain to form a counteralliance.

KING GEORGE'S WAR

Meanwhile, the hostilities between Britain and Spain, the latter now joined by France, continued in America, where the struggle was generally known as King George's War, after the reigning King George II (ruled 1727–1760). George was the last British king to personally command in battle, fighting in the European phase of the War of the Austrian Succession. Events in Europe were fluctuating too violently for any country to risk committing substantial forces to the American front. The British made disorganized raids on Spanish territories on the mainland and in the Caribbean, but were beaten back, as much by tropical disease as by the Spanish. The only notable reversal in King George's War occurred in 1745, when New England colonial forces captured the French-held Cape Breton Isle and its fortress of Louisbourg, which commanded the St. Lawrence estuary.

British and French troops continued to skirmish elsewhere. In India, the French took the British town of Madras in 1746. The next year, the British Navy defeated two French fleets off the Atlantic coast, and thereby prevented them from carrying reinforcements to overseas French territories.

By 1748, amid general frustration and exhaustion, peace negotiations at Aix-la-Chapelle (Aachen) brought about an end to the war and a restoration of conquered territory. Britain handed back Louisbourg and regained Madras in return. The only real winners were Prussia, which held on to Silesia, and Maria Theresa, whose right to succeed her father was generally recognized. Eight years of conflict had revealed that British superiority at sea was counterbalanced by French supremacy on land. The resulting stalemate left virtually all the disputes between the European powers unresolved, not the least of them the battle for control of North America.

THE DIPLOMATIC REVOLUTION

The period from 1749 to 1756 saw intense negotiation and counternegotiation, as the leading participants prepared for the inevitability of renewed conflict. By the time war broke out again in 1756, the alliances of the War of the Austrian Succession were reversed in a series of changes known as the Diplomatic Revolution. When the Seven Years' War broke out, the chief enemies were the same: Prussia versus Austria, and Britain versus France. Britain, however, now supported Prussia instead of Austria, and France was allied with Austria rather than Prussia.

The break between Britain and Austria was caused by Britain's refusal to support Maria Theresa's demands for the return of Silesia. The British had backed the Austrians in the earlier war mainly because they were the enemies of France, but they had no interest in becoming embroiled in Austria's territorial disputes. Early in 1756, Britain and Prussia signed the Convention of Westminster, and the French—who were furious with Friedrich for allying Prussia with the hated British—hastened to negotiate a defensive alliance with Austria.

At this point, a new player appeared on the scene. The empress of Russia, Elizabeth (ruled 1741–1762), was deeply mistrustful of the British and Prussian agreement. She tried to persuade the French and Austrians to join Russia in an offensive triple alliance to crush Prussia's growing power. With hostilities between the British and French in North America becoming increasingly serious, the French hesitated, unwilling to encourage a European war that would overstretch French resources.

While they tried to decide, Friedrich of Prussia suspected that a coalition of powers was planning to attack him. With characteristic boldness he struck first, taking military action on the principle that "negotiations without arms produce as little impression as musical scores without instruments." In August 1756 the Prussians invaded Saxony, thereby provoking the French into action and bringing into being the alliance that Friedrich wrongly suspected already existed. The Seven Years' War was under way.

Like the earlier War of the Austrian Succession, the Seven Years' War involved action both in Europe and America. On the European front, the Prussians battled their various enemies and struggled to hold on to Silesia. Across the Atlantic, the British and French fought the decisive struggle for control of North America. Both Prussia and Britain emerged victors.

The two wars were interdependent. Britain provided Prussia with an annual subsidy, maintained the so-called Army of Observation in Germany to protect Prussia against a French attack, and made periodic assaults on the French fleet and coast. The purpose of these moves was to reduce French pressure on Prussia. In return, the Prussians' military activities pinned down French troops in Europe and prevented them from throwing all their effort into the North American campaign.

THE STRUGGLE FOR NORTH AMERICA: THE ASCENDANCY OF BRITAIN

Although the British and French were officially at peace until the declaration of war in 1756, fighting between them had continued ever since the end of the War of the Austrian Succession. In India, the British and French East India companies struggled for commercial dominance, as the Moghul empire (the Muslim empire ruling most of north and central India in the 16th and 17th centuries) continued to break up. The British soldier and administrator, Robert Clive (1725–1774), defeated the French in 1751 and captured a string of French strongholds; he subsequently overcame the local ruler of Bengal at the Battle of Plassey (1757), to establish the British East India Company's control over all Bengal and neighboring provinces. The British victory at Plassey thus played a key role in establishing British control in India and laid the foundation for their eventual Indian empire.

BRITISH AND FRENCH COLONISTS IN NORTH AMERICA

The most important stage for Anglo-French rivalries, however, was North America, where the culminating struggle—the American side of the Seven Years' War—is often called the French and Indian War.

The attitude of the two nations toward their American colonies was very different. The 13 British colonies in North America grew rapidly, as immigrants from the home country arrived in increasing numbers. By the time war officially broke out, the colonial population numbered around a million and a half. Some of the communities were already the size of a small European city. In 1760, for example, Philadelphia had some 23,000 inhabitants and a well-

Miniature illustration of an employee of the British East India Company. Mid-18th century. Miniature painting was a popular art in Moghul India. This example, by a local artist, shows the Englishman, in a cloudless landscape, impeccably dressed in the style of his London contemporaries. Like many Company employees, however, he has to some degree, "gone native"—he sits cross-legged on the ground, smoking a water pipe.

Victoria & Albert Museum, London/Art Resource

developed commercial life; by 1776, it was the third or fourth largest city in the British Empire.

By contrast, the French were much less enthusiastic about emigrating to Canada or Louisiana, areas that presented formidable environmental challenges to 18th-century immigrants. Unlike the bustling British settlements, the French colonies consisted of large empty spaces with only a scattering of inhabitants. Although smaller, the French com-

SIGNIFICANT DATES

War in the Colonies

1713	Treaty of Utrecht
1739	War of Jenkins' Ear
1740–1748	War of the Austrian Succession
1746	French take Madras from British
1756–1763	Seven Years' War
1757	British victorious at Battle of Plassey
1758	French lose Guadeloupe to British
1759–1760	British take Quebec and Montreal
1763	Treaty of Paris

munities were efficiently run and on occasion more profitable than the British. Without the distractions of urban life, the new settlers concentrated on sugar planting, fur trading, and other commercial operations.

These differences significantly affected French and British relations with the Native American populations. In order to establish settlements and encourage further immigration from the homeland, the British set up large land investment schemes, making land available by driving native residents from their traditional hunting grounds. The French, by contrast, were interested in trading rather than building settlements. As a result, they were more likely to find native residents cooperative.

THE FRENCH AND INDIAN WAR

This cooperation became of considerable importance when French forces began to seal off the Ohio Valley, to block the British on the Atlantic seaboard and prevent them from moving westward. In the years before the official outbreak of war, the French built a north-south chain of forts along the Ohio and Mississippi valleys, to connect their settlements in Louisiana with those in Canada. The Iroquois and other local tribes supported the French attempts to keep out the British.

In 1754, in an encounter near Fort Duquesne (site of the future city of Pittsburgh), French and Indian fighters combined to defeat a force of Virginian levies under the command of the young George Washington (see Topic 59). The colonial troops had been dispatched by the Ohio Company of Virginia, a land investment company. The following year, the British government sent regular British soldiers to America for the first time. Once again the French and Indian combined forces proved more effective. Ambushing the British troops nine miles from Fort Duquesne, they killed the expedition's general and captured his men. The French maintained the initiative. In 1757 the distinguished French commander, Louis Joseph de Montcalm (1712–1759), took Fort William Henry, and a year later defeated a British expedition at Ticonderoga.

Yet by the time of the British defeat at Ticonderoga, the French were losing their superiority. The autocratic British politician William Pitt (1708–1778), despite George II's implacable hostility toward him, took charge as secretary of state in 1756. The king dismissed him in 1757, but the disastrous news from America forced his reappointment, and Pitt took full and determined control over foreign and military affairs.

THE BATTLE FOR CANADA

When Pitt came to power, his strategy was to concentrate on driving the French from Canada. British forces attacked from three different directions: up the St. Lawrence via Louisbourg, into the Ohio Valley against Fort Duquesne, and from the Hudson Valley via Ticonderoga. The last of these attacks was frustrated by Montcalm's victory, but the other two succeeded. By 1758, the British were in control of Louisbourg and Fort Duquesne; the latter was renamed Fort Pitt, in honor of the prime minister.

The British continued to advance. In 1759, the young general James Wolfe (1727–1759) led his troops up the St. Lawrence to Quebec, which was defended by a force under Montcalm. On the night of September 12, advancing soldiers silently climbed the cliffs west of the city, to the Plains of Abraham. After a short, bloody battle, in which Montcalm and Wolfe were both fatally wounded, the French fled. The following year, the British besieged Montreal, while back in Europe the British fleet decimated that of France. With France unable to send reinforcements, Montreal fell, and with it all of Canada.

WAR IN THE CARIBBEAN

With the accession of George III (ruled 1760–1820) in 1760, a triumphant but war-weary Britain began to move toward peace negotiations with France. Peace talks actually began, but in 1761 the new Spanish king, Charles III (ruled

Painting showing British troops storming Quebec on the Plains of Abraham. Late 18th century. The British are visible on the left, disembarking and climbing up, as dawn breaks, to take the city from the west. Their victory in the ensuing battle, in which the commanders on both sides were killed, saw the French lose control over Canada.

1759–1788), talked the French into renewing their old alliance and opposing British colonial expansion in the Caribbean. Early the following year, Britain declared war on Spain, and the colonial war entered its final phase.

The French had already lost Guadeloupe to Britain in 1758. Now the British added the important French islands of Martinique and Grenada, and the neutral St. Lucia and St. Vincent, to their Caribbean holdings. Spain lost Havana, Cuba, while the Spanish position in the Pacific was badly shaken by the capture of Manila in the Philippines by a British expedition sent from India.

THE TREATY OF PARIS

Between February and August of 1763, the negotiations of the Treaty of Paris among Britain, France, and Spain formalized the new distribution of territory. In America, France ceded to Britain the territories of Canada, Cape Breton Island, and all of Louisiana east of the Mississippi (except for New Orleans). In return, the French received two small islands, St. Pierre and Miquelon, which are still French territory and became an overseas department in 1976.

In Asia, Spain regained Manila. As for India, both Britain and France agreed to restore their mutual conquests, returning to the positions they had occupied in 1749. French influence in India was effectively ended, however, because the terms of the treaty prohibited them from rebuilding their fortifications.

In 1759, with the war at its height and with news pouring in of British victories, Pitt observed that "peace will be as hard to make as war." His successor as prime minister, the Earl of Bute (served 1762–1763), feared that if Britain assumed too dominant a position, the rest of Europe would band together against her in resentment. The terms of the Treaty of Paris reflected the British concern to provide at least some satisfaction to France and Spain.

The greatest loss of all to France had been Canada; perhaps French authorities took some comfort in Voltaire's description of the former French possession as a "wretched country, covered with snow and ice eight months out of twelve, and inhabited by savages, bears, and beavers." France had lost its North American empire, but French commercial power remained formidable.

THE SEVEN YEARS' WAR AND THE SUCCESS OF PRUSSIA

Friedrich's gamble in invading Saxony in 1756 and launching a preventive war seemed at first to pay off. He followed one of his favorite maxims, "If you must go to war, fall on your enemy like thunder and lightning." After capturing Dresden, he advanced on the Hapsburg territory of Bohemia. By bringing about the very alliance of Austria,

Engraving of British Government offices in Calcutta. Late 18th century. Calcutta was founded by the British East India Company in 1690; Fort William, the nucleus of the magnificent buildings seen here across the river, was begun in 1696. The contrast between the colonial palaces and the squalor of the lives of the locals seen in the foreground is perhaps unconsciously ironic.

Corbis-Bettmann

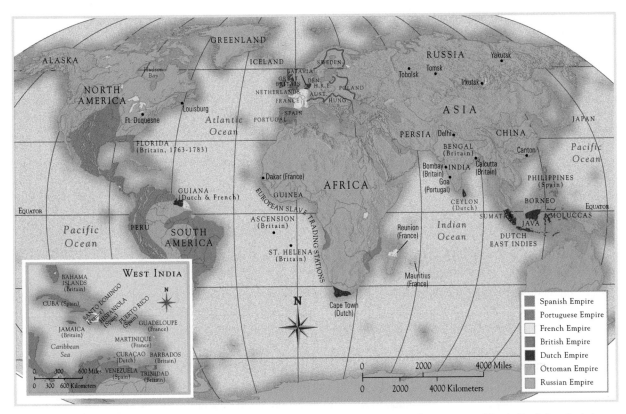

Map 56.1 European Possessions Overseas, c. 1780. India was divided between the British, Portuguese, and Dutch; South America between the Spanish and Portuguese. Note the large Spanish holdings in North America. The Ottoman Empire now controlled most of the Middle East and North Africa. The dismemberment of most of these holdings after the end of World War I and the collapse of the Ottoman Empire continued to bring instability to the region (and the world) in the early 21st century.

France, and Russia that he had moved to prevent, however, he undid the benefits of his surprise attack. In 1757 an Austrian army drove the Prussians out of Bohemia. Thereafter the fighting followed the same pattern. Friedrich kept his troops moving, beating back repeated attacks by the allies, and winning impressive tactical victories, but he never managed to break the strategic stalemate. Prussia's long-term prospects seemed doomed. Either the fighting would continue indecisively, with the Prussians gradually losing territory, or the allies would make a breakthrough and crush their enemy.

THE END OF THE SEVEN YEARS' WAR

At the beginning of 1762, with Prussian resources stretched to the breaking point and on the verge of collapse, rescue arrived from the most unexpected of directions. Friedrich's old enemy, the Russian Empress Elizabeth, whose suspicion of Prussia had helped create the anti-Prussian alliance, died at St. Petersburg. Her nephew and liberal successor, Peter III (ruled December 1761–June 1762), had long admired Friedrich's enlightened domestic policies. On his accession he ordered the immediate suspension of Russian attacks on the Prussians, and in May 1762 the Prussians and Russians signed a peace treaty whereby all conquests were returned. Friedrich's luck was all the greater in that six weeks after signing the treaty Peter was deposed by his ambitious wife,

Catherine II (see Topic 59)—while under arrest, Peter was assassinated by a group of guardsmen under mysterious circumstances.

With Russia out of the action and France fully occupied in dealing with Britain, the alliance collapsed, leaving Maria Theresa no choice but to accept the loss of Silesia. The Treaty of Hubertusburg (1763) between Prussia, Austria, and Saxony restored the prewar situation, with the Austrians recognizing Prussian possession of Silesia. Saxony regained its independence, but Friedrich paid no compensation for the damage Prussia had inflicted.

Unlike the War of the Austrian Succession, the Seven Years' War significantly changed the balance of power in Europe by reinforcing Prussia's status; at the same time, it underlined the growing importance of colonial strength. Even though the Treaty of Paris sealed Britain's victory on terms that were not excessively vindictive, Britain clearly emerged from the colonial wars as the indisputable imperial leader in Europe.

The triumph did not last long. Within 10 years of the Peace of Paris, Britain's 13 North American colonies were beginning their successful attempt to break away. Their loyalty to Britain had been assured by the threatening presence of France on American soil. With the French driven out and the British asserting their control with ever more unpopular taxes, conditions were right for the Revolutionary

War—in which, ironically enough, the colonists received assistance from France (on the American Revolution, see Topic 59).

Prussia was the other main victor, but its emergence as a major power was bought at considerable cost. Friedrich spent the first half of his reign (23 years) in virtually continuous war, devoting much energy during the second half to keeping the peace by skillful, if ruthless, diplomacy.

Furthermore, the Prussian Army's invincibility did not long survive Friedrich's death. It fell behind in training and equipment and was decisively crushed by Napoleon's French troops at Jena (1806). Yet the Prussian successes of the mid-18th century proved its right to be taken seriously as an important power and foreshadowed events a century later, when Prussia, against the will of a declining Hapsburg Austria, succeeded in uniting Germany.

Putting Wars for Empire in Perspective

At a casual glance, the history of the 18th century seems as filled with conflict as the bloody 16th century. There are important differences, however, between the destructive wars of the earlier period, often fueled by religious hatreds, and the 18th century's careful search for a stable balance of power. European countries fought one another for specific political and economic goals, and not to wipe out whole groups or classes.

When it became clear that the war aims would—or, as the case might be, would not—be achieved, the combatants stopped fighting and made peace. The various treaties of the century sought not so much to reward the winners and punish the losers, as to recreate and maintain the balance. The prudence of 18th-century European statesmen was, of course, dictated by realism rather than charity. In so fluctuating a world, yesterday's enemy might well become tomorrow's most important ally.

The 18th century's other distinction was that of spreading both war and diplomacy beyond the boundaries of Europe to a global context. Battles fought in the Philippines or along the Mississippi affected the political and economic developments of countless European citizens. The wider horizons required new resources: Britain's success in the conflicts outside Europe was largely the result of the strength and efficiency of its navy, an indispensable force in empire building.

The careful diplomatic balance achieved at Paris and Hubertusburg was destined to be of short duration. Along with the growth of international trade and revolutionary developments in industry, the revolutionary political movements of the late 18th century wrought vast changes in European political life. One factor remained constant, however. Starting with the 18th-century wars for empire, European political and economic life was permanently linked to that of the rest of the world.

Questions for Further Study

1. How did the European powers use the wars in the colonies to continue their struggle for domination in Europe?
2. What role did the British Navy play in Britain's success in the colonial wars?
3. What have been the lasting effects of the 18th-century colonial wars in Africa, Asia, and the Americas?
4. How did war and diplomacy interconnect in settling the colonial disputes of the 18th century? Was the process different from the relationship between war and diplomacy in earlier periods?

Suggestions for Further Reading

Anderson, Fred. *Crucible of War: The Seven Years War and the Fate of Empire in British North America*. New York, 2000.

Anderson, M.S. *The War of the Austrian Succession 1740-1748*. New York, 1995.

Bearce, George D. *British Attitudes Toward India*. Westport, CT, 1982.

Brewer, John. *The Sinews of Power*. New York, 1989.

Browning, Reed. *The War of the Austrian Succession*. New York, 1995.

Davis, L., and R. Hittenback. *Mammon and the Pursuit of Empire: The Political Economy of British Imperialism*. Cambridge, MA, 1987.

Ehrman, John. *The Younger Pitt : The Consuming Struggle*. Stanford, CA, 1996.

Evans, Eric J. *William Pitt the Younger*. London, 1999.

Mommsen, W. P.S. Falla, trans. *Theories of Imperialism*. Chicago, 1982.

Mori, Jennifer. *William Pitt and the French Revolution 1785-1795*. London, 1997.

Peters, Marie. *The Elder Pitt (Profiles in Power)*. London, 1998.

Raudzens, George. *Empires: Europe and Globalization, 1492-1788*. Sutton, 1999.

Sen, Sudipta. *Empire of Free Trade: The East India Company and the Making of the Colonial Marketplace*. Philadelphia, 1998.

InfoTrac College Edition

Enter the search term *American Revolution* using Key Terms.

EUROPEAN SOCIETY IN THE EIGHTEENTH CENTURY

In 1789, European society was struck by the great upheaval known as the French Revolution. The leaders of that tumultuous event, who used language as an essential aspect of politics, believed that they were building a new, radically different social order. For this reason, they called the world that had existed before the revolution the *Ancien Régime*—the "Old Regime." Historians still use the term to describe the way of life and the institutions that characterized Europe before 1789.

Although the society of the Old Regime was based on traditional notions of hierarchy and privilege, what appeared on the surface to be a stable social order was being undermined by powerful forces. European economic life and population were both expanding rapidly. Major innovations were introduced in agriculture and manufacturing that would bring revolutionary transformations. The social structure, which for centuries had seemed to be ordained by God, adjusted to new conditions, especially as the nobility was forced to make concessions to a middle class that was growing in wealth and insisted on sharing power and status. These social realities were rationalized and justified by the intellectual climate of the times, which questioned the principles on which the social structure of the Old Regime rested.

Royal absolutism, itself based on the idea of a stable society, also underwent change. Many of the rulers cloaked their power in the trappings of "enlightened" monarchy while seeking to increase government efficiency and control. To sustain the increasing centralization of government and pay for the frequent colonial and European wars of the period, rulers constantly squeezed more and more taxes from their subjects, taxes that eventually sparked rebellion in the New World against Britain and threw the Old Regime in France into crisis. The great revolutionary upheaval that erupted in 1789 was the climax of a process that had been underway for decades.

SOCIETY AND THE OLD REGIME

The Old Regime was an intricate network of political, economic, and social relationships. Its political character was defined by the system of absolute monarchy, with its divine right theory and increasingly centralized state bureaucracy. The economic life of Europe was overwhelmingly rural and agrarian, burdened by isolation and chronic food shortages, and while evolving financial practices often produced instability, restrictive mercantilist policies still constrained commerce. The social patterns of the 18th century had their roots in the Middle Ages.

THE NATURE OF THE OLD REGIME

Unlike modern society, in which status is defined largely by wealth and economic function, in most countries during the Old Regime a person's position was fixed by birth and heredity within one of three "estates": (1) the clergy, either of the Roman Catholic or the Protestant churches, the upper levels of which were often linked by family ties to the nobility; (2) the noble elites, who possessed an array of legal powers and privileges; and (3) the overwhelming bulk of society, consisting of the rural peasantry and several groups that lived in the towns—the artisans who were members of highly restrictive guilds, manual laborers, and a small but growing commercial middle class, whose ranks would be swelled in the course of the Industrial Revolution.

The social system of the Old Regime was deliberately based on the notion of inequality and difference, and during the 18th century the hierarchical structure of society actually grew more rigid. In some parts of Europe, so-called sumptuary laws, which regulated extravagance in food or dress, were designed to make social distinctions visible by prohibiting people in one order from wearing clothes worn by those in a higher order. In other countries, members of the middle class were forbidden to marry into noble families, while nobles generally could not be members of guilds or engage in commerce.

Such laws were, however, largely unnecessary, because the social hierarchy was maintained by the constraints of the community of which one was a member. Most 18th-century Europeans had access to special privileges and bore certain responsibilities only in so far as they were members of a given group or community—the nobility or the clergy, a town, a village, or a guild. The nobles, for example, were exempt from direct taxation and could expect certain services from the peasants who worked their land, while the church collected an annual offering known as the *tithe*. In a similar fashion, members of artisan guilds enjoyed the exclusive right to engage in their craft, while inhabitants of a particular village might have access to certain grazing lands or forests. Tradition was the moral basis of 18th-century society. Most people, guided by a belief in a divinely sanctioned order and the experience of their ancestors, did not want or expect change. If people—whether nobles or peasants—expressed grievances against the existing order, it was usually because their traditional rights had been undermined by the ever-expanding power of the central government.

Despite these rigid patterns of thought and behavior, the society of the Old Regime was neither uniform nor static. It was distinguished by the startling contrast—sharper perhaps than in modern industrial societies—between the lives of people in each of the social orders. The highest ranks of society displayed refined tastes and manners, lived on magnificent estates, and enjoyed a luxurious standard of living; the less fortunate peasants and the urban destitute lived in extreme poverty. Sharp differences also existed within the orders as well as from region to region. Although some nobles were very wealthy, others were hardly distinguishable from the wealthier peasants in their communities. Within the church, the economic and social differences between a bishop and a village priest were sharp. Similarly, whereas most peasants in Western Europe lived well above the subsistence level and enjoyed some legal status, those in Eastern Europe generally tended to be serfs or existed in dire economic straits. In countries with strong commercial economies, such as Britain and the Netherlands, the middle classes were growing rapidly in wealth and status, whereas they hardly existed in the Holy Roman Empire or Russia.

THE GROWTH IN POPULATION

One of the most powerful sources of change in the 18th century stemmed from shifting demographic patterns. Europe's population had experienced periods of growth throughout its history, although disease or warfare had at times depopulated parts of the Continent. About midcentury, however, the population began to increase at a startling rate. Population figures for this period can only be estimates rather than exact numbers because most countries did not conduct census surveys until the 19th century, and accurate figures were available only much later. Nevertheless, it is clear that between 1700 and 1800, the number of inhabitants in Europe almost doubled, from slightly more than 100 million to about 190 million, and by 1850 the population had increased to more than 265 million. The demographic growth pattern, which continued well into the 19th century at rates varying from 40 to 60 percent, was more rapid in Western and Central Europe but occurred almost everywhere, in rural as well as urban areas.

In England (including Wales), the population increased from 5.5 million to more than 9 million in the century after 1700, and reached 14 million by 1831. France, the most populous western European country at the beginning of the 18th century, grew from 16 to 17 million to more than 24 million by the time of the Revolution of 1789. Even in 18th-century Russia, the demographic pattern repeated itself, with the population growing from 18 to 30 million.

The causes of this dramatic explosion in population are much debated. One theory holds that in traditional agricultural societies the birthrate tends to remain relatively high, so that declining mortality rates explain population growth. Yet although the annual death rate generally declined from the 18th century onward, in many areas of Southern and Eastern Europe, as well as in large cities, the rate of deaths did not fall below that of births until after 1850. Similarly,

Map 57.1 Growth of European Population, c. 1800–1850. The map shows the impact of the First Industrial Revolution. The greatest increase is in areas convenient for shipping (northwest and southern France, the Low Countries, and Scandinavia), rich in natural resources (Poland, northern Italy), or both of these (the Baltic states and, preeminently, England and Wales). Southern Europe was to remain underpopulated until after 1945.

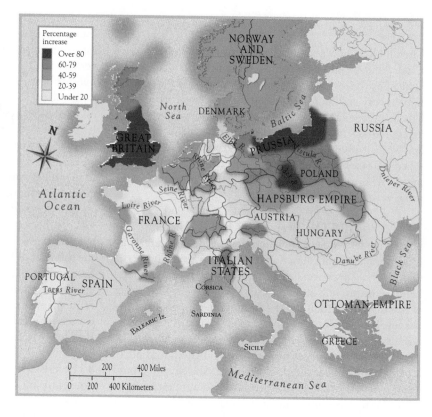

strong population growth occurred before the most important advances in medicine could have affected infant mortality and adult health. Nor did the Industrial Revolution cause the demographic explosion because the upward movement of population began before industrialization.

Food supply appears to have been the most significant factor in the growth of population. Until the 18th century, English demographic growth reflected a relationship between marriage patterns and the availability of food. In periods of population growth, when the demand for food was greater, prices for basic staples rose. Because even in good times the poorer classes lived close to the edge of subsistence, higher food prices—which meant, in effect, a reduction in real wages—tended to discourage marriage in order to avoid the financial burden of maintaining a family. On the other hand, population decline lowered the demand for food and deflated prices, which in turn made marriage and children more feasible.

Over the course of the 18th century, fundamental changes transformed the society of the Old Regime. The depressed economic conditions prevalent in the 17th century slowly improved. Along with the demographic growth, rapid commercial and financial expansion took place. Most significant of all, Europe was about to experience two far-reaching revolutions, one in agriculture and one in industry (see Topic 60).

MARRIAGE AND THE FAMILY

The family remained the basic unit of European social life. The traditional family was a patriarchy, with the husband wielding authority over wife and children. In upper- and middle-class families, the interests of the family as a whole were generally regarded as taking precedence over those of its individual members, and marriages were usually arranged according to considerations of finance and status.

Throughout Europe, the nuclear family, consisting of parents and children, had been the rule among the upper classes since the 16th century. When finances permitted, married couples set up independent households separate from parents, but young people generally delayed marriage until at least their mid-twenties in order to accumulate sufficient savings. Among noble families, the first-born son usually married at a younger age because his inheritance rights imposed the responsibility to father future heirs.

In Western Europe, where most lower-class couples married in their mid-twenties, the illegitimacy rate was surprisingly low. In mid-century, however, the number of illegitimate children began to increase. In Central Europe, for example, the illegitimacy rate appears to have increased fivefold between 1700 and 1800. The increase in illegitimacy may have been the result of the breakdown of village communities and the weakening role of churches in everyday life.

In any case, the average married couple had five children, and more of them survived infancy and childhood than in earlier times. Several factors, however, acted as a break on the birthrate: About half of all women between the ages of 15 and 44 remained unmarried. Moreover, birth control—achieved by such devices as sheepskin condoms, the vinegar douche, and sponges, and by the application of

Jan Steen, *The Village School,* c. 1665. One of the pupils, whose written exercise lies crumpled on the ground, is about to be punished by having his hand struck with a wooden spoon. Steen's many paintings of "childish" errors often have a moralistic or satirical tone, whereby the children's behavior seems to be symbolic of adult foolishness.

Reproduction of *The Village School* by Jan Steen. Courtesy of the National Gallery of Ireland

herbal potions—was increasingly practiced by the upper classes. Members of noble families generally married younger, but after 1650 declining revenues and the need to keep estates intact contributed to a decline in the average number of children from six to two.

Along with the other developments that began to transform Western society, attitudes toward children began to change. Rousseau, for example, believed that childhood was a stage in human development, and that childhood experiences often proved crucial to adult behavior. Parental kindness and love did not begin in the Old Regime, but a new spirit of humanism and compassion increasingly led parents to treat their offspring as children rather than as small adults in their dress, in matters of discipline, and in recreation.

Economically, children were viewed both as a burden and as an opportunity, especially among the lower classes. In peasant families, they were expected to work in the fields or in cottage industries at an early age, and in the towns teenage males were apprenticed in shops. Nevertheless, large numbers of children represented an expense, and in hard times could be a serious burden on poor families. As a result, many parents resorted to infanticide or placed unwanted children in foundling homes, which were supported by private charities. In some large cities, perhaps 30 percent or more of all children were given up by their parents or by unwed mothers. If

such unfortunate children survived—mortality rates were shockingly high in these institutions—they were usually sent to workhouses or otherwise exploited.

AGRICULTURE AND THE WORLD OF THE PEASANTRY

European society in the 18th century was still overwhelmingly rural, and the peasantry represented the largest portion of the population—between 80 and 85 percent. Peasant life was harsh and often unrewarding. Few rural dwellers, except those in military service or on religious pilgrimage, ever traveled much beyond the village where they were born. They ate more or less the same kind of foods that their ancestors had eaten hundreds of years earlier. The staple item in peasant diets was black bread, which provided considerable nourishment. This was supplemented by soups made of grains and vegetables, especially beans, peas, and turnips, and by rice and pasta. By the 18th century, potatoes and tomatoes introduced from the Americas had become important ingredients in the peasant diet. Meat and fish were rarities, especially on the Continent.

Peasants and tenant farmers were constantly dependent on nature because the productivity of the grain harvest was the crucial fact of life. If the harvest failed, the result could be severe hardship if not starvation. Ironically, in such circumstances rural dwellers found it more difficult to obtain food than did people in towns, where municipalities generally kept reserve supplies. The yield ratio—that is, the relationship between the quantity of seed planted and the quantity of the crop harvested—generally went up in Europe in the 18th century.

The village and the immediate countryside around it represented the universe within which the peasants lived and died. Sons learned their father's trade, families intermarried, and loyalty was concentrated in the extended family. The church was the center of civic and religious life, and the priest was often the only local person who had a minimum of literacy. For the peasant, the village community functioned as the real government because it was responsible for public order, charities, maintaining roads, and enforcing access to common pasture lands and forests. In Western Europe, where rural society was organized around the villages, the owners of small plots would often decide communally what crops to plant. In Eastern Europe, where the land was held in the form of huge estates, the noble landowners made such decisions.

FREE PEASANTS AND SERFS

Conditions among the peasantry varied widely from one part of Europe to another. In Western and Central Europe—Britain, France, the Low Countries, Spain, northern Italy, and portions of Germany—most rural dwellers were legally free peasants. In places such as Portugal, southern Italy, Sardinia, and Sicily, their lives were overshadowed by stark

Le Nain, *Family of Country People,* c. 1640. 3 feet 8 inches by 5 feet 2 inches (1.14 by 1.56 m). The painting shows the hardships of peasant life during the Thirty Years' War; the family here is eating simple black bread and soup. The fact that the figures shown here—and in other paintings by the same artist—seem to exhibit a calm, stoic dignity and piety has led some scholars to speculate that these works were intended to reassure wealthy patrons.

poverty and the exactions of absentee landowners. In France, slightly more than half of the free peasants owned their own land, and these were generally small and inefficient plots. The rest of the free peasants were tenant farmers or day laborers. On the eve of the French Revolution, free peasants still owed nobles tithes as well as special fees—known as *banalités*—for the use of the lord's mill, wine press, and baking oven. Such obligations were bitterly resented.

Moreover, in addition to these feudal obligations, the peasantry also bore the burden of taxation.

The farther east they lived, the greater the degree of authority landowners exercised over peasants. In Eastern Europe, serfs rather than free peasants predominated. These legally unfree peasants lived and worked on huge estates owned by powerful nobles. At a time when serfdom was being eliminated in most western regions of the Continent, in

Map 57.2 Grain Production in the 18th Century. England's commercial supremacy derived from the fact that while it became a center for manufacturing and commerce (see previous map), its agriculture continued to flourish. Other notable farming lands—Sicily, southern Spain, southern Greece—lacked political stability and a thriving population to exploit their natural resources,

the 16th and 17th centuries, it became the widespread practice in Eastern Europe. As in the Middle Ages, peasants in Eastern Germany were bound to their lord's estates and could neither marry nor move without their master's consent. By contrast, Russian serfs were bound personally to the landlord, much as slaves, and could be transferred from one estate to another. Russian monarchs from Peter the Great to Alexander I rewarded loyal nobles with huge tracts of state land and the serfs who lived on them. Throughout Eastern Europe the oppressed peasantry and serfs often rose in rebellion against their landlords.

Aristocrats, Urban Classes, and the Poor

In sharp contrast to the precarious and harsh existence of the peasantry stood the aristocracy, the social elite that controlled most of the wealth and status in society. The nobles, who were by far the smallest class in terms of numbers, were long established in their legally sanctioned privileges and their estates. The middle class, on the other hand, although larger than the nobility, was not yet socially pervasive or powerful. In the larger cities of Europe, such as Paris or Rome, most of the population was poor, a social fact that presented unexpected challenges to governments and represented a new political element as the Old Regime drew to a close.

THE ARISTOCRACY

Aristocrats were by birth at the top of the social hierarchy. Although they represented only a small portion of the overall population—ranging from less than 2 percent to perhaps as much as 5 percent, depending on the country—the nobles dominated society. Among the legal privileges they enjoyed were immunity from certain forms of punishment, exemption from direct taxation, and judgment by their peers.

Since the Middle Ages, the European aristocracy had performed vital military and governmental functions. Feudal lords first received their estates from the king in return for serving as military officers and providing a specified number of soldiers. As the power of the monarchs

Gainsborough, *Husband and Wife in a Landscape*. **Mid-18th century.** This example is typical of "Grand Manner portraiture," of which Gainsborough was a master. The couple seems to be on a hunting excursion—the husband has his gun and hunting dog—but the elegant way in which both are dressed is hardly appropriate. As always, Gainsborough appears to be more interested in the landscape and the weather than in his apparent subjects.

The National Gallery, London

grew and centralized states developed, nobles continued to hold a virtual monopoly on the highest ranks of the officer caste in most countries. Similarly, nobles had once served as advisers to medieval kings, and in the modern state system they controlled the upper levels of the royal administration. In the late 17th and early 18th centuries, some sovereigns, such as Louis XIV of France and Friedrich Wilhelm I of Prussia, flooded their bureaucracies with commoners in a deliberate effort to weaken the hold of the nobility on the state, although the policy was reversed after 1750.

The major source of noble wealth was revenue derived from their landed estates. Sometimes they obtained money, which was always in short supply, through inheritance, marriage, or a royal pension. Most nobles were unwilling to earn income from such business activities as trade or finance, and in some countries they were prohibited from doing so. But as some nobles found their revenues from agriculture diminishing by the end of the century, they were more willing to take advantage of the nonagricultural resources available on their lands and set up mining operations, foundries, and other commercial activities.

Like the peasantry, the aristocracy was not a compact or uniform social group. In England, many landowners rented their land to tenant farmers. In Prussia, on the other hand, the Junkers managed their estates directly with a labor force still consisting of serfs, as in Russia. Yet because the number of noble landowners was declining in Prussia—by 1789 some two-thirds of the Junkers no longer possessed estates—the legal code of 1794 prohibited non-nobles from owning land; in Russia, on the other hand, increasing numbers of nobles were being given large estates by the monarchy.

The nobility, especially those of ancient lineage, jealously guarded their privileges and status, but financial difficulties or state policy often led to new blood entering the ranks. Some noble titles, for instance, were inseparable from the ownership of particular estates, so that commoners who were able to buy that property were also buying noble status. In France, about 3,700 offices were held by royal appointment, which automatically gave noble status to their holders. During the course of the 18th century, the king ennobled between 6,500 and 10,000 people.

For the most prestigious noble families, the center of life was at the royal court, where proximity to the sovereign

Painting of *The Oyster Luncheon*. 1731. The luxury and abandon of this scene, as the waiter brings yet another tray of oysters to an already sated group of diners, makes an obvious contrast to the peasant family in the picture on p. 590. The statue of Venus and Cupid in the niche on the right refers to the fact that oysters were considered an aphrodisiac.

was an exclusive privilege. Those nobles who lived at Louis XIV's palace at Versailles enjoyed special honors, although their lives were constantly guided by the will, and sometimes the whim, of the king.

In country houses, where an extended noble family could live in relative privacy, the interior layout was designed for several particular purposes. Hosts would greet their guests in a grand entrance hall on the ground floor, while common spaces—a drawing room, a dining room, a library or study, and perhaps a conservatory—were designed for entertaining. A large staircase off the entrance led to the upstairs quarters, including the bedrooms and rooms reserved for family activities and other private circumstances. Servants were housed in their own wing of rooms, while gardeners usually lived in separate cottages on the estate.

CITIES AND THE MIDDLE CLASS

In the 18th century, urban dwellers were a minority of the population in most countries, with the exception of states with longstanding commercial experience such as England and the Dutch Republic. London was the largest European city, with a population of about 1 million, while Paris was only half that size. Some 20 cities, including Rome, Amsterdam, St. Petersburg, and Vienna, had more than 100,000 inhabitants. The rapid growth of Europe's cities came in the 19th century, when industrialization drew large numbers of rural dwellers to urban centers.

The social and economic differences between Eastern and Western Europe also affected the role and importance of cities in each region. In Eastern Europe, cities tended to be smaller in size, less cosmopolitan, and subject to more direct government control. In the West, they had larger populations and more diverse ones and often enjoyed a greater degree of municipal self-government. In commercial cities, such as Amsterdam, Venice, and Frankfurt, elite oligarchies of nobles and merchants still dominated city councils.

Although rural dwellers greatly outnumbered those who lived in cities, urban centers exerted considerable influence on European society. In addition to serving as the seats of national and regional governments, large cities were centers of education and culture, of foreign ideas and influences, and of economic activity. Peasants in the hinterland often resented the towns as parasites exploiting the countryside by draining food and other resources while serving as dangerous sources of immorality for village youth.

THE URBAN POOR

Poverty was a serious problem in 18th-century society, especially in the cities, where streets were sometimes lined with beggars. For the poor, urban living conditions were often worse than in the country, and the death rate remained high throughout the 18th century. This was particularly true of children, who were more susceptible to disease caused by overcrowding, bad water, and the almost universal lack of sewers. By the end of the century, perhaps 10 percent of the entire populations of Britain and France lived on charity or begging. Some cities, such as Venice, where as much as 20 percent of the city's population was without employment,

Hogarth, *Gin Lane*. 1750. Hogarth's engravings convey a grim picture of contemporary London life. Here the path to destruction, caused by excessive alcohol, leads downward. On the left, a couple pawns their last possessions (the pawnshop is indicated by the three balls hanging outside and by the inscription over the door: "Gripe, Pawnbroker"). Below, on the top step, a mother under the influence of her Gin cheerfully neglects her child, while below at the bottom right we see the results: beggary.

granted municipal licenses to the poor to beg and live off the largesse of the many well-to-do tourists who flocked to the city each year. Despite a tradition of Christian teaching that the poor were God's blessed children, changing social mores made the attitude among the middle classes more harsh. Some political economists, for example, insisted that charity only induced the poor to lead useless lives and encouraged crime. The role of the state in dealing with the problem was still affected by such prejudice, as witnessed by the fact that in the mid-1700s in France beggars and vagrants were still subject to arrest and imprisonment, although their only crime was unemployment. Private charitable groups, particularly religious orders, provided much needed assistance, but poverty remained an ugly and pervasive reality of life in 18th-century Europe.

WOMEN AND THE OLD REGIME

Women were subordinate to men in every society of the Old Regime and had few legal rights of their own. In many societies, women could not own property directly or sue on their own in courts of law. In such cases, fathers, husbands, or other male relatives would manage estates or represent women. In Britain, a husband exercised total control over his wife's property, unless marriage contracts stipulated otherwise. In most cases husbands could file for separation but wives could not, although courts in France and England began to offer some measure of protection for women whose spouses mismanaged their estates. Some women, of course, exercised power as rulers, while the authority of others varied within a particular family setting. But for most women, their role was limited to family responsibilities, reproduction, and the rearing of children, along with work that could be performed in the home. By the end of the 18th century, however, some aspects of the lives of women had begun to change. In aristocratic and upper-middle-class circles, women played an increasingly important role in intellectual life, while among the working classes the Industrial Revolution began to bring many women out of the home and into the factory.

Childbirth and its attendant risks remained a constant issue for most young women of all classes. Because the church maintained the view that sexual activity between husband and wife was legitimate only for the purpose of having children, it condemned all forms of contraception except abstinence. Nevertheless, the increasing use of birth control, especially among the upper classes, enabled some women to limit or escape the burdens of childrearing. Although abortion was similarly prohibited by the church, it too was widely practiced.

WOMEN AND WORK

In the countryside, wives and daughters generally worked in the fields alongside male family members, particularly to harvest crops, and were central to the so-called **cottage industry,** where families worked in the home to produce textiles and some finished goods (see Topic 60). While husbands planted and tended cereal crops, women often raised vegetables for family consumption, made cheese and butter, cared for livestock, and sold excess eggs and milk in village markets.

In cities, women from the laboring class worked as household servants for the wealthy—40 percent of all British working women fell into this category—or worked as seamstresses and laundresses. Some women also sold vegetables, fish, and other foodstuffs in city markets, where such women were important elements in the urban economy. Among the lower rungs of the middle classes, wives and daughters served as salesclerks in family shops or helped their artisan husbands informally in craft workshops. Much female work of this kind was undertaken as part of a family business, usually within or near the home: Women's labor was regarded as a nonessential contribution to the labor of males. In reality, however, among the poor and laboring classes, women's labor often made the difference between survival and destitution.

UPPER-CLASS WOMEN

Among the upper-middle and noble classes, the role of women was far different. In both groups, family wealth freed them from having to earn an income. In middle-class and gentry families, women managed household establishments, while aristocratic women, who had large retinues of staff, enjoyed considerable leisure, which was used either for personal improvement such as music and reading or for social visits.

Wealthy women played an increasingly large role in the organization and functioning of their homes in the late 18th century. Interior decor became more comfortable and "feminine" in appearance, while wives would often entertain female friends in the afternoons over tea or cards. In the evenings, after formal dinner parties, the men usually remained in the dining room or retired to the library for tobacco and brandy, while the women retired to the drawing room for conversation and sweets. During the 18th century, however, some aristocratic women presided over a mixed company of men and women in their own salons, where intellectual discussions took place (on the salon, see Topic 54).

In the royal courts of Europe, women played still other roles and encountered different opportunities. There, in the extravagant world of luxury, high politics, and intrigue, wives of noblemen were expected to be accomplished in the social graces, not only in order to preside at elaborate dinners and balls, but also to flatter and influence men of influence. Yet despite the privilege that aristocratic women enjoyed, they shared with their lower-class sisters a series of proscriptions and burdens that were mapped out by convention, by their parents, and by the cultural constructs of gender. Not least of the difficulties they faced were the repeated dangers of pregnancy and childbirth.

The position of courtesan held a particular fascination with the opportunities it offered to those women, regardless of the status into which they were born, who were willing to bear the degradation of having sex with their patrons. Prostitution had, of course, always existed in European society, and courtesans obtained rewards by their physical attraction. An en-

PUBLIC FIGURES AND PRIVATE LIVES

JEANNE BÉCU DU BARRY AND LOUIS XV

Giraudon/Art Resource

© Chateau de Versailles, France/Giraudon/Superstock

One of the most successful courtesans in 18th-century Europe was Marie Jeanne Bécu, the Comtesse du Barry (1743–1793), mistress to the French sovereign, Louis XV. Her life was a case study in the limits and constraints of women in the Old Regime.

She was born Jeanne Bécu, the illegitimate daughter of a young woman from the village of Vaucouleurs. In 1748, her family moved to Paris, where the mother worked as a cook in the home of a wealthy businessman. Jeanne was taken into a convent at the age of seven, where she learned the rudiments of reading and writing, and left when she was 16. Beautiful and quick-witted, she worked as a clerk in a millinery shop and had several affairs with married men. In 1763, she met in a gambling house the self-styled Count Jean du Barry, an adventurer who moved both in the Paris underworld and in aristocratic circles. Du Barry ran a profitable business as a procurer of young women for his noble friends. Jeanne served as hostess in his home, where she befriended many important aristocrats.

In 1768 she married Jean's brother, the real Count du Barry, in order to appear at the court, where she met the 58-year-old king privately at Versailles. Louis was particularly lonely at the time because his wife had died a month earlier, and he was without an official mistress. Madame de Pompadour (1721–1764), the immensely influential royal mistress for 20 years, had died some years earlier. Louis was captivated.

Jeanne could not become the new royal mistress until she was officially "presented" at court, a move blocked by a conspiracy between the foreign minister the Duke de Choiseul—who hoped his own sister would become the royal mistress—and the Austrian ambassador, who was trying to persuade Louis to marry an Austrian princess. The anti–du Barry party did everything it could to prevent the presentation, but to no avail—in April 1769, she entered the royal chamber, resplendent in formal dress and diamonds. She was given her own apartment in the palace and a retinue of servants, and over the years Louis bestowed sumptuous gifts on her, including a chateau.

Jeanne du Barry chose not to exercise her influence in political matters, preferring instead to be a patron of the arts. As a result, she remained immensely unpopular at a court that was increasingly bent on extravagance and intrigue. On the death of Louis in 1774, she was banished to a nunnery, where she remained for two years, and then was allowed to move to her private estate. She lived there with a lover, the Duke de Brissac, until the outbreak of revolution in 1789, traveling to London in order to aid the noble émigrés living in exile. By the time she had returned to France, she had lost much of her famed beauty. In December 1793, during the Reign of Terror, she was condemned as a counterrevolutionary and guillotined.

terprising young woman could become the lover and companion of a wealthy aristocrat or a royal patron, perhaps even of the king himself. Yet courtesans had to cultivate many other talents, including the art of flirtation; literary, musical, and conversational skills; and highly polished social charms.

Regardless of religious proscriptions or secular laws against illicit sex, courtesans were institutionalized by the 18th century in the courts and in society at large. Sexual in-

fidelity had become more commonplace in aristocratic circles, and married couples—men and women alike—felt free to have affairs. In some cities, courtesans were highly paid professionals who had agents and paid special taxes. In the royal courts, talented young women were actually taken under wing and trained by aristocratic male mentors, who could then present their ward to a royal patron in return for any future influence she might have.

Putting European Society in the Eighteenth Century in Perspective

As the 18th century opened, the Old Regime appeared to be safely and permanently entrenched, much as it had been for centuries—a world of privilege, tradition, and hierarchy. Yet before the century was out, that well-ordered society and many of its values had been turned upside down by a revolutionary upheaval that shook all of Europe.

In retrospect, the period was rent with the forces of change. The commercial and financial life of Europe was expanding rapidly, while the population was growing at an unprecedented rate. Both in agriculture and manufacturing, revolutionary transformations were taking place that would have far-reaching repercussions. Even the social structure, which had appeared fixed by divine sanction, was undergoing important adjustments as the old aristocracy was forced to make room for an increasingly aggressive middle class that wanted a share of power and privilege. Throughout Europe, a new intellectual ferment was questioning many of the fundamental premises that underlay the social structure of the Old Regime.

Absolutist government, which rested on the notion of secure social foundations, was undergoing change. Some rulers sought to justify their authority by appearing to be "enlightened" and disinterested sovereigns, and all of them struggled to improve the efficiency of their bureaucracies and the power of their arms. To support the growth of central government and the luxury of the royal court, to fight the all-too-frequent wars that marked the century, rulers made more incessant demands for taxes, demands that ultimately produced a rebellion in the New World against the Old, and the political crisis of the Old Regime in France.

Questions for Further Study

1. In what ways was privilege built into the social system of the Old Regime?
2. How was society changing in the 18th century?
3. What differences existed between the aristocrats and the upper reaches of the middle classes?
4. What does the life of Jeanne Bécu du Barry reveal about the lives of women in the Old Regime?

Suggestions for Further Reading

Earle, Peter. *The Making of the English Middle Class: Business, Society, and the Family in London, 1660–1730.* Berkeley, CA, 1989.

Epstein, S.R., ed. *Town and Country in Europe, 1300-1800.* New York, 2001.

Houston, Robert A. *Literacy in Early Modern Europe: Culture and Education, 1500–1800.* New York, 1988.

Macfarlane, Alan. *Marriage and Love in England: Modes of Reproduction, 1300–1840.* New York, 1986.

Martin, A. Lynn. *Alcohol, Sex, and Gender in Late Medieval and Early Modern Europe.* New York, 2001.

O'Brian, Patrick, ed. *Urban Achievement in Early Modern Europe: Golden Ages in Antwerp, Amsterdam and London.* New York, 2001.

Pollock, Linda A. *Forgotten Children: Parent-Child Relations from 1500 to 1900.* Cambridge, MA, 1984.

Roche, Daniel. M. Evans, trans. *The People of Paris: An Essay in Popular Culture in the Eighteenth Century.* Berkeley, CA, 1987.

Rogers, Katherine. *Feminism in Eighteenth-Century England.* Urbana, IL, 1982.

Stone, Lawrence. *The Family, Sex and Marriage in England, 1500–1800.* New York, 1977.

Traer, James F. *Marriage and the Family in Eighteenth-Century France.* Ithaca, NY, 1980.

InfoTrac College Edition

Enter the search term *Old Regime society* using Key Terms.

THE AGE OF REASON

Toward the end of the 17th century, scientists and intellectuals began to circulate to a wider public the ideas and principles behind 17th-century science. During the 18th century, philosophers applied the same scientific attitudes to broader questions of human behavior. The school of thought that developed was called the Enlightenment, and the period during which it flourished—1740 to 1790—is often known as the Age of Reason.

The center of Enlightenment thinking was France, where a group of intellectuals known as the *philosophes* developed a consistent view of the world. The highest power, they believed, was reason used critically because only by its means could true knowledge be gained. Reason, in turn, reflected the rational essence of Nature, which is ordered, operating according to logical and unchanging laws.

At the same time, Enlightenment thinkers were believers in practical information and experiment. The chief expression of this conviction was the *Encyclopédie*, a vast multiauthored work describing the contemporary state of science, technology, and philosophy. Despite government interference, the 17 volumes of the *Encyclopédie* appeared between 1747 and 1771, and its sales throughout Europe helped spread the ideas behind the Enlightenment.

The leader in the Enlightenment battle against organized religion was Voltaire. Poet, novelist, and historian, Voltaire also wrote on science and philosophy. The most famous intellectual of his time, in the last 25 years of his life Voltaire constantly attacked organized religion—he called it "the infamous thing"—which he believed caused so much bigotry and fanaticism.

Other thinkers dealt with scientific and social issues. Georges Buffon was the first modern classifier of the animal world, while Marie-Jean Condorcet used his work as a mathematician to reinforce his belief that the human race was capable of systematic progress. In Italy, Cesare Beccaria studied new approaches to criminals and their punishment. The Scottish economist Adam Smith, in writing *The Wealth of Nations* (1776), founded economics as a social science.

Although he was one of the contributors to the *Encyclopédie*, Jean-Jacques Rousseau strongly contested the *philosophes'* notion that civilization would lead to an improved society. On the contrary, he held that humans were good but civilization was evil. The way to happiness, therefore, lay in a return to a simple, natural life. An advocate of free love and unrestrained emotion, Rousseau devised a social contract that proposed a new kind of relationship between individuals and their government.

THE SEEDS OF THE ENLIGHTENMENT

The intellectual movement known as the **Enlightenment,** which reached its peak in the latter part of the 18th century, represented the fusion of several currents of thought from the late 17th century. The scientific revolution had led the way in seeking to understand how the world works, revealing in the process that many of the teachings of traditional Christianity about natural science and astronomy were simply wrong (see Topic 48).

THE PHILOSOPHY OF JOHN LOCKE

One of the fathers of the Enlightenment was the English philosopher John Locke (1632–1704). In *An Essay Concerning Human Understanding* (1690), Locke discussed the origin and nature of knowledge. At birth, he argued, the human mind was a blank tablet—a *tabula rasa*—that was filled up by sense impressions gained through direct experience. As a result, all human beings were born as equals, whereas status and privilege usually determined the kind of experiences that each person underwent. Education was, therefore, of prime importance in creating a just and equitable society.

In a truly revolutionary move, Locke rejected the traditional Christian teaching of original sin and the traditional political system of monarchy. Instead, he believed in the essential goodness of humanity and argued that political power should have a broad popular base. In his *Two Treatises on Civil Government* (1690), written in the wake of the English Revolution, Locke posited the contract theory of government, according to which individuals living in a state of nature entered freely into a political compact in order to protect the essential individual rights of life, liberty, and property. Citizens would act loyally toward government, but if government broke its part of the contract by undermining these liberties, then the people had the right to change it.

As the scientific revolution had demonstrated, it was possible for humans to make progress in understanding the workings of nature by using reason. Similar beneficial change could be created in society by following the same positive course. Although many of the rationalists who followed Locke abandoned the traditional beliefs of Christianity, and some rejected the very notion of God, Locke was not an atheist and strongly advocated a degree of religious freedom—although not for Catholics, Jews, or atheists.

By the early part of the 18th century, these ideas had begun to crystallize. Thinkers increasingly rejected the past and looked forward to social and political reform. Custom and tradition, far from being valuable, were the shackles that bound the human race and prevented progress. Hope for humanity lay not in contemplating the rewards of the next life—the existence of which in any case could not be objectively demonstrated—but in concentrating on improvements in the real world. With this optimistic attitude, civilization could reach new heights and redress many of the existing injustices.

THE *PHILOSOPHES:* THE BATTLE AGAINST SUPERSTITION

The center of Enlightenment thought was France, where its representatives fought a constant battle against the weakening absolutism of Louis XV and the power of the Catholic Church. Important Enlightenment movements developed in Germany and Italy, and Enlightenment ideas also circulated in North America, especially toward the end of the century, where they influenced the first pronouncements of the founding fathers. Eastern Europe was relatively little affected, its rulers being fully aware of the subversive character of Enlightenment doctrines. Furthermore, most Eastern European countries had a low level of literacy and only a small middle class to be affected by intellectual developments.

In France, the movement's leaders were the **philosophes.** Literally translated, the word means "philosophers" in French, but the *philosophes* were not so much original thinkers as popularizers and propagandizers, who circulated

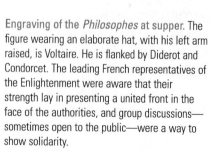
Engraving of the *Philosophes* at supper. The figure wearing an elaborate hat, with his left arm raised, is Voltaire. He is flanked by Diderot and Condorcet. The leading French representatives of the Enlightenment were aware that their strength lay in presenting a united front in the face of the authorities, and group discussions—sometimes open to the public—were a way to show solidarity.

The Granger Collection

the ideas of others in the form of pamphlets, plays, novels, or works of history.

Few Enlightenment thinkers completely ruled out the possibility of the existence of a divine force in the universe; even the highly skeptical Edinburgh philosopher David Hume (1711–1776) argued only against the provability of such a power. Most of them, however, attacked the power of the clergy and all traditional superstition. In place of the Christian God stood nature—or Nature—whose laws benevolently governed the universe. The same order that existed in astronomy and physics could be found in morality, or politics, or even economics. Only by seeking to understand these natural laws and following them could humans achieve happiness. By emphasizing happiness, rather than salvation, the *philosophes* rejected the traditional Christian view that misery in this life would receive compensation in the next.

The concern with general well-being led to protests at the ill-treatment of prisoners and the insane, and condemnation of slavery. Most Enlightenment thinkers were pacifists and internationalists, who saw patriotism—along with religion—as the cause of most wars. Above all, they believed in freedom. The France of Louis XV, although less repressive than that of his predecessor, still maintained restrictions on freedom of speech, religion, trade, and work. For all their fervor, however, the *philosophes* were not revolutionaries. They advocated not immediate democracy, but a gradual transition by means of rulers who were "enlightened despots" such as Friedrich II of Prussia (see Topic 59). They did not aim at radical change, even though many of their ideas inspired the leaders of the French Revolution. Furthermore, Enlightenment thought circulated chiefly among the urban aristocracy and educated middle classes.

In addition, few of the *philosophes* had much time for women's rights, even though some of them reached their audience by means of the salons of the more advanced women of the day. By contrast with centuries of earlier thinkers, they acknowledged women's ability to reason, and encouraged female education, but on the whole they accepted the conventional notion of women as inferior to men. The only real attempt to argue for fundamental change, Mary Wollstonecraft's *Vindication of the Rights of Women* (1792), found few sympathizers.

DIDEROT AND THE *ENCYCLOPÉDIE*

One of the leading French *philosophes*, Denis Diderot (1713–1784), sought to provide an organized basis for Enlightenment thought by preparing an immense encyclopedia. He intended the work to describe the contemporary state of science, technology, and philosophy, and at the same time to establish a classification system for human knowledge. Working with the physicist and mathematician Jean Le Rond d'Alembert (1717–1783) as his co-editor, Diderot began work on the project in 1747; the last of its 17 volumes of text and 11 of engravings appeared in 1771. The *Encyclopédie*, with its articles by various contributors, provided a wealth of information on a bewildering range of subjects, from metallurgy to political economy to the raising of asparagus.

Implicit in this philosophy was the idea that no political or religious system should try to limit or control the minds of individuals. The authors of the *Encyclopédie* opposed all corporate privilege, in fact, and believed that no group—the guilds, for example—had exclusive rights to any area of knowledge. As the leading German philosopher of the Enlightenment, Immanuel Kant (1724–1804), pointed out, the very essence of the Enlightenment was to "dare to know." If this meant rejecting established wisdom or resisting authority, then the *philosophes* were prepared to do so. Voltaire had to leave France, Hume was threatened with excommunication (and thus ostracism), and Diderot spent time in jail. Church and government authorities both tried to stop publication of the *Encyclopédie*, or at least censor it, but Diderot succeeded in completing his project.

The *Encyclopédie* sold not only in Europe's great cities, but also in small provincial towns. It helped an entire generation to see their lives in an entirely fresh way and led them to challenge hitherto unquestioned assumptions. Its

Illustration from the *Encyclopedie*. Mid-18th century. The scene shows a scientific laboratory, in which various experiments are being conducted. In the foreground a kneeling figure seems to be performing a dissection, while at the table behind others are mixing liquids. The various vessels on the shelf above are numbered and named in the accompanying text.

tone of optimism, and its conviction that humans had their destiny in their own hands, powerfully influenced the Declaration of Independence of the new American nation.

CHARLES-LOUIS MONTESQUIEU

A more specific influence on the political growth of America was the political philosophy of one of the contributors to the *Encyclopédie*, Charles-Louis Montesquieu (1689–1755). Aristocratic by birth, Montesquieu argued against the abolition of monarchy. His ideal system of government was based on a division of powers among king, lords, and commons. This separation of powers would, he believed, create a series of "checks and balances" capable of safeguarding personal liberty. The framers of the American Constitution adapted the principle, transforming Montesquieu's three divisions into the executive, judicial, and legislative branches of government.

Montesquieu's other important contribution to the study of politics was his book *The Spirit of the Laws* (1748). In it he claimed that different forms of government were appropriate to different geographic conditions. Small states such as Venice or 5th-century B.C. Athens were best suited by a republican government, whereas vast countries like Russia required an absolute monarchy. Pioneering in its aims, Montesquieu's work was the first serious attempt to examine the relationship between politics and environment.

"THE INFAMOUS THING": VOLTAIRE AND NATURAL MORALITY

Perhaps the most versatile genius produced by the Enlightenment—if less original than Diderot—was François-Marie Arouet (1694–1778), best known to us as Voltaire, his pen name. As a writer, Voltaire moved with ease from drama to satire to history. His studies included science and politics. He was an honored guest at the courts of Louis XV and Friedrich II, but also spent time in prison. Above all, Voltaire was fully committed to the great issues and battles of his times. An enemy of all forms of tyranny, he spent most of his life in exile.

His early satirical writings pilloried French aristocratic society and won him a jail sentence in the Bastille (1717–1718). Undeterred, he continued with an epic poem on Henry IV of France, which he published in 1723. After he spent another few months in prison in 1726, the authorities released him on the condition that he left France.

Voltaire chose to spend his exile in England, where the system of government seemed to him far more just and liberal than in France. Returning home in 1729, he wrote his *Letters on the English* (first published in English in 1733; in French in 1734), extolling English social and political liberalism and religious toleration, and praising the ideas of Newton and Locke. In advocating the experimental approach to science, he held that doubt is the beginning of wisdom and the basis of tolerance.

His contemporaries were enraged by the book's attack on French society and political institutions, and the uproar it

created drove him out of Paris into the country. He spent most of the next 15 years living in isolation with his mistress, Madame du Châtelet (1706–1749). A woman of considerable learning, and a prolific writer on scientific subjects—among her works was a translation of Newton's *Principia*—she exercised an important intellectual influence on Voltaire. The two of them returned briefly to Versailles in 1744, but life at the court of Louis XV was sterile and frustrating, and they soon withdrew.

The death of Madame du Châtelet in 1749 came as a bitter blow, and the following year Voltaire accepted an invitation to visit the court of Friedrich II at Potsdam. At first he established a close friendship with the king and worked on a history of the age of Louis XIV, his most important historical work. Two such powerful temperaments were probably bound to clash before long, however. The king made it clear that royal friendship had its limits: When Voltaire dared to criticize his patron's verse, the king abruptly dismissed him. In 1753, Voltaire left Prussia in disillusionment and circulated throughout Europe his own version of the falling-out.

The last 20 years of his life were spent in the village of Ferney, near Geneva, where he set up his own court. A pro-

Pigalle, *Voltaire*. 1770–1776. Height 4 feet 9½ inches (1.47 m). The head, modeled from life, shows the venerable philosopher at the age of 76. The position of the statue is based on an ancient Roman statue. The contrast between the thoughtful face and the active movement of the rest of the body perhaps symbolizes Voltaire's intellectual vigor.

Giraudon/Art Resource

cession of the leading figures in European political and intellectual life came to visit him, to discuss, and above all to listen to the sage of Ferney. Voltaire returned to Paris only in 1778, but the hero's welcome he received proved too much for his poor health, and the excitement probably hastened his death.

"THE INFAMOUS THING"

Voltaire's writings touched on all of the great questions raised by Enlightenment thinkers, but the most frequently recurring theme is the importance of freedom of thought. From the beginning of his career he castigated bigotry and intolerance, and to the end of his life he poured out a stream of pamphlets condemning prejudice and fanaticism: "The superstitious man is ruled by fanatics and he becomes one himself." Many of the letters in his vast correspondence ended with the phrase he made famous: "Crush the infamous thing!" The "thing" in question is organized religion, together with the intolerance bred of superstition.

The chief agents of prejudice, he believed, were the Christians, both Catholic and Protestant. Voltaire ridiculed the notion of the Bible as the inspired word of God. Rather, he saw it as a collection of anecdotes and contradictions that had no relevance to the modern world. Furthermore, it had provided the basis for centuries of disputes and persecutions that were as violent as they were pointless. The results, he said, were self-interested priests and false traditions.

Voltaire's attacks on organized religion were particularly bitter. His book *Candide* contains a famous scene based on an actual historical event; after the earthquake that destroyed most of Lisbon in 1755, killing more than 30,000 people, some of the victims who managed to survive the devastation were solemnly burned alive by the "wise men," the priests and monks, in a superstitious attempt to avert further disaster. Yet his position was fully in line with the Enlightenment's chief aims and goals, and most Enlightenment thinkers actively campaigned against the outward manifestations of organized religion.

Yet Voltaire was no atheist. The God in whom he believed created the world but could not be tied down to any single religion. Like many of the *philosophes*, the sage of Ferney held that only natural morality—the true religion common to all humans—could cure the ignorance and arrogance that plagued the world: "The only book that needs to be read is the great book of Nature."

SCIENCE AND SOCIETY: SOCIAL AND ECONOMIC THOUGHT

Many of the *philosophes*, including Voltaire, took an active interest in science and mathematics. Marie-Jean Condorcet (1743–1794), who helped in the preparation of the *Encyclopédie*, was a mathematician with a special interest in probability theory. Believing as he did in the inevitability of human progress, Condorcet looked forward to a time when even human biology might improve. Condorcet's optimism

was tested by his experience. He played an important role in the French Revolution but incurred the hostility of the extremists for his moderate opinions. After two years in hiding, he was arrested and thrown into prison, where he committed suicide.

The naturalist Georges-Louis Buffon (1707–1788) also believed in the possibility of physical progress. He ran a series of experiments to try to extend the human lifespan to 120 years or more. Buffon is best known for his work on the classification of the animal kingdom, and he also directed the royal gardens in Paris (the present *Jardin des Plantes*). The 44-volume *Natural History* (1749–1804), whose production he led, was one of the major scientific achievements of the 18th century.

CESARE BECCARIA AND PRISON REFORM

The center of the Enlightenment in Italy was Milan, where the brothers Alessandro (1741–1816) and Pietro (1728–1797) Verri headed a group of liberal intellectuals and published the influential journal *Il Caffè* (*The Cafe*). Among the younger members of the group was the economist and criminologist Cesare Beccaria (1738–1794), who derived an interest in political and social issues from his reading of Montesquieu.

In 1764, at the age of 26, Beccaria published *On Crimes and Punishments*, the first systematic treatment of rational criminal punishment. The work was an instant success and was translated into a variety of languages. Eventually its ideas led the way to criminal reform in many European countries, including Russia, and helped shape the U.S. system of criminal justice. Beccaria's main thesis was that his contemporaries' attitude toward criminals was unreasonable and inefficient. The harsh system of punishments, with long prison terms or death sentences for relatively minor crimes, was based on the belief that criminals were hopelessly evil. Because they were believed incapable of repentance, they deserved no mercy. Furthermore, the penalties were applied inconsistently.

As a child of the Enlightenment, Beccaria believed that all humans were capable of improvement. Prisons should thus be places for rehabilitation, whose occupants were adequately housed and fed and given the chance to work, rather than centers of futile and vindictive punishment. His book argued passionately against the death penalty and torture, pointing out that such savage penalties do not stop crime; in any case, torture was uncivilized, and capital punishment was an abuse of the natural rights of humans.

ADAM SMITH AND FREE TRADE

In his economic lectures, Beccaria anticipated the ideas of the leading economist of the 18th century, the Scot, Adam Smith (1723–1790). While traveling in Europe, Smith met and was influenced by members of a French school of economists known as the *physiocrats*. Their most famous principle was **laissez faire**—"let it be": the natural laws of economics require only noninterference to be successful. Smith also visited Voltaire at Ferney.

On returning home, Smith retired to his native town of Kirkcaldy, near Edinburgh. He spent the next 10 years

PERSPECTIVES FROM THE PAST

THE AGE OF REASON

The Enlightenment was known as the Age of Reason because the *philosophes* argued that superstition, faith, and tradition should be replaced by logic, scientific inquiry, and a secular spirit of the quest for knowledge of the natural laws that governed the universe. These principles informed the works of all the major writers of the era.

On Method

René Descartes (1596–1650) was one of the leading figures of the scientific revolution. Perhaps his greatest contribution to the Enlightenment is the set of principles he enunciated in 1637 on the proper method to be followed in pursuing "scientific" truth.

I believed that the four [principles] following would prove perfectly sufficient for me, provided I took the firm and unwavering resolution never in a single instance to fail in observing them.

The *first* was never to accept anything for true which I did not clearly know to be such; that is to say, carefully to avoid precipitancy and prejudice, and to comprise nothing more in my judgment than what was presented to my mind so clearly and distinctly as to exclude all ground of doubt.

The *second*, to divide each of the difficulties under examination into as many parts as possible, and as might be necessary for its adequate solution.

The *third*, to conduct my thoughts in such order that, by commencing with objects the simplest and easiest to know, I might ascend by little and little, and, as it were, step by step, to the knowledge of the more complex; assigning in thought a certain order even to those objects which in their own nature do not stand in a relation of antecedence and sequence.

And the *last*, in every case to make enumerations so complete, and reviews so general, that I might be assured that nothing was omitted.

The long chains of simple and easy reasonings by means of which geometers are accustomed to reach the conclusions of their most difficult demonstrations, had led me to imagine that all things, to the knowledge of which man is competent, are mutually connected in the same way, and that there is nothing so far removed from us as to be beyond our reach, or so hidden that we cannot discover it, provided only we abstain from accepting the false for the true, and always preserve in our thoughts the order necessary for the deduction of one truth from another. . . .

From Brian Tierney, Donald Kagan, and L. Pearce Williams, eds., *Great Issues in Western Civilization,* 4th ed., Vol. II. McGraw-Hill, Copyright © 1992.

Natural Law

Most of the philosophes believed that the universe and the human condition were based on natural law, and that a discovery of truth could be achieved by understanding those laws. The following extract is from an article by Denis Diderot written for his Encyclopédie.

In its broadest sense the term [natural law] is taken to designate certain principles which nature alone inspires and which all animals as well as all men have in common. On this law are based the union of male and female, the begetting of children as well as their education, love of liberty, self-preservation, concern for self-defense.

It is improper to call the behavior of animals natural law, for, not being endowed with reason, they can know neither law nor justice.

More commonly we understand by natural law certain laws of justice and equity which only natural reason has established among men, or better, which God has engraved in our hearts.

The fundamental principles of law and all justice are: to live honestly, not to give offense to anyone, and to render unto each whatever is his. From these general principles derive a great many particular rules which nature alone, that is, reason and equity, suggest to mankind. . . .

Man, by nature a dependent being, must take law as the rule of his action, for law is nothing other than a rule set down by the sovereign. The true foundations of sovereignty are power, wisdom, and goodness combined. The goal of laws is not to impede liberty but to direct properly all man's actions.

From *Encyclopedia*: Selections by Denis Diderot, D'Alembert.

The Principles of Morals

David Hume (1711–1776), perhaps the most important English philosopher of the 18th century, sought to understand the world beyond the senses. In this essay from 1751 on the nature of morals, he revealed his belief that morality was capable of scientific, rational analysis.

There has been a controversy started of late, much better worth examination, concerning the general foundation of MORALS; whether they be derived from REASON or from SENTIMENT; whether we attain the knowledge of them by a chain of argument and induction, or by an immediate feeling and finer internal sense; whether, like all sound judgment of truth and falsehood, they should be the same to every rational intelligent being; or whether, like the perception of beauty and deformity, they be founded entirely on the particular fabric and constitution of the human species. . . .

It must be acknowledged, that both sides of the question are susceptible of specious arguments. Moral distinctions, it may be said, are discernible by pure *reason*: else, whence the many disputes that reign in common life, as well as in philosophy, with regard to this subject; the long chain of proofs often produced on both sides, the example cited, the authorities appealed to, the analogies employed, the fallacies detected, the inferences drawn, and the several conclusions adjusted to their proper principles? Truth is disputable; not taste: what exists in the nature of things is the standard of our judgment: what each man feels within himself is the standard of sentiment. Propositions in geometry may be proved, systems in physics may be contro-

verted; but the harmony of verse, the tenderness of passion, the brilliancy of wit, must give immediate pleasure. No man reasons concerning another's beauty; but frequently concerning the justice or injustice of his actions. . . .

David Hume, *An Inquiry Concerning the Principles of Morals*, Section I.

A Call for Toleration

Voltaire used his brilliant style and sense of irony to debunk many aspects of the Old Regime and its dependence on superstition. In the following essay, he tried to point out that a major step toward toleration was often just a matter of putting oneself in the other person's place.

One does not need great art and skilful eloquence to prove that Christians ought to tolerate each other—nay, even to regard all men as brothers. Why, you say, is the Turk, the Chinese, or the Jew my brother? Assuredly; are we not all children of the same father, creatures of the same God?

But these people despise us and treat us as idolaters. Very well; I will tell them that they are quite wrong. It seems to me that I might astonish, at least, the stubborn pride of a Mohammedan or a Buddhist priest if I spoke to them somewhat as follows:

This little globe, which is but a point, travels in space like many other globes; we are lost in the immensity. Man, about five feet high, is certainly a small thing in the universe. One of these imperceptible beings says to some of his neighbours, in Arabia or South Africa: "Listen to me, for the God of all these worlds has enlightened me. There are nine hundred million little ants like us on the earth, but my ant-hole alone is dear to God. All the others are eternally reprobated by him. Mine alone will be happy."

They would then interrupt me, and ask who was the fool that talked all this nonsense. I should be obliged to tell them that it was themselves. I would then try to appease them, which would be difficult. . . .

From Lynn Hunt, Thomas R. Martin, Barbara H. Rosenwein, R. Po-chia Hsia, Bonnie G. Smith, eds., *Connecting with the Past*, Vol. I. D.C. Heath, Copyright © 1995.

working on his most famous publication, *The Wealth of Nations* (1776), while involving himself on an almost daily basis in Edinburgh's intellectual and cultural life. In *The Wealth of Nations* he worked out his theory of the division of labor, money, prices, wages, and distribution; the classic system of economics he described laid the foundations of the science of political economy.

Smith argued that if market forces were allowed to operate without state intervention, an "invisible hand" would guide self-interest for the benefit of all. This was another example of Enlightenment optimism. He was in favor of open competition and strongly opposed to price rings (the predecessors of the modern cartels), observing: "People of the same trade seldom meet together even for merriment or diversion, but that the conversation ends in some conspiracy against the public, or in some contrivance to raise prices."

THE OUTSIDER: ROUSSEAU AND THE SOCIAL CONTRACT

Enlightenment belief in the blessings of civilization found one eloquent dissenter: Jean-Jacques Rousseau (1712–1778). Tormented and quarrelsome, Rousseau's unstable temperament shaped most of his life. He lost his mother at birth and was separated from his father at the age of 10. After a brief period as an engraver's apprentice, he met and fell in love with a French noblewoman, Madame de Warens (1700–1762). The two settled down in the country for almost 10 years (1732–1741), a period Rousseau later recalled in his autobiographical *Confessions* (1765–1770) as idyllic.

In 1741 he set out for Paris, where he devoted himself to music. In the 1750s, Diderot commissioned him to produce some articles on music for the *Encyclopédie,* and his short opera *The Village Soothsayer* (1752) was an instant success. In 1745 he began an affair with an illiterate servant girl, Thérèse Levasseur.

The first of his major philosophical works, *Discourse on the Sciences and the Arts,* appeared in 1750. It laid out one of his basic principles: the savage, "natural" condition is superior to civilization. Rousseau was convinced that the growth of society had corrupted the natural goodness of the human race and destroyed the freedom of the individual. Humans, in short, were good; society was bad.

THE SOCIAL CONTRACT

Rousseau soon became identified with the notion of the "noble savage," but he never advocated a return to some form of primitive existence. Instead he urged the creation of a new social order. In 1762 he published *The Social Contract,* one of the most radical political works of the 18th century, and one that proved immensely influential on modern political theory.

Rousseau's ideal was a society in which there was no hereditary, privileged aristocracy. All members should have joined freely, surrendering their individual rights to the group. The "rulers" would be the servants of the community, answerable to the people's will, and instantly removable if the people so decided. Unlike his contemporaries, Rousseau claimed that if the people really governed themselves, there would be no need for checks and balances, separation of powers, or protection of rights.

Clearly such a system could operate only in a small society. In any case, Rousseau did not intend *The Social Contract* to be taken as a practical program, although in the bloodiest days of the French Revolution, the extremist Robespierre claimed to be following Rousseau's recommendations in unleashing the Reign of Terror. Its purpose was to set out the basic theory of democratic government. For conservatives, Rousseau was a dangerous emotionalist and an anarchist, whereas for liberals and democrats, a forerunner of totalitarian dictatorship. Few political thinkers have inspired more controversy.

ROUSSEAU AND THE ROLE OF WOMEN

For all the importance of *The Social Contract,* most of Rousseau's readers were more interested in the social ideas expressed in his novels than in his political philosophy. His two most popular books, *The New Heloise* (1761) and *Émile* (1762), were bestsellers throughout Europe. These works reveal Rousseau's ideas about education, society, and the role of women. The first of them owed much of its popularity to its praise of the open display of emotion, while the other dealt with education, recommending that children be protected from the harmful effects of civilization and exposed instead to the moral influence of nature.

In both books, women are assigned specific social roles as nurturers and educators. Julie, the heroine of *The New Heloise,* inspires her children with a sense of right and wrong—law enforcer rather than lawmaker. In *Émile,* the two children who are the tale's principal characters are both given unconventional educations, but their training is not the same. Émile, the boy, learns knowledge and self-control so that he can become confident and in charge of his own destiny in the wider world. Sophie, his future partner, is educated for the domestic sphere, where she will serve as Émile's faithful and obedient companion. For all Rousseau's revolutionary political thinking, he was quite prepared to institutionalize the traditional "separate spheres" for women and men. Women, he believed, far from receiving a natural education, should be kept away from nature lest they became disruptive.

Putting the Age of Reason in Perspective

For many Enlightenment thinkers, their movement marked humanity's coming of age. The power of pragmatism and critical reason, they believed, had replaced what they regarded as the childish superstitions of the Middle Ages. Their strenuous opposition to the Old Regime and all of its works was to help bring it crashing down, and by undermining respect for established authority they laid the foundations for the increasing intellectual freedom of the 19th century. Some of their ideas, such as Rousseau's praise of open emotional expression, were taken up by the romantics.

On the other hand, most of the *philosophes* fully realized that further human progress would be neither smooth nor painless. Many of them were concerned about the desperate state in which most of Europe's population lived. Smith and Hume both wrote about the conditions of the rural and urban poor, and the French physiocrat Jacques Turgot tried to redistribute taxes more fairly and abolish compulsory labor. Hume even argued on his deathbed that "man will never be enlightened." Most Enlightenment thinkers, in fact, aimed to bring about progress on a limited scale, through their local societies and academies, in the hope that someday the total accumulation of their efforts might produce significant change.

The upheavals of the French Revolution and the subsequent Napoleonic era seemed to bear out Hume's skeptical conclusion. Yet in the long run the Enlightenment proved decisive in changing basic attitudes in Western culture. Never again did traditional religion occupy the position it held before the 18th century. From the end of the 18th century, democracy became an increasingly admired political ideal, even if it could not be attained in practice. Science and technology maintained their role as catalysts of social change, while the *Encyclopédie* illustrated the immense value of knowledge and practical information.

Condorcet once described the intellectuals of his time as a "class of men less concerned with discovering the truth than with propagating it." For all the immensity of the task, the leaders of the Enlightenment led the way to the social and political revolutions of the 19th century.

Questions for Further Study

1. What were the main goals of the Enlightenment? How did its philosophers set about achieving their aims, and how successful were they?
2. What effect did Enlightenment thinking have on European economic development?
3. How did the ideas of Voltaire and Rousseau differ? Which of the two was closer to the ideals of the Enlightenment?
4. How far did Beccaria's attitude toward prison reform anticipate or inspire modern approaches?

Suggestions for Further Reading

Behrens, C. *Society, Government, and the Enlightenment: The Experiences of Eighteenth-Century France and Prussia*. New York, 1986.

Chartier, R. *The Cultural Origins of the French Revolution*. Durham, NC, 1991.

Hampson, N. *The Enlightenment*. London, 1982.

Munck, Thomas. *The Enlightenment: A Comparative Social History 1721-1794*. New York, 2000.

O'Hagan, Timothy. *Rousseau*. New York, 1999.

Rendall, J. *The Origins of Modern Feminism: Women in Britain, France and the United States*. New York, 1984.

Roche, Daniel. Arthur Goldhammer, trans. *France in the Enlightenment*. Cambridge, MA, 1998.

Sklar, J. *Montesquieu*. Oxford, 1987.

Scott, H.M. *Enlightened Absolutism*. Ann Arbor, MI, 1990.

Spencer, S. *French Women and the Age of Enlightenment*. Bloomington, IN, 1984.

InfoTrac College Edition

Enter the search term *Enlightenment* using the Subject Guide.

Enter the search term *Voltaire* using Key Terms.

Enter the search term *Diderot* using Key Terms.

Enter the search term *Rousseau* using Key Terms.

PART VII

THE MODERN AGE

The 18th century produced two revolutionary transformations with profound historical consequences: the Industrial Revolution and the French Revolution of 1789.

Each in its own way led to fundamental structural and ideological changes in European and world civilization and gave birth to the modern age.

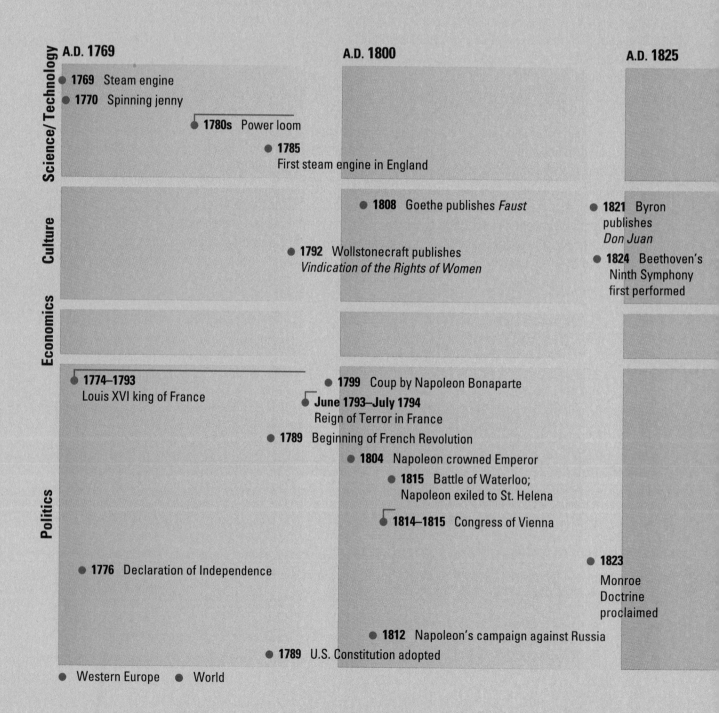

Science/Technology

A.D. 1769

- **1769** Steam engine
- **1770** Spinning jenny
- **1780s** Power loom
- **1785** First steam engine in England

A.D. 1800

A.D. 1825

Culture

- **1808** Goethe publishes *Faust*
- **1792** Wollstonecraft publishes *Vindication of the Rights of Women*
- **1821** Byron publishes *Don Juan*
- **1824** Beethoven's Ninth Symphony first performed

Economics

Politics

- **1774–1793** Louis XVI king of France
- **1799** Coup by Napoleon Bonaparte
- **June 1793–July 1794** Reign of Terror in France
- **1789** Beginning of French Revolution
- **1804** Napoleon crowned Emperor
- **1815** Battle of Waterloo; Napoleon exiled to St. Helena
- **1814–1815** Congress of Vienna
- **1776** Declaration of Independence
- **1823** Monroe Doctrine proclaimed
- **1812** Napoleon's campaign against Russia
- **1789** U.S. Constitution adopted

- Western Europe ● World

In its simplest form, the Industrial Revolution saw machines and steam power assume functions that had always been the exclusive province of human and animal labor. As a result, the West entered a long period of unprecedented economic growth in which living standards for many people improved. The social structure that characterized modern Europe was no longer

A.D. 1850

A.D. 1900

- **1830** First successful steam railway in England
- **1859** Darwin publishes *On the Origin of Species*
- **1851** Crystal Palace Exhibition
- **1876** First internal combustion engine
- **1869** Work on Suez Canal finished
- **1839** Daguerre demonstrates photographic process
- **1876** Bell invents telephone
- **1895** Marconi invents wireless
- **1887** Pasteur establishes Institute in Paris
- **1900** Freud publishes *The Interpretation of Dreams*
- **1905** Einstein formulates the theory of relativity

- **1848** Marx and Engels publish *Communist Manifesto*
- **1896** Herzl publishes *The Jewish State*
- **1838** Dickens publishes *Oliver Twist*
- **1869** Mill publishes *On the Subjection of Women*
- **1876** Wagner's *Ring* first staged at Bayreuth
- **1870** First Impressionist exhibition in Paris
- **1879** Isben's *A Doll's House* first performed
- **1903** Women's Social and Political Union formed

- **1846** Repeal of the Corn Laws in Britain
- **1871** Gold Standard begins

- **1830** Revolutions in France and Italy; Belgium becomes independent
- **1860** Garibaldi's expedition to Sicily
- **1861** Kingdom of Italy created
- **1900** Assassination of Umberto I
- **1901** Death of Britain's Queen Victoria
- **1870–1871** Franco-Prussian War; Bismarck unites Germany
- **1875** France inaugurates Third Republic
- **1837** Coronation of Queen Victoria
- **1878** Berlin Congress on the Balkans
- **1852** Louis Napoleon becomes Emperor in France
- **1914** Outbreak of World War I
- **1849–1861** Victor Emmanuel II rules Piedmont-Sardinia
- **1848** Revolutions in Italy, France, Austria, Germany
- **1864–1876** First International
- **1889–1914** Second International
- **1894** Dreyfus convicted of treason
- **1867** *Ausgleich* creates Dual Monarchy
- **1839–1842** The Opium War
- **1862–1867** French campaign in Mexico
- **1904** Russo-Japanese War
- **1908** Young Turks introduce liberal constitution
- **1861** Land-bound serfs emancipated in Russia
- **1829** Greece becomes independent
- **1861–1865** American Civil War
- **1905** Revolution in Russia
- **1853–1856** Crimean War
- **1899–1902** Boer War
- **1853** Admiral Perry arrives in Tokyo
- **1895** Jameson Raid
- **1912–1913** Balkan Wars

物人加利墨亞北　ペルリ像

determined solely by birth and inherited privilege, although these factors remained important. Instead, under the dual impact of industrialization and the French Revolution, economic class, defined by the relationship of individuals to labor and capital, became an increasingly important social determinant.

Europe's transition from tradition to modernity was accelerated at the end of the 18th century by the French Revolution, which radically altered centuries of political and social tradition. The revolution swept away the remnants of feudalism in France and the social system of the Old Regime that had rested on the hereditary privilege of the nobility. The events that took place in France from the late 1780s to the mid-1790s ushered in the age of "mass politics," in which social elements that had never been active in politics, such as the peasantry, workers, women, and the urban poor, now became participants in the making of history. The famous rallying cry of those who made the Revolution—"liberty, equality, fraternity"— entered the Western political consciousness as the ideal slogan of liberal political systems.

In the second half of the 19th century, two events of global importance were rapidly making themselves felt in Europe: the last stage of Western imperialism, which resulted in the European conquest of most of Asia and Africa; and the emergence of the United States as an economic and political world power.

By the opening of the 20th century, European civilization was moving rapidly toward a critical phase in its history. Increasing nationalist tensions and imperial competition had divided its great powers into competition with alliance systems, while social tensions and extremist political programs—anarchist, syndicalist, and Marxist— raised serious questions about future stability. The outbreak of World War I in 1914 signaled the end of the era of European dominance in world history.

THE POLITICS OF ENLIGHTENMENT: EUROPE AND AMERICA

The Enlightenment had a far-reaching impact that extended beyond Western Europe—its ideas spread as far west as the New World and as far east as the steppes of Russia. Nor was the Age of Reason only an intellectual revolution. In the course of the 18th century, the thought of the *philosophes* also affected political developments and lay behind a variety of reform impulses in states as diverse as Russia, Prussia, and Austria.

The *philosophes* were practical people who wanted to see improvement in the condition of human society through meaningful reforms. Despite the legacy of Rousseau, however, few *philosophes* were democrats who trusted the common people to rule themselves. Some *philosophes,* who evolved the principles of "enlightened absolutism," were convinced that strong—although not absolute—rulers were needed to maintain order, protect the "natural rights" of individuals, and implement reforms. In this sense, the ideal ruler was one who exercised authority fairly and impartially, permitted domestic tolerance for religious beliefs and free expression, and created conditions in which science and the arts would flourish. Other *philosophes* looked to the educated, reasonable members of the mercantile classes, who gathered in the academies and literary societies. For most reformers of the period, whether supporters of monarchs or the enlightened middle class, change should come from above, not from below.

To what degree did the monarchs of the 18th century fulfill such expectations and qualify as "enlightened"? The question has been often debated by scholars, who have examined the policies of the leading monarchs of the age in order to test the theory. Were Josef II of Austria, Friedrich the Great of Prussia, and Catherine the Great of Russia genuinely inspired by the *philosophes* and did they actually apply the principles of the Enlightenment in ruling their states?

THE POLITICAL THOUGHT OF THE *PHILOSOPHIES*

Political ideas stemmed from the same set of intellectual assumptions that inspired other aspects of the Enlightenment. Whereas scientists such as Sir Isaac Newton and economists such as Adam Smith emphasized adherence to natural laws, in politics the equivalent concept was natural rights. In the 17th century, John Locke had identified these rights broadly as life, liberty, and property—rights which no legitimate ruler should abridge or deny. Should a monarch cease to protect such inalienable rights, the people had a further right to change their government, for the monarch had violated the compact formed between ruler and ruled.

POLITICAL IDEAS IN THE AGE OF REASON

Those *philosophes* who thought most consistently about political reform stressed not only toleration but the practical fact that no one system of government was best for all countries. In *The Spirit of the Laws* (1748), Montesquieu insisted that tradition and environment helped to determine the form of government best suited for a particular society. He argued that the larger the political unit, the more power had to be exercised by the monarch. In Britain, a state of moderate size, the hereditary nobility in the House of Lords was balanced by the elected representatives in the House of Commons. Like most other enlightened thinkers of his age, Montesquieu believed that by themselves the common people were "extremely unfit" to govern a nation. In the case of his own country, he suggested that France might have been better off if the Bourbon monarchs had kept the political power of the aristocracy intact. In Britain, Montesquieu

also saw the principles of the separation of powers and checks and balances at work: Parliament checked the powers of the monarch, while within Parliament the House of Lords and the House of Commons checked each other. In the government as a whole, the balance was maintained by means of the separation of powers. Montesquieu could not have known, of course, that over the next century and a half the principle of separation of powers would decline in Britain as the House of Commons gathered more power unto itself, including control over the cabinet, which was becoming an instrument of legislative authority.

More radical in nature were the theories of Jean-Jacques Rousseau, which had a great influence on Enlightenment political ideas. Nature, he believed, dignified people, whereas civilization corrupted them. Hence, social and political institutions should adhere more closely to nature. In *The Social Contract* (1762), Rousseau sought to establish a new version of government by contract by reconciling individual liberty with government. Whereas Locke and other contract theorists had stressed agreement between a ruler and the people's willingness to be governed, Rousseau emphasized the agreement of society as a whole to be ruled by its "general will," to which every person submits. "In our corporate capacity," he argued, "we receive each member as an indivisible part of the whole." When an individual puts selfish interests before the needs of the community, that individual is forced to obey the general will—"forced," in Rousseau's words, "to be free."

Rousseau insisted that determining the general will was the responsibility of all the people and should not be left to an elected body, while the power to implement the general will could be delegated to a smaller group. He did not believe that any society could be governed by a genuine democracy, in which the people themselves both made and carried out the laws. Yet Rousseau's ideas were idealistic, and he maintained a deep personal dislike for royal absolutism. Holders of executive power, he argued, were the officers of the people, not their masters, and could be removed. Placed in the perspective of later history, however, his notion of the general will may appear to offer a justification for totalitarian government. He seems, for example, to be insisting that the whole of the general will is more precious and moral than its individual parts. Some later critics have argued that for Rousseau the welfare of the nation was greater than that of its citizens—an argument used, for example, by 20th-century dictators who claimed that they had a superior understanding of the general will and could set it above individual interests. In any case, this concept of the general will provided a rationale for some rulers who wanted to implement reforms.

Many of the English and Scottish intellectual colleagues of Montesquieu and Rousseau shared their concern for the nature of legislative authority. Those who did not agree believed that the only real responsibility of government was to administer the laws of nature instituted by God and that such authority was too often in the hands of individuals whose personal interests conflicted with the general welfare of society. Only hereditary monarchs, argued some philosophes, could reconcile their personal interests with those of the nation. Legitimacy—the right to rule—was maintained as long as royal policies were both reasonable and natural, and many monarchs of the period saw in the concept of enlightened despotism a useful justification for their powers, a more modern justification than divine right theory.

JOSEF II AND THE FAILURE OF THE AUSTRIAN ENLIGHTENMENT

The victory of Friedrich the Great in the War of the Austrian Succession exposed the weaknesses of the Hapsburg empire (see Topic 56). The young and inexperienced Empress Maria Theresa proved, however, to be a practical champion of reforms designed to strengthen imperial government. Advised by talented ministers, the empress increased the taxes on the nobility and reduced the power of their local assemblies. The central bureaucracy was modernized and staffed with experts, and the non-German populations of the empire were forced to accept both German administrators and language. Most important, however, Maria Theresa took measures to improve conditions among the peasantry, most of whom still lived and worked as serfs.

The taxes that peasants paid and the amount of labor they owed to their landlords were now limited, in contrast to the trends elsewhere in Europe.

Although the empress was a devout Catholic—Catherine the Great of Russia scornfully called her "Lady Prayerful"—she imposed heavier taxes on the church, confiscated monastic property, and expelled the Jesuits. Despite these reforms, all of which were intended to increase the power of imperial government, Maria Theresa was not sympathetic to many of the critical ideas of the Enlightenment. She prohibited the publication or circulation of the works of Voltaire and Rousseau and suppressed all books that she deemed dangerous to the established order.

JOSEF II AND THE AUSTRIAN EMPIRE
Not Maria Theresa but her eldest son, Josef II, was the Austrian monarch most responsible for bringing "enlightened absolutism" to the Hapsburg realm. Josef (ruled 1765–1790) ruled as co-regent with Maria Theresa but was constantly held back and dominated by his mother until her death in 1780. Stricken with grief when his wife died, Josef became a compulsive worker, impatient with bureaucratic delay and entrenched interests. A serious-minded man, he declared that he would make philosophy the guide for all imperial laws. During the decade that he ruled alone, he promulgated some 17,000 measures. Although his policies

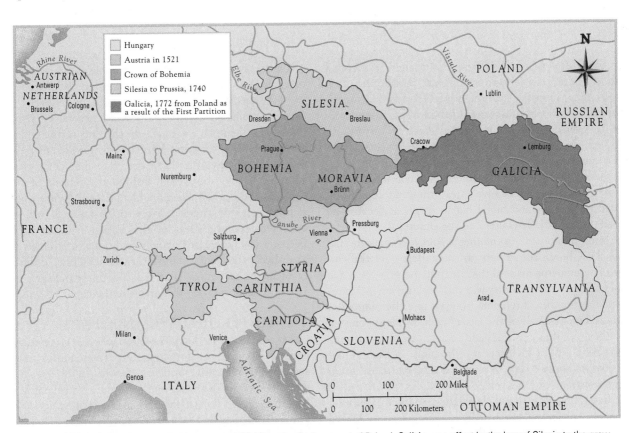

 Map 59.1 The Austrian Empire, 1521–1772. The gain of a large part of Poland, Galicia, was offset by the loss of Silesia to the growing state of Prussia. The region indicated as Hungary was split, by the early 21st century, into the independent states of Croatia, Slovenia, the remains of Yugoslavia (its capital, Belgrade, just to the south of Austria-Hungary on this map), and Romania. The southern half of the Tyrol became Italian after World War I. Go to http://info.wadsworth.com/053461065X for an interactive version of this map.

Giraudon/Art Resource

Martin van Maytens, *The Empress Maria Theresa and her Family.* Mid-18th century. The Empress is seated to the right, facing her husband, Francis I. The couple had 16 children. The oldest son, standing to his mother's right, became Josef II. Their youngest daughter, seen in the center in her crib, was Marie Antoinette, who grew up to marry Louis XVI of France and be executed by the guillotine.

were more often than not similar to his mother's, Josef ruled with less caution or concern for the established order.

In 1781, Josef II issued the Edict of Toleration, which gave Lutherans, Calvinists, and Orthodox Christians freedom to worship for the first time in Austrian history. He also improved the condition of his Jewish subjects, lifting the requirement that they live within the ghetto and wear the yellow star that had once branded them as inferior, and allowing them to enter universities—these reforms he regarded not as just and moral but as practical because he hoped to make the Jews useful to the empire.

Josef reinforced his mother's policy of making the Catholic Church subservient to the authority of the empire. The emperor insisted that he, not the pope, was the final ecclesiastical authority within Hapsburg lands. He reduced the number of religious holidays and the number of nuns and monks, calling the latter "useless." He suppressed one-third of all monasteries and convents, selling or renting these lands for the support of hospitals in Vienna, but encouraged those orders that were dedicated to education and charity.

In dealing with the plight of the peasantry, Josef took the policy of reform initiated by his mother to its logical conclusion. He emancipated the serfs and abolished most of their feudal obligations to the landowners and removed the traditional noble right to administer justice among the peasants. He tried collecting a single tax on agricultural land, a revolutionary step because the large noble estates were to be taxed on the same basis as the small peasant holdings.

Like the *philosophes*, Josef II believed in the leveling effect of popular education and provided teachers and textbooks for all primary schools. By the end of the century, more children attended school in Austria—about one in four—than in any other European state. The emperor also accepted, at least in symbolic fashion, the concept of social equality, and opened a large public park in Vienna, known as the Prater, to citizens of every social status. A new legal code reflected the ideas of the Italian reformer Cesare Beccaria (see Topic 58) about equality before the law and abolished both capital punishment and the use of torture. Noblemen found guilty of crimes, like commoners, were often sentenced to sweep the streets of the capital.

THE LIMITS OF AUSTRIAN REFORM

Other aspects of Josef's policies often reflected an unenlightened absolutism. He maintained the old mercantilist policies such as high protective tariffs on imports. In other ways, he continued many of his mother's programs—weakening the influence of the nobility by appointing commoners to important positions and furthering the Germanization of the empire by speaking German and patronizing German writers. Josef also tried to reduce the administrative and cultural autonomy of non-German areas of the empire such as Hungary and Bohemia.

Josef's enlightened reforms and centralizing policies sparked domestic opposition from all directions. The nobility spoke out bitterly against laws enforcing equality and forced him to revoke the single-tax decree. The religious faith of the peasants, who remained oblivious to most of his other reforms, led them to resent his suppression of the Catholic Church. The Hungarians and Bohemians resorted to rebellion to protect their local rights against encroachments from Vienna. Josef was both an absolutist and a realist. More often than not, he dealt with his opponents simply by insisting on having his way.

Josef II died of exhaustion and overwork, believing that his policies had been right but that he had failed to accomplish great things. The judgment of one contemporary was that he had "governed too much and reigned too little." Certainly not all of Josef's reforms succeeded—some of them, such as the abolition of serfdom, were repealed after he died—but many others remained intact.

Josef's lasting reforms were reinforced by the policies of his younger brother, Leopold II (ruled 1790–1792), Grand Duke of Tuscany, who succeeded to the imperial throne and proved to be an enlightened absolutist in much the same tradition. In the 25 years that he served as ruler of Tuscany, he had made considerable reforms in the government of the Italian duchy, including legal reforms suggested by Cesare Beccaria. Leopold sought to bring his subjects into public affairs and, unlike the other enlightened monarchs of the day, was interested in representative government as it was unfolding in the newly created United States of America.

"FIRST SERVANT OF THE STATE": FRIEDRICH THE GREAT OF PRUSSIA

In many ways, Prussian King Friedrich II (ruled 1740–1786), known as "the Great," appeared to be the best example of an enlightened despot. In his youth he had tried to escape from the harsh discipline of his father, Friedrich Wilhelm I (see Topic 52), who tried his son as a deserter and executed his son's companion and probable lover. A young man of sensibility and studious habits, he devoted the next 10 years of his life to literary pursuits and music. Playing his flute, which he carried with him everywhere, remained one of his favorite pastimes. He studied the writings of the *philosophes* and corresponded with many of them, favored French writers, and in 1750 invited Voltaire to live for three years at Potsdam Palace, outside Berlin.

Like Josef II of Austria, Friedrich worked hard at being king and drove his ministers and servants relentlessly. He avoided luxury and overindulgence, often wore dirty, ill-fitting clothing, and appeared obsessed with achieving success. In the conduct of foreign affairs and warfare, he proved to be a man of genius and cunning. Friedrich was one of the most efficient and successful monarchs of the 18th century, but there is no doubt that he practiced the art of despotism as much as he believed in the ideas of the Enlightenment.

Königin Friedrich der Große.

Engraving of Friedrich the Great. Late 18th century. The king is shown on the battlefield, mounted on horseback, giving orders to his staff. When not on duty, Friedrich cultivated the arts. He was an enthusiastic music lover who played the flute, and in 1750 invited the French Enlightenment philosopher Voltaire to stay in his palace at Potsdam. Voltaire stayed for three years.

THE CONTRADICTIONS OF ENLIGHTENED ABSOLUTISM

In economic affairs, Friedrich's policies were marked by deep-seated contradictions. He improved Prussian agriculture by importing from Western Europe the ideas of crop rotation and the iron plow, as well as new crops such as the potato and clover. He reclaimed land from swamps and, after the conquest of Silesia, established farms there and settled the region with immigrants from other German states. In the aftermath of the Seven Years' War, Friedrich worked to restore ruined forests and supplied the peasants with tools, seed, and animals. Like his Austrian counterpart, Friedrich did not accept the doctrine of a *laissez-faire* (free market) economy and resorted to mercantilist protectionism to stimulate Prussian industry, especially for such items as metals and textiles needed by the army. In Prussia, as elsewhere in Europe, the consumption of coffee grew rapidly in the 18th century. When it became apparent, however, that this new consumer fad required the export of Prussian currency, he put a heavy import duty on coffee beans and set up a corps of special agents to stop coffee smuggling. Moreover, Friedrich considered coffee and tea signs of the degeneration of modern society and insisted that his soldiers drink beer instead. Friedrich's military ambitions imposed a heavy tax burden on his subjects.

Despite his adherence to Enlightenment notions of equality, Friedrich believed in the maintenance of social hierarchy. At the same time, he was convinced that the same patriotic duties were expected of both monarch and subjects—the king, he said, was merely "the first servant of the state." The elite Junker class of landowners exercised a monopoly of social prestige in Prussia, but Friedrich did not spare them from the consequences of his absolutism. Only Junkers received appointments as army officers, but he discouraged marriage among them in order to avoid having to pay their widows military pensions. He abolished serfdom on the royal estates but not elsewhere in his realm, although in 1773 he did prohibit the sale of landless serfs in East Prussia. For practical reasons, he supported a minimum rural literacy and gave the peasants considerable economic assistance. The middle class he generally held in contempt, although he recognized their usefulness as tax payers.

Friedrich was a deist who took pride in his religious tolerance, yet his religious policies were also riddled with contradictions. When the Jesuits were expelled from other states, he invited them to his own Lutheran country. Throughout his realm, the king granted his Catholic subjects almost full equality and even built an impressive Catholic church in Berlin. On the other hand, in 1779, when the writer Gotthold Lessing (1729–1781) made a Jew the hero of his play *Nathan the Wise*, Friedrich kept him out of the royal academy. Whereas Josef considered his Jewish citizens useful, Friedrich pronounced Prussia's Jews to be useless, levied special taxes on them, and discouraged them from entering the professions and the civil service.

Friedrich made sweeping reforms in the Prussian legal system, freeing the courts from political pressures and reducing the use of torture. He also created a system of appellate courts to replace the strange tradition of allowing university faculties to hear appeals from the courts. Finally, he tried to eliminate the widespread practice of bribery by setting up a special gratuities fund to supplement judicial salaries.

Was Friedrich's enlightened absolutism little more than a clever deception to hide his will to dominance behind the fashionable intellectual discourse of the day? In his last testament, Friedrich insisted that he be buried beside his pet dogs. Some, including a number of Friedrich's contemporaries, have seen this gesture as a symbol of his contempt for his fellow human beings. Perhaps that scorn was a result of the difficulties of Friedrich's own life, torn as he was between the severe military traditions of his own Hohenzollern dynasty and the gentler doctrines of the Age of Reason.

ENLIGHTENMENT IN THE EAST: RUSSIA FROM CATHERINE TO ALEXANDER

Like the Austrian Empire, Russia had two monarchs whose policies conformed to the general pattern of enlightened absolutism: Catherine II (ruled 1762–1796) and her grandson Alexander I (ruled 1801–1825). The empire they ruled was a vast country in which feudal traditions were still very strong. In the decades following the death of Peter the Great in 1725, the monarchy suffered from a series of weak and ineffective leaders, and the nobility reemerged as a dominant force.

Having chafed under the harsh reign of Peter the Great, the deeply dissatisfied nobles sought to regain their former status and privileges. In 1730 they began to extricate themselves from servitude to the tsar, and by 1762 gave military service to the tsar only by choice. At the same time, the noble landowners extended their power over the serfs, serving as agents for collecting the poll tax. Masters could still exile their serfs to Siberia and mete out physical punishment at will. Serfs lost the right to gain their freedom by joining the army, and they could neither buy nor engage in commercial activities without permission from their masters.

CATHERINE THE GREAT

Brought up in a German court, Catherine was married at the age of 15 to the Russian Grand Duke Peter. In St. Petersburg, she ingratiated herself quickly with the Russians, learning their language and embracing the Orthodox religion. She soon came to detest her husband, took on a succession of lovers, and conspired to become empress in her own right. In 1762, a palace coup dethroned and assassinated Peter in a plot that probably involved Catherine, who was proclaimed Empress Catherine II, known as "the Great." The new ruler was a devoted student of the Enlightenment, who wrote plays, edited a journal, and read the works of the *philosophes* with great eagerness. Catherine wanted a good press in Western Europe both for herself and for the country she ruled, and she used the *philosophes* for that purpose. She invited Diderot, whose library she purchased, to visit St. Petersburg and granted him a pension. Catherine also corresponded with Voltaire, who did not visit Russia but did accept her financial support, praising her in return as "the north star."

REFORM AND ITS CONSTRAINTS

The empress was no doubt inclined to institute sweeping reforms in Russia, but a combination of personal liabilities—principally the fact that she was both a woman and a foreigner—made it difficult for her to move swiftly or decisively. Because she relied heavily on the support of the nobility, she felt she could not work to eliminate serfdom. On the contrary, in granting huge estates to her supporters, she converted many thousands of state peasants to privately owned serfs.

Painting of Catherine the Great, Empress of Russia. 1762. Under her rule, Russia gained control of the Ukraine and part of Poland, where she established one of her lovers as king. She secularized the property of the clergy and patronized the arts, but the condition of the Russian peasants and serfs became even worse under her rule.

Like Montesquieu, Catherine believed that a country as large as Russia had to be ruled by an autocrat. Once on the throne, however, Catherine appointed a Legislative Commission to codify the complex laws implemented over the previous century, and personally helped write the Commission's guidelines, which were replete with theories taken from Montesquieu's *Spirit of the Laws* and Beccaria's *Crimes and Punishments*. In addition, the more than 500 members of the Commission were elected by all social classes except the serfs and had to compile written statements of grievances from their districts. After a year and a half of inconclusive debate, Catherine closed down the Commission without having codified the laws. This was the last attempt by the Russian monarchy to consult its subjects until the 20th century.

REBELLION AND REPRESSION

In 1775, Catherine faced a great Cossack rebellion under the leadership of Yemelyan Pugachev (1726–1775). With a coalition of soldiers and peasants, Pugachev led a revolt against Catherine. The Cossack leader claimed to be Peter III, the murdered husband of the empress, and promised freedom and land to the serfs. Pugachev moved across southeastern Russia toward Moscow, burning and killing, and slaughtering landlords and priests. The outbreak of famine along the Volga River and betrayal by some of his followers brought an end to the rebellion. Pugachev was taken in an

iron cage to Moscow in 1775, where he was tried and executed. Pugachev's rebellion, which Catherine brutally crushed, reflected the depth of discontent felt for the monarchy as well as for landowners and government officials.

Catherine moved immediately to increase imperial centralization and further repress the serfs. In a major restructuring of local government, she increased the number of provinces from 20 to 50, hoping that the smaller provinces would prove easier to govern. She appointed nobles to most of the new provincial offices while imposing close government supervision on their activities. In 1785, Catherine issued two imperial charters. One charter granted the nobles exemption from taxation and military service and gave them complete control over their serfs. The other charter, which permitted self-government for cities, revealed Catherine's support for the small but growing middle class.

When the empress died in 1796, her son succeeded her as Paul I (ruled 1796–1801). Catherine had always feared that her son might lead a conspiracy against her, so that when Paul became tsar, many thought he would eliminate his mother's reforms. Paul proved, however, to be unpredictable. In his more reactionary moments, he placed the population of St. Petersburg under a strict curfew and prohibited Western sheet music, fearing that it would spread revolutionary sentiments among his subjects. He also continued the practice of giving state lands to his supporters, thereby transforming hundreds of thousands of peasants into private serfs. In 1797 he prohibited serfs from working on Sunday but permitted landlords to increase the amount of their labor.

Paul's policy toward the nobles proved to be his undoing. Attempting to reverse the developments of decades, he made the aristocrats once again subject to imperial service and limited their local powers. He also forced them to subsidize the construction of public buildings and to pay new land taxes. Paul also wanted to modernize his army along Prussian lines, instilling in the officers a sense of responsibility for ordinary soldiers. The elite guards' regiments resented these changes and hatched a conspiracy that murdered Paul in 1801.

THE LIBERAL TSAR

Alexander I (ruled 1801–1825) was educated by a liberal Swiss tutor who instilled in him a respect for the teachings of the Enlightenment. Despite his liberal leanings, however, Alexander made such extensive compromises that his accomplishments were limited. Perhaps one of his most ambitious reforms was a law that created a class of landowning farmers from former serfs who had been freed by their masters. This measure had only limited success, however, because emancipation by landlords was voluntary; fewer than 40,000 serfs were freed out of many millions.

The liberal but hesitant Alexander had the benefit of an exceptionally talented adviser, Michael Speransky (1772–1839), the intelligent and well-educated son of a priest. Inspired by Montesquieu's doctrine of the separation of powers, Speransky presented Alexander with a plan for

HISTORICAL PERSPECTIVES

How Enlightened Were the Enlightened Despots?

JOHN G. GAGLIARDO   Boston University

A vigorous debate on this question has occurred since the term "enlightened despotism" (now, more commonly "enlightened absolutism") first came into historical usage in the 19th century. The debate has revolved mostly around the motivation and purposes of the domestic policies and programs of those European monarchs of roughly the last half of the 18th century to whom the term has been applied. Over the years, many historians have argued that the reform programs of the so-called enlightened despots were neither chiefly called forth by nor primarily intended to serve the higher humanitarian ideals usually associated with the Enlightenment. Such policies were instead not much more than updated versions of periodic earlier efforts to strengthen the political power of absolute monarchy and to improve the economic and military position of their states in the dangerous climate of the 18th-century international system.

These historians hold that the cultivation of power rather than service to the spiritual and material welfare of their peoples was the prime motivator of the enlightened despots. Their frequent appeal to Enlightenment ideals and principles is seen as rhetorical camouflage designed to justify in the name of philanthropic necessity what was in fact a self-interested campaign to regiment and control their societies more tightly in the service of goals that had little to do with social welfare. At the risk of some simplification, the evidence produced for this interpretation points to the fact that nearly all reforms launched by these princes, including those that did bring some humanitarian benefit, also strengthened the fiscal or governmental apparatus of the monarchical state. Moreover, the programs with the strongest "purely" humanitarian content—popular education, charitable enterprises, reform of the brutal criminal jus-

tice system and of prisons, and so on—were persistently underfunded and always the first to be abandoned when money got tight. Some rulers did successfully move to abolish serfdom, and many more to alleviate its burdens, but the record is a very mixed one; and while noble privilege was invaded and curtailed in some respects, no ruler undertook to overthrow the traditional "society of orders" to which the concepts of privilege and legal inequality were fundamental. Even the two reforms most universally demanded by the enlightened community—religious toleration and freedom of the press—were not everywhere realized or well enforced, and some degree of censorship continued to exist in even the most "enlightened" states. This negative interpretation does not deny the achievement of some practical benefits for these monarchs' peoples; it simply asserts that the humanitarian ideas of the Enlightenment were not an important source of their policies, that any popular benefits resulting from those policies were more incidental than purposeful, and that an enlightened absolutism therefore did not really exist at all.

Even without disputing the historical facts of this interpretation, however, it is possible to approach the question from a different perspective—one that puts far more weight on the judgment of those contemporaries who first termed these monarchs "enlightened," and who persisted in doing so through all of the failures, partial successes, and supposedly hypocritical rhetoric of their undertakings. Unless we assume stupidity or willful naiveté in a very large part of the enlightened community, we have to believe on their own testimony that they perceived the enlightened despots as actual executors of many of their hopes for mankind, and applauded them for the overall direction of their regimes (without necessarily keeping detailed lists of every success or fail-

constitutional government. It provided for several elected provincial assemblies and a Duma, or national parliament, which would approve all laws presented by the tsar. These bodies would be elected by the nobility and the middle classes, with the exclusion of the serfs.

Had it been implemented, Speransky's far-reaching plan would have ended absolutism in Russia, but Alexander refused to put it into effect. Speransky had made powerful enemies in his effort to reform the civil service by requiring examinations and promotion based on

ure). Most enlightened thinkers and publicists, after all, were not dreamers or utopians, but informed and intelligent people living in a real world of real problems they wanted corrected. Almost none of them developed schemes for anything resembling a completely new political or social system; and despite much grumbling about the pace or depth of reform, or about the foreign and military policies of even those states they regarded as most enlightened, they also recognized the difficulties of reform. Consequently, they were not uncomfortable with incrementalist approaches to reform as long as they were persistent and real in terms of identifiable progress, however partial. They were, in general terms, "possibilists" rather than revolutionaries, who judged rulers and regimes by their *tendencies* rather than by comparison to some finished blueprint of a perfect society.

The fact that various reform projects corresponding to their own desires also served the self-interest of monarchs by bringing new power and efficiency to their governmental apparatus was not uniformly worrisome to the *philosophes* of Europe, and indeed had positive aspects: it not only illustrated a favorite truth discovered by the Enlightenment—the cunningly beneficial relationship between self-interest and public utility—but also improved the power of rulers to do good; we should not forget, after all, that most enlightened thinkers supported a powerful absolute monarchy as the form of government best able to reform a stubbornly traditional society, *when animated by enlightened rulership*.

What the *philosophes* sought, in broadest terms, was a society more tolerant of diversity (especially in matters of religious faith, with all their secondary social consequences); more humane (in caring for the disadvantaged of all sorts, including accused and convicted criminals); and more efficient and less wasteful (quicker and less expensive justice, rationalized civil codes, and elimination of arbitrary and capricious administrative practices through the greater regularity of a government operating under known and comprehensive laws). Even a brief review of the history of the enlightened despots will reveal much dedicated attention to this agenda—an attention more persistent and successful in some places than in others, but real nonetheless. By the standards employed by the *philosophes* themselves, therefore, the record of reform achievement in these areas, while not of revolution-

ary proportions, is undeniable, and suggests that their positive view of these princes was based on observed fact, not on wishful thinking or on such enlightened rhetoric as the latter employed. (A strong case can be made for the personal adherence of many of the enlightened despots to the basic premises of the Enlightenment—natural law doctrine, for example—which they knew well through some combination of both formal education and their own reading, and personal contacts with leading literary exponents of Enlightenment. This personal culture cannot be ignored in approaching the question of motivation.)

In the final analysis, to be sure, it is necessary to recognize several facts that may qualify the degree of enlightenment of the enlightened despots. Motive, to begin with, is always a murky and perhaps in the end impenetrable question; some of the reforms of the period clearly were continuations of earlier policies more than wholly new initiatives; there was often a considerable gap between announced intentions and results achieved, and what did not get done was at least as impressive as what did; and, finally, there is little evidence that the monarchs of the time had any vision of a breakthrough to an entirely new kind of society that might be made possible by their own efforts. The removal of all these reservations might be necessary to qualify these rulers as "enlightened" by today's standards. Nonetheless, shrewd and critical observers in their own time clearly believed not only that their intellectual receptivity, openness to experimentation, and intentions conformed to the enlightened spirit of the age, but also that their regimes represented a sufficiently progressive chapter in the history of monarchy as to justify dubbing them "enlightened."

In the end, then, if one can accept the reality of mixed motives—a genuine degree of humanitarian concern, combined with the imperative to keep the state both solvent and militarily strong—and if one can recognize the numerous and severe obstacles to all reform in societies that were economically marginal and stubbornly traditionalistic, with much ability to resist change, then a reasonable case for a genuine enlightened despotism can be made. In all essentials, it is the case made by the Enlightenment itself, and it remains a compelling one today.

merit, a system opposed by the many nobles and illiterates who held government office. He had also proposed an income tax for the nobility. Speransky's enemies found an opportunity to undermine him in 1812, when Napoleon invaded Russia; Speransky, who had arranged an alliance with the French ruler, was exiled and the constitutional scheme was abandoned.

Ironically, Alexander proved to be a more liberal tsar in the territories he ruled beyond Russia's borders. In 1809, after he had annexed Finland from Sweden, the tsar allowed the Finns to keep their law codes and a degree of local government. Similarly, when he became king of Poland in 1815, he granted the Poles a constitution and permitted them to have their own army and government officials, as well as to use their own language. It was in Russia that tsarist absolutism failed to temper the repressive regime with the political doctrines of the Enlightenment.

THE GREAT EXPERIMENT: THE ENLIGHTENMENT AND THE AMERICAN REVOLUTION

In the context of the Age of Reason, the American Revolution was an important event in European history. Its immediate causes lay in specific fiscal problems between Great Britain and its North American colonies, but the political ideals that undergirded the American revolt were part of the Enlightenment tradition. Inspired by the thought of John Locke, Rousseau, and other political theorists, colonial leaders such as Benjamin Franklin and Thomas Jefferson posed basic questions about the advantages of monarchy versus constitutional government and about the sources of political authority.

THE ROOTS OF REVOLUTION

After the end of the Seven Years' War in 1763, a victorious Great Britain had to deal with several pressing problems in America. London quickly discovered that its much enlarged empire required considerable financial expenditures and insisted that these be shared with the American colonists, who had benefited most from the war. The problem lay, however, in the fact that the colonists opposed the system under which they were taxed, mainly because their economy was no longer suited to Britain's mercantilist policies.

In 1764 Parliament passed the Sugar Act, which aimed to raise revenue through import duties, followed in 1765 by the Stamp Act, which put a tax on such items as legal documents and newspapers. The American response was that because they were not represented in Parliament, they should not be taxed by that body—"no taxation," they insisted, "without representation." That October, the so-called Stamp Act Congress agreed not to import British goods and issued a protest to the king. In the face of this resistance, Parliament repealed the Stamp Act, while asserting its right to legislate for the colonies.

Over the next decade, a familiar pattern repeated itself: Whenever Parliament passed a revenue measure or an administrative act affecting the colonies, the Americans resisted it, often with violence, and the British would then back down. Relations between colonies and mother country deteriorated steadily. When the colonies resisted a set of four import duties sponsored by Chancellor of the Exchequer Charles Townshend (1725–1767), the British sent special customs agents and soldiers to Boston in 1768 to enforce the laws. Tensions rose, and in March 1770 British troops killed five civilians in what came to be called the Boston Massacre. Parliament repealed all but one—that on tea—of the Townshend duties.

In May 1773 Parliament permitted the East India Company to sell tea directly to American distributors, thereby avoiding American wholesalers. Although the measure lowered the price of tea, colonial merchants viewed it as an oppressive act against American merchants. Some American cities refused to permit the unloading of tea in their ports, and in Boston a cargo of tea was dumped into the harbor. In 1774, British Prime Minister Lord North (1732–1792), determined to assert British authority over the colonies, passed the so-called Intolerable Acts. These laws closed the port of Boston, suspended many rights, and permitted soldiers to be quartered and fed in private homes.

Crisis was at hand. Incensed by what they considered high-handed and unjust treatment, colonists who were critical of Britain formed committees to discuss their common problems. In September 1774 the First Continental Congress met in Philadelphia, where the 56 delegates demanded redress as British citizens, denounced taxation without representation, and agreed to boycott trade until their rights were restored. The result, however, was war rather than negotiation. By May 1775, when the Second Congress met, battles had already been fought at Lexington and Concord. Although the colonists met defeat at Bunker Hill in June, the assemblies of each colony began to meet as sovereign bodies instead of under the king's authority. The revolution had begun.

FRANKLIN, JEFFERSON, AND THE AMERICAN ENLIGHTENMENT

When the Second Continental Congress met that spring, it could boast among its members two of the most illustrious intellects in the American colonies: Benjamin Franklin (1706–1790) and Thomas Jefferson (1743–1826). Both men epitomized the American Enlightenment, and their ideas made important contributions to the course of the revolution and to the political development of the future United States.

Franklin was born in Boston of modest background, the son of a soap and candle maker, and learned the printing trade as a young man. In Philadelphia, he ran his own print shop and published the *Pennsylvania Gazette* as well as *Poor Richard's Almanac*. At the age of 42, he retired from business with enough money to devote his energies to the sciences and public affairs. He had already helped set up a library, an academy that eventually became the University of Pennsylvania, and a discussion group that gave rise to the American Philosophical Society. He published the influential book *Experiments and Observations on Electricity* in 1751 and was a prolific inventor. The embodiment of a trained observer of natural phenomena in the Age of Reason, Franklin's scientific knowledge included astronomy, medicine, geology, and physics. Serving as Pennsylvania's agent in London from 1764 to 1775, he had been an important

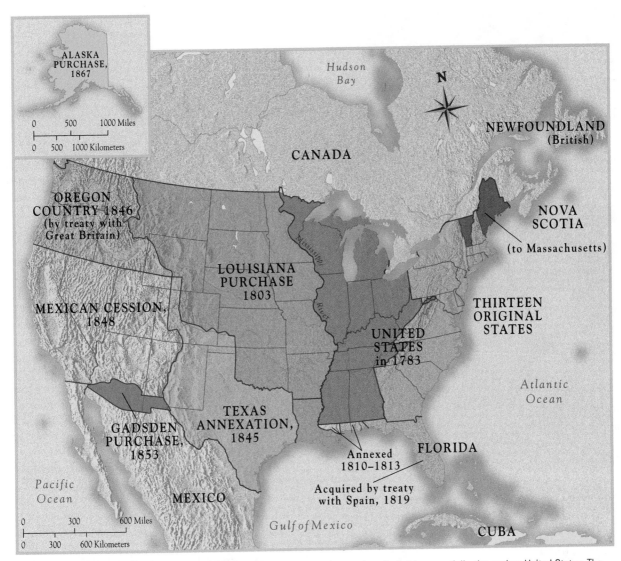

Map 59.2 The United States, 1776–1867. The map illustrates the creation of what is, essentially, the modern United States. The territory labeled as Louisiana had been won from the French by the Spanish in 1762. The French reclaimed it under Napoleon, who sold it to President Jefferson for $15 million, to finance his forthcoming war against the British. Texas, which was originally part of Mexico, became independent in 1836 and joined the United States in 1845. Three years later, following the Mexican War, Mexico ceded the land between Texas and the Pacific coast. The territory just to the south, which provided a rail link to the West, was purchased from Mexico in 1853 for $10 million. The deal was negotiated by James Gadsden, U.S. Minister to Mexico. Go to http://info.wadsworth.com/053461065X for an interactive version of this map.

voice for conciliation with Britain before becoming a member of the Second Continental Congress.

In contrast to Franklin's humble origins, Jefferson was the son of a Virginia planter and educated as a lawyer. The breadth of his interests and learning was even greater than that of Franklin, who had little interest in aesthetics. Jefferson read widely in the arts and humanities as well as in the sciences, played the violin, and read or spoke seven languages. He was an accomplished architect and knowledgeable in mathematics and engineering. His book *Notes on Virginia* (1785) showed him to be familiar with botany, zoology, geography, and archeology. Later in his life, one of the contributions of which he was most proud was the founding of the University of Virginia.

Jefferson first entered politics in 1769 as a member of the Virginia House of Burgesses. In 1774, in response to the Intolerable Acts, Jefferson wrote *A Summary View of the Rights of British America*, in which he rejected Britain's right to govern in America.

Although the Second Continental Congress sought conciliation with Britain, events led the body to plan for self-government because King George III had declared the colonies to be in rebellion. In the winter of 1775, an impassioned and immensely influential pamphlet by Thomas Paine (1737–1809) entitled *Common Sense* influenced many Americans toward independence. A colonial army was created under the command of George Washington (1732–1799).

The Granger Collection

Painting of Thomas Jefferson. Early 19th century. This idealized portrait shows the great American *philosophe* picking up a document containing the Declaration of Independence from a table on which stands a bust of Benjamin Franklin. The scientific instruments and globe to his left are a reminder of his wide-ranging intellectual interests.

In June 1776, the Continental Congress appointed a five-man committee, including Franklin and Jefferson, to write a Declaration of Independence. Jefferson drafted the document, to which Franklin contributed much discussion and some changes of language. The final version was a moving statement of the essential principles of Enlightenment political thought. Both Franklin and Jefferson were familiar with the works of Locke and the French *philosophes*, and the emphasis on natural rights embodied in it could not have been more clear: "We hold these truths to be self-evident, that all men are created equal; that they are endowed by their creator with certain inalienable rights; that among these are life, liberty and the pursuit of happiness." The colonies had invoked the notion of contract theory, in which subjects were free to overthrow an unjust monarch.

On July 2, the Continental Congress declared the independence of the colonies, and on July 4 adopted the Declaration of Independence.

The War of Independence raged on, widening in 1778 into a European conflict when Franklin, then serving as rebel minister to France, persuaded the government of Louis XVI to support the Americans. In 1779 to1780, Spain and the Dutch Republic also joined the war on the side of the colonies. In 1781, after Washington's army decisively defeated British forces at Yorktown, the British agreed to sue for peace. Franklin led the negotiations, which culminated in the Treaty of Paris (1783). The 13 American colonies had won their independence.

THE EARLY UNITED STATES

Perhaps the most successful application of Enlightenment principles to the world of politics in the 18th century took place not in Europe but in the United States. Between 1781 and 1789, the Americans governed themselves through the Articles of Confederation, which provided for a weak central authority in recognition of the difficulties they had experienced at the hands of the British monarchy. In 1787, however, a convention meeting in Philadelphia drafted an entirely new constitution for the United States. A national government was created with powers that transcended those of the individual states, such as the authority to tax, conduct foreign policy, and raise an army. Montesquieu's dual principles of separation of powers and checks and balances inspired the creation of an executive (an elected president), a legislature (a two-chamber Congress, consisting of a Senate elected by the states and a House of Representatives chosen directly by popular vote), and a Supreme Court.

During the early decades of their republic, Americans were as divided over political ideology as their European counterparts. In the United States, political leaders split between Federalists and Democrats, much as Europeans chose conservatism or liberalism. The Federalist party, founded by Alexander Hamilton (1755?–1804), was the first true American political party. Hamilton's support came mainly from prosperous business groups and landowners from the northern states; they wanted a strong central government run by the educated and wealthy elite. They were the strongest supporters of the new constitution and pushed for the addition of the Bill of Rights to the document, which were ratified as 10 amendments in 1790. These amendments guaranteed such basic rights for citizens as freedom of speech, press, assembly, and worship, and trial by jury. The Democratic Republican party, on the other hand, represented small independent farmers, largely from the south. The titular leader of the Democratic Republicans was Jefferson (president from 1801 to 1809), who preached popular control of government.

Putting the Politics of Enlightenment in Perspective

Enlightened absolutism had many weaknesses, not the least of which was the fact that a good monarch ruled as an accident of birth, not by the choice of the people. Nor were any devices built into the system in the event that these monarchs acted as despots without the benefit of enlightened sensibilities. Josef II of Austria proved to be too rigid and wedded to centralized control of an empire that incorporated too many diverse ethnic groups. The Prussian king, Friedrich the Great, was determined to increase the power of the monarchy and reinforced the status and power of the Junkers, who generally opposed the Enlightenment. In Russia, Catherine the Great compromised her reformist principles to satisfy the power of the nobility. Only in the United States, where the political principles of the Enlightenment were applied without a monarch, did democracy thrive.

Questions for Further Study

1. To what degree did the monarchs of the 18th century qualify as "enlightened despots"?
2. What were the political goals of monarchs in Prussia, Austria, and Russia? How did enlightened reforms help them achieve those goals?
3. What cultural and intellectual connections existed between 18th-century Europe and the American colonies?

Suggestions for Further Reading

Beales, Derek. *Joseph II*, Vol. I. Cambridge, MA, 1987.

Blanning, T.C.W. *Joseph II (Profiles in Power)*. New York, 1994.

Brewer, Daniel. *The Discourse of Enlightenment in Eighteenth Century France*. New York, 1993.

Erickson, Carolly. *Great Catherine*. New York, 1994.

Fraser, David. *Frederick the Great: King of Prussia*. New York, 2000.

Furbank, P.N. *Diderot: A Critical Biography*. New York, 1992.

Gianta, Mary A. *The Emerging Nation: A Documentary History of the U. S. under the Articles of Confederation*. Washington, DC, 1996.

Kennedy, Roger. *Burr, Hamilton, and Jefferson*. New York, 2000.

Madariaga, Isabel de. *Russia in the Age of Catherine the Great*. London, 1981.

McCulloch, David. *John Adams*. New York, 2001.

Scott, Hamish M. *Enlightened Absolutism*. Ann Arbor, MI, 1990.

Troyat, Henri. Joan Pinkham, trans. *Catherine the Great*. New York, 1994.

InfoTrac College Edition

Enter the search term *Frederic II* or *Frederick the Great* using Key Terms.

Enter the search term *Joseph II* using Key Terms.

Enter the search term *Catherine the Great* using Key Terms.

Enter the search term *American Revolution* using Key Terms.

THE INDUSTRIAL REVOLUTION

Beginning in the 18th century, life in the West underwent a gradual transformation so far-reaching that the term *revolution* has been employed to describe it. The new era, in which machines and steam power took over functions that were previously the exclusive province of human and animal labor, produced unprecedented and continuing economic growth. Living standards for many Europeans improved, while much smaller numbers of entrepreneurs accumulated huge fortunes. The social structure that came to characterize modern Europe was no longer determined by birth and inherited privilege but by economic class, defined by the relationship of individuals to labor and capital. This "revolution" gave rise by the 20th century to the western European civilization with which we are familiar today—a predominantly urban, industrial, and secular culture that was able to seize world power as a result of its mastery of science and technology.

Europe's transition from tradition to modernity was accelerated at the end of the century by the French Revolution. That political upheaval was, however, largely independent of this wider transformation. Three other sweeping changes had been at work in Europe before 1789: revolutions in population growth, in agriculture, and in the means of production. While the Industrial Revolution—a process rather than an event—unfolded more slowly across a longer period than the French Revolution, its consequences were even more crucial to the way in which most Europeans came to live.

THE ORIGINS OF THE INDUSTRIAL REVOLUTION

Industrialization required certain preconditions: a labor supply, markets, investment capital, raw material, and technological innovation. The rate of industrial development also depended on the political, social, and economic circumstances that prevailed in a given country. The Industrial Revolution began in the 1760s in England, where the prerequisites were present at more or less the same time, and spread to the Continent after 1815.

THE AGRICULTURAL REVOLUTION

The great population explosion that began to unfold in the 18th century provided one essential element in the complex of factors behind the Industrial Revolution. This development was, in turn, closely linked to the improvement in farming and stock breeding that constituted an "agricultural revolution" in the 18th century.

The tremendous increase in Europe's population pushed the price of food higher, and this in turn made life difficult for the poorer peasants. The larger landowners who marketed their crops, however, earned more. As profits grew, so too did the inclination to increase income even further by improving cultivation methods. In the crowded Netherlands, where farmable land was in short supply, the Dutch had pioneered in planting new money crops, particularly turnips, and in reclaiming land through drainage and the construction of dikes.

In the 18th century, English landlords began copying these methods for consumption crops and became enthusiastic proponents of agricultural innovation. There, as on much of the Continent, two medieval practices mitigated against the widespread adoption of new methods and crops: the three-field and the open-field systems. Several English landowners now sought to overcome the problems these practices caused by diversifying crops, trying other kinds of fertilizer, and developing new techniques and equipment.

Jethro Tull (1674–1741), an agricultural inventor, developed a mechanical wheat seeder and used iron plows to dig deeper furrows. Tull's work in agricultural experimentation encouraged others. Charles "Turnip" Townshend (1674–1738) successfully used turnips and other crops on a rotating system; this was a crucial contribution because by rotating crops that required different nutritional properties from the soil, the fallow field could be eliminated. His innovations were interconnected because the new methods increased the quantity of animal feed produced per acre, and the resulting larger livestock herds were a source of manure for wheat and barley planting.

Such ideas were disseminated on the Continent through the writings of the French physiocrats. In England, where King George III (ruled 1760–1820) took a personal interest in agricultural improvements, special journals such as the *Farmers' Magazine* and the *Annals of Agriculture* were published. Similar magazines, filled with reports of experiments and practical advice, appeared later in Italy, France, and other places on the Continent. The influence of British agricultural innovation on the rest of Europe is shown by the publication between 1798 and 1800 of a book by a German professor named Albrecht Thaer, *Introduction to the Knowledge of English Agriculture*.

The open-field system of landholding was the other impediment to the modernization of agriculture. Traditionally, farmers owned property in the form of small, narrow strips of unconnected land. These strips were not fenced in, but rather open to those of other landowners. In addition, villages usually shared common lands on which animals grazed, while the entire community decided what crops to plant as well as the rotation plan. This splintered pattern of landholding, together with the communal decision-making process, made it virtually impossible for innovative cultivators to apply the new methods on a large scale.

THE ENCLOSURE OF THE LAND

In order to create more productive, successful farms that could be effectively managed, some British landowners put together large tracts comprising many contiguous fields that could be enclosed with hedges or fences. This tendency had begun in the 16th century, when farms were converted to sheep pastures and enclosed, in response to the growing wool trade. To achieve this purpose, lands formerly rented to peasants were taken back and consolidated with other small parcels to make larger units. Sometimes common lands and entire villages were enclosed. When poor farmers, who had benefited from the open-field system, objected, the landowners secured the legalization of enclosures through the passage of special acts of Parliament. In the second half of the 18th century alone, more than half a million acres of English farm land were enclosed in this manner.

The enclosure movement eliminated the open-field system and altered English rural life. Small farmers were not only barred from the common fields but were also often left with unproductive pieces of land. Many lost the use of their plots and become workers without property, so that the English

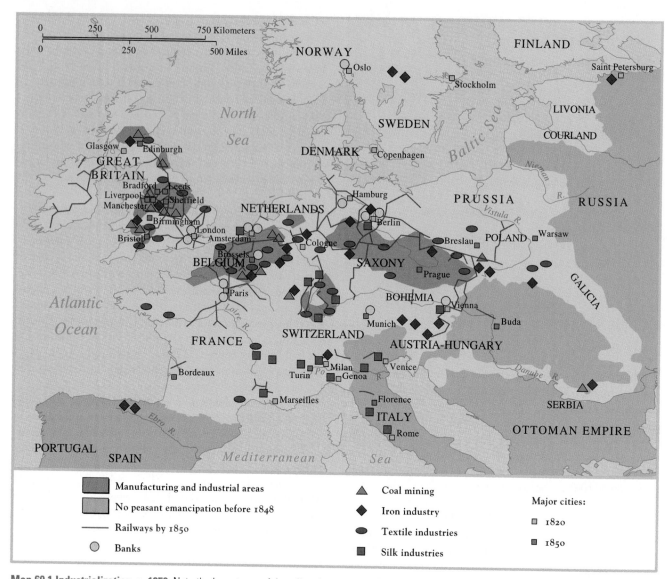

Map 60.1 Industrialization, c. 1850. Note the importance of the railroad network, especially in Britain and northern Europe. There is no railroad in southern Europe, and the only line in Russia had as much political as industrial significance, connecting pro-Western St. Petersburg with pro-Slav Moscow. The French lines to Bordeaux and Marseilles served to connect with maritime traffic across the Atlantic and within the Mediterranean.

yeoman, or independent free landowner, practically disappeared. Around 1700, most people in Great Britain made their livelihoods in agriculture, but by 1800 less than half did so. Although some displaced peasants moved to the cities to seek employment, the enclosure movement did not result in the widespread migration of people from the countryside.

If the enclosure movement did not provide the workforce for the Industrial Revolution, it did have an impact on industrialization. Profits made from commercial agriculture increased the supply of capital available in England, and the example of rational farming managed by entrepreneurial criteria was increasingly followed in much of Western Europe in the 19th century. Moreover, the agricultural revolution, of which enclosure was a feature, increased productivity so significantly that for the first time food could be produced in sufficient quantity to feed both the countryside

and the cities—at lower cost, with less labor, and on a consistent basis.

TECHNOLOGY AND INVENTION IN THE AGE OF STEAM

Initially, the Industrial Revolution primarily affected three critical industries, textiles, mining, and metals, and was specifically concerned with the most important products of each: cotton, coal, and iron. At the heart of the changes in these industries were two essential developments: (1) the invention of machines that could make products or exploit raw materials faster, more efficiently, and in greater quantity; and (2) the harnessing of forms of energy other than muscle power to drive the machinery. Together, these two features resulted in the transfer of production from homes and small shops, chiefly in the countryside, to urban factories. The factory system, both a new means of production and a social factor of great significance, radically transformed the daily lives and the quality of existence for millions of people. The factory remains to our own day the primary unit of industrial production.

THE TEXTILE INDUSTRY

The English had been manufacturing wool for centuries. Next to agriculture, wool production employed more people and accounted for a greater volume of trade than any other industry. Wool, made in virtually every county in England and Wales, provided secondary work and income for farmers and agricultural workers. Yet the first significant technological innovations occurred in the manufacturing of cotton rather than wool. The demand for cotton had increased as a result of the India trade, which supplied most of the muslin and calico used in England. Cotton was not only cheaper than wool, but it was also lightweight and could be cleaned by washing. Moreover, unlike wool, cotton could be dyed or printed by machine in bright, appealing colors. English spinners were unable, however, to make a cotton thread of sufficient strength or quantity, so that production was limited.

Encouragement for the development of new methods of cotton manufacturing came in 1700 when wool merchants, alarmed at the popularity of the competing fabric, secured the passage of import restrictions on printed cottons from India. In 1733, a clock maker from Lancashire named John Kay made an important improvement in the loom called the "flying shuttle," by which one worker could move the shuttle with wooden arms controlled by strings, instead of by hand. This invention speeded up the weaving process and resulted in a much wider fabric at lower cost, although it was slow to be adopted.

Kay's shuttle improved the weaving process, but the problem of spinning still remained. In 1738 Lewis Paul of Birmingham developed a device intended to do for spinning what Kay tried for weaving. Technical defects in both Kay's and Paul's inventions, as well as opposition from the spinners and weavers, created difficulties, and it was only in the 1760s that improved versions of these machines came into widespread use.

In 1770 James Hargreaves (?–1778), a weaver and carpenter, patented the *spinning jenny*, which he had developed several years earlier. With this simple machine, a worker could spin up to eight—and, with further improvements, many more—threads at once. The jenny spread rapidly, and by 1788 there were an estimated 20,000 machines in use in England. In 1768, Richard Arkwright (1732–1792), a barber by trade, invented the *water frame*, a device similar to Paul's early spinning machine. The frame required less skill than the jenny but more power than human hands could provide, so that a large installation with water power was needed. In 1771, therefore, Arkwright built a factory that

eventually employed some 600 workers, mostly children. The water frame provided a major impetus to the creation of the factory system, its rollers and weights automatically spinning out the yarn.

Two additional inventions made it possible for English entrepreneurs to produce cotton fabric on a massive commercial basis. In 1779 Samuel Crompton (1753–1827) invented the *spinning mule*, a steam-powered hybrid of the jenny and the frame able to produce high-quality thread. Crompton, a poor weaver, sold his patent rights for a mere £60, although many years later Parliament awarded him a settlement. In the 1780s, when the demand for cotton increased tremendously, Edmund Cartwright (1743–1822), a clergyman, developed a proto-power loom, which could be driven by horse, water, or steam, although it was not widely used until the 1820s.

As cotton factories and the new technology spread, centers that had once been sparsely populated burgeoned into urban communities. The city of Manchester, located in the county of Lancashire, became the first important center of urban industry, having the advantage of water supply, coal deposits, and the nearby port of Liverpool for shipping goods to customers abroad. By the late 1830s, cotton fabric accounted for half of all British exports. Moreover, in order to capture the Indian market entirely, the British made it illegal for Indians to produce cotton textiles, and between 1820 and 1840 exports to India rose from 11 million yards to 145 million yards.

THE INDUSTRIAL MATRIX: COAL, STEAM, AND IRON

The British textile industry did not grow in a technological vacuum; advances in factory production were dependent on metal processing to build the machines and on the availability of inexpensive energy to power them. This interdependency can be clearly seen in the development of the coal and iron industries, and the steam engine.

For many centuries the fuel for such tasks as heating, brewing, and firing furnaces had been wood or coal, but by the early 18th century, English forests were depleted. Yet water power, on which the early Industrial Revolution was based, also had its limitations because the supply of water—and therefore its force—varied with the seasons, and factories had to be located at particular water sources, which were often far from markets, raw materials, and ports.

Coal, of which Britain had immensely rich deposits, provided a solution to the fuel problem. As the demand for coal increased, however, technical obstacles arose. Deep mining required shafts as deep as 200 feet below the surface, and the extensive networks of underground tunnels needed pumps for removing water and for ventilation. The first effective pumping machine was invented in 1705 by a blacksmith named Thomas Newcomen. Here steam was condensed inside a cylinder housing a piston.

Newcomen's steam pump increased coal production, but it could be used only for pumping, not for turning wheels, so that it had little application in factories. It was

James Watt (1736–1819), a mechanical engineer from Scotland, who succeeded in designing the first steam engine capable of operating factory machinery. He came to his discovery by accident when he was asked to repair one of Newcomen's machines for the University of Glasgow. Realizing the great waste of energy in heating and cooling the cylinder for every stroke, Watt made a simple but important design change: He installed a separate condenser in order to save heat. Watt received a patent for his steam engine in 1769 but continued to improve it. In 1782 he developed an even more effective engine that used the pressure of steam, rather than atmospheric pressure.

In perfecting the steam engine, Watt, a mechanical genius, would not have succeeded without the entrepreneurial daring and business sense of Matthew Boulton (1728–1809) of Birmingham. Watt moved there—the center of Britain's metal and iron industry—and developed his invention with Boulton's capital. John Wilkinson, a local weapons maker, and other skilled technicians helped Watt to design further improvements, including a gear mechanism.

Watt's new prime mover, which was twice as efficient as Newcomen's, was the great breakthrough in the Industrial Revolution and intensified the interdependency of the various industrial sectors. The rotation device enabled the steam engine to power new iron industrial machinery as well as coal-mining pumps. Its first widespread application was in the cotton factories, the rapid growth of which required both ever-larger quantities of coal and more machines. In turn, the increased demand for steam engines and the machinery they powered provided the impetus behind the takeoff of the British iron industry and machine tools.

The manufacture of iron, however, faced technological problems of a different sort. The steam engine enabled the blast furnaces used in iron smelting to achieve higher temperatures, but coal could not be used for this purpose because its impurities mixed with and contaminated the iron. In 1709, Abraham Darby (1678?–1717) succeeded in using coke—coal from which most of the gases have been removed—to smelt iron ore. In 1784, Henry Cort (1740–1800) took the process another major step forward with his "puddling process." As fuel for this method of melting and mixing the ore, Cort used coke. In addition, iron made by the puddling process had a greater purity.

Once England's plentiful supply of coal could be used as a source of fuel for smelting, the iron industry began to expand. Other innovations followed quickly. Cort designed the rolling mill, which eliminated the need for ironmasters to beat the semi-molten iron into industrial shapes, and thereby dramatically increased productivity while lowering costs. In 1815, James Neilson overcame the last obstacle to the unfettered use of coal with his "hot blast" process, which eventually enabled coal instead of coke to be used in smelting. This innovation, in turn, produced a critical need for cheap transportation, a problem solved between 1770 and 1800 by the extensive network of canals built by the British.

FROM COTTAGE TO FACTORY: THE GROWTH OF INDUSTRIAL CAPITALISM

Until the Industrial Revolution introduced the factory system, textile manufacturing was largely a rural affair. The rise of the factory toward the end of the 18th century transformed not only the system of production and the daily lives of millions of workers, but also the size and appearance of Europe's cities. Moreover, the large amounts of investment capital required to build the industrial system created a new form of capitalist enterprise and altered the relationship among business, finance, and government. It also expanded the distance between worker and management.

Engraving showing the working of flax into cloth. 18th century. Like many cottage industries in the period preceding the Industrial Revolution, the manufacture of cloth required the participation of all the family members—here Irish. Only the youngest is exempt from work and plays with the family pet in the foreground.

THE COTTAGE SYSTEM

Traditionally, poor farmers added to their incomes by processing, spinning, and weaving linen, wool, and later cotton cloth in their homes. All members of the peasant family—husbands, wives, children, and grandparents—participated in the various stages of the work. The cloth thus produced was not intended for domestic consumption, but for commercial markets. This so-called cottage industry spread widely in the 18th century, especially as unemployment increased as a result of population growth in the countryside.

Cottage industry became a vital part of the British rural economy, but was not without its problems. Because cloth making was a secondary occupation for most peasants, who worked long, hard hours tilling the soil, they were not inclined to keep to production quotas. Quantity remained low and, especially after cotton came into vogue, the workers could not keep up with the rising demand.

THE RISE OF THE FACTORY

The textile industry was the first sector to be affected by the factory system in a major way, but in all industries conversion to factory production was slow, because of both the enormous capital required and worker resistance to the machines and the work environment outside the home. It was also impossible before the age of Watt, cheap iron, and machine tools.

At first, most factories remained modest in size and number. In 1782, Manchester had only two cotton mills, whereas 20 years later the city boasted 52. In the late 1830s, by which time there were 100,000 power looms operating in England, Manchester had the largest cotton factories, which employed an average of 300 workers each. Between 1800 and 1850, the city's population rose from some 75,000 to more than 300,000.

The growth in population had reduced the scarcity of labor by the end of the 18th century. Nevertheless, although rural laborers were attracted by the higher pay, they moved to the urban factories with reluctance and only during periods of unemployment. Because most factory equipment required little or no skill or muscle to operate, many of the early factory workers seem to have been drawn from the unskilled urban classes. Only later, in the first decades of the next century, did large-scale migration from the countryside to the cities take place. The concentration of labor under one roof brought an entirely different mode of work and labor organization. "Factory discipline" was imposed on workers who, especially in the countryside, had controlled their own work pace, schedules, and leisure time. Time, once measured by the rising and setting of the sun for rural laborers, was now determined by precise rules laid down by employers. Most factories had bell towers, and later clocks, over their entrances to control the rhythm of life for industrial workers. Starting before sunrise, often at 5:30 A.M., factory employees usually worked for 12 to 14 hours, and sometimes more, until British factory legislation in the 1840s lowered the workday to 10 hours. Workers who arrived late were either locked out or fined.

Factory conditions were inflexible, grueling, and dangerous. The long hours and monotony of tasks often led workers to fall asleep or collapse, and the incidence of industrial accidents was high, especially among children. Extremes of temperature from summer to winter, together with high humidity, filth, and polluted air, made the factories unhealthy places for workers. Foremen controlled the discipline inside the factories, imposing fines and layoffs on unruly or slack workers and sometimes meting out physical punishment. During the 19th century, such harsh working conditions were exposed and criticized by social reformers and government investigators, but improvements came slowly (see Topic 71).

In the factories, as in the cottage, work was divided according to gender and age. Men did not only the heavier

A print from Gustave Dore and Blanchard Jerrold, *London.* 1872. Dore has chosen a viewpoint from which London's overcrowded working-class neighborhood appears at its most "satanic"—a word used by the poet William Blake to describe industrial conditions in the 19th century. The result is an eerie evocation of the views of ancient Roman ruins in the engravings of Piranesi, Dore's great 18th-century predecessor.

Three engravings showing work in a coal mine. 1832. The three scenes are captioned: Woman Draging (i.e., dragging) Coal, Old Women at Work, and Children Picking Up. They come from an official government report that sought to record actual working conditions in Britain's mines, and that eventually put an end to child labor.

tasks, but were also usually assigned the more skilled technical work. Women and children, on the other hand, were relegated to simpler, repetitive work. In the early stages of the Industrial Revolution, most factory workers were women and children—even in the late 19th century, women continued to represent some 30 to 40 percent of the industrial workforce. Employers paid women and children less than men and preferred them because of the assumption that they would conform more easily to discipline. Workers often secured employment for their entire family in the same factory. The division of labor into specialized tasks speeded up productivity and required less worker training. Artisans and skilled craftsmen who were drawn to the factories in hard times resented this simplification of the production process, but when they protested they were usually replaced with women and children (see Topic 64).

INDUSTRIALIZATION AND THE EUROPEAN ECONOMY

As industrialization spread to parts of continental Europe, it proved to be particularly sensitive to political developments. Periods of war and peace, as well as government tariff regulation, affected markets and prices. Such fundamental transformation destabilized long-established social arrangements and intensified the impact of business and financial cycles on the immediate lives of ordinary people.

THE PACE OF INDUSTRIALIZATION IN GREAT BRITAIN

At the end of the Napoleonic Wars, three-fourths of the population of Europe still continued to earn their living from agriculture. Even in England, where industrialization was most advanced, two-thirds of the people lived and worked in rural areas. As late as 1815, more spinning was done by hand than by machinery, and half the cotton mills were still powered by water. Not until the 1820s did England develop a full-fledged industrial system.

Production figures for major industrial sectors reveal the pace of British industrialization. The output of pig iron, for example, jumped from a mere 17,000 tons in 1740 to 127,000

tons in 1786, and then rose to 248,000 tons in 1806. Thereafter, iron production generally registered steady increases, so that by 1835 it had reached more than 1 million tons, and by 1850 more than doubled to 2.285 million tons. Between 1815 and 1840, the mining of coal doubled, from 16 to 34 million tons per year, and in 1850 had increased to more than 50 million tons. Similarly, the amount of raw cotton consumed by England's textile mills almost doubled every 10 years between 1820 and 1850. In 1852, when the cotton consumption figure stood at 336,000 tons, cotton factories contained more than 20 million spindles and employed 500,000 people. By 1840, half of British workers were industrial.

In 1825 the British built the earliest steam railway that carried passengers; France followed in 1828, Belgium in 1835, and the German Confederation in 1839. The railroads provided a major stimulus to industrial and financial expansion. Private investors made huge fortunes by speculating in railroads, which also stimulated the demand for machinery, engines, and iron. Together with improved roads, canals, and bridges, the railroads created national—and international—markets, speeding up the movement of raw materials and finished goods as well as increasing worker mobility. Railroads made the industrial process more efficient because they linked factories with mines and ports and the countryside with urban centers.

By midcentury, Britain had become the wealthiest nation in the West—not only the "workshop of the world," but also its shipper, for it carried one-third of the world's trade on its ships. Its output of coal, iron, and textiles exceeded the total production of all other European countries combined. Britain's role as the world's leading industrial power was maintained until late in the 19th century.

THE EXPANSION OF INDUSTRIALISM

The Industrial Revolution spread to several other European states during the early part of the century. On the whole, industrialization moved more slowly on the Continent than it had in Britain, and it varied widely from country to country because of differences in social mobility, political cohesiveness, and resources. Moreover, most continental societies faced greater resistance to industrialism from traditional values. Nevertheless, industrial development began to transform Europe in the 1830s.

Engraving of the opening of the Stockton-Darlington railway. 1825. The pace of the steam engine, the first to carry passengers, can be judged from the leisurely gait of the horse and rider in front of it; the man is waving a flag to warn of the train's approach. Note that the passengers are riding in goods wagons.

Belgium, which had won its independence from the Netherlands in 1830, led the way. The small country had coal and iron deposits of its own as well as a long tradition of textile manufacturing and trade with Britain. Moreover, its entrepreneurs readily received English technological innovations. The British machine firm of Cockerill, which had a factory branch in Belgium early in the Industrial Revolution, sold machinery and steam engines to neighboring countries. France, the German Confederation, Russia, and even Sweden outproduced Belgium in charcoal pig iron, but between 1815 and 1850, Belgium mined more coal than they did. The new nation-state planned and built its railroads with lines linking it to France, the German Confederation, and the Netherlands. In 1840, 10 percent of its population of 4 million were industrial workers, making Belgium the first industrialized country on the Continent.

France ranked as the major industrial power on the Continent throughout the first half of the 19th century, second only to Britain in iron and textile production. Its familiarity with technology dated to the late 18th century, when drawings and entries on traditional machines and industrial processes were published in Diderot's *Encyclopédie*. Napoleon had encouraged scientific inquiry and technological experimentation, and by 1810 the Creusot works were using coke for iron smelting. Lille in northeastern France contained rich coal and iron deposits, and much of the country's industry developed there.

Under the liberal monarchy of Louis Philippe after 1830, private business received some encouragement and

support. Railways, roads, and canals were built and improved with capital from private banks. Along with cotton mills in Normandy and Alsace, France also had an important silk manufacturing center at Lyon and almost doubled its cotton and iron production between 1830 and 1850. Moreover, by midcentury the country had more steam engines than the rest of continental Europe combined. Despite such gains, however, the Prussians were already generating more horsepower, and although more than a million French workers were employed in large-scale industries, half of all Parisian workers—where a total of 400,000 were employed by midcentury—were still in small preindustrial shops.

The German states, which after unification became Europe's new industrial giant in the late 19th century, were hampered by political division. The Prussians took the lead in trying to overcome this disability by eliminating all internal tariffs within their borders in 1818. More important for long-range development, Prussia advanced the 1834 tariff union, which included most of the important German states and did much to increase trade and industry. The coming of the railroads in the mid-1830s was the major factor in sparking industrialization.

The German Confederation was rich in mineral resources, but its early industries imported much of their iron from the French region of Lorraine. German coal and iron mines in the Ruhr, the Saar, and in Silesia were first developed in the 1830s. The firm of Friedrich Krupp (1787–1826), founded in 1810, developed iron and machine factories in

Essen in the same period, although at the time the company used steam engines in the 1840s, it employed fewer than 200 people. The Krupp Works later went into armaments manufacturing. Nevertheless, during the first half of the 19th century, the German states lagged behind France and Russia in pig iron production and were only slightly ahead of Belgium in coal mining. Despite such limited beginnings, before the achievement of national unification in 1870 to 1871, the Germans began to challenge Britain's industrial supremacy.

INSTABILITY AND CRISES IN THE EUROPEAN ECONOMY

During the first years of the Industrial Revolution, profits were extremely high in Britain for those enterprises that did not fail: Although wages rose steadily, prices for food and manufactured goods remained high. The Napoleonic Wars helped create an artificial demand for arms and other industrial goods, but this situation collapsed in 1815 with the coming of peace. Prices dropped, reducing profit and investment. The results were especially harsh for the working class. Some 300,000 veteran soldiers were suddenly added to the labor market. To make matters worse, in 1815 the powerful landowners secured passage of restrictionist tariffs on grain, known as the Corn Laws. This legislation increased the cost of food and kept it high, thereby reducing spending power for manufactured goods. In Europe, where the economy had been artificially sustained by Napoleon's Continental System, the end of hostilities brought similar distress, with conditions in southern Italy possibly the worst in Europe.

The European economy recovered temporarily in 1820. Britain established its currency on the gold standard, and good harvests drove down the price of food. But the rapid expansion of industry in the early 1820s led to uncontrolled speculation and a bust. For the next several decades, economic depressions and bad harvests followed each other in succession in 1825–1826, 1838–1839, and 1846–1847.

The response from manufacturers was to keep profits up by cutting costs. Despite the periods of economic crisis, real wages for British workers had risen during most of the first half of the 19th century, and the savings came in the area of wages. Lowered wages, extended factory work hours and discipline, and cyclical unemployment constituted a general trend in labor-management relations. Factory owners also redoubled their efforts to introduce labor-saving devices, expecting that increased mechanization would reduce production costs.

WORKERS, MACHINES, AND LABOR PROTEST

As machines found their way into more and more factories and industrial sectors, their impact on the lives of workers became more evident. To the workers it was clear that technology and factory production represented a new economic system that would deeply alter their daily lives. The response came in the form of a radical worker movement that sought to destroy the machine and hold back the tide of what they regarded as the increasing repression of the industrialists.

THE LUDDITES AND LABOR RESISTANCE

Workers were no mere passive observers of the process of mechanization. In 1753, the home of John Kay was destroyed by spinners protesting his flying shuttle. Similarly, Hargreaves' spinning jennies and Arkwright's water frame had also been subject to industrial sabotage by workers.

The most celebrated incident in the movement to smash machines took place in 1811, when stocking knitters in Nottingham began protesting wage cuts. Calling themselves followers of the mythical Ned Ludd, the "Luddites" organized themselves into groups of 50 or so men and wrecked knitting frames with heavy hammers and metal pikes. In January 1812, after the passage of a law making machine breaking an offense punishable by hanging, the Luddites issued a statement from "Ned Ludd's Office, Sherwood Forest," declaring their intention to continue their operations. That year the movement spread to the woolen trade and cotton towns. In all, perhaps as many as 1,000 mills were destroyed in the Nottingham area, and some factory owners killed.

The British authorities saw the Luddite movement as a plot against the government and an "insurrection of poor against the rich." A parliamentary committee investigating the uprisings agreed to the use of troops, despite the eloquent appeal of the English poet Lord Byron (1788–1824) in the House of Lords that the machine breakings "have arisen from circumstances of the most unparalleled distress." In January 1813, 17 Luddites were hanged in York. Although the machine breaking continued sporadically over the next several years, including a major incident near Manchester as late as 1829, the movement was eventually crushed.

Later, the Luddites were viewed as irrational primitives intent on holding back progress. More recently, however, some historians have concluded that these workers were not against technology as such, but rather against the social changes that the new technology reinforced. Along with their violent assaults on the factories and machines, the Luddites issued rational statements about wages, market conditions, and other technical issues affecting their livelihoods. In a period when trade unions were outlawed as conspiracies by association, the Luddite movement constituted a form of organized protest against employers and their efforts to replace labor with machines in order to lower costs of production.

The Luddites in England were not an isolated case. Throughout the 19th century, similar worker movements incorporated machine breaking in their labor tactics in other countries, including those of the silk weavers in Lyon in 1831 and linen weavers in Silesia in 1844. Yet the labor movement was to take quite another direction, especially after the rise of socialist parties and trade unions in the second half of the century. In the plight and the protests of the Luddites, however, there came together the central issue: the human consequences of the Industrial Revolution.

Putting the Industrial Revolution in Perspective

On one level, the term *Industrial Revolution* refers to a series of technological innovations between the mid-18th and the early 19th centuries that enabled human beings to produce food and manufactured goods faster, in greater quantity, and more cheaply. The revolution in production was possible because the new machines were made of cheap iron and run by a new form of energy—the use of coal to produce steam power. In industry proper, these advances were applied first to the making of textiles and iron.

In another sense, however, the Industrial Revolution is associated with a complex set of social and economic changes that transformed European civilization. These changes involved not only population growth, but also the way in which millions of ordinary men and women led their daily lives. The shift from the cottage industry to the factory system altered the relationship between worker and work as well as between worker and entrepreneur. The formation of an industrial labor force affected how society was structured and had important implications for gender relations, family structure, and sexuality. The revolution in industry also brought a radical change in how and where people lived, drawing people from country to city, and affecting housing, health, and general living conditions.

For two centuries after the start of the Industrial Revolution, the West—Europe and the United States—exercised unchallenged economic and political hegemony over the rest of the world. This unique position was mainly the result of technological achievements and industrialization.

Questions for Further Study

1. What did population growth and agriculture have to do with the Industrial Revolution?
2. Which were the most important inventions of the Industrial Revolution? How did one invention stimulate a demand for still more inventions?
3. How did the factory system change labor and social life?
4. By what process did industrialization spread from England to the Continent?

Suggestions for Further Reading

Ashton, Thomas S. *The Industrial Revolution: 1760-1830*. New York, 1999.

Bland, Celia. *The Mechanical Age: The Industrial Revolution*. New York, 1995.

Crafts, N.F.R. *British Economic Growth During the Industrial Revolution*. New York, 1986.

Dennis, Richard. *English Industrial Cities of the Nineteenth Century*. Cambridge, MA, 1984.

Grassby, Richard. *The Idea of Capitalism before the Industrial Revolution*. Lanham, MD, 1999.

Hopkins, Eric. *The Rise of the Manufacturing Town: Birmingham and the Industrial Revolution*. Gloucester, 1998.

Lloyd-Jones, D., and M.T. Lewis. *British Industrial Capitalism Since the Industrial Revolution*. Long Beach, CA, 1998.

Mokyr, Joel, ed. *The Economies of the Industrial Revolution*. London, 1985.

More, Charles. *Understanding the Industrial Revolution*. New York, 2000.

Tuttle, Carolyn. *Hard at Work in Factories and Mines: The Economics of Child Labor During the British Industrial Revolution*. Boulder, CO, 1999.

Wrigley, Chris, and Eric Hobshawn. *Industry and Empire: the Birth of the Industrial Revolution*. New York, 1999.

InfoTrac College Edition

Enter the search term *Industrial Revolution* using Key Terms.

Enter the search term *industrial development* using the Subject Guide.

REVOLUTION IN FRANCE: LIBERTY, TERROR, REACTION

Before 1789, no one had foreseen anything like the French Revolution, a political and social upheaval vast in its repercussions: the most important event in Western history in the modern era. It swept away the social system of the Old Regime that had rested on noble privilege. After it, feudalism ceased to exist in France, while power and influence were opened to those with wealth and ability. The events that took place in France from the late 1780s to the mid-1790s shaped, by trial and error, the very concept of "revolution" as a means of solving fundamental political and social problems. They ushered in the age of "mass politics," in which once politically passive social groups, such as the peasantry, workers, women, and the urban poor, could be active participants in making history. The revolutionary slogan, "liberty, equality, fraternity," became a permanent part of the Western political vocabulary as the ideal expression of political liberalism.

In France, the Revolution gave birth to the nation-state, whose sovereignty was seen not as the will of a king, but as the expression, first, of the nation and then of the people. The new state mobilized and claimed the allegiance of all citizens. Beginning in 1793, citizen soldiers extended these revolutionary ideals, together with French conquest and occupation, beyond the borders of France. The Napoleonic Wars provoked staunch resistance, which stimulated nationalism throughout the Continent. Within a generation, the Revolution profoundly and permanently changed the face of Europe.

SIGNIFICANT DATES

The French Revolution

1774–1793	Louis XVI rules as king of France
May 5, 1789	Estates General meets
June 17, 1789	National Assembly formed
July 14, 1789	Bastille stormed
August 4, 1789	Feudalism abolished
August 26, 1789	Declaration of Rights of Man and Citizen
October 5, 1789	March to Versailles
1790	Civil Constitution of the Clergy
June 1791	Flight to Varennes
April 20, 1792	War against Austria
August 10, 1792	Attack on Tuileries Palace
September 1792	"Massacres" in Paris
January 21, 1793	Louis XVI executed
March 1793	Vendée uprising begins
June 1793–July 1794	Reign of Terror
October 1793	Marie Antoinette executed
February 4, 1794	Slavery abolished
March 1794	Widespread arrests and executions, including Danton
July 27, 1794	Thermidor
November 1799	Coup by Napoleon Bonaparte

THE THIRD ESTATE AND THE "RIGHTS OF MAN"

The Revolution had its distant roots in the underlying social trends that had characterized the Old Regime. In a more immediate sense, however, it came as a result of a fiscal crisis that was mishandled by an inept king and his ministers.

THE CALLING OF THE ESTATES GENERAL

By the end of the 18th century, the Seven Years' War and intervention in the American Revolution, together with the high costs of the royal court, had brought the French government to the edge of bankruptcy. In 1783, after a string of failures, King Louis XVI (ruled 1774–1792) appointed Charles Alexandre de Calonne (1734–1802) as finance minister. Calonne proposed a single land tax on the First Estate (the clergy) and the Second Estate (the nobility). Both estates had been largely exempt from direct taxation but together controlled perhaps one-third of all French agricultural land and a comparable portion of French income.

In February 1787, Louis XVI called a special Assembly of Notables, consisting mainly of great lords and prelates, to endorse Calonne's measures. The assembly insisted on preserving the basic distinctions between the three social orders. Louis then replaced Calonne with the former archbishop of Toulouse, Loménie de Brienne (1727–1794), hoping that he could convince the stubborn nobility and

his fellow clergymen to accept the taxation. Brienne took the tax reform to the Parlement of Paris, the judicial body empowered to approve new laws, but he, too, failed to win its backing of the notables. Instead, Parlement demanded the convocation of the Estates General.

Exasperated by the intransigence of the privileged orders, Louis declared that royal prerogative alone made the new taxes legal and ordered the closing of the Parlement. Nobles protested, and some lawyers from the Parlement stirred up provincial riots. It was, however, the middle-class bankers who forced Louis to capitulate, refusing to lend the government more money. Finally, in August 1788, the king agreed to call the Estates General.

The Estates General represented the three traditional principal social orders of clergy, nobles, and the Third Estate of peasants, workers, and bourgeoisie. The convening of the assembly was decisive in the coming of the French Revolution because it brought the less privileged middle classes into the political process.

Delegates were elected in the winter and spring of 1789. The elections provided an opportunity for a public analysis of national problems because the delegates circulated lists of ills that reflected regional concerns. Most of these documents, called *cahiers de doléances* (grievance reports), were not statements of revolutionary principle. Rather, they were specific complaints concerning provincial abuses, corruption, and administrative waste. Only in Paris and other principal cities did some of the *cahiers* reflect such Enlightenment ideas as social justice and legal equality.

As the Estates General prepared to meet, Louis XVI reacted ineptly, attempting unsuccessfully to maneuver between the interests of two increasingly competing social groups, the nobility and the bourgeoisie. The nobles, who were intent on regaining a role in government and preserving their privileges against the monarchy's encroachments, fully expected to dominate the proceedings. The middle classes, aspiring to share power and status as they grew in wealth and numbers, sought to end the monopoly of special privileges enjoyed by the nobles and the clergy.

THE TENNIS COURT OATH AND THE NATIONAL ASSEMBLY

Each estate had roughly the same number of representatives, but the Third Estate, led by lawyers and business groups, represented 98 percent of the population of France, including workers and peasants. It asked, therefore, for double the number of representatives and to vote by head—thus enabling the Third Estate to control the outcome because some clergy and liberal nobles wished to support reforms. The aristocrats, on the other hand, demanded that each estate have one vote, giving the First and Second Estates the ability to determine all decisions. The king agreed to double the number of representatives, but did not give in on the issue of voting by head rather than by order. In January 1789 the Abbé Emmanuel Sieyès (1748–1836) published a pamphlet entitled *What Is the Third Estate?*, describing the political agenda of the middle classes: "What is

David, *The Tennis Court Oath.* 1789. David was an enthusiastic supporter of the French revolution, and much of his work served to establish an "official" style for Revolutionary art. This oil sketch, a preparatory study for a more finished work, captures all the excitement of the occasion. Early in 1793, David's wife left him because of his vote in favor of the execution of Louis XVI.

the Third Estate? *Everything.* What has it been in the political order up to the present? *Nothing.* What does it ask? *To become something."*

When the approximately 1,700 deputies gathered at Versailles in May, the hostility of the court to the delegates of the Third Estate was clear. After the opening ceremonies, each order was assigned its own chamber. Louis' refusal to bend on the voting issue provoked the first major act of revolutionary defiance on the part of the Third Estate, which found another spokesman in the skillful and persuasive politician Honoré Gabriel de Mirabeau (1749–1791), a renegade noble who had won election as a deputy for the Third Estate. On June 17, with Sieyès and Mirabeau to guide it, the Third Estate, along with some clergy, constituted itself as the National Assembly and called on the other two orders to meet with it as a single body. This defiance prompted the king to lock the delegates of the Third Estate out of their meeting hall. The outraged deputies gathered instead in a tennis court and swore not to disband until they had written a constitution for France.

The so-called Tennis Court Oath, taken on June 20, forced the weak-willed monarch to back down again, especially after many of the clergy and liberal nobles joined the middle class. Louis remained indecisive, but at a special session of the Estates General on June 23, he declared that the deputies could discuss constitutional matters only in separate chambers. Threatening to dismiss the Estates General if he were not obeyed, he commanded the deputies to separate immediately into the three traditional orders. To the king's aide, who repeated the royal command at the end of the session, Mirabeau is said to have responded, "Go and tell those who sent you that we are here by the will of the people, and that we will go only if we are driven at the point of the bayonet." On the 27th, the ever-hesitant Louis announced that

the three estates would meet together as the National Assembly in order to draft a constitution. The king had precipitated the end of absolute monarchy in France.

THE PEOPLE AND THE REVOLUTION

The creation of the National Assembly was the first real revolutionary event because the inclusion of the middle classes constituted the end of government controlled exclusively by the nobility and the monarchy. Despite the domination of the Third Estate, the National Assembly was a rather conservative body. Its members, drawn from a minority of the French people, were wedded to the protection of property, the maintenance of social order, and the preservation of the monarchy, but they also wanted a role in government decisions. The summer of 1789, however, saw the entrance of two genuinely revolutionary forces into the already complex political situation: the peasantry of the countryside and the lower classes of the cities. These forces, perceived as a common threat by most of the delegates to the National Assembly, were to push the Revolution in a more radical direction.

Food shortages and economic hardship sparked social unrest in the rural regions of France, where farm prices had fallen and taxes had increased during the last 20 years. A disastrous harvest in 1788 produced severe grain losses and a spiraling rise in the price of bread, the basic staple of most French households. In the countryside the peasants stopped paying taxes and the "seignorial dues," which they had been obliged to render to their landlords, the church, and local nobles since medieval times. Acts of organized violence erupted as early as May as peasants burned local castles and town halls in order to destroy tax and dues records. In July, these revolts merged with the "Great Fear," a series of panics that swept the countryside, fueled by rumors that the no-

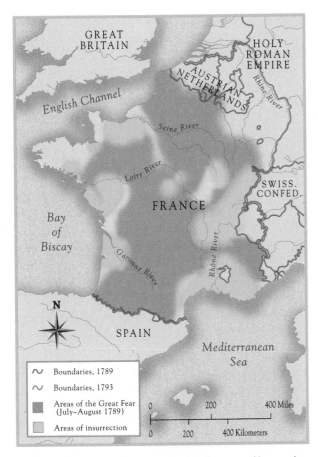

The areas of insurrection are those where the harvests of 1788 had been especially disappointing; they correspond to France's potentially richest farmland. Note that the French Revolutionary forces' victory over a joint Austrian-Prussian army at Valmy in September 1792 extended French territory in the Northeast. Go to http://info.wadsworth.com/053461065X for an interactive version of this map.

bles and their hired brigands were killing peasants and destroying the new crop about to be harvested. As rural social order deteriorated, peasants sought not only to seize the food they had grown and the land on which they worked, but also to destroy the manorial system under which they and their ancestors had suffered for centuries.

In the cities, where food shortages and the increase in bread prices coincided with growing unemployment, demonstrations and riots broke out. In Paris, a city of more than half a million people, the royal government had 5,000 troops and police to maintain public order, but as unrest grew, Louis XVI gathered another 20,000 soldiers outside the city. Groups of citizens, consisting mainly of artisans, small shopkeepers, housewives, and wage earners, had been organizing themselves on the ward level ever since the elections to the Estates General. Now, fired by signs that the king was turning against the Revolution, they formed a citizen militia and attacked barracks in search of weapons. Later the militia became the National Guard, commanded by the Marquis de Lafayette (1757–1834), a liberal and respected hero of the American Revolution. Lafayette designed a flag that combined the red and blue of Paris with the white of the royal family, thus producing the "tricolor."

On July 11, Louis suddenly dismissed his finance minister Necker, the only nonnoble minister in the government and a man regarded as protector of the people. Parisian crowds, intoxicated by alcohol and revolutionary oratory, erupted in anger. This insurrection climaxed on July 14 with the storming of the Bastille. Rumor spread that arms were stored in the Bastille, an old fortress used to house special prisoners and defended only by 80 retired soldiers and 30 Swiss guards. When the crowd broke into the courtyard, about 100 citizens were shot and killed. With help from renegade government troops who joined the insurgents with cannon, the fortress surrendered. The enraged mob

Map 61.2 Revolutionary Paris. The main areas affected were, of course, those connected with the royal family: the Royal Palace, the Palace of the Tuileries, and the Tuileries Gardens. Note the nearby location of the Jacobin Club. The Bastille, stormed on what has since become France's National Day, July 14, is over to the east. Built as a fortress in 1370, it was used for political prisoners. Almost completely empty at the time of its destruction, it nevertheless remained a powerful symbol of oppression.

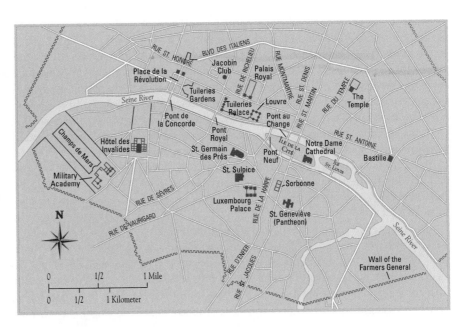

Sketch of the armed women of Paris marching on Versailles on October 5, 1789. The caption reads: "Departure of the heroines of Paris for Versailles," with the date. The weapons they are brandishing—old-fashioned spears and axes, with an ancient cannon in the foreground—must have come from a storage room in the Municipal Hall of Paris, which they ravaged before setting out for Versailles.

Depart des Heroines de Paris pour Versailles le 5 Octobre 1789.

massacred the commander and several guards, cutting off their heads and parading them through the city on pikes. The fall of the Bastille became a powerful symbol of the unfolding revolution.

The peasant violence and the fall of the Bastille were dramatic evidence of the revolutionary spirit of the common people. Radical delegates in the National Assembly, heeding the temper of the people, seized the initiative. Late on August 4, an exceptionally hot and humid night, a liberal aristocrat who owned no land called on the nobles and clergy to renounce all their feudal rights and dues. Frightened by the growing disorder in the country, and caught up in the passionate scene, the delegates of the First and Second Estates rose one by one to surrender their ancient privileges. By the next morning, feudalism had been all but eliminated in France.

Later that month, the National Assembly issued a set of general principles on which to base the constitution that it was drafting. The "Declaration of the Rights of Man and of the Citizen," issued on August 27, reflected Enlightenment thought as well as the ideas that had inspired the leaders of the American struggle for independence. Proclaiming that all people were born "free and equal in rights," the document identified "liberty, property, security, and resistance to oppression" as the most important of these rights. Citizens were to enjoy freedom of worship, equal access to public office, and equality before the law, while government was to protect these rights and tax its citizens only according to their income.

The framers of the Declaration assumed that laws and government were the expression of popular will—that is, that "sovereignty" resided in the nation. This assertion was to have important European consequences. In defining political sovereignty in national terms, the Declaration elevated nationalism to a sacred doctrine that, in its extreme

form, claimed blind devotion and loyalty. Under the threat of foreign invasion, the doctrine of revolutionary nationalism would succeed in mobilizing millions of Frenchmen.

Popular unrest continued unabated through the fall, despite the Declaration and reform decrees issued by the National Assembly. In Paris the supply of grain from the bad harvest of the previous year had all but run out. Hunger, together with encouragement from radicals and suspicions against Louis XVI and his queen, the unpopular Marie Antoinette (1755–1793), aroused the people to action. On October 5, a large group of housewives demanding bread caused a disturbance at a baker's shop. Joined by several more women from the market, they moved on to the municipal hall, which they ransacked. Eventually a force of several thousand women began marching to Versailles, their ranks swelling along the way. Lafayette followed them with the National Guard. The next day, after a violent skirmish with palace guards, the mob forced Louis, Marie Antoinette, and their son to follow them back to Paris, where they took up residence in the Tuileries. The crowd chanted, "we have the baker, the baker's wife, and the baker's child." A few days later, the National Assembly also moved to Paris. With the king a virtual prisoner of the Revolution, the mob could keep an eye on both the royal family and the National Assembly.

THE ASCENDANCY OF THE MODERATES

In the two years between the Declaration of the Rights of Man and the adoption of the constitution in 1791, the National Assembly governed the nation. Its policies changed France in several fundamental ways that reflected the interests and values of the middle classes that dominated the assembly.

PROPERTY AND THE CHURCH

Economic issues were at the center of the assembly's actions. The Declaration of the Rights of Man stressed that "Property being a sacred and inviolable right, no one can be deprived of it unless a legally established public necessity evidently demands it, under the condition of a just and prior indemnity." Having made private property secure, however, the assembly still had to deal with the huge debt that had brought the royal government into crisis in the first place. Rather than repudiate the debt, which was owed to the middle-class bankers and merchants, the bishop of Autun, Charles Maurice de Talleyrand (1754–1838), proposed another solution. In November 1789 the assembly endorsed his proposal to confiscate and sell off all lands belonging to the Catholic Church.

With the anticipated revenue from the sale of church property as backing, the assembly issued bonds, called *assignats*, to finance the debt. The assignats were so popular that they were soon used as currency, and the assembly issued even more, thus fueling inflation. Nevertheless, the sale of church land had a long-range stabilizing effect because it enlarged the number of property owners in France. Buyers of the land, mainly the middle class and the wealthier peasants, were thereby tied more closely to the successful outcome of the Revolution. Petitions from the landless peasantry for the division of the large estates were ignored.

The church found further reason for declaring itself an enemy of the Revolution. The abolition of ecclesiastical tithes and the confiscation of the land made the Catholic Church in France financially dependent on the government. The following July, therefore, the assembly passed the "Civil Constitution of the Clergy," a measure that placed the church under the jurisdiction of the state. Priests and bishops were henceforth popularly elected—even by Protestants and Jews—and paid government salaries.

The Civil Constitution, which undermined the independence of the church and the authority of the pope in the most fundamental ways, generated considerable controversy. When it became clear that some bishops and priests would resist, the assembly went even further by requiring the clergy to swear an oath to abide by and support the constitution. Half of all French priests—the more affluent—and most bishops refused to take the oath. The papacy naturally supported the protests of the clergy. With these and other measures, the Revolution had created a rift between the state and the church in France that continued into the next century.

Economic liberalism, together with the interests of the middle classes, influenced the assembly's policies. Several direct taxes—on land, on income from commerce and manufacturing, and on rents—were voted, but they proved difficult to collect. In order to stimulate trade and business, the assembly abolished internal tariffs and monopolies granted by the crown, and standardized weights and measures by introducing the metric system. The old guilds were abolished in order to lift restrictions on professions and crafts, but the assembly passed the so-called Le Chapelier Law (June 14, 1791), which outlawed worker unions and the right to strike.

THE CONSTITUTION OF 1791

It was not until September 1791 that the assembly completed the constitution under which France was to be governed. Although it did not address all the ills of the Old Regime, the constitution did reflect the theories of Enlightenment reformers who wanted government to be rational, efficient, and just. Local administration was standardized, and a simplified judicial system with elected judges and prosecutors was introduced. The former patchwork of provincial subdivisions was replaced by 83 *départements* of roughly equal size, each further subdivided into smaller administrative units in which local assemblies were elected.

The Constitution of 1791 transformed the French government into a limited, rather than an absolute, hereditary monarchy. The king still appointed and dismissed his ministers at will, but the power to legislate was invested in a body called the Legislative Assembly, which was chosen by indirect election. The king could temporarily veto its measures, although the Legislative Assembly could override the royal veto by approving a bill in three successive assemblies. No one who had served in the National Assembly was permitted to participate in the new body, with the result that its members were more radical and less experienced.

The Constitution was by no means a radical democratic document. The Declaration of the Rights of Man proclaimed that all citizens were free and equal, but the right to vote was limited in several important ways. The population was divided into two categories, "active" and "passive," a distinction based on wealth. Only French males who were 25 years of age or older, and who paid taxes equivalent to three days' wages, had the franchise. These men voted for electors, who in turn chose the deputies. Higher income qualifications were required of electors, and deputies had to be property owners. Of the approximately 26 million French people, 4.25 million could vote, only 50 thousand were eligible to serve as electors, and even fewer as deputies. This formula of limited male suffrage, which was to be the pattern of European constitutions throughout most of the 19th century, essentially placed political power in the hands of men of property.

WOMEN AND MINORITIES

The status of women and minorities in revolutionary France provides further evidence of the moderate outlook of the National Assembly. Some deputies had, for example, argued in favor of abolishing slavery, but economic interests—those of the shipowners, merchants, and sugar refiners who derived their profits from the sugar colonies in the French West Indies—prevailed. Slavery and the trade in slaves were preserved. In September 1791, the deputies voted to allow assemblies in the colonies to determine whether to give political rights to their free blacks and mulattoes. The

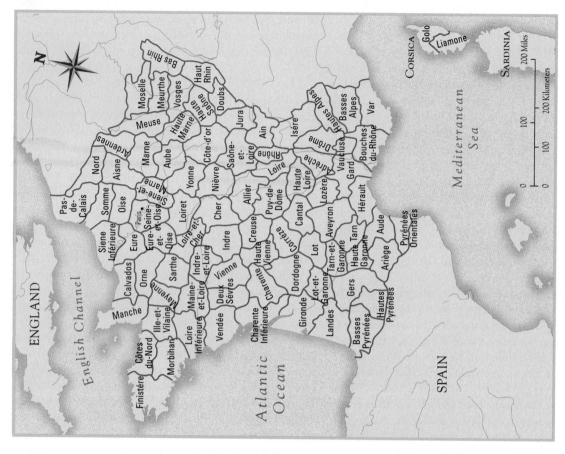

BEFORE 1789

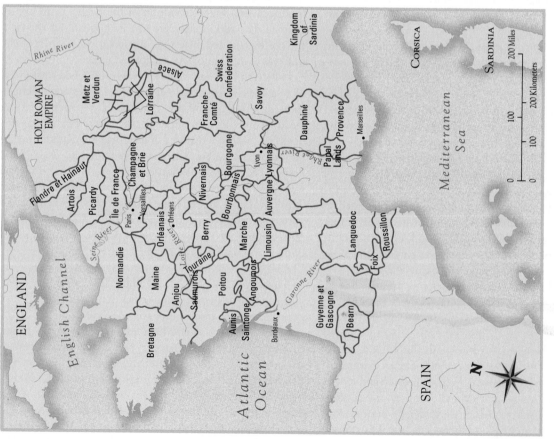

AFTER 1789

Map 61.3 Administrative Changes in France, Before and After 1789. Note the "rationalization" whereby all the départements (provinces) are roughly equal in size after the reorganization. Normandy, for example, now consists of six separate districts. The divisions shown on the right-hand map correspond, more or less, to the provincial administrative units of France today.

results were deeply disappointing to these groups, and in Haiti, the French part of Santo Domingo, the blacks rose up in rebellion.

Under the leadership of François Dominique Toussaint L'Ouverture (c. 1744–1803), a former slave who served as an officer in the French forces, the blacks formed guerilla bands. When the English invaded Haiti in 1793, Toussaint's black forces maintained an uneasy alliance with the mulatto André Rigaud and cooperated for a time with the remaining French authority. But in 1801, Toussaint conquered the entire island of Hispaniola (Haiti was the western portion of the island, while Eastern Hispaniola had been under Spanish control), abolished slavery, and proclaimed himself governor. Although the French captured Toussaint, the revolt continued. Napoleon tried to retake Haiti but was eventually forced to withdraw his troops. Aided by U.S. President Thomas Jefferson, who feared that Napoleon would use Haiti as a naval base from which to invade Louisiana, in 1804 Haiti became the second nation in the Western Hemisphere—after the United States—to win independence.

Jews fared better than slaves and free blacks at the hands of the Revolution. Most enlightened monarchs had taken steps to integrate Jews into the state in the 18th century, but in France their status varied from region to region. The National Assembly had first debated Jewish rights as part of efforts to define "active citizenship" for voting purposes, but without result. In January 1790, an exception was made for the Jews of Bordeaux, Bayonne, and Provence, whose economic status and social contacts enabled them to claim "elite" status among their people. Some Parisian Jews, who were rigorous supporters of the Revolution, then succeeded in securing the endorsement of voters for emancipation from most of the city's districts. In September 1791 the assembly passed a law enfranchising all Jews.

Women played an active role in some of the leading events of the Revolution. Yet the Declaration of the Rights of Man was just that—a document that proclaimed civil equality among men. Enlightenment *philosophes* were divided on the question of women's rights. A few, such as the Marquis Marie Jean de Condorcet (1743–1794), supported the "admission of women to the rights of citizenship" on the basis of natural rights; most either ignored the issue or, like Rousseau, saw women as childbearers and incapable of participating in public affairs.

Frenchwomen, inspired by Revolutionary ideals, seized the initiative. They took their demands into the streets, presented arguments before the National Assembly (to which they could neither elect deputies nor stand for election), wrote political tracts, and established their own political organizations. Individually and in groups, they asserted their right both to political participation and to education, property, and equality in marriage.

Olympe de Gouges (1748–1793), who claimed to be the illegitimate daughter of a nobleman but was raised by a butcher, wrote in 1791 what became a classic statement of feminist principles, the "Declaration of the Rights of Woman and the French Citizen," deliberately modeled on the docu-

ment issued by the National Assembly (see Topic 64). In it, she underscored the fact that the framers of the original Declaration had violated revolutionary principles by creating a double standard in politics. De Gouges argued that equality between men and women conformed to the natural order, and she appealed to Marie Antoinette, "mother and wife," to assume leadership in the women's movement, a mistake that later caused her to be executed as a royalist sympathizer.

Between 1790 and 1793, legislation partially corrected what the Declaration of the Rights of Man had ignored. Illegitimate children and their mothers were now able to sue fathers for support, and the ancient system of primogeniture was abolished by giving all children the right to inherit equally. New laws enabled wives as well as husbands to seek legal remedy in divorce, while another law permitted civil marriage and lowered the age of legal consent for women to 21. Despite these gains, the Jacobin leaders, inspired by Rousseau, did not admit women to the category of "active" citizens.

THE RADICALS IN POWER: THE REIGN OF TERROR

Within two years of the meeting of the Estates General, the social order and political structure of France had been radically changed. Yet this period represented only the first, more moderate phase of an ongoing revolutionary process. The upheaval grew more extreme over the next several years as conservative opponents, whose world of privilege, monarchy, and tradition had collapsed, and radical patriots, who felt that change had not gone far enough, pressed the Revolution from both sides. Meanwhile, the Revolution also aroused active opposition from the conservative powers of Europe, especially Austria and Prussia.

REVOLUTION WITHIN A REVOLUTION

The crisis of the Revolution began as a result of a failed effort by Louis XVI to leave France. Escape plans had been underway ever since October 1789, when the royal family was forced to move to Paris. In June 1791, Louis XVI, encouraged by French emigrés, attempted to flee with his family to Belgium but was caught at Varennes and brought back to the capital. By maintaining secret contacts with monarchist supporters in the Assembly as well as with emigré nobles and the Austrian government, Louis had proven himself an enemy of the Revolution. The constitution then being drafted rested on the premise of a monarch committed to the constitution. Louis' actions had the effect, therefore, of undermining the document even before it was adopted. The king's capture, together with radical threats against the monarch, drew a sharp reaction from abroad.

On August 27, 1791, Emperor Leopold II (ruled 1790–1792) of Austria (Marie Antoinette's brother) and King Friedrich Wilhelm II (ruled 1786–1797) of Prussia issued the Declaration of Pillnitz, in which they threatened to intervene in France if the royal family or the monarchy were in danger. Both radicals and moderates began clamoring for war against these external enemies of the Revolution.

The flight to Varennes aroused the ire of the Parisian radicals, who condemned the king as a traitor to the Revolution. The moderates in the assembly, on the other hand, had been weakened by the death of Mirabeau. They spread the story that the king, whom they regarded as a force for stability, had been kidnapped. The split between radicals (the "left") and moderates (the "right")—the terms *left* and *right* derived from the seating arrangements in the assembly—had grown sharper ever since 1789. For some time the radicals had been organizing political clubs through which to discuss and spread their ideas. The most influential of them, the Jacobin Club (which took its name from its meeting place, the former St. Jacques monastery of Dominican friars, who were known as Jacobins), consisted chiefly of educated members of the Third Estate such as the physician-turned-journalist Jean Paul Marat (1743–1793) and the lawyer Georges-Jacques Danton (1759–1794). The views of the Jacobins, who corresponded with branches in the provinces, grew increasingly radical.

The more radical Legislative Assembly elected in 1791 pushed through laws against the noble emigrés and the refractory clergy and spearheaded the call for a declaration of war against Austria, which was passed on April 20, 1792. Soon France was at war with Prussia as well.

The war, depicted at home as a crusade against the enemies of the Revolution, started out poorly. As a Prussian army repelled the French troops and pushed its way across the border, its commander, the duke of Brunswick, announced that he would take any action, including the destruction of Paris, to prevent harm from befalling the royal family. Brunswick's threat both energized the spirit of resistance and emboldened the radicals. On August 10, the communal leaders of the capital staged an uprising that changed the course of the Revolution. A large crowd, angry at the king's attempt to escape, broke into the Tuileries. While the Parisians fought a bloody battle with the king's Swiss guard, Louis and Marie Antoinette fled to the Legislative Assembly for safety. The wrath of the people frightened the deputies, and after suspending the king's powers, many of them left the city. Parisian militants forced those deputies who stayed behind to schedule elections to a new body, known as the National Convention, and to dissolve the Legislative Assembly.

JACOBINS, SANS-CULOTTES, AND THE NATIONAL CONVENTION

The Revolution now faced three serious problems: a dangerous and expanding war, deepening economic crisis, and the growing anxieties of the Parisian masses. To these dangers were soon added a royalist uprising and a widening factional division within the ranks of the Jacobins. Under these combined pressures, the temper of the Revolution accelerated and reached its most extreme form in the "Reign of Terror" that engulfed France.

Most deputies elected to the Legislative Assembly were royalists or constitutionalists, but leadership soon passed to two radical groups that emerged out of the Jacobin Club—the Girondists and the Mountain. A group of deputies around Jacques Brissot (1754–1793) and the *philosophe* Condorcet, known as Girondists, after the region of France from which many had come, formed a fiery cadre of brilliant orators. The Girondists had supported the war and extreme measures against the nobles and the clergy, but drew back from popular violence and feared that the radicalization of the Parisian masses would result in anarchy.

In early September 1792, with Paris rife with rumors of counter-revolutionary plots, common citizens unleashed a startling massacre. Crowds of workers, shopkeepers, and artisans stormed the prisons, from which they believed thousands of royalists would break out in the event of foreign invasion. Popular courts were improvised, which condemned and brutally ordered the executions of more than 1,000 prisoners, many of whom were common criminals and prostitutes. These "September Massacres," for which no rational explanation can be adduced, set the tone for the next two years of the Revolution.

News of a French victory at Valmy helped calm the atmosphere of tension in Paris. The National Convention, elected on the basis of universal male suffrage, met for the first time the following day. Among its deputies was a group of extremist Jacobins elected from Paris, including Danton, who had helped incite the storming of the Tuileries; Marat, who had cheered on the September Massacres; and Maximilien de Robespierre (1758–1794), who became the principal architect of the terror that was to come.

These men formed a nucleus of radical Parisian Jacobins known as the "Mountain," so-called because its members sat high up in the chamber of the convention. The Mountain believed the war would consolidate support at home for radical domestic measures against the counter-revolution. The Girondists outnumbered the Mountain, but Robespierre and his colleagues quickly learned to outmaneuver opponents with help from the crowds of Paris. The Mountain and the Girondists, who attacked each other with increasing bitterness, were soon locked in a deadly battle for control of the convention and the support of the several hundred centrist deputies, known as the Plain.

The fate of Louis XVI was the first major issue over which the Mountain and the Girondists fought for mastery of the Revolution. As one of its first acts, the convention abolished the monarchy and declared France a republic. But what was to be done with the deposed king? While the Girondists sought to spare Louis, the Mountain demanded his execution. In the trial that took place in December, the Mountain prevailed. Louis XVI was found guilty by an overwhelming margin, although he was then condemned to death by a vote of 361 to 360. He was beheaded by guillotine on January 21, 1793. Marie Antoinette's turn followed in October, after a trial in which her allegedly promiscuous sexual conduct formed part of the charges against her.

The leaders of the Mountain, men skilled in oratory and the manipulation of popular sentiment, understood from the beginning that the radicalization of the Revolution was the result of direct action by the common people of Paris—

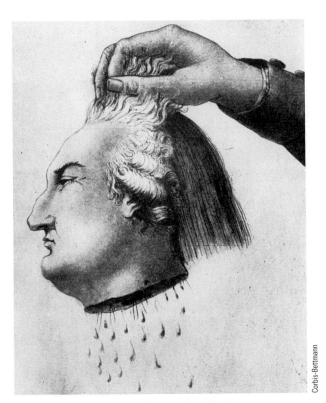

Engraving of the head of Louis XVI after he had been guillotined. The image caused havoc throughout Europe, as his fellow
monarchs—and the ruling class in general—were forced to think
the unthinkable. The long-term consequences were the extremely autocratic regimes imposed in France and throughout much of the rest
of Europe 22 years later, at the Congress of Vienna.

In the offensive launched by Austria and Prussia in 1793,
French troops suffered serious reverses after initial victories. In
March their commander, General Charles Dumouriez, de-
fected to the enemy. Unrest at home worsened the crisis. The
convention voted to impose a military draft, just as food riots
erupted once again in Paris. That same month the peasants of
the Vendée, in western France, rose in revolt against the
Parisian leaders of the anticlerical Revolution. In the spring
and summer, Lyon, Marseilles, and Bordeaux followed suit. In
all cases, royalist agitators channeled local discontent into
counter-revolutionary insurrections.

The Mountain and the sans-culottes drove the convention into action to deal with these challenges. In March
"surveillance" committees were set up in towns and villages
to crush counter-revolutionaries. The following month saw
the establishment of the 12-member Committee of Public
Safety, which functioned as the executive branch of government. The committee was quickly dominated by
Robespierre and his fellow radicals, and for the next year or
so they acted as the real government of France.

With domestic power secured, the committee turned its
attention to the war, which was going against the French. The
military effort was now placed under the direction of Lazare-

the *sans-culottes*, or people "without breeches," so-called because, unlike the aristocrats who wore knee breeches, the
working populace wore long trousers. In the sans-culottes the
Mountain recognized a unique political force that, if properly
guided and manipulated, could be used as an avenue to power,
while the sans-culottes saw a chance to fight for the right to
work, the introduction of price controls, and other measures
of economic protection. Over the next year and a half, the
Mountain regarded the sans-culottes as its constituency, implementing extremist policies in their name and, in turn, being goaded on by them to impel the Revolution further.

THE JACOBINS IN POWER

The National Convention came into being as the fate of
the Revolution hung in the balance. A week after the execution of the king, the convention declared war on Great
Britain. By April, revolutionary France was also at war with
Austria, Prussia, the Netherlands, Spain, and Piedmont-
Sardinia. At stake, however, were not the traditional issues
of power politics. In December 1792 the convention had
proclaimed its intention of helping the other peoples of
Europe to free themselves from the tyranny of kings and the
oppression of the Old Regime. The monarchs of Europe responded, therefore, not only to French military aggression,
but also to the dangerous ideology of revolution that its
armies promised to export.

David, sketch of Marie Antoinette on her way to execution.
October 1793. As the artist's note below describes, this is a "Portrait of
Marie Antoinette, Queen of France, conducted to the scaffold, drawn by
the pen of David, a spectator of the convoy." He adds that his vantage
point was the window of Citizeness Jullien, whose husband was a
Representative, and thus presumably taking part in the convoy.

THE HISTORIANS' FRENCH REVOLUTION

JACK R. CENSER   George Mason University

The tumultuous political storms of the French Revolution as well as the complexity of the event have made agreement among historians extremely elusive. To understand the current controversies requires a survey of how earlier scholars interpreted its causes and development. Early in this century the most visible battle was the struggle between two French historians, Alphonse Aulard (1849–1928) and Albert Mathiez (1874–1932). Like many other scholars of his day, Aulard ignored social and economic factors and focused on ideas and politics. In his best-known book, *The French Revolution: A Political History* (1901), he approvingly chronicled the rise of republicanism. But what is most notable about Aulard's work was his overwhelming commitment to the moderate Georges Danton rather than to the Jacobin Maximilien Robespierre as the representative man of the Revolution. Aulard and his followers were especially concerned about rescuing Danton's reputation from charges of corruption. By cheering on revolutionary republicanism and embodying it in Danton, Aulard could praise a government vaguely similar to the moderate reformist Third Republic—the regime of his own day to which he wished to lend support (on the Third Republic, see Topic 73).

Mathiez, who had been Aulard's student, broke with the older man in nearly every way. Interested more in social and economic than political factors, Mathiez also glorified Robespierre and the Jacobin dictatorship. Mathiez's politics—sometimes socialist, occasionally communist—doubtless influenced this perspective, so contrary to his mentor's. In particular, in Robespierre's speeches about equality Mathiez could find forerunners of his own 20th-century positions.

Although Aulard and Mathiez both demonstrated extraordinary knowledge of the historical sources, the tendency of each to praise his personal hero often made their work unconvincing. Such history seemed to approach propaganda and encouraged the emergence of an entirely new focus. It was mainly the avowedly Marxist Georges Lefebvre (1874–1959) who supplied a fresh perspective in the 1930s. This histori-cal vision, whose later champions would include Albert Soboul (1914–1982), generally maintained—like other Marxists—that antagonisms among different social classes led to the founding of a new order.

But by the beginning of the 1980s new findings of North American and English historians had largely undermined this widely accepted view. First, it seems that before 1789 there may have been little social conflict between aristocracy and bourgeoisie. Furthermore, under the Old Regime, nobles proved as likely as commoners to support Enlightenment notions that challenged, at least in theory, both the absolute monarchy and the social organization of the Old Regime. Such positions suggested that an independent revolutionary middle class, vital to Lefebvre's position, did not exist. Historians also found problems in the Marxist interpretation of the revolutionary decade.

In the last 20 years, new general interpretations have come along to replace Lefebvre and Soboul's. Of all these overviews of the French Revolution, François Furet's remains the most influential. To Furet, ideas possessed the power that Lefebvre attributed to social class. Thus he presented a story of competing ideologies. Ways of thinking—not class interests—played the determining role. Furet began by describing (and defending) the ideology that undergirded the French Old Regime. Although revolutionaries criticized this philosophy for protecting a system of special privileges, Furet argued that they did not understand the benefits of such privileges. Under the Old Regime, he claimed, residency in a city or participation in a craft guild, just like the rank of nobility, guaranteed individuals' freedom (here defined as lack of oppression). But such traditional privileges came under attack, ironically, from the monarchy, and French society became particularly interested in the appeals of new political ideologies. In this changeable situation, Rousseauian notions of equality, best explained in *The Social Contract*, emerged as the strongest competitor to tradition according to Furet, and gradually upstaged defenders of the system of privileges.

According to Furet, the events of the Revolution settled this ideological conflict. First, the financial crisis in 1787 had undermined royal authority, but it took two years for the people to appreciate fully what had happened. Then, in the midst of the Revolution, with the exercise of power believed to be responsible for the ills of society, "language was substituted for power, for it was the sole guarantee that power would belong only to the people, that is, to nobody." With politics reduced to a struggle over language, Rousseauian thinking, already ascendant, emerged dominant. In these circumstances, politicians could no longer wield power in the traditional sense. Although some resisted, in the end they were forced to compete in the arena of ideas and language. The most influential revolutionary leaders clearly understood that if they were to play the game of politics, they had no choice about its rules. Leadership passed to those who promised the greatest subservience to the people and the greatest equality. Once extreme notions of equality that denied individual differences dominated political debate, the coming of the Terror seemed inevitable. Fortunately, Furet went on, the Thermidorians broke the tyranny of language and returned politics to competition among classes and political groups.

Like Furet, Lynn Hunt is interested in language and owes much to him, but she tends to focus on subtle shifts in word usage and grammar rather than on the clash of ideas. For Hunt, language and image serve as barometers of revolutionary sentiment. In her pathbreaking work *Politics, Culture, and Class in the French Revolution* (1984), Hunt scrutinized the everyday language used to express the ideology of "democratic republicanism," which she found at the core of the revolutionary spirit. Her concern was first to uncover and then to explain its underlying structure, which she calls grammar. To do so, she turned to a range of theoretical writings, particularly those regarding theatricality. She also borrowed insights from the works of literary critics, anthropologists, and linguists. She used their theories to help her arrange and rearrange the content of revolutionaries' language, to uncover their basic values, the deeply imbedded categories of revolutionary thinking. Revolutionaries' intentions, she argued, could be inferred especially well from their symbolic usages. Hunt's interest in discourse analysis strongly shaped her overview of the French Revolution. Within revolutionary thought, she argued, there was no past, only a "mythic pres-

ent," composed of belief in the nation and the Revolution. Revolutionaries, ever fearful of conspiracies, spoke and wrote first as if actors in a comedy, cheering their successes; then as if in a romance, struggling with good and evil; and finally as if in a tragedy, watching things fall apart. In all three stages, Hunt believes their thought to be transparent, that is, hostile to artificiality. It was also ever vigilant and always subservient to the people. Through the revolutionaries' use of symbols, they developed this litany of new beliefs.

Another important tendency emerges collectively in the works of four recent historians: William Doyle, D.M.G. Sutherland, Simon Schama, and John Bosher. Although they do not constitute a formal school, these historians share common concerns, including similar strategies to describe and explain the Revolution. Politics take center stage, and extensive political chronologies fill their works. Yet they also consider social, intellectual, and economic factors, a commonsense approach typical of historians for whom political and literary theories are relatively unimportant. In particular, they make no attempt to deal with current debates about the relation of discourse to reality. They simply accept that these factors coexist, one alongside the other. Although these authors differ about some specific aspects of the Revolution, their views accord on some important issues. They all find redeeming value in the Old Regime and also believe that overall the Revolution failed to advance the good of humanity. This simultaneous praise for the Old Regime and attack on the new provides an especially strong blast against the claims of many participants and later historians. Such considerable concurrence of opinion should not obscure considerable disagreements over the Revolution. For example, Schama and Bosher argue that France experienced its problems in large part because of the machinations of ruthless and unscrupulous Jacobins. To the contrary, Sutherland and Doyle tend not to blame the revolutionaries but to point to outside problems, especially those of the war and counter-revolution.

To some degree the variations in these four interpretations matter less because of their distance from Furet's and Hunt's emphasis on ideas. But the interpretations mentioned here hardly exhaust the list of new approaches that continue to tumble forward. Fertile as the Revolution was for contemporaries, it also shows no sign of withering for historians.

Nicolas Carnot (1753–1823), a military engineer who had served in the Legislative Assembly and was now appointed to the Committee of Public Safety. In August, Carnot proclaimed the mobilization of the entire nation—a *levée en masse* that drafted all single males, from every social class, between 18 and 25. Because most high-ranking officers had been nobles, the Revolution produced a critical shortage of military leaders. To solve this problem, noncommissioned officers were elected, while higher ranks were to be appointed on the basis of talent. Within six months, more than 800,000 soldiers were raised, and France seized the military initiative once again.

The 1793–1794 period, during which the "Reign of Terror" triumphed, has gone down in history as the most infamous phase of the French Revolution. Under the rule of the Mountain, the government was rigidly centralized and all internal dissent was silenced. Along with the economic controls imposed, the committee passed the "law of suspects," whereby the local surveillance committees were given authority to arrest citizens suspected of disloyalty and try them by revolutionary tribunals. Local branches of the Jacobin Club, reporting back to the central club in Paris, acted as watchdogs of the Revolution in the provinces. Over the following months, domestic revolutionary armies were created to crush the peasant uprisings in the Vendée and put down the rebellion of the southern cities.

In July 1793, a young woman named Charlotte Corday (1768–1793), inspired by Girondist rhetoric, assassinated Marat in his bath, convinced that she had rid France of an evil influence. For her deed, Corday was guillotined. With Marat dead, Robespierre came to be regarded as the leader of the Mountain and now assumed direction of the Committee of Public Safety. Under his command, the committee not only orchestrated a campaign of systematic terror to purge the enemies of the Revolution but also undertook to transform the lives of all citizens.

ROBESPIERRE AND THE REPUBLIC OF VIRTUE

Robespierre was a complex man, selfless in his absolute commitment to preserve the republic, single-minded in his determination to protect the Revolution. A self-righteous, ascetic young bachelor, a lawyer by profession, he had earned a reputation among his colleagues as "the Incorruptible" (yet despite his radicalism, he refused to alter his elegant prerevolutionary dress). Robespierre asserted that revolutionary times required two qualities—virtue and terror. The republic created by the Revolution would, he believed, engender civic virtue in all citizens, who should devote themselves to the service of the nation and their fellow citizens. He took from the writings of Rousseau the vision of an ideal republic—a "Republic of Virtue"—in which both poverty and excessive wealth would be eliminated, and in which reason, trust, and justice would reign.

For all his idealism, Robespierre was cold-blooded in ordering the execution of the Revolution's enemies—or his own. His fanaticism led him to believe that terror was another name for revolutionary justice. Its purpose was to purify the nation and impose obedience on it by impressing citizens with the severity of republican discipline. The justification for the Terror was that immediate liberties had to be sacrificed to the future of a free republic.

The Terror was used against a wide variety of people, many of whom simply disagreed with the policies of the Committee of Public Safety. The victims of the guillotine included former nobles and priests, peasants and workers, members of the convention, and some of Robespierre's colleagues in the government. By the winter of 1794 the Terror was turned against republican politicians, both on the right and the left. In March, extreme radicals in Paris known as the *enragés* (the "wild men") were beheaded for plotting to destroy the republic. The next month came executions of conservative republicans, including Danton. In June, Robespierre had a law approved to convict suspects without evidence. In all, nearly 30,000 people were executed before the Terror was over.

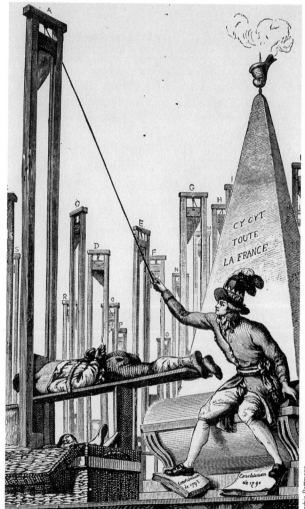

Satirical print. 1794. Amid a forest of guillotines, the figure of Robespierre pulls the cord by which the blade is lowered to execute . . . the executioner. As he does so, he treads beneath his feet two books labeled "Constitution of 1790" and "Constitution of 1792." The pyramid behind is a funeral monument dedicated to the memory of "All France."

Along with the Terror came deliberate efforts to demonstrate in tangible ways that the Revolution had remade history and created an entirely new world. Beginning in September 1792, government documents were dated from "Year I of the French Republic." In October 1793, a new calendar was put into effect (used until 1806), based on "reason" and "nature." The new dating system began with the first day of the republic. There were 10 days in a week, three weeks in a month, and 12 months in a year. The remaining five days were declared republican holidays. The months were named after seasons and the weather, such as Brumaire (fog) and Thermidor (heat).

Not only did the calendar symbolize a new era in human history, but it was also part of a larger effort to dechristianize the nation. In place of established religions, the Revolution now proclaimed the worship of Reason. Churches were systematically closed and the clergy persecuted, and the Cathedral of Notre Dame in Paris was turned into a "Temple of Reason." In May 1794, Robespierre abandoned the worship of Reason because he believed it too difficult for common people to understand. In its place he substituted the deistic Cult of the Supreme Being, which he hoped would promote civic morality.

The transformation of everyday life went further. New forms of public discourse were adopted—"citizen" became the proper term of address for all French people—and streets, buildings, and even cities were renamed according to the revolutionary vocabulary. In dress, trousers of the sans-culottes were adopted by men, while more severe dresses with high necklines and flattened skirts became the style of female attire. Prostitution and gambling, identified by revolutionary propagandists as typically aristocratic vices, were repressed, and a cult of veneration for the virtuous mother became the order of the day.

RETURN FROM THE BRINK: FROM THERMIDOR TO THE DIRECTORY

The dictatorial rule of Robespierre and the Committee of Public Safety was sustained by the need for strong government in the midst of the war and domestic instability. In 1793 to 1794, the French armies once again went on the offensive and won a series of important victories. In June 1794, French troops occupied the Austrian Netherlands, as they had done once before, and annexed the territory. Similar successes on the Rhine frontier and the Pyrenees led to the negotiation of peace terms with Prussia, Spain, Piedmont-Sardinia, and Austria. Having also crushed provincial rebellions against the republic, by the late summer of 1794 the government of the radical Jacobins had achieved its most important success.

THERMIDOR: THE REVOLUTION IN REVERSE

Ironically, the end of the military crisis proved to be the undoing of the rule of the radicals. Once relieved of its foreign enemies, many leaders of the Revolution began calling for relief from the stringent domestic policies of the Committee of Public Safety. Moreover, Robespierre and his colleagues had alienated far too many political forces and social groups on the right and the left, and by mid-1794 found themselves isolated. The moderates in the National Convention, who once cowed before the Terror, now reasserted themselves.

Robespierre pushed the growing discontent to the breaking point and provoked his enemies into the "Thermidorian Reaction" that at last ended the Terror. On July 26 he went before the convention to denounce unnamed conspirators in the government who were plotting against him and against the Revolution; he had followed the tactic in the past in preparation for purging opponents. This time, however, members of the convention organized against him. The next day, the ninth of Thermidor, as Robespierre rose to speak again, he was shouted down and a special decree ordering the arrest of his supporters was passed. On the tenth of Thermidor, Robespierre and 60 of his colleagues were guillotined. The Revolution had devoured its most fanatical children.

The social policies of Thermidor also altered the general atmosphere of the nation. The emphasis on civic morality, with its attendant campaigns against gambling, pornography, and prostitution, disappeared, while the middle classes reverted to their former styles of dress and speech. Many Catholic priests returned to France as freedom of worship was restored.

Even Thermidor, however, was not without its own violence, for a "white terror" in the form of street fighting and massacres now struck the Jacobins and their supporters as well as the sans-culottes. Along with the reaction came an extremely poor harvest in 1795 that resulted in food shortages worse than those of 1789. The result was an abortive uprising followed by a bloody repression.

THE DIRECTORY

Following the fall of Robespierre, the convention issued a third constitution, which operated from 1795 to 1799. The system of universal male suffrage adopted in 1793 was now abandoned, and the country returned to a franchise similar to that incorporated in the 1791 Constitution, based on property and wealth—an exception was made for soldiers, who were entitled to vote regardless of whether they owned property. A two-chamber legislature was established, consisting of a Council of Elders and a Council of Five Hundred. The new document created a five-person directory to function as a plural executive branch of government.

The Directory sought to reestablish political consensus by assuming a moderate position that eschewed extremists on both sides. Thus, while it eliminated the popular democracy of the radical phase of the Revolution, it also opposed a complete resurgence of either royalism or Jacobinism. With stability as the goal, the directors refused to tolerate any organized political opposition that could threaten their rule, although their efforts to repress the extremists did not include a return to wholesale terror.

Despite its aim of restoring stability to the French body politic, the Directory's rule proved to be unstable. Coups and plots continued to challenge the new government, and a wide range of political ideologies flourished just below the level of organized political opposition. The renewal of war with the monarchs of Europe once again brought reliance on the army. When elections in the spring of 1799 went against the candidates sponsored by the Directory, the legislature replaced four of the Directory's five members with a group led by the Abbé Sieyès, who had championed the middle classes in 1789. In turning to the ambitious and brilliant General Bonaparte for support, Sieyès introduced a new factor into the ever-changing course of the French Revolution.

Putting the French Revolution in Perspective

The importance of the Revolution transcended France because its repercussions would be felt for many decades to come throughout Europe and on a worldwide scale. In its aftermath, the society of the Old Regime was increasingly undermined and eventually replaced in most of Western and Central Europe. The social changes that the Revolution had introduced with such drama and violence were reinforced by the long-range repercussions of industrialization. In the 1790s, France had joined Great Britain as the second major European state to apply the ideas of resistance and to depose—indeed, behead—its ruler. Coming on the heels of the recent American Revolution, the revolution in France had forever altered politics in the West. By the late 19th century, the liberal ideas of the French moderates characterized most European governments, while the radical experiment with mass politics would become the predominant pattern of political discourse as the 20th century opened. Perhaps more than anything, the French Revolution had given vivid and tangible proof of the Enlightenment belief in the possibilities of change for the human condition.

Questions for Further Study

1. What were the causes of the French Revolution?
2. What role did the bourgeoisie play in the Revolution? Why was the concept of property important to the revolutionary leaders?
3. How did the sans-culottes affect the course of the Revolution? What was their relationship to the Jacobins?
4. What caused the reaction against the Reign of Terror?

Suggestions for Further Reading

Allen, Rodney. *Threshold of Terror: The Last Hours of the French Monarchy in the French Revolution.* Gloucester, 1999.

Andress, David. *French Society in Revolution, 1789-1799.* New York, 1999.

Blanning, T.C.W. *The French Revolution: Aristocrats Versus Bourgeois?* Atlantic Highlands, NJ, 1987.

Censer, Jack, and Lynn Hunt. *Liberty, Equality, Fraternity: Exploring the French Revolution.* University Park, PA, 2001.

Cobban, Alfred. *The Social Interpretation of the French Revolution.* New York, 1999.

Correa, Manoel Pio. *The Dawn of the French Revolution.* Lewes, 2000.

Furet, François. E. Forster, trans. *Interpreting the French Revolution.* New York, 1981.

Hunt, Lynn. *Politics, Culture, and Class in the French Revolution.* Berkeley, CA, 1984.

Jones, P.M. *The Peasantry in the French Revolution.* Cambridge, MA, 1988.

Landes, Joan. *Women and the Public Sphere in the Age of the French Revolution.* Ithaca, NY, 1988.

Schama, Simon. *Citizens: A Chronicle of the French Revolution.* New York, 1989.

Sutherland, Donald M.G. *France, 1789–1815: Revolution and Counterrevolution.* Oxford, 1986.

InfoTrac College Edition

Enter the search term *French Revolution* using Key Terms.

EUROPE IN THE NAPOLEONIC ERA

The Directory brought welcome relief from the excesses of the Revolution, but it did little to solve France's underlying political problems. In turning to the young general, Napoleon Bonaparte, to overturn the results of the elections of 1799, its moderate leaders launched the final stage of revolutionary transformation.

Napoleon's rapid ascent to power, based like much of his career on a potent combination of military virtuosity and personal charisma, saw him assume the title of first consul in 1799. His Consulate brought about widespread domestic reform in France. He reorganized the institutions of law, religion, education, and the economy. Peace at home was generally restored, together with public self-esteem. With his coronation as emperor in 1804, Napoleon moved to the wider stage of continental Europe. Britain was protected by its superior naval power, but virtually the whole of the rest of Europe fell more or less under Napoleonic rule. Even Russia had to negotiate an alliance that reduced the tsar to the status of a junior partner.

The Napoleonic empire was short-lived. The attempt to blockade all trade with Britain was a predictable failure, and French domination of Spain proved costly in men and resources. In 1812, while still embroiled with the Spanish rebels, Napoleon launched an expedition to the other end of Europe, against Russia, where massive losses, combined with the blizzards of the harsh winter, devastated the French Army. Other European nations were emboldened to unite with Russia in a war of liberation.

The end came quickly. In 1813, Napoleon retreated back to France. The following year the European allies invaded Paris, forced the emperor to abdicate, and shipped him off to the island of Elba. His last attempt to return to power lasted no more than 100 days. He escaped back to France in March 1815, but was finally defeated at the Battle of Waterloo that June.

With the triumph of the European powers and a Bourbon monarch once more on the throne of France, the forces of the Revolution seemed exhausted. Yet by the end of the Napoleonic period, Europe had been transformed. Revolutionary political and social concepts permeated all levels of society throughout the Continent. Furthermore, the desire for national independence, born out of resistance to Napoleon, was to become a dominating theme in the history of the 19th century.

THE RISE OF BONAPARTE: FROM CONSUL TO EMPEROR

Napoleon (ruled as first consul 1799–1804 and as emperor 1804–1814) was unquestionably a figure whose decisions and actions irrevocably changed the lives of countless people. He was known to many of his contemporaries, both admirers and enemies, simply as "The Man"; decades after his death in exile, English children were scared into obedience by the mere mention of his name—"Old Boney."

Many believed that they had reason to be grateful to him. In Italy and the Rhineland his troops threw down the walls of the ghettoes and allowed the Jews to emerge into freedom for the first time since the Counter-Reformation. In other cases his social and political policies undermined some of the achievements of the Revolution: Some of the civil liberties of women, to which revolutionary legislators had been more sympathetic, were removed by the Napoleonic Code of Law.

NAPOLEON THE ADMINISTRATOR

It is misleading to look for a broad, consistent philosophy behind the details of Napoleon's actions. Some of the contradictions that marked his rise and fall were present even in his childhood and early career. He was born in 1769 in Corsica, an island ruled by France but predominantly Italian-speaking; Napoleon never managed to speak French without an accent. In his youth, moreover, the first political ambitions of the future emperor of France were to free Corsica from French control.

At the military academies he attended in France (he was sent to his first at the age of nine), he set out to shock his aristocratic fellow students by spectacular displays of bad behavior, which were intended to show his contempt for their genteel world. His own family was noble but impoverished, and he was proud of achieving success by his own merits. Yet his career was one of contradictions. Once in power, he introduced reforms that helped others of ability to overcome the disadvantage of their nonaristocratic birth and rise to positions of influence, yet he also created a new aristocracy and made family members the rulers of states throughout Europe.

For all his love of the unconventional, Napoleon's intellectual interests marked him as a child of the Enlightenment, and he eventually ruled as an enlightened absolutist. Like many of his contemporaries, he was an enthusiastic reader of history and a keen student of mathematics. His distinction lay in the imagination and speed with which he was able to transform theoretical ideas into practice: Even Napoleon's enemies recognized his outstanding administrative gifts.

His talent for organization and demand for efficiency were formidable, and he was famous for his ability to dictate three letters on different topics to three secretaries simultaneously, without losing concentration or creating confusion. When he applied these skills to major issues, he produced rapid and significant results. Thus his interest in law culminated in the Napoleonic Code, a massive program of legal reform that was destined to have wide-reaching effects—both for better and for worse—far beyond the borders of France.

NAPOLEON'S EARLY CAREER

His rise in the army was helped by the need for talented officers because many former commanders, drawn from aristocratic families, had either fled or had been demoted during the Revolution. Nonetheless his astonishing ability to make a rapid decision and then act on it soon drew attention.

Among those impressed was General Paul Barras, one of the five leaders of the Directory. In 1795, at the National Convention to set up the Directory's constitution, monarchist leaders mounted a huge public demonstration against the convention. When called on to deal with the emergency, Barras summoned Napoleon, whom he had seen in action at the siege of Toulon in 1793, and the crowds were scattered by cannon fire.

In return for his help, Napoleon asked for command of the French forces in northern Italy, which offered the chance of winning military glory in more conventional style. With a dazzling series of moves, he defeated the Austrians and occupied Milan. Exceeding his orders, he pushed into north-central Italy and in October 1797 he personally negotiated the Treaty of Campo Formio, whereby Austria recognized the new state of the Cisalpine Republic, made up of Lombardy, Genoa, and several smaller duchies, in return for control over Venice.

Within the next two years, as French armies moved through Italy, French-controlled republics also sprang up in the Papal States, Naples, and Tuscany. The strategically important Kingdom of Piedmont was occupied and eventually annexed to France. By the end of his command, Napoleon had demonstrated his abilities as statesman, as well as military leader.

Napoleon's sense of drama and love of excitement had a great appeal for the Italians, whose own dreams of independence he astutely encouraged. The leaders of the Directory back in Paris were less enthusiastic at the growing popularity of the young hero (to say nothing of the prospect of a liberated and united Italy), and Napoleon's next move was cunningly designed to enhance his domestic standing. France's greatest enemy was Britain. Even Napoleon was not yet prepared to undertake an armed invasion of the British Isles, but why not attack British interests elsewhere?

THE EGYPTIAN CAMPAIGN

The expedition he led to Egypt in the spring of 1798 was aimed at interfering with British colonial trade and striking a symbolic blow at the British Empire. Furthermore he hoped to find in North Africa an appropriate setting for sensational new heroic exploits, while avoiding the full might of the British Navy.

In the end, the expedition proved disastrous. The French fleet was destroyed by British forces under Admiral Nelson (1758–1805) at the Battle of the Nile, and the

David, *Napoleon Crossing the Alps.* 1800. 8 feet 10 inches by 7 feet 7 inches (2.44 by 2.31 m). David transferred his revolutionary enthusiasm to his new hero, Napoleon, shown here in one of his early successes, when he crossed the Alps and surprised and defeated an Austrian army. The future Emperor, who later made David official court painter, appears calm and masterful on his charging horse, and points the way forward. With the return of the monarchy in 1815, David paid for his support for Napoleon: Louis XVIII exiled him.

French army was left stranded. Napoleon hastily abandoned his troops in order to return to France as quickly as possible and try to limit the damage to his reputation. He and his supporters concealed the military catastrophe as best they could by adroit manipulation of the news from Egypt.

The ease with which he succeeded in reinstating himself was largely because of the chaotic political situation in Paris. During his absence, further French moves in Italy had provoked Britain, Austria, and Russia into forming a coalition against France. The subsequent military crisis, which led to a series of French setbacks in Italy, undermined the credibility of the Directory and led to violent conflict between conservatives and democrats. Napoleon's reappearance on the scene provided the conservatives with a popular hero to lead a political coup.

THE BRUMAIRE COUP

On November 9, 1799, Napoleon seized power and appointed himself first consul, with virtually supreme power; two other consuls were named, but they were never given any real authority. This act is generally known as the Brumaire Coup because its date, according to the revolutionary calendar, was 18 Brumaire VIII. Among the coup's supporters was the Abbé Sieyès (see Topic 61), the former revolutionary and advocate of national sovereignty, who now called for "Confidence from below, authority from above."

The conservatives intended the takeover to institute a republican oligarchy, but the first consul had other ideas. He maintained control of the armed forces, and thus of both internal security and foreign affairs. A carefully picked Council of State was put in charge of all national legislation. Regional governments, corresponding to the departments established by the revolutionary government, became subject to strict surveillance by the appointment of prefects, officials sent from Paris to act as agents of the central government and report back to Napoleon.

Napoleon tried to obtain the appearance of popular support, using censorship where necessary to block the circulation of opposing views, but, for all the rhetoric of his public statements, he was, in his own way, as absolutist as

Old Regime rulers. The constitution he and his advisers drafted included two national legislative bodies with vague general powers, for which all French adult males could vote (women lost most of the rights they had gained under the Revolution). Although the councils had no power to introduce new laws, Napoleon's proposed constitution was overwhelmingly approved by a popular referendum.

THE CONSULATE

The years of the Consulate—1799 to 1804—saw a return to stability in France. The authority of the central government was restored, and citizens could count on the protection of the law. The achievement of a balanced budget and the efficient collecting of a more justly assessed tax burden (there were no more exemptions for the aristocracy and the clergy) reestablished the economy on a sound footing. By 1802, the average Frenchman paid less taxes than in 1789 and received more and better services. The Bank of France, an institution Napoleon founded, was privately owned but state controlled; it took charge of government funds and distributed paper currency.

Napoleon ended the Revolution's battle with the Catholic Church by negotiating a concordat, signed by the first consul and Pope Pius VII in 1801. This agreement proclaimed Catholicism the "preferred" religion in France, but maintained the freedom of religion established during the Revolution. Among its provisions, it held that the church would renounce its claims to the land and other church property confiscated by the National Assembly. Napoleon's own attitude toward religion was practical, to say the least: He is said to have claimed that "God is always on the side of those with the most cannon." The concordat was intended to reassure traditional Catholics in France, who had been shocked by the atheism of many of the revolutionary leaders. On the whole, however, it strengthened the power of the state and was never popular with the Catholic clergy. The pope later renounced it.

THE CODE NAPOLEON

Amid this whirl of reform, the foundations were laid for radical changes in law and education, two areas that had been of particular interest to Napoleon in his youth. With his customary genius for bureaucratic efficiency, he supervised the drawing up of a systematic and consistent body of laws, the Code Napoleon. Among the code's aims was the creation of a rational system for buying, selling, and holding property, which established sound general principles and yet did not interfere with individual rights.

On the other hand, in dealing with family questions, the code was far less egalitarian: It awarded husbands complete control over their wives, children, and possessions. Furthermore, women's occupations were to be limited as far as possible to the marital, maternal, and domestic spheres, with men in complete charge of public matters. Those women who worked were required to give their wages to their husbands; any woman operating a business—selling in a market, for example—could do so only with the permission of her husband, who had a legal right to all her profits.

The code's bias did not go unnoticed: As one woman wrote in the early 19th century, "From the way the Code treats women, you can tell it was written by men." Its effects spread far beyond France. Many new nations, both in the Old and New Worlds, which came into being in the 19th century adopted the Code Napoleon as the basis of their legal systems. In the process its attitude toward gender roles became widely diffused and enforced.

In education as elsewhere, Napoleon aimed to strengthen the power of the central authority. The University of France was founded to supervise educational institutions throughout the country, and new categories of schools were introduced: professional and technical academies, and a nationwide high school system. As in the case of financial and legal reform, the chief beneficiaries of these new schools were the middle classes and their families; they had begun to win a new status for themselves before the Revolution, and now their progress was confirmed.

The return of law, order, and prosperity ensured Napoleon's popularity, and in 1802 he was acclaimed "consul for life"; the popular vote gave him more than 95 percent support The only real failure of the Consulate occurred far enough away from France to make little impact. Although Napoleon won back the North American territory of Louisiana from Spain, he was unable to occupy and develop it and eventually sold the territory to the United States for $15 million.

With security and stability ensured at home, wider horizons beckoned again: the dream of European conquest. For this enterprise, however, a more grandiose title was in order. In 1804, in the cathedral of Notre Dame, he crowned himself emperor with a laurel wreath, symbol of ancient Rome, before crowning his wife, Josephine, in more opulent style. His goal was to recreate the Roman Empire and unite Europe under his rule. The artistic legacy of the Napoleonic period, produced in a style known as *Empire*, provided an appropriate background for these conquests, with its triumphal arches, columns, and "antique" dresses.

EUROPE AND THE FRENCH IMPERIUM

Within a few months of Napoleon's coronation, France was faced for a third time by a hostile coalition of Britain, Austria, and Russia, an alliance formed the previous year to combat the spread of French influence. The most potentially threatening of these three were the British, who joined the coalition even though Napoleon had, in fact, signed a peace treaty with them in 1801. This treaty, the Peace of Amiens, had been negotiated unenthusiastically on both sides. Both Britain and France refused essential concessions—a British withdrawal from Gibraltar and Malta in return

Engraving showing an invasion of England by French aerial forces. Early 19th century. The invasion, of course, never happened. The print is presumably satirical; not even Napoleon's worst enemy could have thought him capable of such a clumsy and hare-brained scheme. Yet it underlines the genuine panic in England at the time.

Corbis-Bettmann

for a French evacuation of the Low Countries—and the treaty soon collapsed.

Napoleon's first strategy for undermining his opponents was to eliminate their strongest member by direct attack. The invasion he launched against England, however, was soon discouraged by the presence of the massed forces of the British Navy in the English Channel. Furthermore, in October 1805 any future threat of a French naval offensive was eliminated by British victory over the combined French and Spanish fleets at the Battle of Trafalgar. Under the command once again of Admiral Nelson, a tactician as brilliantly unorthodox at sea as Napoleon was on land, the British Navy devastated the French and Spanish forces. The battle cost Nelson his life but effectively guaranteed the security of the British Isles from invasion, and limited Napoleon's enterprises to continental Europe.

THE CONQUEST OF CONTINENTAL EUROPE

With characteristic boldness, Napoleon was quick to regain the offensive. French troops moved across Europe at astonishing speed. After occupying Vienna, they took on the combined Austrian and Russian armies at Austerlitz and crushed them; in the battle the French pretended to retreat, only to trap their enemies into taking up an overexposed position, and Napoleon won one of his most famous victories. The Austrians had little choice but to negotiate a peace settlement, the terms of which were distinctly unfavorable to them. The Russians, who were badly shaken, retreated back east in the hope of better luck in the future.

Throughout the hostilities the Prussians had remained neutral, unwilling to come to the aid of their Austrian neighbors and unable to see that their turn was next. With Austria disposed of, Napoleon could turn his attention north, and by the time the Prussians finally declared war, it was too late for them to put up much resistance. The legendary Prussian army, a mere shadow of its former glory, was soundly whipped in October 1806, at the Battle of Jena. Napoleon was master of central Europe.

Formally declaring the end of the Holy Roman Empire, he reorganized its many kingdoms and principalities into a series of new states. Some of these were placed under the rule of family members: his youngest brother, Jerome, was given Westphalia, while Marshal Joachim Murat, the husband of his sister Caroline Bonaparte, became ruler of the Grand Duchy of Berg. Napoleon's purpose in dividing up his conquests among the family was partly to establish dynasties, while it enabled him to retain control in his own hands. His brother Louis became king of Holland, but when he began to show too much interest in the welfare of his Dutch subjects, Napoleon deposed him and made Holland French territory.

THE FRENCH IN EASTERN EUROPE

Among the newly created states was the Grand Duchy of Warsaw, made up of that part of Poland which had been carved out by the Prussians. By appearing to favor the cause of Polish independence, Napoleon could claim to be the champion of national aspirations, as he had in his earlier days in Italy. More to the point, he provided himself with a base from which to move against his last unconquered enemy, Russia. After an indecisive battle at Eylau, which was fought in a raging blizzard and produced terrible casualties on both sides, the Russians were finally defeated at Friedland in June 1807. Within weeks Tsar Alexander I and Emperor Napoleon I met at Tilsit to sign an agreement that divided Europe in half. In return for a relatively free hand in extending Russian influence into the Ottoman-controlled Balkans, Alexander accepted Napoleon's annexation and reorganization of Western Europe and agreed to restrict trade with Britain. The terms were in France's favor, but the tsar had little choice.

ITALY AND SPAIN

With eastern and central Europe reshaped, it was then the Mediterranean region's turn to provide thrones for the Bonaparte family. Parts of Italy, including Piedmont, Tuscany, the Papal States, and several smaller duchies, had already become French territory. Napoleon merged the former Cisalpine Republic, together with other parts of central Italy, into the Kingdom of Italy, governing himself as king through his stepson. In southern Italy, his brother Joseph became king of the Kingdom of Naples in 1806.

In 1808, Napoleon sent Murat to Naples and transferred Joseph to Spain in an attempt to secure power in Iberia. Since 1795 the Spanish had been only fitful partners with the French in their joint attempt to undermine British influence in Europe and the colonies. Napoleon's solution to dealing with his supposed allies was, as might be expected, radical and direct. In 1808 the Spanish king and his son were paid off, and Joseph led French troops to Madrid to oversee the introduction of the new regime.

For once, Napoleon's political instincts deserted him. By a blatant takeover, the former supporter of nationalist causes provoked a nationalist uprising that was to last for years. The popular riots of early May 1808 were soon put down by bloody and brutal troop action on the part of the French, but the memory of the repression galvanized the forces of rebellion. Regular Spanish troops combined with local civilian forces to challenge French occupation of their country, and bitter fighting dragged on until the French were finally driven out of Spain in 1814.

Napoleon's move backfired in several ways. The genuine popular resistance he provoked among the Spanish encouraged nations elsewhere in Europe to resist French strong-arm tactics, while the conflict in Spain provided a golden opportunity to Napoleon's greatest enemies, the British, who dispatched a force to drive the French out of the Iberian peninsula, in a campaign known as the Peninsular War.

The war trapped a large part of the French Army in a hopeless struggle against a mixture of British troops, the local anti-French forces, and several thousand Spanish guerrilla fighters, these latter inspired by memory of the horrors of the May brutalities. The term *guerrilla* is the Spanish word for "little war"; the development in the Peninsular War of "guerrilla tactics"—hit-and-run, ambush, sabotage, surprise attack—against larger and better-equipped forces proved highly influential in many subsequent conflicts around the globe.

In 1808, with all of western and central Europe at Napoleon's command, the problem of Spain must have seemed relatively unimportant; in the end it proved one of the chief causes of his downfall because more than 200,000 troops embroiled in the fighting there were urgently needed elsewhere.

Goya, *Executions of May 3, 1808.* 8 feet 8¾ inches by 11 feet 3¾ inches (2.66 by 3.45 m). 1814. The painting, showing the execution of citizens of Madrid who had protested the French occupation of their city, was commissioned by the Spanish government after the French withdrawal as a memorial. Goya dramatically highlights the victims, while the sinister killers remain in shadow.

THE GRAND EXPERIMENT: OCCUPATION AND REFORM

The Napoleonic empire lasted for a shorter time than just about any empire of comparable size in Western history. In 1808 the French controlled, in one way or another, much of Central and Western Europe (with the exception of the British Isles). By 1813 Napoleon's domination was over. Yet for the brevity of its duration, French imperial rule had a profound and lasting effect on European life.

THE IMPERIAL ADMINISTRATION

In order to administer these vast territories, Napoleon introduced throughout Europe many of the reforms that had succeeded so well in France. The old ranks and privileges were abolished, and family status no longer assured a successful career: The Napoleonic bureaucracy offered the possibility of advancement in public life to those of talent and ability, regardless of their origins. Many of the special powers of the church were curtailed, or—as in the case of church courts—abolished. Under the Code Napoleon, which was valid in the conquered territories, all were equal in the eyes of the law.

Financial reorganization and the implementation of a coherent tax system helped improve local economies. In the process, those involved in trade and commerce were more able to pursue their business and advance their interests. In one area, however, even the emperor failed to remove old barriers. Despite his attempts to abolish customs tariffs for the importation of goods across national boundaries, the various European economic groups maintained their rival tariff systems. With the end of Napoleonic rule, the concept of European free trade disappeared, until it was revived almost 150 years later in the years of rebuilding after World War II.

All of these various reforms were, of course, principally intended to strengthen French rule over her empire. The local populations were free to pursue their own careers, protect their property rights, and work as they pleased, but they were not free to govern themselves. The efficient working of the system was intended to maintain control by a centralized government in Paris that, in turn, was responsible to the emperor. A prosperous Europe, in addition, would pay taxes to pay for the French armies of occupation and finance future military adventures.

NAPOLEON AND LIBERTY

Although the reasons for the Napoleonic reorganization of Europe were practical, they were underpinned by broader philosophical principles. Napoleon had, after all, come to power with the claim that he would implement some of the ideals of the Revolution, with its doctrines of liberty and equality. Many of his reforms, both in France and throughout the empire, did produce a more free and just society.

In many cases, even after his fall, the old vested interests of the aristocracy were unable to impose themselves again. Furthermore the spirit of national independence and self-determination, which both the Revolution and Napoleon claimed to support, was an intoxicating one; in Germany, in particular, resistance to Napoleon played an important role in stimulating nationalism. The very peoples who finally united to overthrow the empire did so following the vision of freedom that the Revolution seemed to offer, and that the Napoleonic reforms made at least partly real. After Napoleon, Europe could never return to the old social and political ways.

THE JEWS UNDER NAPOLEON

In the case of one people, however—the Jews—progress did not survive the end of the Napoleonic era. As early as 1791 the National Assembly had decreed that French Jews possessed the rights of full citizens. Napoleon, with his enlightened attitude toward religious tolerance, continued to work for the integration of the Jews into society. The Cisalpine Republic that he founded in 1797 provided for their freedom of worship, and the concordat signed with the Catholic Church in 1801 contained nothing to undermine the Jews' new civic status in France.

In the years of conquest, as French armies moved through Europe, they freed Jews from their ghettoes and extended full rights to them, although the Jews were often required to pay heavy taxes in return. Jewish candidates were able to stand as candidates for election to public office, and Jewish intellectuals were nominated as members of learned societies such as the Italian Academy of Sciences.

With a characteristic care for detail, Napoleon tried to regularize the position of the Jews, a people who transcended national boundaries, by convening an international congress. In 1806 Jewish representatives were summoned to Paris from all parts of the empire to discuss such questions as divorce and mixed marriages, and Jewish difficulties in entering the professions. A Napoleonic decree

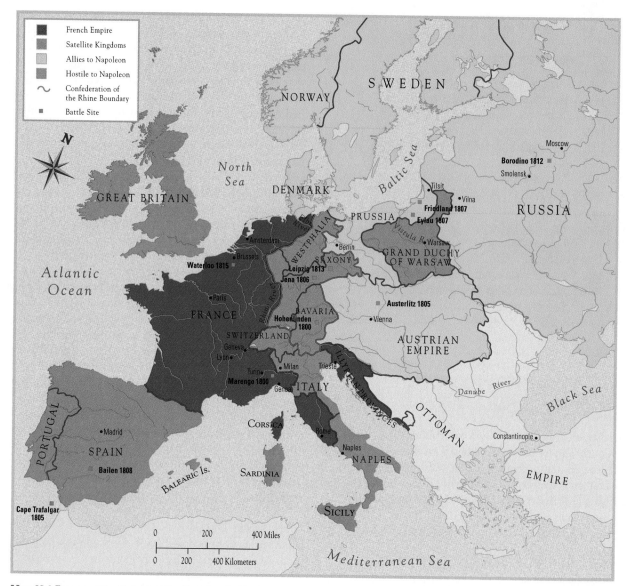

Map 62.1 Europe at the Height of the Napoleonic Empire. The extent of Napoleon's conquests has to be measured against the very limited period during which he held them. Crowned Emperor in 1804, he was forced to abdicate a decade later, in March 1814, when his former allies, including Austria, Prussia, and Russia, took Paris. His fate was sealed by the impossible task of attacking Russia while fighting in Spain.

emerged two years later; it established local administrative councils in Jewish communities throughout the empire, which were answerable to a central council in Paris.

With the defeat of Napoleon, however, the entire system collapsed. In France the Jews retained their rights, but elsewhere in Europe they were repressed even more ferociously, precisely because they had been set free by the hated French conquerors, and in gratitude had exchanged their yellow stars for the French *tricouleurs*. The walls of the ghetto at Rome were thrown up again and the Jews confined there as soon as Napoleon's downfall seemed assured. The Jews of Italy finally won their freedom in the mid-19th century, following the Italian struggle for independence, but many of those in central and eastern Europe could only hope to find theirs by emigrating to the New World at the end of the century.

THE EUROPEAN COALITION AND THE COLLAPSE OF FRANCE

Napoleon was finally overthrown by a third coalition of the European powers, although their success was as much the result of the emperor's miscalculations as of their own military prowess. Both in economic and foreign policy, the French undermined their own strength.

THE CONTINENTAL SYSTEM

In the aftermath of Trafalgar, with the British unshaken in their naval power, Napoleon tried to find a way to undermine Britain economically. His device was the Continental System, introduced for the first time in 1806; among its other policies, it prohibited the importation of British goods into continental Europe. The aim was to destroy the commercial life of a country that Napoleon referred to as "a nation of shopkeepers." When the British in turn imposed their own countermeasures, the ensuing naval blockade and counter-blockade involved virtually all trading nations, including neutral powers such as the United States.

Although the barriers created by the Continental System stimulated the British to exploit alternative markets, including some in South America, they undoubtedly proved disruptive to business. The riots and popular demonstrations that racked England in 1811 were a direct result of the unemployment caused by the trade war. In the end, however, the consequences for the economies of continental Europe were much more disastrous. It became increasingly difficult to obtain the raw materials essential for manufacturing. The economic life of great ports and business centers such as Amsterdam was paralyzed. Production declined and unemployment rose. The Continent, including France, lost more than Britain by the boycott, and the general resentment at French interference did much to fuel the European powers' final military resistance to Napoleon.

THE RUSSIAN CAMPAIGN

Against this background of developing restlessness, the emperor made his fatal mistake—a campaign against the Russians. The most obvious pretext for his invasion was revenge for Alexander's flouting of the Continental System. The Russian economy was heavily dependent on the export of agricultural produce in exchange for manufactured goods, and one of Russia's most important trading partners was Britain. French demands that Baltic ports remain closed to British ships caused a serious economic crisis in Russia, and Alexander began to break the embargo.

Napoleon's response was to muster the "*Grande Armée*," the largest army the world had seen—more than 600,000 in number; many of the troops were conscripts from countries under French rule and thus neither professional soldiers nor enthusiastic supporters of the French cause. In the spring of 1812, the emperor and his army set out to conquer Russia. After the long march to the Russian border, the French force advanced into the heart of the country. The Russians avoided battle and retreated toward Moscow, destroying their own spring crops as they went. The French lines of communication became ever longer and more tenuous, and supplies increasingly difficult to obtain.

The Russians finally took a stand at Borodino, some 70 miles southwest of Moscow. In the battle that followed, both sides suffered terrible losses. Although Napoleon pushed on to Moscow, the Russian army maintained its discipline. The tsar refused to sue for peace and retreated to positions east and south of Moscow. On the evening after the French entered the ancient Russian capital, a mysterious fire broke out, destroying many of its buildings, and leaving the French soldiers with little in the way of shelter. The city's population had fled, taking with them all available supplies.

For once Napoleon's decisiveness deserted him. Weeks passed as he waited in vain for signs that Russian resistance was crumbling. Only at the end of October did he finally order retreat, but the delay proved fatal. Loaded with plunder, his troops trudged into the depths of a Russian winter. As rivers overflowed, swollen by the seasonal rains, the French army was engulfed in mud and battered by blizzards. Disease and hunger ran rampant, while the weary soldiers were harried by mounted Russian Cossacks, who rode out of the storms to wreak yet more havoc.

Six weeks later the survivors staggered back across the border into Germany, the pitiful remnants of the mighty

Contemporary engraving of Napoleon's retreat from Moscow in 1812. Early 19th century. As the column of the retreating *Grande Armée* stretches endlessly into the distance, troops are forced to abandon a cannon and—worse—provisions, in order to make progress through the snow. The winter of that year was one of the most severe on record.

expedition—of the original force of more than 600,000, only 100,000 were left. Napoleon hastened back to Paris to build a new army, apparently neither discouraged by the horrors of the retreat nor deterred by the human misery his campaign had inflicted on so many. The Prussian conscripts deserted.

THE END OF THE EMPIRE

At last the spell was broken, and European statesmen began to plan a war of liberation that would see the end of French domination; one of their leaders was Prince Klemens von Metternich of Austria, a figure who was to play a crucial role in the post-Napoleonic era. In March 1813 a treaty was signed between Russia and Prussia, and Europe waited in suspense to see whether Austria would join the allied coalition against France or remain neutral. The news that the Austrian emperor had finally declared war on France was accompanied by tidings of further French losses in Spain, where the Peninsular War still dragged on.

Faced with the collapse of his empire, Napoleon managed to recruit an army, but only by including underage conscripted troops. In October 1813 at Leipzig, in central Germany, his forces were defeated, and he was driven back to France. As the European powers began to close in, the British joined the coalition. Terms were offered to Napoleon that allowed him to remain emperor. When he rejected the terms, the allies invaded France.

In March 1814 Paris was taken and Napoleon forced to abdicate. A brother of Louis XVI was recognized as king of France and took the title of Louis XVIII (ruled 1814–1824). Meanwhile the allied powers summoned a congress to meet in Vienna a few months later, to negotiate a settlement for the rest of Europe. Somewhat at a loss as to what to do with the former emperor, they exiled him to Elba, a tiny island off the coast of Italy.

Napoleon was set up as ruler of the island in a modest villa and permitted to organize a miniature court, for which he designed the uniforms and prescribed the ceremonials. The rooms of the villa were decorated with paintings showing scenes from his campaigns; on the wall of one of them visitors can still see an inscription, in the former emperor's handwriting, which says: "Napoleon can be happy everywhere."

His happiness seems to have lasted no more than 10 months. As the allies gathered at Vienna and bickered among themselves about reshaping Europe, "The Man" escaped and returned to France, where in the famous "Hundred Days" he reawakened popular enthusiasm and raised an army. Only on June 18, 1815, was he finally defeated at the Battle of Waterloo, in Belgium. At one stage in the fighting Napoleon's army came within sight of victory, and afterward he bitterly blamed his marshals for the loss.

This time the allies were taking no chances. He was shipped out to the remote island of St. Helena far off in the south Atlantic, where he lived out the last six years of his life in seclusion.

Putting the Napoleonic Era in Perspective

During the Napoleonic period, Europe underwent a transformation. In France, the confused and often brutal measures of the Revolution and its aftermath gave way to the relative order of the Consulate. Even before the Revolution the middle classes had demonstrated their special role in French society, and the effect of Napoleonic reform was to strengthen their position. Preservation of the land settlement, reform of secondary and higher education, and the establishment of a civil service all played a crucial role in middle-class achievements later in the 19th century.

As Napoleon's power spread throughout continental Europe, it brought to an end the rule of the Old Regime. A system of states that was the product of centuries of development became irrevocably dismantled. The period immediately following his overthrow saw a strongly conservative reaction, but the ideas of individual and national freedom that were released into the mainstream of European thought remained a powerful force in 19th-century politics. Even some of the most reactionary rulers were forced to compromise with the advocates of liberty.

Britain, Napoleon's most bitter enemy, was the only country in Europe to have no firsthand experience of his reforms. Nonetheless the Napoleonic Wars produced major changes in British life as well. During the years of war the country's economy suffered the strains imposed by the Continental System, but industrial production was high, and on the whole hatred and fear of "Old Boney" kept internal divisions within bounds. With the coming of peace, Britain plunged into a period of economic depression. As a consequence of the trade blockade, manufactured goods had piled up unsold. The return home of soldiers from the Peninsular War and other campaigns flooded the market with workers for whom there were no jobs. The social unrest that followed introduced elements of revolutionary struggle into British life and politics.

As for the Russians, the Napoleonic Wars succeeded in introducing them into the mainstream of European events, and they played a decisive role in liberating the Continent. Yet the spirit of revolution had little immediate effect on Russian society. Even Tsar Alexander I, who flirted briefly with liberal notions, soon returned to conservative orthodoxy. The chief memory left by Napoleon's invasion was that of the heroic Russian resistance. Whether in Tolstoy's epic narrative of *War and Peace,* or in the clashing national anthems of Tchaikovsky's *1812 Overture,* future Russians commemorated the victory against Napoleon as one of their country's proudest achievements.

Questions for Further Study

1. What were the main features of Napoleon's administrative and legal reorganization in Europe? How many of them had a permanent effect?
2. What were the chief economic consequences of the Napoleonic Wars? Which European countries were most affected by them?
3. To what extent did Napoleon undermine his own achievements by his miscalculations? What were his principal mistakes?

Suggestions for Further Reading

Applewhite, H.B., and D.G. Levy. *Women and Politics in the Age of the Democratic Revolution.* Ann Arbor, MI, 1990.

Asprey, Robert B. *The Rise of Napoleon Bonaparte.* New York, 2000.

Bergeron, L. *France under Napoleon.* Princeton, NJ, 1981.

Connelly, O. *Napoleon's Satellite Kingdoms.* New York, 1970.

Gates, David. *The Napoleonic Wars, 1803-1815.* New York, 1997.

Godechot, J., B. Hyslop, and D. Dowd. *The Napoleonic Era in Europe.* New York, 1971.

Hesse, Carla. *Publishing and Cultural Politics in Revolutionary Paris, 1789–1810.* Berkeley, CA, 1991.

Holtman, R. *The Napoleonic Revolution.* Baton Rouge, LA, 1979.

Schom, Alan. *Napoleon Bonaparte.* New York, 1997.

Woloch, Isser. *The French Veteran from the Revolution to the Restoration.* Chapel Hill, NC, 1979.

InfoTrac College Edition

Enter the search term *Napoleon* using Key Terms

Enter the search term *Napoleonic Wars* using Key Terms.

RESTORATION AND RESISTANCE IN THE AGE OF METTERNICH

The years following Napoleon's defeat saw conflicting attempts to remodel European politics and society. Conservative statesmen aimed to construct a balance of power that left no single state in a dominant position. At the same time, they tried to restore the social patterns of prerevolutionary life and stamp out the vestiges of revolutionary ideology.

Set against these goals were two important new forces in European political thought: liberalism and nationalism. For liberals, successful government required that an increased portion of those being governed play some part in the process of political decision making. Those who most eagerly took up the liberal cause were those most likely to benefit from it: the middle classes. Many liberals believed that their goals could best be obtained by the creation of self-ruling nation-states to replace the tangled network of principalities, monarchies, and empires typical of pre-Napoleonic Europe. Nationalism thus served the liberal interest; many saw a nationalist revolution as the essential prelude to the formation of a liberal government.

At the Congress of Vienna, the five chief European powers—Austria, Britain, France, Prussia, and Russia—agreed to redistribute territory while paying little heed to the interests of those whose frontiers were being redrawn. The conservative statesmen at Vienna believed that society could be successfully governed only by maintaining the distinctions and privileges that had evolved over time. Their aim was to enforce the agreements they reached by organized intervention. The concept of united action against the forces of revolution is known as the Concert of Europe. Far from strengthening unity, however, the Concert of Europe soon proved discordant.

The political scene in France after Napoleon was shaped by conflict between Louis XVIII's cautiously reforming conservatism and the ultra-right wing. Although the restoration of the Bourbons brought relative peace and prosperity, tension between the two extremes soon began to develop. Louis was succeeded by his arrogant younger brother, who reigned as Charles X until his ultra-royalist policies and political maneuverings forced him into exile in 1830. His replacement, Louis Philippe, avoided the same mistake by increasing the power of the middle class.

In Britain there was no need to restore the old order because it had never been seriously challenged. The number of those eligible to vote was severely limited, and the right was tied to property ownership. Both houses of Parliament were predominantly aristocratic, as were members of the two political parties, the Tories and the Whigs. Popular unrest provoked by the economic depression following the Napoleonic Wars led to demands for parliamentary reform. From 1829 to 1835, Parliament passed a series of reform bills that, while far from radical, marked a significant change.

THE CONGRESS OF VIENNA AND THE SEARCH FOR STABILITY

Against a background of pomp and ceremony, the leaders of the great powers of Europe gathered in Vienna to restore the Continent to what they conceived to be its rightful order.

LEADERS AT THE CONGRESS OF VIENNA

The central figure in the deliberations was Prince Klemens von Metternich (1773–1859), Austrian foreign minister from 1809 to 1848. An urbane aristocrat whose name has become synonymous with cunning intrigue and the manipulation of power, Metternich's aim at the Congress was to return Europe as far as possible to its pre-Napoleonic state, and to prevent any future outbreaks of "the virus of revolution." For decades Metternich's political and social views made him the chief spokesman of European conservatism.

Metternich's only equal as a diplomat was the French representative, Prince Talleyrand, whose years of service to a bewildering variety of masters—the church under the Old Regime, then the various revolutionary governments, and most recently Napoleon—had made him a wily negotiator. Talleyrand was sent to Vienna to secure a deal for France that would not only involve the fewest possible penalties for his former master's misdeeds, but would also restore French influence on the European political scene.

The British spokesman, Lord Castlereagh (1769–1822), was, like the other two, his country's foreign minister. Less occupied with the finer details than his colleagues, Castlereagh's chief concern was to see that the final agreement posed no threat to Britain's position as the leading European power. Although less dominating than Metternich, Castlereagh was probably the most influential member in framing the final decisions of the Congress.

In such professional company the Prussian king, Friedrich Wilhelm III (ruled 1797–1840), played a lesser role. The remaining great power, Russia, was represented by its ruler, Tsar Alexander I. In the early part of his reign, the tsar demonstrated some interest in the ideas of the Enlightenment, but after the defeat of Napoleon he turned to mystical visions of converting his fellow rulers to Christian virtue. By the time of the Congress he was as staunchly conservative as Metternich, but the Austrian, who was more interested in balancing self-interest and expediency, and violently anti-Russian, had little patience with Alexander's grandiose and incoherent notions.

THE RESHAPING OF EUROPE

The guiding principle at Vienna was "legitimacy," the idea that the status of rulers and their borders should revert to that of 1789, before the Revolution. The concept was suggested by Talleyrand for two reasons: it legitimized the return of a Bourbon monarch to France, and it avoided the loss of any French territory as punishment for Napoleon's aggression. Metternich adopted the idea of legitimacy as a means of justifying his reactionary policies, but it was applied selectively. In the case of France, Talleyrand obtained what he wanted, together with the restoration of Bourbon monarchies in Spain and Naples and the kingdom of Piedmont-Sardinia.

The other participants aimed to redraw frontiers in order to compensate France's conquerors, while providing a secure balance of power. Furthermore, Metternich and his colleagues were determined to block any future French attempt at expansion. To that end the Dutch Republic was combined with the Austrian Netherlands (Belgium), to

Colored engraving showing participants in the Congress of Vienna. 1815. The seated figure at the center—who was also central to the decisions made at Vienna—is Prince Metternich. All of the serious discussions and conclusions, which affected the lives of millions of Europeans, took place privately among the chief diplomats. The Congress never met in full session or allowed public attendance.

form the Kingdom of the Netherlands. This arrangement also satisfied the British concern that the vital North Sea ports remain in neutral hands.

In return for their giving up the Netherlands, the Austrians received two provinces in northern Italy, Lombardy and Venetia. Through dynastic connections, Austria played a decisive role in the policies of the restored Grand Duchy of Tuscany and the Kingdom of the Two Sicilies. The strong Austrian presence just to the south of the Alps served as another barrier against French expansion. As for Italy, which had been divided into a series of small kingdoms and duchies and the Papal States, it remained, as Metternich put it, "only a geographical expression."

To block France on the Rhine frontier, Prussia received a chunk of German territory on the river's left bank. Prussia's claim to all of Saxony, however, caused serious disagreement. The tsar agreed to back the Prussians on Saxony if they in turn would support his taking the lion's share of Poland. Both Castlereagh and Metternich objected to the enlargement and strengthening of two of their chief rivals. In consequence, Metternich, Castlereagh, and Talleyrand formed a secret pact, whereby the three powers would go to war rather than see the deal struck. In the end a compromise was worked out: Prussia took about half of Saxony, and Russia was given most of Poland.

Nowhere was the principle of legitimacy less observed than in Germany and central Europe. Napoleon's organization of the numerous states and kingdoms into 39 (37 states, Austria, and Prussia) was retained, and they were brought together into a larger unit called the German Confederation, which thus replaced the Holy Roman Empire. Although an appearance of German political unity was obtained, the confederation had little power, and in any case it was dominated by Austria.

The final agreement, as Metternich intended, left no clear winner, and everyone with something. Britain, which was more interested in trade outside Europe, received territories in South Africa and South America, and Ceylon. The mere description of the decisions of the Congress, which never once met in formal session, emphasizes the element of game playing. In the elegant drawing rooms of the Hapsburg capital, the fates of millions were decided by a handful of aristocratic diplomats, who were profoundly unsympathetic to the dawning hopes of liberals and nationalists.

Yet the achievements of Metternich and his colleagues have more positive aspects. In the first place they negotiated rather than fought, which was a notable improvement after a generation of bloodshed. Second, the temptation to punish France for the excesses of Napoleon was avoided. Finally, the balance worked out at Vienna, for all its defects, provided a relative degree of stability in Europe for the next 100 years. This stability made possible precisely the revolutionary changes that Metternich so feared.

THE RESTORATION AND THE CONSERVATIVE ORDER

Metternich and his fellow conservatives were not merely trying to preserve the past for its own sake: their views reflected a coherent philosophical position, most cogently expressed in the writings of Edmund Burke (1729–1797). His *Reflections on the Revolution in France* (1790), which appeared as early as the Revolution's second year, came to have a significant influence on conservative thought throughout Europe.

An outspoken opponent of the doctrines of the French Revolution, Burke believed that society should evolve slowly, in accordance with existing varieties of rank and status. Radical change, by its very unpredictability, was seen as dangerous. The intellectual movement from which the Revolution had sprung, the Enlightenment, emphasized the power of reason. Conservative thinkers argued just the opposite. Society was far too complex, and susceptible to human emotions and weaknesses, to be organized by any kind of rational scheme—a point of view that had much in common with the Romantic movement in the arts (see Topic 65).

The conservative rulers of the restoration believed in preserving the existing institutions at all costs. If that required censorship, limits to free speech, and the execution of dissenters, those were necessary prices. So rigid an attitude inevitably proved self-defeating. Even in Metternich's Austria, with its spies and police, its border controls and censorship of books and even music, the forces of change were irresistible.

RUSSIA UNDER ALEXANDER AND NICHOLAS

The country whose rulers most thoroughly repressed attempts at reform was Russia. By comparison with western Europe, Russia was still overwhelmingly an agricultural nation, made up of peasants and their aristocratic masters. There were few cities of any size, and thus no urban middle class. The Orthodox church, far from defending the rights of its adherents, reinforced the policies of the tsar. Once Alexander had recovered from his early bout of liberalism, he proved a formidable conservative, both at home and abroad. Censorship was strict, and the universities were carefully watched to crush the growth of any dangerous new ideas.

The only real challenge to authority came when Alexander died in 1825. A group of army officers inspired by Western ideas staged a revolt; they are known as the *Decembrists*, after the month of their attempt. The young liberals had little chance of success because their uprising was poorly organized and soon crushed, but they gave Alexander's successor, Nicholas I (ruled 1825–1855), an excuse to tighten his grip even further; his reign brought the introduction of many conspicuously reactionary measures. He strengthened the army and police, and increased the power of the state bureaucracy. Little was done to improve the lives and working conditions of Russia's vast peasant population, and all of their attempts at rebellion were suppressed.

THE GERMAN CONFEDERATION AND THE HAPSBURGS

The two rival major powers in central Europe, Austria and Prussia, shared a common fear: the rise of German nationalism. Charlemagne's original attempt to unite Germany, the Holy Roman Empire, had long since broken up into more than 300 separate states, and the idea of a united Germany had been impossible for centuries. With Napoleon, however, the separate states were consolidated under French rule in the Confederation of the Rhine, one of the consequences of which was a burst of German nationalism.

Even the archconservative Metternich could hardly propose a return to the multitude of separate states. The creation in its place of the German Confederation was intended to prevent Germany from achieving any real political union by giving Austria, the confederation's permanent president, an edge over Prussia.

THE BURSCHENSCHAFTEN

Signs of nationalist unrest began to occur in Germany during the war against Napoleon. Shortly after 1815, the nationalist mood intensified with the appearance of groups of student activists known as *Burschenschaften* (Brotherhoods) in university circles. In 1817, the 300th anniversary of Luther's publication of his Ninety-Five Theses was celebrated by the Burschenschaften at the Wartburg Festival. The occasion was supposed to be a religious one, but the heady effects of speeches, song, and beer began to take over. To cheers from the crowd, a French officer's staff and a Prussian military text were symbolically burnt.

The Austrian and Prussian authorities anxiously waited for further trouble. Two years later, when a fanatical student murdered a reactionary writer, Metternich seized his opportunity and summoned the rulers of the leading German states to a meeting at Carlsbad. The Carlsbad Decrees of 1819 abolished the Burschenschaften, tightened censorship, and put students and professors suspected of liberal tendencies under careful watch.

PRUSSIA AND THE CUSTOMS UNION

The ruling family of Prussia, the Hohenzollern, shared Metternich's contempt for liberalism. The chief instrument of their power in Prussia was still the army, which, together with the bureaucracy, was in the hands of the landed nobility, the Junkers. Any gesture toward nationalism would have been regarded by these warlords as a betrayal of Prussian virtue, yet ironically it was the Prussians who began to advance German economic unity.

Their motive was commercial self-interest. With the acquisition at the Congress of Vienna of the German territory on the left bank of the Rhine, Prussia consisted of two separate and unconnected parts. In 1819, to help facilitate

Print showing the student demonstrations in favor of a liberal constitution at the Wartburg Festival. 1817. The buildings are those of the university; note the characteristic half-timbered architecture. In the foreground the Prussian police can be seen repressing with some violence a protest that had started out as peaceful.

the movement of trade, Prussia began to negotiate treaties with the neighboring German states, and encouraged them to adopt the Prussian system of unified tariffs. The leading advocate of removing tariff barriers was the German economist Georg Friedrich List (1789–1846), who later became a naturalized U.S. citizen.

By 1834 almost all German governments were members of the Prussian *Zollverein* (customs union); the notable—and predictable—exception was Austria. The formation of the Zollverein proved to be a major step in building a united German nation, and helped Prussia emerge as its eventual leader.

REPRESSION IN THE HAPSBURG EMPIRE

Prussia and the other German states were at least linked by a common language. The fear of nationalism, which obsessed Metternich and his Hapsburg masters, was based on the multilingual and multicultural nature of their state. With the acquisition in 1815 of parts of northern Italy, Italians joined Hungarians, Serbs, Croatians, Slovenians, Czechs, Slovaks, and others under Austrian rule.

The danger of a nationalist uprising took precedence over all other political considerations. Plans for internal reforms included the establishment of local councils of landholders and a decentralization of the bureaucracy, but they foundered on the necessity of maintaining a police state, albeit an extremely inefficient one. Censorship, surveillance by both police and spies, and the close supervision of universities and libraries combined to produce a regime second only to Russia for severity of repression.

THE CONCERT OF EUROPE

Not content with governing their own countries, Europe's conservative leaders felt the duty to go to the help of one another whenever a reactionary regime was challenged: the French Revolution had taught them that an uprising in one state could threaten another. Two of those present at the Congress of Vienna proposed schemes to present a united front against the forces of revolution. Tsar Alexander asked for support for his Holy Alliance, whose members would use Christian principles to govern their states and defend their interests in Christian brotherhood. Most European governments joined, although with little enthusiasm.

Metternich's Concert of Europe seemed a far more formidable affair: a military alliance among Austria, Britain, Prussia, and Russia, which guaranteed to maintain the Vienna agreement for 20 years. This international "force for order" was to meet at regular intervals to survey the situation and strengthen its resolve, as well as intervene to crush revolutions wherever they should occur. Metternich had called the tsar's Holy Alliance a "sonorous nothing"; in the long run the Concert of Europe had little more lasting influence than Alexander's scheme.

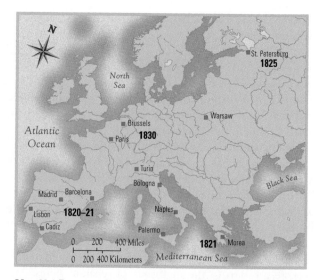

Map 63.1 European Revolutionary Movements, 1820–1830. The Morea, in southern Greece, is better known today as the Peloponnese; it is joined to the rest of Greece (and to Europe) by a narrow strip of land now cut by the Corinth Canal. The region was one of the first to become involved in the struggle for Greek independence.

THE CONSERVATIVE ORDER CHALLENGED: SPAIN AND ITALY

The first signs of trouble appeared in Spain. With the expulsion of the French in 1814, the restoration of Ferdinand VII (ruled 1808, 1814–1833) at first seemed cause for celebration, but it did not take him long, in true Bourbon style, to abandon the constitution and set up all the apparatus of repression. The king had liberal leaders arrested, closed down the universities, revived censorship, and even restored the Inquisition.

Popular resentment came to a head in 1820, when an army that was formed to put down uprisings in the Spanish colonies in America turned on Madrid instead, and forced the king to accept a return to the Spanish Constitution of 1812, a liberal document adopted during the Napoleonic occupation and modeled after the French Constitution of 1791. The reforms did not last long, but news of the successful Spanish revolt had a galvanizing effect on revolutionaries in Italy.

For the Italian states, Napoleonic rule had meant more enlightened rule and fairer taxes. With virtually the whole of Italy now under the Bourbons, the Hapsburgs, or their supporters, the various states slid again into absolutism. Ruthless government repression put down all traces of public protest. In response, Italian nationalists soon began to form secret societies; their members, known as the *Carbonari* (the name means "charcoal burners," and may have been intended to emphasize support for the underprivileged), advocated free and independent Italian states governed by constitutional monarchies.

When word reached Naples in 1820 of the events in Spain, a group of young army officers led a revolt against the hated Neapolitan Bourbon king, Ferdinand I (ruled 1759–1806, 1815–1825). As in the case of their Spanish counterparts, at first the move succeeded, and the king of Naples was forced to introduce a liberal constitution based on the Spanish Constitution of 1812. A similar uprising erupted in Piedmont in 1821, where young Prince Charles Albert (see Topic 66) led the rebels. Here was exactly the kind of situation that Metternich had envisaged. With the agreement of Prussia and Russia, an Austrian army was dispatched to Naples and then to Piedmont. The rebels were crushed; those who did not manage to escape were either executed or thrown into prison. The Spanish liberals' turn was next. This time French troops stamped out the revolt, suppressed the constitution, and restored the Bourbons.

The interventions in Italy and Spain successfully fulfilled Metternich's scheme to oppose change, but they were the last effective antirevolutionary action taken by the Concert. The British, protesting against interfering in other nations' affairs, objected to the French actions, while the Spanish king's bloodthirsty treatment of his liberal opponents horrified the French soldiers: France withdrew from an active role in the alliance. Austria's only remaining dependable allies were Russia and Prussia, and the Concert's next test was too severe even for them.

THE MONROE DOCTRINE

The troops who started the Spanish uprising had been on their way to the Spanish New World colonies to put down rebellions led by, among others, Simón Bolívar (1783–1830). Replacing Ferdinand on his tottering throne did nothing to end the unrest in America, and Metternich decided that the principle of suppressing revolts in Europe should be extended to European possessions abroad. With his encouragement, therefore, Alexander prepared to launch a great fleet to bring the colonies to their senses and return them to Spanish rule.

The British, quite apart from their opposition to interference in another nation's business, had every reason to wish the rebels well: They were causing trouble to Spain, Britain's chief trade rival in America, while providing new markets for the sale of British goods. George Canning (1770–1827), who became foreign minister in 1822, therefore proposed to the United States that a joint British–United States declaration should condemn the involvement of the Holy Alliance—a name in itself offensive to American susceptibilities—in the affairs of the Western Hemisphere.

The Monroe Doctrine, announced by President James Monroe (served 1817–1825) to Congress in December 1823, consisted of a unilateral U.S. statement: Any attempt by European nations to interfere in the Americas would be regarded by the United States as an "unfriendly act." With Britain, still Europe's supreme naval power, supporting the United States' position, Alexander chose to abandon the expedition.

THE GREEK WAR OF INDEPENDENCE

In the case of Spain's American colonies, at least the tsar was sympathetic to Metternich's urgings, if powerless to act.

In a contemporary nationalist uprising on Europe's eastern frontiers, the Greeks' struggle to win independence from their Turkish rulers and found their own state, the Russians found themselves for the first time on the side of the rebels. The Greeks' revolt began in 1821, only to be met by brutal Turkish reprisals. In 1824 the massacre of some 90 percent of the Greek population of the island of Chios shocked many Europeans, who were accustomed to thinking of Greece as the birthplace of European civilization; in addition, leaders of the Romantic movement such as Lord Byron did much to foster sympathy for the Greek cause. The Russians, furthermore, shared the Greeks' Christian Orthodox religion; Russia had been converted to Christianity by two Greek missionaries. To add a practical consideration to the demands of religious brotherhood, if Russia managed to defeat Turkey on behalf of the Greeks, her own position in the Mediterranean would be reinforced by winning control of the straits of the Bosphorus, an aim dating back to the reign of Peter the Great.

In such circumstances the founder of the Holy Alliance could hardly stand by idle. Britain, unwilling to see Russia use the Greeks' cause to gain a power base at the Turks' expense, surrendered its objections to involvement in other people's business; by joining the Russian forces, the British were able to keep a careful eye on their "allies." Against the agonized protests of Metternich, in 1827 Britain, Russia, and France intervened on the side of the Greeks. By 1829 the defeated Turks had no choice but to concede independence to a small mainland Greece. Thus by supreme irony one of the most reactionary members of the Concert of Europe joined with the two powers who had left the original alliance, in support of the very cause the allies had come together to combat in the first place: nationalism. Furthermore, the victory of the Greeks and their supporters violated the principle of legitimacy established at the Congress of Vienna. If the Greek War of Independence did not kill off Metternich's cherished notion entirely, it certainly dealt it a death blow.

FRANCE AND THE POLITICS OF COMPROMISE

Louis XVIII, the Bourbon king restored to the throne of France, was by temperament a political moderate. His brother, Louis XVI, had died on the guillotine, and the so-called Louis XVII, Louis XVI's son and heir, died in prison without ever reigning. Any notion that his return to France might be the signal for popular demonstrations in favor of the Bourbons was soon scotched by the enthusiasm with which Napoleon's escape from Elba was greeted. In any case, Louis, who was almost 60 and too fat and gouty to walk without help, had no wish to be deposed from what he called "the most comfortable of armchairs."

Shortly after occupying that chair, he issued a charter, which laid out the principles by which he intended to rule.

Delacroix, *Liberty Leading the People.* 8 feet 6 inches by 10 feet 8 inches (2.6 by 3.24 m). 1830. Many of Delacroix's other paintings reveal his revolutionary spirit: He campaigned ardently for the cause of Greek independence. This scene represents the Paris Revolution of 1830. Liberty, wearing a scarlet cap of a kind worn by freed slaves in the ancient world, leads a diverse assortment of citizens over the bodies of their fallen comrades.

SIGNIFICANT DATES

The Congress of Vienna and Its Aftermath

1814–1815	The Congress of Vienna meets
1818	First meeting of the Concert of Europe at Aix-la-Chapelle
1819	Peterloo Massacre
1820	Spanish Army revolts against Bourbons
1821	Revolt in Piedmont; Greeks begin struggle for independence
1823	Monroe Doctrine proclaimed
1824	Massacre of Chios; coronation of Charles X of France
1829	Greece becomes independent
1830	Revolution in France and Italy; Belgium becomes independent
1832	Reform Bill passed in Britain

Napoleon's legal system and centralized bureaucracy were to remain in force, along with the Napoleonic tax structure. The country was to be governed by a parliament consisting of two chambers: the Chamber of Peers, made up of the aristocracy, and the Chamber of Deputies, elected by the votes of a tiny wealthy minority. The king could dissolve the Chamber of Deputies, appoint and dismiss his own ministers, and deal directly with foreign countries. Because he was also head of the army, the authority of either chamber of Parliament was, to say the least, limited.

THE ULTRAROYALISTS

Far from using his own concentration of power in the interests of the nobility, Louis fought to oppose the often reactionary demands of the "ultraroyalist" aristocrats who had trickled back into France. Eager to avenge the injuries inflicted on them by the Revolution, they returned to reclaim their lands and privileges. If the aristocrats expected to see their property automatically restored to them by Louis' charter, they were bitterly disappointed. Peasants and middle-class citizens who had bought land from nobles were confirmed in their possession.

Although the aristocracy was enraged by the charter, middle-class liberal reformers were far from completely satisfied. It gave the middle classes little actual political power because political representation was based on land, rather than business wealth, so most of them could neither vote for, nor take part in, the two chambers of Parliament. Nonetheless Louis, steering a moderate course between "ultras" and reformers, maintained a precarious peace.

Among the more autocratic leaders of the rebellious nobles was the king's younger brother and eventual successor, the count of Artois (ruled 1824–1830). While he was alive, Louis managed to keep his brother under control, and tried to persuade him of the need for moderation if the Bourbon family was to remain in power. In 1824 Louis died, and the new king, Charles X, did not take long to demonstrate the truth of the saying that "the Bourbons learnt nothing and forgot nothing" from the Revolution. Charles's coronation at Reims became the excuse for an ornate ceremony in medieval style, to symbolize his intention to return to past glories.

THE REVOLUTION OF 1830

Within a few years Charles had so alienated vast sections of public opinion that in the spring of 1830 even the chamber turned against him. The king dismissed it and called new elections. Despite press censorship and official pressures, another liberal majority was returned. In July 1830 Charles again dissolved the chamber and produced an electoral system that would guarantee him a majority: only some 25,000 people—the richest men in France—could vote. All freedom of the press was suspended.

The result was revolution. In the July uprisings, the workers and students of Paris blocked the streets with barricades. Among the first groups were workers in the printing trade. With the army unwilling to fire on the crowds, and in the absence of any firm political support, the last Bourbon king of France abdicated and took off to England, where he died, unmourned, in exile.

The revolutionaries had fought to bring back a republic, but France's political and business leaders were more cautious. Remembering the excesses of the Revolution of 1789, they decided to avoid the extremes of absolute monarchy and popular republic by creating a constitutional monarchy. In this way they hoped to achieve stability and at the same time maintain their own influence. The same sense of compromise governed their choice for the new king. The duke of Orléans was an aristocrat, the descendant

A print showing the outbreak of revolution in Paris. 1830. The scene is at the Pont Neuf (one of the bridges that cross the river Seine in the heart of Paris). Soldiers armed with bayonets and rifles are pitted against a mob of demonstrators who are, for the most part, unarmed. Tensions on both sides had been heightened by the unusually hot summer weather (the riots occurred at the end of July).

of a cousin of Louis XVI who had served on the convention and voted for Louis' execution in 1793. The duke thus had both noble and appropriately revolutionary family credentials, and had lived an unexceptionable middle-class life. After promising to honor the Constitution of 1814, he was duly crowned as Louis Philippe (ruled 1830–1848).

The Revolution of 1830, fought by workers, students, and artisans, abolished the absolute power of the king, but its chief beneficiaries were the middle-class property owners, who now controlled the legislature.

CONSERVATISM CHALLENGED: POLITICAL UNREST AND CONSTITUTIONALISM IN BRITAIN

The tumultuous events that swept continental Europe in the early 19th century reinforced the innate conservatism of British politicians. The Tory party, Britain's conservatives, had held virtually uninterrupted power since the 1780s and guided their country to victory over Napoleon. Their parliamentary opponents, the Whigs, shared the Tories' aristocratic background. Whatever differences there might be on niceties of policy, neither party had any interest in a wider sharing of power or in a more equitable distribution of property.

The country was governed by two houses of Parliament, the Lords and the Commons. Members of both houses, virtually always landed aristocrats, were elected by a tiny minority of around 5 percent of the adult male population, themselves property owners. The counties and boroughs that these members represented were traditional aristocratic strongholds; the growing industrial centers of central and northern England sent no members to Parliament.

THE PETERLOO MASSACRE

In the aftermath of Waterloo and the economic depression that beset Britain, popular unrest began to mount. The misery of living and working conditions in northern cities such as Manchester, together with the fear of unemployment, inspired radical leaders to press for wider parliamentary representation The violence of government reaction proved its own undoing, however. In 1819 a crowd of some 60,000 gathered in St. Peter's Fields, in the center of Manchester, to attend a political demonstration in favor of reform. Troops of the Manchester and Cheshire Cavalry fired on the assembly, killing 11 people and wounding more than 400. Radical leaders and critics in the press, in reference to the decisive Battle of Waterloo, dubbed the event the "Peterloo Massacre," and its victims became the first martyrs of the struggle for reform.

The Peterloo Massacre proved significant in another respect: more than one-quarter of those injured were women, demonstrating alongside men for political change. By the second decade of the 19th century, the development of industry had begun to change the part that gender played in the division of labor. Machines provided their own energy and required no special strength on the part of their users; they could be operated by women or men. The growing cities provided a greater range of employment for women, which often led to their exploitation.

PRESSURE FOR REFORM

In Parliament, the demand for social and political reform fell on deaf ears. The Six Acts of 1819, passed in the year of Peterloo, limited the right of public assembly, censored literature, and imposed a tax on newspapers. So extreme a response alarmed many moderate Tories, whose general inclination was to aim for compromise. Some feared that government stubbornness could lead to revolution, whereas others were genuinely interested in social reform. Under pressure from George Canning, Robert Peel, and other moderates, the criminal code was reformed, and workers were allowed to form unions, although not to strike. The tariffs on cheap imported grain, controlled by the Corn Laws—which had raised the tax after the Napoleonic Wars—were reduced; these taxes, which protected English landowners while keeping the price of bread high, had long been a source of popular resentment.

Reform of Parliament was a different matter. No Tory majority backed by the Anglican Church and the aristocracy would agree to revising the conditions of parliamentary representation. Many members of Parliament were either directly appointed by wealthy landowners or were elected by "rotten" or "pocket" boroughs—districts where electors were bullied and bribed to vote for the candidate of their landlord's choice; thus the election was in the "pocket" of the landowner. In the case of the "rotten" boroughs, members represented districts that were virtually unpopulated or had actually been abandoned.

It fell to the Whigs, with the support of the rising manufacturing and trading classes, to lead the cause of reform. They were inspired not by democratic principles but by the pragmatic belief that change would be "in the interests of the realm"; this characteristically British formula was bolstered in many cases by the ideas of utilitarian thinkers such as Jeremy Bentham (see Topic 66). Furthermore, they hoped that middle-class members of Parliament would represent both middle- and working-class interests. In this way the workers would be satisfied and make no further protests, and a revolution could be avoided.

In 1830 an alliance of the Whigs and reform-minded liberals succeeded in defeating the Tories and forming a government. (Toward the end of the 19th century, the Whig party changed its name to the Liberal party.) The Whig prime minister, Earl Charles Grey (1764–1845), hastily forced through Parliament the Reform Bill of 1832.

Although the bill was to have momentous importance for British democratic life, it was intended to preserve the existing situation as far as possible. The vote was extended, but only on the basis of property; about 400,000 new electors were added to the voting rolls. Electoral districts were redistributed: the "rotten" boroughs were abolished and their seats given to the industrial cities of the north. No attempt was made, however, to create an equal balance between population size and political representation. As in France under Louis Philippe, the chief victors in 1830s Britain were the industrial middle classes, and their accession to a share in power promoted a whole series of social reforms. Liberal legislation reorganized the church, reformed the divorce laws, and introduced the Poor Law of 1834. In 1833, on behalf of a reform society, a private member of Parliament successfully introduced a bill abolishing slavery throughout the British Empire.

In the years between then and 1847, the criminal code was further reformed, reducing the number of capital offenses to three; 20 years earlier there had been hundreds of crimes for which those found guilty had been executed. Working conditions for women and children were improved. Government grants were awarded to schools. In 1846, a Tory administration finally repealed the hated Corn Laws. The British had achieved the beginnings of revolutionary change without a revolution.

Putting the Age of Metternich in Perspective

The years following Waterloo saw the apparent triumph of conservatism throughout most of Europe. The decisions of the Congress of Vienna and the subsequent formation of the Concert of Europe seemed to doom the liberal and nationalist causes to defeat right from the start. Effective power either remained in aristocratic hands, as in Prussia and Austria, or was returned there, as in France, Spain, and the kingdoms of Italy.

Yet, with the single exception of Russia, liberalism and nationalism were to have a profound effect on virtually every country in Europe, including Britain. Even where its manifestations were repressed, as in the Hapsburg empire, the demand for reform built to an irrepressible force. Further attempts to produce changes a generation after the Congress of Vienna led to violent action. In Britain, by contrast, political compromise led to a gradual process of reform that proved a continuous one.

In many cases one of the chief factors was economic. The growing demands of the rising industrial class in France proved fatal to the rule of Charles X, although his own misjudgments helped hasten his fall. Prussia's plans for economic expansion led to the formation of a customs union that in turn prepared the way for a united Germany.

In some countries the repression of nationalist uprisings inspired the forces of protest. The struggle to form a united Italy, known as the *Risorgimento,* had its roots in the Carbonari movement, born in opposition to Bourbon rule. The Greeks actually managed to achieve their freedom from the Turks, largely because the great powers—for selfish reasons of their own—decided to intervene.

Thus a battle that seemed definitively won in 1815 continued to rage at one level or another over the following decades. It says much for the persistence of the liberals and nationalists that so much progress was made so quickly. On the other hand, the conservatives were determined and stubborn opponents: When the next round of protests came, in 1848, it led to violent revolution.

Questions for Further Study

1. How successful was the Concert of Europe in maintaining conservative policies in European affairs?
2. What role did Russia play in European politics following the Congress of Vienna? To what extent was this role influenced by internal Russian developments?
3. What were the main stages of the Greek struggle for independence, and why was it successful?

Suggestions for Further Reading

Billinger, Robert. *Metternich and the German Question: States' Rights and Federal Duties 1820-1834.* Washington, DC, 1991.

Blakemore, Steven. *Burke and the French Revolution.* Athens, GA, 1992.

Carr, R. *Spain, 1808–1939.* Oxford, 1982.

Chapman, Tim. *The Congress of Vienna: Origins, Processes and Results.* New York, 1998.

Church, C. *Europe in 1830: Revolution and Political Change.* London, 1983.

Dakin, D. *The Greek Struggle for Independence, 1821–1833.* Berkeley, CA, 1973.

Dwyer, Philip G. (Compiler). *Charles-Maurice de Talleyrand 1754-1838.* Westport, CT, 1996.

Gildea, Robert. *Barricades and Borders, Europe 1800–1914.* Oxford, 1987.

Kroen, Sheryl. *Politics and Theater: The Crisis of Legitimacy in Restoration France, 1815-1830.* Berkeley, CA, 2000.

Matthews, Andrew. *Revolution and Reaction: Europe 1789-1849.* New York, 2001.

Seward, Desmond. *Metternich: The First European.* New York, 1991.

Talmon, J.L. *Romanticism and Revolt.* New York, 1979.

InfoTrac College Edition

Enter the search term *Metternich* using Key Terms.

THE NEW SOCIAL ORDER: WORKERS, WOMEN, AND THE MIDDLE CLASS

In the mid-18th century, Europe was still an overwhelmingly rural society. Life for most people centered around traditional values associated with labor in the fields, the family, and the church. The authority of the nobility on their lands and over the peasants was largely unquestioned. The extended family, with several generations of relatives living and working together, prevailed. In agrarian families, women remained subservient to males, their roles limited to childbearing and rearing, to household duties, and to occasional participation in fieldwork and home-based textile making. Peasants, nobles, and clergy were the major social categories, while the merchant capitalist class and those who lived in towns represented a small percentage of the population.

One hundred years later, much of that traditional way of life had changed. The development of technology and factory-based manufacturing pushed Europe increasingly toward an urban, industrial civilization. The structure of society grew more complex as two new groups—industrial workers and the middle class—joined the social order in ever-larger numbers, creating the modern class structure. As rural dwellers migrated to the cities in search of work, traditional values and family bonds began to break down, replaced by the urban nuclear family of parents and children. The status and role of women in this emerging industrial society also assumed new dimensions as tens of thousands of them left home for work in the factories.

By the middle of the 19th century, the general contours of European society as we know it today were formed. The years from 1789 to 1850 represented, then, a period of social transition, marked by great mobility and flux, and accompanied by growing political instability.

EUROPEAN SOCIETY IN TRANSITION

Although advanced industrialization brought many changes to Europe, it also intensified some earlier social and demographic trends. Moreover, as the French Revolution had shown, the political aspirations of different social groups could lead to violence. Now, however, the new emerging social classes began to struggle over competing economic interests. The political struggles of the period after 1789 were largely the result of growing class consciousness among both industrial workers and the middle class. In addition, while urban life had always presented governments with special challenges in public policy, the dramatic growth in the size and number of cities in the 19th century raised new dilemmas of planning and infrastructure and presented problems of enormous dimension in areas such as health, housing, transportation, and social control.

POPULATION PATTERNS IN THE AGE OF INDUSTRIALIZATION

During the 18th century, Europe began to experience a tremendous growth in population. As industrialization spread, numbers continued to increase, although not at a uniform or regular rate. The population of Europe grew by 40 percent between 1800 and 1850, from about 190 million to some 265 million. On the Continent (excluding Russia) the sharpest population rise occurred in the periods 1800–1820 (14 percent) and 1820–1830 (11 percent).

The agricultural revolution had enlarged the food supply in England, and during the 1820s and 1830s improved farming methods were gradually adopted on the Continent. Crop failures were less frequent, but when they did occur, as in the Irish potato famine of the 1840s, they still caused widespread distress. A lower incidence of disease and improvements in diet slowly helped raise the average life expectancy. Nevertheless, the basic staple of most diets, which for most people were extremely limited and unbalanced, consisted of bread, grains, or potato. In the town of Ghent, for example, an average of 2,435 calories per day were consumed by each citizen, but 80 percent of that total—1,479 from cereals and potatoes and 428 from beer—came from cereal carbohydrates.

Earlier marriage patterns and lower annual death rates slowly altered the general demographic profile of 19th-century Europe. Initially, younger age groups increased at a faster rate than the rest of the population, but during the second half of the century medical advances allowed older people to live longer. Moreover, the peasantry and working class tended to have more children than those higher up in the social hierarchy.

Population growth and higher living standards expanded the market for manufactured goods and provided a labor supply for the factories. The combination of economic factors and political conditions in the 19th century produced massive shifts in Europe's population. Initially, factories in cities drew much of their labor from the urban poor, but increasingly after 1815 the cities attracted rural workers,

especially the young. The volume of migration from villages to cities intensified as people flocked to the factories to take advantage of higher salaries and new opportunities. Typically the migrant was a male between the ages of 15 and 30, although women also moved.

The numbers of people moving from country to city during the 19th century ran into the tens of millions. In addition to the permanent migration to urban areas, seasonal migration in agriculture was also common in many European countries, and it has been estimated that some 900,000 seasonal migrants were in France in 1852 alone. Migration between countries was more difficult, although in 19th-century Europe only Turkey and Russia had passport regulations. Nearly 400,000 foreign workers were employed in France at midcentury. Poverty and political repression also drove an estimated 50 million Europeans abroad during

Table 64.1	The Growth of European Cities, 1800–1850 (in 1000s)	
CITY	1800	1850
Barcelona	115	175
Belfast	37	103
Berlin	172	419
Birmingham	74	233
Bordeaux	91	131
Bristol	64	137
Brussels	66	251
Budapest	54	178
Cologne	50	97
Cracow	24	50
Dresden	60	97
Edinburgh	83	202
Glasgow	77	357
Kiev	23	50
Leeds	53	721
Leipzig	30	63
Liverpool	80	376
London	1,117	2,685
Lyon	110	177
Madrid	160	281
Manchester	90	303
Marseilles	111	194
Milan	135	242
Moscow	250	365
Munich	40	110
Naples	427	449
Paris	547	1,053
Rotterdam	53	90
Sheffield	31	135
St. Petersburg	220	485
Stuttgart	18	47
Vienna	247	444

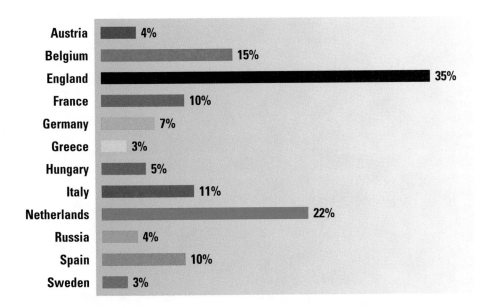

Graph 64.1
The Urban Population of Europe in 1850 (Percentage of people living in cities of 20,000 or more)

Austria 4%
Belgium 15%
England 35%
France 10%
Germany 7%
Greece 3%
Hungary 5%
Italy 11%
Netherlands 22%
Russia 4%
Spain 10%
Sweden 3%

the 19th century, many of them emigrating to the United States and Latin America.

THE RISE OF THE CITY

The most far-reaching population change in 19th-century Europe was the dramatic rise in the number and size of its cities. By 1850, many rural districts in England and the Continent were sparsely populated as millions moved to industrial towns and cities. Industrialization, together with the expansion of financial enterprises and government, spawned an urban revolution of unprecedented dimensions.

At the opening of the 19th century, London alone among European cities had a population of more than a million. Paris, the second largest city, had half that number, while only five other cities could boast 200,000 or more. Within half a century, however, London had reached 2.6 million, Paris more than 1 million, and some 30 additional cities had in excess of 200,000 inhabitants. Most urban centers had at least doubled—and many trebled—in population. Glasgow, Leeds, Liverpool, and other British manufacturing cities experienced massive growth, while on the Continent, Berlin, Brussels, Budapest, and Munich saw increases almost as startling.

Despite the rapid urbanization pattern, however, Europe remained a predominantly rural or small-town society throughout the 19th century. One estimate classified 14.5 percent of Europe's population as urban in 1800 (counting cities of 5,000 or more), a figure that rose to only 22.3 percent by 1850. England, Europe's industrial leader, had the most highly urbanized population: in 1850, 35 percent of its people lived in cities, whereas in that same year only 10 percent of the French and 7 percent of the German population fell into the urban category (counting cities of 20,000 or more). Even as late as 1910, only 43 percent of Europe's population was urban.

Nevertheless, the industrial cities defined the character of European civilization and its new social hierarchy. The huge concentration of people in these burgeoning centers created unprecedented dilemmas for their inhabitants. Some of the new industrial cities had mushroomed rapidly without planning from hardly more than small towns, whereas others had grown from already sizable foundations. In all cases, local and national administrations were unprepared to deal with the seemingly insurmountable array of problems confronting them. Public transportation was nonexistent during the first half of the century, so that workers had to live close to the factories. In older towns, workers crowded into inadequate housing in conditions of extreme congestion—in Paris, the number of people living in an average house rose from 21.9 in 1800 to 35.2 in 1851. Entire families lived in one or two tiny rooms, often in cellars or attics, most without heat, toilet facilities, or water. New working-class housing, thrown up in the form of cheaply constructed, densely packed tenements, was little better.

Sulfurous fumes from the burning of cheap coal and factories hung over the narrow alleys, while soot, garbage, and human excrement often filled the streets. Public water supplies were limited and generally unsafe. In the 1850s, only one in five houses in Paris had its own water, and most people in Berlin still used public fountains. Sewers, when they existed at all, were often merely open drains that emptied into the nearest river. In Britain, the first Public Health Act was passed only in 1875, while in France it was not until 1894 that sewage systems were required in all towns. The failure to separate the water supply from the sewage disposal caused periodic outbreaks of epidemic. Ancient Rome of the 1st century A.D. had a cleaner water supply than most European cities in the 19th century.

Such conditions presented serious health hazards in the form of infectious diseases, especially for the urban poor. Cholera and typhoid, which are carried by polluted water, and typhus, which is spread by lice, were common. In Western Europe alone, tens of thousands of people were killed by a cholera epidemic in 1831 to 1832. For the poor—

Engraving of Manchester, England. Mid-19th century. One of the chief manufacturing towns of Northern England, Manchester was notorious for its slums and pollution. The factories—the largest is on the right—have huge chimneys that belch their smoke and grime over the workers' housing estate in the center (the tightly packed rows of narrow houses).

the bulk of the population—the quality of urban life was generally worse than in the countryside during the first half of the century. The mortality rate was higher and the birthrate lower in the cities, and within large cities such as Paris or London death rates were higher in working-class areas than in fashionable districts. Reform movements to deal with issues such as health and urban welfare began in England in the 1830s (see Topic 71), and efforts to improve the infrastructure of the cities spread through the Continent in the 1840s and 1850s. Not until the end of the 19th cen-

tury, however, did conditions in most of Europe's cities begin to approach modern standards.

THE EMERGENCE OF CLASS STRUCTURE

In 1844, the young German Friedrich Engels (1820–1895)—who later became a close friend and collaborator of Karl Marx—wrote a now-classic book, *The Condition of the Working Class in England*. In this study of the laboring people, Engels explained how the Industrial Revolution had created both a "middle class" and "an integral, permanent class," the

Print by Boisieu showing peasants begging. Early 19th century. If life in the cities was grim for industrial workers, the transfer of most able-bodied men and women to the urban centers in search of a better life left the countryside abandoned to neglect. As this image shows, the only inhabitants left to try to scratch a living from the earth were children who were too young to work and the elderly.

"proletariat," or working class. The first he defined as the "possessing" or property-owning class (distinguishing, however, between them and the old landowning aristocracy) and the second as the "propertyless" class.

At the time Engels wrote, the term *class* had only recently come into use to describe the new social categories produced by industrialization. Before the Revolution of 1789, European society had been based on legally defined status groups known technically as "orders," membership in which was determined by birth and legal privilege. The social hierarchy of the Old Regime was a pyramid, with a series of wide levels stretching from the poor and the peasantry at the bottom to the apex of princes and king at the top, all linked by ties of authority and obligation.

By the beginning of the 19th century, social classes were increasingly identified by income and occupation. Less tangible indicators, such as aspirations and values, were also important factors in determining one's class, but wealth or property, and how a person earned a living, became the chief measure of status. Class identification along these lines was, however, neither absolute nor clear-cut, and the transition from the old hierarchy to the new structure evolved throughout the century.

Titles of nobility and access to the royal court at first kept the old aristocracy at arm's length from the rising business magnates. Yet by the end of the 18th century, impoverished nobles and the wealthiest industrialists began to see mutual advantages in arranging marriages between their families, a trend that accelerated in the next century. Monarchs often bestowed titles on businessmen and received them at court, while some more enterprising nobles made the transition from living off land rents to capitalist agriculture and investment in industry. In the same way, successful artisans and skilled laborers began to accumulate sufficient resources and property, and move up into the ranks of the middle classes. Thus the new class structure revealed an unprecedented degree of mobility. Yet, although the pyramid of the Old Regime no longer existed, a different urban social hierarchy emerged in which the new distinctions of income and wealth between categories were at least as sharp.

THE CONDITION OF THE WORKING CLASS

As Engels recognized, the European working population consisted not only of factory employees, but represented a much broader category that also included artisans, domestic

The Marble Hall, Kedleston Hall, Derbyshire, England. 1775–1790. The architect, Robert Adam, created a light, airy version of Neo-Classicism, based on his studies in Italy. This grand hall, with the two "antique" statues flanking the rear door, might have come from one of Adam's important London commissions. In fact, however, he built it for a relatively modest country house in Northern England—an indication of the prosperity of the English landed gentry and aristocracy.

servants, cottage industry workers, and agricultural laborers. The complexities of social change created by the Industrial Revolution increased or further defined differences in status, income, and attitude within the worker hierarchy. All working-class persons, however, were linked by the factor of dependency—that is, they depended on others for employment, for the kind of work they did, and for the conditions under which they labored. Beyond this common denominator, the differences among them reflected the degree and nature of their skills.

THE WORKING-CLASS HIERARCHY

As a whole, the working class constituted some 80 percent of Europe's urban population at midcentury (more than 90 percent if rural laborers and peasants are included). Industrial workers accounted for a small portion of that number, and only after 1850 did factory workers begin to dominate the production system. In France, which was at that point much less industrialized than England, 27 percent of the labor force was in industry, but factory workers were less than 5 percent. Moreover, industrial workers were unevenly distributed; they formed most of the population of new industrial towns such as Manchester or Birmingham but represented only a small portion of the inhabitants of older, large cities like London.

The number of factory workers was relatively small in the early 19th century, but they were the fastest growing urban class. In the first stages of industrialization, most factory laborers came from rural areas; they went to the factories with great reluctance and kept their ties to the countryside. Among the first generation of industrial workers, as many as 25 percent went back to their rural areas in the summer to harvest crops.

Skilled factory labor was generally scarce in the first half of the century, so that industrial pay was higher than rural wages. Even among industrial workers, however, differences were clearly delineated, often according to the level of skill commanded. Unskilled workers, by far the largest group, earned too little to maintain the average working-class family of father, mother, and three children. This situation accounts for the presence of large numbers of women and children in the labor force, both in the factories and as servants. Domestic servants made up an increasingly large portion of the working population. Among the unskilled were manual laborers such as ditch diggers and construction helpers, teamsters, dock workers, and factory employees assigned the simplest tasks.

Women and children were a strong presence in the lower ranks of the workforce, especially in the textile industry. Women constituted between 40 and 50 percent of all workers in cotton mills and children from 15 to 25 percent. Perhaps as many as one-third of all teenage girls in England were domestic servants. Because employers knew that most, although by no means all, women and children worked to supplement family income, they were paid the lowest wages in the workforce. Women earned half as much as men in the same jobs, and children half as much as women.

Higher up in the social hierarchy were semiskilled workers, who earned an average of 1.5 times the lowest rates, including tradesmen such as carpenters (as opposed to cabinetmakers), plumbers, and brick masons. As machinery came into wider use in the factories, the number of semiskilled industrial workers increased.

Skilled workers were the elite, representing only some 15 percent of the labor force. Their pay was at least twice that of the unskilled category, and some—such as expert machinists and iron puddlers—earned as much as five times the lowest rates. A few skilled workers eventually made their way into the lowest rung of management as foremen. Technological developments expanded the number of skilled workers as the need grew for machine toolmakers, railroad engineers, and other specialists.

ARTISANS UNDER STRESS

The artisans engaged in highly skilled crafts—jewelers and goldsmiths, glassblowers, cabinet and instrument makers, bookbinders and printers—were the "aristocracy" of the skilled workers. Strong traditions of group identity and quality craftsmanship bound them together. Through their guilds, which were centuries old, artisans had established work standards, pay scales, and conditions of employment in small workshops. Industrialization adversely affected artisans, who outnumbered factory workers in the first half of the 19th century, even in countries such as Britain, France, and Prussia. They were, however, widely distributed in large European cities such as London, Paris, and Vienna, where the demand for high-quality luxury goods actually grew as middle-class wealth expanded.

At first, factory production hurt specialty textile manufacturing, such as the finishing of wool cloth or lace making, and artisans in the cottage industry were most severely displaced by the new mechanical inventions in weaving. By midcentury mechanization and the factory system threatened to make the skills of artisans virtually obsolete. As a result, the guilds tried to tighten their control over the craft trades and to make advancement more difficult, but new laws and capitalist economic policy often made this impossible. The revolutionary government in France had abolished the guilds in 1791, and in Britain the guilds disappeared gradually in the 1830s. By 1850, they were eliminated in many of the German and Italian states as well as in the Low Countries and Spain.

As a group, artisans felt distinct from factory workers and the middle class. Industrial laborers increased three or four times as rapidly as artisans, but direct contact between the two categories was limited. Artisans inhabited long-established residential sections in cities, and their sense of dignity and higher status led them to regard ordinary workers as beneath them. Clinging resolutely to their traditional ways of life and work methods as the factory system spread, they tried to maintain tight family unity—artisan wives, for example, did not generally work in factories—and to limit the number of children they had in order to sustain their living standards. In addition, artisans tended to take great interest in education and self-improvement and had disciplined savings habits.

THE STANDARD OF LIVING

When he visited the English manufacturing towns in the 1840s, Engels came away with a devastating impression of the condition of the working class:

> Thus the working class of the great cities offers a graduated scale of conditions of life, in the best cases a temporarily endurable existence for hard work and good wages, good and endurable, that is, from the worker's standpoint; in the worst cases, bitter want, reaching even homelessness and death by starvation.

Throughout the 19th century, wages stayed ahead of the rise in the cost of living, except during periods of economic slump. This was especially true in England, where per capita real income doubled. Wages also rose on the Continent as industrialization spread after 1850. By comparison with the countryside, real wages in the cities were higher. Even Engels, who believed that working-class conditions would steadily deteriorate, admitted that the situation was complex and that his examples stressed the worst cases.

On the other hand, unskilled workers outside the factory system and cottage industry laborers suffered seriously from the dislocations. The housing conditions for factory workers that Engels described in the British cities were indeed miserable, and the mortality rate rose among urban workers. Food consumption was hardly above subsistence for most urban workers, although they had better diets than peasants. The high consumption of alcohol among workers, which was regarded as a serious problem by contemporary social observers, reflected the stress of daily life and the limited opportunities for leisure-time activities. In working-class families, wives and children usually worked to buy basic necessities rather than luxuries. Moreover, the uncertainty of employment was a constant source of demoralization. Chronic poverty remained widespread, affecting as much as 10 percent of the population of Britain.

Living standards among artisans were equally complex. Those with skills in demand earned high wages and increased their real income, whereas many less fortunate craftsmen who faced factory competition experienced declining pay and rising work hours. Wages for most artisans were higher than for most workers, and they generally enjoyed more material comfort. Yet the position of artisans was especially vulnerable in times of economic hardship, when the demand for their high-quality products collapsed more quickly than that for basic necessities.

THE COMFORTABLE BOURGEOISIE

The middle class was as complex and varied as the other social groups, perhaps more so, and during the first half of the 19th century it underwent considerable growth and change.

The category was so broad as to include at the top those whose wealth rivaled that of the old nobility, and at the bottom those whose income was scarcely higher than that of the best-paid skilled worker. In fact, the wide range of economic status found within this social category suggests a range of middle classes rather than just one.

Certain general characteristics, however, help define the middle classes as a social unit. By midcentury, they made up perhaps 20 percent of the urban population of Europe, although the figure was lower in eastern and southern Europe, where industry and commerce were less advanced. Their numbers grew steadily along with industrial and economic development, as did their wealth. Most, although not all, owned some form of property. Their income afforded them a degree of comfort that was unattainable by the working classes.

The middle classes were the most mobile sector within the new urban social hierarchy. By midcentury, most members of the group had risen above their origins, and they regarded themselves as distinct from both the working classes and the titled nobility. Wealth and new status led the middle classes to demand participation in government alongside the aristocracy; the leaders of most political revolutions in Europe between 1789 and 1848 were from the middle classes.

THE STRUCTURE OF THE MIDDLE CLASSES

During the first phase of the Industrial Revolution, most entrepreneurs came from relatively modest backgrounds: small businessmen, engineers, and artisans with their own shops. Three distinct segments are discernible among the middle classes. The upper level, consisting of large-scale industrialists, bankers, and merchants, was the smallest but wealthiest sector, making up less than 5 percent of the middle class. Together with the aristocracy, this group earned one-third of all income. As a result, the upper middle class was able to enjoy a sumptuous existence, with private mansions in exclusive areas of the city and villas in the country, a retinue of servants, and luxuries that imitated the lifestyle of the aristocracy.

The middle range of the bourgeoisie consisted of small manufacturers, moderate-sized merchants, and businessmen, as well as professionals. This group usually lived either in rented apartments in genteel urban neighborhoods or owned their own homes in newer sections of the cities. The professionals included lawyers, physicians, and university professors, and a rapidly growing number of accountants, engineers, and chemists. Although most lawyers and physicians had adequate but not spectacular incomes and little property, they had more advanced education than other middle-class groups. The professionals also stood apart from the business elements because of their involvement in political and social reform. From this same segment came most of Europe's intellectuals and artists, who often rebelled against the social conventions and material values of their class.

The largest and fastest growing element within the bourgeoisie was the lower-middle class, consisting mainly of small shopkeepers and the relatively new white-collar workers, especially civil servants such as teachers, postal clerks, and secretaries. This group accounted for approximately half of the entire middle-class population. Their income was considerably less than the two higher bourgeois strata, and they owned little or no property. Nevertheless, they lived modestly but comfortably in decent apartments, managed to save money, and gave their children elementary educations.

Much of the wealth generated by industrial and economic growth—almost one-half of all income—went to the middle classes. That wealth was unevenly distributed among the three levels of the bourgeois class. In England, for example, the savings of taxpayers in the highest income bracket increased fourfold between 1800 and 1850, while those of the lower-middle class grew much more slowly. For manufacturers, the need for capital investment and rising pay scales for workers were offset by steadily falling production costs. For the shopkeepers, cheaper goods and the expanding purchasing power of all classes meant more customers. In the complex social environment of the cities, the lives of the middle classes contrasted vividly with those of the working class.

HOW THE MIDDLE CLASSES LIVED

The bourgeoisie lived comfortably. The homes of the lower and middle classes, whether owned or rented, were furnished with solid, sensible furniture that conveyed a cozy, respectable well-being. In Austria and Germany before 1850, the popular style of middle-class furniture was known as *Biedermeier*, constructed of sturdy, light-colored woods with simple, clean lines. In England, darker, carved pieces of what was later called Victorian furniture were to be found in bourgeois homes, while in France after midcentury the so-called Empire style—a heavier, less elegant variation of the neoclassical style favored during Napoleon's reign—prevailed. Success was partially measured by a family's number of servants and by the elaborate dinner parties that were provided for guests. The middle classes ate well, and in fact virtually half of all their income was spent on food and servants.

The lower ranks of the middle classes generally prized education, not as an end in itself but as a means of preparing children for adult responsibilities. Two standards of education, which were determined by gender, prevailed. Boys were taught practical subjects such as mathematics and accounting or technical skills, whereas training for girls was usually limited to music, poetry, sewing, and household management. This educational hierarchy, in turn, reflected the bourgeois separation of the outside male world of work from the protected sphere of domestic life that was thought to be the proper sphere of women. For most of the century, classical education in universities was largely the preserve of the sons of the wealthiest families and the aristocracy.

The middle classes centered their lives principally around work and the family. Hard work was thought to be the moral responsibility of every person, regardless of rank or status. The middle-class ethic held that those with the requisite energy and drive could succeed and prosper, while the poor had only

Painting showing a French middle-class family at home. Mid-19th century. Note the relative segregation of the sexes. The women talk to one another or to the child standing center-left. The three men on the right seem to occupy a separate space where "serious" matters are discussed as they peruse what is probably a newspaper.

themselves to blame for their plight. This attitude was partly a product of Enlightenment thought and the French Revolution, both of which had encouraged the notion that advancement depended on talent and ability rather than on birth or privilege. Habits of self-discipline and work were instilled in children from an early age because it was believed that these traits built character and would help develop strong and responsible adults. The work ethic reinforced the middle-class belief in *laissez-faire* economics and the spirit of free competition. Thrift, and the importance and sanctity of private property, which all classes were encouraged to accumulate, were also central to the bourgeois worldview. Such attitudes contributed to the cult of material and spiritual progress that became a hallmark of middle-class thinking.

WOMEN IN A REVOLUTIONARY AGE

During the first half of the 19th century, the two major developments of the period—the French Revolution and the Industrial Revolution—deeply affected the status and role of women in European society.

WOMEN, LAW, AND GOVERNMENT

The early revolutionary governments of France had legislated some basic legal rights for women in such matters as marriage, consensual age, divorce, and inheritance. These advances did not, however, survive the republican experience because the Napoleonic Code of 1804 reestablished a patriarchal society, giving power to males in family matters. A married woman had to assume her husband's nationality, could not take part in court proceedings or sue for paternity rights or support, and—unlike the husband—could be punished for adultery. Women were denied not only legal identity as independent human beings but also those very "rights" of citizenship that the Revolution of 1789 had proclaimed so loudly.

Property laws further marginalized women in ways that were important to the new middle-class ideology of wealth. The Napoleonic Code allowed women to have virtually no control over their property, even when prenuptial contracts required that dowries be kept separate from other family resources. Wages earned by married working women passed to the husband, as did profits made by women who owned tiny shops or market stalls. Because the pattern of government in the 19th century was moving toward liberal institutions in which political rights hinged on property ownership, such measures were crucial to the status of women. The Napoleonic Code provided the basis for legal reform and precedent throughout much of Europe and the Americas. Implicit in its provisions regarding women were certain assumptions about gender differences—that women were "weaker" than men both physically and in character, and therefore required their protection. According to the jurists who wrote the code, women's place should remain within the one "natural" sphere of their competency, the home.

WOMEN AND THE INDUSTRIAL REVOLUTION

The industrial transformation of Europe brought contradictory results for women as it affected patterns of work and home life. On the one hand, it widened the scope of activities for some women, and on the other it reinforced the separation of men's and women's roles that were endorsed by the Napoleonic Code. Women had, of course, always worked. In almost all cases, however, their occupations were carried out as part of a family production unit, usually within the home, and their labor was viewed as a supplement to male labor rather than having any intrinsic value.

Industrialization changed female work patterns significantly. In the new textile factories women constituted a major portion of the labor force, and many also worked in tobacco and food processing. On the other hand, while they were an important element in the industrial working class, factory labor was not the typical work experience for women. At midcentury, for example, 40 percent of all British working women were servants and 20 percent textile workers, while 40 percent of Frenchwomen still worked in agriculture and only 10 percent in textiles.

Division of labor based on gender had existed in cottage industry and agriculture, and it continued in the factories, as men and women were separated by task and by area in the workplace. This was done not only because of differences in skill or physical strength, but also because factory owners assumed that males and females working in proximity to each other, often dressed in scanty clothing, would lead to immorality and thereby hamper productivity. Wherever women worked in the factories, they were almost always supervised by men.

Industrialization did not always tear working families apart. In the early stages of the factory system, entire families—husbands, wives, and children—often worked together. Moreover, throughout the century most women in the factories were young and single. Some factory owners provided dormitories or boardinghouses where single women employees were able to live and eat at low cost, and in England the Factory Acts of 1842 and 1844 limited the number of hours per day women could work. Some married working-class women earned extra income by sewing or doing laundry, but the growth of mass-produced consumer goods formerly made at home, such as ready-to-wear clothing, soap, and candles, limited such work in the cities.

For some women, a less respectable but profitable source of income was prostitution. Prostitutes in European cities numbered in the tens of thousands, and brothels were to be found in many neighborhoods. It has been estimated that by 1850 there were perhaps 80,000 prostitutes in London alone and 50,000 in Paris. Some women engaged in prostitution only when they were unemployed or when their regular employment hit a slow season. Migrants from the countryside also turned to prostitution to support themselves when they first arrived in the city, as did women who had been abandoned by their husbands or lovers. Most prostitutes, though, were single young women in desperate straits rather than women from very poor families.

Once working in this occupation, women often found that their income could be measurably improved over the meager factory wages they could earn. Some worked independently as streetwalkers, whereas others operated on a fee basis out of brothels. Beginning with the Napoleonic Code, many European governments regulated the prostitution business, requiring that prostitutes register with the police and submit to medical examinations. Despite periodic roundups and police raids, the 19th-century middle classes seem to have regarded prostitution as a "necessary evil"—the double standard of the period held that while women had no sexual drive, the "natural" sexual energy of men needed release.

MARRIAGE, FAMILY, AND SEX

The family remained the focus of life for most women, including not only wives but also servants and unmarried female relatives. Nevertheless, the ways in which women conducted their lives and defined their roles changed. The increasingly complex urban environment and the factory system also affected marriage patterns, sexual behavior, and family structures.

MARRIAGE AND THE FAMILY

Industrialization was one cause of a growing conflict for women between the private sphere and the workplace. The low pay scale for female workers meant that single women without family support experienced severe difficulties in maintaining themselves. Moreover, the spreading social ideology of the middle classes established norms of expected behavior for women that proscribed activity beyond that of wife and mother.

PERSPECTIVES FROM THE PAST

THE RIGHTS OF WOMEN

Throughout most of the 18th century, most women in middle-class and working families remained subservient to males, their roles limited to childbearing and rearing, to household duties, and to occasional participation in fieldwork and home-based textile making. But under the impact of industrialization, the status and role of women in the emerging industrial society began to assume new dimensions as tens of thousands of them left home for work in the factories. Moreover, as a result of the Enlightenment and the French Revolution, women increasingly struggled to achieve political and social rights, and in the half-century after 1789 developed theoretical and political arguments for those rights.

Wollstonecraft's *Vindication of the Rights of Women*

Mary Wollstonecraft (1759–1797), an English writer and the wife of anarchist philosopher William Godwin (see Topic 65), was a woman of the Enlightenment. In her Vindication of the Rights of Women (1792), *she based her argument on the belief in reason. Wollstonecraft chastised the framers of the French Constitution of 1791 for limiting the rights of citizenship to men and lectured them that women were equal to men as rational beings. She also replied in detail to Rousseau's position on female inferiority, stressing the need for educational equality.*

Consider—I address you as a legislator—whether, when men contend for their freedom, and to be allowed to judge for themselves respecting their own happiness, it be not inconsistent and unjust to subjugate women, even though you firmly believe that you are acting in the manner best calculated to promote their happiness? Who made man the exclusive judge, if woman partake with him the gift of reason.

In this style, argue tyrants of every denomination, from the weak king to the weak father of a family; they are all eager to crush reason; yet always assert that they usurp its throne only to be useful. Do you not act a similar part, when you *force* all women, by denying them civil and political rights, to remain immured in their families groping in the dark? For surely, sir, you will not assert that a duty can be binding which is not founded on reason? If, indeed, this be their destination, arguments may be drawn from reason; and thus augustly supported, the more understanding women acquire, the more they will be attached to their duty—comprehending it—for unless they comprehend it, unless their morals be fixed on the same immutable principle as those of man, no authority can make them discharge it in a virtuous manner. They may be convenient slaves, but slavery will have its constant effect, degrading the master and the abject dependent.

But, if women are to be excluded, without having a voice, from a participation of the natural rights of mankind, prove first, to ward off the charge of injustice and inconsistency, that they want reason—else this flaw in your new constitution will ever show that man must, in some shape, act like a tyrant; and tyranny, in whatever part of society it rears its brazen front, will ever undermine morality.

From Mary Wollstonecraft, *Vindication of the Rights of Women.*

Women and Poverty

By the mid-19th century, the struggle for women's rights had extended well beyond Enlightenment ideals to more concrete economic issues. In 1841, the Belgian utopian socialist Zoe Gatti de Gamond argued that the abolition of poverty among women would be a major step toward social justice.

The most direct cause of women's misfortune is poverty; demanding their freedom means above all demanding reform in the economy of society which will eradicate poverty and give everyone education, a minimum standard of living, and the right to work. It is not only that class called "women of the people" for whom the major source of all their misfortunes is poverty, but rather women of all classes.

From that comes the subjection of women, their narrow dependence on men, and their reduction to a negative influence. Men have thus materialized love, perverted the angelic nature of women, and created a being who submits to their caprices, their desires—a domesticated animal shaped to their pleasures and to their needs. Using their powers, they have split women into the appearance of two classes; for the privileged group, marriage, the care of the household, and maternal love; for the other, the sad role of seduced woman and of the misfortunate one reduced to the last degree of misery and degradation. Everywhere oppression and nowhere liberty.

The question is not to decide whether it is fitting to give women political rights or to put them on an equal footing with men when it comes to admission to employment. Rather the question exists above all in the question of poverty; and to make women ready to fill political roles, it is poverty above all that must be effaced. Nor can the independence of women be reconciled with the isolation of households, which prevents even the working woman from being independent.

The system of Fourier, imperceptibly and smoothly introducing associations within society, resolves all the difficulties in the position of women; without changing legislation or proclaiming new rights, it will regenerate them, silence the sources of corruption and reform with one blow education and morals with the single fact that results naturally from the associational principles of his system: a common education and the independence of women assured by the right to work; independence rendered possible by the association of households, attractive and harmonious work, and the multiplication of wealth.

From Bonnie G. Smith, *Changing Lives: Women in European History Since 1700.* © 1989 D.C. Heath and Company. Used by permission of Houghton Mifflin Company.

Nationalism and Feminism

The Italian feminist and socialist Anna Maria Mozzoni (1837–1920) worked to secure basic rights for women in the context of the movement for Italian unification. In 1864, three years after the creation of the Kingdom of Italy, she wrote about the contributions that free women could make to national life and argued that the new national laws did not recognize women's rights.

The revision of the Civil Code by the Italian Parliament has placed in my mind the following argument: woman, excluded by worn out customs from the councils of state, has always submitted to the law without participating in the making of it, has always contributed her resources and work to the public good and always without any reward.

I begin with the principles that all rights and all duties have as their foundation and rationale to serve as the force which gives the conscience its ostensible legitimacy. This principle holds for each human being of whatever sex and I do not see for what reason this faculty should be in one case exercised freely and sometimes with force and in the other case buried and entirely suffocated. This occurs so much that in the miserable conditions in which society has cast her, woman, deprived of half her wealth, weakened because of the degrading work actually given her, finds herself dragged down to the fatal necessity to destroy herself through trade in her unhappy body.

Humanity and the nation, civilization and morality, need women on their side.

From Bonnie G. Smith, *Changing Lives: Women in European History Since 1700.* © 1989 D.C. Heath and Company. Used by permission of Houghton Mifflin Company.

European marriage patterns varied according to region and economic status. Among the urban working classes, poverty often prevented or delayed marriage. On average, working-class women married in their midtwenties and men somewhat older, although the age for both began to reduce as living standards improved among low-income groups. Working couples usually married out of mutual attraction and love, so that when circumstances mitigated against a formal marriage, couples often lived together in common-law unions. City dwellers generally abandoned the rural tradition of long courtship, and parental consent ceased to be as important.

Middle-class customs differed from those of the working class in several ways. Among bourgeois families, marriages were largely viewed as serious financial undertakings. Although arranged marriages were rapidly disappearing, parents were concerned about the economic prospects of possible sons-in-law or the dowries of daughters-in-law. The correct social environment, in which daughters could meet eligible men, was therefore vitally important. Longer courtships were also the rule for the middle classes, and marriage plans often included prenuptial contracts and inheritance agreements. Because the middle classes valued financial security so much, their sons tended to wait until their incomes were sufficient to support a family. As a result, men were almost always older than their wives. Before marriage, parents carefully guarded the virginity of their daughters, whereas sons usually had considerable sexual experience by the time they became husbands.

Except among the wealthiest groups, the size of families began to shrink by midcentury. The significant decline in the birthrate in most Western European countries was caused by a combination of factors. Efforts to sustain or improve an acceptable standard of living limited family size, especially among the middle classes, for whom educational expenses were a growing priority. Parents also restricted the number of children they had because declining infant mortality meant that more children survived into adulthood. Moreover, technological and medical advances in the 1840s made possible new and inexpensive birth control devices, although they were not yet widely available. Until then, *coitus interruptus* (withdrawal) and vinegar solutions had been the only widely practiced birth control methods, but thereafter condoms, vaginal sponges, and diaphragms were increasingly available as a result of the vulcanization of rubber. As early as the 1820s, birth control information was being distributed in England, although its proponents risked fines and imprisonment.

The typical early 19th-century family was a "patriarchal" unit in that the husband had legal authority over the wife and children. In actual practice, however, the influence of the wife within the family grew stronger as her role was confined to the home. Wives kept the family's budget and determined how much of its income would be expended. Mothers controlled the rearing of children on a daily basis, including such matters as education and religious training. Affection between spouses and the nurturing care of children were the guideposts of the ideal bourgeois family, while the home was to be a tranquil haven from the harsh realities of the world.

SEX AND THE NEW SOCIETY

Sexuality is a difficult subject to study because of the scarcity of accurate information about the intimate lives of past generations. Moreover, 19th-century middle-class morality made any discussion of sex a taboo. Nevertheless, government and church statistics on marriages, births, and family sizes, as well as private sources such as diaries and letters, provide some evidence.

Although men and women have always had sex, the circumstances in which it took place, attitudes toward it, and how people dealt with its consequences have changed over time. Clearly, for example, premarital sex was widespread among working-class couples because illegitimacy rates rose significantly in the early 19th century. In Austria, for example, as many as one in three peasant children was born out of wedlock. The migration of young men and women to the cities, away from the restraints of family and village community, made for freer sexual behavior. In the first decades of the 19th century, almost 40 percent of all births in Paris were illegitimate, while in Vienna illegitimate births outnumbered legitimate ones. By 1840, perhaps as many as one in three European babies was born out of wedlock.

Before 1850, celibacy among unmarried men and women seems to have been more prevalent in the middle than in the working classes, partly because of the greater bourgeois concern for financial security and moral conduct. Nevertheless, after midcentury the illegitimacy rate reversed itself. This was not, however, because premarital sex declined: It has been estimated that in the years after 1850, one in three working-class women was pregnant at the time of marriage. Rather, marriage had grown more popular among the working classes as their income grew and they absorbed notions of respectability.

Gender influenced attitudes about sex. The middle class professed to adhere to a strict code of morality, particularly for women, who were conditioned to remain chaste. Sex was supposed to be a distasteful obligation for women, but necessary for purposes of procreation. The flavor of this 19th-century bourgeois convention is reflected in the premarital advice that Queen Victoria—the British sovereign who had nine children—is said to have given her daughter: During sexual intercourse, the royal mother suggested, "Close your eyes and think of England."

The anecdote about Victoria underscores the nature of the double standard that developed during this period. Not only were women not supposed to enjoy sex, but medical opinion of the time held that they did not have orgasms; men, on the other hand, were virile creatures who had to expend their natural urges in the sexual act. Fidelity in marriage was publicly expected of both men and women, but law and custom imposed it only on wives. There are, of course, numerous contemporary accounts testifying to the fulfilling sexual relationships that many wives had with their husbands, but the prevailing ethos of conduct made it impossible for women to express their needs openly. The double standard largely reinforced the increasingly exclusive roles of mother and wife to which women were limited.

Putting the New Social Order in Perspective

The transformations that took place in the half century following the French Revolution, with their attendant stresses and upheavals, shaped the character of European society. High-density population, large, rapidly growing cities, and a complex and changing social structure were the outward manifestations of this great transformation. The large and expanding working class received only a small portion of national wealth, while dependency and discipline in the workplace, together with widespread urban poverty, marked the material lives of much of the new industrial labor force. For the new middle classes, however, increasing comfort and influence were the order of the day. Although women participated in both the political and the industrial revolutions of the period, their role in society was steadily circumscribed by an ideology that stressed family and home above all else. From these and related developments of the period from 1789 to 1850 came the political and social struggles of late 19th-century Europe.

Questions for Further Study

1. What was the impact of the Industrial Revolution on European society?
2. How would you describe the way in which most workers lived? How did life change for most people in the period under discussion?
3. In what ways was middle-class life different from working-class life?
4. Was the role of women in society different after the French Revolution? If so, in what ways? If not, why not?

Suggestions for Further Reading

Applewhite, Harriet B., and D.G. Levy, eds. *Women and Politics in the Age of the Democratic Revolution*. Ann Arbor, MI, 1990.

Bronstein, Jamie L. *Land Reform and Working-Class Experience in Britain and the United States, 1800-1862*. Stanford, CA, 1999.

Chase, Karen, and Michael Levenson. *The Spectacle of Intimacy: A Public Life for the Victorian Family*. Princeton, NJ, 2000.

Coleman, William. *Death Is a Social Disease: Public Health and Political Economy in Early Industrial France*. Madison, WI, 1982.

Corbin, Alain. J. Phelps, trans. *The Lure of the Sea: The Discovery of the Seaside in the Western World, 1750–1840*. Berkeley, CA, 1994.

Davidoff, Leonore, and C. Hall. *Family Fortunes: Men and Women of the English Middle Class, 1780–1850*. Chicago, 1987.

Himmelfarb, Gertrude. *The Idea of Poverty: England in the Early Industrial Age*. New York, 1984.

Landes, Joan. *Women and the Public Sphere in the Age of the French Revolution*. Ithaca, NY, 1988.

Lynch, Katherine A. *Family, Class, and Ideology in Early Industrial France: Social Policy and the Working Class Family, 1825–1848*. Madison, WI, 1988.

Marsden, G., ed. *Victorian Values: Personalities and Perspectives in 19th-Century Society*. New York, 1990.

O'Grada, Cormac. *The Great Irish Famine*. Houndmills, Ireland, 1989.

Sewell, William H. *Work and Revolution in France: The Language of Labor from the Old Regime to 1848*. New York, 1980.

Shapiro, Ann-Louise. *Housing the Poor of Paris, 1850–1902*. Madison, WI, 1985.

Sutcliffe, Anthony. *Towards the Planned City: Germany, Britain, and the United States, 1789–1914*. New York, 1981.

InfoTrac College Edition

Enter the search term *Victorian* using Key Terms.

THE ROMANTIC VISION: ART AND CULTURE IN A REVOLUTIONARY WORLD

In the latter part of the 18th century, the chief source of artistic inspiration was the world of Classical Antiquity, in particular that of Republican Rome, with its emphasis on virtue and patriotism.

With the revolutionary changes that had swept over most of Europe by the early 19th century, a new artistic vision was thrust forward: Romanticism. Although Romantic artists produced works of a bewildering variety of types, they shared certain characteristics. Instead of exalting the power of reason, they explored the irrational, probing the world of emotion. In contrast to earlier artists, the Romantics were openly subjective, even autobiographical. Two aspects of life had a special appeal: nature, with its mysterious unpredictability, and the exotic, in the form of remote times and faraway places.

One of the early centers of Romanticism was Germany, where the philosophy of Immanuel Kant sought to describe the nature of artistic experience. The literary giant of the age was Goethe. Although many of his works were Classical, they provided inspiration to the Romantic writers who followed him.

In England the Romantic poets expressed many of the concerns of their times. William Wordsworth used a simple and direct style to explore the relationship between humans and the natural world around them. George Gordon Byron, who became the symbol of Romantic melancholy, supported the liberal causes of his day, including the Greek struggle for independence.

Romantic painters often used their art to protest against the violence of the times. The leading French Romantic artist was Eugène Delacroix, whose subjects ranged from political support for Greek independence to fantastic depictions of ancient Assyria.

Perhaps the supreme expression of Romanticism can be found in music, the most intuitive and emotional of the arts. The towering figure of Ludwig van Beethoven dominated the age. Firmly grounded in the Classical tradition, he extended the range of his music to include the detailed depiction of emotion, the evocation of nature, and the striving for universal human peace.

NEOCLASSICISM AND THE REDISCOVERY OF ANTIQUITY

Toward the end of the 18th century, with the growing interest in rational humanism, as evidenced in the work of the French Encyclopedists, and the increasing challenge to centuries-old social patterns, a new artistic style began to develop: **Neoclassicism,** a revival of the art of ancient Greece and Rome. To some degree its inspiration was intellectual, even philosophical. The history of ancient Rome, in particular, contained many tales of stern patriotic virtue, and Greek and Roman Stoic philosophers emphasized the notions of duty and lack of self-interest.

THE DISCOVERY OF HERCULANEUM AND POMPEII

An even more direct stimulus to the development of the Neoclassical style, however, came from the chance discovery of the ancient cities of Campania, which lay just to the south of Naples. Buried by an eruption of the volcano Vesuvius in A.D. 79, they had virtually disappeared from history. A series of random events led to the discovery first of Herculaneum, in 1711, and then, in 1748, to that of Pompeii, the better preserved site.

The houses and villas of Pompeii, with their frescoes and fountains, public baths, theaters and shops, provided an incomparably vivid picture of life almost two millennia earlier. Visitors from all over Europe traveled to the excavations, sketching the paintings and taking back copies of ancient objects. Among those who were most impressed was the greatest German writer of the age, Johann Wolfgang von Goethe, who commented that "There have been many disasters in this world, but few which have given so much delight to posterity."

Thus, at just the time that artists were searching for a language to express their new—if age-old—ideals, the discoveries at Pompeii and the other sites provided exactly what they were looking for. *The Oath of the Horatii*, painted by the French artist Jacques-Louis David (1748–1825) in 1784–1785, was a call to patriotic action. The subject, drawn from the early history of Rome, uses weapons, costumes, and even poses based on those in Pompeian frescoes. One of the greatest literary achievements of the times, the vast and learned *Decline and Fall of the Roman Empire*, written by Edward Gibbon (1738–1794), provided a more general setting for this revival of interest in ancient Rome; the first volume was published in 1776. Along with the writings of the *philosophes*, works such as these provided the intellectual background to the French Revolution. Gibbon believed that the decline of Rome was largely caused by the rise of Christianity. His negative attitude toward Christianity—and, indeed, toward religion in general—was shared by the greatest *philosophe* of the day, Voltaire.

The Neoclassical style forecast and underpinned the revolutionary changes that shook Europe at the end of the 18th century, but it could not express the immensely varied consequences of those events. In order to do justice to the new world they were helping to construct, artists forged a new means of expressing themselves: **Romanticism.**

David, *The Oath of the Horatii*. 1784. 10 feet 10 inches by 14 feet (3.3 by 4.25 m). The story of the Horatii, three brothers who swore to defend Rome, even at the cost of their lives, evokes a spirit of patriotism. David's work captures the tumultuous political mood of the period just before the French Revolution and highlights its artistic style: Neoclassicism, in part inspired by the excavations at Pompeii begun a generation earlier.

ROMANTICISM AND THE DISCOVERY OF SELF

The 18th century had exalted the power of human reason. The successes and, more significantly, the failures of the Revolution demonstrated the limits of human ability to construct a better world, and the uncertainties of history were reflected in the arts. Beethoven, one of the towering musical figures of the period, was inspired by Napoleon's early career to compose a symphony subtitled *Eroica*—"The Heroic"—dedicated to the Frenchman; Beethoven's democratic convictions led him to see Napoleon as the champion of liberty. When his hero had himself crowned emperor in 1804, Beethoven struck out the dedication on the title page in disgust.

THE CONCERNS OF ROMANTICISM

One of Beethoven's most quoted remarks provides a valuable insight into the perceptions of Romantic artists: "There will always be thousands of princes, but there is only one Beethoven." The chief concern of the Romantics was themselves: their emotions, their reactions to the world around them, and their own individuality—all viewed in a context where freedom and social equality were the highest

Waldmuller, *Ludwig van Beethoven*. 1823. 28 by 22¼ inches (72 by 58 cm). This is a photograph of the original painting, which is now lost. Beethoven is seen a year before the first performance of his *Ninth Symphony*. The irascible composer, with his casual dress and hair, and tightly compressed lips, allowed the artist only one sitting—and that only at the insistence of his publisher.

good. Artists used painting, music, and literature not to satisfy their patrons or to set forth generally accepted truths, but to express themselves.

In the quest for subjective emotional revelation, practitioners of all the arts turned to the irrational. Rejecting their 18th-century predecessors' emphasis on reason, they explored the power of dreams and the subconscious. This led in turn to a new vision of nature. The natural universe was no longer seen merely as a background for human activities, but as a mysterious world of its own, whose unpredictable workings corresponded to the fluctuations of human emotion. The desire to escape the constraints of their own objective situation produced another rich source for Romantic artists: remoteness of time or place. The Druids of ancient Britain and the medieval world of knights in armor inspired operas and paintings. Writers and artists depicted the mysterious East and the wilderness of America.

The political enthusiasms of most Romantic artists were democratic and libertarian, and figures such as Byron and Delacroix publicly supported liberal causes. But the Romantic movement also had much in common with the other political philosophy of the day, conservatism. Both Romantics and conservatives distrusted the ability of human reason to create a better world. The conservative solution was to reconstruct the old political and social order, whereas Romantic artists tried to escape all confinements in the search for self-expression. Neither group had much sympathy for the chief proponents of liberalism, the middle classes.

THE ROMANTIC MOVEMENT IN GERMANY

Romanticism flourished throughout Europe, but nowhere did it affect as many aspects of culture as in Germany. Moral philosophy and theology, sociology and education, the natural sciences and chemistry were all influenced by the Romantic movement. In addition to its cultural and intellectual interest, Romanticism presented an escape from the realities of German political life. After the Congress of Vienna, when the promise of political freedom had withered, thinkers and artists turned to the interior world of their own emotions in search of free expression. If hope had disappeared in the external universe, it could perhaps be regained in contemplating the ideal and the infinite.

The philosophical foundation of the German Romantic movement had been constructed by the writings of Immanuel Kant (1724–1804), who questioned the very nature of the real world. According to Kant, our impressions of external events are derived from our internal mental processes. Thus, what appears to be objective is, in fact, subjective. Kant was a rationalist, but his ideas, together with the high value he put on aesthetic pleasure, inspired a host of Romantic artists. In some cases his doctrines were pushed to extremes; the German dramatist Heinrich von

By permission of the Houghton Library, Harvard University

Johannot. Illustration for a mid-19th century edition of Goethe's *The Sufferings of the Young Werther*. 1852. Werther, the epitome of the hopeless young Romantic hero, has just declared his love to a shocked (and married) Charlotte. Note the piano with the open music upon it: Music played an important role in spreading the ideas of the Romantic Movement.

Kleist (1777–1811) used Kant's theories on the limits of objective knowledge to prove that all knowledge is an illusion and that the true will always be mistaken for the false. A stormy, even unstable personality, Kleist wrote both comedies and tragedies in which appearance and reality are constantly confused; only unqualified love and trust provide the hope of escape from disaster.

THE WORK OF GOETHE

Kleist's pessimism is in strong contrast to the ethical and aesthetic worldview of the leading literary figure of the age, Johann Wolfgang von Goethe (1749–1832). Poet, critic, dramatist, and novelist, Goethe also wrote on botany and zoology and played an active role in politics. Many of his plays and poems are Classical in style, and throughout his long life he followed Classical principles of balance and order. Yet his works are touched by many of the characteristics of Romanticism; his early writings belong to a movement known as "Storm and Stress."

His first great success, the novel *The Sorrows of Young Werther,* is a largely autobiographical account of an unhappy love affair. Many of his lyric poems express emotional

reactions to human experience and to the world of nature; and among the enormous range of influences he absorbed were the writings of Hafiz (?1326–1390), the Persian poet of love and wine. Goethe was profoundly influenced by his travels in Italy, which he described in the *Italian Journey;* the journal provides an engrossing guide to the rich variety of his intellectual interests.

Goethe's most famous work, *Faust,* was published in two parts. The first, which appeared in 1808, deals with the nature of human experience and responsibility as seen in the relationship between Faust and Gretchen. In Part Two, published in 1832, at the end of his life, Goethe meditated on no less a subject than the nature and future of civilization. Despite all the sufferings and faults that beset humanity, the divine spark that drives us in quest of knowledge—a search symbolized by Faust's pact with the devil—will guarantee our salvation.

The leading German Romantic painter was Caspar David Friedrich (1774–1840). Friedrich's mysterious landscapes seem to express the vastness and uncertainty of the world around us, in which isolated figures contemplate a dizzying emptiness or a remote seashore. In a sense Friedrich seems to deny the Romantic premise of the importance of the individual, yet in portraying the irrationality of human existence he illustrates one of the most important ways in which the Romantics broke with their predecessors.

"SPIRIT OF THE AGE": THE ENGLISH ROMANTIC POETS

Many of the chief poets of the early 19th century in England embodied an aspect of Romanticism in their works. William Wordsworth (1770–1850), often held to be the founder of the English Romantic movement, personally witnessed the confusion of revolutionary France. He visited there in 1790, the year after the fall of the Bastille, and was inspired by the political idealism of the times—"Bliss was it," he wrote, "in that dawn to be alive." The later course of the Revolution, however, together with the ensuing war between England and France, undermined much of his enthusiasm for politics. He withdrew to the quiet of the English countryside, and by 1799 he had settled in the Lake District in northwest England, which his poetry was to make so famous.

The theme of his best works was the natural world and its relation to human experience. In language of deliberate simplicity, he aimed to express the calm remembrance of powerful emotions and to draw from this contrast an understanding of human nature. He was strongly influenced by his sister Dorothy (1771–1855), whom he called "sister of my soul"; her *Grasmere Journal* contains vividly evocative descriptions of cloud and light, and of the local wildflowers.

Very different from Wordsworth's "emotion recollected in tranquility" were the stormy romances of George Gordon, Lord Byron (1788–1824). His mysterious and gloomy heroes and his own unconventional life provided the Romantic

Friedrich, *Cloister Graveyard in the Snow.* 1810. 4 feet by 5 feet 10 inches (1.21 by 1.78 m). The original painting was destroyed in Berlin during World War II. The tiny humans in the foreground, even the collective human achievement of the huge abbey, now in ruins, are dwarfed by vast bare trees encircling the scene.

movement with one of its archetypal characters: the Byronic hero. Works like *Childe Harold's Pilgrimage,* set against exotic backgrounds, fed the public appetite for Romantic melodrama, while in *Don Juan,* Byron struck a note of sophisticated irony. One of the most famous figures of his times, he shocked English public opinion by his relationship with his half-sister Augusta, and left London to resettle in Italy.

With his move to the Continent, Byron's fame and influence spread throughout Europe, where the writers inspired by his tormented heroes included the Russian Alexander Pushkin (1799–1837). The character who gives his name to Pushkin's novel *Eugene Onegin* is truly Byronic. Byron's support for libertarian causes led him to identify with the Greek fight for independence, and he died in 1824 while training soldiers in Greece.

PAINTING AND POLITICS

Neoclassical paintings such as David's *Oath of the Horatii* had set the stage for the heroics of the Revolution. Reality proved far less picturesque, and the early Romantic painters chronicled the brutality and suffering of war and violence.

ROMANTIC PAINTING IN FRANCE

Romantic artists often responded in their works to political cruelty and injustice. In 1816 the newly restored government of Louis XVIII was shaken by scandal. *The Medusa,* a French government ship, was wrecked off the coast of Africa. The vessel was ill-equipped with safety boats, and the captain and ship's officers were incompetent to deal with the emergency—it was later learned that they owed their ap-

pointments to political influence. A raft was thrown together, and passengers and crew spent days drifting under the tropical sun before the raft was spotted. Of the original 149 who were evacuated from the abandoned ship, 15 survived.

In *The Raft of the Medusa,* Théodore Géricault (1791–1824), a young French liberal, produced a dramatic rendering of the conditions of the last survivors at the moment of their sighting. The painting was put on public exhibition in 1819 and produced a sensation. Géricault used violent lighting contrasts to enhance the emotional effect of the scene. Other works of Géricault explore the Romantic obsession with madness and death, many of them painted directly from observation in mental institutions.

The greatest of all French Romantic artists, Eugène Delacroix (1798–1863), combined a virtuoso use of color with elaborate composition to create another masterpiece of Romantic political protest in *The Massacre at Chios.* The painting, which illustrates the Turkish slaughter of 20,000 of the Greek inhabitants of the island of Chios in 1824, was intended to rally support for the cause of Greek independence. Delacroix drew his inspiration from the writings of his distinguished English contemporary: "To set fire to yourself, remember certain passages from Byron," he recorded in his journal.

A work by Byron also inspired *The Death of Sardanapalus.* In this orgy of violence, the Assyrian king is seen seated atop his own funeral pyre. The Medes are at the gates of his capital, and he has chosen to destroy his possessions (including his wives) rather than let them fall into enemy hands. For all the brutality of the scene, the painting has a dreamlike quality, echoed in the brooding figure of Sardanapalus himself. Delacroix's own sense of detachment is suggested by his nickname for the work: *Massacre No. 2.*

Géricault, *The Raft of the Medusa.* 1818. 16 feet 1¼ inches by 23 feet 6 inches (4.91 by 7.16 m). For all the apparent confusion of the scene, the artist has produced a careful pyramidal composition. The viewer's eye is led diagonally from the hopeless group in the bottom left-hand corner to the top right, where a survivor desperately waves his shirt to attract a passing ship.

Delacroix, *The Death of Sardanapalus.* 1826. 12 feet 1 inch by 16 feet 3 inches (3.68 by 4.95 m). Unlike Neoclassical artists, who aimed for calm, orderly control, the Romantics preferred raw emotion. Delacroix's free, almost violent brushstrokes depict the cruelty and suffering of the story, with a painful contrast between the rich fabrics and jewels and the pale, naked bodies of the victims.

PUBLIC FIGURES AND PRIVATE LIVES

MARY WOLLSTONECRAFT AND PERCY BYSSHE SHELLEY

The Granger Collection

The Granger Collection

It is hardly surprising that Mary Wollstonecraft's life (1797–1851) should have been an unconventional one, given the independent spirits of her parents. Her father was William Godwin (1756–1836), the anarchist philosopher. Her mother, also named Mary, maintained herself by keeping a school and by writing and translating; her best-known work is *Vindication of the Rights of Women*, which appeared in 1792 during a crucial phase of the French Revolution. After a trip to revolutionary Paris, Mary set up house with Godwin. Four years later, in 1797, they married in order to protect the rights of the unborn child that she was by then carrying. A daughter was born to them that year and named after her mother.

The young Mary Wollstonecraft's early life was clouded by her mother's reputation. After his wife's early death, Godwin proudly published her last works, which included *Maria, or The Rights and Wrongs of Women*, a novel that made a powerful case for sexual rights for women. He followed this up by writing her full and frank biography. Given the climate of the times, an outburst of public outrage was inevitable.

Brought up by her father and his second wife, Mary Wollstonecraft first met Percy Shelley when she was 16 and he 22—and already married for three years. Of all the English Romantics, none was more politically committed than Shelley (1792–1822). The son of a landed aristocrat, he was expelled from Oxford because of his publication of atheist beliefs. He had established something of a reputation for his unconventional ideas and behavior. This was reinforced when in 1814 Shelley and Wollstonecraft ran off together to Italy, and invited his wife to join them and live together.

A few months later Shelley's wife committed suicide, and shortly thereafter he and Wollstonecraft married. From 1818 to 1822 they were at the center of a group of English poets living in Italy that included Byron and Keats. One of Shelley's greatest works, *Adonais*, was dedicated to Keats's memory. Shelley never developed a consistent and practical approach to social and political issues. He preferred instead to express large-scale visions of the human condition and of ways of improving it.

While Shelley developed a series of warm if idealized relationships with women in his circle, he encouraged his wife to write fiction. Her first book was *Frankenstein*, one of the best of all horror stories. This remarkable novel describes a character, Dr. Frankenstein, so arrogant and certain of himself that he circumvents the normal processes of procreation and makes a monster in his laboratory. A creature so abnormally produced is bound to act without love, and the monster—which at one point has been reading *The Sorrows of Young Werther*—ends by destroying its maker and mournfully seeking to obliterate its own vital spark. If the negative message of this is that a world without women is doomed to violence, the positive aspect is that maternal love is the key to happiness. The overriding theme of this complex work is the relationship between nature and science, especially when science is out of control—a growing issue for the 19th century.

Shelley was drowned in 1822 off the west coast of Italy, under circumstances that still remain mysterious. The following year Wollstonecraft returned to England, where she continued to write novels, two of which (*Lodore* and *Falkner*) include sympathetic portraits of Shelley. Surviving her husband by almost 30 years, she wrote other romances; among them is *The Last Man*, set in the 21st century, in which humanity is destroyed by a plague that leaves only a single survivor.

BEETHOVEN AND THE HEROIC IDEAL

The composer Ludwig van Beethoven (1770–1827) is the supreme example of an artist whose works passionately advocate liberty and universal peace. Deeply stirred by the lofty principles of the French Revolution, he was equally appalled by its degeneration into dictatorship. His one opera, *Fidelio*, is subtitled *Conjugal Love:* It describes how a devoted wife rescues her husband, a political prisoner, and sees just punishment meted out to his oppressor.

With his detailed depiction of nature in the *Pastoral* Symphony, daring use of harmony in the last string quartets, and introduction of words into the hitherto instrumental form of the symphony (Ninth Symphony), Beethoven served as the inspiration for generations of Romantic musicians. His own musical roots, however, were firmly imbedded in the Classical tradition.

Born in Bonn, Germany, he spent most of his creative life in Vienna, winning his first successes there as a virtuoso pianist. It was in writing for this instrument that he began to explore a freedom of form and a range of emotional content that were truly revolutionary. He subtitled the *Moonlight* Sonata "almost a fantasy."

The age of 32 marked a turning point in Beethoven's life because he realized that his increasing deafness was incurable. Driven to despair, he contemplated suicide. With the emotional crisis past, and determination renewed, his works took on a new heroic tone. One of the first fruits of this middle period was the Third Symphony, the *Eroica* (The Heroic), which was originally dedicated to Napoleon. In the Fifth Symphony the ominous sounds of "Fate knocking at the door," which open the work, give way to a triumphant conclusion in the final movement.

The music of his last years is in a deeper, more complex style, marked by emotional intensity and abrupt contrasts. At one end of the scale, the *Missa Solemnis* (Solemn Mass) and the Ninth Symphony, with its setting of Schiller's *Ode to Joy*, express the search for universal unity and peace. At the other extreme, the last string quartets lay bare the most intimate and profound personal emotions; a section of one of them is explicitly described as a "song of thanksgiving for recovery from an illness."

Beethoven's visionary final works were far beyond the comprehension of his contemporaries, yet he was widely acclaimed as the greatest composer of his time. When he died in 1827, 10,000 people are said to have attended his funeral. The first musician to become a public figure, Beethoven played a vital part in creating the image of the artist as hero, voicing the feelings of all humans, not just a privileged few.

THE ROMANTICS AFTER BEETHOVEN

Beethoven's symphonies and sonatas, large-scale instrumental works, served as one model for Romantic musicians: the French composer Hector Berlioz (1803–1869) wrote a *Fantastic Symphony*, which uses the orchestra to portray his own drug-induced hallucinations, and other major writers

Delacroix, *Frédérick Chopin.* 1838. 18 by 15 inches (45 by 38 cm). Chopin was then at the height of his powers; his famous *24 Preludes* appeared the following year. Composer and painter were close friends, and Delacroix was a keen music-lover. Rather surprisingly, perhaps, he preferred Mozart to Beethoven.

Copyright Réunion des Musées Nationaux/Art Resource, NY

of symphonies included Felix Mendelssohn (1809–1847) and Robert Schumann (1810–1856).

Another form that appealed to Romantic composers was the small, intimate song or piano piece. The first great writer of *Lieder* (the German word for "songs") was Beethoven's younger contemporary Franz Schubert (1797–1828), who composed more than 600 songs to a wide variety of verse—some of it by Goethe. Schubert's lyric gifts also emerge in his chamber music, written for performance in the home. Like Schubert, Robert Schumann wrote songs on Romantic texts. Both composers produced superb piano miniatures, in Schumann's case often linked together into sets and inspired by literary characters and themes.

Beethoven had begun his career as a virtuoso performer, and the Romantic love of the spectacular encouraged the development of brilliant displays of instrumental skill. The most famous pianist-composers of the first half of the 19th century were Frédéric Chopin (1810–1849) and Franz Liszt (1811–1886), both of whom came to Paris from Eastern Europe to make their careers. Chopin's music alternates between dreamy, often brooding, melancholy and fiery liveliness. Essentially retiring and introverted by temperament, his performances were generally given in the upper-class drawing rooms of Louis Philippe's Paris. Liszt was more robust, his music more rhetorical. Among the sources of inspiration for this arch-Romantic were Dante's *Divine Comedy*, the Faust story, and poems by Byron.

The cult of the virtuoso reached its peak in the figure of Niccolò Paganini (1782–1840), perhaps the most astonishing violinist of all time. So impressive was his technical prowess that audiences whispered that, like Faust,

he had sold his soul to the devil—a rumor that Paganini, enterprising showman that he was, did nothing to discourage. In his compositions he exploited every conceivable violin technique, producing solo pieces and concertos that, in his own time at least, only he had the skill to perform.

Putting the Romantic Vision in Perspective

The French Revolution and the Napoleonic conquests opened up possibilities for social and political change that threatened the survival of the old aristocratic order throughout Europe. The process came to a halt at the Congress of Vienna, where Metternich and the other conservative statesmen endeavored to reconstruct the Old Regime and combat the cause of liberalism. The artistic and intellectual revolution of the period could not be so easily checked. Many of those Romantic artists who had been inspired by the Revolution's original aims were disillusioned at its consequences, but that did not mean that painters, poets, and composers could go back to creating in prerevolutionary styles.

The Romantic movement was born of a desire for freedom, both personal and political. With liberty came a sense of a new status: Beethoven, Goethe, and Byron were among the most famous figures of their times, and the public exhibition of an important new painting was a major event. Artists occasionally reacted against their privileges and responsibilities because having to please a middle-class public could be just as frustrating as working for an aristocratic patron.

In response, there began to develop a process of artistic alienation—the artist as rebel rather than as hero. Furthermore, creators who felt that they no longer needed to satisfy a specific audience were free to develop as they pleased. The notion of an "avant garde," whose ideas were always ahead of the public, grew throughout the 19th century, and with the rise and diffusion of popular culture, "high" art began to follow a course of its own.

But in the early decades of the 19th century, this evolution had not yet occurred. Artists were at the forefront of the campaign for reform, and their voices were still heard when political reformers could be—and were—silenced.

Questions for Further Study

1. Which characteristics of Romanticism are common to all the arts? What form do they take in the various artistic media?
2. What factors—cultural, social, historical—favored the development of the novel in the 19th century?
3. What role did nationalism play in the Romantic movement?

Suggestions for Further Reading

Boime, A. *Art in the Age of Bonapartism, 1800-1815.* Chicago, 1990.
Brown, David Blaney. *Romanticism.* New York, 2001.
Cairns, D. *Berlioz: Servitude and Greatness.* New York, 1999.
Canaday, J. *Mainstreams of Modern Art.* New York, 1981.
Chissell, J. *Clara Schumann: A Dedicated Spirit.* London, 1983.
Cooper, Barry. *Beethoven.* Oxford, 2000.
Cooper, Wendy A. *Classical Taste in America, 1800-1840.* Baltimore, MD, 1993.

Eisenmann. S.E. *Nineteenth-Century Art: A Critical History*. New York, 1994.

Eisler, Benita, *Byron: Child of Passion, Fool of Fame*. New York, 1999.

Porterfield, Todd. *The Allure of Empire: Art in the Service of French Imperialism. 1798-1836*. Princeton, NJ, 1998.

Roston, Murray. *Changing Perspectives in Literature and the Visual Arts, 1650-1820*. Princeton, NJ, 1990.

Wolf, B. *Romantic Re-vision: Culture and Consciousness in Nineteenth-Century Painting and Literature*. Chicago, 1982.

InfoTrac College Edition

Enter the search term *Romanticism* using the Subject Guide.

Enter the search term *Goethe* using Key Terms.

Enter the search term *Beethoven* using Key Terms.

THOUGHT AND ACTION: THE REVOLUTIONS OF 1848

In the 30 years following Waterloo, a widespread reshaping of values and priorities occurred, based on a series of intellectual and philosophical positions. In Britain the new industrial middle class found justification for their social and economic overturning of the old order in the writings of Thomas Malthus and Jeremy Bentham, both of whom advocated the primacy of the individual over society as a whole.

The most important systematic political philosophy to develop was socialism. Its general aims were an equitable distribution of wealth and social and political equality. Methods to achieve this goal, however, varied widely. "Utopian" socialists such as François Charles Fourier and Robert Owen put their faith in natural human goodness. By contrast, the more militant "scientific" socialists Marx and Engels advocated revolution: Their *Communist Manifesto* appeared during the revolutions of 1848.

The 1830 revolution in France and the British electoral reforms of the 1830s raised hopeful expectations for many elsewhere in Europe, but on the whole they were disappointed. The chief beneficiaries were the industrial middle class. The workers, who had erected the barricades in Paris, and demonstrated in the streets of Britain, won nothing. The growing discontent at the suppression of national freedom, and at the lack of representative government, led to a wave of revolutionary uprisings, which swept over most of Europe in 1848.

As in 1830, France led the way. The frustrations of the industrial poor provoked savage street fighting in Paris. Within days Louis Philippe abdicated, and the Second French Republic was proclaimed. Others were quickly fired up by the success of the French revolutionaries. Student liberals in Vienna and nationalists in Hungary, Czechoslovakia, and Italy rebelled against Hapsburg rule and local monarchs. Street riots in Berlin scared the Prussian king, Friedrich Wilhelm IV, into appointing a liberal government. The only countries not affected were Britain, where hasty compromise averted revolution, and Russia, which was still firmly under repressive tsarist rule.

Judged in terms of immediate success, the 1848 revolutions were a failure, and conservative forces returned to power throughout Europe. Yet the causes for which the rebels of 1830 had fought and lost the struggle—nationalism, liberalism, and socialism—were by no means doomed. A new realism replaced the idealism of much pre-1848 political thought. For the rest of the century both socialist and nationalist issues dominated the European political scene, with increasing success.

LIBERALS, NATIONALISTS, AND SOCIALISTS: REVOLUTIONARIES AND THEIR IDEALS

The conflicts that shook European society throughout the 19th century were largely the result of a growing challenge to the conservative order. The three ideologies inspiring this opposition were liberalism, nationalism, and socialism. The first two played a part in the struggles immediately following the Congress of Vienna, whereas the early development of modern socialism dates to the 1830s and is best understood as a result of the gradual rise of the working classes.

LIBERALISM

Liberals could trace their ideas back to the Enlightenment and the moderate stages of the French Revolution, and both Romanticism and nationalism helped shape their views of government. Political **liberalism** held that a representative system, generally in the form of constitutional monarchy, was the wisest form of government because it allowed for stability, the participation of the middle classes, and the protection of basic freedoms such as equality before the law and freedom of speech.

Liberalism varied greatly from country to country in the 19th century, but nowhere was it intended to be a democratic doctrine. As a political system of the middle classes, liberalism was based on a belief in the importance of private property, education, and the wisdom of the leisured classes. Liberals believed in change, but change that was the result of balanced, orderly growth as society in general underwent moral and material progress.

Liberal economic theory lay at the core of political liberalism. The 18th-century thinker Adam Smith (1723–1790) had argued that prosperity would result from economic forces that were allowed to operate freely without government intervention. David Ricardo (1772–1823) expanded on Smith's theory, especially in his *Principles of Political Economy and Taxation* (1817). He expounded the "iron law of wages," which held that the price of labor, like commodities, depended on supply and demand. When the number of available workers is high, their pay will be low—around a mere subsistence level. Ricardo believed that labor, like land, is a commodity that should not be regulated but allowed to fluctuate with the marketplace.

MALTHUS AND THE MALTHUSIANS

The economic inequities of the Industrial Revolution that Ricardo found inevitable were reinforced by the pessimistic predictions of Thomas Robert Malthus (1766–1834). Malthus held that human suffering and poverty were unavoidable, a natural result of overpopulation; this in turn resulted because people increased in number faster than food could be produced to feed them. Unless there was some conscious check on population growth, only famine or plague could restore the natural equilibrium. Even an increase in agricultural production would lead only to a rise in population and a repetition of the whole cycle.

Despite his gloomy predictions, Malthus viewed himself as a humanitarian, believing that if society would only listen to his conclusions and take action to reduce population growth, it could reduce the quantity of human suffering. Nonetheless, in general he remained pessimistic, opposing any attempt by government or employers to alleviate the poverty and misery of the workers or the unemployed: Charity, he believed, would make the situation worse by allowing more people to survive. Some economic liberals, however, tended to adopt a more positive attitude toward the Malthusian predictions. If human suffering was inevitable, middle-class manufacturers should not be surprised if their workers starved while they themselves grew rich, and liberals could reconcile themselves to manifest social injustice because it was unavoidable. Revolutionary concepts of equality were replaced by the realities of the marketplace, and the field of political economy became known as the "dismal science."

Although the harsh views of this "classical economics" were systematized into social theories later in the 19th century, other liberals rejected them. Original liberal notions of general freedom of thought and action crystallized into the concept of the "greatest good for the greatest number." The "utilitarianism" of political reform—its practical benefits as opposed to its theoretical desirability—was first clearly expounded in the writings of Jeremy Bentham (1748–1832).

According to Bentham, the criterion for judging a policy was not its natural appropriateness, but its utility. That which is good avoids pain and gives pleasure. Individuals can make their own estimates of what is to their advantage, while governments should aim for the same end result for their societies. The correct calculation of pleasure and pain would lead to a just society. Democratic government is useful because it satisfies the largest number of people, an argument that steps back from the doctrine of universal liberty. The broader implications of Bentham's ideas were explored in midcentury by John Stuart Mill (see Topic 67).

The more immediate implications of Bentham's utilitarianism inspired a group of liberals known as the philosophic radicals. In their pursuit of the greatest good for the greatest number, they pressed for widespread social reform. By 1832, the year of Bentham's death and passage of the Reform Bill, the philosophic radicals were leading campaigns to reform the legal system, education, prisons, and welfare.

NATIONALISM

The concerns of nationalism were of a different order. In its simplest form, **nationalism** is an awareness of cultural and territorial identity—the identity, that is, of people who share a common language, history, and traditions in a given region. The French Revolution and Napoleon's conquests were both major stimuli to the emergence of nationalism. Not only did the Revolution identify popular will with national sovereignty, but it also succeeded in mobilizing French citizens in defense of the revolutionary nation-state.

National consciousness in Germany, Italy, and Eastern Europe was generated by French conquests in those regions. Under the impact of French invasion, two intellectuals, Johann Gottfried von Herder (1744–1803) and Johann Gottlieb Fichte (1762–1814), appealed to fellow Germans to seek for the common roots and culture of their *Volk* (people). With the growth of national awareness came a call for national self-determination, as peoples living under foreign rule began to demand political independence and unity.

Cultural campaigns were often as useful as political ones in instilling national consciousness. In Germany, Jakob and Wilhelm Grimm compiled Germanic folktales as well as German dictionaries and grammar books. In Hungary, Lajos Kossuth (1802–1894), future revolutionary leader, promoted the cause in articles appearing in the daily newspaper he edited from 1841 to 1844. He wrote these articles in Magyar, which had become the official government language in Hungary only in 1826. Frantisek Palacky (1798–1876), a Czech historian, fanned national consciousness with his five-volume *History of Bohemia*, which he began publishing in the 1830s.

The Polish poet Adam Mickiewicz (1798–1855) was deported to Russia for his political activities. On his release he settled in Paris, where in 1834 he published *Pan Tadeusz*, an epic poem set in the Polish Lithuanian villages where he grew up.

GIUSEPPE MAZZINI

Like Mickiewicz, the Italian patriot Giuseppe Mazzini (1805–1872) spent most of his life in exile. The most important proponent of nationalism in the 19th century, Mazzini was a leading figure in the struggle to unify Italy, but his nationalist philosophy became a European as well as an Italian doctrine of liberty. A passionate, idealistic revolutionary, he believed in national self-determination as in a religion; he was sometimes called the "high priest" of Italian nationalism.

A member of the *Carbonari* in his youth, Mazzini took part in its conspiracies during the late 1820s. After spending time in jail, he rallied the cause of Italian unity first from Switzerland and, when the Swiss government banished him, from France and later from London. In 1831 he created a revolutionary group of his own called *Giovine Italia* (Young Italy) with a tight organization and a specific program: popular insurrection led by youthful enthusiasts, Italian unity and independence, and—most subversive of all, from the point of view of the authorities—a republican government based on popular will and democratic principles. Mazzini, a determined foe of the papacy as well as of kings, was a Romantic who hoped that a united Italy would establish its capital at Rome. From there, Italy would inspire a new "Europe of the Peoples," based on universal brotherhood, a sense of duty, and social justice.

Mazzini's breadth of vision made him impatient with the necessities of practical politics, and his relations with other Italian leaders were generally stormy. In the 1830s and 1840s, Young Italy fomented countless ill-conceived conspiracies and uprisings, each of which failed, but in the process Mazzini had given a generation of idealistic Italians a strong sense of their common destiny. Throughout Europe, too, his example was followed as nationalist organizations modeled after Young Italy sprang up among other subject peoples.

THE RISE OF SOCIALISM

At the same time as the Industrial Revolution was permanently changing European society, the first critics of industrialism began to appear. Their fundamental objection was that the growth of manufacturing did nothing to produce a more equitable distribution of wealth and contributed to the exploitation of millions of workers.

The idea of a community in which the products of common labor are divided among all, according to their needs, was not a new one, although it had in general been limited to relatively simple societies. In modern Europe, this notion was first applied to industrial society in the 1820s, under the general name of **socialism.** Socialists further advocated that economic equality should be accompanied by similar political and social reform.

The earliest socialist thinkers were derided by their more militant successors as **utopians** because their ideas were regarded as naive and impractical; later socialists tried to argue from objective, "scientific" principles, or, like Marx, from the notion of historical inevitability. Like many of the utopians, Count Henri de Saint-Simon (1760–1825) was noble by birth. For all the oversimplification of his beliefs—he proposed a massive plan of social reorganization based on the rule of technical experts and scientists—Saint-Simon coined what was to become one of the central teachings of the socialist creed: "From each according to his capacity, to each according to his work."

In Saint-Simon's ideal society, work had the highest value, and industrialists and technicians would replace theologians or philosophers as leaders. In the coming industrial age, he believed, the government of humans would give way to the administration of things. Religion also had a part to play because it "should direct society toward the great aim of the most rapid amelioration of the lot of the poorest class."

After his death a cooperative farming and manufacturing community was organized in his name in Paris. In theory, women and men had equal status, and the community had a male and female leader. Before a suitable woman could be chosen, however, the community was closed down by the authorities because it had extended equal rights to sexual as well as working relations. Women followers of Saint-Simon continued to meet, forming the most sophisticated women's movement of the times. They organized a women's newspaper and discussed the formation of a women's association, which would not imitate male organizations but take its own explicitly female form.

Another form of ideal community was proposed by Charles Fourier (1772–1837). Fourier believed that most of the ills of society were the result of the unsuitable physical and social conditions under which most people lived. Thus the way to create a better society was to produce a more favorable environment. Fourier proposed to provide this in the shape of self-sufficient agricultural communities called "phalanxes," each with a limited population and economically self-sufficient, on pieces of land set aside for the purpose. Members of the community would receive wages according to their abilities and contributions.

Among Fourier's followers was Flora Tristan (1801–1844). In her speeches, letters, and diaries, Tristan proclaimed that at the root of industrial misery was the competition between women and men workers. The working class, she urged, should unite in the cause of women, and thereby help all workers.

In Britain, the chief proponent of utopian community life was Robert Owen (1771–1858). A prominent cotton manufacturer, in his own factories he cut the normal workday nearly in half, provided child care for working parents, and increased both productivity and profit. Owen believed that the price of manufactured products should be based on three factors: the cost of the raw material, the cost of labor, and an added amount to provide capital for future supplies.

Owen actually created a model community, to demonstrate that by minimizing profits and improving working conditions, he could still increase productivity; the community had its own housing and clubs and a system of workers' benefits. Inspired by Owen, several groups of craftspeople—weavers, glove makers, and others—set up unions and cooperative workshops, and working-class newspapers were founded. An industrial dispute put an end to the practical side of "Owenism," when tailors struck to protest the hiring of women to work part-time in their own homes. Their successful action destroyed the ideal of solidarity, which later socialists developed.

By the time of the 1848 revolutions, socialism had taken a new turn. In France and Germany, societies were formed calling for the abolition of all private property: communism. In 1844 two young Germans, Karl Marx (1818–1883) and Friedrich Engels (1820–1895), helped found the Communist League, whose purpose was to overthrow the middle class (their term was the "bourgeoisie"); Marx used the term "Communist" to avoid confusion with the utopian socialists who, he believed, failed to see the historical laws that made revolution inevitable.

Engels, the son of a wealthy cotton manufacturer, met Marx in Paris, where they worked together on an analysis of the state of contemporary society and a radical prescription for its reform. Their conclusions were outlined in *The Communist Manifesto*, published in 1848 for the gathering of Communists held in that year, in the midst of the revolutions. In the years after 1850, their ideas spread throughout Europe (see Topic 71).

A TIME FOR CHANGE: THE ROOTS OF DISCONTENT

The year of revolutions, 1830, began with a nationalist victory. At the Congress of Vienna, Belgium (the former Austrian Netherlands) had been made part of the kingdom of Holland. Inspired by the French success in deposing the Bourbons, in August 1830 the Flemish citizens of Brussels staged a revolt in favor of Belgian independence. The

Engraving showing the English king (William IV), his majesty symbolized by the lion, surrounded by his Whig ministers. The engraver has dated his work April 15, 1832, and labeled it "A Memento of This Great Public Question of Reform." The occasion was the passing of the Reform Bill in that year, and among those shown are some of the bill's sponsors, Lords Grey, John Russell, and Brougham.

Mary Evans Picture Library

SIGNIFICANT DATES

Between the Revolutions of 1830 and 1848

1830	Belgium achieves independence; revolution in France makes Louis Philippe king
1831	Mazzini forms Giovine Italia
1834	Mickiewicz publishes *Pan Tadeusz*
1838	The Chartists circulate their "People's Charter"
1844	Marx and Engels found the Communist League
1846	Repeal of the Corn Laws
1848	*The Communist Manifesto* published

Dutch held back, while Britain and France discouraged the threatened intervention of Russia and Austria, and Belgium became an independent state guaranteed by international treaty.

Elsewhere, however, there were less encouraging signs of progress. A revolt in Poland was crushed by the Russians, and Mazzinian-inspired revolts in Italy were put down by Austrian troops. In a few German states minor upheavals did result in the granting of liberal constitutions, but Metternich was determined to prevent the rise of a nationalist movement that could benefit Prussia and encouraged states to repress any uprisings. The Diet of the German Confederation duly followed Metternich's instructions.

As for the Hapsburg possessions in eastern Europe, the failure of revolt there is explained by the strength of the Austrians' control and the ferocity of their reprisals at the first sign of rebellion. In addition, unlike Britain and France, and even Belgium, southern and eastern Europe had no industrialized middle class to organize and lead a revolution.

BRITAIN: THE REPEAL OF THE CORN LAWS

The first signs of popular discontent arose, ironically enough, in the one Western European nation that managed to avoid open revolutionary conflict: Britain. The Reform Bill of 1832 (see Topic 63) had gone some way toward satisfying popular demands for increased parliamentary representation,

but many were disappointed by it. In 1838 a group of radical reformers drew up a "People's Charter," which called for wholesale parliamentary reform; among the provisions were universal adult male suffrage, a secret ballot, and the abolition of property qualifications for members of Parliament. The **Chartists,** as supporters of the proposals were called, also campaigned against the revised Poor Laws (in theory, laws to protect the needy), which had been passed in 1834. As one of them wrote, "The new poor law is a law to punish poverty; making working men dislike the country of their birth, brood over their wrongs, and hate the rich of the land." The Chartists twice presented their Charter to Parliament, which rejected it out of hand both times.

The repeal of the hated Corn Laws in 1846 went some way to redressing the general sense of grievance, and its effects help explain the sudden collapse of the Chartist movement. In 1848 a final petition demanding reform, accompanied by some 6 million signatures (many bogus), was carried to London by a mob so threatening that the government prepared to disperse it by force. In the end the crowd broke up peacefully, and so did the Chartist movement. Subsequent campaigns for reform were conducted by more orthodox means. Thereafter Britain remained untouched by events on the Continent, except for its function as refuge for political exiles. Among those who could have met one another in London in the 1850s were Marx and Metternich, but there is no evidence that they did.

Print of Chartists at a protest meeting in London. April 1848. One of the banners waved by the demonstrators on the platform, who are presenting their petition, reads: Voice of the People. Note the armed troops, some on horseback, to control proceedings. In the end, the meeting broke up peacefully—unlike demonstrations elsewhere in Europe in the same year.

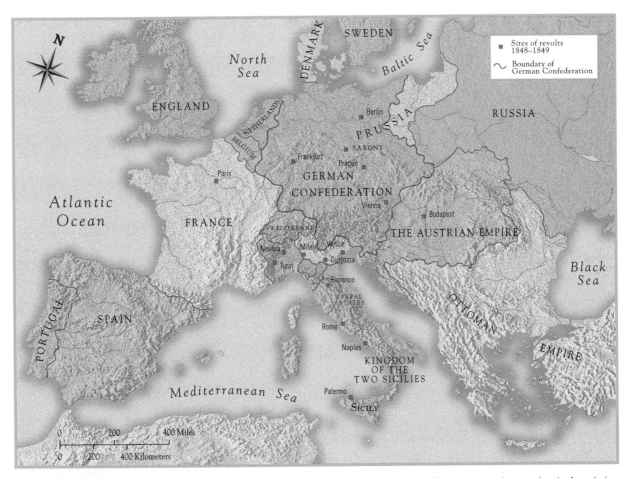

Map 66.1 The Revolutions of 1848–1849. Repressive regimes in Spain, Russia, and the Ottoman Empire prevented any outbreak of revolt; in Britain, the government reached a peaceful settlement of protesters' demands. The first rebellion occurred in Sicily in January 1848, spreading throughout Italy. In France, Louis Philippe abdicated at the end of February, and by March Germany and Austria were in turmoil.

REVOLUTION IN FRANCE

By the early spring of 1848 the general frustration symbolized in Britain by the Chartist movement was spreading throughout Europe. Growing unemployment, and bad harvests in 1846 and 1847, increased tensions. The first uprisings took place in Italy, where Sicilians demonstrated against their Bourbon rulers. A month later, the explosion hit France, where on the surface the political scene seemed relatively calm. Both Louis Philippe and his chief minister, François Guizot (who served as premier of France 1847–1848), followed a policy of order and prosperity at home and peace abroad. Guizot, a self-proclaimed liberal, believed that the Constitution of 1830, which extended political power to the property-owning classes, provided a proper balance between liberty and order. Cautious and rigid, he opposed any further broadening of the franchise, hoping to combine industrial growth with political stability by preserving the status quo.

As elsewhere in Europe, however, industrialization had brought with it the rise of a large and underprivileged urban proletariat. The slum dwellers of Paris and France's northeastern industrial cities began to demand the right to form labor unions and to vote. When they received neither, workers protested at their living conditions and demanded reform; socialist ideas were increasingly circulated at political banquets.

A mass protest, in the form of a banquet, announced for February 22, 1848, was banned the day before by government decree. When a crowd in Paris gathered to protest against the restriction, street brawling broke out and workers began to build barricades. Louis Philippe tried to pacify the mob by dismissing Guizot, but in the rioting around the prime minister's residence, a shot rang out. The troops guarding the house lost their nerve and fired on the crowd, killing several demonstrators. The reverberations of their bullets echoed throughout Europe.

EUROPE AT THE BARRICADES: THE PATTERN OF REVOLT

For two days Paris was racked by street fighting. Workers erected some 1,500 barricades. The troops of the National Guard either disappeared or joined the rioters. Louis Philippe had been brought to power by the 1830 revolution, and on February 25, 1848, he left it by the same route, abdicating like his predecessor and leaving for England. Always a moderate, he prevented a bloodbath by refusing to call out the army and by leaving so quickly.

THE SECOND REPUBLIC

A provisional government assumed power and, to appease the demonstrators, proclaimed the Second Republic, its leaders chosen by acclamation from the crowds outside the Hotel de Ville (city hall). The poet Alphonse de Lamartine, an overnight convert to the republican cause, led the government, with a cabinet that included the socialist Louis Blanc, a token worker named Albert Martin, and a radical republican, Alexandre Ledru-Rollin. The provisional government announced April elections for a new National Constituent Assembly.

The overthrow of the monarchy had temporarily united the competing political factions. Once the king was gone, the politicians took over and rival forces openly waged a struggle for power. The liberals favored a moderate extension of the vote. The republicans advocated permanent abolition of the monarchy and radical reform. Blanc, the only real socialist in the government, proposed a system of "national workshops" to pay the unemployed a small stipend and put them to work. The government set up a version of the scheme, but organized it so badly that the plan proved disastrous. Thousands of workers flocked to Paris to join the workshops, at immense cost to the taxpayers, while Blanc complained that the scheme had been deliberately set up in such a way as to guarantee its failure.

Despite the political battles, the provisional government managed to make some positive steps. The new republic adopted universal male suffrage, abolished the death penalty, and rejected participation in any foreign wars. It also improved relations with the Catholic Church. The elections in April took place in relative calm, with around 85 percent of those eligible to vote actually doing so. The result was a triumph for the moderate and conservative republicans. Even the monarchists did better than the socialists, who won only a handful of seats.

REVOLUTION IN THE HAPSBURG EMPIRE

While France began to rebuild some form of order, news of the cataclysmic events there reached Vienna. On March 12, workers and students finally threw off years of repression and rampaged through the city. The imperial palace was invaded. Under pressure from the emperor, Ferdinand I, Metternich resigned. The architect of conservative Europe hastily disguised himself and fled into exile in England, never returning to Austria. The emperor followed him, although only as far as Innsbruck, and a hastily convened liberal National Assembly drafted a constitution. Among other measures, peasant feudalism was abolished.

Elsewhere in the Hapsburg empire, Austrian rule faltered. Before the end of March, Milan and Venice rose up against their foreign rulers, while disturbances in Piedmont,

Tuscany, Naples, and the Papal States forced the granting of constitutions. Taking advantage of these developments, Charles Albert (ruled 1831–1849), king of Piedmont-Sardinia, declared war on the Austrians with the aim of removing them from the affairs of the peninsula.

Charles Albert was an enigmatic and unstable man who, during the abortive Piedmontese revolt of 1821, had led an unsuccessful campaign against Austria. Now he planned to redeem himself and, once having driven out the hated foreigners, unite northern Italy under his rule. The constitution that he issued in February 1848 was a slightly modified version of the Spanish Constitution of 1812. Although it provided for representative government based on limited male suffrage, it also gave the monarch considerable powers and left the question of parliamentary authority vague. Thirteen years later, it would provide the basis for the constitution of a united Italy.

In Hungary, where Kossuth led the Magyar nationalist party, the Austrians agreed to the March Laws, guaranteeing a large measure of Hungarian self-rule. One of the new government's first acts, the reaffirmation of Magyar as the

Barrikade am Altstädter Brückenturm zu Prag am 16. Juni 1848.
Nach einer gleichzeitigen Darstellung der „Leipziger Illustrierten Zeitung".

Print showing barricades being erected by demonstrators in Prague. 1848. The crowd is blocking the Bridge Tower of the Charles Bridge (Vltava in Czech, Moldau in German), then—as now—the chief place to cross the river dividing the city. Their hope is to cut off the authorities on one side in the Town Hall from those on the other side in Prague's Castle Fortress.

country's official language, alienated Hungary's ethnic minorities, in particular the Croats.

Such divisiveness did not augur well for the revolution's success. In Bohemia too there were ominous signs of the national rivalries that were to prove fatal to the cause of reform. The Czech majority and the German minority feuded over rival national conferences: a pan-Slavic one to be convened in Prague and a pan-German one meeting in Frankfurt. By mid-1848, the Hapsburg empire may have seemed on the brink of collapse, but the revolutionary gains were precarious.

RIOTS IN BERLIN

In Berlin, the Prussian capital, Friedrich Wilhelm IV (ruled 1840–1861), the Hohenzollern king, had come to power

SIGNIFICANT DATES

The Revolutions of 1848

France

February 22–24, 1848	Louis Philippe abdicates; Provisional Government formed
February 26	National Workshops begin
April	Constituent Assembly
June	Workers Revolt in Paris
November	Second Republic founded
December	Louis Napoleon elected president

Germany

March 1848	Riots in Berlin; King Friedrich Wilhelm IV promises reforms
May	Frankfurt Assembly meets
December	Prussian constitution issued
March 1849	Friedrich Wilhelm refuses crown of Germany
June	Frankfurt Assembly dispersed

Italy

January 1848	Uprising in Sicily
January–March	Constitutions issued in Naples, Piedmont, Tuscany, and Rome
July	Austrians defeat Charles Albert
November 1848– February 1849	Uprising in Rome, republic proclaimed
March	Charles Albert defeated and abdicates
March–August	Revolutions crushed in Italy

Austria

March 1848	Revolt in Vienna, Metternich dismissed; Milan revolts
June	Revolt in Prague put down
October	Movement in Vienna crushed
April–August 1849	Hungarian independence proclaimed; crushed by Russians

supporting liberal reforms but had never carried them out. Now, in March, when he heard that Metternich had fled Vienna, the king issued a manifesto promising a constitution. Events took an unexpected turn, however. Crowds of demonstrators celebrating the news from abroad were provoked into bloody violence when government troops fired shots at them. Barricades went up in Berlin and the king eventually relented, appointing a liberal government and announcing a national assembly. This decision left both conservatives and radicals angry, the former because they wanted to see the demonstrations crushed, and the latter because they had already been fired on.

By May, liberals throughout the German states had sent delegates to an assembly at Frankfurt, where the Diet of the German Confederation had its seat. The Frankfurt Assembly was a well-meaning gathering of middle-class professionals—lawyers, professors, bureaucrats—convened to create a united German nation. The absence of any working-class representation, however, was a dangerous indication of the narrow base of the German revolutionary movement.

HOPES CRUSHED: THE REACTIONARIES TRIUMPHANT

Within less than a year the fires of revolution were spent. The revolutionaries were dead or in exile, and the reactionaries were back in power. In France the return to order was self-imposed: In the April elections for the National Assembly, the middle class and the peasants, fearful of "socialist excesses," had voted for moderate candidates.

The assembly proceeded to draw up a constitution establishing the Second French Republic. Rule was divided between a one-chamber parliament, which retained legislative control, and a president, who had executive and administrative powers. Both instruments of government were to be elected by universal male suffrage; a bill for women's suffrage was defeated by 899 votes to 1.

THE ELECTION OF LOUIS NAPOLEON

In December 1848 elections were held for president. Among the candidates was Louis Napoleon Bonaparte (1808–1873), the late emperor's nephew, who claimed that he could restore the glory of France's imperial days.

A complex and eccentric figure, Louis Napoleon had acquired liberal ideas during his youth and something of a revolutionary pedigree. After living in exile in Germany and Switzerland with his mother, he had taken part in uprisings in Italy in 1830–1831. In 1840 he had been arrested for plotting a seizure of power in France, but escaped from prison and fled to England. A wily politician with a skillful instinct for creating popular poses, while in prison he published a pamphlet entitled *The Extinction of Pauperism*, which won him support among the workers.

Amid utter confusion, the country prepared to vote. To the great surprise of many, Louis Napoleon swept the elections with 70 percent of the vote, becoming the republic's first president. A clever manipulator of opinion, he had played on the glamour of his name, promising to repeat his uncle's achievements—or at least some of them—and restore France to greatness. Moreover, he appealed to workers and revolutionaries as easily as he did to conservative peasants and monarchists. Less than four years later, in 1852, he overthrew the constitution, seized power, and crowned himself Napoleon III (the so-called Napoleon II, the dictator's son, died in 1832 without ever ruling). Thus France returned from the heady days of February 1848 to 20 years of authoritarian rule.

REVOLUTION CRUSHED IN CENTRAL AND SOUTHERN EUROPE

The reassertion of Hapsburg rule was made possible by two factors: the innate strength of the Austrian Army and the continued destructive feuding among various ethnic groups. In Bohemia, divided by rivalry between the Czech majority and the German minority, the anti-German Czechs summoned a confederation of Slavs to gather in Prague and refused to send a delegation to participate in the pan-German assembly meeting in Frankfurt. The German minority resented their government's refusal to allow them to participate in the Frankfurt discussions. Austrian forces took advantage of the mutual hostility between Slavs and Germans to reassert control in Prague. The troops were ordered in, moreover, not by the emperor, but by the new Austrian government, which for all its liberalism had no intention of presiding over the breakup of the empire.

In northern Italy the excitement of freedom soon gave way to the all-too-familiar inability of the Italian states to cooperate. The troops of Piedmont, left to fight alone, were no match for General Radetzky and the Austrian forces, and in July concluded an armistice. In March 1849, under the urging of the Piedmontese radicals and his own desire for vindication, Charles Albert denounced the armistice and declared war on Austria for a second time.

Within a week the struggle ended in defeat. Abdicating in favor of his son, Victor Emmanuel II (ruled as king of Piedmont 1849–1861; and as king of Italy 1861–1878), from whom he had extracted a promise never to abrogate the constitution, he went into exile and died a few months later.

Even before then, Hapsburg rule had been restored in Vienna. At the end of October 1848, forces loyal to the emperor occupied the city, and the government resigned. The new Austrian chief minister, Prince Felix von Schwarzenberg (1800–1852), proceeded to dissolve the National Assembly and impose his own authoritarian constitution throughout the empire.

As for Prussia, where a middle-class National Assembly had been elected and was drafting a liberal constitution, as soon as Friedrich Wilhelm realized that the Hapsburgs were back in power, he dissolved the assembly and reasserted his authority. In the face of the Prussian Army, street demonstrations by radical workers were soon put down. The riots also confirmed middle-class distaste for the socialists and scared them into accepting the king's rule.

The one continuing sign of liberal activity was the assembly in session at Frankfurt to discuss the future of a united Germany. One of the chief issues to divide the delegates was whether Austria should be included in the future German state. Those in favor constituted the *Grossdeutsch* ("Great Germany") faction; the others were called the *Kleindeutsch* ("Little Germany") party. After months of lofty debate, the matter was resolved in the end by the reactionaries' return to full control in Vienna: Hapsburg Austria could have no place in a liberal Germany.

In March 1849 the victorious "Little Germany" delegates offered the leadership of the German world to Friedrich Wilhelm. The Prussian king contemptuously refused it, proclaiming disdainfully that he had no need of a "crown from the gutter." The delegates despondently returned home. Just over a year after the first riots in Paris, the last sparks of reform were extinguished.

THE REVOLUTIONARY EXPERIENCE AND ITS MEANING

By midcentury even the most ardent revolutionaries had to admit that their prospects were not promising. For a few months the whole of Europe seemed on the brink of irreversible change, only to slide back into reactionary hands. The reformers' failure was, of course, partly because of their opponents' superior strength. In the long run the Austrian Army and the Prussian Junkers had an advantage that not even the most fiery rebel could withstand.

Yet with hindsight it was clear that the revolutionaries were largely responsible for the abruptness of their failure. In virtually all cases, leadership was indecisive and divided. Much of the actual fighting, with its consequent loss of life, involved the workers. With the battles over, and the time come for debating future moves, the middle class took over. The two factions never really shared a common interest because the workers wanted to overturn existing society, whereas the others—who had not wanted a revolution in the first place—were concerned to reassert earlier gains. In addition, the more extreme forms of socialism were used by conservatives to scare middle-class revolutionaries back into obedience. As a result of their experience in 1848, both parties learned to mistrust the other.

One of the principal goals of the revolutions, the promoting of national identity, turned out to be a double-edged sword. Divisions among ethnic minorities, which had often existed for centuries, allowed the Austrians to divide and rule. Broader national rivalries prevented the coordination of revolutionary movements across frontiers. Where, as in Germany or Italy, there was no actual difference of nationality, political disagreements and local rivalries stood in the way of united opposition to conservative regimes.

Yet the experience of 1848 was not entirely in vain. At least some German and Italian nationalists drew the obvious conclusion that only united opposition could cause the collapse of a hated regime, and applied it with varying degrees of success in their struggles for unification later in the century. A few measures enacted by liberal assemblies—the abolition of serfdom in Austria and Hungary, for example—remained in force. Some former conservative leaders remained in exile; Metternich was one who never returned to power. More intangibly, those who continued to press for reform learned to value realism, rather than idealism. Political theories and notions of human rights, or the rights of nations, could be put into practice only by organized and efficient leadership. The events of 1848 had demonstrated to even the most idealistic revolutionaries that utopianism was not enough.

Putting the Revolutions of 1848 in Perspective

The French Revolution anticipated the beginning of the modern world, but the revolutions of 1848 seemed to reinstate the old order. Yet although the conservatives were back in power, the society over which they ruled was undergoing a period of profound upheaval. Vast numbers of people were bitterly unhappy with the systems under which they lived. The causes of their dissatisfaction were only too clear. Most of them lived crowded together in cities, which increasingly became Europe's dominant social and economic units. Each country's wealth and political power remained in the hands of a tiny minority. The citizens of many parts of Europe remained under foreign domination.

For many of those who felt themselves oppressed, socialism offered the hope of escape. The rewards of liberalism seemed limited to one segment of society, whereas the triumph of nationalism still appeared distant. Under the influence of socialist ideas, working-class people began to take practical steps to organize themselves. Trade union and cooperative leaders forced industrialists to take them seriously. Many socialist theorists encouraged the feminist movement, which first developed in the 1850s in Britain.

Thus out of the ashes of 1848 arose the industrial world of the late 19th century. The conflicts that permeated it involved in increasing measure citizens who had hitherto played little part in shaping history: the industrial working class.

Questions for Further Study

1. What were the principal aims of liberalism and socialism, and how did they differ?
2. How did the political developments of the 1830s and 1840s in Britain differ from those in continental Europe?
3. What caused the rise of nationalism in the 19th century? How successful were its early leaders, and what were their methods?

Suggestions for Further Reading

Barer, Shlomo. *The Doctors of Revolution: Nineteenth Century Thinkers Who Changed the World*. New York, 2000.

Beecher, J. *Charles Fourier: The Visionary and His World*. Berkeley, CA, 1986.

Calhoun, C. *The Question of Class Struggle: Social Foundations of Popular Radicalism During the Industrial Revolution*. Chicago, 1982.

Church, C. *Europe in 1830: Revolution and Political Change*. London, 1983.

Droz, J. *Europe Between Revolutions, 1815–1848*. Ithaca, NY, 1980.

Seidman, S. *Liberalism and the Origins of European Social Theory*. Berkeley, CA, 1983.

Sperber, Jonathan. *The European Revolutions, 1848-1851*. New York, 1994.

Thompson, D. *The Chartists: Popular Politics in the Industrial Revolution*. New York, 1984.

InfoTrac College Edition

Enter the search term *Chartism* using the Subject Guide.

Enter the search term *Habsburg* and also the term *Hapsburg* using Key Terms.

Mary Evans Picture Library

Commemorative plate issued to honor Queen Victoria's Jubilee in 1887—the fiftieth anniversary of her coronation. The queen is faced by Edward, Prince of Wales (who succeeded his mother as Edward VII in 1901). The chief territories of the British Empire are symbolized in the corners: Australasia, Canada, India, Cape Colony (South Africa). Around the disc under the figure of Britannia is inscribed: "The Empire on Which the Sun Never Sets."

nor German aristocrat, was tranquil and loving. Albert's death in 1861 so devastated Victoria that for some time she hid from public life in Windsor Castle, earning the popular title of "the widow of Windsor." For years afterward she continued to have Albert's shaving kit put out each morning. As wife, mother, and widow, Victoria provided her subjects with an exemplary model for their behavior.

JOHN STUART MILL AND THE FEMINIST CAUSE

The placid, confident image that Victoria presented was only one aspect of her age. The rapid development of urban society and the political and economic issues it raised continued to perplex many liberal thinkers. In 1848 the greatest liberal philosopher of his times, John Stuart Mill (1806–1873), published *Principles of Political Economy*, in which he studied the effects of the growth in size and importance of the working class. Mill was also concerned with the theoretical principles of liberalism: *On Liberty*, published in 1859, is the most complete statement of his belief in the inherent value of individuals and their actions, while it also warns against the "tyranny of the majority." Mill took this conviction to its logical consequence both in his own lifestyle and in supporting the cause of women's suffrage.

The young Mill's interest in political philosophy had been first stimulated by his father, who subjected the child to a grueling training in the principles of Jeremy Bentham. After a period in which he became interested in the Romantic ideas of Coleridge, Saint-Simon, and other thinkers, Mill turned to politics, liberalism, and the philosophical thinking behind the French Revolution.

Among Mill's closest and most intimate friends was Harriet Taylor (1807–1858), whom he first met in 1829, and to whose influence and help he attributed many of his most important works. They labored together for the cause of women's rights, a movement that became organized in London in the mid-1850s. In contrast to Victorian attitudes toward gender, their partnership and subsequent marriage represented an early example of the feminist ideal of equality of status.

Mill's relationship with the smart and cultivated Taylor had the reluctant sanction of her husband but caused much public gossip. Combined with his open support of the feminist movement, it made them favorite figures of fun for newspaper cartoonists. In 1833 Taylor and her husband separated, but neither she nor Mill would take the daring step of living together. Only in 1852, two years after her husband's death, did Taylor and Mill marry. Mill conceived of marriage as a voluntary business partnership between equals, one that was dissolvable, and he tried, perhaps excessively, to avoid the conventional relationship between husband and wife in which the power of the male predominated. Before their marriage, he even gave Taylor a kind of contract in which he renounced his rights, financially and sexually, as a husband.

After Taylor's death, Mill devoted considerable energy to the cause of women's rights. In *On the Subjection of Women* (1869), which incorporated many of Taylor's ideas, he stated many of the key doctrines of feminism: Injustices in society were the result of the inequality of the sexes; if men were no longer tyrants and women slaves, happiness would increase both at home and in society. Two years before the book's publication, at the time of the great reform debate, Mill was one of the 73 members of Parliament who voted for a provision to introduce female suffrage; 193 voted against, and the measure failed to pass.

With the defeat of the bill, the feminist movement split over whether men should be allowed to continue to serve on its committees. Mill remained an active member of the campaign, however. *On the Subjection of Women* became one of feminism's classic texts, and his death in 1873 was seen as a major setback for the cause.

LIBERALS, CONSERVATIVES, AND THE POLITICS OF REFORM

The campaign for female suffrage waged by Mill and Taylor was part of a larger battle for electoral reform that dominated British political life for almost two decades. The issue of electoral reform brought together on the same side two groups: traditional middle-class liberals and workers. Many of those employed in the textile and manufacturing industries had achieved a measure of economic independence;

now they felt unjustly excluded from the political system. The middle-class liberals, for their part, resented the hold that the landed gentry maintained on many institutions. The Anglican Church, for example, was dominated by the younger sons of aristocratic families and supported by public taxes paid by all citizens, even those who were not members of the Church of England.

THE REFORM BILL OF 1867

In general the Whigs were sympathetic to the cause of reform, but Lord Palmerston (1784–1865), the Whig prime minister for most of the period between 1855 and 1865, was more interested in rousing patriotic fervor at home and supporting nationalist movements abroad. The two rising politicians of the age, the Whig William E. Gladstone (1809–1898) and the Tory Benjamin Disraeli (1804–1881), were more responsive to public demands. In 1866, together with the Whig Prime Minister Lord John Russell, Gladstone introduced a reform bill to widen the suffrage. The bill was defeated and the government fell. The following year a Tory government led by Disraeli introduced its own, more radical reform bill. Disraeli, a consummate politician, realized reform was inevitable and stepped in to claim the credit for it.

The Second Reform Bill of 1867 effectively doubled the number of electors. All adult males paying 10 pounds rent per year in the cities, or 12 pounds per year in the country, could now vote; in effect the measure enfranchised the upper working classes—the "skilled workers"—and the lower middle classes. Parliamentary seats were redistributed, with an increased number going to the populated and industrial north. The results of Disraeli's bill were a long way from universal suffrage: In addition to the poor, half of Britain's citizens—women—remained unenfranchised. The measure was sufficient, though, to satisfy most of the reformers.

Gladstone and Disraeli continued to lead their parties, by now known respectively as the Liberals and Conservatives, in a series of governments that promoted the liberal causes of representative government and free trade. Apart from joining other Western European countries in the Crimean War against Russia (see Topic 74), Britain avoided involvement in European affairs. Closer to home, the question of whether to grant home rule to Ireland became increasingly controversial. The Irish nationalist leader Charles Stewart Parnell (1846–1891) led the battle from within Parliament in the years following 1877, finally convincing Gladstone to adopt a home rule policy (on the Irish question, see Topic 73).

LOUIS NAPOLEON AND THE SECOND FRENCH REPUBLIC

With the election of Louis Napoleon as president in 1848, after decades of political infighting, ideological debate, and upheaval, the French were ready to unite behind a figure who seemed to promise peace and provide conditions for the growth of prosperity. If their new leader was also able to become an international figure of consequence and place France back on the world stage, so much the better. Napoleon I had, after all, come close to conquering all of Europe. Who could tell what his nephew might accomplish?

A printed Trade Union membership certificate. 1851. Guarded by an angel, a working woman and man receive the homage of the Military and Britannia, while below are individual workers and scenes of factory life. The motto, "Be United and Industrious," is followed by a list of the fields the Union represents; they include engineers, machinists, millwrights, smiths, and pattern makers.

Hulton Getty Collection/Tony Stone Images

SIGNIFICANT DATES

Britain and France from 1846 to 1871

1846	Repeal of Corn Laws
1848	Louis Napoleon elected president
1852	Louis Napoleon becomes emperor
1856	Paris Peace Conference on Crimean War
1860	Chevalier-Cobden Treaty
1862–1867	French campaign in Mexico
1866	Gladstone's unsuccessful First Reform Bill
1867	Disraeli passes Second Reform Bill
1869	Mill publishes *On the Subjection of Women*
1870–1871	Franco-Prussian War

LOUIS NAPOLEON AND PUBLIC OPINION

Hopes like these, which Louis Napoleon adroitly fanned, persuaded the electors to trust him when, in the early months of his presidency, he imposed a series of repressive measures. Socialists were expelled from the assembly, press censorship was introduced, and public meetings were restricted. To distract attention, and to win the support of the majority, he appealed to the interests of large sections of the population. Thus the Catholics were pleased when the schools were returned to church control and when a French military expedition overthrew Mazzini's Roman Republic to restore the pope to power (see Topic 66). Other French patriots were also encouraged to see their country reasserting a role in international affairs.

For all his aristocratic origins, Louis Napoleon fully realized the need to establish a broad power base, and he set out to win over the middle class and the workers. The middle class was distracted from its loss of liberties by the enactment of laws encouraging business and trade. The introduction of state-supported old age insurance won him support among the poor. In 1851 he felt sufficiently sure of himself to dissolve the assembly and proclaim a temporary dictatorship; the alleged excuse was that of protecting the rights of the "masses."

Louis Napoleon's confidence was justified. In a plebiscite held in December 1851, an overwhelming majority awarded him unlimited power to create a new constitution. A year later another popular vote approved his assumption of the title Napoleon III, emperor of the French; more than 90 percent of the electors voted in favor. The Second Republic became the Second Empire.

A few lone voices of protest were heard, the most notable that of Victor Hugo (1802–1885), the leading writer of the day. Hugo at first supported Louis Napoleon, but when he realized the authoritarian direction in which the president was moving, he changed his mind. In July 1851 he publicly denounced the intentions of the "Little Napoleon." After trying unsuccessfully to organize opposition, Hugo went into exile in the Channel Islands, from where he published works that bitterly attacked the emperor. He returned to France only after the fall of the empire.

NAPOLEON III AND THE SECOND EMPIRE

It is worth underlining the implacable hatred of Hugo and other French intellectuals for Napoleon III because this feeling was far from generally shared. For the first half of his reign, the emperor maintained an iron grip on the state while remaining popular and admired. In the 1860s he permitted the transformation of his authoritarian regime into a more liberal rule. With the relaxation of control, opposition to the emperor began to grow in Parliament, in part because it was safer to oppose him and in part to urge him toward more liberal government, but he retained his general popularity.

Photograph of French Emperor Napoleon III and the Empress, Eugénie. Mid-19th century. Eugénie's interest in high fashion—note the elaborate costume she wears here—and her husband's constant infidelity were in strong contrast to royal behavior across the Channel, in Victorian England.

Louis Napoleon remains a complex character. Fully aware of the havoc that his uncle had wreaked on most of Europe, he had no hesitation in playing on French thirst for glory and their highly selective memories. In personal dealings he impressed most of his contemporaries as gentle and charming, albeit a womanizer. Others found him a sensualist, sinister and insincere. Like Napoleon, he claimed to rule as tribune, rising above factions, and expressing the popular will. Yet he lacked his uncle's administrative brilliance, and his attempts to win an empire proved disastrous. Above all, it is difficult to see a consistent vision behind his rule—except that of retaining power by a constant series of manipulations. He was helped by the fact that a weary country seemed willing to be manipulated.

POLITICS IN THE SECOND EMPIRE

The element of deception was present from the beginning of Louis Napoleon's reign, in the new constitution introduced in January 1852. Like Napoleon's constitution of

1799, it provided for a legislative body to be elected by universal male suffrage. This body had no real power or influence and could approve only measures that were drawn up by a Council of State, itself appointed by the emperor. In any case, elections were controlled and candidates carefully selected. The emperor kept charge of the army and of foreign and economic policy. When he desired to "consult" his subjects he could call a referendum, the result of which would be a foregone conclusion.

It is difficult to imagine a more complete rejection of liberal politics, yet this authoritarian regime was combined with a liberal economic policy that explains much of the widespread middle-class support for Napoleon III's rule. Private citizens were encouraged to invest by a law that limited their liability if the company in which they had bought stock ran into debt. The fundamental liberal doctrine of free trade was honored in the signing of a pact with Britain in 1860—the Chevalier-Cobden Treaty—which reduced tariffs on both sides.

All of these measures were intended to stimulate the economy and win the backing of the business classes. Meanwhile, other means were used to discourage any possible protests at government high-handedness. For the first decade of the Second Empire, no political opposition was tolerated, the press was censored, and the universities, tra-

ditional centers of rebellion, were kept under careful observation. In the years after 1860 there was a steady process of relaxation of these restrictions in an effort to cut off popular resentment before it had a chance to become dangerous. Open debate in the assembly was permitted, and the proceedings were made public.

While the middle classes were happily making money, and the intellectuals were effectively silenced, the urban proletariat was provided with new social benefits. Medical facilities, public housing, and homes for the elderly were built, and in the process many jobs were created. A workers' insurance scheme offered security against loss of earnings in case of injury or ill-health, while a new law recognized workers' rights to certain limited strike action. As for the rural population, whose votes had helped put Louis Napoleon in power in the first place, they were delighted with the general national prosperity and political stability.

THE "EMPIRE" STYLE
Napoleon III, like many another authoritarian ruler, set out to provide an appropriate setting for his reign. His most lasting legacy, the rebuilding of Paris, served a dual purpose, in fact. The broad boulevards, elegant squares, and public parks, designed by Baron Georges Haussmann (1809–1891), give the city its special, personal character. At the same time

An early photograph of Boulevard de Sebastopol, Paris. 1859. Part of Haussmann's remodeling of the city in the mid-19th century, its great width was intended to prevent any future revolutionaries from blocking it with barricades, as had occurred in 1830 and 1848. The cart in the foreground is delivering containers, probably holding milk.

the streets were intended to be too wide for any future revolutionaries to construct barricades, while the broad, direct routes facilitated the coordinated movement of troops if the need to put down riots ever arose.

The plan was controversial at the time, and remains so still. The shady gardens continue to provide rest and refreshment in warm weather, but the formal squares, crossed by roads leading in several different directions, are apt to become jammed with traffic. The great monumental vistas—Place de la Concorde, Place de l'Étoile, with its Arc de Triomphe (Arch of Triumph)—were intended as backdrops for imperial ceremonies, rather than as parts of a living city. Haussmann's ideas, which included such practical innovations as clean water supply and sewage systems, influenced designers of other 19th-century urban projects such as those in Rome, Washington, D.C., and Mexico City.

From clothes to furniture, clocks to table settings, the richly elaborate "Empire" style appeared in just about every aspect of daily life. One of its prime promoters was the emperor's Spanish wife, Eugénie (1826–1920). Her ornate silk gowns became famous—and much imitated—throughout Europe and confirmed France's reputation as the center of high fashion. In contrast to Victoria and Albert, pillars of bourgeois respectability across the Channel, Napoleon and Eugénie set out to create an image of glamour and luxury, a picture that was only slightly marred in the public eye by Napoleon's philanderings. Eugénie's dignified behavior in the face of her husband's conduct won her the approval of many feminists, who applauded her encouragement of improved education for women. On the other hand, the empress was inclined to be narrow-minded, leading the unsuccessful fight to ban Gustave Flaubert's novel *Madame Bovary* (see Topic 72).

The excitement generated by the Second Empire and its prosperity subdued early attempts at criticism, but over the long term Napoleon III had to deal with his liberal opponents. Throughout the 1860s, he continued to make concessions to them, which only fed the demands for more reforms. By 1869, opposition had crystallized in the form of a renewed republican party, which at one point actually named a premier. The government introduced an amended constitution, entrusting virtually complete power to Parliament, which was approved by a great margin—even including the opposition leaders, who supported the government. The sudden collapse overnight of the Second Empire was attributable not to Napoleon III's political difficulties at home but to his failure to win success in France's overseas ventures.

FRANCE AND THE POLITICS OF EMPIRE

Louis Napoleon came to power with the claim that he could renew France's imperial glory. For all his domestic achievements, his mismanagement of foreign policy fatally undermined his popularity. He used the magic name "Bonaparte"

to evoke memories of a French empire, but a string of French military losses was more likely to bring Waterloo to mind, and his disappointed subjects did not forgive him.

Matters began promisingly enough. The overthrow of the Roman Republic in 1849 was an early, if easy, victory. It was followed by France's leading role in the Crimean War, in which Russia was defeated. The ensuing peace conference met in Paris in 1856, expansively hosted by the emperor, who used it to demonstrate to his subjects his growing international prestige.

THE FRENCH IN ITALY

Among the other European powers represented at the Paris Peace Conference was the small Italian state of Piedmont-Sardinia (see Topic 69). Its prime minister, Camillo di Cavour, was trying to rally support for freeing the northern Italian provinces of Lombardy and Venetia from Austrian rule. In 1858, Napoleon III promised Cavour French aid in a war against Austria, in return for which France was to gain Nice and Savoy. More than territorial expansion, the emperor seems to have been motivated by a desire to enhance French prestige. When the war broke out the following year, Napoleon sent troops, and the combined French and Piedmontese forces did drive the Austrians out of Lombardy. At this point, to the general disgust of the supporters of Italian independence, Napoleon III suddenly signed an armistice with the Austrians and withdrew his troops (see Topic 69).

Whatever the consequences of French interventionism were for the Italians, its effect on morale in France was predictable. By opposing Catholic Austria, the emperor had offended Catholics back home. By deserting the Italian cause, he confirmed the liberals' mistrust of him. Furthermore, the fighting, although brief, had been ferocious and the losses heavy. The only gains were Savoy and Nice, which France obtained from Piedmont in 1859–1860.

The expansion of French power outside Europe offered easier prospects. Charles X had begun the occupation of Algeria and Napoleon III completed it. French settlements were founded in West Africa and Indochina, although control of Indochina was not completed until the Third Republic. In the Pacific region, New Caledonia was occupied. The prestige that these conquests generated was not matched by any tangible benefits, and Napoleon showed little interest in matching the commercial success of the British Empire. In the long run, the French colonies in Africa and Asia proved disastrous for many nations other than France. The bloody history of Southeast Asia in the years following World War II, and the violence that ravaged New Caledonia in the late 1980s, are legacies of Napoleon III's attempts to build an empire.

THE FRENCH IN MEXICO

Napoleon III's attempt to conquer Mexico was even more disastrous. Mexico had recently won its independence from Spain, and its government was ruled by the revolutionary leader, Benito Juárez. French forces were originally sent in 1862 as part of a joint expedition that also included British and Spanish troops; the motive was to compel the new regime to pay debts it allegedly owed to the countries involved. When it became clear that the French intended to annex the country, the British and Spanish troops returned home. Mexico City was captured; Juárez and his government retreated into the countryside, and the French installed as emperor a Hapsburg prince, Maximilian (1832–1867), archduke of Austria and brother of the reigning Hapsburg emperor.

The United States invoked the Monroe Doctrine of 40 years earlier, prohibiting the Europeans from interfering in the affairs of their former colonies in the Western Hemisphere. In 1865, Union troops lately victorious in the American Civil War were dispatched toward Mexico, and once again Napoleon III threw in his hand. In 1867 the last French soldiers set off back to France. The hapless Maximilian refused to leave and remained in the hands of Juárez's men. They shot him. His young wife Carlota

(1840–1927) had returned to Europe at her husband's request in a vain attempt to secure aid from Napoleon III and the pope. The news of Maximilian's failure and impending execution drove her hopelessly insane, and she spent the remaining 60 years of her life in seclusion near Brussels.

Napoleon III's final defeat was at the hands of Prussia, the culminating act in the German drive for national unification (see Topic 69). From the French viewpoint, the Franco-Prussian War of 1870 was an unmitigated disaster. It ended France's role as the leading power of continental Europe. More immediately, France was invaded by the Prussian Army, Napoleon III was taken prisoner, and Paris was besieged for four terrible months in the winter of 1870. When news of the emperor's surrender of the army at Sedan reached Paris in September 1870, the Second Empire was declared dead, and liberal republicans formed a provisional government. Its first needs were to survive the starvation of the Prussian siege and to begin the painful process of rebuilding the state.

Putting the Liberal State in Perspective

Britain and France experienced the radical transformations of the years from 1850 to 1870 in very different ways. In one a constitutional monarchy and a parliamentary government presided over the peaceful extension of political power. In the other a charismatic leader offered high hopes but eventual calamity. Britain saw the victory of traditional liberalism and the triumph of compromise. In France, Napoleon III offered something to everyone, with a liberal economy and an authoritarian, aggressive state.

To judge with hindsight is notoriously easy, and the early years of the Second Empire seem to have had a genuine sense of exhilaration, especially when contrasted with the more stolid virtues of the Victorian age in Britain. The French desire for renewed self-esteem, fueled by the domestic successes of Napoleon III's early reign, led to their emperor's attempts to satisfy them abroad. Nor was he responsible for the tragedy of the Franco-Prussian War, which formed part of Bismarck's schemes for the birth of the new German nation. In any case, by 1870 the political balance of power in Europe was radically changed.

Yet the long-term consequences of Britain's success and France's defeat were to prove dire. The blow to French self-esteem left wounds that were reopened in 1914 and again in 1940, in the opening phases of the two world wars, when Anglo-French cooperation was vital. At the same time, pride in the achievements of Victorian Britain was easily converted into a belief in the divine right of the British Empire. The result was an aggressive, arrogant world power. A weakened France left Germany as Britain's chief rival on the European, and eventually world, scene. The German challenge to British superiority became increasingly strident. Eventual conflict between the two seemed inevitable, and in response militarism continued to grow during the last quarter of the 19th century.

Questions for Further Study

1. What are the main factors accounting for the differences in the political life of Britain and France from 1850 to 1870? How much were the differences the result of differing styles of leadership?
2. How did the Second Empire affect the social and cultural climate in France? What permanent changes, if any, did it leave?
3. What was Louis Napoleon's foreign policy, and what consequences did it have?
4. Why was Disraeli more successful than Gladstone in passing a reform bill, and what did his measure accomplish?

Suggestions for Further Reading

Bresler, Fenton. *Napoleon III: A Life*. London, 1999.

Christiansen, Rupert. *Tales of the New Babylon. Paris 1869-1875*. London, 1994.

Gould, Andrew C. *Origins of Liberal Dominance: State, Church, and Party in Nineteenth Century Europe*. Ann Arbor, MI, 1999.

Jenkins, Roy. *Gladstone*. New York, 1995.

Joyce, P. *Visions of the People: Industrial England and the Question of Class, c. 1848–1914*. New York, 1991.

Mokyr, J. *Why Ireland Starved: A Quantitative and Analytical History of the Irish Economy, 1800–1850*. London, 1983.

Plessis, Alain. *The Rise and Fall of the Second Empire, 1852–1871*. Cambridge, MA, 1985.

Price, R. *A Social History of Nineteenth-Century France*. New York, 1988.

Robb, Graham. *Victor Hugo*. London, 1997.

Seidman, S. *Liberalism and the Origins of European Social Theory*. Berkeley, CA, 1983.

Thompson, F.M.L. *The Rise of Respectable Society: A Social History of Victorian Britain, 1830–1900*. Cambridge, MA, 1988.

InfoTrac College Edition

Enter the search term *John Stuart Mill* using Key Terms.

Enter the search term *Victorian* using Key Terms.

AUSTRIA AND RUSSIA: CONSERVATISM ENTRENCHED

In the decades after 1848, most of Western Europe felt the growing effects of liberalism and nationalism. In Eastern Europe, however, the Hapsburg monarchy fought to limit the consequences of the revolutionary uprisings of 1848 by centralizing the empire. In Russia, which was virtually untouched by the ferment into which the rest of Europe was plunged, the first signs of a relaxation of autocratic rule appeared. Yet despite early reforms, political repression reemerged by the 1880s.

With the overthrow of Metternich in March 1848 and the abdication of Ferdinand I, the new emperor, Franz Josef, hoped that strong central government would provide the empire with greater authority. Yet ethnic divisions ran too deep for bureaucratic solutions. The non-German-speaking peoples were united in only one respect: their resistance to the German-speaking rulers who governed them from Vienna. In everything else, from territorial borders to school systems, they struggled for independence both from Hapsburg rule and from each other.

The chief opponents of Vienna's supremacy were the Magyars of Hungary. In order to meet some of their demands and still preserve the empire, in 1867 the Austrians—weakened by their defeat in the Austro-Prussian War of 1866 and plagued by economic problems—devised the *Ausgleich* ("Compromise"), which created the Dual Monarchy. This was an uneasy attempt to provide an artificial bureaucratic solution to an impossibly complex dilemma. The Austro-Hungarian empire survived for almost half a century, but its suppression of Slavic minorities fueled continuing resentments.

By the 19th century, the Russian Empire consisted of 15 separate countries and several tribal nations, speaking more than 100 separate languages. The tough, authoritarian Nicholas I died during the Crimean War of 1853–1856. His successor, Alexander II, at first favored the liberalization of Russian society—if only to prevent spread of the "contagion" of revolution. An additional strong motivation was the military ineptness of his army. In 1861 the land-bound serfs were emancipated, but the success of this long-awaited reform was limited. At the same time, the Emancipation Edict created unrealistic hopes for real change that were further aroused by Alexander's reforms in education and local self-government.

A surge of socialist and intellectual enthusiasm produced by the mood of progress led to open advocacy of extreme radicalism and nihilism, aimed at dismantling the state. The official backlash was inevitable. When Alexander II was killed by a terrorist bomb in 1881, his son and successor Alexander III used harsh, autocratic methods to eradicate all liberalism in Russia.

THE AUSTRIAN EMPIRE: A MULTIETHNIC STATE IN THE AGE OF NATIONALISM

In the generation after 1848, in Western Europe, the spirit of nationalism inspired and brought to birth the new nations of Germany and Italy. During the same period, the unity of the Austrian empire was increasingly threatened by the ethnic minorities it governed. They resented the rule of their German-speaking masters, who made up a minority of 23 percent of the population. Austrian domination was chiefly maintained by a careful manipulation of the divisions between the various nationalities. The national and cultural diversity of the territories under Hapsburg rule was, of course, one of the leading factors in the outbreak of revolt there in 1848. Even within each of the three principal geographic areas—Austria, Hungary, and Bohemia—ethnic tensions were exacerbated by the reassertion of Austrian control.

Map 68.1 Nationalities in Central and Eastern Europe, c. 1900. Belgium, Germany, Italy, and Greece were all created in the 19th century. In 1900, Poland did not exist as an independent nation, but was split between Germany and Russia. It was refounded after World War I, when—with the fall of the Hapsburg and Ottoman Empires—a new state was created from the territory of the Slovenians, Croats, and Serbs: Yugoslavia (Land of the Southern Slavs). The Yugoslav Federation began to fall apart toward the end of the 20th century, with NATO's campaign against Serbian domination of Kosovo. In 2003, its new name became The Federation of Serbia and Montenegro—the only two remaining parts of the original federation.

PAN-SLAVISM

The broadest of nationalist causes in Eastern Europe was Pan-Slavism, which involved peoples beyond the borders of the Austrian empire. Those considering themselves Slavs included Czechs, Slovaks, Slovenes, Serbs, Croats, and Ruthenians (Ukranians), all of whom were under Austrian rule. The Poles, who were also Slavs, were divided. Some lived in territories governed by the Hapsburgs, whereas others were in that part of Poland that remained under Russian control (there were also Poles resident in Prussia). To complicate the situation, a growing number of Russian intellectuals began to identify with the cause of Pan-Slavism and consider themselves not Russian but Slav.

All of these peoples spoke related languages and could thereby distinguish themselves from the other groups in Eastern Europe and, more specifically, in the Hapsburg empire. These were the Magyars (Hungarian speakers whose ancestors had settled there in the 9th century), the Italians, and—above all—the German-speaking ruling class. Yet for all their numbers and nationalist fervor, the various Slavic peoples never managed to forget their own differences and cooperate to throw off Hapsburg rule.

The Austrians adroitly exploited national rivalries. Not the least of these was the traditional hostility between the Magyars and the Slavic peoples living in Hungary. In Hapsburg Poland, where Polish nationalist feeling was strong among the aristocracy, the authorities used tensions between the nobles and their serfs to create a class war and keep the country divided.

Yet the events of 1848 provided a warning: Even conservative Austria could not maintain a monolithic indifference to the dissatisfactions of its subjects. The sense of a turn of direction was symbolized by the departure from the scene of the two figures who represented the old regime: the emperor Ferdinand I and his chief minister, the orchestrator of the Concert of Europe, Prince Metternich. The crown was assumed by Franz Josef (ruled 1848–1916), then barely 18 years old, while the government of the empire passed into the hands of the archconservative Prince Felix Schwarzenberg (1800–1852). Even Franz Josef's most fervent supporters could hardly have imagined that he would remain Austrian emperor for the better part of 70 years: He died in 1916, in the middle of World War I.

Schwarzenberg intended to forge the basis of unity throughout the empire in two ways: a single system of laws and taxes, and the administration of that system by an absolutist, centralized bureaucracy. His new constitution imposed political uniformity even on regions like Bohemia and Hungary that had won a measure of independence. The railway, which had already begun to revolutionize communications in Western Europe, connected many of the chief urban centers under Hapsburg rule. Roads across the Alps, into the Austrian provinces of northern Italy, were improved.

Schwarzenberg died in 1852, before he was able to see his schemes fully implemented, and things reverted to their former state: German-speaking regional administrators, who were only nominally responsible to Vienna, continued to run the affairs of peoples whose cultures they looked down on and whose languages they chose not to speak. Bureaucratic inefficiency, coupled with insensitivity to minority feelings, produced resentment and frustration among Austria's subject peoples.

FRANZ JOSEF AND CONSTITUTIONAL REFORM

In 1859 events in northern Italy brought about a crisis. French forces, with the help of Piedmont-Sardinia, defeated the Austrians and drove them out of Lombardy (see Topic 69). Franz Josef, by now old enough to be his own master, and realizing the risk of further rebellions elsewhere in his empire, sought to forestall them by introducing a revised constitution. This document decentralized the government and gave considerable powers to regional assemblies. The reform drew a united burst of hostility from all sides. In the various regions, the nationalists could not agree on who should represent whom; the liberals in Vienna were appalled by the monarch's high-handedness; and bureaucrats throughout the empire protested at the confusion.

In the face of such opposition, within a few months the emperor reversed himself. In February 1861 yet another new constitution was introduced, which created a two-chamber parliament in Vienna: the *Reichsrat*. Having held up the promise of local independence, Franz Josef was now withdrawing it. To make matters worse, his electoral system guaranteed the German speakers a majority in the parliament's lower chamber. Anger among the ethnic minorities ran high, and Hungary's Magyars refused to send representatives. By the fall of 1865 the emperor was forced to admit failure and suspend the constitution.

In the midst of political crisis, troubles abroad once again distracted attention. In his struggle to create a united German nation, Bismarck's plans required the elimination of the only other serious candidate for German leadership, Austria; he therefore sought a military confrontation because Prussian supremacy was most easily established on the battlefield. By the end of the Austro-Prussian War of 1866 (see Topic 69), Austria's defeat left its prestige in the German-speaking world considerably undermined.

THE *AUSGLEICH*: ILLUSION OF THE DUAL MONARCHY

The fiercest and most persistent opposition to Austrian rule was in Hungary, where the temporary successes of 1848 fueled an active Magyar independence movement. In 1867, Hungarian nationalist leaders seized on Austria's weakness and forced through a political compromise; the German word for "compromise," *Ausgleich*, is used to refer to the Austro-Hungarian agreement.

HUNGARY AND COMPROMISE

In 1867, after Austria's defeat by Prussia, under the *Ausgleich* Hungary became an autonomous state with its own parliament, with Franz Josef as its king. This inaugurated the Dual

Monarchy, whereby the emperor of Austria ruled simultaneously as king of Hungary. Theoretically, joint ministries of the two states, known as the "Delegations," decided questions of finance, foreign policy, and war. In practice, however, most of Hungary's domestic policies were now established internally. The Magyar business class and landowning nobility took control of the Hungarian economy. Foreign policy and defense remained under the control of the Delegations.

As part of the agreement, the Romanian, Serbian, and Croatian minorities in Hungary were left to Magyar rule. Most of the other Slavic minorities in the empire, including the Slovenes, Slovaks, and Ruthenians (Ukranians), remained under the Austrians. The Czechs and Poles were given some privileges as a means of buying their collaboration. In this way the Austrians hoped to eliminate the risk of a Pan-Slavic union. The Hungarians were not a Slavic people, and their treatment of Slavic minorities was notable for its harshness. A few years later, when the idea of a triple monarchy was voiced, in which the Slavs would have been represented, German speakers and Hungarians alike opposed it.

In Vienna the emperor played liberals and nationalists off against one another. The result was an impotent Austrian parliament, riven by ethnic divisions. Sessions were notorious for violent fighting among the delegates, not always only verbal, and were often paralyzed by noise. Effective power was held by the ethnic German bureaucrats, who continued to implement conservative policies. In combined numbers the minorities actually formed a majority in each half of the Dual Monarchy, but they remained as far as ever from self-government.

The *Ausgleich* was an attempt to buy off the Magyars at the expense of the other ethnic groups. In the long term so precarious a compromise was doomed to failure. The crisis finally came with World War I, when the collapse of the Austro-Hungarian empire, with its labyrinthine interweaving of alliances, brought with it conflict throughout Europe. Yet viewed as a desperate expedient, the Dual Monarchy achieved its limited objectives. For all their mutual mis-

trust, Austrians and Magyars shared a common interest in making the compromise work.

Nonetheless, the price of survival was a heavy one, and it was mainly paid by the nationalist minorities. The legacy of hatred and rivalry lasted late into the 20th century. Furthermore, the climate of growing frustration and resentment proved all too fertile for the growth of anti-Semitism. Peoples divided by so much still shared in common their irrational discrimination against the Jews. Franz Josef's Vienna became at the same time a center for Jewish cultural life and a breeding ground of anti-Semitism.

RUSSIA UNDER THE TSARS: THE EMANCIPATION OF THE SERFS

The only two major powers in Europe untouched by revolution in 1848 were the British and Russian empires. Britain's way of dealing with the demand for political change was a policy of compromise. Russia's method was the precise reverse: repression. From the time of the Congress of Vienna in 1815, Tsar Alexander I maintained strict authoritarian control at home while generally assuming the role of defender of the conservative cause in Europe. His only significant departures from this approach, his initial support for Poland and for the Greeks in their war of independence,

Cartoon showing the hierarchical structure of the Russian state. Under the Double Eagle, symbol of the Romanovs, the tsar and tsarina sit enthroned. Below, in descending order, come the aristocracy, the church, the army, and the gentry (prosperous middle classes). The entire weight rests on the backs of the people, who are beginning to show ominous signs of protest.

David King Collection, London

were sufficiently striking to worry Metternich. All domestic attempts at protest, such as the Decembrists' revolt in 1825, and periodic peasant rebellions, were ruthlessly repressed and only reinforced the hostility of Tsar Nicholas I (ruled 1825–1855) to any form of liberalism. Russia's only contributions to the events of 1848–1849 were to help the Austrians regain control in Hungary and to put pressure on Prussia to end the Frankfurt Assembly.

One consequence of so rigid a political stance was economic stagnation. While the rest of Europe underwent the transformation of industrialization, Russia remained primarily an agricultural country, dependent on the labor of serfs, who were virtual slaves tied to the land of the great estate owners. A few factories were opened, but the technological progress that was reshaping Western Europe made little impact in Russia.

The first impetus for change came as the result of Russia's defeat in a relatively limited conflict, the Crimean War, fought on the Crimean peninsula, which projects into the Black Sea. Formerly part of the crumbling Ottoman Empire, Crimea had been conquered by Russia in 1783. In 1853, Nicholas I decided to use it as the base for further seizure of Ottoman territory in order to gain access to the Mediterranean and establish a presence in the Middle East.

This action drew the opposition of most of the Western European powers, and when the Turks declared war on Russia, Britain and France joined them in a triple alliance against Nicholas. Superior equipment and more efficient transport gave the Western allies an advantage that allowed them to cut short Russian ambitions. At the Paris Peace Conference of 1856, the terms negotiated underlined Russia's loss of military prestige.

ALEXANDER II AND THE SERFS

A year before the conference, Nicholas I died and was succeeded by the more moderate Alexander II (ruled 1855–1881). One of Alexander's first acts was to issue a manifesto promising reforms in working conditions, education, and the legal system. His motives were practical as much as humanitarian. Limited but controlled changes imposed from above were better than revolution from below. In any case, although a few aristocratic intellectuals already opposed serfdom on liberal grounds, most Russian nobles reluctantly accepted reform because they were convinced that the old system was making their country uncompetitive. Russia needed to develop urban manufacturing centers; even in farming the easy availability of serf labor had stood in the way of technological progress.

The Granger Collection

Early photograph showing the allied forces of the British, French, and Turkish navies anchored in the Bay of Balaclava, on the Crimean coast. 1855. The battle fought here on October 25, 1854, was commemorated in a famous poem by the British Poet Laureate Alfred Lord Tennyson: *The Charge of the Light Brigade.* The severity of the cold drove the sailors to invent a type of knitted cap that became known as a "balaclava."

In a climate of hesitation and uncertainty, the tsar emancipated most of the serfs in 1861, one year before Lincoln's Emancipation Proclamation that freed slaves in areas in rebellion in the United States. (Alexander's emancipation of the serfs affected some 52 million, while the number of slaves freed by Lincoln was around 3 million.) Domestic serfs had to continue their service for two more years and were then freed without any land. The others received most of the land they worked, but they had to redeem it by paying with interest for it over a long period, often at inflated prices. The most productive pastures, furthermore, generally remained in the hands of the aristocrats. Control of the land and farming was entrusted to the *mir*, or village commune, whose representatives assigned and redistributed holdings and decided what should be grown. The former serfs paid the landowners for their land and paid taxes to the government; these "redemption dues" were collected by the *mir* and handed over to the state.

Far from satisfying liberal hopes, the Emancipation Decree's limited provisions increased resentment. The serfs had no economic independence and no political rights. Instead of working for an aristocratic landowner, they were now tied to their village commune and spent most of their lives working to pay off their debts. (Freed serfs, on the other hand, could leave to go elsewhere, thus providing a potential labor force for the coming Industrial Revolution in Russia.) Peasant opposition continued to take the form of open rebellion, which was put down by official intervention.

Photograph of the Russian mathematician, Sofia Kovalevskaya. Of Ukranian origin, the young Kovalevskaya went to study in Stockholm because women were not permitted to attend universities in Russia. In Stockholm, she became the first woman to win a doctorate in mathematics and became a professor there as well. Besides her scholarly papers, she published an autobiographical sketch and several novels.

REFORM AND REACTION UNDER ALEXANDER II

Alexander II's other reforms were more successful in addressing class grievances. In 1864 the *zemstvos* were introduced. These were local regional administrative councils, whose elected members were responsible for the roads, primary schools, and welfare institutions of their districts. Although the *zemstvos* had no influence on issues outside their immediate sphere of influence, and never led to the formation of a national assembly, they provided a forum for public debate and permitted middle-class professionals such as doctors and lawyers to take part in civic life. All effective power, however, remained in the hands of the tsar and his ministers.

Educational reorganization ranged from a notable increase in the number of primary schools to the relaxation of controls in the universities. Alexander initiated secondary-level education for girls, and special university courses for women were introduced. Even though some of the changes were short-lasting, they broke down centuries of custom. In 1861, the Medical Surgical Academy in St. Petersburg admitted women for the first time, only to ban them again three years later. Thereafter, women who wanted a medical career left Russia to study in Western Europe. Zurich, one of their most popular refuges, developed a small Russian community, which later became a center for political dissidents—among them Lenin.

Alexander II's reforms affected other aspects of Russian life. The legal code was revised. The new system introduced some Western liberal ideas by relaxing punishments for some crimes, although it never challenged the authority of the state. Modernization of the army led to greater efficiency. Most of the recruits were peasants, and the education they received while enrolled helped increase the general spread of literacy. Beginning in the 1870s, planning and construction began on a vast railroad system, including the vital trans-Siberian line, which was intended to consolidate links within the vast spaces of Russia and to help in the delivery of exports to the West.

The results of Alexander II's reforms were to strengthen both extremes of the political spectrum. In response, police repression was used to control any protests that the apparent relaxation provoked. A rebellion in the Polish territory under Russian rule was ferociously repressed in 1865. Ten years later the *zemstvos* were prohibited from even debating national political issues, and censorship was strengthened in the press and in the universities.

THE RADICAL MOVEMENT

The hopes encouraged by the new measures led at the same time to the growth of a radical socialist movement. The intellectual father of Russian socialism was Alexander Herzen (1812–1870), an early advocate of the "Westernization" of Russian society. Herzen spent 1848 in revolutionary Paris and saw the failure there of socialism at the barricades. From exile in London, he wrote and published works in which he hailed the peasant commune as the best basis for socialism in Russia. By building on these ideas, the Russians could avoid capitalism, which he believed disfigured Western society, and move directly from an agricultural to a socialist society.

Herzen's writings and his journal, *The Bell*, inspired some intellectuals to live in peasant communities and try to sow the seeds of revolution. Those participating in this "back to the people" movement were called *Narodniki*. The innate conservatism of both the peasants and the authorities stood in the way of any success, however, and Herzen's followers were further inhibited by his strict advocacy of nonviolence.

By the 1870s Herzen's ideas were regarded as old-fashioned, and there developed in reaction a new radical socialism. Younger intellectuals called themselves "nihilists," or believers in nothing. Under the influence of the anarchist philosopher Michail Bakunin (1814–1876), they proposed to use violent means to overthrow the state and revolutionize society (on Bakunin and the anarchists, see Topic 77). Although most nihilists limited themselves to talking about action, in 1877 Vera Zasulich (1849–1919), a young radical, killed the governor of St. Petersburg for mistreating prisoners. Two years later, some nihilists formed a secret society called "The Will of the People." The organization included many young female activists—a third of its executive committee consisted of women. Its aim was to bring down the government by assassinating the state's leading figures. As socialist extremists moved further from their popular roots, the Pan-Slavic movement encouraged contempt for Western liberalism. The result was an increasing sense of isolation among Russia's intellectuals.

Alexander II's response to the restlessness and threats was at first to return to a policy of repression. By the end of his reign, however, he had reached the conclusion that he needed to give way to liberal sentiment. The change came too late. In March 1881, the Will of the People assassinated the tsar in a bombing plot coordinated by Sophia Perovskaia

Print showing the assassination of Tsar Alexander II on March 13, 1881. Late 19th century. Tragically, Alexander II was the only Russian ruler who tried to promote reform. Six foiled attempts had been made on the tsar's life, including a bomb on the imperial train and another one in the Winter Palace. The fatal explosion illustrated here came while he was driving through St. Petersburg.

(1853–1881) and others. Most of those involved in the plot were captured and hanged, and Perovskaia was the first woman executed in Russia for terrorism. On the dead tsar's desk was found legislation for providing Russia with a constitution, awaiting his signature.

The tsar's son and successor, Alexander III (ruled 1881–1894), blamed his father's death on excessive political reform. He had no intention of making the same mistake and initiated a period of harsh, autocratic rule. Using the police, the army, and the Orthodox Church, he kept a careful watch on all levels of society. Most local control was taken away from the *zemstvos* and given back to the landowning aristocrats. Local governors were appointed with wide powers. The persecution of Russia's Jewish population was encouraged. Almost a generation was to pass before socialist and liberal reformers had regained the strength to renew their protests.

Putting Austria and Russia in Perspective

At a time of widespread economic growth and rapid social change throughout Western Europe, Austria and Russia succeeded in maintaining conservative and authoritarian rule. In both cases, liberal causes met with little success; even the emancipation of Russia's serfs created as many problems as it solved. In both countries, nationalism, far from leading to reform, served the purposes of state repression. The Austrians, with Hungarian help, used nationalist divisiveness to keep the regime's opponents divided. In Russia, the strength of Pan-Slavic sentiment presented a barrier to the introduction of Western-style reforms.

Several common factors help explain the ability of the conservatives to retain power. Russia and the Austro-Hungarian empire were, at least in comparison with

Continued next page

the rest of Europe, economically underdeveloped. In consequence, they lacked the great urban centers where a large working class was built up and reform movements traditionally developed.

In vast countries, covering huge geographic areas, communications were poor. Intellectual life was limited to a handful of cities. Vienna was really the only Austro-Hungarian cultural center on the level of the capitals of Western Europe, and Prague was the empire's other artistic center. In Russia, artists and thinkers were divided between Moscow and St. Petersburg. Many creative artists from Eastern Europe left their homelands to make their reputation abroad: the Hungarian Franz Liszt, the Pole Frédéric Chopin, the Russian Ivan Turgenev—all won their fame in Paris. Even as nationalist an author as Fyodor Dostoyevsky wrote most of his greatest works while living in Western Europe.

The result was an isolationism in political thinking as well as in culture that affected both of the countries involved and also those parts of Europe from which they were isolated. To most observers in London, Brussels, or Rome, Russia was a remote and mysterious land, with its own version of Christianity and a unique set of political institutions. As for the Austro-Hungarian empire, few in the West were likely to fight for the liberation of the Serbs or the Slovaks. The only genuine support for the independence of a people in Eastern Europe, the Greeks, was inspired by a kind of historical Romanticism. Vienna did play a key role in the formation of late 19th-century culture, but the Hapsburg capital always had an air of exoticism, and in any case showed the empire's multiethnic character at its best.

Yet, ironically enough, when these two conservative giants collapsed, they did so along with much of the rest of the world. It took World War I and its aftermath to depose the Austro-Hungarian emperor and tsar of Holy Mother Russia. The process and its consequences were cataclysmic.

Questions for Further Study

1. What political and economic factors created the differences between the speed of reform in Western Europe and in Austria and Russia?
2. What part did intellectual developments in Russia play in changing Russian society?
3. What was the impact of ethnic differences and the Pan-Slavic movement on the Hapsburg empire? What lasting effects, if any, was it to have in the 20th century?
4. In what ways did the Crimean War influence international European affairs in the mid-19th century?

Suggestions for Further Reading

Cahm, C. *Peter Kropotkin and the Rise of Revolutionary Anarchism*. New York, 1989.

Geraci, Robert P. *Window on the East: National and Imperial Identities in Late Tsarist Russia*. Ithaca, NY, 2001.

Hillyar, Anna, and Jane McDermid. *Revolutionary Women in Russia, 1870-1917: A Study in Collective Biography*. New York, 2000.

Okey, Robin. *The Habsburg Monarchy: From Enlightenment to Eclipse*. New York, 2001.

Palmer, Alan. *Twilight of the Hapsburgs, The Life and Times of Emperor Francis Joseph*. London, 1994.

Riasanovsky, N.V. *Russia and the West in the Teaching of the Slavophiles*. Boston, 1980.

Schorske, Carl E. *Fin-de-Siècle Vienna: Politics and Culture*. New York, 1981.

Stites, R. *The Women's Liberation Movement in Russia: Feminism, Nihilism, and Bolshevism, 1860–1930*. Princeton, NJ, 1978.

Taylor, A.J.P. *The Habsburg Monarchy, 1809–1918*. Baltimore, MD, 1990.

InfoTrac College Edition

Enter the search term *Crimean War* using Key Terms.

DIPLOMACY AND WAR: THE AGE OF NATION BUILDING

In the period from 1815 to 1849, those revolutions that had been influenced by a combination of Romanticism and nationalism produced little in the way of concrete political change. After midcentury, however, nationalism shed its Romantic idealism in favor of power politics and emerged as the most effective political ideology in Europe. The ability of post-1850 leaders to forge national unity depended more on diplomacy and war than on cultural awareness or insurrection.

The amalgam of power politics and nationalism resulted in the creation of national states in Italy and Germany between 1850 and 1871. This was largely the work of two men—the Piedmontese prime minister Camillo Cavour and the Prussian minister-president Otto von Bismarck. Both were realists who wanted to achieve results and cared little about the morality of their means.

Cavour, the architect of Italian unification, enhanced Piedmont's prestige among the great powers by strengthening his country's economy and joining Britain and France in the Crimean War. Over the following years, Cavour seized the initiative in the wake of Giuseppe Garibaldi's conquest of southern Italy and, using the Piedmontese army and the benevolent support of Great Britain, forged the Kingdom of Italy.

The territorial completion of the Italian state took place against the backdrop of German unification. Bismarck, who became minister-president of Prussia in 1862, strengthened the Prussian Army and the power of its king at the expense of constitutional liberalism. In 1866, he waged a brilliant war against Austria that excluded Austrian influence from German affairs and created a Prussian-dominated North German Confederation. Finally, in 1870–1871, Bismarck eliminated French opposition to a unified Germany by defeating Napoleon III in another war and bringing all the states of Germany together in a single German empire; Italy, taking advantage of Napoleon's withdrawal of French troops from Rome, seized the Papal States and made Rome the new Italian capital.

While the peoples of Germany and Italy struggled to create new nation-states, the American people fought over the issue of national unity. In the Civil War of 1861–1865, regional loyalties combined with economic interests and moral issues to divide the young republic. As in Europe, the victory of the industrialized North under the leadership of Abraham Lincoln over the agrarian South reflected the triumph of power politics.

ITALY, GERMANY, AND THE UNITED STATES: PATHS TO UNIFICATION

The revolutions of 1848–1849 represented the first major efforts to create national states in Italy and Germany, but the armies of Austria (and, in the case of Mazzini's Roman Republic, of France) proved triumphant. Yet the setbacks of 1849 were not without result. The ill-fated military campaigns of Charles Albert (see Topic 66) had at least positioned the Kingdom of Piedmont-Sardinia as the one Italian state committed to fighting for national independence. Similarly, Prussia emerged as the unquestioned leader of the German unification movement, especially because of its role in forging economic unity through the *Zollverein*, or customs union. Together and separately, Piedmont and Prussia would challenge the dominance of the Austrian empire in central Europe.

Cavour and Bismarck revolutionized the European state system, but their methods reflected the most conservative aspects of 19th-century liberalism. They preferred monarchy to republicanism, had little faith in democratic principles, and manipulated both popular opinion and constitutional process to achieve their goals, believing that history was made from above, by political and economic elites, rather than from below, by "the people."

In the midst of this process of unification in Italy and Germany, the United States also faced its own serious crisis of national unity—the Civil War (1861–1865). In the 1840s and 1850s, American nationalism under the guise of

"Manifest Destiny" expanded the boundaries of the United States west to the Pacific coast and south to Mexico. Like Cavour and Bismarck, the American president Abraham Lincoln struggled to impose centralized authority over regional forces that challenged the unity of this far-flung national state. Yet, although Lincoln also resorted to war and enhanced his executive power in order to preserve the American republic, his political faith derived from democratic principles.

PIEDMONT AND THE ITALIAN QUESTION

The regimes restored to power in Italy in 1815 fell into three geographical-historical categories. The first was northern Italy, which consisted of the provinces of Lombardy-Venetia, given to Austria by the Congress of Vienna, and the Kingdom of Piedmont-Sardinia. The Hapsburgs administered Lombardy-Venetia through a viceroy, and because of the relative prosperity of the region, its citizens deeply resented Austrian domination. Piedmont, ruled by the House of Savoy, lay in the militarily vital northwest corner of the peninsula, along the French border. The Savoy kings, descended from an old and distinguished dynasty, had for centuries sought to extend their domain across northern Italy.

The second, all of southern Italy, known as the Kingdom of the Two Sicilies, was ruled by the Bourbons of Naples. The kingdom stretched from Naples to Sicily, a vast region of poor peasantry who toiled on the estates of noble absentee landlords. Here, too, the Hapsburgs had considerable influence, as a result of dynastic connections. The Bourbon king, Ferdinand II (ruled 1830–1859), was scornfully dubbed "King Bomba" because he had ruthlessly bombed Sicilian cities in order to crush the 1848 insurrections.

The third, central Italy, included the Papal States and a group of small principalities, the most important of which was the Grand Duchy of Tuscany, also under the influence of Austria. The Papal States were territories of the Catholic Church. Their subjects experienced considerable political repression and widespread poverty, but the rule of the pope was supported by French troops stationed in Rome and the ever-vigilant Austrian Army of Italy.

THE DEBATE OVER UNIFICATION

In addition to the opposition of the monarchs themselves, the movement for Italian unification—known as the *Risorgimento* ("resurgence")—was hampered by strong sectional loyalties. Moreover, Italian patriots were deeply divided about how to achieve the common goal of Italian unity and independence. Three major currents of thought proposed different solutions. The Young Italy organization founded by the nationalist leader Giuseppe Mazzini (see Topic 66), called for a popular revolution and the establishment of a republic based on democratic principles and universal suffrage.

SIGNIFICANT DATES

Italian Unification

1820–1821	Revolutions in Naples and Piedmont
1831	Young Italy formed by Mazzini
1831–1848	Charles Albert reigns as king of Piedmont-Sardinia
1848–1849	Revolutions in Italy; Piedmontese *Statuto* decreed
1854–1856	Crimean War; 1856 Paris Peace Conference
1858	Treaty of Plombières
1859	Austro-Piedmontese War
1860	Garibaldi's expedition to Sicily
1849–1861	Victor Emmanuel II rules as king of Piedmont-Sardinia
1852–1861	Cavour prime minister of Piedmont-Sardinia
1861	Kingdom of Italy created
1861–1865	American Civil War; Lincoln serves as president
1866	Austro-Prussian War; Italians seize Venice
1870–1871	Franco-Prussian War; Italians seize Rome
1846–1878	Pius IX rules as pope
1861–1878	Victor Emmanuel II rules as king of Italy

Map 69.1 The *Risorgimento*.
Even before the main drive of the *Risorgimento*, Victor Emmanuel II, with a force led by Garibaldi, took Lombardy from the Austrians in 1859. Most of the Papal States became part of the new Kingdom of Italy the following year, but Rome was untouched until 1870. The reigning pope, Pius IX, refused to accept the notion of a united Italy and withdrew into the Vatican, which is still to this day sovereign papal territory. Go to http://info.wadsworth.com/053461065X for an interactive version of this map.

For those who saw the Catholic Church and monarchy as the twin pillars of a united Italy, the liberal priest Vincenzo Gioberti organized a "Neo-Guelph" movement (during the Middle Ages, the popes and their allies called themselves Guelphs in the struggle with the Holy Roman Emperors). Gioberti, a Piedmontese by birth, wanted a confederation of Italian states with the pope as its political head and the king of Piedmont-Sardinia as its military defender. Although the Neo-Guelph movement received momentary encouragement with the election of Pius IX—born Giovanni Mastai-Ferretti (ruled 1846–1878)—as pope in 1846, most contemporaries believed it impossible to preserve the territories of the Catholic Church in the context of a united Italy because not only did they cut the peninsula in half, but an ecclesiastical state could not easily coexist within a temporal state.

The third, and ultimately successful, solution for Italian unification was known simply as the "moderate" program. Led by Count Cesare Balbo (1789–1853) and other liberal aristocrats from Piedmont, the moderates rejected both the radical strategies of the Mazzinians and the pro-papal ideas of the Neo-Guelphs. Most of the moderates were Piedmontese patriots who had supported the reforms that Napoleon Bonaparte had brought to Italy, and their more practical and realistic approach was to succeed.

CAVOUR AND THE TRIUMPH OF THE MODERATES

The Austro-Piedmontese war of 1848–1849 greatly strengthened the position of the moderates. Although Charles Albert had been soundly defeated in 1849, Piedmont was the only Italian state to preserve its constitution in the wake of the revolutions. The new Piedmontese king, Victor Emmanuel II (ruled as king of Piedmont 1849–1861, as king of Italy 1861–1878), successfully maintained his father's constitution in the face of Austrian threats; however, Camillo Cavour rather than the king brought the moderate program to fruition.

Count Camillo Benso di Cavour (1810–1861) was born into the Piedmontese nobility, but like many liberal statesmen of his day he was more bourgeois than aristocratic in his values. Cavour was distinctly unimpressive in appearance—he was round in girth and short in stature and wore sober frock coats and wire-rim spectacles—and an uninspired public

S. E. M. LE COMTE DE CAVOUR

Engraved portrait of Camillo di Cavour. 1855. This portrait shows Cavour five years before the creation of Italy, when he was President of the Council of Ministers of the Kingdom of Piedmont. His name and title are written in French, the official language of Piedmont, and the one preferred by Cavour even when he became Italy's first Prime Minister.

speaker. Moreover, he thought of himself first as a Piedmontese and only latterly as an Italian—in fact, he wrote more often in French than in Italian. Cavour possessed a razor-sharp intellect and proved to be one of the 19th century's most adept practitioners of the art of diplomacy. Calculating and single-minded, he never allowed moral principles to interfere with practical considerations. His experience in industry, banking, and farming made him an advocate of economic liberalism.

Cavour won election to the Piedmontese Chamber of Deputies in 1848. Two years later Victor Emmanuel II appointed him minister of agriculture and trade, and his efficiency and experience gained him the prime ministership in 1852. In order to carry out an ambitious program of reform aimed at improving the country's economy, he forged an alliance of moderate forces in the Chamber of Deputies. Realizing that by itself Piedmont was unable to oust the Austrians, he sought to gain the backing of Europe's great powers for Italian unification under Piedmontese leadership. Although he eventually created the Kingdom of Italy, Cavour had a more limited conception of unification than either Mazzini or Gioberti. At first, his goal was merely to

expand Piedmontese territory throughout northern Italy, without involving either the Papal States or the Kingdom of the Two Sicilies.

To gain the favor of Britain and France, Cavour brought Piedmont into the Crimean War in 1854. Piedmont had no political stake in Near Eastern affairs, but its military alliance with the Western powers enabled Cavour to take part in the Paris Peace Conference of 1856. There Cavour convinced the British to condemn Austrian interference in Italian affairs and established a friendship with the French emperor.

In July 1858 the two ambitious politicians secretly concluded the Treaty of Plombières, which secured French assistance against Austria. They agreed that if the Franco-Piedmontese alliance proved victorious, Piedmont would annex Lombardy and Venetia and create a kingdom of northern Italy. This kingdom would then join with the other Italian states in a federation under papal leadership. Napoleon's reward would be the French annexation of Savoy and Nice, both of which were Piedmontese territory. Because Napoleon was sensitive to European opinion, however, he insisted that Austria should appear the aggressor, and Cavour agreed to stage an incident designed for that purpose.

In April 1859, Cavour goaded the Austrians into making unacceptable demands against Piedmont. Napoleon immediately went to war against Austria and sent a large army to Italy to fight alongside the Piedmontese. The allies drove quickly through Lombardy, but before the invasion of Venetia could begin, Napoleon—who was horrified at French losses, under pressure from domestic opponents, and nervous about Prussian military movements on the Rhine—unexpectedly signed a separate armistice with the Austrians. Cavour, outraged at Napoleon's perfidy and Victor Emmanuel's acquiescence, submitted his resignation as prime minister, although he soon returned to office.

CAVOUR VERSUS GARIBALDI: UNIFICATION ACHIEVED

Cavour's machinations had largely determined the first phase of the *Risorgimento*. In 1860, however, he began to respond to events as leadership of the unification movement was unexpectedly grasped by Giuseppe Garibaldi (1807–1882). Unlike the unscrupulous and plotting Cavour, Garibaldi was an uncomplicated idealist—he had, noted the British poet Alfred Lord Tennyson, "the divine stupidity of a hero." The son of a sea captain, from whom he inherited a love of adventure, Garibaldi had already become a popular figure who fought on behalf of Italy's common people. A populist in the Mazzinian mold, Garibaldi wanted a democratic republic, but his first goal was to secure Italian unification.

In the 1830s, after the failure of an uprising in which he participated, Garibaldi fled to South America, where he and his Brazilian wife Anita took part in several revolutions. While fighting in the jungles of Brazil and Uruguay,

Photograph of Giuseppe Garibaldi. Mid-19th century. One of the leading figures in the struggle to unite Italy, Garibaldi was born in Nice, which passed under French rule in 1860. The photograph shows him wearing the South American poncho he had acquired during his years of fighting revolutionary campaigns in Brazil and Uruguay.

Garibaldi developed the tactics of guerrilla insurrection. With the outbreak of the 1848 revolutions, he came back to Italy and raised a volunteer army in support of Charles Albert's war against Austria. When that campaign collapsed, he joined Mazzini in Rome and coordinated the defense of the republic. In 1859 Garibaldi led another volunteer force in the Austro-Piedmontese War.

GARIBALDI AND THE RED SHIRTS

Garibaldi was able to seize the initiative from Cavour because he conceived of Italian unity as embracing all existing regions, including the south. He planned an invasion of the Bourbon kingdom, starting from the island of Sicily and working his way northward. Cavour, who learned of the plans in the spring of 1860, worried that Garibaldi would try to take Rome—a move that would certainly bring intervention by Napoleon III. Cavour decided, therefore, to make his own plans. While supplying weapons to Garibaldi and supporting his efforts to recruit an army of about 1,000 "Red Shirts," he also secretly ordered the Piedmontese Navy to sink Garibaldi's ships if they turned toward Rome. (The term "Red Shirts" was derived from the fact that while in South America the only uniforms Garibaldi could afford to provide for his men were red butcher's shirts; he dressed his men the same way.)

In May 1860, Garibaldi's expedition reached Sicily. The Bourbons had a considerable garrison stationed there, far outnumbering the Red Shirt forces, but Garibaldi managed to outflank them. With additional troop strength recruited from the local population, he conquered all of Sicily. He then landed on the mainland in September and seized the city of Naples, where he established a temporary government for the former Kingdom of the Two Sicilies.

As Garibaldi moved up the mainland, Cavour sent a Piedmontese army down into the Papal States—but while claiming that he wanted to secure the papacy against a possible attack from Garibaldi, he quickly occupied the Papal States, leaving Pope Pius IX only Rome and the territory immediately around the city.

The most dramatic moment in the *Risorgimento* took place in October, when the armies of Garibaldi and King Victor Emmanuel II met at Teano, north of Naples. The meeting between the leader of the radical movement and the king, the symbolic head of the moderates, could have resulted in a disastrous civil war. The day was saved, however, because Garibaldi, who placed the unity of Italy above all else, surrendered the lands he had conquered to Victor Emmanuel.

Engraving showing meeting between Victor Emmanuel II, the first king of Italy, and Garibaldi. 1860. Garibaldi is on the right. The image does not try to give a realistic depiction of the actual historical encounter, but rather to present the culminating moment of Italy's *Risorgimento*—and the end of Garibaldi's career as revolutionary leader.

PERSPECTIVES FROM THE PAST

THE *RISORGIMENTO*

The Italian movement for liberation and unification was in one sense an ideological struggle among a series of competing philosophies of government and society. From the time of the Congress of Vienna in 1815, Italian patriots argued about the methods that should be employed to achieve their goals and the kind of state that should govern a unified nation.

Young Italy

The nationalist leader Giuseppe Mazzini founded the Young Italy society in 1831 as a vehicle for co-ordinating patriotic revolution throughout Italy. His goal was the creation of a unified republic.

It was during these months of imprisonment that I conceived the plan of the association of Young Italy (*La Giovine Italia*). I meditated deeply upon the principles upon which to base the organization of the party, the aim and purpose of its labors—which I intended should be publicly declared—the method of its formation, the individuals to be selected to aid me in its creation, and the possibility of linking its operations with those of the existing revolutionary elements of Europe.

We were few in number, young in years, and of limited means and influence; but I believed the whole problem to consist in appealing to the true instincts and tendencies of the Italian heart, mute at that time, but revealed to us both by history and our own previsions of the future. Our strength must lie in our right appreciation of what those instincts and tendencies really were.

All great national enterprises have ever been originated by men of the people, whose sole strength lay in that power of faith and of will, which neither counts obstacles nor measures time. Men of means and influence follow after, either to support and carry on the movement created by the first; or, as too often happens, to divert it from its original aim. . . .

At that time even the immature conception inspired me with a mighty hope that flashed before my spirit like a star. I saw regenerate Italy becoming at one bound the missionary of a religion of progress and fraternity, far grander and vaster than that she gave to humanity in the past. . . .

Why should not a new Rome, the Rome of the Italian people—portents of whose coming I deemed I saw—arise to create a third and still vaster Unity; to link together and harmonize earth and heaven, right [law] and duty; and utter, not to individuals but to peoples, the great word Association—to make known to free men and equal their mission here below?

From Denis Mack Smith, ed., *The Making of Italy 1796–1870.* Harper & Row. Copyright © 1968. Reprinted with permission of Denis Mack Smith.

Gioberti's Neo-Guelph Idea

Vincenzo Gioberti's notion that only the pope could act as symbolic leader of a federated Italy of autonomous princes was widely accepted by Catholics and monarchists but its credibility collapsed in the wake of the 1848 revolution, when Pius IX abandoned the patriotic cause.

I propose to prove that Italy contains within herself, above all through religion, all the conditions required for her national and political resurrection or risorgimento, and that to bring this about she has no need of revolutions within and still less of foreign invasions or foreign exemplars. And to begin with I say that Italy must first and foremost regain her life as a nation; and that her life as a nation cannot come into being without some degree of union between her various members. This union can be interpreted and established in various ways, but, however it is achieved, it is a necessity, and if it fails our nation will be weakened and enfeebled beyond repair. . . .

Supposing we succeeded in putting an end to the present division in Italy by revolutionary means? Far from achieving the union we desire, we would be opening the door to fresh disorders.

For political union cannot bring happiness to a people if it is confused and vacillating instead of tranquil and stable. The principle of public peace and security must be sought in the sovereign power, whatever form it may take; because without sovereignty there is no order, and without order there is neither peace nor security nor free living nor any other civil good. The sovereign power is based partly on moral force, that is to say on law, and partly on material force, that is to say on the army; and although, given human wickedness, arms are needed to protect public opinion, they cannot replace it, for it is impossible to restrain a few malcontents unless there is a general consensus among many men of good will. Only moral authority can justify a sovereign power, it being inconsistent that others should be expected to obey a system of rule that they think it morally legitimate to offend or annihilate. . . .

That the Pope is naturally, and should be effectively, the civil head of Italy is a truth forecast in the nature of things, confirmed by many centuries of history, recognized on past occasions by the peoples and princes of our land, and only thrown into doubt by those commentators who drank at foreign springs and diverted their poison to the motherland.

From Denis Mack Smith, ed., *The Making of Italy 1796–1870*. Harper & Row. Copyright © 1968. Reprinted with permission of Denis Mack Smith.

Cavour's Realism

Count Camillo di Cavour, prime minister of Piedmont and architect of Italian unity, was above all a realist with a practical sense of the possible. In this famous article, dealing ostensibly with railroads, he explained the idea of a gradual program of moderate development for unification under the leadership of the Piedmontese monarch.

If the future holds a happy fortune for Italy, if this fair country, so one may hope, is destined to regain her nationality, it can only be the consequence of a remodeling of Europe, or as a result of one of those great providential explosions in which the mere ability to move troops quickly by rail will be unimportant. The time of conspiracies has passed; the emancipation of peoples cannot result from mere plots or from a surprise attack. It has become the necessary consequence of the progress of Christian civilization and the spread of enlightenment. Once the hour of deliverance sounds, the material forces which governments possess will be powerless to keep conquered nations in bondage. Moral forces are growing daily which sooner or later, with the aid of providence, must cause a political upheaval in Europe; and governments will then have to yield. . . .

All history proves that no people can attain a high degree of intelligence and morality unless the feeling of its nationality is strongly developed. This remarkable fact is a necessary consequence of the laws which govern human nature. The intellectual life of the masses moves within a very limited range of ideas. Among the ideas which they are capable of acquiring, the noblest and most elevated are first those of religion, then those of country and nationality. . . .

[I]t seems likely that the precious triumph of our nationality cannot be realized except by the combined action of all the live forces in the country, that is to say, of the national rulers openly supported by every party. The history of the last thirty years, as well as an analysis of the various elements in Italian society, will prove that military or democratic revolutions can have little success in Italy. All true friends of the country must therefore reject such means as useless. They must recognize that they cannot truly help their fatherland except by gathering in support of legitimate monarchs who have their roots deep in the national soil. . . .

But more than by any other administrative reform, as much perhaps as by liberal political concessions, the building of the railways will help to consolidate the mutual confidence between governments and people, and this is the basis of our hopes for the future. These governments have the destiny of their peoples in trust, and railway building is therefore a powerful instrument of progress which testifies to the benevolent intentions of each government and the security they feel. On their side the people will be grateful for this and will come to hold their sovereigns in complete trust; docile, but full of enthusiasm, they will let themselves be guided by their rulers in the acquisition of national independence.

From Denis Mack Smith, ed., *The Making of Italy 1796–1870*. Harper & Row. Copyright © 1968. Reprinted with permission of Denis Mack Smith.

Garibaldi remained a controversial figure in the *Risorgimento*, finally retiring to self-imposed exile on the island of Caprera. The Kingdom of Italy was established in March 1861, with Victor Emmanuel II as its sovereign and Cavour as its first prime minister. Charles Albert's *statuto* of 1848 became, with minor modifications, the Italian constitution.

As soon as the new nation had been proclaimed, it found itself overwhelmed with an array of serious domestic challenges. Italy lost its most adept political leader when Cavour died that May. Deeply rooted regional loyalties delayed the development of a sense of national identity, a fact poignantly underscored by the comment of one Piedmontese nobleman in 1861: "We have made Italy—now we must make Italians." The challenges of nationhood would sorely test the new Italian leadership over the next half-century.

BISMARCK AND THE STRUGGLE FOR POWER IN PRUSSIA

The Vienna settlement of 1815 did not completely restore the prerevolutionary situation in Germany. The Holy Roman Empire, which Napoleon dissolved, was too unwieldy to resurrect. Instead, a new German Confederation comprising 39 independent states was established. All members were represented in a parliament, known as the "Diet," which assembled periodically at Frankfurt. Austria, technically a part of the confederation, dominated German affairs. Religious differences reinforced Austrian control: Because Prussia and the surrounding northern states were Protestant, Austria could present itself as the protector of the southern Catholic states.

PRUSSIAN AMBITIONS AND THE GERMAN CONFEDERATION

On the surface, the parallels between the German and the Italian situations seemed obvious. Prussia's role was similar to that of Piedmont in Italy: Prussia was the only state ca-

pable of challenging Austrian preponderance in the German Confederation. The House of Hohenzollern, Prussia's autocratic dynasty, had greatly expanded its domains over the centuries, and King Friedrich Wilhelm IV (ruled 1840–1861) thought in terms of extending Hohenzollern authority throughout most of Germany. The major difference between the two ambitious states was one of scale and power because although Piedmont had not been strong enough to best Austria by itself, Prussian industrial and military resources made it a formidable antagonist.

In 1849 Friedrich Wilhelm issued a conservative constitution. This established a parliament with two chambers, similar to that of the Piedmontese constitution of 1848: an upper house, the *Herrenhaus*, appointed by the king, and an elected lower house known as the *Landtag*. Elections were in theory on the basis of universal male suffrage, but a complicated method of indirect voting kept poorer citizens greatly underrepresented and gave the advantage to the upper classes. Royal power remained far-reaching.

Friedrich Wilhelm had turned down the Frankfurt Assembly's offer of the German crown in March 1849 (see Topic 66) because he refused to accept the principle of popular sovereignty. He did not, however, reject the notion of German unification under Prussian leadership from above, although he preferred to achieve the goal in cooperation with Austria. In 1849, the Prussian chief minister, Josef von Radowitz (1797–1853), presented the king with a unification plan that called for the creation of a single German government based on the federal system, headed by Prussia but in permanent union with Austria. Austria rejected the Prussian proposal outright, and Friedrich Wilhelm backed down. In November he dismissed Radowitz and, in the face of an Austrian threat to go to war, humiliated himself by agreeing to a series of terms dictated at a meeting in Olmütz.

BISMARCK: THE IRON CHANCELLOR

The "humiliation of Olmütz" weakened Prussia's self-appointed role as the leader of German unification. Not only did Friedrich Wilhelm's foreign policy fail to inspire confidence, but the unhappy monarch was also afflicted with periodic bouts of insanity. In 1858 his brother Wilhelm was made regent, and in 1861 he succeeded his brother as king.

Wilhelm I (ruled 1861–1888 as king of Prussia, 1871–1888 as emperor of Germany), a soldier by training, was no less conservative and autocratic than his brother. In February 1860, he sent a controversial military reform bill to the Landtag. With the shadow of Olmütz still looming, he proposed a new budget meant to double the size of the Prussian Army and raise the terms of required military duty from two to three years. He also wanted to abolish the reserve militia because he regarded its unprofessional civilian soldiers with disdain.

For the middle-class liberals who represented a majority in the Landtag, the reorganization bill presented a unique opportunity to assert the budgetary authority of parliament over the king, as well as to strike a blow against the influence of the military. Liberal opposition succeeded in

SIGNIFICANT DATES

German Unification

1834	Zollverein created
1840–1861	Friedrich Wilhelm IV rules as king of Prussia
1848–1849	Revolutions in Germany; 1849 Prussian constitution issued
1861–1888	Wilhelm I rules as king of Prussia
1866	Austro-Prussian War; North German Confederation created
1862–1870	Bismarck serves as minister of Prussia
1870–1871	Franco-Prussian War; German empire created

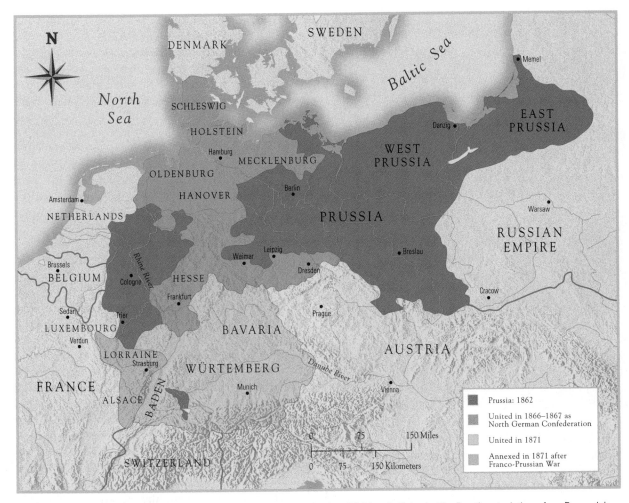

Map 69.2 Unification of Germany. Note the disputed territories of Schleswig-Holstein. The Prussians took these from Denmark in 1866; North Schleswig was returned to Denmark after World War I. To the south, the new state of Germany conquered the French region of Alsace-Lorraine as a result of the Franco-Prussian War of 1870–1871. Returned to France in 1919, it was conquered again by the Germans during World War II, only to be turned back over to France after the war. Go to http://info.wadsworth.com/053461065X for an interactive version of this map.

forcing Friedrich Wilhelm to withdraw the measure. Wilhelm dissolved the Landtag and called for new elections, but he was further embittered when an even larger liberal majority was returned. So frustrated was the king that he came close to renouncing the throne. Finally he decided to appoint Count Otto von Bismarck (1815–1898) as his new minister-president in an effort to resolve what had become a major constitutional crisis. Bismarck's own views on unification seemed well suited to the moment. He envisioned a Prussian-dominated Germany from which Austria would have to be ejected by force, and he detested the liberals.

Bismarck was the exact opposite of Cavour: A towering and vigorous man, he seemed the embodiment of the patri-archal landowning class of Junkers from which he came. Yet, while more conservative than Cavour in his politics, he had none of the narrowness of vision of the Prussian elite; his service in the Frankfurt Diet had given him a deep awareness of German affairs, while his experience as Prussian ambassador first to Russia and then to France had

broadened his knowledge of European diplomacy. Flexible rather than rigid, he could nevertheless be unbending in the face of opposition. He cared little for constitutions and disdained liberals as impractical idealists. Like Cavour, Bismarck thrived on the intricacies and maneuverings of power politics.

Prussian liberals proved to be Bismarck's most bitter enemies. He understood, however, that the industrial and financial expertise of the middle classes was essential to a strong Prussia, and that they were the major advocates of national unification. At first Bismarck saw unification only in terms of Prussian dominance over the Protestant states of the north, and only gradually did his perspective widen to embrace all of Germany. He understood, too, that unification required the elimination of Austria from German affairs.

Bismarck saw the king's army reorganization bill as essential to the extension of Prussian power because he was determined to give Prussia a military force capable of defeating the Austrian empire. Bismarck sidestepped the Landtag alto-

The Granger Collection

Colored photograph of Otto von Bismarck. Late 19th century. The leaves in the vase on the table are from an oak tree, symbol of strength. Known as the "Iron Chancellor," Bismarck's long grip on power allowed him to introduce many sweeping social reforms, including the first workman's insurance scheme in Europe.

gether by raising funds for the army through the sale of bonds in government railroads and the sale of mines and iron works. The liberals attacked Bismarck's subversion of the constitution, but both he and the king ignored them. More difficult to ignore were the liberal views of Victoria, the princess of Hohenzollern (1840–1901), the English-born wife of Crown Prince Friedrich (1831–1888), the heir apparent, who ruled for only three months as German emperor before his death in 1888. This daughter of Britain's Queen Victoria was highly cultured and politically aware, and encouraged her husband to favor a unified German state free from military influence.

Bismarck viewed the liberal opposition as shortsighted obstructionists who failed to understand power politics. He proclaimed unabashedly that only "iron and blood," not parliamentary speeches, would unify Germany. Constitutional theory, he told the Landtag, must give way to the necessities of military strength. Bismarck was certain that victory on the battlefield would convince the liberals that his budget manipulations were irrelevant.

THE SEVEN WEEKS' WAR

The war with Austria that Bismarck wanted began to take shape in the 1860s, and had its roots in the so-called Schleswig-Holstein question. Years later, the British prime minister of the day, Lord Palmerston, remarked that the Schleswig-Holstein affair was so complicated that only

three people had ever fully understood it: One of them was dead, a second had become insane, and the third—Palmerston himself—had forgotten the details.

The international status of these two duchies, both administered by the Danish king, was uncertain. Holstein, predominantly German-speaking, was a member of the German Confederation, but Schleswig, inhabited by Danes as well as Germans, was not. A crisis broke out in 1863, when Denmark annexed Schleswig. On Bismarck's suggestion, Prussia and Austria fought a joint war to reclaim the two provinces. After peace had been made, Austria and Prussia agreed to a joint administration of Schleswig-Holstein. As Bismarck anticipated, disagreement over the future status of the provinces increased tensions between the two powers. In 1865, the Convention of Gastein placed Holstein under Austrian administration and Schleswig under Prussian authority. Disputes between Austria and Prussia followed, and Bismarck soon found a suitable pretext for war with Austria.

Bismarck first cleared the way by ensuring that none of the other powers would intervene on Austria's side. Tsar Alexander II was likely to stay neutral because Bismarck had assisted the Russians in crushing a revolt in their area of Poland in 1863. He was uncertain, however, of Napoleon III, and in 1865 he met secretly with Napoleon at Biarritz to discuss the situation. Napoleon assured Bismarck that he would remain neutral in a war between Prussia and Austria. In 1866 Bismarck, encouraged by his negotiations with Napoleon, offered Italy the province of Venetia in return for Italian help in the war he was preparing against Austria.

On June 1, 1866, Bismarck ordered the Prussian Army into Holstein after alleging that Austria had violated the Convention of Gastein. The Austrians responded by pushing the German Confederation into war against Prussia. Elated, Bismarck announced the end of the confederation and declared war against Austria.

Bismarck couched Prussian aggression in nationalist rhetoric, asserting that the future of Germany hung in the balance. Moving troops by rail, and employing the new breech-loading "needle" gun—Prussia was the first nation to do so—Count Helmuth von Moltke (1800–1891), chief of the Prussian general staff, stunned all of Europe by swiftly reducing one of the most powerful empires in Europe to total defeat. The effect of the Austro-Prussian War—known as the Seven Weeks' War—was to shift the balance of power in central Europe.

Bismarck dealt reasonably with vanquished Austria. The Treaty of Prague, signed in 1866, did not require Austria to pay reparations, and no part of its territory other than Venetia—ceded as promised to the Italians—was lost. On the other hand, Vienna had to agree to the dissolution of the German Confederation and to renounce its interest in Germany. Prussia annexed Schleswig-Holstein and some of the other states in northern Germany.

Bismarck then forced all German states north of the river Main into a new North German Confederation, with the king of Prussia as its president and Bismarck as its chancellor. While its member states still controlled local affairs, military and foreign policy was in the hands of the central government. The confederation's parliament had two chambers, an upper house known as the *Bundesrat*, representing the states, and a lower house, the *Reichstag*, elected by universal male suffrage. The constitution granted extensive powers to the king of Prussia.

THE BIRTH OF THE SECOND REICH

Bismarck no doubt saw the North German Confederation as a temporary expedient, but he had not counted on the reaction of Napoleon III. The French emperor, who had not expected such a complete Prussian victory, was stunned by the rapid Austrian defeat, which left him no time to intervene.

THE FRANCO-PRUSSIAN WAR, 1870–1871

Coming on the heels of the failure of Napoleon's intervention in Mexico (see Topic 67), the emperor's domestic opponents attacked him where he was most vulnerable—on the issue of French prestige. Napoleon saw belatedly that he would have to oppose the creation of a unified Germany on France's borders. Bismarck, on the other hand, believed that he could use a war with France to arouse nationalism and rally the other German states around Prussia's leadership in order to complete the unification process.

Relations between France and Prussia deteriorated as both sides fanned popular sentiment through press campaigns. As with Austria, an obscure diplomatic issue provided the excuse for war—the question of whether a member of the Hohenzollern family would be made king of Spain. Much to Bismarck's dismay, Wilhelm I backed down in the face of French pressure. But the French, pressing their diplomatic victory too far, demanded a formal guarantee that no Hohenzollern would ever again become king of Spain. Wilhelm I met with the French ambassador at the resort town of Ems in July 1870, but politely refused the French demand for such a guarantee, and sent Bismarck a telegram recounting the details of the meeting. Bismarck, who was unwilling to see an excellent pretext for war disappear, carefully abbreviated the wording of the so-called Ems Dispatch so as to make it appear that the king had abruptly rejected the French proposal. Bismarck then made the telegram public. With the enthusiastic help of the popular press in both countries, the doctored telegram enraged public opinion and gave Napoleon III little choice—he announced hostilities on July 19, 1870. The Franco-Prussian War had begun.

Once again the devastating precision of Prussia's armies stunned Europe. Despite its defeat in 1866, Austria remained neutral, principally because Bismarck had imposed such moderate peace terms on Vienna. Bismarck could also claim that the war was a "German," rather than a Prussian, struggle because the other German states were bound to Prussia by military alliances. The war was over in six months. On September 1, 1870, the Prussians struck a devastating blow against France at Sedan, capturing 100,000 French troops and taking Napoleon prisoner. In Paris, Napoleon was dethroned and a republic proclaimed on September 4. Although the outcome of the war was certain, for five months Republican France refused to give in and

Painting of the proclamation of King Wilhelm of Prussia as Emperor of Germany. Late 19th century. The Prussian king had personally led the victorious Prussian troops at Sedan. He then proceeded to Versailles, where he became the first head of a united Germany on January 18, 1871. His chief minister, Bismarck, dressed in white uniform, stands at the front of the crowd.

the Prussians laid siege to Paris. The French surrendered in January, and two months later Parisian radicals led the desperate population in a rebellion against the republican government and proclaimed the Commune (see Topic 77).

Against the backdrop of the terrible siege of Paris, Bismarck staged the last act in the unification of Germany. On January 18, 1871, Wilhelm I was crowned German emperor in a ceremony held in the symbolic heart of former French glory—the Hall of Mirrors of the Palace of Versailles. The "Second Reich"—German nationalists counted the Holy Roman Empire as the "First" Reich—had been created.

Adolphe Thiers (1797–1877), the provisional head of the French government, negotiated with the German empire. The Treaty of Frankfurt was far different in spirit and intent from the generous terms Bismarck had given Austria five years earlier. Germany annexed most of the strategically vital province of Alsace and a large portion of Lorraine—areas in eastern France that held rich iron mines and flourishing textile mills. Although the inhabitants were mainly German-speaking, most preferred French rule. For the next five decades the loss of Alsace and Lorraine rankled deeply in the French psyche. The Prussians marched triumphantly through Paris and, to make matters worse, France was required to bear the humiliation of German occupation until it had paid a huge indemnity of 5 billion francs, a sum that amounted to more than twice the cost of the war for Prussia.

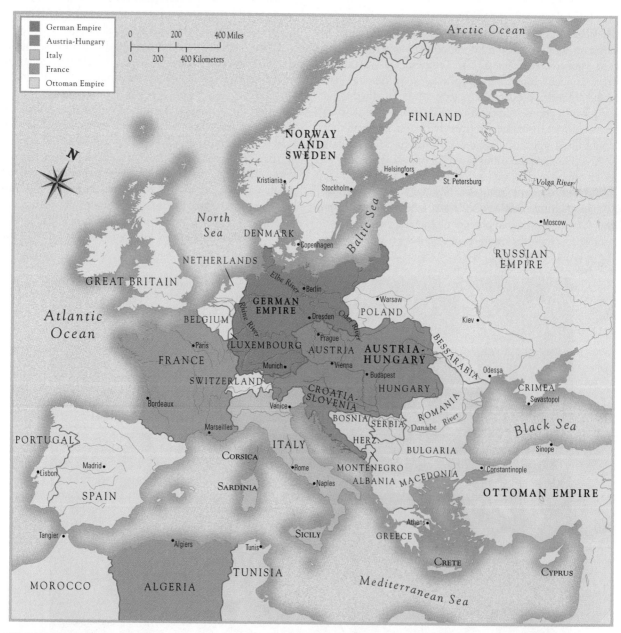

Map 69.3 Europe in 1871. There are three new 19th-century countries between northeast France and Germany: Belgium, the Netherlands, and Luxembourg. The last two became independent in 1815, after the defeat of Napoleon. Belgium, which was originally a province of the Netherlands, broke away in 1830. Note that the largest power in terms of territory is the Ottoman Empire; its collapse after World War I created massive problems in the Balkans, North Africa, and the Middle East, many of which continue to plague those areas in the 21st century.

Photograph of President Abraham Lincoln with George B. McClellen and staff at Antietam. September 1862. The bloody battle fought at Antietam repulsed the Confederate General Robert E. Lee's first thrust north toward the beginning of the Civil War. Union forces halted Lee's army before they could reach Washington and drove them back across the river Potomac.

The Franco-Prussian War was one of the most far-reaching events of the 19th century. Bismarck had succeeded in unifying Germany under Prussian control, not through the spirit of liberal nationalism that had wanted it in 1848–1849 but in alliance with the conservative elites who had made Prussia into an autocratic, military state. Bismarck's armies had defeated the two most powerful states on the Continent, and the German empire had emerged as the most powerful state in Europe. The European balance of power was irrevocably altered.

NATIONALISM, REGIONALISM, AND THE AMERICAN CIVIL WAR

The struggle for political unification that transformed Europe in the 19th century was also played out in the New World, where the recently created United States underwent a process of expansion and crisis (see Topic 59). European radicals, struggling against the Vienna settlement of 1815, were encouraged by the triumph of democratic principles in the United States, in particular by the adoption of the Bill of Rights. In 1828, while the Restoration was still firmly entrenched in Europe, Americans gave their democratic system a still broader popular base by sending Andrew Jackson (president 1828–1835) to the White House.

NATIONALISM AND THE CIVIL WAR

American nationalism grew steadily in the first half of the 19th century, especially after the War of 1812 with Great Britain. Moreover, Americans not only believed that their national interests conflicted with those of Europe's great powers, but also thought of their political culture as fundamentally different from that of the Old World. A thirst for expansion further fueled nationalist sentiment as Americans pushed west and south from the original 13 states, bringing enormous areas such as the Louisiana Purchase and the Northwest Territory under the control of the United States. America's "Manifest Destiny," claimed imperialists, was "to overspread the continent allotted by Providence for the free development of our multiplying millions." In this aggressive spirit, President James Polk (served 1845–1849) fought the Mexican War in 1846–1848 and, with the seizure of Texas and California, extended the boundaries of the United States to the Rio Grande and the Pacific coast.

This rapid expansion deeply divided Americans because it raised the issue of the extension of slavery to the new territories. Tensions mounted between the southern states, where slavery was a key element in the plantation-based agriculture of the region, and those in the North, where industrialization was taking hold. Although slavery was only one element in a complex web of sectional disputes, it became the chief focus of the Civil War (1861–1865).

European nationalist leaders, particularly those in Italy, watched the Civil War closely. Because Abraham Lincoln (president 1861–1865) led the federal government in the struggle to maintain the American union, Italians regarded him as one of the most important statesmen of the century. Cavour and Garibaldi had been long-time admirers of the American political system; Garibaldi had lived in New York in the early 1850s, and on several occasions Cavour seriously contemplated emigrating to the United States. Whereas Cavour expressed dismay that the Civil War might set back the cause of national unification, Garibaldi was more interested in the moral urgency of suppressing slavery. In 1861 Lincoln actually offered Garibaldi command of an army corps, but the offer was never formalized: The American president was not prepared to accept Garibaldi's demands that he be given supreme command of the Union army and that slavery be abolished immediately. Cavour did not live to see the northern victory over the Confederacy, which eliminated slavery in the United States and successfully preserved the union.

Putting the Age of Nation Building in Perspective

In the two decades after the revolutions of 1848–1849, nationalism achieved its greatest successes. National unity in the United States was preserved, Italy and Germany were created, the Hungarians had forced the Hapsburgs to grant them a measure of autonomy within the Austrian state, and the inhabitants of the Balkans were beginning to stir against Turkish domination.

By the end of the 19th century, however, nationalism had taken on a new and significantly different meaning. The idealistic vision of Mazzini, who had seen nationalism as a liberating force that would create an era of international cooperation among free nations, all but disappeared as a new brand of chauvinist patriotism gained sway. Cavour and Bismarck, who applied the methods of power politics to the task of national liberation, had forged domestic alliances with conservative elites—army officers, businessmen, and aristocrats—in order to achieve their goals. These conservative forces now controlled the destinies of the newly unified states and ushered in a period of intense national rivalry. After 1871, competition among nations for prestige and dominance increasingly shaped international relations.

Questions for Further Study

1. What were the principal programs for Italian unification? How did they differ?
2. What methods did Bismarck employ in his efforts to unify Germany? With which Italian leader would he be most readily compared?
3. What were the consequences of the way in which Italy and Germany were unified?
4. In what ways was the unification experience of the United States different from that of Italy and Germany?

Suggestions for Further Reading

Brueilly, John, ed. *Nineteenth Century Germany: Politics, Culture and Society 1780-1918.* London, 2001.
Crankshaw, Edward. *Bismarck.* New York, 1981.
Davis, John A., ed. *Italy in the Nineteenth Century: 1796-1900.* New York, 2000.
Di Scala, Spencer. *Italy from Revolution to Republic,* 2nd ed. Boulder, CO, 1998.
Hamerow, Theodore S. *The Social Foundations of German Unification, 1858–1871.* 2 vols. Princeton, NJ, 1969.
Mack Smith, Denis. *Cavour.* New York, 1985.
Mack Smith, Denis. *Garibaldi.* Englewood Cliffs, NJ, 1969.
Mack Smith, Denis. *Mazzini.* New Haven, CT, 1994.
Pflanze, Otto. *Bismarck and the Development of Germany.* 3 vols. Princeton, NJ, 1990.
Williamson, D.G. *Bismarck and Germany, 1862–1890.* New York, 1998.
Woolf, Stuart. *A History of Italy, 1700–1860.* New York, 1986.

InfoTrac College Edition

Enter the search term *American Civil War* using Key Terms.

TECHNOLOGY AND THE EUROPEAN ECONOMY

By 1850 Britain, long in the vanguard of the Industrial Revolution, had established its superiority over the rest of Europe in virtually all facets of economic life—technology, the factory system, energy production, commerce, and trade. A proud and self-satisfied nation determined to show off its achievements to the rest of the world in the Great Exhibition of 1851. The exhibition at the Crystal Palace was not only a British event, but rather the first world's fair. Other European countries and the United States also displayed their machines and products. The Exhibition's international nature underscored the spread of industrialization. The British economy maintained its lead until overtaken by Germany and the United States in the 1890s, but between 1850 and 1873, the rapid pace of its early growth slowed as continental Europe and the United States began to close the gap.

The two decades after 1850 were years of rapid industrialization on the Continent. Production levels in key sectors such as coal, iron, and textiles increased enormously. France, Germany, and other countries adopted—and sometimes improved—the new machines and factory organization already in place in Britain.

The railroad came into its own in this period. Europe and America experienced something of a "railroad revolution," as country after country built dense networks of rail lines, creating national markets for the first time. The railroad boom became a major sphere of investment and banking activity and stimulated the further expansion of heavy industry.

Agriculture, having improved significantly since the late 18th century, also entered a phase of increased productivity. New farming regions were opened up in Eastern Europe, and increased mechanization went hand in hand with land reclamation and new fertilizers.

The accelerating growth of the continental economy in this period required significant change in the way in which Europeans conducted business. Old laws hampered modern financial operations, while huge amounts of capital were needed to buy machinery and to build factories and railroads. Industrial expansion encouraged the development of the modern corporation and banking systems and contributed to the decline of trade barriers.

By the 1870s, the industrial and financial world looked quite different from that of 1850. Europe was poised on the edge of the era of modern capitalism and global economy.

THE GREAT EXHIBITION OF 1851: THE PROMISE OF TECHNOLOGY

While visiting the Paris Exposition of 1849, Henry Cole (1808–1882), an English civil servant, conceived the idea of organizing an event in London that would reveal Britain's industrial superiority. With a population half the size of France, Britain produced two-thirds of the world's coal and more than half its iron and cotton cloth; its manufactured goods flooded markets everywhere, and its ships carried the bulk of the world's trade. Britain's per capita income was 50 percent higher than France's and more than twice that of Germany.

THE CRYSTAL PALACE

Prince Albert, Queen Victoria's husband, sponsored the exhibition through the Society of Arts, of which he was president. A competition was announced for the design for the exhibit pavilion, to be located in Hyde Park. After considering and rejecting some 245 projects, the organizers turned to Joseph Paxton (1803–1865), a horticulturalist and self-trained landscape architect. He had achieved fame for the gardens and landscaping he supervised for the duke of Devonshire, including the construction of a glass-roofed conservatory supported by cast-iron columns.

Paxton came up with an imaginative concept: a long, three-story building consisting of numerous round-headed bays in the neo-Gothic style that was then popular. The roof was in the form of an enormous arc. In the interior, galleries for individual exhibits lined either side of the huge central space. Most daring of all, the pavilion would be built entirely of glass (a material never before used for major construction) and held together by wrought-iron framing supports—in effect, a "crystal palace."

The genius of Paxton's idea derived in part from the requirement that the entire building had to be erected in

<table>
<tr><td colspan="2">**S I G N I F I C A N T   D A T E S**</td></tr>
<tr><td colspan="2">**Technology and the Economy**</td></tr>
<tr><td>1830</td><td>First successful steam railway opened in England</td></tr>
<tr><td>1843</td><td>End of British ban on exporting machinery</td></tr>
<tr><td>1844</td><td>Bank Charter Act in England; 1846, Bank of Prussia</td></tr>
<tr><td>1851</td><td>The Crystal Palace Exhibition</td></tr>
<tr><td>1852</td><td>Crédit Mobilier</td></tr>
<tr><td>1856</td><td>Incorporation with limited liability</td></tr>
<tr><td>1840–1860</td><td>Railroad boom</td></tr>
<tr><td>1865</td><td>Belgium, France, Italy, and Switzerland form the Latin Monetary Union</td></tr>
<tr><td>1871</td><td>Gold standard begins</td></tr>
<tr><td>1850–1900</td><td>Second Industrial Revolution</td></tr>
</table>

nine months. His design made it possible to accomplish this because the building could be put together from prefabricated, interchangeable parts assembled in modules. A triumph of civil engineering in the age of iron, the Crystal Palace covered an area of almost 20 acres and utilized 2,224 wrought-iron girders, 3,300 cast-iron columns, and 300,000 panes of glass—some being, at the time, the largest ever made. Sixteen huge semicircular arches of wood, reaching more than 100 feet high, provided additional support.

Londoners marveled as the structure went up, and Victoria and Albert made numerous visits to the construction site. Despite dire predictions of disaster from skeptics, the Crystal Palace did not collapse. The queen officially opened the exhibition on May 1, 1851, with some 500,000 people crowding Hyde Park for the occasion. "The sight," Victoria recorded in her diary, "was magical—so vast, so glorious, so touching."

INDUSTRIAL CIVILIZATION ON DISPLAY

Within Paxton's palace were displayed more than 100,000 industrial products from around the world, submitted by 7,351 exhibitors from the British Empire and 6,556 from other countries. The items were grouped into categories such as raw materials, machinery, textiles, metal and ceramic products, and the fine arts.

Not unexpectedly, the machine displays most interested the public. Visitors saw the full range of 19th-century industrial items, from railroad locomotives and steamship engines to machine tools of all sorts, from power looms to printing presses and envelope-making machines, from hydraulic turbines to fireplaces. The American exhibit attracted particular attention because it was the most forward-looking and included such practical items as ice-making machines, a Cyrus McCormick reaper, a sewing machine, and Colt revolvers made from standardized parts. From California came a device for winnowing gold, and from Canada a hand-operated fire pump.

Engineering and architectural firms exhibited a variety of construction schemes, including lighthouses, iron bridges, and a model for a canal across the Suez isthmus. Amid the products and inventions were also coal and iron ores, and the German firm of Krupp—described as "a manufacturer of Essen"—startled the public with a two-ton block of cast steel, the largest steel ingot ever seen. Weapons and scientific objects intermingled with telegraph machines, cameras, and cooking utensils. For the mid-19th-century consumer, the exhibition presented a feast of incredible items that delighted and awed spectators.

The Crystal Palace show was a major success. The queen came several times a week. The duke of Wellington was a frequent visitor, and was called on for advice when a peculiar problem developed. The Palace had trees inside it, and the sparrows that nested in them constantly bespattered the visitors. Wellington's recommendation was "sparrow hawks"—trained birds that would kill the sparrows and then fly out of the building.

Engraving of the exterior of the Crystal Palace, Hyde Park, London. 1851. The Crystal Palace was the first cast-iron frame building and the first for which structural units were prefabricated and then assembled on the site. Its architect, Sir Joseph Paxton, took as his model a conservatory (greenhouse) he had constructed in the gardens at Chatsworth, England.

More than 6 million people, including streams of English schoolchildren, saw the exhibition (the Crystal Palace was dismantled after the exhibition and moved to another location, where it remained until a fire destroyed it in 1936). German princes and other dignitaries headed a long list of foreign notables and thousands of other pilgrims, all intent on seeing the wonders of the industrial age. Europeans had enjoyed a singular glimpse of the promise of technology.

CONTINENTAL INDUSTRY COMES OF AGE

The pace of industrialization in continental Europe between 1850 and 1873 was unprecedented. This expansion, best measured by production figures in coal, iron, textiles, and steam power, sometimes increased as much as 10 per-cent each year in the so-called industrial inner zone of France, Belgium, and Germany. Resources, government policies, political instability, and capital availability all affected the rate of growth.

ECONOMIC GROWTH: WAGES, PRICES, AND DEMAND

These developments, often called the Second Industrial Revolution, took place in the context of a significant demographic change. The rapid and sustained growth in Europe's population that had accompanied the first Industrial Revolution slowed down considerably after 1850. Population did continue to grow because more and more children lived to maturity, but now at a reduced rate. Significantly, the lower birthrate did not have an adverse impact on the demand for consumer goods. On the contrary, the number of potential consumers had become less important than the volume of consumption, which rose on a per capita basis. Two factors account for this rising demand.

Table 70.1	Real Wages, 1848–1872 (1850 = 100)		
YEAR	BRITAIN	FRANCE	UNITED STATES
1848	90	82	100
1850	100	100	100
1852	102	95	90
1854	96	84	88
1856	96	76	85
1858	102	100	83
1860	103	97	97
1862	105	103	86
1864	117	111	76
1866	116	111	83
1868	110	103	93
1870	118	113	120
1872	122	108	132

Adapted from Walt W. Rostow, *The World Economy: History and Prospect* (Austin and London: University of Texas Press, 1978), 157.

First, as Europe's population aged, more emphasis was placed on industrial products than on food, and the general increase in prosperity produced rising sales. Second, the opening of new markets overseas, especially in the United States, India, and East Asia, also stimulated demand.

focus on products instead of food.

Prices for both industrial goods and food generally went up between 1848 and 1873, when a long depression brought an end to this growth. Contributing to this pattern were the discovery of gold in California and Australia, which increased the money supply and investment; inflationary cycles during the Crimean War, the U.S. Civil War, and the wars of German unification; the high costs of capital investment required for technological improvement and for the developing of new farmlands; and the overall rise in wages.

Despite the steady increase in prices, real wages—that is, actual purchasing power—grew in the more advanced countries. This increase in prosperity and wealth was an important spur to industrial development.

THE TEXTILE INDUSTRY

Industrialization affected the production of textiles after 1850 on the Continent as fully as it had in Britain at the opening of the century. Although heavy industry experienced more significant developments, the manufacture of textiles continued to be important because of the great demand and the huge number of workers employed. Improved machinery was introduced into regions where preindustrial methods had prevailed, steam power became more widespread, and advances in chemistry were applied to the finishing of cloth, both cotton and wool.

By midcentury, Great Britain had completed its transformation to a fully mechanized textile industry. The self-

Colored print of women workers with a male overseer in a mill. Mid-19th century. The scene—the women chatting as they work, the well-lit hall, the sense of space and order—are a far cry from the true nature of industrial production. In reality, factories were overcrowded, dark, and polluted. A print such as this one must have been made to decorate the parlor of a mill owner's wife.

acting mule—a steam-powered, fully mechanized spinning machine—had all but replaced hand-operated spinning jennies. Cotton remained the predominant fabric in terms of demand and quantity, a position enhanced by the expanded supply of cheap raw material from the United States. The wool industry was mechanized later than cotton making, but in the 1850s it, too, changed as wool combing became a mechanical process.

In 1843 Britain lifted the ban on the exporting of machinery. As a result, spinning machines were widely introduced in Alsace, the center of the French cotton industry, as well as in Switzerland, Germany, and even Russia. Those factories producing higher-quality fabrics adopted the most technically advanced equipment. By 1870, France and Germany had made great progress in mechanization, although Britain still remained ahead.

THE EXPANSION OF COAL PRODUCTION AND STEAM POWER

Because coal was the major fuel source for 19th-century industries, the quantity produced helps reveal the rate of industrial expansion. Between 1850 and 1870, the world's volume of coal increased almost threefold, from some 81 million tons to 213 million. Until the 1890s, when the United States began to take the lead, Britain remained the greatest coal-producing nation in the world. Because many of France's coal deposits were of an inferior quality, one-third of its supply was imported. Many German states, however, possessed rich mineral resources, and after 1840 coal production rose rapidly. By the time of unification in 1871, Germany turned out 2.5 times the amount of coal as France, and its output had reached almost one-third of Britain's. The British consumption pattern, which was fairly typical of the period, revealed that iron makers and steam-driven factories used more than half of all British coal, while the rest went for heating, export, and as fuel in railroad engines and steamships.

For most countries, a critical problem in coal production was transportation. Many British coalfields were near the coast, so that the coal could be brought directly to ships, but in France transport costs increased the cost of coal tenfold. The exploitation of inland deposits required cheap transportation, which canals and inland waterways only partially provided. It was the railroad that created a national market—that is, the condition that prevails when the price of a particular item is generally similar in all regions of a country. Once markets were easily accessible, new mines were developed in areas such as Pennsylvania, the Donets

Basin, northern Britain, and the Ruhr. In the 1840s, French mining engineers discovered a major extension of their northern coalfields, which brought production up from less than 5,000 tons in 1851 to more than 2 million in 1870.

The increase in coal supplies went hand in hand with the development of more efficient steam engines, which drove the new machinery. Great increases in horsepower were achieved by the introduction of high-pressure steam engines fitted with elaborate valve systems. The amount of steam energy generated in Europe followed the established pattern: Britain was in first place, with Germany second and France third. A French tariff on imported steam engines curtailed their adoption, and French mills continued to rely on waterpower years after British and German manufacturers had converted to steam. Even in Germany, only 62,000 horsepower was generated by 1855, although within 20 years it increased tenfold. World production of steam shot upward between 1850 and 1870, from some 4 million horsepower to more than 18 million.

IRON AND ITS LIMITATIONS

British breakthroughs in cheap iron making also moved across the channel in full force by midcentury. The Belgians were the first on the Continent to adopt British methods: Instead of costly charcoal, coke was used in the blast furnace to smelt ore into cast iron. The "puddling" process, whereby the molten cast iron was constantly stirred in order to remove impurities, produced a cheap but tough wrought iron that would bend without breaking under tension (see Topic 60). In addition, in the mid-1840s rolling mills had been designed that permitted large-scale production of iron "I" beams, which could be used in making rails for railroads.

In 1845, 90 percent of Belgian cast iron was made in coke blast furnaces. By contrast, in France, Germany, and the United States, where wood for charcoal was cheaper, the transition to coke took place much more slowly, primarily because of the shortage of good coal and the distance between the coal and iron deposits. In the 1850s, when railroads brought the two materials together, France tripled its iron output within two decades. Coke smelting was introduced into Germany only in the 1840s, but the new technique took hold rapidly, and by 1862 Prussia was making almost 90 percent of its iron with coke.

The production of pig iron in major western areas between 1850 and 1870 increased about 70 percent each decade, with worldwide volume increasing threefold as the United States became a major producer.

Because cast iron made in coke blast furnaces was so brittle, it could be used only under compression for such items as columns, as in those of Paxton's Crystal Palace. Wrought iron was used for all purposes where tension bending was involved, such as the construction of suspension bridges. The demand for a stronger metal became intense after midcentury, with the tremendous expansion of railroads throughout the Continent. The answer was steel, provided it could be made cheaply. Steel had been manufactured in limited quantities since the 18th century, but

Table 70.2	Coal Production (in millions of tons), 1850–1870			
YEAR	BRITAIN	FRANCE	GERMANY	UNITED STATES
1850	50	4.4	6.9	2.5
1860	81	8.3	16.6	15.2
1870	112	13.3	34	42.5

Painting of a coke-smelting operation in Upper Silesia, Poland. Mid-19th century. The region is still Poland's most important industrial region. Before the exploitation of natural gas, much coal gas was produced by coke furnaces. After more than a century of production, Silesia is one of the most polluted regions in Europe; its chief river—the Oder—has been severely affected.

Table 70.3	Pig Iron Production (in thousands of tons), 1850–1870			
YEAR	BRITAIN	FRANCE	GERMANY	UNITED STATES
1850	2,285	406	210	560
1860	3,890	898	529	821
1870	6,059	1,180	1,260	1,690

Table 70.4	The Railroad Revolution (in miles), 1840–1870			
YEAR	BRITAIN	FRANCE	GERMANY	UNITED STATES
1840	838	360	341	2,820
1850	6,620	1,890	3,640	9,020
1860	10,430	5,880	6,980	30,630
1870	15,540	9,770	11,730	53,400

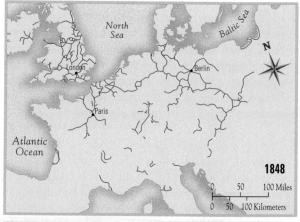

Map 70.1 The Railroad Explosion. Even in Britain, where railroad construction first began, the explosion during these three decades is astounding. The four concentrations are in central and northern England, around Paris, in northwest Germany, and around Milan. Southern Italy and Spain are barely affected; in the latter, Barcelona had not, by 1879, yet begun to develop as a major industrial region.

further technological breakthroughs were needed before the age of steel could be realized (see Topic 75).

THE RAILROAD ERA

The world's first commercially successful steam railway opened in Great Britain in 1830, from Liverpool to Manchester. By 1835 the commercial benefits of the railroad had been proven because in three hours goods could now travel the same distance that once took 36 hours by canal. Within 20 years Britain had more than 8,000 miles of rail lines that crisscrossed the country in all directions. Fifteen years later, the figure had almost doubled. Because of its small size and intense commercial life, Britain had a traffic density on its rails greater than any other country.

THE RAILROAD BOOM

Britain had undergone its industrial revolution before the coming of the railroad, using waterways for moving coal and iron—the only country to have done so. On the Continent and in the United States, industrialization took place along with the development of railroads. The two decades after 1850 saw the expansion of railroads on such a massive scale as to create the "railroadization" of Western Europe.

By 1840, Belgium had essentially completed its main rail lines of more than 200 miles, whereas the much larger territories of France and Germany each had fewer than 400 miles. The boom hit in the decades between 1840 and 1860, when a combination of political leadership and commercial factors pushed railroad building to the extreme. In France, an 1842 law called for close cooperation between government and private capital in realizing a national plan of trunk lines radiating from Paris. Napoleon III, a railroad enthusiast, encouraged rail construction with state support, and the Crédit Mobilier made large-scale financing possible. By 1870, France had almost 10,000 miles of rails. In Germany, after initial reluctance, Prussia eventually took the lead in railroad building, and Berlin became the kingdom's rail hub. The Prussians, who paid particular attention to the military uses of the railroad, quickly outstripped France in total mileage.

THE IMPACT OF THE RAILROAD

Railroad lines were built and operated according to varying national policies. The British railroads were built with private capital, just as their turnpikes and canals had been private enterprises. Other governments built the rail lines themselves, subsidized private enterprise, or combined these approaches. Belgium and Austria both decided on public ownership, whereas the French solution was a compromise. The state provided the land, planned the layout, and prepared the roadbed, and then granted long-term leases to private companies to run the lines.

Regardless of the particular national strategy, the impact of the railroad on economic and industrial development was enormous. It substantially lowered transportation

Monet, *Gare Saint Lazare.* 1877. 2 feet 5¾ inches by 3 feet 5 inches (1.02 by .77 m). The Saint Lazare railway station is in the heart of Paris, near the Grands Boulevards, and therefore a major center for commuters. It may seem an odd choice of subject for an Impressionist painter, but Monet was fascinated by the effects of light on smoke. Cezanne said of him: "Only an eye, but my God, what an eye!"

costs for regional, national, and international markets. Railroads also stimulated the adoption of new technologies in the iron, coal, and machine engineering industries and created a huge demand for these and other products. The need for more durable rails would act as a major inducement for the birth of the modern steel industry.

The enormous amounts of capital required to build railroads deeply affected systems of finance and business cycles in the second half of the 19th century. Railroads opened up vast new tracts of farmland, especially in the United States, where much European capital was invested. Investments in railroads, along with speculation in real estate, became a veritable craze at times, and widespread speculation caused both huge profits and financial panics. Investment banks were often started in order to raise capital, international loans were granted, and trading in rail bonds and stocks contributed to the rise of modern exchanges. In many instances the capital accumulated in railroad speculation was then available for reinvestment in other industries.

The political and social consequences of railroad construction were equally far-reaching. Lines linking once isolated regions contributed to the rise of national spirit and helped the process of domestic consolidation after unification. Generals rethought modern military strategy in the light of the rapid transportation of troops and war materiel now possible. Railroads encouraged the growth of cities and changed their appearance as rail lines and stations dotted the urban landscape. Moreover, people—ordinary, working-class citizens—now had for the first time the possibility of traveling long distances at relatively modest cost, both for leisure and for work, and the railroads offered an opportunity for some to escape the inner cities and live in healthier, more pleasant suburbs.

MODERNIZING THE EUROPEAN ECONOMY: TRADE, FINANCE, AND THE CORPORATION

Two facts dominated the changing character of the European industrial economy in the period from 1850 to 1873: technological modernization and the expansion of markets. These developments required money on a scale hitherto unknown—money to make the capital improvements dictated by the new technology, and money to operate the burgeoning industries in order to meet the production requirements of an increasingly international demand.

Barriers to European trade were generally lowered after midcentury. In the 1850s, international waterways such as the Danube, the Rhine, the Elbe, and the Baltic and North Seas were opened to free commerce by the elimination of levies and restrictions. But the most important move in this direction came in the following decade as a result of a series of commercial treaties among the leading industrial nations. The gradual adoption of the gold standard made international trade still easier in the latter part of the century, although the trend toward free trade was reversed after 1870.

THE RISE OF THE CORPORATION

The pressures of expanding markets and industrialization meant that after 1850 business units had to be much larger than the old firms and partnerships. Joint-stock or corporate forms of business organization provided clear advantages. In joint-stock firms, several people pooled their capital in a common enterprise, usually with transferable shares. If incorporated, such enterprises are recognized by law as single units, or bodies (*corpora*), which can sue and be sued inde-

Engraving of the *Great Eastern* ship laying the Transatlantic Cable in 1866. One of the great engineering feats of the 19th century, it provided a communication link between Europe and the Americas. Its impact on international trade, banking, and money exchange made possible the development of a world economy.

Hulton Getty Collection/Tony Stone Images

pendently of their members. Thus, shareholders could have "limited liability" that protected their individual property.

Because unbridled speculation had resulted in a major financial crash in the early 18th century, Britain had passed the Bubble Act of 1720, which required special acts of Parliament to grant a joint-stock charter. This restriction was repealed in 1825, and further changes made it much easier to form such companies. In 1856, incorporation with limited liability became a simple matter of registration, and in the next decades France and Germany followed suit, while in the United States individual state governments chartered companies. The corporation soon became widely utilized by railroad companies in Europe and America, and by the end of the 19th century, corporations took over most industries.

THE GOLD STANDARD AND BANKS

The rise of large corporations controlling huge assets and doing business across national boundaries created a need for new sources of money and a variety of banking institutions. In addition, the worldwide movement of capital was intensified and facilitated by the development of a new international monetary system based on gold.

As in the case of industrialization, Great Britain moved toward the gold standard before the rest of Europe. In 1821, the Bank of England made its notes convertible into gold, and the British pound sterling was guaranteed at a specific gold weight. In 1865, Belgium, France, Italy, and Switzerland formed the Latin Monetary Union, which sought to encourage a world currency system by adopting the franc as a common unit and minting coins of uniform weight in each country. Greece was the only other nation, however, to join the group, and in the 1870s the union gave up its efforts in favor of the gold standard, which the German empire had adopted in 1871. By the eve of World War I, all the other major powers had followed suit.

Although most currencies eventually based their standard on gold, it was not the actual medium of exchange. Rather, gold became a form of reserve money, housed in banks, which in turn issued notes and bank certificates for circulation. Three kinds of banks evolved in the second half of the 19th century: central, commercial, and investment banks. Central banking appeared in Britain with the Bank Charter Act of 1844, which required the Bank of England to increase the quantity of its banknotes only if it increased its bullion reserves by the same amount. A new Issue Department received a monopoly on printing all future banknotes in England, while a Banking Department established a commercial checking system. Because the Banking Department maintained its reserves at from 30 to 50 percent, while smaller banks kept much smaller reserves, the Bank of England became the lender of last resort in times of emergency—in effect, a kind of bankers' bank.

The Bank of France, founded by Napoleon Bonaparte in 1800, received a monopoly on the issue of banknotes in 1848. Although the bank was privately owned, the government maintained close supervision of its activities, and it, too, kept high levels of reserves to support its notes. In Germany, central banking began when the Bank of Prussia, established in 1846, was converted into the Reichsbank in 1875. Both the Bank of France and the Reichsbank served an important business function by discounting bills of exchange (that is, exchanging them for cash), and established numerous branch banks for that purpose.

Unlike central banks, the chief function of commercial banks is to serve commerce and industry directly by providing short-term loans to businesses. Commercial banks became joint-stock companies in the 19th century and tended toward a high degree of monopoly: the so-called Big Five (Barclays, Lloyds, Midland, National Provincial, and Westminister) dominated British commercial banking, while four firms—including Crédit Lyonnais and Société Générale—monopolized most of French commercial banking, and the Big Four "D" banks—such as the Deutsche Bank and the Dresdner Bank—controlled such operations in Germany.

Investment banks, on the other hand, were concerned principally with extending long-term credit in the form of stocks and bonds. Investment banks arose in order to provide capital for plants and equipment for railroads and large industrial firms. In the early 19th century the principal "investment" bank of Europe was the House of Rothschild, which engaged mainly in financing government loans. Five brothers operated the firm, one in each of five major cities—Frankfurt, London, Paris, Vienna, and Naples. These and other international bankers facilitated the financing of railroads by marketing stocks and bonds.

Yet such investment banks tended to be cautious in underwriting new industries, and by the mid-19th century other avenues were needed. Napoleon III, unhappy over his dealings with the Rothschilds, promoted one of the most interesting experiments in investment banking—the Crédit Mobilier. Founded by the Pereire Brothers in 1852, it accumulated capital by selling its own stocks and bonds, and then lending the capital to make long-term loans to start new businesses; once the firms were established, the Crédit Mobilier would also sell the securities of the new enterprises to investors. It was highly successful for a time in promoting railroads, utilities, and industrial firms. Given the nature of its operations, the Crédit Mobilier was vulnerable in financial crises because it had little liquid assets. The company went bankrupt in 1867 and was liquidated in 1871. Similar institutions were established in Germany in the 1850s and in Britain in the following decade. Even the Rothschilds joined the trend, establishing the Credit-Anstalt in Austria. Later the American investment banks of J.P. Morgan and Kuhn, Loeb and Co. were to become giants on the international banking scene.

The national and international money markets established between 1850 and 1873 played a critical role in the industrialization of the Continent. The capital raised, invested, and circulated by these new banking institutions provided the financial basis for the remarkable growth of the European industrial economy, particularly in the decades after 1870, and in the creation of a global capitalist system.

Putting Technology and the European Economy in Perspective

The 20 years after 1850 represented an important phase of maturation for the European economy. The essentials of the industrialization process had reached the Continent. The growth rate maintained generally high levels as production in textiles, coal, and iron rose steadily—and sometimes dramatically.

The revolution in transportation, caused chiefly by the railroad, deeply affected every aspect of European civilization, from industrial and financial growth and market expansion to the shape of cities and the way in which millions of people led their daily lives. Along with the equally far-reaching revolution in banking and business organization, the railroads pointed the way toward an age of capitalist enterprise in which the links between technology, heavy industry, and the world of finance grew increasingly close.

As industrial and agricultural profits reached new heights in this era, the wealth of Europe was reflected in the improvement of real wages and living standards. Rather than a sign of crisis, the declining birthrate meant the emergence of new patterns of consumption and higher levels of comfort for many Europeans. The Great Exhibition of 1851, with which the period opened, symbolized the beginning of an age of enthusiastic and self-conscious materialism for European civilization.

Questions for Further Study

1. How did technology transform the European economy in the 19th century?
2. How did the development of railroads influence industrial and economic policy?
3. To what conditions did the rise of the corporations respond?

Suggestions for Further Reading

Auerbach, Jeffrey. *The Great Exhibition of 1851: A Nation on Display.* New Haven, CT, 1999.

Bordo, Michael, and Anna J. Schwartz. *The Gold Standard and Related Regimes: Collected Essays.* New York, 1999.

Cameron, Rondo. *A Concise Economic History of the World.* New York, 1989.

Carter, E.C., et al., eds. *Enterprise and Entrepreneurs in Nineteenth and Twentieth Century France.* Baltimore, MD, 1976.

Elon, Amos. *Founder: A Portrait of the First Rothschild and His Times.* New York, 1996.

Freeman, Michael J. *Railways and the Victorian Imagination.* New Haven, CT, 1999.

Henderson, William O. *The Rise of German Industrial Power, 1834–1914.* Berkeley, CA, 1975.

Hobhouse, Hermione. *The Crystal Palace and the Great Exhibition: Art, Science and Productive Industry.* London, 2002.

Hobsbawm, Eric J. *The Age of Capital, 1848–1875.* New York, 1979.

Lottman, Herbert P. *The French Rothschilds: The Great Banking Dynasty Through Two Turbulent Centuries.* New York, 1995.

Milward, Alan S., and S.B. Saul. *The Development of the Economies of Continental Europe, 1850–1914.* Cambridge, MA, 1977.

Trebilcock, Clive. *The Industrialization of the Continent.* New York, 1981.

InfoTrac College Edition

Enter the search term *industrial revolution* using Key Terms.

MIDDLE-CLASS VALUES AND WORKING-CLASS REALITIES

Family = important

By the mid-19th century, the focus of European life had decisively shifted from the country to industrial cities. In this urban context the aristocracy slowly lost some of its traditional authority, while the middle classes, which were involved in trade and industry, grew in wealth and power. Bourgeois attitudes toward work and private life established a norm for all levels of society. At the bottom of the social scale, the condition of the workers and urban poor seemed, if anything, even worse than that of agricultural laborers. Yet the sheer concentration of their numbers, and the manifest unfairness of their grim living conditions, led to pressure for reform.

The moral tone of the midcentury was set by those who had gained most from the confrontations of earlier years: the middle classes. From the security of their financial independence, manufacturers, merchants, and professionals praised the virtues of hard work, honesty, and self-reliance. Material success, they claimed, could be achieved by combining these merits with a healthy dose of personal ambition. The high self-image sustained by the bourgeoisie was accompanied by a rigid code of behavior, laying out the duties of public and private conduct.

At the heart of the middle-class world view lay the family. The house provided the setting for domestic life and was defined as women's narrowly circumscribed sphere of influence. By contrast, all other activities were largely restricted to men. Thus bourgeois women were enshrined at the center of a cult whose effects on all aspects of their lives were claustrophobic. Yet even within the middle classes, there were rebels. The mid-1850s saw the formation of some of the earliest feminist groups. For many of the working-class poor, living in urban squalor, the bourgeois prescription for domestic happiness was meaningless. By the middle of the century, charity workers and social reformers had begun to attack some of the more basic problems. Public health, working conditions, education, and housing were all the subject of increasing government action.

Pressure for reform began to come not only from middle-class humanitarians but also from the working classes themselves. Earlier worker protests had lacked a coherent sense of direction. In the mid-19th century the cause of the rights of the working class was given a philosophical basis and powerful expression in the writings of Karl Marx. His aggressive socialist vision of a newly ordered society, first published on the eve of the 1848 revolutions, prepared the way for the working-class parties that played a growing role in late-19th-century politics.

Map 71.1 European Urbanization, 1860.
The world's largest city at this time was London. Cities that grew significantly in size during the mid-19th century include Brussels, Hamburg, and Madrid. Cities that became important urban centers by the end of the century (and so are not shown on this map) include Milan, Stuttgart, Frankfurt, Copenhagen, and Budapest.

THE URBANIZATION OF EUROPE

The rapid transformation of European life from an agricultural to an urban society had begun in the early 19th century. In the two decades after 1850, the trend continued, but with some differences. Earlier the most dramatic urban growth had occurred in British towns, where industrial development had been concentrated. Although urban growth continued in Great Britain, after midcentury the pace slowed down. The most startling increase in urban populations took place on the Continent, especially in German cities. In Berlin, for example, the number of inhabitants doubled between 1850 and 1870 from some 400,000 to more than 800,000. In London during the same period, however, the population grew by little more than 40 percent, from 2,685,000 to 3,890,000.

THE SOCIAL IMPACT OF CITIES

Despite its uneven character, urban growth, especially in Western Europe, continued to produce revolutionary changes in social customs and patterns. By the 1870s, almost one-third of all Europeans, regardless of class, gender, or income, lived in cities. Some of these cities were capitals that combined manufacturing and government offices, as in the cases of London and Berlin, whereas others were major industrial centers, such as Glasgow and Düsseldorf. In most cases the problems of urban life were the same.

The consequences of so vast and rapid a change in the lifestyles of millions of people were naturally complex and far-reaching. Viewed from the perspective of the early 21st century, with its fears of urban chaos and collapse, it is tempting to accentuate the drawbacks of city life at the expense of its very real benefits. Widespread application of new technologies and improved medical methods benefitted increasing numbers of people. The continual growth of national prosperity helped underwrite public welfare programs. Furthermore, the rise in the general level of education created a wider audience for intellectual debate and cultural entertainment.

At a more mundane level, great cities like London, Paris, or Vienna provided public gardens, fireworks, and dance halls, pleasures that were easily accessible to the working class. The infinite variety of daily experience, street entertainments ranging from Moroccan dancers to mechanical men, the "busy idleness" of the throngs of people, all offered novelty to those who flocked from the provinces to enjoy the excitement of metropolitan existence. One visitor to Paris called it "a glass beehive, a treat to the student of humanity"—the essence of existence there was "the consciousness of being observed."

Yet inevitably behind the passing scene there lay the other side of city life: grinding poverty, overcrowding, squalor. Nor were such conditions limited to the northern industrial cities. When the novelist Charles Dickens (see Topic 72) first arrived in the Italian city of Genoa in 1844, he was horrified at "the unusual smells, the unaccountable filth, the disorderly jumbling of dirty houses, one upon the

Table 71.1	The Growth of European Cities (in thousands of people), 1850–1870	
CITY	1850	1870
Berlin	419	826
Glasgow	345	522
Hamburg	132	240
London	2,685	3,890
Moscow	365	612
Paris	1,053	1,852
Rome	175	244
Sheffield	135	240
Vienna	444	834

urban conditions became bad

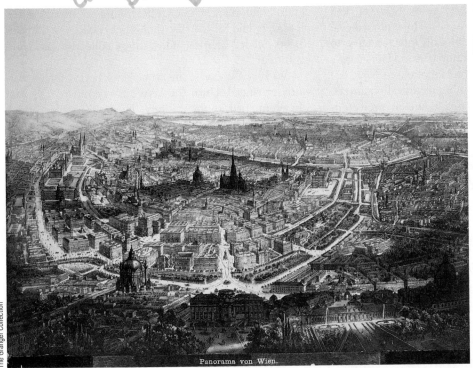

The Granger Collection

Panorama von Wien.

Engraving of bird's-eye view of Vienna. Mid-19th century. The city planners of Vienna consciously designed it to serve as Imperial capital. At the heart of the circular center is St. Stephen's Cathedral. The center is delineated by a broad series of streets called collectively the Ring Roads (Ringstrasse), on which all the chief buildings stand—the large building in the lower left is the State Opera—and the whole of the center is enclosed by the Danube Canal.

roofs of another. I never, in my life, was so dismayed!" Many agricultural workers drawn from declining rural centers by the hope of making their fortunes in the cities found themselves drifting into marginal jobs: rag picking, scissor grinding, collecting human excrement. Others took to crime. More fortunate were those who found employment in domestic service, thanks to the growing demand of prosperous middle-class householders for servants. Nor did urban existence always prove fulfilling in social terms. One migrant to London described it as "a wilderness of human beings."

The faster people crowded into the cities, the worse urban conditions became. At the same time, increasing industrial production created ever-greater pollution, especially in the great mining and textile cities. "Muck means money," one Manchester cotton manufacturer is said to have observed. For his employees it also meant blackened windows, clothes, and lungs. The general replacement of wood by coal as a means of heating increased pollution further; it also meant that those who could not afford to buy coal lived in cold, damp conditions, with inevitable consequences for their health.

Further difficulties were presented by the urgent need for urban planning. Some big industrial and commercial cities began to grow only in the late 18th century; they included the manufacturing centers of the Midlands and northern England, the Ruhr district of northern Germany, and Madrid. In these, at least, coherent planning was theoretically possible. Athens, one of the oldest cities in Europe, is the only European capital whose present center was laid out in the 19th century. After centuries of neglect under the Turks, it was completely rebuilt by the German architects whom Otto (ruled 1832–1862), the first king of independent Greece, brought with him from Bavaria.

Keystone Mast Collection/California Museum Photography/University of California, Riverside

A late 19th-century poor Russian village. Living standards in Eastern Europe remained well below those of the West. Note the unpaved streets, even in the center of this village, the poorly clad children, and the bare feet of the men. The problems of rural communities were increased by the movement of young women and men to the towns to find work.

young people moved into towns to find work

Most of the chief 19th-century cities, however, had been centers of population for centuries. Those of medieval foundation often still had their city walls intact, adding to the complexity of organized expansion. Baron Haussmann's rebuilding of Paris during the Second Empire (see Topic 67) had involved the demolition of medieval quarters. Haussmann's work in Paris inspired a similar project in Vienna, where walls were torn down to make way for the famous *Ringstrasse* in the 1870s.

Further difficulties lay in anticipating and providing for the new needs of urban life. The arrival of the railways required that cities be organized around station terminals and the various branch lines. Increased street traffic made it necessary to build wide avenues and to separate pedestrians and vehicles by constructing sidewalks. By the end of the 19th century, when it was clear that still more transport facilities were needed, subway systems were be-

gun in London and Paris. Underground sewers and water-pipes were laid for the first time since the Roman Empire. Streets needed lighting, and garbage collection had to be organized.

With the increase in crime, city police forces were vastly expanded. Until the 19th century, order was generally maintained by the military. The police served principally as government spies, on the lookout for those regarded as opponents of the regime. As property holders came to demand protection, and the anonymous crowds of the big cities needed controlling, the police began to serve to maintain civic order; Sir Robert Peel established the first British police force in London in 1829 (see Topic 67).

The teeming cities of 19th-century Europe provided the stage on which the political and social battles of the remainder of the century were fought: the struggle for the suffrage, women's rights, and social justice.

Map 71.2 European Nationalities. Future problems loom ahead in the Balkans, and in the Basque region, trapped between southeast France and Spain. Belgium, too, divided between French and Flemish speakers, was to undergo periods of disturbance in the late 20th century. For the most part, the Scandinavian countries maintained their ethnic and linguistic independence.

VICTORIAN VIRTUES: THE THEORY AND PRACTICE OF THE BOURGEOISIE

The attitudes toward life developed by the prosperous middle classes in Western Europe are often summed up under the general term "Victorian." "Victorian morality" is practically synonymous with a rigidly puritan lifestyle, involving pure women and upright men, whose duty was to produce children to serve the public good. Living in respectable homes, gathering daily for family prayers, spending their Sundays in decorous inactivity, Victorian families often seem to have lived in numbing respectability. The outward impression is of stern and decisive husbands and fathers, and women trapped as tightly in their domestic role as they were in their whalebone and steel corsets.

VICTORIAN RELIGION

The age was marked by a revival in religious observance, especially among women, who attended church services more regularly than men. What little opportunity middle-class wives, in particular, had for lives outside the home was often found in prayer societies and charitable organizations. In Catholic countries, including France and Italy, women who seemed unlikely to marry often entered convents; in the eyes of many, a cloistered life was the only respectable alternative to marriage. One of the most important aspects of child raising was religious education: the catechism, prayer, and regular church attendance.

The virtues that the devout hoped to encourage in their families were those that would maintain a tranquil home life. Children were taught to accept their destiny, forgive their enemies, and help those less fortunate than themselves. A home strengthened by these virtues would, in turn, protect against the snares of the world outside: impiety, greed, and, most dangerous of all, sexual immorality. As for the poor, who clearly had little chance of enjoying the benefits of domestic bliss, they could best be helped by the distribution of hot soup and improving religious tracts. So determined a program of self-denial and gloom did not make for an agreeable existence. Florence Nightingale (1820–1910), the "Lady with the Lamp" who revolutionized the care of the sick, wrote that "Life is a hard fight, a struggle, a wrestling with the Principle of Evil."

Yet the conventional version of bourgeois life provides a one-sided impression of 19th-century society. The battle to maintain such exalted standards of virtue was probably won by only a few. Even at the time, the traditional picture of Victorian morality was recognized for what it was: a decorous façade behind which life remained as varied as it had always been. The young Queen Victoria grew up at a time when London's social life was dominated by luxurious whores and dissolute dandies, yet in the same years, Thomas Bowdler produced an edition of Shakespeare censored for family reading (the term *bowdlerized* derives from his name), and the Society for the Suppression of Vice was founded; the English wit Sydney Smith (1771–1845) suggested that this latter group should have been called the Society for Suppressing the Vices of Persons Whose Income Does Not Exceed Five Hundred Pounds per Annum.

THE "NECESSARY EVIL"

Loose living and zealous puritanism continued to coexist throughout Victoria's reign. The spread of bourgeois propriety did nothing to decrease prostitution in the period after 1850. An English clergyman remarked in 1858 that England was "the most religious in pretension but in reality the most immoral and licentious under the sun." One source in 1857 claimed that the number of prostitutes in London was around 80,000, an estimate generally accepted by contemporary observers. If each prostitute received only 25 customers per week, the number of weekly male visits to a prostitute amounted to some 2 million—in a city whose total male population was about 1.3 million.

A phenomenon so widespread could hardly be ignored or concealed, and bourgeois society debated at length both prostitution and other social problems, including child abuse, alcoholism, infanticide, wife beating, and a thriving subculture of pornography. In the case of prostitution, some governments intervened. In 1860 Cavour introduced to the new nation of Italy a system of state control that he had worked out in Sardinia. Based on the assumption that prostitution was a "necessary evil," the system regulated dress, living conditions, and the scale of payments. Cavour's system became popular with its clients, and by 1880 almost two-thirds of Italian prostitutes worked in officially regulated "closed houses," with the women having regular health controls.

During the 1860s and 1870s, social reformers in France and Germany tried to construct brothels along the same humanitarian lines as hospitals or factories. The overwhelming majority of those employed in them were working-class women. The brothels served a double purpose: to free middle-class (and other) men from excessive passion, so that they could return purged to a tranquil domestic life, and to guarantee the virtue of pure women.

High society had its own share of courtesans. One of the most famous and admired was the French Marie Duplessis (1824–1847). Fragile and melancholy in appearance, she was described by one admirer as "a young woman of exquisite distinction, a pure and delicate type of beauty." Her affair with the dramatist Alexandre Dumas *fils* (1824–1895), and her subsequent premature death of tuberculosis at the age of 23, inspired his play *The Lady of the Camellias*, which in turn formed the basis of the opera *La Traviata* by Giuseppe Verdi (see Topic 72). In both play and opera, the heroine dies in poverty. The real-life character earned enough in her short career to leave quantities of jewelry, silver and porcelain, furniture, works of art, a horse and carriage, and a pony. The sale of her estate after her death took four days and raised almost 100,000 francs.

THE BOURGEOISIE WAY OF LIFE

If state control and the laws of the marketplace took care of one basic human appetite, middle-class households became

midday meal = social gathering

increasingly adept at satisfying another one. During the period from 1830 to 1865, the midday meal developed into the major social occasion of daily life, with children and governess taking their place at the parents' table. Preceded by a lavish breakfast and a glass of wine with a biscuit in the middle of the morning, lunch became a hot meal—it had previously consisted of a cold collation. Working-class men often could not return home at midday, and a hot supper was generally kept for them.

Outside the house, the middle classes sought to maintain the same practice of elaborate meals. Even boarding schools provided lavish spreads. In September 1853, the French Ministry of Public Education circulated a list of standard meals to be served in state institutions, organized by days of the week. On Tuesdays, lunch consisted of meat soup, boiled beef, veal or mutton stew, poultry or game in pastry, and cold pâtés, while at dinner—a lighter meal, as was customary by midcentury—roast mutton and stewed fruit were served.

Thus behind the theoretical austerity and self-sacrifice of the bourgeois ideal, the middle classes used their growing prosperity to live as comfortably as possible. As the century progressed, new discoveries extended life's pleasures and conveniences to the less prosperous. Mechanized manufacturing made cheap shoes and clothing widely available. The wealthy had their clothes made for them, but their income was often based on the mass production and sale of ready-made garments, known as "reach-me-downs," stacked on the shelves of clothing stores. In the 1870s new processes of food preserva-

tion were developed, including canning and bottling. In 1870 margarine was invented as a substitute for those who could not afford butter, which was twice the price. A decade earlier, in 1860, the invention of the earth closet provided a more healthy sanitary system. The absence of drains meant that water closets did not become widespread, even in middle-class homes, until the turn of the 20th century.

While preaching resignation and simplicity, the middle classes schemed and planned to lead lives of ever-increasing complexity. Yet the façade of Victorian virtue certainly had its effects and claimed its victims. Its central tenet, the sanctity of home and family, left women trapped in performing an increasingly burdensome role.

WOMEN AND THE CULT OF DOMESTICITY

Middle-class morality revolved around a basic principle: The privacy of domestic family life, presided over by women, offered protection and tranquility. This simple belief served in practice to reinforce a whole series of prejudices and to bolster the high self-esteem of the new bourgeoisie. In the first place, the cult of domesticity drew immediate attention to the greatest strength of the middle classes: their strong financial position. The working class and the poor were automatically excluded from being homeowners, while many of the aristocracy were forced to reduce their expenditures, in

A middle-class English woman seated before her vanity (dressing table), c. 1860. Her air of idleness reflects the role assigned to women of her class in the cult of domesticity. Unable to work—as her social inferiors did—or to lead the active social lives of the upper classes, she could only superintend the running of the home by giving instructions to the cook and other servants.

James Helme/Royal Photographic Society

part because of their unwillingness to engage in commercial ventures. In any case, those great lords or princes who still maintained estates or palaces lived in splendor and opulence, but hardly in comfort. A middle-class home was intended to impress not by its frescoes or the grandeur of its salons, but by the convenience and ease of its appointments. Far more important than the possession of ancient treasures was the latest plumbing device or heating system. By comparison with the gilded elegance of the 18th century, 19th-century furniture was solid, and the chairs and couches stuffed—even overstuffed.

If their homes provided one way of defining their position, the difference between the lifestyles of middle-class and working-class women offered a second. The latter were compelled by necessity to seek labor, whether in factories or in the kitchens of bourgeois families, or in the brothels that served, paradoxically, to maintain middle-class respectability. They spent considerable time away from their own families, in the case of those in domestic service actually living in the houses of strangers.

Bourgeois women, by contrast, were virtually forbidden to work, or to spend significant amounts of time away from home. The more their status came to depend on their inactivity, the more the idea of an actively employed woman became discouraged. Thus the financial progress of the middle classes left bourgeois women theoretically superior, but in practice even less free than ever.

The exaltation of domesticity reinforced the controlling role of bourgeois husbands and fathers, for whose benefit the whole system operated. By entrusting the care of the home, although not the physical labor, to their womenfolk, Victorian males assured themselves a monopoly on all other forms of activity: business, finance, higher education, politics, and public life. The only appropriate interests for women in public life, such as philanthropy and moral reform, evoked their maternal role.

If women's sphere—or, as one writer described it, "kingdom"—was the home, they needed guidance in administering it. Handbooks on the new "domestic science" began to circulate widely. One of the most successful was the *Book of Household Management* (1861), by Isabella Beaton (1836–1865). Her advice on hiring and managing the servants, supervising the household accounts, and practicing a host of bewildering social customs (the use of finger bowls, for example) was read, if not always followed, by more than one generation of Victorian housewives. She also provided information on hygiene and health. Most important of all, she helped her readers to keep their husbands at home by maintaining an agreeable atmosphere and pleasing them with tasty, nourishing meals. The world of restaurants and clubs, a specifically male preserve, was seen as a potential threat to domestic peace.

THE FEMINIST MOVEMENT

Not all 19th-century women accepted the role assigned to them, although in some cases the form their protest took was a tacit acknowledgment of the advantages in being a man. The French novelist George Sand (Aurore Dudevant) dressed as a man and smoked cigars and a pipe. George Eliot (Mary Ann Evans), one of the leading literary figures of Victorian England, refused to marry the man with whom she lived, while her French contemporary, Daniel Stern (Marie d'Agoult), gave birth to several illegitimate children (whose father was the composer Franz Liszt). All of these unconventional women wrote novels, which they published under male pseudonyms (see Topic 72).

A far greater threat to male supremacy was the emergence, in midcentury England and America, of an organized feminist movement. In general, feminism arose as a result of the social changes produced by industrialization, which had pushed countless women into the workforce. In a more immediate sense, however, middle-class women rebelled against the repressive nature of the cult of domesticity. This was the theme of *A Doll's House* (1879), by the Norwegian playwright Henrik Ibsen (1828–1906): Its heroine, a repressed housewife who leaves her husband for the challenges of the larger world, shocked middle-class audiences of the day.

Like Ibsen's character, many bourgeois women resisted their exclusion from the world beyond the home, although in less dramatic ways. Women tried, for example, to find more meaningful lives by putting their time and energies into religious and charitable activities. Both American and British women joined the abolitionist cause, and after 1850 volunteered in ever-larger numbers to work in hospitals and working-class slums. By the end of the century, women were gravitating toward careers in nursing, teaching, and social work.

Participation in campaigns against slavery increased female consciousness of their own oppression. An important step in this direction came in 1840, when delegates to an international antislavery congress gathered in London. The American abolitionist Elizabeth Cady Stanton (1815–1902) and the other women present were outraged when they were required to observe the proceedings from an upstairs gallery, separated off from the male delegates. In 1848, Lucretia Mott (1793–1880) joined Stanton in spearheading the first women's rights convention, which met in Seneca Falls, New York. The participants announced a "Declaration of Sentiments" that demanded equal rights to divorce, to own property, and to hold jobs, as well as to vote.

These demands were echoed by early British feminists, particularly Barbara Smith Bodichon (1827–1891), whose London address gave their organization its name: the Langdon Place Group. The *English Women's Journal*, which she helped found, led to the creation of an employment agency in order to help women find jobs. By the 1860s, feminist groups had begun the long battle for the vote. Ironically, many of the leading opponents of the female franchise were Liberals, who feared that women would mainly vote for the Conservatives.

On the Continent, the cause of feminism advanced much more slowly. In France, Napoleon III was hostile to feminism, which he regarded as another form of revolution. The prominent working-class leader Pierre-Joseph Proudhon (see Topic 77) actually opposed women's rights, asserting that women's physical, mental, and moral inferiority justified their being restricted to the home. Nevertheless, a real feminist movement under the leadership of Juliette Lamber and Jenny d'Hercourt did operate as a kind of underground political opposition to the repressive policies of the Second Empire. In the German states, Louise Otto-Peters (1819–1895) headed the All German Women's Union, formed in 1865, and founded the feminist newspaper *Neue Bahnen* (New Roads), which proclaimed that "Work, liberating and liberated work, is the motto of our organization."

Italian feminists were among many whose high hopes in unification were disappointed by subsequent events. Nor was Cavour's official regulation of prostitution greeted with any enthusiasm by feminists who had fought in Garibaldi's army to liberate their people. Anna Maria Mozzoni

(1837–1920), the best-known feminist in Italy, criticized the laws that regulated women's rights and family relations and attacked the Catholic Church. She also translated Mill's *On the Subjection of Women*. In 1868, Italian feminists began publishing *La Donna* (Woman), a newspaper that advocated Mazzini's notion of women as citizen-mothers.

THE URBAN POOR AND SOCIAL REFORM

Unlike the middle classes, the working-class urban population seemed to have gained little from the Industrial Revolution. Many had given up the bare livelihood of a rural existence for the even grimmer task of scraping a liv-

Urban working-class alley in Yorkshire, England. Late 19th century. Note the overcrowding and the poor state of maintenance of the buildings. The woman in the center is probably going to fetch water from the common well. Even in Victorian England, the richest and most developed nation in the world at the time, most people lived without running water and used common outhouses as toilets.

Culver Pictures

Engraving of an English working-class schoolroom. Mid-19th century. The school seems hopelessly crowded, with children of both sexes and all ages. Nonetheless, the general spread of education—in particular, literacy—helped raise living standards over time. The village school-master, seen here in the center, became one of the most important figures in communities where, in many cases, few of the adults could read or write.

ing in overcrowded and polluted cities. Those engaged in work in middle-class homes were able to contrast their lot with that of their employers. Others could see the shops filled with luxury goods and the streets crowded with carriages. City life made class differences only too visible.

The struggle to improve the conditions of the poor was a long one, fraught with setbacks. In Britain, the Poor Law of 1834, passed after much controversy, aimed to make public assistance unappealing: Paupers and unemployed were required to live in workhouses, where conditions were minimal and treatment harsh. As late as 1900 in Britain, then the most prosperous country in the world, one in every five people received a pauper's funeral.

The problem lay partly in the speed and complexity of urban growth. Another factor was the lack of sympathy on the part of artisans and successful workers, who saw the urban poor as a threat to their own upward mobility. Those who could see their way to social advancement eagerly accepted middle-class notions of property as the only real indication of status. As a result, they had little time for those with no hope of escape from the squalor of poverty, with its slums and chronic alcoholism. Middle-class attitudes blamed poverty on the poor themselves.

By the end of the century, working-class support for social reform at the bottom of the scale began to grow, partly because of the politicization of workers' movements. In the 1850s and 1860s, however, the poor were mainly dependent

on government actions and the charity of middle-class benefactors.

PRIVATE CHARITY

The most common form of relief was that provided by private organizations, whose numbers multiplied rapidly by midcentury. By the 1850s, more than 450 charitable groups were operating in London. Many charities were inspired by religious motives. The Society of St. Vincent de Paul, founded in Paris in 1835, was active throughout France, Italy, Spain, and the Catholic parts of the Austrian empire. Its members, successful, educated men, visited the poor and improved their lot both by financial help and by teaching them thrift. As well as helping the needy, organizations such as this did much to inform the better-off of the terrible conditions of many of their fellow citizens.

The Society of St. Vincent de Paul was unusual in that its membership was restricted to men. The overwhelming majority of those engaged in practical charitable work were middle- and upper-class women. Often inspired by religious motives, they tried to establish direct personal contact with those from whom they were isolated both psychologically and physically—middle-class residential areas were kept at a distance from the poorer parts of cities. In addition to fulfilling Christian teachings of charity toward all, their work also became an extension of their domestic role, expressing "the flow of maternal love," applied to a broader notion of family.

Other groups had more specific goals. In France, maternal societies provided help to mothers in need; during the Second Empire, the Empress Eugénie became actively involved in their work. Around 1850 the Italian reformer Laura Mantegazza established day care centers for the children of working mothers, and a few years later set up schools for the illiterate. In Spain, Concepción Arenal (1820–1893) campaigned for prison reform and wrote a guide for those engaged in charitable work, *The Visitor of the Poor* (1860).

The active participation of so many women in relief work made an enormous contribution to public welfare at a time when government aid was limited. It also caused many women to question the bourgeois assumptions that lay behind the cult of domesticity. After seeing the conditions under which the poor lived, it was difficult to return unchanged to their material comforts, which were often enjoyed at the expense of others. Furthermore, women came to realize that, far from being helpless and best confined to the home, they could play a vital part in producing social reform.

KARL MARX AND THE VISION OF A NEW SOCIAL ORDER

One of the chief aims of 19th-century reformers was to redress social injustice. Those who had most to gain from reform—the workers and the needy—were in no doubt about their own plight, but for the first half of the century they were unable to articulate their case. When working-class protests were heard, they were often misdirected or unsustained. The Luddites' destruction of machinery (see Topic 60) did nothing to hold back the Industrial Revolution. The Chartists mounted a more organized campaign but failed to carry it through.

What was lacking was an overarching vision of the radical social reordering needed to change the entrenched system. The middle class was too satisfied with its victories to theorize about the rights of others, and the establishment certainly had no interest in overturning an order from which they benefited. When serious and sustained workers' protests did finally make themselves heard, toward the end of the century, they were based on a world view based largely on the writings of Karl Marx and Friedrich Engels.

Both men came from prosperous middle-class families, although Marx's financial position deteriorated with the death of his father. After studying at the universities of Bonn and Berlin, and obtaining a doctorate from the University of Jena, Marx—already a radical in his ideas—took up journalism. Hoping to be able to influence contemporary society, in 1842 he became editor of *The Rhineland Gazette*, a well-known liberal newspaper. Within a year his articles had won him the enmity of the Prussian government and of his own publishers, and he moved to Paris, the center in continental Europe of political exiles and radical debate.

There he renewed an earlier friendship with Engels, who had firsthand experience of the appalling conditions under which industrial workers lived. The Engels family owned a cotton mill near Manchester, and Engels wrote a searing account of his observations there, *The Condition of the Working Class in England* (see Topic 66). Marx and Engels joined forces to diagnose the cause of society's ills, and to provide a prescription for their cure. On the eve of the revolutions of 1848 they published the *Communist Manifesto*. At the time the work made little impression, and with the end of the revolution in Paris, Marx made his way to London. He lived there in exile for the rest of his life, continuing his collaboration with Engels, who also provided him with financial support. The first volume of *Das Kapital* appeared in 1867; Engels edited the other two volumes (1885, 1894) after Marx's death.

THE *COMMUNIST MANIFESTO*

Marx and Engels intended their work to accomplish two ends: to explain the nature of contemporary society by looking back to the pattern of European history, and to provide a practical means for correcting its faults. Thus the *Manifesto* is at the same time a broad philosophical statement and a handbook to revolution.

The Marxist theory of history takes its departure from the ideas of the German philosopher Georg Hegel. Hegel believed that "dialectic"—the clash of ideas in thesis and antithesis—would lead to a "synthesis," and that this resolution of conflict would mark a new stage in historical evolution. The clashing ideas were purely intellectual, however, and the resolution would always be a positive one. Rejecting Hegel's abstraction, Marx claimed that history was propelled forward by conflict not over ideas, but over economic interests, and that all aspects of society were determined by materialist factors, in particular by the means of production.

This "dialectical materialism" was responsible for changes in the past. The economy of the Middle Ages had depended on the feudal system, whereby large numbers of serfs worked for a small, landowning, hereditary aristocracy. With the rise of commerce and trade, a new middle class began to develop. The "dialectic," or struggle, between aristocracy and middle class was resolved in the triumph of the bourgeoisie, first in England and the Netherlands in the 18th century, then in the American War of Independence and the French Revolution, and finally and decisively in the middle-class victories of the 19th century.

This Marxist analysis reveals his belief that historical change depends not only on economic factors, but also on an inherent and inevitable class struggle. Just as the middle class overcame the aristocracy, so in the next stage the workers—the proletariat—would overcome the middle class. In order to accomplish this goal and throw off their oppressors, the workers of the world needed to organize and unite, under the inspiration of their newly developed class consciousness. In the new order, the "dictatorship of the proletariat" would abolish existing political systems, make all production public, and bring about a classless society in which the state would "wither away."

The struggle would be made easier by the inherent defects in the middle-class economic system of capitalism.

Marx argued that because capitalism by its nature required competition, those capitalists who succeeded would do so at the expense of others. Those who went out of business would join the proletariat. Because successful employers would be forced to cut wages and expenditures to remain competitive, the poor would continue to get poorer and the rich richer. In the end the capitalist system would collapse.

MARX AND MARXISM

The accuracy of Marx's historical and economic analyses has frequently been challenged. Furthermore, never did he or Engels really describe the precise nature of the society to be brought about under the dictatorship of the proletariat. Many developments that Marx did not live to see, such as mass communications, the spread of popular democracy, and expanding technologies, outdated some of his conclusions. The poor have not all continued to get poorer, and the capitalist system has not collapsed. Nor did Marx's rigorously economic determinism leave any place for the part played in history by individual human characteristics or even pure random chance.

Yet after its early neglect, the *Manifesto*, along with Marx's other writings, went on to influence, directly or indirectly, countless millions of lives, and served as the inspiration for revolutionary movements throughout the world. The degree to which Marxist ideas have ever been applied in practice can be debated, as can the relationship between Marx's communism and the Communist party that came to power in Russia following the Bolshevik Revolution of 1917. Nevertheless, generations of political, social, and economic reformers turned to his writings.

Much of the appeal of **Marxism** lay in its positive view of the social role of workers and other underprivileged citizens, who had been accustomed to think of themselves as the dregs of society, beyond hope. Marx had less enthusiasm for them intellectually, believing them basically unable to discern their own interests, and thus in need of a "vanguard of intellectuals" to lead them. The socialist parties that were formed in the late 19th century drew much of their pride and energy from Marx's essentially optimistic view of their role in history and the inevitability of their eventual success, although by no means were all of them Marxists. Nor, like some other thinkers, did Marx seek to reverse the Industrial Revolution and return to a problem-free (and nonexistent) rural past. The lot of most human beings was to be improved by means of greater productivity: Marx was the prophet of modernism, not its enemy. In addition, although he overstressed the role played by economics, his assertion of the need for radical economic change drove many to challenge the status quo. Finally, he made two claims for his analysis that were bound to appeal to many. It was, he said, scientific, and therefore intellectually sound. Furthermore, given his determinist view of history, sooner or later his long-term predictions were bound to come true; any setbacks or defeats would be only temporary.

Neither Marx nor Engels claimed that the dictatorship of the proletariat would be achieved quickly, but they and their followers believed that history was on their side. By the end of the 19th century, with the spread of socialism and the rise of the trade unions, many who were not Marxists began to share their conviction.

Putting Middle-Class Values and Working-Class Realities in Perspective

By 1870, the certainties of bourgeois existence were coming under increasing challenge. Just as Marx was undermining economic attitudes, so Darwin's work questioned the entire basis of traditional morality (see Topic 72). Increasing numbers of middle-class women were becoming restless with the position assigned to them in society. These developments took place at a time when governments in Western Europe were beginning to come under pressure to extend the franchise beyond the aristocracy and the prosperous middle class.

In Britain, Victoria continued her apparently everlasting reign, but the social situation was in a state of growing ferment. Elsewhere in Europe instabilities began to develop. The French Second Empire came abruptly to an end. Germany and Italy were faced with the new uncertainties of nationhood. The Austro-Hungarian empire lived on the brink of perpetual crisis. The only country where social conditions seemed likely to remain unchanged for centuries, as they had for centuries past, was Russia. By one of the ironies of history, amid the cataclysm of World War I, Russian society was overturned and remade by self-proclaimed followers of the obscure German philosopher of the mid-19th century.

Questions for Further Study

1. What factors influenced the urbanization of Europe? How did urbanization affect social patterns?
2. Describe the principal values of the middle classes. How did they affect daily life?
3. What roles did "Victorian" values assign to women?
4. How did Marx explain the inevitability of the proletarian revolution? What would happen after the revolution?

Suggestions for Further Reading

Accampo, Elinor. *Industrialization, Family Life, and Class Relations: Saint Chamond, 1815–1914.* Berkeley, CA, 1989.

August, Andrew. *Poor Women's Lives: Gender, Work and Poverty in Late-Victorian London.* Madison, NJ, 1999.

Berlanstein, Lenard R. *The Working People of Paris, 1871–1914.* Baltimore, MD, 1984.

Girouard, Mark. *Cities and People: A Social and Architectural History.* New Haven, CT, 1985.

Himmelfarb, Gertrude. *The Idea of Poverty: England in the Early Industrial Age.* New York, 1984.

Joyce, P. *Visions of the People: Industrial England and the Question of Class, c. 1848–1914.* New York, 1991.

Jones, Gareth. *Outcast London.* Oxford, 1984.

Marsden, G., ed. *Victorian Values: Personalities and Perspectives in 19th-Century Society.* New York, 1990.

Miller, Michael. *The Bon Marché: Bourgeois Culture and the Department Store, 1869–1920.* Princeton, NJ, 1981.

Pilbeam, Pamela M. *The Middle Classes in Europe, 1789–1914.* Chicago, 1990.

Ross, Ellen. *Love and Toil: Motherhood in Outcast London, 1870–1918.* New York, 1993.

Shapiro, Ann-Louise. *Housing the Poor of Paris, 1850–1902.* Madison, WI, 1985.

Sutcliffe, Anthony. *Towards the Planned City: Germany, Britain, and the United States, 1789–1914.* New York, 1981.

Taithe, Bertrand. *Defeated Flesh: Medicine, Welfare, and Warfare and the Making of Modern France.* Lanham, MD, 1999.

Walkowitz, Judith. *City of Dreadful Delight.* Chicago, 1993.

InfoTrac College Edition

Enter the search term *Marxism* using Key Terms.

Enter the search term *Victorian* using Key Terms.

Enter the search term *family nineteenth century* using Key Terms.

ARTS, IDEAS, AND SOCIAL CONSCIOUSNESS

By mid-19th century, European artists and thinkers were already beginning to take a critical look at the society produced by industrialization and political reform. The enormous speed with which the world was changing, not only politically but also as the result of developments in science and technology, encouraged analysis of the present and speculation about the future. At the same time, the rapidly rising literacy rate made new ideas circulate with ever-increasing speed.

The scientific study of human society—sociology—was enthusiastically advocated by Auguste Comte, whose optimistic belief in the power of human achievement inspired the rise of new fields of research: psychology, anthropology, and the social sciences in general. Charles Darwin's work on evolution presented a more serious challenge to conventional notions of the world. Plants and animals (humans included), he claimed, had not been created in their present form by divine plan but had evolved over millions of years.

The diffusion of world views that seriously questioned the teachings of Christianity increased debate by instilling tension between religion and scientific discovery. Furthermore, with the rise of the secular nation-state, Christian churches had to work out new ways of coexisting with civil powers.

In literature the most popular form of the day was the novel. No longer seeking merely to entertain, writers aimed to make public the chief issues of the times—social injustice, religious intolerance, evolving political patterns. Many of the leading novelists attracted a mass readership and succeeded in influencing substantial bodies of opinion.

Musicians also promoted political causes, in particular that of nationalism. In Russia and among the peoples of Eastern Europe, traditional folk music was used as the basis for works that set out to reinforce ideas of national consciousness. The leading musician in Italy, Giuseppe Verdi, became the symbol of the unification of Italy. Many of his operas made indirect reference to political events and won popular support for the *Risorgimento*.

In the visual arts, Romanticism gave way to a new movement, realism. Some painters produced realistic, unglamorized depictions of peasant and working-class life, whereas for others art was a means for revealing social injustice. Interest in realism was stimulated around midcentury by the invention and spread of photography.

AUGUSTE COMTE AND THE PHILOSOPHY OF POSITIVISM

The chief artistic and intellectual movements of the early 19th century, Romanticism and utopian socialism, were inspired by the ferment of change that the revolutionary spirit of the times seemed to open up. Released from the bondage of traditional patterns of society, artists and thinkers explored possibilities for a new future. Even where, as in Germany, the old ways soon reestablished themselves, Romanticism continued to offer an escape from the realities of political power. Amid the hopes and delusions of postrevolutionary France, the utopian socialists tried to prescribe for a future ideal society (see Topic 66).

By midcentury, Romanticism was giving way to realism, while new currents of thought examined humanity's place in the universe. Auguste Comte (1798–1857) arrived at an overarching view of civilization, which sought to rationalize the development of human understanding. Comte had spent many years as private secretary to the utopian Saint-Simon and inherited his predecessor's optimistic confidence in the progress of society.

THE PHILOSOPHY OF POSITIVISM

By the time of his death in 1857, Comte's philosophy of positivism was established as an international movement. His basic belief was that knowledge must be derived from experience or observation, and not from speculation. It was impossible to know why things happen, let alone what would happen in the future; the only certainties could be found by learning how things actually occur in the world. Study of this "positive" knowledge would eventually lead to an improved, "positive" society, based not on beliefs but on scientific facts.

Comte divided the history of civilization into a series of "progressive" stages. In the first, the "theological," people had tried to explain the world in terms of nature deities. Then came the "metaphysical" stage, in which religion served to find hidden causes and understand abstract principles. By his day a new age was dawning, the "positive," in which society would achieve its highest form. Traditional religions such as Christianity played an important role in the growth of civilization, but would in due course be replaced by a new "religion of humanity."

Reduced to its essence, Comte's positivism seems no more convincing than other optimistic philosophies—that of the 17th-century German Gottfried von Leibnitz, for example. Its appeal to his contemporaries lay in two factors. In the first place he warned that the progress from the "metaphysical" stage to "positivism" would involve struggle. The outward sign of this struggle was the upheaval of industrialization, with its social injustices and human misery. Thus his followers could accept the troubles of their times as the inevitable price to be paid for progress. The message was especially welcome to those members of the prosperous middle classes who felt pangs of guilt at the ignoble foundations on which their wealth seemed to rest.

Second, Comte's insistence on the scientific observation of human society created a new and intriguing way of looking at the world: sociology (Comte coined the term). During the second half of the 19th century, the scientific study of different forms taken by various societies led to widespread interest in the social sciences. Economics, psychology, anthropology, political science, sociology, history—all are ways of trying to satisfy Comte's requirement and provide objective, "positive" knowledge about society.

CHARLES DARWIN AND THE CASE FOR NATURAL SELECTION

Comte's positivism saw traditional religion as benign, although in the end to be superseded by humanism. The publication in 1859 of Charles Darwin's *On the Origin of Species* presented a far more severe challenge to established Christian beliefs, and its implications still remain controversial.

As a young man, Darwin (1809–1882) began to study medicine, his father's profession. He soon changed his mind and decided to become a minister of religion, although without abandoning his interest in natural history. In 1831 the offer of an unpaid position as naturalist aboard the H.M.S. *Beagle*, about to sail on an expedition to South America, tempted him away from his theological studies at Cambridge. The voyage lasted five years, and Darwin's work on South American fossils and bird and animal life gave him the basis for his theory of natural selection.

Like many important intellectual ideas, natural selection did not suddenly appear in a vacuum. Other scholars and scientists had begun to look for natural rather than divine explanations for the order of creation. In 1809 the French biologist Jean Lamarck (1744–1829) proposed a hypothesis whereby animals that changed their characteristics because of the environment, or the acquisition of new habits, could transmit these changes to their offspring. The theory was unsound. A man who develops strong muscles as a result of hauling sacks of flour will not pass on his physique to his sons and daughters. Nevertheless, Lamarck's notion began to question the traditional religious teaching that life had been created according to a divine and unchanging scheme.

In his geological studies, Darwin was inspired by his contemporary Charles Lyell (1797–1875), whose *Principles of Geology* (1830) argued that all geologic phenomena could be explained by natural causes. A general philosophical rationale was provided by the writings of Malthus (see Topic 66) and the struggle for existence they describe. This struggle became, for Darwin, the basis of the process of natural selection.

Although all members of a species are generally similar, no two living creatures are identical. The random differences between individual members are transmitted to their offspring in a process that is, as we now know, genetic. Some variations are apparently irrelevant, whereas others—

strength, speed, natural markings—are likely to improve the chances of survival. According to Darwin's theory of the "survival of the fittest," the characteristics that are most likely to help in the struggle for life will, over millennia, be strengthened by the simple fact that the members of the species possessing them have a better chance of surviving.

When Darwin published his conclusions in 1859, encouraged by the independent formation of a similar theory by Alfred Wallace, he did not intend them as an open challenge to religion. He avoided speculation about the origins of life, or on why so many species have characteristics that cannot apparently be explained by this process. Nor did he emphasize natural selection as the most important of his ideas. Instead, the avowed tone of his publication was one of optimism at the notion of the "rising swell of the Great Chorus of Being."

THE IMPACT OF DARWINISM

Inevitably, however, Darwin's work was seen as inextricably opposed to Christian teaching. The fittest survive, by implication, only because the overwhelming majority of living organisms are destroyed, a principle that Darwin clearly extended to the human species. This concept was impossible to reconcile with belief in an all-loving God—and one, at that, who created the world according to His own scheme and humans in His own image. Church leaders were horrified, and controversy raged. Darwin's publication of *The Descent of Man* (1871), which claimed that humans and anthropoid apes were both descended from a common apelike ancestor, was hardly likely to still the debate.

The theological implications of Darwinism remain unresolved. Many Christians, and others, managed to reconcile the idea of natural selection with the Bible's account of creation by taking the biblical description as poetic rather than literal. There continue to be those whose understanding of the Bible leads them to reject Darwin's theory of evolution by natural selection.

Darwinism also had widespread influence in social thinking and the arts, often in ways that went far beyond the intentions of its originator. For Darwin, survival was a fact that of itself was morally neutral. A species was neither "better" nor "worse" for having won the struggle. Self-styled "Social Darwinists," however, began to use the notion of the survival of the fittest to imply the survival of the best (see Topic 78).

For contemporary poets and novelists, Darwin suggested new insights into the human condition. Romanticism drew attention to the uniqueness of the individual, but Darwin's work put existence into a very different perspective. The vision was not always a comforting one. In his famous poem, "In Memoriam," the eminent Victorian poet Alfred, Lord Tennyson (1809–1892) gloomily accepted the notion of a "Nature, red in tooth and claw," which proclaims: "A thousand types are gone; I care for nothing, all shall go." Under such conditions, life was "as futile, then, as frail!"

The immediate impact of Darwin gradually abated, and by the end of the 19th century the new disciplines of psychology and sociology probably had a greater influence on European intellectual life than the religious implications of natural selection. Yet the theory of evolution remains an important and controversial topic, and not only for theologians. Modern scientists, using methods of genetic research and the study of the physicochemical composition of DNA, are rapidly revising Darwin's conclusions. Darwin would surely not have been surprised: He predicted that future scientists would modify his theories as they explored the many unanswered questions concerning natural selection.

SCIENCE AND RELIGION IN A CHANGING WORLD

The theory of evolution was not the only idea to present problems for 19th-century organized religion. With the advance of science and the growth of the secular state, Christian leaders found themselves facing serious challenges. For centuries the various branches of Christianity had at least agreed on a central body of teaching, and they regarded themselves as uniquely qualified to expound it. Lutherans and Catholics alike agreed on the importance of the Scriptures. Biblical accounts had been attacked since the 17th century by scientists like Galileo and philosophers such as Voltaire, but now increasing numbers of laypeople exposed to the new ideas began to question truths that had been held immutable since the Middle Ages.

Some of the doubts came from biblical historians, who were trying, as they thought, to save Christianity from being too closely tied to the teachings of the Bible. The French scholar Ernest Renan (1832–1892) pointed out historical inconsistencies in the Scriptures, emphasizing that the human fallibility of its authors did not invalidate its general message. His most widely read book was *The Life of Jesus*, which appeared in 1863. It perfectly expresses the intellectual spirit of the times by substituting a heightened appreciation of the poetry and human achievements described in the Bible for blind faith. Renan's purpose was to emphasize the continuing relevance of the Christian story to modern life, and he described Jesus as "an incomparable man." The authorities of the Collège de France, however, under the influence of the Catholic party, forbade him to teach his version of Christianity.

A far more hostile opponent of Christianity was the English philosopher Thomas Henry Huxley (1825–1895). An energetic defender of Darwin, Huxley invented the term *agnosticism*: the belief that the existence and nature of God are unknowable. He was a pioneer in the field of popular scientific education and a champion of free speech and investigation. Among the critics of Darwin whom Huxley lambasted in his newspaper articles was the British prime minister, William Gladstone, a deeply religious man who was one of Darwin's most vocal opponents.

The German philosopher Ludwig Andreas Feuerbach (1804–1872) took an even more extreme position. The most fiery and uncompromising prophet of philosophical materialism, Feuerbach attacked belief in an afterlife and declared that all deities are merely personifications of human fears. Religion, he claimed, prevented the full understanding and enjoyment of physical and moral reality. Expressing one of the 19th century's most typical ideas, he wrote that "the characteristic of the modern age is that man sees himself as divine and infinite, and that the individual feels these qualities within himself in his individuality."

Meanwhile, science and technology did not so much challenge traditional religion as ignore it. Furthermore, by visibly improving the lives of countless people, advances in these areas were seen as a source of "progress" and material well-being. The work of Louis Pasteur (1822–1895) on bacteria revolutionized standards of public health and nutrition. Joseph Lister's (1827–1912) discovery of the value of carbolic acid as a disinfectant vastly improved surgical techniques. The development of the telegraph and the subsequent laying of a transatlantic cable from Europe to America between 1858 and 1866 produced miraculous changes in communication.

None of these innovations was hostile to Christianity, but to some puzzled believers they seemed to make religion increasingly irrelevant to modern life. The Catholic Church responded by taking the offensive, motivated by reasons of dogma, and also by its loss of temporal power in

Culver Pictures

Painting of Louis Pasteur conducting an experiment. Late 19th century. The great French chemist and microbiologist is shown checking the results of his experiment against written observations. Among his discoveries was that bacteria cause anthrax, and he devised treatments for hydrophobia in humans and rabies in dogs, as well as developing vaccination procedures.

Italy as a consequence of Italian unification. In 1864 Pope Pius IX issued the *Syllabus of Errors,* in which he castigated materialism, freedom of thought, and the belief that all religions are equally valid. Five years later, in 1869, he summoned the first church council since the Counter-Reformation and proclaimed the doctrine of papal infallibility. According to this teaching, when the pope speaks "ex cathedra," from his position as head of the church, on any issue of faith or morals, he is infallible. Pius was speaking precisely from this position in condemning what he saw as dangerous modern tendencies.

The pope's assertion of authority met with a mixed reception, not least in Italy where tensions already existed between church and state. Protestants, lacking a central authority or a body of established dogma, were left with their consciences to guide them to an accommodation with new ways of thinking. Some turned to social commitment and tried to contribute to progress by active work among the poor. They emphasized the ethical teachings of Jesus rather than faith in miracles and belief in original sin.

CHRISTIANITY AND THE STATE

At the same time as the Catholic Church was fighting its moral battles, it was involved in a more temporal struggle. The papacy had never been sympathetic to the cause of Italian unification, which had sought to incorporate the Papal States into the new Italian nation. In 1871, the year after the seizure of Rome, the Italian parliament passed a law designed to define and guarantee the pope's status. Pius IX, who never accepted the loss of the Papal States, refused to accept the Italian government's stand. Instead, he withdrew into the Vatican, causing serious liabilities for the Italian government (see Topic 73).

Elsewhere in Europe, political leaders and religious authorities found themselves in conflict. The governments of France and Spain, both predominantly Catholic countries, denounced the dogma of papal infallibility as proclaimed by the Vatican Council in 1870. In Germany, Bismarck's *Kulturkampf* (battle over culture) saw the introduction of several anti-Catholic laws between 1872 and 1875, which expelled the Jesuits and gave the state control over seminaries and the appointment of priests and bishops. Bismarck was concerned about a possible alliance of Catholic powers and wanted to limit outside influence in Germany (see Topic 73). The strength of the Catholic Center party forced the eventual repeal of the measures. Even the Church of England, whose official head was the monarch, found itself increasingly losing the special privileges it had accumulated over the centuries.

THE WRITER AS CRITIC: SOCIAL REALISM AND THE NOVEL

With the spread of education and an increase in literacy throughout most of Europe, public demand for literature increased. The most popular form was the novel, and the most successful writers of the 19th century were those who managed both to entertain and to instruct their readers. As industrialization and the growth of urban life intensified social discontent, authors turned from the self-centered images of Romanticism to deal with the practical problems of the day in a realistic style. Not content merely to describe society's injustices, in many cases they fought to correct them. In the process they criticized many of the mid-19th century's conventional beliefs.

The realities of social existence were memorably expressed by several women writers, many of whom took male names to reassure some readers who might not have otherwise taken them seriously. In England, George Eliot (1819–1880; her real name was Mary Ann Evans) dealt with questions of morality and philosophy, as well as creating, in *Middlemarch* (1871–1872), an unforgettable picture of provincial life. The French writer George Sand (1804–1876; in real life Aurore Dudevant) tackled just about every issue of the day, including women's rights. Her contemporary, the English poet Elizabeth Barrett Browning, called Sand "true genius but true woman."

Perhaps the most devastating attack on middle-class values and society is that found in *Madame Bovary*, the masterpiece of Sand's friend Gustave Flaubert (1821–1880). When the work first appeared in print in 1856–1857, its reception did much to confirm Flaubert's low opinion of his times: He was prosecuted for offenses against public morals, although in the end he was acquitted. The story's main character, Emma Bovary, has been brought up on a diet of romantic novels, which leave her unsatisfied by the dull reality of her respectable life in the provinces. Married to a boorish country doctor, she embarks on a shoddy affair and ends up fatally in debt. Flaubert's understated, impersonal recounting of the banal tragedy is filled with carefully observed details.

The most successful English novelist of the period was Charles Dickens (1812–1870), whose rich, many-layered books are filled with characters both realistic and bizarre—a far cry from the restraint of Flaubert or the measured tone of Eliot. Dickens' style is poetic, with an endlessly imaginative use of language. His finest works combine insights into human behavior with searing indictments of the flaws and social inequities of his times. *Bleak House* (1853) attacked the British legal system, which was notorious for its interminable, inhumane delays and incomprehensible proceedings. The book played a part in the movement that led to legal reform in the 1860s. In *Hard Times* (1854), Dickens analyzed the ills of industrialized society and powerfully underlined the fact that education without humanity can destroy those whom it seeks to help. Often unpopular with the establishment, Dickens won a huge and affectionate audience both in Europe and in America. The arrival in New York of a ship carrying the latest episode of one of his works attracted crowds to the docks.

Not all authors met with so appreciative a reception. The Russian novelist Nikolai Gogol (1809–1852), of Ukranian birth, spent many years abroad, most of them in Rome, where he wrote his satirical masterpiece, *Dead Souls*

Cruikshank, illustration from Charles Dickens, *Oliver Twist.* 1838. The scene shown is that in which Oliver Twist, the workhouse "brat," dares to ask for a second bowl of gruel (a kind of thin, watery porridge): "Please sir, I want some more." Both author and artist were trying to draw the public's attention to the terrible conditions existing in workhouses and other public institutions.

(1842). Gogol's readers saw his satires of bureaucracy and serfdom as blows in the struggle for progress. He was, however, more concerned to castigate moral evil than social or political error. Gogol's contemporary and fellow Russian, Ivan Turgenev (1818–1883), was a liberal who advocated the importation of Western ideas into his country. Among his early writings was a series of depictions of peasant life. His novels dealt with the great issues facing Russian society: the emancipation of the serfs in *On the Eve* (1860—a year before the emancipation became law); nihilism in *Fathers and Children* (1862); and populist revolution in *Virgin Soil* (1877). The last of these was written in Paris because, discouraged by the lack of sympathy on the part of Russian readers and critics, Turgenev spent the last 21 years of his life in Germany and France.

MUSIC AND THE RISE OF NATIONAL CONSCIOUSNESS

Around the middle of the 19th century, composers in many parts of Europe became eager to write music that openly proclaimed their nationality. In Bohemia, Bedřich Smetana (1824–1884) gave the Czech people a new sense of identity and self-confidence by the musical style he developed, and by his choice of nationalistic subjects for his operas and symphonic poems. In addition to *The Bartered Bride* (1866), his best-loved work, with its sparkling dances and lyrical songs, he wrote a set of six orchestral pieces called *Ma Vlast* (My Fatherland). The most popular, "Vltava," paints a musical picture of the river Vltava, flowing from its bubbling source through the Czech landscape, and finally rolling majestically into Prague.

His younger contemporary, Antonin Dvořák (1841–1904), became famous for his Slavonic dances and rhapsodies. Much of his music, including the symphonies and string quartets, uses traditional Czech folk rhythms like the polka. The famous *New World* Symphony (Ninth Symphony, 1893), composed during Dvořák's stay in America to commemorate the 500th anniversary of Christopher Columbus's landing in the Americas, is far more Czech in character than American, although his interest in folk music of all kinds led him to collect American spirituals and incorporate them in his later works.

The greatest Italian composer of the century, Giuseppe Verdi (1813–1901), became a symbol of his country's *Risorgimento*. He began his career at a time when Milan, the center of Italian operatic life, was under Austrian rule. Although forbidden by the Austrian censor from depicting politically suggestive subjects on stage, he found ways to allude to the nationalist cause. His opera *Nabucco* (1842) shows the captivity of the Jews under the Babylonians in the 6th century B.C. His Italian audience, under Austrian captivity, had no difficulty in identifying themselves with the plight of the suffering Jews, and the work was greeted with wild enthusiasm at its first performances.

Even Verdi's name helped remind Italians of the great struggle in progress. One of the leaders of the *Risorgimento* was Victor Emmanuel II of Piedmont, who became the first king of united Italy (see Topic 69). For the excited spectators, who cried "Viva Verdi!"—"long live Verdi!"—after performances of his works, his name also stood for Vittorio Emmanuele, *Re d'Italia*—Victor Emmanuel, king of Italy. At the request of Cavour, Verdi was elected to the new national parliament and served as a deputy from 1861 to 1865.

The nationalist movement in Russia was more concerned with establishing the importance of Russian culture than with political questions. The key figure in the birth of an independent Russian musical tradition was Mikhail Glinka (1804–1857), whose opera *A Life for the Tsar* (1836) was the first Russian stage work to make widespread use of folklike melodies. From an artistic point of view, Glinka's achievement was surpassed by the most original Russian composer of the 19th century, Modest Moussorgsky (1839–1881). Intensely imaginative, but tormented by a lifelong addiction to alcohol, Moussorgsky combined his musical career with political activism.

Bequest of Mrs. H.O. Havemeyer, 1929. Photo©1985 The Metropolitan Museum of Art

Daumier, *The Third-Class Carriage*, c. 1862. 2 feet 1¾ inches by 2 feet 11½ inches (64 by 89 cm). While first- and second-class railway carriages had padded seats and were closed, passengers in third-class carriages sat crowded on benches, and the windows had no glass. Much of Daumier's art attempts to show his middle-class audience the plight of the poor.

In the late 1860s, Moussorgsky completed his most important work, *Boris Godunov*, which was finally staged in 1874. The opera tells the story of Tsar Boris, who is haunted by his murder of the true heir to the throne and finally driven mad by guilt. The music incorporates folk motifs and powerfully evokes the spirit of Russian Orthodox Christianity. The chief character of the work is not so much Boris as the chorus, which represents the long-suffering Russian people, somehow surviving the crimes and indifference of their rulers.

On a more limited scale, musicians in Scandinavia also turned to their national musical heritage. The Norwegian Edvard Grieg (1843–1907) produced arrangements of Norwegian folk songs and provided incidental music for the Ibsen play *Peer Gynt*. Although his works were written within the general Western tradition, pieces like the popular Piano Concerto (1868) incorporate fresh, folklike melodies.

Even the most mainstream musicians of midcentury exploited their native resources. The Germans Robert Schumann (1810–1856) and Johannes Brahms (1833–1897) used German folk songs, and the mighty music dramas of Wagner (see Topic 79) were based on German legends. In France, the most popular composer of the Second Empire was Jacques Offenbach (1819–1880), whose exhilarating operettas, such as *La Vie Parisienne* (Life in Paris, 1866), often commented on contemporary society and politics.

THE IMAGE OF SOCIETY IN THE VISUAL ARTS

French painters and sculptors of the period showed a similar interest in the political and social world around them. Just as Offenbach mocked the excesses of his contemporaries, Honoré Daumier (1808–1879) pilloried the follies of the times in paintings, lithographs, and sculpted statuettes. More bitter than his musical contemporary, Daumier often expressed anger at the abuse of power. He shared with Dickens a deep resentment of the injustices of the legal system and the corruption of those working in it. In a series of lithographs, he showed the indifference of lawyers to their clients' sufferings. Many of his small sculptures depict the leading politicians of Napoleon III's Paris, characterized by greed and self-satisfaction.

The paintings of Gustave Courbet (1819–1877) also show realistic scenes, although they are less explicitly political in tone. Rejecting the full-blown Romanticism of Delacroix for naturalistic depictions of the world, Courbet preferred to paint peasants and workers. A socialist, he produced plain and unromantic scenes of village life. In *The Stone Breakers* (1849), his avoidance of the sentimental and underlining of realistic details are a visual parallel to the literary realism of his contemporary Flaubert.

Courbet, *The Stone Breakers.* 1849. 5 feet 3 inches by 8 feet 6 inches (1.59 by 2.6 m). The Revolutions of 1848 had drawn new attention to the sufferings of those on the margins of society. Courbet's choice of subject—the most menial of occupations—for a work of "high art" was as much political as aesthetic; his use of "dirty" shades of grey and brown underlines the drudgery of the men's task.

Thomas Eakins *Swimming*, 1885, oil on canvas. Purchased by The Friends of Art, Fort Worth Art Association, 1925; acquired by the Amon Carter Museum, 1990, from the Modern Art Museum of Fort Worth through grants and donations from the Amon G. Carter Foundation, the Sid W. Richardson Foundation, the Anne Burnett and Charles Tandy Foundation, Capital Cities/ABC Foundation, Fort Worth Star-Telegram, the R.D. and Joan Dale Hubbard Foundation, and the people of Fort Worth. Amon Carter Museum, Fort Worth, Texas

Eakins, *The Swimming Hole*. 1885. The figure swimming in the bottom right-hand corner is Eakins. His painting combines an interest in anatomy (based on his interest in Classical art) with an attempt to depict forms in movement inspired by the newly invented art of photography. Eakins' contemporaries were critical of his insistence on accuracy of observation; he is probably now held to be the greatest of 19th-century American artists.

The increasing tendency of artists to approach their subjects naturalistically was further stimulated by one of the most important inventions of the century: photography. In 1839, Louis Daguerre (1787–1851) gave the first public demonstration of a type of photographic process in Paris. The new technique was soon improved and hailed with excited enthusiasm by artists as different as Delacroix and Ingres, in part because, as Ingres observed, photographs provided "an exactitude that I shall like to achieve." The impact of photography on art and culture in general was vast and far-reaching. As the American painter Thomas Eakins perceptively realized, it represented no less a convention than traditional art. By stimulating painters to examine the actual process of literal observation, it inspired one of the most important artistic movements of the late 19th century, Impressionism (see Topic 79).

Putting Arts, Ideas, and Social Consciousness in Perspective

In the early 19th century, artists and thinkers often saw themselves as leaders in the battle for social and political change. As time wore on, they became commentators on the process, rather than participants. Several factors were responsible for this gradual alienation from politics. In the first place, philosophical and intellectual developments such as the evolution controversy and the growing interest in psychology created a barrier between "advanced" intellectuals and the general public. The level of popular education was increasing, but not sufficiently to deal with these basic challenges to widespread beliefs.

Second, the increasing complexity of the industrialized world ruled out the broad, simple solutions of the early revolutionaries. Whatever the defects of urban life— and Dickens, Daumier, and others did not hesitate to point them out—nobody could seriously advocate that the process of modernization be suspended or reversed. Thus artists, whose ability to influence economic or technological developments was inevitably limited, began to describe rather than prescribe.

Furthermore, at least some of the goals of the early years of the century had been achieved. By the 1870s the new nations of Germany and Italy had been created, Hungary had obtained a measure of independence, political compromise had been relatively peacefully achieved in Britain, and even in Russia, the last bastion of conservatism, the serfs had been emancipated. All of these developments brought their own problems with them. The rise of Germany entailed the humiliating defeat of France, and both the Austrians and their subjects were unhappy with the compromise of the Dual Monarchy. Yet many liberal aims had been fulfilled, few wept for Napoleon III, and the rapid rate of industrial transformation held out hope of further progress. Artists needed to absorb and reflect on the significance of their world and reveal its true essence in their works, before they could move on.

Thus, in all the arts, midcentury was a time for reacting to contemporary society and its problems, and relating it to an ever-wider public. The thirst for novels, opera performances, more easily affordable art objects in the form of prints and lithographs, and the immediate popularity of photography were all signs that public enthusiasm for culture, far from diminishing, was rapidly increasing. In part, the demand was caused by the greater spread of affluence in Western Europe. The middle classes of Victoria's Britain or the Second Empire in France were among the first worshipers at the shrine of conspicuous consumption, that cult which came to dominate Western society a century later. Yet in turning to the arts to seek explanations for their own lives and times, the public expressed a need that many artists fulfilled.

The spread of culture was not limited to Europe. In America the importation of European culture provided a stimulus to the growth of an indigenous artistic legacy. Paradoxically, the more the United States became exposed to European ideas and works of art, the more distinct was the voice with which American artists and intellectuals spoke. In response to the crisis of faith produced by Darwin, American thinkers developed the philosophy of Pragmatism: Truth was whatever "worked." Painters like Winslow Homer and Thomas Eakins used the new realistic style to illustrate their own landscape and people. Walt Whitman sang of himself and his country.

As the century neared its end, and the first ominous signs of future conflict began to appear, the arts increasingly reflected contemporary uncertainties. In the generation after Turgenev, Verdi, and Daumier, the language and structure of art were to be questioned and, in many cases, rejected. The mood of growing political concern is perceptible in artistic developments between 1880 and 1914. In the 1870s, however, artists could still touch many people by revealing to them the nature of the world in which they lived.

Questions for Further Study

1. How did the role of artists change in the course of the 19th century? What effects did this have on the subjects and style of their works?

2. What were the philosophical and moral implications of Darwin's theories? How has reaction to them evolved since his time?

3. What was the impact of nationalism on the arts? Did it have a stronger influence on some art forms than on others?

Suggestions for Further Reading

Ackroyd, Peter. *Dickens*. London, 1991.

Barger, M. Susan, and William B. Wright. *The Daguerreotype: Nineteenth-Century Technology and Modern Science*. Washington, DC, 1991.

Barzun, J. *Darwin, Marx and Wagner*. Chicago, 1981.

Bowler, P.J. *Evolution: The History of an Idea*. Berkeley, CA, 1989.

Dale, P.A. *In Pursuit of a Scientific Culture: Science, Art, and Society in the Victorian Age*. Madison, WI, 1990.

Eisenmann, S.F. *Nineteenth-century Art*. New York, 1994.

Longford, E. *Eminent Victorian Women*. New York, 1981.

Mainardi, Patricia. *The End of the Salon: Art and the State in the Early Third Republic*. Cambridge, 1993.

Rosenberg, Alexander. *Darwinism in Philosophy, Social Science, and Policy*. New York, 2000.

InfoTrac College Edition

Enter the search term *Charles Darwin* using Key Terms.

Enter the search term *Victorian* using Key Terms.

POLITICS AND NATIONAL DEVELOPMENT IN EUROPE, 1870–1914

In the last decades of the 19th century, despite a century's battles for broad-based political participation, huge numbers of Western Europeans still had no vote. The liberal reforms of midcentury gave political power to those with money or property but left the majority of citizens disenfranchised. In another respect, political discrimination even transcended class because no women could vote in national elections anywhere in Europe. Behind the apparent diffusion of political power, elite interests remained entrenched. A resurgent aristocracy continued to resist the spread of democracy, the rise of the workers, the women's movement, and ethnic nationalism, and thereby preserved domestic divisions within each country.

Instability in domestic politics was less manifest in Britain than elsewhere in Europe. Between 1867 and 1914, the extension of the suffrage was accompanied by social reform. Yet in the years immediately preceding World War I, British political life began to show signs of the turmoil already visible on the Continent. Strikes and industrial agitation led to clashes between workers and police. The suffragist campaign to obtain the vote for women became increasingly militant. In Ireland, the demand for national independence met with a combination of repression and reform.

Nowhere in Europe was there a greater contrast to the stability of Victorian England than in France. The bloodshed of the Paris Commune was followed by bitter political conflict between republicans and monarchists as the Third Republic was founded in 1875. For most of the rest of the 19th century, French politics were dominated by the moderate wing of the republicans. Periodic crises challenged government authority—first anarchists, then the threat of a coup led by General Boulanger, labor unrest, and finally the Dreyfus Affair.

The new national governments of Germany and Italy were both intent on crushing perceived internal enemies. In Germany, Bismarck waged campaigns against Catholics and socialists, undercutting the socialists by introducing his own social welfare legislation. Kaiser Wilhelm II, who dismissed Bismarck in 1890, was determined to reassert the power of the monarchy. Nevertheless in 1912 the German Socialist party became the largest single party in Parliament. In Italy, a very limited number of citizens could vote. Moreover, the similarity of the two chief parliamentary groupings reflected the dominance of upper-class elites. Under both parties, anarchists and socialists were crushed with equal severity.

Similar social conflicts unfolded in other parts of Europe. In the poorer regions of southern and eastern Europe, rural and working-class resentments led to revolts. Governments were brought down in Greece and Portugal, and mass protests erupted in Bulgaria and Spain. In the wealthier north, dissatisfaction focused on the demand for political and social reform. Sweden, Belgium, and the Netherlands all experienced strikes and demonstrations. In a climate of massive disaffection, some political leaders welcomed the outbreak of war in 1914 as a distraction from domestic unrest.

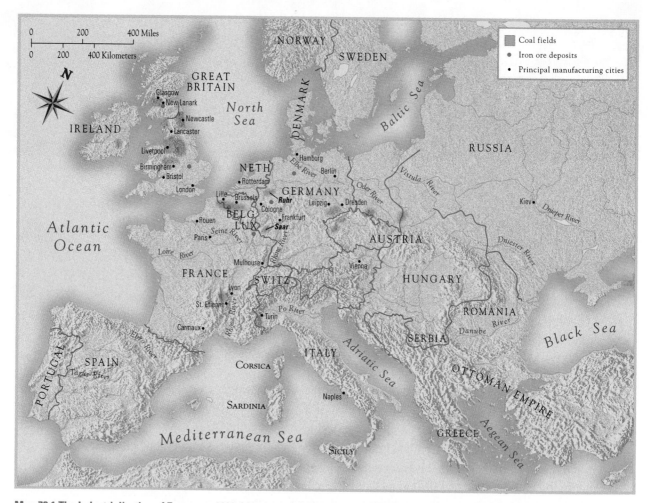

Map 73.1 The Industrialization of Europe, c. 1860. Most heavy industry is still concentrated in Britain and northern Europe. Note the two new industrial regions in northwestern Germany: the Ruhr and the Saar. The former became a center for coal-mining and iron and steel production. Goods were transported to the Rhine via canals, and then onward. The Saar, also rich in coal, iron, and steel, is like Alsace-Lorraine in that control of it has passed between France and Germany. Since 1957, it has been a German state.

POLITICAL REPRESSION AND PARLIAMENTARY RULE

By the 1870s many liberals in Western Europe looked with satisfaction at the world they had created. Revolutions earlier in the 19th century had accomplished many of their goals: the property-owning middle classes had the right to vote; social welfare legislation was introduced by many governments; the nationalist cause triumphed in Germany and Italy; and industrial development, together with scientific and technological advances, was almost daily improving the lives of thousands of people.

Yet only a few decades later, in the early years of the 20th century, the general mood of optimism was replaced with the fear that government and society were on the brink of collapse throughout Europe. When the Great War came in 1914, most of the participants were facing internal crises that seemed impossible to resolve without serious and wrenching changes. The issues varied from country to country, but the results were the same: mass demonstrations put

down by police violence, the resurgence of deep class divisions, and economic dislocation.

The earlier optimism had been ill-founded. For all the achievements of the 19th century, serious problems remained in European society, many inherent in the very advances that had been made. Thus nationalism led to dangerous rivalry for national superiority. The social welfare measures that had been passed were generally inadequate and only drew attention to the widespread poverty and misery still existing. Scientific and technological progress created new problems and aggravated old ones, even as it solved others. By reducing infant mortality and prolonging life expectancy, and by constructing huge new cities with the means to travel around them, the advances led to overcrowded urban squalor.

THE RIGHT TO VOTE

For all the revolutions and reforms, effective political power remained in the hands of a restricted few. Most countries of Western and Central Europe were governed by constitu-

Striking match-workers in England. 1888. The strikers won their cause and went on to found a union of match-workers. In the past, guilds had protected the interests of skilled workers, but the growing numbers of unskilled workers produced by the Industrial Revolution had nobody but themselves to protest bad working conditions or poor pay. The result was the growth of the union movement, whereby unity of action (or inaction) protected collective rights.

tional monarchies, in which royal power was limited through a combination of constitutional guarantees and parliaments. These political systems had been the result of the triumph of bourgeois liberals in the revolutionary upheavals of the first half of the 19th century.

Parliaments consisted of two chambers, an upper and a lower. In Britain, members of the House of Lords either inherited their titles or were appointed by the monarch. The French Senate was elected by regional bodies. The German *Bundesrat* represented the constituent states of the empire, while the Italian Senate was appointed by the king. The lower houses were generally elected through limited male suffrage, although France and Germany had universal male suffrage for their lower houses. The guiding principle of parliamentary liberalism was that by national elections the citizens of a country would choose representatives to formulate and enact national policies.

Parliamentary government distinguished countries such as Britain and Italy from autocratic monarchies such as Russia. Yet by 1900 only in France did more than one-quarter of the citizens have the right to vote. In Britain, about one person in six was enfranchised, whereas of the Italians, new citizens of a new country, about one in fourteen could vote. The right to vote depended on three criteria: gender, financial worth, and literacy. At the beginning of the 20th century, women had no vote in the election of any national assembly in any European country. The suffragist campaign (see Topic 77) became increasingly active in the years before World War I, especially in Britain, but only in Finland (1906) and Norway (1907) did women actually win the right to vote before World War I.

The other criteria, money and literacy, were deliberately applied in order to restrict the vote to the middle classes and the aristocracy, and to exclude the peasants and working classes from the political process. Even "enlightened" liberals did not advocate universal suffrage. Around midcentury the British historian and parliamentarian Thomas Macaulay (1800–1859) called it "utterly incompatible with the existence of civilization," and declared that if the people at large were given the vote, they would "plunder every man in the kingdom who had a good coat on his back and a good roof over his head." Restricting the suffrage to the wealthy was a way of protecting established interests.

Liberals and conservatives alike justified this limitation in several ways. In the first place, it was claimed that wealth was in itself a sign of intelligence, and that poverty indicated both stupidity and moral laxity. The rich saw themselves as being more involved in society, and thus having more at risk. Finally, in clear contradiction to this last argument, they asserted that their wealth provided them with the security to be able to make political decisions without consulting their own self-interest.

Throughout Europe complex electoral systems were devised that not only limited the vote to the prosperous, but also gave additional votes according to the degree of prosperity. As late as 1911, British citizens who met property requirements in more than one constituency could vote in each of them—some cast as many as 20 votes. In other cases education was a criterion. In 1893 Belgium introduced a system whereby all males 25 or older received one vote, wealthy ones a second vote, and those with a higher education a third. By this means the effectiveness of universal male suffrage was virtually annulled because the wealthy and educated could always outvote the rest.

So determined a grasp on power led in the end to widespread resentment on the part of the disenfranchised masses. Many who had fought for reform, or in the nationalist cause, found themselves still shut out from any political rights. The sense of frustration found release in the bitter and often bloody industrial disputes that shook most of Western Europe in the years before World War I, and in the increasing militancy of the suffragist movement.

One other effect of frustrated nationalism was to drive some political extremists to terrorism and assassination as a means of undermining existing regimes. **Anarchists,** who are generally associated in the public mind with political violence, advocated the overthrow of all governments (see Topic 77). A rash of assassinations around the turn of the 20th century, including the Empress Elizabeth of Austria (1898), King Umberto I of Italy (1900), and U.S. President William McKinley (1901), coincided with alleged terrorist activities in Spain, Ireland, and elsewhere.

GREAT BRITAIN: FROM VICTORIA TO EDWARD

In general, British political life remained relatively tranquil until around 1910, at least partly because of the sense of continuity and security provided by the monarchy. When Victoria died in 1901, most of her mourning citizens could not remember a time when she had not been queen. Although her son and successor, Edward VII (ruled 1901–1910), lacked his mother's immense prestige, his famous (for some, infamous) appetite for pleasure and self-indulgence gave its own character to his reign. Later, the Edwardian Era came to be looked on nostalgically as a last time of comfort and sunny confidence, before the darkness of war.

In 1867 the Conservative Prime Minister Benjamin Disraeli, with Liberal support, passed the Second Reform Bill, widening the suffrage. William Gladstone, the Liberal leader, returned to power in 1880, and during the 1870s and 1880s both parties collaborated on several liberalizing measures, instituting secret balloting in elections, legalizing trade unions, providing elementary education for most children, and initiating slum clearance projects.

In 1884, under Liberal leadership, Parliament accepted the principle of universal male suffrage. Yet once again theory and reality did not coincide because only those males with an independent place of residence were qualified to vote. Given the living conditions of the time, around one

in five adult males was excluded. In another issue that arose at the same time, one group of voters managed for once to impose their wishes on Parliament. Charles Bradlaugh (1833–1891) was elected by the constituency of Northampton. On taking his seat in the House of Commons, he refused to swear the oath required of members on the grounds that he was an atheist. Bradlaugh was barred and reelected six times before finally being seated in 1886; atheists could thereafter enter Parliament.

IRELAND AND HOME RULE

For most of the period between 1870 and 1914, the most divisive issue in Britain was Ireland. Irish farmers and laborers had long resented the fact that about half the island belonged to absentee landlords, most of them Anglo-Protestants. Bad harvests in the late 1870s, and the subsequent eviction of many of the tenant farmers, led in 1879 to the formation of the Irish National Land League under the leadership of the fiery Irish parliamentarian, Charles Parnell (1846–1891). The League's slogan was: "The land of Ireland for the people of Ireland."

Gladstone tried to compromise. Those deemed agitators were arrested—Parnell was jailed in 1881—whereas tenant farmers were offered some measure of protection from eviction and excessive rent increases. An already tense situation became complicated the following year when the government's representative in Dublin was murdered by

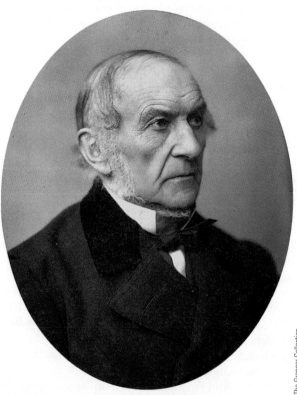

The Granger Collection

Benjamin Disraeli and William Gladstone. Second half of 19th century. The two dominant figures of British political life in Victorian England had very different relations with Victoria. The queen admired "Dizzy" for his charm and open flattery (it was Disraeli's suggestion that she take the title of Empress of India) and disliked Gladstone's seriousness and air of moral superiority. Servants removed all chairs when Gladstone had an audience with Victoria, so that he had to remain standing in her presence.

members of a secret society, although the group was not connected to the League. Public outrage forced Gladstone to impose three years of virtual martial law in Ireland.

In 1886, Gladstone's Liberals finally adopted Home Rule as party policy. The First Home Rule Bill, however, which was introduced in the same year, went down to defeat, precipitating a general election and a Conservative victory. The Conservatives subsequently maintained power almost uninterruptedly until 1906. The same tactics of combined repression and reform were adopted by the Conservative leader, Lord Salisbury (1830–1903). The government improved the terms of low-interest loans available to Irish tenant farmers for buying their own farms, instituted various public works, and introduced industrial and agricultural improvements. At the same time, however, harsh new laws clamped down on Irish nationalist activities. Salisbury's measures bought a brief period of calm, but resentment at the inequities remained.

THE STRUGGLE FOR REFORM

Successive Conservative governments introduced moderate reforms in the structure of local government, the civil service, and education. Yet Conservative hostility toward the trade unions led to a wave of strikes, and in 1900 to the formation of a new political party, the Labour party. In the general elections of 1906, 29 Labour members were elected and the Conservatives overwhelmingly defeated. The Liberals who swept back to power set out to redress working-class grievances by wholesale social reform. In 1909 the Liberal chancellor of the exchequer, David Lloyd George (1863–1945), prepared a budget that required extra revenue for social programs and for increased military spending. He proposed to raise the funds by a system of progressive taxes, according to which the more wealthy would pay a higher rate. His bill passed the House of Commons but was rejected by an outraged House of Lords.

Seizing his opportunity, the Liberal prime minister, Herbert Henry Asquith (1852–1928), dissolved Parliament and fought an election on the two issues of the budget and the power of the House of Lords to block the government. In a famous speech during the election campaign, Lloyd George derided the noble members of the upper chamber, who inherited their seats from their fathers: "They need not be sound, either in body or in mind. They only require a certificate of birth, just to prove they are the first of the litter. You would not choose a spaniel on these principles."

Returned victorious to office, the Liberals carried their budget in both chambers, and in August 1911 drove through a bill that effectively removed the Lords' power of veto. The Liberal actions, far from satisfying the desire for thoroughgoing political reform, initiated a period of widespread unrest. Between 1911 and 1914, strikes and demonstrations brought workers and troops into violent conflict. Labour leaders were jailed and strikers killed. During the same period the British suffragist movement pursued the cause of votes for women by increasingly militant means. Its members interrupted meetings, cut telephone wires, and smashed

and burned public buildings. With violence erupting again in Ireland, Britain was plunged into a state of national disorder. The outbreak of war postponed the resolution of a crisis whose roots lay far back in the self-confidence of the Victorian Era.

FRANCE AND THE DILEMMAS OF THE THIRD REPUBLIC

If Britain's journey from the 1870s to the eve of war began in peace and prosperity, France began with a decade of social and political turbulence. After the Prussian victory at Sedan in September 1870, the French republic had been proclaimed (see Topic 69). Its provisional president was Adolphe Thiers (1797–1877), a liberal with monarchist sympathies.

In March 1871, the National Assembly angered the Parisians by moving the seat of government to Versailles, from where the monarchy had once ruled. When Thiers ordered the confiscation of some 200 cannons, which the people of Paris had financed to fight the Prussians, in an outburst of popular fury, crowds rescued the cannons and killed two generals. In the bloody civil war that ensued, Parisian radicals proclaimed a Commune. The initial demands of its leaders were relatively moderate, but in May the republican government sent troops to crush the rebellion. The "Communards" defended the capital in bitter street fighting that lasted a week. The army shot hundreds of civilians. After the government had recaptured the city, some 20,000 Communards were executed and tens of thousands of others were sent to penal colonies. The brutal suppression of the Commune claimed more lives than any single event in the French Revolution. Press and public meetings remained under strict control, the International was banned, and suspected political agitators were arrested and transported.

THE THIRD REPUBLIC

Meanwhile, the politicians fought over the kind of political system that should govern France. Once again, as in 1849, the chief opponents were monarchists and republicans. In the elections of 1871, the voters returned a clear monarchist majority to the National Assembly. The main issue was that of war or peace, and the conservatives' support for the latter brought them victory.

Had it not been for a bitter split within the monarchist ranks into three factions—the two leading ones were the Bourbons who sought to establish a monarchy and the Orleanists who wanted a return to the empire—France would have seen the reestablishment of conservative rule. In any event, a prolonged standoff between the two royal clans led to an impasse and the creation of the Third Republic. The decision was passed in January 1875 by a majority of one vote, 353 to 352.

A two-chamber parliament consisted of a Senate indirectly elected by local officials and a Chamber of Deputies chosen by universal male suffrage. Parliament had the responsibility of electing a president to serve for seven years, who would appoint ministers, but much of whose power became ceremonial. Marshal Marie MacMahon (1808–1893), a monarchist, served as president until 1879. The stability of the Third Republic, which lasted until 1940, lay, paradoxically enough, in the lack of strong party rivalries and interests. Although ministries changed almost annually, most of them consisted of a reshuffling of the same politicians.

THE OPPORTUNISTS AND THE DREYFUS AFFAIR

By 1879 both chambers of Parliament had a moderate republican majority. The Opportunists were so called because they believed in introducing reforms only when it was "opportune." Their leader, Leon Gambetta (1838–1882), once remarked, "There is no social question." Instead of social reform, they concentrated on limiting the power of forces they thought dangerous: the church, the monarchists, and working-class radicals. The last of these groups, in the absence of serious government attempts at reform, began to develop an increasingly strong independent socialist party.

In the early 1880s a series of bomb attacks and attempted assassinations were attributed to anarchist plotters, and the authorities rounded up several well-known anarchists, including the Russian political theoretician Prince Peter Kropotkin (1842–1921). None of them could be linked to any of the incidents, but several, including Kropotkin, were sent to jail. The arrests aroused widespread protests in France and elsewhere in Western Europe. When demonstrators took to the streets of Paris, the police made more arrests. Among those sentenced was a woman named Louise Michel (1830–1905), known popularly as the "red virgin," one of the leading activists, who played an important part in the Commune. By 1886 public opinion forced the release of all the jailed anarchists.

The anarchist scare was followed by a more serious threat to the government, in the shape of General Georges Boulanger (1837–1891). A dashing army officer, Boulanger appealed to the French weakness for glamorous authority figures, promising to restore real or imagined past glories and offering revenge against Germany. His danger lay in the fact that his supporters included not only monarchists and nationalists, but also disgruntled urban poor. By 1889, Boulanger seemed on the verge of power. At the news that the government was about to press false charges against him, however, the general suddenly took fright and fled to Belgium and the arms of his mistress. He subsequently committed suicide at her grave. His support abruptly melted away, but the very fact that such disparate elements backed him was a clear sign of serious discontent in French society.

At the turn of the 20th century, French public life was rocked by the Dreyfus Affair, a scandal that deeply divided the country and attracted attention throughout Europe. In 1894 Alfred Dreyfus (1859–1935), a Jewish member of the Army General Staff, was tried for espionage on behalf of the Germans, convicted, and transported to Devil's Island, France's notorious prison camp off the coast of South America. His brother Mathieu protested his innocence,

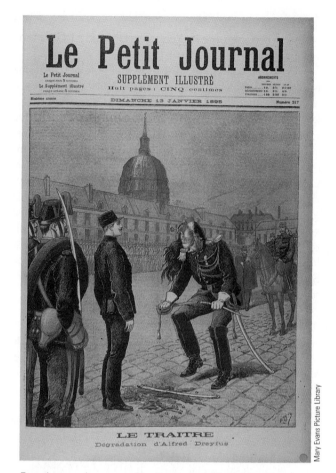

French magazine cover showing the breaking of Captain Alfred Dreyfus's sword. January 1895. *Le Petit Journal*'s position on the Dreyfus Affair is made abundantly clear by the illustration's caption: "The Traitor: The Degradation of Alfred Dreyfus." The official ceremony took place in front of the serried ranks of Dreyfus's fellow officers; Dreyfus stands to attention, under guard.

avowing that his accusers, a group of monarchist army officers, were inspired by anti-Semitism. Both monarchists and nationalists became increasingly openly anti-Semitic in the late 19th century.

In 1897 evidence came to light that demonstrated conclusively that Dreyfus's conviction had been obtained by the use of forged documents. The government was asked to reopen the case. It refused, claiming that his supporters were trying to attack the honor of France in general, and the army in particular. With that, the entire country lined up as either pro-Dreyfus or anti-Dreyfus. On his side were liberals, socialists, and Radical republicans—the most famous of Dreyfus's defenders was the novelist Émile Zola (see Topic 79). Colonel Georges Picquart also defended his military colleague, for which he was forcibly retired from the army and imprisoned. Arrayed against him were monarchists, nationalists, and reactionary Catholics, and also a substantial body of conservative working-class opinion.

When one of the officers accused of forgery committed suicide, the government was forced to act. In 1899 a new court martial reached the absurd verdict that Dreyfus was guilty of espionage, but under "extenuating circumstances."

In the face of widespread public protests, Dreyfus received a presidential pardon, and a further hearing in 1906 cleared him completely. His defender, Colonel Picquart, was restored to active service; Picquart later became a general and served as minister of war from 1906 to 1909. Throughout the whole affair, in which strong opinions were often violently expressed and demonstrators frequently came to blows, the person who seemed least moved was Dreyfus himself. Unemotional, tight-lipped, as patriotic as the most fanatical of his accusers, he formed the still center of a storm that wrecked the Opportunists' grip on power.

THE RADICALS IN POWER

The Opportunists' Radical successors did little to improve on the Opportunists' unimpressive record of social reform. French living and working conditions remained inferior to those in many other parts of Western Europe. Government legislation concentrated on curbing the power of the church with sweeping anticlerical measures, provoked at least in part by the Catholic stand on the Dreyfus Affair. Unauthorized schools and religious orders were prohibited, and in 1905 the union of church and state was dissolved. For the first time since Napoleon's reforms of 1801, all religions had equal status.

The industrial reforms of the 1870s, which included protective legislation for youths, women, and miners, went some way to reduce industrial unrest, and over the following decade, France had fewer strikes than most other Western European countries. Around the turn of the 20th century, however, the climate rapidly deteriorated. On several occasions between 1906 and 1910, militant strikers were ruthlessly beaten back, with deaths and injuries. Other demonstrators were arrested and jailed. France's prime minister, Georges Clemenceau (served 1906–1909, 1917–1920), openly described himself as his country's "number one policeman."

In 1910 and 1911, housewives across France staged massive protests at the steep rise in the price of basic commodities such as eggs and milk. In general, French trade unions did not encourage women members. Now, however, in a mood of growing frustration, and impressed by the energy of the women's lobby, union leaders organized them into consumer associations or enlisted them in the unions. Yet labor's struggle was an uphill one. When the railway strike of 1910 was crushed, most French socialists and political radicals came to believe that it was useless to look to the government to produce any serious reform in living and working conditions. Only direct action, they claimed, could bring about change. The fragile political stalemate between workers and management was barely maintained up to the outbreak of war in 1914.

GERMANY AND ITALY: THE PROBLEMS OF NATIONHOOD

For all the obstacles overcome, Europe's two new nations had yet more problems to solve in the task of achieving stable government and social justice. Political parties needed to be developed that could balance the existing social and economic forces against the requirements of nationhood—and this at a time of growing international tension.

The new German empire, created in January 1871, was in theory democratically based. Of the two chambers of Parliament, the lower house, or *Reichstag,* was elected by universal male suffrage, and the upper house, or *Bundesrat,* was made up of appointed representatives of the 25 states constituting the empire. In practice, however, Germany was among the least democratic nations in Western Europe. Prussia dominated all the other German states by means of its power of veto over constitutional changes, and by the authority of the Prussian king, who was also German emperor. He served as head of the army, and thus controlled foreign policy and the waging of war. Furthermore, German chancellors invariably came from Prussia. Bismarck served as minister-president of Prussia as well as chancellor of the Reich. Had there been a strong tradition of political parties represented in the *Reichstag,* the emperor's position might have been challenged. As it was, even the most influential of his ministers served only at the monarch's pleasure, as Bismarck was to discover. Because the Prussian king continued to favor the interests of the Junker and business classes, the creation of Germany brought no real change in political policies. The consequence of reactionary government was the rise of an increasingly aggressive socialist movement.

CATHOLICS AND SOCIALISTS IN BISMARCK'S GERMANY

Bismarck, who was chancellor from 1871 to 1890, realized the threat posed to traditional interests by socialism. His first target, though, was the Catholic Church, and in particular the Jesuits, whom he believed to be the natural enemies of a Protestant Germany. In the early 1870s he began to wage the *Kulturkampf* (the "struggle for civilization") against the Church. His motives were not only religious. Anxious to cement the new Germany, he resented Catholic influence; in addition, he feared a possible alliance of Catholic powers—Austria, France, Italy—against Germany.

The Jesuits were expelled from Germany, members of religious orders were not allowed to teach in Prussian schools, and political statements by members of the clergy were censored. Bismarck's reforms introduced civil marriage and divorce. The same program applied to Prussian Poland, which was predominantly Catholic. There, in addition to religious legislation, the elementary schools had to teach their classes in German rather than Polish.

Discrimination against Poles continued, but in Prussia the German Catholics fought back. By 1878 Bismarck was forced by public support for the Catholic Center party to incorporate them in his alliance, and to withdraw most of the *Kulturkampf* legislation. Thereafter the church occupied the same position as elsewhere in continental Europe, one of support for conservative interests and opposition to socialism. In addition, Bismarck's questioning of Catholics' patriotism made them especially anxious to appear nationalistic.

Bismarck's battle with the socialists was a far more bitter and drawn-out affair. Government persecution of individual socialist workers' groups backfired. The separate organizations banded together in self-defense, and in 1875 laid the foundations of what was to become the Social Democratic party (SPD), Europe's first real socialist party. To Bismarck's horror, the new party soon had thousands of members, was publishing widely circulating newspapers, and won almost 10 percent of the votes in the elections of 1877.

The following year two unsuccessful attempts to assassinate the emperor gave Bismarck his chance to strike back. Even though the SPD had no connection with the attacks, in October 1878 the *Reichstag* passed an antisocialist law, banning any activity aimed at "the overthrow of the existing political or social order." The law remained in force until 1890. During the interim, thousands of socialists were arrested or driven into exile, and almost 1,300 books, periodicals, and newspapers were banned.

The antisocialist law represented the negative side of Bismarck's campaign. His more positive effort consisted of a series of reforms that he hoped would eliminate working-class support for socialism. Beginning in 1883–1884, he introduced measures that made Germany a model of progressive social welfare. Workers were insured against incapacity resulting from illness, accidents, or old age. Maximum working hours were fixed for men, and limits were established for the employment of women and children. Official inspection of working conditions became mandatory. The aim of all this legislation was to wean workers from socialism.

GERMANY UNDER THE EMPEROR
Whether the bizarre combination of repression and social benevolence would have enabled Bismarck to keep the socialists under control is impossible to say: In 1890 he was dismissed by the new emperor, Wilhelm II (ruled 1888–1918). Wilhelm was a strong believer in the principle of divine right. After an initial period of tolerance, he showed no greater sympathy toward working-class problems than his Hohenzollern ancestors.

The emperor's chancellor from 1900 to 1909 was Bernhard Heinrich Martin von Bülow, who had previously held a wide variety of diplomatic posts. Bülow was anxious to achieve imperial glory for Germany, but his manipulation of foreign affairs led to the formation of an anti-German alliance of Britain, France, and Russia, and eventually to World War I. In 1909, in an argument over the budget, he lost the emperor's confidence and resigned.

Over the previous two decades an increasingly threatening gap had begun to appear between a rapidly swelling socialist party and a ruling class bent on preserving the privileges of the wealthy, the landowners, and the military. In the elections of 1912, the SPD became the largest party in the *Reichstag* and the strongest socialist party in Europe. When war came in 1914, the class divisions that had been endemic to German life throughout the 19th century were no nearer resolution.

Unfinished portrait of Kaiser Wilhelm of Germany. Late 19th century. Having dismissed the venerable Bismarck early in his reign, Wilhelm took Germany's foreign policy into his own hands, undercutting his various ministers' attempts to build alliances. The resulting instability led inevitably to the outbreak of war in 1914. Having led his country to defeat, he abdicated in 1918, but lived on in exile until 1941—long enough to see the start of another world war.

POLITICAL INEQUITY IN ITALY
With the annexation of Rome in 1870, when the patriots of the *Risorgimento* finally achieved their goal, their high expectations were far from matched by reality. The political system under which the new nation was ruled between 1870 and 1922—the period of the so-called Liberal State—left much to be desired. As in Germany, the Italian constitution left significant powers to the king. Parliament consisted of a Senate, appointed by the monarch, and an elected Chamber of Deputies. There were no formal political parties, but in theory the two chief groups stood for opposing positions: the *Destra* (the Right), representing Cavour's conservative tradition, and the *Sinistra* (the Left), the forces that had opposed Cavour. The Sinistra began by championing the poor, especially those of southern Italy, but in practice any real difference between the groups soon disappeared. Both proved to be equally repressive of those they saw as challenging their own elite interests. Before the end of the 19th century, they merged into a single "liberal" party.

In any case, the number of those qualified to vote was so limited that few Italians felt seriously involved in the political process. From 1870 to 1882, only about 2 percent of the population could vote; from 1882 to 1911, the average was around 8 percent. Virtually all voters were drawn from the traditional power bases: the upper and upper-middle classes. In consequence, the Destra and the Sinistra soon came to reflect the interests of the elite. As for the average Italian, frustration at being excluded from political life became expressed in the wry observation that "Things were better off when they were worse off."

POPULAR PROTESTS AND THE ITALIAN SOCIALIST MOVEMENT

Both Destra and Sinistra administrations of the following decades followed the same policy of repressing radical movements. In 1877, the Italian branch of the International was banned outright, its leaders were arrested, and socialist newspapers were destroyed. Both parties were equally anticlerical and antirepublican. Repression reached its height during the premierships of Francesco Crispi (served as prime minister 1887–1891, 1893–1896), especially after the formation of the Italian Socialist party in 1892. In 1894 Crispi passed a series of harsh laws against those guilty of "incitement to class hatred." Crispi, once a radical hero of the *Risorgimento*, emerged as an ambitious prime minister with a bent for dictatorship.

Serious peasant uprisings in Sicily were followed in the fall of 1897 by a wave of strikes and demonstrations that swept through the country and were met with brutal government reaction. The worst violence was in Milan in 1898, where troops fired indiscriminately on unarmed demonstrators. General Fiorenzo Bava-Beccaris, who was decorated by the king for ordering the shootings, became popularly dubbed "the butcher of Milan." Even a Capuchin monastery was raided, and its monks charged with being revolutionaries. The government insisted that the various spontaneous riots formed a single socialist conspiracy to overthrow the regime. With the disorders under control, thousands of "dissidents" were rounded up, ranging from Catholic priests to trade union leaders.

TRASFORMISMO

The antigovernment riots were provoked by a variety of causes—rent increases, land seizures, rises in the price of bread. Beneath them all, however, lay deep popular resentment at the failure of Italy's parliamentary system to resolve the widespread poverty that afflicted the peasantry and the slowly developing working class. By the 1880s a phenomenon known as *trasformismo* developed, which lasted up to 1914. Under *trasformismo*, a politician of the left could hold office under the right by becoming "transformed." In practice this meant that the two chief parties divided up between themselves the advantages of power and handed them out to their respective members. Patronage, and the manipulation of elections, meant that the only politicians who could succeed were those who cooperated with the system.

Faced with such cynicism on the part of their rulers, many Italians lost any remaining faith in the possibility of serious social or political reform. The benefits of the few social welfare measures that were introduced, which included penal, educational, and public health reform, were outweighed by the bitter hostility between workers and government. By the end of the 19th century the only major country in Europe with a more repressive regime was Russia.

GIOLITTI AND THE POLITICS OF COMPROMISE

In 1900, King Umberto I (ruled 1878–1900) was assassinated by an emigrant anarchist named Gaetano Bresci, who had returned to Italy from Paterson, New Jersey, to exact retribution for the bloodshed of 1898. The new king, Victor Emmanuel III (ruled 1900–1946), proved more sensitive to the need for relaxing social tensions. Under the leading Italian politician of the early 20th century, Giovanni Giolitti (1842–1928), a measure of confidence was restored. Far from abolishing *trasformismo*, Giolitti extended it to include those opposition elements that had previously been excluded: the Catholics, and, more crucially, the socialists. Thus the responsibility of power was shared over a wider political base as Giolitti attempted to coopt these new elements into the parliamentary system.

The result of his policies was a notable lessening of social tension, although the compromise was often uncomfortable. Just as Giolitti accepted the necessity of collaborating with the socialists, so he also relied on the support of a substantial group of corrupt right-wing southern Italian and Sicilian politicians who were notorious for their manipulation of elections. To those reproaching him with double dealing, he replied that, "A tailor who has to cut a suit for a hunchback has no choice but to make a hunchback suit."

With the help of a major improvement in the Italian economy, and the reduction of class conflict, Giolitti's government introduced a program of social legislation. Life insurance and the railways were nationalized, with lower prices and better services made available on a broader basis, and the public health system was reformed.

In characteristically Giolittian style, at the same time he sought to mollify Italian nationalists by giving them what they wanted: a colonial war in Libya. Italy's desire to emulate her European neighbors and acquire an empire had already led to trouble at the end of the previous century, when Crispi had been forced to resign in 1896 by the disastrous failure of a colonial expedition he sent to Abyssinia (Ethiopia). In the Battle of Adowa, troops led by Menelik II (ruled 1889–1913) crushed the badly outnumbered Italian expedition, the first African army to defeat a European colonizing force. In the period of increasing international tension that preceded World War I, Giolitti saw a chance to move into North Africa. Libya officially belonged to the Ottoman Empire, but the Turks were in no condition in 1911 to defend their property. Italian forces occupied Tripoli, together with the group of Greek islands known as the Dodecanese (the largest is Rhodes), and the sultan conceded Libya and the islands to Italy.

SIGNIFICANT DATES

Western Europe 1870–1914

1875	France inaugurates Third Republic
1878	Bismarck withdraws *Kulturkampf* reform
1879	Parnell forms Irish National party
1880	Gladstone returns to power
1883–1884	Bismarck introduces social welfare legislation
1886	Gladstone's Home Rule Bill defeated
1892	Italian Socialist party formed
1894	Dreyfus convicted of treason
1900	Umberto I assassinated
1900	British Labour Party formed
1901	Death of Queen Victoria
1905	Finland first European country in which women can vote
1910–1911	Strikes across France
1912	German SPD becomes strongest socialist party in Europe
1901–1914	Giolittian era in Italy

THE PACE OF DEVELOPMENT: NORTH AND SOUTH

Industrialization and the spread of socialism affected the political climate throughout Europe. In general, people in the poorer southern countries continued to fight for political and economic reform right up to World War I. In northern Europe, where a measure of political and economic progress had been won by the 1890s, the remaining goals were social: improvement of working and living conditions, the provision of insurance schemes, and health care.

POLITICAL OPPRESSION IN SOUTHERN EUROPE

Spain, Portugal, and the Balkans remained the poorest, least developed parts of Europe until World War I. In Spain, alternating conservative and liberal governments protected the interests of the ruling classes and exploited the advantages of power, while ruthlessly putting down workers' protests. The system of alternation was called *turno pacifico* ("taking turns peacefully"). In the 1880s the Spanish police used the alleged formation of a terrorist organization called the Black Hand to arrest and imprison thousands, although there is considerable doubt about whether the Black Hand ever really existed. Worker response included massive demonstrations. In 1892 to 1893 some 20,000 Spaniards were jailed on the accusation of having been involved in a series of violent incidents. In 1897 an anarchist assassinated Prime Minister Antonio Canovas del Castillo.

During the first decade of the 20th century, terrorist bombings and police reprisals continued to wreak havoc in Spain's public life. The coming of age of King Alfonso XIII (ruled 1886–1931) in 1902 did little to resolve national problems. A climax of sorts came in 1909, when in the *Semana Tragica* (Tragic Week), 30,000 demonstrators took over the city of Barcelona for several days. The police regained control by firing on the crowds.

Portuguese public life was also controlled by two parties who protected one another's interests, the cynically named Regenerators and Progressives. The system that was devised to make sure they retained power, and thereby access to public funds—the equivalent of the Spanish *turno pacifico*—was called "rotavism." It led to widespread popular disgust at political corruption. In addition to worker protests, an increasingly strong middle-class republican movement began to form, which attributed Portugal's problems to its king, Carlos I (ruled 1889–1908).

In 1908 Carlos and the heir to the throne were both assassinated in Lisbon, and two years later, in October 1910, a republican uprising overthrew the regime and abolished the monarchy. The republicans were joined in the coup by left-wing forces, who shared their hatred of the Catholic Church and the crown, but the republicans soon alienated their allies. Republican Prime Minister Alfonso Costa (served 1913) enforced the violent repression of demonstrators. He also won the dubious distinction of being the only European government leader to secure passage of a bill actually reducing the suffrage. The electoral law of 1913 cut the number of voters in half.

At the other side of southern Europe, in the Balkans, economic conditions were even more wretched, and liberal government proved elusive. In the absence of a hereditary aristocracy, two forces, the ruling princes and kings, and professional city politicians, battled for power. The instruments used in the struggle were the army and the police, which were kept strong by the conscription and heavy taxes imposed on the peasants.

Bulgaria had been part of the Ottoman Empire from 1396 to 1878, when Turkish rule there was restricted by the Congress of Berlin. In 1894, the Bulgarian state spent less money on the combination of education, agriculture, justice, administration, and other public services than went to support the army. Thus living conditions, which had been grim under the Turks, deteriorated still further.

At the end of the 19th century a series of disastrous harvests drove the Bulgarian peasants into open revolt. In 1900 thousands of demonstrators were dispersed only by wildly firing troops. In January 1907, a national railway strike led to widespread rioting. Among the leaders of the protests were students and professors from Sofia University. In retaliation the government closed the university and jailed many of the students. A few weeks later the prime minister was assassinated. By 1914 opposition to the regime was so strong that in the elections of that year only massive rigging, including the kidnapping of antigovernment candidates, kept the government in power.

Greece was the only country in southeastern Europe where some liberal reform was introduced. In 1875 the young liberal politician Charilaos Tricoupis persuaded the king to call the first fair elections in Greece's history. In the absence of any democratic party tradition, the results were predictably confused. Between 1875 and 1882, Greece was governed by 13 different ministries. Tricoupis managed to create somewhat more settled conditions for a few years, during which he encouraged economic development and tried to build a stable civil service.

On the death of Tricoupis in 1896, Greece's political life once again fragmented, with eight elections over the next 12 years. Finally, in 1909, army demands for reform were supported by mass demonstrations in Athens. The government fell, to be replaced by military rule. When that, too, proved unpopular, the Cretan politician Eleutherios Venizelos was chosen to lead a new national assembly, charged with rewriting the constitution. Venizelos's reforms were generally progressive, but they did little to change the basic character of Greek politics.

SOCIAL PROTEST IN THE NORTH

In Scandinavia, political affairs were complicated at the turn of the 20th century by hostility between Norway and Sweden, because Norway was ruled by the Swedish king, although it had its own parliament. After much diplomatic skirmishing, Norway was finally declared independent in 1905. In all three of the principal Scandinavian countries—Norway, Sweden, and Denmark—the early years of the 20th century were marked by significant extensions of the suffrage. Socialist groups in Denmark and Sweden contin-

ued to lead protests, even though the International was banned in Denmark and socialists were harassed in Sweden during the 1880s. In 1893 and 1896, Swedish socialists organized two "People's Parliaments" in Stockholm to agitate for electoral reform. A reform bill finally passed the Swedish Parliament in 1907–1909; a flurry of social legislation followed. Old age pensions were introduced, the penal code was updated, and working hours and conditions were made subject to control.

A similar process occurred in the Netherlands and Belgium: Conservative governments unwillingly introduced electoral reform in response to widespread popular uprisings. The first serious riots broke out in 1886 in Belgium. Although they were violently quashed, they succeeded in making politicians aware of the degree of working-class discontent. Minor reforms were introduced, including restrictions on the employment of women and children. Demonstrations continued to rock Belgium almost annually, until in 1893 a form of universal male suffrage was introduced.

Although protests in the Netherlands were less violent, they proved more effective in the long run. A liberal government, in office from 1897 to 1901, passed many social measures: it was dubbed the "Cabinet of Social Justice." Electoral reform proved more elusive. Large-scale demonstrations were held in 1910, 1911, and 1912, and hundreds of thousands of people signed petitions in favor of extending the suffrage. As elsewhere in Europe, however, it took World War I to effect the change: Universal male suffrage was finally adopted in 1917.

Putting Politics and National Development in Europe in Perspective

By the outbreak of World War I, the optimistic confidence of the mid-19th century was long gone. Those countries that had tried to reconcile the interests of rulers and ruled had discovered it to be an agonizing process. Furthermore, conditions in many areas on the fringes of Europe still remained untouched by liberal reforms. However noble the ideal of a constitutional monarchy and parliamentary democracy might be, it proved almost impossible to implement to general satisfaction. The greater the pressure for change, the stiffer the resistance of those in power became. Because the rulers controlled the instruments of their rule—the police and the army—violent conflict was inevitable. When war came in 1914, the established order in most European countries was faced with serious challenges. Within the ruling classes, not a few regarded the war as an escape from the mounting threat to their authority. Events were to prove them wrong.

Questions for Further Study

1. What were the chief differences between the pace of political reform in Britain, France, Germany, and Italy?
2. What part did the development of socialist parties and trade unions play in the political crises of the early 20th century?
3. Why did the Dreyfus Affair become so important at the turn of the 20th century? What light does it throw on the nature of French society at the time?
4. To what extent were countries in northern and southern Europe faced with the same political problems as those in Western Europe? To what extent, if at all, did they resolve them?

Suggestions for Further Reading

Avrich, P. *Anarchist Portraits*. Princeton, NJ, 1988.
Burns, M. *Rural Society and French Politics: Boulangism and the Dreyfus Affair*. Princeton, NJ, 1984.
Fortescue, William. *The Third Republic in France: Conflicts and Continuities*. New York, 2000.
Hause, S.C., and A.R. Kenney. *Women's Suffrage and Social Politics in the French Third Republic*. Princeton, NJ, 1984.
Johnson, Martin Philip. *The Dreyfus Affair: Honour and Politics in the Belle Epoque*. New York, 1999.
Lovett, Clara M. *The Democratic Movement in Italy*. Cambridge, MA, 1982.
Mommsen, W.J., and H.-G. Husung, eds. *The Development of Trade Unionism in Great Britain and Germany, 1880–1914*. Boston, 1985.
Sheehan, J.J. *German Liberalism in the Nineteenth Century*. Chicago, 1978.
Sturmer, Michael. *The German Empire, 1870-1918*. New York, 2000.

InfoTrac College Edition

Enter the search term *Victorian* using Key Terms.

Enter the search term *anarchism* using Key Terms.

THE CRISIS OF EMPIRE IN EASTERN EUROPE

The trend toward increased democracy in Western Europe was slow, but in most countries reformers made progress. In Eastern Europe, by contrast, liberal and worker demands were ever more rigorously and consistently repressed, with the result that opposition forces never managed to organize themselves. Where parliaments existed, they had little or no real power. In the absence of adequate social welfare legislation in countries that were inherently poor, living standards were far inferior to those in the West. The one serious challenge to a regime, the Russian Revolution of 1905, was led by the only relatively industrialized working class in Eastern Europe.

In the Austro-Hungarian empire, the Dual Monarchy became increasingly paralyzed by conflict between the empire's various nationalities. Power remained firmly in the hands of Emperor Franz Josef. Between 1870 and 1890, a socialist movement began to develop, but the government arrested its members and crushed any sign of rebellion. Civil liberties were repeatedly suspended.

The Hungarians, like the Germans within the empire—a minority but a far more independent one—maintained their control by a blend of nationalist fervor and bureaucratic corruption in favor of the aristocratic landowners. Other ethnic minorities in Hungary were forcibly repressed. When the Magyars threatened to assert themselves even further by nationalizing their army regiments, Franz Josef suspended the constitution.

In the Russian empire, with its large number of separate countries and nationalities, Alexander III intensified the persecution of opponents and minorities. From 1881 until 1891, the government ruled with virtually unlimited powers of repression. Nonetheless, the gradual spread of education and the rise of an urban working class, coupled with a series of disastrous famines and cholera epidemics, produced growing public resentment.

By the 1870s, the Ottoman Empire was in the last stages of disintegration. Turkish territories in the Balkans revolted continuously, and by 1878 the Turks had lost most of their European possessions. Within Turkey contempt for the sultan's corrupt and inefficient rule was compounded by the dawning of a new national pride. In 1908 a group known as the "Young Turks," supporting Western ideas, forced the sultan to introduce an elected parliament. A year later, they deposed him.

The Balkan conflicts brought the great European powers into increasing tension. After 1890, international relations saw shifting alliances that ended with Europe split into two camps: Britain, France, and Russia versus Germany, Austria, and Italy. Repeated diplomatic crises after 1905 raised international tensions to a fever pitch. On June 28, 1914, a Serbian nationalist assassinated the Austrian Archduke Franz Ferdinand at Sarajevo, and the world was plunged into war.

THE SUNSET OF THE AUSTRO-HUNGARIAN EMPIRE

The formation of the Dual Monarchy (see Topic 68) went some way toward relieving tensions between Austria and Hungary, but the basic problem underlying the Hapsburg empire—the conflict among its numerous ethnic groups—remained unresolved. The few gestures in the direction of liberalization only made things worse because as soon as minorities received a measure of political power, they used it to protest their grievances. The only public figure in Austria who seemed to support liberal reform was Crown Prince Rudolf (1858–1889), who was found shot in the royal hunting lodge at Meyerling, together with the 17-year-old Baroness Mary Vetsera. The exact circumstances of their deaths have never been clarified, but it appears that the two may have taken part in a suicide pact.

The sheer number of parties and interest groups ensured that the Emperor Franz Josef remained firmly in control. Both the national parliament, the *Reichsrat*, and the regional parliaments served as little more than debating chambers and were all dissolved by the time of the outbreak of war in 1914. The emperor and his governments ruled by decree. To maintain a sort of balance, Franz Josef shifted between liberal and conservative prime ministers, but the repression of left-wing opposition remained constant. By contrast to Vienna's reactionary political condition, cultural life there was astonishingly rich, varied, and creative (see Topic 79).

Painting of Austrian Emperor Franz Josef at a court ball. 1913. The event is taking place in the gardens of the Imperial Palace, Vienna; the Emperor is standing, in military uniform, at center left. At the time of this image he was 83 years old and had been ruling since 1848. He lived long enough to issue an intransigent ultimatum to Serbia in July 1914 that plunged the world into war a month later.

© Erich Lessing/Art Resource, NY

The conservative Count Eduard von Taaffe (1833–1895) served as prime minister from 1879 to 1893. Following an outbreak of anarchist terrorism in the early 1880s, his government suspended civil rights in Vienna, broke up political associations, and made numerous arrests. Taking his example from Bismarck in Germany, Taaffe tried to head off workers' support for the socialists by offering a program of welfare legislation. One of the measures, the spread of education, exacerbated ethnic tensions because the issue of which language should be used in the empire's various school districts became a major fighting point. His social reforms had already won him the opposition of his fellow conservatives, and the renewed bout of nationalist feuding brought down his ministry.

Taaffe's successors drew the moral that to introduce even minor reform was dangerous, and later governments tried to maintain as inactive a position as possible. Public demonstrations compelled some degree of liberalization in 1896, when a form of suffrage was extended to virtually all adult males. In theory, some 20 percent of the population was thenceforth entitled to vote, but a complex class electoral system ensured that control over elections remained in the hands of the richest 2 percent. The Russian Revolution of 1905 encouraged a fresh outburst of popular resentment: In November of that year, 250,000 people joined demonstrations in Vienna, and protests were also organized in other cities of the empire.

ETHNIC CONFLICTS

Even if the *Reichsrat* had been given far more authority—and it was in any case disastrously divided into warring factions—there would have been scant possibility of its resolving the multiplying nationalist crises that bedeviled the last years of the empire. In Bohemia, Czechs and Germans remained locked in conflict, and Franz Josef's policy of favoring first one and then the other only compounded the mutual hostility. In the summer of 1893 the German-speaking authorities in Prague took advantage of a wave of violence directed against German and imperial signs and emblems to declare a state of emergency. Schools were forbidden to fly Czech flags; when teachers protested, Count Franz Thun, the governor, told them: "If you do not do as you are told, I shall break your necks."

Several years later, in a characteristic attempt to balance both sides, the central government sought to win over the Czechs by requiring that all civil servants should speak both Czech and German. This time it was the turn of the German speakers to riot, both in Bohemia and Vienna.

The same pattern of worsening ethnic clashes occurred throughout the empire. In those parts of northern Italy still under Austrian rule, fighting broke out in 1904 between Italian and German speakers. In the part of former Poland under Austrian rule, where there were very few resident Germans, the Austrians encouraged the Polish upper classes in their repression of the Polish and Ruthenian peasants, who lived as virtual serfs. Revolts against aristocratic landowners occurred in 1899 and 1902, and in 1908 a Ruthenian student assassinated the governor.

NATIONALISM IN HUNGARY

The case of Hungary was rather different, at least in theory. Hungarian nationalists had already won many of the concessions for which other minorities in the empire were fighting: The Magyar language was used in schools, the courts, and public services, and the Hungarians, by the provisions of the *Ausgleich* (see Topic 68), had their own government. These powers were used systematically to defend the interests of the landed aristocracy and to repress the other minorities resident in Hungary, in particular the Romanians.

Despite the rights they had won, many Hungarians continued to demand further concessions from Vienna. In 1903 nationalist politicians began to agitate for the reorganization of the army, with the use of the Magyar language for Hungarian regiments. The scheme inevitably met with a blunt veto from Franz Josef, but the nationalists insisted, and parliamentary proceedings degenerated into uproar, with members overturning benches and tearing down paneling from the walls.

Early in 1906, Franz Josef stepped in and dissolved Parliament with the use of military force. The emperor appointed the new prime minister and guaranteed him the grudging support of the Hungarians by threatening to introduce universal male suffrage if they did not cooperate: The extension of the vote to the lower classes and the other minorities would have meant the end of Hungarian aristocratic supremacy. The emperor's threat was brought home by repeated mass protests in favor of electoral reform in the years from 1906 to 1913. When parliament finally passed a reform bill, in March 1913, it raised the percentage of those eligible to vote from 6 to 8 percent of the citizens; on the eve of war, Hungary's electorate was the most restricted of any European country, including Russia.

By 1914 the Austro-Hungarian empire was irretrievably damaged by decades of bitter interethnic strife. Taaffe, the prime minister of the 1880s, had described his method of government as "muddling through." Much the same could have been said of Franz Josef (who died in 1916), but with the coming of war, the confusion was too great to resolve even by more systematic methods. To the astonishment and bewilderment of many of its citizens, who believed it, for better or worse, to be indestructible, in 1917, after three years of fighting, the Hapsburg empire simply collapsed in defeat.

THE RUSSIAN EMPIRE: INDUSTRIALIZATION AND POLITICAL CRISIS

When Tsar Alexander III (ruled 1881–1894) was brought to power in 1881 by the assassination of his father, Alexander II, one of his first acts was to order the public execution of those implicated in the attack. A crowd of more than 100,000 attended the event, which set the tone for a reign marked by unrelieved reactionary repression. In August of the same year, a "provisional decree" gave the government almost unlimited powers of censorship, arrest, and deportation; the decree was regularly renewed and remained in effect until the last tsar was deposed in 1917.

By the time of Alexander's death in 1894, his policies had effectively suppressed all organized opposition throughout the Russian empire. His son and successor, Nicholas II (ruled 1894–1917), continued Alexander's methods. All minority groups, especially Poles, Finns, and Jews, were subject to the process of "Russification." The Poles were forced to use the Russian language in their schools. In 1899 the Finnish Parliament was stripped of its powers and replaced by direct rule by the tsar.

Yet in 1905 massive public protests forced Nicholas to make major concessions. Several factors contributed to so remarkable a reversal. Nicholas, who was deceptively mild-mannered in appearance, was as committed to maintaining his autocratic rule as his father had been, but less aggressively single-minded in enforcing it. In addition, a series of terrible famines and epidemics of cholera in the 1890s led to widespread poverty and distress in the rural districts, and fueled anger among the peasants.

Perhaps even more significant was the rise of a working-class population, as industrialization began to concentrate large numbers of urban poor in the big centers of production. Although the pace of Russian industrial development lagged behind that in the West, by the end of the 19th century, manufacturing and heavy industry plants existed in Moscow, St. Petersburg, Rostov-on-Don, and throughout southern Russia. Capital from France was used to finance Russian railway and telegraph construction, and the Franco-Russian understanding became ratified into a formal alliance in 1894. With the spread of the railways, raw materials were transported to these new industrial centers, and the finished products were distributed both in Russia and elsewhere in Europe.

The growth of manufacturing and trade, and improvements in transport, produced radical changes in Russian society, which had been stagnant for so long. On the bottom rung of the ladder, the peasants were now joined by urban workers, who were congregated in the big cities. Unlike the rural poor, they could make their presence felt both by mass strike action and by demonstrations in the most important cities of the empire. At the same time, a middle, business class began to appear, which was eager to speed the process of Westernization in Russia.

The new classes sought to change Russia's monolithic regime by forming political parties. The Constitutional Democratic party represented the middle class and progressive landowners, while the Social Revolutionary and Social Democratic parties were led by radicals. The latter two had to operate for the most part underground, and many of their leaders either fled to exile in Western Europe or had to face imprisonment, often in Siberia. The Social Democratic party (SDP) was to play a crucial role in the later Russian Revolution of 1917. In 1903 it split into two groups, the more moderate Mensheviks and the firmly revolutionary Bolsheviks, whose leader was Vladimir Ulianov (1870–1924), better known as Lenin.

The general mood of change also encouraged Russian feminists. The regime made considerable effort to prevent the Russian women's movement from forming links with international groups and discouraged even the most harmless of feminist activities. Nicholas's wife, Alexandra, forbade the reproduction of her portrait on diplomas awarded for women's courses. Under the leadership of Anna Nikitichna Shabanova (1848–1932), however, Russian women began to combine philanthropic activities—the provision of housing and day care centers—with the demand for political rights.

THE REVOLUTION OF 1905

The time was ripe for major political protest, and would-be revolutionaries were unexpectedly given their opportunity by the outcome of the brief but bitter Russo-Japanese War of 1904, which occurred when the two countries tried to expand at the expense of the decaying Chinese empire. The Russians occupied Manchuria during the Boxer Rebellion (see Topic 76) and seemed ready to take Korea. In February 1904, the Japanese attacked the Russian naval base of Port Arthur (now Lu-shun), and in May 1905 destroyed the Russian Baltic fleet in the Battle of Tsushima. The humiliating defeat and the food shortages resulting from an inadequate transport system overworked by the war underlined the Russian government's failings, and protestors were quick to mount demonstrations. Their leader was a 35-year-old Russian Orthodox priest, Georgi Apollonovich Gapon,

who persuaded them that their best hope lay in presenting a petition to the tsar in person, humbly begging him to set right the terrible injustices afflicting them.

On January 9, 1905, a crowd of some 200,000 people moved toward the Winter Palace in St. Petersburg. A few days earlier, Gapon had written to Nicholas, telling him of the demonstration's peaceful intentions and imploring him to accept the petition. The tsar's response was to depart at once for the country, leaving behind ranks of armed police and Cossack soldiers. As the crowd collected in front of the palace, many holding up crosses and pictures of Nicholas and singing "God Save the Tsar," they believed that their ruler would appear on the balcony and hear their pleas.

The palace guards ordered them to disband. As the throng stood in bewilderment, Cossacks and police opened fire. They shot into the dense mass of people until the snow was stained red by the more than 100 dead and hundreds of others wounded. Gapon escaped the massacre of what came to be called "Bloody Sunday" (according to some because as a police informer he was intentionally spared) and fled to Finland. In a letter to the tsar he wrote: "The blood of innocent workers, women, and children forever separates you and the people of Russia. May all the blood still to be shed, executioner, fall on thee and thine own kin!"

For once the regime had gone too far. The strikes and agitations that followed forced even Nicholas to propose a compromise. In March 1905, he offered concessions. His limited reforms, which included the establishment of a Duma, or parliament, elected by a restricted franchise and with limited powers, were greeted with further riots. By the

Theodore Roosevelt with the Russian and Japanese delegations to the peace conference following the Russo-Japanese War of 1904. Roosevelt, who had succeeded to the Presidency after the death of President McKinley in 1901, was elected in 1904, and persuaded representatives of the two sides in the war to come to the United States for peace negotiations. The meeting, at which this photograph was taken, was held in Portsmouth, New Hampshire, in September 1905.

Corbis-Bettmann

Tsarist troops shooting at demonstrators in front of the Winter Palace, St. Petersburg. January 9, 1905. The day became known as "Bloody Sunday." The crowds were waiting in front of the Palace in the belief that they would be received by the Tsar (who had, in fact, left for the country). The photograph became a famous propaganda image for the leaders of the Russian Revolution of 1917.

end of October, public anger was so widespread that Russia's economic life had ground to a halt. Finally, on October 30, 1905, the tsar gave way and issued his October Manifesto. It guaranteed individual freedoms, broadened the electoral basis for the Duma, and gave it legislative power. Crowds danced in the streets.

Then the revolution petered out. In part, the October Manifesto split the demonstrators. The moderates, who became known as the Octobrists, were satisfied, whereas the Social Revolutionaries and Social Democrats saw it as a trick. In part, the mass of the population was simply exhausted by almost a year of chaos. A major factor, however, was the regime's use of massive repression to crush any remaining signs of protest. In the Baltic provinces alone more than 2,000 people were executed.

Meanwhile, Nicholas issued a series of decrees that withdrew almost all of his concessions. An upper house was added to the Duma, with half its members appointed by the tsar, who also retained his power of veto and of appointing ministers; subsequently, a new set of electoral laws gave the Duma a guaranteed conservative majority. At least Russia now had

a parliament, and the aristocracy no longer possessed unlimited powers, but the tsar still controlled the army and Russia's foreign policy, and could dissolve the Duma.

The prime minister from 1906 to 1911, Peter Stolypin (1863–1911), sought to modernize the economy by introducing a land reform program. This program redistributed the holdings of the communes and encouraged private ownership. At the same time, increased foreign investment speeded the process of industrialization. Any chance that labor might organize itself sufficiently to challenge the regime once again was eliminated by Stolypin's ruthless repression of any sign of protest. By the time of his assassination in 1911 by a revolutionary who was also a police agent, all radical organizations had been crushed; their leaders were dead, in jail, or in exile abroad.

Yet the 1905 Revolution proved not entirely in vain, although its long-term effects were psychological as much as practical. The mystical awe with which the tsar was regarded by his subjects was irretrievably damaged. Nicholas's public image was that of a shy, kindly man, who was most at ease with his family (see Topic 81). After Bloody Sunday

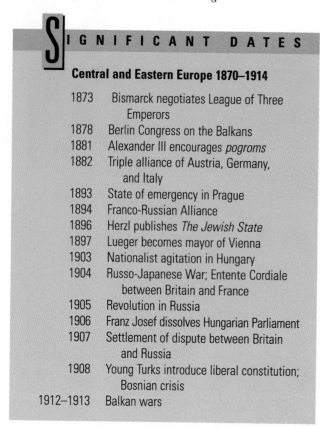

Map 74.1 The Jewish Population of Europe. The absence of Jews in Spain after 1492 produced large concentrations of Sephardic Jews in North Africa, and in the Ottoman Empire and its possessions (including Cyprus). Cities like London, Amsterdam, and Venice, with significant Jewish populations, often had three or even four different synagogues, to cater to the various languages and rites.

and the subsequent extended campaigns of reprisal, even the most loyal of his citizens knew that behind the façade Nicholas was willing to unleash violence. Furthermore, the growing pace of industrialization made further clashes inevitable because a country in the course of rapid modernization remained ruled by an archaic and inflexible autocrat.

EUROPEAN JEWS AND ANTI-SEMITISM

In 1903 the Russian secret police faked and published a pamphlet entitled *The Protocols of the Elders of Zion*. The document, they claimed, proved the existence of a Jewish plot to take over the world. This notorious forgery represented a deliberate move to rekindle a long tradition of anti-Semitism in Russia. Nor was prejudice against the Jews limited to Russia; in the late 19th century, anti-Semitism became a factor in the national politics of many European countries.

RUSSIAN JEWS AND THE *POGROMS*

Millions of Jews had become Russian subjects with the partition of Poland in the late 18th century. In 1791 Jews were confined to towns within a limited area in Russian-occupied Poland known as the Pale of Settlement. The repressive measures introduced by successive tsars in the course of the 19th century culminated in violent anti-Semitic outbreaks against Russia's approximately 5 million Jews. Beginning in 1881, Alexander III encouraged *pogroms* (the Russian word for "devastation"), in which thousands of Jews were beaten or massacred and their property destroyed. In May 1882, the

government required all Jews living in the Pale to leave rural centers and move to already overcrowded cities. During the reigns of Alexander III and Nicholas II, countless Jews escaped the horrors of persecution by fleeing abroad. Some 2 million of them reached the United States.

During the 19th century, anti-Semitism flourished throughout Europe. Some extremists, largely from the radical right, began to develop theoretical justifications for age-old prejudices. Their pseudoscientific theories of racial superiority inflamed extreme nationalist sentiments. The French diplomat Count Joseph de Gobineau (1816–1882) published *The Inequality of the Human Races* (1853–1855), which propounded the theory that the Nordic races were superior. Such notions reached an even more extreme expression in the works of the Anglo-German writer Houston Stewart Chamberlain (1855–1927). His *Foundations of the Nineteenth Century* (1899) offered a racialist glorification of the Germanic past, which depicted history as a struggle between "heroic" Aryans and the "destructive" Semitic peoples. Kaiser Wilhelm II read the book aloud to his children and urged its adoption by officer-training schools. A generation later, Adolf Hitler drew many of his Nazi ideas from Chamberlain's book (see Topic 81).

German Jews in the latter part of the 19th century had received increasing legal rights. In reaction, Adolf Stoecker (1835–1909), Protestant minister at the imperial court, founded the Christian Social Workers' party, which developed a comprehensive anti-Semitic program. In Austria-Hungary, Karl Lueger (1844–1910) took control of the anti-Semitic Christian Social Union in 1890 and became mayor of Vienna in 1897. With his election, Vienna became the first major city in Europe to support a political party that included in its platform hatred for the Jews. Lueger was famous for his declaration: "I'll decide who is a Jew"—an attitude typical of his opportunistic anti-Semitism. Living in Vienna on the eve of World War I, Hitler admired Lueger but thought him too moderate.

In France, where Jews were prominent in politics and culture, public attitudes toward them became polarized by the notorious Dreyfus case. In the process, anti-Semitism rather than the innocence or guilt of Dreyfus emerged as the real issue. Despite the victory of Dreyfus's supporters, anti-Semitism remained a potent force in French right-wing politics. Elsewhere, the path to Jewish emancipation was smoother. In Britain, the last restrictions against Jewish participation in public life were removed in 1858 when Jews could become members of Parliament. In Italy, Jews had taken their place as full citizens following the *Risorgimento*, and many played a prominent part in public and intellectual affairs. One Italian Jew became war minister—at a time when Jews in Germany could not even hold an army commission—and in 1910 Luigi Luzzatti (1841–1927) was appointed prime minister.

THE ZIONIST MOVEMENT

By the late 19th century, many Jews felt threatened from two directions: the continuing persecutions in Eastern Europe and weakening of Jewish tradition through assimilation in the West. To meet these challenges, Jewish leaders organized the Zionist movement, the ultimate goal of which was the creation of a separate Jewish state in Palestine, the home of their ancestors. Zionists believed that only in this way could Jews live in freedom.

The leading exponent of Zionism was Theodor Herzl (1860–1904). Herzl was born in Hungary and studied law in Vienna. While serving as foreign correspondent for an Austrian newspaper in Paris, Herzl covered the Dreyfus Affair. The anti-Semitism associated with the case brought home to him his own sense of Jewishness (he had earlier advocated the mass conversion of Austrian Jews to Catholicism). In 1896, he published an influential pamphlet, *Der Judenstaat—The Jewish State: An Attempt at a Modern Solution of the Jewish Question.*

Herzl urged the formation of an international Jewish movement to secure a homeland in Palestine. In 1897, he presided over the first meeting of the World Zionist Organization, a movement that rapidly spread throughout the world. Encouraged by the enthusiasm of many Jews, Herzl sought the backing of government officials for the Zionist cause. Britain supported the idea with caution, and in 1903 he met with British officials to discuss plans for a Jewish settlement. After Herzl's death, these aims were advanced further by Chaim Weizmann (1874–1952), who succeeded him as head of the Zionist movement. Weizmann secured the co-

operation of Arthur Balfour (1848–1930), British prime minister and later foreign secretary, in the creation of a Jewish state in Palestine. The return to Palestine after 2,000 years was, however, to prove fraught with problems.

THE DISINTEGRATION OF THE OTTOMAN EMPIRE

To the southeast of Russia lay its long-term enemy, the Ottoman Empire. The sultan ruled some 40 million subjects, but his authority was seriously weakened by corruption and the pressures of nationalism. In Egypt, the sultan's strong-willed viceroy, Mohammed Ali (1769–1849), made the territory virtually independent, while elsewhere in North Africa the French seized Algiers. The first major loss of Ottoman territory in Europe occurred in 1829, when the Turks were forced to grant independence to Greece and autonomy to Serbia (see Topic 63).

The Crimean War of 1853–1856, in which the Turks lost additional Balkan territory, was part of a larger international issue known as the "Eastern Question." The war stemmed in part from increasing competition between Austria and Russia over the Balkans, and in part from the longstanding Russian desire to gain control over the Dardanelles Straits so as to secure naval access to the Mediterranean. The latter issue especially concerned the British, who regarded the Middle East as a vital link to their empire in India.

The conflict broke out in 1853, when the Turks declared war following the Russian occupation of the provinces of Moldavia and Walachia. The following March, Britain and France allied with Turkey against Russia. Piedmont soon joined the allies as an active participant, and Austria became an allied nonbelligerent. At the peace conference that met in Paris in 1856, the powers stipulated the neutrality of the Black Sea and forced Russia to withdraw from Moldavia and Walachia.

The Paris conference preserved the Ottoman Empire only temporarily. In the Russo-Turkish War of 1877–1878, the Russians proved so successful that they drove the Turks out of most of their European possessions. This would have made Russia the dominant force in the Balkans, but the other European powers had no intention of letting that happen. At the urging of Britain and Austria, Bismarck convened a congress in 1878 in Berlin, at which the captured land was divided. Russia, which felt cheated out of what it regarded as its just desserts, managed to hold on only to Bessarabia, while Bosnia and Herzegovina were placed under Austrian administration; this last decision proved to have ominous consequences 30 years later.

INTERNAL REFORM IN TURKEY

For many Turks the loss of their European empire was the final proof of the inefficiency and corruption of their rulers. Nationalists began to claim that Turkey could make progress and enter the modern world only by adopting Western approaches to government and society. The move-

Mary Evans Picture Library

Tinted photograph of the Turkish Sultan Abdul-Hamid II. Early 20th century. Known as "Abdul the Damned," the sultan ruled autocratically from his secluded palace. His misgovernment led to a prolonged period of discontent, which he tried to head off by appeals to pan-Islamism. His eventual successor as the first leader of the Turkish Republic, Kemal Ataturk, secularized his country and banned the wearing of the *fez*, the small red felt hat worn here by Abdul.

ment for reform was led by a group of army officers and students calling themselves the Young Turks, who succeeded in 1908 in compelling the sultan, Abdul-Hamid II (ruled 1876–1909), to implement a liberal constitution. The following year the sultan, whose subjects called him "Abdul the Damned," tried to reverse himself. The Young Turks seized their chance and deposed him.

GREAT POWER RIVALRY AND THE BALKANS

The political uncertainties hanging over all three Eastern European empires produced an ominous instability. The various national crises, furthermore, were compounded by increasing tensions among the great powers, whose relations were complicated by a series of fluctuating alliances. Rivalry between the leading European nations led eventually to global conflict, but the first skirmishes took place on the fringes of the Continent, in the Balkans.

THE BISMARCKIAN ALLIANCE SYSTEM

After the unification of Germany, Bismarck had determined to consolidate and develop the empire. In his view, this effort required peace and security for Germany. Over the next

20 years, therefore, he devised a diplomatic system aimed chiefly at isolating France, Germany's acknowledged enemy. He sought to achieve this purpose by binding most of the great powers to Germany in a series of intricate, and sometimes conflicting, alliances.

The first step in building his system was to create a modern version of the old "Holy Alliance" (see Topic 63). In 1873 Bismarck concluded the *Dreikaiserbund*, or League of the Three Emperors, with Austria and Russia, which bound the three conservative powers to consult with each other in the event of international crisis, but the league collapsed as a result of Russia's anger over the outcome of the Congress of Berlin. In 1879, Bismarck, faced with choosing between Austria-Hungary or Russia as principal ally, chose the former; he sought to bolster German security through the Dual Alliance with Austria, which provided that each partner would assist the other in the event of a Russian attack. Bismarck then succeeded in resurrecting the Three Emperors' League in 1881, but now strengthened by a provision that, should one of the three partners go to war with a fourth nation, the others would stay neutral. The next year, Bismarck added still further to this web of agreements by negotiating the Triple Alliance, which pulled Italy into a defensive treaty with Germany and Austria.

Because of Russian suspicions concerning the Triple Alliance, Bismarck conceived the cornerstone of his diplomatic system, the Reinsurance Treaty of 1887 with Russia. This agreement provided for friendly neutrality should either partner be involved in a war with another power (a specific proviso, however, released the partners from this obligation should Russia attack Austria, or Germany attack France). Germany was therefore freed from what Bismarck called the "nightmare" possibility of a two-front war with France and Russia, while Russia was assured that Germany would not combine with Austria against her.

The relationship among these various alliances was dubious at best. There was even direct conflict between the Dual Alliance and the Reinsurance Treaty because Bismarck promised both Austria and Russia that he would support them in the Balkans. Yet, despite the Iron Chancellor's having overstepped the thin line of diplomatic ethics, he had established German security. Moreover, while the delicate balance of his system depended largely on his own diplomatic skills, European peace was maintained for two decades.

REALIGNMENTS AND NEW ALLIANCES

Bismarck's dismissal as German chancellor in 1890 brought about a diplomatic revolution. Kaiser Wilhelm II proceeded to reverse or cast overboard the basic tenets of Bismarck's foreign policy. He refused a Russian request to renew the Reinsurance Treaty because he believed that Germany's proper ally was Austria and that a German-Russian alliance was counter to the spirit of Germany's obligations to the Austro-Hungarian empire. Naturally alarmed, the Russians approached France, which seized the opportunity to end its forced diplomatic isolation. The two nations concluded a defensive alliance in 1894, which was reinforced in 1904.

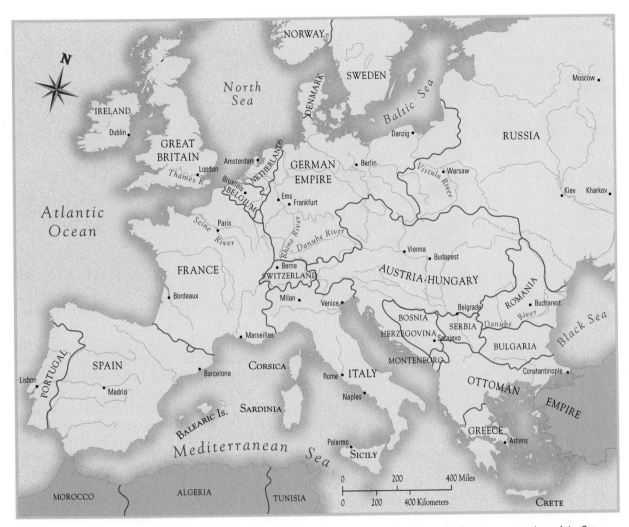

Map 74.2 Europe in 1878, after the Congress of Berlin. The Congress was convened to divide up the European possessions of the Ottoman Empire, following Turkish defeat in the Russo-Turkish War of 1877–1878. It assigned Thessaly, in the north of the Greek mainland to Greece, Bosnia and Herzegovina to Austria, and established Bulgaria as autonomous. The only European territory the Turks retained was the island of Crete. Its inhabitants rose up and drove the Turks out in 1899, and Crete became an independent state for the first time since the fall of Knossos around 1400 B.C., before uniting with Greece in 1908.

Although Britain was not tied to Germany by formal treaty, Bismarck had carefully avoided threatening British interests; he undertook no overseas ventures that might antagonize them and refused to build up the German Navy. Wilhelm, however, was bent on achieving a "place in the sun" for Germany equal to England's empire. In addition to launching German expansion in Africa, he also began a massive naval buildup. The British saw both policies as serious threats to their world interests. Furthermore, Germany sought to play an important role in the Near East by proposing the construction of a railway from Berlin to Baghdad. The German threat to Britain eventually led to the conclusion in 1904 of the "friendly understanding," or Entente Cordiale, between Britain and France, resolving among other issues their longstanding colonial conflicts in North Africa.

The last step in reshaping European alliances occurred in 1907, when Britain settled its colonial differences with France's ally Russia (the British and Russians agreed to neutralize Tibet, to recognize British predominance in Afghanistan, and to divide Persia—modern Iran—into spheres of influence). The so-called Triple Entente, a loose series of agreements among the three powers, came into being. To the Germans' alarm their Triple Alliance was now matched by this potentially more dangerous alignment.

THE BOSNIAN CRISIS

The Russians, now able to rely on British and French backing, were in a far better position to interfere in the Balkans. When they did so, conflict with Austria was inevitable. In the past, Germany had tried to discourage Austrian aggressiveness in Eastern Europe, but now Austria was Germany's only important ally. As a result, Germany had little choice but to support Austria under all conditions.

The Austrians moved first. In 1908 they annexed Bosnia and Herzegovina, which had been placed under

Bulgarian artillery during the First Balkan War. 1912. The Balkan Wars of 1912–1913 drove the Turks from the last Ottoman possessions in Europe, but were instrumental in increasing regional tensions, which contributed to the coming of war in 1914. Issues in the Balkans, which these Bulgarian cannons failed to settle, remained unresolved into the 21st century; they include the problems in Bosnia and Kosovo.

their administration at the Congress of Berlin 30 years earlier. Russia protested, and threatened action, encouraged to do so by the Serbians. Serbia, which had plans of its own to carve a great Slavic kingdom out of the southern parts of the Hapsburg empire, had wanted to include Bosnia in its territory. The Serbs looked to the Russians, fellow Slavs, for support. Russia, however, weakened by its defeat by Japan, racked by internal troubles, and pressured by the British, was in no condition to fight a war. When Germany announced its support for Austria, the Russians were forced to back down and to persuade the Serbians to reconcile themselves to the Austrian action. Both Russia and Serbia were humiliated. As a consequence, the Russians stepped up their preparations for a war that seemed increasingly inevitable, while the Serbians continued to incite Austria's Slavic minorities to revolt against their imperial masters.

THE BALKAN WARS

In September 1911, Italy declared war on Turkey and seized Libya, which it annexed the following year. Encouraged by the weakening of the Ottoman Empire and goaded on by Russia, in 1912 an alliance of four Balkan states—Serbia, Bulgaria, Montenegro, and Greece—invaded the last

Ottoman possession on European soil, the province of Macedonia. The Turks were in no condition to resist, beset as they were by an uprising in Albania. The revolt was just coming to an end when the First Balkan War began.

Austria then entered the struggle, however, in order to keep the Serbs from expanding to the Adriatic. Russian protests led in May 1913 to an international conference in London to settle the matter. As a result, the independent state of Albania was created on the Adriatic; Serbia received other land in compensation but remained deeply frustrated. That June, another war broke out in the Balkans. Serbia, together with Greece, Romania, and Turkey, relieved Bulgaria of much of Macedonia. In the process, Serbia doubled its territory.

The Balkan wars failed to resolve either Serbian ambitions or the growing tensions. Moreover, the struggle for hegemony in the Balkans unsettled both Russia and Austria-Hungary, which began to question the loyalty of their own allies. The Austro-Hungarians harbored resentments over Germany's failure to support them more vigorously, while the Russians were highly critical of their British allies. Within the Triple Entente and the Triple Alliance, the mood seemed grim.

Putting the Crisis of Empire in Eastern Europe in Perspective

The battle over the disintegrating Ottoman Empire thus intensified hostility between Austria on the one side and Russia and Serbia on the other, and served as an indicator of the climate of international tension. The rapid extension of regional conflict in the Balkans to the international level in 1914 would reveal clearly enough the desperate state of relations among the European powers. Torn by rivalry in Europe, Asia, and Africa, beset by domestic crises that, in the case of the ruling classes of the Hapsburg and Russian empires, proved fatal, the nations of Europe plunged from the disaster of uncertainty to the all-too-certain catastrophe of world war.

Questions for Further Study

1. What caused the breakdown of the Hapsburg empire? What part did its collapse play in precipitating World War I?
2. How did resistance to authoritarian rule begin to develop in Russia? How did Russian rulers try to deal with their opponents, and how successful were they?
3. What were the main factors in the spread of anti-Semitism in Europe? What were the long-term consequences?
4. What were the main stages in the crisis in the Balkans of the decade before World War I?

Suggestions for Further Reading

Ascher, A. *The Revolution of 1905: Russia in Disarray.* Stanford, CA, 1988.

Evans, R.J.W., and H.P. von Strandmann, eds. *The Coming of the First World War.* New York, 1989.

Hall, Richard C. *The Balkan Wars, 1912-1913: Prelude to the First World War.* London, 2000.

Jelavich C., and B. Jelavich. *The Establishment of the Balkan States, 1804–1920.* Seattle, WA, 1977.

Kennan, G. *The Decline of Bismarck's European Order: Franco-Russian Relations, 1875–1890.* Princeton, NJ, 1979.

Mckean, R.B. *St. Petersburg Between the Revolutions: Workers and Revolutionaries, June 1907–February 1917.* New Haven, CT, 1990.

Sked, Alan. *The Decline and Fall of the Habsburg Empire, 1815–1918.* London, 1990.

Turfan, M. Naim. *The Rise of the Young Turks: Politics, the Military and Ottoman Collapse.* London, 1999.

InfoTrac College Edition

Enter the search term *Nicholas II of Russia* using Key Terms.

EUROPE, THE UNITED STATES, AND THE WORLD ECONOMY

In the half-century after 1871, European social and economic conditions suggested contradictory trends. Most indices of social development, such as nutrition and health, education, mortality rates, housing, and transportation, revealed a previously unknown degree of physical comfort. This achievement was largely the result of the advances in science and technology. The economy, on the other hand, showed signs of considerable instability. After two decades of virtually uninterrupted growth and prosperity, in which industrial production, profits, and real wages rose to new levels, Europe entered a phase marked by recurrent cycles of alternating recession—in some sectors, of serious depression—and renewed economic vitality.

These economic setbacks were a result of the particular stage of Europe's industrial development and the structural nature of its economy. First of all, after 1870, Europe entered the later phase of the so-called Second Industrial Revolution. Since midcentury, the Continent had been industrializing rapidly, and the industrial zone was spreading. Moreover, new technologies—first in steel, then chemicals and electricity, and finally the internal combustion engine—gave industrialization the main features that would distinguish it well into the 20th century.

This was also the period in which business organization assumed the characteristics of what has been called "monopoly capitalism." The corporation had already emerged as the basic form of industrial and commercial structure. By the end of the 19th century, a few giant corporations dominated many industries. With huge resources at its disposal, "big business" formed monopolies within each industrial sector by gaining control of raw materials, transportation, production, and marketing, while consolidating many smaller concerns or driving them out of the field.

The emergence of the United States as a major industrial power not only had important economic repercussions in Europe, but also reflected the development of a true global economy. Europe increasingly had to compete for worldwide customers as well as in its own domestic markets, and the international flow of investment capital linked the transatlantic economy. One of the first indicators of this growing interdependence was the so-called Long Depression that stretched off and on from 1873 to 1896, with effects in both America and Europe.

THE SECOND INDUSTRIAL REVOLUTION

The 18th-century Industrial Revolution had introduced machines and steam power as a substitute for human muscle and water power, principally in making textiles and iron. In the Second Industrial Revolution, electricity and the internal combustion engine began to offer new sources and ways of producing energy, while two new industries—steel and chemicals—were born. Nonetheless, at the end of the 19th century, coal still provided some 90 percent of the world's energy.

THE AGE OF STEEL

Iron technology had made significant advances since the first Industrial Revolution, but the metal, whether wrought or cast, had basic disadvantages. Pig iron, which is hard and brittle, contains between 2.5 and 4 percent carbon. When cast, it cracks or snaps under tension. Wrought iron, on the other hand, which has a carbon content of less than 0.1 percent, is malleable, so that it wears easily and gives under pressure. Steel combines the characteristics of both forms of iron: With a carbon content within the range of 0.1 to 2.0 percent, it is simultaneously hard and elastic. It resists wear and abrasion and is exceedingly strong in relation to its weight and volume. For rail construction, and many other uses, steel appeared to be the answer, but in the mid-19th century it was not yet commercially available on a large-scale basis.

The first technical breakthrough that made cheap steel possible was the work of the British technician Henry Bessemer (1813–1898), whose converter—patented in 1856—reduced the carbon content of pig iron cheaply and quickly. Bessemer's process forced air through molten pig iron in a converter (a brick-lined crucible housed in a wrought-iron casing) in order to reduce the carbon and produce steel, which could be made at about one-seventh of its former cost.

Improvements in the Bessemer method were made by several technicians. In the 1850s, the Siemens brothers in Germany developed a heat exchanger for blast furnaces that used waste gases from cheap-grade coal to heat the air, thus achieving extremely high temperatures for melting and reducing the carbon content of the pig iron to make steel at a much lower cost. In the 1860s, the Martins, a family of French metallurgists, succeeded in making steel by using the Siemens heat exchanger to fuse a mixture of scrap and pig iron. This Siemens-Martin process was slower than Bessemer's method, but allowed for careful control of the quality of steel. In 1878,

Table 75.1	Steel Production (thousands of tons), 1870–1913		
COUNTRY	1870	1890	1913
Britain	240	3,636	8,500
Germany	126	2,135	20,500
United States	69	4,277	31,300
France	84	683	5,100

Colored print showing steel manufacturing. 1876. The drawings illustrate the process for producing steel named after its inventor, Henry Bessemer; he patented his work in 1856. Bessemer went on to open his own steelworks in Sheffield, England, in 1859, which specialized in the manufacture of guns.

The Granger Collection

two British cousins, Sidney Thomas and Percy Gilchrist, made the final innovations by adding limestone into the molten iron and devising a crucible liner made of lime and magnesium, techniques that eliminated the phosphorus from iron ores and allowed for the use of more abundant, cheaper ores.

The production of inexpensive steel on a large-scale basis made possible by the combination of these technical advances did not really begin until the 1880s. When it occurred, however, it revolutionized industry and commerce. By 1885, the steel rail had taken the place of iron in railroads, and in the early 20th century, steel became the fundamental material of industry, replacing iron not only in railroads but also in ships, buildings, machines, engines, tools, armaments, and tens of thousands of consumer products.

THE CHEMICAL INDUSTRY

Before the age of steel, chemicals had already proven important to the development of the textile industry: In midcentury, British and French chemists began producing dyes from organic sources such as coal tar. Beginning in the 1870s, the Germans made significant advances in applying chemistry to industrial uses by developing synthetics. In Germany, where the government placed a major emphasis on technical and scientific education, universities developed close ties with industry. Public funds were made available for chemical research, and in 1872 British visitors in Germany discovered that the University of Munich alone had more chemistry students than all of the English universities combined. By 1900, German firms produced 90 percent of the world's synthetic dyes.

The scientific principles on which the synthetic dye industry was based were also applied to a wide range of other products. From cellulose, for example, were derived explosives, lacquers, film, celluloid plastic, and artificial fibers. "Artificial silk," or rayon, was patented as early as 1889; bakelite, the first synthetic resin, in 1909; and cellophane was produced in 1912. Building on the research of Justus von Liebig (1803–1873) in the 1840s, German firms also pioneered in artificial fertilizers. Among the new products were pharmaceuticals such as aspirin.

THE ENERGY REVOLUTION

The turn of the 20th century also saw a profound transformation in the forms of energy. Along with important advances in steam power and steam-driven motors came the harnessing of electricity and the invention of the internal combustion engine—developments that not only drove

Gun shop at the Krupp factories, Essen, Germany. Early 20th century. The first Krupp factory opened at Essen in 1811. Field guns produced there in the mid-19th century helped assure Prussia victory in the Franco-Prussian War of 1870–1871. In the years leading to the outbreak of World War in 1914, successive generations of the family sold Krupp arms to at least 46 countries.

modern industry cheaply and more efficiently, but eventually also transformed the daily lives of millions of people.

The expansive working of steam at ever-higher pressures dramatically increased the efficiency and power of steam engines. By the 1890s, for example, big steamships had 30,000-horsepower engines as compared to the 60 horsepower of the first paddle-wheel steamers. The steam turbine after 1884 provided a breakthrough in power.

The internal combustion engine dates to midcentury, when Étienne Lenoir devised the prototype of a motor fired by a mixture of air and coal gas. Steam was finally replaced by electric motors. Labor costs were reduced, and inexpensive gas was obtainable as a byproduct of other industrial processes. Once liquid fuels were developed from petroleum, the internal combustion engine became even more practical because it could be moved from place to place without being tied to the source of the gas supply.

The cost of oil dropped significantly as new sources were exploited at the end of the century in Borneo, Mexico, Texas, and Persia. Ocean liners subsequently adopted oil in place of coal, followed soon after by naval ships. Although Gottlieb Daimler (1834–1900) built the earliest automobile in 1885, it was not until after World War I that gasoline-fueled automobiles gained significant ground. Eventually, France led in auto production in Europe, while the United States was the world's leading producer of cars. Airplanes, first flown successfully in 1903, were driven by internal combustion engines during World War I.

ELECTRIFICATION

Electricity has two crucial characteristics: it can move energy across long distances without great power loss, and it can be easily converted into other forms of energy, such as light, heat, or motion. Electrification depended on the development of the electric motor and generator. During the course of the 19th century, electrical experiments demonstrated its commercial potential, first applied in communications. The electromagnetic telegraph, using very little current, was first demonstrated in the 1830s, and by 1866 underwater telegraph cables had been laid across the English Channel and the Atlantic. Alexander Graham Bell's telephone (1876) and Guglielmo Marconi's wireless (1895) followed, both of which used feeble current.

By the end of the century, electric lighting, which had an important economic impact, came into use. Thomas A. Edison (1847–1931) perfected a high-resistance incandescent lamp, or lightbulb, which made electricity useful for the private home as well as for industry and commerce. Edison also understood that the illumination of hundreds of thousands of homes, as well as city streets, required a central power system. The generation and distribution of power were made possible by theoretical and practical advances achieved during the century.

The first public power station in Europe was built in England in 1881 by the German firm founded by Werner Siemens (1816–1892), who invented the dynamo and built the first electric railroad. By the mid-1890s a series of local

stations had appeared throughout western and central Europe, but with no uniform equipment or standards. Here, too, the Germans took the lead, and in the years immediately before the war, firms such as the General Electric Company (*Allgemeine Elektrizitäts-Gesellschaft*) had begun to adopt the principle of power distribution grids servicing commercial and home customers over large regions. By 1914, Germany led the world in the production of electrical equipment and products. The war created a tremendous demand for even more electrical energy, and after 1919 army engineers had plans to build huge centralized power grids crisscrossing entire countries.

In the years between the Franco-Prussian War and the outbreak of World War I, the Second Industrial Revolution transformed the material basis of much of European civilization. The practical applications of science and technology radically altered the relationship between human beings and their environment. The advent of steel not only made possible new, more precise and durable machines, but also enabled architects and builders to shift the growth of cities from a horizontal direction to a vertical profile—the Eiffel Tower in Paris, built between 1887 and 1889, was the best-known symbol of this development. The chemical industry, for good or ill, reduced human reliance on the products of nature, and electrical power offered a seemingly unlimited source of energy and brightened the world for millions of ordinary people. Advances in transportation and communications "shortened" physical distances and changed the conception of time itself.

THE AMERICAN CHALLENGE AND THE LONG DEPRESSION

By 1871, important shifts were beginning to take place in the industrial and economic development of Europe. For the long term, the two most crucial changes were Germany's steady encroachment on Britain's position as the prime industrial power, and the rise of the United States as a great industrial nation, soon to eclipse Europe's economic position.

The United States eventually surpassed Europe not only in the production of industrial products and manufactured goods, but in agriculture as well. The "invasion" of Europe by American—and Russian—wheat imports had serious repercussions on European agriculture and rural life. American competition, both in industry and agriculture, contributed to economic setbacks in Europe. The transatlantic economy had become so closely intertwined that events on one continent directly affected conditions in the other. Uncontrolled speculation and bank panics, along with agricultural and industrial overproduction, combined to create a serious slump in the Western economy between 1873 and 1896.

THE GROWTH OF AMERICAN INDUSTRY

The Civil War (1861–1865) stimulated American industry by sharply increasing demand for manufactured goods. Over

Table 75.2	Pig Iron and Coal Production (thousands of tons), 1870–1910					
	PIG IRON			**COAL**		
YEAR	GB	USA	GERMANY	GB	USA	GERMANY
1870	5,960	1,690	1,400	117,000	42,000	29,000
1880	7,749	3,835	2,429	147,000	65,000	47,000
1890	7,900	9,200	4,000	181,000	143,000	70,000
1900	8,960	13,800	7,429	225,000	244,000	109,000
1910	10,000	27,300	12,905	292,000	571,000	190,100

the next decades, the United States experienced unparalleled economic expansion as a variety of factors came together. Rich natural resources provided a basis for the technological applications in agriculture and industry that characterized the Second Industrial Revolution. The railroad boom and westward expansion, together with a steady increase in population as a result of the flood of immigration from Europe, provided both employment and labor.

The increase in productivity was even more impressive than in Europe. The timber from America's forests provided an abundant supply of charcoal for making iron, but this advantage delayed the transition to coke as fuel for iron smelting. America's localized and scattered iron industries were inadequate to meet its needs, and as late as 1850 some 60 percent of its iron for railroad tracks was imported from Great Britain. Once the British methods of iron production were adopted, however, the iron industry expanded rapidly. Production was concentrated near the coal mines of Pennsylvania. As in Europe, railroad construction provided a stimulus for iron manufacturing. Production of coal and iron rose in spectacular increments.

American coal and iron production virtually doubled every decade after 1860. By 1890, the United States was producing twice as much iron and coal as Germany. The most revealing figures, however, showed that by that date the United States had actually pulled ahead of Great Britain in iron, and at the turn of the 20th century was producing twice as much iron and coal as the former leading industrial nation in the world. Moreover, American factories turned the world's steel production figures completely around. In 1870, both Britain and Germany each exceeded America's steel production, whereas in 1913 the United States made one-third of the world's steel, more than both European powers together. By World War I, the United States had become the world's leading industrial nation.

AMERICAN WHEAT AND EUROPEAN AGRICULTURE

The opening of the Great Plains to agricultural settlement in the years after 1865 coincided with two technological advances of great significance: the mechanization of farming and the westward expansion of the railroad. Among the important agricultural innovations were the polished steel plow, which enabled farmers to break the tough soil of the prairie; the mechanical, horse-drawn reaper designed by Cyrus McCormick; and the threshing machine. All three inventions had been first patented in the 1830s, but after the Civil War they came into wide use.

Once railroads had penetrated beyond the Ohio Valley and across the plains in the 1860s, the productivity of farms was linked to the rapidly increasing urban consumers of the east and American agriculture became market-based. During the decade before the Civil War, the United States had grown an average of some 137 million bushels of wheat per year. In the 1870s American farmers produced an average annual yield of 338 million bushels, and in the 1890s more than 1.3 billion bushels a year.

The abundance of wheat represented a huge surplus beyond the needs of the domestic market. Improvements in transatlantic transportation—the speed and cargo capacity of steamships and a significant drop in shipping rates—enabled American merchants to flood Europe with the surplus wheat at considerably reduced prices. Nor were American wheat exporters alone. In the 1880s, Canada, Australia, Argentina, and even India also began to send wheat to Europe, and at the turn of the 20th century, Russian wheat production surpassed that of the United States.

In the meantime, European agriculture had undergone its own transformations. There, too, railroads had linked urban markets to rural areas. In addition to higher productivity derived from mechanization and fertilization processes, new areas came under cultivation, especially in Russia (which tripled its wheat production between 1871 and 1914) and the Russian part of Poland, Hungary, and Romania. Markets that Western European farmers once had almost completely to themselves suddenly closed with the influx of new wheat. The result was a severe drop in agricultural prices—by 1894, wheat could be bought in Britain for one-third of its price in 1867.

Individual countries weathered the crisis in different ways. In Britain, free trade policies had eliminated agricultural tariffs in the 1840s, and public opinion demanded continuing low food prices. The depression in agriculture caused by massive food imports hurt British landowners seriously. Many gave up farming, and the total arable land under cultivation dropped by one-half in the two decades after 1875. France, on the other hand, protected its farmers by raising tariff walls against foreign grains starting in 1885. Although French wheat growers did not suffer like their British counterparts, wine makers in France experienced a serious depression because their vines were attacked by an insect pest, phylloxera. The Meline Tariff of 1892 placed almost all French agricultural products under tariff protection. In Germany, where a combination of Junker landowners, small farmers, and industrialists pushed for protection against foreign imports, Bismarck imposed a moderate tariff in 1879.

The crisis in agriculture had contradictory results. The lower wheat prices meant that basic food staples cost less, so that the urban working class did not suffer as it had during the famines of the 1840s; on the other hand, the drop in farming income created widespread hardship in the countryside, where peasants had generally experienced considerable prosperity in the preceding decades. In Britain, the hardest-hit country, the number of people involved in farm labor fell by 40 percent.

THE LONG DEPRESSION

The agricultural crisis caused by the flood of American wheat into Europe was one aspect of the overall slump that hit the transatlantic economy between 1873 and 1896. Although generally known as the "Long Depression," the period actually saw a series of separate economic setbacks and business cycle troughs punctuated by intermittent phases of recovery. The collective downturn of the economy appeared worse than it really was because it came after two decades of sustained growth between 1850 and 1873.

The Long Depression encompassed three interrelated elements: agricultural depression, financial retrenchment, and industrial overproduction and contraction. The beginning of the agricultural depression coincided with a banking panic precipitated in 1873. The financial collapse occurred as a result of rampant speculation, especially in railroads, because the banks had made excessive loans based on securities issued by these firms. The first major bank failure occurred in Vienna, and panic spread from there to Berlin, Rome, London, and other European cities, and then to the United States, where Europeans had also invested heavily in railroads. One of the most catastrophic panics hit after the failure of Jay Cooke & Company, one of the leading American brokerage firms. Jay Cooke (1821–1905) had underwritten massive amounts of railroad stock, which he then resold. As banks failed and credit dried up, manufacturing slowed down. British iron production fell by almost 1 million tons in the 1870s, and the wholesale price index dropped from 130 to 107. Unemployment soared from less than 1 percent to an all-time high of almost 12 percent, before declining again to around 2 percent.

Further recessions, less severe than the previous one, occurred in the 1880s. In 1890, however, another serious depression began with the failure (largely as a result of a revolution in Argentina) of the London banking house of Baring Brothers. Partly because of the gold standard, the financial panic spread to the United States. As British banks called in gold, the gold supply in the U.S. Treasury began to move off to London, and the stock market crashed in 1893. The gold drain became so severe that the investment banker John Pierpont Morgan (1837–1913) formed a private consortium to lend gold to the government, much to the anger of the public and Morgan's immense profit.

Prices, which had fallen irregularly since 1873, collapsed still further. Industrial overproduction was one factor that caused the deflation. The gold standard also contributed to lower prices because a shortage in the quantity

Collection, Brandywine River Museum (acquisition made possible by Beverly and Ray Sacks)

Alice Barber Stephens, *The Woman in Business*. 1897. The illustration, published in *The Ladies Home Journal*, shows women working as clerks in a large department store. The scene here is in the fabric section, with rolls of cloth piled on the shelves behind the assistants. Virtually all of the customers of a department like this would also be women.

of world gold reduced the money supply, which in turn drove prices down. European industry experienced the same problem that had plagued agriculture—excessive supply in relation to demand. The two factors were intertwined because the decline in farming income as a result of the agricultural crisis meant that the rural population—some 60 percent of Europe's total—had less money to spend on consumer goods. Moreover, the techniques of mass production were so successful that the supply of manufactured items pushed ahead of the market. In an era when unregulated capitalism still held sway, overproduction led to cutthroat competition and destructive price wars.

The wholesale price index in most European countries reached its lowest level since midcentury—in Britain, it dropped from the 1873 high of 130 to 76 in 1896. International trade also declined. Industries cut back production and laid off workers. In 1892, Britain produced almost 2 million tons less of pig iron than it had a decade earlier, and unemployment jumped from 2.1 percent in 1890 to almost 7.5 percent in 1893.

Despite the recurrent cycles of economic slump, the Long Depression did not prove to be seriously destructive, and full-scale recovery began in late 1896. Although wages declined slightly during the worst years of the depression, they experienced an overall rise between 1873 and 1900. Moreover, low food and commodity prices offset some of the impact. By the end of the century, demand for consumer goods had risen again, especially in urban centers. Producers began to cultivate buyers and develop marketing strategies, including advertising, sales in large department stores, and mail-order firms such as Sears, Roebuck & Co. Prices recovered as a result of higher demand and protective tariffs. Governments also adopted new regulations to prevent speculative busts of the kind that had set off the panics of 1873 and 1890.

The followers of Karl Marx had predicted that in its final stage of development, capitalism would produce the seeds of its own destruction. The Long Depression, however, proved not to be the crisis of capitalism but rather a series of phases of readjustment that came after decades of extraordinary expansion. Moreover, the precarious nature of *laissez-faire* capitalism taught business leaders important lessons about the advantages of cooperation over unrestrained competition. Marx had also argued that wealth would tend to concentrate increasingly in the hands of fewer people as business moved toward the "monopoly" stage of its evolution. From the setbacks of the post-1873 period, industrial capitalism emerged altered but stronger than ever.

BIG BUSINESS IN THE AGE OF MASS PRODUCTION

The Long Depression encouraged the development of "big business" and the trend toward monopolies, thus bringing to an end the era of "heroic" capitalism that had prevailed since the first Industrial Revolution. By the turn of the 20th century, a few huge companies dominated the field in most major industrial and commercial sectors.

CARTELS, TRUSTS, AND MERGERS

Business combinations generally fall into one of three types: (1) agreements known as *cartels*, in which firms remain separate and autonomous; (2) *trusts* or holding companies, in which financial control is exercised over several firms through a company created for that purpose; and (3) *mergers* or consolidations, in which individual firms are dissolved and their assets are put together into one new company.

Some of these business combinations were formed in order to achieve "horizontal" integration among firms within the same industry or stage of production, such as railroad companies or makers of steel girders. Other combinations sought to integrate companies "vertically," at separate stages of production or in different industries—such a combination, for example, might include coal mines, railroads, blast furnaces, and steel producers all in the same cartel or trust. Whatever the form, business combinations set prices and production quotas, reduced costs, delineated markets, and controlled or eliminated competition.

The legal traditions and economic attitudes of individual countries affected the way in which such combinations were formed. In Britain, Adam Smith's *laissez-faire* theories, together with business failures in the 18th century, reinforced hostility toward monopolies and agreements that restrained trade. In Germany, however, where no such traditions existed, combinations were seen as desirable and even necessary. One of the earliest and strongest German combinations was the cartel of potash companies established in the 1870s. German coal producers also created loose agreements in the 1870s, and during the serious depression of 1893 they formed a famous cartel, the Rhenish–Westphalian Coal Syndicate, which fixed prices by limiting the output of coal for all its members. Steel manufacturers similarly created several cartels, and in 1904 these joined together in the German Steelwork Association, a huge combination that not only set prices by limiting production but also lobbied successfully for protective tariffs. By the turn of the 20th century, two firms, Siemens and the AEG, dominated Germany's electrical industry and made agreements between them that fixed prices, defined areas of influence, and divided product specialization. By 1914, German industry boasted more than 600 cartels.

In Great Britain, the tendency toward monopoly manifested itself less intensely and by means of mergers (which the British called *amalgamations*) instead of cartels. British soap firms, for example, formed a cartel in 1906, but it was quickly replaced by the merging of almost a dozen companies into a giant amalgamation, Lever Brothers. The British-controlled Royal Dutch Shell Company, resulting from the merger of several petroleum firms, became one of the world's largest business combinations.

American businesses followed the European pattern. In the 1870s, the owners of the New York Central and the Erie Railroad created a "pool," or informal combination, to end a rate war that was wiping out profits. The pool divided rail traffic among them at fixed rates. One of the largest and most controversial combinations in the United States was the Standard Oil Trust, formed by John D. Rockefeller (1839–1937) in 1882. Even before the trust, however, Rockefeller had engineered a huge conspiracy to drive competitors out of business by controlling railroad transportation rates. He brought together more than 40 firms engaged in all phases of the oil business. The government saw such trends as a threat to consumer interests, however, and passed the Sherman Antitrust Act in 1890, which outlawed all trusts in restraint of trade, although the measure did not halt the trend toward monopoly. Between 1898 and 1900, monopoly combinations were established among makers of steel products. In 1900, Andrew Carnegie (1835–1919), owner of the largest steel company in America, sold out to John Pierpont Morgan for $500 million. Morgan then formed a giant holding company known as the U.S. Steel Corporation, the

The assembly line at the Ford Motor Company. 1913. The average daily production in that year was of a thousand automobiles, made possible by the moving assembly line. Ford revolutionized automobile production by making cars that could be sold at a price within the reach of the average American—he sold 15 million Model T cars between 1908 and 1926.

Brown Brothers

world's first billion-dollar corporation, controlling three-fifths of the steel business in America.

At the turn of the 20th century, big business came to be identified with the careers of business tycoons who amassed fabulous fortunes through ruthless business practices and preached a philosophy of "rugged individualism." Yet these "captains of industry"—Americans such as Rockefeller, Germans such as Alfred Krupp (1812–1887), or Britons such as William Armstrong (1810–1900)—were really products of a business system that had abandoned unrestrained free market capitalism under competitive pressure.

MASS PRODUCTION AND SCIENTIFIC MANAGEMENT

Railroads and the rise in real wages created huge national markets, and the Second Industrial Revolution met the consumer demand with a tremendous growth in productivity. Mass production resulted from a combination of two interrelated factors—technology and business management. Machine tools—machines for precision cutting and finishing metals, such as planers, boring instruments, grinders, and lathes and other precision instruments—were a prerequisite for the making of interchangeable parts.

The American inventors Eli Whitney (1765–1825) and Samuel Colt (1814–1862) had used crude interchangeable parts to make small arms in what came to be called "the American system of manufacture," but neither adopted the principle of the moving assembly line, which began to come into use at about the time of the Civil War. Henry Ford (1863–1947) finally combined interchangeable parts with moving assembly lines in his automobile plant to take advantage of economies of scale. By using several thousand standardized parts, with workers specializing in particular tasks, Ford was able to turn out a thousand Model "T" cars one day prior to World War I.

Along with the assembly line process, principles of management were devised in an effort to increase the rate of production and to raise the cost-effectiveness of labor in connection with the new factory equipment. Frederick Winslow Taylor (1856–1915), an American mechanical engineer, first proposed "scientific management." After developing high-speed machine tools, Taylor turned to a study of shop management. In 1895 he proposed two revolutionary principles: the establishment of performance standards and the creation of a permanent staff of "planners" who were not shop foremen. Basing his calculations on how long a job took, Taylor urged that workers be paid incentives for producing more than the minimum within the allotted time.

Taylor's theories were developed more fully in *The Principles of Scientific Management* (1911). His idea of task design was based on the notion that workers should be told "not only what is to be done but how to do it and the exact time allowed for doing it." He also advocated a total approach that included plant layout and tool design to maximize efficiency. By 1914, "Taylorism" had spread to Europe and Japan.

The consequences of the new "American" system of manufacture were many. Large-scale production met the growing demand of millions of working-class and middle-class buyers for inexpensive consumer goods. On the other hand, the quality and aesthetic appeal of industrial products generally declined. Corporate profit margins increased dramatically, but mass production eventually led to overproduction and business downturns. For those on the assembly lines, the new productivity standards and work pace depersonalized labor. The results were psychological as well as physical exhaustion and increased worker hostility toward

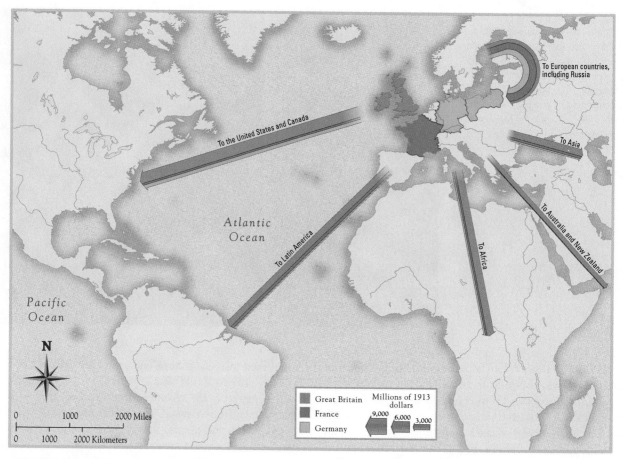

Map 75.1 European Foreign Investment, 1850–1914. Note the heavy preponderance of British investment in all directions. All three leading European powers invested significantly in North America, but only Britain sent capital to Australia and New Zealand. Investment elsewhere in Europe was relatively limited.

foremen and employers. The "management revolution" had an important social impact because the growth of corporate organizations greatly expanded the white-collar group within the lower middle class.

EUROPE AND THE GLOBAL ECONOMY

Between 1870 and 1913, Western Europe and the United States emerged as the focus of the modern industrial-capitalist world. Science, technology, and economic organization all combined to focus extraordinary wealth and power in the grasp of a half-dozen nations. Yet as the circle of industrializing nations slowly widened, important shifts in the international balance of power took place.

THE WORLD DIMENSIONS OF COMPETITION

In the European context, Germany provided the most dramatic evidence of this transformation as it quickly became the new industrial colossus. By 1913, Germany produced more than twice the amount of steel as Britain and also led

all other countries in the chemical and electrical industries. Between 1870 and World War I, Britain's rate of growth slowed to 2.2 percent, while Germany achieved a 2.9 percent annual growth and the United States 4.3 percent. Although Britain remained immensely strong in trade, finance, and industry, statistically it had fallen to the world's third-ranking power.

Moreover, as Belgium and France slipped in terms of their share of industrial manufacturing, Russia, Italy, and Sweden entered the industrial ranks. Russia's industrial growth came late in the century, but it possessed more resources. Between 1860 and 1900, the number of cotton mills rose from less than 40 to more than 700, principally around St. Petersburg and Moscow. Private companies built railroads with government subsidies and foreign investment; by 1900 Russia had more than 35,000 miles of track and a Trans-Siberian line that connected Moscow to the Pacific coast at Vladivostok.

Russian coal production jumped from 1 million tons per year in 1873 to more than 36 million tons by 1913, yet it remained a small fraction of Germany's or Britain's output. Russia did produce iron, but by using fuels and methods long since abandoned in Western Europe. By 1913, how-

Table 75.3	Manufacturing (percent of total of national economies) by Nation							
YEAR	GB	USA	GERMANY	FRANCE	RUSSIA	BELGIUM	ITALY	SWEDEN
1870	31.8	23.3	13.2	10.3	3.7	2.9	2.4	0.4
1913	14.0	35.8	15.7	6.4	5.5	2.1	2.7	1.0

ever, it boasted a steel output equal to two-thirds that of Britain. Russia stood out, furthermore, in the petroleum industry because its rich fields near Baku and Grozny made it the world's leading oil producer until overtaken by the United States at the turn of the 20th century. Moreover, damage to the Baku wells in the war with Japan in 1905 restricted production for years.

Although poor in natural resources, Italy began a phase of rapid industrialization in the 1890s, with heavy industry consuming enormous amounts of imported coal, which jumped from 300,000 tons per year in 1880 to 12 million by 1914. The silk industry had a world market, and railroads and shipping made considerable progress by the turn of the century, when the development of hydroelectricity enabled Italian industry to accelerate. Sweden also began to industrialize, expanding its metalworking and silk industries and increasing exports in wood pulp, dressed lumber, paper, iron ore, and special varieties of coal.

Table 75.3 suggests the changing picture of world industrial production between 1870 and 1913.

INTERNATIONAL TRADE AND INVESTMENT

In the years after 1850, railroads had created not only national but also international markets. Railroads, along with technical advances in steamship construction—steel hulls and fast, powerful steam engines—pushed the volume of world trade steadily upward. Although the British position in industrial production had slipped, it maintained an impressive lead in mercantile shipping. By 1914, Britain could claim 39 percent of the world's commercial tonnage, while Germany and the United States together possessed only 22 percent.

In the half-century after 1870, the volume of world imports and exports increased threefold, despite the slumps occasioned by the Long Depression. Overall trends revealed that Europe's share of this trade declined in that same period, while that of the United States and Japan grew accordingly. U.S. imports and exports were tied closely to Europe in the decades before 1914—60 percent of exports went to Europe, while half of American imports came from Europe. The position of Britain, which retained the largest single percentage of international commerce in 1913—61 percent—had fallen by more than 10 percent since 1870. Trade among European countries represented about two-fifths of all world commerce, although as the 19th century drew to a close, European and American trade with Asia, Africa, and Latin America increased.

Europe's trade with the rest of the world consisted largely of an exchange of manufactured goods for raw materials. Most major countries imported more than they exported. With the exception of Britain, the industrializing nations ran up heavy balance of payments deficits with the suppliers of raw materials. The British, and other countries to a lesser extent, offset the payments imbalance with "invisible earnings," such as shipping and insurance charges and earnings on foreign investments.

International trade grew despite a general move toward protectionism after 1870, both on the part of the United States and of European nations. Trade treaties between individual nations helped overcome tariff barriers, although the exportation of American and Russian wheat to Europe in the 1870s led Germany, France, and other countries to impose tariffs on agricultural goods. Some nations, such as Italy and France, engaged in tariff wars with one another. Industrialists joined the clamor for tariffs as the business slumps took hold, and nationalist rhetoric added to the impulse toward protectionism. Besides Britain, only Denmark, Finland, and the Netherlands retained free trade systems between 1880 and 1913. In addition to the tariff barriers, the existence of some 100 international cartels—in such industries as shipping, armaments, and aluminum—also restricted commercial competition. Nevertheless, neither tariffs nor cartels appear to have seriously hindered the growth of international trade.

During the second half of the 19th century, Europe "exported" huge portions of the capital that had been accumulated in industry and trade. Britain, France, and Germany took the lead in overseas investment, chiefly by buying foreign stocks and bonds or by extending loans to foreign banks and governments.

Britain remained the single most important source of foreign funds between 1870 and 1914, exporting between 4 percent and 9 percent of its national income each year. In 1914, British overseas investments accounted for 43 percent of all exported capital, with France coming in a distant second (20%) and Germany third (13%). Most revealing, perhaps, is the fact that almost half of these funds went to Latin America, Asia, and Africa.

On the eve of World War I, industrialization had ceased to be the preserve either of Great Britain or Western Europe. Competition among nations, rather than the primacy of a single one, had become a principal feature of economic development. Moreover, patterns of trade, investments, and monetary policies revealed the formation of a global economy—one in which Europe played an important but no longer exclusive role.

Putting Europe, the United States, and the World Economy in Perspective

The last three decades of the 19th century and the years immediately before World War I witnessed significant advancements in industrial technology and economic growth, both in Europe and the United States. The Second Industrial Revolution, which was founded on steel, energy, and large-scale manufacturing, drew the two continents into a tightly knit transatlantic economy that became increasingly interdependent. The abundance of American wheat caused a sharp depression in European agriculture in the 1870s, and financial panic in Europe's capitals resounded in New York and Washington.

Changes of far-reaching consequence emerged from the economic slumps that beset Europe and America between 1873 and 1896. Corporations and industries adopted new forms of business organization designed to control economic fluctuations, limit price competition, and stimulate consumer demand. From an era of overproduction—one cause of the Long Depression—came an age of mass production.

The transatlantic economy grew more complex as nations changed their industrial position in an absolute sense as well as their status vis-à-vis each other. The degree of economic competition intensified within Europe, while the industrializing countries expanded the parameters of their operations to Africa, Asia, and Latin America, creating a truly global economy.

It should be remembered, however, that the process by which Europe had achieved its economic ascendancy had not been entirely peaceful. Armed with scientific knowledge, technological skill, and great wealth, Europeans inaugurated an era of imperial expansion after 1870 that enabled them to subjugate and exploit vast portions of the globe (see Topic 76).

From their position at the center of the world economy, Europeans—most of whom enjoyed more physical comforts and a higher standard of living than any people in history—regarded the rest of the world with a sense of superiority. The exploitation of Asia and Africa, which accompanied the Second Industrial Revolution, was intended to promote further European economic expansion. Some imperialists claimed that it also provided a means for extending the "advantages" of Western civilization to less developed regions of the globe.

Questions for Further Study

1. What was the Second Industrial Revolution, and how was it different from the first?
2. How did the development of the American economy affect Europe?
3. To what extent is it accurate to use the term "Long Depression" to describe the European economy between 1870 and 1914?
4. What were the principles of "Taylorism," and why were they important to the modern world economy?

Suggestions for Further Reading

Ashworth, William. *A Short History of the International Economy Since 1850*, 4th ed. London, 1987.

Bensel, Richard Franklin. *The Political Economy of American Industrialization, 1877-1900*. New York, 2000.

Cameron, Rondo. *A Concise Economic History of the World*. New York, 1989.

Carter, E.C., et al., eds. *Enterprise and Entrepreneurs in Nineteenth and Twentieth Century France*. Baltimore, MD, 1976.

Gallarotti, Giulio. *The Anatomy of an International Monetary Regime: The Classical Gold Standard, 1880-1914*. Oxford, 1997.

Henderson, William O. *The Rise of German Industrial Power, 1834–1914*. Berkeley, CA, 1975.

Israel, Paul. *Edison: A Life of Invention*. New York, 1998.

Kanigel, Robert. *The One Best Way: Frederick Winslow Taylor and the Enigma of Efficiency*. New York, 1997.

MacKay, James A. *Alexander Graham Bell; A Life*. New York, 1998.

McCraw, Thomas K., ed. *Creating Modern Capitalism: How Entrepreneurs, Companies, and Countries Triumphed in Three Industrial Revolutions*. Cambridge, MA., 1998.

Milward, Alan S., and S.B. Saul. *The Development of the Economies of Continental Europe, 1850–1914*. Cambridge, MA, 1977.

Pursell, Carroll W. *The Machine in America: A Social History of Technology*. Baltimore, MD, 1996.

Trebilcock, Clive. *The Industrialization of the Continent*. New York, 1981.

Wrege, Charles D. *Frederick W. Taylor: The Father of Scientific Management: Myth and Reality*. New York, 1991.

InfoTrac College Edition

Enter the search term *Henry Bessemer* Key Terms.

Enter the search term *Thomas A. Edison* using Key Terms.

Enter the search term *John D. Rockefeller* using Key Terms.

THE DRIVE FOR EMPIRE: EUROPEAN IMPERIALISM IN ASIA AND AFRICA

The latter half of the 19th century saw an increasingly frenzied drive on the part of many European powers for territorial conquest beyond Europe. Known as the **New Imperialism,** to distinguish it from the earlier phase of European expansion in the 15th century, this surge of aggression resulted in the domination of virtually all of Asia and Africa by a handful of Western powers.

The most direct motivating force was economic, but other factors also encouraged the pursuit of empire. Pressure groups of business, military, and conservative interests promoted colonial expansion as a means of enhancing national prestige in the context of European power rivalries. The various Christian churches saw imperialist conquest as a means of spreading their faith, while some Europeans were genuinely interested in improving conditions in other parts of the world. Many Westerners believed that the exportation of their culture abroad fulfilled a mission to spread a superior culture and "civilize" the world.

The unification of India under British rule represented the crowning achievement of the age of imperialism. Nonetheless, as early as 1857 the "Indian Mutiny," as the British styled it, revealed Indian determination to resist foreign domination. After the unsuccessful rebellion, the British introduced limited political representation, educated Indians of the upper classes in schools under their supervision, and encouraged them to enter government service.

The Western powers had little need for direct rule over China because they found it relatively easy to impose demands on the declining Chinese empire. Racked by internal disorder, China was forced to make continual concessions to Western nations. By 1900, the Chinese emperor allowed a combined European and American military expedition to restore order.

China's problems were compounded by Japan's highly successful adaptation to Western ways. In 1867 the Japanese, who had maintained their isolation from the outside world until as late as 1853, began a wholesale replacement of their feudal system and introduced Western-style reforms. They also emulated the Europeans by seeking their own imperialist conquests.

In Africa, the last quarter of the 19th century saw virtually all of the Western European nations fighting to win territory. In North Africa, the British and French took control of the tangled finances of Egypt, anxious as joint owners of the Suez Canal to protect their investment. In 1882, the British occupied the country; the French found compensation in the Sudan.

In South Africa, conflict was unavoidable. The British Cape Colony became increasingly at odds with two neighboring states settled by the Boers, colonial farmers of Dutch origin who had subdued or pushed out the Bantu. The Boer War broke out in 1899. It took more than three years for the British to defeat their stubborn and determined opponents.

THE IMPERIALISTS: EXPLORATION, COMMERCE, AND COMPETITION

Europeans had been in contact with other parts of the world for centuries, but with the new methods of transport, communication, and warfare available by midcentury, conquest and occupation of distant lands became a serious possibility for the first time.

THE NEW IMPERIALISM AND ITS CAUSES

The New Imperialism differed from earlier European expansion in a variety of ways. The first was the sheer speed—a mere 30 years—with which a handful of nations assumed control of vast portions of the globe. Britain took 4 million square miles, France 3.5 million, Russia 3 million, and Germany, Belgium, and Italy 1 million each. Second, in addition to commercial exploitation, the European powers assumed direct control over conquered territories, making enormous capital investments maintained by colonial bureaucracies and military forces.

The advocates of imperialism claimed a variety of motives as their inspiration, including converting the "heathen," spreading Western civilization, advancing national glory, and exploration for its own sake—as in the daring exploits of Henry M. Stanley (1841–1904) or Sir Richard Burton (1821–1890), who charted much of the African interior. Moreover, the aggressive spirit of capitalism, buoyed by the advances of science and technology, favored an outward drive for expansion.

Yet the deeper causes powering that drive were more prosaic. The pace of industrial growth had been so hectic that European economic interests needed a wider stage. With the vast increase in production and intense competition in European domestic markets, manufacturers had to find new customers. As businesses became more and more profitable, wealthy industrialists looked for ways to invest the capital they had accumulated. By 1870, with industrialization well under way throughout most of Europe, they were turning to other parts of the world where investment often brought quicker and higher profits than at home. Furthermore, mining and processing a country's natural resources—vital supplies for the investing nation—were in themselves forms of imperialism, as the Germans demonstrated by winning control of Chilean nitrates. Thus imperialism represented the domination of nonindustrialized areas of the world by industrialized or industrializing nations.

European prosperity also contributed to the imperialist impulse. With the transformation from an agricultural to an urban society, and the general rise in prosperity, the European demand was increasing not only for staple commodities such as beef and grain, but also for specialty goods not produced in Europe, such as coffee and sugar, as well as luxury items such as ivory and animal skins. Furthermore, manufacturers came to depend on a ready supply of materials not available in the West, including cocoa, rubber, and copper.

By the end of the 19th century, a global economy inextricably linked Western and non-Western interests (see Topic 75). The two sides were not, however, equal partners because modern technology gave the West an enormous power advantage. Moreover, the non-Western nations traded raw materials and food, whereas the West produced sophisticated and expensive manufactured goods, and transported the bulk of the world's trade. Because European economic prosperity depended on maintaining its dominance, the European powers sought to control those regions necessary for their prosperity. Given their military and technological superiority, the most direct means was outright conquest. The superiority of European weapons reinforced the notion of racial superiority. In Nigeria in 1897, 32 Europeans and 500 African mercenaries defeated an army of 31,000 with the use of machine guns; the following year the British killed some 10,000 Muslims with machine guns at Omdurman in the Sudan.

Yet a generation that had seen the abolition of the European slave trade (it ended in 1834), and upheld the importance of "morality," could hardly acknowledge such a motive for acquiring foreign territory. The notion that it was "the white man's burden" to civilize the world—that is, to Westernize it—provided a moral justification for governing other people. Other important factors could be adduced. From the time of the Crusades, there had been a strong belief in the superiority and eventual triumph of Christianity. With the growth of Western power throughout the world, European missionaries, both Protestant and Catholic, could spread their faith, while improving local health care and bringing Western education to local populations. Some religious leaders saw imperial conquest as not only justifiable but also as an obligation, particularly at a time of growing religious doubt at home.

For many European governments, imperialist projects helped distract attention from domestic dissatisfactions. A successful campaign or a heroic victory, appropriately celebrated by the press, could deflect, at least temporarily, demands for broader political participation and for increased social justice. Some classes and individuals for whom urban, industrial life had little appeal were naturally drawn to colonial existence. Aristocrats, by becoming imperial administrators, could take up positions of authority and superiority. Those for whom the cities of 19th-century Europe were anonymous, and for whom industrial employment represented monotonous drudgery, had the prospect of excitement, and maybe financial profit, in the colonies. In Germany, colonial expansion was a safe outlet for German nationalism.

IMPERIALISM AND NATIONAL RIVALRIES

One motive for imperialism that no government ever tried to conceal was *patriotism*—the enhancement of national interests, especially when in conflict with those of a rival nation. France's imperial ambitions increased after 1871 in order to compensate abroad for her defeat by Germany at home. Britain sought to maintain a dominant position in

Egypt after 1882 in order to protect the Suez Canal and offset the risk of the crumbling Ottoman Empire falling under Russian control. Even those smaller countries without the public resources to launch a campaign entered the race. In 1876, the king of Belgium, Leopold II (ruled 1865–1909), joined with a group of financiers to found the International Association for the Exploration and Civilization of Central Africa. Intended in theory to underwrite the explorations of Henry M. Stanley, the association helped Leopold claim "trusteeship" of large tracts of the Congo as possessions of the crown.

With tension among nations rising in Europe, and the pace of imperialism increasing, particularly in Africa, the danger of outright war was clear. In 1884–1885, a conference met in Berlin to lay some ground rules for the acquisition of empire, and thereby avoid clashing interests. The participants agreed that possession of coastal territory brought with it the right to the interior, provided, however, that the claimant was actually occupying the land with military or administrative forces. This arbitrary drawing of borders, with no regard for indigenous African cultures, produced a set of artificial "countries" that satisfied the colonizers, but proved disastrous in the years of decolonization after World War II (see Topic 89).

By the early years of the 20th century, India and virtually the whole of Africa were under European rule, China was at the mercy of Western demands, and Japan had adapted itself to Western political ideas, including that of territorial conquest. For many Europeans, it seemed that imperialism had triumphed and that Western civilization was destined to become the dominant world culture. Yet the European grip on the world was soon shaken by three factors. Growing hostility among the European powers themselves reached its peak in World War I, while the United States played an increasingly prominent role in international affairs. Within the colonial territories, the rise of national consciousness eventually combined with the weakening position of the Western powers to bring an end to imperialism.

THE BRITISH IN INDIA: FROM MUTINY TO NATIONAL CONSCIOUSNESS

Through the East India Company, the British had maintained commercial links with India since the 18th century, and by the middle of the 19th century, with virtually the whole subcontinent informally "ruled" by the Company, British domination was producing considerable resentment.

THE SEPOY REBELLION
The first signs of trouble developed in May 1857, among *Sepoys* (the Hindi word for "troops") in the Company's Bengal Army, stationed near Delhi. A new type of rifle, lately introduced, employed greased bullets. A false rumor

Lord Curzon, Viceroy of India, with his wife and the Raja of Chamba and staff, c. 1900. Curzon served as Viceroy from 1898 to 1905. He tried, as here, to maintain good relations with local rulers, improved the Indian Railways, and appointed a Director-General to uncover India's ancient past. In the end, however, he fell victim to a feud with Lord Kitchener and Nationalist outrage at the partitioning of the state of Bengal, and resigned.

The *Durbar*—a special Anglo-Indian ceremony—which invested Queen Victoria as Empress of India. 1877. The queen had "accepted" the new title the previous year, but it took a few months for India's Viceroy, Lord Lytton, to organize a suitably imposing ceremony, which brought together the princes of the various Indian States; he remarked (somewhat ingenuously): "If we have with us the Princes, we shall have with us the people."

spread that the fat used for the cartridges came from cows and pigs—the former sacred to Hindus, and the latter regarded by Muslims as unclean. In the ensuing revolt, which the British contemptuously labeled the "Indian Mutiny," the rebels seized Delhi, killing many of the British inhabitants, together with large sections of north-central India. In March 1858, with the aid of considerable reinforcements, British troops finally broke the rebellion, and the British government took over direct control of India, ruled by a viceroy. In 1876, Queen Victoria was crowned empress of India. It was clear that, whatever the immediate cause, the "Mutiny" had reflected widespread discontent, and a few measures were taken to redress grievances. Indians received limited political representation at a local government level. Social reforms included the abolition of slavery.

The British made a thoroughgoing attempt to replace traditional cultural patterns with Western values. The government discouraged the rigid barriers of the caste system, whereby members of different castes could not mix in public places or on trains, and put limitations on child marriages. Hindus who became Christians were eligible for government jobs. Although regional variation was unavoidable in so vast a country, a British-type legal system operated nationally, and taxes were collected by the government, rather than by regional princes.

Schools and universities were run along British lines. Instruction was generally in English, which thus became the common language of the educated, who later were to lead the battle for Indian independence. Science and technology replaced traditional Hindu and Muslim learning. The products of this educational system were eligible for posts in the Indian Civil Service. After 1864, Indians

in theory could be appointed to the highest ranks; in practice, appointees (generally Hindus) were restricted to lower positions, where many became familiar with Western notions of bureaucracy.

Improved communications assured effective control of the colony. The authorities constructed a telegraph system during the 1850s, and laid thousands of miles of rail tracks. By 1900, the Indian rail network extended for more than 26,000 miles. These modernizations, together with the introduction of Western farming methods, also increased prosperity for colonial entrepreneurs and the limited but growing number of local business interests.

For most Indians, who were illiterate and living at a bare subsistence level as their ancestors had for centuries, the effects of British rule were mixed. Among those better off, there continued to be considerable resentment. Upper-caste Hindus disliked seeing the caste system challenged. Muslims, who had been accustomed to forming the ruling class, now found themselves discriminated against. Both groups resented the Christian missionary work that often formed part of the school program.

Another challenge to the British came from educated Indians who combined a sense of national identity with a belief in Western ideals of freedom. The Indian National Congress party first met in 1885 to advocate greater Indian participation in the Civil Service. Over the next few decades, it campaigned with increasing vigor for Indian independence, both political and economic. Yet, ironically, the very fact that Congress party leaders represented progressive ideas cut them off from most of their fellow Indians, traditionalists who saw no essential difference between British governors and upper-caste intellectuals. India did not achieve independence until 1947.

Perspectives from the Past

The Drive for Empire

Even at the time, imperialism was the subject of great debate in Europe and the United States among social critics, political and business leaders, and writers. Arguments for and against imperialism disagreed not only about its causes but about its impact and its future.

The Arrogance of European Imperialists

The British journalist and explorer Henry M. Stanley (1841–1904) embodied the arrogant attitudes toward non-Westerners that typified many of his generation. In his memoirs, he explained the "necessity" of his harsh manner in dealing with Africans.

The natives rapidly learned that though everything was to be gained by friendship with me, wars brought nothing but ruin.

When a young white officer quits England for the first time, to lead blacks, he has got to learn to unlearn a great deal. We must have white men in Africa; but the raw white is a great nuisance there during the first year. In the second year, he begins to mend; during the third year, if his nature permits it, he has developed into a superior man, whose intelligence may be of transcendent utility for directing masses of inferior men.

My officers were possessed with the notion that my manner was "hard," because I had not many compliments for them. That is the kind of pap which we may offer women and boys. Besides, I thought they were superior natures, and required none of that encouragement, which the more childish blacks almost daily received.

From Henry M. Stanley, *Autobiography*, ed. Dorothy Stanley. Houghton Mifflin. Copyright © 1909.

The Economic Impulse

In 1898 the American financial expert Charles A. Conant wrote an important article on the economic necessity for American participation in imperial expansion.

This new movement [imperialism] is not a matter of sentiment. It is the result of a natural law of economic and race development. The great civilized peoples have today at their command the means of developing the decadent nations of the world. What this means, in its material aspects, is the great excess of saved capital which is the result of machine production. . . . There must always be savings in a progressive industrial society to repair the wear of existing equipment and to meet new demands, but under the present social order it is becoming impossible to find at home in the great capitalistic countries employment for all the capital saved which is at once safe and remunerative. . . .

For the means of finding new productive employments for capital, it is necessary that the great industrial countries should turn to countries which have not felt the pulse of modern progress. Such countries have yet to be equipped with the mechanism of production and of luxury, which has been created in the progressive countries by the savings of recent generations. They have not only to obtain buildings and machinery—the necessary elements in producing machine-made goods—but they have to build their roads, drain their marshes, dam their rivers, build aqueducts for their water supplies and sewers for their towns and cities. Asia and Africa are the most promising of these countries. Japan has already made her entry, almost like Athene full-armed from the brain of Zeus, into the modern industrial world. . . .

The United States cannot afford to adhere to a policy of isolation while other nations are reaching out for the command of these new markets. The United States are still large users of foreign capital, but American investors are not willing to see the return upon their investments reduced to the European level. Interest rates have already declined here within the last five years. New markets and new opportunities for investment must be found if surplus capital is to be profitably employed. . . .

From Charles A. Conant, "The Economic Basis of 'Imperialism'," *North American Review* (September 1898).

The Marxist Interpretation

Russian radical activist V.I. Ulianov (1870–1924), better known by his pseudonym Lenin, was leader of the Bolshevik (Communist) party. He wrote the most sophisticated early Marxist interpretation of imperialism. Influenced by the ideas of Hobson, Lenin claimed that imperialist economic competition abroad represented the last phase of a dying capitalism.

Imperialism is capitalism in that phase of its development in which the domination of monopolies and finance-capital has established itself; in which the export of capital has acquired very great importance; in which the division of the world among the big, international trusts has begun; in which the partition of all the territories of the earth amongst the great capitalist powers has been completed. . . .

Monopoly has grown out of colonial policy. To the numerous "old" motives of colonial policy the capitalist financier has added the struggle for the sources of raw materials, for the exportation of capital, for "spheres of influence," i.e., for spheres of good business, concessions, monopolist profits, and so on; in fine, for economic territory in general. When the European powers did not as yet occupy with their colonies a tenth part of Africa (as was the case in 1876), colonial policy was able to develop otherwise than by the methods of monopoly—by "free grabbing" of territories, so to speak. But when nine-tenths of Africa had been seized (towards 1900), when the whole world had been shared out, the period of colonial monopoly opened and as a result the period of bitterest struggle for the partition and the repartition of the world. . . .

From all that has been said on the economic nature of imperialism, it follows that we must define it as capitalism in transition, or, more precisely, as dying capitalism. It is very instructive in this respect to note that the bourgeois economists, describing modern capitalism, employ with great fluency such terms as "interlacing," "absence of isolation," etc.; the banks are "enterprises which by their objective and their course of development have a character not purely economic, but are departing more and more from the sphere of private economic management." And the same Reisser, to whom these last words belong, declares with the greatest seriousness that the "prophecy" of the Marxists concerning "socialization" has not been realized!

From V. I. Lenin, *Imperialism: The Highest Stage of Capitalism.* Vanguard Press. Copyright © 1926.

The Hubris of World Power

British Nobel prize–winning poet Rudyard Kipling (1865–1936) was thought of as the official poet of the empire. His famous poem "The White Man's Burden," which appeared in 1899, was an appeal to the United States to help the British and other powers in assuming the "burden" of imperial rule. But in this poem, written two years earlier on the occasion of Queen Victoria's diamond jubilee, he pointed out that all things pass, including world empire.

God of our fathers, known of old—
Lord of our far-flung battle line—
Beneath whose awful hand we hold
Dominion over palm and pine—
Lord God of Hosts, be with us yet,
Lest we forget—lest we forget!

The tumult and the shouting die—
The Captains and the Kings depart—
Still stands thine ancient sacrifice,
An humble and a contrite heart. . . .

Far-called, our navies melt away—
On dune and headland sinks the fire—
Lo, all our pomp of yesterday
Is one with Nineveh and Tyre!
Judge of the Nations, spare us yet,
Lest we forget . . .

If, drunk with sight of power, we loose
Wild tongues that have not Thee in awe—
Such boasting as the Gentiles use
Or lesser breeds without the Law—. . . .

For heathen heart that puts her trust
In reeking tube and iron shard—
All valiant dust that builds on dust,
And guarding calls not Thee to guard,
For frantic boast and foolish word,
Thy Mercy on Thy People, Lord!

From Rudyard Kipling, "Recessional," *Barrack Room Ballads: Recessional and Other Verses.* Robert McBride. Copyright © 1910.

THE OPENING OF CHINA AND THE BOXER REBELLION

For the first centuries of European exploration in Asia, the Chinese succeeded in maintaining their isolation from Western culture. By the early decades of the 19th century, however, internal administrative and financial problems hampered Chinese resistance to the presence of foreign merchants and traders. As the imperial government became increasingly challenged by peasant rebels, it turned to outside help in the struggle to retain control.

Chinese helplessness in the face of European military force became manifest in the Opium War of 1839–1842. British merchants in India had developed the custom of exchanging opium for Chinese tea, porcelain, and other goods. The Chinese wanted silver and gold in return, but the British feared problems with their balance of payments, and traded opium instead. Use of the drug, the harmful effects of which were well-known, was not traditional in China, and the government attempted to prevent its importation. The Chinese emperor even addressed a personal appeal to Queen Victoria, but she turned a deaf ear, feeling that it would be inopportune to give up such a major source of revenue.

The result of the Chinese attempts to ban opium was open war and a British blockade of the Chinese coast. China, with no real sea power, was forced to give way and accept humiliating terms of settlement. Several ports, including Shanghai and Canton, were opened to the British, who also received the island of Hong Kong. Hong Kong's mainland territory was added in 1898, when China gave the British a 99-year lease, which expired in 1997. British merchants continued to trade in ever-increasing quantities of opium: 6,000 cases were shipped to China in 1820, 100,000 in 1880.

Chinese suspicion of Western influences received further reinforcement when peasants led by Christian converts staged a major uprising to demand tax and land reform. The Tai Ping Rebellion lasted from 1851 to 1864, and was finally crushed only with the help of Western forces, including a British contingent led by General Charles "Chinese" Gordon (1833–1885). During its course, several other nations, including France and the United States, took advantage of the government's weakness to force further trade and territorial concessions. In 1860 a Franco-British force occupied Peking (now spelled Beijing), drove out the emperor, and burned the Summer Palace.

Whereas in India a colonial power had taken on direct rule, in China competition among Western imperialists led European powers to seek financial control without taking the country over. As long as a weak central government depended on European troops and advisers, the Chinese were at the mercy of Western demands. Nor, given the Chinese reverence for tradition, was there any move to modernize. With the Tai Ping Rebellion crushed, the government tried to revive traditional principles of Confucianism. Among its tenets was the saying, "Acknowledgment of limits leads to happiness," a dangerous attitude with which to face driving capitalist Europeans.

Before the century was over, China lost territory to its neighbor Japan. The Japanese had followed the opposite tactic of adopting Western ways wholesale, and used them to wrest control of Korea from China in 1894–1895. The shock of defeat by its much smaller rival finally induced the Chinese emperor to initiate a campaign of reforms.

Decapitated bodies of Boxer rebels executed by Chinese officials. 1901. Although the executioners seen here were Chinese, the rebellion was put down by Western allied forces, including British, French, Russian, and American soldiers. The result was to increase internal pressure for change, and by 1911 Imperial rule was swept away.

Mary Evans Picture Library

THE BOXER REBELLION

The attempt at domestic reform came too late, however. In 1898, Tz'u-Hsi (1835–1908), the previous emperor's formidable widow who had earlier ruled as regent, seized power. Bitterly anti-Western, she maintained control through a small clique of conservative ministers. To reinforce her rejection of outside influences, she also encouraged the activities of a secret society, the "Harmonious Fists," called by Europeans the "Boxers." In the Boxer Rebellion of 1900–1901, members of the society killed missionaries and Chinese converts to Christianity, murdered the German minister in Peking, and besieged the foreign embassies there.

A joint European and United States military force suppressed the uprising and demanded yet further concessions. By the terms of the Boxer Protocol, China paid a huge indemnity to the United States and the European powers involved. New treaties gave Britain, France, Germany, and Russia long-term leases on ports, from which they could expand inland. With effective power and no responsibility, the European nations built railroads and developed river transport to open up the interior. The dowager empress grimly held on to what authority she could, finally Westernizing the army and imperial bureaucracy, but the internal pressure for change was too great. Within three years of her death in 1908, open revolution ended imperial rule and replaced it with the Chinese Republic.

JAPAN AND THE WEST

Like China, Japan came under heavy pressure from Americans and Europeans to end its isolation and open itself to international trade. In contrast to their neighbors, however, the Japanese quickly reformed their country along Western lines and adopted Western technologies. So swift was the transformation that by the end of the 19th century Japan, too, had become an imperialist power.

Japan's exposure to international pressure was both later and more violent than that of China. In 1853, the American Commodore Matthew Perry (1794–1858) sailed four vessels into Tokyo Harbor, threatening bombardment and refusing to leave until a Japanese envoy agreed to accept a United States demand for a diplomatic and trade treaty. The next year he returned to conclude the agreement. Britain, the Netherlands, and Russia were quick to follow, claiming their rights to fish in Japanese waters and to trade. With little in the way of naval power, the Japanese had little choice but to concede.

Both progressives and conservatives in Japan began to urge reform, the former inspired by Western models, the latter in the belief that their nation's independence could be assured only by radical change. In 1867 they found a leader in the new young emperor, Meiji (ruled 1867–1912)—a word meaning "the enlightened one," chosen in place of his real name, Mutsuhito. In place of the old feudal system of

Portrait of Commodore Matthew Perry. Mid-19th century. The Japanese artist, faced with the unusual task of painting a Westerner, has produced what seems—to a Western eye—a strangely stylized result. Perry's large face and beetling eyebrows are rendered in a series of flat planes, while the uniform has the fine detail of traditional Japanese design.

© National Gallery of Art, Washington, D.C./SuperStock

regional lords known as *shoguns*, the emperor assumed symbolic leadership, and the country was governed by his advisers, a small group of elder statesmen. Responsible to the emperor rather than to the Diet (parliament), they provided the authoritarian leadership that made rapid change possible.

In looking for a model for their institutions, the Japanese turned to Europe and the United States. Western experts were brought in to help build up a navy, while the new Japanese army adopted German systems of conscription and training. A new constitution, introduced in 1890, was also based on that of Germany. State investment and the rise of a business class encouraged industrialization along Western lines. On the other hand, a new system of universal education, while it included scientific and technical subjects, also laid strong emphasis on patriotism and loyalty to the emperor.

During the last three decades of the 19th century, Japan adopted a variety of aspects of Western culture, including the metric system and the calendar. Christianity made little impact, however. Nor did the Japanese have any interest in taking up the cause of feminism, which was beginning to

ACROSS CULTURES

LAFCADIO HEARN IN JAPAN

The opening up of Japan to the West had profound economic consequences for both sides, but it was also important for its cultural impact. One of the first Western writers to take advantage of the new world that had suddenly become available was Lafcadio Hearn (1850–1904). Hearn was born on the Greek island of Levkas, after which he was named, shortly before Perry's momentous expedition to Tokyo. At the age of 19 he emigrated to the United States, where he worked as a journalist. In 1891, the magazine *Harper's Weekly* sent him to Japan to report to its readers on the exotic culture there. Once arrived, Hearn taught English in Japanese schools, married a Japanese woman, became a Japanese subject and a Buddhist, and remained there the rest of his life.

Courtesy of William Duiker

In 1894 he published a book, *Glimpses of Unfamiliar Japan,* which describes his discovery of Japanese life:

> "Do not fail to write down your first impressions as soon as possible," said a kind English professor whom I had the pleasure of meeting soon after

advance in Western Europe, and Japanese women retained their traditionally inferior status, confined to the home.

Japan's first major adventure abroad, the war with China over Korea (1894–1895), was almost too successful. By its end, the Japanese had taken not only Korea itself, but also the island of Taiwan (Formosa) and a piece of the Chinese mainland. This was too much for Russia, which found support in France and Germany. The European powers had no intention of sharing China with another Asian nation and insisted that the Japanese withdraw from the mainland. Yet the acceptance of Japan as an imperialist country was underscored in 1902, when Britain, the leading colonial power, and Japan signed an alliance. Further success came in the Russo-Japanese War of 1904–1905, when superior Japanese naval power helped lead them to victory.

By the early 20th century, Japan had achieved many of the goals of Western society, including industrialization, prosperity, and imperial conquest, without the upheaval or revolution that marked the modernization of most European countries. The methods—the encouragement of obedience and unquestioning patriotism, and firm repression of any dissent—helped shape the character of modern Japan.

NORTH AFRICA: THE BRITISH AND FRENCH IN CONFLICT

The fiercest competition of all for imperialist conquest occurred in the "scramble for Africa." In 1870, a European presence in Africa was limited to the northern regions

my arrival in Japan: "they are evanescent, you know; they will never come to you again, once they have faded out; and yet of all the strange sensations you may receive in this country you will find none so charming as these." I neglected the friendly advice, in spite of all resolves to obey it: I could not, in those first weeks, resign myself to remain indoors and write, while there was yet so much to see and hear and feel in the sun-steeped streets of the wonderful Japanese city. Still even could I revive all the lost sensations of those first experiences, I doubt if I could express and fix them in words. The first charm of Japan is intangible and volatile as a perfume.

Hearn had arrived in Yokohama, and on one of his first days took a ride through the city in a *kuruma* (a kind of carriage drawn by a runner). He is first struck by the shop signs, "all made beautiful and mysterious with Japanese or Chinese lettering." Then he sees the same kind of writing on the costumes of the people in the streets:

No arabesques could produce such an effect. As modified for decorative purposes, these ideographs have a speaking symmetry which no design without a meaning could possess. As they appear on the back of a workman's frock—pure

white on dark blue—and large enough to be easily read at a great distance (indicating some guild or company of which the wearer is a member or an employee), they give to the poor cheap garment a factitious appearance of splendor.

Later the same day, still under the spell of his new discoveries, he looks across the bay

to the feet of the green wooded hills flanking the city on two sides. Beyond that semicircle of green hills rises a lofty range of serrated mountains, indigo silhouettes. And enormously high above the line of them towers an apparition indescribably lovely—one solitary snowy cone, so filmily exquisite, so spiritually white, that but for its immemorially familiar outline one would surely deem it a shape of cloud. Invisible its base remains, being the same delicious tint as the sky: only above the eternal snow-line its dreamy cone appears, seeming to hang, the ghost of a peak, between the luminous land and the luminous heaven—the sacred and matchless mountain, Fujiyama.

Throughout his life, Hearn wrote books and articles explaining Japanese life and culture to a Western audience, but he never surpassed the sense of rapt wonder of these first impressions of the country he made his home.

above the Sahara and a few coastal ports. By the end of the 19th century, virtually the entire continent was under European rule.

In the north, a new era began with the completion of the Suez Canal in 1869. The construction of the canal was jointly financed by the *khedive* (viceroy) of Egypt, ruling on behalf of the Ottoman Empire, and French investors. The original inventor of the scheme, and the director of the company involved in the canal's construction between 1859 and 1869, was Ferdinand-Marie de Lesseps (1805–1894), who later worked on the Panama Canal project. The immense engineering project was intended to facilitate French commercial expansion to the east because ships bound for India and East Asia would be able to sail directly from the Mediterranean to the Indian Ocean, without having to circumnavigate Africa.

Egypt's participation had resulted in heavy debts to British banks, and by as early as 1875 its financial state was so calamitous that the *khedive* was forced to sell his shares. The British prime minister, Benjamin Disraeli, jumped at the chance to buy into France's engineering achievement and challenge French influence in North Africa. The two great rivals thus found themselves in joint control of Egypt.

When in 1882 a nationalist revolt by the Egyptian Army tried to drive out the foreigners, the French and British planned a joint intervention. The French cabinet fell and France backed off, whereupon the British went ahead on their own, taking the opportunity to reinforce their position. Ships of the Royal Navy bombarded Alexandria, and British troops moved in to take control of the country, leaving the *khedive* as a mere figurehead. The

Map 76.1 Africa on the Eve of World War I. French control is consolidated in West Africa; the British territories are more spread out, ranging from Egypt to the southern part of the continent. Newcomers as colonial powers are Italy (Libya, Eritrea, Somalia) and Germany (Southwest Africa and East Africa). Abyssinia (now generally known as Ethiopia) is the only part of Africa still not colonized by 1914. The Italians occupied it briefly in the 1930s. The borders of the colonial states took (and still take) no account of ethnic, linguistic, or tribal divisions, and are thus responsible for much of the chaos still reigning in Africa in the 21st century.

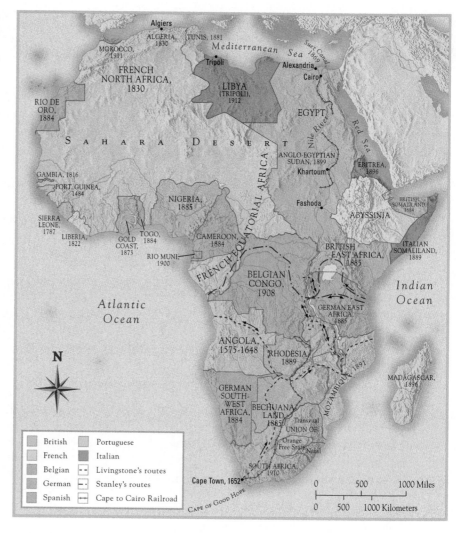

British protectorate over Egypt lasted until well after World War II.

With the British established in Egypt, the French were anxious to strengthen their bases elsewhere in North Africa. They had begun their conquest of Algeria, which was also Ottoman territory, in 1830. In 1881 they took Tunisia, another possession of the crumbling Ottoman Empire. Shortly after 1900, a French military force also entered Morocco, where their control was unsuccessfully challenged by Germany in the years leading up to World War I (see Topic 74). A subsequent Franco-British agreement of 1904 recognized French control of Morocco in return for British rule in Egypt. With the Italian capture of Libya in 1912, by the eve of World War I the whole of Muslim North Africa was in European hands.

The direct confrontation between two imperialist powers, which the British and French avoided in Egypt, reached a crisis point in the Sudan. In 1898, a French military expedition under commander Jean-Baptiste Marchand (1863–1934) making its way toward the Red Sea from West Africa arrived at the Nile settlement of Fashoda, just as British troops led by General Herbert Kitchener (1850–1916) were occupying the southern Sudan. In the

steamy swamplands, two grand imperialist schemes came face to face: the French plan for a territory stretching across the continent from the Atlantic to the Indian Ocean, and the British idea of an equally vast empire running north to south, from Cairo to the Cape of Good Hope. After several weeks of tension, the French troops withdrew on government orders. The French government realized the error of risking war with Britain when their real enemy was Germany. As the radical republican leader, Georges Clemenceau (1841–1929), said, "war with Britain is not worth a few marshes on the upper Nile."

The British had begun the subjugation of the Sudan in the 1880s, but they were opposed by Muslim forces led by Muhammad Ahmad (1844–1885), the self-styled *Mahdi* (the Mahdi were a series of self-proclaimed saviors in the Muslim tradition). In 1885, the Mahdi's army attacked a British garrison in the city of Khartoum, killing General Gordon and massacring its inhabitants. The death of Gordon, who had won popularity in Britain for his role in the suppression of the Tai Ping Rebellion in China and for ending the slave trade in the Sudan, provoked British anger and the collapse of William Gladstone's government. Ten years later, in 1898, Kitchener decisively defeated the

Scottish troops in front of—and climbing on—the Sphinx, outside Cairo, Egypt. Late 19th century. Two eras collide in this image. The sphinx was carved out of a natural rock formation on the spot, in Egypt's Old Kingdom of the 3rd millennium B.C. The British forces of whom these soldiers formed a part established British control over Egypt until the country became independent in 1953.

Hulton Getty Collection/Tony Stone Images

Mahdi forces at Omdurman, where British soldiers mowed the Muslims down with machine guns.

THE DISMEMBERMENT OF CENTRAL AFRICA

European involvement in the affairs of North Africa went back to the days of ancient Rome. Africa south of the Sahara, however, was little known to Europeans before the mid-19th century. Coastal cities such as Lagos and Dakar served as trading centers, principally for slaves, but the interior remained unvisited except by Arab traders and the most intrepid explorers. With the end of the slave trade, two states on the West African coast were settled by freed slaves. Liberia, the oldest black African republic, became independent in 1847, although it remained under informal American influence. Sierra Leone, which became a British colony in 1808, combined an indigenous population with freed slaves from the West Indies and prisoners liberated from slave ships.

With the burst of imperialism after 1870, the Europeans forced their way into the African interior, draw-

ing artificial boundaries, and inventing new countries. By 1900, the British controlled Nigeria in West Africa and a string of territories running south from Egypt, consisting of Kenya, Uganda, and Rhodesia (the territory comprising Rhodesia now forms the two countries of Zambia and Zimbabwe). The French held most of the rest of West Africa, with Dakar, the largest city in Senegal, as their administrative center. They constructed roads, railways, and harbor facilities there, and opened a university. Senegal had sent a deputy to the French parliament as early as 1848, although the first black deputy was elected only in 1914.

The heart of the continent fell to the Belgians, whose ruthless exploitation of the Belgian Congo soon became notorious. In the Horn of Africa on the Red Sea and the Indian Ocean, the Italians seized part of Somaliland (modern Somalia), other portions of which were occupied by the British and French, and Eritrea (now part of Ethiopia). They tried to conquer Ethiopia in 1896 but were driven back by the Ethiopian army at the Battle of Adowa, the first European colonizers to be defeated by indigenous African forces.

Portugal increased its hold on Angola and Mozambique, both of which it had used as trading bases for slaves as early as the 16th century. Unlike other colonizing powers, Portugal was not rich enough to invest in building infrastructure for its colonies (Belgium was in the same position). Work was done by a system of forced labor—virtually a form of slavery—and contracts were farmed out to foreign companies, which had even less interest than the government in the welfare of the indigenous populations.

The Germans were slow in developing a serious colonial drive. Bismarck was one of the few statesmen of the times who remained doubtful of the benefits of imperialism, and he realized that the quest for German colonies would only antagonize Britain. Nevertheless he began the German colonization of Southwest Africa and the Cameroons in 1884, more as an outlet for German nationalism than for economic motives. After Bismarck's dismissal by Kaiser Wilhelm II in 1890 (see Topic 73), Germany embarked on a vigorous imperialist policy. Its only possessions of any size were Southwest Africa (now Namibia), a barren area of little economic value, German East Africa (now Tanzania), gained in 1891, and some important Pacific islands.

THE BOER WAR AND THE UNION OF SOUTH AFRICA

Although the southern part of Africa is farthest from Europe, the history of European involvement there goes back to the end of the 15th century, when Portuguese mariners sailed past the Cape of Good Hope into the Indian Ocean. In 1652, the Dutch East India Company founded a settlement at the Cape, to serve as a supply base for ships, and to search the interior for slaves and precious metals. Over the next century and a half, the Dutch expanded eastward, taking land from the indigenous Bantu, Bush peo-

Leaders of German forces in East Africa. 1889. The two civilian administrators are flanked by German officers; in the rear stand local recruits. Germany lost both of its African territories after its defeat in 1918 in World War I: The League of Nations placed German Southwest Africa (Namibia) under South African control, and German East Africa (modern Tanzania)—the scene of this picture—went to Britain.

ple, and Hottentots, who were either killed off, enslaved, or pushed out of the region. Other slaves were imported from West Africa and Mozambique. The present "colored" people of South Africa are the descendants of children born to unions between Dutch settlers and indigenous people, and Dutch and imported slaves. South Africa's "Indians" are descended from Indian and Malayan workers and merchants imported during the 19th century.

The Dutch colonists, who called themselves the *Boers* (the Dutch word for "farmers"), spoke a Dutch dialect that came to be known as Afrikaans. As they continued to take over good farming land wherever they found it, the only native people to put up any serious resistance were the Bantu. The first Bantu War of the 1770s was only the beginning of a series of bitter conflicts in which the Europeans gradually gained possession of Bantu lands. In the process, the Boers developed their notion of "apartheid," which claimed that the two cultures were separate and irreconcilable. Opposition to any form of multiracialism was thus embedded in Boer political life from the beginning of their destruction of indigenous culture.

The Cape of Good Hope was annexed by the British in 1815. Relations between newly arrived British settlers and the Boers, which were unfriendly at best, were exacerbated further when in 1834 the British authorities banned slavery. From 1835 to 1845, in a migration known as the Great Trek, Boer farmers moved northeastward out of the British Cape Colony in search of new land. They founded two independent republics, the Orange Free State and the Transvaal. The indigenous Zulu warriors who opposed them, armed with shields and spears, were shot down in large numbers, and in the 1870s the British crushed the remaining Zulu forces despite fierce resistance.

A few years later, first diamonds (in 1867) and then gold (in 1886) were discovered in the Transvaal. The conquered peoples provided cheap labor for the mines, but the Boers urgently needed capital to exploit their resources. The British were only too willing to step in. The Cape Colony's aggressive prime minister, Cecil Rhodes (1853–1902), went further. He had first come to Africa as a sickly young man, and quickly made a fabulous fortune in diamonds. Driven by ambition to unite Africa from the Cape to Cairo under British rule, Rhodes set out to subvert the Boer republics. In 1895, having first encouraged a rebellion among white, non-Boer mineworkers, he sent a force of volunteers to raid the Transvaal. The illegal and disastrous Jameson Raid, named after its leader, Leander Starr Jameson (1853–1917), was supposed to spark an uprising of foreigners in the Transvaal and provoke the Boers into outright war. The Boers located the arms caches the British had hidden, and the scheme failed. International outrage at the unprovoked attack on fellow Westerners drove Rhodes from office.

Boer resentment at growing British interference was bound to lead to conflict sooner or later. The Boer War broke out in 1899, and bitter fighting went on until 1902. After taking the offensive, well equipped with arms by Germany, the Boers soon began to give way as British reinforcements were poured into South Africa. For the last two years, Boer efforts were confined to guerrilla fighting, in a struggle that was grim and determined on both sides. The British, for their part, spared no means to discourage the guerrilla combatants, burning their farms and imprisoning their families in detention centers—the first modern concentration camps.

The British finally prevailed, and in 1910 the various territories were incorporated into the Union of South Africa. The legacy of resentment continued to influence relations between the British and the Afrikaaners for decades, while the true losers in the "white man's war" were the native populations. At the same time, the spectacle of two European, "civilized" peoples fighting over land and natural resources to which neither had any right underlined the true nature of imperialism, and the lengths to which Europeans were prepared to go to achieve conquest.

Putting European Imperialism in Asia and Africa in Perspective

By the first decade of the 20th century, the history of Africa had been irrevocably changed. A few regional kingdoms remained, and Ethiopia retained its independence, but the rest of the continent was divided up into a series of colonies, which often fragmented single tribal groups or combined rival peoples.

The impact of Westernization varied according to the policies of the colonizing power. The British tried to introduce educational and health systems on a fairly broad scale, but did not encourage local peoples to become involved in administrative positions. The French, by contrast, aimed to produce an African elite, versed in Western culture; it is no coincidence that many of the leading African writers of the first half

Continued next page

of the 20th century came from French colonies. Other imperialist powers, notably Belgium and Portugal, were almost exclusively concerned with making profits from their colonies.

The overall phenomenon of Western imperialism in Africa and Asia was so vast, affecting so many millions of lives, that generalization about its effects is difficult. For many of the conquering powers the benefits of empire were dubious. With the exception of the British Empire, most of the colonies cost vast sums of money to maintain, and few Europeans actually wanted to live in them. Yet one recurring pattern can be seen: the growth of nationalism. The pursuit of national identity, one of the most powerful forces in the late 20th century, first developed in many parts of the world as a way of resisting the imperialists of the late 19th century and their successors.

Questions for Further Study

1. How did motives for colonization vary among the European powers? How did these differences affect their approach to establishing and governing their colonies?
2. To what extent were economic interests significant in the drive for colonization? How far were economic expectations fulfilled?
3. What effect did European colonization have on the creation of nationalist identities in the colonized territories? What were the long-term effects?

Suggestions for Further Reading

Baumgart, W. *Imperialism: The Idea of British and French Colonial Expansion, 1880–1914.* New York, 1982.

Bierman, John. *Dark Safari: The Life Behind the Legend of Henry Morton Stanley.* New York, 1990.

Christopher, A.J. *Colonial Africa.* Totowa, NJ, 1984.

Conklin, Alice L. *A Mission to Civilize: The Republican Idea of Empire in France and West Africa, 1895-1930.* Stanford, CA, 1997.

Cooper, Frederick, and Ann Laura Stoler, eds. *Tensions of Empire: Colonial Cultures in a Bourgeois World.* Berkeley, CA, 1997.

Doyle, M.W. *Empires.* Ithaca, NY, 1986.

Hobshawm, E.J. *The Age of Empire, 1875–1914.* New York, 1987.

Hochschild, Adam. *Leopold's Ghost: A Story of Greed, Terror and Heroism in Colonial Africa.* Boston, 1998.

Keown-Boyd, Henry. *The Fists of Righteous Harmony, A History of the Boxer Uprising in China in the Year 1900.* London, 1991.

Lewis, D.L. *The Race to Fashoda: European Colonialism and African Resistance in the Scramble for Africa.* London, 1988.

McLynn, Frank. *Hearts of Darkness: The European Exploration of Africa.* London, 1992.

Moon, P. *The British Conquest and Domination of India.* Bloomington, IN, 1989.

Pakenham, T. *The Scramble for Africa.* New York, 1991.

InfoTrac College Edition

Enter the search term *imperialism* using the Subject Guide.

THE SOCIAL ORDER CHALLENGED

The triumph of modern capitalism in the half-century before World War I did not go unchallenged. Opponents of *laissez-faire* economics attacked big business for exploiting the working class in the quest for ever-increasing profits. Social critics insisted that while prosperity enhanced the already privileged existence of the bourgeoisie, grinding poverty oppressed the daily lives of millions. Radical political leaders charged that parliamentary liberalism served the interests of the upper classes through repressive domestic policies designed to maintain the status quo.

Critics of the established order claimed to speak for two distinct but overlapping groups that represented most of Europe's population: the working classes and women. Governments everywhere saw the demands of these groups as dangerous to political stability and social peace and used the coercive apparatus of the state—the police and the armed forces—against the forces of change. Neither working-class nor women's organizations, however, were united in their leadership, methods, or aims, and often there was little cooperation between them.

The divisions within the working-class and women's movements centered on a fundamental disagreement over long-range goals. Moderates wanted to improve conditions by reforming the existing political and social systems. Reformist socialists, trade unionists, and middle-class feminists all sought to extend the suffrage, elect representatives to parliaments or achieve other forms of representation, and pressure governments or business into granting concessions. Radicals, on the other hand, wanted to destroy the existing order completely and replace it with a new society in which the underlying causes of inequality and exploitation would be eliminated—this was the intention of anarchists, revolutionary socialists, and socialist feminists.

By 1914, moderates and radicals found themselves no closer to resolving their differences. Some significant reforms had been achieved, including the right to strike and to unionize, and the adoption of universal male suffrage in almost all countries. Yet capitalism was still fully entrenched, and almost nowhere did women even gain the vote, let alone more deeply rooted personal and legal rights. It took the trauma of the Great War and the subsequent Russian Revolution to shake the liberal-capitalist order to its foundations.

THE FIRST INTERNATIONAL: ANARCHISTS VERSUS SOCIALISTS

In the mid-19th century, the working-class movement found two major theories—among a host of other possibilities—on which to base its revolutionary struggle against industrial capitalism: anarchism and Marxism. Among the early anarchists were the "Mutualists," who followed the ideas of the Frenchman Pierre Proudhon (1809–1865). In *What Is Property?* (1840), Proudhon declared that "Property is Theft!" and asserted that small-scale private ownership of property in a federation of communes was the best guarantee of individual freedom.

The Russian exile Mikhail Bakunin (1814–1876) advocated a different direction: the elimination of the state and all private property by revolutionary violence. By the 1860s, anarchism emerged as the principal rival to Marxism. The worker movement began to divide between anarchist principles and the "scientific" socialism of Karl Marx and Friedrich Engels (see Topic 71). Anarchists and Marxist socialists agreed, at least in theory, that revolutionary violence was the only means of destroying capitalism. Marxists and most anarchists also accepted the idea that private property was the root cause of inequality and exploitation and had to be eliminated.

Where anarchists and Marxists clashed was in their view of the nature and the purpose of the state. Marx declared that the immediate aim of the revolution was for the workers to wrest power from the bourgeoisie by conquering the state and creating a working-class government—the "dictatorship of the proletariat." The anarchists, on the other hand, saw the state as the principal source of oppression, regardless of its nature, and insisted on eliminating it completely, along with other forms of authority. "All exer-

Mikhail Bakunin. Mid-19th century. Bakunin was one of the founders of the political anarchist movement. In 1861, shortly before this photograph was taken, he escaped to England from exile in Siberia. He joined the First International, but quarreled bitterly with Marx and was expelled, together with his followers.

© Sovfoto

cise of power perverts," wrote Bakunin, "and all submission to authority humiliates."

Another theoretical point of disagreement lay in identifying the revolutionary class that would lead the struggle. Marx pinned his hopes on the modern industrial proletariat of advanced nations such as Britain and Germany, which he identified as the only true revolutionary class. Bakunin, on the other hand, argued that the industrial proletariat was already in the process of being indoctrinated by bourgeois values and had lost its revolutionary potential. Instead, Bakunin focused on what he called the "proletariat in rags," those desperately poor elements at the bottom of society—workers in small shops and landless peasants—in preindustrial countries such as Spain, Italy, and Russia.

These ideological currents derived inspiration from the uprising of the Paris Commune, a crucial moment in the development of European radicalism (see Topic 73). European radicals saw the Commune as a class war between workers

Cover of the original edition of *The Manifesto of the Communist Party.* February 1848. Although written and published in German, the work was printed in London, where Marx was living in exile. Under the title and date, there appears for the first time one of the most famous slogans of the 19th and 20th centuries: "Workers of the world, unite." In the Manifesto itself, the sentence continues: "You have nothing to lose but your chains."

and the bourgeoisie. In his analysis of the Commune, *The Civil War in France* (1871), Marx described it as the first example of the dictatorship of the proletariat. But although communists, socialists, and anarchists had fought against the government, so had many more thousands of French citizens with no ideological agenda. Thus the Commune could not be described as a Marxist phenomenon. Nevertheless, the uprising struck terror among European governments, leading many to clamp down on their own radicals and workers.

MARX, BAKUNIN, AND THE FIRST INTERNATIONAL

The International Workingmen's Association—commonly known as the First International—was founded in London in 1864 by a disparate group of radicals that included German Marxists, anarchists, British and Belgian trade unionists, French supporters of Proudhon, and Italian followers of Mazzini. The International sought to act as a clearinghouse for radicalism and to focus revolutionary strategy. Instead, it became the stage for an ongoing debate between Marx and Bakunin, whose personalities and ideas represented the extreme alternatives of revolutionary leadership.

From the outset, Marx tried to run the International, but Bakunin opposed him. In September 1871, after the repression of the Commune, its representatives met at a congress in London, where Marx pushed for the adoption of a platform calling for the seizure of political power by the workers through the creation of socialist parties in all countries. Moreover, he insisted that the International's executive committee be given the power to impose centralized control and ideological uniformity over the International's local sections and federations. Bakunin's anarchist followers and other "antiauthoritarian" radicals lined up against Marx, whose rigid program was supported chiefly by German communists. A year later, at the Hague Congress, the struggle between Marxists and antiauthoritarians further polarized the International, but Marx triumphed by securing the expulsion of Bakunin and the anarchists. Regrouping after the Hague meeting, Bakunin and the antiauthoritarians held their own meeting at Saint-Imier, Switzerland, where they rejected the principle that central committees or congresses could dictate policy to members. Instead of the seizure of political power that Marx demanded, the Saint-Imier delegates called for the destruction of power.

The First International, by then consisting only of Marxists, was officially dissolved in 1876. Over the next 20 years, while the Marxists forged ahead to create socialist parties, militant action remained largely in the hands of the anarchists. Bakunin and a new generation of libertarian leaders worked to arouse the masses. Peter Kropotkin, a Russian prince living in London, called for working-class solidarity, while the Italian Errico Malatesta (1850–1932) shifted his anarchist doctrine away from the collectivist formula of "from each according to his abilities to each according to his labor" to that of anarchist communism, which replaced the word "labor" with "need."

Most anarchists maintained the antiauthoritarian tradition, while some individuals, not all of whom were anarchists, adopted terrorist tactics. In the 1870s, German anarchists made two attempts to kill Kaiser Wilhelm I, and in the 1890s a cycle of retaliation against state repression induced a few practitioners of "propaganda of the deed" to assassinate political leaders and monarchs—among them, French President François Sadi-Carnot in 1894, Prime Minister Antonio Canovas del Castillo of Spain in 1897, the Empress Elizabeth of Austria-Hungary in 1898, King Umberto I of Italy in 1900, and U.S. President William McKinley in 1901. Most anarchist theorists did not believe that such terrorist acts would bring the revolution into being, but saw them as the inevitable result of government oppression. Governments reacted sharply to the assassinations, convening an antianarchist conference in Rome in 1898 to coordinate police efforts on an international level.

Staged photograph of an episode from the Paris Commune. 1871. During demonstrations, the Commune leaders lost control of the crowd, and a mob massacred 62 hostages. This daytime reenactment of the killings may have been intended for use as part of the propaganda campaign against the Communards.

THE SECOND INTERNATIONAL: IDEOLOGY AND SOCIALIST POLITICS

Socialism emerged as a major force in Europe between 1870 and 1914. Mass-based political parties inspired by Marxist principles grew rapidly, and by the 1890s one existed in almost every country, together with a vast network of subsidiary organizations, unions, newspapers, and clubs. Their leaders were optimistic that they were on the verge of attaining a socialist society.

THE RISE OF SOCIALIST PARTIES

The first and most important socialist party in Europe developed in Germany. From the beginning, however, German socialists were divided into two camps—Marxists and those who followed the ideas of Ferdinand Lassalle (1825–1864). Flamboyant and brilliant, Lassalle had taken part in the 1848 revolutions before studying political philosophy and socialist theory. Unlike Marx, who wanted to "smash" the bourgeois state, Lassalle sought to democratize it for the working class. Lassalle had taken from the British economist David Ricardo (see Topic 58) the notion of the "iron law of wages." According to this theory, wage increases resulted in the growth in the number of workers, which in turn created labor competition that drove down wages to the subsistence level. To overcome this tendency, Lassalle urged the formation of worker cooperatives, in which the workers would be the owners and thus control their own earnings. In his view, strikes and unions were futile. In 1863, a year before his death in a duel, he established the General Association of German Workers, which advocated universal suffrage and a program of peaceful, legal means to achieve socialism.

In opposition to Lassalle, Wilhelm Liebknecht (1826–1900) and August Bebel (1840–1913) founded the Social Democratic Labor party in 1869. Although not officially a Marxist party, the group was closer to the ideas of Marx and Engels than those of Lassalle. In 1875, they agreed to issue a joint platform, the "Gotha Program," in alliance with Lassalle's moderate supporters. This policy, which merged aspects of Marxist dogma with the reform strategy of Lassalle, formed the basis of the German Social Democratic party (SPD). Three years later, Bismarck passed the Anti-Socialist Laws designed to stamp out socialism, but the repression actually focused the party's identity, and it struggled underground for years before Kaiser Wilhelm II repealed the laws (see Topic 73).

Marx criticized such blending of his revolutionary ideas with the reformist approach of the Lassallians, but the latter seemed appropriate to the many German socialists who felt that working-class power could be attained peacefully. This was the view of Eduard Bernstein (1850–1932), whose book *Evolutionary Socialism* (1899) was the first major work to "revise" Marxist theory in the light of changing circumstances. Bernstein, an old friend of Engels who had absorbed the views of British moderates known as the Fabians, argued on the basis of the German experience that Marx was wrong in predicting that the status of the working class would inevitably deteriorate. Marxist socialists, he contended, should eschew revolutionary violence and work through the political process to achieve bread-and-butter benefits for workers. He therefore believed that socialist deputies in the *Reichstag* should collaborate with bourgeois political parties to reform German society. Orthodox Marxists in the SPD attacked Bernstein's revisionism and virtually drummed him out of the party.

The success of German "social democracy" and the trade unions in winning worker support acted as a model for socialists throughout continental Europe. Despite efforts to create a Marxist party in Great Britain, socialism there was generally moderate, and a socialist party developed after the trade unions. The most important socialist group was the Fabian Society (1884), named after Quintus Fabius Maximus, a Roman general of the 2nd century B.C. who used evasive tactics instead of direct battles in the Punic Wars. Its founders were middle-class intellectuals such as the writer H.G. Wells (1866–1946) and the dramatist George Bernard Shaw (1856–1950), and among its most important members were Sidney and Beatrice Webb (see Topic 84). In 1900 the Fabians, who favored peaceful political change rather than revolution, combined with the growing trade union movement and other socialist organizations to found the Labour party, in which Marxist elements were a distinct minority.

Belgians, Russians, Austrians, and Italians established their own parties in the two decades after 1870. The first Marxist party in France was formed by Jules Guesde (1845–1922), but several other groups vied for the loyalty of French workers, including the Possibilists, so-called because they rejected Marx's all-or-nothing doctrines, and a group of "Independent" socialist intellectuals. Only in 1905 did French socialists unite under the leadership of Jean Jaures (1859–1914) with a largely Marxist party program.

THE SECOND INTERNATIONAL

In 1889, the centenary of the French Revolution, a large assembly of socialist societies gathered in Paris and founded the Second International. Unlike the First International, whose members were a disparate group of individuals, the Second—known as the "Socialist International"—was based on party affiliation. Marxist revolutionary as well as reformist parties were included, but from the beginning the anarchists were kept out. Through propaganda activities such as "May Day" parades and periodic congresses, the International coordinated socialist activity on a worldwide level in order to raise the consciousness of workers. International congresses were held in 1891, 1893, 1896, 1900, 1904, 1907, 1910, and 1912.

Just as Marx had dominated the First International, the SPD was able to exercise considerable hegemony over the Second, largely because of its more than 1 million members and the large number of deputies it had in the *Reichstag*. Yet

the ideological divisions between Marxist orthodoxy and reformism continued to mark the International's deliberations.

Within the International, the German socialist August Bebel and his French rival Jean Jaures epitomized the cleavage between revolutionaries and reformists. The main controversy that divided them revolved around whether socialists should accept ministerial positions in nonsocialist governments. Bebel and Jaures debated these questions constantly at International congresses.

Bebel led the German Social Democrats with an iron hand for almost 50 years and achieved a series of electoral gains that by 1912 made the SPD the largest party in the *Reichstag*. His orthodox Marxism maintained that socialist parties should be formed to seize power, not to work within parliamentary systems or cooperate with bourgeois parties. He bitterly criticized his French comrades when one of them agreed to serve in a republican cabinet in 1899. Yet, despite its revolutionary rhetoric, in practice the SPD's parliamentary behavior was moderate.

Jaures, an energetic and courageous politician, had helped galvanize the coalition that defended Captain Dreyfus in the wrenching scandal dividing France in the early 1900s. He advocated collaboration between socialists and bourgeois parties in order to obtain reforms. In his polemics with Bebel, Jaures argued that the strength of French parliamentary democracy made it possible for socialists to transform capitalist society peacefully, whereas in Germany that was not possible because the *Reichstag* had no real power. He attacked the SPD for seeking to impose its doctrines on the socialists of all other countries. Later, after the Second International came out in opposition to what it called the "opportunism" of the reformists, Jaures agreed to adhere to a truer Marxist position in the interests of socialist solidarity.

LABOR ON THE OFFENSIVE: TRADE UNIONS, STRIKES, AND REVOLUTIONARY SYNDICALISM

As Bernstein pointed out, events eventually demonstrated the inaccuracy of Marx's conclusion that the material lives of workers would deteriorate. In the decades after 1850, working-class living standards tended to rise as prosperity spread throughout European society. Better conditions, together with the widening of the franchise, in turn made labor leaders less radical and inhibited the appeal of unions for many workers. Labor unionists agreed to operate within the context of capitalist society—hence, the role of unions was not to foment revolution but rather to improve working conditions, raise wages, and secure benefits for their members.

THE RISE OF TRADE UNIONS

After 1870, the development of large-scale unions coincided with economic expansion and the rise of big business. In 1871, when William Gladstone's Liberal government

PUBLIC FIGURES AND PRIVATE LIVES

ANNA KULISCIOFF AND FILIPPO TURATI

INDEX/Pizzi

Culver Pictures

The lives of Anna Kuliscioff (1854–1925) and Filippo Turati (1857–1932) exemplified the trials and achievements of the many European men and women who challenged the established order at the turn of the 20th century. Turati and Kuliscioff combined a lifelong commitment to the welfare of both the working class and women. Their own relationship was one of mutual respect, but the conventional gender patterns of the day compelled them to adopt distinct roles: Turati was able to build an active career both in socialist politics and as a member of the Italian Parliament. Kuliscioff, on the other hand, exerted her indirect influence chiefly through the intellectual discourse of her salon.

Kuliscioff was born Anna Rosenstein in Simferopol, a small town in the Crimea. At 17, the precocious and strong-willed Kuliscioff went to Western Europe to study medicine in Zurich because Russian women were not permitted advanced technical educations at home. In Paris, she impressed the radicals who met her by her commitment to revolution as well as by her beauty. The blonde, blue-eyed Kuliscioff had a brilliant intellect. One of the men attracted to her was Andrea Costa, a handsome young Italian anarchist. They fell in love, and collaborated in the anarchist cause. It was then that she took the alias of Kuliscioff: Many exiled radicals lived under false names as a security measure.

The harsh prison experiences, together with the inability of the anarchist movement to achieve results, prompted Kuliscioff and Costa to move toward socialism and the creation of a working-class political party. They helped establish *Avanti!*, which became the official newspaper of Italian socialists, and Costa soon became the first socialist elected to the Italian parliament. In 1881 Kuliscioff gave birth to a daughter, named Andreina, but the relationship with Costa had cooled.

In 1885, while resuming her medical studies in Naples, Kuliscioff met Filippo Turati. A young man of middle-class background ridden with psychological neuroses, Turati studied law but was drawn to literary and social issues. His interest in politics and in socialism was recent, but Kuliscioff sensed in him a quiet courage and deep humanitarian instincts. Turati went to Milan to help organize the socialists, and she joined him there. They spent the next 35 years together. Their Milan apartment became the headquarters for *Critica Sociale*, an important journal of socialist theory, which they edited.

Turati was the principal strategist of the Italian Socialist party (PSI), which he and Kuliscioff helped found in 1892. Yet Turati evolved his political ideology under Kuliscioff's influence and, after his election as a deputy in 1896, was guided in much of his political dealings by her advice. Kuliscioff no doubt had the superior intellect. She was more decisive and, as outsider to parliamentary politics, less plagued by doubts. One frequent visitor to their salon perceived the gender distinction that marked the couple's relationship when she described Kuliscioff as "the grey eminence behind the red cardinal."

Kuliscioff's interest in women's issues was longstanding and committed. Her lecture on "The Monopoly of Men" (1890) was a point of departure for Italian women—like Zetkin in Germany, Kuliscioff argued that women were oppressed both as workers and as women. At the PSI congress in 1897 she proposed a law regulating female labor, and Turati pushed for such legislation in Parliament. In 1912 she and other Italian women started a newspaper for women, *La difesa delle lavoratrici* (Defense of Women Workers).

Their last years were clouded by the trauma of World War I and the rise of Fascism. Kuliscioff's death in December 1925 devastated Turati. He escaped from the Fascists the following year and fled to Paris, where he died in 1932. Together, they had inspired and led the left-wing struggle for freedom for more than a generation.

granted full recognition to unions and legalized strikes, British trade unionists demonstrated their moderation by disassociating themselves from the violence of the Paris Commune. On the Continent, effective trade unions emerged in the years between the economic depression of the 1870s and the end of the 19th century. Napoleon III, who had once used the army to put down strikes, allowed the formation of French unions in 1864. The French republican government curtailed union activity after the Commune, but the Third Republic finally extended legal status to them in 1884. Although unions were theoretically legal in the Second Reich, Bismarck used the antisocialist laws to suppress them between 1878 and 1890. In 1891 the German Imperial Industrial Code did legalize strikes, but imposed severe penalties on worker violence.

The end to the prohibition of strikes led to a large increase in the number of industrial work stoppages. Between 1880 and 1914, strikes—especially during periods of economic crisis—were a common aspect of industrial life, with hundreds of thousands of workers participating every year. By the late 1880s a "new unionism," different in character and dimension, was emerging. The early efforts at labor organization had involved craft unions, embracing only skilled workers and artisans. Now, however, industrial unions of unskilled workers began to form as a result of long and often bitter strike activity, involving many thousands of workers: They included the strike of Belgian miners and glass workers in 1886, the British match girl strike of 1888, and those of London dock workers and Ruhr coal miners in 1889.

As mass-based unions were established, labor leaders sought to create unified national organizations embracing workers in different industries. French unions formed a national federation in 1895, the *Confédération Générale du Travail* (CGT), while in England the British Trades Union Congress, established in 1868, merged with socialist groups and created the Labour Representation Committee. In 1906 Italian socialist unions set up the *Confederazione Generale del Lavoro* (CGL). By the eve of World War I, European labor unions had a total membership of more than 9 million, including 4 million in Britain, 3 million in Germany, 1 million in France, some 700,000 in Italy, and 250,000 in Russia.

REVOLUTIONARY SYNDICALISM

In the 1870s, elements of the anarchist tradition merged with an aspect of trade union strategy to produce a unique current of radical thought known as **revolutionary syndicalism** (the term is derived from the French word for "union," *syndicat*). Fernand Pelloutier (1867–1901), its principal theorist, propounded the view that the seed of the future stateless society lay in the concept of the union. Syndicalists proposed direct action by the working class to bring about the revolution, with the general strike as their principal weapon. Pelloutier rejected all forms of the state. Instead, he advocated a social organization "limited exclusively to the needs of production and consumption."

Many syndicalists were influenced by the theories of the French intellectual Georges Sorel (1847–1922). A civil engineer by profession, Sorel argued that socialism would be

achieved through the union rather than through political parties. He believed that governments would repress general strikes with violence, and that the workers would respond with revolution. Sorel's major theoretical work was *Reflections on Violence* (1908), in which he posited the "myth of violence" as a force in history. Such all-encompassing strikes were attempted on several occasions—in 1893 in Belgium, in 1902 in Belgium, Sweden, and Spain, in 1903 in the Netherlands, in 1904 in Italy, and in 1909 in France and Sweden—but had little success. Nevertheless, socialist and syndicalist theorists continued to believe in the efficacy of the strike.

WOMEN AND THE VOTE

The rise of socialism after midcentury coincided with the development of *feminism*, a term just then coming into use. By the 1870s, European women interested in liberation strategies had the option of joining a variety of organizations. Women not inclined to direct political activism had worked in an array of reform movements, from the older temperance societies and private charities to settlement houses and educational groups. For those more urgently committed to improving women's rights and gender relations through political action, the choices were challenging. They could opt for Marxist-based movements associated with political parties striving to create socialist societies or "bourgeois" movements that sought rights for women within the framework of capitalist society.

POLITICS AND THE WOMEN'S MOVEMENT

Like their male counterparts in liberal or socialist politics, feminist leaders debated aims and strategies. What united them was a commitment to break down the institutional and cultural legacies of a patriarchal society in which women's identities and rights had been long submerged under a system of male dominance. Laws in every country still limited the equality of women in such basic social institutions as marriage and divorce, or property ownership and in-

---

S IGNIFICANT DATES

The Suffrage Movement

1868	British women given the right to vote in local elections
1869	National American Women's Suffrage Association
1879	Bebel's *Women in the Past, Present and Future*
1884	Engels' *The Origins of the Family, Private Property, and the State*
1903	Emmeline Pankhurst founds Women's Social and Political Union
1904	International Women's Suffrage Alliance
1906	Finland gives women right to vote

heritance. Yet the issue around which women of all social classes and nationalities rallied in the last decades of the 19th century was suffrage.

The right to vote was central to the privileges and responsibilities of citizenship in parliamentary systems of government. Some women viewed the right to vote as their reward for having served as coparticipants with men in the development of modern society, whereas others saw the vote as a means to improve conditions for themselves as well as for the working classes. By the eve of World War I, the suffrage issue had become the foundation for the first mass-based women's political movement, in the United States as well as in Europe. Hundreds of thousands of women joined suffrage groups in France, Britain, Italy, Russia, and other countries.

British women were given the right to vote in local elections in 1868. The following year American activists Susan B. Anthony (1820–1906) and Elizabeth Cady Stanton (see Topic 71) founded an organization that later became the larger National American Women's Suffrage Association, with a membership of more than 2 million. By the 1870s, local governments in Finland and Sweden granted some women the vote, as did some American states in the 1890s, but in these cases suffrage was limited to single women who owned property. In no European country—Finland was the exception—did women have the franchise in national elections before World War I.

Most nonsocialist women's movements included suffrage in their platforms. French women had a popular if controversial hero in Louise Michel, a former schoolteacher turned political activist who had suffered years in prison at hard labor

for her role in the Paris Commune (see Topic 73). Under the Third Republic, the French feminists Maria Deraismes (1828–1894) and Hubertine Auclert (1848–1914) began to organize French women around the suffrage issue, despite strong resistance from republican leaders. Auclert gained notoriety for her symbolic acts of protest, which included refusing to pay taxes and overturning voting urns. In 1909 a French Union for Women's Suffrage was founded.

As early as the 1880s American leaders had proposed the creation of an international organization to advance women's suffrage, but only in 1904 did an organizing conference meet. It gave rise to the International Women's Suffrage Alliance (IWSA). Like the Second International of socialist parties, the IWSA sponsored several world congresses in the years before World War I.

THE SUFFRAGE WAR IN BRITAIN

British women created several suffrage organizations in the late 19th century. The first group of prominence was the National Union of Women's Suffrage Societies (NUWSS), led by Millicent Garrett Fawcett (1847–1929). Working-class women in the textile mills set up associations of their own that underscored the middle-class interests of the NUWSS. The best-known suffrage movement, however, was the Women's Social and Political Union (WSPU), founded by Emmeline Pankhurst (1858–1928) in 1903.

Pankhurst's uncompromising militancy made the suffrage issue a cause célèbre in the early years of the 20th century. While a student in Paris, she had been impressed by French feminists. Later she and her husband campaigned in England

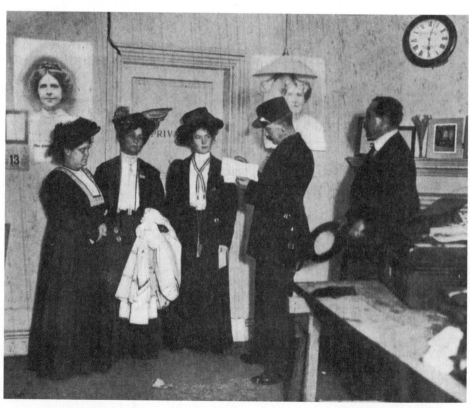

The arrest of the British sufragette leader, Emmeline Pankhurst. 1908. The arrest followed the appearance of a manifesto written by Mrs. Pankhurst—the middle woman in the group of three—urging people to storm the House of Parliament; the police officer is here seen reading her charge. Predictably, the affair only rallied her supporters and stirred up publicity.

on behalf of women's rights to control their own property. Pankhurst, who had joined women in the London match girl strike, believed that Fawcett's NUWSS was too timid. She concluded that only direct, violent action would secure women the vote. The WSPU campaigned against political candidates who refused to endorse female suffrage. With the help of her daughters Sylvia and Cristabel, Pankhurst declared war on the British government, organizing suffragist marches against Parliament and rallies before the royal palace.

When Prime Minister Herbert Asquith (served 1908–1916) refused to endorse women's suffrage in 1911, Pankhurst led a systematic assault on London's most exclusive shops, breaking windows to draw attention to the suffrage cause. Yet, despite a nine-month prison sentence, her activities became still more dramatic. One of her followers slashed a famous painting that feminists found offensive, while another assaulted Winston Churchill (1875–1965), then a young antifeminist politician serving as home secretary. A WSPU member chained herself to the gate outside the official home of the prime minister, shouting at passersby, and a few militants even started fires. As a result of a bomb plot against David Lloyd George, chancellor of the exchequer in Asquith's cabinet, Pankhurst was given a three-year prison term. Even prison, however, did not dampen her enthusiasm for the cause—to the dismay of government authorities, she and her daughters repeatedly declared hunger strikes.

Enemies of women's rights criticized such tactics, but the suffragists succeeded in making the vote for women a public issue that would not go away. The final victory in the suffragist war was not won until after World War I, but Pankhurst's struggles symbolized the determination of countless other women in all countries to secure their rights.

THE SOCIALIST PATH TO FEMINISM

Most socialist parties and labor unions recognized the importance of gaining the adherence of women, who in some countries accounted for almost half the industrial workforce. In Germany, Eleanor Marx, the daughter of Karl Marx, was among those who recruited women into separate organizations affiliated with the SPD. By 1914, the party had some 175,000 women involved in its activities.

SOCIALISM AND FEMINISM
Socialist parties generally supported women's suffrage, along with civil—as opposed to religious—marriage and the right to divorce. Birth control was a more problematic issue because socialists long viewed birth control as associated with the ideas of Thomas Malthus and the notion that workers were to blame for their own poverty. Nevertheless, many socialists did not see gender issues as separate or distinct from working-class concerns, and notions of masculinity often excluded women from socialist or union activism. Although some women won positions of prominence within labor or socialist movements, few actually held important executive posts—exceptions to the rule were the Russian exile Angelica Balabanoff (1869–1965), who served on the executive committee of the Italian Socialist party and later was secretary of the Third (Communist) International, and Ottilie Baader (1847–1925), a longtime member of the SPD's executive committee.

The SPD produced two important theoretical works on the women's question: Bebel's *Women in the Past, Present and Future* (1879) and Engels' *The Origins of the Family, Private Property, and the State* (1884). Each traced the suppression of women to the development of the principle of private property—men, they argued, oppressed women to guarantee the legitimacy of children, which they deemed necessary in order to transfer property to their sons. Bebel saw in the relationship of wives to their husbands a parallel with the worker's relationship to employers, concluding that women were oppressed both as workers and as women.

The most important proponent of feminism within the SPD was Clara Zetkin (1857–1933), an incisive thinker and the editor of *Die Gleichheit* (Equality), a women's paper. A committed revolutionary socialist, Zetkin strongly disliked revisionism and denounced reformists as bitterly as Bebel and others did. She decried collaboration between the socialist women's movement and bourgeois feminism as loudly as they condemned cooperation between socialist and bourgeois parties.

Zetkin had two related concerns: to keep working-class men and women united in the socialist movement, and to prevent bourgeois feminists from drawing working women into their movement. She paid close attention to the economic status of women, stressing that they were not paid for their work as homemakers and mothers. She agreed with the arguments of Engels and Bebel that under capitalism women had become simply a form of male property. She was convinced, therefore, that the liberation of women could be achieved only within the larger socialist effort to eliminate private property. On the other hand, Zetkin joined other socialists in aiming to avoid a division of the working class along gender lines, and stressed the need to focus on women as workers rather than as wives.

Putting the Challenge to Social Order in Perspective

In the half-century between 1870 and 1914, Europe witnessed the emergence of two major but unequal forces—socialism and feminism. Each stood in stark opposition to

Continued next page

the prevailing values and power structure of the age. Anarchism and socialism posited drastic solutions to the problems of capitalist society, and the alternatives appealed to an increasing number of Europeans. The Marxists eventually gained command of the socialist movement, but their ranks were also split as revisionists challenged the assumptions of Marx's strategies. The creation of huge political parties and labor unions nevertheless gained the adherence of millions of workers, while syndicalists proposed to bring down the capitalist system with the general strike.

To the elites governing society, the women's movement appeared to be almost as dangerous. Many women rallied around the issue of the suffrage, creating national groups and an international organization devoted to gaining the vote. Other, more radical feminists emphasized broader questions of gender relations and political revolution. Some women combined feminism and socialism in their militancy, creating further disputes over strategy and theory within their ranks.

Although there was little unity of position within either movement, both fought with great determination to eliminate economic and social injustice in European society, providing a rich legacy that was inherited by later generations of men and women.

Questions for Further Study

1. What theoretical and practical differences separated anarchism from socialism?
2. What issues were of most importance to socialist parties?
3. Why did the idea of the strike assume political importance?
4. Why were many women drawn to radical movements? What was the difference between the goals of suffragettes and those of women socialists?

Suggestions for Further Reading

Adams, Carole. *Women Clerks in Wilhelmine Germany: Issues of Class and Gender.* New York, 1988.

Berlanstein, Lenard R. *The Working People of Paris, 1871–1914.* Baltimore, MD, 1984.

Cahm, Caroline. *Peter Kropotkin and the Rise of Revolutionary Anarchism.* New York, 1989.

Franzoi, Barbara. *At the Very Least She Pays the Rent: Women and German Industrialization.* Westport, CT, 1985.

Pugh, Martin. *The March of the Women: A Revisionist Analysis of the Campaign for Women's Suffrage, 1866–1914.* New York, 2000.

Ross, Ellen. *Love and Toil: Motherhood in Outcast London, 1870–1918.* New York, 1993.

Taylor, Barbara. *Eve and the New Jerusalem: Socialism and Feminism in the Nineteenth Century.* New York, 1983.

Thoennessen, W. *The Emancipation of Women: The Rise and Decline of the Women's Movement in German Social Democracy.* London, 1973.

Tickner, Lisa. *The Spectacle of Women: Imagery of the Suffrage Campaign, 1907–1914.* Chicago, 1988.

Wheen, Francis. *Karl Marx.* London, 1999.

InfoTrac College Edition

Enter the search term *Marxism* using Key Terms.

Enter the search term *anarchism* using Key Terms.

Enter the search term *socialism history* using Key Terms.

SOCIETY IN TRANSITION: THE MODERNIZATION OF EUROPE

With the coming of the Second Industrial Revolution, European society underwent major changes, developing a structure that in the course of the 20th century spread throughout much of the world. The concentration of large numbers of people in ever-growing cities, many of them living at an adequate economic level and possessing the right to vote, produced a new element—the proletarian masses.

The rise of an urban proletariat had an important effect on the role of the middle classes. By 1900 many businessmen saw working-class advancement as a threat to their own interests. As a result, the wealthiest and best educated—the upper middle class—developed alliances with the old aristocracy. The formation of this upper-class elite left the remaining members of the middle classes with considerably reduced influence. Society became increasingly polarized.

Behind the changes in social structure and within classes lay vast changes in population patterns. Improved medical care reduced the rate of infant mortality and extended life expectancy. At the same time, all over Western Europe birthrates were dropping, partly because of the introduction of contraceptive methods, which helped parents to plan their families. On the whole, there seemed to be a general resolve to limit the size of families. In Eastern Europe, where social change was slower, the population continued to increase, and by 1910, population growth was higher there than in Western Europe. This represented a reversal of the situation 50 years earlier.

The political and social battles of the 19th century, along with the general rise of prosperity, had enlarged the numbers of people who were able to vote. Both liberals and the new conservative elite concurred in the need for the education of these new electors, in order to prepare them for the duties of citizenship. As a result, state-run systems of mass education were introduced, with important political consequences. Increasing popular literacy played some part in strengthening trade union activities and protest movements. The principal thrust of school curricula, however, was to encourage nationalism, in order to encourage loyalty to the state and its ruling classes. The spread of mass peacetime military conscription also increased the sense of national consciousness. The growing mood of strident nationalism in Europe provided an appropriately belligerent setting for the events leading to World War I.

THE CHANGING SOCIAL STRUCTURE

As in earlier periods of the 19th century, industrialization continued to affect social patterns in important ways in the decades after 1871. By the eve of World War I, factories had swelled cities with many more workers and middle-class inhabitants, so that much of Europe reached the halfway mark in the transition from a rural to an urban society.

POPULATION GROWTH AND URBANIZATION

Between 1870 and 1910, Europe's population (excluding Russia) rose by 44 percent, from approximately 230 million to 330 million. This growth was not, however, constant everywhere because the size of families in Western Europe tended to diminish. Throughout the latter part of the 19th century, in fact, the birthrate declined rapidly, and only a reduction in the mortality rate allowed for population increase.

The pace of urbanization intensified toward the end of the 19th century because of three factors: (1) the continuing shift of people away from the countryside, (2) the increase in the number and size of cities, and (3) the cities' growing population density. In Britain, the most highly urbanized nation, city dwellers in 1914 constituted almost 80 percent of the population, as compared to about 60 percent 50 years earlier, while France similarly increased its urban population from 33 to almost 45 percent. Because Germany

underwent a dramatic rate of industrialization in this period, the proportion of people living in cities there virtually doubled to 55 percent, while 90 percent of the country's overall population increase was in urban areas. In the years between 1870 and 1900, most large European cities, including the older capitals, doubled their populations and continued to increase sharply over the following decade.

The railroad contributed greatly to urbanization. The physical appearance of cities began to change as the construction industry was revolutionized by developments in civil engineering and building materials. The use of steel and reinforced concrete made it possible for architects to design skyscrapers: The first of these tall buildings, New York's 130-foot-high Equitable Life Assurance Society Building, was built in 1870. By combining steel and wrought iron with glass, European city planners created new forms of public space, such as the enclosed galleries built in London, Paris, Milan, and Naples.

THE GROWTH OF THE URBAN PROLETARIAT

Most of the political and social progress made in the first part of the 19th century was a result of the informal alliance of middle-class liberalism and working-class protest. By the end of the century, however, conditions were changing. The cooperation between the two classes had depended on the tacit understanding that middle-class reformers would decide what was in the best interests of the workers. With the gradual improvement in conditions of urban life and the extension of the franchise, the urban masses were becoming a political force in themselves.

The emergence of an urban proletariat in Western European society profoundly affected old alliances. Trade unions and socialist parties were no longer dependent on the goodwill of the middle class for reforms because an increasingly active membership provided them with new bargaining power. The wealthier members of the middle class, in turn, began to see the various protest movements as a challenge to their business interests. In their search for allies, they turned to their former opponents, the aristocracy. The combination of rich industrialists and aristocrats who were prepared to compromise formed a new upper-class elite.

Although the influence of the aristocratic ruling classes had declined, they still retained considerable prestige. Marriages between the daughters of wealthy businessmen and impoverished heirs to noble titles provided both sides with gains. Although money was beginning to replace birth as the ultimate social status symbol, the combination of both was the most desirable aim of all. In some cases European aristocrats turned to America in search of rich brides. In 1874, Lord Randolph Churchill (1849–1895) married Jennie Jerome, a member of a prosperous New York family. Their elder son was Winston S. Churchill.

With an increasingly militant working class at one end of the social spectrum, and a new alliance of upper-class elites at the other, the median segment of the middle classes lost influence. Growing religious skepticism undermined

Table 78.1	Population Growth (in thousands) of Selected European Countries		
COUNTRY	1870	1900	1910
Britain	22,712	32,528	36,070
France	36,103	38,451	39,192
Germany	41,059	56,367	64,926
Hungary	15,512	19,255	20,886
Spain	16,622	18,594	19,927
Sweden	4,169	5,137	5,522

Table 78.2	Population Growth (in thousands) for Major European Cities		
CITY	1870	1900	1910
Amsterdam	624	511	574
Belfast	174	349	387
Berlin	826	1,889	2,071
London	3,890	6,586	7,256
Milan	262	493	579
Paris	1,852	2,714	2,888
Rome	244	463	542
Stockholm	136	301	342
St. Petersburg	667	1,267	1,962

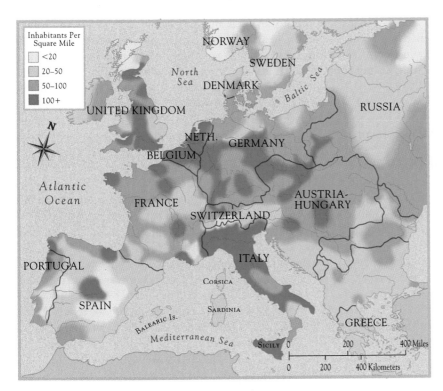

Map 78.1 Europe's Population, c. 1890. The heavy concentrations generally relate to the presence of raw materials or rivers—or often both. Northern Italy is crossed by the River Po. The area between France and Germany is rich in coal, and was a leading producer of iron and steel. Britain had the densest population of all: Note the mining areas of northern Scotland and South Wales.

bourgeois Victorian morality. Social elites developed ever more elaborate and glamorized forms of traditional "high" culture such as opera houses and art galleries. New York's Metropolitan Museum of Art was founded in 1870, and the Paris Opera opened in 1875. At the same time, the working classes began to enjoy their own forms of popular culture. London's first music hall, a place for popular shows, was built in 1849, and held 100 people. By 1890 London had some 500 music halls; the largest offered continuous performances to a changing audience of as many as 45,000 in a single evening.

The class structure of European society became increasingly polarized between two extremes. The rise of the masses created vast new commercial possibilities that business entrepreneurs were quick to exploit. At the same time, it posed a potential threat to governments, which they sought to defuse by developing ways to manipulate and control mass responses. Meanwhile, as conditions for most citizens continued slowly but perceptibly to improve, the very rich became even richer.

WEALTH, POVERTY, AND SOCIAL DARWINISM

For those living in Europe at the turn of the 20th century, the age seemed, and for the privileged few was, one of unprecedented luxury and extravagance. In Paris, the *Belle Époque* (Beautiful Age) brought lavish banquets and balls. The city's cabarets and nightlife, vividly depicted in the art

of Impressionist painters such as Auguste Renoir (1841–1919), were as famous as its parade of elegant courtesans, described by Parisian wits as *les grandes horizontales* (the great recliners). No less a figure than the eldest son of Queen Victoria, the future Edward VII, entertained his mistress at Maxim's, a glamorous Parisian restaurant.

When Edward became king in 1901, his reign introduced a similar mood of opulence to Britain. The Edwardian Era was marked by extravagant "house parties," weekends in the country at which the nobility and eminent industrialists ate, drank, and shot together. On December 18, 1913, at Hall Barn in Buckinghamshire, seven marksmen killed 3,937 pheasants, still a record for a single shoot. The Austrian Archduke Franz Ferdinand, whose assassination in 1914 finally precipitated the outbreak of war, was also an enthusiastic shot. Shortly before his death he expressed satisfaction at having killed his 3,000th stag.

The English well-to-do, like American travelers of later days, were famous in continental Europe for their demand for hygiene and efficient plumbing. Individual water closets with flushing toilets, rare in England before 1900, became increasingly common in the larger towns, although only the largest establishments were equipped with more than one. Even a big upper-class English house, the scene of weekend parties, generally had only one bathroom, which was usually reserved for the family. Fixed baths were first made of porcelain, but by 1910 cast-iron tubs were becoming popular. Bathroom fixtures included showers, either in the bath itself or independent, and heated towel rails. As overnight guests took their morning tea and biscuits, a maid would draw the curtains, light the fire, and set out a portable bath in front of the hearth, to be filled from a hot water can. The comfort of the upper classes required the existence of a household of servants, although the growing introduction of inventions such as vacuum cleaners and washing machines began to reduce the size of domestic staffs.

THE URBAN POOR

The lives of most of the population were in stark contrast to those of the rich. In the London district of Bermondsey at the turn of the 20th century, an observer noted that one water pipe served for 25 houses, with the water turned on for only two hours a day and not at all on Sundays. The same 25 families had one water closet among them, outside of which queues of people lined up every morning before going to work.

Despite the material progress of the 19th century, large sectors of the populations of all European countries continued to live in poverty. A survey conducted around the turn of the 20th century in London, the capital of the richest country in the world, found the proportion of paupers to be 30.7 percent. In eastern and southern Europe, conditions were even worse. In 1900, the average life expectancy in Spain or the Balkans was less than 35 years.

Even those whose earnings allowed them to live above the level of bare subsistence were subject to the constant threat of insecurity. The loss of a job through illness or age brought inevitable ruin to a family. The first country to introduce health insurance and pensions was Germany, where Bismarck enacted legislation in 1883 to combat the appeal of socialism among workers. In Britain, early voluntary insurance programs had been run by some of the trade unions, and the government introduced national policies only in 1911. Even these measures, however, did not cover large categories of workers, including the domestic servants, on whom the upper classes depended, and the self-employed. The uncertainties of illness, accident, or premature death hung over most working homes.

Yet the lives of urban workers did undergo some improvements. Between 1880 and 1914, wages rose considerably, and purchasing power almost doubled in England, Germany, and France. Mass production and marketing, combined with fast transport, reduced the price of many goods. The production and sale of food continued to increase and its price to decline (see Topic 75). By 1891, nearly 600,000 workers in England were employed in the food trades. At the same time, there were 40 percent more grocers and fishmongers than 10 years earlier, and 82 percent more jam and preserve makers. Most workers' families ate vegetables and some form of meat (often a poor one) on a regular basis. One student of working-class conditions noted that "puddings and tarts are not uncommon, and bread ceases to be the staff of life. In this class no-one goes short of food."

Working-class children in the East End of London, c. 1900. This area of London has always been one of the poorer districts; a high proportion of the residents were (and still are) Jewish.

One of the results of the gradual improvement in material conditions was increased leisure time. The increased pace of production meant that most factory workers no longer needed to put in 12- or 14-hour days to maintain output. Workers and trade unions fought for shorter working hours, in order to devote more time to their families and leisure activities. In the earlier years of the Industrial Revolution, factory employees had time for little but working and sleeping. By 1900, many urban workers still put in 10-hour days or more, with Sunday free. In Britain some had Saturday afternoon free as well, in what became known as the "English weekend."

Leisure pursuits increased as fast as people had the chance to enjoy them. Technical advances in paper making and printing made possible mass-circulation newspapers and magazines, which higher literacy made available to a growing readership. They stirred patriotic fervor and popular enthusiasm for imperialism by running dramatic stories of adventure and conquest in exotic places. Popular writers of the day reached mass audiences with science fiction tales and detective stories. The Frenchman Jules Verne (1828–1905) incorporated the latest scientific developments in fantasies such as *Twenty Thousand Leagues Under the Sea* (1870), while the British writer Sir Arthur Conan Doyle (1859–1930) created Sherlock Holmes, the most memorable fictional detective in Western literature. Amusement parks and dance halls offered the chance for relaxed entertainment. Cycling led to a new exercise craze and had a special appeal to middle-class women. Competitive team sports became popular. In Britain in the 1880s, associations were founded to organize athletics, boxing, lawn tennis, rowing, swimming, hockey, and football events. In 1896, the first modern Olympiad took place in Athens, reviving the Olympic Games of ancient Greece.

The increased use of leisure time for simple relaxation and fun was accompanied by a decline in religious observance. Sunday became a day to spend in the country or at the seaside, rather than at church. Virtually the only country in Europe where church attendance actually increased was Ireland, where the Catholic Church symbolized opposition to the hated Protestant British rulers. During the reign of Pope Leo XIII (ruled 1878–1903), official Catholic teaching sought to reconcile church dogma with science and liberalism. Leo's famous encyclical, *Rerum Novarum* (1891), on the condition of the working classes, tried to counter anticlericalism by linking the church to the working class. Churches began to organize their own leisure activities, including youth groups, for the urban masses. On the whole, however, the trend away from organized religion continued.

SOCIAL DARWINISM

Those who were struck by the increasing gulf between the modest improvements in the living conditions of the workers and the extravagance of the wealthy found a handy explanation in the philosophy of **Social Darwinism.** Charles Darwin's *Origin of Species* (1859) (see Topic 72) taught that

life is a fierce and constant struggle, in which only the fittest survive. Darwin had been concerned with the natural process of evolution, but a rising business class was all too ready to apply his arguments to commercial progress. The bitter strife of competitive industry, they claimed, would lead slowly but inevitably to the upward movement of civilization. Thus Social Darwinists asserted that those who were emerging at the top were evidently the fittest and thus qualified to survive and continue the process.

The philosophical underpinning of this world view was to be found in the writings of the British philosopher Herbert Spencer (1820–1903). His version of evolution argued that species develop from simple to complex forms, in a process of automatic improvement, and that any attempt to interfere with change (including economic change) would stand in the way of progress. Spencer's most enthusiastic followers were to be found in the United States, where a Rockefeller remarked that "the growth of a large business is merely the survival of the fittest."

In contrast to the Social Darwinists, increasing numbers of people found new ways of alleviating the plight of the urban poor. Beatrice Potter Webb (1858–1943), a British social reformer, investigated conditions in London's slums to demonstrate their misery. Social workers, both government employees and private individuals, developed organizations to provide practical assistance and training to the needy. The most famous such institution was the Salvation Army, which was formed in 1878 by William Booth (1829–1912). The organization grew out of a mission he founded in 1865.

PATTERNS OF GENDER AND SEXUALITY

As society as a whole underwent profound change, many women and some men began to question traditional attitudes toward family and gender roles. In the late 19th century, increasing numbers of women had jobs outside the home. Most women worked in textile and clothing factories, or in domestic service, the most common field of female employment. The number of single female employees rose steadily. By the eve of World War I, more than 90 percent of working women were unmarried.

Traditional attitudes toward the division of labor within the family, however, remained unchanged. Working-class men played no role in domestic life, apart from providing their wives at intervals with a sum of money to cover expenses. Some men even left their wives to pay for household needs, requiring them to earn money by working themselves or by taking in boarders. Working women remained wholly responsible for all domestic duties.

Domestic violence was common, frequently the result of heavy drinking. The center of working-class life was generally the café or pub, where friends could meet. Alcohol offered an escape from grinding poverty and the rigors of overwork and

Women secretaries working in a corporate office in New York. Early 20th century. As increasing numbers of women entered the workforce, rather than replacing men they took jobs that had not previously existed. The growth of large corporations required huge numbers of secretaries, receptionists, and other office workers, and women began to acquire the skills—typing, shorthand—necessary for these new positions.

Corbis-Bettmann

a temporary warmth for those whose houses were unheated. Returning drunk to a cold home, many men took out their frustrations on their family, beating their wives and children.

In other cases, the violence was sexual. Within the confines of her home, a woman ran the risk of assault by relatives or boarders. With increased numbers of women at work, the phenomenon of sexual harassment on the job developed, whereby a woman was threatened with the loss of her work if she did not submit to sexual advances. Some women gave in under pressure, but as more acquired their working independence, women employees sometimes stood up and defended their rights. Single women living and working in large cities were subject to rape and other forms of sexual violence.

Violence against women in late-19th-century cities riveted the lurid fascination of a mass public. In London, poor working-class women were the victims of a notorious killer nicknamed Jack the Ripper, a man whose real identity has still not been definitively established. In the months from August to November of 1888, he perpetrated a series of gruesome murders, all of them involving single women. Similar, if less spectacular, killings occurred in Paris and the main German cities. For many contemporary observers, the moral to be drawn from the violence was not that single women needed better protection, but that women who did not follow traditional patterns of behavior were likely to suffer for their daring.

SEXUAL RIGHTS AND THE MIDDLE CLASSES

The work of the Austrian psychoanalyst Sigmund Freud (see Topic 79) made sexual behavior a subject for explicit discussion among the educated. In the flood of investiga-

tion and imaginative writing that followed, some long-standing attitudes came into question. Homosexuality and lesbianism were studied more sympathetically. The German psychiatrist Magnus Hirschfeld (1868–1935) wrote of homosexuality as a "third sex," and under his influence the Scientific Humanitarian Committee was formed in Berlin for the study of homosexual culture. In Paris, the salon of Natalie Barney (1876–1972) became a center for women whose rebellion against conventions took the form of lesbianism.

Nevertheless, society as a whole still condemned sexual minorities, and laws were passed that made sexual relations between men illegal. In 1885 the British Parliament enacted the Criminal Law Amendment Act, which for the first time prohibited "indecent" sexual relations between adult consenting males and prescribed a sentence of up to two years in prison with hard labor. One of the most prominent public figures to be punished under this law was the Irish writer Oscar Wilde (1854–1900), who was prosecuted for his relationship with Lord Alfred Douglas (1870–1945). The middle-class refusal to see women as sexual beings was reflected in the fact that the law was restricted to men. When this omission was pointed out to Queen Victoria, she is reported to have replied, "No woman would do that."

Freud's theories promoted a new openness toward sexual behavior. This led in turn to new attitudes toward the relationship between the sexes. No longer regarded as either untouchably pure or mere reproductive machines, women began to change their self-perceptions. Many played an increasingly aggressive role in the feminist movement (see Topic 77). Among those campaigning for a change of atti-

Oscar Wilde (left) and Lord Alfred Douglas, c. 1893. At the time, Wilde was writing a series of extremely successful light comedies, the most famous of which is *The Importance of Being Earnest* (1895). In that same year, as a result of a libel suit brought by the Marquis of Queensbury, Lord Alfred Douglas's father, Wilde was tried on charges of sodomy, convicted, and imprisoned for two years.

tudes was the German Helene Stocker (1869–1943), who believed that a new way of talking and thinking about sex would make sexual relations more ennobling. Other women took the opposite extreme, claiming that traditional relations between the sexes were the curse of civilization and should be completely overthrown. In her book *The Great Scourge* (1913), Cristabel Pankhurst (1880–1958) described marriage as a dangerous institution and men as the scourge of society.

BIRTH CONTROL

The growing use of methods of contraception in the late 19th century was another vital factor in changing society and the nature of family life. With the reduced rate of infant mortality, parents no longer needed to produce more children than they could support, under the assumption that some would die early. Furthermore, with the spread of education and the ability of more families to accumulate savings, parents preferred to have fewer children, who were better educated, to whom to leave their property.

Methods of contraception varied, and knowledge of them spread both by word of mouth and by active campaigning. British laws forbade the publication of birth control material, but in 1878 the Fabian reformer Annie Besant (1847–1933) joined Charles Bradlaugh (1833–1891) in challenging the law. After 1880 they circulated tens of thousands of birth control leaflets. On the Continent, one of the early promoters of birth control was Arletta Jacobs (1851?–1929), the first woman who was awarded a medical degree in the Netherlands. In her work among the poor in Amsterdam, she encouraged the use of the "Dutch cap," a form of individual cervical covering first invented in

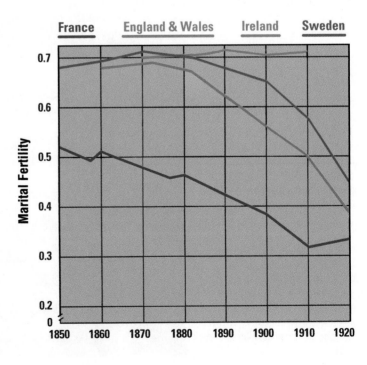

Graph 78.1 Fertility Rates in Selected Countries, 1850–1920. Declining fertility rates between 1850 and 1920 reflected the increasingly common practice of birth control.

Germany. One of the most common methods for dealing with unwanted pregnancies was abortion.

Inspired by the writings of the early-19th-century economic philosopher Thomas Malthus (see Topic 66), Neo-Malthusian leagues were formed in many countries. They advocated population control as a means of improving marital relations and promoting social harmony. Although the Neo-Malthusians encouraged working-class support, the movement was basically a middle-class one.

The effect of contraception on population growth was dramatic. Around 1870, the average English family contained 6.6 children; 50 years later, the number had fallen to just over two. The most extreme declines occurred in the countries of Western Europe, where by 1910 the birthrate had fallen by 30 percent or more; the only exception was Ireland, where it actually rose slightly. In Southern and Eastern Europe, birthrates did not begin to decline until after World War I, with the result that on the eve of war, Western Europe was actually surpassed in population growth.

Although contraception was used by working-class couples, the predominantly middle-class advocacy and adoption of birth control were reflected in birth patterns. In the period from 1879 to 1893, the number of children born to families in Rotterdam varied according to social class: For every three children whose parents were professionals, there were six whose fathers were laborers or artisans. In London at the turn of the 20th century, the birthrate in the working-class East End was one-third higher than in more fashionable districts.

Yet as the use of contraception spread, it had far-reaching consequences for all levels of society. Free of the necessity of continual childbearing, growing numbers of women strove to take their place alongside men in the workplace and in public life.

THE INTEGRATION OF SOCIETY: LITERACY AND MILITARY SERVICE

Between 1870 and 1914, most European governments deliberately indoctrinated large groups of citizens with a sense of national consciousness, especially the workers and peasants who had traditionally been marginalized. Universal elementary education and compulsory military service provided two important instruments for national integration.

PUBLIC EDUCATION

Beginning after 1880, most Western governments took the first steps to introduce mass education. In France, the government of Jules-François-Camille Ferry (served as prime minister 1880–1881, 1883–1885) established free compulsory secular education as part of anticlerical legislation. By 1890, primary education for males and females up to the age of 12 was compulsory in many countries. In Austria, for example, the number of children attending primary schools rose from 1.9 million in 1870 to 4.2 million in 1914, while in Britain during the same period enrollment increased from 1.4 million to 6.2 million. The possibilities of secondary education for women began to increase, but universities were still mainly reserved for men. At the first lecture of the Greek scientist Angeliki Panajiotatou (1875–1954), students shouted at her: "Back to the kitchen!" In 1881, Spain's first female medical students were violently attacked in protest.

Although both liberals and conservatives agreed on the need for the spread of education, their motives differed. For those who encouraged upward social mobility, education—in particular the basic ability to read, write, and perform simple calculations—was an essential key to advancement.

Jennie Brownscombe, *The New Scholar.* 1878. The scholar in question, making her way hesitatingly toward the schoolhouse, is a young girl. The last quarter of the 19th century saw a growing awareness in most European societies of the importance of education, which became compulsory, at least at the elementary level. Activists in the women's movement stressed the importance of equal education for both sexes as a fundamental part of their wider battle.

In some countries, notably France and Italy, secular leaders also encouraged state-run education as a means of offsetting the influence of the Catholic Church.

Conservative governments, on the other hand, saw public education as a way of maintaining control over the masses. As growing numbers of citizens acquired the right to vote, they needed to be directed toward using their powers in a way that was acceptable to the authorities. General literacy did play some part in helping protest groups to circulate written campaign material and win new members; however, compulsory education mainly promoted carefully devised state programs.

The chief goal of these programs was to instill strong feelings of national pride. Official textbooks presented the view of national history and development that favored each state's image, often by denigrating other nations. On many occasions the very language used, or not used, for lessons became a nationalist issue, as in parts of the Austro-Hungarian empire. After leaving school, former students would read similar nationalistic messages in popular newspapers, which celebrated their country's achievements and vigorously bemoaned any perceived slight to national honor.

MILITARY SERVICE

Although obligatory military service dates back to the ancient world, it first began to evolve in modern Europe in the late 18th century; it was introduced by the radicals in France in the fall of 1792 and took the form of mass conscription. Prussia's successes in the 1860s were largely attributable to its custom of maintaining a large body of trained soldiers, even in peacetime. After the Prussian victory over the French in 1870, France took a lesson from its enemy and introduced the military draft. Austria followed suit, as did many other continental nations. Britain did not introduce peacetime conscription until just before World War II, although military service was required during World War I.

The effects of conscription reinforced those of compulsory education. Recruits were generally sent away from their home district in order to break their local loyalties. In their place, military training encouraged recruits to develop a broader sense of identification with the military itself and, ultimately, with the nation-state.

The increasing appetite for nationalist victories, nourished by imperialist conquests, distracted attention from discontent at home. It also succeeded in uniting large masses of each country's population in a common enthusiasm. Socialist leaders opposed nationalism and called for class solidarity to transcend frontiers, but members of the urban proletariat generally showed no less fervor for national interests than their rulers. As a result, there developed a popular demand for diplomatic and military victories that played a significant part in the buildup to war. When World War I came, furthermore, even the socialist parties that had condemned nationalism rallied to the national cause.

Putting Society in Transition in Perspective

By 1914, European society was beginning to shed some of its traditional characteristics. Class patterns created by 19th-century reforms were shifting, as social groups changed alliances. Rich tradesmen and impecunious aristocrats—former enemies— joined forces. The ranks of the lower middle class swelled with the growth of government and corporate bureaucracies. With the coming of universal male suffrage, the working classes, whose condition slowly improved, began to emerge as a potentially powerful political force.

Radical changes in birthrates modified ways of family life that had been constant for centuries. The hitherto universally accepted notion of male dominance was under increasing attack. The taboo on open discussion of sexual matters had begun to be challenged. Traditional habits of religious observance were yielding to secular pressures. Popular literacy made it possible for large numbers of people to follow debate on the great issues of the times.

Questions for Further Study

1. How was the condition of the aristocracy and the middle class changing after 1870?
2. In what ways was science applied to social analysis?
3. To what degree did sexual practices conform to social expectations?
4. What is meant by the modernization of society? What factors were most important to that process?

Suggestions for Further Reading

Accampo, Elinor. *Industrialization, Family Life, and Class Relations: Saint Chamond, 1815–1914*. Berkeley, CA, 1989.

Duberman, Martin, M. Vicinus, and G. Chauncey. *Hidden from History: Reclaiming the Gay and Lesbian Past*. New York, 1989.

Girouard, Mark. *Cities and People: A Social and Architectural History*. New Haven, CT, 1985.

Hopkins, Eric. *Industrialization and Society: A Social History*. New York, 2000.

Joyce, P. *Visions of the People: Industrial England and the Question of Class, c. 1848–1914*. New York, 1991.

McLaren, Angus. *Birth Control in Nineteenth-Century England*. New York, 1978.

Miller, Michael. *The Bon Marché: Bourgeois Culture and the Department Store, 1869–1920*. Princeton, NJ, 1981.

Moch, Leslie P. *Moving Europeans: Migration in Western Europe Since 1650*. Bloomington, IN, 1993.

Pilbeam, Pamela M. *The Middle Classes in Europe, 1789–1914*. Chicago, 1990.

Ross, Ellen. *Love and Toil: Motherhood in Outcast London, 1870-1918*. New York, 1993.

Shapiro, Ann-Louise. *Housing the Poor of Paris, 1850–1902*. Madison, WI, 1985.

Sutcliffe, Anthony. *Towards the Planned City: Germany, Britain, and the United States, 1789–1914*. New York, 1981.

Wiener, Joel H., ed. *Papers for the Millions: The New Journalism in Britain, 1850s to 1914*. New York, 1988.

InfoTrac College Edition

Enter the search term *Social Darwinism* using Key Terms.

ART AND SCIENCE: THE MODERNIST REVOLUTION

The decisive break with the past that World War I was to produce was foreshadowed in the artistic and intellectual developments of the preceding decades. Richard Wagner, the prophet of the "art work of the future," was also the high priest of Romanticism. In many cases the new ideas made return to former ways impossible. The philosophy of Henri Bergson and the psychoanalytical theories of Sigmund Freud conditioned vast areas of 20th-century behavior; the writings of Friedrich Nietzsche anticipated darker aspects of 20th-century political life.

In literature, Freud's ideas stimulated writers to explore the human subconscious, probing neuroses and repressions. Sympathy for the growing tide of political protest in Western Europe led some writers, including Émile Zola, to adopt an increasingly realistic style. By contrast, others sought refuge from the harsh realities of the times in devising complex, symbolic language. By the early 20th century, in the works of Marcel Proust and James Joyce, the very use of language itself represented a revolutionary break with the past.

Painters, too, explored new attitudes toward their art, increasingly rejecting traditional pictorial values in favor of abstract qualities. The Impressionists emphasized how things appeared to their eyes rather than how they really were. Their abstract treatment of form reached a point of no return around the turn of the 20th century in the works of Paul Cézanne. It was only a step from there to the total breakdown of formal realism that Cubism and Futurism represented.

Just as Cubism opened a new chapter in painting by rejecting centuries of traditions, so the revolutionary musical style of atonality broke with 400 years of Western musical history. Devised by Arnold Schoenberg, it abandoned traditional harmony (or "tonality") in search of a new musical language. Not all composers accepted Schoenberg's method, but many agreed that the times required a break with the past. Igor Stravinsky, in his revolutionary masterpiece *The Rite of Spring,* experimented with new approaches to rhythm.

At the same time as artists were forging the ideas of Modernism, science was making its own contribution to the changing world. Einstein's "special theory" of relativity, first formulated in 1905, not only conditioned developments in modern physics but also opened the way to the nuclear age.

Thus the intellectual and cultural life of the generation before World War I reflected forces of disruption that were also operating on a much larger scale. At a time when traditional philosophies or religious belief seemed inadequate for the restless spirit of the age, artists sought refuge for their own disturbed visions in reshaping the world of their art.

The revolutionary artistic and intellectual movements of the late 19th century abruptly thrust Western culture into the Modernist era. Even so, they did not represent a complete novelty that appeared overnight. In the case of **Modernism,** the transformation of Western culture was symbolized to a remarkable degree by the life and art of Richard Wagner (1813–1883).

Wagner is best known today for his huge music dramas, the name he coined for his operatic works. In his time, he was also involved in many of the political issues that shook the second half of the 19th century, from the revolutions of 1848—he fought on the barricades in Dresden, later fleeing to Switzerland—to Prussia's nationalist war against France in 1870. A tireless campaigner on behalf of a bewildering array of causes from vicious anti-Semitism to wholehearted vegetarianism, he also wrote extensively on the arts. Among his early writings of significance was *The Artwork of the Future*, which appeared in 1849.

Many features of his operas are firmly within the German Romantic tradition and are based on his own versions of traditional Teutonic myths. Like many Romantic artists, Wagner incorporated elements of the natural world in his works, such as the surge of a great river or the radiant beauty of spring sunshine. Furthermore, his music often reflects the characteristic Romantic preoccupation with death.

Yet this supremely Romantic creator was, at the same time, the most revolutionary artistic figure of his day, in many ways a true Modern. His musical style pushed the harmonic language of the mid-19th century to its limits, paving the way for the atonality of the early 20th century. His use of a short theme *(Leitmotiv)* to represent an individual, object, or concept allowed him to explore depths of psychological penetration. The use of these themes often reveals a character's subconscious thoughts or motivations. In the opera *Tristan und Isolde* (1865), he depicted virtually every shade of sexual love with a frankness generally unknown in works for public performance until our own time. His last stage work, *Parsifal* (1882), portrays the renunciation of sex with insights that can only be called Freudian. His advocacy of the *Gesamtkunstwerk* (Total Work of Art), a creative work that connects music, the visual arts, words, and movement into one experience, foreshadowed the achievement of Sergei Eisenstein (1898–1948) and other important filmmakers.

THE CYCLE OF *THE RING*

Most remarkably of all, his most complex work, *Der Ring des Nibelungen* (The Ring of the Nibelung, 1851–1874), can be seen as a diagnosis of the flaw at the heart of industrial society: the corrupting influence of power and money. This tetralogy (made up of four separate operas) is in many respects the climax of Romanticism, with its gods, giants, and magic dragon. Yet, as productions in the 21st century continue to reveal, by drawing on the world of myth supple-

Beckman, *Richard Wagner at home in Bayreuth.* 1880. Wagner's wife, Cosima, sits on the left, beneath her portrait. On the right are her father, the composer Franz Liszt, and the philosopher Friedrich Nietzsche. Behind Cosima, on the floor, is a sketch for the stage setting for Act One of *Parsifal*, Wagner's last stage work, which he was composing at the time; Bayreuth staged the first performance in 1882.

mented by acute psychological insight, it also makes a powerful commentary on the development, and eventual crisis in 1914, of European civilization.

Even in his own lifetime, Wagner aroused enormous controversy. Today his music continues to divide opinion between those for whom a performance of his greatest works provides a supreme aesthetic experience and those who find them long and bombastic. Yet there can be little debate over his influence on Western culture, for better or worse. Many subsequent composers followed him, many reacted against him, but few ignored him. His work was an inspiration to the French poet Charles Baudelaire (1821–1867) and the Symbolist poetic movement, which arose from Baudelaire's writings at the turn of the 20th century. More generally, by raising the importance of the arts to a level where they acquired an almost "sacred" function, he revolutionized aesthetic attitudes. The theater he had built at Bayreuth, in Germany, for the staging of his works soon became known to friends and foes alike as the "Temple on the Green Hill." Finally, in showing the power of mythic symbols to express universals, he anticipated much important 20th-century thought.

PHILOSOPHERS OF INSTINCT AND LIFE: NIETZSCHE, BERGSON, AND FREUD

Among Wagner's most passionate admirers in the 1860s was the German philosopher Friedrich Nietzsche (1844–1900). A brilliant Classical scholar, he heralded Wagner's works as the first since the time of the Greeks to develop a philosophy of culture based on tragedy. In 1876, however, he abruptly reversed his opinion and rejected Wagner and the idea of aesthetic redemption. The romantic illusions of art, Wagner's in particular, contributed to a mood of human weakness and self-deception, which would lead to a crisis in European civilization. Only strong, free spirits would survive the inevitable collapse, with its basic message that "God is dead."

Nietzsche expanded his vision of a new world order in the remaining years of his active life. Civilization, he claimed, is nothing more than a collective fantasy. Religion, morality, the arts, even science, are all ways of distracting attention from reality, which lies in the "will to power." Only those who reject all moral restraints, and use their unbridled energy in their "will to power," can win independence. An individual who rejects all illusions in a free assertion of the will can establish a new order of nobility and goodness. Such a person would be an *Übermensch* (Superman). The most poetic description of these new humans appears in *Also sprach Zarathustra* (Thus Spoke Zarathustra, 1883–1892). In the process of the emergence of a new race of Supermen, all the weak and helpless should be cast aside, together with Judaism and Christianity, which traditionally protect the downtrodden.

Nietzsche's profound and original analysis of the crisis in Western culture proved increasingly influential as his ominous predictions seemed to be coming true. The rise of Fascism and Nazism in the 1920s was explained by some as the realization of his ideas. It is true that Nietzsche despised militarism and nationalism as much as he did democracy or equality. In any case, his concept of the new world in which his Supermen would live seems poetic at best, and often shadowy. Yet the anger he expressed toward contemporary society, and the ruthlessness with which he contemplated the tearing down of all barriers, provided a dangerously heady brew. Nietzsche may be more prophet than instigator of 20th-century dictatorships and racial persecution, but a distorted version of his concepts served to fuel them.

HENRI BERGSON
No less original are the writings of Henri Bergson (1859–1941), one of the most influential intellectual forces in the early 20th century. Bergson urged a move from reason and abstraction to the subjective, and to a kind of inner reflection he called "intuition." This attitude required, in turn, a new attitude toward time, which was not merely quantifiable in terms of physics but became "experienced duration." Unlike Nietzsche, Bergson esteemed the creative process highly. In *Creative Evolution* (1907), he describes it as the expression of an *élan vital* (vital impulse). Nor did he reject the value of religion and morality, although he distinguished between "closed," or formal, elements and "open," or spiritual, ones.

Bergson's overall contribution to the intellectual life of his time was to free it of an excessive dependence on intellectualism and rationalism. Furthermore, the Existentialist philosophers of the later 20th century (see Topic 92) built their notions of the self providing its own sense (and justification) on Bergson's emphasis of the dynamic power of the subconscious. Contemporary authors were also quick to exploit the literary device of recording the stream-of-consciousness thought processes of their characters. Among the most successful were Marcel Proust (1871–1922), James Joyce (1882–1941), and Virginia Woolf (1882–1941).

FREUD AND PSYCHOANALYSIS
Nietzsche addressed himself to the political ills of European culture, and Bergson was concerned with providing the means of intellectual renewal. The Viennese physician Sigmund Freud (1856–1939) sought to understand nothing less than the human subconscious and unconscious. In the process he developed ideas that have revolutionized the way humans see themselves and their relationships with others. His theories remain controversial, and some of his successors challenged specific points of interpretation while accepting the general direction of his research. Nonetheless, Freud probably played a larger part in the formation of the characteristically 20th-century Western view of human existence than any other single individual.

Regardless of the accuracy of his analyses, Freud was one of the first figures to write frankly and explicitly about human sexual behavior, discussing it in clinical and not moral terms. At a time when society in general preferred to ignore open discussion of sex, Freud openly claimed that all individuals were born with a strong sexual identity, with genital, anal, and oral drives. These components, however, had no inherent gender identity. The quality of masculinity or femininity was acquired during childhood, as a result of specific experiences, in particular those involving the relationship with parents. Freud described the most powerful of these in terms of the Greek myth of Oedipus. Children are aware of parental power to block their sexual functioning; in the act of rejecting this power, they achieve a "normal" gender identity.

In a society where the family was conventionally regarded as a bastion against worldly vice, Freud taught that family relationships based on incest were at the root of the human psyche and were often the cause of emotional disturbance. Nor was sex simply an anatomical function because it was strongly affected by psychological and cultural factors. The challenge to traditional middle-class attitudes could hardly have been stronger.

Yet even more shocking for many of his contemporaries was Freud's claim that society's repression of women's sexual drives was responsible for many cases of female "hysteria." Far from being a sign of weakness or sickness, the symptoms of women prone to fits or fainting attacks were caused by abnormal sexual development. Whatever the accuracy of his diagnosis, in making this claim Freud broke new ground. He demonstrated that women's sexual drive is equally as powerful—and potentially as fulfilling or destructive—as that of men.

Freud was cautious in exploring some of the implications of his insights. Although he portrayed women as trapped by the conventions of society, he approved of their maintaining a passive domestic role to offset the more aggressive male function. As for homosexuality, he believed that although all children pass through a homoerotic phase, "normal" children emerge from it. His contemporary, Havelock Ellis (1859–1939), by contrast saw homosexuality as merely another form of human sexual behavior. Freud's subsequent work continued his research into the nature of the human subconscious by studying various forms of neurosis and the significance of dreams. In doing so, he established methods of psychoanalysis that subsequently led to the foundation of a variety of analytical techniques. At the end of his career he wrote *The Future of an Illusion* (1927) and *Civilization and Its Discontents* (1930), two magisterial works that offered a broad analysis of modern culture.

The achievement of founding the new and important discipline of psychoanalysis was outstanding enough, but Freud's contribution to the modern world goes much further. Ever since his time, it has been impossible to ignore those aspects of human behavior that cannot be explained by reason. Furthermore, his demonstration of the existence of deeply buried forces in the human personality, capable of

both dynamic and destructive acts, was confirmed by the carnage of two world wars.

VARIETIES OF LITERARY EXPERIENCE: REALISM AND SYMBOLISM

Writers throughout Europe continued to produce realistic novels in the tradition firmly established earlier in the 19th century by Flaubert and Dickens (see Topic 72). With increasing social and political tensions, however, the treatment of the issues of the day became more polemical.

The French writer Émile Zola (1840–1902) set out to dissect society in order to understand its workings, comparing the novelist's "enquiries" with the experiments of a scientist. Zola believed that individual lives were principally shaped by heredity and environment. As a result, many of his characters are destroyed by forces of nature that they are seemingly powerless to control, and Zola's work is often called, in fact, naturalistic rather than realistic.

His best novels deal with specific social ills: alcoholism in *The Dram Shop* (1877), prostitution in *Nana* (1880), and industrial exploitation in *Germinal* (1885). The brutal, often lurid evocation of life at its most grim horrified many of his readers and led to accusations of distortion and pornography. Zola made his own accusations when, in 1898, he became one of the antigovernment forces in the Dreyfus Affair, wading into the fray at considerable risk to himself (see Topic 73). In a short but powerfully worded pamphlet, *J'accuse!* (I Accuse, 1898), he attacked the army's handling of the case and rallied liberal and intellectual support on Dreyfus's side.

Whereas Zola's bleak world contains shafts of hope, the novels of Thomas Hardy (1840–1928) offer a picture of unrelieved despair, in which one character after another is broken on the wheel of an unrelenting fate. The background of most of his stories is English country life. He actually invented a county, "Wessex" (bearing a close resemblance to the English West Country county of Dorset), to provide their realistic setting.

Hardy wrote at a time when industrial progress had wrecked traditional agricultural life, and he saw modern efficiency as a profoundly destructive force. Yet for all his nostalgia at the passing of a way of life, he showed the confining conventions of rural existence to be no less devastating. The heroine of *Tess of the D'Urbervilles* (1891) is destroyed by a rigid code of social behavior that ends with her execution (by hanging) at the hands of a self-righteous society. In his last novel, *Jude the Obscure* (1896), the chief character sees every one of his attempts to emerge from obscurity relentlessly frustrated by the workings of destiny. Hardy has sometimes been criticized for his uncompromising pessimism, an angry man shaking his fist at an indifferent Creator. Yet the hopeless tone of his works is tempered by their passionate and sensitive concern for the sufferings of humanity.

The novels of Mrs. Humphry Ward (1851–1920; her real name was Mary Augusta Arnold) present a much more optimistic view of contemporary society, albeit one that reflected her own comfortable background. Coming from a well-to-do family, she actively campaigned against the feminist movement. Like Hardy's, her books contain realistic and well-drawn accounts of agricultural life, as well as urban settings. One of their recurring themes is the nature of religion, reflecting contemporary doubts about the meaning of Christianity. In *Robert Elsmere* (1888), a young clergyman loses his faith in the divinity of Jesus, leaves the church, and devotes himself to helping the poor in the slums of London's East End. In addition to producing a stream of highly successful books, Mrs. Ward devoted considerable time to her own charitable activities.

The primitive, brooding world of Grazia Deledda (1871–1936) is a far cry from the intellectual doubts of cultivated Londoners. Deledda was born and grew up in Sardinia, and most of her books and stories are set in the island's wild landscape. They describe the struggles of inarticulate peasant folk to surmount the obstacles provided by nature and destiny. In her best books, which include *Ceneri* (Ashes, 1904), she offers a lyrical picture of the gaunt beauty of her island, while conveying the harsh lives of its inhabitants.

Germany's leading novelist of the age was Theodore Fontane (1819–1898), who brought to his fiction a lifetime's experience in many spheres: He served as a war correspondent in the Franco-Prussian War of 1870, had a career in the Prussian civil service, and was a businessman. His masterpiece was *Vor dem Sturm* (Before the Storm, 1878), which describes conditions—real and psychological—in Prussia in 1812–1813, the years marked by Napoleon's collapse and defeat. *Effi Briest* (1895) provides a sensitive and complex picture of a 19th-century loveless marriage. Effi's husband, a minor Prussian aristocrat, feels compelled to fight a duel with his wife's long-abandoned lover not because of jealousy or personal anger, but because of his "social conscience."

THE SYMBOLISTS

At the opposite extreme from these realistic writers, the **Symbolists** aimed to use poetry as a means of escaping from reality. In often difficult and obscure verse, they endowed words with a rich, magic quality that transcends their mundane significance.

The Symbolist movement was born in France in the early 1870s. Among the small group of writers groping for new forms of expression was Arthur Rimbaud (1854–1891), who claimed that a poet should sharpen his perceptions by undergoing every kind of experience, and then transmit what he perceived without any conscious control. In poetic terms this meant abandoning traditional notions of rhyme and meter. Rimbaud called his collection of passages entitled *Les Illuminations* (Illuminations; written 1872–1873, published 1886) "prose poems."

Rimbaud's own life was equally unconventional. Rebellious and violently anti-Christian, he set out to shock the bourgeois world of the Third Republic. At the time of writing *Les Illuminations*, he was in a relationship with a fellow poet, Paul Verlaine (1844–1896). After a bitter quarrel, in the course of which Verlaine shot Rimbaud in the wrist, the younger poet Rimbaud abandoned writing altogether. At the age of 19, he set off on a series of wanderings through Europe and the East, exploring, trading, and gunrunning.

The leading German Symbolist poet, Stefan George (1868–1933), was associated for a while with Baudelaire, Verlaine, and other writers in Paris, and with the Pre-Raphaelite group in London. In 1890, claiming to despise the decadence of his age, he withdrew to Munich, where he lived among a circle of admiring disciples, self-consciously dedicated to a life of the spirit. His attacks on materialism and naturalism dominated German intellectual debate, while in his lyric poems he sought to revitalize German poetry by the use of classicism.

The Belgian Maurice Maeterlinck (1862–1949) was one of the few dramatists to write successful Symbolist plays. They involve legend, allegory, and fairytale to create a sense of mystery and brooding; their characters are passive victims of nameless, unseen forces. The best known, *Pelleas et Melisande* (1892), which was turned into an opera by Debussy, takes place in a kind of dream world, filled with mysterious silences and symbolic events, in which even the characters do not know what is real. In one scene, a flock of sheep being led unknowingly to the slaughter symbolizes the helplessness of the human condition in the face of fate.

IMPRESSIONISM, POSTIMPRESSIONISM, AND EXPRESSIONISM

The restless search for new forms of expression in the visual arts produced a flurry of styles in rapid succession: Impressionism, Postimpressionism, and Expressionism. The burst of "isms" culminated in the birth of Cubism and Futurism just before World War I, and the complete overturning of traditional ways of painting.

Just as Rimbaud tried to communicate experience directly, without shaping it, the **Impressionists** (the name was derisively applied to them by an unenthusiastic critic) sought to give a literal impression of light and color. Avoiding any kind of organized form, and hoping to paint without interpreting their subject, they tried to reproduce the overall visual impact of what they saw. Thus, when Claude Monet (1840–1926) painted a pool with water lilies, he was concerned to record glowing colors and reflecting lights, rather than an actual pond with real flowers.

Archivo Inconografico, S. A./CORBIS

Monet, *Nympheas (Water Lilies)*. 1920–1921. 6 feet 6 inches by 19 feet 7 inches (1.98 by 5.97 m). This is one of a series of paintings Monet produced in the garden of his villa at Giverny, outside Paris. The artist creates no formal or intellectual composition but uses very light and fluid brushstrokes to convey the "impression" of what he sees—plants, water, and, above all, light.

Cincinnati Art Museum (John J. Emery Endowment, 1928)

Cassatt, *Mother and Child,* c. 1889. 29 by 23½ inches (74 by 60 cm). By turning the mother's face away from the viewer, the artist concentrates attention on the child. Mary Cassatt, born in Allegheny City, Pennsylvania, came to Paris in 1866, where her work was included in some of the early Impressionist exhibitions.

Van Gogh, *The Starry Night*. 1889. 29 by 36¼ inches (73.7 by 92.1 cm). The artist creates the impression of irresistible movement by his use of line and shape. The combination of vertical spirals in the cypress trees and the horizontal spirals in the sky produces a sense of rushing speed. The result is a mood of desperate ecstasy. Van Gogh committed suicide the following year at the age of 37.

Several of the leading Impressionist painters were women. The American Mary Cassatt (1844–1926) settled in Paris to study with the Impressionists. Like her close friend Edgar Degas (1834–1917), she preferred to paint spontaneous scenes from daily life. Her unsentimental depictions of mothers and children, like Degas' scenes of women bathing, show their subjects caught unawares, in a moment of intimacy.

POSTIMPRESSIONISM
Although many artists continued to work in the Impressionist style—Monet used it right up to his death— the restless spirit of the times drove other painters to find new approaches. The Postimpressionists are so called because they all rejected Impressionism, but they have little else in common. The range of Postimpressionist artists emerges most vividly in the work of the two greatest: Paul Cézanne (1839–1906) and Vincent van Gogh (1853–1890). Cézanne's monumental landscapes and ordered still lifes achieve an abstract sense of balance that derives from their use of geometric forms. He advised his fellow painters to "treat Nature in terms of its geometrical

shapes, the sphere, the cylinder, and the cone." At the opposite emotional extreme, van Gogh depicted the "terrible passions of humanity," in works filled with swirling lines and violent color contrasts.

EXPRESSIONISM
Although the emotional intensity typical of van Gogh's work was partly a result of his own tragic life, it also reflected the uneasy climate of the times. Another school of painting developed in the first decade of the 20th century, which pushed the sense of explosiveness even further. The **Expressionists,** who were mainly German, used their art to express strong emotions. The tone of the Expressionist movement had been set at the end of the 19th century by the Norwegian Edvard Munch (1863–1944). Munch said of his famous and horrifying painting *The Scream,* "I hear the scream in nature." His German successors used similarly bold images to capture the expression of extreme states of mind, often those of loneliness and alienation. The alarming, even hysterical mood of their paintings reflects all too clearly the mood of the age.

Munch, *The Scream*. 1893. 35½ inches by 28¼ inches (91 by 74 cm). This is perhaps the key work of the Expressionist movement. Munch once said: "I hear the scream in nature," and in his painting the anguish of the human figure seems to be echoed by the entire world around him. The lurid colors heighten the sense of morbid tension.

THE MODERNIST REVOLT: CUBISM, FUTURISM, AND ATONALITY

During the years from 1908 to 1914, the hectic speed of cultural change reached a breakneck pace. A mere catalogue of some of the main events conveys the sense of upheaval. In 1908, the Cubist paintings of Pablo Picasso and Georges Braque challenged centuries of pictorial conventions, and Schoenberg was the first composer for 300 years to write music with no tonal center. In 1910, the Futurist works of Umberto Boccioni attempted to combine time and space, and Wassily Kandinsky produced the first purely abstract work of art. In 1913, the first volume of Marcel Proust's stream-of-consciousness novel appeared, and a year later Joyce, who revolutionized the use of language in his later books, published his first prose work.

CUBISM

If Cézanne had laid the foundations for a new way of painting, two young artists working in Paris between 1908 and 1914 built on them to create **Cubism.** The French Georges Braque (1882–1963) and his Spanish fellow artist Pablo Picasso (1881–1973) challenged the idea, universal since the Renaissance, that works painted on a two-dimensional surface should try to show three dimensions. They aban-

Braque, *Violin and Palette*. 1909–1910. 36⅛ inches by 16⅛ inches (92 by 43 cm). In this classic Cubist painting, the artist depicts a violin with the front, sides, and back visible at the same time, on a single flat plane, without any sense of three dimensions. Cubist painters like Braque and Picasso painted familiar objects (the violin is perfectly recognizable as such) but used them to make abstract designs.

doned traditional perspective, and in a series of experimental canvasses tried to find new ways of seeing their subjects geometrically. In some of Picasso's early Cubist works, he used the entire surface of the painting as a geometric grid. The image to be depicted was then broken up into separate squares and located in various places. Braque developed the technique of simultaneously showing aspects of an object that could in reality be perceived only separately. In one well-known picture, he showed the front, back, and sides of a violin on a single plane.

THE FUTURIST MOVEMENT

In Italy, the Modernist revolt in the arts took a dramatic form with the appearance of the Futurist movement. In their first manifesto (1909), the **Futurists** boldly rejected all traditional forms of culture. They turned instead to the cult of the machine and the technological future. Filippo T. Marinetti (1876–1944), its founder, proclaimed that "a roaring automobile, which runs like a machine-gun, is more beautiful than the Winged Victory of Samothrace. . . . We wish to glorify war."

Umberto Boccioni (1882–1916), the greatest of Futurist artists, developed an aesthetic theory called Dynamism that sought to express energy in terms of motion and light. His *Unique Forms of Continuity in Space* (1913) seeks to convey a sense of accelerating movement in sculpture. Boccioni and his fellow Futurists glorified violence and war as means of overthrowing established values, and they greeted the coming of World War I with great nationalist enthusiasm. The most original phase of Futurism ended with the death of many of its leading exponents in the course of fighting.

ATONALITY IN MUSIC

Many composers of the turn of the 20th century followed Wagner's example in their increasingly free attitude toward conventional rules of harmony. The Frenchman Claude Debussy (1862–1918) wrote music that drifts from key to key, with frequent dissonances. His abandonment of traditional forms for shifting sound pictures led his contemporaries to compare his works to Impressionist paintings, while his opera *Pelleas et Melisande* (1902), based on Maeterlinck's play, allied him for a while with the Symbolists.

Yet even Debussy's shimmering, evanescent works do not represent a dramatic break with the past. The decisive move came in 1908, when the Austrian Arnold Schoenberg (1874–1951) wrote his *Three Piano Pieces*, Op. 11. Schoenberg was convinced that the traditional system of harmony, which had been used in Western music for 300 years, had lost its value. Pursuing Wagner's experiments to their ultimate conclusion, he wrote piano pieces that were "atonal"—that avoided any sense of a fixed tonal center, or key.

In the period immediately preceding World War I, Schoenberg's free atonal works eerily echo the instability and morbidity of the times. His musical composition, *Pierrot Lunaire* (1912), employing texts of symbolist poems, uses a cross between song and speech to create an Expressionist mood of macabre fantasy. Schoenberg also produced several Expressionist paintings. In the 1920s, Schoenberg and his followers developed new ways of organizing their musical material to replace those that they had rejected. The most important was the famous 12-tone system, or serialism.

Critics reviled Schoenberg's atonality as a "perversion." His great contemporary Igor Stravinsky (1882–1971) met with even less sympathy. When in 1913 Stravinsky's ballet *Le Sacre du Printemps* (The Rite of Spring) was first performed in Paris, the composer was accused of "the destruction of music as an art." Throughout his long career, Stravinsky continued to write in an astonishing variety of styles, many of which used a version of traditional harmony; years later he finally adopted serialism. His revolutionary contribution to music lay in his new approach to rhythm. In *Le Sacre*, Stravinsky replaced the more or less regular beat of conventional music with a combination of constantly fluctuating rhythmical patterns. The sense of barbaric energy, whipped up by a vast orchestra, drove its first hearers, sophisticated Parisians though many of them were, to unprecedented scenes of shouting and stamping.

DEVELOPMENTS IN LITERATURE

The Modernist movement in literature was to emerge at the end of World War I, but its character was already established. In 1913, the French novelist Marcel Proust (1871–1922) published the first volume of his seven-part work *À la recherche du temps perdu* (Remembrance of Things Past; the work was written between 1907 and 1919, and published between 1913 and 1927). Semiautobiographical, Proust's work explores the nature of time and memory and the role of the subconscious. Its narrator sets out to recreate his past life. In the process, he realizes that all past experiences remain within us but can be called up again either by the perceptions of our senses or by the agency of art. Thus, for all the futility of individual human effort, art can recreate the past and transcend death.

The Irish writer James Joyce (1882–1941) took the stream-of-consciousness style used by Proust's narrator to even greater lengths. His first work of fiction, *Dubliners*, appeared in 1914. It sets out many of the themes that were to dominate his later books: the need to escape one's environment (in this case Dublin), the loss of illusions, or the acknowledgment of failure. Although *Dubliners* includes realistic treatments of the lower-middle-class setting, it also foreshadows the subtlety of Joyce's later work. In *Ulysses*, begun at the beginning of the war and finished in 1922, he used a stream-of-consciousness technique to describe a single day in the lives of two Dublin men. The resultant blend of fantasy, surrealism, and pastiche, filled with complex wordplay, proved to be one of the 20th century's most influential novels.

SCIENCE FROM CERTAINTY TO RELATIVITY

The astonishing technological advances of the late 19th century were accompanied by new discoveries in all branches of science, especially in physics. These developments, which profoundly altered human perceptions of the nature of the physical world, may have seemed theoretical and of little relevance to everyday life. Yet discoveries made shortly after 1900 eventually ushered in the atomic age.

Virtually all scientists working at the end of the 19th century accepted the view that matter consisted of indivisible atoms that responded to fixed natural laws, which were observed by Sir Isaac Newton (1642–1727) in the 17th century. According to Newton, absolute time passed uniformly, and absolute space was immovable—both "were unrelated to any outward circumstances."

Yet classical physics failed to account for certain observations. In 1895 the German physicist Wilhelm Roentgen (1845–1923) discovered X-rays when he observed the highly energetic, invisible electromagnetic radiation emitted by certain wavelengths. These rays produced a form of energy capable of penetrating opaque materials. Other scientists discovered similar rays produced by uranium. The British physicist Ernest Rutherford (1871–1937) built on this work to develop a theory of radioactivity. He argued that radiation was caused when atoms of radioactive substances disintegrated. In 1911, Rutherford proposed his nuclear theory of the atom and the potential energy within it.

To explain the phenomenon of radioactivity, the German physicist Max Planck (1858–1947) developed in the early years of the 20th century his quantum theory. According to this theory, energy is not infinitely subdivisible but exists as a series of discrete bundles, or quanta. In light of this discovery, Newton's laws of motion as graduated and continuous could not be correct.

EINSTEIN AND RELATIVITY

The most shattering theoretical advances in physics were made by the German physicist Albert Einstein (1879–1955). His theory of relativity, which was first formulated in 1905, was to have far more general consequences and represented an even more decisive break with past ideas of stability. Because everything in our universe is in motion, any observation will be affected by the observer's relative position. Thus space and time, far from being uniform, are relative. The change of relative position governs the measurement of space; the duration of movement, in the space crossed in that spatial change, governs the measurement of time. All energy and matter are related in this space-time continuum.

The notion that it is not possible to distinguish between space and time, or between matter and energy, was startling enough. Einstein's famous equation, $E = mc^2$, went on to prove the relationship between mass (m), energy (E), and the speed of light (c). This theory played a vital part in the development of nuclear physics because it explained the nature of nuclear energy.

Putting the Modernist Revolution in Perspective

Einstein's demonstration of the relativity of forces that had always been regarded as unchanging was a major blow to the idea of a stable universe. Intensifying challenge to the established political order, struggles for wide-ranging social reform, the shattering of centuries of artistic traditions—all these were now joined by a view of the material world based on perpetual change. By 1914, European society and culture were on the brink of the most complete and wrenching shift of all.

Questions for Further Study

1. In what ways did art and literature at the turn of the 20th century reflect the changing role of women?
2. How did the ideas of Freud and Einstein revolutionize Western culture?
3. What similarities are there in developments in music, painting, and literature in the early years of the 20th century? How are they linked with parallel historical events?

Suggestions for Further Reading

Antliff, Mark. *Cultural Politics and the Parisian Avant-Garde*. Princeton, NJ, 1993.

Broude, N. *Impressionism: A Feminist Reading*. New York, 1991.

Calder, N. *Einstein's Universe*. New York, 1980.

Fried, M. *Manet's Modernism, or, The Face of Painting in the 1860s*. Chicago, 1996.

Gay, P. *Freud: A Life for Our Times*. New York, 1988.

Golding, J. *Cubism: A History and an Analysis*. Cambridge, MA, 1988.

Lipton, E. *Looking into Degas: Uneasy Images of Women and Modern Life*. Berkeley, CA, 1986.

Miller, Arthur I. *Einstein, Picasso: Space, Time, and the Beauty that Causes Havoc*. New York, 2001.

Richardson, J. *Pablo Picasso*. Vols. I, II. New York, 1991, 1996.

Robb, Graham. *Rimbaud*. New York, 2000.

Smith, Paul. *Impressionism: Beneath the Surface*. New York, 1995.

Tadier, J-Y. *Marcel Proust: A Life*. New York, 2000.

Tanner, Michael. *Wagner*. New York, 1996.

InfoTrac College Edition

Enter the search term *Nietzsche* using Key Terms.

Enter the search term *Sigmund Freud* using Key Terms.

PART VIII

THE CONTEMPORARY ERA

Conflict, doubt, and pessimism dominated the mood of much of the 20th century. The political and diplomatic crises of the early 20th century reinforced the collapse of the old moral order—the first half of the 20th century was domi-

nated by two gigantic military conflicts. The Great War of 1914–1918 wreaked unimaginable destruction and death on the European world, shattering permanently the notion of Western superiority and dominance. In its wake, as Europeans experi-

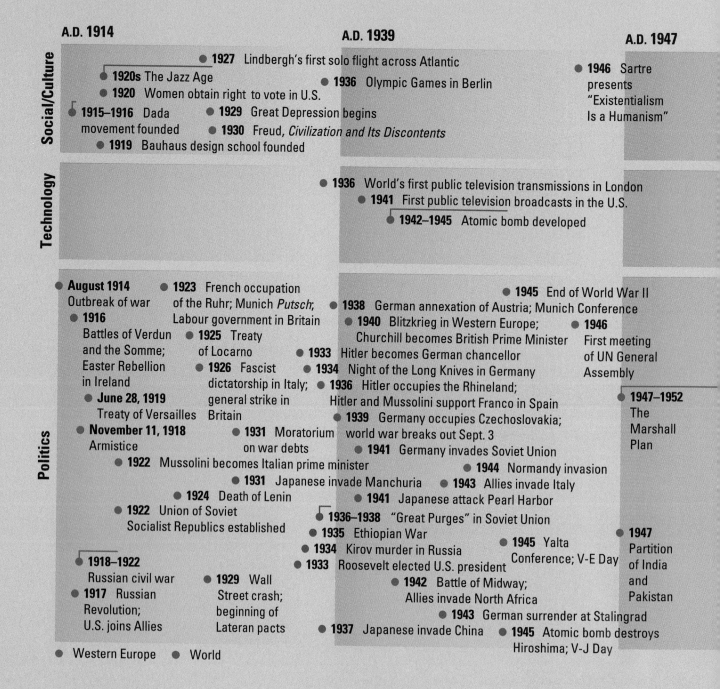

A.D. 1914   **A.D. 1939**   **A.D. 1947**

Social/Culture

- **1927** Lindbergh's first solo flight across Atlantic
- **1920s** The Jazz Age
- **1920** Women obtain right to vote in U.S.
- **1936** Olympic Games in Berlin
- **1915–1916** Dada movement founded
- **1929** Great Depression begins
- **1930** Freud, *Civilization and Its Discontents*
- **1919** Bauhaus design school founded
- **1946** Sartre presents "Existentialism Is a Humanism"

Technology

- **1936** World's first public television transmissions in London
- **1941** First public television broadcasts in the U.S.
- **1942–1945** Atomic bomb developed

Politics

- **August 1914** Outbreak of war
- **1916** Battles of Verdun and the Somme; Easter Rebellion in Ireland
- **June 28, 1919** Treaty of Versailles
- **November 11, 1918** Armistice
- **1922** Mussolini becomes Italian prime minister
- **1924** Death of Lenin
- **1922** Union of Soviet Socialist Republics established
- **1918–1922** Russian civil war
- **1917** Russian Revolution; U.S. joins Allies

- **1923** French occupation of the Ruhr; Munich *Putsch*; Labour government in Britain
- **1925** Treaty of Locarno
- **1926** Fascist dictatorship in Italy; general strike in Britain
- **1931** Moratorium on war debts
- **1931** Japanese invade Manchuria
- **1929** Wall Street crash; beginning of Lateran pacts

- **1938** German annexation of Austria; Munich Conference
- **1940** Blitzkrieg in Western Europe; Churchill becomes British Prime Minister
- **1933** Hitler becomes German chancellor
- **1934** Night of the Long Knives in Germany
- **1936** Hitler occupies the Rhineland; Hitler and Mussolini support Franco in Spain
- **1939** Germany occupies Czechoslovakia; world war breaks out Sept. 3
- **1941** Germany invades Soviet Union
- **1944** Normandy invasion
- **1943** Allies invade Italy
- **1941** Japanese attack Pearl Harbor
- **1936–1938** "Great Purges" in Soviet Union
- **1935** Ethiopian War
- **1934** Kirov murder in Russia
- **1933** Roosevelt elected U.S. president
- **1942** Battle of Midway; Allies invade North Africa
- **1943** German surrender at Stalingrad
- **1937** Japanese invade China

- **1945** End of World War II
- **1946** First meeting of UN General Assembly
- **1947–1952** The Marshall Plan
- **1945** Yalta Conference; V-E Day
- **1947** Partition of India and Pakistan
- **1945** Atomic bomb destroys Hiroshima; V-J Day

● Western Europe   ● World

mented with new forms of social and cultural energy, they also invented new forms of political control that in their worst manifestations produced totalitarian regimes in the Soviet Union as well as in Fascist Italy and Nazi Germany. The economic chaos of the Great Depression not only helped bring the new totalitarian movements to power, but also threw Western society into deep crisis.

The ultimate consequence of the totalitarian nightmare was World War II (1939–1945), in which

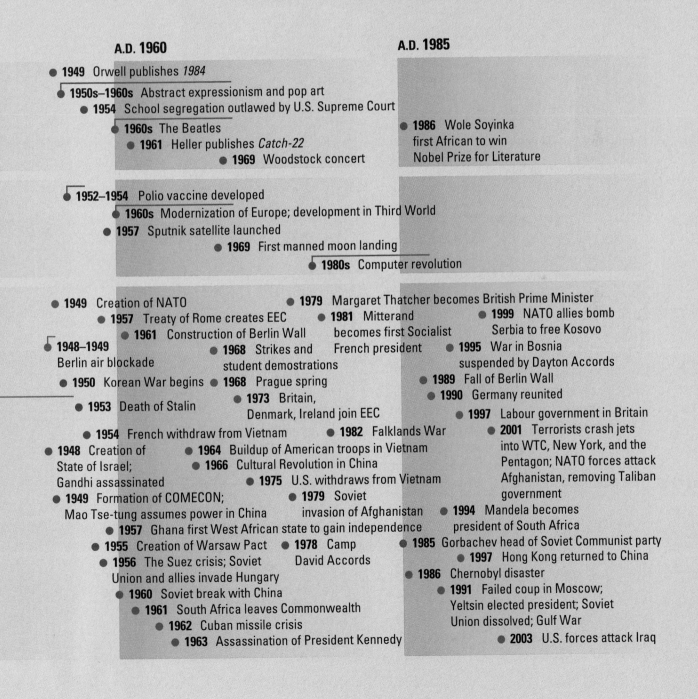

A.D. 1960

A.D. 1985

● **1949** Orwell publishes *1984*

● **1950s–1960s** Abstract expressionism and pop art

● **1954** School segregation outlawed by U.S. Supreme Court

● **1960s** The Beatles

● **1961** Heller publishes *Catch-22*

● **1969** Woodstock concert

● **1986** Wole Soyinka first African to win Nobel Prize for Literature

● **1952–1954** Polio vaccine developed

● **1960s** Modernization of Europe; development in Third World

● **1957** Sputnik satellite launched

● **1969** First manned moon landing

● **1980s** Computer revolution

● **1949** Creation of NATO

● **1957** Treaty of Rome creates EEC

● **1961** Construction of Berlin Wall

● **1948–1949** Berlin air blockade

● **1950** Korean War begins

● **1953** Death of Stalin

● **1954** French withdraw from Vietnam

● **1948** Creation of State of Israel; Gandhi assassinated

● **1949** Formation of COMECON; Mao Tse-tung assumes power in China

● **1957** Ghana first West African state to gain independence

● **1955** Creation of Warsaw Pact

● **1956** The Suez crisis; Soviet Union and allies invade Hungary

● **1960** Soviet break with China

● **1961** South Africa leaves Commonwealth

● **1962** Cuban missile crisis

● **1963** Assassination of President Kennedy

● **1979** Margaret Thatcher becomes British Prime Minister

● **1981** Mitterand becomes first Socialist French president

● **1968** Strikes and student demostrations

● **1968** Prague spring

● **1973** Britain, Denmark, Ireland join EEC

● **1982** Falklands War

● **1964** Buildup of American troops in Vietnam

● **1966** Cultural Revolution in China

● **1975** U.S. withdraws from Vietnam

● **1979** Soviet invasion of Afghanistan

● **1978** Camp David Accords

● **1999** NATO allies bomb Serbia to free Kosovo

● **1995** War in Bosnia suspended by Dayton Accords

● **1989** Fall of Berlin Wall

● **1990** Germany reunited

● **1997** Labour government in Britain

● **2001** Terrorists crash jets into WTC, New York, and the Pentagon; NATO forces attack Afghanistan, removing Taliban government

● **1994** Mandela becomes president of South Africa

● **1985** Gorbachev head of Soviet Communist party

● **1997** Hong Kong returned to China

● **1986** Chernobyl disaster

● **1991** Failed coup in Moscow; Yeltsin elected president; Soviet Union dissolved; Gulf War

● **2003** U.S. forces attack Iraq

the struggle for mastery assumed more horrific proportions than in the Great War, reaching its nadir in the racial policies of the Nazi dictatorship and the Holocaust. This second conflict was a truly global one, and its implications for the future were enormous.

The last half of the 20th century in Europe saw the passage from the grim certainties of the Cold War to the increasing unpredictability of its final decade. The fall of the Berlin Wall in 1989 and the collapse of the Soviet Union brought to an end a period in which Europe was firmly divided into two blocs. Western Europe, much of which emerged shattered from World War II, re-

built its cities and the institutions of its sovereign states with help from the Marshall Plan organized by the United States. The Western European nations based their transatlantic alliances on the North Atlantic Treaty Organization (NATO). At the same time, they sought a closer form of unity among themselves by forming the European Economic Community (EEC), intended to provide an economic union with a single currency, the Euro, which might eventually lead to forms of political cooperation.

Meanwhile, in Eastern Europe, the Soviet Union led the postwar recovery, in the process imposing client regimes. The defensive organization uniting the Soviet Union and the countries of Eastern Europe was the Warsaw Pact. Yugoslavia, the only significant East European country to defy Stalin and leave the Soviet bloc, subsequently became one of the leading members of a third bloc—that of the "nonaligned nations."

Relations between East and West were ultimately conditioned by each side's capability to wreak destruction on the other by use of atomic weapons. A series of crises, beginning with the Berlin Blockade of 1948, and continuing with Soviet invasions of Hungary and Czechoslovakia, saw the two blocs develop the art of "brinkmanship," with neither side finally willing to push the dispute to outright confrontation. Meanwhile, the United States was embroiled in a series of conflicts outside Europe. They included the Korean and Vietnam wars, and—in a clash that seemed to bring the world to the edge of nuclear war— the Cuban missile crisis.

By the end of the 20th century, in a world where technology and culture were ever more global, European history was inextricably linked with that of the rest of the globe. The original EEC membership of six grew to fifteen by 1997, with the possibility of adding Eastern European members by 2004. Problems dominating the end of the century included unemployment, increas-

ingly aging populations, terrorism, and the threat of ecological disasters. The collapse of the Soviet Union, and the future of its former members—most importantly Russia—raised new questions about the role Europe will play in the next century.

The nature of NATO, originally intended to counterbalance the Soviet bloc, underwent radical change with its invitation to, and eventual inclusion of, former members of that bloc: the Czech Republic, Hungary, and Poland. Other former Eastern European nations looked likely to join later. In the absence of UN agreement, NATO conducted the campaign to liberate Kosovo in 1999.

The terrorist attacks on the United States on September 11, 2001, added a further dimension to widespread alarm about international terrorism. General worldwide unity in the face of this threat was shaken by a further turn in the crisis in Iraq, where weapons inspections had been suspended since 1998. In November 2002, the Security council of the UN unanimously backed a resolution calling for the return of inspections, and over the following months the prospect of war against Iraq led by the United States and Britain led to divisions between the United States and other European countries, and to a split within Europe itself.

THE GREAT WAR

Today, historians refer to the events of 1914–1918 as World War I, but those who experienced the conflagration called it the Great War. At the time, there was nothing to compare with it. The last conflict that had engulfed all of Europe—the wars of Napoleon—had ended a century earlier. Thereafter, wars were localized or of short duration. In the Great War, the European battles were fought as far west as France, as far east as Russia, and as far south as Italy and the Balkans. Fighting also took place in Africa, the Middle East, and East Asia. Few expected the war to last more than a few months. Nevertheless, in all the belligerent countries, many idealistic young men enlisted with enthusiasm. "It's all great fun," the English poet Rupert Brooke (1885–1915) wrote to his family in the first winter of the war.

As the realities of the catastrophe into which Europe had stumbled were driven home, participants came to regard it with a bitter sense of irony. "Great" hardly described the horrors of the battlefield, the destruction of life and property, and the social and political upheavals caused by the fighting. The war burned itself deep into the human psyche, with consequences that made themselves felt for much of the rest of the 20th century.

The immediate cause of the Great War was a murder in a province of the Austro-Hungarian empire in June 1914. Monarchs and their ministers mismanaged the resulting diplomatic crisis, and in August the guns began firing. In another sense, however, the war was the culmination of historical developments, including nationalism, militarism, and imperialism. Decades of international tensions fed the roots of the 1914 crisis.

Europe's great powers aligned themselves into two military blocs: Britain, France, and Russia—the "Allies"—on one side, Germany and Austria-Hungary—the "Central Powers"—on the other. As the war unfolded, each side drew other states into its camp. The Central Powers fought a two-front war. On the Eastern front, they cut Russia off from vital supplies, and under the pressure of great losses and internal opposition, the tsarist autocracy finally collapsed in 1917. On the Western front, both sides became locked in the terrible stalemate of trench warfare. The entrance of the United States on the side of the Allies in 1917 brought about the collapse of the Central Powers and the end of the war.

The signing of the armistice of November 1918 ended the fighting, but the impact of the war continued to reverberate throughout the rest of the 20th century. Tens of millions of human beings had died. The effects on society of "total war," in which civilians played as vital a role as soldiers in the outcome, were first seen on the home front. Governments mobilized entire populations—men, women, and children—behind the war effort, reorganized national economies, and bolstered civilian morale as a vital military operation. Gender and class lines were blurred, family life reshaped, social values altered, and liberal ideals suspended.

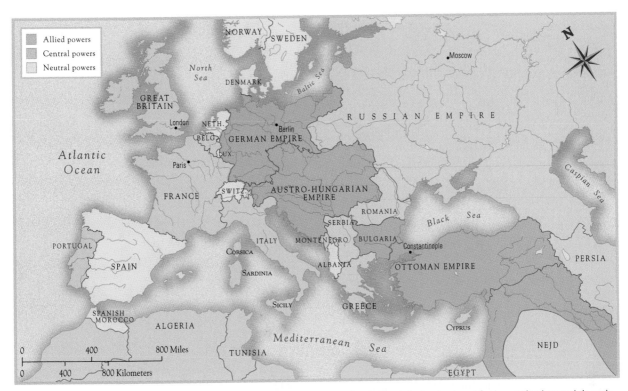

 Map 80.1 The European Alliances, 1914. The Scandinavian countries, Holland, Switzerland, and Spain remained neutral throughout the war. Spain, Sweden, and Switzerland did the same in World War II. Italy did not send troops before 1915. Turkey, an enthusiastic supporter of the Central Powers, saw defeat sweep away the remnants of the Ottoman Empire; it remained neutral for most of World War II. Albania had become an independent state in 1913, only to become swept up in the fighting and occupied by the Central Powers. Go to http://info.wadsworth.com/053461065X for an interactive version of this map.

THE ORIGINS OF THE FIRST WORLD WAR

Since the mid-19th century, technological developments had changed the way in which modern wars were fought, while the likelihood of war was enhanced by the growing political influence of military officers. Arms manufacturers, who derived economic benefits from hostilities, also influenced government policy.

MODERN WEAPONS AND MILITARY COMPETITION

During the last third of the 19th century, several factors contributed to a huge increase in armaments: the intense competition among the great powers for colonial territories, the rise of nationalist tensions in the Balkans, the hardening alliance systems, and repeated diplomatic crises.

Each major country had its own armaments manufacturers, most of which also sold weapons on the international market to all parties. Krupp, the German firm, and Armstrong-Whitworth, the British company, poured large sums into research and development and made large profits. Other industries often combined with armaments makers to influence defense programs. They backed nationalist and imperialist organizations that supported the arms race and, to-

gether with anti-foreign propaganda and the popular press, pressured politicians to vote for larger military budgets.

Military strategy continued to be based on the infantry soldier. By the 1870s, Britain was the only great power without a peacetime draft. When war broke out in August 1914, Russia's million-man army was the largest, followed by Germany with about 850,000, France with 700,000, and Austria-Hungary with 450,000; Britain, relying on naval superiority for defense, had only 250,000 men under arms. Strategists believed that reserve training would allow each of the great powers to mobilize a force more than five times the size of its standing army. During the war, the number of men actually brought under arms more than doubled these estimates—Russia eventually mobilized 12 million, Germany 11 million, France 8 million, and Britain and the British Dominions 9.5 million.

Sheer numbers themselves were not decisive because the quality of training and weaponry, military planning, transportation facilities, and industrial productivity all affected a country's ability to wage war. Most governments adopted the German practice of maintaining a permanent general staff, which was responsible for military strategy, training, and weapons development.

Handheld infantry weapons were greatly improved during the 19th century. By the 1870s most armies had substituted the breech-loading rifle for the muzzle-loading musket.

In the 1880s, the introduction of the magazine rifle permitted more rapid firing. But the most significant change came with the development of the machine gun, which fired several hundred rounds per minute. Its considerable weight—about 100 pounds—made it effective only when fixed in position, but the machine gun greatly enhanced defensive operations and, during World War I, caused enormous casualties.

Special alloys of hardened steel and the use of ferro-concrete enabled countries to build huge fortresses as protection against invasion, and even the most sophisticated technological advances in heavy weapons systems failed to undermine the effectiveness of such defenses. Siege howitzers could pound enemy positions and reduce cities to rubble from long distances, but after months of the heaviest artillery bombardment in history, fortresses such as Verdun did not fall to the enemy.

Other developments took place at sea, where Britain and Germany engaged in a feverish "naval race" that heightened tensions between them. With the passage of the Naval Defense Act in 1889, Britain aimed to make its fleet twice as large as the combined size of the two next biggest navies. The competition began when Admiral Alfred von Tirpitz (1849–1930) became German naval secretary in 1897. Tirpitz was an Anglophobe, and under his direction Germany passed a series of naval bills between 1898 and 1912 designed to build a battle fleet two-thirds the size of Britain's. Tirpitz's "risk theory" held that such a fleet would be so powerful that in the event of war Britain would not risk attempts to destroy it.

Britain responded to Germany with a massive naval buildup and the creation of a North Sea Fleet. In 1906, the British revolutionized naval warfare with the *Dreadnought*, a large, heavily armored, and highly maneuverable battleship. Driven by powerful turbine engines, it carried 12-inch guns that could strike targets many miles away. Despite these advantages, *Dreadnought*-class ships were by no means invincible—other countries copied the technology, and both torpedo boats and destroyers could sink even the *Dreadnought*. By 1914, heavy-oil engines and storage batteries made possible the building of submarine fleets that challenged conventional naval warfare.

The Germans did copy the *Dreadnought* idea, and by the eve of World War I had 18 such ships to Britain's 29. Germany's naval strength rose from seventh to second place. Berlin brushed aside proposals to limit naval construction, and British fears of German ambitions grew accordingly. Secretary of War Richard Haldane (1856–1928) went to Berlin in 1912 to seek an accommodation with Germany, but the mission proved unsuccessful. As a result, Britain and France then reached an important agreement: Britain concentrated its naval forces in the North Sea, France in the Mediterranean. Although no formal alliance was made, self-interest now bound the two nations as never before.

MILITARY STRATEGY AND THE SCHLIEFFEN PLAN

Despite the new weapons, military planners continued to employ strategies inspired by the theories of the Prussian General

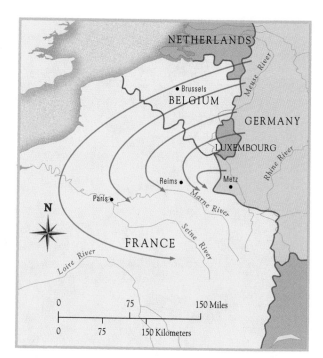

Map 80.2 The Schlieffen Plan. Schlieffen had drawn up the plan in 1905, to fight a hypothetical war against France and Russia; it assumed that both powers would not attack simultaneously, thereby allowing the Germans to defeat first the French and then the Russians. Already flawed, the plan was further weakened when it was modified by Moltke. After losing the first major battle of the Great War, in the valley of the River Marne in September 1914, Moltke was dismissed. Go to http://info.wadsworth.com/053461065X for an interactive version of this map.

Karl von Clausewitz (1780–1831), who advocated offensive operations designed to achieve victory with speed, mobility, and surprise. Based on accurate maps, railroad transportation, and precise timetables, such plans aimed at moving huge numbers of troops rapidly over large areas. The so-called Schlieffen Plan, developed by General Alfred von Schlieffen (1833–1913), chief of the German General Staff, was the most famous. Although his strategy anticipated that Germany would be at war with both Russia and France at the same time, Schlieffen thought principally in terms of how to defeat the French in the West. He devised his plan in 1905, while Russia was still reeling from its defeat by the Japanese and from domestic uprisings. He argued that since Russia, which was weak and disorganized, would require at least a month to mobilize its armies, Germany should concentrate on a quick victory against France, after which it could deal easily with Russia.

Schlieffen held that because French fortifications such as those at Verdun were too formidable, Germany's only alternative was to launch a surprise attack against France through the level terrain of the Low Countries. Keeping the Russians at bay in the East, two separate German armies would form a large pincer in the West, with one larger arm closing around the French from behind. Schlieffen's plan held several strategic risks: He banked on the assumption that Russia would not attack until its mobilization had been completed, that the Belgians would offer no serious resistance, and that the timing would go according to schedule. Furthermore, the German authorities believed that military needs would outweigh the political repercussions of violating Belgian neutrality. In 1906, von Schlieffen was succeeded by Count Helmuth Johannes von Moltke (1848–1916), the plodding and insecure nephew of the brilliant strategist who had executed Prussia's victories during the struggle for German unification. The younger Moltke so changed Schlieffen's original plan as to enhance the risks of disaster. He increased the strength of the left wing significantly, partly by weakening the Russian Front, and thereby changed the fundamental thrust of the assault.

The French, who had gained a sense of the Schlieffen Plan, developed their own "Plan XVII," which called for a holding action against the German armies in Belgium while attacking Germany with a superior force through Lorraine. The logic of "military necessity" made both the German and French generals overconfident. Strategies such as the Schlieffen Plan increased the chances of war because their success hinged on the ability of the general staffs to deploy millions of soldiers and a huge quantity of equipment on a war footing *before* the outbreak of hostilities—hence, while civilian authorities attempted to resolve diplomatic crises through negotiation, the military demanded immediate mobilization so as to be able to strike first.

Map 80.3 The Balkans, c. 1914. The Balkans saw the final retreat of an Ottoman occupying power from European soil. At the same time, however, tension between Serbia (spurred on by Russia) and Austria-Hungary—worsened by squabbling among the other Balkan powers—led to the assassination of Archduke Franz Ferdinand on June 28, 1914. Within weeks, Europe had plunged into war.

FROM CONFRONTATION TO CRISIS: THE COMING OF WAR

Between 1882 and 1914, countries chose membership in one of the two great alliance systems in order to gain a measure of security against their enemies. Thus Great Britain, France, and Russia were aligned in the Triple Entente, and Germany, Austria-Hungary, and Italy were grouped in the Triple Alliance. Yet the increasingly tense character of diplomatic relations, especially after 1905, produced the opposite effect. Based on the assumption that powerful alliances supported them, countries tended to be less cautious during international disputes. Such disputes restricted the maneuverability of the blocs as allies strove to demonstrate their support for each other. Thus the alternatives available to the great powers narrowed dangerously during international confrontations.

ASSASSINATION AT SARAJEVO

Relations between the Triple Alliance and the Entente deteriorated as one international face-off followed another. The Balkans, the scene of considerable turmoil as a result of the Bosnian crisis of 1908 and the wars of 1912–1913, proved to be the seedbed of the Great War because the clashes between Russia and Austria-Hungary destabilized the region (see Topic 74).

These forces clashed head-on at Sarajevo, the capital of the Austrian possession of Bosnia, in the summer of 1914.

On the morning of June 28, the Archduke Franz Ferdinand (1863–1914), heir to the Austro-Hungarian throne and nephew of Emperor Franz Josef, was shot and killed while riding through the streets of Sarajevo in an open car. His wife, the former Countess Sophie Chotek (1868–1914), was also killed. The royal couple was on an official tour of Bosnia, and at the moment of their death had been returning from a reception at the town hall.

Seven young men—five teenagers and two in their twenties—took part in the assassination conspiracy. A student named Gavrilo Princip (1895–1918) fired the fatal shots. All were members of a nationalist organization called "Young Bosnia." They had made Franz Ferdinand their target because he was known to favor autonomy for the Slavs of the empire, much as the Magyars enjoyed. Were Franz Ferdinand to come to the throne and implement this policy, Serbian ambitions would be crushed. Serbia bore indirect responsibility for the murder. Officers in the Serbian Army had provided the assassins with rudimentary training and weapons. Princip and his friends had been in contact with a Serbian terrorist group known as the "Black Hand," which had been supported by the Ministry of War. Perhaps most damning, although members of the Serb cabinet had known that an attempt on Ferdinand's life would be made, they did almost nothing to stop it.

Archduke Franz Ferdinand with his wife, Sophie, in Sarajevo. June 28, 1914. The picture was taken shortly before both passengers were assassinated by Gavrilo Princip. The Austrian authorities had planned to change the route back from the Town Hall reception, but the instructions were never passed on to the Archduke's escort.

Gavrilo Princip. 1914. Several conspirators were involved in the plot, and when Princip heard a bomb explode, he assumed (wrongly) that the couple were dead. He went for a coffee and came back to find himself exactly in front of the royal car. Tried by an Austrian court (by the time the trial began, the Great War was well underway), which could not give a death sentence to anyone younger than 21, he was imprisoned and died of injuries—probably as a result of torture—in 1918.

Austrian officials were not unduly upset at the murder because many thought Ferdinand's political ideas were dangerous. Moreover, his marriage to a minor aristocrat had angered the emperor and the royal court, who felt that the archduke had married beneath his station. Despite these private misgivings, Austria-Hungary decided to use the event as a pretext for extracting retribution from Serbia. Count Leopold von Berchtold (1863–1942), the wealthy aristocrat who served as Austrian foreign minister, advocated a march on Belgrade. But the army chief of staff urged caution because an attack against Serbia could mean war with Russia. Berchtold then turned to Berlin, hoping to secure assurances that Germany would back Austria-Hungary if war broke out.

HOW EUROPE STUMBLED INTO WAR

On July 5, Wilhelm II gave Count Berchtold what he wanted: the infamous "blank check," by which Germany pledged military assistance in the event of war between Austria-Hungary and Russia. The German chancellor, Theobald von Bethmann-Hollweg (served 1909–1917), confidently predicted that Russia would not intervene if Austria acted quickly. Unknown to him, however, on July 21 French President Raymond Poincaré, on a visit to St. Petersburg, encouraged Russia to be firm. On both sides, the inevitable logic of the alliance systems took hold.

Over the weeks that followed the German assurance of support, Berchtold deliberately kept Berlin ill-informed of Austrian plans. Finally, on July 23, Vienna issued an ultimatum that clearly threatened to violate Serbian sovereignty. The Austrians insisted that the Serb government suppress all anti-Austrian activities and that Austrian officials be permitted to investigate the assassination in Serbia. At 5:55 P.M. on July 25, Belgrade—which had already ordered mobilization—responded with some concessions, but refused to accept all of Vienna's demands. At 9:23 P.M., the Emperor Franz Josef ordered Austro-Hungarian mobilization.

The two mobilizations shocked Europe's diplomats into action. The German ambassador in St. Petersburg persuaded the Russians to suggest talks with Berchtold to end the crisis. British Foreign Secretary Sir Edward Grey (1862–1933) appealed to the kaiser to hold the Austrians in check and called for mediation talks. Bethmann-Hollweg, who misunderstood the gravity of events because of Berchtold's deceptions, failed to forward Grey's proposals to Vienna, and when Wilhelm returned from a cruise on July 27, he angrily asked his chancellor, "How did it all happen?"

That night, the chastened German minister wired Berchtold that Austria must agree to discuss the Serbian concessions. But in Vienna, a declaration of war had been drafted, and Berchtold got the aged Emperor Franz Josef to sign it by falsely claiming that the Serbians had already begun to attack. On the morning of July 28, Austria delivered its declaration of war to Serbia, while in Berlin the kaiser decided that he would attempt to mediate the dispute between Austria-Hungary and Serbia. The next day, Bethmann-Hollweg telegraphed sternly to Berchtold that "We [Germany] must refuse to let ourselves be drawn . . . by Vienna into any general conflagration because she has ignored our advice." Had such a message been delivered on July 5 instead of the "blank check," events might have taken a different course.

On July 28, the French ambassador assured the Russians that France would stand by its ally. Tsar Nicholas II, who had been persuaded to order partial mobilization, telegraphed to Kaiser Wilhelm: "Very soon I shall be forced to take extreme measures that will lead to war." The royal cousins exchanged telegrams, signed "Willy" and "Nicky," which were so friendly that Nicholas countermanded the mobilization order. But when Wilhelm learned that Russian mobilization had been under way, he exploded in anger and ended the discussions. The tsar signed a full mobilization decree on July 29. Although Germany had not been a party to the events in the Balkans, General Helmuth von Moltke, bearing in mind the time constraints of the Schlieffen Plan, urged immediate mobilization.

Events rushed forward. On July 31, Austria-Hungary mobilized against Russia; Germany issued two ultimatums—one demanding that Russia call off its mobilization, the other giving France 18 hours to decide whether it would remain neutral if Germany and Russia fought; France ordered mobilization. On August 1, Sir Edward Grey promised that Britain would keep France neutral if Germany would not act.

Throughout the crisis, France had pressed Britain for a clear statement of support, but without result. Instead, Sir Edward Grey had asked for assurances from both France and Germany that the international treaty guaranteeing Belgian neutrality would not be violated. France agreed, but the Germans avoided a clear answer. On August 2, Germany demanded free passage for its troops through Belgium, but

King Albert I (reigned 1909–1934) refused, declaring that "Belgium is a country and not a road." The next day, Grey got an endorsement from the House of Commons to defend Belgian neutrality if it were violated. In the meantime, Germany had declared war on France and its armies were marching. Using an unhappy choice of words to describe the treaty on Belgian neutrality, on August 4 Bethmann-Hollweg expressed his chagrin that Britain would go to war over "a scrap of paper." War between Britain and Germany began at midnight.

For two tension-ridden months, Europe's statesmen had stumbled their way through a mounting crisis. With the failure of the diplomats, the generals now took command. In a mood of deep despondency, Grey gazed out of the window of his London office at the streetlights. "The lamps are going out all over Europe," an aide heard him say; "we shall not see them lit again in our lifetime." It is a measure of the bitter irony surrounding these events that Grey did not remember having made that remark.

FIGHTING THE WAR

From the first, the Schlieffen Plan broke down. Belgian resistance slowed the German advance, a British force of 100,000 quickly joined the French Army, and the Russians moved against East Prussia sooner than expected. Surprised by these developments, von Moltke made further changes—instead of retreating on the left flank to draw the French away from the real battle zone, German reinforcements were sent to Lorraine. More crucial still, von Moltke weakened the assault against France by withdrawing troops from the West to halt the Russian attack.

As the Germans advanced to within 30 miles of Paris, General Joseph Joffre (1852–1931), the French commander-

SIGNIFICANT DATES

The Great War

August 1914	Outbreak of war
September 1914	Failure of Schlieffen Plan
November 1914	Turkey joins Central Powers
April 1915	Chlorine gas used at Ypres
May 1915	Italy joins Allies; *Lusitania* sunk
1916	Battles of Verdun and the Somme
March 1917	Russian Revolution; November, Bolshevik coup
1917–1918	Offenses on Western front
April 1917	U.S. joins Allies
November 11, 1918	Armistice
January 1919	Paris Peace Conference opens
June 28, 1919	Treaty of Versailles

PERSPECTIVES FROM THE PAST

WORLD WAR I: WHO WAS RESPONSIBLE?

Ever since the outbreak of World War I in August 1914, diplomats, politicians, and scholars have debated the question of responsibility: Did the blame for the war rest on one country, as the Allies claimed for Germany, or did some or all of the European powers share responsibility collectively? Were the causes of the war systemic—that is, was it the result of the kind of diplomatic system that prevailed in Europe, with its secret military alliances? Did the clash of imperial interests globally contribute to the war, or did the arms race and the influence of military industrialists bring about the disaster? At the time, each of the major states involved in the war issued its own diplomatic documents, and later statesmen and generals published their memoirs, all in an effort to explain the causes of the war in a way that would be advantageous to their own nations or to their personal interests. The selection of documents that follows may shed some light on the vexing question and on the difficulties of sifting historical truth out of official records.

The German Response

On July 5, 1914, Count A. Hoyos of the Austrian Foreign Ministry and Ambassador Count L. de Szogyény saw Kaiser Wilhelm in Berlin, where they asked whether they could count on German support if Austria took strong action against Serbia. The next day, Theobald von Bethmann-Hollweg, German foreign minister, described the kaiser's response to his ambassador, Heinrich von Tschirschky, in Vienna:

Finally, as regards Serbia, His Majesty, of course, cannot take any position in regard to the questions pending between that country and Austria-Hungary, as they are outside his authority. But Emperor Francis Joseph can rely on His Majesty's taking his stand loyally at the side of Austria-Hungary in accordance with his duties as an ally and his old friendship.

Quoted in Luigi Albertini, *The Origins of the War of 1914*, trans. I. M. Massey, II. Oxford University Press. Copyright © 1952.

Austria-Hungary's Ultimatum to Serbia

During conversations in Vienna as to the nature of the Austro-Hungarian response to Serbia, Austrian Foreign Minister Count Leopold Berchtold told German Ambassador Heinrich von Tschirschky

that he would advise Emperor Franz Josef "so to formulate these demands that their acceptance appears impossible." When Russian Foreign Minister Sergei Sazonov heard the text of the ultimatum (technically the Austrians called it a "timed note" rather than an ultimatum), he exclaimed, "This means a European war." The following terms were presented to Serbia on July 23:

The Royal Servian Government further undertakes:

1. To suppress any publication which incites to hatred and contempt of the Austro-Hungarian Monarchy and the general tendency of which is directed against its territorial integrity;

2. To dissolve immediately the society called Narodna Odbrana [The People's Defense], to confiscate all its means of propaganda, and to proceed in the same manner against all other secret societies and their branches in Servia which engage in propaganda against the Austro-Hungarian Monarchy. . . .

3. To eliminate without delay from public instruction in Servia, both as regards the teaching body and the methods of instruction, everything that serves, or might serve, to foment the propaganda against Austria-Hungary;

4. To remove from the military service, and from the administration in general, all officers and functionaries guilty of propaganda against the Austro-Hungarian Monarchy whose names and deeds the Austro-Hungarian Government reserves the right of communicating to the Royal Government;

5. To accept the cooperation in Servia of representatives of the Austro-Hungarian Government in the suppression of the subversive movement directed against the territorial integrity of the Monarchy;

6. To take judicial proceedings against accomplices in the plot of the 28th of June who are on Servian territory. Delegates of the Austro-Hungarian Government will take part in the investigation relating thereto;

7. To proceed without delay to the arrest of Major Voja Tankositch and of the individual named Milan Ciganovitch, a Servian State employee, who have been compromised by the results of the preliminary investigation at Sarajevo;

8. To prevent by effective measures the participation of the Servian authorities in the illicit traffic in arms and explosives across the frontier; to dismiss and punish severely the officials of the frontier service at Schabatz and Loznica who have been guilty of having assisted the perpetrators of the Sarajevo crime by facilitating their passage across the frontier;

9. To furnish the Imperial and Royal Government with explanations regarding the unjustifiable utterances of high Servian officials, both in Servia and abroad, who, notwithstanding their official positions, did not hesitate after the crime of the 28th of June to give utterance, in published interviews, to expressions of hostility to the Austro-Hungarian Government; and finally

10. To notify the Imperial and Royal Government without delay of the execution of the measures comprised under the preceding heads.

The Austro-Hungarian Government awaits the reply of the Royal Government at the latest by 6 o'clock on Saturday evening, the 25th of July.

James Brown Scott, ed., *Diplomatic Documents Relating to the Outbreak of the European War*, Part I. Oxford University Press. Copyright © 1916.

The French Response

French President Raymond Poincaré and Foreign Minister René Viviani had been in St. Petersburg on an official visit in late July, and the Austrians had deliberately waited until after their departure before submitting the ultimatum to Serbia. On July 24, Maurice Paléologue, French ambassador in St. Petersburg, gave a luncheon for the English ambassador and Sazonov, and later wrote in his memoirs that he had said the following to his guests:

. . . I had no hesitation in advocating a policy of firmness.

'But suppose that policy is bound to lead to war?' said Sazonov.

'It will only lead to war if the Germanic powers have already made up their minds to resort to force to secure the hegemony of the East. Firmness does not exclude conciliation. But it is essential for the other side to be prepared to negotiate and compromise. You know my own views as to Germany's designs. The Austrian ultimatum seems to me to provoke the dangerous crisis I have anticipated for a long time. Henceforth we must recognize that war may break out at any moment. That prospect must govern all our diplomatic action.'

The English ambassador, Sir George Buchanan, reported to London the following:

The French Ambassador gave me to understand that France would not only give Russia strong diplomatic support but would, if necessary, fulfil all the obligations imposed on her by the alliance.

Paléologue, *An Ambassador's Memoirs*, 3 vols.

British Response to the Crisis

Sir Edward Grey, British foreign secretary, consistently took a rather detached and almost fatalistic attitude toward the unfolding diplomatic crisis. On

July 24—a day on which the cabinet spent almost all its time discussing the Irish problem rather than the diplomatic crisis—he told German Ambassador Lichnowsky that Britain was in no position to rein in its Russian ally following the Austro-Hungarian ultimatum:

I said that if the Austrian ultimatum to Servia did not lead to trouble between Austria and Russia I had no concern with it; . . . I was very apprehensive of the view Russia would take of the situation. I reminded the German Ambassador that some days ago he had expressed a personal hope that if need arose I would endeavor to exercise moderating influence at St. Petersburg, but now I said that, in view of the extraordinarily stiff character of the Austrian note, the shortness of the time allowed, and the wide scope of the demands upon Servia, I felt quite helpless as far as Russia was concerned, and I did not believe any Power could exercise influence alone.

The only chance I could see of mediating or moderating influence being effective, was that the four Powers, Germany, Italy, France and ourselves, should work together simultaneously at Vienna and St. Petersburg. . . .

The immediate danger was that in a few hours Austria might march into Servia and Russian Slav opinion demand that Russia should march to help Servia; it would be very desirable to get Austria not to precipitate military action and so to gain more time. But none of us could influence Austria in this direction unless Germany would propose and participate in such action at Vienna.

From *British Documents on the Origins of the World War, 1898-1914*, ed. by G.P. Gooch and Harold Temperly, Vol. II. Copyright © 1938.

The Serbs rejected outright only the sixth clause of the ultimatum, and the kaiser thought that their carefully worded response made war avoidable—"every reason for war drops away. . . . On the strength of this, I should never have ordered mobilization." Nevertheless, on July 26 General Helmuth von Moltke, chief of the German General Staff, drafted for his files an ultimatum demanding free passage for German troops through Belgian territory. When Austria-Hungary declared war against Serbia on July 28, Moltke wrote a memorandum to the German chancellor on the military necessity for swift action, and the next day he sent the Belgian ultimatum, sealed inside two envelopes, to the German Embassy in Brussels with orders to be opened only upon instructions from Berlin. Here is Moltke's memorandum:

Austria, if she enters Serbia, will be faced not only with the Serbian Army but with strong Russian superiority; she will thus not be able to wage war with Serbia without making Russian intervention certain. That means she will be forced to mobilize the other half of her army, for she cannot possibly put herself at the mercy of a Russia ready for war. The instant Austria mobilizes her whole army, the clash between her and Russia will become inevitable. Now that is for Germany the *causus foederis*. Unless Germany means to break her word and allow her ally to succumb to Russian superior strength, she must also mobilize. That will lead to the mobilization of the remaining Russian military districts. Russia will then be able to say, "I am being attacked by Germany" and that will make her sure of the support of France who is bound by treaty to go to war if her ally Russia is attacked. The Franco-Russian agreement, so

---

in-chief, retreated in orderly fashion. In September, Joffre counterattacked along the Marne River, pushing the Germans back. Once the Germans halted, however, the front line stabilized. Following the Battle of the Marne, each side tried unsuccessfully to outflank the other by moving northward around the enemy in what has been called the "race to the sea"—when that tactic failed, the combatants moved southward, so that the front soon consisted of a 400-mile line stretching from the North Sea to Switzerland. For

the remainder of the war, the Western front hardly moved more than a few miles in either direction.

STALEMATE IN THE WEST

The Battle of the Marne shattered German hopes for a quick victory. General Erich von Falkenhayn (1861–1922) replaced von Moltke as chief of staff. For the next four years, each side slaughtered the other repeatedly in futile attempts to wear the enemy down and achieve a breakthrough.

often praised as a purely defensive alliance brought about only to meet German plans of aggression, comes thereby into operation and the civilized states of Europe will begin to tear one another to pieces. . . .

From Helmuth von Moltke, *Essays, Speeches, and Memoirs of Field Marshal Helmuth von Moltke*, J. R. Osgood McLlvane and Company. Copyright © 1893.

The Russian Decision to Mobilize

The Russians, who responded to the Austrian declaration of war with alarm, had two military contingencies. They could declare partial mobilization for operations along the Austro-Hungarian frontier, or general mobilization along both the Austro-Hungarian and the German borders. Tsar Nicholas II signed both edicts and on July 29–30 shifted back and forth twice between ordering general and then partial mobilization. But Russian military commanders put increasing pressure on Foreign Minister Sazonov and the tsar, pointing out that partial mobilization would jeopardize Russia's ability to carry out general mobilization in the event of an enemy declaration of war. The following account of the fateful meeting with Nicholas on July 30 is from the memoirs of Baron von Schilling, head of the Chancery of the Russian Ministry of Foreign Affairs:

During the course of nearly an hour the Minister [Sazonov] proceeded to show that war was becoming inevitable, as it was clear to everybody that Germany had decided to bring about a collision, as otherwise she would not have rejected all the pacificatory proposals that had been made. . . . Therefore it was necessary to put away any fears that our warlike preparations would bring about a war and to continue these preparations carefully, rather than by reason of such fears to be taken unawares by war.

The firm desire of the Tsar to avoid war at all costs, the horrors of which filled him with repulsion, led His Majesty . . . to explore every possible means for averting the approaching danger. Consequently he refused during a long time to agree to the adoption of measures which, however indispensable from a military point of view, were calculated, as he clearly saw, to hasten a decision in an undesirable sense. . . .

Finally the Tsar agreed that in the existing circumstances it would be very dangerous not to make timely preparations for what was apparently an inevitable war, and therefore gave his decision in favour of an immediate general mobilization.

From Baron M. F. Schilling, *How the War Began In 1914*, translated by William C. Bridge. Allen and Unwin. Copyright © 1925.

On Friday, July 31, Germany presented two ultimatums: one to Russia that it would mobilize unless the tsar suspended all military operations within twelve hours; and one to France asking whether Paris would remain neutral in the event of a German-Russian war and, if so, to permit German occupation of French frontier fortresses. At five p.m. on Saturday, having received no answer from either the Russians or the French, the Germans began mobilization. An hour later, the German ambassador in St. Petersburg handed the Russians the text of their declaration of war.

Despite some differences in military and industrial capability, the Allies and the Central Powers were each sufficiently strong to prevent victory or defeat.

The assumptions behind modern military strategy collapsed as armies constructed a web of trenches that eventually measured a combined length of 25,000 miles. These trench systems were cordoned by miles of barbed wire, with a fearful "no man's land" dividing them. Behind the trenches, a vast transportation network moved millions of soldiers and hundreds of millions of tons of equipment in preparation for assaults. To all except the generals who commanded the front, the principal tactic adopted by both sides was horrific in its simplicity: long-range artillery pounded the enemy for days. Then, at a prearranged moment, officers led the infantry soldiers out of the trenches to attack. Machine guns cut them down as they scrambled through exploding shells that blasted craters in the earth and filled the air with dirt and smoke. Eighty percent of all

French soldiers rush out of the trenches on the Western front in Word War I. Note that the most foreward soldier was shot at the moment this photograph was taken. The greatest number of casualties on the Western front were the result of such futile advances.

casualties were caused in this manner—between August and November 1914 alone, more than 1,640,000.

The Great War produced few "heroes" in the traditional sense of the word. Each assault caused tens of thousands to die anonymously on the battlefields, while millions more huddled in the trenches amid mud, slime, and the stench of rotting corpses. New weapons, such as poison gas and tanks, were employed—the Germans first used chlorine gas at Ypres in April 1915, and the Allies responded in kind—but it failed to prove decisive and only introduced a fiendish element into the conflict. Yet the generals refused to see the futility of their tactics, instead waging a war of attrition.

This war attained grotesque dimensions in 1916. The Germans deliberately sought to bleed the French into defeat by unleashing a major assault on Verdun. They correctly expected the French to defend the fortress at any price. More than 1 million German artillery shells fell on Verdun on February 21, the opening day of the attack. In August, daily German casualties began to exceed French losses and the kaiser replaced von Falkenhayn with General Paul von Hindenburg (1847–1934), who had been called out of retirement to command the Eastern front. When the siege was finally lifted in December, 700,000 had died—600,000 French soldiers and 100,000 Germans.

Aerial photograph of French troops passing through the ruins of Verdun. 1916. The German failure to dislodge the French forces in the trenches near Verdun—the fighting lasted almost 11 months—cost 700,000 lives. By the end, no significant advantage had been gained by either side.

The most fearsome battle of the Great War, which began while Verdun was still under siege, took place along the Somme River. General Douglas Haig (1861–1928), the British commander, had for some time planned a "big push" at the Somme, and the bloodletting at Verdun failed to dissuade him. The British first pounded the Germans with an immense artillery attack that began on June 24, sublimely confident that the three-quarters of a million soldiers they had amassed would then be able to occupy the enemy trenches. But when the offensive opened on July 1, the damage to German installations proved to be superficial: 20,000 British were killed and 40,000 wounded.

Haig refused to call off the battle, which raged on throughout the summer. In September, for the first time, he used tanks, which the British had been developing, but they proved unreliable. A snowstorm ended the Somme offensive in November, but not before the blood of more than 1 million had soaked the battlefields: Haig's "big push" had cost the British and French 600,000 casualties, and the Germans 500,000. When David Lloyd George (1863–1945) became prime minister in 1916, he tried to end these costly offenses but gave in when Sir William Robertson (1860–1933), chief of the Imperial General Staff and a man with powerful political and newspaper connections, insisted that they continue.

CRISIS IN THE EAST

In the East, the imbalance between the combatants and the huge space over which supplies and armies had to move pre-

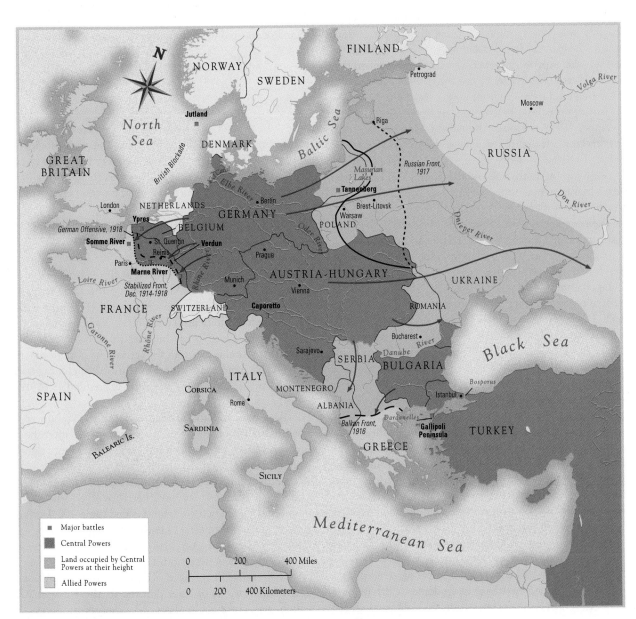

Map 80.4 The Great War, 1914–1918. The most bitter fighting and the greatest losses occurred at the point where the two sides met in northeastern France, in the valleys of the rivers Somme and Marne. From April 1915, the weapons used included chlorine gas. The Central Powers' campaign in the east against Russia took an unexpected turn in 1917, with the outbreak of the Russian Revolution. The result was that Russia was the only Allied power to sign a peace treaty with Germany before the end of the war, in 1917. It was nullified the following year at the war's end.

vented the kind of stalemate that had bogged down the fighting on the Western front. When the war broke out, the Russians had moved against Germany before completing mobilization and achieved a surprise advantage in East Prussia. At that point, von Moltke had shifted four divisions from the Western theater to stop the Russians.

Rather than fighting the numerically larger Russian forces along all points, Hindenburg, who had taken command of the Eastern front with General Erich Ludendorff (1865–1937) as his deputy, chose to take on sections of the Russian armies individually. In this way, they won an important engagement at the Battle of Tannenberg, where the Germans took over 100,000 prisoners, and another at the Masurian Lakes. By the time the Battle of the Marne had been determined in the West, the Russian "steam roller" had been stopped. Farther to the south, along the Austro-Hungarian front, Germany's principal ally was less successful because the Russians drove through Galicia and invaded Hungary. In the Balkans, the Austrians also experienced reverses as the Serbs repulsed their armies and retook Belgrade. By the end of 1914, the results of the fighting on the Eastern front were inconclusive.

Turkey's declaration of war against the Allies in November 1914 seriously weakened Russia's position. Tensions between the two countries, already sharp, were exacerbated by the presence of the Armenians, a Christian people living on both sides of the Russo-Turkish border. The Armenians had suffered centuries of persecution by both the Russians and the Turks. In 1915, after failing to secure their support against Russia in the war effort, the Turks forcibly relocated the Armenians in the Anatolian interior. In the process, more than a million Armenians died of disease, starvation, and slaughter.

Upon entering the war, the Turks closed the Dardanelles Straits in order to stop vital supplies from reaching Russia. In March 1915, British and French naval forces attempted to open the straits, but the plan failed. In April, the Allies landed along the Gallipoli peninsula, which juts out from the southern coast of European Turkey and guards the straits, but the Turks were able to trap the invading forces below from their higher ground. After suffering great losses, the expedition was recalled.

In the spring of 1915, von Falkenhayn launched a major offensive against the Russians. The Germans pierced the Russian line and moved forward, taking Warsaw and pushing east from the foothills of the Carpathian Mountains. Because the Russians lacked machine guns and heavy artillery, the offensive cost them some 2.5 million men killed, wounded, or taken prisoner.

The Allied position was strengthened in May 1915 by Italy's declaration of war against Austria-Hungary. The previous month, Italy had concluded a secret agreement with the Allies that ended months of bitter domestic debate over the war. In return for its intervention, the Treaty of London pledged to give Italy the Trentino, the southern Tyrol, Istria, and the city of Trieste, as well as territory along the Dalmatian coast—all territories under Austrian rule. The new front thus opened along the Italian-Austrian border re-

lieved some German pressure against Russia. That October, Bulgaria threw in its lot with the Central Powers, and the following August Romania joined the Allies.

The year 1917 brought major crises to the Allies. In March, revolution broke out in the Russian capital and forced the abdication of Tsar Nicholas (see Topic 81). A provisional government dominated by Alexander Kerensky (1881–1970) proclaimed a continuation of the war, but the Russian people demanded peace. Convinced that the imminent collapse of Russia would soon end the two-front war, the Germans erected a fortified defense system on the Western front known as the Hindenburg Line. While the German armies waited, the French flung themselves at the Hindenburg Line in April in a wasted effort that cost 250,000 casualties. Between July and November, Haig led another huge assault at Ypres, but the fighting in the muddy fields of Flanders resulted in an additional 300,000 British casualties.

THE HOME FRONT

The Great War placed tremendous stress on society. Europeans found it difficult to absorb the psychological impact of the carnage. As each side suffered millions of casualties, the excitement that had greeted the outbreak of war in 1914 turned to horror. At home, morale began to waver under the joint pressures of the fighting and the demands increasingly placed on civilian populations.

DOMESTIC OPPOSITION

The war aroused opposition from pacifists, women's groups, churches, and the left. Almost all of the socialist parties, however, had voted for war credits in 1914—only in Italy did they adopt the neutral position of "neither sabotage nor support"—and leaders of churches in belligerent countries rallied to national interests. Governments of national unity brought all major parties into coalitions, including socialists. In August 1917 Pope Benedict XV (ruled 1914–1922) issued an appeal for peace.

As the terrible toll of dead and wounded mounted, opposition took more direct forms. In May 1917, after the failure of a bloody offensive, some French regiments that had suffered heavy casualties ignored orders to attack, and revolts broke out in other units. A total of between 30,000 and 40,000 soldiers may have been involved in such incidents, and the French command issued some 400 death sentences against mutineers. One British camp in France experienced a riot, and even the Germans had to deal with individual cases of desertion. During the summer, the crew of one German ship staged a hunger strike to protest the better food rations of their officers. In the Russian Army, which was chronically short of weapons, uniforms, and food, mutiny and desertion were widespread.

Incidents of civilian revolt were deeply troubling to wartime governments. The British faced a critical problem in Ireland, where support for the war effort clashed with anti-British sentiment. During Easter of 1916, Irish nationalists tried to capitalize on the war to stage a rebellion against British rule. The Irish politician Sir Roger Casement (1864–1918) arranged for the Germans to supply arms to the rebels from a U-boat, but British destroyers intercepted the vessel and Casement was captured. After a week of street fighting, the rebellion was crushed and 15 nationalist leaders, including Casement, were hanged.

The March 1917 revolution in Russia, provoked in part by conditions at the front, sent shock waves throughout Europe. In July, Matthias Erzberger (1875–1921) of the German Center party introduced a peace resolution in the Reichstag. The resolution, which called for a peace based on understanding and rejected territorial acquisitions achieved by force, passed by a margin of almost two to one. The following month, revolutionary socialists staged an antiwar uprising in the Italian industrial city of Turin. Some 50 workers were killed and 200 wounded when the government used army units to restore order.

Morale on the home front was as vital to victory as the willingness of soldiers to fight. The war made tremendous demands on national economies and the workforce. In order to deal with continued shortages of food and clothing, most nations imposed rationing as well as limited wages and prices, and most labor unions adopted voluntary restraints. Industrial commissions, composed of business and labor leaders, government officials, and experts, directed national production. Every country was caught off guard by the "technical surprise" of the war—that is, the insatiable demand for raw materials and weapons that increased beyond all expectations every day of the fighting. Stockpiles of artillery shells, for example, that prewar estimates assumed would last for six months were consumed in a single day at the front.

WOMEN AND THE WAR

The wartime economy created an artificial prosperity that greatly affected women. At first, many female workers found themselves unemployed because the demand for consumer goods traditionally made by women, such as dresses and textiles, declined. But the drafting of millions of young men created a labor shortage. By the second year of the war, women were working in heavy industry and munitions plants, and by 1918, perhaps one in three industrial workers was a woman. Women appeared on streetcars and subways as drivers, ticket takers, and conductors. In addition to the home front, they served in combat zones as ambulance drivers and military nurses, and were active in assisting civilian refugees.

Governments proclaimed female labor essential to the war effort, although the women were not always welcomed by male workers and were paid lower wages. Nor were women taught technical skills beyond those required for their immediate work because industry and labor unions considered female labor a temporary measure. Many munitions factories provided day care centers for working mothers, but after 10- or 12-hour shifts, they still had to care for their families.

Yet the war made a great difference in the lives of many women and in how men perceived them. Not only did many women earn wages for the first time, but they often experienced a degree of social independence that they were unwilling to give up when peace came. Single women appeared in public, attended theaters and ate in restaurants alone, dated more freely, and dressed with fewer constraints. The criticism and ridicule that some working women experienced resulted in part from sexual tensions that accompanied changing female roles. The unprecedented requirements of "total war" made it impossible to maintain a traditional gender separation between the male warrior and the female wife or mother. "Girls are doing things," wrote the poet Nina Macdonald, "They've never done before . . . All the world is topsy-turvey/Since the War began."

Official propaganda attempted to mitigate the impact of the war on gender roles, as in the case of the British nurse Edith Cavell (1865–1915). Volunteer nurses were in high demand because of the terrible casualty rate of trench warfare. These women faced daily the searing psychological experience of dealing with bloodshed, mutilation, and death.

A propaganda cartoon showing the German execution of the English nurse Edith Cavell. 1915. As matron of the Berkendael hospital near Brussels, she helped some 200 British, French, and Belgian soldiers to escape to the Dutch border. When arrested by the Germans, she admitted what she had done and was shot. This British drawing emphasizes the beastly nature of her executioners—pigs wearing German helmets.

Working near the front lines, they, like the soldiers they assisted, confronted serious physical dangers. Although a professional nurse, Cavell was a British patriot who used her position at a Red Cross facility in Belgium to aid captured Allied soldiers. The Germans tried Cavell for espionage and executed her.

CIVILIAN POPULATIONS AND TOTAL WAR

Inevitably, society became regimented under the pressures of the war. Governments demanded complete loyalty and dedication from all citizens in order to wage total war. Civilians were subjected to military requirements, which took precedence over matters not essential to the war effort. Fundamental legal rights, such as freedom of the press and habeas corpus, were set aside. Generals wielded more authority than civilians in government deliberations. In Germany, General Ludendorff practically dictated domestic policy until 1918. Political leaders asked their populations for more and more sacrifices, and to justify the steadily mounting cost in lives and money, governments developed war aims that stressed lofty ideals such as democracy, justice, and permanent peace.

Domestic propaganda created the impression that class differences diminished as all social groups pulled together for the general good. Working-class women rolled bandages together with duchesses; businessmen and labor leaders served together on production committees; and in the trenches peasants died along with intellectuals and shopkeepers. Peasants constituted the majority of all draftees, whereas officers came from the upper classes. Because lieutenants and captains were the first out of the trenches in assaults against the enemy, the casualty rate among social elites was disproportionately high. In most armies, lower-rank officers and drafted soldiers tended to work together in the face of common peril.

In the war of attrition, great stress was put on efforts to undermine enemy civilian resistance. Cities of no military significance were bombed by long-range artillery and Zeppelins, and blockades attempted to keep food, medicines, and other vital supplies from reaching the enemy. Turkey's control of the Dardanelles Straits severely restricted Russia's access to Allied supplies, and Britain's dominance of the sea was effective in cutting off Germany and Austria-Hungary from much maritime trade. France and Britain, on the other hand, had access to American and other overseas sources of food and materiel, even during the height of submarine warfare. Germany was the first to adopt a ration system, and most of the other belligerents followed suit.

THE WORLD CONFLICT

The conflict widened steadily as more nations intervened and, alongside the main theater of operations in Europe, a peripheral war was fought in the Middle East, Africa, and the Pacific. In 1917, the balance of power among the belligerents finally shifted as the United States abandoned its neutrality and joined the Allied cause.

THE GLOBAL DIMENSIONS OF WAR

The military outcome of the Great War was to be determined in Europe, but both sides were concerned about global strategic issues. Britain was especially interested in the Middle East because of the importance of the Suez Canal to its Indian realm, and tried to wrest control of the region from the Turks.

After their failure to seize Baghdad in November 1915, the British sought to foment a revolt against the Turks by openly encouraging Arab independence. They supported Hussein ibn-Ali (1856–1931), of the Holy City of Mecca, who declared himself ruler of an Arab kingdom embracing the region between the Red Sea and the Persian Gulf. Hussein raised an army in 1916 and declared a holy war against the Ottoman Empire. At the same time, however, the French and the British planned to divide the Middle East between themselves. The Sykes-Picot Agreement, named after British diplomat Mark Sykes and French diplomat Georges Picot, stipulated that Lebanon and Syria would come under French authority, and that Palestine and Iraq would fall within the British sphere. In 1917, the archeologist T.E. Lawrence (1888–1935), then a British officer, worked with Hussein's son, Prince Faisal (1885–1933), in organizing an Arab Army. Together, Hussein and "Lawrence of Arabia" succeeded in taking Jerusalem and Damascus. Despite Britain's pro-Arab stance, however, in November 1917 Foreign Secretary Arthur Balfour angered Arab leaders when he announced support for the Zionist goal of establishing a Jewish state in Palestine.

The British also occupied the German colonies of South-West Africa (Namibia) and Togoland (Togo). The Germans managed, however, to keep the Allies busy in German East Africa (Tanzania) until 1918, using local African recruits to wage a guerrilla campaign. In Asia, the British believed their interests were endangered by their Japanese allies, who immediately occupied the German islands in the north Pacific. To prevent further Japanese expansion, troops from New Zealand and Australia seized Samoa and New Guinea. In 1917 the Chinese government also joined the Allied cause, yet when Japan ousted the Germans from the port of Tsingtao, it refused to return the stronghold to China.

THE UNITED STATES AND THE EUROPEAN WAR

Public opinion in the United States was divided over the war, but President Woodrow Wilson's (served 1913–1921) own sentiments leaned toward Britain, although publicly he argued for strict neutrality. In the end, Germany's reliance on the submarine acted as the catalyst for American intervention.

International law proscribed attacking neutral ships not carrying war contraband. In 1915, however, each side attempted illegally to keep all goods from reaching the other, although only the British blockade proved to be effective.

Germany's U-boat fleet was a powerful weapon in this campaign, but submarines sank enemy ships by underwater torpedo, not by surface battle, and could not lose the advantage of surprise in order to determine whether a vessel's cargo contained war materiel. As a result, unarmed merchant ships as well as citizens of neutral countries fell victim to U-boat attacks, which caused significant shipping losses.

The United States reacted sharply against the U-boat campaign, especially after more than a hundred Americans were among the almost 1,200 passengers killed when the Germans sank the British passenger liner *Lusitania* in May 1915. The crisis caused a debate inside the German government, with Chancellor Bethmann-Hollweg arguing for a cessation of submarine warfare and Admiral von Tirpitz insisting that it was Germany's only chance for victory.

In September 1915, the kaiser limited submarine operations, but he was finally convinced that the military advantage of submarine warfare outweighed the danger of antagonizing American opinion. In late January 1917, Wilhelm therefore ordered unrestricted U-boat attacks to be resumed. During February, the U-boats destroyed 781,500 tons of Allied shipping.

In protest, President Wilson severed formal ties with Germany on February 3, 1917. Toward the end of that month, the British passed on to American authorities an intercepted coded telegram from a German Foreign Ministry official, Arthur Zimmermann (1864–1940), to the German minister in Mexico. The Zimmermann telegram proposed an alliance between Mexico and Germany in the event of American belligerency, with Mexico receiving Texas, New Mexico, and Arizona as its compensation. Wilson's outrage reached the breaking point in March 1917, when the Germans torpedoed two American ships. By the end of the month, an additional 500,000 tons of Allied shipping had been lost. On April 2, he asked for a declaration of war against Germany, which Congress passed overwhelmingly four days later.

General John J. Pershing (1860–1948), commanding the American Expeditionary Force (AEF), brought the first U.S. troops to France in July. The contribution of the United States to the Allied cause came in the form of industrial supplies as well as soldiers. American intervention also struck an important blow for morale at a critical moment. In March, Russia had been shaken by revolution; that October, Italy was almost overrun by the Central Powers during the disastrous rout of Caporetto, and lost a half-million soldiers in their efforts to halt the enemy at the Piave River; in November, the Bolshevik coup augured the eventual withdrawal of Russia from the war.

At the beginning of 1918, President Wilson declared the famous "Fourteen Points," which he believed would provide the basis for a permanent peace—hence, the slogan, "the war to end all wars." Wilson's goals included elimination of the arms race and secret diplomacy, adherence to the principle of self-determination for all peoples, and freedom of the seas. One legacy he left to the future would be the idea of a world organization, known later as the League of Nations, designed to preserve peace.

PEACE AND ITS CONSEQUENCES

While Wilson issued the Fourteen Points, Germany still planned for a decisive breakthrough on the battlefield. Teenagers were being called up as its manpower was depleted, and the supply of food and equipment grew critically short. Moreover, on January 28, 400,000 Berlin workers stopped working to demand peace and democracy, and the strike spread to other industrial cities. On the other hand, Russia finally withdrew from the war in March 1918 after Germany and the Bolshevik regime concluded the Treaty of Brest-Litovsk (see Topic 81).

GERMANY SUES FOR PEACE

The end of the fighting on the Eastern front allowed General Ludendorff to strengthen German forces in the West and to attempt a large offensive against the Allies. The last-ditch attack, initiated on March 21, succeeded at first in pushing the enemy back to the Marne. By June, however, the Allies, now reinforced by large numbers of American soldiers, broke the advance and shattered all hopes for a German victory. In mid-July, the Allies counterattacked.

In September 1918, General Ludendorff reluctantly told the Crown Council that German forces had to go on the defensive, and by the end of the following month they were in retreat along most of the Western front.

A new, more liberal German government was formed in late September under Prince Max of Baden (served as chancellor October–November 1918), who then asked Wilson for armistice terms derived from the Fourteen Points. The American president, however, insisted that Kaiser Wilhelm abdicate before an armistice was concluded. During the weeks that followed, Germany's allies withdrew from the war, and a full-scale mutiny among German sailors at Kiel sparked revolutions in Berlin and elsewhere. Still the kaiser vacillated, until on November 9, Prince Max forced the issue by publicly announcing the abdication. Wilhelm II left secretly the next day for the Netherlands, where he spent the rest of his days in exile. The armistice agreement, concluded in a railway car at Compiègne, went into effect at 11 A.M. on November 11, 1918. The Great War was over.

THE POLITICS OF PEACE MAKING

The armistice ended the fighting, but technically the great powers still remained at war until peace treaties were signed. The making of peace proved to be difficult because the price of war had been so high. Almost three dozen nations had fought in the Great War. Some 11 million people—soldiers and civilians—had been killed as a direct result of the fighting, and 20 million were wounded or disabled; countless others died of disease, starvation, and forced relocation. The monetary costs of the conflict forced Europe to reverse its former position as a capital exporter: henceforth, the United States was Europe's creditor. The economic transition to peace was made more difficult by the fact that widespread physical destruction had weakened Europe's capacity to produce food and industrial goods.

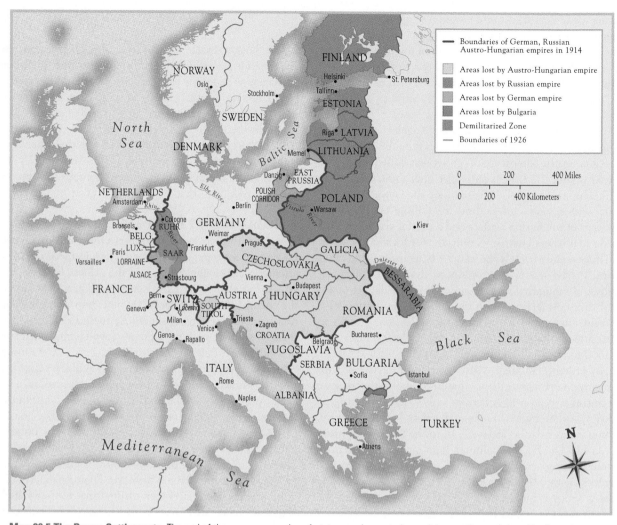

Map 80.5 The Peace Settlements. The end of the war saw a series of states newly created out of the wreckage of three Empires: the Hapsburg (Austro-Hungarian), the Russian, and the Ottoman. Some of these countries still exist, including Austria and Hungary. (At the end of the 20th century, some agreed to split: Czechoslovakia became the Czech Republic and Slovakia. Yugoslavia broke up, but with disastrous consequences.) In 1919, Alsace-Lorraine returned to France, while the Saar became a demilitarized zone, and was to become one of the trouble spots that helped ignite World War II.

Wartime propaganda raised public expectations that both domestic governments and the peacemakers were unable to fulfill. National interests and broad Wilsonian principles clashed at the conference table, although both sides had agreed to make peace on the basis of the Fourteen Points. Moreover, the generally conservative mood of the victorious nations stood in sharp contrast to the radical revolution unfolding in Russia.

The international conference called to make peace gathered in Paris in January 1919. It included delegates from some three dozen states as well as leaders hoping to gain recognition from the great powers, such as Prince Faisal and his Arab delegation. The immediate purpose of the Paris Peace Conference was, of course, to arrange peace treaties with the defeated Central Powers and their allies.

Not since the Congress of Vienna of 1814–1815 had so many heads of state and their ministers assembled in one place to discuss common problems. In a dramatic departure

from America's isolationist past, Woodrow Wilson crossed the Atlantic to argue for the ideals he had publicly declared. His erstwhile colleagues were experienced and shrewd statesmen—French Premier Georges Clemenceau (1841–1929), British Prime Minister David Lloyd George (1863–1945), and Italian Prime Minister Vittorio E. Orlando (1860–1952). Each leader was accompanied by a staff of advisers and experts in matters ranging from economics and international law to linguistics and cartography.

Despite the rhetoric of democracy that marked Allied propaganda, decision making at the Paris Peace Conference operated according to traditional principles of power politics. An informal executive group of the "Big Five"—the United States, Britain, France, Italy, and Japan—was supposed to settle basic positions, but in reality both Italy and Japan were excluded from the inner core of the "Big Three," consisting of Clemenceau, Lloyd George, and Wilson. Their ideological antipathy to Communism led them to exclude the new

Bolshevik regime in Russia from the conference, and public opinion among their political constituencies at home demanded that the Germans not be accorded equal status with the other participants. The new German republican government was invited, therefore, merely to send observers. Peace would be dictated to the defeated enemy, not negotiated.

THE PEACE TREATIES AND THE LEAGUE OF NATIONS

Discussions surrounding the German question divided the Allies from the outset, and the final settlement with Germany—the Treaty of Versailles—represented an unhappy compromise. The French, painfully aware of the experiences of both 1870 and 1914, wanted to carve an independent state out of German territory in the Rhineland that would protect France's eastern border against attack. Clemenceau and Wilson clashed head-on over this issue, the American president insisting that the French proposal ran counter to the spirit of self-determination. They finally reached a compromise, one that the French accepted reluctantly and that proved in the long run to be unworkable. In return for an American commitment to sign a military alliance with France, Clemenceau agreed that Germany would be forbidden to keep a military force in the Rhineland and in an area 50 kilometers east of the Rhine River. The Allies would occupy this "demilitarized" region for a period of 15 years. The coal mines and factories of the Rhineland's Saar district formed part of the arrangement because Britain and France wanted to use these economic resources to offset the huge debt they had incurred to the United States. The Allies agreed that during their occupation, the newly founded League of Nations would administer the Saarland in order to ensure the delivery of fixed amounts of goods and raw materials to them.

Although Germany did not permanently lose the Rhineland, it did lose other territories. In the west, France received the provinces of Alsace and part of Lorraine, which Germany had taken from it in 1871, and Belgium obtained several strategic towns and fortresses. In Eastern Europe, where the Allies created a series of new independent states, Germany lost additional territory: Poland received portions of East Prussia and Upper Silesia, and the port city of Danzig (now Gdansk, Poland) was made a free city under League of Nations authority. From territory formerly in the Austro-Hungarian empire, Czechoslovakia was given the German-speaking area of Bohemia known as the Sudetenland. Because the new state of Austria consisted chiefly of the German-speaking portion of the old Hapsburg empire, there was considerable sentiment both in Germany and Austria for a union (known in German as *Anschluss*) between the two countries. In November, the provisional Austrian assembly declared itself to be a part of Germany, but the Allies expressly prohibited *Anschluss*.

These territorial losses clearly implied that the Allies held Germany responsible for the war, as did the economic provisions of the settlement, which required Germany to pay reparations for costs inflicted on Allied civilians. The concept of responsibility was directly incorporated into the peace treaty with Germany in the form of Article 231. This "war guilt" clause made Germany liable for all financial losses suffered by the Allies "as a consequence of the war imposed upon them by the aggression of Germany and her allies." Reparations were eventually set at $35 billion.

The Versailles Treaty also imposed rigid military restrictions on Germany. The army was limited to 100,000 volunteer officers and soldiers, and the General Staff and all officer-training schools were eliminated. The navy was permitted a few ships under 10,000 tons and no submarines. Offensive weapons, such as tanks, long-range artillery, military airplanes, and chemical weapons, were similarly forbidden.

The Treaty of Versailles was both unconventional and unusually harsh. Contrary to any precedent in international

The signing of the Treaty of Versailles. June 28, 1919. The ceremony took place in the Great Hall of the Palace of Versailles, just outside Paris; the photograph shows the members of the delegations and others, who were allowed to be present, at the signing itself, which is taking place at the long table in the rear.

affairs, the Allies charged Kaiser Wilhelm with war crimes and demanded a trial, although the Dutch government granted him political asylum. Then, too, the unstated purpose of the peace settlement was clearly to destroy Germany's status as a first-rank world power, but the statesmen at Paris failed to consider the human suffering it would cause or its long-range political impact. In 1919 one prominent British expert at the conference, John Maynard Keynes (1883–1946), denounced the Versailles Treaty in a book entitled *The Economic Consequences of the Peace*. Keynes warned that the economic provisions of the treaty would make Germany unstable and endanger the peace, arguing that the reparations payments were unreasonable because of the loss of coal and iron deposits as well as other vital assets that Germany was forced to sustain (on Keynesian economic theory, see Topic 82).

The text of the Versailles Treaty was made known just as the infant German republic was struggling to establish itself against serious odds. When the Germans balked at the terms, the Allies said they would continue to fight. On June 28, 1919, two German political leaders, Hermann Muller of the Majority Socialists and Johannes Bell of the Center party, signed the document in the Hall of Mirrors of the Versailles Palace.

The Paris Peace Conference completely recast Eastern Europe, including the Balkan region where the Great War had begun. The Dual Monarchy was dismantled in conformity with the notion of self-determination (see Topic 84). In addition to Poland, which was created from former German, Austro-Hungarian, and Russian territory, Austria and Hungary—both considerably reduced in size—became separate states, as did Czechoslovakia. The new nation of Yugoslavia was created out of the former states of Serbia and Montenegro and the provinces of Bosnia, Herzegovina, Slovenia, and Croatia. Greece was enlarged at the expense of Bulgaria and Turkey, the latter retaining a small area around Istanbul and Asia Minor itself. Although Turkey kept control of the Dardanelles, they were henceforth open to the peacetime commerce of all nations.

When Woodrow Wilson first suggested the idea for a League of Nations, the other Allied statesmen had not given it an enthusiastic reception. Wilson persisted, however, and the League's charter (known as the Covenant) was included as an integral part of the individual treaties. The League sought to preserve peace through collective security, largely by providing a forum for discussion and arbitration. The League had limited authority in administering international agreements, as in the case of the free city of Danzig and the Saarland. Through the mandate system, it also supervised the administration of Germany's former colonies by France and Britain, which were to prepare the mandates for independence.

Serious weaknesses doomed the League from the start. It could fight aggression only with the moral force of its decisions because it could not enforce even its economic sanctions against sovereign nations. Germany and Russia were not invited to join the international body, and despite Wilson's key role in its conception, the U.S. Congress rejected the Treaty of Versailles and membership in the League.

Putting the Great War in Perspective

The Great War vastly changed the nature and focus of international power. Europe's economy never fully recovered from the physical destruction to farmland and factories, the dislocation of trade, and the draining of its resources. Nor did the European psyche, which was deeply wounded by the trauma of a war of attrition, regain its equilibrium. In politics, the impact of the war was equally devastating. Even before peace was restored, three historic empires—Russia, Austria-Hungary, and Germany—had collapsed. Within a few years, the world's first socialist government had been established by Lenin in Russia and the first fascist state in Italy by Mussolini. Britain and France, once the dominant Western powers, never regained their former positions of world influence because their hold on their imperial domains steadily weakened and the United States began to emerge as the arbiter of world affairs. The Great War was truly the great divide in European history.

Questions for Further Study

1. Is the question of "responsibility" for the war a useful one for historians?
2. How would you describe the causes of the war?
3. In what ways was the fighting in World War I different from that of previous wars?
4. How did the war affect social conditions behind the lines?
5. Was the Paris Peace Conference a success or a failure?

Suggestions for Further Reading

Beckett, I.F.W. *The Great War, 1914–1918*. New York, 2001.

Chickering, Roger, and Sig Forster, eds. *The Great War, Total War: Combat and Mobilization on the Western Front, 1914–1918*. New York, 2000.

Evans, R.J.W., and H.P. von Strandmann, eds. *The Coming of the First World War*. New York, 1989.

Fussell, Paul. *The Great War and Modern Memory*. New York, 1975.

Gilbert, Martin. *First World War*. London, 1994.

Higgonet, Margaret R., J. Jenson, S. Michel, and M.C. Weitz, eds. *Behind the Lines: Gender and the Two World Wars*. New Haven, CT, 1987.

Hynes, Samuel. *A War Imagined: The First World War and English Culture*. New York, 1991.

Joll, James. *The Origins of the First World War*. London, 1984.

Kocka, Jurgen. *Facing Total War: German Society, 1914–1918*. Cambridge, MA, 1984.

Mappin, John M. *Christmas in the Trenches, 1914*. Montreal, 1994.

Schmitt, Bernadotte E., and H.C. Vederler. *The World in the Crucible, 1914–1919*. New York, 1984.

Verhey, Jeffrey. *The Spirit of 1914: Militarization, Myth, and Mobilization in Germany*. New York, 2000.

Welsh, David. *Germany, Propaganda, and Total War, 1914–1918: The Sins of Omission*. New Brunswick, NJ, 2000.

Winter, J.M., and R.M. Wall. *The Upheaval of War: Family, Work, and Welfare in Europe, 1914–1918*. New York, 1988.

InfoTrac College Edition

Enter the search term *Russia Revolution* using Key Terms.

Enter the search term *World War, 1914–1918* using the Subject Guide.

Enter the search term *Versailles Treaty* using Key Terms.

RADICAL EXTREMES: THE RUSSIAN REVOLUTION AND THE RISE OF FASCISM

Between 1917 and 1919, Europe experienced a series of events that shaped the course of the 20th century. To the east, imperial Russia was struck by two successive revolutionary upheavals in the spring and fall of 1917 that toppled the centuries-old tsarist autocracy and set in its place the first self-proclaimed socialist state in history. Two years later, in central and southern Europe, equally significant events took place: Italy gave birth to Europe's first Fascist movement, while Germany followed six months later with the founding of the Nazi party.

Russia had been ill-prepared to fight the Great War. After three years of social and economic strain, riots and demonstrations at home forced Tsar Nicholas II to abdicate in March. A provisional government led by liberals took power, first under Prince Georgi Lvov and then under the moderate Alexander Kerensky. Their refusal to take Russia out of the war proved their undoing. In November, V.I. Lenin led his radical Marxists, known as **Bolsheviks,** in a successful coup.

Lenin proclaimed the founding of the Communist state, eventually called the Union of Soviet Socialist Republics (U.S.S.R.). Over the next three years, after withdrawing Russia from the war, the Bolsheviks struggled to secure their power through a bloody civil war with political opponents and a military campaign against foreign intervention. Upon Lenin's death in 1924, a power struggle ended with the victory of Joseph Stalin, who ruled the Soviet Union as a dictator for 25 years.

In Italy in March 1919, a former socialist and war veteran named Benito Mussolini, once hailed as "Italy's Lenin," created a radical movement of another kind, known as **Fascism.** Its program combined left-wing and right-wing elements, and it took advantage of the postwar atmosphere of nationalist frustration and fear of Bolshevik revolution that pervaded Italian political life. Mussolini came to power in 1922 on a wave of systematic violence carried out by his paramilitary "Black Shirt" squads. Three years later, after a major political crisis, Mussolini proclaimed a dictatorship.

In Germany, the fascist seizure of power took longer. There, in September 1919, Adolf Hitler—would-be artist and himself a war veteran—joined and soon dominated the National Socialist German Workers' party. The **Nazis,** as its members came to be called, capitalized on the political weakness of the new German state, known as the Weimar Republic, as well as on the economic and social dislocation following Germany's defeat in World War I.

Hitler's propaganda stressed a combination of extreme nationalism, working-class rhetoric, and middle-class values, but the core of his new ideology was a rabid racism that took the form of virulent anti-Semitism. Hitler, too, created a paramilitary organization of "Brown Shirts," which he used against his political enemies. After a failed coup in 1923, it took another decade of political maneuvering, violence, and propaganda, combined with the disaster of the Great Depression, before Hitler came to power in 1933.

REVOLUTION, LEFT AND RIGHT

The upheaval in Russia in 1917 was a revolution on the extreme left, inspired by the theories of Karl Marx and Lenin's Bolshevik political strategies. The fascist revolutions in Italy and Germany began with a blend of socialist and nationalist principles, but by the 1920s, fascism became symbolic of extreme right-wing political values.

Both Bolshevism and fascism entailed revolutionary change. The existing governments fell in a context of social upheaval and civil war. In the aftermath of the revolutionary seizure of power in the countries involved, new political and economic structures were created. Lenin, Mussolini, and Hitler were revolutionary leaders who came from segments of society with hitherto little influence and who rose to power on a wave of mass support. Each, whether of the left or the right, was a masterful manipulator of public opinion who sought to evoke blind obedience and ideological fervor from his followers. These men represented a new kind of political power, claiming authority from popular will or historical inevitability and maintaining it in part by modern technology and new systems of mass communications. The political movements they brought to power established a new form of rule known as *totalitarianism*, which used terror and repression to stamp out political opposition and minorities, backed up by educational programs and massive propaganda campaigns designed to impose conformity of thought.

Although inspired by opposite political ideologies, both left-wing and right-wing revolutionaries wanted to create economic systems dominated by state planning and control. Under the Bolsheviks, private property rights were abolished and the state dictated production levels in accordance with socialist principles. In the fascist regimes of Italy and Germany, however, capitalism and private property continued to exist, although they were subject to government regulation.

Between the two world wars, European political life was largely dominated by the struggle between the ideologies of communism and fascism. Supporters of both camps battled one another in bloody confrontations while threatening established governments almost everywhere in Europe. By the early 1930s, traditional liberal democratic notions were under siege from both right and left.

THE MARCH REVOLUTION AND THE BOLSHEVIK SEIZURE OF POWER

The Russian Revolution of 1917 consisted of two separate upheavals—the first in March, the second in November—which occurred against the background of the enormous strains caused by World War I. The first stage saw the overthrow of the centuries-old monarchy of the tsars and the establishment of a provisional government. In November, the Bolsheviks staged a coup d'état and seized power in their own right, laying the basis for a communist state. In their determination to demonstrate the irreversible break with the past, Bolshevik leaders ordered the execution of Tsar Nicholas II and his family.

THE CRISIS OF TSARIST RUSSIA

The first serious threat to the autocratic rule of the tsars had come in 1905, when working-class protestors managed to extract limited political concessions from Nicholas (see Topic 74). The problems of the imperial government were compounded by the character and personality of the tsar and his wife, Alexandra (1872–1918). Nicholas lacked sufficient strength of will or keenness of intellect to be an effective ruler. He believed in absolutism and divine guidance, but was too easily influenced by those around him. Nor was Nicholas comfortable with change. The Tsarina Alexandra, a German princess by birth, was even more of an absolutist than her husband, and she counseled Nicholas not to give in to pressures for reform. Deeply religious, to the point of superstition, Alexandra's views were reinforced by Gregori Yefimovich Rasputin (1871?–1916), a bizarre holy man of peasant origins. As a young man he gained such an unsavory reputation that he was given the nickname of "Rasputin," meaning a debauchee. When he arrived in St. Petersburg in 1905, he came to the attention of the tsarina for his mystical powers and his supposed ability to improve the hemophiliac condition of her young son. Soon he exerted enormous influence over the royal family and in political affairs. Rumors of corruption and sexual license within the court helped erode public confidence in the imperial government.

SIGNIFICANT DATES

The Russian Revolution

March 8, 1917	Women's march in Petrograd
March 10, 1917	General Strike
March 12, 1917	Provisional government
March 15, 1917	Nicholas II abdicates
March 1917	Petrograd Soviet formed
April 20, 1917	Lenin's "April Theses"
May 16, 1917	Kerensky heads provisional government
July 1917	Coup against provisional government fails
November 6–7, 1917	Bolshevik coup
January 1918	Lenin closes Constituent Assembly and establishes dictatorship
March 15, 1918	Treaty of Brest-Litovsk
1918–1922	Russian civil war
March 1921	New Economic Policy introduced
December 1922	Union of Soviet Socialist Republics established
1924	Lenin dies
1929	Trotsky exiled

Although Nicholas had no military experience, he assumed personal charge of Russia's armies in 1915. The Tsarina Alexandra actually ran the day-to-day operations of the government while her husband was at the front. Food shortages and the lack of basic necessities aroused civilian restlessness in the cities, and advisers and court officials urged reforms in order to bolster morale. But at Rasputin's insistence, Alexandra refused any concessions and temporarily closed the Duma (legislative assembly). In a desperate effort to end his pernicious control of government policy, three noblemen killed Rasputin in December 1916. His death was as strange as his life. At a private party arranged for the purpose, he was fed a cake containing an enormous amount of poison, but he remained alive; in the end, the assassins finally had to shoot him and fling his body into a river. When the corpse was recovered, the authorities determined that he had died of drowning.

THE FIRST REVOLUTION

By 1917, some 7 million soldiers were dead, wounded, or missing. In early March, workers joined housewives in protests against the lack of food. When the socialists staged a massive Woman's Day demonstration, thousands of workers moved into the city avenues and squares. Nicholas demanded that the demonstrations be crushed, and on March 11 soldiers fired at the demonstrators. Soon, however, the troops joined the rioters. As the tsar became the target of popular outrage, the Duma formed a provisional government led by Prince Georgi Lvov (1861–1925). Nicholas was persuaded to abdicate when it was clear that the army's loyalty could not be guaranteed. Lvov announced plans to hold elections for a constituent assembly and for the introduction of universal suffrage for males and enacted basic civil liberties. To gain popular support, the provisional government promised to distribute land to the peasants, mandated an eight-hour day for workers, freed the tsar's political prisoners, and proclaimed that Jews would no longer be persecuted.

Although the provisional government gained the support of a wide stratum of Russians, its leadership was undermined by the Soviet (Council) of Workers' and Soldiers' Deputies, a radical organization consisting of worker representatives established in Petrograd. (The city of St. Petersburg had been renamed Petrograd in 1914, to replace the German word for city, *burg*, with the Slavic *grad*. The name was changed again in 1924, when Stalin ordered it replaced by Leningrad, in honor of the late revolutionary leader.) The Petrograd Soviet quickly came to direct the activities of hundreds of similar councils that were created in industrial factories, the armed forces, and in rural villages across Russia.

The Soviets were formed mainly by socialists, who were divided, however, into Social Revolutionaries and members of the Marxist-inspired Social Democratic Workers party. The Social Revolutionaries were agrarian radicals who believed that Russian society could best be changed by the peasants through established village councils. Members of the Social Democratic Workers party had split into two groups, the Mensheviks and the Bolsheviks. *Menshevik* means "minority" and *Bolshevik* "majority." The terms had nothing

to do, however, with their size but rather were derived from a vote that had been taken in 1903 on matters of party organization, in which the Mensheviks had gotten a minority of the vote. Both shared an adherence to Marxist principles, but they disagreed over fundamental questions of strategy. The reformist Mensheviks wanted to create a mass-based party as socialists had done in Western Europe. The Mensheviks expected to bring about a socialist society by peaceful reform, but not until industrial capitalism had spread more fully and had created a large urban working class.

The Bolsheviks disagreed with both principles. Their leader, Vladimir Ilyich Lenin (born Vladimir Ilyich Ulianov, 1870–1924), fought against the reformist ideas of the Mensheviks. He believed that such peaceful tactics were not possible under tsarist absolutism and insisted that revolutionary violence alone could achieve socialism. Lenin also disagreed with Marx's notion that revolution was not feasible in an agrarian society like Russia's that had only an infant industrial working class. Moreover, Lenin saw the party not as a mass movement but as a small elite of professional revolutionaries. Such a vanguard would not only provide the party with discipline and leadership, but would also be able to seize power when circumstances were favorable. Although the Soviets lacked a uniform ideological position, they competed with the provisional government by backing the demands of the urban workers and rural peasants. The Duma, on the other hand, which supported the government, was dominated by liberal elements who favored a constitutional monarchy. Because the Bolsheviks were not in the government, they could distance themselves from the Lvov regime.

The provisional government and the Duma stubbornly refused to make peace with the Germans, declaring it their duty to fight alongside the Allies. In May, after the government announced once again its determination to pursue the war effort, popular pressure persuaded some members of the government to resign. This crisis was compounded by the government's inability to meet the demands of the workers or the peasants' cry for land.

THE BOLSHEVIK SEIZURE OF POWER

Under the skillful leadership of Lenin, the Bolsheviks took full advantage of the government's failure to secure popular support. Despite his unassuming appearance, Lenin had an immense appeal, not only to party militants but also to workers. Possessed of a brilliant mind, he had become an opponent of the tsarist regime at the age of 17, when his brother was executed for attempting to kill Tsar Alexander III. He later became a militant in the Social Democratic Workers party and spent years in prison and in Siberian exile because of his antigovernment activism. In 1900 he escaped to Western Europe, from where he directed the Bolshevik faction of the party and led the split with the Mensheviks over tactics for achieving a socialist state.

Lenin was in Switzerland at the time of the March revolution, but the Germans, hoping that the Bolsheviks would disrupt the Russian war effort, allowed him to cross their country by railway to reach Russia. Not until April did

Lenin arrive in Petrograd, but he immediately went on the offensive. Instead of supporting the provisional government, he ordered his fellow Bolsheviks to plan for another revolution. The seizure of power in Russia, he said, would be the first step toward upheaval in the industrialized societies of Western Europe.

The collapse of the government's offensive against the Central Powers in July 1917 sparked a large-scale military insurrection in Petrograd. Lvov, who quelled the mutiny, accused the Bolsheviks of treachery and arrested some of their leaders. Lenin escaped in disguise to Finland. Yet the uprising suggested the need for the provisional government to broaden its support. Alexander Kerensky (1881–1970), a moderate Social Revolutionary, therefore became head of government. Like Lvov, however, Kerensky quickly lost credibility by refusing to make immediate peace with the Germans. In September, Kerensky followed this mistake with another—permitting a reactionary officer, Lavr Kornilov, to strike at the Soviets. Kerensky panicked, however, when he thought that Kornilov intended to seize the government and he provided arms for the Soviet's Red Guards. Kornilov's attempt was forestalled.

By now, Kerensky's ability to govern rested on the Soviets, which Lenin sought to take over. Bolshevik support grew rapidly as he launched a campaign for "peace, land, and bread" that contrasted sharply with the government's inability to achieve any of these. Lenin then demanded "all power to the Soviets." When the Bolsheviks won control of the Soviets of both Petrograd and Moscow, Lenin made his way back to Russia.

Lenin prepared to take power with the help of Leon Trotsky (real name Lev Bronstein, 1879–1940), whose keen mind and organizational genius made him the mastermind of the Bolshevik victory. Trotsky, who headed the Petrograd Soviet, first gained crucial advantage by securing appointment as the council's military commander of the capital. He then persuaded government soldiers to join with the Soviets. Together, on the night of November 6, Trotsky's forces quickly took control of the railroads, power stations, telephone building, bridges, and important government departments. At the same time, Soviet sailors moved the ship *Aurora* along the Neva River and trained its guns on the Winter Palace, Kerensky's headquarters. Kerensky fled. While these events transpired, the Bolsheviks announced that the Soviets had taken power and had made Lenin the new head of government. In one sudden blow, the Bolsheviks had won.

THE SOVIET UNION IN THE MAKING

THE LENINIST DICTATORSHIP

The first goal of Lenin's regime was to satisfy the people's demands for an end to war and hunger. Lenin nationalized the land, and the Soviets were to convert the large estates into collective farms. In fact, however, many peasants had already taken plots of land and were allowed to keep them. These measures did not, however, address the burning problem of hunger because the small landowners refused to send their crops to the cities. The civil war, combined with successive harvest failures, exacerbated the problem and contributed to mass starvation.

Lenin also found the restoration of peace difficult. Germany demanded severe terms from the Soviets, and some Bolsheviks even suggested continuing the war as a revolutionary struggle against the West. But Lenin was determined to make peace. The Treaty of Brest-Litovsk, negotiated by Trotsky and concluded on March 15, 1918, gave to Germany all the land it had conquered from Russia during the war, including the Baltic regions of Finland, Estonia, Latvia, and Lithuania, as well as the Ukraine and eastern Poland. Despite the heavy price, the return of peace was greeted with deep satisfaction by millions of Russians.

Russia had no experience with democracy, either on the national level or among the local peasant councils. Only the Soviets practiced a form of democracy, and in factories and army units workers and soldiers elected officials and exercised some authority. The lack of democratic tradition conformed to Lenin's purposes because his idea of a centralized, highly disciplined party would prevail in the aftermath of the November revolution. The Bolsheviks never claimed to admire Western-style democracy. Lenin's dictatorial views were made clear when elections for a constituent assembly were held in November: The Social Revolutionaries won nearly twice as many delegates as the Bolsheviks, and Lenin closed the assembly down after only one meeting. In its place he created a "dictatorship of the proletariat." The Communist party—the new name assumed by the Bolsheviks—now ruled Russia.

The Bolsheviks began to put their political and economic policies into practice in 1918. The capital of the country was moved from Petrograd to Moscow, deep in the interior. There, a centralized state bureaucracy controlled by the Communist party was established. All peasants were now forced to surrender their crops to urban markets. When it was clear that the factory committees were failing to meet the government's demand for higher industrial production, party trade unions replaced the worker committees. Every branch of industry was nationalized and placed under centralized state control. Dozens of state trusts were created within several years, and each was placed under the authority of a Supreme Council of National Economy that coordinated economic planning and production.

THE CIVIL WAR

Lenin argued that these measures—he called them "war communism"—were needed because the new Communist government had to fight for its existence against foreign and internal opponents. Reactionaries, moderates, and Social Revolutionaries formed legions known as the "White Army" to bring down the regime. Then, too, a host of ethnic minorities and nationalities sought independence from Russia. In 1918, some 100,000 soldiers from the United States, France, Great Britain, Japan, and other nations in-

Map 81.1 Russia, 1918–1919. Virtually all of the territory ceded by Russia by the treaty of Bresk-Litovsk was regained by Russia and added to form the Soviet Union—Georgia and the Ukraine after 1920, and the Baltic Republics of Estonia, Latvia, and Lithuania in 1940. In 1939, Stalin's forces invaded Finland but were driven back by fierce resistance.

vaded Russia in an effort to topple the Communists from power. Finally, peasants launched a counter-revolutionary war against the Red Army that was confiscating their crops.

The Treaty of Brest-Litovsk hurt the Allied military position because the Germans were now able to move their troops from the Eastern to the Western front. The German Army pierced Allied lines and advanced against Paris. Although the Germans were turned back, Allied governments worried that Communist revolution might affect their own war-torn societies. On July 16, 1918, after the British and French sent some 20,000 troops to Archangel and Murmansk on the Arctic Sea, the Bolsheviks killed the imperial family lest the White Army or the Czechs try to rescue them.

The United States intervened ostensibly in response to the plight of thousands of Czech prisoners of war in Siberia

who broke out of their prison camps and seized the railroad in order to get home, where they hoped to fight for Czech independence. To support the Czechs, the United States agreed to a combined landing of American and Japanese soldiers at Vladivostok, on the Pacific coast. That winter, British troops captured the railroads between the Caspian and the Black seas, and a French-Greek operation seized Odessa.

After the armistice was concluded in November, Allied troops stayed in Russia. Yet Lenin's immense prestige, together with the Communist party's internal discipline, kept the Red Army intact, while the White Army was deeply divided by ideological differences. The Bolsheviks dominated the center of Russia and fought along interior lines, while the enemy forces were stretched out along an immense border.

By late 1920, the Red Army victory was so complete that the Allies withdrew their forces from Russia. The

Map 81.2 The Russian Civil War. By keeping their fighting forces concentrated in the area between Petrograd (from 1914 to 1924 the name of St. Petersburg) and Moscow, the Bolsheviks forced their opponents, the White forces, to split up their troops in order to attack from different directions. When the Allied forces withdrew in 1920, the Bolshevik victory was assured.

Bolsheviks succeeded in recovering much of the territory they had lost to the Germans. The Soviet state now began to take shape. Some ethnic minorities and border nationalities had achieved a measure of self-determination during the civil war, but the Soviets now reestablished command of Russian Armenia, Azerbaijan, and Georgia. In December 1922, Lenin created a centralized Russian-dominated federal system of "autonomous" states united into the Union of Soviet Socialist Republics.

THE NEW ECONOMIC POLICY

The civil war, together with disease and starvation, killed millions of Russians. Farms and urban centers had been destroyed, and the transportation network was in shambles. Engineers, doctors, and other professionals were desperately needed, and the shortage of raw materials was critical. Industrial production fell to less than one-fifth of its pre-1914 level. Crop failures and hoarding contributed to persistent starvation. The Bolsheviks, who now had responsibility for government policies, lost more popular backing.

In the wake of worker and peasant unrest, a military uprising at Kronstadt broke out in March 1921. Lenin moved to regain control of the situation. He introduced a New Economic Policy (NEP), which represented a compromise with socialist theory. The NEP allowed a measure of private ownership in retail shops and small industries. In the countryside, it stopped crop confiscation and permitted peasants to sell their goods competitively. Communists debated the

NEP hotly because it created a new category of middle-class peasants known as *kulaks* ("big peasants"), in contradiction to the socialist ideal of a society with no class distinctions. Viewed as a temporary expedient, the NEP did not end state ownership and management of banking, large industries, and transportation. The program had limited success, and only by 1928 did industry and farming return to prewar production levels.

The Soviet constitution provided for an All-Union Congress of Soviets, a representative body that in theory wielded supreme authority. The Congress elected a Council of People's Commissars, an Executive Committee, and a Presidium that presided when the Congress was not in session. In 1936 the name of the Congress was changed to the Supreme Soviet, and that of the People's Commissars was altered in 1946 to the Council of Ministers. The party, however, actually governed the Soviet Union. The party's Central Committee, with some 50 members, gathered only occasionally and chose a 10-member Politburo. Executive power rested in a Secretariat of from one to three members, selected by the Politburo.

THE RISE OF STALIN

Lenin had two strokes in 1922 that prevented him from exercising leadership on a regular basis. Many thought that Trotsky, his closest collaborator, would be his successor, but Trotsky's ambitions led important party officials to oppose him. Late that year the party leaders created a *troika*—a three-person executive—that included the general secretary of the party, Joseph Stalin (real name Joseph Djugashvili, 1879–1953).

Although most of the Old Bolsheviks—those who had led the 1917 Revolution—were from the middle class, Stalin was a man of the people, born in the region of Georgia. Stalin's father had been a shoemaker and his grandfather a serf. He became a Bolshevik when he was about 20, when he adopted the underground name of Stalin ("man of steel"). Like Lenin, he spent years in prison and in Siberia, but Stalin never lived abroad. As a result, he was more provincial in outlook and lacked perspective. His thirst for power was limitless, and he was shrewd and ruthless. He used his position as general secretary of the party to create a cadre of bureaucrats who owed allegiance to him.

In December 1922, after his second stroke, Lenin began to think about his successor, but he was anxious about Stalin, just as others were becoming concerned about Trotsky. He dictated to his wife and confidant, Nadezhda Krupskaya (1869–1939), a political testament in which he analyzed the strengths and weaknesses of Stalin and Trotsky as possible successors. He was uncertain about whether Stalin was capable of exercising power prudently, and when he learned that Stalin had used brutal methods in subduing the anticommunist opposition in Georgia, Lenin added a codicil to his testament rejecting Stalin and advising his comrades to select another leader.

After Lenin's death in 1924, Krupskaya tried unsuccessfully to have his testament and the codicil read to a

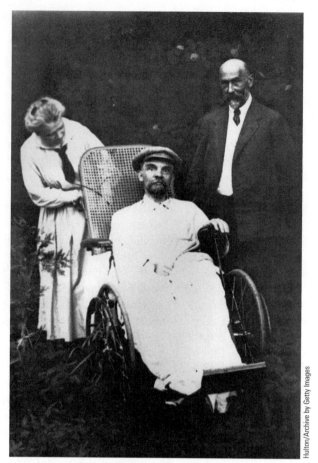

Hulton/Archive by Getty Images

Lenin in a wheelchair. 1923. Lenin's illness and incapacity did much to facilitate Stalin's rise to power. After suffering two strokes in 1922, he remained nominal leader of the Soviet Communist Party for the next two years, until his death in 1924. As this image shows, he was unable to play any significant part in day-to-day activities. The woman present is his sister, Maria Ulyanova. The identity of the man, perhaps a doctor, is unknown.

Hulton/Archive by Getty Images

Stalin and Serge Ordzkonikidze, Commissar for economics. 1924. At the time, Stalin had just become party leader. His companion and close friend had joined the Communist Party as early as 1902. After the 1917 Revolution he became chairman of the Party's Caucasian bureau and was instrumental in bringing Georgia, Stalin's native region, into the Soviet Union in 1922.

party congress. Instead, Stalin presented to the congress his theory of "Socialism in One Country." He wanted the Soviet Union to build an industrial economy that would preserve socialism inside the country and eschew the export of revolution elsewhere. In his power struggle with Trotsky, Stalin outmaneuvered the hero of the civil war, and in 1925 won the backing of party members in removing him as war commissar. In 1929, Trotsky was forced into exile. One by one, Stalin then disposed of the Old Bolsheviks, including those who had supported him against Trotsky. For years Trotsky stood as a symbol of opposition to Stalin's brutal regime, until in 1940 a Stalinist assassin murdered him with an axe in Mexico City.

For the next 20 years, Stalin was the absolute ruler of the Soviet Union, wielding more power than the tsars. Krupskaya lived through the terror of Stalin's purges and held a position on the party's Central Committee until her death in 1939, but the fact that Lenin had rejected Stalin remained secret. Under Stalin, Lenin's goal of creating a workers' democracy disappeared, replaced by a program of forced modernization aimed at making Russia a world power. For that goal, the Russian people paid a heavy price.

"MUTILATED VICTORY": ITALY FROM WAR TO FASCISM

Italy entered World War I a year later than the other European powers. From the summer of 1914 to May 1915—the period known as the "interventionist crisis"—the country remained neutral while negotiating with both sides the highest price for its support. By the Treaty of London, which promised her extensive territorial gains in the event of an Allied victory, Italy joined the war in 1915 alongside Britain, France, and Russia (see Topic 80).

At war's end, however, Italy found itself in a difficult position. Politicians and intellectuals had agonized over the question of intervention. Millions of men, mainly peasants, had been drafted, and many of them had been killed or wounded. The fighting had drained the national treasury, and the government had made generous

SIGNIFICANT DATES

The Rise of Fascism

1883–1945	Life of Benito Mussolini
1902–1904	Mussolini in Switzerland
1912	Mussolini becomes editor of *Avanti!*
August–November 1914	Mussolini breaks with PSI; founds *Popolo d'Italia*
April–May 1915	Pact of London; Italy's entrance into war
1915–1917	Mussolini serves at front and is wounded
November 1918	Armistice
March 1919	*Fascio di Combattimento* formed
September 1919	D'Annunzio invades Fiume
1920–1922	Fascist violence
October 29, 1922	Mussolini becomes prime minister
1924	Fascist electoral victory; Matteotti crisis
1924–1926	Fascist dictatorship created

promises to the lower classes in order to maintain morale. By late 1919, inflation had struck, and angry veterans wanted jobs at a time when some 2 million Italians were out of work.

At the Paris Peace Conference, the Italians were denied most of the territory that had been promised them, including the entire Dalmatian coast. Instead, Dalmatia was given to the new nation of Yugoslavia. When Italy demanded the port of Fiume (now Rijeka) as compensation, the Allies refused. This blow to Italian national prestige was especially hard for the veterans. Irate nationalists fanned the flames of patriotism, blaming government for having accepted a "mutilated victory."

MUSSOLINI THE REVOLUTIONARY

One of the most outspoken critics of the government was Benito Mussolini (1883–1945), who had become an ardent interventionist during the war. Mussolini was a native of the Romagna region in northeastern Italy, where his father had been a blacksmith and a socialist agitator. Prone to violence even as a child, he had been expelled from several schools before becoming a schoolteacher. By 1901, he too had joined the Socialist party. He spent the years 1902–1904 in Switzerland as a draft dodger, and he completed his political education there. Neutral Switzerland was refuge for hundreds of revolutionary exiles from all over Europe, especially Russian radicals such as Lenin who had escaped the tsar's police. There Mussolini helped organize workers and gave speeches on behalf of the Italian Socialist party (PSI).

Back in Italy again in 1904, Mussolini began to make a name for himself among revolutionary socialists. He proved to be a powerful orator and writer. When Italy and Turkey fought over Libya in 1911–1912 (see Topic 73), he joined other pacifist socialists in condemning imperialism, spending several months in prison for his antiwar activities. In 1912 he took part in a revolutionary socialist coup against the reformist leaders of the PSI, and became editor of *Avanti!*, the official Socialist party newspaper.

During the interventionist crisis, Mussolini did an about-face. Arguing that the war would spark revolution, he pressed for Italian intervention on the Allied side, for which the PSI expelled him. He then began publishing an interventionist newspaper, *Il Popolo d'Italia*, and volunteered for military service, serving at the front and being promoted to sergeant. In 1917 he was wounded and mustered out of the army, returning to politics. During the last years of the war, Mussolini's thinking underwent a further evolution as he replaced the Marxist doctrine of class struggle with the principle of nationalism.

Benito Mussolini posing for a sculptor. October 1922. The day before this picture was taken, the king had appointed Mussolini prime minister. Always conscious of the power of the image—both literal and metaphorical—Mussolini promoted his own image by copies of this work and other similar ones. At a time before television, they provided a visible symbol of his message.

THE BIRTH OF FASCISM

Mussolini soon emerged as spokesman for the war veterans, repeatedly condemning Italy's lost peace. Some of his thunder was stolen in September 1919 by the flamboyant nationalist poet Gabriele D'Annunzio (1863–1938), who led war veterans in the seizure of Fiume. When the Italian government refused to accept Fiume from his hands, D'Annunzio proclaimed it an independent state. Italy expelled him from the city a year later, but the expedition had inflamed nationalist feeling and suggested the ease of staging a military takeover. From D'Annunzio, Mussolini learned something about the choreography of political propaganda, and eventually took as his own D'Annunzio's Roman salute, with its outstretched arm and cry of *"Viva il Duce!"*—*Duce,* from the Latin *dux,* is the Italian word meaning "leader."

Meanwhile, the liberal government had become the target of popular resentment. In November 1919, national elections based on universal male suffrage were held, and the liberals lost the majority they had held in Parliament since 1861. Instead, the PSI and a new Catholic party became, respectively, the two largest parties. But with the socialists and Catholics refusing to form a coalition government, King Victor Emmanuel III felt free to choose liberal prime ministers.

This political crisis unfolded in a context of massive social unrest—almost 2,000 industrial and agrarian strikes took place in 1919. Peasants seized land in the South, and others organized associations in the northern Po Valley; in September 1920 some 500,000 workers, supported by socialist leaders such as Antonio Gramsci (1891–1937), occupied factories in the major industrial cities of the North. Such labor tensions, together with the success of the PSI, frightened many middle-class Italians into thinking that Bolshevik revolution was imminent.

Fascism was born in these unstable conditions. Mussolini founded the movement in Milan on March 23, 1919, at an unimpressive rally of little more than 100 followers who were later called the "Fascists of the first hour." The members of this *Fascio di Combattimento* ("combat group") were war veterans, nationalist intellectuals, and former interventionist socialists and syndicalists like Mussolini. He took the movement's name from the Latin *fasces* (sticks bound around an axe handle and used in ancient Rome as a symbol of unity and authority), a common term for left-wing radical movements at the time. A program issued later that year combined left-wing ingredients such as the eight-hour workday, worker participation in management, a republican constitution, and the vote for women and 18-year-olds, with right-wing demands for an aggressive foreign policy and strong secular, nationalist education. Later, under pressure from conservative supporters, the program underwent a pronounced shift to the right.

THE STRUGGLE FOR POWER

Most active members of the Fascist movement were from the lower middle class, especially young veterans inspired by the spirit of bravery and comradeship they had experienced in the war, and bound by loyalty and discipline. These men generally stood against the established order, resentful of privilege and wealth, and committed to avenging the "mutilated victory" of 1919. They made up the rank and file of the armed Fascist squads, whose bludgeons and daggers, black-shirted uniforms, and skull and crossbones insignia represented a new, dangerous element in European politics.

Organized in military fashion and led by powerful regional chieftains, these so-called *squadristi,* many of whom were simply brutish thugs, plunged Italy into a bloody nightmare of violence aimed not only against Fascism's political enemies, but also against those perceived as defeatists and pacifists. Armed with military weapons, they went on "punitive expeditions" against socialists and labor union activists, terrorized peasant groups, and broke up strikes.

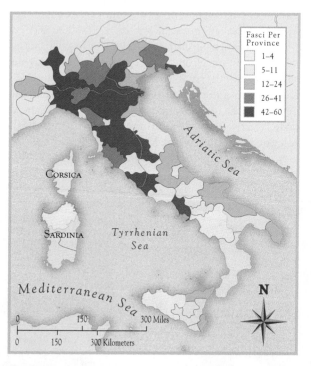

Map 81.3 Fascist groups (Fasci) in Italy, May 1922. The heartland of Fascism was central Italy: the regions of Emilia and Romagna, the latter where Mussolini was born. There were concentrations in the northwest, around Genoa, Turin, and Milan, and on the west coast farther down, around Rome and Naples. The rural south and Sicily were barely affected. Life there was so hard, and most people so poor, that nothing seemed able to offer hope of improvement.

THE FASCIST VICTORY AND MUSSOLINI'S DICTATORSHIP

Because of the "Red Scare" that swept over Italy in 1920–1921, the war against the socialists enabled Mussolini to secure financial support from landowners and industrialists. The liberal government, secretly anxious to see the weakening of the PSI, failed to stop the Black Shirt violence. In 1921, the Fascists began attacking the state, raiding municipal halls, provincial councils, and railroad and telegraph stations. Soon they threatened to take over the central government. Fascism had grown rapidly; the number of recruits, which had numbered not quite 1,000 in the summer of 1919, jumped to 250,000 by 1922. Fascist violence, combined with official inaction, gave the appearance that the movement was the only viable force capable of governing the nation.

FROM DUCE TO PRIME MINISTER

Mussolini played a shrewd game, preserving the public fiction that he was an ordinary, respectable political leader while goading on his Black Shirt followers. In 1921 he changed the Fascist movement into the Fascist National party (PNF). In the elections that year, Mussolini and 34 other Fascists won seats in the Chamber of Deputies. Giovanni Giolitti, the liberal prime minister (see Topic 73), failed, however, to understand that Fascism was no ordinary political party. He tried unsuccessfully to entice Mussolini into the government as part of a moderate-conservative front called the National Bloc, but the Fascists would not be drawn into traditional establishment politics—they wanted nothing less than full power.

In late 1922, Mussolini's hardline Fascists convinced him to attempt the seizure of power. They planned a "March on Rome" to force King Victor Emmanuel III into appointing a Fascist government. At the end of October, while Mussolini remained in his office in Milan, the Black Shirt chieftains launched a three-pronged drive toward Rome with some 50,000 men. The regular army could have mustered much stronger forces to protect the capital, but the king, afraid that the country would be thrown into civil war or that the military would go over to the Fascists, failed to declare a state of emergency. The prime minister, Luigi Facta (served February to October 1922), resigned, and the king then collapsed in the face of the Fascist threat. On

October 29, Victor Emmanuel offered Mussolini the prime ministership. Traveling to Rome by train, Mussolini, having discarded his Fascist uniform, took the oath of office as the youngest prime minister in Italian history.

The March on Rome never really happened. Mussolini became prime minister in accordance with the provisions of the Italian constitution. Nor was he yet a dictator, for only half of his cabinet members were Fascists, and of the more than 500 deputies in Parliament, the party could still count only 35. As a result, Mussolini worked to solidify his position. He asked for and received special powers to rule by decree and to censor the press, and in 1923 he convinced the liberals to enact legislation aimed at giving the Fascist party control of Parliament. The so-called Acerbo Law provided that the party that made the strongest showing in a national election would—provided it received at least 25 percent of all votes cast—receive two-thirds of all seats in the Chamber of Deputies. In the 1924 elections, the Fascists won the required number of votes by renewed violence and poll fixing. With the party now dominant in Parliament, Mussolini felt more secure, but relations with the Italian Army remained unresolved. He secured the backing of the military only after agreeing to turn the Black Shirt squads into a Fascist militia, controlled by the regular army.

Still, Mussolini hesitated to move toward full dictatorship. An unexpected political crisis later in 1924 changed the situation. Giacomo Matteotti (1885–1924), a bold and popular Socialist deputy, began to expose the illegal manner in which the Fascists had stolen the recent election. That summer Fascist agents murdered him, possibly on orders from Mussolini. A wave of public indignation exploded, and the non-Fascist press turned against the prime minister. Even the king wavered in his support of Mussolini, and some liberal statesmen urged that he be dismissed. Leaders of the anti-Fascist opposition withdrew en masse from Parliament and called themselves the "Aventine Secession," in memory of the secession of the Roman people in the years of the ancient

Mussolini on the balcony of Palazzo Venezia, Rome. 1930s. Mussolini deliberately chose Palazzo Venezia as the location of his office because of the huge piazza Venezia where mass rallies such as this one could be staged. Furthermore, it is located right in the heart of the city, close to the ancient Forum Romanum and the Capitoline Hill, and was (and still is) dominated by the Monument to Victor Emmanuel II, the first king of Italy; the monument is called the Altare della Patria (Altar of the Nation).

THE NATURE OF FASCISM

STANLEY G. PAYNE University of Wisconsin–Madison

Fascism was the only completely new force among the major radical movements active in European affairs after World War I. Although ingredients that made up fascism were not themselves new, they had never coalesced into a specific form before 1919. Moreover, fascism was also difficult to understand or to categorize. Although fascists strongly opposed the movements of the left, such as communism and socialism, they denied that fascists were of the right. Fascists claimed to represent a synthesis of both the left and right, and some fascist movements even called themselves "national socialists," as distinct from Marxist or international socialists. Communists, in turn, usually denounced fascism as the instrument of the "most reactionary and violent" sector of the bourgeoisie, but fascists always claimed to be a popular force that united people of diverse social and class backgrounds in the service of the nation.

Fascism was even more confusing because fascist leaders boasted of being activists and pragmatists, relatively indifferent to doctrines or ideology. Later, after World War II, the understanding of fascism even sparked controversy among professional historians. Some would complain that the term "fascist" was applied too loosely and vaguely as a mere political epithet, or used to encompass a wide variety of political movements that were mutually contradictory. Others sought to explain the nature or historical meaning of fascism according to social, economic, philosophical, or even psychological factors.

The term "fascism" was derived from the Italian *fascio*, meaning a union or league, and commonly adopted by new Italian political forces in the later 19th and early 20th centuries. Thus a new group of radical Italian nationalists led by Benito Mussolini found it natural to call themselves the "Fasci Italiani" in 1919 and later transformed the term into an adjective when they organized the "Italian National Fascist Party" two years later, giving rise to "fascist" and "fascism." The movement soon developed a mass member-ship, enabling its leader to become prime minister in October 1922 and to convert Italy's government into a one-party dictatorship in January 1925.

Its nearest major counterpart, the National Socialist German Workers' party (known to their enemies as "Nazis") sprang from a small group organized in Munich in 1917, then reorganized under Adolf Hitler three years later. Whereas Mussolini came to power relatively rapidly, the same process took Hitler much longer, although he built an even larger and more potent political movement along the way. By the time that Hitler took power in 1933, other new radical nationalist parties had appeared in most other European countries. They became strong mass movements, in one form or another, in only four other countries: Hungary (the Arrow Cross), Romania (the Iron Guard), Austria (the Austrian Nazis), and Spain (Spanish Phalanx).

Although these individual fascist-type movements sometimes differed a good deal among themselves, they also shared certain fundamental characteristics and goals, which as a whole tended to set them off from other kinds of political forces. The fascists were first of all unique because they were opposed to nearly all of the existing political sectors. They were antiliberal, anticommunist (as well as antisocialist in the social democratic sense), and also anticonservative, although sometimes willing to undertake temporary alliances with rightist groups.

What differentiated fascists from the right was their rejection of philosophical as well as economic conservatism and their determination to replace the established social elites of the right. They differed profoundly from the left in their rejection of internationalism and egalitarianism or equal rights, as well as in their antipathy to socialized materialism. They sought to remake Europe in the form of a nationalist/imperialist "New Order," profoundly different from the liberal 19th century or the new Marxist-Leninist system of the Soviet Union.

Fascist movements drew support from highly diverse social sectors. In their earliest phase, followers came from former military personnel and small sectors of the radical *intelligentsia*, sometimes university students. Although some fascist movements enjoyed a degree of backing from the upper bourgeoisie, the broadest sector of support was often provided by the lower middle class. In Germany and Hungary, considerable support also came from workers, while university students were especially important in Italy, Germany, Spain, and Romania, and poor farmers were often recruited in Romania.

A bewildering variety of theories and interpretations have been advanced since 1923 to explain fascism. Among them are (1) theories of socioeconomic causation, primarily of Marxist inspiration; (2) the application of modernization theory, which posits fascism as a phase in modern development; and (3) the theory of totalitarianism, which interprets fascism as one aspect of the broader phenomenon of 20th-century totalitarianism. None of these theories is entirely convincing. The diversity of the basis of social recruitment and political backing makes any simple theory of social determinism implausible, while the fact that numerous societies have undergone modernization without succumbing to fascism seriously weakens any theory drawn primarily from modernization. The theory of "totalitarianism" is of little help because it tends to ignore the differences between fascism and communism, as well as the differences in historical milieu between the countries in which these two diverse movements triumphed.

Probably the only way to account for fascism is by a "historic" approach that isolates the five key variables in the historical situation of countries in which the main fascist movements emerged. The main *national* variable was one of military defeat, frustration, disunity, and status deprivation. The main *political* variable had to do with countries that were just beginning, or had only recently begun, the transition to direct political democracy. (Conversely, stable and satisfied countries, and those in which political democracy had already existed for a generation or more, were not susceptible.) The key *cultural* variable was the influence of currents of new philosophical idealism and vitalism (propitious to fascism) in a nation's cultural life, as contrasted with materialism and rationalism. The key *economic* variable was either depression or underdevelopment in a context where problems seemed both national in scope and to some extent international in origin. The key *social* variable involved widespread discontent not merely among the young and sectors of the lower classes, but among the lower middle class as well. No one or two or even three of these variables by themselves sufficed to produce a significant fascist movement. Only in those few countries where all five variables were present at approximately the same time were conditions propitious for the emergence of major fascist movements.

Does fascism have a future? Worried foes sometimes fear so, but it is doubtful that the specific forms of early 20th-century European fascism can be revived. Broad cultural, psychological, educational, and economic changes have made the reemergence of something so murderous as Nazism in a modern industrial nation almost impossible, just as international interdependence seems to rule out war among the major European and industrial countries. The prevailing culture of materialism and consumerism militates against extreme positions, and any appeal to mass vitalist and irrationalist politics.

Movements and regimes most similar to fascism during the second half of the 20th century have been more important in certain "Third World" countries than in the West. There, nationalist one-party dictatorships have not been uncommon. More than a few governments in Africa, Asia, and the Middle East have preached their own versions of national socialism (for example, "Arab socialism") and have propagated doctrines based on violence and grounded in mysticism, idealism, and willpower. There too the "cult of personality" and charismatic dictatorship have sometimes been popular. Nonetheless, it is not possible to refer to more than specific features and tendencies. The nationalist movements and dictatorships of the Third World have also developed unique identities and profiles of their own, and in no instance have literally copied or revived European fascist movements. The exact characteristics of interwar Europe, like those of any particular historical epoch, cannot be precisely repeated or reproduced. New authoritarian movements of the 1990s would have to develop qualities appropriate to their own times to achieve support, for a literal revival of the past—particularly of a past so discredited as that of fascism—is doomed to sterility.

Roman Republic, some two and a half millennia earlier. While Mussolini wavered, the more intransigent Fascist chieftains confronted him and forced him to abandon all pretense of democratic rule. Going before a special session of Parliament on January 3, 1925, Mussolini delivered the most important speech of his life, in which he took total responsibility for everything that had happened and announced that he would restore order to Italy. In the following weeks, the "second wave" of Black Shirt terror was unleashed against the anti-Fascists. In this way, Mussolini silenced the opposition and either arrested or forced into exile its most prominent leaders. Between 1925 and 1929, he began to build the Fascist state.

THE GERMAN REVOLUTION AND THE WEIMAR REPUBLIC

Nazism is the German variety of generic fascism—scholars refer to Italian Fascism with a capital "F," and to the generic phenomenon with a lowercase "f." To contemporaries, the two seemed virtually the same. Each was, after all, a radical movement with utopian ideologies that mixed nationalism with socialist and syndicalist ideas, each worshiped an all-powerful *Duce* or *Führer*, and in both instances the average militant was a lower middle-class veteran. Moreover, Fascism and Nazism boasted paramilitary armed squads and both exalted violence, which they used against Marxists and their other political enemies, including liberal democracy.

There were, however, differences. Nazism was based on a theory of racism, whereas a more conventional form of extreme nationalism lay at the heart of Fascist philosophy—

a fact that has something to do with the more pervasive and systematic violence that marked the Nazi regime. Hitler's Nazi government is also considered a more efficient example of totalitarianism than Mussolini's Fascist state, and this difference may be partially explained by Germany's more advanced levels of technical education and industrialization.

THE WEIMAR REPUBLIC

At the end of 1918, Germany was poised at the edge of a revolution as far-reaching as that in Russia. Defeated on the battlefield, Germany's society and economy were exhausted. Moreover, its political system—based on the old Prussian constitution and an all but absolute emperor—had lost its credibility. As a result, left-wing agitation erupted, and soldiers and workers set up groups that resembled the Russian Soviets. Sailors at the northern ports, inspired by revolutionary ideas, staged mutinies in late October. The most dramatic event took place on November 8, when the Independent Socialist Kurt Eisner (1867–1919) formed a Bavarian Republic in Munich. Eisner was assassinated and the radical experiment crushed following bitter street fighting with right-wing reactionaries.

In Berlin, events took a similar turn. Kaiser Wilhelm II abdicated on November 9, 1918, following pressure from the Allies, and Prince Max, the imperial chancellor, resigned. Philipp Scheidemann (1865–1939) and Friedrich Ebert (1871–1925), leaders of the Social Democratic party, formed a provisional government. Then, in order to forestall the more radical Revolutionary Marxists, otherwise known as Spartacists (from Spartacus, a gladiator who led a rebellion of slaves against Rome in the 1st century B.C.), Scheidemann announced the birth of the German Republic. Scheidemann became president and Ebert his chancellor.

The republic quickly became the target of Marxist and right-wing radicals, each of which tried to take power from it. In order to protect the republic, Ebert struck a deal with the German officer corps: In return for protecting the republic against its enemies, the government would pledge to maintain the army intact. The agreement worked only too well. Between January 6 and 15, 1919, the Spartacists, led by Rosa Luxemburg (1870–1919) and Karl Liebknecht (1871–1919), attempted a coup in Berlin known as "Spartacist Week." Government troops, assisted by illegal paramilitary organizations known as the *Freikorps*, put down the revolution with considerable bloodshed. Luxemburg and Liebknecht were arrested, but they were both mysteriously killed on the way to jail. The Freikorps, composed of veterans, were to provide Nazism with some of its first members.

In the midst of this instability, delegates to a National Assembly gathered in the city of Weimar to create a permanent government for Germany. The delegates represented a large number of political parties, including the Social Democrats, the Catholic Center party, and the liberal Democratic party; together these three parties constituted the moderate "Weimar Coalition" that was to govern the nation throughout the 1920s. In July 1919 they approved a

SIGNIFICANT DATES

The Rise of Nazism

1889–1945	Life of Adolf Hitler
1909–1913	Hitler in Vienna
1914–1918	Hitler serves in army and is wounded
November 9, 1918	Kaiser Wilhelm II abdicates; German Republic established under provisional government
November 11, 1918	Armistice
January 6–15, 1919	Spartacist Week
June 1919	Treaty of Versailles
September 1919	Hitler joins the DAP
1920	DAP becomes the NSDAP, or Nazi party
March 1920	Kapp *Putsch*
1923	French occupation of Ruhr
November 1923	Munich *Putsch*

constitution that created the German Republic, one of the most progressive European governments in interwar Europe. Because of its association with the liberal city of Weimar, the republic came to be known as the Weimar Republic.

The constitution, inspired in part by the example of the United States, embodied modern notions of social justice and popular democracy. "Political authority," read its first article, "derives from the people." The head of state was a president, elected for a seven-year term by universal suffrage, and a British-style cabinet government over which a chancellor, appointed by the president, presided. Legislative power resided in a parliament, consisting of a lower house called the *Reichstag*, and an upper chamber, the *Reichrat*, that represented the various German states. A bill of rights protected civil liberties. As a safeguard, Article 48 permitted the president to enact special powers in the event of national emergency.

In the summer of 1920, elections for the *Reichstag* were held. Ominously, the Weimar Coalition lost significant popular support, its share of the vote falling in subsequent elections from more than 75 to less than 50 percent. Instead, the smaller, extremist parties gained considerable strength. Because the centrist parties were unable to secure a majority thereafter, the republic experienced 20 governments between 1920 and 1933.

At best, most Germans regarded the Weimar Republic with skepticism. The very circumstances of its birth were the cause of considerable concern. The kaiser had, after all, abdicated because the Allies wanted him to, not because the German people had expressed their will. The Allies had also pronounced Germany "guilty" of having caused war, but many Germans did not believe that their weakness had really lost it. Reactionary elements, especially monarchists and the military, invented the "stab in the back" myth, ac-

cording to which internal traitors had destroyed Germany's war effort. Hitler would tell the people that these traitors were Jews and Marxists. Finally, of course, the Allies had forced Germany to accept the Treaty of Versailles.

The serious economic difficulties that plagued Germany after 1919 further undermined public confidence in the republic. The economic provisions of the Versailles Treaty had deprived Germany of vital resources and income, and unemployment was widespread. Lacking the resources to deal effectively with the crisis, the government printed millions of dollars worth of paper money, which made the *mark* worthless and sparked rampant inflation. When the French occupied the Ruhr Valley in 1923 in order to extract late reparations payments from Germany, the economy declined further. The cost-of-living index rose on a daily basis, wiping out the value of salaries and pensions. Millions of working- and middle-class Germans were ruined by the inflation, and life in the Weimar Republic took on a real sense of desperation.

HITLER AND NATIONAL SOCIALISM

Like Fascism in Italy, Nazism was a product of the postwar crisis. Yet to an even greater degree than was the case with Mussolini and his movement, Adolf Hitler shaped and dominated the Nazi party.

ADOLF HITLER

The most infamous man in German history actually began life as a subject of the Austro-Hungarian empire. Hitler (1889–1945) was born in Braunau, Austria, the son of an unimportant customs bureaucrat. As a youth, Hitler was

Crowds in Munich, welcoming the news of the outbreak of war. August 1, 1914. Among those present was the young Adolf Hitler, who is shown in the inset (*top right*). Hitler had gone to Munich in 1913, frustrated in his efforts to become an artist in Vienna. He served in the Bavarian regiment and was awarded the Iron Cross.

Robert Hunt Library

estranged from his father, who tried to discourage him from studying art. The boy was bright but was not a good student. He failed to graduate from high school and remained intent on becoming an artist.

Hitler moved to Vienna in 1909 and remained there until the eve of World War I. He first sought to develop his aesthetic inclinations there by studying at the Vienna School of Architecture. Despite limited talent as an architectural draftsman, however, Hitler was twice disappointed when his application to school was rejected. Thereafter, he led a squalid, frustrated life trying to earn a living by painting street scenes and working at menial jobs. Vienna served for Hitler the same purpose that Switzerland had for Mussolini: It provided an opportunity for study and practical experience, during which he developed his political ideas and his notions about race. Reading widely but without purpose, he was exposed to the kinds of extremist, irrational prejudices that proved to be the foundation of his Nazi philosophy.

Vienna was a microcosm of the ethnic diversity of the Austro-Hungarian empire, and it was in that environment that Hitler discovered racism. At the turn of the 20th century, Vienna bred a number of political leaders who tried to capitalize on racial fears and on Austrian anti-Semitism. Such men were among Hitler's first political heroes. Karl Lueger (1844–1910), the leader of the reactionary Christian Social party, won election as mayor of Vienna—"the greatest German mayor of all times," Hitler wrote of him years later—on an anti-Semitic platform. Lueger's example taught Hitler how a radical movement could achieve power by making a campaign against the Jews the basis of mass-based urban politics. Another contemporary, Georg von Schoenerer, was a parliamentary deputy who preached Pan-Germanism and described the Germans as a higher race who deserved to dominate the other peoples of Europe. From such views he derived his belief that all Germans everywhere had to be united into a "greater Germany." Racial theories soon dominated Hitler's mind, and by the time he left Vienna, he had become convinced that Jews and Marxists were the cause of Western cultural and political corruption and the cause of Europe's degeneracy.

At the start of World War I, Hitler immediately joined the German Army. He saw frontline combat, for which he earned a corporal's rank, and was injured in a poison gas attack at the end of the war. While undergoing recovery, he was approached by Captain Ernst Roehm (1887–1934), later a major Nazi leader, and recruited to work for the army in Munich as a civilian investigator.

THE NAZI PARTY

In September 1919, while engaged in gathering information on extremist politics for Roehm, Hitler joined the German Worker's party (DAP). The tiny organization was founded by an anti-Marxist, anti-Semitic worker who wanted the working classes to become fervid nationalists. Hitler soon dominated the party and emerged as a brilliant public

speaker and a powerfully inspiring leader, despite a somewhat comical appearance. He was able to conjure up a unique intensity of emotion in his audiences that eventually captured the loyalty of millions of Germans. In 1920 the party was rebaptized as the National Socialist German Workers' party (NSDAP), soon known popularly as the "Nazi" party—"Nazi" is derived from the German pronunciation of the first two syllables of the German word for "National." He gave talks at rallies all over Munich, increasing the party's membership and shouting his political and racial ideas to all who would listen. His appeal grew as he made the "stab in the back" legend and the Treaty of Versailles the cornerstones of his platform. His devoted followers called him the *Führer* (leader), and by 1930 his tiny party had become a large and vocal force in Weimar politics.

The Nazi party soon had a daily newspaper, the *Völkischer Beobachter* (The People's Observer). Its official platform contained 25 points, chief among them being the creation of a "Greater Germany," an end to the hated *Diktat*—the Treaty of Versailles—and the creation of a prosperous and loyal working and middle class. The platform also aimed to remove the rights of citizenship from Jews. Hitler never believed in the importance of the socialist rhetoric in which the Nazis couched their appeals to the workers. "Left-wing" Nazis like Gregor Strasser (1892–1934) were important in spreading Nazism among the industrial workers of the North, but once they had served their purposes, Hitler purged them from the party.

In 1921, Roehm created and took charge of the SA (*Sturmabteilung*), a paramilitary unit that wore brownshirted uniforms with the swastika as its symbol. The swastika symbol was used in a variety of ancient cultures, from Egypt to China, and it appeared later in Estonia, where the Freikorps saw it during the fighting in 1918–1919. The Ehrhardt Brigade used it on their steel helmets in Berlin during the Kapp *Putsch,* and Hitler no doubt saw it when the brigade came to Munich in 1920. Soon the swastika appeared on armbands, flags, and uniforms because Hitler saw it as the symbol of "the mission of the struggle for the victory of the Aryan man."

The SA's rank and file came from the lower middle class, especially war veterans and Freikorps members, many of whom were little more than hooligans. Roehm told his followers that only through violence would the Nazis achieve power. Later, in 1925, Heinrich Himmler (1900–1945) organized the elite guard unit called the SS (*Schutzstaffel*), whose black uniforms and lightning bolt symbols became dreaded symbols of Nazi brutality. Like Mussolini, Hitler used torch-lit parades, impressive ceremonies, and other techniques that Joseph Goebbels (1897–1945) eventually made into the most effective propaganda machine in history.

In 1923, a year after Mussolini's March on Rome, Hitler tried to take power, but only on a local level. The French occupation of the Ruhr and the severe inflationary cycle that erupted that year had been psychologically and

Hitler with Field Marshal Erich von Ludendorff. 1923. Ludendorff was the chief-of-staff of the Eighth Army during World War I. In 1918, his forces defeated, he fled to Sweden. The following year he returned to Germany, where he took part in reactionary conspiracies. This picture was taken in Munich at the time of the Munich *Putsch,* in which Hitler used the veteran soldier to try to add respectability to the uprising.

economically devastating to most Germans (see Topic 82). In Munich, Hitler sought to exploit these conditions by plotting a *Putsch* that he thought would be supported by municipal authorities. He also enlisted the retired General Erich von Ludendorff to bring a measure of national prestige to the attempt. The abortive coup took place on November 8, but it ended less than 24 hours later when the police intervened. Hitler and several others were arrested, and although he was sentenced to five years in prison, he spent only nine months in jail. While serving his time, Hitler dictated *Mein Kampf* (My Struggle), a long and discursive book in which he laid out his political and racial theories and explained how he intended to conquer. The Munich fiasco also taught him that he had to adopt a legal strategy for achieving power that would go hand in hand with Nazi violence.

In 1924, Hitler and Roehm vied with each other for control of the Nazi party, whose membership now reached some 25,000. Roehm tried to make the SA the focus of the party's power, whereas Hitler sought to make the SA the party's tool. Hitler proved the more skillful of the two, driving Roehm into exile and restoring his own authority over the party. Hitler's new strategy had only limited success, electing some 12 deputies in 1928. Economic conditions in Germany improved after 1924, and the political unrest that had weakened the Weimar Republic quieted down. Although Hitler succeeded in raising Nazi membership to more than 175,000, his prospects for obtaining power legally seemed dim. It would require another five years and the impact of the Great Depression before Hitler came to power (see Topic 83).

Putting the Russian Revolution and the Rise of Fascism in Perspective

Between 1917 and 1933, three new political regimes came to power in Europe— the Soviets in Russia, the Fascists in Italy, and the Nazis in Germany. Together they posed a major challenge to the Western notion of parliamentary democracy. In all three cases, absolute dictators now controlled the destinies of their countries. Each proclaimed that he would completely reorganize society according to a utopian ideology that stressed community, discipline, and sacrifice for the general good. Whereas the communists in Russia rejected capitalism, the fascists claimed to represent an alternative to both capitalism and communism. As the Great Depression imposed suffering and misery on millions of Europeans, many lost hope with traditional governments and turned in desperation to these radical extremes.

Questions for Further Study

1. What is meant by "Leninism"? How does it differ from conventional socialism?
2. Why did revolution come to Russia instead of to England or France?
3. What were the origins of fascism? How did fascism differ from Bolshevism? How did Italian Fascism differ from German Nazism?
4. Is it useful to speak of a generic "fascism" that combines the Italian and the German varieties?

Suggestions for Further Reading

Bullock, Alan. *Hitler, A Study in Tyranny.* New York, 1964.

De Felice, Renzo. *Interpretations of Fascism.* Cambridge, MA, 1977.

De Grand, Alexander. *Italian Fascism: Origins and Development,* 2nd ed. Lincoln, NE, 1989.

Figes, Orlando. *A People's Tragedy: The Russian Revolution 1891–1924.* London, 1996.

Fitzpatrick, Sheila. *The Russian Revolution.* New York, 1982.

Griffin, Roger, ed. *Fascism.* Oxford, 1995.

Kershaw, Ian. *Hitler,* 2 vols. New York and London, 1999–2000.

Mack Smith, Denis. *Mussolini.* New York, 1982.

Marples, David R. *Lenin's Revolution: Russia, 1917–1921.* New York, 2000.

Nicholls, A.J. *Weimar and the Rise of Hitler.* New York, 2000.

Occleshaw, Michael. *The Romanov Conspiracies.* London, 1993.

Payne, Stanley. *A History of Fascism.* Madison, WI, 1995.

Pipes, Richard. *The Russian Revolution, 1899–1919.* London, 1990.

Steinberg, Mark D., and Vladimir L. Khrustalev. *The Fall of the Romanovs.* New Haven, CT, 1995.

Stille, Alexander. *Benevolence and Betrayal: Five Italian Jewish Families Under Fascism.* London, 1992.

InfoTrac College Edition

Enter the search term *Russia Revolution* using Key Terms.

Enter the search term *Bolshevik* using Key Terms.

Enter the search term *socialism history* using Key Terms.

Enter the search term *Mussolini* using Key Terms.

Enter the search term *Hitler* using Key Terms.

THE EUROPEAN ECONOMY: BOOM AND BUST

The impact of the Great War was felt for decades to come. The political upheavals wrought as a consequence of the war changed Europe's map, altered relationships among the great powers, and created new kinds of political systems. No less dramatic were the effects of the war on Europe's—and the world's—economy.

Wartime government controls, together with the demands of the military, created an artificial economic situation in every belligerent country. Once peace came, economies had to readjust suddenly to peacetime production as well as to free-market conditions. The European economy responded with a brief but intense postwar boom, followed by collapse. Thereafter, despite periodic adjustments in economic conditions, the 1920s saw considerable prosperity and growth. The new prosperity greatly affected social developments as millions enjoyed the unprecedented economic expansion and the spread of mass-produced consumer products.

Not that the 1920s were without economic difficulties. Two long-range financial legacies of the war, reparations and war debts, made recovery more difficult and fueled international tensions. A series of agreements attempted unsuccessfully to settle these touchy questions, but only the Great Depression put an end to both issues in any real sense. Moreover, the wartime economic dislocations, together with the peace settlements and inflationary cycles, destabilized Europe's major currencies, causing them to drop in value in international exchange. Governments attempted to deal with this problem by instituting deflationary policies and balanced budgets at home. This was combined with a return to the gold standard.

In the 1920s, the United States and Great Britain made extensive foreign loans, generally to countries with weak economies, thus adding an element of instability to the world financial markets, while the unchecked speculative boom in the American stock market only added to the stresses on the economic system. Nor was the boom of the 1920s universal: Chronic agricultural depression marked most regions, whereas some countries, such as Germany, Great Britain, Italy, and Japan, hardly shared in the prosperity of the period.

When the New York stock market crashed in October 1929, the first major crack in the world economic system appeared. By 1930, the Great Depression had begun, shattering industrial productivity and making conditions in the already depressed agricultural sector worse. The Great Depression proved to be the most serious, deep-seated economic crisis in modern history, causing enormous human misery and putting huge pressures on political and social stability. Lasting well into the decade, governments adopted strategies of public spending and public works projects to cope with the massive unemployment. In addition, the widespread suffering attendant on the Depression led governments to expand public assistance programs and pass legislation that created the modern welfare state.

Table 82.1	Share in World Exports for Selected Countries (in percent)	
COUNTRY	1913	1925
Great Britain	13.9	12.4
Germany	13.1	7.0
France	7.2	7.2
Italy	2.6	2.4
Russia	4.2	1.0
USA	13.3	16.0
Canada	2.4	4.4
Japan	1.7	3.0

THE ECONOMIC CONSEQUENCES OF THE WAR

The economic impact of the war took a variety of forms, from the direct physical destruction of factories, railroads, and farms to the disruption of trade and the financial drain on national budgets. The peace settlements, responsive as they were to nationalist pressures, made the economic terms of the peace treaties political issues of great importance that were to hound international relations throughout the decade.

READJUSTMENT AND BOOM

In 1919, Europeans found it necessary to deal with two industrial issues: the need to change over from the production of war material to peacetime consumer goods, and the task of raising production back up to prewar levels. In the period from 1914 to 1920, industrial output had declined by 39 percent in Germany, 34 percent in France, 26 percent in Italy, and 12 percent in Britain. These production drops were the result of a combination of circumstances, especially lower demand caused by the closing of foreign markets and the lack of raw materials. In countries overrun by armies, the physical destruction was an equally important factor. Belgium, for example, lost half of its steel mills and the bulk of its railroad lines.

Four years of fighting had undermined Europe's industrial supremacy. The productive capacities of the United States, Canada, and Japan expanded as each country took a larger share of the world's exports, and new home industries had begun to spring up in Latin America, India, and most of the British Dominions. The resulting change in the pattern of world trade reflected the fact that Europe's economic status had been significantly altered. The wartime naval blockades, the shortage of commercial carriers, and the loss by European nations of overseas markets all contributed to this changed trade pattern, although in the case of Russia the Bolshevik Revolution, the civil war, and the loss of territory to newly created nations explained the drastic drop of that country's exports.

Another important change in Europe's economic posture was in its role in international finance. The belligerent nations had borrowed huge amounts of money to finance the war. As a consequence, Germany's national debt rose from roughly 5 billion to more than 100 billion marks. In Germany's case, this money had been raised entirely by floating domestic war bonds. Although the British and French were equally burdened (the British and French debts, when measured in real purchasing power, were about the same size), about 25 percent of their increased debts came from American loans—by doing so, the two Western powers, once the world's greatest creditor states, had become debtor nations, even though they continued to lend money to the other Allies during the war. Countries on both sides had also resorted to the increased printing of paper money, thus fueling inflation.

Despite these problems, the years 1919 to 1920 saw an economic boom in Europe and the United States, characterized by high profits and low unemployment. The sudden prosperity resulted because the stock of consumer goods had been depleted during the war, whereas with peace the demand for these goods rose sharply. As a result, prices—and profits—grew, and producers borrowed heavily at increasing rates of interest to expand their operations. A speculative boom followed as businesses recapitalized and expanded. Official British figures put unemployment at only 2.4 percent, or about half the prewar levels. The boom was short because by the summer of 1920 the supply of consumer goods caught up to the demand, especially as prices rose so high as to discourage some buying. To encourage sales, prices were lowered, but this did not work. As the price index fell precipitously, production slackened off, unemployment increased, and numerous bankruptcies were declared. By the end of 1921, British unemployment stood at 17 percent.

The postwar depression was temporary and was followed in a few years by a longer period of increasing prosperity. For Europe, however, the significant fact was that although the world's productive capacity grew in the 1920s, a greater proportion of that capacity lay elsewhere.

REPARATIONS, INFLATION, AND WAR DEBTS

The Allies hoped to meet their war debt obligations by reparations from Germany, which had been forced by the Treaty of Versailles to make such payments. Yet the onerous economic terms imposed on Germany by the peace treaty made it virtually impossible for Germany to make its reparations payments.

PROBLEMS OF GERMAN RECOVERY

The payment of reparations was a political as well as an economic issue. To complicate matters, the French regarded reparations as a means of keeping Germany in a weakened state. Article 231 of the Treaty of Versailles had stipulated that Germany would pay reparations because it was responsible for having caused the war, a position that the German people strongly resented. Moreover, the Allies could not agree on a specific sum in 1919 and created a Reparations Commission that would eventually determine the amount and collect the payments. At the time they signed the treaty, therefore, the Germans did not know how much they would be required to pay.

In April 1921, the Reparations Commission settled on a figure equivalent to $33 billion, a staggering sum in view of the fact that Germany had lost some 15 percent of its total productive capacity, 36 percent of its coal supply, 72 percent of its iron ore, more than 90 percent of its merchant shipping, and almost all of its foreign investments. In a brilliant book entitled *The Economic Consequences of the Peace*, the British economist John Maynard Keynes (1883–1946) argued that the harsh economic terms of the Versailles settlement would make it impossible for Germany to meet its obligations and would have an adverse effect on the European economy as a whole.

Germany paid its first installment late, and only after a loan from British bankers. By 1923, the Germans had made additional payments only in kind and then announced that they could not continue payments at all. The French and Belgians then occupied the Ruhr Valley, sparking passive resistance in the mines and factories of the region and prompting the German government to begin printing paper currency recklessly. The mark, 100,000 to the dollar in June, reached a low of 6.3 trillion by November. Wages could not keep up with prices, and every day saw a stampede to convert the almost worthless currency into real goods. The most serious result of this hyperinflation was to ruin the entire German middle class, whose savings and pensions were wiped out, thus making the soil in which the Nazi party grew more fertile; it was in the midst of the inflation crisis that Hitler attempted his Munich *Putsch* (see Topic 81).

German woman using paper money to light a kitchen stove. 1920s. Inflation, which occurred throughout Europe after 1918, was so severe in postwar Germany that it was cheaper to burn money than wood. Before the war, the U.S. dollar was worth 4.2 German marks; by 1918, 8.4 marks were necessary to buy one U.S. dollar; by the end of 1922, 7,000 marks were worth one U.S. dollar.

REPARATIONS AND WAR DEBT SETTLEMENTS

The German economy was stabilized beginning in late 1923, when the government issued new currency tied to the gold standard in the context of an international settlement of the reparations problem. A committee of financial experts headed by the American Charles G. Dawes (1865–1951) agreed to a two-year moratorium on reparations, the return of the Ruhr to Germany, and a $200 million loan to the beleaguered Germans. Germany committed itself to making regular payments on an increasing scale.

A large part of the international loan was sold in the United States, where it was underwritten by the House of Morgan. The success of this loan stimulated a frenzy of foreign loans, not only to European countries but to South America as well. Moreover, as confidence was restored in the economy, the Germans borrowed lavishly from abroad for public works projects and to rebuild their industrial base.

In 1929, another committee, also chaired by an American, Owen D. Young (1874–1962), devised a revised reparations arrangement. The Young Plan also involved an international loan, this time for $300 million, and the creation of a Bank for International Settlements, through which Germany would pay its reparations over a period of 59 years.

War debts similarly plagued international relations. By 1919, European nations owed the United States almost $10 billion in war debts, including some $4.7 billion from France, $4.2 billion from Great Britain, and $1.6 billion from Italy. In addition, however, significant debts existed among the smaller Allies—France and Italy, for example, were in debt to Britain, and Belgium and Yugoslavia to France. Russia owed $2.5 billion to Britain and $900 million to France, but these loans were repudiated by the new Soviet government.

Some economists had suggested that all war debts be canceled, and British leaders repeated the idea formally to the United States in the early 1920s. American authorities, however, refused, insisting that they were willing to negotiate the debts owed to them, but with each individual nation. The European Allies had hoped that the combination of war debts and reparations would create a three-tiered financial relationship: German reparations payments would be made to countries such as Belgium and France, which would use that income to pay their war debts to Great Britain, which would in turn repay the wartime American loans. The United States insisted on keeping the reparations and war debt issues separate. Beginning in 1923, the United States began to settle the debt question with some 13 countries, beginning with Great Britain.

RECOVERY AND PROSPERITY

After the collapse of 1921–1922, the European economy underwent a period of recovery, centered principally around the stabilization of Europe's major currencies. The end of runaway inflation and the new currency in Germany, capped by the settlement of reparations in the Dawes Plan, marked the beginning of this process.

CURRENCY STABILIZATION

The 19th century had been a period of relative monetary stability, with major paper currencies retaining their relative values and readily convertible into silver or gold. The war changed all this, however, lowering the buying power of Europe's major currencies, and doing so unequally. Wartime inflation had struck every belligerent country, and in the first postwar boom of 1919–1920, price inflation rose higher, although nowhere so drastically as in Germany. Moreover, the gold standard, adopted in the late 19th century (see Topic 75), collapsed during the war, and currencies fell still further in value. By the end of the war, the monetary systems of Germany, Austria, Hungary, and Russia were virtually destroyed. International monetary conferences attempted to restore some stability in the

1920s, and the German rescue operation was the most dramatic of these efforts.

In Britain, where the commitment to restoring the prewar parity of the pound to the dollar—$4.86—was a moral as well as a financial question, recovery was slow in coming and never fully realized. The British had lost important markets to the Americans and Japanese, and by 1921 were exporting half the value of goods traded in 1913. To get its huge national debt under control, Britain imposed heavy taxation at home and reduced government expenditures. Although the pound fluctuated, in the second half of 1923 it recovered to about $4.30, and when it almost reached parity in January 1925, the government passed the Gold Standard Act that pegged the pound at $4.79. In retrospect, the pound was clearly overvalued, and this had the effect of making British exports even more difficult to sell abroad. Britain never fully regained its prewar prosperity.

In 1919, the French franc stood at only half its prewar value of 19¢, and by 1926 fell to 2¢. French leaders insisted on the importance of reconstruction, even at the price of larger deficits and more foreign loans. In less than two years, 10 finance ministers tried unsuccessfully to resolve the chaos of French finances. When Premier Raymond Poincaré (see Topic 84) came to office in July 1926, he finally took stern measures to stabilize the franc at 25 to the dollar, or one-quarter of its prewar value. This cheap franc helped sell French goods abroad.

THE ERA OF PROSPERITY

After the stabilization of inflated currencies and the settlement of war debts, the pace of economic development picked up. New industries developed or expanded, with industrial growth taking place mainly in the production of consumer goods that were designed to make life easier or more enjoyable. A host of new appliances invaded the middle-class home, from vacuum cleaners and electric mixers to refrigerators and radios. In Britain alone, there were perhaps 36,000 radio sets in 1922, but by the end of 1929 that number had jumped to almost 3 million. The output in rayon, plastics, chemicals, and aluminum also rose substantially. The production of electrical energy doubled in the 1920s, and by the end of the next decade had doubled again in the major industrial countries.

The automobile was by far the most important product of the period, both from the economic viewpoint as well as in terms of its social impact. Automobiles had been appearing on European roads since the early 20th century—France alone produced some 16,500 in 1902—but they had not come into mass use before the Great War. The war, however, greatly increased the demand for automobiles and trucks. Henry Ford's ability to produce the Model T inexpensively and in great quantity made the automobile the biggest selling wholesale product in the United States by 1928. European manufacturers copied Ford's methods, lowering production costs by using standardized parts on the assembly line and concentrating production in fewer companies. High protective tariffs shielded European producers

Table 82.2	Registered Motor Vehicles, 1913–1938 (in 1000s)			
	BRITAIN	GERMANY	FRANCE	U.S.
1913	208	93	125	1258
1921	464	91	236	10,494
1926	1,042	319	891	22,053
1930	1,524	67	1,460	26,532
1938	2,422	1,816	2,251	29,443

from American cars in the 1920s. The automobile industry acted as an important stimulus to other industries and raw materials, including metals, rubber, gasoline, and lubricants—the world's production of crude petroleum increased from 400 million barrels in 1914 to 1.5 billion in 1938. Road construction came into its own in the 1920s as a result of the spreading use of the automobile.

In the late 1920s, industrialization began to spread to less developed nations, especially to the Soviet Union and the countries of Eastern Europe. In addition, industry everywhere underwent a process of rationalization, whereby less economical plants with older equipment and production methods were closed down and production either shifted to new factories or concentrated in more efficient ones. This change was accompanied by the introduction of new labor-saving machinery, the standardization of parts, and the adoption of mass-production assembly-line techniques. The process was easier in those countries, such as France and Belgium, where physical destruction required that new factories be built or in planned economies such as the Soviet Union and Fascist Italy.

Britain did not participate fully in the era of prosperity. Unemployment never fell below 1 million, and the British share in world trade never returned to prewar levels.

Moreover, while the United States outproduced Britain in the new industries, the former "workshop of the world" faced serious handicaps in traditional industries such as coal mining, steel, and textiles. Production declines were registered in all three industries during the two decades following the war. That British industries could no longer compete as they had once done was fully revealed by the steady abandonment of the free trade that had been followed since the 19th century.

France was troubled less by trade patterns than by the need for industrial reconstruction. Reparations, together with the recovery of Alsace-Lorraine and the new, modernized factories that were built in the northern portions of the country, stimulated French industrialization. As a result, France emerged in the interwar era with a greatly expanded industrial sector. Germany relied on massive foreign loans to rebuild and modernize its industry. The Germans also experienced a boom in construction, especially by public funds, after 1924. On the other hand, in the entire period from 1923 to 1936, unemployment fell below 7 percent only once, in 1925, when it registered 6.9 percent, and it soared to 18 percent in the following year. In 1929, with the boom in full swing, some 2 million German workers were without jobs. For Europe as a whole, figures show that the number of unemployed rose from around 3.5 million in the first half of the decade to perhaps as high as 5.5 million during the era of prosperity.

Hence, although the second postwar economic boom stretched across the second half of the 1920s, it was by no means general and all-pervasive. European production as a whole regained the 1913 level only in 1925, whereas in the same period it had increased by 25 percent in North America and 20 percent in Asia. Textiles, once the most important product of Europe's Industrial Revolution, stagnated in the face of cheaper Japanese production. Moreover, Europe's share of world industrial production shrank steadily, from 57.6 percent in 1913 to 47.1 percent

Map 82.1 Industrialized Zones of Europe, c. 1930. Note the rise of industrialization in northern Portugal and around Barcelona; the latter became the most prosperous region in postwar Spain. The undeveloped area between Lyon to the north and Marseilles and Milan to the south contains the Alps, hardly a landscape lending itself to industry. Russia appears almost completely untouched, but that was to change by the time of World War II.

A young boy working in a coal mine in northern England. 1920. With the decline in British production of coal and steel, the conditions in British mines began to deteriorate as less money was available for investment in them. The use of young, inexperienced laborers as illustrated here—their wages were lower—increased the unemployment that led to the General Strike of 1926. In contrast, these two privileged British boys are dressed in school formal wear for the annual Eton-Harrow cricket match.

in 1928, while that of the United States rose from 32 percent to 39.3 percent. In the same period, Europe's share of world trade declined from 54.5 percent to about 49.2 percent. From 1913 to 1939, per capita real income actually grew in Western Europe, but the growth was slower than it had been during the Long Depression of the late 19th century (see Topic 75).

THE CRASH: WALL STREET AND THE FINANCIAL COLLAPSE

There is no agreement among economists or economic historians about the underlying causes of the Great Depression, nor is there consensus about where it began or why it was so widespread. On some points, however, experts do agree. In view of the crucial role played by the United States in world affairs after 1917, its economic policies, both internally and externally, had much to do with the coming of the Depression as well as its longevity. Unlike the pre-1914 era, the new international financial system had shown itself to be unstable, and the United States would not play the role that Britain had once played as watchdog of the system. Then, too, postwar recovery proved to be less than universal, and much of the newly generated wealth was poorly distributed. Moreover, there were signs that the economy was far from perfect well before the stock market crash of 1929.

AMERICA IN THE TWENTIES
In the United States the age of postwar prosperity was known as the "Roaring Twenties," a term that captured the sense of modern, fast-paced life in a society marked by uncontrolled speculative investment, soaring profits, and the thirst for material well-being. Two Republican presidents,

Warren G. Harding (served 1921–1923) and Calvin Coolidge (served 1923–1929), identified the nation's welfare with that of private business and followed a policy of noninterference in the workings of the economy. "This is a business country," proclaimed Coolidge, "and wants a business government." Federal spending was slashed, as were taxes for the highest income levels. Laws regulating business monopoly were eased, and the stock market was permitted to soar upward virtually without regulation.

The United States was not immune from the kind of flaws that marred European prosperity. A boom in Florida land speculation had burst in 1925, and in 1927 the industrial production index fell as a result of Ford's decision to close down his automobile plants in order to change over from the Model T to the Model A. Nevertheless, between 1923 and 1929, corporate profits increased by 62 percent, while real income for the average worker rose only 11 percent. One-third of all personal income went to the richest 5 percent of the population, and workers were unable to share in the prosperity or to buy the huge quantity of industrial goods being produced. Overexpansion and large inventories of unsold goods led to job layoffs and business slowdowns even before the crash.

The economic growth of the 1920s had been financed largely by credit—business, personal, and international. Those who extended credit for business expansion assumed that borrowers could repay their loans with their profits while continuing to purchase capital goods. Similarly, stock investors bought heavily on a credit system known as "margin trading," which permitted them to pay out only a small part of the cost of their securities by borrowing most of the price from the brokers, who were themselves operating on bank credit. These practices fueled the unchecked financial speculation that led to the 1929 crash. Consumer credit was widely available in the form of installment plans. The ease of obtaining credit encouraged overspending for major purchases such as automobiles, appliances, and even houses. High sales expectations induced retailers and wholesalers to pay their suppliers with borrowed money. The danger, of course, lay in the fact that a call for repayment by any creditor would require everyone in the system to pay their debts in cash. Because most investors borrowed more than they could repay, the system was fraught with potential disaster.

AMERICA, EUROPE, AND THE CRASH

On the international level, the credit system of the 1920s was equally precarious. Lavish loans were extended to many small nations, especially in Latin America and Eastern Europe, despite their inability to repay the obligations. The decision of one creditor state to withdraw funds from a foreign bank or call in its loans threatened at any moment to upset international finances.

In the six years from 1924 to 1930, the United States loaned 6.4 billion dollars abroad, mainly in short-term loans liable to sudden recall. Then, starting in June 1928, the American loans suddenly began to dry up. This shift in foreign lending was primarily because as profits soared on the stock market, investors removed their resources from loans and put them into securities. (High interest rates in the United States also attracted foreign capital.) The problem, of course, was that the market value of securities was being inflated far beyond their actual worth. In 1928–1929, the average price of stocks on the New York Stock Exchange rose by 60 percent. The halt to U.S. lending placed a severe financial strain on several debtor countries, where economic activity began to decline.

The crash was precipitated when the Bank of England raised its interest rates at the end of September 1929, largely in order to attract capital back to London—the same day that the New York Stock Exchange reached its peak. Prices began to slip on October 3 and gave way to panic on October 24, known as "Black Thursday," as orders to sell exceeded orders to buy. A frenzy of selling swept the floor of the exchange, and panicked brokers demanded payment of margin payments, which triggered bankruptcies among thousands of small investors. Confidence was partially restored when a group of powerful bankers pooled resources to buy securities. The next week, on "Black Tuesday," October 29, the market fell even more precipitously. Many who had bought cheaply the previous week were now forced to sell at great losses. As the collapse continued into November, increasingly larger investors went under. The spiral of ever-rising prices reversed itself as the market collapsed.

Given the fragile nature of the international financial system, the impact of the crash was bound to be felt abroad. American creditors called in their overseas loans. In May 1931 the *Creditanstalt*, which held two-thirds of all Austrian assets, failed, despite a loan from the Bank of England. The panic spread across Europe. Investors withdrew their capital from Germany, the largest recipient of foreign loans, and banks also began to fail there. In June 1931, U.S. President Herbert Hoover (served 1929–1933) declared a moratorium on all international debt payments. By July, British banks began to suffer, and in September the government there took the country off the gold standard.

THE GREAT DEPRESSION

The stock market crash did not cause the Great Depression because the economy was already in deep trouble, but the panic brought a sudden halt to the years of economic optimism and led to a scramble for liquidity. Banks that had invested heavily in securities failed, and businesses cut back as sales and orders declined, both at home and abroad.

The scene outside the New York Stock Exchange. Late October 1929. The worst day of the stock market crash was October 29. Over the preceding days, increasing numbers of people had begun to collect outside the New York Stock Exchange on Wall Street, drawn by a sense of horrified fascination. The ensuing Great Depression brought economic collapse on a worldwide scale.

Table 82.3	Percentage of the Labor Force Unemployed (selected countries, 1929–1936)			
	BRITAIN	GERMANY	SWEDEN	U.S.
1929	10.4	13.1	10.7	3.2
1930	16.1	22.2	12.2	8.7
1931	21.3	33.7	17.2	15.8
1932	22.1	43.7	22.8	23.6
1933	19.9	26.3	23.7	24.9
1934	16.7	14.9	18.9	26.7
1935	15.5	11.6	16.1	20.1
1936	13.1	8.3	13.6	16.9

Unemployment figures shot up throughout the world as the financial panic gave way to general economic depression.

INDUSTRY AND AGRICULTURE

As the financial crisis spread to business, large corporations slowed down or stopped production because markets for industrial goods and raw materials soon disappeared. Compared to 1929, world industrial production dropped by 38 percent and global trade by two-thirds. The human impact of the Great Depression was devastating, creating unprecedented misery. The ranks of the unemployed had grown so large that the fabric of society was on the verge of being torn apart. As early as 1931, one-third of the entire German labor force—more than 6 million people—was jobless. The next year, when the Depression was at its worst, the number of unemployed in the United States reached 13 million.

The Depression caused widespread demoralization, both on the individual level and throughout society in general. In many instances, desperation grew into anger against existing governments and often expressed itself in radical political movements. Throughout the 1920s, agriculture had been suffering from a chronic state of depression. One-fifth of Europe's wheat fields had been taken out of cultivation by the war, and the resulting rise in prices had encouraged farmers in North America to increase their output and to buy more land at relatively high prices. European output increased substantially for a variety of reasons. Improvements in mechanization now permitted a farmer to reap and bind five times more grain than was possible before the war. Political changes also affected agriculture. In the new countries of Eastern Europe, the bulk of the population was still agrarian: Three-quarters of the population of Yugoslavia, Romania, and Bulgaria, and two-thirds of all Poles, lived by farming. Between 1913 and 1939, cultivated areas increased by more than 17 million acres. Many of the large landed estates that had once dominated the economic life of the region were broken up and small plots distributed to peasants.

Parisians standing in line to receive free food allowances during the Great Depression. 1930s. The sign listing the food available provides the names and addresses of the various shops where supplies—meat, vegetables, bananas, mandarin oranges—could be collected. It also adds that only one "confection" or package would be available to each "customer."

Graph 82.1 Industrial Production in the Great Depression

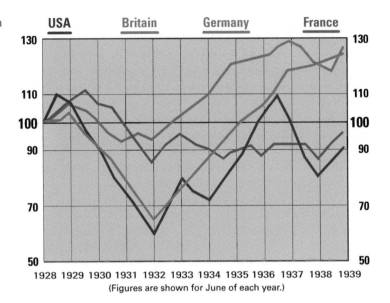

(Figures are shown for June of each year.)

Despite these reforms, however, the fall in agricultural prices—some 30 percent between 1925 and 1929—resulting from overproduction and competition from abroad hurt farmers everywhere. European governments tried to protect their farmers by raising agricultural tariffs, a move that damaged producers elsewhere. With the coming of the Great Depression, prices fell even more sharply, making a bad situation worse. In general, agricultural interests suffered heavier losses than industrial interests during the Depression.

THE NEW ECONOMICS AND THE NEW DEAL

For many contemporaries, the Great Depression represented a crisis that confirmed longheld beliefs about the evils and weaknesses of capitalism. Karl Marx had asserted the inevitability of class conflict, and during World War I, Lenin had foreseen the collapse of capitalism as Western nations competed with each other over colonies and markets. Now, Marxists and others seemed about to be proven correct. Prime Minister Ramsay MacDonald of Great Britain (see Topic 84), a socialist, announced in 1930 that capitalism had to be blamed for the Depression: "We are not on trial," he said, "it is the system under which we live. It has broken down . . . everywhere, as it was bound to break down."

Government reaction to the Great Depression differed from country to country. In would-be totalitarian regimes such as Fascist Italy and the Soviet Union, governments created jobs for the unemployed and already provided a range of social services, including health care and other benefits (see Topic 83). In democratic states, however, where the principles of *laissez-faire* economics and limited government intervention prevailed, the policy adjustments caused by the economic collapse were more wrenching to tradition (see Topic 84).

First reactions, even under MacDonald's Labour government, included government spending cuts and tight fiscal policies, but when it was clear that such deflationary approaches only worsened conditions, the democracies turned increasingly to methods that were already in place elsewhere, including public works projects and extensive social insurance programs. Public officials took a more active role in shaping the economic and social affairs as the Depression forced governments to deal with the devastating impact of the collapse on millions of their citizens.

Even before the Depression had struck, the British economist John Maynard Keynes began to evolve theories about the economic responsibilities of government. A brilliant and eclectic thinker, Keynes was a member of the Bloomsbury Circle of intellectuals and artists (see Topic 86), a high-ranking civil servant, and taught at Cambridge University. He served as chief economist with the British delegation to the Paris Peace Conference in 1919.

As Keynes observed the already depressed conditions under which the British working class suffered in the second half of the 1920s, he began to rethink the entire basis of prevailing economic principles, and in the process offered a powerful critique of both *laissez-faire* capitalism and socialism. Keynes published his ideas in a variety of articles and books, including *The End of Laissez-Faire* (1926), and brought his arguments together in *The General Theory of Employment, Interest and Money* (1936). The classical theory of capitalist economic policy had long been that the laws of supply and demand would, if left to operate without interference, establish a healthy equilibrium of prices, wages, and production. But the chronic state of unemployment that dogged the British economy, together with his analysis of the Depression, led Keynes to conclude that the economics of free enterprise was imperfect and misguided. Instead, he argued that government should intervene actively in the economy, manipulating such controls as the interest rate, monetary expansion, and public works programs, to correct the weaknesses of capitalism. According to his theory, in times of economic dislocation, governments could stimulate demand by priming the economic pump through public spending, which would in turn spark production and create jobs. Whether consciously or not, as bad times dragged on, most governments eventually adopted Keynesian principles in dealing with the Depression, and his ideas came to dominate economic thinking for generations to come.

It was in the United States, rather than in Europe, that Keynesian theories found their first widespread application among the democratic states of the West. As we have seen, nowhere had the principles of the free enterprise market economy been more freely or completely practiced than in the American economy of the 1920s, and nowhere was the collapse more extreme. The Hoover administration had initiated several programs to deal with the financial crisis as well as with the effects of the Depression. It was, however, with the election of Franklin D. Roosevelt (served 1933–1945) as president that American society underwent a major transformation.

Roosevelt's "New Deal" policies were aimed at bringing America out of the Depression by reforming the capitalist system to save it from destruction. His economic advisers, who were familiar with Keynesian ideas, pushed for massive government intervention in the economy. Roosevelt introduced far-reaching laws to regulate banking and investment and created a host of government programs to stimulate business recovery, help the devastated farmers, strengthen labor organization, and create jobs. He also introduced several basic social welfare programs into American national life, including Social Security and unemployment compensation. The New Deal programs did stimulate recovery and cushioned the impact of the Depression for millions of citizens, although by the eve of World War II, employment had not returned to pre-1929 levels. Nevertheless, the improvement in economic conditions was so successful that American voters eventually endorsed the New Deal reforms by reelecting Roosevelt to an unprecedented third term.

As soon as he was elected, Roosevelt had sent a special envoy to Fascist Italy to study how Mussolini's corporate state was coping with the Depression. The president's political opponents on the right charged that he was replacing capitalism with socialism, whereas those on the left accused him of fascism; however, the ideas of Keynes provided both the inspiration and the theoretical justification for the most radical transformation in modern Western economic thought. Reformers in Great Britain, France, and other democratic states eventually adopted similar programs, although not always with such enthusiasm as the New Dealers in the United States.

Putting the Great Depression in Perspective

Despite the optimism that had greeted the end of the First World War, and the flashes of fast living and prosperity that marked the postwar era, the economic life of the interwar years was also characterized by partial recovery, instability, and uneven development. The momentary boom of 1919–1920 was followed by a longer period of recession and readjustment, after which some countries enjoyed a wave of prosperity while others went through a variety of economic experiences that ranged from the doldrums to real crisis. The legacies of reparations and war debts were partially responsible for the difficulties of recovery and for making the international financial system uncertain. The crisis of the Great Depression, when it came in 1929, should not have been totally unexpected.

The Depression was responsible in many instances for major change: in politics, for a radicalization of popular opinion that resulted in the rise of extremist movements and, in the case of Germany, contributed to the Nazi seizure of power; in social and economic policy, for an abandonment of the principles of *laissez-faire* economics by most Western nations and the inauguration of an era of government activism. The economic crisis weakened democracy and made other, totalitarian alternatives attractive to many millions of people who experienced the trauma of a world turned upside down.

Questions for Further Study

1. What effect did World War I have on the European economy?
2. What caused the Great Depression?
3. How did governments respond to the Great Depression?

Suggestions for Further Reading

Cameron, Rondo. *A Concise Economic History of the World.* New York, 1989.

Clavin, Patricia. *The Great Depression in Europe, 1929–1939.* New York, 2000.

Evans, Richard J., and D. Geary. *The German Unemployed: Experiences and Consequences of Mass Unemployment from the Weimar Republic to the Third Reich.* New York, 1987.

Feinstein, C.H., Peter Tamin, and Gianni Toniolo. *The European Economy Between the Wars.* New York, 1997.

Galbraith, John K. *The Great Crash, 1929,* rev. ed. Boston, 1979.

Holtfrerich, Carl-Ludwig. *The German Inflation, 1914–1923.* Berlin, 1986.

Jackson, Julian. *The Politics of Depression in France, 1932–1936.* New York, 1985.

James, Harold. *The German Slump: Politics and Economics, 1924–1936.* Oxford, 1986.

Keynes, John M. *The Economic Consequences of the Peace.* London, 1919.

Kuromiya, Hiroaki. *Stalin's Industrial Revolution: Politics and Workers, 1928–1932.* New York, 1988.

Maier, Charles S. *Recasting Bourgeois Europe: Stabilization in France, Germany, and Italy.* Princeton, NJ, 1975.

InfoTrac College Edition

Enter the search term *Great Depression* using Key Terms.

MUSSOLINI, HITLER, STALIN: THE TOTALITARIAN NIGHTMARE

The years between the two world wars saw the development of a new kind of antidemocratic political system known as **totalitarianism.** The totalitarian state was a unique development in political theory, although in practice it is doubtful that a true totalitarian society was achieved in any of the three nations—Fascist Italy, Nazi Germany, and the Soviet Union—in which leaders aspired to create one.

Mussolini became dictator of Italy by 1925, and over the next 20 years he sought to make his government the first totalitarian regime in history. Alongside the preexisting constitutional structure that had governed the country since unification, he created new Fascist institutions, which he empowered with theoretically supreme authority. After coming to terms with the Catholic Church, which exercised a powerful influence over Italian loyalties, he set about regimenting Italian society in an unparalleled fashion: revamping the educational system and dragooning all Italian youth into special organizations designed to indoctrinate and train them according to Fascist ideology.

In order to mold popular consensus and extract obedience, the Fascist state combined positive image making with an atmosphere of terror. Mussolini did this through twin policies: by building a vast propaganda machine that shaped the values, ideas, and information received by the entire population, and by creating an elaborate police state that rounded up anti-Fascists and employed paid informants, torture, and internment programs.

Hitler built his totalitarian state in much the same manner. In Germany, where official theory was more clearly articulated, the degree of control exercised by the government was more effective and the party permeated the government bureaucracy and daily life more completely. Moreover, whereas Mussolini was largely uninterested in art and viewed it as propaganda, Hitler had clear and definite views about the kind of style and image he wanted German art to project.

There had been no real tradition of anti-Semitism in Italian Fascism, and Fascist racial policies were not as drastic as Nazi programs, nor were they implemented with any degree of enthusiasm. Most Italians greeted them with revulsion. Hitler's anti-Semitic policies, on the other hand, were at the core of Nazi belief. They began by stripping Jews of their rights as citizens and ended with the horrors of the Holocaust.

The totalitarian state in Stalin's Russia also reflected differences that derived from ideology and national circumstances. In his obsession to modernize Russia's economy, Stalin pushed his country into a vast experiment in social regimentation that aimed at maximizing agricultural and industrial productivity. Stalin was so driven to accumulate all power in his own hands that he destroyed an entire generation of Soviet leaders to safeguard it. To combat the resistance against his development plans, and in a blind effort to wipe out his enemies, Stalin resorted to mass exterminations, labor camps, and purges that were unparalleled in their scope.

SIGNIFICANT DATES

Fascist Italy and Nazi Germany

October 1922	Mussolini becomes prime minister of Italy
1926	Ministry of Corporations created
1929	Lateran Pacts
1930s	Fascistization of Italian society and culture
1930	Nazi electoral victories
January 1933	Hitler becomes chancellor
1930s	Regimentation of German life
1933	Mussolini sets up Institute for Industrial Reconstruction
June 30, 1934	Night of the Long Knives
1935	Nuremberg Laws
1938	Night of the Broken Glass
1938	Mussolini creates Chamber of Fasci and Corporations
October– November 1938	Anti-Semitic laws passed in Italy

THE NATURE OF TOTALITARIANISM

The historical examples of Fascist Italy and Nazi Germany on the one hand and of the Soviet Union on the other suggest that totalitarianism is a politically neutral concept, linked neither to the left nor the right. Totalitarianism is a type of government that seeks to exercise total control over the citizens of a given country and to put into practice a set of beliefs designed to alter human society radically.

A set of common characteristics is usually found in all totalitarian regimes. Totalitarian states are dictatorships in which the ruler claims to exercise authority in the name of a political ideology. Mussolini, Hitler, and Stalin were radicals, each bent on forcing millions of citizens to conform to his values and each with a vision of an ideal future society. In the name of ideology, the most extreme crimes and horrors were committed and rationalized. In each case, the dictator became the object of secular worship in order to justify his unlimited power.

Totalitarian governments are dominated by one political party and by the suspension of the most basic civil liberties. So intertwined are the dominant political party and the state bureaucracy that lines of authority are blurred. Totalitarian regimes are police states, in which force, violence, and terror are used against their own citizens. Such governments normally control the educational systems and mass media, and create an array of social institutions to indoctrinate and mobilize the population. Regardless of whether a particular regime rests on a socialist or capitalist footing, all totalitarian governments aim to centralize and shape economic policy.

ITALY UNDER MUSSOLINI: REGIMENTATION IN THE FASCIST STATE

Mussolini's totalitarian state continued to evolve over the entire two decades that he was in power. Yet within less than three years he had established the basic structure of the regime: the one-party state, a secret police to arrest and a military tribunal to try anti-Fascists, press censorship, and loyalty oaths for government employees.

THE FASCIST STATE

Mussolini's regime grafted Fascist institutions onto already established government. Technically, the Italian constitution was the fundamental legal document of the realm and King Victor Emmanuel III still ruled, with the right to appoint and dismiss the prime minister (see Topic 73). Mussolini allowed traditional forms to persist alongside his own, to preserve the fiction of legitimacy. He created, however, a Fascist Grand Council that included party and state officials and was the supreme organ of state. Mussolini personally selected the members of the Grand Council as well as candidates for Chamber of Deputies elections. The Grand Council abolished Parliament altogether in 1938 and put in its place the Chamber of Fasci and Corporations.

Ever since Italy had seized Rome from the papacy in 1870, the Vatican had refused to recognize the existence of the Italian state. One of Mussolini's most popular decisions was to make peace with the Catholic Church. There were two chief reasons for this result. Millions of Italians were devout Catholics and were loath to divide their loyalties between church and state; and the church was perceived as acting as a stable, conservative influence in modern society. In 1929, therefore, he and Pope Pius XI (ruled 1922–1939) concluded the Lateran Pacts, according to which the Vatican City became an independent state ruled by the pope inside the confines of Rome. Mussolini further agreed to pay the Vatican a large sum of money in compensation for the lost papal territory around Rome. Perhaps more important, however, the church's popular youth organizations could now operate without harassment, and the Vatican had its own newspaper and radio station. Mussolini also implemented compulsory religious instruction in public schools. This "concordat" was an important success for Mussolini, who not only guaranteed himself the public support of the church, but also instantly won the admiration of Catholics everywhere.

THE MAKING OF CONSENSUS

Mussolini enjoyed considerable popular support, at least until his foreign adventures in the mid-1930s. Such consensus was the result of a dual policy of coercion and socialization. The Fascist police system was a complicated affair, consisting of several traditional Italian police units as well as a special division of "political police" and a network of paid informants. In addition, tens of thousands of anti-Fascists were rounded up and placed under surveillance or sent to

Map 83.1 Interwar Europe. Note the independent, demilitarized region of the Saar, which Hitler was to reunite with Germany in 1935, after a plebiscite (or people's vote). Danzig, on the border between northeast Germany and Poland, passed between periods of German and Polish rule; in the interwar years it was a free city, self-governing. Since World War II, under the name Gdansk, it has returned to Polish rule. By 1940, Stalin had added Estonia, Latvia, and Lithuania to the Soviet Union.

domestic exile in remote and barren parts of Italy. As effective as this structure was, it proved less gruesome than the mass killings in Hitler's or Stalin's police states.

The Fascists devised numerous methods for forging consensus among intellectuals and artists. Some were appointed to a new Royal Academy, others were given secret government subsidies or government employment, and others were simply ignored as long as they did not openly oppose the regime. In the 1930s Mussolini created a Ministry of Popular Culture that controlled newspapers, radio, theater, film production, and book publishing.

The Fascist party played a crucial role in regimentation. A host of organizations provided Italian youth with political indoctrination and physical training. Although many parents refused to send their children to party groups, by the mid-1930s more than 3 million were enrolled. Popular leisure time programs, including cultural events, vacations, and light entertainment, were provided by the "after-work" organization, known as the *Dopolavoro.*

Millions of Italians joined the party in the 1930s, for job opportunities if not out of conviction.

Under the fanatical direction of party secretary Achille Starace (1889–1945), the regime even tried to change the way in which Italians behaved in their daily lives. Starace, who became something of a joke among many Italians, ordered civilians not to use words of foreign origin, to salute each other instead of shaking hands, and to wear black shirts instead of dresses and business suits.

Party propaganda exalted Mussolini as the *Duce* of Fascism, the wise, strong, and all-powerful leader who would make Italy great again. Absurd slogans, plastered on public buildings and taught to schoolchildren, were intended as secular chants to the myth of the *Duce:* "Better one day as a lion than a hundred years as a sheep," or "Believe! Obey! Fight!" The regime merged Fascist themes with ancient Roman images, and Mussolini—portrayed in official sculpture and painting as the new Caesar—promised to restore the glories of the imperial age.

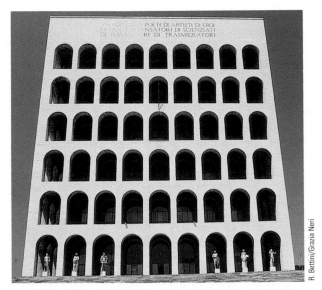

The Palace of Civilization, Rome. The building, which lies in an area to the south of the city called EUR, was completed by 1937. EUR stands for Esposizione Universale di Roma, or Rome's Universal Exhibition, which Mussolini planned for 1942—the coming of war meant that the exhibition never took place. The style is the official Fascist one, a modernized form of Classicism. Locals dubbed it "the square Colosseum."

The other side of life in Mussolini's Italy was represented by the many ordinary Italians who opposed Fascism. When Mussolini declared his dictatorship, many anti-Fascists were beaten or arrested, but a remarkable number of prominent political leaders managed to escape abroad, where they regrouped and established resistance organizations. Inside the country, many others engaged in minor acts of opposition or were involved in underground networks. Not all such people were active anti-Fascists, but

during World War II, hundreds of thousands of Italians participated in the armed resistance.

HITLER'S GERMANY: RACE AND REPRESSION IN THE NAZI REGIME

The coming of the Great Depression in 1930 gave the Nazis the huge popular following that Hitler needed. In 1925, Field Marshal Paul von Hindenburg, the hero of World War I, was elected president of the Republic. Hindenburg, already in his late seventies, was an upright, stolid patriarchal figure who gave Germany an aura of stability. Yet not even Hindenburg's prestige could stave off the terrible economic plight that struck Germany, which experienced a more severe setback than any other European state in 1930. With industrial production at 39 percent of its former level and some 6 million people out of work, the economic crisis devastated the German working class and wiped out the incomes and savings of much of the middle class.

THE NATIONAL SOCIALIST VICTORY

Such extreme conditions undermined popular consensus for the centrist parties that had stabilized the Weimar Republic since its birth, and created the conditions under which the Nazis could come to power. In their desperation, the German electorate turned to extremist forces on the right and the left. The Nazis increased their seats in the *Reichstag* dramatically, first to 107 in September 1930 and then to a startling 230 in July 1932, making it the largest single party in Parliament. The Communists jumped from 54 to 89. Hitler stood at the edge of power.

In 1932 Germany experienced a three-way race for the office of president. The aged Hindenburg was persuaded to run again, and against him were arrayed the Communist

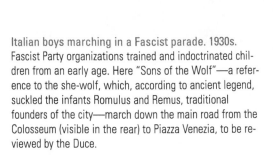

Italian boys marching in a Fascist parade. 1930s. Fascist Party organizations trained and indoctrinated children from an early age. Here "Sons of the Wolf"—a reference to the she-wolf, which, according to ancient legend, suckled the infants Romulus and Remus, traditional founders of the city—march down the main road from the Colosseum (visible in the rear) to Piazza Venezia, to be reviewed by the Duce.

candidate Ernst Thaelmann and Hitler. Hitler won enough votes to enter a runoff election with Hindenburg, who won. Nevertheless, Hitler had attracted some 13 million voters, many of them from the working class. In the November parliamentary elections that same year, the Nazis dropped down to 196 seats, while the Communists increased their strength to 100. In Germany, as in postwar Italy, the specter of the radical left frightened many middle-class citizens into the arms of the right. Conservative forces grew more comfortable with the notion of a Hitler-led government and began to provide the Nazis with money and support, thinking that once in office Hitler would become tame. Hindenburg was finally persuaded to ask Hitler to form a cabinet.

Hitler took office as chancellor on January 30, 1933. He immediately dissolved Parliament and prepared for elections. At that moment, the *Reichstag* building burned down in a mysterious fire, and Hitler accused the Communists of responsibility. The German people went to the polls angry, while the Nazis unleashed another round of violence on their enemies. The Nazis won 44 percent of the seats in the *Reichstag*, enabling them to form a coalition with the Nationalists, who held 8 percent.

Armed with a majority, Hitler then invoked Article 48 of the constitution and proclaimed a state of emergency. He ejected the Communists from Parliament and had the rump *Reichstag* grant him extraordinary powers. All political parties except the Nazis were outlawed, and when Hindenburg died in August 1934, Hitler merged the offices of president and chancellor into his own hands. Adolf Hitler had become dictator of Germany.

Hitler's totalitarian state took shape more rapidly than Mussolini's. Within a year of coming to power in 1933, he had established most of the institutions that characterized Nazi Germany. The Nazi restructuring of German life was in many respects more radical. Hitler, who liked to think in sweeping historical clichés, called his creation the "Third Reich" (the first *Reich* was the Holy Roman Empire, from 800 to 1806, and the second was imperial Germany, from 1871 to 1918) and predicted that it would last a thousand years.

THE THIRD REICH

Hitler made himself the supreme leader (*Führer*) of the German state. So powerful was he that the very concept of sovereignty—the legitimate right to rule—emanated not from the people or a deity, but from himself. The German legal system was completely Nazified. Thenceforth, the higher interests of the state provided the basis for all laws. Nazi "justice" was meted out by People's Courts in the name of the *Führer*.

The German Republic, like the Second Reich before it, had been a federal arrangement composed of a variety of state governments, such as Prussia and Bavaria. Hitler removed these states, substituting in their place a highly centralized government. In keeping with the Nazi theory of the "conquest of the state," appropriate party leaders assumed command of equivalent positions in the government ad-

ministration. Hitler retained the *Reichstag* but removed all real authority from it.

Hitler could neither remain in power very long nor carry out his strategy for world hegemony without the support of the German Army. But most of the German officer corps, with a long tradition of status and aristocratic privilege behind it, considered Hitler and his Nazi entourage low-class thugs. From their perspective, the generals saw Hitler as a temporary expedient who would serve a useful purpose in destroying the Republic and restoring the army to its former position of strength. Like Mussolini, Hitler had to compromise with the generals, and like Mussolini he did so by sacrificing his own storm troops, the SA.

Ernst Roehm, the deposed leader of the SA, had come back to Germany on Hitler's urging in 1930 and had been instrumental in the seizure of power (see Topic 81). But Roehm had always resented the power and pretensions of the generals, and after 1933 he demanded that Hitler replace the German Army with the SA. For Hitler, the choice between the SA and the army was clear, and he secured a pledge of loyalty from the generals in return for the destruction of Roehm's forces. The agreement was executed on the night of June 30 in a series of surprise raids of SA camps throughout Germany. The purge, known as the "Night of the Long Knives," ended with the coldblooded murder of Roehm and his followers.

The Nazi police state was as complex as Mussolini's structure. The secret police (*Gestapo*) sought out anti-Nazis and other internal political enemies. Information and confessions were extracted by torture and blackmail, but the victims of Nazi terror were often summarily executed or incarcerated without formal charges. As early as 1933, Hitler opened the first concentration camp at Dachau, where political prisoners were kept. Almost a dozen more were subsequently constructed. Heinrich Himmler, who served both

Hitler arriving at a rally organized by the Nazi Party. 1934. The careful choreography of these mass rallies, which Hitler had learned from Mussolini, and the rhetoric of Hitler's speeches did much to consolidate the impression that the Nazis had broad popular support. At this 1934 rally at Nuremberg, in Bavaria, southern Germany, Hitler announced the anti-Jewish laws.

Jesse Owens starting a race at the Berlin Olympic Games of 1936. Owens' victories in the 100- and 200-meter dash, the 400-meter relay, and the broad jump, shattered Hitler's attempt to demonstrate "Aryan"—that is, White—"Supremacy." Thus the Games, seen by the Nazis as a propaganda coup, undermined the foundations of Nazi ideology.

as head of the Gestapo and the SS, ran the camps, where prisoners were either used as slave labor, were allowed to die of hunger, or were otherwise brutalized. During World War II, the death camps became the most horrible manifestation of Nazism.

HITLER, MUSSOLINI, AND RACIAL POLICY

Hitler's own twisted contempt for Jews, Slavs, gypsies, and other ethnic groups that he considered "inferior" became the basis of Nazi ideology. Yet, in making racism a part of his political program, he called on an extensive European tradition of prejudice and hatred. The Nazis mixed these traditions with 19th-century Pan-German sentiment, believing with Hitler that the German "Master Race" would inevitably rule the world. Hitler's obsessive hatred for the Jews was the focus of a huge and systematic effort by the Nazi state of unparalleled evil—their mass extermination.

Anti-Semitism became official policy almost immediately. Jews were purged from government employment in

April 1933. Two years later, in 1935, the so-called Nuremberg Laws stripped Jews of their rights as citizens and made it a crime for them to marry "pure" Germans. Jews were forbidden to practice medicine or law and could no longer attend or teach in universities (see Topic 88). The regime then launched a moral and physical assault against the Jewish communities of Germany.

Those Jews who recognized the danger tried to leave Germany, but too many found it impossible. In 1938, a Polish Jew killed a German diplomat in Paris, and the crime became the excuse for the unleashing of a premeditated attack against German Jewish synagogues, homes, and businesses. Many Jews lost their lives in the carnage, and the government then levied heavy taxes on the victims. After this destruction—known as *Kristallnacht* (Night of the Broken Glass)—it was increasingly difficult for Jews to flee the country, and those who managed to get away found in many cases that the Western powers were not disposed to take them in. While some Western leaders criticized German policy, their warnings fell on deaf ears.

In November 1938, Mussolini reversed himself on the question of the Jews. Before that, he had claimed repeatedly that Fascism was not anti-Semitic. The decision to introduce anti-Semitic legislation was a purely political one—his desire to align Italy in a united front with Germany. The measures that Mussolini enacted, although thoroughly reprehensible, were not nearly as severe as those in Germany. Italy's 50,000 Jews had to abandon most professions and universities, but Italian-born Jews retained their citizenship. Mixed marriages were forbidden, and Jews were not allowed to own land. On the other hand, unlike Nazism's immutable "scientific" racism, Fascist laws enabled some Jews—such as early members of the Fascist movement, war veterans, and children of mixed marriages who did not profess Judaism—to escape their provisions.

THE REGIMENTATION OF GERMAN LIFE

To Nazi ideologues, the German churches, whether Catholic or Protestant, competed with the state for control over the minds of the German people. Parents were pressured not to send their children to religious schools, and the authorities deliberately encouraged anti-Christian cults based on old Teutonic deities. Hitler persecuted the churches, confiscated their newspapers, and arrested their priests and bishops. The state tried without success to impose a "German Christian" church on Protestants. A group of clergy under the leadership of Pastor Martin Niemoeller (1892–1984) and others was the center of Protestant resistance. Niemoeller was an outspoken critic of Hitler and was interned in a concentration camp in 1937. Many Catholic priests were similarly engaged in anti-Nazi activities and offered refuge to Jews and other victims of Nazi persecution. In 1937, Pope Pius XI issued the encyclical *Mit Brennender Sorge* (With Burning Sorrow) to reject Nazi racism.

Nazism presented itself as a revolutionary force in German society, promising prosperity and equality. Its propaganda was most successful among the middle classes, who

Two people passing a Jewish storefront with the windows broken. November 1938, the morning after *Kristallnacht*. The shop next door displays a Swastika in the window, to confirm its allegiance to the Party. The Night of the Broken Glass was followed by a notable increase in the persecution of the Jews under Nazism.

saw the regime as having saved them from the despair of the Great Depression. The Nazi party instituted the same array of social and leisure organizations as Mussolini had created in Italy, including "Strength Through Joy," similar to Mussolini's *Dopolavoro*. The *Hitler Jugend* (Hitler Youth) indoctrinated young Germans with Nazi ideas and the virtues of discipline and obedience. The educational system, from elementary schools to universities, was reorganized and the faculties purged. Hitler did actually break down some of the social distinctions that had existed, especially for middle-class German men, and both the government and the party bureaucracies offered opportunities to many for rapid advancement.

Joseph Goebbels (1897–1945), one of Hitler's closest associates, a brilliant manipulator of public opinion, was minister of Propaganda and Enlightenment. Goebbels imposed rigid controls on all aspects of intellectual and artistic life, including the mass media, literature, publishing, music, and art. Books that were banned by the government were burned in dramatic public bonfires.

Hitler was, for obvious reasons, especially concerned with art and architecture. Modernism and abstraction were anathema to him, examples of what he called "decadence." He purged the art academies and the museum staffs and in 1937 opened an "Exhibition of Degenerate Art," in which were displayed the works of the Cubists, Expressionists, and other modern movements. He insisted that art inspire German values. Official painting presented versions of Nazi mythology: Germanic knights, idealized peasant families, nudes in classical poses, and beautiful youths enraptured by the Nazi ideal. In architecture, Hitler closed down the Bauhaus, which had been the center of Europe's functional international style (see Topic 86), and worked closely with

Albert Speer (1905–1981), the government's official architect, in designing monumental structures in the neo-Greek Revival style.

THE DICTATORS AND THE DEPRESSION: LABOR, BUSINESS, AND ECONOMIC POLICY

Mussolini and Hitler pursued similar economic policies, which were designed to make their countries self-sufficient and capable of waging modern war. Although neither dictator wanted to end private property, both imposed state intervention in the economy that went far beyond the measures taken by the Western powers during the Great Depression.

MUSSOLINI'S CORPORATE STATE

The Fascists, who came to power in part because they opposed Marxism, appeased business interests by outlawing strikes and traditional labor unions. They also permitted manufacturing associations to bargain with Fascist unions and the government. Such measures did not sit well with Fascist syndicalists, and in 1926 Mussolini created the Ministry of Corporations. Corporativism was to be a system of institutional arrangements in which capital and labor were integrated into units. In this arrangement, each unit, or corporation, was supposed to regulate a particular sector of industry or the economy, supervised by the disinterested power of the state. The theory behind this unique concept was that class conflict, which Marx had said was inevitable, would be overcome.

Between 1929 and 1932, the minister of Corporations was the Fascist intellectual Giuseppe Bottai (1895–1959), who tried unsuccessfully to use state authority to dictate to both management and labor. Mussolini insisted that the "corporate state" remain a fiction because the private sector had grown too powerful. The corporate system, advertised to the world as a "third way" between capitalism and communism, served only as a propaganda device.

The effects of the Depression were not as severe in Italy as they were in Germany. Nevertheless, it did wipe out many of the gains that the boom of the 1920s had created. Unemployment stood at 1 million in 1933, stock prices fell by 39 percent, and the previously balanced budget went into deficit. The policy of "autarchy," designed to make Italy self-sufficient in agriculture and some industries, tended to force workers into unprofitable areas of production and to drive up prices. Although wheat production went up, other kinds of crops went down. Higher tariffs, used to protect Italian manufacturers, pushed the cost of living up and created shortages.

Another novel aspect of Fascist economic policy was the Institute for Industrial Reconstruction (IRI), established in 1933. The IRI bought up the large stockholdings of big banks and companies on the edge of bankruptcy, thus making the government a major stockholder. By 1939, the government owned 70 percent of pig iron production and 45 percent of steel manufacturing, and could control both.

Spending on public works projects, used by most governments in Europe and America to alleviate effects of the Depression in the 1930s, doubled. Mussolini had swamps and marshes drained to produce more farmland, roads and rail lines were constructed, and thousands of government buildings and subsidized housing projects sprang up the length of the peninsula. Nevertheless, the Depression, combined with Mussolini's economic policies, meant a decline in the standard of living for most Italians.

THE NAZI ECONOMY

Hitler's efforts to fight the Great Depression with public works projects were even more extensive. Here, too, swamps were drained and forests replanted, public housing was built, and highways extended across the country. Agriculture was important to the Nazis, not only because of their "back to the soil" movement, but also to make Germany self-reliant in the event of war. Government subsidies were extended to farmers along with long-term loans.

As in Italy, German workers lost most of their economic rights, although unemployment virtually disappeared and the standard of living improved. In 1936 Hitler launched a Four-Year Plan that regulated all sectors of the economy, from prices to wages and from factory regulations to production levels. A National Labor Front took the place of labor unions and strikes were forbidden, while industrial associations were recognized as part of the state structure. Private industry remained intact, although government regulations were more stringent. Although most workers had more stable jobs, they generally worked longer hours and earned lower wages.

STALINIST RUSSIA: STATE PLANNING, COLLECTIVIZATION, AND THE POLICE STATE

Stalin's totalitarian dictatorship differed in several respects from those in the West. In the first place, according to Marxist theory, the state was supposed to be temporary. Then, too, instead of having to create a new revolutionary regime, when Stalin came to power in the late 1920s, the communist state was already in place. Politically, his aim was simple—to consolidate and strengthen his personal power (see Topic 81).

Stalin was, of course, committed to Communism and had always considered Lenin's NEP program a temporary makeshift. His ambition was to make the Soviet Union a great industrial giant and to socialize agriculture as well as industry. To achieve these goals, Stalin would remake the country's society. The fundamental techniques in his drive to industrialize and modernize the Soviet economy were similar to those employed in Italy and Germany: state intervention and centralized planning. Here, however, the degree of regimentation and coercion of the working class was even greater.

THE PLANNED ECONOMY

Stalin devised the idea of a Five-Year Plan, the first of which unfolded between 1928 and 1932. Under this plan, every national resource was mobilized to achieve a fundamental transformation. Stalin eliminated all vestiges of private property and instituted industrial quotas that were determined by an agency of the Communist party. The emphasis was placed on heavy industry and transportation, which received the greatest resources, so that the production and availability of consumer goods suffered and rationing was imposed.

The quotas established for every individual worker and production unit were almost always too high. Stalin's plan anticipated more than doubling industrial manufacturing and tripling steel making. Although workers and plant managers who reached their goals were rewarded, those who failed to meet the quotas were penalized. Most Russian workers were unskilled and not accustomed to the pace and discipline imposed by the Five-Year Plan, and managers had to learn on the job.

SIGNIFICANT DATES

The Soviet Union Under Stalin

1924	Stalin begins to emerge as Soviet dictator
1928–1932	First Five-Year Plan
1928–1933	Collectivization of Soviet agriculture
1934	Kirov murder
1936–1938	"Great Purges"

The first Plan achieved only part of its goals, largely because of the unreasonably high quotas. Equipment was overused and often of poor quality, so that mechanical breakdowns were not unusual, and parts were difficult to obtain. The same could be said for the products themselves because quantity was stressed at the expense of quality.

Despite these setbacks, Stalin, who had learned some lessons, announced the second Five-Year Plan in 1932, which moved at a more reasonable rate (the Second Plan covered the years 1933–1937, and the Third 1938–1942). By 1938, iron and steel production had increased four times and coal three and one-half times. On the eve of World War II, the Soviet Union was the third nation in the world in industrial output, being surpassed only by the United States and Germany, and was ahead of Great Britain in steel and iron.

In the agricultural sector, Stalin placed the entire Soviet harvest under government control. Surpluses were sold abroad to buy the sophisticated machinery needed at home. To achieve these goals, Stalin decided to destroy the entire class of landowning peasants known as the *kulaks*, who had prospered under the NEP. The *kulaks*—a term of derision used to describe greedy money lenders—were sufficiently prosperous to hire farm laborers and to extend loans to the local villagers. The elimination of the *kulaks* enabled the government to consolidate small farms into huge agricultural collectives, where modern equipment and farming techniques were used efficiently.

COLLECTIVIZATION AND THE PEASANTRY

The **collectivization** program required that all peasants turn their land and livestock over to the state, keeping only their houses and personal property. As in industry, every collective received production quotas. Peasants shared the work as well as the profits or losses the cooperative earned. The peasants staunchly resisted collectivization and fought back against the state by hiding or burning their crops and killing their animals. The resulting shortages of food caused deep concern in Moscow. In the Russian countryside, a massive rebellion soon consumed an untold number of lives—Stalin himself admitted later to 10 million.

Collectivization wreaked havoc on Soviet agriculture. The *kulaks*, who were generally the best farmers, were either killed or deported to Siberia, and half of all farm animals were destroyed. Grain production hardly increased in the decade after 1928. Collectivization also produced a terrible famine in 1932–1933, and it killed an estimated 3 million persons. The heavy price paid by Russian peasants brought Stalin a political success because he could now claim that socialism had reached the countryside. By 1933, more than half of all farming families had joined collectives, and five years later the figure had passed 90 percent.

SOVIET SOCIETY UNDER STALIN

The ambitious plans that Stalin set transformed the Soviet Union. Thousands of factories were built in the 1930s, and the industrial expansion swelled the size of older cities and created new urban centers in isolated regions of Siberia and Asiatic Russia. Millions of people were moved en masse from rural regions to the new cities to supply the workforce.

Life everywhere was difficult for the average Soviet citizen. Housing was primitive and in short supply, and the steady rise in prices produced a serious drop in the standard of living. In the decade following the start of the Five-Year Plans, for example, the purchasing power of an industrial worker declined by some 40 percent. The constraints of political indoctrination were oppressive. Adults and children alike became captive audiences for party lecturers, and the government-operated mass media were filled with official information. Mass organizations for the young, women, and workers assisted in the indoctrination process. In addition to selling the virtues of Communism, Soviet propaganda stressed a theme that was crucial to the dictatorship: the creation of the cult of Stalin. Stalin's face became familiar to all Russians as his photograph and portrait appeared everywhere.

Some important positive advances were made in Soviet life during Stalin's dictatorship. Nearly every able-bodied citizen found a job, although most involved unskilled heavy labor. The government provided free education and medical care, cheap housing, and pensions. In education the progress was more impressive. Stalin sought to wipe out illiteracy and brought free elementary schooling to the far reaches of the country. For those with superior skills, higher education was available. Education, especially of a technical nature, could lead to higher salaries, privileges, and status. A managerial class eventually joined the political and intellectual elites, giving the lie to the notion of a "classless society."

THE STALINIST TERROR

Although the police state was a pervasive feature of life in the fascist dictatorships, neither Hitler nor Mussolini used it in quite the same way as Stalin, who unleashed a reign of terror on a vast scale against the Soviet population at large.

The suppression of the peasants during the collectivization and the Five-Year Plans caused considerable unrest, not only among ordinary Soviet citizens but in the inner circles of the Communist party and the state administration as well. Stalin decided in the mid-1930s to use his domestic security forces to crush any signs of discontent and eliminate possible opposition to his rule. The so-called Great Purges were so indiscriminate that even high-ranking military officers suffered the fate of dissidents. For two years, between 1936 and 1938, millions of Soviets suffered imprisonment, forced labor, and death at the hands of a ruthless dictator.

Stalin first struck in late 1934, when one of his most trusted followers, Sergei Kirov (1888–1934), was murdered. Stalin no doubt had Kirov killed and then used the murder as a pretext for wide-scale purges. Announcing a plot against him by Trotsky's followers, he held several infamous show trials in Moscow. In 1936, the court accused 16 prominent Old Bolsheviks of conspiracy and ordered their execution. The next year, less important party leaders were similarly eliminated, followed by the court martial of General

Mikhail Tukhachevsky (1893–1937) and other high-ranking officers. Soon, vast numbers of innocent people, including government and party bureaucrats and intellectuals, workers and factory foremen, fell victim to the ever-expanding purge. In the end, Stalin completed the process by having officials of the NKVD—the internal security unit—eliminated as well. The statistics of Stalin's terror can only be estimated, but perhaps as many as 8 million people were held in prisons or work camps, 90 percent of whom eventually died, and the total number of deaths may have exceeded 10 million.

When the Great Purges were over, Stalin had succeeded in clearing out entire categories of the Soviet leadership. The officials whom he appointed to the vacant positions represented a new breed of bureaucrat, not tied to the Old Bolsheviks or to the Revolution of 1917, but bound only by loyalty and fear to Stalin. Stalin's power was now virtually without limits.

WOMEN AND TOTALITARIANISM

The interwar totalitarian dictatorships were the first national governments to implement clear policies regarding the position of women. These programs responded in part to the ideologies of each movement, and in part to the economic and social priorities of the regimes. Fascism was a philosophy of conquest, in which women were subsumed to men's desires, whereas the earliest Soviet laws had accepted the notion of women's equality. Yet both forms of totalitarianism allowed only limited scope for women to develop their potential in society or to share in the exercise of power.

FASCISM AND WOMEN

Among the "Fascists of the First Hour" in 1919 were to be found several Italian women, including the female Black Shirt leader Regina Teruzzi and Mussolini's lover, Sarfatti. Nevertheless, Fascists in general held most women in contempt, regarding them primarily as wives, mistresses, and mothers. Mussolini was never loyal to the many women in his life, and yet his public reputation as a womanizer inflated his popular image.

Fascists considered it the natural duty of men to possess women sexually. In official lore, Fascists were by definition young and virile warriors, and all Italian males were to be "new men," ruthless, hard, and heroic. Women, on the other hand, were to be pure and subservient keepers of the hearth. The regime's propaganda machine reinforced a stable and traditional patriarchal social order of the kind that was familiar to most Italians. The Fascist party ran separate youth organizations for all males and females ages six through seventeen.

Because Mussolini wanted to increase Italy's population, the regime encouraged large families. Adolescent females were given instruction in caring for a home and children, and the state gave mothers free birthing and medical assistance, hygiene care, and prizes to the families with the largest number of children.

For a brief period before coming to power, Mussolini had demanded women's suffrage, but he later changed his mind. During the 1920s and 1930s, fewer and fewer women were active in the industrial workforce, a trend accelerated by the large unemployment figures of the Great Depression. Some specialized fields, such as nursing and teaching, were regarded as suitable for women, but females were largely discouraged from entering the professions. By law, husbands retained superior rights over children and property, and divorce went unrecognized.

WOMEN AND THE NAZI STATE

Like Mussolini, Hitler found little room for women in his Nazi movement or in his government. He did not marry until just before his suicide in 1945, and although for several years he had maintained a liaison with Eva Braun, the relationship may have been purely platonic. The *Führer* demanded that women provide Germany with children who would become workers and soldiers. Government policies and party programs encouraged larger families and modern medical care for mothers and children.

The Nazi party deliberately recruited women, and in the early 1920s about one in five members of the NSDAP was women. After the seizure of power, women never achieved important positions in the regime. Nazi women, on the other hand, supported Hitler's goal of restoring family values and were active in community work designed to foster such attitudes. At first, women were not encouraged to work in factories or agriculture, but when Hitler began to re-arm Germany, they moved into the labor force in larger numbers.

Nazi aesthetics had an element of repressed sexuality, whether in painting, sculpture, or film. Hitler had always railed against cultural decadence and pornography, but prized the nude in art. Women were portrayed as the embodiment of the ideal German female, virtuous and pure, while male bodies were presented as athletes and warriors. In the propaganda films of the great director Leni Riefenstahl (see Topic 86), there is, among the thousands of semi-clothed young Germans whom she idolized, an underlying if unacknowledged sexual tension. She subsumed that tension in images of perfect beauty, choreographing them in dances of dominance and power.

SOVIET WOMEN

Marx and Engels had both seen the repression of women as a function of the suppression of the working class, arguing that in capitalist societies women were a form of property. Lenin agreed, and as early as 1918, the party had set up a special Women's Bureau to mobilize women into the party. Alexandra Kollontai (1872–1952), an early Bolshevik leader, pushed for sexual freedom and laws that would make her feminist ideals a reality. The Soviet constitution embodied full rights and equality for women, yet although Russian women did gain the right to divorce and abortion in the 1920s, reality never matched the official rhetoric.

A woman driving a tractor on a Soviet collective farm. 1930s. Stalin promoted the idea of women as workers in farming and heavy industry. It fitted well with Soviet theories of equality, although in practice women workers received lower salaries than men. State collective farms, such as the one shown here, provided virtually all of the Soviet Union's domestic food production.

© Sovfoto

Under Stalin, the position of Soviet women changed. He played down talk of gender equality, but his drive to industrialize and increase production brought women into the workforce in large numbers, just as the collectivization of agriculture did for rural women. Low salaries encouraged women to seek employment in even the heaviest kind of work. The acute shortage of trained professionals and technicians also led Stalin to make education available to Soviet women. Although women had greater access to employment and education in the Soviet Union than in the West, they did not receive equal pay for equal work. Nor were they relieved of the burdens of child rearing and housekeeping.

Putting Mussolini, Hitler, and Stalin in Perspective

The totalitarian experience in interwar Europe had profound repercussions. In their effort to control the minds and the values as well as the loyalties of their subjects, these regimes succeeded in mobilizing millions of people in an unprecedented fashion. Programs of indoctrination and socialization drew formerly isolated sectors of Europe's population into the mainstream of national life and politicized them for the first time. Never before were the lives and deaths of such vast numbers of citizens so directly affected by government actions.

Mussolini, Hitler, and Stalin were major figures of the period, whose personalities and policies dominated public events for years. Their revolutions were designed to destroy ordinary politics of the kind familiar to most Westerners, and each of their regimes was built with the intention of implementing a particular world view and a philosophy of life. That philosophy preached the attainment of utopia through dominance, power, and control. The human suffering that resulted has perhaps never been equaled in modern history.

Questions for Further Study

1. Is the concept of "totalitarianism" useful for historians? Why? Why not?
2. What similarities and differences existed between the Fascist state and the Nazi state?
3. What was the nature of totalitarian economic policy? How did the fascist dictators respond to the Great Depression?
4. What factors explain Stalinist terror?
5. What role did women have in totalitarian societies? Was it different from their role in democratic societies?

Suggestions for Further Reading

Cannistraro, Philip V., and B.R. Sullivan. *Il Duce's Other Woman*. New York, 1993.

Conquest, Robert. *Stalin, Breaker of Nations*. New York, 1991.

De Grand, Alexander. *Fascist Italy and Nazi Germany: The Fascist Style of Rule*. London, 1995.

Gentile, Emilio, trans. Keith Botsford. *The Sacralization of Politics in Fascist Italy*. Cambridge, MA, 1996.

Kerhsaw, Ian. *The Hitler Myth: Image and Reality in the Third Reich*. New York, 1987.

Kershaw, Ian. *The Nazi Dictatorship: Problems and Perspectives of Interpretation*, 2nd ed. London, 2000.

Koonz, Claudia. *Mothers in the Fatherland: Women, the Family, and Nazi Politics*. New York, 1987.

Lee, Stephen J. *Stalin and the Soviet Union*. New York, 1999.

Mack Smith, Denis. *Mussolini*. New York, 1982.

Peukert, Detlev J.K. *Inside Nazi Germany*. New Haven, CT, 1987.

Pipes, Richard. *Russia Under the Bolshevik Regime, 1919–1924*. London, 1994.

Tannenbaum, Edward R. *The Fascist Experience: Italian Society and Culture, 1922–1945*. New York, 1972.

Tucker, Robert C. *Stalin in Power*. New York, 1990.

InfoTrac College Edition

Enter the search term *Mussolini* using Key Terms.

Enter the search term *Hitler* using Key Terms.

Enter the search term *Stalin* using Key Terms.

THE WESTERN DEMOCRACIES AND EASTERN EUROPE

In the 20 years between the two world wars, the viability of European democracy was put to the test by a variety of destructive forces. The rise of fascism, and particularly the success of the movements in Italy and Germany, combined with the triumph of communism in Russia, appeared to forecast the wave of the future. With the 1929 crash and the resultant Great Depression, the social and economic systems of the two great Western democracies, Britain and France, came under tremendous stress.

In the 1920s, the prevalent trend in domestic politics was the search for stability, a goal that proved impossible in the context of postwar conditions. Readjustment to peacetime economies had been difficult, and alternating cycles of unemployment, inflation, and depression jarred Britain and France. Working-class discontent grew significantly, and even the formation of Britain's first socialist government—that of Ramsay MacDonald in 1924—failed to quell the unrest or its causes. Drift rather than decisive action remained the order of the day.

In France, where the Depression hit later than elsewhere, the right and the left also alternated in power and produced equally unimpressive results. The first postwar elections returned a conservative majority, but its strident nationalism over the Ruhr invasion in 1923 frightened many Frenchmen into voting for the left, and the Socialists formed a coalition with the Radicals. When the Depression finally did arrive in France in 1932, retrenchment and the lack of clear policies made matters worse. The outbreak of serious riots in 1934 and the growing polarization of French politics created a crisis of confidence unequaled since the Dreyfus Affair.

Despite the unimpressive record of government in responding to the Depression, the economic collapse did cause liberal democratic governments to readjust their thinking about the obligations of the state to its citizens. As a result, they inaugurated an era of social intervention and economic activism that has marked Western society ever since. The United States, with the election of Franklin D. Roosevelt and the implementation of his vigorous New Deal programs, went further than either Britain or France in restructuring the government-citizen relationship. By the end of the 1930s, the institutional basis of the modern welfare state had been built.

In Eastern Europe, the prospects for democracy were equally uncertain. There, upon the ruins of the old Austro-Hungarian, German, and Russian empires, a series of newly created, independent states arose after World War I. From the start, these new countries were burdened with serious problems: illiteracy and the lack of social modernization, and economies that rested primarily on agriculture. Moreover, the myriad of nationalities the region comprised meant that every nation had ethnic minorities within its borders to cause unrest and tension, as well as constant friction with neighbors over borders and nationality issues.

GREAT BRITAIN AND THE IRISH QUESTION

It is difficult to speak of a British "recovery" from the trauma of World War I because in the domestic arena the country experienced the next 20 years as one long, continual series of trials and failures. A government—whether of the left or the right—that was unable to cope adequately with the economic dislocations of the postwar period and the accompanying labor unrest, could hardly deal successfully with the Great Depression. Although the British did succeed, at long last, in coming to terms with Ireland's future as an independent state, the agonizing ordeal of the Irish people continued in a devastating civil war.

THE POSTWAR DRIFT

The British electorate, like that in France, was in a decidedly conservative mood as World War I drew to an end. Wanting a harsh settlement with defeated Germany, the 1918 khaki election—so-called because of the large number of veterans who participated—returned a strong Conservative majority to the House of Commons. The Conservatives permitted Liberal Prime Minister David Lloyd George to continue in office at the head of a coalition government, but they held the real power. In the autumn of 1922, however, the Conservatives pushed Lloyd George out, chiefly over his Irish policies, and formed a cabinet under the elderly Scotsman, Andrew Bonar Law (served 1922–1923).

In the elections of 1922, the working class was in an especially aggressive mood because the Labour party doubled its strength, making it the second party in Parliament. Nevertheless, the Conservatives gained even more ground and elected Stanley Baldwin (served 1923–1924, 1924–1929, 1935–1937). The following year, further elections increased the strength of the Liberals, who were now in a position to form a coalition with the Conservatives or Labour. Instead, Herbert Asquith (1852–1928), the Liberal leader, declared that Labour should have an opportunity to form a government. The decision was an important one for two reasons: The liberals would never again head the government, and Ramsay MacDonald, who led the new Labour ministry, became the first socialist prime minister in Western Europe.

Ramsay MacDonald (served 1924, 1929–1931, 1931–1935), the man who held that distinction, was a Scotsman of working-class origin. Although good-looking and eloquent, MacDonald possessed little leadership ability or firmness of character. Not only did he prove indecisive, but once in office he also felt it necessary to convince everyone that the country had little to fear from the Labour party. His recognition of the Soviet Union did not, however, endear him to those on the political right.

MacDonald fell as a result of scare tactics. The opposition accused the government of not prosecuting a communist editor who advocated sedition, and during the election a letter was circulated, allegedly from Grigori Zinoviev, head of the Comintern (the communist international organization), suggesting connections with the Labour party. The letter was a fake, but it was sufficient to give the Conservatives a huge majority.

Baldwin came back to 10 Downing Street, heading the British government for the next five years. During that time, he offered the country what he described as "sane, common-sense government," and his manner inspired public confidence. In reality, however, this meant an almost total failure to come to grips with the problems of inflation, industrial slump, and unemployment that were plaguing British society.

The low point of Baldwin's second ministry was the general strike of 1926, during which he succeeded in exasperating class tensions and antagonizing the workers. After a royal commission appointed to investigate conditions in the coal industry failed to satisfy either the miners or the owners, in the face of a threatened general strike, the mine owners shut down operations. For nine days in May 1926, some 2.5 million workers in all fields of endeavor struck, while the government organized middle-class volunteers to run basic services. Some local violence and considerable anger marked the strike, and when negotiations collapsed, Baldwin forced the unions into a settlement that virtually gave up the miners' demands. When the general strike ended, the miners stayed out on their own for another six months, embittered at the government for having engineered their defeat.

THE NATIONAL GOVERNMENT

In the wake of the 1926 strike, working-class sentiment against Baldwin intensified, and when he called elections in 1929, he was swept out of office. Labour campaigned on the unemployment issue and blamed the Conservatives for

London during the General Strike. 1926. The scene is at the entrance to the street known as Whitehall, which contains many government buildings, and leads to Buckingham Palace. Armored vehicles patrol the neighborhood, guarded by soldiers armed with machine guns. Note that many of the men are wearing circular metal battle helmets.

Britain's economic troubles. Labour won more seats than the Tories but lacked a majority and had to form a coalition with the Liberals. In addition, Labour was still burdened with Ramsay MacDonald as its leader.

The second MacDonald government faced a deteriorating economic situation. During 1930 alone, unemployment jumped from 1 million to 2.5 million. The government's response was simply to increase government financial support for the unemployed (known as the "dole"). This caused a huge increase in the deficit. The next year, experts advised MacDonald that only a cut in expenditures—that is, a reduction in the dole—would prevent bankruptcy. An atmosphere of crisis spread, causing heavy withdrawals from banks and the virtual depletion of the country's gold reserves. American financiers refused to extend further credits to Britain without cutbacks. In August 1931, MacDonald told his cabinet that unemployment benefits would have to be cut; when they balked, he asked them to resign. Instead of submitting his own resignation, however, King George V (ruled 1910–1936) persuaded MacDonald to form a new, broad-based coalition with himself as prime minister and Stanley Baldwin as second in command. In fact, the Conservatives dominated this so-called National Government, with MacDonald as their pawn. Labour, stunned by what they considered MacDonald's betrayal, expelled him from the party.

From 1931 to 1935, MacDonald and Baldwin ran the government. Together, they added Britain to the growing number of countries that were abandoning the gold standard. The international value of the pound did drop from $4.86, but held at $3.40, thus defying the warnings of conventional economists. Parliament also approved a 10 percent reduction in unemployment benefits. The financial crisis began to ease, and the government called for new elections for a vote of confidence. Despite a coalition effort, the Conservatives took the lion's share of votes—out of 556 seats in Parliament, they won 472 while Labour lost some 85 percent of its seats.

MacDonald continued to serve as prime minister until 1935. With the National Government ratified, it pushed through Parliament a program of tariff protection, thus ending Britain's longstanding tradition of free trade. When failing health led to MacDonald's retirement, Baldwin moved to Downing Street, where he remained until 1937.

Britain came through the Depression with minimal damage to its political traditions, despite the lame policies of the Labour and Conservative ministries. Conditions in some parts of England, and in Wales and Scotland, remained depressed, but something of an economic revival began to take hold by the end of the decade. The coming of World War II interrupted that process, and in its aftermath Britain seemed to pick up where it had left off.

THE QUEST FOR IRISH INDEPENDENCE

The Irish question remained one of the most vexing and agonizing issues in modern British history. Since the 17th cen-

Map 84.1 Ireland. Formerly part of the United Kingdom, in 1922 the British split the six Northern counties, which were predominantly (but by no means entirely) Protestant, from the rest of Ireland. The south became the Irish Free State and later (1949), the Republic of Ireland. Northern Ireland became a province of Britain. The battle by members of the Irish Republican Army (IRA) to reunite the island, and the counter-campaign by Protestant "Loyalists" led to some of the worst terrorist incidents in Europe in the last decades of the 20th century.

Irish Republican Army (IRA) members patrolling the streets of Dublin. Summer 1922. The IRA had as its core members the survivors of the Easter Rising of 1916. As can be seen here, most of them dressed in civilian clothes, although a few wore a form of military dress. The IRA continued to lead the fight for a unified Ireland into the 21st century.

tury, Ireland had been virtually a British colony, ruled by a small Protestant gentry that insisted on maintaining ties with England. The Protestant minority comprised the six counties of Ulster in the northeastern portion of Ireland. The larger section of the island, in the south and west, comprised Catholics who increasingly demanded Home Rule—that is, Irish control over domestic affairs. The Liberal party under William Gladstone had incorporated Home Rule in its platform, but the Conservatives opposed it.

In the late 19th century, two efforts to get Home Rule approved in Parliament failed. The extension of the suffrage to Irish males, however, resulted in the election of a growing Irish Catholic delegation to Parliament. A third Home Rule bill passed in 1914 but was then postponed because of the war. Among Irish nationalists, extremists grew impatient and sparked the 1916 Easter Rebellion (see Topic 80), which intensified feeling on both sides—the Irish, especially, being provoked by Britain's overreaction to the Rebellion.

In the 1918 elections, Irish nationalist sentiment triumphed when some 70 candidates were sent to Parliament by a new party, Sinn Fein (Gaelic for "We Ourselves"). Its members abandoned Home Rule in favor of complete freedom and, instead of taking their seats in Parliament, proclaimed themselves an Irish Parliament called Dail Eireann. That January, they declared Ireland independent.

The government of Lloyd George responded slowly to the Sinn Fein's actions, but by the end of the year was lending the "Black and Tans"—a special army of volunteers in Ireland that distinguished itself by its exceptional brutality—official support. As this cruel war escalated and casualties

grew, public opinion in Britain began to turn against the repression. Finally, in the summer of 1921, Lloyd George agreed to meet with Irish leaders, and the result was the signing of a formal treaty in December that created the Irish Free State out of the Catholic regions as a self-governing nation with Dominion status. Protestant Ulster became an autonomous region within the United Kingdom, under the name of Northern Ireland.

The Irish Free State did not satisfy a radical minority of Irish nationalists, who united under the leadership of Eamon De Valera (1882–1975). Born in New York City, De Valera was raised in Ireland and became an ardent republican who played an active role in the Easter Rebellion. Refusing to recognize the treaty, his followers organized the clandestine Irish Republican Army (IRA) and carried on a terrorist civil war to prevent the separation of Northern Ireland. The bombings, raids, and deaths escalated on both sides of the border. In 1923, De Valera's forces were overwhelmed and he was imprisoned. The next year, however, he started a new party, Fianna Fáil, continued the struggle, and won power in 1932. De Valera was elected prime minister five years later and declared the country independent, renaming it Eire. During World War II, Eire remained neutral, and in 1949 it left the British Commonwealth and became the Republic of Ireland. The 1921 Irish settlement remained unchanged, and the tragic civil war continued in Ulster.

FRANCE: THE QUEST FOR STABILITY

The somber mood of British public life in the 1920s contrasted sharply with the more exuberant tone of life in France. In the aftermath of World War I, Paris regained its position as the capital of the European avant-garde (see

Topic 85). But if France led the way in cultural life, its politics left much to be desired. The relative stability of Britain's governmental experience contrasted sharply with the tense, unstable French political arena. One reason for this difference was the extensive damage the country suffered in the war and the considerable resources needed to rebuild. The French had not managed their war financing well, and between 1914 and 1919 the circulation of bank notes had increased sixfold. War debts to Britain and the United States added to the pressure, and politicians wavered in their determination to raise taxes both to meet the deficit and to reconstruct the economy. Once the Depression hit in 1932, the strain on financial resources increased still further.

THE ERA OF STABILITY

Because the electoral system was based on proportional representation, a myriad of political parties competed for power. Pressure on the republic was particularly strong from the right, which formed a coalition known as the Bloc National to compete in the postwar elections. In 1919, the French people chose a solidly conservative, highly nationalist Chamber of Deputies—the "Blue Horizon Chamber," so named after the large number of veterans in blue uniforms represented in it.

In 1923, however, Premier Raymond Poincaré (served 1912, 1922–1924, 1926–1929) occupied the Ruhr Valley in order to force payment of German reparations. The resulting war scare, combined with high inflation, led voters to turn to the left. The radical socialist Édouard Herriot (served 1924–1925, 1932), supported by the *Cartel des Gauches* (Cartel of the Left), succeeded Poincaré but lasted only one year. Herriot, who was ignorant of financial matters, did nothing to deal with the country's enormous war debts, nor could he control the rising inflation that seriously hurt the working and middle classes. The ineffective Herriot stepped down, but by 1926 the French franc, once among the most stable currencies in the world, had lost 90 percent of its value on the international market. More se-

rious still was the fact that the middle classes lost three-quarters of their savings.

Poincaré came back into office in 1926 and established a "National Union" ministry that included six former premiers. Aloof, sober, and unimaginative, yet with a strict sense of duty, he was the right man for the moment. Poincaré did nothing dramatic to deal with the economic crisis. Rather, he moved carefully and precisely, collecting taxes more effectively, making administrative savings, ending overspending in government programs, and generally presenting an air of confidence and stability that had been lacking in the body politic. Gradually, the franc was stabilized and the sense of relief that resulted helped soothe national tensions. Poincaré remained in office for three years, longer than any other interwar premier, and retired in 1929.

DEPRESSION POLITICS

Between 1929 and 1932, a large number of premiers held office, but none of them had Poincaré's stature or his commitment to the republican tradition. When the Depression struck France in 1932, unemployment in France was not as severe as in other countries, but it did have a destabilizing effect on political life. Herriot returned to the premiership for six months, and was quickly followed by four others. Once again the government failed to deal effectively with the crisis, and when the restored prosperity of the late 1920s dissolved, social tensions reemerged.

The most dramatic proof of the instability of French politics was the upheaval following the mysterious Stavisky scandal. Serge Stavisky (1886?–1934) was a master financial swindler who sold millions of worthless bonds. His trial in December 1933 and subsequent suicide caused a sensation. The radical right exploited the scandal, spreading accusations that high government officials were implicated with him in the affair and that the government had then covered up their involvement. The findings of the official investigation supported these charges. On February 6, 1934, huge crowds organized by right-wing forces filled the streets

Socialist French leader Léon Blum (in the center, wearing glasses) and Communist leader Maurice Thorez, with other members of the French Popular Front. July 1937. Blum was the first Socialist—and the first Jew—to become Prime Minister of France. From 1940 to 1945, he was imprisoned by the Vichy (French collaborationist) government, but he returned briefly to political life as the head of a provisional government from 1946–1947.

of Paris demanding the ouster of Premier Édouard Daladier (served 1933, 1934, 1938–1940). When they attempted to break into the Chamber of Deputies, police fired on the crowd, killing 11 people. The Daladier government collapsed in a storm of indignation.

Not since the Dreyfus Affair at the turn of the 20th century (see Topic 73) had the people of France been so violently divided, nor the republic so completely called into question. Nor did subsequent governments have any more success than their predecessors in dealing with the effects of the Depression. France was the only country to remain stubbornly on the gold standard. Moreover, social unrest increased as a result of the government retrenchment and the lowering of salary levels.

The danger from the right grew so threatening that the French communists—taking their cue from the Comintern, which the year before had endorsed alliances with other leftist parties—formed a "Popular Front" with the socialists and Radicals, and presented a joint platform in the 1936 elections. The Front won a huge victory and formed a government under socialist Léon Blum (served 1936–1937). A cultured and sensitive man, Blum brought union officials and employers together and produced an agreement that laid the basis for the welfare state, including minimum wages, the 40-hour workweek, and collective bargaining.

Blum's reforms reduced social stress, but he was the target of attack from enemies to his right and his left. Bigots pointed to the fact that he was Jewish as evidence of the decline of France, while conservatives gathered strength from business interests and eventually slowed down his programs. Meanwhile, the communists attacked him for not going far enough. The Blum government resigned in June 1937. By the eve of World War II, the French people were deeply divided over the future of the republic. For many, the widening appeal of the radical right, and especially the coming to power of Adolf Hitler in Germany, was deeply troublesome.

THE SPREAD OF FASCISM

Blum's dilemma was repeated elsewhere in Europe. By the mid-1930s, European political life was polarized between the extremes of communism and fascism. Every country experienced, to one degree or another, an increasingly bitter ideological war, and the danger was especially fierce from the right. From the British Isles to the shores of the Black Sea, fascism—which had already come to power in Italy and Germany—appeared to be on the ascendancy.

Great Britain and France spawned their own native varieties of fascism, although they neither created a mass following nor seriously challenged the power base of those democratic societies. In Great Britain, several small groups inspired by Mussolini's Black Shirts were started in the 1920s but never amounted to very much. In the early 1930s the rich and well-educated Sir Oswald Mosley (1896–1980) founded the British Union of Fascists. A great fan of Mussolini, Mosley based his organization on the Italian model. Like Mussolini, he had been a prominent member of the British socialist movement, having served as a Labour minister. Mosley became increasingly interested in Hitler's regime after 1933. The British Union attracted many disreputable thugs, and Mosley extolled the use of violence, a fact that led the government to try to limit the movement by placing a ban on the wearing of political uniforms. The Union did not, however, represent a serious threat to British political stability.

In France, conservative and reactionary movements drawing inspiration from the country's monarchist past were established as early as the turn of the 20th century. In 1898, the poet and journalist Charles Maurras (1868–1952) started the *Action Française* (French Action), a group that stressed extreme nationalism and advocated anti-Semitism. Maurras wanted a restoration of the monarchy and a return to a corporative society based on hierarchy and aristocracy. The government banned the movement in 1936.

A rally of the British Union of Fascists. 1930s. The movement's leader, Sir Oswald Mosley, is at the head of the procession. Originally a member of the Labour party, Mosley fell in love with Mussolini's style of Fascism. His party imitated many of the Italian Fascist ways, including the wearing of shirts of a specific color (Italian Fascists, and so Mosley's followers wore black shirts), and the fascist salute, seen here.

© CORBIS/Bettmann

In the interwar period, an array of proto-fascist political groups, some directly modeled on Mussolini's Fascism or Hitler's Nazism, appeared in France. The most notorious of these were the *Jeunesses Patriotes* (Young Patriots) and the infamous *Capoulards* (Hooded Men). At the height of the Depression, the *Parti Populaire Française* (French Popular Party) attracted some 500,000 followers. The sheer number of such radical movements, each with its own ideology and platform, mitigated against the creation of a united right.

The Spanish monarchy, which was incapable of guiding the country's transformation into the 20th century, proved no barrier to the formation of a fascist movement. By the early 1920s, a dictatorship was created by General Miguel Primo de Rivera (1870–1930). The dictator's son, José Antonio Primo de Rivera, organized a real fascist movement, the *Falange*, in 1931. When the Spanish Civil War erupted, the movement was taken over by General Francisco Franco (1892–1975) and eventually merged into his own party (see Topic 87).

The Austrian case is a good example of how fascist movements competed against each other. The situation there was complicated by the fact that two paramilitary groups, the Social Democratic *Schutzbund* (Alliance for Defense) and the Christian Socialist *Heimwehr* (Home Guard), not only espoused conflicting ideologies, but also opposed the Austrian Nazis. The *Heimwehr*, headed by Prince Ernst Rudiger von Starhemberg (1899–1956), fought to undermine the country's republican government but wanted to preserve Austrian independence. Chancellor Engelbert Dollfuss (1892–1934) tried to play the *Heimwehr* off against the Nazis and the Social Democrats, inviting it to join the "Fatherland Front" that worked against the *Anschluss* (union) of Austria and Germany. As fascist movements spread across Europe in the 1930s, the prospects for democracy looked grim indeed.

THE NEW SHAPE OF EASTERN EUROPE

At the Paris Peace Conference, the Allied statesmen had made a deliberate decision to create a group of new states in Eastern Europe from the ruins of four empires—Austria-Hungary, Germany, Russia, and Ottoman Turkey. Eastern Europe provided a test case for the principle of self-determination that President Wilson advocated so strenuously. Yet other reasons that had to do more with power politics than justice compelled the creation of these new nations: They would serve a useful purpose for the Allies in acting as a buffer along the western border of the Bolshevik Russia and along the eastern frontiers of Germany.

These newly created nations—Austria, Hungary, Poland, Czechoslovakia, Yugoslavia, and the Baltic republics of Latvia, Estonia, and Lithuania—are known as "successor states" because they took the place of the older

Map 84.2 Ethnic Groups in Central and Eastern Europe. Many of these ethnic enclaves caused conflicts that, in some cases—Yugoslavia, for example—continue to rage. The presence of a German minority in Czechoslovakia gave Hitler a pretense to invade that country in 1938. The Hungarians in Romania continue to charge successive Romanian governments with discrimination. The German-speaking population of northern Italy has struggled, sometimes violently, to maintain their rights.

empires. With the inclusion of Greece, Romania, Bulgaria, and Albania, Eastern Europe consisted of a dozen independent states.

THE STATES OF EASTERN EUROPE

The governments of the successor states began as models of the parliamentary system. Each was either a Western-style republic or a constitutional monarchy. Yet, by the eve of World War II, most of these nations had yielded to authoritarianism. They found that the combination of domestic and foreign policy problems was so demanding that parliamentary government was not adequate to their needs.

Because of history and geography, the new states of Eastern Europe had remarkably mixed populations. Along with the dominant ethnic and religious group in each country, one or more minority nationalities coexisted in uneasy rapport. In Czechoslovakia, Poland, Hungary, Yugoslavia, and Romania, these minorities were large groups. The minorities posed serious problems for the governments, most of which wanted to forge cohesive social and political units out of their populations. The minorities, on the other hand, sought to maintain their distinctiveness and to protect their separate identities. In some instances, such as the case of Nazi Germany and the German minority in Czechoslovakia, a foreign power deliberately appealed to these minorities over the heads of their governments. On the whole, most states in the area treated their minority populations unfairly. (The exception was Finland, where the Swedish minority enjoyed constitutionally assured rights.) The result was continuing tension that kept domestic tranquility off balance.

After the euphoria of independence had subsided, the successor states found themselves burdened with the legacy of the past. For one thing, their efforts to develop their economies were blocked by a wide range of liabilities. Before World War I, Eastern Europe had been largely a semicolonial region in which the great powers made investments and sold manufactured goods, while the area supplied raw materials and agricultural goods. With the coming of independence, however, these new states lost what had been guaranteed markets for their products. Hence, while they lacked sufficient revenue, the resources they now needed in order to undertake industrialization were expensive. The entire infrastructure and financial structure of the region mitigated against rapid development: local capital was virtually nonexistent; trading and business practices were antiquated; and roads, railways, and communication systems required building from the ground up. Moreover, in an area that was overwhelmingly agricultural, farming techniques and mechanization were outdated.

In Austria and Czechoslovakia, a small but thriving middle class, mainly of German and Jewish origin, had existed for some time, but the other states lacked managers and experts. Wealth and status were concentrated in the hands of a relatively small but powerful landowning aristocracy, as well as in the ranks of the church hierarchy. The workforce in such traditional agricultural societies—that is, the bulk of the population—consisted of millions of poor peasants whose lives were not much better than their serf ancestors. As a result, poor health care and nutrition, high birth and death rates, and illiteracy made the task of national development still more difficult, and in the long run weakened the strength of the new parliamentary governments.

THE FAILURE OF DEMOCRACY

Under these circumstances, the prospects for democratic government in Eastern Europe were bleak. The fact that most of these societies lacked formal experience with parliamentary government undermined the opportunities for stable political progress. To make matters worse, while authoritarian traditions were strong in many states, the new parliamentary systems generally spawned numerous political parties, a fact that made for instability and a poor legislative record.

Nationalism represented by far the most serious political problem facing the Eastern European states. Nationalist sentiment in the region was fierce, especially in Poland, Bohemia, and Hungary, each of which had an old nationalist heritage. World War I had intensified the nationalist animosities among the states of the region. Austria, Hungary, and Bulgaria were "revisionist" states that were unhappy with the peace settlements and wanted to regain lost territories. The older independent nations of Greece, Albania, and Romania, on the other hand, wanted to keep what they had gained from the war. Finally, the new countries of Poland, Czechoslovakia, Estonia, Latvia, and Lithuania indoctrinated their citizens with patriotic fervor in an effort to create a loyal population willing to fight to preserve independence. The result was an intricately intense web of national fears and animosities that made regional cooperation difficult and kept international relations tense.

Liberal democracy did not fare well in these circumstances, and in virtually all cases eventually collapsed in the face of authoritarianism. The Hungarian case was one of the saddest. In 1919, the communists set up a socialist dictatorship in Hungary under Béla Kun (1885–1937), which was put down by a Romanian army sanctioned by the Allies. Admiral Miklós Horthy (1858–1957) was made regent of the country, remaining as a figurehead until the Nazis deposed him in 1944. Horthy appointed Count Stephen Bethlen prime minister (served 1921–1931), and he ran the government with only a pretense of parliamentary responsibility for a decade. Then followed General Julius Gombos (prime minister 1932–1936), the head of the anti-Semitic Race Defense party, who made a farce of Hungary's representative system and worked closely with Mussolini and Hitler in foreign affairs.

In the 1920s, dictators or authoritarian leaders took power in Albania, Lithuania, Yugoslavia, and Poland. In the latter country, Marshal Jozef Pilsudski served as president from 1918 to 1922. When internal divisions paralyzed the state, Pilsudski staged a "march on Warsaw" in 1926 and seized the government, making himself dictator. In the following decade, a combined leadership emerged under army officers and a fascist-like organization.

In Eastern Europe, unlike Britain and France, parliamentary government could not withstand the strains of the Depression. In 1930 the controversial Romanian monarch, King Carol II (1893–1953), returned to his country after having deserted his throne and family to live in Paris with

Mustafa Kemal Atatürk. His dictatorship forced an independent Turkey into internal reform and Westernization. Here he is shown in traditional Turkish dress.

Marshal Pilsudski. 1920s. The future dictator of Poland began his political career as a leader of Poland's Socialist party at a time when an official nation of Poland did not exist. He led Polish troops against both Russians and Germans, and in 1920 became the first Marshal of the newly created Polish state. For the rest of his life he ran the country either as authoritarian dictator, minister of war, or commander-in-chief of the army—often in combination.

a mistress. Carol deposed his son Michael and ruled as a dictator, being deposed by Hitler in 1940. Over the next several years, dictators also took power in Austria, Estonia, Latvia, Bulgaria, and Greece.

The one successor state in central Europe that was able to prevent its democratic system from succumbing to dictatorship was Czechoslovakia. The Czech state was relatively prosperous, and the government had implemented important reforms, including the breakup of the large estates. Its founder and first president was Thomas Masaryk (1850–1937), a former professor of philosophy and a humane man of principle. He served as president for 17 years. His successor, Edouard Benes (1884–1948), was a close associate of Masaryk. Together, such upright leaders might have resolved the country's serious domestic problems had it not become the target of Hitler's aggression.

Putting the Western Democracies and Eastern Europe in Perspective

The record of European democracy in the interwar period was mixed. In Western Europe, Great Britain and France, along with most of the smaller states, maintained their political systems intact. After World War I, most of them had instituted universal suffrage and had begun to develop social programs designed to integrate their citizens into a uniform national experience. During the Great Depression, this trend accelerated as the governments created the basic institutions of the welfare state, designed to insulate their citizens from the worst aspects of the crisis.

The Western democracies successfully resisted the lure of fascism, although such movements appeared in virtually every country. Only in Italy and Germany did fascism seize power before World War II, although in Spain a right-wing dictator came to power in the 1930s after a tragic civil war. The experiment with democracy in Eastern Europe, however, proved a dismal failure, as the enthusiastic hopes of the Allied statesmen of 1919 were dashed by the rise of authoritarian dictatorship.

Questions for Further Study

1. What were the chief political concerns in postwar England and France?
2. What were the origins of the Irish question?
3. To what conditions did fascism appeal?
4. Why was democracy so tenuous in postwar Eastern Europe?

Suggestions for Further Reading

Arthur, Max. *The Royal Navy, 1914–1939: A Narrative History*. London, 1996.

Brendon, Piers. *The Dark Valley: A Panorama of the 1930s*. New York, 2000.

Chazan, Naomi, ed. *Irridentism and International Politics*. London, 1991.

Gilbert, Martin. *A History of the Twentieth Century*, Vol. 1: 1900–1933; Vol. 2: 1933–1951. New York, 1997.

Jackson, Julian. *The Popular Front in France: Defending Democracy, 1934–1938*. New York, 1988.

Jelavich, Barbara. *History of the Balkans: Twentieth Century*. New York, 1983.

Kitchen, Martin. *Europe Between the Wars: A Political History*. London, 1988.

Marin, Benjamin F. *France and the Apres Guerre, 1918–1924: Illusions and Disillusionment*. Baton Rouge, LA, 1999.

Roberts, Mary L. *Civilization Without Sexes: Reconstructing Gender in Postwar France*. Chicago, 1994.

Weber, Eugen. *The Hollow Years: France in the 1930s*. London, 1995.

InfoTrac College Edition

Enter the search term *Ramsay MacDonald* using Key Terms.

Enter the search term *Eamon De Valera* using Key Terms.

Social Values and the Lost Generation

In 1914, European social conditions still reflected the manners and mores of the Victorian Age, but the Great War began a process of social transformation that profoundly changed the way in which most Europeans lived. Daily life became more open to change and more democratic, social and sexual codes relaxed, and people felt less tied to tradition. The new yearning for personal freedom and modern life was reflected in the public behavior of the so-called Jazz Age, in which fast-paced, expressive dancing and music became the rage. The postwar era also saw the rise of a new mass culture in which millions with greater leisure enjoyed the automobile, radio, motion pictures, and sports as part of everyday experience.

The new social values reflected the shift to an urban-based, industrial, nonagrarian society. In the 1920s and 1930s, the most important social factor was the expansion of the white-collar class, a social category composed of people who worked for a living and did not own significant property, but who thought and behaved like the middle class. At the same time, the upper ranks of the bourgeoisie and the old aristocracy increasingly joined together in support of social stability and authoritarian government in the face of the new political and organizational power of the industrial working classes, whose cause was now championed by the Soviet Union and the growing strength of socialist parties.

The year 1929 marked a phase in social development that was different in tone and spirit from the 1920s. Social stress increased significantly in the 1930s, as the effects of the Great Depression made themselves felt. The spirit of class conflict, already noticeable in the previous decade, became more intense, especially among the middle classes, whose security and savings were decimated by the economic collapse, and among the working classes, who experienced widespread misery. As optimism and opportunity gave way to fear and insecurity, Europe underwent a loss of social momentum. The birthrate declined because young people delayed marriage and the rearing of families. Along with the economic difficulties of the decade, Europe's political future seemed dark as totalitarian dictatorships held millions in their grip and the threat of war loomed.

MOBILITY AND STATUS: SOCIAL CLASS UNDER STRESS

Since the first Industrial Revolution in the 18th century, two broad trends had characterized European development: the rise of cities in what had been a predominantly rural society, and the diversification of a once overwhelmingly agrarian economy with the growth of the industrial and service sectors. In the 20th century, these trends matured. As a result, class structure became more complicated as wealth and status shifted and tensions among the classes increased.

TRENDS IN EUROPEAN SOCIETY

Industrialization drew millions of Europeans from the countryside to the cities. By 1910, Great Britain was the most urban European nation, with some 65 percent of its population living in cities, while Belgium, Germany, and the Netherlands each counted slightly less than half their populations in the urban category. France was still only around 38 percent urban, and in Italy, Denmark, Austria, and Hungary about one-third of the people lived in cities with 20,000 or more inhabitants. In the agrarian countries of southern and eastern Europe, much smaller proportions of the populations were urban—Bulgaria, for example, was only 9 percent urban.

On the Continent, only the Netherlands reached the 50 percent mark before World War II, but everywhere the trend was apparent. The position of cities with more than 100,000 inhabitants was strengthened in some countries: Between 1910 and 1930, the proportion of Germans living in such large cities rose from 21 to 37 percent, while for Italians the increase was from 11 to 17 percent. In 1910 there were seven European cities with populations over 1 million, while in 1940 the number had more than doubled.

Another indicator of a society's development is the distribution of the working population among the three "sec-

Table 85.2	The Working Population of Selected Countries by Sector (in percent of entire population)					
	1910			**1930**		
	A	**I**	**S**	**A**	**I**	**S**
Britain	9	51	40	6	46	48
Germany	37	41	22	29	40	31
France	41	33	26	36	33	31
Italy	55	27	18	47	31	22
Hungary	58	20	22	53	24	23
Poland	77	9	14	66	17	17

Source: Adapted from Gerold Ambrosius and William H. Hubbard, *A Social and Economic History of Twentieth-Century Europe* (Cambridge, MA: Harvard University Press, 1989), 58. A, I, and S stand for agricultural, industrial, and service.

tors" of agriculture, industry, and services (the latter including such work categories as trade, banking, public administration, and education). All European countries have followed the same general pattern, although at different rates of development. The percentage of people employed in agriculture has fallen steadily, that of industry first rose and then fell, while the service sector has increased constantly. In 1910, 41 percent of the European workforce was in agriculture, 34 percent in industry, and 25 percent in the service sector. By 1930, agriculture remained at 41 percent, but industry had declined to 30 percent, and services had grown to 29 percent. This trend continued throughout the rest of the century; by 1950 the services represented 31 percent of the workforce and in the 1980s Europe entered the "postindustrial" era when the service sector reached 50 percent. As in the case of urbanization, this pattern differed widely, depending on the region of Europe and the country. In Eastern Europe, for example, the agricultural sector stood at 75 percent in 1910 and by 1930 had fallen only to 64 percent.

The same general pattern could also be discerned for a variety of other social indicators, including rates of literacy, mortality, industrial production, and income. In the case of literacy, important gains had been made since the last decade of the 19th century, when systems of universal primary education were widely introduced. By 1900, 95 percent of the British and French people could read and write, whereas in Italy almost half the population could not. After 1918, a wave of democratization swept school systems in many countries. Between 1920 and 1940, the proportion of secondary school students doubled in countries such as Britain, Germany, Italy, Sweden, and Austria. By 1921, the number of illiterates in Italy had been almost halved, and a decade later the illiteracy rate there had fallen to 21 percent. By the 1930s one-third of all secondary school students in Western Europe were girls. With the exception of the Soviet Union, however, higher education remained a class prerogative, and in the more developed nations of Europe only 2 percent of the college-age population attended university. In the 1930s, 25 percent of university students in Britain were women, but the percentage was much less in other countries.

Table 85.1	Populations of Major Cities of Interwar Europe (in thousands)	
CITY	**1920**	**1940**
Berlin	3,801	4,332
Brussels	685	913
Budapest	1,185	1,163
Glasgow	1,052	1,132
Hamburg	986	1,682
London	7,488	8,700
Madrid	751	1,089
Milan	836	1,116
Moscow	1,050	4,137
Paris	2,907	2,830
Prague	677	928
Rome	692	1,156
Vienna	1,866	1,918
Warsaw	931	1,266

CLASS BOUNDARIES, WEALTH, AND STATUS

Class distinctions are determined by a variety of factors, ranging from legal differences in the case of the aristocracy to manner of dress, and they generally involve lifestyles and attitudes. Income and wealth are, however, among the most crucial factors, not only of class but also of the broader question of social equality. Measured by gains in per capita national product and real wages, a process of leveling has characterized European development during the 20th century, although the greatest gains in a more equal income distribution have been made since World War II.

One important change was that the economic significance of the very wealthy declined. In 1913, British society was still marked by an immense gulf between rich and poor: The richest 1 percent of the population controlled 70 percent of all personal wealth. By 1930, that proportion had declined to about 60 percent, and by 1945 to some 50 percent. In France, similar changes took place. Real wages followed the broad economic trends of the postwar period (see Topic 82). In Western Europe they dropped sharply after the bust of 1921, rose until the Great Depression, and then rose again beginning in the mid- to late 1930s, depending on the particular country. After 1950, they jumped significantly. Nevertheless, living standards continued to differ considerably among classes. For workers and the lower middle classes, the bulk of all income—as much as 80 percent—still went for basic necessities such as food, clothing, and shelter, as well as taxes. Moreover, poverty grew significantly during the Great Depression, when mass unemployment affected millions in all but the highest social classes.

Contrary to the trend begun in the 19th century, the post-1919 period did not see the continuing growth of the working class. Instead, the fastest growing group was the white-collar worker, whose ranks swelled with the expansion of government and private-sector bureaucracies. Self-defining attitudes put most of these employees in the lowest levels of the middle classes, but in fact many earned salaries that were the same or even lower than factory workers. In Germany, one in four white-collar workers had come from a working-class family. In this respect, the Depression stimulated considerable social instability because unemployment forced many white-collar workers to go back to the factories.

Generally, upward mobility within the middle classes declined in the interwar period. A few speculators made huge fortunes, but most of the bourgeoisie experienced slow gains, if any, in income and status, and for many people living standards actually declined as inflation and then depression wiped out their savings. In Germany, where they were hardest hit, inflation destroyed more than half of the capital of the lower middle class. The professional classes were in oversupply in some countries, and many college graduates were unemployable.

Because the condition of the middle classes declined in the 1930s, the gap between them and the upper classes widened. Despite the decline in the position of the wealthiest portion of the population, most of this group weathered the Depression relatively unscathed. The aristocracy, which maintained its status and power most fully in eastern and southern Europe, experienced some difficulties. This was especially true of those who derived their income from landed estates because the agricultural depression and land reform both weakened the landed nobility. Political reforms, particularly in the new nations of Eastern Europe, also weakened aristocratic power. Only in the Soviet Union, however, was the aristocracy actually wiped out, and in countries such as Britain and France it retained significant influence.

In those countries in which the nobility was weakened, the status of the peasantry generally improved. In agrarian countries where parliamentary democracy was introduced, peasant political parties developed and reforms gave many peasants their first opportunity to own their own land. In Czechoslovakia, slightly more than 10 percent of the land was divided, and in Romania significant progress was made, whereas much less land distribution took place in Poland and Hungary. Such changes did not always mean a real improvement in peasants' lives because they tended to use antiquated farming methods and generally were forced into debt to meet the costs of their own production. By the late 1920s, peasants everywhere faced increasing economic hardships.

Millions of workers were without jobs for most of the Depression years, having to subsist on limited public assistance. For them, the 1930s were demoralizing and without hope. Most countries saw considerable labor agitation. A minority of workers supported the communists, but most gravitated either to socialist parties or trade unions, using the strike as their principal instrument of protest. Radical political movements such as Italian Fascism were in part a response to worker demands and in part a reaction against them. As the Great Depression descended, the middle and upper classes grew more agitated and insecure, not only about their own condition but also about working-class demands. The result everywhere was heightened social tension and class conflict. The Depression, like the Great War, proved to be a profoundly unsettling experience for European society.

NEW YORK, PARIS, AND BERLIN: THE AGE OF CABARET

The postwar years were filled with contradictions. While government leaders spoke of a return to "normalcy" after the deprivations and sacrifices of wartime, popular opinion clamored for a new era of expressive freedom and self-indulgence unlike anything known before the war. In the United States, the era of Prohibition was simultaneously the era of the "speakeasy." One reflection of the relaxed social conditions that prevailed in the postwar period was the popularity of the nightclub. Although not an entirely new social institution, the modern nightclub offered an ideal backdrop for the culture of the Jazz Age.

Hine, *Skyboy*. 1931. Although born in the Midwest, Lewis Hine spent most of his career in New York. His first collection was of portraits of Ellis Island immigrants (1905). This picture shows a young worker high above Manhattan, hanging by a cable, as he takes part in the construction of the Empire State Building. By leaving out any trace of scaffolding, or of the building itself, Hine underlines the precariousness of the boy's position.

Avery Architectural and Fine Arts Library, Columbia University in the City of New York

PROHIBITION AND THE JAZZ AGE

In the United States, where a sense of Protestant moralism remained strong, the Eighteenth Amendment, passed in January 1919, prohibited the consumption or sale of "intoxicating beverages," and later that year the Volstead Act made traffic in such beverages illegal. The anti-alcohol campaign reflected the more conservative values of rural America, but in the big cities life assumed a frenetic and modern pace despite—and in part because of—Prohibition.

The Eighteenth Amendment was widely ignored by average Americans, and some used the demand for whisky and beer to reap huge profits from bootlegging. Illegal clubs, known as "speakeasies," served these beverages to private customers—in New York City alone there were some 5,000 of them by 1922. Gangsters such as Al "Scarface" Capone (1899–1947) in Chicago and Arthur "Dutch Schultz" Flegenheimer (1902–1935) in New York built powerful criminal organizations on the profits from bootlegging. With their machine guns, big automobiles, and flashy lives, these hoodlums became folk heroes to some Americans, especially when Hollywood immortalized them in the new talking films. In the literary imagination, the hero of "Roaring Twenties" America was the protagonist of the novel *The Great Gatsby* (1925), by F. Scott Fitzgerald (1896–1940). A wealthy young man of mysterious origins who made a fortune in bootlegging, Jay Gatsby grew famous by giving fabulous parties at his elaborate Long Island estate. Fitzgerald lived a dissolute life not dissimilar to Gatsby, and his female characters were "flappers," young women with men's hairstyles and short, slinky dresses who used lipstick and smoked and drank in public.

A woman dressed in the style of the postwar era. 1920s. Note the short hair, unemphasized breasts, baggy trousers (this "new woman" does not wear a skirt), and male-style long coat. She wears no jewelry, but—supreme symbol of the age—she is smoking a cigarette, which is inserted into a long cigarette-holder.

Hulton/Archive by Getty Images

The nightclub became the quintessential entertainment spot of the era, and New York City was the nightclub capital. The first nightclub opened in New York in 1921, and they spread rapidly. High society frequented the clubs, especially those in Harlem, which was then the scene of a major black cultural movement known as the Harlem Renaissance.

One of the most famous of Harlem's nightclubs was the Cotton Club, owned by a mobster. Duke Ellington and Fats Waller (1904–1943) performed there, as well as singers such as Ethel Waters (1896–1977) and the dancer Josephine Baker (1906–1975). But although the best black entertainers could be seen at the Cotton Club, black patrons were prohibited. "Everyone rushed up to Harlem at night," remembered one socialite, "to sit around places thick with smoke and the smell of bad gin, where Negroes danced about with each other until the small hours of the morning." While wealthy white audiences packed the Harlem clubs night after night, the black writer Langston Hughes (1902–1967) underscored the exploitation and racism involved in this experience with his cynical comment, "the Negro was in vogue."

The 1929 crash brought the flashy era of the Harlem nightspots to an end because the clubs there had been driven largely by white money. The end to Prohibition in 1933 destroyed the speakeasies, which had attracted many of their high-society customers by the very allure of illegality. As the grim realities of the Depression set in, the "Gatsby" set's fascination with Harlem dissipated, and blacks there were left to the miseries of ghetto impoverishment.

EUROPE AND THE IMAGE OF AMERICA

In the 1920s, America and its popular culture became the rage in Europe. European travelers to the United States brought back images of a super-modern society of skyscrapers and machines that looked to the future. In Fascist Italy, young Italians of anti-Fascist sentiment gravitated toward American culture as an escape from the conformity of the reactionary regime, and Mussolini eventually prohibited jazz as a "corrupting" influence.

Europeans became especially fascinated with black American culture. Foremost among the cultural imports was jazz (see Topic 86), whose chief admirers were the French. In this respect, Europe's counterpart to New York was Paris, the city that since the second half of the 19th century had been the premier European center of the cultural avant-garde.

In the 1920s, many Americans made Paris their home, attracted by the Bohemian atmosphere and liberal attitudes that the city extended to even the most unconventional behavior. Paris drew many expatriate American intellectuals. The writer Gertrude Stein (1874–1946) had been there since 1904 and, together with her lover Alice B. Toklas (1877–1967), held court at one of the most famous cultural salons of the century. Stein was one of the first to appreciate the genius of the painter Pablo Picasso and other artists, and her apartment became a mecca for young American

Scene at the Paris bar La Boule Blanche. 1930. Most of the customers are young African Americans. From the time of the 1920s and the so-called Harlem Renaissance, black Americans began to travel in Europe, attracted by the far greater mobility they could enjoy there. Paris offered many attractions. It was already a multiracial city, and—perhaps most enticingly of all—the great Josephine Baker had made her life and career there (see next illustration).

writers—Stein called them the "lost generation"—searching for their own cultural identity. F. Scott Fitzgerald lived in Paris much of the time, as did the writer Ernest Hemingway (1899–1961). Black American entertainers flocked to Paris, where they performed in a host of cabarets famous since the 1880s, foremost among them the Moulin Rouge, immortalized by the artist Toulouse-Lautrec. Parisians found black Americans, especially women, exotically sensuous. In 1925, an all-black musical called *La Revue Nègre,* which ran first in New York, was booked to play in Paris at the Théâtre des Champs-Elysées. When Josephine Baker arrived in Paris as the lead in the review, she joined a group of black musicians who played the blues in the bohemian quarters of the city. The singer Bricktop was already there and owned a popular nightspot. Baker became an overnight hit and remained in Paris for the next 50 years, opening her own cabaret, the Chez Joséphine, and marrying an Italian count. Duke Ellington made his first European tour in the late 1920s and was wildly acclaimed.

If Paris had long been a major cultural center of Europe, Berlin had no such heritage. Rather, the city of almost 4 million inhabitants had been the capital of the former German empire and its economic life. Yet in the 1920s, Berlin transformed itself into the center of an extraordinary flowering of modern culture, and also earned a reputation as one of Europe's most notorious fleshpots. "Sex," said the actress Louise Brooks, "was the business of the town."

The atmosphere in postwar Berlin was iconoclastic and innovative, and the city drew creative young Germans attracted by the counterculture of modernity. Bars, restaurants, prostitution houses, and music halls sprang up, offering free-wheeling entertainment. The city became especially known for its hundreds of bars frequented by lesbians and gays, whose experiences were chronicled in a series of short stories by British-born author Christopher

Poster advertising the appearance of Josephine Baker at the Folies Bergere. 1930s. Baker, who was born in St. Louis, Missouri, began her career on Broadway, but from her first appearance in Paris in 1925 she became a sensational star there, with her exotic singing and dancing, extravagant costumes and gestures, and the erotic appeal of her image. In 1937 she became a naturalized French citizen, and she worked with the French Resistance during World War II.

Isherwood (1904–1986). American jazz became the rage here, too, and cabarets, originally imported from France, flourished. In Berlin, however, the cabarets assumed an original aspect, for in many of them light music and comedy were used to convey serious political and social satire. The cabarets also inspired the artist George Grosz (1893–1959), a communist supporter. His brilliant talent created political drawings that savagely assaulted reactionary forces, especially the Nazis, whom he passionately hated.

As in America, in Europe, too, conditions in the 1930s altered the social atmosphere. The Great Depression, the

rise of Hitler, and the looming threat of war combined to bring an end to the era of rampant pleasure seeking and the spirit of the age of cabaret.

GENDER, SEXUALITY, AND THE FAMILY

The great popularity of the nightclub among the middle and upper classes reflected the greatly changed attitudes about women, gender, and sexuality. Women not only attended the cabarets but also acted in public places generally much as men did, for they drank, smoked, danced, and enjoyed themselves, often without male companions. Women's fashions, revealing portions of the body that had been kept hidden during the Victorian era, paralleled the emergence of a "new woman"—independent, accomplished, and interested in self-fulfillment. Such attitudes and behavior would have been inconceivable for most women 20 years earlier. The changing status of women in society was part of a broader social transformation that included major shifts in sexual standards and behavior, in marriage and birth patterns, and in the way in which the household was organized.

THE NEW WOMAN: OPPORTUNITIES AND LIMITATIONS

World War I had begun the process of altering gender roles because hundreds of thousands of women had moved into the factories to replace the men who served in the armies (see Topic 80). In the aftermath, women gained new freedoms and privileges. The contribution of women to the war effort was in part responsible for the passage of female suffrage laws in the immediate postwar period. Denmark and Iceland, both neutral during the war, actually gave women the vote in 1915, and the Netherlands followed in 1917. In 1918, Britain was the first major European state to enact female suffrage, although it was limited to women older than 30. The first women candidates who ran in the elections that year were all defeated. The Weimar Republic gave German women the vote in 1919, while Belgium did so for war widows only. In the new states of Eastern Europe, women also achieved the vote, while in France and Italy voting remained a male preserve until after World War II.

Despite the politically conservative mood of most Western European countries in the postwar era, women's attitudes and their social position changed significantly, creating a clash of opinion between those who wanted to restore prewar social values and those who demanded the modernization of society. Women seemed more ubiquitous in postwar society, both because millions of men had been killed in the war and because women increasingly did things once reserved only for men—women became journalists, took part in professional sports, flew airplanes, and entered mainstream politics. Women's public conduct became more relaxed, and many now demanded careers of their own. The role of women in the professions and the arts assumed greater importance, and the modern middle-class housewife emerged in the 1920s.

Women changed their physical appearance in several ways. In dress, they began to reveal their arms, legs, and shoulders. The length of their skirts was shortened by about 12 inches, and sleeves, which were once wrist-length even in summer, disappeared. Women who thought of themselves as modern adopted varying degrees of male appearance—short, bobbed hair, flattened breasts, and a slim figure, and wore slacks and trench coats. Scanty bathing suits were fashionable, and the ideal of a suntanned body replaced the Victorian preference for pale skin. The cosmetic business grew to a mass industry as millions of women began to use lipstick, rouge, and mascara, items once identified only with prostitutes.

In the 1920s, the gains in employment made by women during the war were generally pushed back. With the coming of peace, many governments encouraged women to return to the home and allow men to take their place in the workforce, a policy that unions and even reform-minded socialists supported. The percentage of women working declined almost everywhere. Some of the women who lost their jobs went back to low-paying work as domestics or in agriculture, occupations in which they could not qualify for unemployment insurance. In Britain, unemployment insurance payments were lower for women than for men and not enough for a woman to live on. The expansion of bureaucracies and the growth of department stores did give many women new job opportunities as office workers or salesclerks, and the spread of the telephone led many women to become operators. In factories, where men sometimes outnumbered women nine to one, women were relegated to the most menial jobs. Only in the Soviet Union, where the desire to industrialize took precedence over everything else, did women constitute a major portion—as high as 45 percent—of the workforce.

In those countries where unemployment was high in the 1920s, women workers suffered more than men. The Great Depression made the plight of working women even worse. As conditions deteriorated, increasing numbers of women were forced out of jobs, in both democratic and authoritarian countries. In 1931, British Labour Minister Margaret Bondfield (1873–1953) excluded most women from unemployment insurance. In Fascist Italy and Nazi Germany, women were encouraged as a matter of ideology to be wives and mothers, not workers (see Topic 83).

VARIETIES OF SEXUALITY

If women demanded the development of a modern outlook, much of the new mentality focused on sexuality. In the Victorian era, the prevailing middle-class attitude had been the exercise of sexual restraint for men, virtue for women, and the general repression of overt sexual references in daily life (see Topic 71). These conventions began to change with the war, when men and women mingled more freely in an atmosphere of "living for today." Modern medicine and postwar psychology both undermined the earlier emphasis on restraint by stressing the benefits of release and self-expression. Finally, the rise of consumerism led to the discovery of the power of sex as an advertising device, while mass culture, especially the movies, promoted sex symbols on the silver screen.

The struggle against gender tradition inevitably contributed to a more open discussion of sex, but the issue often aroused bitter debate. One of the most controversial figures in the postwar encounter with sexuality was Marie Stopes (1880–1938), a British paleobotanist and birth control advocate. A university lecturer and author, in 1921 Stopes founded the Mothers' Clinic for Constructive Birth Control. She argued that sexual pleasure was an important part of marriage and life in general and should not be limited to procreation; the search for physical pleasure, she said, was a woman's right. In 1918 she published *Married Love*, vividly describing the sexual joy that could be attained in marriage. In 1926, she also wrote *Sex and the Young*, which countered Victorian assumptions about the innocence of youth.

The year 1926 also saw the appearance of *Ideal Marriage: Its Physiology and Technique*, by the Dutch physician Theodor von de Velde. The book was one of the most authoritative sex manuals and became an international bestseller. Its popularity, like that of Stopes' books, was because it provided women with detailed practical information.

Europeans not only read such works, but also increasingly practiced birth control and abortion. Between 1850 and 1914, Europe's population increased steadily. After the war, however, marriage and birthrates changed in a manner that suggests deliberate efforts to control fertility. The bloody battles of the war, together with disease and undernourishment, killed some 11 million people, or about 3 percent of Europe's population. The war also disrupted the pattern of marriages and births. In the interwar period, mortality rates fell and life expectancy grew, yet the birthrate declined everywhere. Several factors explain the change: economic hardships and unemployment, especially after the Depression, the diffusion of birth control information, and the changing role of women. In many countries, politicians expressed concern about the population decline, and France, Italy, and Germany passed laws restricting birth control information and abortions. Nevertheless, it has been estimated that perhaps as many as 1 million German women had abortions each year in the 1920s. On the other hand, nations as diverse as France and Sweden, Fascist Italy, and Nazi Germany instituted programs to encourage large families.

Sexual minorities also encountered a freer atmosphere in the postwar era. Gays and lesbians came "out of the closet" in increasingly larger numbers, and many prominent intellectuals and artists made their orientation known publicly. The German psychiatrist Magnus Hirschfeld (1868–1935) founded his famous Institute for Sexual Science, where homosexuals had access to counseling and psychological support in coping with a society that still retained deep hostility

Radclyffe Hall (on the right) with Lady Trowbridge, c. 1930. Hall took advantage of what she perceived as a more open climate of public opinion about sexuality, and in 1928 published *The Well of Loneliness,* a novel dealing with lesbian relationships. She was accused of obscenity, tried, and the book was banned. Many eminent authors, including E.M. Forster and Virginia Woolf, supported her appeal to the High Court, but it was refused. The book finally appeared in 1949.

toward them. The problem of lesbian identity was directly discussed in the novel *The Well of Loneliness* (1928), by the British writer Radclyffe Hall (1880–1943). Although the book was banned by the government, it appeared in many languages throughout the world.

THE LIFE OF THE FAMILY

The family as it had developed over the 19th century had also begun to undergo profound changes after World War I, and many of the trends continue to this day. Men and women both postponed marriage longer than ever before, and when they did marry they had fewer children. The average size of the family declined steadily as the number of offspring dropped by almost half.

Within the family, the dynamics of gender moved slowly away from the patriarchal model of the Victorian

bourgeoisie. Husbands increasingly shared household responsibilities and became more directly involved in child rearing. Nevertheless, most working-class and middle-class women continued to have major responsibility for managing the household. Technology and consumerism did, however, change the role of the housewife. The 1920s saw the beginnings of modernization in the middle-class home, primarily through the introduction of new machines and the application of technology to household tasks. Electric washing machines and irons transformed those tasks, while the vacuum cleaner came into general use. Such machines made strenuous work less demanding for the average housewife, although some experts have argued that they also raised the standards to which women had to aspire.

The most dramatic change came in the kitchen. During World War I, working women, often without the responsibility of feeding husbands, sons, or brothers, adopted lighter meals that were quick and easy to prepare, and the widespread availability of preservatives and canning after the war encouraged a continuation of such practices. A host of new cookbooks catered to the modern diet, with a new emphasis on nutrition and health. Electric mixers and juicers were introduced, and gas or electric stoves and ovens replaced wood-burning stoves, while electric refrigerators eliminated the need for hauling ice and for daily shopping.

In the mid-1920s, industrial design altered the way in which both home appliances and the home looked. The International Exposition of Modern Decorative and Industrial Arts, held in Paris in 1925, presented the first views of streamlined everyday objects and furniture, while the so-called International Style of architecture, developed in Europe by Walter Gropius and Le Corbusier and in the United States by Frank Lloyd Wright, stressed simplicity, modern building materials such as steel, reinforced concrete, and glass, and functionalism (see Topic 86). By the 1930s, a "streamlined modern" style had shaped the design of everything from vacuum cleaners to airplanes to railroad engines and refrigerators, while kitchens became laboratory-like in their cleanliness, organization, and functionalism. The modern household, like the modern family, assumed a new, more progressive aspect.

Putting the Lost Generation in Perspective

The social transformations that took place in the 20 years between 1919 and 1939 explain much about how Europeans and others live today. As the West began to emerge out of the Industrial Revolution and toward the postindustrial world, the composition and status of social classes also changed. The middle classes grew increasingly complex, especially with the growth of the white-collar group, and while the condition of the working classes improved, that of the upper classes deteriorated. The result was a general leveling of society, at least in terms of a more equal distribution of income and standard of living. The social impact of the Great Depression, by threatening the well-being and security of the middle and the work-

Continued next page

ing classes, increased class tensions and encouraged the radicalization of domestic politics.

Despite the grim aspects of life between the wars, the era was one of self-conscious modernity, in which many of the repressive features of Victorian society were replaced by values that stressed nonconformity, free expression, and individualism. Women enhanced their social equality, advanced sexual freedom, and won the vote in most democratic countries; in the totalitarian dictatorships, however, the status of women regressed under the impact of a self-consciously male-dominated ideology. Everywhere, working women experienced a mixture of new opportunities and exclusion from the workforce.

The 1920s especially were an age of hedonism marked by a desire for fast-paced, unconventional public behavior. Behind the glitter of the jazz clubs and cabarets lay evidence of a society bent on excess and overindulgence after the shattering experience of a war that had upset tradition more than any single event since the French Revolution. By the 1930s, a more sober, solemn mood set in as society grappled with the ravages of the Great Depression.

Questions for Further Study

1. What was the impact of World War I on European society? How did that impact manifest itself in the 1920s?
2. What were the chief characteristics of popular culture and leisure-time activities in the postwar period?
3. In what ways did postwar society reflect the changing role of women?

Suggestions for Further Reading

Anderson, H., and R. Beardon. *A History of African American Artists from 1792 to the Present*. New York, 1993.

Bridenthal, Renate, A. Grossmann, and M. Kaplan, eds. *When Biology Became Destiny: Women in Weimar and Nazi Germany*. New York, 1984.

Brinnin, John Malcolm. *The Third Rose: Gertrude Stein and Her World*. New York, 1987.

Douglas, A. *Terrible Honesty: Mongrel Manhattan in the 1920s*. New York, 1995.

Grossmann, Atina. *Reforming Sex: The German Movement for Birth Control and Abortion Reform, 1920–1950*. New York, 1995.

Gruber, Helmut. *Red Vienna: Experiment in Working-Class Culture, 1919–1943*. New York, 1991.

Kent, Susan. *Making Peace: The Reconstruction of Gender in Postwar Britain*. Princeton, NJ, 1994.

Maier, Charles S. *Recasting Bourgeois Europe: Stabilization in France, Germany, and Italy*. Princeton, NJ, 1975.

Roberts, Mary L. *Civilization Without Sexes: Reconstructing Gender in Postwar France, 1917–1927*. Chicago, 1994.

Winter, J.M., and R.M. Wall, eds. *The Upheaval of War: Family, Work and Welfare in Europe, 1914–1918*. Cambridge, MA, 1988.

InfoTrac College Edition

Enter the search term *prohibition* using Key Terms.

Enter the search term *Jazz Age* using Key Terms.

Enter the search term *suffragists* using Key Terms.

CIVILIZATION AND ITS DISCONTENTS: PSYCHOANALYSIS AND THE ARTS

World War I led many Europeans to question the basic values of their society and culture. Concepts such as patriotism, the glory of war, aristocracy, rationalism and technology, and the notion of progress itself were tarnished by the carnage of the trenches. Profound doubts arose about the ability of Western civilization to survive. Some artists reacted by seeking refuge in frivolity, often combined with a spirit of cynicism. Others sought to understand human motives by exploring ideas that had been developed before the war, in particular psychoanalysis.

Freud's emphasis on irrationality and the nature of the unconscious proved especially fruitful. The French critic André Breton ushered in a movement called Surrealism, which affected literature and the visual arts, while the English writer Virginia Woolf used her novels to explore the "stream of consciousness" of her characters. In drama, the American Eugene O'Neill made explicit the Freudian theme of the relations between parents and children.

Woolf was one of the leading members of an intellectual circle known as the Bloomsbury Group, whose members were responsible for many important cultural developments. In his poem "The Waste Land," T.S. Eliot analyzed the failure of modern civilization. The philosopher Bertrand Russell and the economist John Maynard Keynes also had contacts with the world of Bloomsbury. In painting, the two leading movements represented opposite attitudes. The Dadaists fought against the idea of any kind of meaning, while the Surrealists explored the meaning of dreams. Meanwhile, other painters continued to explore the possibilities of Cubism.

With the spread of modern urban culture, some artists and designers tried consciously to create a style that would be valid in a wide variety of settings. At the *Bauhaus* in Germany, Walter Gropius and his colleagues devised the International Style, which had a great influence on the urban landscape of the 20th century.

Artists were profoundly affected by the growing popularity of the movies and the radio. Among the most widespread influences of the day was jazz, originally a form of music indigenous to America. Jazz became popular among all those with access to a radio or a phonograph. The leading composers of the day, including Igor Stravinsky and Paul Hindemith, incorporated jazz elements in their music.

The interwar years were overshadowed not only by the horrors of World War I, but also by the growing realization that further conflict seemed to lay ahead. The Spanish Civil War drove many artists and writers to protest the brutality of fascism. Yet if art could warn, it could not prevent. With the outbreak of World War II, Freud's insistence on the power of the irrational seemed frighteningly justified.

STREAM OF CONSCIOUSNESS: LITERATURE AND PSYCHOANALYSIS

World War I brought into question many of Europe's most cherished values. Some, such as a belief in the inherent superiority and leadership qualities of noble birth, were already challenged in the 19th century. Others, most notably the importance of patriotism and national pride, retained their potency and their potential destructiveness. Technological progress, the proud achievement of the late 19th century, was now revealed as morally neutral. Its ability to cause good or ill was vast and depended on how it was used: Tanks, planes, and poison gas were responsible for the slaughter of millions of troops.

For some the shock to civilization marked the beginning of the end. The Irish poet William Butler Yeats (1865–1939) spoke for many who were fearful of the future when he wrote: "Things fall apart: the center cannot hold; Mere anarchy is loosed upon the world." The sense that Western civilization was deteriorating permeated *The Decline of the West* (1918–1922), a massive historical study by the German philosopher Oswald Spengler (1880–1936). According to Spengler, history moved in cycles. Western culture, he believed, had passed its high point and was on the way down.

Those of less apocalyptic temperament sought escape from recent memories in the lighthearted, even trivial. The English novelist Evelyn Waugh (1903–1966) caricatured the dizzy world of London's "bright young things" with a mixture of attraction and repulsion. In Paris, Picasso designed sets for a ballet, *Parade,* with music by Erik Satie (1866–1925), which included sound effects such as whistles, automobile horns, and typewriters to evoke everyday life.

LITERATURE AND THE UNCONSCIOUS

Among those to look deeply at the problems of the modern age was Sigmund Freud, who published *Civilization and its Discontents* in 1930 (see Topic 79). Freud's work earlier in the century proved an increasing source of inspiration to artists searching to understand the motives for human behavior. By stressing the importance of the unconscious and the inner meaning of dreams, he underlined the power of the irrational to affect apparently rational thought processes.

Exploration of the unconscious was the chief goal of Surrealism, an artistic movement that influenced both writers and painters. The high priest of Surrealism was the French poet André Breton (1896–1966), who published his *Manifesto of Surrealism* in 1924. In his poems he intermingled the everyday and the fantastic, probing the con-

Picasso, Curtain for the ballet *Parade*. 1917. 34 feet 9 inches by 56 feet (10.6 by 17.3 m). The ballet was produced by the great Russian impressario Serge Diaghilev for his Paris season that year. The plot was by one of the leading poets of the day, Jean Cocteau. The music, by Eric Satie, included whistles, car horns, and typewriters—sounds that were symbolic of everyday life. Most critics thought, though, that Picasso's brilliant sets stole the show.

nections between dream and reality, the subjective and the objective.

The novels of Virginia Woolf (1882–1941) use the "stream of consciousness" technique to deal with themes of time, change, and human personality. Instead of providing a chronological account of her characters' lives, she moved back and forth in time, describing the effect of the past on present consciousness. In *To the Lighthouse* (1927), the central section of the three parts into which the novel is divided is called "Time Passes." It provides an impressionistic rendering of the effects of the passage of time on people and things. In further refining the techniques of Joyce and Proust (see Topic 79), Woolf paid special attention to the experiences of women. Her book *Mrs. Dalloway* (1925) described a single day in the life of the novel's heroine. Woolf's own frustration at the exclusion of women from intellectual life found expression in a later polemical work, *Three Guineas* (1938), which described a fascist-like world dominated by men, in which individual rights, freedom, and justice were suppressed.

The great American dramatist Eugene O'Neill (1888–1953) used psychology and symbolism to illuminate another of Freud's revelations: the complexity of the relationship between parents and children, and the fundamental importance of early family experience in creating human personalities. In *Mourning Becomes Electra* (1931), ancient Greek tragedy became reenacted in Civil War New England, with Aeschylus's idea of the unavoidability of fate given modern form as psychological destiny.

The World of Bloomsbury

Amid the confusion of the interwar years, a group of writers and intellectuals in England sought to maintain a coherence of thought and action. They were called Bloomsbury after the area of London in which many of them lived and worked. The name acquired further cultural resonance from the fact that the Bloomsbury district also contained the British Museum. Virginia Woolf and her husband, Leonard Woolf (1880–1969), were at the center of the Bloomsbury Group. From the basement of their house they operated a publishing company, the Hogarth Press, which circulated works by many of the most influential writers of the time. Among the offerings in Hogarth Press editions were the first complete English translations of the works of Freud, and the first English translations of the German poet Rainer Maria Rilke (1875–1926) and the Italian novelist Italo Svevo (1861–1928; real name Ettore Schmitz).

ELIOT AND "THE WASTE LAND"
Although an American, and on the periphery of the Bloomsbury circle, the poet T[homas] S[tearns] Eliot (1888–1965) was among the writers the Woolfs published. His most famous work, *The Waste Land*, appeared on their list in 1922, and over the following years Eliot acted as informal adviser to them.

After studying at Harvard, Eliot moved to London, where he eked out a living by teaching and writing reviews, and working in a bank. *The Waste Land* placed him immediately at the center of the modernist movement. Its theme was the spiritual and moral chaos of postwar Europe. Abandoning traditional forms, the style of the poem conveys the bleakness of its theme in broken lines and fragmented images. The overwhelming mood of the work is one of alienation and exile, expressing the disillusionment of an entire generation.

In subsequent works, Eliot moved from the despair of *The Waste Land* to an affirmation of traditional culture. The foundation of his growing optimism was Christianity. The most fully worked-out meditation on his Christian faith appeared in the *Four Quartets* (1944). Not only the most widely read poet of his generation, Eliot was also an enormously influential literary critic.

THE INFLUENCE OF BLOOMSBURY
Bloomsbury's cultural influence extended far beyond poetry. Lytton Strachey (1880–1932) brought new life to the writing of biography by taking an irreverent look at pillars of the Victorian establishment. His *Eminent Victorians* (1918) caught the postwar mood of cynicism by depicting Florence Nightingale as an interfering busybody, and General Charles George "Chinese" Gordon as an alcoholic. In a slightly later work, he even took on Queen Victoria.

The art critic and painter Roger Fry (1866–1934) was one of the leading champions of Cézanne and the other Postimpressionist painters; the exhibitions he organized of their works helped inspire public interest and enthusiasm for them. The historical writings and translations of Arthur Waley (1889–1966) introduced Chinese and Japanese culture to a wide audience. Although many of them are now superseded, his versions of Chinese poetry and the great Japanese novel *The Tale of Genji* (written around 1000 A.D. by Lady Murasaki) opened up new cultural horizons for many readers.

Other influential figures who maintained links with Bloomsbury included John Maynard Keynes (see Topic 82), a major pioneer in the development of modern economics. The leading philosopher of the day, Bertrand Russell (1872–1970), although not an inner member of the group, was in contact with many who were. Far more closely involved—she had a love affair with Virginia Woolf—was Victoria Sackville-West (1892–1962), whose unconventional marriage to the critic and diplomat Harold Nicolson (1886–1968) illustrated the iconoclastic spirit of the world of Bloomsbury.

Movements in Modern Art: Dada, Surrealism, and Abstraction

The years before World War I saw a succession of "isms," including Fauvism, Cubism, and Futurism, as artists tried to build on the innovations of their predecessors. The

PUBLIC FIGURES AND PRIVATE LIVES

VITA SACKVILLE-WEST AND HAROLD NICOLSON

Daughter of a eccentric English aristocrat, Vita Sackville-West became one of the most flamboyant and well-known figures of her era. Passionately attached to her family and its ancestral home, Knole, her two absorbing interests were literature and gardening. After meeting her for the first time around Christmas 1922, Virginia Woolf wrote of Vita: "Not much to my severer taste—florid, mustached, parakeet-colored, with all the supple ease of the aristocracy, but not the wit of the artist." Two years later, under the spell of her infatuation, Virginia described Vita's legs: "Oh they are exquisite—running like slender pillars up into her trunk, which is that of a breastless cuirassier."

In 1913 Vita married Harold Nicolson, an eligible young man in the diplomatic service, whose early emotional relationships included several lighthearted homosexual affairs. When they first met in 1910, Vita was involved in a romantic crush on another young girl. While maintaining their own independent lifestyles, they brought up two sons and wrote. Nicolson published literary criticism, including an influential monograph on Tennyson. From 1935 to 1945, he served in Parliament.

Throughout their marriage, Sackville-West and Nicolson kept diaries and exchanged a flood of correspondence with one another during their frequent separations. Their relationship has been described, in fact, as one of the best-documented marriages in history. They constantly brooded on their own lives and on the question of relations between men and women, as well as on the issue of feminism. In 1934, Nicolson recorded in his diary a discussion about women's lives and their approach to freedom: "V says that in every revolution there is a transitional stage. That women have for centuries been suppressed and that one cannot expect them to slide quite naturally into freedom. This saddens me."

Twenty years later, Vita summed up her feelings about her marriage in a letter to a friend: "We have gone our own ways for about 30 years; never asked questions; never been in the least curious about that side of our respective lives, though deeply devoted and sharing our interests. I love him deeply, and he loves me. . . ."

To some extent, the openness of their marriage was facilitated by the well-to-do British social world in which they moved and by Sackville-West's utter indifference to convention. Both of them drew considerable strength and satisfaction from their independent literary work. Nicolson's early pleasure in his political career gave way to a growing sense of not being taken seriously enough, but his diary reveals a keen if somewhat detached interest in diplomatic affairs. Certainly they both took their duties as parents seriously. In a letter to her elder son, in fact, Vita spelled out the oddness and success of an unlikely union: "Two of the happiest married people I know, whose names I must conceal for reasons of discretion, are both homosexual." Their son had little doubt about whom his mother meant.

---

movement of the immediate postwar period, Dada, rejected the past and sought to begin again.

THE DADAISTS

The **Dadaist movement** was born out of anger, frustration, and despair. In 1915, as war raged, a group of artists met around a café table in Zurich, Switzerland, to protest the madness of their times. Their response was to reject the past and all its works, and to create meaningless nonsense. The very word "Dada" seems to have been chosen for its similarity to childlike babble. The leading Dada poet, the Romanian-born Tristan Tzara (1896–1963),

SURREALIST ART

Unlike the Dada pursuit of the meaningless, **Surrealism** set out to discover the deeper meanings that lay beneath the surface of the conscious mind. According to Breton's Surrealist *Manifesto* of 1924, artists should set out to express "the real functioning of thought without any control by reason." One of the leading exponents of Surrealism, the Spanish painter Salvador Dalí (1904–1989), described his works as "hand-painted dream photographs." Like many others of the period, Dalí was obsessed with the nature of time. His best-known work, *The Persistence of Memory* (1931), has become virtually an icon of Surrealism. The work combines precisely painted detail with melting watches to create a sense of quiet alarm.

CUBISM AFTER WORLD WAR I

Both Pablo Picasso and Georges Braque, the co-inventors of Cubism, continued to explore the possibilities of the style, while generally moving away from the highly analytical character of their prewar work (see Topic 79). In works such as the *Three Musicians* (1921), Picasso still used flat planes, but the figures have a liveliness and color—even humor—that was absent in earlier Cubist work. One of the chief exponents of this freer, "Synthetic Cubism" was Picasso's fellow Spaniard Juan Gris (1887–1927), who applied the technique to still-life subjects.

By contrast, the Dutch artist Piet Mondrian (1872–1944) moved toward ever-greater abstraction. Art, he believed, should have "balance, unity, and stability." Using pure colors and clean lines, he constructed rectangles of varying dimensions that seem almost to be street plans; Mondrian wrote, in fact, that "the new style will spring from the metropolis." The spare, abstract repose of his works had a considerable influence on many aspects of modern design, from fashion to advertising.

Duchamp, *L. H. O. O. Q.* 1919. 7¾ inches by 4⅞ inches (20 by 12 cm). Duchamp was one of the leading artists of the "Dada" school, which aimed to fight the "scientific" and "rational" warmongers with nonsense and ridicule. In this famous (or, perhaps, notorious) assault on high culture, he adds a moustache to one of the most revered faces in Western art and captions it with an off-color expression.

BAUHAUS: THE INTERNATIONAL STYLE IN BUILDING AND DESIGN

Mondrian was one of a group of Dutch artists who joined forces in a movement known as *De Stijl* (Dutch for "The Style"). At the end of World War I, De Stijl architects constructed buildings according to Mondrian's principles of geometric balance. The Schroder House in Utrecht, designed in 1924 by Gerrit Rietveld (1888–1964), has a façade whose severely geometric lines form the three-dimensional equivalent of a Mondrian canvas. In addition to buildings, Rietveld also designed furniture, using a similar spare geometric style.

GROPIUS AND THE BAUHAUS

The most comprehensive attempt to devise an all-embracing design style for modern living developed in Germany in the 1920s. In 1919, the German architect Walter Gropius (1883–1969) was commissioned to organize a German art school. The result, the **Bauhaus** (Building Institute), became

wrote a manifesto in 1918 calling for the destruction of memory, the end of good manners, and the practice of the spontaneous.

Dada's most original, and iconoclastic, figure was the French Marcel Duchamp (1887–1968). An early proponent of Cubism, he created a sensation in New York in 1913 with his *Nude Descending a Staircase*. Duchamp invented the Dada form of sculpture, the "ready-made," by taking ordinary objects—a snow shovel, a urinal—and putting them on display. ("Ready-made" sculptures enjoyed a revival after World War II; among those producing them was Picasso.) No masterpiece of high culture was safe from his scorn, as his notorious defacement of a copy of Leonardo's *Mona Lisa* vividly illustrated. For all the anger, however, the sheer energy of the Dada movement soon worked itself out. Duchamp abandoned art for chess in 1923, and many Dada artists went on to produce Surrealist paintings.

Dalí, *The Persistence of Memory.* 1931. 9½ by 13 inches (24.1 by 33 cm). This is perhaps the most famous image produced by any of the artists of the Surrealist school. The painting gains its fascination from the combination of almost photographic realism (Dalí had a magnificent touch) with objects that defy the laws of nature. The luminous colors add to the weird effect.

Picasso, *Three Musicians.* 1921. 7 feet 7 inches by 7 feet 3¾ inches (2.7 by 2.23 m). In the early years of the 20th century, Picasso and Braque had invented a new style of painting, which they called Cubism. In its earlier, "analytical" phase this produced paintings that so distorted the forms that they were barely recognizable. After 1918, Picasso began to use what he called "synthetic Cubism," which, as in this painting, broke up the forms without destroying them.

the 20th century's most influential school of architecture and design. The innovations of Gropius and his colleagues derived from a new attitude toward the nature and function of a building, based on the possibilities of advanced construction techniques. The three principal ingredients were a reinforced concrete base, a structural framework made of steel, and glass panels for walls. By using the principle of cantilevering (projecting beams to support balconies) Bauhaus architects were able to construct upper stories that overhung their supporting bases.

The most visually daring of these elements was the use of glass for walls. Because glass reflects light, as well as transmitting it, changing weather patterns outside a building, along with illumination inside, affect its appearance. At times both inside and outside are visible simultaneously, creating the equivalent of the Cubist effect whereby two different views can be seen at the same time. At other times the glass walls produce a mirror-like effect, reflecting the buildings around. In Bauhaus architecture, in fact, the wall became a decorative rather than structural element, acting as a curtain against the outside environment.

The inventors of the Bauhaus style intended it to serve for constructions in any urban setting. Their "International Style" became widely diffused throughout Europe and was carried to the United States when Gropius and his colleague Mies van der Rohe fled there in the late 1930s.

The Bauhaus philosophy of design affected far more than architecture. Its governing principle, that of unadorned utility, characterized the forms of a wide variety of objects and processes. Printmaking and metalwork techniques laid emphasis on clarity of line and ease of production. Mass-produced tubular chairs combined simple comfort and convenient storage capacity. Household appliances were streamlined, and easy to use and to clean.

The characteristically "modern" look of most post–World War II industrial production owed much of its inspiration to the Bauhaus group. Followers of the school praised the clean lines, efficiency, and practical advantages. Others, who were less convinced, lamented the uniformity and lack of character of the International Style. In architecture, at least, a reaction against Bauhaus simplicity began to develop in the 1980s, when the Postmodernist movement reintroduced elements of decoration (see Topic 93). Yet in the late 20th century the urban landscape of most large cities throughout the world remained firmly conditioned by Bauhaus ideas, and modern design continued to pay homage to the Bauhaus principle: "Less is more."

Mies van der Rohe and Philip Johnson, the Seagram Building, New York. 1956–1958. Height 512 feet (156.2 m). The character of this Modernist building can be seen by comparing its clean, sleek lines with the far more ornate buildings in the background. It has been one of the most imitated buildings of the 20th century, but not always with happy results.

Ezra Stoller © Esto

THE JAZZ AGE: MUSIC, RADIO, AND THE MOVIES

The years after World War I saw the rapid spread of mass communications. Radio, first invented by Guglielmo Marconi (1874–1937) at the turn of the 20th century, became an increasingly popular source of information, culture, and simple entertainment. It linked city and country dwellers, it crossed over national boundaries, and it spanned the Atlantic. By the outbreak of World War II, more than 300 million people had access to radio sets. In most European countries, radio networks were state-controlled. Transmissions throughout the 1930s reinforced government attitudes, especially in Fascist Italy, Nazi Germany, and Soviet Russia. During World War II, radio broadcasts were used for psychological warfare.

The effect of radio on popular culture, especially music, was to produce a growing standardization of "consumer product," whereby listeners in remote regions or countries could hear the latest Berlin cabaret song or Broadway hit almost as soon as their first local audiences. At the same time, radio also won new listeners for symphonies and operas. In the United States, nationwide transmissions of Metropolitan Opera broadcasts began in 1931. That same year, when Arturo Toscanini (1867–1957), one of the towering figures in European musical life, fled Fascism and went to America, he became the chief conductor of a radio orchestra, the NBC Symphony.

THE MOVIES

Scarcely less revolutionary was the impact of the movies. Like radio, the movies had been around before World War

I, but their great age was the 1920s and, with the coming of sound, the 1930s. In the decade before World War II, giant picture palaces sprang up in the big cities, and few rural communities did not have access to a movie theater in a provincial center nearby. Between 1933 and 1942, annual cinema attendance in Germany rose from a quarter of a billion to 1 billion. Over the same period in Britain it remained constant at around 1 billion.

As in the case of radio, movies could and did serve propaganda purposes. Weekly newsreels, feature films, and documentaries poured out of government propaganda ministries. The most notorious examples of film at the service of the state are the works of the German Leni Riefenstahl (1902–1987). Her *Triumph of the Will* (1936) set out to glorify the Nazi party and its doctrines of mass ritual and racial superiority, using highly controlled and sexually charged images of young athletes and physical beauty.

Despite the politicians' efforts, most people went to the movies for entertainment. With the rise of Hollywood in the 1930s, and the cult of the superstar, the cinema reached new heights of popularity. One of the most successful types of film, the musical, became possible with the improvement of sound techniques and the introduction of color processing.

The first sound film, *The Jazz Singer* (1927), had seemed to many to mark a setback in movie history. The first sound cameras were immobile and permitted only very limited flexibility. Many of the stars of the silent screen, furthermore, feared the effect of the sound of their voice on their adoring public: Adroit publicists cleverly managed to capitalize on this issue and turned the first sound appearance of Greta Garbo (1905–1990) into an international event. By the 1930s, however, the movie industry had developed improved methods, and musicals such as *Showboat* (1936; original stage version 1927) played to audiences of millions.

Riefenstahl, still shot from the diving sequence of *Olympia*. 1938. The film, much of it shot at the Berlin Olympic Games of 1936, shows the intensely original camera angles that Riefenstahl used. They were to be much imitated by later documentary film-makers.

JAZZ

It is no coincidence that the movie chosen to inaugurate the new age of sound was *The Jazz Singer*. Not only did it provide even wider circulation for jazz music, but by casting a white actor, Al Jolson (1886–1950), as a black jazz musician, it also illustrated the degree to which a black musical idiom had been appropriated by white America (see Topic 85).

Jazz grew out of the black culture of the southern United States. Complex in rhythm, making frequent use of syncopation (the stress of normally unstressed beats), jazz was at first improvised. It took its mood from the work songs, laments, and spirituals (religious folk songs) of the slaves and black communities of the Deep South; its distant origins were derived from the folk music of Africa. The first organized performances were given by street bands of black musicians in New Orleans and other southern cities around 1900.

In the 1920s, as the black populations of the northern cities began to grow, jazz found a wider audience. Listeners in Chicago, New York, and other centers developed a taste for the blues singing of Bessie Smith (c. 1898–1937) and the trumpet playing of Louis Armstrong (1900–1971). White musicians took up the idiom, often forming big bands that developed a commercialized form of jazz known as "swing." The popularity of bandleaders such as Benny Goodman (1909–1986) or "Count" Basie (1904–1984) would be further spread by radio and phonograph records.

In a short time the new music spread to Europe. In Paris there grew up a cult following for "*le jazz hot*," and one of the jazz world's most celebrated figures, the singer and dancer Josephine Baker, settled there permanently (see Topic 85). She was later to play a part in the French Resistance movement during World War II. Cabaret artists in Berlin included jazz numbers in their acts, and in 1933 recordings by Benny Goodman and his band created a sensation in Britain. So pervasive was the influence of jazz that some spoke of "the Jazz Age," a phrase derived from the title of a collection of short stories by F. Scott Fitzgerald, who was one of the chroniclers of the expatriate American community in Paris.

European composers soon began to explore the possibilities of jazz in their own music. Igor Stravinsky incorporated elements of "ragtime" (one of the early stages in the development of jazz) in his work *The Soldier's Tale* (1918). In the slow movement of his Violin Concerto of 1931, he made use of a blues-like theme. In Germany, Kurt Weill (1900–1950) developed a sophisticated blend of jazz and popular music to create works filled with powerful social criticism. The best-known is *The Threepenny Opera* (1928), the most ambitious *The Rise and Fall of the City of Mahagonny* (1929). (In Weill's later works, written after his move to the United States in 1935, he drew on the Broadway musical tradition.)

The most consistent attempt to combine jazz and traditional musical forms occurred in the work of the American composer George Gershwin (1898–1937). His *Rhapsody in Blue* (1924), a piano concerto in all but name, was written for the jazz band of Paul Whiteman (1890–1967); Gershwin played the solo part at the sensationally successful first performance in New York. His full-length "American folk opera," *Porgy and Bess* (1935), incorporated jazz and spiritual music. Received with only limited enthusiasm at first, the work enjoyed increasing success at its revivals in the 1970s. By the 1990s it had entered the repertory of such traditional companies as the Metropolitan Opera, New York, and Glyndebourne, England.

COMING SHADOWS

Over the restless energy of the Jazz Age there began to fall the shadow of war. The sense of trouble ahead emerged in the work of several European artists and writers. The German satirical artist George Grosz savagely chronicled the corruption and militarism of post–World War I Germany, before fleeing to the United States in 1933. The brutalities of the Spanish Civil War (1936–1939) provoked widespread protests. Among the most eloquent commentaries were those of the English poet W.H. Auden (1907–1973) and Picasso—his painting *Guernica* (1937) commemorated the bombing of the small Basque town by German planes fighting for Franco's fascist forces (see Topic 87).

One of the first to warn of the dangers of Nazism was the eminent German writer Thomas Mann (1875–1955). Mann's reverence for the conservative, philosophical, and musical traditions of German culture permeated his first successful novel *Buddenbrooks* (1901), a sensitive and moving picture of German provincial family life. In the 1920s he began to diagnose the sick state of contemporary society; his novel *The Magic Mountain* (1924) used the metaphorical background of a tuberculosis sanatorium to describe the intellectual and moral uncertainties of the postwar years. In 1933, while Mann was abroad, the Nazi regime denounced him and confiscated his property.

Mann settled in Switzerland, from where he continued to issue warnings, some of them in the form of broadcasts to Germany. In 1939, on the eve of war, he took up a visiting professorship at Princeton University. Many other leading German and Austrian intellectuals and artists sought refuge in the years preceding and during the war in the United States; they included Albert Einstein and Arnold Schoenberg, both of whom were Jewish. Mann was one of the few major non-Jewish European figures—Toscanini was another notable example—to protest their country's regime and go into exile.

Putting Psychoanalysis and the Arts in Perspective

With the benefit of hindsight, it is clear that the sense of instability that permeated the culture of the interwar years—Dada, Eliot's alienation, the Surrealists' rejection of reality—represented not only a reaction against the values of life before World War I but also a greater sense of doubt. If old political and social realities were dead, there was nothing firm with which to replace them. An understanding of the unconscious proved a difficult foundation on which to rebuild civilization. Nor did Freud's insistence on the power of the irrational provide much comfort for those who had already seen its capacity for destruction.

Thus the arts of the years between the wars reflected the agitated mood of the times. The new freedom from traditional restraints opened up exciting possibilities in painting, music, and fiction. New means of communication created a vast public for art at all levels. Yet for all the vitality and variety of the Jazz Age, its spirited energy failed to hide completely a sense of foreboding. The Great War had shown one terrible direction civilization could take, and a repeat of the "war to end all wars" seemed increasingly likely.

In 1918, a week before the armistice ending World War I was signed, a young Englishman, Wilfred Owen (1893–1918), was killed in action. A year earlier, he had been invalided out of the fighting in France and spent some time in a military hospital. While there he wrote poems describing the horror and human sacrifice of war. One of them contains the line: "All a poet can do today is to warn."

Questions for Further Study

1. How did both poets and painters use symbolism and surrealism? What other styles influenced more than one art medium?
2. How did the ideas of Freud influence the arts between the world wars?
3. Is Owen's observation, "All a poet can do today is to warn," a true reflection of the role of the arts in the 20th century? How far is it still true today?

Suggestions for Further Reading

Ackroyd, P. *T.S. Eliot*. London, 1984.

Barron, Stephanie, ed. *Exiles and Emigres: The Flight of European Artists from Hitler*. Los Angeles, 1997.

Berman, M. *All That Is Solid Melts into Air: The Experience of Modernity*. New York, 1981.

Bohn, Willard. *The Rise of Surrealism: Cubism, Dada, and the Pursuit of the Marvelous*. New York, 2001.

Cantor, N.F. *Twentieth Century Culture: Modernism to Deconstruction*. New York, 1988.

Douglas, A. *Terrible Honesty: Mongrel Manhattan in the 1920s*. New York, 1995.

Fer, Briony, David Bachelor, and Paul Wood. *Realism, Rationalism, Surrealism: Art Between the Wars*. New Haven, CT, 1993.

Harrison, Charles, Francis Frascina, and Gil Perry. *Primitivism, Cubism, Abstraction: The Early Twentieth Century*. New Haven, CT, 1993.

Hayman, R. *Kafka: A Biography*. New York, 1981.

Hughes, R. *The Shock of the New*. New York, 1981.

Smith, Angela. *Katherine Mansfield and Virginia Woolf: A Public of Two*. New York, 1999.

Taylor, Brandon. *Avant-Garde and After*. New York, 1995.

InfoTrac College Edition

Enter the search term *Sigmund Freud* using Key Terms.

THE ROAD TO WAR

International relations in the interwar period fell into two broad phases. In the first, from 1919 to 1931, the major Western powers put their hopes for peace on the League of Nations and a general spirit of reconciliation; in the second, from 1931 to 1939, Japan and the two fascist powers of Europe—Italy and Germany—unleashed one act of aggression after another, demonstrating the helplessness of the League and testing to the limits the policy of appeasement adopted by Britain and France. The Nazi invasion of Poland in September 1939, coming in the wake of Adolf Hitler's violation of earlier agreements, pushed the West to the wall and triggered war.

In the 1920s, many Western statesmen believed that they could create a condition of permanent peace by simply willing it into existence. International efforts at disarmament and the abandonment of war as an instrument of national policy were well-intentioned, but belied the fact that the 1919 peace settlements had created an imbalance of power in the world. Germany and Italy demanded a revision of the settlements, while France recognized the danger to its own interests but could not convince Britain that alliances rather than the League of Nations were needed.

Appeasement had begun in 1931, even before Hitler came to power, when the West protested Japan's aggression against China but did nothing. Mussolini's invasion of Ethiopia in 1935 was the crucial test case for the efficacy of the League. On the other hand, wars in East Asia and in Africa were not perceived as immediate dangers to Europe. The intervention of the fascist powers in the Spanish Civil War should have been a clearer lesson about the direction of German and Italian policy, but the ideological nature of the conflict there made Britain and France prefer not to intervene.

When Hitler moved against Austria and the Czech Sudetenland in 1938, the Western powers rationalized his demands as legitimate goals based on the argument of self-determination. Only in 1939, when it became clear that the appetites of the dictators would not be quenched by appeasement, did Britain and France conclude that war was necessary.

THE ILLUSION OF PEACE

The League of Nations (see Topic 80), with which President Woodrow Wilson hoped peace would be permanently preserved, rested on the concept of "collective security," which meant that its members guaranteed each other's security. But the European powers did not find this arrangement sufficient for their purposes, and during the 1920s a variety of separate treaties created the illusion of stability. When the U.S. Senate refused to ratify the Treaty of Versailles and Wilson's commitment to offer the French an assistance pact, France arranged a military alliance with Poland in 1921 and with the so-called Little Entente of Czechoslovakia, Yugoslavia, and Romania. In doing so, France attempted to link the preservation of the peace settlement in the West with that in the East.

THE SPIRIT OF LOCARNO

In the 1920s, Europe entered a period of relative stability and sought alternative ways of guaranteeing security. In 1923, the Draft Treaty of Mutual Assistance came before the Assembly of the League. It stipulated that in the event of hostilities, the League Council should determine the aggressor, and that members were then obliged to offer military assistance. This treaty would have made military sanctions by the League automatic instead of optional. France, worried about future German aggression, was enthusiastic, but Britain opposed it.

Unable to strengthen the League, France turned to efforts aimed at securing a guarantee of her border with Germany. This aim succeeded, in part, because of the poli-

cies of German Foreign Minister Gustav Stresemann (1878–1929), who sought reconciliation with the great powers. In 1922, Germany had already proposed a mutual pledge with France not to resort to war and had signed the Treaty of Rapallo with the Soviet Union, in which each side had agreed to stay neutral in the event of an attack. The Rapallo agreement made the international community uneasy because it ended the diplomatic isolation of both Germany and the Soviet Union.

In October 1925, Britain, France, Germany, Poland, and Czechoslovakia met at Locarno, Switzerland, and signed several agreements. The Treaty of Locarno stipulated that any changes in the French-German and the Belgian-German borders would come as a result of negotiations; meanwhile, France concluded a treaty with Poland and Czechoslovakia that guaranteed the eastern borders. Germany further agreed to submit all frontier disputes to arbitration. The next year, Germany became a member of the League of Nations.

The mood of international cooperation was expanded further with the Pact of Paris. In 1927, French Foreign Minister Aristide Briand (1862–1932) proposed to U.S. Secretary of State Frank B. Kellogg (1856–1937) that each country renounce war as an instrument of national policy. This Kellogg-Briand Pact, signed in 1928, was eventually endorsed by all of the great powers (except the Soviet Union) and a total of 65 nations. Making war "illegal" did much to foster an illusion of international peace but did little for its reality.

By the end of the decade, a more self-confident Germany had rejoined the community of nations, and many of the conditions imposed on her by the peace settlement had been removed. In June 1930, Allied troops left the Rhineland. By then, France had begun the construction of the Maginot line of fortifications along the frontier with Germany, and in September the Nazis had 107 deputies in the *Reichstag*.

SIGNIFICANT DATES

The Road to War

October 1925	Treaty of Locarno
1928	Kellogg-Briand Pact
1931	Japanese invade Manchuria
October 1933	Hitler withdraws from League
March 1935	German Air Force announced
1935	Mussolini proposes Stresa Front
October 1935	Ethiopian War
March 1936	Hitler occupies Rhineland
1936	Mussolini and Hitler support Franco in Spain
October 1936	Rome-Berlin Axis
November 1936	Anti-Comintern Pact between Germany and Japan
1937	Japanese invasion of China
March 1938	German annexation of Austria
September 1938	Munich conference
March 1939	Germany occupies all of Czechoslovakia
August 1939	Nazi-Soviet Non-Aggression Pact
September 1, 1939	Germany invades Poland

EUROPE, JAPAN, AND THE LEAGUE OF NATIONS

In the 1920s, few observers anticipated that the first real challenge to the League of Nations would come from East Asia. But in 1931, Japan embarked on a program of deliberate expansion that tested the willingness of the Western powers to stand behind treaty obligations, even when the participants in the dispute were Asian nations.

JAPAN AS A WORLD POWER

Japan had burst on the international scene during the Sino-Japanese War of 1894–1895, when it defeated China in a struggle over Korea. To Europeans, even more startling was Japan's smashing victory over Russia in the 1904–1905 war. The Japanese eyed China and adjoining territories as a natural sphere of interest. During World War I and the Civil War in Russia, Japan moved on to the Chinese mainland and captured markets that were once controlled by the Western powers.

Map 87.1 Japanese Expansion. Note in particular Japanese expansion into Korea. Manchuria had been one of the areas contended in the Russo-Japanese war of 1904–1905. By 1932, the Japanese had obtained domination of the whole region and created a puppet state. The Russians took back control there in 1945, before withdrawing and leaving Chinese communists and Nationalists to fight over the territory; the Communists eventually, in 1948, won control. Go to http://info.wadsworth.com/053461065X for an interactive version of this map.

In the 1920s, Japanese factories supplied most of Asia with a host of consumer products, but the foundations of its economy were fragile. Japan had created modern industrial and financial institutions, mainly by large family-owned trusts, but it lacked raw materials. Political economists argued that Japanese power would depend on securing both raw materials and markets.

Japan's government was modeled on the European example. In 1889, a constitution had been adopted and, in 1925, universal male suffrage went into effect. Nevertheless, Parliament's authority was limited, and ministers served at the pleasure of the emperor, whose powers were supreme. Militarism had a strong influence in society, and high army officers wielded significant influence in government circles.

In the postwar period, Japanese imperialist expansion was widely discussed in military circles. Not only was expansion for economic gain proposed, but some also insisted that the future of Asia was in the hands of Japan, the only local power capable of freeing it from European influence.

THE MANCHURIAN CRISIS

The Japanese first turned their attention to Manchuria, which had been wrested from Russian control in the Russo-Japanese War of 1904–1905. On paper, Japan allowed Manchuria to revert to China, but in reality the region became a Japanese protectorate. Border tensions between the Soviet Union and Japan occurring over the years culminated in September 1931 in a bomb explosion on the south Manchurian railroad, a few miles from the Japanese garrison at Mukden. The Japanese used the incident as a pretext for occupying strategic points in southern Manchuria. The Chinese government appealed to the League of Nations and

Street scene in the Chinese city of Shanghai under Japanese occupation. 1934. Two years earlier the Japanese had occupied Manchuria. In 1934, they first bombed and then took Shanghai; the picture shows some of the sacks piled up by the local population to reduce damage from bomb blasts. The armed soldiers are part of the Japanese army of occupation.

also to the United States under the terms of the Kellogg-Briand Pact. Secretary of State Henry L. Stimson insisted that the matter be settled peacefully but took no real action. In January 1932, by which time Japan had conquered all of Manchuria, Stimson announced that the United States would not recognize the Japanese gains.

China, which was otherwise powerless, announced an economic boycott, but Japan responded with a temporary occupation of Shanghai. In March, Japan proclaimed the territory an independent nation called Manchukuo ("Land of the Manchus"), and eventually installed Henry Pu Yi (1906–1967), the last emperor of China, as its ruler.

The League of Nations sent a commission to Manchuria headed by Lord Victor Lytton (1871–1947). The commission's report, issued in October, condemned the Japanese invasion and exposed the pretense of Manchukuo. Japan, a member of the League, withdrew from that international body and invaded the Chinese mainland southwest of Manchuria. By mid-1935, the Japanese had penetrated deep into China. Neither the League nor the United States took any action beyond verbal protests. The League of Nations had been dealt a deadly blow.

In July 1937, after a two-year hiatus, the war between Japan and China was renewed. The Japanese took the cities of Shanghai, Nanking, and Canton and drove Chinese forces under General Chiang Kai-shek (1887–1975) deep into western China. In Nanking, the Japanese troops killed perhaps 300,000 civilians in reprisal for their resistance. The invasion finally came to a halt when the Japanese reached the mountains of western China, while in the north a guerrilla resistance was led by the communists. The Japanese occupation of China proved brutal.

AUSTRIA, ETHIOPIA, AND THE AXIS

The failure of the League to stop Japan's aggression in China lent encouragement to European dictators. In 1934, Hitler attempted to seize Austria, but Mussolini prevented him from doing so. The following year, however, Mussolini tested the mood of the powers in the West by invading Ethiopia in October 1935. Before that conflict was over, Hitler had violated the Versailles Treaty by remilitarizing the Rhineland. Again, neither the League nor the Western powers acted. The era of appeasement had begun.

THE AUSTRIAN COUP AND THE STRESA FRONT

Upon coming to power, Hitler began immediately to strengthen Germany's military position. In October 1933, Hitler withdrew Germany from the League. The following

The funeral of the Austrian chancellor Engelbert Dollfuss. July 28, 1934. The picture was taken as the gun carriage bearing the coffin is passing Vienna's city hall. Dollfuss tried to maintain an independent Austria through his friendship with Mussolini but was shot and killed by rebels in the Austrian Nazi party.

AP/ Wide World Photos

year he made his first move toward the creation of his "Greater Germany." In July, the Austrian Nazis, some 100,000 strong, attempted to seize power in a coup supported by Hitler. Chancellor Engelbert Dollfuss (1892–1934), who had befriended Mussolini in an effort to keep Austria independent of Germany, was assassinated, but martial law was proclaimed in Vienna and the coup failed. Kurt von Schuschnigg (1897–1977), one of Dollfuss's collaborators, became the new chancellor, and Mussolini sent Italian troops to the Brenner Pass to dissuade Hitler from invading Austria. Mussolini later reminded the European powers that he could not always be the one to "march to the Brenner," by which he meant that they too would have to take responsibility for controlling Hitler's expansionist ambitions.

In March 1935, Hitler demonstrated his complete contempt for international agreements by announcing that Germany would no longer abide by the disarmament clauses of the Treaty of Versailles. Secret German rearmament had been going on ever since 1933, but now Hitler reintroduced peacetime conscription. Taking their cue from Mussolini, Britain and France met with Italian representatives at Stresa, in northern Italy, and agreed to Mussolini's proposal for common action against Germany. But British and French unwillingness to take the idea of the "Stresa Front" beyond mere words made it useless. Instead, in June, Britain signed a naval pact with Hitler that permitted Germany to build a fleet equal to one-third of British strength. The French and Italians both felt betrayed.

THE ITALIAN INVASION OF ETHIOPIA

In the meantime, Mussolini had been laying his plans for colonial conquest. For this he had been preaching to Italians that Fascism would restore the grandeur of the Roman Empire and give Italy its rightful position in international affairs. Since the summer of 1934 he had been preparing for the military conquest of Ethiopia (then known as Abyssinia). The country was one of two independent states in Africa. The Italians had tried unsuccessfully to conquer it in the 1890s but were disastrously defeated by Ethiopian troops at the Battle of Adowa. Mussolini now promised to "wipe clean the stain of Adowa."

In January 1935 Mussolini persuaded French Foreign Minister Pierre Laval (1883–1945) to give Italy a free hand in Ethiopia, but the British balked. In September British Foreign Minister Sir Samuel Hoare (1880–1959) assured the League that Britain would resist Italian aggression. On October 3, Mussolini launched his attack. Ethiopian Emperor Haile Selassie (1892–1975) went before the League and warned that Europe would be next if Mussolini was not stopped. Less than a week later, the League voted to condemn Italy and imposed economic sanctions. The sanctions, however, omitted petroleum from its list of proscribed materials. Moreover, Germany, the United States, and Japan did not participate in the sanctions. Toward the end of the year, Laval and Hoare met in Paris, where they agreed to offer Mussolini a compromise—he could have two-thirds of Ethiopia. When news of the Hoare-Laval Agreement became public, a storm of public indignation broke.

During the Ethiopian War, Hitler had been active. On March 7, 1936, he remilitarized the Rhineland in direct violation of the Treaty of Versailles and denounced the Treaty of Locarno. In October, Mussolini, who felt betrayed by the Western powers, sent his foreign minister, Count Galeazzo Ciano (1903–1944), to Berlin to arrange a treaty with Germany. The result was the signing of an agreement to collaborate on anticommunist propaganda in their foreign policies. Proclaiming this the beginning of a "Rome-Berlin

Ethiopian soldiers marching off to fight Mussolini's invading forces. 1935. Note that the Ethiopian forces are barefoot and carrying old-fashioned rifles. The Italian troops against whom they were to do battle were, of course, armed with the most modern European weapons. The Italian occupation lasted from 1935–1936 through 1941, when Italy's military defeats in World War II forced its withdrawal, and Haile Selassie, the Ethiopian emperor, returned to his throne.

Map 87.2 The Ethiopian War. The Ethiopian War of 1935–1936 represented Mussolini's attempt to remove memories of Italian humiliation there at the end of the 19th century: The Italian army was the only Western colonial force ever to be defeated by indigenous troops. Attacking from the Italian colonies of Eritrea and Somaliland, and using heavy air power and modern European weapons, the Italians soon won control of the capital, Addis Ababa. Ethiopia was liberated in 1941.

munist, and anarchist forces on the other; an internecine struggle among these antifascist forces; an internal Spanish political struggle for power; and finally, as a test of wills between the Axis powers and the Western democracies, it represented the real prelude to World War II.

The war broke out in July 1936 and raged on until March 1939. Its origins lay in the political culture of modern Spain. In September 1923, General Primo de Rivera staged a coup d'état and created a military dictatorship, although King Alfonso XIII (ruled 1902–1931) continued to rule in name. In 1930, Alfonso dismissed the unpopular general and in 1931 restored the constitution. In the elections that followed, the republican forces won a landslide in the cities, and the king, interpreting the vote to be against him, left the country, although he never abdicated. The Spanish Republic was proclaimed on April 14, 1931.

The Constituent Assembly was divided over the policies of the government, from those on the left who wanted social revolution to Catholics on the right who hated the Republic. The new democratic government began to initiate major social and economic reforms, including civilian control of the army, land reform, and regional autonomy. By late 1933, when the first *Cortes*, or parliament, met, the conservative majority under the leadership of the clerical José Gil Robles (1898–1980) began to undo the reforms and move Spain toward fascist dictatorship.

In 1936 the Republicans, syndicalists, anarchists, and communists joined together in a Popular Front to halt the

Axis," Mussolini moved increasingly close to Germany over the next two years.

THE MARCH OF FASCISM: THE SPANISH CIVIL WAR

Ever since Lenin had created the Communist International (Comintern) in 1919, European communist parties had been instructed by Moscow not to participate in political coalitions with bourgeois parties. The spread of fascism, however, gave Stalin pause. In September 1934, the Soviet Union joined the League of Nations. When the Comintern held its 1935 world congress, Italian and French communists suggested that the policy be reversed in order to fight fascism. The result was that communist parties now joined with socialists and democrats in what came to be known as "Popular Fronts." The most prominent Popular Front government was that of Léon Blum in France (see Topic 84). Over the next four years, the Popular Front concept was sorely tested in the tragedy of the Spanish Civil War.

THE SPANISH LABYRINTH

The civil war in Spain was a struggle fought on several levels at once: an ideological war between fascism on one side and an international alliance of democratic, socialist, com-

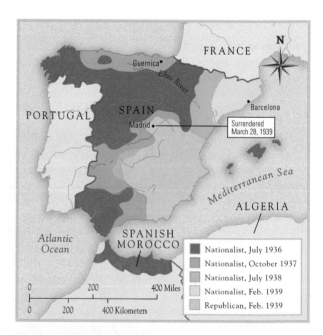

Map 87.3 The Civil War in Spain. This conflict between liberal and conservative forces in Spain saw the gradual victory of the latter, under the leadership of General Franco. His victory, aided by supplies from Hitler and Mussolini, was delayed when the Soviet Union began sending aid to the Republicans. Nevertheless, Franco took Madrid in 1938 and Barcelona, one of the Republicans' chief strongholds, in 1939. The most notorious episode in the war was the German air force's systematic destruction of the town of Guernica.

Fighting during the Spanish Civil War. 1936. This picture of a Loyalist fighter carrying a wounded friend to safety through a trench filled with dead bodies, became one of the most widely circulated images of the War. Robert Capa, the photographer, was one of the pioneers of war journalism; he went on to take a famous series of pictures of the Normandy landings in World War II.

Robert Capa © 2001 by Cornell Capa/Magnum Photos

reaction and succeeded in winning power. They immediately began to push for radical change, seizing landed estates and staging revolutionary strikes. Then, after a well-known reactionary deputy was assassinated, the forces of counter-revolution responded. On July 17, a military garrison in Spanish Morocco revolted under the leadership of General Francisco Franco (1892–1975). Other generals on the mainland joined in support. At the end of July, the rebels set up their headquarters in Burgos, in the north, and proclaimed a Junta of National Defense. Franco was named its *caudillo*, or chief.

Franco was a shrewd, calculating man, wedded to tradition and authority but with no precise ideology of his own. He gathered under his leadership nationalists, monarchists, and members of the fascist *Falange*. He also had the support of landowners, business interests, and Catholics. The Popular Front forces were as disparate a group as Franco's, although the left—composed of socialists, communists, a Trotskyite group, and the Anarcho-Syndicalists—dominated.

With the backing of most of the regular army, Franco's forces—known as the Nationalists—quickly hemmed the Republicans into four areas: Madrid, Valencia (where the government had fled), Barcelona, and the Basque provinces. For the next two and a half years, Spain was racked by a cruel and bloody civil war that was complicated by foreign intervention.

INTERVENTION AND IDEOLOGY

Foreign nations quickly took sides in the Spanish conflict. Blum's French government supported the Popular Front, while Mussolini and Hitler made common cause with the Nationalists. In November the two dictators officially recognized Franco's government, while the first antifascist volunteers organized by the Comintern began to arrive in the form of the International Brigades. The French Popular Front sent equipment and the Soviet Union fighter planes, equipment, and advisers. Hitler supplied Franco with tanks, planes, and military advisers, while Mussolini sent troops.

In March 1937 the antifascist forces won a major moral victory when the International Brigades repulsed the Nationalists at Guadalajara. By the end of 1937, the war had reached a stalemate.

With the Spanish participants more or less evenly matched and deadlocked, foreign intervention became decisive. Portuguese dictator António Salazar (1889–1970) sympathized with Franco, British Prime Minister Stanley Baldwin expected the Nationalists to become the future government, and even Blum was careful not to antagonize the right wing in France by openly supporting the Republicans. As a result, when Blum suggested the formation of a Non-Intervention Committee, Britain readily agreed. The purpose of the committee was to prevent foreign powers from intervening and to withhold military assistance from both sides. The committee, composed of representatives from 27 states, met in September 1936. The League of Nations backed its position.

Despite such appeals for neutrality, volunteers continued to arrive from abroad while the fascist powers poured in men and supplies. In effect, nonintervention meant that the legitimate government of Spain was prevented from purchasing supplies from abroad, while the Nationalists received significant illegal help. Morally, the Axis intervention aided the Republicans, especially after German planes bombed the town of Guernica in April 1937, inspiring Pablo Picasso's famous painting by that name (see Topic 86). In September, unidentified submarines—now known to have been mostly Italian—attacked ships carrying goods to the Republicans. When Britain and France called a conference at Lyon to prevent such actions, Germany and Italy boycotted the meeting, whereupon the Western powers jointly patrolled the Spanish waters and the piracy stopped.

By the spring of 1938, Franco—supported by some 100,000 Italian troops—launched a major offensive against the government. Franco had the advantage, especially because the Republican forces had become bitterly divided. Stalin had decided on a policy of no support for socialist revolutions in Spain, in order to reassure Western opinion. It

Picasso, *Guernica.* 1937. 11 feet 5½ inches by 25 feet 5¼ inches (3.49 by 7.77 m). The artist's outrage at the bombing of civilians in Guernica is visible throughout the painting. On the left, a bull (symbol of Spain and also of Picasso) stands guard over a woman with the broken body of a child. In the center, a horse screams over a dismembered corpse, while other figures lament to the right. To emphasize the grim, somber spirit of his work, Picasso limited himself to black, white, and shades of grey.

was a cynical policy that persuaded no one and undermined the Spanish left. Before the war was over, communist forces were killing Anarcho-Syndicalists by the thousands and Stalin's advisers had taken command of communist groups.

In mid-1938 the Soviet Union abandoned the Republic, convinced that Britain and France would not help. With the end of Soviet support, Franco succeeded in cutting government holdings in half. In the months that followed, the Nationalists proceeded to take more and more territory and began the systematic bombing of civilian populations. Barcelona fell in January 1939, followed by Madrid in March. The struggle was a particularly bitter one on both sides. The Republicans had killed priests and nuns, and now tens of thousands of Spaniards met the fate of brutal reprisals from Franco's victorious forces. Many thousands more fled Spain, and Franco imprisoned hundreds of thousands of opponents. When it was over, the civil war had bled the country of perhaps 1 million lives.

The civil war was a devastating blow for the democratic forces of Europe. The defeat of the Republicans became a symbol of fascist victory, and the war deeply divided opinion abroad. Mussolini and Hitler had shown that they could defy international opinion and the Western powers with impunity.

THE PRICE OF APPEASEMENT: AUSTRIA AND CZECHOSLOVAKIA

The year 1938 proved to be crucial. Hitler had been planning for some time to strike at Austria, determined to bring about *Anschluss* (union) with Germany. No sooner was that goal accomplished than Hitler began working against

Czechoslovakia, whose German minority provided the pretext for aggression there. In the case of the Czech crisis, however, the Western powers did not merely stand by—they actively participated in the dismemberment of an independent country.

Even before Hitler moved against Austria, political conditions in Britain and France mitigated against Western opposition. In Britain, the government of Neville Chamberlain (served as prime minister 1937–1940) was doggedly determined to do whatever it could to prevent war. Chamberlain embarked, therefore, on a policy that came to be known as "appeasement," by which the British were willing to make major concessions to Hitler for the sake of peace. The foreign minister, Anthony Eden (1897–1977), was a staunch opponent of the fascist dictators, and in 1938 he resigned in protest against appeasement. Thereafter, Chamberlain really conducted his own foreign policy. In France, the resignation of Blum's Popular Front in 1937 eventually brought to the premiership Edouard Daladier (served 1933, 1934, 1938–1940). Claiming that he would prepare France for war, he assumed the defense ministry. Yet French resolve, already softened by the fear of war, hinged to a great degree on Britain.

ANSCHLUSS

In February 1938, Hitler began to pressure Austria, using the Nazi radio and press to agitate for union with Germany. The *Führer* insisted that Chancellor Schuschnigg come to Berchtesgaden, his retreat in the Bavarian mountains, where Hitler proceeded to harangue the hapless Austrian leader for hours. After Hitler's bullying, Schuschnigg consented to concessions—he would appoint a Nazi as minister of the interior (who controlled the police) and issue an amnesty for imprisoned Austrian Nazis.

Once back in Vienna, however, Schuschnigg's resolve returned, and he began to mobilize public opinion against Germany. The chancellor decided to hold a plebiscite to secure public endorsement of his anti-German position. Hitler exploded and sent an ultimatum to Vienna demanding that the plebiscite be canceled. When Schuschnigg refused, Hitler moved German troops to the border. Faced with the prospect of invasion, Schuschnigg resigned. The Germans began marching against Austria even before Schuschnigg's successor, the Nazi Arthur Seyss-Inquart (1892–1946), had invited the Germans into his country, which Hitler then annexed to Germany. In April, a rigged plebiscite registered 99.75 percent public approval.

In Britain, Chamberlain had already written Austria off to appease Hitler, and France was caught between governments. The most interesting reaction came from Italy. In 1934, Mussolini had sent troops to the Brenner to prevent what he now congratulated Hitler for accomplishing. Hitler had not bothered to inform the *Duce* of his plans, but Mussolini pretended to ignore the slight. In any case, by then Mussolini's Italy was in no position to stand up to the Third Reich. Hitler rejoiced that he had added this strategically important nation to his realm, and no doubt remembered the difficulties of his youthful days spent in Vienna.

CZECHOSLOVAKIA AND THE SUDETENLAND

When the Paris Peace Conference of 1919 decided on the creation of Czechoslovakia as an independent state, it burdened the new republic with a serious problem: the mountainous rim of territory known as the Sudetenland, where some 3 million German-speaking people lived. In truth, Thomas Masaryk, the founder of the Czech state, had insisted on having the area, arguing that Bohemia and Moravia were a historical and economic unit and should not be broken up. Moreover, a border drawn strictly along linguistic lines would have been impossible.

The Sudeten Germans received better treatment at the hands of the Prague government than most ethnic minorities in Eastern Europe. After 1933, however, Nazi agents, led by Konrad Henlein (1898–1945), worked feverishly to arouse German sentiment and to push for an autonomous Sudetenland independent of Czechoslovakia. Nevertheless, most Czechs, including President Eduard Benes, knew that the real intention behind Hitler's rhetoric was annexation.

A week after the annexation of Austria, Henlein's followers inflamed the Sudetenland question. Consultations between Britain and France followed. The French, who were bound to Czechoslovakia by a defensive treaty, were prepared to come to Czechoslovakia's aid, but Chamberlain announced in the House of Commons that Britain would not commit itself to supporting France in such an event. Chamberlain was convinced that any effort to coerce Hitler would result in war. With support for this position within

Map 87.4 The Dismemberment of Czechoslovakia. Note the Sudetenland in the north and west of Czechoslovakia. Originally the term referred to the Sudetes Mountains, but it came to be used for those parts of the Bohemian and Moravian lands where German speakers predominated, which were included in the Czech state created in 1919. The Sudetenland was ceded to Nazi Germany at the Munich Conference of 1938 and restored to Czechoslovakia in 1945. It now forms part of the new Czech Republic.

the French cabinet, Premier Daladier agreed to follow Britain's lead.

In April, Henlein increased his demands for autonomy. When Benes refused, the Nazis erupted in open violence, hoping no doubt to provoke German intervention. Czechoslovakia partially mobilized. When Chamberlain actually warned that Britain might have to get involved, Hitler backed off publicly but ordered plans for a military attack on Czechoslovakia. In the meantime, Chamberlain sent a mediator to Prague to arrange a compromise. When the Czechs agreed to Henlein's demands, the Nazi leader broke off the talks. On September 15, a distraught Chamberlain boarded a plane—the first time in his life—and flew to Berchtesgaden to make a personal appeal to Hitler. In a three-hour meeting, Hitler insisted that he would now settle only for outright German annexation of the Sudetenland and convinced the prime minister to join with France in trying to extract this concession from Prague. Chamberlain was undaunted, not understanding that he was about to be a party to the dismemberment of a sovereign state. He wrote at the time that Hitler "was a man who could be relied upon when he had given his word."

THE MUNICH TRAGEDY

On September 19, the French and British governments told Benes that he had to concede the Sudetenland, warning that they would not be responsible for the consequences if the Czechs refused. Without the support of the Western powers, Benes had no choice but to give in. Chamberlain flew to Germany again, this time to Godesberg on the Rhine, where Hitler now raised his demands still further, presenting the prime minister with a strongly worded memorandum insisting on immediate occupation of the territories in question. Chamberlain was wounded and disillusioned. On September 24, the Czechs mobilized and the French called up reservists. Four days later, the British Navy was mobilized. Chamberlain wrote to Mussolini and Hitler asking for a four-power conference to resolve the crisis. Mussolini convinced Hitler to attend, and the four statesmen—Hitler, Mussolini, Chamberlain, and Daladier—met in Munich on September 29. The Soviet Union was not invited.

The Munich conference was brief. The participants agreed to the terms of the Godesberg Memorandum, but now also to guarantee Czechoslovakia's borders. On September 30, Chamberlain and Daladier presented the terms of the agreement to the Czechs, who had no choice but to accept. Benes resigned as president.

When Chamberlain arrived in England that day, he held aloft a piece of paper on which he and Hitler had indicated that henceforth they renounced war. "This," he declared in one of the most haunting phrases of the age, "means peace in our time."

Chamberlain may have believed his own words, but he nevertheless embarked on a massive rearmament program for Great Britain. The end came with a kind of numbed disbelief. On March 14, the new Czech president, Emil Hacha (1872–1945), was summoned to Berlin, where he was subjected to six hours of continuous verbal abuse from Hitler and his entourage. When Hermann Goering, one of Hitler's associates, threatened to reduce Prague to rubble, Hacha agreed to surrender his country, and Hitler's troops carved up the remainder of Czechoslovakia. Chamberlain was stunned, and British opinion suddenly hardened against the man who could so callously violate a solemn agreement.

The Czech fiasco created a mood of fatalism in Europe, as both sides now began to prepare for war. Hitler clearly did not believe that the Western powers would act, and by the end of March 1939 he was already making it clear that Poland was his next target. A much sobered Chamberlain assured the Poles that Britain and France would protect them, and the next month gave similar guarantees to Romania, Greece, and Turkey. On April 3, Hitler secretly told his generals to be ready for an assault against Poland in September. Mussolini, who had remained an observer of Hitler's triumphs, invaded Albania on April 8. Britain introduced peacetime compulsory military service for the first time in its history. On May 22, Mussolini and Hitler concluded a military alliance that Mussolini dubbed the "Pact of Steel." The pact bound each partner to render assistance to the other in the event of war.

THE NAZI-SOVIET PACT

One more shock awaited the Western powers. The Soviet Union now controlled the balance of power in Europe. In planning for the attack against Poland, Hitler wanted to prevent interference from Stalin and thereby avoid the danger of a two-front war. Since the Spanish Civil War, the Soviet Union had suspected that the Western powers would not stand against the fascist dictators. Yet, while talking secretly with Hitler, Stalin also carried on covert negotiations with the West. He insisted that any mutual defense pact include guarantees for the Baltic states, but these nations feared the Soviet Union as much as they did Germany and would have nothing of it.

On May 3, Stalin appointed a new foreign minister, Vyacheslav Molotov (1890–1986), a man with a much narrower sense of Russian national interests than his predecessor,

The participants in the Munich Conference. September 29, 1938. The figures are from the left: Chamberlain (the British Prime Minister), Daladier (the French Prime Minister), Hitler, Mussolini, and Ciano (Italian Foreign Minister and Mussolini's son-in-law). One delegation is notable by its absence: the Soviet Union was not included.

Map 87.5 The Expansion of Nazi Germany. The first territory to be taken by the Nazis in peacetime was the Rhineland, which was demilitarized after World War I and reoccupied by German troops in 1936. The final blow to peace was the German invasion of Poland, in September 1939, which drove the Western powers into declaring war. At the same time, by the terms of a secret treaty between Hitler and Stalin, the Soviet Union annexed eastern Poland.

Maxim Litvinov. Because Litvinov was Jewish, Molotov's appointment was a clear signal to Hitler that accommodation was possible. In Molotov's view, an alliance with Britain and France would most certainly lead to war against Germany, but with little advantage for the Soviet Union. Stalin was interested, on the other hand, in reaching an agreement with Hitler to divide Poland, thus providing a buffer between the two countries. In talks with Molotov, the Nazis suggested not only that the Soviets remain neutral in the event of a German war with the West, but that the Soviet Union and Germany divide Eastern Europe between them.

On August 23 Germany and the Soviet Union signed a trade agreement, a 10-year Non-Aggression Pact, and a secret protocol. The news took almost everyone, including Mussolini, by surprise because communism and Nazism had been such deep ideological enemies for so long. The real import of the pact, however, lay in the "Secret Additional Protocol" added to the treaty. The protocol created spheres of influence in Eastern Europe. Western Poland and Lithuania were to fall to Germany, while eastern Poland, Finland, Estonia, Latvia, and the Romanian province of Bessarabia would go to the Soviet Union.

If Hitler hoped that news of the pact would frighten Britain and France into abandoning support for Poland, he miscalculated. On August 25, Britain signed a mutual assistance pact with Poland. When German troops invaded Poland at the beginning of September, the Western powers declared war.

Putting the Road to War in Perspective

From 1931 to 1939, the Western powers remained on the defensive against policies of aggression and expansion by Japan, Italy, and Germany. The repeated violation of the League of Nations charter made a shambles of the spirit of internationalism that

Continued next page

had spread in the 1920s and meant, inevitably, a return to power politics. In this circumstance, however, Britain and France were unwilling to see the outbreak of another world war and adopted appeasement as the way to avoid it.

That Britain and France were militarily unprepared for war as late as 1938 added an element of sober logic to the policy of appeasement. In retrospect, that policy appears more foolish and morally reprehensible than it did at the time. Yet in the atmosphere of reconciliation that began with Locarno, European statesmen had begun to accept German and Italian arguments that the 1919 settlements had been unfair. In negotiating with Hitler, Chamberlain tacitly admitted the justice of Germany's demands for union with Austria and the Sudetenland.

Yet Mussolini and Hitler were no ordinary statesmen. They did not believe in the sanctity of treaties or conventional notions of balance of power. In dealing with such men, Chamberlain and Daladier were at a supreme disadvantage in not understanding the ideological imperatives that drove them. After appeasement had given up too much and the dictators were still not satisfied, the realization dawned on the West that war was inevitable.

Questions for Further Study

1. To what extent were the origins of World War II to be found in World War I? In the peace conference?
2. What was the policy of "appeasement"? Was it a logical and credible policy in the 1930s?
3. To what degree was the Rome-Berlin Axis inevitable?
4. Did fascist ideology affect foreign policy? How do you explain the Nazi-Soviet Non-Aggression Pact in light of the ideological clash between fascism and communism?

Suggestions for Further Reading

Burgwyn, H. James. *Italian Foreign Policy, 1919–1940*. New York, 1996.

Caputi, Robert J. *Neville Chamberlain and Appeasement.* Selinsgrove, PA, 2000.

Carroll, Peter N. *The Odyssey of the Abraham Lincoln Brigade: Americans in the Spanish Civil War*. Stanford, CA, 1994

Chung, Iris. *The Rape of Nanking: The Forgotten Holocaust of World War II*. New York, 1997.

Davis, Richard. *Anglo-French Relations before the Second World War: Appeasemeny and Crisis*. New York, 2001.

Iriye, Akira. *The Origins of the Second World War in Asia and the Pacific*. London, 1987.

Kitchen, Martin. *Europe Between the Wars: A Political History*. London, 1988.

Klemperer, Victor. *I Shall Bear Witness: The Diaries of Victor Klemperer, 1933–1941*. London, 1998.

Lamb, Margaret, and Nicholas Tarling. *From Versailles to Pearl Harbor: The Origins of the Second World War in Europe*. New York, 2001.

Low, Robert. *La Pasionaria: The Spanish Firebrand*. London, 1992.

Preston, Paul. *Franco*. New York, 1994.

Robertson, E.M. *Mussolini as Empire Builder*. London, 1977.

Thomas, Hugh. *The Spanish Civil War*. New York, 1987.

Watt, D.C. *How War Came: The Immediate Origins of the Second World War, 1938–1939*. New York, 1989.

InfoTrac College Edition

Enter the search term *World War, 1939–1945* using Key Terms.

Enter the search term *Hitler* using Key Terms.

Enter the search term *Mussolini* using Key Terms.

THE SECOND WORLD WAR

The outbreak of World War II in September 1939 brought almost six years of unparalleled death and destruction. Hitler's armies rolled quickly across Poland, which he and Joseph Stalin proceeded to divide between them. Soviet forces then occupied the Baltic states and attacked Finland. Until the spring of 1940, however, no real fighting between Germany and the West occurred. The Nazi **Blitzkrieg** began in April, when the Germans smashed Norway and Denmark, and the following month attacked Belgium, the Netherlands, and France. By mid-June, France had fallen, and Italy had joined Germany in the war. When months of aerial bombardment could not induce the British to surrender to Hitler, the Axis (the alliance of Germany and Italy) turned toward North Africa and the Balkans and occupied both regions. The high tide of Axis power came in 1941, when Hitler began his assault against the Soviet Union and the Japanese attack at Pearl Harbor brought the United States into the war.

The year 1942 saw a crucial shift in the fortunes of war, as Soviet troops stopped the German advance and American forces struck back at the Japanese in the Pacific. But even while the Allies won some headway, the most horrible of tragedies unfolded: In Germany and the occupied regions of Eastern Europe, the Nazi extermination of the Jews began to take shape. By the end of 1942, the Allies had invaded the Axis stronghold in North Africa, and in 1943 Hitler's armies surrendered at Stalingrad. In 1943, Mussolini was overthrown by an internal coup, and the Allies launched the invasion of Italy. The Allied leaders—Churchill, Roosevelt, and Stalin—met for the first of a series of wartime conferences that determined not only military strategies but also the shape of the postwar peace settlements. In June 1944, the Western powers finally opened a second front in Europe by invading France. By the spring of 1945, Mussolini and Hitler were dead and the war in Europe was over.

The war in Asia came to an end several months later. The Allies began to advance in the Pacific in the second half of 1942. American and Australian forces slowly reclaimed the captured islands of the Pacific, and by 1944 U.S. aircraft were bombing mainland Japan. In August 1945, Japan surrendered after the United States dropped two atomic weapons on its cities.

World War II proved to be the most costly conflict in history, both in human lives and in material terms. In response to the tremendous suffering that the Axis powers had caused, the Allies held a series of tribunals in which Axis leaders were tried for "war crimes," and a new international organization—the United Nations—was created in an effort to maintain the peace so dearly won.

FROM *BLITZKRIEG* TO THE BATTLE OF BRITAIN

By late 1939, no amount of appeasement could prevent war. On August 11, the Germans informed their Italian allies that Hitler was determined to resolve the Polish question at any cost. Mussolini sought to temper German demands in order to prevent the outbreak of a general European conflict, but German Foreign Minister Ribbentrop declared unabashedly that the *Führer* wanted war, not compromise.

BLITZKRIEG IN POLAND

With the signing of the Nazi-Soviet Non-Aggression Pact on August 23 (see Topic 87), Hitler positioned himself for the assault on Poland: The Soviets had been neutralized and the Poles isolated. The Germans wanted to strike a quick knockout blow before the fall rains limited the effectiveness of their tanks. At dawn on September 1, without a formal declaration of war, the Germans struck against Poland. Britain and France went to war on September 3.

The Polish campaign was the first demonstration of the new German strategy known as *Blitzkrieg*, or "lightning

SIGNIFICANT DATES

World War II

September 3, 1939	World War II breaks out; *Blitzkrieg* against Poland
April–May 1940	*Blitzkrieg* in West
May 10, 1940	Churchill becomes prime minister
June 10, 1940	Italy declares war on France
June 22, 1940	Surrender of France
April 1941	Germany occupies Yugoslavia and Greece
June 22, 1941	Germany invades Soviet Union
December 7, 1941	Japanese attack Pearl Harbor
June 4, 1942	Battle of Midway
November 1942	Allied invasion of North Africa
February 2, 1943	German surrender at Stalingrad
May 1943	Axis surrender in North Africa
June 1943	Allied invasion of Sicily
July 5–12, 1943	Battle of Kursk
July 25, 1943	Coup against Mussolini
September 1943	Allied invasion of Italy; Italian armistice with Allies
June 6, 1944	Normandy invasion
February 1945	Yalta conference
April 28–30, 1945	Mussolini shot and Hitler commits suicide
May 7, 1945	Surrender of Germany
July–August 1945	Potsdam conference
August 6, 1945	Atomic bomb destroys Hiroshima
August 14, 1945	Japan surrenders

war." *Blitzkrieg* was the brainchild of Heinz Guderian (1886–1954), a German officer who had experienced the senseless war of attrition on the Western front during World War I. In 1933, Guderian won Hitler over to the idea that the outcome of the next European war would be determined by a combination of rapid-moving, heavily armed armored tanks, supported by aircraft and motorized infantry units. *Blitzkrieg* involved the close coordination of these three kinds of forces. The armored tank (*Panzer*) divisions would drive wedges into the enemy's territory and rapidly cut off its troops from behind. The *Luftwaffe* (air force) would simultaneously destroy the enemy's air force before turning against its communications system and infantry troops. The German motorized infantry, moving behind the *Panzers*, would then secure the overrun territory while the tanks continued to press forward. When the regular infantry had moved up, the motorized troops would rejoin the *Panzers*.

Panzer divisions under the command of Guderian pushed through Poland ahead of the mobilized units and foot infantry. German dive bombers, called *Stukas*, assaulted civilians not only with bombs and machine guns, but also with shrill sirens that struck terror in their victims. Polish military forces lacked modern military equipment, especially tanks, heavy artillery, and transportation units. Hitler's *Luftwaffe* had 10 times more operational planes than the Polish Air Force, and Poland's 39 divisions were no match for Germany's 60 divisions. After a few days, the Germans broke through Polish lines. On September 17, the Soviet Union invaded Poland from the east in conformity with the intent of the Nazi-Soviet Pact and overran the rest of the country.

Warsaw was surrounded by German armies and on September 25, Hitler ordered his bombers to reduce the city to ruins. The capital surrendered on September 27. The next day Ribbentrop and Soviet Foreign Minister Molotov met to partition Polish territory. The Soviet Union occupied a little more than half the country, including one-third of the population, while Germany took the bulk of the population and the core of the industrial and farming regions. The western half of the German area was annexed into the Reich along with Danzig, thus pushing the frontiers beyond Germany's 1914 borders. The rest was placed under Nazi occupation as the "Government General" of Poland. Poland ceased to exist as an independent nation. General Wladyslaw Sikorski (1881–1943) formed a new Polish government, first in France and then in London, the first of many such governments in exile.

THE FALL OF WESTERN EUROPE

While the *Blitzkrieg* ravaged Poland in the East, a strange, tension-filled peace known as the "Phony War" prevailed in the West. Hitler, planning to attack Western Europe in the fall of 1939, had moved his troops from Poland to the Western frontiers in October but did not order them into battle. Leading German generals believed that an all-out war with the West at that moment was premature. Bad weather and the capture of German military plans by

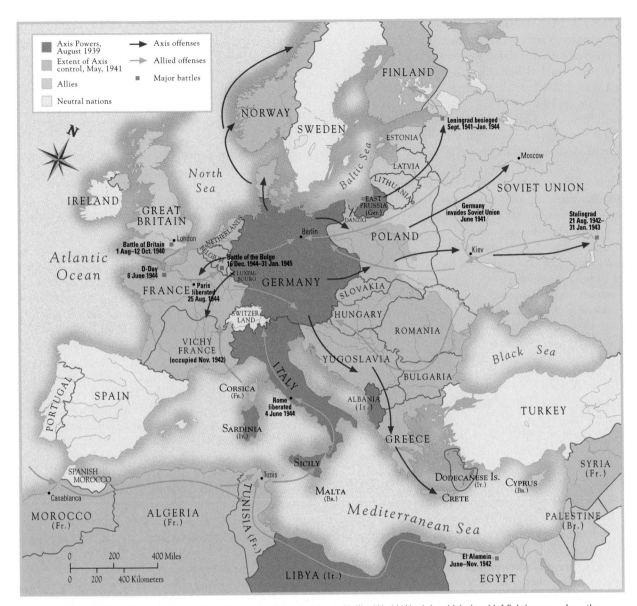

Map 88.1 The Second World War, Europe and North Africa. Unlike World War I, in which the chief fighting was along the French-German border and in Russia, World War II involved virtually the whole of Europe and spilled over into North Africa—and of course, with the Japanese entry, was to involve much of the rest of the world (see Map 88.3). Note the neutral countries. Hitler and Mussolini had expected Spain to join the Axis Powers, in return for the assistance they had provided him, but both Spain and Portugal remained neutral. Republican Irish hostility toward Britain kept them out of active participation, while Turkey, although pro-Allies, had suffered too much damage by participating in World War I. Go to http://info.wadsworth.com/053461065X for an interactive version of this map.

Belgian authorities in January 1940 caused a delay in the attack until the spring.

French military leaders expected that their defense system would suffice to ward off any German attack. This Maginot Line consisted of an intricate system of fixed fortifications, built in the 1930s, that ran from the Swiss border northward to where Luxembourg and Belgium joined. Its weakness lay in the fact that it gave the French a false sense of security that retarded military modernization. In any case, a German attack was likely to come through Belgium. British Prime Minister Chamberlain, still hoping for a negotiated settlement, doubted that Hitler would attack in the West. Instead, he believed that the German economy would collapse under the stress of a major war and instituted, together with the French, a naval blockade. Unlike the blockade imposed during World War I, this one did not prove effective because of a far-reaching economic agreement between Berlin and Moscow that provided Germany with essential resources such as oil, grain, and rubber. The British used the respite provided by the Phony War to build up their air force.

Stunned by Hitler's overwhelming victory in Poland, Stalin began to worry about Soviet security and tried to create a buffer zone between his own country and Germany. By mid-October 1939, he had forced Latvia and Estonia to accept Soviet bases and soldiers on their territories. When the Finnish government refused to grant similar concessions, the Soviets attacked Finland in late November. This so-called Winter War lasted longer than Stalin anticipated, requiring the use of some 45 divisions to crush the stubborn Finnish resistance. Only in March 1940 did the Soviets finally force an armistice, whereby Finland conceded extensive territories and military bases.

The Allies had seriously considered sending help to the Finns, largely because they worried that the mines and strategic location of Scandinavia might make the region a target of German operations. At the beginning of April, Hitler's armies quickly invaded and overran Denmark, whose 15,000-man army collapsed after a day of fighting. Geography made Norway more difficult to take, and the Allies landed troops there to assist the Norwegians. After several weeks, however, Norway fell, and Hitler set up a collaborationist regime under the leadership of Vidkun Quisling (1887–1945), a name that became identified with treason.

With Scandinavia secured, Hitler turned next to the Low Countries. The long-awaited war against the West began on May 10 with the invasion of Belgium, the Netherlands, and Luxembourg. In terms of troop numbers, the Allies actually had some superiority. Germany had 136 divisions (42 of which were held in reserve), while the Allies counted 144 divisions—101 French (36 involved in the Maginot Line defense), 11 British, 22 Belgian, and 10 Dutch. The Allies also had more tanks, although the Germans concentrated theirs in armored divisions while the French dispersed them. Similarly, the French actually possessed 4,360 aircraft to Germany's 3,270, but French air strategy had been so inadequate that when Hitler attacked they could put only one-fourth of their planes in the air. The French proved indecisive against Hitler's *Blitzkrieg*, but the country's premier, Paul Reynaud (1878–1966), was a strong-willed leader who had warned repeatedly that France needed to adopt modern military strategies.

The capture of secret German documents in 1939 was partially responsible for Hitler's decision to adopt an entirely new plan for the assault against Western Europe. The original plan provided for a heavy concentration of strength in a northern spearhead to push through the Netherlands, Belgium, and northern France, while a support group moved through southern Belgium and Luxembourg. The revised plan, designed to overcome the possibility of stalemate similar to that of World War I, called for making the southern force the armored spearhead of the assault. Once the southern army group had broken into France, it could push on to Paris, swing behind the Maginot Line, or—and this in the end was the decision—rush to the English Channel in order to cut off Allied forces.

Only in recent years has it become known that by the outbreak of the war the Allies possessed the ability to break the German codes. Before Hitler came to power, German engineers had developed an incredibly sophisticated coding machine known as Enigma, capable of creating literally billions of different coding patterns. When the Germans attempted to deliver an Enigma machine to their embassy in Warsaw, Polish intelligence agents intercepted it and, unknown to the Germans, had it reproduced. The Poles then discovered how the machines operated and in July 1939 turned copies of Enigma over to the French and British. Tragically, the French failed to exploit Enigma; although it provided numerous deciphered German messages concerning the new invasion strategy, the generals remained convinced by the documents captured in 1939 that the original attack plan was still operative. The British, on the other hand, created a top-secret intelligence network, known as Ultra, that monitored and decoded Enigma messages throughout the war.

The recast invasion plan worked brilliantly. When British and French forces entered Belgium, they were quickly outflanked and the Germans broke through the French lines at Sedan on May 13. "We are beaten," a tearful Reynaud telephoned to British Prime Minister Winston S. Churchill (1874–1965), who had replaced Chamberlain the very day the German attack began. A week later, Guderian's swiftly moving armored divisions reached the English Channel in order to encircle the Allies between the two converging German armies. The British Expeditionary Force retreated quickly to the French Channel ports of Boulogne, Calais, and Dunkirk, from where they hoped to evacuate. Guderian drove toward the same destination, but just as he reached the outskirts of Dunkirk he was ordered to halt. Despite the German conviction that such a massive escape was not possible, on May 26, 338,000 Allied soldiers began leaving France. Although Dunkirk proved an amazing success as an evacuation operation, it symbolized an unprecedented military defeat for the British.

Reynaud reorganized his government, appointing General Maxim Weygand (1867–1965) as military commander and the venerable Marshal Henri Pétain (1856–1951) as vice-premier. Neither man, however, believed that France could be saved, although Weygand was at least determined to fight to the last. After Dunkirk, the Germans made rapid headway. On June 5, they sent 95 divisions across northern France, with one spearhead driving into Normandy and the other toward Paris.

When Mussolini joined Hitler in the Pact of Steel in May 1938, the dictators bound themselves to provide each other with total assistance in the event of war. But Mussolini had informed the Germans that Italy would not be prepared for full-scale war until 1943, and had, therefore, remained neutral in 1939. The dazzling success of Hitler's *Blitzkrieg* shocked the *Duce* into acting, lest the war end before Italy could claim a part in the victory. Mussolini declared war on France on June 10, 1940. In the meantime, Paris fell to the Germans on June 14 and the government, which fled south, grew deeply divided over whether to continue to resist. Reynaud proposed fighting from French possessions in North Africa, but Weygand and Pétain secured the cabinet's support to sue for an armistice. Pétain took Reynaud's place as premier on July 16. While he awaited Hitler's response to his request for peace terms, the

The French Prime Minister in the Vichy government, Pierre Laval (on the right) and Marshal Henri Pétain. 1940. Pétain was 84 when this picture was taken and one of the French heroes of World War I; he was in charge of the defense of Verdun in 1916. He became head of the Vichy government. In 1945 he was tried for treason and sentenced to life imprisonment, dying in 1951. Laval was also tried and shot.

Germans pushed deeper into France and Mussolini's armies attacked in the southeast.

Hitler demanded severe terms for an armistice, which he insisted be signed on the same site in Compiègne, northeast of Paris, where the Allies had forced terms on Germany in 1918. The document, executed on June 22, 1940, provided for German occupation of two-thirds of France, comprising the north and central portions of the country and the city of Paris. Alsace-Lorraine was given to Germany for the second time in less than a century. The remaining southern third of French territory, together with the colonial empire, continued to be headed by Pétain, whose government ruled from Vichy in collaboration with the German authorities. The Third Republic, founded in the wake of the Prussian victory of 1871, thus came to an ignominious end.

While Pétain headed a rump state in the name of the humiliated French, national honor was kept alive by General Charles de Gaulle (1890–1970), the undersecretary of war who opposed both the armistice and the Vichy government. De Gaulle had taught military history at the Saint-Cyr military academy, where he was educated. An advocate of tank warfare from whose books the Germans had learned some of their tactics, the strong-willed general had never been popular among his more traditional fellow officers. Refusing to recognize the armistice, he flew to Britain and appealed to the French people to continue the fight under his leadership. In London, he set up a government in exile, the Free French National Committee, and recruited an army of volunteers.

THE BATTLE OF BRITAIN

Germany's *Blitzkrieg* gave Hitler control over as much of Europe as Napoleon had once ruled. Victory was, however, not yet his because Britain remained still at war, although Hitler believed that the British had no choice but to make peace. The British rejected all offers of a settlement. Churchill, the new prime minister, was a pugnacious leader in the face of adversity, a brilliant speaker, and a tireless proponent of British national interests. Out of office for much of the 1930s, he had been a staunch advocate of rearmament and a bitter critic of appeasement.

Hitler saw no alternative but to force Britain into submission, but he recognized that an invasion would be virtually impossible as long as British air and naval power remained intact. Nevertheless, in July Hitler ordered his strategists to develop an invasion plan, Operation Sea Lion, to begin on September 15. Before the invasion could start, however, German leaders agreed that the *Luftwaffe* would destroy the Royal Air Force (RAF) fighter planes; bombers could then strike British ships, coastal defenses, and ground troops. Reichsmarshal Hermann Goering was supremely confident that his *Luftwaffe* could destroy the RAF and bomb the British people into surrendering without an invasion. Preparations for Operation Sea Lion were known to the British through Ultra reports.

Goering failed to appreciate the British spirit of resistance and overestimated the strength of the *Luftwaffe*. The two chief German air fleets consisted of 1,200 bombers, which lacked sufficient range and bomb capacity, and 280 *Stukas*. The latter, which had proved so effective elsewhere, were decimated by British fighters and withdrawn. For daytime missions, the German bombers had to be escorted by Messerschmitt fighters, whose range was equally limited. In all, the two German air fleets had 980 Messerschmitts of various kinds. Because the RAF boasted only 650 Hurricane and Spitfire fighters, its commanders insisted on keeping large numbers of their planes in reserve. Aircraft production soon increased significantly, however, and the British also developed a radar system.

After a month of preliminary bombing of British shipping, the Germans began to attack airfields in mid-August to destroy the RAF. During the Battle of Britain, RAF pilots engaged in intense combat with the *Luftwaffe*, losing more than 800 fighters but destroying 668 German fighters and 500 bombers during the first two months. On September 7, Goering began raids on London, but it was soon clear that the Germans could not destroy the RAF. Hitler canceled Operation Sea Lion in mid-September, although the bombing of civilian targets in Britain continued through the spring of 1941. The Battle of Britain cost the RAF 1,265 planes and the *Luftwaffe* 1,882 aircraft.

St. Paul's Cathedral, London, seen through the smoke of the German *Blitzkrieg* on the city. January 1941. Sir Christopher Wren's church, with its famous dome, was built where earlier churches had been destroyed by the Great Fire of London (1666). It was damaged by the bombing seen here, but rebuilt after the war according to Wren's original design.

© CORBIS

THE PARALLEL WAR AND BARBAROSSA

When it was clear that the Battle of Britain was a standoff, Hitler began operations against British forces in the Mediterranean. It was Mussolini, however, who forced Hitler's hand in campaigns designed as his own "parallel" war, but that the German leader considered merely a sideshow toward a much larger goal: the invasion of Russia.

NORTH AFRICA AND THE BALKANS
In September 1940, Italian forces in Libya invaded Egypt. The Italian thrust came quickly to a halt at Sidi Barrani, 50 miles across the border, where they wanted to build a supply base. In early December, British General Archibald Wavell (1883–1950), commanding half the number of troops but with double the tank strength, counterattacked. The British pushed the Italians out of Egypt and across the North African desert, taking huge numbers of prisoners.

The Italian defeat was so sweeping that it forced Hitler to intervene. He sent General Erwin Rommel (1891–1944) to North Africa with meager forces consisting of one light motorized and one *Panzer* division, information that came to Wavell through Ultra. In March, Rommel attacked, driving the British back into Egypt, but because his supply lines were stretched thin he could not move further. The war in North Africa had turned into a stalemate. In East Africa, however, the British won a clear victory, overrunning Italian possessions in Eritrea, Ethiopia, and Somaliland.

In October, while the North African campaign was under way, Mussolini ordered an attack against Greece—an ill-advised move taken against the opinions of his generals.

The attack deeply angered Hitler because it threatened German domination of the Balkans. The Italian invasion met with torrential rains, and the tough if small Greek army fought back fiercely. Italian forces suffered huge casualties as they overextended themselves into the mountains. Churchill also sent some 58,000 troops to help the Greeks. That April, Hitler moved to rescue Mussolini from disaster in Greece, while simultaneously invading Yugoslavia, and by the end of the month had conquered both countries. In late May, these successes were followed by a remarkable airborne conquest of Crete.

OPERATION BARBAROSSA
Even as the Battle of Britain began, Hitler turned his mind eastward to the Soviet Union. He had long regarded Eastern Europe and Russia as providing the necessary *Lebensraum* ("living space") that Germany required for the Reich to dominate Europe. For Hitler, the Nazi-Soviet Pact of 1939 was a temporary expedient. His long-range plans called for the destruction of Bolshevism and the seizure of Soviet oil and food resources. Once he had defeated the Soviet Union, he believed, Britain would be forced to capitulate. The invasion of Russia proved, however, to be a fatal error that eventually cost Hitler victory.

Convinced that Britain was near collapse and that the U.S.S.R. was too weak to stop him, Hitler told his generals in July 1940 to plan for "Operation Barbarossa," an attack on the Soviet Union. The generals shared with Hitler a gross misconception of the difficulties ahead and sorely underestimated Soviet military strength. The Germans assembled some 145 divisions along the long Russian front, while the Soviets had more than 230 divisions. Hitler disagreed, however, with the generals over strategy: The latter wanted to focus on taking Moscow, not only the Soviet capital but also an important industrial and rail center, whereas Hitler wanted to aim both at Leningrad in the north and the Ukraine in the south. In the end, Hitler approved an ambitious plan that consisted of three army groups, each aimed at one of the targets.

The invasion, which began a month later than scheduled on June 22, 1941, caught the Soviets completely off guard. German planes took off before the start of hostilities and within hours destroyed some 1,200 Soviet aircraft. The northern army group got to within 80 miles of Leningrad in five days, while the center army group captured almost 500,000 prisoners and was 200 miles from Moscow within a month. Only in the south, where the Soviets fought strenuously, was progress slower than expected. In mid-July, however, Hitler overruled his generals and weakened the center army group by shifting armored divisions to Leningrad and the Ukraine. In September, Hitler ordered the siege of Leningrad, which he intended to starve into surrender. The population suffered gruesome deprivations and huge casualties as it fought with the Soviet army to defend the city. Only in 1944 was the siege finally lifted. In the south, the Germans succeeded in encircling Soviet forces near Kiev and took 600,000 prisoners. At the end of the month, Hitler changed strategy again, this time ordering an all-out drive toward Moscow and a simultaneous push deep into the industrial regions of the Ukraine. Hundreds of thousands of additional Russian soldiers were captured along with vast amounts of material. As the Germans moved forward, Stalin had more than 1,500 Soviet factories dismantled and moved to the east of Moscow along with some 2 million workers.

The coming of heavy rains toward the end of October halted the advance of Hitler's armies, which had come as close as 40 miles to Moscow. German supply lines were in serious jeopardy when winter set in, but on November 15, Hitler and his generals began what they believed would be the final assault on Moscow; however, extreme temperatures, as low as –40°F, and heavy snows forced the Germans to stop. On November 28, the Nazi armies sustained their first setback when a Soviet counteroffensive in the south forced them to abandon positions. On December 5, Marshal Georgi Zhukov (1896–1974) attacked the German flanks north and south of Moscow, but instead of making a tactical withdrawal, Hitler ordered his forces to fight on. It was Stalin's turn now to make a serious error. He overruled Zhukov, who wanted to make an all-out offensive at the Moscow front, and dispersed the Red Army along all sectors, a decision that made it possible for the Germans to resist the counteroffensive.

Both sides suffered enormous losses, and the war on the Eastern front, like the war in North Africa, ground temporarily to a stalemate. The failure of the German attack against the Soviet Union resulted in a major shake-up of the German high command, and Hitler now assumed the role of commander-in-chief of the army. By the beginning of 1942, victory over both Britain and the Soviet Union had eluded Hitler's grasp.

THE JEWS AND HITLER'S "NEW ORDER"

Hitler's dream of creating a Greater Germany went far beyond any traditional thirst for territory. His aims were determined by the racial concepts that were the basis of Nazi ideology. It is difficult to say precisely what form Hitler's empire would have taken had he won the war, but Nazi policies in conquered territories suggest the fiendish nature of the "New Order" he hoped to create.

HITLER'S "NEW ORDER"

By the end of 1941, Hitler held sway over as much European territory as any ruler in modern history. In addition to an expanded Germany that included Austria, portions of Czechoslovakia, and half of Poland, his troops occupied northern France, Belgium, the Netherlands, Luxembourg, Denmark, Norway, Greece, part of Yugoslavia, and a vast segment of the Soviet Union. At the height of the war, Vichy France, Italy, Hungary, Romania, Albania, Bulgaria, Slovakia, Croatia, and Finland were allied with Germany. Moreover, much of North African territory was in Axis hands. Spain, Portugal, the Irish Republic, Sweden, and Switzerland remained neutral.

Map 88.2 The Holocaust. Note the closeness of many of the concentration camps to major cities: Munich, Warsaw, Berlin. The camps in Eastern Europe, although administered by the SS, used local workers.

According to Nazi plans, the Germans of the Third Reich were to be the rulers of the new Europe, and Germany its core. The so-called Aryans whom the Nazis extolled as the superior race also included Germanic peoples such as the English, the Scandinavians, and the Dutch, and Hitler hoped one day to incorporate most of them in Greater Germany. At first, Hitler allowed those Germanic states that he conquered to administer themselves, but resistance to Nazi occupation led to direct German control.

Hitler's attitude toward the Latin peoples of Europe, including the Italians, the French, and the Spanish, was mixed. Although the Latins were not in the elite Germanic category, Nazi ideologues argued that they had some Aryan blood. His admiration and friendship for Mussolini led him to treat Italy with special regard, and after Mussolini adopted anti-Semitic policies in 1938, Fascist theorists there claimed that Italians were an Aryan race.

Despite such gradations, the Nazis generally considered all non-Germans to be inferior, and some—such as the Slavs of Eastern Europe, who were low in the Nazi racial hierarchy—were thought useful only as a source of manual labor. The Third Reich regarded the populations and resources of other European nations as German resources. In occupied areas, inhabitants were conscripted into forced labor squads—more than 2.5 million Poles and Russians, for

example, were brought to Germany as forced workers and industrial equipment and agricultural produce were confiscated on a grand scale. By 1944, some 7 million foreign workers were eventually conscripted to Germany, where they were overworked and treated poorly.

Hermann Goering, who supervised economic policies in occupied areas, announced blatantly, "I intend to plunder, and plunder copiously." Occupation was generally more severe in the East than in Western Europe, where local populations were assessed for the cost of occupation troops but most private property was not actually confiscated. Policies were often confused because Nazi authorities such as the army, the SS (see Topic 81), and the Gestapo often vied with each other for control. Regardless of which Nazi officials ruled, however, their policies were harsh and brutal.

The most horrendous aspect of Hitler's New Order was its policies toward the Jews — policies that resulted in the planned extermination of millions of innocent people. This Holocaust, as the destruction of the European Jews is known, formed part of Hitler's original scheme; as early as 1922, he was outspoken about his intentions. In September 1935, the Nazis passed the so-called Nuremberg laws, stripping Jews of their rights as citizens. The systematic destruction of Europe's Jews began in the wake of the attack against the Soviet Union.

Jews from the Warsaw ghetto being rounded up. April 1943. The process of transporting Jews from Poland's ghettos had been speeded up in 1942. Those in the Warsaw ghetto, realizing that shipment east meant certain death, managed to resist by staging a revolt. Finally, in the spring of 1943 German troops, visible in this picture, invaded the ghetto and rounded up the survivors.

Some time in the spring or summer of 1941, Hitler made mass murder, which came to be known as the "Final Solution," official policy. By the end of the war, as many as 6 million Jews—three-fourths of all Jews in Europe—may have been murdered. The Holocaust also consumed others, including political enemies and resisters, gypsies, and homosexuals.

Nazi cruelty engendered resistance almost everywhere, although before the German defeat at Stalingrad, this was on a small scale and mainly led by Communists. In occupied territories active underground movements sprang up in opposition to German authority. Sometimes resisters engaged in symbolic acts of defiance, but more often they were involved in intelligence gathering, sabotage, and other meaningful acts that helped the Allied war effort. The attack against the Soviet Union pulled hundreds of thousands of additional Communists into the underground, and after 1943 resistance forces became mass movements, increasingly armed by the Allies.

In France, where the resistance forces were generally called the *Maquis* (meaning "underbrush"), several groups fought against both Vichy and the Nazis. In 1943, French resistance leaders unified them into a single National Resistance Council and a Military Action Committee, and by the time of the Allied invasion some 200,000 armed resisters were in the field. Yugoslav and Russian partisans achieved significant military successes, and hundreds of thousands of German soldiers were bogged down in antiresistance operations. After Mussolini was overthrown by a coup in the summer of 1943, the anti-Fascist armed resistance played an equally significant role in northern Italy, where perhaps 250,000 partisans fought.

Nazi victims did not all go to their slaughter passively. In Warsaw, the Nazis had herded some 400,000 Jews together into the overcrowded ghetto, where SS-Chief Heinrich Himmler planned to starve and work them to death. In the spring of 1943, however, Himmler tired of the slow process and ordered the ghetto and its inhabitants destroyed. A group of Jewish survivors, led by the youth of the ghetto, fought heroically against the Nazis for 42 days.

The Nazis tried to keep their crimes secret, but word began to leak out as early as late 1941, and by the following year the U.S. government knew about the death camps. Nevertheless, Churchill and Roosevelt decided that the Jewish problem would have to await the opening of a second front. Only when the Allies liberated the camps in 1945 did the full horror of what had happened become public knowledge. What made the horror even more difficult to comprehend was the fact that so many millions of human beings were destroyed with careful deliberation and according to scientific principles by a state whose people had otherwise made such significant contributions to the civilization of Europe.

AMERICAN INTERVENTION AND THE WAR IN ASIA

While the war raged for two years in Europe, the United States maintained a guarded neutrality. Isolationism remained deeply rooted in American public opinion. In 1935 Congress passed a law that ensured U.S. neutrality during Mussolini's invasion of Ethiopia, and in 1937 an even

Piles of corpses in a trench at Belsen concentration camp. 1945. The soldiers are from the Allied forces that liberated the camps. Some 115,000 people—mostly Jews—were killed at the camp, named after the nearby German village of Belsen, in Lower Saxony.

AKG London

Perspectives from the Past

The Destruction of the European Jews

The most horrendous aspect of Hitler's New Order was its policies toward the Jews—policies that resulted in the planned extermination of millions of innocent people. This Holocaust, as the destruction of the European Jews is known, made an already gruesome and inhumane war even more terrible.

Hitler's Plans for the Jews

Hitler's anti-Semitism had been one of the principal forces in his early development (see Topic 81). During his rise to power he made the "Jewish question" a central issue of the Nazi platform. Although he did not explain the exact nature of his plans for the Jews, he did talk of creating a Germany free of Jews. In an interview as early as 1922, he was outspoken about what he would do once he took full power.

His eyes no longer saw me but instead bore past me and off into empty space; his explanations grew increasingly voluble until he fell into a kind of paroxysm that ended with his shouting, as if to a whole public gathering: "Once I really am in power, my first and foremost task will be the annihilation of the Jews. As soon as I have the power to do so, I will have gallows built in rows—at the Marienplatz in Munich, for example—as many as traffic allows. Then the Jews will be hanged indiscriminately, and they will remain hanging until they stink; they will hang there as long as the principles of hygiene permit. As soon as they have been untied, the next batch will be strung up, and so on down the line, until the last Jew in Munich has been exterminated. Other cities will follow suit, precisely in this fashion, until all Germany has been completely cleansed of Jews."

Quoted in Gerald Fleming, *Hitler and the Final Solution.* University of California Press. Copyright © 1984.

An Eyewitness Account

Here is the terrible testimony of Mrs. Rivka Yosselevscka, who as a young girl survived one of the innumerable episodes of killings in Russia.

When it came to our turn, our father was beaten. We prayed, we begged with my father to undress, but he would not undress, he wanted to keep his underclothes. . . .

Then they tore the clothing off the old man and he was shot. I saw it with my own eyes. And then they took my mother, and she said, let us go before her; but they caught mother and shot her too; and then there was my grandmother, my father's mother, standing there; she was eighty years old and she had two children in her arms. And then there was my father's sister. She also had children in her arms and she was shot on the spot with the babies in her arms. . . .

And finally my turn came. There was my younger sister, and she wanted to leave; she prayed with the Germans; she asked to run, naked; she went up to the Germans with one of her friends; they were embracing each other; and she asked to be spared, standing there naked. He looked into her eyes and shot the two of them. . . . Then my second sister was shot and then my turn did come. . . .

We were already facing the grave. The German asked "Who do you want me to shoot first?" I did not answer. I felt him take the child from my arms. The child cried out and was shot immediately. And then he aimed at me. First he held on to my hair and turned my head around; I stayed standing; I heard a shot, but I continued to stand and then he turned my head again and he aimed the revolver at me and ordered me to watch and then turned my head around and shot at me. Then I fell to the ground into the pit amongst the bodies; but I felt nothing. The moment I did feel I felt a sort of heaviness. . . . Then I felt that I was choking; people falling over me. I tried to move and felt that I was alive and that I could rise. I was strangling. I heard the shots and I was praying for another bullet to put an end to my suffering, but I continued to move about. I felt that I was choking, strangling, but I tried to save myself, to find some air to breathe, and then I felt that I was climbing towards the top of the grave above the bodies. I rose, and I felt bodies pulling at me with their hands, biting at my legs, pulling me down, down. And yet with my last strength I came up on top of the grave, and when I did I did not know the place, so many bodies were lying all over, dead people; I wanted to see the end of this stretch of dead bodies but I could not. It was impossible. They were lying, all dying; suffering; not all of them dead, but in their last sufferings; naked; shot, but not dead. Children crying "Mother," "Father". . . .

From the English transcript of the Eichmann trial, May 8, 1961, as reproduced in Raul Hilberg, ed., *Documents of Destruction: Germany and Jewry 1933–1945.* Copyright © 1971, Raul Hilberg.

The Final Solution

At the end of July 1941, Hermann Goering sent the following order to Heydrich:

Complementing the task already assigned to you in the decree of January 24, 1939, to undertake, by emigration or evacuation, a solution of the Jewish question as advantageous as possible under the conditions at the time, I hereby charge you with making all necessary organizational, functional, and material preparations for a complete solution of the Jewish question in the German sphere of influence in Europe.

In so far as the jurisdiction of other central agencies may be touched thereby, they are to be involved.

I charge you furthermore with submitting to me in the near future an overall plan of the organizational, functional, and material measures to be taken in preparing for the implementation of the aspired final solution of the Jewish question.

Quoted in Raul Hilberg, ed., *Documents of Destruction: Germany and Jewry 1933–1945.* Copyright © 1971, Raul Hilberg.

The Nazis established death camps in order to murder Jews in large numbers by rational, systematic methods. Camps were built in Auschwitz, Chélmno, Bełzec, Treblinka, and at numerous other sites. These policies were discussed and approved at the Wannsee Conference of high German officials in January 1942. The text of the discussion was carefully sanitized by SS officer Adolf Eichmann (1906–1962), who took the minutes.

Chief of Security Policy and Security Service, SS-Lieutenant General Heydrich, opened the meeting by informing everyone that the Reich Marshal [Göring] had placed him in charge of preparations for the final solution of the Jewish question, and that the invitations to this conference had been issued to obtain clarity in fundamental questions. The Reich Marshal's wish to have a draft submitted to him on the organizational, functional, and material considerations aimed at a final solution of the European Jewish question requires that all of the central agencies, which are directly concerned with these problems, first join together with a view to parallelizing their lines of action.

The implementation of the final solution of the Jewish question is to be guided centrally without regard to geographic boundaries from the office of the Reichsführer-SS and Chief of the German Police (Chief of Security Police and Security Service).

The Chief of Security Police and Security Service then reviewed briefly the battle fought

Continued

thus far against these opponents. The principal stages constituted

    a) Forcing the Jews out of individual sectors of life *[Lebensgebiete]* of the German people

    b) Forcing the Jews out of the living space *[Lebensraum]* of the German people

In pursuance of this endeavor, a systematic and concentrated effort was made to accelerate Jewish emigration from Reich territory as the only temporary solution possibility. . . .

The disadvantages brought forth by such forcing of emigration were clear to every agency. In the meantime, however, they had to be accepted for the lack of any other solution possibility. . . .

In lieu of emigration, the evacuation of the Jews to the east has emerged, after an appropriate prior authorization by the Führer [Hitler], as a further solution possibility.

While these actions are to be regarded solely as temporary measures, practical experiences are already being gathered here which will be of great importance during the coming final solution of the Jewish question. . . .

In the course of the final solution, the Jews should be brought under appropriate direction in a suitable manner to the east for labor utilization. Separated by sex, the Jews capable of work will be led into these areas in large labor columns to build roads, whereby doubtless a large part will fall away through natural reduction.

The inevitable final remainder which doubtless constitutes the toughest element will have to be dealt with appropriately, since it represents a natural selection which upon liberation is to be regarded as a germ cell of a new Jewish development. (See the lesson of history.)

In the course of the practical implementation of the final solution, Europe will be combed from west to east. If only because of the apartment shortage and other socio-political necessities, the Reich area—including the Protectorate of Bohemia and Moravia—will have to be placed ahead of the line. . . .

Quoted in Raul Hilberg, ed., *Documents of Destruction: Germany and Jewry 1933–1945.* Copyright © 1971, Raul Hilberg.

Eichmann rounded up his victims and used railroads to ship them to death camps in Poland, the largest at Auschwitz. After Jews were killed in the gas chambers, the Nazis processed all usable items, including clothing, gold teeth, eyeglasses, and even human hair, and burned the bodies in ovens. Here is a description of the first testing of gas on Russian prisoners by Rudolf F. Hess, commandant of Auschwitz:

While I was away on duty, my deputy, Fritzsch, the commander of the protective custody camp, first tried gas for these killings. It was a preparation of prussic acid, called cyclon B, which was used in the camp as an insecticide and of which there was always a stock on hand. On my return, Fritzsch reported this to me, and

stronger measure prevented the government and U.S. manufacturers from shipping armaments and vital war materiel to belligerents on any side of a conflict. On the other hand, President Franklin D. Roosevelt was deeply concerned over the dangers of Nazi-Fascist aggression in Europe and Japanese ambitions in East Asia.

THE CRISIS OF AMERICAN NEUTRALITY

A move away from neutrality first appeared with the Japanese invasion of China in 1937, when the Roosevelt administration came out openly against Japan. The president, in his famous "Quarantine Speech" delivered in October, asked that the world community oppose violations of international law. There was, he declared ominously, no escaping responsibility through "mere isolation or neutrality."

When war erupted in Europe, most Americans supported the Western democracies but still opposed intervention. Nevertheless, Roosevelt moved to strengthen U.S. defenses and to make America what he called the "arsenal of democracy." In November 1939, he persuaded Congress to repeal the arms embargo and permit the sale of war supplies to Britain through a "cash and carry" program—the measure did, however, prohibit U.S. ships from transporting the arms to avoid German submarine attacks. Congress also approved a huge defense budget and in September 1940 instituted the draft. After he had won reelection that year, the president introduced the Lend-Lease Bill into Congress; Britain was about to exhaust its financial resources, and the law, passed in March 1941, allowed the president to lend or lease arms, with payment to

the gas was used again for the next transport. . . . Protected by a gas-mask, I watched the killing myself. In the crowded cells death came instantaneously the moment the cyclon B was thrown in. A short, almost smothered cry, and it was all over. . . . I have a clearer recollection of the gassing of nine hundred Russians. . . . While the transport was detraining, holes were pierced in the earth and concrete ceiling of the mortuary. The Russians were ordered to undress in an anteroom; they then quietly entered the mortuary, for they had been told they were to be deloused. The whole transport exactly filled the mortuary to capacity. The doors were then sealed and the gas shaken down through the holes in the roof. I do not know how long this killing took. For a little while a humming sound could be heard. When the powder was thrown in, there were cries of "Gas!", then a great bellowing, and the trapped prisoners hurled themselves against both doors. . . . The mass extermination of the Jews was to start soon and at that time neither Eichmann nor I was certain how these mass killings were to be carried out. . . . Now we had the gas, and we had established a procedure.

Quoted in Yehuda Bauer, *A History of the Holocaust*. Franklin Watts. Copyright © 1982.

At his trial for crimes against humanity in Jerusalem in 1957, Eichmann gave this chilling explanation of his "moral" universe:

I did not take on the job as a senseless exercise. It gave me uncommon joy, I found it fascinating to have to deal with these matters. . . . My job was to catch these enemies and transport them to their destination. . . . I lived in this stuff, otherwise I would have remained only an assistant, a cog, something soulless. . . .

I thought it over, and I realized the necessity for it, I carried it through with all the fanaticism that an old Nazi would expect of himself and that my superiors undoubtedly expected from me. They found me, according to their experience, to be the right man in the right place. . . . This I say today, in 1957, to my own disadvantage. I could make it easy for myself. I could now claim it was an order I had to carry out because of my oath of allegiance. But that would be just a cheap excuse, which I am not prepared to give. . . .

To be frank with you, had we killed all of them, the 10.3 million, I would be happy and say, Alright, we managed to destroy an enemy. . . .

I suggested these words ["Final Solution"]. At that time I meant by this the elimination of the Jews, their marching out of the German Nation. Later . . . these harmless words were used as a camouflage for the killing.

Quoted in Gideon Hausner, *Justice in Jerusalem*. Herzl Press. Copyright © 1966.

---

be made after the war. That summer, lend-lease was extended to the Soviet Union.

Under Roosevelt's leadership, the United States inched its way closer to active intervention on the side of the Allies. In January 1941, British and American military officials met in Washington, D.C., to develop plans in the event the United States entered the war. In April and July, U.S. military forces took possession respectively of Greenland and Iceland, two Danish possessions in the North Atlantic. In August, Roosevelt met Churchill on a British battleship off the coast of Newfoundland. Despite Roosevelt's suspicions that Churchill was intent on maintaining the British Empire, the two leaders issued an important statement known as the Atlantic Charter. The document described a joint postwar policy that affirmed the right of all peoples to self-government, rejected any territorial acquisition as a result of the war, and called for the destruction of Nazism. For the United States, still a neutral nation, the Atlantic Charter represented a virtual announcement of war goals.

WAR IN ASIA

Japan, rather than Germany, actually provoked American intervention (see Topic 87). In September 1940, Japan joined Germany and Italy in a Tripartite Pact, aimed indirectly at the United States, that gave Japanese expansionism the endorsement of the Axis. Japanese leaders now took advantage of the war in Europe to build their own empire in Asia—one that they hoped would reach from Manchuria in the North to embrace all of Southeast Asia, including

Indochina, Indonesia (the Dutch East Indies), Singapore, and the Philippines. Japanese strategists, claiming that they would free Asia from Western control, conceived of this empire as the "Greater East Asia Co-Prosperity Sphere," a far-flung economic zone in which Japan's industrial and technological superiority would be combined with the vast resources and labor supply of East Asia.

In 1940, Japan pressed the Dutch government to grant trade concessions and forced the French to cut off supply lines to China through their colony in Indochina. The American reaction was to impose an embargo in July on the export of such items as steel and aviation fuel to Japan. Working against pressure from Japanese military leaders, Premier Fumimaro Konoye (1891–1945), a moderate aristocrat, began talks with the United States in 1941 in an effort to reach a peaceful agreement. When the German attack against the Soviet Union removed the danger of Soviet action in East Asia, Japan overran Indochina. Roosevelt responded by freezing Japanese assets in the United States and announcing a severe trade embargo, including the shipment of oil.

Konoye resigned in October and was replaced by Tojo Hideki (1885–1948), an army general who favored war with America. His colleague, Admiral Isoroku Yamamoto (1884–1943), commander of the Fleet, believed that such a war could succeed only if Japan destroyed the U.S. Pacific Fleet in a surprise attack. Emperor Hirohito (ruled 1926–1989) ordered that negotiations continue, while Tojo's cabinet decided on war if the diplomatic effort failed. In November 1941, Washington insisted that Japan withdraw completely from China and Indochina before it would lift economic sanctions. The Japanese considered this an ultimatum, and at the end of the month they secretly decided on war. The Americans, who had broken the Japanese diplomatic code, knew that war seemed likely but probably did not anticipate the assault on Pearl Harbor, although debate on the background to the attack continues.

The Japanese launched their surprise attack on the morning of December 7. The target was the U.S. naval base at Pearl Harbor, in the Hawaiian Islands. Hundreds of planes from Japanese aircraft carriers caught the Americans by surprise, sinking four of eight U.S. battleships, three destroyers, and four smaller ships, and destroying 160 planes. The United States, its military strength in the Pacific severely damaged, was at war.

Immediately after Pearl Harbor, the Japanese also struck against the British fleet near Singapore and the U.S. Air Force base in the Philippines. Japan overran Malaya, Burma, the Dutch East Indies, and the Philippines, campaigns made possible by its control of Indochina. Thailand was forced to let Japan use its military bases, and by 1942, Japan had seized most of the islands in the western Pacific.

The aftermath of the Japanese attack on Pearl Harbor, on the island of Oahu, Hawaii. December 7, 1941. The picture shows one of the 19 American ships that were either damaged or sunk as a result of the Japanese bombing, which also destroyed 188 U.S. planes. There were 2,200 American casualties, with negligible losses to the Japanese.

The Granger Collection

Japanese occupation policies were no less brutal than those of the Nazis in Europe because the Japanese regarded other Asians with their own attitude of racial superiority. By the beginning of 1942, Japan controlled most of East Asia, and its new empire appeared invincible.

TURNING THE TIDE: THE RUSSIAN ADVANCE AND THE ECLIPSE OF JAPAN

With America's entrance into the war in December 1941, the Axis powers now faced an informal alliance consisting of Great Britain, the United States, and the Soviet Union (the three powers were allies only in the European theater because the U.S.S.R. and Japan were not at war). From December 22 to January 14, Churchill and his chiefs of staff met in Washington with Roosevelt and American officials to develop a grand strategy. The two nations agreed that the defeat of Germany and victory in Europe would be the first goal, to be followed by the defeat of Japan. The Allies accepted two other essential points: a second front in the West to relieve the Russian war effort, and a cross-channel invasion of the European continent. The Anglo-American conference ended with a "United Nations Declaration" in which the 26 countries fighting against the Axis endorsed the principles of the Atlantic Charter, accepted the premises of the Anglo-American conference, and agreed to postpone political questions until after military victory.

The Allies disagreed over both strategy and broader political issues. The Americans believed that victory could be achieved only by a direct frontal assault on Hitler's "Fortress Europe" through an invasion of France. The British, however, feared that a premature landing there would spell disaster, and Churchill pushed for an attack against what he called the "soft underbelly" of Europe—either in the Balkans or in Italy. A compromise was reached, whereby the Allies would first seize North Africa and use it as a base for a campaign against the "underbelly," followed then by an invasion of France.

Strategic disagreements combined with political mistrust because each of the three leaders came from a totally different political background. Stalin, a lifelong communist, worried that the two Western statesmen were intent on keeping the Soviet Union from sharing in the postwar settlement and from expanding into Eastern Europe. Even Roosevelt and Churchill had doubts about each other—Roosevelt believed that Churchill was driven by the desire to extend Britain's empire into the Mediterranean, while Churchill thought the U.S. president naive about international politics. Nevertheless, the three men forged an alliance of convenience to defeat the Axis.

THE SOVIETS PUSH WEST

The fortunes of war began to turn against the Axis in 1942, in North Africa, Europe, and the Pacific. That fall, British

General Bernard Montgomery (1887–1976) won a decisive victory over Rommel's desert forces at El-Alamein. In November, while the fighting was still raging at El-Alamein, a joint Anglo-American army commanded by U.S. General Dwight D. Eisenhower (1890–1969) landed in Morocco and Algeria, and by May 1943 had captured all of North Africa.

It was in the Soviet Union, however, that Hitler suffered his greatest setbacks, the accumulated weight of which proved decisive. The *Führer's* decision not to pull back his forces in the winter of 1941–1942 proved crucial in draining his eastern armies. The Germans were fighting the Red Army on a front line that stretched almost 2,000 miles. Hitler then decided to abandon the Moscow campaign and concentrate his strength in a huge offensive in the south. The aim of this strategy was to seize the vital oil fields in the Caucasus. The drive began in late June 1942 by attempting to encircle the Soviet forces in the region where the Don and the Volga rivers flowed close to each other, near the industrial city of Stalingrad. The Soviets withdrew toward Stalingrad under the impact of the German attack, leaving Hitler to believe that the Soviet war effort was on the verge of collapse. Yet the strategic withdrawal induced the Germans into dividing their strength in pursuit of several different objectives.

As one German force made its way toward Stalingrad in late August, Marshal Zhukov prepared to defend the city. Stalingrad was important primarily as a symbol—Stalin was determined that the city named after him would not fall to the Germans, and Hitler became obsessed with the goal. After the Germans reduced most of the city to rubble, they and the Soviets fought desperately in street-to-street fighting that took a terrible toll on both sides. By November, the Germans held almost the entire city, a success won at the price of having exposed themselves along a dangerously overextended line. The Soviets, who had been steadily building up their forces, counterattacked, and on November 23 they surrounded the city and trapped the entire German Sixth Army as well as a *Panzer* corps. Hitler refused irrationally to permit a withdrawal; as the situation worsened and the cruel Russian winter set in, he ordered his troops to fight to the last man. Nevertheless, the remaining soldiers of the Sixth Army surrendered on February 2, 1943, the Germans having lost more than 300,000 men. Thereafter, the Germans would be on the defensive in the East. A major turning point in the war had been reached at Stalingrad.

Faced with a significant inferiority in manpower, the Germans were now forced to adopt a defensive posture involving carefully planned withdrawals at key points along the Russian front. In July, Hitler approved an attempt to eliminate a Russian bulge that extended into the German line at Kursk. Marshal Zhukov, whose intelligence agents learned of the German plans, prepared a defensive position. In the Battle of the Kursk Salient, July 5–12, the Russians outnumbered the Germans in all areas: 1.3 million to 900,000 men, 3,300 tanks to 2700, and 20,000 artillery pieces to 10,000. After a week of exceptionally heavy German losses, Hitler ordered an end to the attack. The

© Sovfoto

Stalingrad during the raging battle for control of the city. November 1942. The siege began on Sunday, August 23, as the German air force carpet-bombed the city. Hand-to-hand fighting, as seen here, continued in the increasingly ravaged streets until February 2, 1943, when the last German soldiers surrendered.

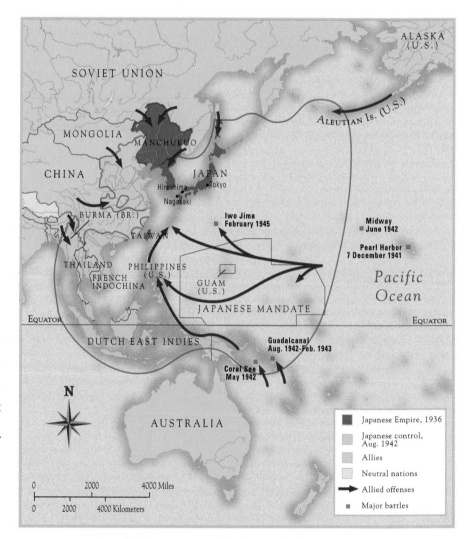

Map 88.3 The War in Asia.
With the attack on Pearl Harbor and America's entry into the war, Britain and America, together with Australia and New Zealand, were united in fighting the Japanese. The Soviet Union only declared war on Japan in August 1945, after the bombing of Hiroshima. After the bloody fighting in the Pacific islands and the Philippines, the Allies finally gained the initiative. Go to http://info.wadsworth.com/ 053461065X for an interactive version of this map.

Germans reeled under heavy counterattacks that fall, and the Soviets began pushing the enemy westward.

JAPAN ON THE DEFENSIVE

The Japanese position in the Pacific began to weaken in the summer of 1942, when American forces struck two major blows. On May 4–8, U.S. carriers stopped the Japanese advance toward New Guinea in the Battle of the Coral Sea, an engagement fought by aircraft from ships that never made visual contact with each other. Then, in June 1942, the U.S. Navy attacked a Japanese force approaching the American base at Midway, northwest of the Hawaiian Islands, winning a decisive victory that passed the initiative to the Allies in the Pacific.

The war in the Pacific became the primary responsibility of the Americans, assisted by Australia and New Zealand. Roosevelt divided military command between General Douglas MacArthur (1880–1964), the commander-in-chief of Allied forces in the Southwest Pacific, and Admiral Chester Nimitz (1885–1966), who commanded the rest of the Pacific theater. Together they began a costly strategy of "island-hopping," in which they retook the Pacific islands in a continual series of bloody invasions. Beginning in 1943 with battles in New Guinea, the Solomon Islands, and the Bismarck Archipelago, in 1944 they pushed northward, taking Saipan in June. In October, the Americans won a major victory at the Battle of Leyte Gulf in the Philippines, which struck a death blow to Japanese naval power.

In 1945, the Americans retook the Philippines, and in February Nimitz launched an invasion of Iwo Jima, a small but heavily defended volcanic island some 660 miles from Tokyo. Iwo Jima was taken after five terrible weeks of battle, followed in June by the seizure of Okinawa, which cost 12,000 U.S. lives. In these and other confrontations, the Japanese fought almost to the last man. During the Battle of Leyte Gulf, the Japanese also introduced a new weapon known as *kamikaze*, or "divine wind" ("Kamikaze" was the name for the typhoon that destroyed the Mongol fleet hoping to invade Japan in the 13th century)—suicide missions in which pilots deliberately smashed their planes into enemy ships. Despite the determination of its military commanders to hold out, Japan's naval power had practically disappeared, its cities were bombed and gutted by U.S. planes, and its population was on the edge of starvation. By the spring of 1945, Japanese authorities were beginning to probe the Allies for peace terms. The collapse of Japan was imminent.

YALTA, POTSDAM, AND THE DIVISION OF EUROPE

In January 1943, while the campaign in North Africa was still underway, Roosevelt and Churchill held a meeting in Casablanca, Morocco. The two leaders agreed to a cross-channel invasion of France in 1944, and chose Italy as the target for the "soft underbelly" assault in the Mediterranean.

THE FALL OF MUSSOLINI AND THE INVASION OF NORMANDY

On July 10, Eisenhower commanded an Allied invasion of Sicily, and its success led to widespread dissatisfaction among Fascist leaders over Mussolini's conduct of the war. On the evening of July 25, at a meeting of the Fascist Grand Council, a group of dissidents—including Count Ciano, Mussolini's son-in-law—voted no confidence in the *Duce*. During an audience with King Victor Emmanuel III the next morning, Mussolini was arrested. Marshal Pietro Badoglio (1871–1956) was named prime minister, a position Mussolini had held for more than 20 years. Badoglio opened secret talks with the Allies for an armistice. Hitler immediately sent German troops into Italy and around Rome in anticipation of an Allied assault against the mainland. In September, as the Allies made their first landings on the mainland, Badoglio signed an armistice by which Italy abandoned the Axis to fight on the side of the Allies.

Shortly before the armistice, the *Führer* sent a special mission to rescue Mussolini, who then set up a new Fascist government in northern Italy known as the Italian Social Republic (RSI). The *Duce* had little autonomy, however, because German military authorities made most important decisions. Over the next year and a half, Italy was cut in two—Mussolini ruled in the region north of Rome, while Badoglio and the king governed southern Italy.

In November, while the Allies pushed their way up the Italian mainland, the foreign ministers of the chief Allied powers gathered in Moscow. They again insisted on the unconditional surrender of Germany and Japan as well as the postwar occupation of Germany. The Moscow meeting was prelude to the conference in Teheran, where Stalin met for the first time with Roosevelt and Churchill. The three leaders agreed on basic aspects of "Operation Overlord," the assault against France planned for the spring of 1944, and Roosevelt announced the appointment of Eisenhower as supreme commander of the Allied forces.

The landings on the Normandy coast on June 6, 1944, were part of the largest sea-to-land operation ever undertaken. Within a week of D-Day, some 300,000 soldiers—three-fourths of them American—and endless supplies had landed and began spreading out through Fortress Europe. On July 20, an unsuccessful attempt on Hitler's life was made by army officers who wanted to make peace. Field Marshal Rommel, implicated in the plot, was forced to commit suicide. Paris was liberated on August 25, and by mid-September, Eisenhower's forces had advanced steadily, pushing the Germans to the borders of France. In December, Hitler ordered a powerful counterattack that struck hard at Allied positions in the Ardennes forest, but at the cost of seriously weakening the Eastern front. This Battle of the Bulge was his last important military offensive.

In January 1945, the millions of Soviet soldiers who were pushing westward overran Hungary, Poland, and Czechoslovakia and entered German territory. American and British forces crossed the Rhine in March, and over the next two months the noose tightened around the Third Reich.

THE END OF THE SECOND WORLD WAR

With victory in Europe in sight at last, in February 1945 the three Allied leaders gathered once again, this time at the Black Sea resort of Yalta in the Soviet Union. In a show of unity, they repeated what had now become fundamental Allied policy: unconditional surrender; the occupation, disarmament, and de-Nazification of Germany; and the establishment of the United Nations. The three great powers were already engaged in a struggle among themselves to win the peace and create spheres of influence in Europe. In this context, the controversial Yalta meeting has been viewed by some as a shortsighted capitulation to Soviet demands, but Roosevelt and Churchill had little choice. For one thing, the Red Army had reached Eastern Europe, Germany, and the Balkans at the time of the conference. Furthermore, the United States and Britain had already approved a democratic, capitalist government for postwar Italy without consulting the Soviets, and Stalin felt free to act with the same independence in Eastern Europe. Finally, Roosevelt felt he had to make concessions in order to induce the Soviet Union to declare war on Japan. Roosevelt and Churchill therefore agreed in principle to Stalin's demands that portions of eastern Poland be given to Russia and German territory be transferred to the new Polish state. For his part, Stalin agreed to the "Declaration on a Liberated Europe," a purposefully vague statement about free elections and self-determination.

Within two months of Yalta, the war in Europe ended. On April 25, U.S. and Soviet forces linked arms on the Elbe River. Mussolini was captured by Italian partisans and executed on April 28, two days before Hitler committed suicide. Admiral Karl Doenitz (1891–1980) became head of state and officially surrendered to the Allies. Berlin, the capital of the thousand-year Reich, lay in ruins, and Germany surrendered unconditionally on May 7, 1945. Roosevelt, who died on April 12 of a cerebral hemorrhage, did not live to see V-E Day—Victory in Europe.

Italian partisans patrolling Milan after its liberation. Spring 1945. Note that women were in the forefront of the undercover struggle against the Germans. A few weeks after this picture was taken, the body of Mussolini (he had already been shot) was brought to Milan and hung upside-down in one of the main squares.

Hulton/Archive by Getty Images

The war in the Pacific ended after the Big Three had held still one more conference, this time at Potsdam, Germany, in July–August 1945. Of the original leaders, only Stalin remained because the United States was represented by its new president, Harry S Truman (1884–1972), and Britain by Clement Attlee (1883–1967), who had replaced Churchill as prime minister. At Potsdam, the political divisions between the Soviet Union and its Allies surfaced openly for the first time, and some have seen in this meeting the origins of the Cold War (see Topic 91). Truman accused Stalin of having gone back on the promises made at Yalta by setting up communist-dominated regimes in Eastern Europe.

Also at Potsdam, Truman revealed to the other powers that the United States possessed a powerful new weapon, the atomic bomb. Scientists had been working feverishly on the top-secret Manhattan Project since 1942, and the bomb was tested in the New Mexico desert on July 16. That same month, although the Japanese agreed to all of the Allied terms of surrender except the deposition of the emperor, Truman approved the use of the atomic bomb against Japan, a much-debated decision. The president explained that he and his military advisers believed that the bomb was the only way to avoid massive American casualties during an invasion of Japan. Yet Truman may well have wanted to impress the Soviets with America's new power. At the same time, he could end the Pacific war before the Russians declared war on Tokyo and claimed the right to take part in a Pacific peace settlement.

On August 6, the *Enola Gay*, an American B-29 bomber, dropped a five-ton atomic weapon on Hiroshima, reducing the city to rubble and killing one-fourth of its inhabitants—almost 80,000 people. Truman warned the Japanese that another nuclear explosion would come if they did not surrender. The Soviets officially entered the war against Japan two days later, and on August 9, the Americans dropped an atomic bomb on Nagasaki. On August 10, Emperor Hirohito ordered his government to prepare to surrender and declared to his people that they must now endure "the unendurable" pain of defeat. Americans celebrated August 14 as "V-J Day," although the Japanese signed the surrender document officially on September 2 aboard the U.S.S. *Missouri* in Tokyo Bay.

The controversy surrounding the decision to use atomic weapons on civilian populations should be seen in the wider context of the saturation bombing of German and Japanese cities. The Germans had begun bombing London and other British cities in 1940, and by 1942 the British began to respond in kind: that May, hundreds of bombers struck against Cologne, leaving the city in ruins; the next year some 50,000 inhabitants of Hamburg were killed as a result of massive incendiary bomb raids, while as late as February 1945—six months before the dropping of the atomic bombs—British planes killed more than 100,000 civilians in Dresden. In Asia, American B-29 bombers began the large-scale bombing of Japanese cities in late 1944. The atomic bombing of Japan was the last, terrifying consequence of modern warfare.

Map 88.4 Postwar Europe.
The most obvious feature of the map of postwar Europe is the division of Germany into West and East, with the British, French, and Americans administering West Germany, and the Soviet Union controlling East Germany. The former German capital of Berlin, in the Soviet zone, was similarly split. A new West German capital was created at Bonn, in the British Zone. To the east, the Soviet Union maintained its control over the Baltic states (Estonia, Latvia, and Lithuania) and over Byelorussia and Bessarabia, the latter taken from Romania in 1944. With the reunification of Germany and the breakup of the Soviet Union at the end of the 20th century, this map no longer reflects current national boundaries. Go to http://info.wadsworth.com/053461065X for an interactive version of this map.

Since the Casablanca Conference of 1943, the Allies had demanded unconditional surrender from the Axis and the elimination of fascism. To ensure that history would not repeat itself, they forced a series of social and political reforms on the defeated enemy states, drafting democratic constitutions and implementing far-reaching changes in the educational systems. They also insisted on purging fascists and militarists from government bureaucracies. As the horrors of the Holocaust became widely known in 1945, the Allies decided to try the chief enemy war leaders and punish them for their "crimes against humanity." The Nuremberg Military Tribunal was the most famous of these trials. Among the most prominent fascist leaders, some committed suicide, while others were executed or given long prison terms. Hitler and Mussolini escaped the judgment of the victors, if not of history.

Putting the Second World War in Perspective

World War II was the most terrible conflict in history. Before it was over, perhaps as many as 50 million people had perished, nations had vanished, and the battles had destroyed property and economic life around the globe.

The great powers fought World War II as a "total war," mobilizing their societies and economies toward the single goal of victory. The war became the focus not only

Continued next page

of private industry and farmers, but also of ethnic groups, writers, the scientific establishment, the entertainment industry and filmmakers, universities, and every other resource that could be useful to the military effort. As in the First World War, traditional social arrangements were altered and some trends accelerated. Millions of men from all walks of life were drafted or volunteered to serve in the armed forces, while women joined in noncombatant positions or moved to fill assembly-line jobs in factories making munitions, tanks, planes, and ships. Rationing, wage and price controls, and government production quotas became the norm. The vast intervention of government in the daily lives of citizens required by this huge effort established the foundations for the welfare state that was to evolve in the postwar period.

Once again, as they had done at the end of the First World War, the winners put their hopes in the idea of an international organization to preserve the peace that had been won with such difficulty. At the Moscow foreign ministers' meeting in October 1943, the Allies had agreed to create a United Nations when the fighting was over. The new body, formally endorsed by 50 sovereign states in July 1945, took the place of Woodrow Wilson's old League of Nations, which had proven unable to prevent aggression in the years between the wars. But although the nuclear superpowers, not the United Nations, would dominate world affairs over the next half-century, Europe was to remember the harsh lessons of the past as it reshaped its future.

Questions for Further Study

1. What were the principles of modern warfare embodied in *Blitzkrieg*?
2. Can the Holocaust be explained historically? What in your opinion is the explanation?
3. What were the principal contributions of the United States to the outcome of the war? Of the Soviet Union?
4. What factors were behind the expansionist policies of the Japanese?
5. Was the use of the atomic bomb necessary and/or justified?

Suggestions for Further Reading

Axell, Albert. *Stalin's War Through the Eyes of his Commanders*. London, 1997.

Beevor, Antony. *Crete: The Battle and the Resistance*. London, 1991.

Costello, John. *Love, Sex and War: Changing Values, 1939–1945*. London, 1985.

Daws, Gavan. *Prisoners of the Japanese: POWs of World War II in the Pacific*. New York, 1994.

Fest, Joachim C. *Plotting Hitler's Death: The Story of the German Resistance*. New York, 1996.

Gilbert, Martin. *The Holocaust: The History of the Jews of Europe During the Second World War*. New York, 1985.

Hilberg, Raul. *The Destruction of the European Jews*, rev. ed. New York, 1985.

Jackson, Julian. *France: The Dark Years, 1940-1944*. New York, 2001.

Lamont-Brown, Raymond. *Kamikaze, Japan's Suicide Samurai*. London, 1997.

Lee, Cecil. *Sunset of the Raj: Fall of Singapore, 1942*. Edinburgh, 1994.

Loth, Wilfred. *The Division of the World, 1941–1955*. New York, 1988.

MacKay, Robert. *The Test of War: Inside Britain, 1939-1945*. Philadelphia, 1999.

Mazower, Mark. *Inside Hitler's Greece: The Experience of Occupation*. New Haven, CT, 1993.

Purdue, A.W. *The Second World War*. New York, 1999.

Reuth, Rolf Georg. *The Life of Joseph Goebbels, The Mephistophelian Genius of Nazi Propaganda*. London, 1993.

Tobin, James. *Ernie Pyle's War: America's Eyewitness to World War II*. New York, 1997.

Waller, John W. *The Unseen War in Europe: Espionage and Conspiracy in the Second World War*. New York, 1996.

Weinberg, Gerhard. *A World at Arms: A Global History of World War II*. New York, 1994.

Wistrich, Robert S. *Hitler and the Holocaust*. New York, 2001.

InfoTrac College Edition

Enter the search term *World War, 1939-1945* using Key Terms.

Enter the search term *Holocaust* using the Subject Guide.

Enter the search term *Hitler* using Key Terms.

THE END OF EMPIRE: DECOLONIZATION AND THE THIRD WORLD

World War II wrought major transformations around the globe, especially in regions that had been held in the grip of European domination. Nationalist movements for independence had begun to develop in some of the European colonies of Africa and Asia as early as the beginning of the 20th century. With the disruption of the war, and the resulting military and financial weakness of the great powers, the European grip over their colonial possessions was loosened.

World War II had been waged in the cause of freedom from oppression, and by 1945 Britain's new Labour government saw imperial domination as neither acceptable nor feasible. Involved in repairing the ravages of war and building a welfare state at home, it was not eager to invest resources in maintaining colonial possessions. India and Pakistan, the chief British colonies in Asia, became independent in 1947. Subsequent Conservative governments continued the process of decolonization, and most of Britain's West African territories were self-governing by 1960.

Postwar French leaders were less willing to give up their empire. Bitter fighting between French troops and nationalist guerrillas continued in Indochina until 1954, and in Algeria, France's principal North African colony, until 1962. In both cases the French finally negotiated a withdrawal. The struggle over Algeria deeply split public opinion in France and produced considerable political upheaval.

The withdrawal of the European powers from the Middle East was accompanied by the founding of a new nation there, Israel. The subsequent history of the region has been dominated by fighting between Israel and its Arab neighbors, together with feuding among the Arab states. The volatile situation was further complicated by the conflicting interests of the two superpowers—the United States and the Soviet Union—which were concerned to preserve their access to a region that contains about half of the world's oil supplies.

Elsewhere in Asia and Africa, former rulers struggled to maintain control. After several years of bloody fighting, the Dutch finally recognized Indonesia's independence in 1949. Alarmed by a series of riots in 1959, Belgium suddenly withdrew from the Congo, leaving a vacuum that plunged the region into a state of confusion threatening Western economic interests there.

By the late 20th century, European colonial holdings were reduced to a handful of small territories. One of the first indicators of autonomous politics among developing countries came when a group of nations describing themselves as "nonaligned"—uncommitted, that is, to alliance with either the United States or the Soviet Union—joined together in a loose association. The problems in providing aid to these countries were formidable, and the results were mixed. Furthermore, the collapse of Communist regimes in Eastern Europe in 1989–1990, and the subsequent Western efforts to help economic reconstruction there, threatened to divert resources from other regions of the globe.

THE LEGACY OF EMPIRE: COLONIES IN A CHANGING WORLD

The dismantlement of the European colonial empires in Asia and Africa was hastened by World War II, but long before the war, effective nationalist movements were developing in several countries.

GANDHI AND INDIAN NATIONALISM

The Indian National Congress party, founded in the late 19th century (see Topic 76), was led by Mohandas Gandhi (1869–1948), whose policy of nonviolent civil disobedience became an inspiration to liberation movements throughout the world. Born into a wealthy Hindu family, Gandhi studied law in London. He went to South Africa to practice and discovered brutal discrimination there against Indian laborers who had been imported by the British. In seeking to devise a strategy that would enable weak victims to overcome their oppressors, he organized peaceful protest marches and nonviolent resistance to police actions.

In 1915 Gandhi returned to India, where his emphasis on the spiritual values of nonviolence exerted a profound influence on sophisticated nationalist leaders and, more important, on the Hindu rural masses. His own austere lifestyle (he was known as the *Mahatma,* or saintly one) was combined with the organization of mass demonstrations, at which thousands of peaceful protestors surrounded government offices or lay down on railway lines. Gandhi was frequently arrested, but time after time public indignation, exacerbated by the Mahatma's hunger strikes, forced the authorities to release him.

In 1935, as a result of the demonstrations, the British introduced a new constitution, which extended the right to vote to 35 million people and provided a limited measure of Indian participation in government. Although Gandhi favored trying out the new system of government, more radical leaders, who were anxious to obtain complete independence, pressed for continued opposition to Britain. With the onset of World War II, and the refusal of the nationalists to support the British cause, Gandhi and others were arrested. In 1939, India found itself under British military rule and at war with the Axis through no choice of its own.

Although lacking a charismatic leader of the stature of Gandhi, nationalist movements elsewhere in Asia began to agitate for independence. In Indochina one of the chief organizers of the struggle against the French was Nguyen That Thanh (1890–1969), better known as Ho Chi Minh, the name (meaning "He who enlightens") he took in 1940. Like Gandhi, he was to play a crucial role in his country's liberation after the war. In response to popular demonstrations and rioting, the French introduced some reform measures, but made it clear that they intended to retain power. The Dutch authorities in their colony of Indonesia similarly tried to discourage nationalist uprisings, but their arrest of popular leaders only led to increased agitation.

AFRICA BETWEEN THE WARS

By contrast with their limited concessions to nationalist movements in Asia, the colonial powers in Africa showed few signs of relinquishing their grip. At the same time, however, the capital investment that had marked the early years of the 20th century, most of which went to regions north of the Sahara, had almost completely faded. Europeans seeking prosperity abroad after World War I continued to make for North America rather than the African colonies.

In the face of increasing political neglect and economic decline, Africans in many parts of the continent began to form nationalist organizations to achieve independence. One of the first leaders to emerge in North Africa was Habib Bourguiba, one of the founders in 1934 of a liberation party seeking independence for the French Protectorate of Tunisia. Although the authorities imprisoned Bourguiba and banned his organization, his campaigning led to Tunisia's independence after World War II.

Protest demonstration in India led by Gandhi. 1930. The Mahatma is visible in the center, wearing a white shirt draped over his shoulders and glasses. The campaign of civil disobedience, of which this protest formed a part, forced the British to call a Round Table Conference in London the following year, which Gandhi attended.

© CORBIS/Bettmann

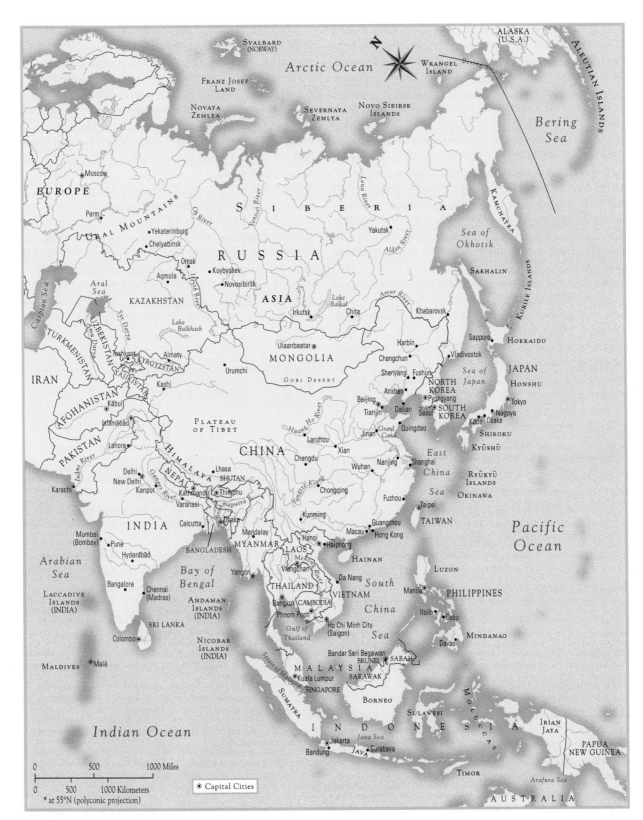

Map 89.1 Contemporary Asia. The map reflects the unification of Vietnam in 1975 and the continuing division of Korea. The fall of the Soviet Union brought independence to Kazakhstan and the other Central Asian republics. Note the location of Afghanistan, scene of much fighting in 2001–2002, where the fundamentalist Muslim Taliban government was driven from power. Peace in the region depends largely on international efforts to replace it with a stable regime.

In the European colonies of West Africa, increasing numbers of Africans were frustrated by their continued exclusion from political participation despite their Western-style educations. In 1918, the West African National Congress was formed to fight for the creation of national parliaments in the British-held territories. These new bodies would replace the existing legislative councils, which generally consisted of British civil servants with a handful of African "advisers."

African leaders in the French colonies strove to advance the cause of black African nationalism by demonstrating the richness of the African cultural tradition. Leopold Senghor (1906–1989), who was to become Senegal's first president in 1960, used both poetry and prose to expound the idea of *negritude*, a version of socialism that incorporates black African values.

The efforts of Senghor and other African intellectuals to promote the intrinsic importance of black African culture were reinforced by the development of similar ideas in the United States and the West Indies. The American William E.B. Du Bois (1868–1963) helped create the National Association for the Advancement of Colored People (NAACP) in 1909. His advocacy of Pan-Africanism stressed the common destiny of American and African black people. Marcus Moziah Garvey (1887–1940), born in the British West Indies, founded the Universal Negro Improvement Association (UNIA) in 1914. Two years later, he went to the United States, where he started UNIA branches in Harlem (New York City) and other northern ghettos. Like Du Bois, he preached pride of race and black self-sufficiency and planned a "Back to Africa" movement to establish a black-governed country in Africa.

Only in South Africa was there no overt sign of a developing nationalist movement. With the discovery of diamonds and gold in the 1870s and 1880s and the growth of mining operations (see Topic 76), unskilled African laborers began to live in "shantytowns" on the outskirts of the large industrial centers. By comparison with white workers, the black laborers, who were not unionized and underpaid, endured unspeakable conditions. Nonetheless, dependent as they were on employment by white mine owners, they were able to accumulate enough money to buy the consumer goods manufactured and sold to them by white South Africans. Thus the industrial development of South Africa created a black urban proletariat that was politically and economically under the control of the white bourgeoisie.

The white inhabitants, made up of the descendants of British and Dutch settlers (the latter known as Boers), retained complete political control and economic power. By the policy called *apartheid* ("separateness"), legally enacted in 1948, this minority maintained strict racial segregation, with separate and inferior housing, education, and public services for nonwhites. The apparatus of a repressive police state enforced the dominance of the whites. Although those of Asian descent received limited political rights, the black majority remained disenfranchised.

In both Asia and Africa, the end of World War II in 1945 brought renewed demands for national independence. After the years of fighting, most European powers were in no condition to resist for long. Given the importance of reconstruction at home, taxpayers were unwilling to see large amounts of money diverted to support colonial empires. In any case, public opinion, convinced that the war had been fought in the name of freedom and liberation, was less sympathetic to the notion of imperialism. Nor, after the experience of two world wars, could Europeans seriously claim a right to rule on the grounds of moral superiority.

Both of the superpowers encouraged the process of decolonization. The United States favored the granting of self-determination to European colonies, while the Soviet Union (and, after 1949, the People's Republic of China) provided help to revolutionary nationalists in Africa and Asia. Once begun, the drive for independence gained rapid speed: In less than 20 years from the end of the war, almost all of the European empires were gone.

THE DISSOLUTION OF THE BRITISH EMPIRE

The Labour government of postwar Britain, faced with the problems of reconstruction, and committed to implementing a massive program of domestic social welfare, was only too eager to avoid further conflict in India. One of the most divisive issues on the subcontinent was the rivalry between Hindus and Muslims, which led to violent rioting. The creation in 1947 of two independent states, a mainly Hindu India and a predominantly Muslim Pakistan, only exacerbated tensions. The following year, Gandhi's attempts to conciliate the two sides led to his assassination by a Hindu fanatic who resented his tolerance of Muslims.

BRITISH DECOLONIZATION IN AFRICA

By 1945, most British politicians realized the necessity of preparing the populations of their colonies for independence. In introducing advances in health care, housing, and sanitation, colonial administrators aimed at social as well as economic improvements. Educational opportunities were also enlarged. As early as 1943, Britain had formulated a scheme to set up universities in the colonies. By contrast, other colonial powers showed less concern for their subjects. Belgian fears that educational advances could be destabilizing led them to invest only in primary and vocational schooling.

The first British colony in Africa to win independence was Ghana, formerly known as the Gold Coast, because of the early coastal trade in gold. In 1945, its American-educated nationalist leader, Kwame Nkrumah (1901–1972), formed a mass political movement with the slogan "Self-Government Now." After a decade of strikes and riots, the British yielded to the inevitable, and Ghana became independent in 1957.

Ghanaian wearing a shirt with a portrait of Kwame Nkrumah, the country's first president. 1960s. One of the first generation of leaders in the battle for the decolonization of Africa, Nkrumah's rule in Ghana was overthrown by a military coup in 1966. Nkrumah then fled to Guinea, where he was granted asylum.

Two starving children in Biafra, the break-away Nigerian province. 1970. The rebels were defeated as much by drought and starvation as by the central government. Pictures such as this one did much to focus the world's attention on the terrible hardships under which many civilian Africans, especially children, were living.

The decolonization of other British West African possessions followed swiftly. Like many former colonies, Nigeria, which achieved independence in 1960, was subsequently beset by rivalries among its many tribal groups. Different cultures had evolved in the northern and southern regions of the country. The cultural disparity was compounded by both colonial rule and religious missionaries. In the north the Hausa had been converted to Islam by Mali traders in the 14th century, while the southern and coastal Ibos—Christians and animists—were affected by the fact that their territory contained Nigeria's colonial capital, Lagos. More involved with the British colonial administration, the Ibos were in general better educated and more active in their new country's government. In 1967, tribal hostilities led the Ibos east of the Niger River to secede as the Republic of Biafra. Only in 1970, after bitter fighting, did the central government manage to reincorporate the rebel province into the Nigerian state.

In the British colonies of East Africa, resistance by white settlers complicated the granting of independence. In 1965, as the tide of nationalism swept through Africa, the white government of Southern Rhodesia refused to grant black majority rule and illegally issued a "unilateral declaration of independence" from British control. Only in 1980, after years of conflict, international pressure, and eventually

negotiation, did the country become legally independent, under the name Zimbabwe.

In Kenya, the final years of British rule were marked by the rise of the Mau Mau, a secret society made up of members of the dominant Kikuyu tribe. The aim of the Mau Mau was to drive out the British and all other white settlers and set up an independent Kenya. After more than a decade of terrorist activity, the movement's aims were undermined by peaceful acquisition of independence. In 1960 Kenya became self-governing, under the leadership of Jomo Kenyatta (1893?–1978).

THE COMMONWEALTH

As Britain's possessions obtained their independence, most chose to retain a link with their former rulers by joining the Commonwealth of Nations. This free association operates without any constitution or specific treaty. Members are linked by common economic and cultural interests and, more broadly, by a shared heritage that includes the English language; they all recognize the British sovereign as symbolic head of the Commonwealth. Nations involved range in size from India (population 800 million) to the tiny Pacific kingdom of Tonga (population 95,000). Commonwealth prime ministers and leaders meet at regular intervals. Their conferences discuss issues of mutual concern and sometimes succeed in bringing moral pressure to bear as a means of settling differences.

The most intractable problem facing the Commonwealth was political repression in South Africa. Black resistance to apartheid was led by the African National Congress (ANC), which was formed in 1912. Throughout the 1950s, the ANC embraced both moderates and radicals, including Marxists, and pursued both political and terrorist tactics, organizing strikes and demonstrations against the government that culminated in the massacres by the police at Sharpeville in 1960. The authorities continued to refuse any form of negotiation with the ANC. They outlawed it and arrested its leader, Nelson Mandela (born 1918).

South Africa withdrew from the Commonwealth in 1961 over criticism of its apartheid policies. Over the years, various commissions of Commonwealth statesmen and resolutions passed at conferences tried to induce the South African government to dismantle its police state and introduce a democratic system of government. A program of economic sanctions was introduced, backed by the European Economic Community and the United States.

Bowing to continual international pressures, the South African government began a fitful dismantling of apartheid. Prime Minister F.W. de Klerk (born 1936), who came to power in 1989, began a new policy of tentative negotiation with the ANC and released Nelson Mandela, leader of the ANC, from prison. Economic sanctions by the Commonwealth, the European Community, and the United States seemed to play some part in encouraging the South African government to open the subsequent talks with black leaders. Tribal and racial violence persisted, however, allowing the authorities to maintain their authoritarian controls. Nevertheless, by 1991 most of the laws sustaining apartheid had been repealed, and in April 1994 Mandela was elected president of South Africa.

LAST VESTIGES OF EMPIRE

By the early 1980s, little remained of the British Empire except a few scattered possessions and nostalgic memories. In 1982, one of these last British holdings, the Falkland Islands in the South Atlantic, demonstrated the continuing allure of British imperial power. At the same time the Falkland crisis illustrated the use by the Argentine regime of nationalism and expansionism as a means of bolstering its unpopular dictatorship—a practice not uncommon in the Third World.

When Argentina's military government invaded and conquered the territory (it lies about 500 miles off the Argentine coast), renaming the islands the Malvinas, Conservative Prime Minister Margaret Thatcher sent British troops to drive out the Argentine forces and retake the islands. Her success in reasserting British rule over the barren, sparsely populated islands won her government massive popular approval. Her opponents claimed that the Falklands War was a cynical diversion to distract public opinion from problems at home. At all events, the mood of patriotism the war stirred up, enthusiastically endorsed by the press, was in the best—or worst—19th-century tradition.

By the early 1990s, the last British holding of any importance was Hong Kong, a Crown Colony on the South China coast. Hong Kong had been acquired during the 19th

Decolonization After World War II

1946	France creates French Union
1947	Partition of India and Pakistan
1948	UN votes to divide Palestine into Jewish and Arab states
1949	Indonesia becomes independent
1954	French withdraw from Vietnam
1955	First conference of nonaligned nations at Bandung
1956	Tunisia becomes independent
1957	Ghana first West African state to become independent
1960	Nigeria and Kenya become independent
1961	South Africa withdraws from Commonwealth
1965	Rhodesia declares unilateral independence
1967	Secession of Biafra
1975	United States withdraws from Vietnam
1978	Camp David Accords
1982	Falklands War
1987	Palestinian *Intifada* begins
1991	Gulf War
1994	Mandela elected president of South Africa
1997	Hong Kong returned to China

century, on terms that foresaw its return to Chinese rule in 1997. A major financial center, and one of the world's busiest ports, Hong Kong is a free trade area, while relying heavily on China for water and food supplies. In 1984 Britain agreed to honor the original agreement and hand the territory over to China in 1997, on condition that it would remain capitalist for 50 years and have a high degree of autonomy. In 1988, the first draft of the Chinese Basic Law for Hong Kong was made public; it suggested that China felt free to interpret "autonomy" as it saw fit. The early 1990s saw increasing waves of business and professional people leaving the colony for Australia, Canada, and the United States. Meanwhile, the British government wrestled with the problems, moral as well as practical, involved in denying subjects of Hong Kong (who were technically British) admission to Britain. At midnight on June 30, 1997, Hong Kong returned to China and the HMS *Britannia* sailed out of its harbor carrying on board its last British governor, Chris Patten.

THE FRENCH IN INDOCHINA AND AFRICA: THE AGONY OF WITHDRAWAL

Like the British government, postwar French leaders were forced to adjust their imperial ambitions in the light of the calamitous state of the economy. In the hope of maintaining some measure of control over their colonies, in 1946

France created a federation known as the French Union. Some of its members, however, successfully demanded their independence: Syria in 1946, Morocco and Tunisia in 1956. By 1958 the Union had become the French Community, a loose alliance of France, its few remaining possessions, and those African nations that formed French Equatorial and West Africa.

Yet in two places—Indochina and Algeria—French pride in imperial rule, coupled with a desire to efface memories of their disastrous defeat by the Germans in 1940, led to prolonged and bitter conflict. Both former colonies obtained their independence only after struggles that were fought not just on the field but also in French public opinion.

THE BATTLE FOR INDOCHINA

French suppression of independence movements in Vietnam, Laos, and Cambodia was encouraged by the United States, which was fearful of the spread of communist regimes in Southeast Asia. During World War II, Ho Chi Minh, the founder of the Vietnamese Communist party, had led the resistance to Japanese occupying forces. In 1945 he declared his country a republic, only to see it reclaimed by the French the following year. From 1946 to 1954 the French waged an increasingly bloody and hopeless war against Ho Chi Minh's Vietminh guerrilla forces, whose activities were aided by the support they received from the peasantry. The increasing casualties provoked growing protests at home. At the Battle of Dien Bien Phu in 1954, the French Army, besieged for 55 days, lost 15,000 troops to the Vietminh. Later the same year, at an international conference convened in Geneva, the French formally withdrew from Vietnam. It was agreed to divide Vietnam on a temporary basis: The Vietminh were to take the north, while Vietnamese supporters of the French were to move to the south. Within two years free elections would be held and the country reunited. The United States refused to sign the Geneva Accords, and over the next few years discouraged any attempt at reunification, creating a South Vietnamese state with its own government. The claim that this "independent" state was under attack by equally "independent" North Vietnam justified increasing American intervention, leading to the Vietnam War. Only in 1975 did the last U.S. troops leave Saigon, and the following year a unified republic was proclaimed.

THE FRENCH SETTLERS AND ALGERIA

With the rest of their former empire melting away, the French determination to hold on to their most important North African colony, Algeria, became increasingly grim. Nor was the issue only one of French national pride. The longstanding community of French residents in Algeria, faced with the possibility of losing their rights and property, became more vocal in urging the government to maintain French rule. Meanwhile, under the impact of growing terrorist and guerrilla attacks, French troops and their commanders resorted to violent countermeasures.

Back home in France, as governments fell over the "Algerian question," intellectuals and socialists furiously protested army brutalities and called for France to leave Algeria to the Algerians. By 1958, tension between army officers and the indecisive authorities was so high that a group of soldiers staged an insurgency and seized control of Algeria. Both government and rebels turned in desperation to Charles de Gaulle (see Topics 88 and 90). The French National Assembly invested him with extraordinary powers as president for a period of six months (in fact, he remained France's leader for 10 years).

Although the insurgents believed that the former general would be sympathetic to their revolt, de Gaulle moved quietly to dissolve the rebellion and began to promote the cause of Algerian self-determination. In January 1961, a referendum in its favor was approved by some 75 percent of French voters. Those army elements most implacably opposed to Algerian independence went undercover in the Secret Army Organization (OAS) and staged a series of

Khrushchev, Mao Tse-tung, and Ho Chi Min together at a banquet. 1959. This rare picture of the three leaders was taken the year before the "Great Break" between China and the Soviet Union. Ostensibly this break was caused by a border war between the two powers, but in fact it marked China's disapproval of the beginnings of Khrushchev's opening to the West.

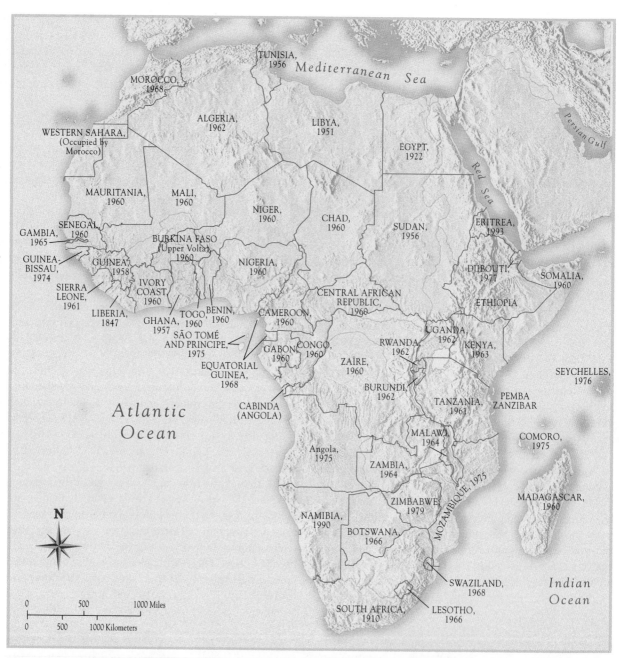

Map 89.2 Independent Africa. War continues to plague many of the continent's central regions. The Democratic Republic of the Congo (formerly Zaire) is the center of a conflict involving many of the other countries in the region, notably Rwanda, Burundi, and Uganda, together with a series of rebel groups. Peace negotiations in 2002 opened the possibility of hope both here and in Sudan, where another of Africa's most intractable conflicts has raged for decades, but the outcome in both cases seems doubtful.

terrorist attacks both in Algeria and in France. By 1962, however, de Gaulle's firmness put an end to the OAS, and Algeria was declared independent.

ISRAEL AND THE MIDDLE EAST

The Arab states of North Africa and the Middle East, many of which achieved independence after World War II, demonstrated a wide range of political perspectives and systems of government. Yet one characteristic united virtually all of them: implacable opposition to the founding and continued existence of the state of Israel.

THE FOUNDING OF ISRAEL

The Zionist movement was founded in the 19th century (see Topic 74), and grew rapidly after World War I. In the 1930s, increasing numbers of European Jews sought to escape the horrors of persecution by emigrating to Palestine, where they swelled the population of the *Yishuv*, as the Jewish community was called, to almost half a million—one-third of the overall population of Palestine. The British, under whose rule the League of Nations had placed

Israeli soldiers in the Negev Desert. Spring 1948. On May 14, 1948, Israel declared itself an independent state. The following day, Egypt, Iraq, Jordan (then called Transjordan,) Lebanon, and Syria attacked the new state, but within a month Israeli troops, including the ones seen here, had occupied most of the territory of the former British mandate, Palestine.

Robert Hunt Library

Palestine, resisted the settlement of Jewish immigrants there, as did the surrounding Arab nations. After World War II, mounting violence, and terrorist attacks by both Arabs and Jewish settlers, led in 1947 to a United Nations decision to divide Palestine into separate Jewish and Arab states of roughly the same size. Later that year, the British withdrew. Against a mounting swell of Arab hostility, in May 1948 the Jewish settlers proclaimed the existence of the State of Israel. The new nation's first task was to beat off an attack mounted by the surrounding Arab countries—Egypt, Iraq, Jordan, Lebanon, and Syria—which had refused to accept the United Nations decision. The Israelis' successful campaign, which left them in control of most of Palestine, ensured the survival of their state. At the same time, however, it created the problem that embittered future Arab-Israeli relations and lay at the heart of the unrest in the Middle East: the fate of the Arab refugees displaced by Israel's victory.

Refugee settlements were established, under United Nations administration, in southern Lebanon, on the West Bank of the river Jordan, and in the Gaza Strip. Over the following decades these camps continued to pose political and social problems, while also proving to be the breeding ground for Palestinian guerrilla and terrorist groups. Tension rose further when, in the Six-Day War of 1967, Israel won control of the West Bank and Gaza Strip territories, and thus assumed direct administration of the refugee settlements. In December 1987, frustrated by the lack of progress on the issue of Palestinian independence, and angered by Israeli plans for development on the West Bank territory, Palestinian Arabs launched an uprising, known as the *Intifada*, which won their case considerable attention in Europe and the United States.

ISRAEL AND HER NEIGHBORS
The general pattern of unremitting hostility toward Israel on the part of her Arab neighbors, exemplified by another Arab-Israeli war in 1972, was broken in 1977, when the Egyptian president, Anwar Sadat (1918–1981), traveled to Israel and subsequently succeeded, with the help of U.S. President Jimmy Carter, in negotiating an Egyptian-Israeli peace treaty; the agreement, signed in 1978, became known as the Camp David Accords. Apart from a brief reduction of tension, and the return to Egypt of some of the territory captured in 1967, the agreement did little to produce any lasting improvement in Middle East affairs.

The Camp David Peace Accord. 1978. The agreement was reached when U.S. President Jimmy Carter (*center*) brokered a negotiation between Israeli Prime Minister Menachem Begin (*left*) and Egyptian President Anwar Sadat (*right*). This triple handshake followed the signing. Like many later such "historic" agreements, Camp David brought little real improvement in Middle East relations, and two years later Sadat was assassinated by a group of Egyptian army officers.

AP/Wide World Photos

Relations with Lebanon, Israel's neighbor to the north, were further complicated by the fact that Palestinian guerrilla groups, notably the Palestinian Liberation Organization (PLO), were using the country as a base. In 1982, Israeli forces invaded southern Lebanon and succeeded in driving the guerrillas out. The result, however, was to produce even greater conflict in Lebanon, a country already racked by religious and political civil war. Multinational attempts at peacekeeping operations, including the sending of French, Italian, and Syrian troops, as well as U.S. Marines, proved fruitless; the international forces withdrew in 1984, and most of the Israeli troops were gone by 1985.

With almost 50 years behind it, Israel's future remained overshadowed by two apparently irresolvable issues: the refusal of most Arabs to recognize the country's right to exist, and Israel's own refusal, on security grounds, to surrender territory won in 1967. In 1988, Yasir Arafat (born 1929), the leader of the PLO, declared that his organization accepted the United Nations' resolutions recognizing the legitimacy of Israel; no other Arab leaders followed, and the Israelis dismissed the declaration as a propaganda move. As for territorial concessions, in the late 1980s Israel began moving in the reverse direction, by extending settlements into the West Bank area. With the liberalization of the Soviet Union in the late 1980s, and the revolutions of 1989 in Eastern Europe, Arab spokesmen began to voice fears that waves of Russian and other Jewish immigrants would prove permanent occupants for these new settlements.

Israel's problems were compounded by domestic political divisions. In the elections of 1988, support for the two chief political parties, Labour and Likud, was almost equally divided. The right-wing Likud party managed to put together a government that included support from conservative religious forces, making the prospects of compromise even more remote.

The upheaval of the Gulf War of early 1991, fought under UN auspices to free Kuwait after Iraq had occupied it in August 1990, produced some significant shifts in a situation that had seemed deadlocked for a generation. Hard-line Arab states such as Saudi Arabia and Syria seemed on the verge of following Egypt's earlier lead and recognizing Israel, while Israeli restraint in not responding to Iraq's missile attacks won general approval. Furthermore, American influence in the Middle East was sufficiently strong to allow the United States to play a significant role in working toward a settlement of the Palestinian question. Yet the problem of who would represent the Palestinians in any negotiations leading to such a settlement remained crucial. The PLO had backed Iraq in the conflict, and as a result it lost many of its supporters, not least among the Arab countries that had supported the mission to free Kuwait. In the confusion that followed the Gulf War, however, the Palestinians seemed bereft of any other spokesmen. Secret negotiations in Oslo led to a public reconciliation in 1993 between Labour Prime Minister Yitzhak Rabin and Yasir Arafat, but Rabin's subsequent assassination and the return of the Likud party to power seemed bound to set back progress toward peace.

BELGIUM, THE NETHERLANDS, AND PORTUGAL: END OF EMPIRE

The dismantling of the British and French empires presented a multitude of problems, but most political leaders recognized the irresistible force of nationalism. Other imperial powers were less willing to relinquish their possessions. The Dutch colony of Indonesia was occupied by the Japanese during World War II. At the end of the war, the Indonesian nationalist leader Sukarno (1901–1970) declared his country a republic. When the Dutch tried to reconquer it, they encountered bitter resistance. By 1949, they were forced to withdraw and recognize Indonesia's independence.

Belgium's departure from the Congo was equally violent and even more precipitated. In 1959, demonstrations there in favor of independence developed into violent riots. Within a year the Belgians were gone; the result was chaos. Whereas elsewhere in Africa the British and French had tried to prepare their colonies for independence, the Belgians had limited the education of their subjects and prevented any African participation in political affairs. The elections held in May 1960, a month before the Belgian withdrawal, were the first ever held in the country. There were no Congolese doctors or army officers, and the only teachers were at the primary school level. The number of African university graduates living in the country totaled 16.

Belgian financial interests assumed that, in the light of such complete inexperience, the citizens of the new Republic of the Congo would leave their old colonial masters in control. Instead the army mutinied; in the growing confusion the mineral-rich province of Katanga broke away from the rest of the country, encouraged to do so by Belgian investors. The Katangese rebellion ended in 1962, but the country returned to stability only in 1965, when Joseph Mobutu (1930–1997; later took the name Mobutu Sese Seko) led an army coup.

Mobutu's rule led to hopes for reform, which were at first fulfilled. The mining production of minerals increased, and the educational system improved. In 1971 Mobutu changed the country's name to Zaire, one of the names for the Congo River, as a symbol of the new spirit of "Africanness." Yet general poverty remained widespread; in 1988, the per capita annual income was $180, 10 percent of that in 1960, and the eighth lowest in the world—despite Zaire's considerable natural resources. Meanwhile, the ruling class became notorious for its corruption, and Mobutu amassed a fortune estimated at between $3 and $5 billion. The country's economic survival was assured only by massive support from Europe, the United States, and international financial agencies, which were anxious not to lose access to valuable mineral resources. Only in 1997 was Mobutu finally driven from power by an army led by one of his longtime opponents, Laurent Kabila. Abandoned by his former Western protectors, Mobutu died shortly afterward in exile.

No European country held on to its colonies longer than Portugal. Like the Belgians, the Portuguese exploited their natural assets, while doing nothing to provide lasting political or economic stability. Only a political revolution at home, which ended 40 years of dictatorship, finally brought independence to Portugal's African colonies—Guinea-Bissau in 1974 and Angola and Mozambique in 1975. The lack of any preparation for nationhood led to bitter civil war in the latter two nations, exacerbated by interference by South Africa.

EUROPE AND THE THIRD WORLD

With the end of European colonial power, many of the new nations in the so-called Third World (the poorer, developing countries of Africa and Asia) faced the task of building politically viable systems against a background of economic instability and social injustice. In response to this need for assistance, Western governments created several international agencies whose task was to help developing nations. The International Monetary Fund (IMF), an organization affiliated with the United Nations, began operations in 1947. Led by the "Group of Ten" (that is, Britain, France, West Germany, Italy, Belgium, the Netherlands, Sweden, Japan, Canada, and the United States), its purpose was to provide international credit and stabilize exchange rates. The World Bank, a specialized agency of the United Nations, was also established to perform similar functions.

The results of massive loans by richer, industrialized Western nations to the Third World were mixed. The steep rise in oil prices after 1973 prompted heavy borrowing. By the early 1980s, Third World debts amounted to more than $400 billion. When rising interest rates combined with inflation to produce a general worldwide recession, many countries found themselves unable to repay even the interest on their loans, let alone the principal. The first government to temporarily suspend payments was Mexico, and others soon followed. Banks and international agencies were forced to renegotiate loans and impose tough (and often highly unpopular) conditions before extending further credit. The economic hardship these measures created proved dangerously destabilizing in many Third World countries. Their difficulties increased in the late 1980s and early 1990s, when the newly democratic countries of Eastern Europe attracted Western capital and investment away from Africa, Asia, and Latin America.

Under the threat of serious global economic crisis, several international movements developed. The major Western nations began in the 1970s to hold regular meetings on financial and trade problems. The intention was to coordinate policy on issues such as interest rates and export regulations. Differences among the group's members prevented the agreement on a common policy of economic assistance to developing countries, however, and international development remained largely controlled by banks and private corporations.

THE NONALIGNED MOVEMENT

In the 1950s and 1960s, in response to what they regarded as the inadequate response of Western governments, Third World nations created their own organizations. In 1955, at a conference in Bandung, Indonesia, leaders of countries claiming to belong neither to the Western nor the Soviet bloc met to proclaim their independence. Among the governments represented were those of Egypt, Yugoslavia (Tito had broken with Moscow), and India. The group met intermittently over the following years. In 1960, the Organization of Petroleum Exporting Countries (OPEC) was formed. A more formal alliance, the "Group of 77," was born in 1964, as the result of the United Nations Conference on Trade and Development (UNCTAD), which was held at Geneva. The organization, which eventually acquired more than 100 members, represented the interests of nonaligned countries. When oil prices rose steeply in 1973 as a result of an OPEC agreement, a special session of the United Nations General Assembly was held at which Third World countries, coordinated by the Group of 77, succeeded in passing two resolutions. The first called for a New International Economic Order (NIEO), whereby all nations would be equal; the sec-

Leaders of the Nonaligned Movement at a meeting in the Indonesian city of Bandung. 1955. The three central figures were the leaders of the Movement: (*from left*) Egyptian President Gamal Abdel Nasser, Indian Prime Minister Jawaharlal Nehru, and Yugoslav President Josip Brod Tito.

© CORBIS/Bettmann

ond called for the transfer of Western technology to poorer countries and the end of Western exploitation.

In further meetings held in the 1970s and 1980s, the economic imbalance between the prosperous Northern Hemisphere and poorer Southern countries became the subject of intense discussion. A few actual decisions were made:

By the Lome Convention of 1975, 46 former European colonies could export their products to the European Community free of tariffs. On the whole, however, prosperous Western nations were unwilling to surrender the advantages of cheap labor and natural resources provided by Third World countries or to share their own wealth.

Putting Decolonization and the Third World in Perspective

At the end of World War II, European domination of world affairs seemed over. Quite apart from the moral responsibility for two global conflicts, the European nations had lost the economic capacity to maintain their prewar power. Many of them—Germany, Italy, France—were faced with rebuilding workable political systems. All of these nations, even the most stubborn, eventually withdrew from their imperial possessions.

For most of the new nations born in Africa, the Middle East, and Asia, the euphoria of independence was followed by the grinding problems of political and economic reality. Many of them had been deliberately left unprepared for self-government. For all the talk, furthermore, there was little concerted economic assistance from their former rulers. Relations between the richer countries and the Third World were further complicated by the growing power of the big multinational corporations, which often moved into developing countries as Western governments moved out. The multinationals often operated on financial assets greater than the national budgets of the countries in which they set up factories; they exploited natural and labor resources, while being concerned almost exclusively with profit. Not surprisingly, their activities drew considerable resentment.

For the Europeans, however, the loss of empire provided the chance to concentrate on rebuilding at home. The economic chaos of the immediate postwar years gave way to an economic rebirth that was slowed only by the oil crisis of the 1970s. By the 1990s, political tensions were lowered by the collapse of Communist regimes in Eastern Europe, and economic expectations were raised by the prospect of vast new markets developing there. With its emergence as an economic power potentially as great as the United States or Japan, Europe was in a position to provide vitally needed aid to its former colonies.

Questions for Further Study

1. What part did the United States and the Soviet Union play in the process of decolonization?
2. How did the European powers differ in their handling of independence movements? How far were they motivated by political factors, and how far by economic ones?
3. To what extent have international organizations—the UN, the World Bank, OPEC, the Nonaligned Movement—been able to provide help to developing nations? What are the future prospects?

Suggestions for Further Reading

Adu Boahen, A. *African Perspectives on Colonialism.* Baltimore, MD, 1989.

Alexander, Peter F. *Alan Paton, A Biography.* Oxford, 1994.

Camberlain, Muriel Evelyn. *Decolonization: The Fall of the European Empires.* Malden, MA., 1999.

Davidson, B. *Modern Africa.* London, 1984.

De Klerck, F.W. *The Autobiography: The Last Trek, A New Beginning.* London, 1999.

Gilbert, Martin. *Israel: A History.* London, 1998.

Herring, G.C. *America's Longest War: The United States and Vietnam, 1950–1975*. New York, 1986.

Lockman, Z., and J. Beinin, eds. *Intifada*. Boston, 1989.

Mandela, Nelson. *Long Walk to Freedom*. London, 1994.

Newsom, David D. *The Imperial Mantle: The United States, Decolonization, and the Third World*. Bloomington, IN, 2001.

Richards, A., and J. Waterbury. *A Political Economy of the Middle East*. Boulder, CO, 1989.

Sampson, A. *Black and Gold*. New York, 1987.

InfoTrac College Edition

Enter the search term *decolonization* using Key Terms.

Enter the search term *Khrushchev* using Key Terms.

THE POLITICS OF STABILITY IN WESTERN EUROPE

Faced with the devastation created by World War II, the nations of Western Europe strove to reconstruct political and economic institutions, and—literally—to rebuild cities and industries. With the old guard of European statesmen discredited by the failures of the 1930s, many of the political and financial leaders who rose to power represented a new generation.

The task of reconstruction was complicated in many countries by the need to reject the past as decisively as possible. In Germany, Italy, and Vichy France, an entire ruling class was replaced and, in some cases, tried for its complicity in Fascist and Nazi crimes. New, or in some cases renewed, political parties found themselves in unlikely coalitions: in Belgium, France, and Italy the first postwar governments included Communists, Socialists, and liberal Christian Democrats. In Britain, despite Churchill's personal popularity, his Conservatives lost decisively to the Labour party.

On the international scene, growing tensions between the Soviet Union and the United States polarized European loyalties, and the Cold War came to dominate political life. After the Berlin crisis of 1948–1949, Western Europe and the United States formalized their alliance in the North Atlantic Treaty Organization (NATO), which was signed in 1949. To build Western Europe's ability to withstand Communist pressures, and to make possible its economic recovery, the United States launched the European Recovery Program, generally known as the "Marshall Plan," which operated between 1947 and 1952, providing massive financial aid to 17 Western European countries.

In Britain, the postwar Labour government established a welfare state (assistance for the needy), expanding social services and nationalizing key industries. Subsequent Conservative governments continued Labour's social policies and took Britain into the Common Market. After an economic boom in the early 1960s, chronic inflation and strained labor relations undermined British industrial competitiveness and brought down successive Conservative and Labour governments.

The French Fourth Republic, which lasted from 1946 to 1958, was marked by political instability. It was replaced by the strongly presidential Fifth Republic, created by Charles de Gaulle; the former general left retirement to lead his country for the following decade. Conservative in domestic policies, de Gaulle encouraged an independent French line in foreign affairs, which involved loosening ties with the United States. De Gaulle resigned in 1969. After another decade of conservative government, in 1981 François Mitterand, a Socialist, was elected president.

At the end of the war, the Allies divided Germany into four zones of occupation. In 1949 three of these became the German Federal Republic and the fourth the German Democratic Republic. Berlin, the former capital of Germany, lay in the Soviet zone but was divided between the Soviets and the other Allies. West Germany's postwar boom, the so-called Economic Miracle, created under the leadership of the Christian Democrat Konrad Adenauer, saw the country become Europe's leading economic and industrial power. With the collapse of the East German communist regime in 1989, the dream of a reunited Germany became a reality.

THE NEW GENERATION IN POWER

The reconstruction of postwar Europe began under the most daunting of conditions. Through a continent whose chief cities were scarred by bomb devastation, there streamed millions of refugees: the former occupants of the Nazi concentration camps, people displaced by wartime action, increasing numbers fleeing from Soviet-occupied Eastern Europe. Food supplies were woefully inadequate. The destruction of war had created havoc in rail and road transport. Inflation and economic chaos made cigarettes the most stable currency for buying necessities—when goods were available.

Behind the difficulties of day-to-day survival lay other, more general fears. Already by the last year of the war the Grand Alliance was under a strain, and as the Soviet Union moved toward taking over Eastern Europe, the shadows of the coming Cold War began to close in. To make matters worse, the possibility of renewed conflict threatened horrors even greater than those of the recent past. In the new age of the atom bomb a third world war, played out once again on the battlefields of Europe, might well be the end of the Continent.

A decade or so later, much of Western Europe's industry was more productive than ever. In West Germany and Italy, democratic governments replaced the dictatorships of the years between the wars. British, French, and Belgian transport systems were reconstructed. In most West European countries, more people led more prosperous lives than ever before. One of the paths to solving Europe's problems proved to be treating them, in fact, as broad European issues rather than simply national concerns. Beginning in the early 1950s, national leaders began to work toward European collaboration and cooperation, at least in economic matters (see Topic 94).

NEW LEADERS

Each country faced its own particular problems, but many shared certain broad trends. Among the most significant was a major change of leadership, both in politics and in other aspects of public life—business, the law, education. For most of continental Europe, politicians, judges, and administrators were irrevocably tainted by their wartime actions and collaboration. There were practical limitations to the rebuilding of society. The Nuremberg Trials of 1945–1949 tried to establish as a principle of international law the responsibility of individuals for their actions, but the ordinary business of daily life had to continue. Many card-carrying Nazis and Fascists lost their positions, or even their lives, but many others quietly transferred their allegiances. At the same time, inconvenient aspects of recent history were buried or forgotten. Until 1983, French school textbooks made no mention of the Vichy collaborationist government, and only in 1997 did French bishops acknowledge the failure of the Roman Catholic Church to condemn the treatment of French Jews by the Vichy regime.

With the coming of peace, those who had been active in Resistance movements, or in fighting against the Axis,

Konrad Adenauer, Chancellor of West Germany, and Charles de Gaulle, President of France. 1963. In the century before these two great statesmen came to power, their countries had fought three terrible wars as adversaries. The personal respect and friendship they shared, clearly visible in this picture, played a large role in the reconciliation between their two countries—and in the establishment of peace in Europe.

came forward to play a part in shaping the freedom they had fought to save. Many of this new generation of leaders came from the parties of the left. Communists served in the immediate postwar governments of France, Belgium, and Italy. Socialists reinforced their position in the Scandinavian countries. In Britain, the election of 1945 brought a socialist government to office. Britain's wartime government had been a coalition one, and the Conservative leader, Winston Churchill, was a national hero. Nonetheless prewar Conservative leaders were seen as responsible for not having prevented the outbreak of war and for having left the country so unprepared.

The result of the perceptible shift to the left was a new emphasis on technical and leadership skills. The last traces of aristocratic power disappeared from political life and the business world. Noble birth did not prevent a career in public life, but it certainly ceased to guarantee one. At least one British politician gave up his hereditary title rather than abandon his seat in the House of Commons. The doings of Europe's aristocracy—marriages in Monaco or Westminster Abbey—retained their glamour and fascination for many, but almost exclusively as a kind of branch of the entertainment industry.

Efforts to remove the old business families proved less successful. After the war, the head of the leading German armaments producer, Alfred Krupp (1907–1967), spent three years in jail for war crimes, but although the company was reorganized, it still retained most of its original holdings. Nonetheless, in the business world as in politics, expertise in engineering or economics became more important than family connections.

Thus, as Europe faced the difficult problems involved in reconstruction, leadership passed to an increasingly broad-based and highly qualified "meritocracy." Most of the new generation accepted a more limited role for their own country and for Europe in international affairs. The only European leader who continued to sound the note of national pride was de Gaulle, one of the few survivors of an earlier generation.

THE POLITICS OF RECONSTRUCTION

The immediate task of postwar governments was a double one: to restore democratic institutions and to reconstruct shattered economies. Following Britain's lead, many countries introduced welfare state programs, which aimed at improving the lives of their less affluent citizens.

THE WELFARE STATE
Although a few social welfare programs were launched in the late 19th century, and expanded during the Great Depression, the notion of a complete welfare state only appeared after World War II. In Britain, the Labour government of 1945 to 1951, led by Clement Attlee (1883–1967), passed legislation to provide virtually free medical care to all and to expand unemployment insurance and educational opportunities. In an attempt to put basic facilities under the control of all citizens, Labour nationalized the steel and mining industries and the railways.

By the 1950s, most other Western European nations had introduced similar schemes. Subsidies for housing, financial support for child raising, the provision of education beyond the primary level, all improved the opportunities for poorer citizens. Measures such as these, together with increasing government control of industry, enlarged the power of the state.

POLITICAL PARTIES
European political life after the war was characterized by the development of democratic multiparty systems, in which government generally alternated between two main parties. The chief exceptions were Spain and Portugal, where dictatorships established well before World War II remained in place. Most politicians avoided extremes. The horrors of Fascism and Nazism had completely discredited the radical right. A small neo-Fascist party remained active in Italy, although for many years it was regarded as not constitutionally legitimate by the other political forces. Otherwise, apart

from a few fanatical terrorist groups, extreme right-wing politics was unrepresented in the decades immediately following the war. By the 1980s, an extremist party began to collect some support in France, campaigning principally on the issue of immigration restrictions. All official conservative parties were fully committed to maintaining democratic government and rarely dismantled welfare legislation introduced by socialist predecessors. The only notable exception was Thatcher's government in Britain in the 1980s.

On the left, no major communist or socialist movement in Western Europe publicly advocated extreme views in theory or tried to put them into practice when in power. Communists never achieved control of national governments, but where they won administration of a city or region they proved no more doctrinaire—and no more or less efficient—than their opponents. The socialists who came to power showed the same concern for individual liberties and the democratic process as their conservative rivals. Extreme differences of ideology and opinion still existed, but no political leader posed a radical challenge to the prevailing system, as Hitler, Mussolini, or Stalin had done.

THE UNITED STATES IN EUROPE

The international background against which the process of European renewal began to unfold was dominated by growing tension between the world's two superpowers and former allies—the United States and the Soviet Union. In the last year of the war, while the Allies began to make plans for the future of Europe, Stalin took advantage of the reigning confusion to move Soviet troops into the chief Eastern European countries. By 1947, pro-Soviet regimes were firmly installed in Bulgaria, Czechoslovakia, Hungary, Poland, and Romania. The Baltic states of Estonia, Latvia, and Lithuania remained under Soviet rule, incorporated into the Soviet Union. In 1945, when the Allies had divided Germany into four zones, the most eastern zone came under Russian occupation. Berlin, the former capital of Germany, lay in the Soviet zone but was divided between them and the other Allies.

If Stalin were planning further aggressive expansion, the "Eastern Bloc" he had created would provide an effective base. At the same time he built a psychological division between two Europes: one free and democratic, the other repressed. The "Iron Curtain," a memorable phrase of Winston Churchill's, left both sides in mutual fear and incomprehension. The nations most likely to be affected by Soviet aggression were those of Western Europe, in particular the western zones of Germany. Yet the Allies had disarmed the Germans at the end of the war, and in any case no European state was in a condition to confront Stalin.

THE MARSHALL PLAN
This vacuum was filled by the United States. Regimes that seemed under threat from the Soviets received American

Soldiers and barbed wire in front of the Brandenburg Gate, Berlin. 1960s. From the end of World War II until 1989, the Brandenburg Gate marked the dividing point between West and East Berlin, and—as this picture shows—was heavily fortified on both sides. The sign reads: "Attention. Here you are leaving West Berlin."

backing. In some cases U.S. intervention helped prevent communist takeovers. In 1947, President Harry S Truman (served 1945–1952) sent massive American military assistance to Greece, thereby securing the defeat of communist guerrillas and the installation of a parliamentary system. Elsewhere, as in Iran, American support for regimes that were strongly anticommunist but also strongly repressive embarrassed some Western observers and led the Soviets to accuse the United States of doing its own empire building. The American efforts to "contain" communism in those areas the United States already controlled came to be known as the "Truman Doctrine."

In a similar vein, the United States introduced its European Recovery Program, which operated from 1947 to 1952; the scheme is better known as the Marshall Plan, after its originator, U.S. Secretary of State George C. Marshall (1880–1959). Seventeen European countries, which formed the Organization for European Economic Cooperation, received some $13 billion in money and materials, to help their economic recovery.

The plan was clearly intended to combine humanitarian concerns with a strong dose of self-interest. Its provisions undoubtedly gave vital and much-needed aid to war-ravaged Europe and brought about improvements in the daily lives of countless ordinary citizens. For the Soviets, however, the help represented yet another case of American economic imperialism. It also created the possibility of U.S. control over its allies' politics. In countries such as France and Italy, where communist parties made a strong showing immediately after the war, governments receiving aid were also under American pressure to "control the spread of communism" in their internal politics. In any case, strong economic growth certainly reinforced the capitalist system and undercut support for the left among voters. On balance, the Marshall Plan not only provided much-needed financial assistance but also became an important element in America's politics of stabilization in Western Europe.

THE BERLIN CRISIS

The confrontation between the two superpowers—the "Cold War"—was most direct at the heart of Europe, in Germany. The three allied zones there soon began to function as a single unit, with local and national elections and a unified economy. The Soviet response to the revival of German strength was to blockade access by rail, river, or road to West Berlin, which was completely surrounded by Soviet-controlled territory. The Berlin blockade lasted from late June 1948 to mid-May 1949. During that period, the United States and Britain mounted a massive airlift to provide the West Berliners with food, water, and other essential supplies. The total number of flights amounted to around a quarter of a million, carrying 2 million tons of goods, at a cost of $224 million.

By the end of the blockade, the Americans had made their point. They would defend the interests of their allies, at whatever price, but would seek to do so without open conflict whenever possible. In May 1949, a separate West German nation, known as the Federal Republic of Germany, was established at Bonn, which became its capital. In response the Soviets formalized the existence of their zone of Germany as a separate country, called the German Democratic Republic, with its capital in East Berlin. East Germany hailed the division of the country as irreversible, while West Germany's leaders at first refused even to recognize the existence of East Germany and maintained the goal of eventual reunification.

Map 90.1 Europe During the Cold War.
The two opposing sides are divided by what Winston Churchill called, in a speech in 1946, an "Iron Curtain." The map does not, of course, show the chief NATO power, the United States. Albania left the Warsaw Pact in 1968. The Pact broke up with the fall of the Soviet Union, but NATO continued to operate; among its missions in the early 21st century was the liberation of Kosovo, itself the result of the collapse of Yugoslavia.

One of the planes in the Berlin airlift flying over a group of children. 1948–1949. The coordination of the Berlin airlift was one of the opening confrontations of the Cold War. While not using force to oppose the Soviet right to block roads in their own territory, the Allies found a peaceful means to thwart Soviet intentions and show support for those Germans living under their control.

AKG London

THE CREATION OF NATO

Even before the blockade was over, the Western allies had formed an organization specifically directed at the "threat of armed communist attack in Europe or the North Atlantic or Mediterranean area." The nations that joined the North Atlantic Treaty Organization (NATO) in April 1949 were Belgium, Britain, Canada, Denmark, France, the Netherlands, Iceland, Italy, Luxembourg, Norway, Portugal, and the United States. Greece and Turkey became members two years later, West Germany in 1955, and Spain in 1982. The terms of the treaty affirmed that an attack on any one member would be regarded as an attack on all.

Among the provisions of NATO was that American forces would remain in Europe, both in Germany and elsewhere. The popularity of the American presence rose and fell on both sides of the Atlantic as the intensity of the Cold War fluctuated. In the decade following the end of World War II, the United States' "umbrella" protection, by now nuclear, was widely regarded as essential to the continued security of Western Europe. In the 1960s, as new trouble spots developed outside Europe—the Middle East, Vietnam—complaints began to be heard in the United States about the high cost of European security to American taxpayers. At the same time, some European political movements started to agitate for the closing of U.S. military facilities in their countries. In 1966, de Gaulle actually expelled NATO forces from French territory. Throughout the 1980s, the Greek government threatened to close American bases in Greece. With the apparent collapse of the Soviet Bloc in the revolutions of 1989, heated debate began to rage about the future role of NATO and of its Soviet equivalent, the Warsaw Pact (see Topic 91).

GREAT BRITAIN: BEYOND THE WELFARE STATE

British politics following World War II were dominated by alternating Labour and Conservative governments. Other forces included a small Liberal party and a Social Democratic party (founded in 1981). In the early 1980s, these two groups formed an alliance that seemed at first able to challenge Labour and Conservatives, but by the end of the decade, with the Conservatives in power, the Labour party remained the only real alternative.

The first postwar Labour government, following both its socialist principles and the spirit of the times, began the dismantlement of Britain's former imperial possessions and laid the foundations of the welfare state. Conservative governments followed from 1951 to 1964, continued the granting of independence to colonies, and led the country into a period of economic prosperity.

Sir Anthony Eden, who served as prime minister from 1955 to 1957, resigned as the result of the Suez crisis of 1956, which clearly illustrated the limits on postwar Britain's freedom to follow an independent course in foreign affairs. When Egypt's President Gamal Abdel Nasser (1918–1970) nationalized the Suez Canal, hitherto under joint Franco-British ownership, Britain and France invaded Egypt to regain possession. Under strong U.S. pressure, and with UN intervention, the occupying forces withdrew, and the canal reopened under Egyptian control. Eden, who had served earlier as Churchill's foreign secretary, was professionally and physically wrecked by the crisis; at its height, his wife later observed, it felt as if the canal itself were flowing through their living room.

By 1964, Britain's economy was facing serious problems. The government's failure to enable industry to compete in international markets, coupled with rising unemployment and chronic inflation, persuaded the electors to turn to Labour. For the next fifteen years each party in turn failed to solve the country's economic difficulties. In 1971, after years of heated controversy and debate, Britain became a member of the Common Market.

THE CONSERVATIVES UNDER THATCHER

The Conservative leader from 1975 was Margaret Thatcher (born 1925), who served continuously as prime minister from 1979 to the end of 1990. From the beginning she announced an abrupt change of direction: no concessions. In her first year in office, steel, railway, and national health service workers all struck. All their strikes collapsed. The price was massive unemployment and social unrest.

Thatcher's own personal popularity, dimmed by the disastrous state of the economy, received a sudden boost from the Falklands War of 1982 (see Topic 95). In the following year's election, the Conservatives won the largest number of seats any party had gained since 1935. In part, this was the result of the extreme program on which Labour had fought the election. Among other pledges, Labour promised to withdraw from the Common Market, abandon Britain's nuclear weapons (a longstanding cause of furious debate in the party), nationalize more industries, and suppress foxhunting.

With her huge parliamentary majority, Thatcher pushed forward to rein in the welfare state and develop a free-market economy. The unsuccessful coal miners' strike of 1984–1985 reinforced her reputation for getting her way. (The letters of one of her nicknames, "Tina," stood for "There Is No Alternative.") Her admirers praised her firmness; her critics pointed to the increasing gulf between the prosperous and the poor and to the growing violence on the part of the jobless and hopeless in Britain's big cities.

Reelected in 1987, her government began to run into increasing trouble as the economy went into decline again. Once the Conservatives' biggest asset, Thatcher came under increasing fire for her uncaring, confrontational attitude. When in 1990 she insisted on pushing through an unpopular reorganization of the local taxation system—the new method became known as the "Poll Tax"—rioting broke out not only in London but also in hitherto firmly Conservative provincial regions of the country.

With her leadership of the party increasingly open to challenge, the annual election by Conservative Members of

Parliament of their leader was held in December 1990. These contests were generally a formality, and Thatcher was out of the country at the time of the first ballot, representing Britain at a Paris summit conference. Amid general surprise, she failed to gain the necessary percentage of votes for outright victory, and after a day or so of uncharacteristic hesitation, withdrew her candidacy. John Major (born 1943) became the new prime minister and leader of the Conservative party. Thus a handful of Tory Members of Parliament, voting in secret, brought to an end the Thatcher years.

Postwar Britain, despite victory, had to face adjustment to a world position far below that of the preceding centuries. Firmly overshadowed by U.S. policy on the international scene, surpassed as a European economic power by Germany and France, and in the mid-1980s by Italy, Britain's own commitment to a European identity remained less than wholehearted. The left wing of the Labour party continued to fight, unsuccessfully after the 1983 debacle, for a promise that Labour would negotiate Britain's withdrawal from the Common Market. Thatcher for her part had remained deeply suspicious of growing European economic interdependence and firmly opposed to any form of political union. With her replacement by Major, Britain seemed likely to reverse its anti-European stance and move toward a policy of cooperation rather than isolation, although the Conservative party remained deeply divided. With the victory of Tony Blair's New Labour party in 1997, British official attitudes toward European unity became far more positive.

FRANCE IN THE FOURTH AND FIFTH REPUBLICS

By contrast with Britain, France's modern political history has been marked by discontinuity. The 19th century saw a constant alternation of republican and monarchical rule. As a result, by the 20th century, French politics became conditioned by the average citizen's distrust of the state and its agencies. Unlike the British, the French tended to defend themselves against collective action, rather than turning to the state for help.

THE FOURTH REPUBLIC

In comparison with its European competitors, by the beginning of World War II French industry was relatively stagnant. Between 1870 and 1940, German gross national income had increased five times, and British three and a half; that of France rose only 80 percent. Reconstruction thus involved not only repairing war damage, but also strengthening the economy as a whole. The architect of the plan to modernize France, Jean Monnet (1888–1979), began a series of five-year schemes to rebuild basic industries and develop exports. The first Monnet Plan covered the period from 1947 to 1952. Even before it went into effect, the government had nationalized key industries, including electric-

ity, gas, rail transportation, and the Renault automobile plants (their former owner was accused of collaboration with the Germans). Economic reform was accompanied by an extensive program of social legislation, including accident and unemployment compensation, medical care, maternity benefits, and family allowances.

The constitutional framework that governed France from 1946 to 1958 was that of the Fourth Republic. Parliament exercised supreme power, and the conflicting interests of various parties and political groups threw up and then destroyed a continual series of governments: The 20 different cabinets of the Fourth Republic's 12 years were a sign of serious political uncertainty.

DE GAULLE AND THE FIFTH REPUBLIC

By 1958, the combination of political instability and public agitation over the Algerian crisis clearly indicated the need for major reform. Charles de Gaulle, leader of the Free French movement in exile during World War II, served as president during the transition to the Fourth Republic and retired from active political life in 1953. Yet because he stood as a powerful symbol of French national determination, in June 1958, at the height of the Algerian crisis, he returned as prime minister, with authorization to prepare a new constitution. De Gaulle remained France's leader until 1969, when he resigned on the failure of a referendum to give him further powers for constitutional reform.

By contrast with the Fourth Republic, the Fifth Republic vested strong powers in the president, who became not only the symbol but also the instrument of executive authority. The original constitution of the Fifth Republic called for the president to be chosen by an electoral college, but in 1962 de Gaulle successfully campaigned for presidential election by a direct popular vote. Independent of any political party, presidents have exercised a wide range of powers, including the designation of prime ministers, the dissolution of Parliament, and control of French foreign policy. De Gaulle claimed, in fact, that "the President elected by the nation is the source and holder of the power of the state."

Already in the early years of the Fifth Republic the multiple parties of the postwar period began to coalesce into two main groups: on the left, communists, socialists, and radicals; on the center-right, Gaullists and various centrist parties, including the Union for French Democracy (UDF) and Rally for the Republic (RPR). In the early 1980s, the National Front (FN) began to attract increasing attention as a party of the extreme right, campaigning mainly on the issue of immigrant workers.

Under de Gaulle, France pursued generally conservative policies at home, while seeking to maintain an independent line in foreign affairs. Growing resentment of U.S. domination led to France's withdrawal from NATO in 1966. Deeper signs of unrest at the President's paternalistic style of government became manifest in the student and worker uprisings of two years later; 1968 was marked, in fact, by student protests throughout much of Europe.

The following year, when de Gaulle resigned, his former prime minister, Georges Pompidou (served 1969–1974, died in office), won election as president. Both Pompidou and his successor Valéry Giscard-D'Estaing (served 1974–1981) continued de Gaulle's conservative financial policies, while failing to prevent rising inflation and unemployment.

MITTERAND AND THE SOCIALISTS

In 1981, for the first time the voters turned to a socialist to head the Fifth Republic. With the Communist party in decline, and the parties of the right divided, François Mitterand (served 1981–1995) won election in May 1981 as president. One month later he called a general election in which the Socialist party won a clear majority and the Communists lost half of their members of Parliament.

Mitterand's government began by introducing generous new social legislation that increased minimum wages, family allowances, and housing subsidies. After a year, however, it was clear that the program had backfired. The French were spending more and more money on imported goods, while exports lagged. As a result, unemployment remained high. At the end of 1982, despite union and communist protests, the government changed direction. State spending was lowered, wages were frozen, and state and industrial employees were dismissed. The austerity program succeeded in lowering inflation and balancing the budget, but it disappointed, and actually hurt, many who had voted socialist.

The general election of 1986, fought two years before Mitterand's term expired, saw the Socialist party hold most of its strength—it lost 5 percent of the support it had won in 1981. On the right, however, the two major parties, the RPR and the UDF, put together a temporary agreement that gave them jointly a majority of seats in Parliament. The RPR leader, Jacques Chirac (born 1932), became prime minister, facing Mitterand with two years of "Cohabitation" with a premier who was a political opponent. The Socialist president maintained his right to control French foreign policy, while the conservative Chirac began to privatize the economy, selling off state-owned enterprises to private investors.

In 1988 Mitterand stood again for the presidency, with Chirac running as his principal opponent. This time the socialist represented stability and the conservative change. The voters chose the former. Chirac lost and resigned as prime minister. On both left and right, candidates began to look toward the presidential election of 1995. The two leading candidates were Jacques Chirac and the Socialist Lionel Jospin. On the final ballot, Chirac emerged as the winner, although—to the surprise of many observers—Jospin won more votes in the first round than any other candidate (although not an absolute majority). Two years later, when President Chirac called a snap general election, the socialists astonished most observers by winning and formed a government with the support of Communist and Green deputies.

SIGNIFICANT DATES

Western Europe After 1945

1947–1952	The Marshall Plan
1948–1949	The Berlin Blockade
1949	Creation of NATO
1951	European Coal and Steel Community formed
1956	The Suez crisis
1958	De Gaulle returns to power
1961	Construction of Berlin Wall
1968	Strikes and student demonstrations
1971	Britain enters Common Market
1979	Thatcher becomes British prime minister
1981	Mitterand elected first Socialist French president
1982	Kohl becomes West German chancellor
1983–1986	Craxi serves as Italian prime minister
1989	Fall of Berlin Wall

WEST GERMANY: REBUILDING THE INDUSTRIAL GIANT

In 1945 Germany lay in ruins, split among its conquerors. Ten years later, the Federal Republic of Germany joined NATO and attained full sovereignty. At the end of 1989, the communist regime in the German Democratic Republic collapsed; a government installed after free elections in March 1990 began negotiations to prepare for reunification in late 1990.

GERMAN ECONOMIC RECOVERY

This astonishing reconstruction of a nation that seemed shattered beyond repair was made possible in part by West Germany's rapid financial recovery. By 1960, West German national income had surpassed that of France; in 1964 it overtook that of Britain; by 1973, German and American workers were paid the same. By the late 1980s the only country in the world to exceed West Germany (population 61 million) in total exports was the United States. At the same time as rebuilding industry, creating jobs, and providing housing, the postwar German government found shelter and employment for more than 14 million Germans who were fleeing from or had been expelled from Eastern Europe. All of these achievements were accomplished against a background of relative social peace, broken only by recurrent bursts of extremist terrorism.

The political scene in West Germany provided a firm and generally tranquil foundation for this rebirth. The two main parties, the conservative Christian Democrats and the left-wing Social Democrats, alternated in power, each on occasion forming a coalition with the much smaller liberal

The main street, the Kufurstendam, of a booming West Berlin. 1965. With the construction of the Berlin Wall in 1961, the contrast between West Berlin, with its broad streets and luxury shops, and the poverty of East Berlin grew even more marked. Note the prominent sign over the large building to the left advertising Mercedes-Benz automobiles, one of the prestige products of West Germany.

Robert Hunt Library

Free Democratic party. Politicians resigned or were removed from office generally as the result of personal scandal rather than for political reasons.

KONRAD ADENAUER

The tone of German public life—serious and responsible—was set by West Germany's first chancellor, Konrad Adenauer (served 1949–1963). No newcomer to politics, Adenauer was mayor of Cologne during the Weimar Republic. Having avoided involvement with the Nazis, he was an appropriate choice to provide his country with authoritative leadership. A venerable figure of lofty dignity, he was 73 when he became chancellor. Adenauer did much to repair Franco-German relations by the cooperative relationship he established with de Gaulle.

American aid in the form of the Marshall Plan certainly contributed to the German economic revival, but other important factors were also involved. Management was efficient and the labor force hardworking. Trade unions concentrated on increasing production rather than seeking to improve conditions for their members. The influx of refugees from Eastern Europe provided cheap and plentiful labor, with a strong incentive to improve their conditions by hard work. German Economic Minister Ludwig Erhard (served as West German chancellor 1963–1966) skillfully balanced a free-market economy with welfare programs for the workers and government incentives for management. Unlike Britain, France, and Italy, the government nationalized no important services or industries.

In foreign policy, Adenauer maintained close relations with the United States, while beginning to work toward European cooperation. In 1951 the foundations of the

Common Market were laid with the establishment of the European Coal and Steel Community (see Topic 94), of which Germany was a member. In the same year Adenauer addressed the painful issue of German responsibility for the Holocaust. Germany signed an agreement with Israel, pledging to make financial reparation over the following 12 years. As for East Germany, and the "German Question," at first Adenauer's government recognized neither East Germany nor the Soviet Union.

By the mid-1950s, West Germany was ready to assume the status of a fully sovereign state. In 1955 it joined NATO, and the following year the Western Allies declared the occupation formally over. Later in 1955, Adenauer traveled to Moscow to establish diplomatic relations with the Kremlin. In March 1957 West Germany became one of the founding members of the Common Market. Toward the end of Adenauer's chancellorship, in 1961, relations with the Soviet Union grew tense with the construction of the Berlin Wall—built by the East Germans to cut off their citizens from access to the West.

"OSTPOLITIK"

Under Adenauer's successors, West Germany began to try to improve relations with the governments of Eastern Europe. The policy of *Ostpolitik* ("politics looking east") was the special creation of the socialist Willy Brandt (1913–1992), who served first as foreign minister and then, from 1969 to 1974, as chancellor. Brandt was especially qualified to open up relations with Eastern Europe because as mayor of West Berlin from 1957 to 1966, he had dealt directly with the problems of isolation. In 1972 a treaty was finally signed between the two German states, which established mutual recognition. Brandt's *Ostpolitik* marked a major step in easing East-West relations and paving the way for eventual reunification.

Under the leadership of Helmut Schmidt (born 1918), Brandt's successor as head of the Social Democrats and chancellor from 1974 to 1982, the German economy remained strong. Beginning in the late 1970s, however, the general calm of German life became increasingly shattered by terrorist outbreaks. The revolutionary Red Army Faction claimed responsibility for a rash of bombings of NATO installations and the murder of prominent industrialists. The other social problem that helped bring down Schmidt's Socialist government and return the Christian Democrats to power in 1982 was that of the *Gastarbeiter* ("guest workers")—the large and increasing number of foreign workers living in West Germany.

Helmut Kohl (born 1930), chancellor from 1982, favored a move toward a free-market economy. Under continued opposition from employers and unions, which were both unwilling to change the status quo, most of his initiatives failed, and by the end of the 1980s the German economy had begun to falter. Growth was slow and unemployment relatively high. Kohl's most visible initiative was his immediate espousing of the cause of German reunification after the events of November 1989. Leading the East German Christian Democrats' campaign in the elections of March 1990, and appearing at packed rallies where he was hailed as a second Bismarck, Kohl helped his East German counterparts to achieve an overwhelming victory. His long period in office finally ended in 1998, when a financial scandal in which he seemed personally implicated brought the Social Democrats to power. (see Topic 95).

By the early 1990s, after nearly half a century of rehabilitation, West Germany moved toward leading a renewed and reunited Germany. While the United States and West Germany's European allies underlined the need for safeguards, the Soviet Union expressed fears of future aggression. Yet the general realization that the choice of reunification was and should be essentially a German one underlined the degree to which 50 years of responsible leadership had changed the defeated country of 1945. For many years it was said that the key to German reunification lay in Moscow. Now, for the first time, it lay in Bonn.

ITALY'S ECONOMIC MIRACLE

With the collapse of Fascism in 1943, Italy faced the choice of either restoring the monarchy or introducing a republican form of government. In June 1946 a referendum decided by a narrow margin to abolish the monarchy, which had collaborated with Mussolini. The republican constitution, which went into effect on January 1, 1948, was based on those of other Western democracies, with two chambers of parliament and universal suffrage. Unlike France of the Fifth Republic or the United States, the

Alcide de Gasperi addressing a crowd, c. 1950. He is the man wearing glasses in the lower center, speaking into a microphone. De Gasperi, head of the Christian Democratic party, was Italy's second postwar prime minister. He had been imprisoned by the Fascists from 1927 to 1929 and served in the first government formed after the Fascist collapse in 1943.

president had few powers; the prime minister became head of the government.

PARTY POLITICS IN ITALY

Unlike Britain or Germany, Italian political life was made up of a host of parties, most of which were represented in Parliament as a result of a system of proportional representation. Governments depended on the formation of coalitions, which either made up a parliamentary majority, however precarious, or which could count on opposing parties not voting against them. Because virtually all parties, even the small ones, had internal divisions, the making and unmaking of coalition cabinets became an endless process. Between 1950 and 1980, 35 governments held office, some lasting no more than a few weeks.

Yet, by contrast with the confusion of the French Fourth Republic, the Italian economy was strengthened, major social changes such as divorce and abortion were introduced, and the scourge of terrorism was brought under control. By the 1980s Italy was one of the "Club of Seven," one of the seven most wealthy and industrialized nations in the world. Italian automobile manufacturers controlled the largest share of the European market, and Italian fashion and leather goods were popular throughout the world. A founding member of the Common Market, Italy was one of the countries that pressed most enthusiastically for greater European union.

By far the most powerful force in postwar Italian political life was the Christian Democratic party, whose members led virtually every Italian government from 1945 to 1981, with various assortments of coalition partners. A loose association of factions representing shades of opinion from center left to fairly far right, the Christian Democrats confirmed the Italian propensity for individualism, negotiation, and compromise. Although the party was promoted and supported by the Catholic Church, Christian Democratic governments introduced the referenda that legalized divorce and abortion—both vigorously opposed by church leaders.

Italy's second largest party, the Communists, continued throughout the postwar period to attract the votes of almost one-third of the country's electors. Although never admitted to any of the national coalitions, the Communists held seats on the important parliamentary committees that administered much of the day-to-day running of the country. They also won control of many city and regional governments. In the mid-1970s the Communist Enrico Berlinguer (1922–1984) and the Christian Democrat leader Aldo Moro (1916–1978) began to talk cautiously of the "historic

compromise," and in 1977–1978 the Communists supported a Christian Democrat government. Then Moro was captured and murdered by extreme left-wing terrorists known as the "Red Brigades," in one of the grimmest periods of Italy's *anni di piombo* ("years of lead"). Talk of cooperation faded, and following the collapse of the Soviet Union, the Communist party split up.

The Socialist party, the third largest in Italy, began to increase its share of the vote in the late 1970s and 1980s. Its leader, Bettino Craxi (born 1934), was strong enough to head Italy's longest-lasting government since World War II, from 1983 to 1986. Thus, for all of its political fragmentation, the Italian system permitted a surprising degree of political stability. At the same time it also achieved the intentions of its creators, by never allowing a single individual to attain significant power—the success of Mussolini had taught a grim lesson. It was no accident that Italian politics never produced an Adenauer or de Gaulle, a Mitterand or a Thatcher. Significantly enough, Craxi's fall from popular favor in the late 1980s was because he was perceived as being too strong.

Putting the Politics of Stability in Western Europe in Perspective

By 1990, Western Europe had enjoyed four and a half decades of peace and prosperity, broken only by the steep rise in oil prices in the mid-1970s. Democratic government was introduced in Spain and Portugal, and Greece's brief period of dictatorship in the late 1960s was over. The success of the Common Market was demonstrated by the number of nations seeking to join it. The challenge of the next decade was to achieve economic unity as painlessly as possible, and, as some believed, to look toward Western European political unity in the future.

Then, in a few weeks at the end of 1989, the division between Eastern and Western Europe, which had seemed permanent, fell apart. The road to a Europe united from the Atlantic to the Urals was infinitely long and filled with wrong turnings. Many did not want to make the journey. Yet even the remote possibility of accomplishing a small part of it was an indication of the degree of European recovery after two disastrous world wars.

Questions for Further Study

1. How did the major Western European nations emerge from World War II? How did their populations see the role of the state?
2. What part did social protest and mass demonstrations play in postwar political life in Western Europe?
3. What were the immediate effects of the fall of the Berlin Wall? What are its long-term consequences likely to be?

Suggestions for Further Reading

Annan, Noel. *Changing Enemies: The Defeat and Regeneration of Germany.* New York, 1996.

Bark, D.L., and D.R. Gress. *A History of West Germany: Vol. II. Democracy and Its Discontents, 1963–1988.* Oxford, 1989.

Bashevkin, S., ed. *Women and Politics in Western Europe.* London, 1985.

Hughes, H.S. *Sophisticated Rebels: The Political Culture of European Dissent, 1968–1987*. Cambridge, MA, 1988.

Koff, Sondra Z., and Stephen P. Koff. *Italy from the First to the Second Republic*. New York, 2000.

Lewis, R. *Margaret Thatcher: A Personal and Political Biography*. London, 1984.

Mazey, S., and M. Newman, eds. *Mitterand's France*. New York, 1987.

McCullough, David. *Truman*. New York, 1992.

Richie, Alexander. *Faust's Metropolis, A History of Berlin*. New York, 1998.

Seldon, Anthony, and Daniel Collings. *Britain Under Thatcher*. New York, 2000.

Spotts, F., and T. Wieser. *Italy, A Difficult Democracy*. New York, 1986.

Thatcher, Margaret. *The Downing Street Years*. London, 1993.

Tiersky, Ronald. *Francois Mitterand: The Last French President*. New York, 2000.

InfoTrac College Edition

Enter the search term *Soviet Union relations with the United States* using the Subject Guide.

Enter the search term *Cold War* using the Subject Guide.

Enter the search term *Charles de Gaulle* using Key Terms.

THE SOVIET UNION AND EASTERN EUROPE

With the end of World War II, the Soviet Union faced the daunting task of domestic reconstruction. In accordance with Stalin's policies, priority was given to heavy industry and weapons production. Governmental bureaucratic decisions controlled centralized state industrial development. In foreign affairs, relations between East and West grew tense and confrontational, as the Cold War dominated international relations.

In the period immediately following the war, most of the governments in Eastern Europe were taken over by Soviet-backed Communists. By 1948, these "Eastern bloc" countries were under firm Soviet control. Only Yugoslavia succeeded in breaking away from Soviet influence. The countries of Eastern Europe were bound to the Soviet Union economically by the COMECON organization, and militarily by the Warsaw Pact, although individual countries developed along different paths.

After Stalin's death in 1953, his eventual successor, Nikita Khrushchev, denounced the crimes of "Stalinism" and assumed sole power in 1958. Khrushchev encouraged the beginnings of East-West détente. Partly as a result, Soviet relations with China became strained and were eventually broken. In 1964, the failure of Soviet agriculture, coupled with the diplomatic consequences of the Cuban missile crisis of 1962, brought about Khrushchev's downfall.

The Soviet Union was ruled from 1964 to 1982 by Leonid Brezhnev. Brezhnev's policies were cautious. Amid intermittent signs of détente, the massive Soviet arms buildup continued. The power of the bureaucracy was intensified, and agricultural and industrial production remained backward.

Both Khrushchev and Brezhnev maintained a repressive policy in Eastern Europe. Soviet troops put down the Hungarian Revolt of 1956, and Warsaw Pact forces intervened to end the attempts at liberalization in Czechoslovakia in 1968. When in the late 1970s, unrest in Poland led in 1980 to the formation of an independent trade union, Solidarity, a Soviet-backed government imposed martial law and arrested Solidarity's organizers.

With the rise of Mikhail Gorbachev in 1985, Soviet policy underwent a dramatic change. In an attempt to revitalize the Soviet economy, Gorbachev turned to more open, reformist policies. By decentralizing and privatizing sectors of the economy, democratizing party rule, and encouraging individual creativity, he aimed at raising productivity and improving the lives of Soviet citizens.

The degree of change in Soviet policy was demonstrated by the freedom with which the countries of Eastern Europe were able to overthrow their governments in the revolutions of 1989. In the spring of 1990, free elections were held in Czechoslovakia, East Germany, and Hungary, all of which led to center-right, pro-Western governments. Later in the 1990s, many Eastern European countries returned former communist leaders to power.

THE SOVIET UNION FACES RECONSTRUCTION

World War II left havoc throughout Europe, but the problems that faced the Soviet Union were especially daunting. Estimates of the number killed are impossible to confirm, but the figure generally given of 22 million does not seem exaggerated. Innumerable towns and villages were in ruins. Leningrad suffered massive damage during its long siege by the Germans, and many industrial plants elsewhere in the Soviet Union had been obliterated. Living conditions were grim: Around 25 million Soviets were homeless, and many of those who did have shelter had to share kitchen and bathroom facilities with other families for decades.

Soviet victory in the war was largely the result of the industrialization of the Soviet Union in the 1930s. Furthermore, the German invasion reinforced Russian fears of foreign interference. Thus Stalin's top priority in 1945 was to rebuild the heavy steel and iron industries and to step up armaments production: "In industry lies power." The relatively little attention paid to the manufacture of consumer goods meant that the standard of living of most Soviet citizens remained low.

Cartoon by Walt Kelly showing the two sides in the Cold War as groups of picnicking children, c. 1950. Note the weapons in the picnic baskets. The woman in the Eastern group with a large moustache is a caricature of Stalin. The artist worked in the 1930s for the Walt Disney Studio and in 1945 created the "Pogo" comic strip.

Control of planning and production was kept firmly in the hands of the Communist party, itself subject to Stalin. The system was that of a "command" economy in which all decisions were centralized and carried out by the state bureaucracy. Capital investment, production levels, and pricing, matters that in a free-market economy are decided by private industries or even individual factories, remained subject to state control. Multiyear plans, and more detailed annual and even monthly production quotas, were imposed on all industrial enterprises and state collective farms. In practice, however, plans and deadlines were rarely met. The weight of bureaucratic obstructionism and inactivity led to growing inefficiency and the stifling of initiative and creativity.

STALINISM

By the end of the war, Stalin was able to use the Soviet Union's victory to enhance his image as his country's savior. The purges of the 1930s removed any chance of serious opposition, but the secret police state remained firmly entrenched. Spies and police terror ensured that even his immediate subordinates feared their master, whose bursts of suspicion and sudden changes of mood were notorious. Prisons and labor camps remained the fate for political and intellectual dissidents. Both in the Soviet Union and in the Eastern bloc countries, art, music, and literature served to glorify Stalin's "genius." In 1949, when the dictator celebrated his 70th birthday, the gifts he received were sufficient to fill a warehouse. Yet, to the end of his life, he remained insecure and untrusting, capable of turning on his closest supporters.

STALIN AND THE SOVIET BLOC

World War II led to German invasion and occupation of Eastern Europe. Bulgaria, Hungary, and Romania became allies of Germany; Poland was divided between the Soviet Union and Germany at the outset of war and then occupied by the Germans. At the end of the war, Bulgaria, Hungary, Poland, and Romania, together with the Soviet zone of Germany (the future East Germany), all fell under the control of the Red Army. In Stalin's mind, Soviet control of Eastern Europe would guarantee protection against future threats. The governments that were formed there, known as "national fronts," originally consisted of coalitions between local politicians and Moscow-backed Communists. In 1947, however, local communist parties seized power and created one-party regimes.

The postwar Government of National Unity in Czechoslovakia was made up of both Communist and noncommunist parties and enjoyed broad popular support. Its program of economic reform included land redistribution. In 1948, however, the Czech Communist party engineered a coup that placed its country also under Soviet domination. The only Eastern European nation to retain its independence was Yugoslavia, where Josip Broz Tito (1892–1980) had led Communist partisan resistance to the brutal German occupation. After the war, Tito suppressed all noncommunist opposition to establish a one-party Communist state but managed to avoid becoming part of Stalin's empire.

THE STALINIZATION OF EASTERN EUROPE

In all of the Soviet Union's Eastern "satellites," the Stalinist totalitarian system of government imposed the Communist party as sole political force and the Kremlin as leader: All policy decisions and choices were made or at least approved by Moscow. Eastern bloc countries introduced constitutions based on Stalin's Soviet Constitution of 1936, developed elite leaderships, severely restricted individual liberties, including religious worship, established central planning, and imposed Soviet-approved culture. Industries in each of the states were nationalized.

Methods used in the Soviet Union in the 1930s suppressed all traces of indigenous opposition in Eastern Europe. In the late 1940s and early 1950s, local Communist leaders in Hungary and Bulgaria were purged, tried for "treason," and executed. Other show trials took place in Romania and East Germany. In Czechoslovakia in 1952, 14 party leaders, 11 of whom were Jewish, were tried; all but three were subsequently executed. Stalinist control became further reinforced by the creation of several organizations. The formation of the Council for Mutual Economic Assistance (COMECON) in 1949 subordinated the economies of Eastern Europe to that of the Soviet Union. Because Soviet industry was geared to the production of armaments, iron, and steel, the Soviet Union came to rely on Eastern Europe for consumer and other manufactured goods, which were increasingly traded for Soviet raw materials and energy supplies. In the 1970s, COMECON helped Eastern European countries to invest capital in developing technology and equipment for the processing of Soviet natural resources. In its initial stages, however, the organization was chiefly a means for ensuring the dependence of the Eastern bloc on the Soviets.

Soviet military domination of the region was formalized in the Warsaw Pact treaty, signed in 1955, which represented the Eastern European equivalent of NATO. The original members were the Soviet Union and Albania, Bulgaria, Czechoslovakia, East Germany, Hungary, Poland, and Romania. Albania's idiosyncratic Communist regime, led by Enver Hoxha (1908–1985), broke with Moscow in 1961 to form a temporary alliance with Communist China, the Soviet Union's ideological and political rival. The Albanians formally withdrew from the Warsaw Pact alliance in 1968, claiming as their reason the invasion of Czechoslovakia in that year by Warsaw Pact forces.

YUGOSLAVIA: STALIN VERSUS TITO

In 1945, no Eastern European political leadership more enthusiastically espoused communism than Yugoslavia, where the Communist party's heading of the resistance to the Germans had won it considerable popular support. Tito, the former resistance leader, nationalized the economy and introduced centralized planning and collectivized agriculture. As Stalin increased his control of the rest of Eastern Europe, the Yugoslavian leadership began to emphasize nationalism and to resist Soviet pressures to conform to Moscow's directives. Stalin is said to have told Nikita Khrushchev in anger: "I will shake my little finger and there will be no more Tito. He will fall."

In 1948, when Yugoslavia was expelled from the Communist Information Bureau (COMINFORM), Tito held firm to an independent line and began to establish contacts with nations describing themselves as "nonaligned." Strict party control was maintained within Yugoslavia, but communist policy became increasingly modified. By the time of Stalin's death in 1953, the Yugoslavs had introduced "self-management" in factories. In foreign affairs, they firmly rejected Soviet domination in favor of neutrality toward the West.

Tito's success in creating the first nationalist Communist state received official acknowledgment after Khrushchev's denunciation of Stalin in 1956, when Khrushchev admitted that "the ways of socialist development vary in different countries and conditions." Future Soviet actions made clear, however, that the rest of Eastern Europe was to be denied the possibility of trying out variations of their own.

THE SOVIET UNION FROM KHRUSHCHEV TO BREZHNEV

The death of the "Wisest of the Wise" was followed by a power struggle in the Soviet Presidium from which Nikita Khrushchev (served 1958–1964) emerged victorious. The Ukrainian-born Khrushchev was groomed by Stalin to succeed him, and in 1953 he became party secretary.

DE-STALINIZATION

At the Party Congress of 1956, Khrushchev began his campaign of "de-Stalinization." For the first time a Soviet leader attacked some of the Soviet Union's most sacred myths. In a fiery and revolutionary speech, he denounced Stalin's excesses and "cult of personality," accusing him of crimes against his political opponents. As Khrushchev subsequently moved to take over the premiership, he abandoned two of Stalin's chief doctrines: the notion that the closer the Soviet Union moved to true Communism, the more intense the class struggle would become; and the labeling of political opponents as "enemies of the people." Both of these concepts had been important in Stalin's reign of terror. Khrushchev's own rivals, rather than being purged, were dismissed or demoted as "antiparty."

Khrushchev's policies were generally conservative, but the release from Stalinist oppression triggered a period of economic growth. By the 1960s only the United States surpassed the Soviet Union in overall wealth and production.

Nikita Khrushchev pounding the lectern during a speech at the United Nations General Assembly. September 1960. In the course of his fiery speech, Khrushchev took off a shoe to pound the desk, and Harold MacMillan, the British Prime Minister who was also present, drew laughter and applause when he said: "I'd like a translation, please."

His rule also saw several technological breakthroughs. In 1957 the Russians launched *Sputnik I*, the first artificial satellite, and in 1961 they put the first man in space.

Khrushchev's foreign policy was marked by a thaw and increased openness toward the West. Unlike Stalin, who rarely left the Soviet Union, Khrushchev traveled to Western Europe and the United States and United Nations Assembly, where his much-publicized encounters with government leaders and ordinary citizens humanized the Soviet Union's image. The increasing rapprochement with the West was accompanied in 1960 by a diplomatic break with China. The direct cause of the split was a longstanding border dispute between the two nations, but a deeper reason lay in Chinese resentment of Soviet approaches to the West; a Chinese newspaper article of the time referred to the "filthy Soviet revisionist swine." With accusations such as these hurled by both sides, the idea of a united world Communist movement seemed increasingly improbable.

THE CUBAN MISSILE CRISIS

Amid the general relaxation of tension between East and West, the Cuban missile crisis of 1962 came as a fearful warning of the precariousness of peace in the nuclear age. In 1959, Cuba's revolutionary leader Fidel Castro (born 1926) seized power and set up a Communist state less than 100 miles off the U.S. mainland. The following year, when Castro accepted Soviet military aid, America broke off relations with Cuba and supported an unsuccessful invasion of the island by a band of Cuban exiles.

In October 1962, American intelligence sources reported that Soviet forces in Cuba were constructing nuclear missile sites, from which nuclear warheads could be launched well into the heart of the continental United States. The American president, John F. Kennedy (1917–1963), promised reprisal against the Soviets for any missile dispatched from Cuba against the United States and blockaded the seas around the island to prevent the delivery of the warheads.

For the week of October 22 to 28, 1962, amid frantic diplomatic activity, the world faced the most serious crisis of the Cold War. While Khrushchev and Kennedy established direct communication by telephone, Soviet actions gave contradictory signals: Soviet ships sailing toward Cuba turned back, but work continued on the missile sites. Finally, the Soviet Union agreed to dismantle the missile launchers in return for an American promise not to invade Cuba. Khrushchev's face-saving proposal that the Americans should also dismantle some missiles of their own in Turkey led eventually to their removal, but as part of an existing United States–Turkish policy.

The appearance of Soviet weakness that the Cuban adventure created did much to undermine Khrushchev's power. Together with the Sino-Soviet split and growing restlessness in Eastern Europe, it reflected an uneasy instability in Soviet foreign policy. Khrushchev's opponents drew further ammunition from the continuing poor performance of Soviet agriculture, where new technologies he had introduced failed to produce significant improvements. The Central Committee and the Presidium voted him out of office in October 1964. His retreat into quiet retirement represented another stage in the Soviet Union's development of an orderly system of transition.

THE BREZHNEV ERA

The years in power of Leonid Brezhnev (served as first secretary of the Communist party 1964–1982; chief of state 1977–1982) were generally a period of stagnation. The Soviet bureaucracy assumed ever-greater powers, and the state continued to throw its most massive efforts into armaments manufacture. By 1981, the Soviet Union was probably the most fully armed power in history. Yet poor agricultural yields continued to create food shortages. In 1972 and 1975, the Soviet Union had no choice but to purchase large supplies of grain from the United States.

Despite firm attempts to muzzle it, the issue of human rights in the Soviet Union created some attention. Soviet Jews, some 3 million in number, were subject to discrimination at home. At times, Jews were permitted to emigrate, although at other times the government arbitrarily removed their rights. One of the most vocal Soviet dissenters was the writer Alexander Solzhenitsyn (born 1918), who was denied permission to leave the Soviet Union to accept the

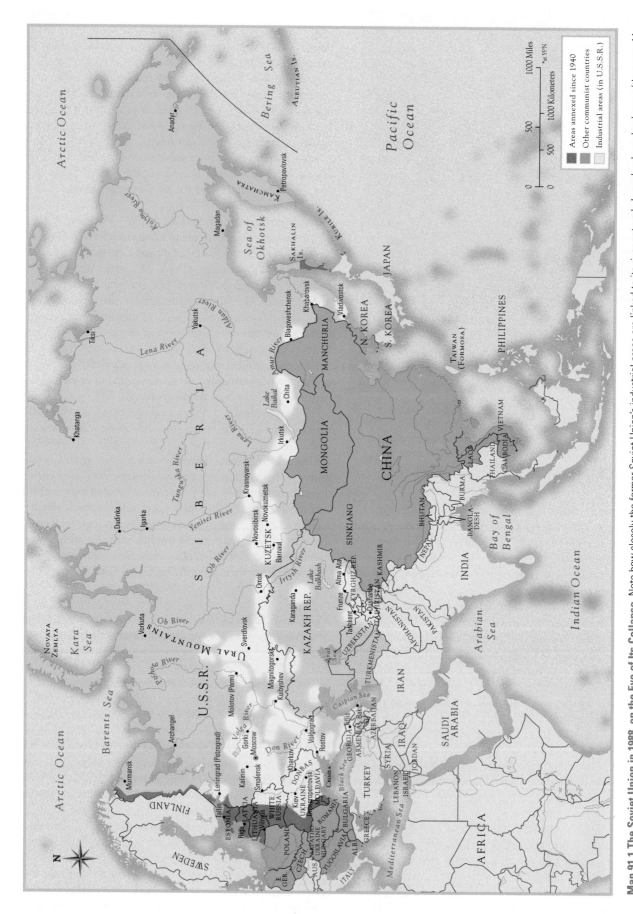

Map 91.1 The Soviet Union in 1988, on the Eve of Its Collapse. Note how closely the former Soviet Union's industrial areas are linked to its river network. In such a huge land-mass (there are 11 time zones, compared with the four in the United States), transport has always been a major problem. The industrial regions in the south of the Central Asian republics follow the line of the ancient Silk Route.

Nobel Prize awarded him in 1970. (An earlier Nobel Prize winner, Boris Pasternak, received similar treatment in 1958.) His *Gulag Archipelago* exposed the brutality of Stalin's labor camps. In 1974, Solzhenitsyn was arrested and deported, and he continued his denunciation of the Soviet regime from his exile in the West.

In foreign policy outside Europe, the Brezhnev years saw the extension of Soviet influence in Africa and Asia. Cuban troops with Soviet arms and support helped set up a Marxist regime in Angola. Similar forces assisted the revolutionary government of Ethiopia to put down rebellions. The biggest, and most disastrous, Soviet adventure was the invasion in 1979 of Afghanistan, to support a Marxist regime Moscow had installed there. In 1988, after years of fruitless fighting between the Soviet troops and United States–backed guerrillas, the Soviet forces withdrew.

REPRESSION AND RESISTANCE IN EASTERN EUROPE

For all the signs of growing détente between the superpowers that intermittently marked the years after Stalin, the Soviet grip on Eastern Europe remained tight. Both Khrushchev and Brezhnev left no doubt that they were prepared to use brute force to remove any government not fully under Soviet control.

THE HUNGARIAN UPRISING OF 1956

Khrushchev's speech to the Moscow Party Congress of 1956 acknowledged that the Yugoslav-Soviet break had been

SIGNIFICANT DATES

The Soviet Union and Eastern Europe After 1945

1948	Communist party coup in Czechoslovakia
1949	Formation of COMECON
1953	Death of Stalin; Khrushchev in office
1955	Creation of Warsaw Pact
1956	Hungarian uprising
1957	*Sputnik* satellite launched
1960	Soviet break with China
1961	Soviets put first man in space
1962	Cuban missile crisis
1968	Prague spring
1974	Deportation of Solzhenitsyn
1979	Soviet invasion of Afghanistan
1980	Solidarity labor union formed in Poland
1985	Gorbachev general secretary of Soviet Communist party
1989	Fall of Berlin Wall

avoidable and hinted that different forms of socialist development were legitimate. Events later that same year proved the emptiness of his words. Late in October 1956, mass demonstrations in favor of political change, including withdrawal from the Warsaw Pact alliance, broke out in Poland. The situation was resolved peacefully, when a faction of the official party threw its support behind the reformist leader Władysław Gomułka (served 1956–1970). Gomułka managed to convince the Soviet leadership that the central institutions of party government remained intact and that Poland intended to keep unchanged its close ties with the Soviet Union and membership in the Warsaw Pact. Throughout the 1960s, Gomułka continued a policy of cautious social and economic reform.

The Hungarians were encouraged by the Polish success. Within days, crowds gathered in Budapest and in Hungary's other big cities, demanding similar changes—withdrawal from the Warsaw Pact among them. The Central Committee of the Hungarian Communist party turned to Imre Nagy (1896–1958). During an earlier period as premier, from 1953 to 1955, Nagy had been openly critical of the Soviets and was ousted by the Stalinist party secretary. Now he was restored to office. In an atmosphere of considerable nervousness, Soviet troops entered Budapest to keep the situation under control, only to be withdrawn four days later. Nagy and the new party secretary, Janos Kadar (1912–1989), were given the chance to set up a regime that was acceptable to Moscow, as Gomułka had done a few days earlier in Poland. On October 30, the Soviet government issued a statement affirming the principle of noninterference.

The same day Nagy, perhaps under the influence of his more extreme supporters, declared that a multiparty system would be introduced, and moved to make the Hungarian army independent of the Soviets. One day later, Nagy announced Hungary's intention of withdrawing from the Warsaw Pact. On November 1, he proclaimed Hungary neutral. On November 4, Soviet tanks again entered Budapest. They were met with mass uprisings, which they crushed. With the revolt under control, the troops arrested thousands of Hungarians. Many were executed, others deported to Siberia. As for Nagy, the Soviets seized him from the Hungarians and executed him. (In 1989, Nagy was officially rehabilitated, and his remains received a solemn state funeral.)

Kadar, Nagy's former associate, became premier and helped the Soviets eliminate the remaining rebel leaders. He served as prime minister from 1956 to 1958, and again from 1961 to 1965, and remained party secretary until 1988. Although Kadar permitted a certain flexibility—the so-called goulash communism—he remained close to Moscow. His death in 1989 came at exactly the same time as the collapse of the Communist regime in Hungary.

World reaction to the brutal extinction of the 1956 uprising was one of shock, but became confused by the fact that the events occurred in the middle of another international crisis, that involving the Suez Canal (see Topic 90). In the course of a few days in the fall of 1956, the two superpowers asserted themselves, albeit by very different means. The

Soviet tanks in Budapest. November 4, 1956. As the picture shows, the civilian population of Budapest tried to remain calmly defiant, but mass arrests and deportations, together with the execution of Imre Nagy, the prime minister, soon put an end to resistance. Approximately 65,000 Soviet troops remained in Hungary until the collapse of the Communist regime there in 1989.

United States reined in its allies by opposing the British and French takeover of the Canal; the Soviet Union made it only too clear that it would tolerate no true independence in Eastern Europe.

THE PRAGUE SPRING OF 1968

Unlike Hungary and Poland, Czechoslovakia remained under continuous Stalinist rule. Its president from 1957 to 1968 was Antonín Novotny (1904–1975), a hard-line supporter of Moscow. By the late 1960s, however, with the centrally planned economy performing increasingly poorly, dissent began to grow. The Slovaks, in particular, claimed that Czech regions were receiving preferential treatment. Matters came to a head at the beginning of 1968, when reformers within the official Communist party ousted Novotny and replaced him with Alexander Dubcek.

As spring approached, Dubcek and his supporters carried out an ever-increasing process of democratization. They allowed independent political movements to develop, reduced censorship, promised to guarantee individual freedoms, and proposed to create a federation giving equal rights to Czechs and Slovaks. A special congress was scheduled for September to reform the party along democratic lines.

Soviet reaction began with press criticism and escalated in July with Soviet troop movements in bordering countries. In the same month, all of the Warsaw Pact members except Czechoslovakia (and Albania, which had broken with Moscow earlier) met to discuss the conditions that would legitimize intervention. These conditions were made public a few months later and constituted the "Brezhnev Doctrine." They stated that "when internal and external forces hostile to socialism seek to reverse the development of any socialist country whatsoever in the direction of the restoration of the capitalist order . . . this becomes a common problem and concern of all socialist countries."

In August 1968, Warsaw Pact forces moved into Czechoslovakia (Romania did not take part in the invasion). Dubcek and the others who had tried to introduce "socialism with a human face" were purged, and the staunchly pro-Soviet Gustav Husak was put in charge. Husak rigidly enforced Stalinist policies of state planning, which, together with inept management, undermined the economy. By the late 1980s, with Gorbachev's reforms in effect in the Soviet Union, Czechoslovakia remained the only bastion of orthodox Stalinism in Eastern Europe. In 1989, in the regime's last weeks, Dubcek emerged from retirement to play a part in leading the revolution.

POLAND AND THE BIRTH OF SOLIDARITY

In Poland, Gomułka's program of cautious reform failed to prevent food shortages and a steep rise in the prices of the available supplies. In 1970, Gomułka resigned and was replaced by Edward Gierek (born 1913). The problem of the

Demonstrators in Prague rally round the stand taken by their leader, Alexander Dubcek. August 1968. The picture was taken in the heart of Prague's Old Town, one of the few urban areas in Central Europe not to suffer heavy bomb damage in World War II: note the 19th-century buildings. The movement known as the "Prague Spring" was crushed within a few days by the Soviets with the help of troops from other Warsaw Pact members.

scarcity of food remained unsolved, however, and in the late 1970s public unrest led to the creation in 1980 of an independent trade union movement, "Solidarity." Solidarity led a series of strikes to demand lower prices; toward the end of the 1970s, the staggering size of the national debt had forced the government to raise the price of basic supplies to more realistic levels.

After beginning as a protest against the rising cost of living, the Solidarity movement began to press for political reform, including the establishment of independent trade unions. In 1981, Gierek was driven out of office and at the end of the year, under Soviet pressure, Poland's new leader, General Wojciech Jaruzelski (born 1923), imposed martial law and arrested Solidarity's leaders. In the year of their release, 1983, Solidarity's head, Lech Wałesa (born 1943), received the Nobel Peace Prize for his contribution "to ensure workers' rights to establish their own organizations."

Solidarity maintained a low profile for the next five years. With the beginnings of reform in the Soviet Union, however, the trade union returned to the fray. In 1987, with the economy still in poor shape, the government announced reforms that included a reduction in central planning and wage incentives. For the first time a popular referendum was held to approve the plan. Massive public rejection of the government's proposals, the result of general lack of confidence, led to further rises in food prices. In a mood of widespread hostility, a wave of strikes broke out throughout the country.

In 1988, Solidarity was revived. The movement's leaders sat down with government representatives and other political forces and negotiated an end to the strikes. Subsequent talks led to the establishment of a noncommunist prime minister— ending the Communist party's monopoly on power—and the holding of free elections. Thus Poland set the lead in breaking Soviet control of Eastern Europe.

THE GORBACHEV ERA: *GLASNOST* AND *PERESTROIKA*

The liberalization of Eastern Europe would have been inconceivable in the Brezhnev era. With the death of Brezhnev and his two elderly successors, however, power passed to a new generation of Soviet leadership. The changes inaugurated by Mikhail Gorbachev (born 1931), general secretary of the Soviet Communist party from 1985 to 1992, produced radical and far-reaching reforms in the Soviet Union, freed Eastern Europe from dependence on Moscow, and began to end the Cold War.

Gorbachev was born in the Stavropol region of southern Russia and began his political career as party first secretary there in 1970. In 1978, he was called to Moscow to take over the controversial task of running Soviet agriculture. Within two years he was promoted to the Politburo, becoming its youngest member.

Gorbachev's election as party leader in 1985 signaled a dramatic change in direction. The conservatives in the Kremlin, led by Yegor Ligachev (born 1921), continued to oppose the Gorbachev reform program, but most of the Brezhnev generation of political leaders were forced into retirement. Gorbachev's most vocal opponents in the early 1990s were those who felt that the pace of change was too slow; their leader was Boris Yeltsin (born 1931).

THE REFORMS OF GORBACHEV

By the mid-1980s the Soviet economy was still stubbornly resisting all attempts at improvement. Sluggish and backward, it was responsible for keeping the quality of life of most Soviet citizens well below that of capitalist countries and even inferior to that of some Eastern European nations. In the 1950s, the Soviet annual growth rate was around 6 percent; by the

1980s it had fallen to 1.5 percent. Gorbachev's economic reforms were intended to free industry from the stifling hand of centralized state planning by encouraging decentralization, reducing bureaucratic inefficiency, and using market incentives to encourage increased output.

He symbolized these goals in two words: *glasnost* (openness) and *perestroika* (restructuring). The first signified an opening up of Soviet society, so that individuals could use their initiative to break through the heavy weight of bureaucracy and general apathy. *Glasnost* also signaled an openness to comment and criticism. With *perestroika*, the institutions of the state were to be restudied and, if necessary, restructured.

The Soviet economy was in so desperate a state, and its habits so deeply ingrained, that little progress was visible. Food supplies and consumer goods remained in short supply, and living conditions showed no real sign of improvement. Yet the more general effects of *glasnost* and *perestroika* transformed Soviet society and wrought important change in international relations.

Within the Soviet Union, the Gorbachev era brought greater freedom for political dissent and open discussion of problems. Political dissidents, including the distinguished physicist Andrei Sakharov (1921–1989), were released. Artists, musicians, and writers had a new freedom of expression. Heated parliamentary debate accompanied the passage of reform measures. Yet the new democratic spirit had its limitations. By 1990, Gorbachev had assumed virtually supreme power, ruling as the Soviet Union's first president to be "elected" by Parliament.

In international relations, the need to reduce Soviet spending on armaments produced a new flexibility in negotiations to reduce weapons. A series of summit meetings between Gorbachev and American President Ronald Reagan (born 1911) produced the signing of a treaty to reduce intermediate-range nuclear weapons in 1987. Further arms talks on both conventional and nuclear weapons seemed likely to produce more agreements. Soviet involvement in Africa, Asia, and the Caribbean was reduced, economic aid to Cuba was cut, and in 1988 Soviet troops began to withdraw from Afghanistan.

THE REVOLUTIONS OF 1989

In the last three months of 1989, almost half a century of Soviet and Communist domination in Eastern Europe collapsed. Inspired by the sight of free elections in Poland, increasing crowds of peaceful demonstrators drove their governments from power.

THE FALL OF 1989

The long process of negotiating shared rule in Poland ended in August 1989, when Tadeusz Mazowiecki, a Solidarity member, became prime minister; his cabinet included both Solidarity representatives and Communists. Over the late summer months, thousands of East Germans, "voting with their feet," began to pour westward. Many sought visas at the West German Embassy in Budapest but needed to find a way out of Hungary to travel through Austria to West Germany. In September, the Hungarians opened their border with Austria to allow them to leave. October, ironically, saw the celebration of the 40th anniversary of the founding of East Germany. As parades marched through East Berlin, at a ceremony attended by an impassively smiling Gorbachev, the stream of refugees became a flood. By the end of the month, East Germany's leader, Erich Honecker (1912–1997), after a series of anxious meetings with Gorbachev during the latter's visit, quit as party chief. Meanwhile in Hungary, the party was being liberalized. Already in the previous June the government had signaled its change of attitude by staging the imposing ceremonies that accompanied the hero's reburial accorded to Imre Nagy. Their facilitating the exit of East German refugees was another sign of yielding. Now, as the crisis intensified in East Germany, the Hungarian Communist party changed its name and announced free multiparty elections for the following year.

In November, the already hectic pace intensified. In a last desperate attempt to deter its people from leaving their country, the East German authorities began to tear down the Berlin Wall—hated symbol of oppression. As the world watched in disbelief, East and West Berliners danced and drank champagne on the spot where armed

U.S. President Ronald Reagan and Mikhail Gorbachev, Chairman of the Praesidium of the Supreme Soviet, in New York. 1988. Reagan was in the last year of his second term as President, while Gorbachev was to fall from power in 1991. The two men had first met in Finland, one year earlier, and their apparent ease in working together helped bring an end to the Cold War.

Markel/Liaison

guards had patrolled hours earlier. Far from quieting the excitement, the removal of the wall increased the upheaval, as evidence of massive corruption at the highest level of the party began to circulate. Within weeks the Communists abandoned their positions, and a coalition of political representatives began to prepare for free elections early in the following year.

Inspired by success elsewhere, the people of Czechoslovakia began their own mass demonstrations. At first, the government responded with tough police action, but once again the sheer force of events drove the Communist party from power. A weary but jubilant Dubcek addressed the crowds, and the playwright Václav Havel (born 1936) emerged as the dominant figure in his country's political rebirth. Again, elections were promised for the following year.

Even Bulgaria, a country with virtually no experience of democratic politics, deposed its aging Stalinist dictator, Todor Zhivkov (born 1911); he was subsequently accused of corruption.

REVOLUTION IN ROMANIA

The only remaining Soviet bloc country unaffected by the ferment was Romania, where Nicolae Ceausescu (1918–1990) and his wife Elena presided over a bizarre form of Communist dictatorship. Ceausescu's relations with Moscow had been strained for years. In the 1980s, as his country lurched from one economic crisis to another, he poured resources into grandiose construction projects. Much of Bucharest was bulldozed to make space for a new "imperial" capital, with a vast palace, in which Nicolae and Elena were each to have two immense office suites. In the countryside, villages were destroyed, and their inhabitants forcibly gathered together in "collectives." Overseeing all of this was the dreaded secret police, infamous for their cruelty.

At first, the apparatus of repression seemed sufficient to deter protest demonstrations. In mid-December 1989, when protestors began to gather, police fired on the crowd; around 200 people were killed. The violence provoked an immediate reaction. Angry demonstrators stormed through Bucharest. Gun battles broke out between army units sympathetic to the crowds and the secret police force. Ceausescu and his wife fled. Captured by army forces, within hours they received a military trial, were sentenced to death, and summarily executed.

The path toward democratic government in Romania remained fraught with obstacles. Many of those remaining in power were compromised by their complicity with the Ceausescus. The holding of genuine free elections seemed problematic. Yet at least a start had been made on dismantling a regime that—even for Eastern Europe—had found new extremes of repression.

Latvians watching a statue of Lenin come down. 1991. The plinth on which the statue had been standing is visible in the background. The end of Communist rule in the three Baltic states—Latvia, Lithuania, and Estonia—was complicated by the large number of Russians living in them; in Latvia about one-third of the population was Russian.

Putting the Soviet Union and Eastern Europe in Perspective

The end of World War II found the Soviet Union and the United States facing one another as opposing powers, anxious to demonstrate their own supremacy, and fearing one another's military capacity. With its political stability and economic dynamism, the United States was able, in a gesture of enlightened self-interest, to help Western European reconstruction of economies and democratic institutions. While Stalin consolidated his dominion over Eastern Europe, his natural paranoia was reinforced by the American success.

Khrushchev aimed at achieving recognition of his country's superpower status by a combination of promises and threats. During his rule, the Soviet Union extended its activities to the Third World, which Stalin had largely ignored. Thus the struggle of former colonies in Africa, Asia, and Central America for national independence became the battleground for confrontation between the two superpowers.

The same policy was continued under Brezhnev. No less than 14 Soviet-backed revolutionary movements around the world achieved power in the second half of the 1970s. At the same time, the Soviet Union claimed military parity by building huge numbers of nuclear missiles, while investing unprecedented sums in its naval forces. In Eastern Europe, the Brezhnev Doctrine maintained rigid control until the upheavals of 1989.

Fundamental to Gorbachev's attempt to modernize the Soviet state was the realization that it could not afford massive spending abroad to support friendly regimes and equally vast sums at home on an armaments buildup. The maintenance of revolutionary movements and governments drained national resources and brought in return little power or prestige. To cut the military budget required better relations with the United States—an end to the Cold War—and a stable and independent Eastern Europe.

To move on so many fronts at the same time inevitably presented enormous risks. In the first place, domestic opposition to the Gorbachev reform plan from both right and left remained an unpredictable factor. Second, the very existence of the Soviet Union came under threat, not from outside, but from the growing demands of individual republics for independence (see Topic 95). Third, old rivalries and hostilities between the various Eastern European nations and ethnic groups, stifled under the grey weight of Stalinism, soon began to emerge. Yet another complication was the reunification of Germany, with its effect on the balance of power in Europe, and on plans for European unity.

Yet by the early 1990s, many Europeans, both West and East, were more hopeful about the future of the old Continent than at any time in the 20th century. The arms buildup to World War I, the tensions and failures of the interwar years, and the grim confrontations of the Cold War were replaced by talk of the common house of Europe (see Topic 95). It was at least possible that at some future time NATO and the Warsaw Pact would no longer be needed—or at least would no longer serve their original purpose. The Western European union of 1992 began to appear not as the final stage in European unification, but as a beginning.

Questions for Further Study

1. What were the main stages in the "de-Stalinization" of the Soviet Union? How far was the process reversed under Brezhnev?
2. How did the Communist regimes of Eastern Europe differ in their relationship to the Soviet Union?
3. What factors helped prepare the countries of Eastern Europe for the collapse of Soviet influence? Were they chiefly political, economic, or social?
4. To what extent were Gorbachev's reforms in the Soviet Union a reaction to a process that could not be halted?

Suggestions for Further Reading

Banac, Ivo. *With Stalin Against Tito: Conformist Splits in Yugoslav Communism*. Ithaca, NY, 1889

Cohen, S. E., and K. Van Den Heuvel. *Voices of Glasnost. Interviews with Gorbachev's Reformers*. New York, 1989.

Bills, Scott L. *Empire and Cold War: The Roots of the US-Third World Antagonism, 1945–1947*. London, 1990.

Conquest, Robert. *Stalin, Breaker of Nations*. London, 1991.

Davies, R.W. *Soviet History in the Gorbachev Revolution*. Bloomington, IN, 1989.

Garton Ash, T. *We the People: The Revolutions of 1989*. London, 1990.

Hanson, Philip. *From Stagnation to Catastroika: Commentaries on the Soviet Economy, 1983–1991*. Westport, CT, 1992.

Hosking, G. *The Awakening of the Soviet Union*. Cambridge, MA, 1990

May, Ernest R., and Philip D. Zelikow, eds. *The Kennedy Tapes: Inside the White House during the Cuban Missile Crisis*. Cambridge, MA, 1997.

Roberts, Geoffrey K. *The Soviet Union in World Politics: Coexistence, Revolution, and Cold War*. New York, 1999.

Rothschild, A. *Return to Diversity: A Political History of East Central Europe*. New York, 1990.

Saxonberg, Steven. *The Fall: A Comparative Study of the End of Communism in Czechoslovakia, East Germany, Hungary, and Poland*. Amsterdam, 2001.

Selbourne, D. *Death of the Dark Hero: Eastern Europe 1987–1990*. London, 1990.

Service, Robert. *A History of Twentieth-Century Russia*. London, 1998.

White, Stephen. *Communism and Its Collapse*. New York, 2001.

InfoTrac College Edition

Enter the search term *Khrushchev* using Key Terms.

Enter the search term *Cold War* using Key Terms.

Enter the search term *Soviet Union relations with the United States* using the Subject Guide.

MOBILITY AND SOCIAL CHANGE: TOWARD THE CONSUMER SOCIETY

Throughout most of Europe, the postwar years saw the restructuring of society by increasing state support for the lives of large numbers of citizens. Social welfare legislation proved so popular that even when, in the 1970s, national economies began to decline, governments avoided cutbacks.

Several groups played a special role in forming postwar society. Many intellectuals, who had seen left-wing movements as the only real defense against fascism and capitalist dictatorship, grew increasingly disillusioned with the political alternatives available. Others preferred action to words. Growing dissatisfaction with capitalist society led to widespread protests, which reached a head in 1968 with violent student and worker demonstrations. On the whole, the "Spirit of '68" consisted of a release of accumulated tensions without producing any major change of direction. The 1970s and 1980s brought a general relaxation in the polarization between left and right. The only major exception in Western Europe was Britain, where confrontation between government and trade unions continued to influence political life.

Perhaps the most significant changes in late-20th-century society were produced by the women's movement. As women became an increasingly important part of the workforce, and began to play a part in running industry and government, their traditional role became increasingly questioned and rethought. The battle for equal rights was fought at a variety of levels, and few elements of society remained untouched, from campaigns for national office to individual families.

The whole structure of family life in Western society entered a period of considerable turmoil. Greater sexual freedom, coupled with vastly improved methods of contraception, caused many people to rethink the institution of marriage. The birthrate declined. Perhaps more significantly, divorce became widespread and by 1980 had more than doubled.

The increase in prosperity created new attitudes and expectations. Urban-industrial society became virtually the only form of life. Within the cities, young workers and professionals—without family responsibilities, and therefore with more money to spend—were barraged by publicity, as advertising assumed ever-greater importance for most corporations. Many workers from the Third World, attracted by Western prosperity, settled in Western Europe. Their arrival provided cheap labor for unpopular jobs but also led to an increase in racism and the resurgence of the far right.

By the early 1990s, society in Western Europe was moving into a postindustrial phase. As machines, in particular the computer, revolutionized the processes of industrial production, more and more people were working in service industries rather than in factories. This "new industrial revolution" seemed bound to lead to radical changes in the lifestyles and social roles of both individuals and institutions.

LIFE IN THE WELFARE STATE

The spread of the welfare state ushered in profound changes in the lives of ordinary citizens. Social policy was no longer only a means of improving the lives of the workers because the expanded concept of welfare aimed to achieve a broad social balance. An all-party agreement in France in 1946 looked to the extension of social security to "promote the solidarity and renewal of French society." The Basic Law of West Germany, formulated in 1948, declared that the state was a "social state" with a "social market economy." Not all of these egalitarian aims were achieved in practice. In West Germany, different classes received different treatment: Blue-collar workers and white-collar salaried employees had separate insurance funds.

Welfare systems spread rapidly in the 1950s and 1960s. In 1950, the only Western European countries where more than 70 percent of the population were covered by welfare legislation were Britain, Denmark, Norway, and Sweden. By 1975, the only countries where coverage was still below 70 percent were Greece, Portugal, and Spain. Although Eastern Europe dismissed the notion of welfare as a "bourgeois capitalist concept," these governments tended to introduce legislation providing insurance and pensions, which had been initially reserved for state employees.

THE WELFARE STATE AND THE FAMILY

The welfare state affected life from birth to death. In Sweden in the 1970s, public doctors treated 99.7 percent of all newborn babies, and all parents were required by law to submit their children to a medical checkup when they reached the age of four. Children throughout Western and Eastern Europe went to state-subsidized schools and then on to public universities. Unlike the United States, there were very few private European universities.

A young couple could generally count on some form of subsidized housing and help in bringing up their children. Welfare legislation introduced in France in 1946 gave women benefits and maternity leave before and after pregnancy and provided day care centers and after-school programs. Most European countries followed suit. At work, employees were covered by national insurance schemes, which would allow them treatment by a national health service. On retirement, they spent the last years of their lives drawing a state pension.

Nor did the welfare state cover only basic expenses. The state ran, and therefore controlled the cost of, energy, communications, and transport. Culture and the arts were also subsidized, and most postwar governments in Europe had a Ministry of Culture. One of France's most distinguished literary figures, André Malraux, served in such a post, and ministers of culture played important if controversial roles in Eastern European politics. State support for the arts continued into the 1980s. In the opera season of 1987–1988, La Scala (Milan) received public funds to cover 74 percent of its expenses; similar grants were 78 percent for the Munich opera, 76 percent for Vienna, and 82 percent for Paris. In the same period, the Metropolitan Opera House in New York could count on 2 percent.

THE WELFARE CRISIS

In 1950 the average proportion of the gross national product devoted by Western European countries to social welfare was 9.4 percent. By 1977 this figure had risen to 22.4 percent. The expense of health care alone more than doubled. At the same time, the average age of the European population continued to rise. Improved medical techniques, which were more widely available, enabled increasing numbers of people to survive to retirement age; on retirement, they began drawing pensions and continued to need state medical care.

The vast rise in costs coincided with the economic recessions of the 1970s. The enormous growth of the 1950s and 1960s turned stagnant, and most Western European countries were badly hit by the 1970s oil crises. The welfare state, which had seemed a permanent feature of postwar European life, became subject to agonized debate. Conservatives argued that social welfare was too expensive and too inefficient and should be dismantled, while private enterprise and individual initiative should be encouraged. On the other side, radical critics claimed that social legislation emphasized material welfare without creating a sense of community.

Throughout the 1980s, both conservative and socialist governments in Western Europe cut back benefit levels. Nonetheless welfare was so integral a part of the lives of millions that most countries continued to devote large proportions of their annual budget to it, hoping to cover the costs with higher taxes and increased production. Only in Thatcher's Britain was there a sustained attempt to shift back the cost of welfare to the private sector. The results produced furious public debate about the consequences for Britain's educational and medical systems and about the general issue of social justice.

THE INTELLECTUALS' DILEMMA: EXISTENTIALISM OR COMMITMENT

In the euphoria of victory in 1945, the intellectual map seemed easy enough to interpret. Of the two chief movements of the 1930s, the radical right was discredited beyond repair. The left was triumphant because Communists and Socialists had been among the leaders in resistance struggles throughout Europe, both West and East. Furthermore, the Soviet Union, the supreme Communist power, had been one of the principal architects of military victory.

Yet as the Soviets moved to occupy Eastern Europe and set up their puppet governments there, doubts began to arise. Even before the war, some intellectuals had seen the darker side of the Russian Revolution and its consequences. In 1940, Arthur Koestler (1905–1983) published *Darkness at Noon*, a novel that drew on the Moscow purges of the 1930s to indict the excesses of Stalinism.

PUBLIC FIGURES AND PRIVATE LIVES

SIMONE DE BEAUVOIR AND JEAN-PAUL SARTRE

The most overarching attempt to find a path forward for modern society was that of the existentialists. More an attitude than a coherent system of philosophy, existentialism began in the 19th century with the ideas of the Danish theologian Søren Kierkegaard (1813–1855). According to Kierkegaard, individual humans are more important than collective abstractions—"The crowd is untruth."

The most important exponent of the existentialist view after World War II was the Frenchman Jean-Paul Sartre (1905–1980). Sartre's intellectual position was reinforced by his experiences; after being a prisoner of war, he lived through the German occupation of France and played a part in the Resistance. After the war, his writings served as inspiration to a generation of intellectuals. His existentialist works tried to come to terms with the problems of living in a world without God, where there is no ultimate significance to existence. People are alone, forced to decide who they are, "condemned to be free." In such a world, it was necessary to come to terms with freedom and try to devise a system of behavior.

It was typical of Sartre's commitment to intellectual enquiry that he both wrote about and explored in his actual life the issue of feminism. His inspiration in this was Simone de Beauvoir (1908–1986). Together, they became the most celebrated intellectual couple in the postwar period.

De Beauvoir grew up conventionally enough in a Parisian middle-class family. After World War I, when she needed to find some means of supporting herself, against her family's wishes she decided to become an academic. De Beauvoir and Sartre met at the Sorbonne and fell in love. For the rest of Sartre's life, they maintained an intense emotional and intellectual union. Refusing to marry, they also remained independent, often living separately and having other love affairs.

De Beauvoir's most widely read book, *The Second Sex* (1949), dealt with the nature of womanhood and analyzed the way in which women are locked into gender definitions. For many women, the traditional feminine role had its attractions. The "independent woman," by contrast, preferred the harder but more rewarding life of work, self-definition, and significant interaction with the male "Other." *The Second Sex* was widely read, at least in part because of de Beauvoir's relationship with Sartre. Some readers were shocked (or claimed to be) by her frank discussion of issues such as misogyny and lesbianism. Others accused Sartre of having written the book. His influence on her thought emerged more consistently, however, in her four volumes of memoirs, in which she described her own self-creation by means of her relationships with Sartre and others.

De Beauvoir and Sartre illustrated by the example of their own public lives the possibilities opened up by collaboration between individual men and women on equal terms. (In private, de Beauvoir seems to have been rather more conventionally bourgeois, often abandoning her feminism to cater to Sartre's wishes.) Both of them inspired countless individuals to question the basic premises that underpinned society and to search for new and more satisfying ways to face the uncertainties of the modern world. De Beauvoir, although criticized by early feminists for underestimating the need for radical change, became in the late 1960s one of the women's movement's most important leaders.

THE INTELLECTUAL AND SOCIETY

As many began to face disillusionment with all forms of social organization, some artists and thinkers turned with increased despair to the search for meaning in a hostile world. The works of the Irish playwright Samuel Beckett (1906–1989) presented an enigmatic vision of a world beyond logic. In his best-known play, *Waiting for Godot*, two bizarre characters wait for an event that never takes place: the arrival of Godot. Is Godot God? Does his nonarrival illustrate the hopelessness of life?

Other intellectuals sought to illuminate aspects of the modern dilemma. The Swedish filmmaker Ingmar Bergman used his films to explore the disappearance of religious faith and the demands of contemporary despair. As knowledge of the atrocities of the Nazi death camps began to come to light, some writers tried to give voice to the experience. In some cases they were actual survivors. The Italian Primo Levi (1919–1985) and the Romanian-born Elie Wiesel (born 1928) both wrote works meditating on their experiences in the camps.

Not all thinkers took so hopeless a view of the possibilities for change. Among the first postwar writers to take a role in government was André Malraux (1901–1976), one of the most distinguished figures in French 20th-century culture. Although never a Marxist, Malraux had impeccable left-wing credentials. He fought for the Republicans in the Spanish Civil War, was one of France's leading antifascists before World War II, and was active in the Resistance. He served as minister of information from 1945 to 1946 and as minister of culture from 1959 to 1969.

Many on the left accused Malraux of betraying their cause by taking the Gaullist (that is, right-wing) side in the Cold War. Malraux insisted that he was defending society against Stalinism. In perhaps his most profound literary work, *The Voices of Silence* (1951), he claimed that art— "the essential, eternal assertion of human freedom over destiny"—transcended history.

In some cases intellectuals used their work to fight for social and political change without actually playing an active role. Few voices spoke out more powerfully or authoritatively about the evils of Stalinism than Alexander Solzhenitsyn (born 1918), who based his descriptions of Stalin's labor camps on his own experiences there. At first suppressed, then expelled, Solzhenitsyn moved from epic denunciations of Stalinism to broader criticism of the nature of modern society.

In Britain, social criticism became symbolized in the figure of the "angry young man"—classless, disillusioned, rebellious. The archetypal example appeared in *Look Back in Anger*, a play by John Osborne (born 1929), first performed in 1956. Osborne and others bitterly questioned the comfortable assurances of the welfare state and of middle-class society. A more specific issue that several writers addressed was that of feminism. Sylvia Plath (1932–1963) and Doris Lessing (born 1919) both moved to England—Plath from the United States and Lessing from southern Africa. Their works explore feminine consciousness from a variety of angles.

STUDENTS, WORKERS, AND POWER: 1968 AND ITS AFTERMATH

By the mid-1960s, the driving force of European renewal had begun to run out of steam. After the initial excitement of reconstruction, society began to show deep signs of protest and grievance. The two chief groups to lead demonstrations against the state were students and workers.

THE STUDENT UPRISINGS OF 1968

The wave of student demonstrations that peaked in the spring of 1968 was by no means limited to Western Europe. Similar protest rallies took place in Eastern Europe, in Africa, and in the United States; in the latter, there were passionate demonstrations against American participation in the Vietnam War.

The war in Vietnam also figured in the European protests, but there were also more local causes. By the late 1960s, the "baby boom" of the war years had led to overcrowded classrooms and teaching facilities. Furthermore, the increased number of students qualifying meant that job opportunities were becoming more scarce. To some extent the problem became seen in terms of class warfare: Few university professors and not enough students were from the working classes.

The most spectacular demonstrations occurred in Paris in May 1968. When clumsy police actions tried to prevent student sit-ins and classroom occupations, the situation erupted. Students occupied the main university quarter and set up street barricades—in the spirit of 1848—to prevent police access. The general goals of the demonstrators remained vague. They felt that society should be changed but were inspired by no coherent ideology. "Be realistic: demand the impossible!" was one of the popular slogans.

This lack of an overall strategy diminished the long-term effect of the protests. When order was restored, most governments reformed university structures and increased the influence in academic affairs of students and younger faculty members. On the whole, though, the student demonstrations gave voice to a general sense of uncertainty about contemporary society without producing a real change of direction. When, 30 years later, former participants gathered throughout Europe to remember and commemorate the events of their youth, the mood was generally more of nostalgia than of political protest. Many of those involved admitted that they had become as "bourgeois" as those against whom they had protested.

LABOR PROTESTS

One direct effect of the student demonstrations, however, was to galvanize workers into protest action. In the inflation-ridden 1960s, wages often failed to keep up with prices. Factory work, with its unending assembly-line monotony, provided little work satisfaction. In many countries, trade unions seemed less concerned with the welfare of their members than with waging their own political battles.

French riot police beating students at the Sorbonne, the University of Paris. May 1968. The picture was taken near the Luxembourg Gardens. The excessive use of violence and tear gas by the police, visible here, won some public support for the young demonstrators, but the protesters scared and alienated others, who helped achieve the victory of de Gaulle in elections later the same year.

The problems came to a head in France in 1968, as workers followed the example of the students and took to the streets; at the height of the protests, some 10 million were involved. A frightened government increased wages. One month later, the government consolidated its power when de Gaulle and his party swept to victory in a general election. Many of those who voted for him, including Communists, were also voting against the radical student protestors who had challenged the values of postwar society.

WOMEN IN A CHANGING SOCIETY: THE CHALLENGE OF FEMINISM

After World War II, women gained the right to vote in every European nation except Switzerland and the principality of Liechtenstein (Swiss women eventually got the vote in the 1970s). Women have been particularly active in Socialist and Communist political parties, where a long tradition of support for women's rights attracted them. In the 1950s and 1960s, politically active women tended to involve themselves in the great international issues of the day: the dangers of nuclear testing, oppression in Eastern Europe, and the Vietnam War.

Beginning in the late 1960s, new feminist groups began to form to deal specifically with the treatment of women. The first international meeting of the new women's movement was held at Oxford, Great Britain, in 1970. By the end of the decade, hundreds of groups throughout Europe debated women's issues from widely different and sometimes conflicting positions. Some of these distinctions were the result of the specific situation of women in individual countries.

EUROPEAN WOMEN, EAST AND WEST

The Soviet Union was the first government in history to include female emancipation in its constitution. Liberal divorce laws, state child care facilities, and legalized abortion also existed. Yet the reality of gender relations there was far from ideal. As late as the 1980s, Soviet women earned only two-thirds of male income for the same work. Almost half of the women in the labor force held unskilled manual jobs. Although women held almost one-third of all membership cards in the Communist party, they represented only a tiny minority in party or government posts.

In Western Europe, conditions for women varied. In 1970, women in most European countries earned a little more than half the wages earned by men in equivalent positions. In technical professions, such as medicine and engineering, Soviet women held a significantly higher percent-

Five women who were political leaders in the 1970s. *Top:* Sirimavo Bandaranaike of Sri Lanka (1971); Golda Meir of Israel (1973); *center:* Indira Gandhi of India (1977); *bottom:* Margaret Thatcher of Great Britain (1979); Vigdis Finnbogadottir of Iceland (1980). Indira Gandhi (no relation to the Mahatma Gandhi) was assassinated in 1984; the others either retired or lost power.

age of positions than American women. Yet legislation favoring equality and women's rights had been passed in virtually every Western nation. Even in southern countries such as Italy, where the influence of the Catholic Church was still pervasive, divorce laws were enacted.

FEMINISM IN WEST GERMANY

Women in West Germany faced two problems in organizing themselves as a separate and distinct category. In the first place, postwar German society encouraged conformity and the avoidance of anything that could be construed as extreme. Second, in the shadow of the Berlin Wall, the Marxist and Socialist origins of 19th-century feminism created instant suspicion. The first major feminist initiative in West Germany proved, in fact, a failure. In 1971, a national conference of women began a drive to legalize abortion. Not only was the law's anti-abortion stance intensified, but pro-abortion groups became subject to police harassment, and those suspected of political activism found themselves without jobs.

One of the consequences of official opposition to the feminist movement was that the most extreme of its leaders took to terrorist activities to fight their battles. Ulrike Meinhof (1934–1976) was one of the leading journalists to promote the feminist cause. In 1970, she helped found the Red Army Faction, which was responsible for a burst of murder and arson over the next decade. Meinhof was captured in 1972 and died in her cell four years later under mysterious circumstances.

Other women found a more congenial setting in the Green Movement, which aimed at defending the environment. Claiming that the destruction of nature represented a negative aspect of male supremacy, they helped the Green party become a significant force in West German political life. Some women expected the Greens to respond by promoting feminist causes in return. On the whole, however, the predominantly male leadership resisted attempts to become involved in women's issues.

ITALIAN FEMINISM

The Italian feminist movement had greater success in spearheading reform. In 1945, Italian women were among those least well off in Western Europe. They were a source of cheap labor and had little legal protection. In the 1950s, married women could not apply for a passport or travel abroad without their husband's permission.

The first victory of the Union of Italian Women was the successful campaign to introduce divorce; a popular referendum legalized it in 1970. If West German women had to contend with conservatism and fear of communism, Italian feminists were faced with the opposition of the Catholic Church in many of their battles. Only after mass demonstrations, which included women chaining themselves to the gates of the Vatican, did the Christian Democrat government make the distribution of contraceptive information legal. Even more impressive was the success in 1978 of the campaign to legalize abortion.

By the late 1980s, the European women's movement was facing conservative reaction. Pope John Paul II reaffirmed the Catholic Church's traditional view of women. In Britain, Margaret Thatcher, the country's first woman prime

Poster from *Guerrilla Girls: The Advantages of Being a Woman Artist.* 1988. The group was formed in New York in 1984, to draw attention to what they believed to be racist and sexist attitudes on the part of those running major art institutions. Its members remain anonymous and wear gorilla masks when they appear in public. The poster itself is, of course, ironic: It lists the disadvantages of being a woman artist.

THE ADVANTAGES OF BEING A WOMAN ARTIST:

Working without the pressure of success.
Not having to be in shows with men.
Having an escape from the art world in your 4 free-lance jobs.
Knowing your career might pick up after you're eighty.
Being reassured that whatever kind of art you make it will be labeled feminine.
Not being stuck in a tenured teaching position.
Seeing your ideas live on in the work of others.
Having the opportunity to choose between career and motherhood.
Not having to choke on those big cigars or paint in Italian suits.
Having more time to work when your mate dumps you for someone younger.
Being included in revised versions of art history.
Not having to undergo the embarrassment of being called a genius.
Getting your picture in the art magazines wearing a gorilla suit.

A PUBLIC SERVICE MESSAGE FROM GUERRILLA GIRLS CONSCIENCE OF THE ART WORLD
5 3 2   L a G U A R D I A   P L A C E ,   # 2 3 7 •   N Y , N Y   1 0 0 1 2
w w w . g u e r r i l l a g i r l s . c o m

Courtesy of Guerrilla Girls

minister, began to cut social benefits giving women the possibility of self-support. The scourge of AIDS, a sexually transmittable disease, encouraged monogamous relationships. Originally believed to affect only homosexual males, AIDS also spread by means of heterosexual contact and by the exchange of hypodermic needles used in drug abuse.

Yet the feminist challenge had changed perceptions about gender differences and their effects throughout large sections of Western society. No politician could afford to ignore the "woman's question" or fail to pursue the women's vote. At the humblest level, few families were unaware that new ways of viewing old stereotypes were in the air. As so often is the case, revolution sometimes brought reaction, but in the last decade of the 20th century, the issue of feminism showed no sign of disappearing.

SEX, MARRIAGE, AND THE FAMILY: NEW DIRECTIONS

The postwar period saw a loosening of centuries-old sexual attitudes. Women's fashions emphasized breasts and legs, rather than concealing them. In the 1960s women sunbathers of all ages wore bikinis, and a decade later "topless" sunbathing became increasingly common in Europe. Even Spain, which under Franco had long been a bastion of conservative social attitudes, permitted the new fashion after the dictator's death. Books, magazines, and films encouraged women to take pleasure in sex and provided them with detailed instructions on how to do so.

In the mid-1950s the appearance of *Playboy* magazine and other similar publications heralded a change in the male sexual image. Instead of emphasizing the man's role as husband and father, they glamorized the attractions of personal gratification and sexual freedom. Partial or even total female nudity became acceptable in publicity posters and images, and sex shops opened up in many northern European capitals.

Attitudes toward "alternative" sexual patterns remained mixed. Sweden decriminalized homosexuality between consenting adults in 1944, as did Britain in the early 1960s. Most Western European countries had never had specific legislation, in fact, that treated homosexuality as a crime. In the 1960s, gay and lesbian activists joined women, blacks, and other groups struggling for civil rights and organized vocal protest movements. Yet in general, although awareness and tolerance increased, homosexuality remained frowned on and a barrier to public office. The appearance and rapid spread of AIDS, which was at first mistakenly associated exclusively with homosexuality, increased prejudice against gays and lesbians.

CONTRACEPTION AND THE BIRTHRATE

For both men and women, especially young ones, the appearance of the birth control "pill," and the wide diffusion of other contraceptive methods, meant that more-or-less casual sexual contacts no longer ran the risk of producing unwanted pregnancies. As a result, many began to have sexual relations at an early age. In Scandinavia in the 1980s, the average for a girl was fifteen years, two months; for a boy fifteen years, five months.

The new ease of contraception meant that married couples had even greater freedom in planning their families. Increased numbers of women, freed from the burdens of repeated pregnancies, joined the workforce. The birthrate, which soared during the "baby boom" of the war and the postwar period of the "economic miracle," declined steeply after 1964. In France, the rate of births per 1,000 population fell from 22 in 1950 to 14 in 1980; in Czechoslovakia for the same period, the fall was from 18 per 1,000 to 12. Even Italy, with its traditionalist family attitudes, and Spain (after Franco's death) followed suit. More permissive legislation on abortion, introduced in most of Eastern Europe (1956–1957), Britain (1967), and France (1975–1979), further reduced the birthrate.

By the 1980s, the rate became stabilized in most European countries at "zero population growth": the annual number of births equaled that of deaths. The average in Western Europe was 1.7 children per woman, that in Eastern Europe 1.9 to 2.2. One of the chief effects of this change was the disappearance of large families. Except for Ireland and Albania, the relative number of third births fell from 15 to 20 percent in 1950 to 9 to 12 in 1980. The two-child family became more than ever the most common family unit.

PATTERNS OF MARRIAGE AND DIVORCE

In the years of renewed prosperity after the war, the rate of marriage rose steeply. In 1950, the proportion of unmarried women in their late forties was 20.5 percent in Norway and 16.6 percent in England. By 1975 the number had fallen to, respectively, 5.9 and 7. Ireland again proved the exception: In the 1980s, 25 percent of Irish women never married.

Along with the increase in marriage rates went a corresponding rise in divorce. The factors involved were many and complex. With marriages often contracted at an early age, and a higher life expectancy, couples were faced with longer periods of living together, with the increased possibility of friction. In the early 20th century, the average marriage lasted 20 years, before being terminated by the death of one of the partners. By 1980 the average duration of marriages unbroken by divorce was 35 years.

The drastic fall in the birthrate enabled increasing numbers of women to develop their own careers or at least to contribute to the family income. The consequent rethinking of traditional family roles, encouraged by the women's movement, inevitably changed conventional attitudes. As a result, legal discouragement of divorce, together with cultural disapproval, greatly lessened. On average in the 1980s, in both Eastern and Western Europe, the rate of marriages ending in divorce was around 25 percent. The highest rate was in Denmark and Sweden (almost 50 percent) and the lowest in Poland (around 11 percent). Divorce remained difficult in Portugal and impossible in Ireland and Spain; Italy legalized divorce in 1971.

Thus the phenomena of a high rate of marriage and an increasing number of divorces coexisted in European society. Many of those who ended one marriage contracted another. Others chose to return to a single life, and the number of those living alone rose dramatically. In 1980, more than half the households in Paris, Vienna, and West Berlin consisted of only one person; 25 percent of the cities' populations lived alone. In this as in other respects, the late 20th century was marked by a strong break with past social habits.

THE AGE OF CONSUMERISM: AFFLUENCE AND ITS CONSEQUENCES

The general increase in prosperity of the postwar years transformed the lives of most of Western Europe's citizens. Some of this boom, at least, made its way across the Iron Curtain into Eastern Europe: By the 1980s, East Germans and Czechs could buy McDonald's hamburgers and Italian Benetton sweaters. The spread of technology made for more leisure time. Among the ways of passing it was travel, facilitated by postwar developments in air transport and packaged vacations.

The concentration of society in great cities and their suburbs forced traditional agricultural life patterns into further decline, partly because of continued migration from country to city, a tendency that was especially strong in Greece and southern Italy. An additional cause was the inability of traditional farming methods to provide food for increasing populations. As a result, governments encouraged the development of "agribusinesses"—large corporations that mass produced and marketed food products such as milk, eggs, and poultry.

As goods began to circulate within the Common Market, they crossed national lines. A shopper in a small-town West German supermarket could expect to find olive oil from Spain, Greece, and Italy; chocolates from Belgium; flowers from the Netherlands; tea from Britain; cheese from France; and smoked salmon from Ireland. In some cases the free flow of goods caused resentment. In the "wine wars" at the end of the 20th century, French protestors overturned and emptied trucks containing inexpensive Italian wine.

As wages and the number of wage earners rose, young workers and professionals attracted the attention of marketing organizations. Many young people continued to live at home until they married—far more than in the United States—and thus had considerable disposable incomes. Companies began to direct their products and advertising at this new "youth market," rather than toward the traditional family one. By the end of the 20th century, attendance at "family films" declined, while discotheques mushroomed even in small provincial centers.

The "youth cult" led to a new emphasis on physical fitness and changing eating patterns. In traditionally meat-eating countries such as Germany and Britain, the consumption of red meat fell, and in France the "nouvelle cuisine" (new

cooking) provided a lighter approach to the preparation of elaborate dishes. Vegetarian and macrobiotic restaurants became more common. At home, as more family members worked, meals ceased to be an important and extended period for family life and exchange. They shrank in size, and working women turned increasingly to prepared or frozen food for their families, which microwave ovens—by now an essential tool in many kitchens—heated up in a few minutes.

IMMIGRATION

As standards of living rose in Western Europe, immigrants began to arrive from Third World countries. Earlier immigration had seen waves of movement from the poorer parts of Europe—principally the Mediterranean region—to the richer northern countries. In the late 1940s and 1950s, large numbers of Italians from the rural south migrated to Belgium, where they worked in the mines. By the late 20th century, as one of the four most industrialized European nations, Italy attracted immigrants from North and Sub-Saharan Africa and from the Philippines.

In many cases, immigrants took menial and unpopular jobs as hospital orderlies, road workers, and garbage collectors. Many worked illegally and received less than official minimum wages. On some occasions, local authorities made efforts to allow ethnic groups to maintain some form of identity, while encouraging community participation. The Turkish *Gastarbeiter* ("guest workers" in German) were an example of relatively peaceful integration.

Elsewhere racial tension proved pervasive. Britain, as head of the multiracial Commonwealth, attracted widespread immigration, both black and white. Whereas Australians and Canadians were easily absorbed, Caribbean and Pakistani immigrants often had difficulty finding acceptance. A generation of immigrants' children born in Britain grew up regarding themselves as British but often resented by their neighbors. Successive governments introduced legislation to combat various forms of racism. Nonetheless, race riots broke out at intervals. In some cases they were provoked by the National Front, an extreme right-wing organization that rose to prominence in the general election campaign of 1979. At other times, ethnic minorities held their own demonstrations, to protest discrimination.

Similar problems developed elsewhere in Europe. A French version of the National Front campaigned in favor of "France for the French." In the 1986 general election, there seemed a possibility, although it remained unfulfilled, that center-right candidates would seek its support. In 1990 Italy, one of the European countries most open to Third World immigrants, was the scene of growing racial tension, as African street vendors were banned from the streets of Florence. Government officials and social workers in most countries remained only too aware of the possibility of increased tensions, but the best that seemed possible was an uneasy truce.

EUROPE IN THE POSTINDUSTRIAL ERA

By the early 1990s, it seemed that European life, like that of North America, was entering a new phase. The computer

Günter Behnisch, Hysolar Institute Building, University of Stuttgart, Stuttgart, Germany. 1987. The architect designed the building as part of a research project on the technology of solar energy. The apparently chaotic appearance of the structure is a deliberate attempt to break with architectural tradition. From the time of ancient Egypt, buildings have aimed to convey a sense of stability and security. Here, the building threatens to fall to pieces before our eyes.

Behnisch and Partner

technology developed over the preceding decade now controlled most heavy industrial production. Following the example of Japan, industries from automobile manufacturing to printing used machines, appropriately programmed, to make their products. In countries where the trade unions were traditionally powerful, including Britain and Italy, automation led to bitter strike action.

In this new postindustrial era, more and more people were working in "service industries." Banking, insurance, communications, entertainment—these and others replaced traditional manufacturing jobs, whether at the labor or management level. With the rise of the personal computer, many ordinary tasks—depositing a check, buying a pair of shoes or a plane ticket, registering for school—could be done without leaving home.

Some of the effects of these broad changes were already visible. The ability to work at even the most complex jobs from their own homes enabled growing numbers of women to combine family and career. Yet on the whole the postindustrial revolution had a considerable way to go. As it spread and intensified, it seemed bound to lead to radical changes in social and political life.

Putting Mobility and Social Change in Perspective

In the second half of the 20th century, many long-cherished social institutions came under attack. In public life, authoritarian leadership gave way to a search for consensus. Most European nations made a determined attempt to achieve a consistent standard of social welfare. Women continued to battle for equal rights. At home, traditional roles and gender relationships gave way to a period of uncertainty about the rules and function of family life.

By the late 20th century, two competing tendencies drove society. On the one hand, the forces of mass communication, ease of transport, and sheer economic necessity produced a "global village." The search for some form of political and economic unity, or at least community of interests, was accompanied by the spread of social and cultural uniformity. Yet, at the same time, there developed growing pressure toward the assertion of national and ethnic identity, real or imagined. From Wales to Lithuania to Lombardy, Corsica to Croatia, minorities campaigned, often violently, for some form of independence. The long-term effects on society of the inevitable conflicts between the two forces at play remained difficult to predict.

Questions for Further Study

1. What have been the main changes accomplished by the feminist movement since World War II? What has their effect been on Western society?
2. What role has nationalism played in the evolution of postwar European life? How far, if at all, has it been linked with racism?
3. In what ways do Western European and American attitudes toward politics, society, and culture differ? How do people in former Soviet bloc countries compare with either?

Suggestions for Further Reading

Anderson, Benedict. *Imagined Communities*. New York, 1991.

Brinker-Gabler, Gisela, and Sidonie Smith, eds. *Writing New Identities: Gender, Nation and Immigration in Contemporary Europe*. Minneapolis, 1997.

Caute, D. *The Year of the Barricades: A Journey Through 1968*. New York, 1988.

Feenberg, Andrew, and Jim Freedman. *When Poetry Ruled the Streets: The French May Events of 1968*. Albany, NY, 2001.

Fukuyama, Francis. *Trust: The Social Virtues and the Creation of Prosperity*. London, 1995.

Gillis, J.R. *Youth and History: Tradition and Change in European Age Relations, 1770–Present*. New York, 1981.

Hellman, J.A. *Journeys Among Women: Feminism in Five Italian Cities*. New York, 1987.

Hughes, J.H. *Sophisticated Rebels: The Political Culture of European Dissent*. Cambridge, MA, 1988.

Mead, M. *Culture and Commitment: The New Relationship Between the Generations in the 1970s*. New York, 1978.

Outhwaite, William, and Tom Bottomore. *The Blackwell Dictionary of Twentieth Century Social Thought*. Oxford, 1993.

Schlesinger, J.R. *America at Century's End*. New York, 1989.

InfoTrac College Edition

Enter the search term *Green parties* using Key Terms.

CULTURE IN THE AGE OF UNCERTAINTY

In the immediate postwar period, with Europe in ruins, American culture assumed a dominating role in Western civilization. Just as the United States, as the Western superpower, led in the reconstruction of the Western European economies, so American ideas, styles, and themes became widely diffused throughout all levels of European life.

The area to be most radically affected was popular culture. The rapid spread of American popular music, movies, and television programs, of Coca-Cola and blue jeans, made an impact that extended from the smallest Irish hamlet to the Greek islands. Over the following decades pop culture even penetrated behind the Iron Curtain, where enthusiasm for American ways and products provided a way of rebelling against conformist regimes.

In the world of painting, American artists led the way in the move toward abstraction of the 1940s and the return to realism in the early 1960s. Painters like Johns and Warhol invented a vision of "the American scene," and then diffused it. American emphasis on technology encouraged sculptors to use metals such as stainless steel welded into shapes combining weightiness with grace.

Several influential European architects had fled to the United States in the late 1930s. The most important of these, Mies van der Rohe, set the style for much urban architecture in the late 20th century. The clean lines and repetitive forms of city skyscrapers spread in both Western and Eastern Europe, often with deadening aesthetic and human consequences.

In music, a vast gulf opened up between average music lovers and the avant-garde. Most performers limited themselves to the basic repertory of the Classical, Romantic, and early 20th-century eras. Advanced contemporary composers found their public increasingly shrinking. In the field of pop music, commercial interests combined with social statement (on occasion, at least) to achieve global circulation. The distribution of music videos, and worldwide telecasts of concerts such as the Live Aid concert of 1987, or the Mandela concert of 1990, reached a public of proportions inconceivable before the late 20th century.

The leading literary movement of the latter part of the century was postmodernism, a term more easily used than explained. The postmodernists generally rejected the modernist preoccupation with alienation and self-analysis. Using unconventional literary forms, they created works containing meanings to be teased out by the reader—the text itself, not the author, was the point.

By the 1990s Europe had withdrawn from the cultural shadow of the United States. Yet popular culture, and in particular pop music, remained under strong American domination. In the arts, however, the age of mass communications not surprisingly produced a constant exchange of cultural influences, which tended to extend increasingly to non-Western culture.

THE AMERICANIZATION OF EUROPE

In the early part of the 20th century, Americans turned to Europe as cultural arbiter. European artists and intellectuals set the pace and style of cultural development, headed American publishing companies and symphony orchestras, and helped American art collectors to build their holdings. French fashions, British automobiles, Italian aristocrats—all represented old world elegance and charm. Even in Hollywood, the most quintessential of American settings, many of the most glamorous stars and directors were European: Greta Garbo, Rudolph Valentino, Fritz Lang, Alfred Hitchcock.

By the end of the war, with Europe's leading cultural nations either vanquished and in ruins or exhausted from the conflict, roles became reversed. A weary Europe looked to America for spiritual recharging. The wide-open spaces, the sense of unflagging optimism, and the illusion of innocence attracted a continent that was war-torn and deeply insecure. Other, more practical factors helped reinforce the Americanization of Europe. From Scotland to Hungary, many families had relatives in the United States, and so thought of it as a possible future home. The affluence and plenty of American life, represented by the cigarettes and nylons so freely dispensed by American servicemen, made a special appeal in the bare postwar years. Most important of all, American intervention had been decisive in helping the Europeans to put their own house in order; American troops seemed likely to stay around for the foreseeable future to help maintain that order.

As the Marshall Plan helped the Western European nations rebuild their economies, Europe's debt to the United States continued to be both cultural and financial. With the diffusion of television, American programs and personalities became as familiar to audiences in Manchester, Munich, or Milan as at home. The art-buying market moved from Paris to Manhattan. American universities attracted the leading scholars in fields as diverse as nuclear physics and art history, while European universities began to offer courses in a new area: American Studies.

The process had, in fact, begun before the war. Many European artists and intellectuals fled to the United States in the 1930s to escape persecution or war. W.H. Auden, Arnold Schoenberg, Thomas Mann, Mies van der Rohe, and Albert Einstein—all major influences in modern culture—spent the war in America.

POPULAR CULTURE: THE UNIVERSAL LANGUAGE

The aspect of life most overwhelmingly influenced by American ways was popular culture. In the 19th century, each country sought to develop its own national characteristics in the arts, and nationalism was a powerful force in art and politics alike. In the second half of the 20th

century, the lifestyles of Europeans came to follow American models. As prosperity returned to Western Europe, blue jeans, T-bone steaks, and supermarkets became the symbols of progress, followed in turn by fast food and disco nightclubs. In Eastern Europe, political and economic realities precluded such open Americanization. American pop music, however, provided at least temporary refuge from the bleakness of life under Stalin and Brezhnev.

The most singular feature of this popular culture was its universality. Never before had personalities, products, and fashions had so wide a diffusion. One obvious explanation was the phenomenon of mass communication, in particular television. Although introduced on a limited scale before World War II, television became generally available only in the 1950s. By 1980, one in every five Poles owned a television set, while in France, Italy, and West Germany the figure was one in three. Its impact was instant. When a few years later space satellites made international telecasting possible, the "global village" became even smaller. The daily lives of countless millions of people, many of them in remote parts of the globe, could suddenly share common experiences. In some cases these were great public events: the Kennedy funeral, royal weddings, the dismantling of

East German McDonald's, a year before the fall of the Berlin Wall. 1988. The sign above the door indicates that, unlike McDonald's elsewhere, beer is served here. Note the teenagers with mohawks outside. The arrival of fast-food chains in Eastern Europe foreshadowed the collapse of Communist regimes there.

the Berlin Wall, the death of Princess Diana. In other cases television coverage contributed, for better or worse, in forming public opinion: the Vietnam War, the Tiananmen massacres of 1989, the Palestinian *Intifada*. More important, however, was the general sense of a shared culture, operating on the most basic day-to-day level.

The spread of American-style popular culture was not without its critics. Some charged the sheer act of watching television with causing physical damage. In 1964, surveys showed that television-watching habits in the United States, Britain, and Japan were much the same. A report to the American Academy of Pediatrics of the same year accused television of causing fatigue, headache, loss of appetite, and vomiting, all of which could be cured only by abstinence. Others claimed that exposure to violence would adversely affect children and adults alike.

More serious critics feared that the relentless Americanization of everything from fast foods to buildings would lead to monotonous conformity and the loss of individual character. Furthermore, giant U.S.-based conglomerate corporations came to wield enormous power, especially in developing countries. As the Cold War dragged on, and the United States became embroiled in Vietnam, European critics of America became more vocal. With political disillusionment came cultural doubts and talk of urban wastelands and "Coca-Cola-ization."

In the arts, global communications led to a growing internationalization of styles and movements. Yet, in popular culture, American models, promoted by American salesmanship, continued to appeal. The opening of a McDonald's in Moscow in 1989 served as clearly as any summit meeting to proclaim the end of the Cold War.

THE VISUAL ARTS: FROM ABSTRACT EXPRESSIONISM TO CONCEPTUAL ART

Just as Paris dominated the art world at the beginning of the 20th century, so did New York in the years after World War II. Among the factors was the flight to the United States of several leading European avant-garde artists, including Hans Hoffmann (1880–1966), Josef Albers (1888–1976), and George Grosz (1893–1959). An important role was played by the American patron and collector Peggy Guggenheim (1898–1979), whose Art of This Century Gallery in New York became an important center for modern art.

ABSTRACT EXPRESSIONISM AND POP ART
Jackson Pollock (1912–1956), one of the leading members of the New York School, held his first one-man show at this gallery in 1943. The works he exhibited there were in a

Digital image © The Museum of Modern Art/Licensed by SCALA/Art Resource, NY

Jackson Pollock, *Number I*. 1948. 5 feet 8 inches by 8 feet 8 inches (1.7 by 2.6 m). In theory, Pollock based his style on Freudian ideas of free association and the Surrealist artists' adaptation of this in art called *psychic automatism*. In practice, however, even his most apparently random paintings are carefully constructed: Note the black spiral line that binds this composition together.

Andy Warhol, *Mick Jagger.* 1975. 40 inches (102 cm) square. Warhol incorporated into high art the world of media, money, and fashion. Are his portraits of entertainment celebrities, generally lightly retouched silkscreen prints, a celebration of popular culture? A subtle manipulation of it? The results seem banal, but perhaps that is Warhol's message.

Christo and Jeanne-Claude, *Valley Curtain.* Rifle, Colorado, 1970–1972. Spans 1,250 feet (381 m). Christo and Jeanne-Claude's work, like this Valley Curtain in Rifle, Colorado, uses fabric to create temporary works of art in rural and urban sites. The project used 142,000 square feet of woven nylon fabric and 110,000 pounds of steel cables. Among the couple's more recent projects was the wrapping of the Reichstag (Parliament Building) in Berlin, and they plan a similar scheme for Central Park, New York.

style that came to be known as **abstract expressionism.** The paintings made no reference to recognizable subjects—they were abstract—and sought to express interior states of feeling, as the early 20th-century German Expressionists had. Pollock's paintings used elements of random dripping, splashing, and pouring to produce intricate webs of color, filled with energy and movement.

In the mid-1950s, a new generation of painters was moving in exactly the opposite direction, toward the literal representation of mundane objects. Paintings of the American flag, beer cans, and toothbrushes by Jasper Johns (born 1930) were intended to reject the emotional and intellectual portentousness of abstract expressionism in favor of the symbols of popular culture.

The high priest of the cult of pop art was Andy Warhol (1930–1987), whose depictions of soap boxes and Coca-Cola bottles helped reinforce the image of American conspicuous consumption. Some claimed that Warhol's apparent high seriousness, especially in his notorious icons of Marilyn Monroe and other celebrities, masked a severe social critic. Whatever Warhol's attitude toward his subjects, his deliberately banal paintings and silk screen prints perfectly captured the spirit of an era that they contributed to create.

CONCEPTUAL ART

By the 1970s, some artists were trying to break away entirely from what they saw as the straitjacket of any tradition, old or new. **Conceptual artists** aimed to create "objects" or experiences that were not intended to be bought or sold or put in a museum. Their works, often consisting of unlikely materials such as cornflakes or ice, were installed and then dismantled.

The most spectacular environmental artists, Christo and Jeanne-Claude (both born 1935), devised projects involving hundreds of people and vast quantities of material. Their *Valley Curtain* stretched 1 million square feet of orange fabric across Rifle Gap in Colorado. Their major project was the *Running Fence*, 18 feet high and 24½ miles long, which ran through the farmland north of San Francisco in Marin and Sonoma Counties for two weeks in 1976; it had taken four years to bring the project to fulfillment.

ARCHITECTURE AND THE ENVIRONMENT

By the nature of their profession, architects are as much concerned with the practical use of their buildings as with aesthetic considerations. In general, the architecture of the second half of the 20th century tried to balance the two not necessarily opposing elements of form and function.

The foundations of much modern architecture were laid in the 1920s by Ludwig Mies van der Rohe (1896–1969) and his fellow members of the Bauhaus, an influential school of design and architecture, founded in Germany in 1919 (see Topic 86). The Bauhaus taught that

"less is more," and when Mies fled Germany for the United States in the late 1930s, he brought this approach with him. The austere lines, absence of fussy decorative details, and use of reinforced concrete in works such as the Seagram Building, New York, influenced innumerable skyscraper structures throughout Europe and the United States.

Not all buildings in this "International Style" achieved the elegance and practicality of Mies's best work. Many of his followers' steel, concrete, and glass public and office buildings filled the urban landscape with the same forms endlessly repeated. Nor did they always wear well; as metal discolored and concrete cracked, indifferently built International Style constructions brought their own touch of desolation to Eastern European and Third World capitals.

By the 1970s, both architects and public were beginning to be weary of stark concrete piles. The Pompidou Center for Arts and Culture, which opened in Paris in 1977, made a complete break with the idea of less as more. Its architects, Renzo Piano and Richard Rogers, covered the surface of the building with decoration that was also functional—heating ducts, elevators, and escalators.

Few architects were prepared to go as far as this in decorating their buildings, but in the 1980s decorative design came back into fashion with the postmodern style (the name is little more than a convenient label). Postmodernist architects continued to build large structures with simple, basic lines, but added decorative elements derived from Classical architecture: arches, columns, pediments.

Thus the late 20th century witnessed a modernist form of Neoclassical revival and a return to greater variety in architecture. Public interest in the effects of construction and reconstruction on the environment became increasingly vocal. The vast new building plan for Paris, which reached its first stage of completion in time for the Bicentennial of the French Revolution in 1989, was greeted with furious debate. In Britain, Prince Charles became embroiled with the country's leading architects, as he lambasted many of London's new buildings. Not surprisingly, of all the contemporary arts, architecture aroused the most enthusiasm and condemnation.

CONTEMPORARY COMPOSERS IN SEARCH OF AN AUDIENCE

By contrast with architecture, advanced developments in contemporary music left many music lovers and performers bewildered or indifferent. The long-playing record, stereo sound, and then digital recording on tape and compact disc made music increasingly available to an ever-wider public. Concert audiences grew, and regional opera companies sprang up throughout Europe and the United States. Yet the music that audiences wanted to hear, and performers to play and sing, was overwhelmingly drawn from the standard repertory of Baroque, Classical, Romantic, and early 20th-century works. A leading contemporary composer accused

Piano and Rogers, Georges Pompidou Center for Arts and Culture, Paris. 1977. The architects reversed the normal building practice by putting heating ducts, elevators, escalators, and structural supports on the outside, where they are visible. Its industrial style for the National Museum of Modern Art was highly controversial at the time, but the area around it has taken on a lively air, with street performers and musicians.

opera houses of being only museums, endlessly repeating the same dead works. Certainly, few operas written and performed since World War II succeeded in winning themselves a permanent place in the repertory.

In a way that has no parallel with the other arts, the musical world of the second half of the 20th century was characterized by a growing tendency to look back to earlier times, in a series of revivals. In the 1950s, listeners discovered Baroque music, especially that of Vivaldi, and, under the inspiration of the operatic soprano Maria Callas (1923–1977), the world of 19th-century Italian bel canto opera. The 1960s saw the growing popularity of the music of Gustav Mahler, which was up until then virtually unknown. By the 1990s, the early music and original instrument movement was in full swing, as musicians tried to reconstruct the original performing conditions of works ranging from Bach to Verdi by using authentic instruments.

THE MUSICAL AVANT-GARDE

Viewed from the end of the 20th century, the break between audiences and contemporary music seems to go back to the early 1900s, when Arnold Schoenberg rejected tonality in favor of other systems of musical organization (see Topic 79). One of the postwar period's leading composers, the Frenchman Pierre Boulez (born 1925), extended Schoenberg's ordering of pitch to other musical elements: length of notes, volume, method of performance. The purely abstract structures that resulted deliberately avoided any kind of subjective emotional expression.

In the 1950s and 1960s, as technology came to dominate modern life, composers turned to machines to generate their works. Composers of electronic music produced artificial sounds by means of an electronic oscillator; the invention of the Moog synthesizer provided an easy means of combining and changing these sounds. The leading composer of electronic music, the German Karlheinz Stockhausen (born 1928), tended increasingly to combine electronic sounds with these produced by conventional instruments.

Faced with the dilemmas of the contemporary musical scene, the American John Cage (1912–1992) produced pieces that seemed to question the very nature of music. Many of his works, in reaction against the rigid ordering of Boulez and Stockhausen (or Bach and Brahms, for that matter), used elements of chance. The performers tossed coins or shuffled the pages of the work to determine in what order the sections should be played.

THE MINIMALISTS

In the 1980s, several young American composers found a very different solution to the search for a new musical style. One of the first was Steve Reich (born 1936), who built substantial pieces out of the extended repetition of simple chords and rhythms; the use of these basic elements earned the music the stylistic label of "minimalist."

The most successful minimalist composer was Philip Glass (born 1937). Glass was influenced by Indian and West African music, and some of the repeated rhythmical structures in his pieces derive from classical Indian pieces. The seemingly endless repetitions produce either a mood of hypnotic concentration or growing irritation, depending on the individual listener. Glass's best-known works were three large-scale stage pieces—*Einstein on the Beach, Satyagraha,* and *Akhnaten*—performed between 1975 and 1985. His collaborator, the American dramatist Robert Wilson, described their "apparent motionlessness and endless durations during which dreams are dreamed and significant matters are understood."

POPULAR MUSIC

The worldwide appeal and circulation of pop music continued unabated in the decades after World War II. Between 1965 and 1973, "Yesterday"—a John Lennon and Paul McCartney song originally recorded by the immensely popular British group, the Beatles—appeared in some 1,200 other versions. By the late 1970s, the Beatles had sold more than 100 million record albums and an equal number of singles.

Throughout the 1980s and 1990s, rock music took changing forms, mirroring the mood of the times. Acid rock tried to reproduce musically the experience of hallucinogenic drugs, using advanced electronic sound effects. Performers of glitter rock aimed to challenge all of the social conventions by their outrageous costumes and makeup. The bitter violence of punk rock grew out of the hopelessness of the working-class youth in postindustrial Britain.

Other popular musicians used their songs for open political protest. Bob Dylan (born 1941; real name Robert Zimmerman) combined American folk idioms and the blues style. Protest singers were among the first to incorporate non-Western music; by the late 1980s, pop music had absorbed elements from the Caribbean, West Africa, and Latin America.

The internationalization of pop music was matched by its ever-wider circulation. With the coming of the videocassette and world television broadcasting, concerts of pop music became global events. In many cases these were inspired by political, or at least humanitarian, motives. The first was the Live Aid concert of 1987, which was intended to raise money for aid to Third World countries. Among its successors was the Mandela concert, held in London in 1990 to greet and acclaim the recently released South African black leader, Nelson Mandela.

Music has provided the best evidence for the formation of a global culture. The same pop music echoed from continent to continent, while audiences in Europe, America, India, and Japan filled concert halls to hear the great masterpieces of European music. Ironically, at a time when the demand for music had never been greater, avant-garde composers seemed searching for the right direction in which to advance their art.

POSTMODERNISM

By the 1980s, several writers had moved beyond the modernist preoccupation with alienation and self-analysis. Critics tended to collect them under the name of postmodernists, although it was not always clear what specific characteristics they had in common. Nor was the term exactly helpful in defining the nature of their work, although it indicated a change of direction. The postmodernists did not break with their modern past; they built on it. Less concerned with traditional plot and character lines, and less interested in rational organization, their visions were more private, and their works created isolated worlds with their own meanings and significance.

Among the leading writers to be labeled postmodernist was the Italian Italo Calvino (1923–1985), whose works

The Beatles. Mid-1960s. This English rock-music group dominated popular music throughout the world in the 1960s. Their concert tours were accompanied by scenes of mass adulation. The group disbanded in 1970. The murder of John Lennon (*second from right*) in New York in 1980 by a demented fan caused worldwide mourning.

Robert Hunt Library

draw heavily on fantasy. He produced science fiction and historical allegory, explored the genre of the folk tale (*Italian Folktales*; 1956, revised 1980), and toward the end of his life wrote experimental fiction (*If on a Winter's Night a Traveler*; 1979).

Other postmodernists reveal a wide variety of influences. The complexity and ingenious wordplay of the American Thomas Pynchon (born 1937) recalls the style of James Joyce. The short stories and novels of Donald Barthelme

(1931–1989) evoke a mood of surrealism. The grand old man of postmodernism, the Argentinean Jorge Luis Borges (1899–1986), created his own unique blend of essay and short story.

Although in the 1990s traditional fiction was far from dead, postmodernist writers seemed to be exploring a variety of different directions. Without breaking with the past—an impossible aim, in any case—their work suggested rich new possibilities for future literature.

Putting Culture in the Age of Uncertainty in Perspective

Western culture in the second half of the 20th century was shaped by two contrasting forces: unity and diversity. Instant communication and ever-advancing technology made possible a global culture, whereby events and ideas could span the world in minutes. People on every continent could watch the same television programs, admire the same sports stars, share the same fashions and food—and they did. Yet the very speed of communication meant that styles and ideas became outdated and were replaced with dizzying speed. The appetite for variety grew as it was fed, and the 200 or so television channels of postindustrial society offered a choice so bewildering as to be no choice at all.

Faced with this homogenized culture, people in many parts of the world found a renewed sense of national or ethnic identity. For many European countries, the 1970s and 1980s were a period of nationalist sentiment and active nationalist movements. Belgium, Britain, Italy, and Spain all saw separatist demonstrations. By 1990, it was clear that the fall of communism in Eastern Europe would lead to renewed tensions among rival ethnic groups.

The battle to promote national identity was often fought with cultural weapons. Welsh nationalists won a notable victory in establishing their right to a fixed number of hours per week of television programs in the Welsh language. The language issue remained a sensitive one in countries as different as Canada and Yugoslavia; it even arose in the United States, as Spanish became increasingly widespread. Virtually nowhere on Earth seemed untouched by nationalist sentiments. When in 1990 even remote Mongolia began to liberalize, one of the state's first moves was to reintroduce the Mongolian alphabet, which had been replaced by a form of the Russian one. Thus by the 1990s Western culture, by now part of global civilization, enjoyed both the advantages and disadvantages of postmodern times: the freedom and constraints of pluralism.

Questions for Further Study

1. In what ways have technological developments (the communications revolution, computers, etc.) changed the nature of Western culture? What are the effects of the speed of these developments?

2. What are the main characteristics of pop culture? What forms do they take in music, the visual arts, and popular entertainment?

3. How does culture reflect the historical experiences of the world after World War II? In comparison with earlier periods, have the role and function of the artist changed?

Suggestions for Further Reading

Anfam, David. *Abstract Expressionism*. New York, 1990.

Broude, Norma, and Mary D. Garrard. *The Power of Feminist Art: The American Movement of the 1970s History and Impact*. New York, 1994.

Docker, J. *Postmodernism and Popular Culture*. New York, 1994.

Gianetti, L., and S. Eyman. *Flashback: A Brief History of Film*. Englewood Cliffs, NJ, 1991.

Glass P., and R.T. Jones. *Music by Philip Glass*. New York, 1987.

Hampton, W. *Guerrilla Minstrels: John Lennon, Joe Hill, Woodie Guthrie, Bob Dylan*. New York, 1986.

Hertz, Richard, ed. *Theories of Contemporary Art*, 2nd ed. Englewood Cliffs, NJ, 1993.

Jones, Amelia, ed. *Sexual Politics: Judy Chicago's Dinner Party in Feminist Art History*. Berkeley, CA, 1996.

Katz, Adam. *Postmodernism and the Politics of "Culture."* Boulder, CO, 2000.

Kostelanetz, Richard. *John Cage (Ex)plain(ed)*. New York, 1996.

Lewis, Samella S. *African American Art and Artists*, rev. ed. Berkeley, CA, 1994.

Malthy, R. *Passing Parade: A History of Popular Culture in the 20th Century*. Oxford, 1989.

McRobbie, Angela. *In the Culture Society: Art, Fashion, and Popular Music*. New York, 1999.

Sandler, Irving. *Art of the Postmodern Era*. New York, 1996.

Stiles, Kristine, and Peter Selz, eds. *Theories and Documents of Contemporary Art: A Sourcebook of Artists' Writings*. Berkeley, CA, 1996.

Tinkom, Matthew, and Amy Villarejo, eds. *Keyframes: Popular Cinema and Cultural Studies*. New York, 2001.

InfoTrac College Edition

Enter the search term *Jackson Pollock* using Key Terms.

Enter the search term *van der Rohe* using Key Terms.

THE PATH TOWARD EUROPEAN INTEGRATION

In the aftermath of World War II, some European political leaders began to see cooperation, and not competition, as essential to survival. In 1952, the first stage of European integration saw the combining of the coal and steel industries of all the major Western European nations except Britain—France, West Germany, Italy, Belgium, the Netherlands, and Luxembourg.

In 1957, the same nations signed an agreement in Rome to create an economic unit by eliminating tariffs and trade barriers among member states. This European Economic Community (EEC) proved so successful that it led to an economic boom in Western Europe. In consequence, more optimistic politicians began to see economic union as the prelude to some future time when Europe could achieve political union.

The only major Western European industrialized power that at first refused to join the EEC was Britain, largely because of doubts about surrendering its sovereignty in a future united Europe. As the EEC continued to prosper, however, Britain's Conservative government opened prolonged and difficult negotiations to become a member. In 1973, Britain joined the EEC, and Ireland was also admitted.

The EEC soon developed a complex—some said too complex—institutional apparatus, including a dual executive: a Council of Ministers and the European Commission. A European Parliament whose members are elected directly in their home countries is seen by enthusiastic European federalists as a step toward future political unity. The remaining EEC institutions are the European Court of Justice and the European Council, which provides a forum for the heads of governments and their foreign ministers to meet at regular intervals.

In 1981, Greece joined the EEC, and in 1986 Spain and Portugal became members. In the same year, the Single European Act was ratified, which listed a series of future goals. The most immediate was the creation by the end of 1992 of a European community with no frontiers or trade barriers.

Relations with Switzerland and Austria were complex. As neutral nations, both had avoided participation because of its eventual political implications. In 1995, however, Austria became a member together with Finland and Sweden. With the revolutions of 1989, the notion of European unity suddenly took on far more vast dimensions.

Thus by the early 1990s, Europe already provided a market and economic force to compete with the United States and Japan. The chances of any form of political union that would be acceptable to all of its members still seemed distant, but the divisive and destructive national rivalries that had riven the first half of the 20th century had been replaced by constructive cooperation. In 2002 a single European currency, the Euro, began to circulate, replacing the national currencies of 12 of the member states.

THE FIRST STEPS TOWARD EUROPEAN UNITY

For the first four centuries of the Christian era, most of Europe was united under the strong political and legal rule of the Roman Empire. With the decline and fall of the Roman Empire, individual rulers fought over territory, religion, and dynastic questions. The empire of Charlemagne (742–814) imposed unity on a part of Europe, but the authority of his successors in the Holy Roman Empire as leaders of Europe was challenged by the papacy.

Over the centuries, plans for European integration occasionally emerged. The Duc de Sully (1560–1641), finance minister to the French king Henry IV, produced a "Grand Design" for a council of Europe, backed by a European peacekeeping army. A hundred years later, the French political reformer the Abbé de Saint Pierre (1658–1743; real name Charles-Irénée Castel) advocated the creation of a "European Republic," with a European senate; another of his visionary ideas was the establishment of an international peacekeeping organization. All of these proposals foundered on the realities of dynastic and colonial rivalries.

TOWARD EUROPEAN INTEGRATION

The modern notion of a Europe united both politically and economically dated back to the troubled years between the two world wars, when some politicians saw a federal United States of Europe as a means of preventing renewed hostilities. Moves were made toward introducing some degree of economic cooperation, but in 1930 the French politician Aristide Briand argued that a limited customs union would not work. Economic union was possible only if each member's security was guaranteed, but security depended on political decisions. Thus an economic partnership required setting up political institutions and structures. With these in place, a "common market" (the term was Briand's own) could be estab-

lished. The growing nationalism of the 1930s swept away all such notions of cooperation.

During the war, many of those fighting to free Europe from Hitler's "New Order" began to look to the idea of federalism as a hope for the future. *Libérer et fédérer* ("Liberate and federate") was one of the slogans of the French Resistance movement, and freedom fighters in the Netherlands, Italy, Czechoslovakia, and Poland developed similar goals. In July 1944, resistance leaders from various countries, meeting in Geneva, called for the creation of a European Federal Union.

After the war had proved yet again the futility and destructiveness of national rivalries, politicians began to talk seriously about the idea of a European federation. One of the leading promoters of the cause of European integration was the French economist Jean Monnet (1888–1979), who became known as the "father of Europe." Another important figure was the Belgian politician Paul-Henri Spaak (1899–1972), author of the report that eventually established the EEC. The Belgians, in fact, helped lead the way in demonstrating the possibilities of European cooperation. In 1947, Belgium, the Netherlands, and Luxembourg—the so-called Benelux countries—agreed to form a customs union. From 1948 all tariffs between the three partners were abolished, and a standard tariff became imposed on outside imports.

The chief spokesmen for European cooperation were fervent believers in the ideal of a united Europe, but even Winston Churchill and Charles de Gaulle, strong defenders of national sovereignty, spoke approvingly of federation. During the war, Churchill had proposed a postwar European state, governed by a joint council and with its own armed forces. In 1945, de Gaulle called for some form of all-European association "between Slavs, Germans, Gauls, and Latins."

The supporters of European unification saw that the only way to achieve progress was to advance slowly and cautiously, with the goal of maintaining peace. The industries

The European Community headquarters under construction in Brussels. 1980s. Belgium, one of the smallest members of the EU, has two official languages: the top line on the sign is in French, and the one below it in Flemish. Underneath, to the left, is the circle of gold stars on a blue background, which is the EU's symbol and flag.

Photo News/Gamma

most vital to a war effort were those of coal and steel production. If countries would surrender control of these to a supranational authority, an important step would have been taken toward making future conflict less likely. In 1951 an agreement was signed to form the European Coal and Steel Community (ECSC); the agreement went into effect the following year. The member states were France, West Germany, Italy, and the Benelux countries. Thus six nations, which only a few years earlier had been locked in bloody conflict, agreed to share their goods rather than fight over them.

Encouraged by the success of the ECSC, the same nations tried to establish a European Defense Community (EDC), to create a European army and establish a common European foreign policy. In the end, however, neither France nor Italy was prepared to give up control of its defense forces or independent policies. In 1954, the attempt was abandoned.

THE TREATY OF ROME

By 1957, confidence and growing experience led to the next step. On March 25 of that year the Treaty of Rome, signed by the same members, created two new bodies: the European Atomic Energy Community (Euratom), and the EEC. (The ECSC subsequently became absorbed into the EEC, which in turn became the European Union.) The ceremonies took place on Rome's Capitoline hill, ancient center of the first and only power to unite most of Europe under a single rule, the Roman Empire.

THE EUROPEAN ECONOMIC COMMUNITY

From the beginning, the EEC proved a success. The long-term goal of the Treaty of Rome was to achieve some sort of political union. Its terms claimed that its purpose was "to establish the foundation of an ever-closer union among the people of Europe." The aims of the EEC, however, were strictly practical and limited to what could actually be accomplished. It sought to create one large economic market—the Common Market—for its members, by eliminating tariffs and customs barriers among them. Common tariffs and trade restrictions were erected toward nonmembers. Within the EEC, labor and capital could in theory circulate freely (in practice, some countries maintained restrictions), and a Common Agricultural Program (CAP) established equal price levels for agricultural products. Agricultural prices were to become a divisive issue in the future, bringing the farming-intensive countries of southern Europe into conflict with the northern industrial members, who were unwilling to pay huge farming subsidies.

The treaty laid down a timetable for bringing these policies into effect. The first steps toward bringing the national customs tariffs of the EEC's six members together took place at the beginning of 1961; EEC countries then had until July 1, 1968, to eliminate all customs duties

Map 94.1 The European Common Market and the Soviet-Led COMECON, c. 1970. The Soviet organization disappeared with the end of the Soviet Union and had in any case been weakened by unrest in Eastern Europe after the Soviet invasion of Prague in 1968. Members who will eventually join the European Common Market—now the European Union—are Sweden, Finland, and Greece. Twelve of the fifteen members (excluding Britain, Denmark, and Sweden) now use a common currency, the Euro.

among one another and establish common tariffs toward outsiders.

BRITAIN AND THE COMMON MARKET

The most obvious absentee from the negotiations that led to the signing of the Treaty of Rome was Britain. For all the British approval of the general idea of a European federation, politicians there were unwilling to embark on a journey whose ultimate destination—however distantly—was political union. Even Churchill had no doubt that Britain was in some important way different from the continental nations. His attitude summed up the position of many of his fellow citizens: "We are with Europe, but not of it. We are interested and associated, but not absorbed."

The possible loss of national sovereignty became a hotly discussed public issue. The nations of continental Europe accused the British of insularity and lack of commitment to the European ideal. The British counterattacked by pointing out that their insularity had saved them from invasion and occupation for hundreds of years. When the foreign ministers of the future EEC met in 1955 to formulate a common policy, they officially invited Britain to take part. The British government refused.

THE EUROPEAN FREE TRADE ASSOCIATION

As the success of the EEC became apparent, Britain and other European nations began to look toward forming a similar organization that could both liberalize trade among themselves and act as a bargaining force with the EEC. In 1959, a group of seven countries created the European Free Trade Association (EFTA); it came into force the following year. The founding members of EFTA were Austria, Britain, Denmark, Norway, Portugal, Sweden, and Switzerland. Finland became an associate member in 1961 and a full member in 1985; Iceland joined in 1970.

EFTA's goals were avowedly completely nonpolitical, and none of its members had any intention of forming a supranational union. This factor was important not only to Britain but also to the neutral nations of Austria and Switzerland. Even in economic terms, EFTA was less binding than the EEC; although tariffs on industrial goods were eliminated among its members, they remained in place on agricultural and fishing products. The provision on fishing was especially important for the Scandinavian members and the British, who often found themselves in fierce competition for the catch and sale of fish.

Barely had EFTA come into being than opinion in Britain began to swing in favor of joining the EEC. The trade barriers that the EEC had erected against outsiders left British trade in a dangerously uncompetitive position. Then, as wartime memories receded, the idea of peaceful cooperation took precedence over defensiveness. No less important a consideration was the fact that France and Germany—under the leadership of the two senior statesmen, Konrad Adenauer and de Gaulle—were tending to dominate the decision making. Both Britain and the other EEC members could see the potential advantage of a British counterbalance in the community.

In 1961, Britain formally applied for admittance; it was followed by Denmark, Ireland, and Norway. Negotiations began later the same year. The bargaining was hard. As head of the Commonwealth, Britain was concerned to safeguard the reciprocal trading rights existing between itself and the various Commonwealth nations. Nor had the earlier British refusal, followed by the abrupt reversal that led to its application, created a sympathetic atmosphere for negotiating. France, in particular, resented what it saw as the British attempt to obtain "special treatment."

After a period of increasing tension, the French blocked Britain's entry; in January 1963, de Gaulle announced at a press conference that Britain was not yet ready to join the Common Market. Among his reasons was the fear that British membership would undermine the ability of continental nations to control their own affairs. As he put it, with Britain in the EEC, "in the end there would appear a colossal Atlantic Community under American dependence and leadership which would soon swallow up the European Community."

It took 10 more years before Britain was finally admitted. In 1969, the year in which de Gaulle stepped down as head of state, the EEC members agreed to reopen negotia-

SIGNIFICANT DATES

The Formation of the European Union

1947	Benelux countries form customs union
1951	Creation of European Coal and Steel Community
1957	Treaty of Rome establishes EEC
1959	Creation of EFTA
1963	Britain's application to EEC blocked
1973	Britain, Denmark, and Ireland join EEC
1981	Greece becomes member of EEC
1986	Spain and Portugal join EEC; Single European Act passed

tions. One of the leading British representatives at earlier sessions had been the Conservative Edward Heath (born 1916). In 1970, he became prime minister, and two years later his government signed the treaty that was to admit Britain. On January 1, 1973, the EEC received three new members: Britain, Denmark, and Ireland. The first two withdrew from EFTA. Norway, which was also offered membership, rejected it in a popular referendum. By 1990, three more states had joined: Greece in 1981, and Spain and Portugal in 1986.

THE ORGANIZATION OF THE EUROPEAN UNION

The devisers of the European Union's (EU) institutions tried to take into consideration the fact that members would often find their own interests in conflict with those of the EU as a whole. They therefore created an organization that would balance national interests against intergovernmental cooperation. The vast bureaucracy that developed (in 1989 there were 18,000 civil servants—or "Eurocrats"—working for the EU) is a frequent cause of criticism. Jobs and subsequent promotions are assigned on the basis of nationality rather than merit, and Eurocrats can be moved to other positions or dismissed only under exceptional circumstances.

THE EXECUTIVE OF THE EU

The EU has a dual executive. The European Commission, which meets in Brussels, represents the supranational component. According to the Treaty of Rome, it acts in the general interest of the European Community. Its commissioners, who are appointed for four years by the member states, must judge for themselves what the interests of the Community are; they cannot receive instructions from the governments that nominate them. The commission can initiate policy and make recommendations; it cannot make policy.

That task is performed by the Council of Ministers, the second half of the executive, which guards national interests.

HISTORICAL PERSPECTIVES

SOVEREIGNTY, LAW, AND UNITY

MARY VOLCANSEK   Texas Christian University

The treaties establishing the European Community followed the standard model of modern democratic governments by instituting three separate powers—executive, legislative, and judicial. An underlying assumption was that the judicial arm, the European Court of Justice, would be the more passive, because judges typically, by virtue of age and training, are expected to respect tradition more often than boldly to break new ground. The Court of Justice, hidden away in the Duchy of Luxembourg, has often shattered conventional assumptions about the behavior of courts as its judges defined the limits of national sovereignty and pushed for greater unity through its interpretation of the treaties. The Court, which now hears more than 500 cases each year, has significantly contributed to European integration, particularly in its decisions announcing the supremacy of European law over that of individual member states, the legal rights of individuals, human rights protected by the treaties, and rules that foster economic integration.

The relevance of community law for individual nations was firmly fixed by the Court of Justice in 1964 by its decision in *Costa* v. *ENEL*. That case stands as the source from which the authority of the court and of community law flows. Flaminio Costa was a lawyer and a small stockholder in Italy's electric company ENEL, an operation that was nationalized by the Italian government in 1962. He refused to pay his elec-

tric bill of less than three dollars and filed a lawsuit charging that the Italian government had violated the article in the Treaty of Rome relating to national monopolies. The Italian judge hearing the case followed Costa's recommendation that he seek an interpretation of that specific treaty article from the European Court of Justice. The European Court declared that community law was superior to the laws in any member state and was absorbed into the legal systems of each nation. Community law was declared to supersede any existing national law or constitution. That stark assertion of supremacy provided a legal basis giving force to all laws passed by the Community and transforming the founding treaties into the "constitution" of the Community.

If the treaties are a constitution and regulations passed by other institutions of the Community are lawful in any nation, how can an individual secure the protections offered by them? The Court of Justice's answer was to create the doctrine of "legal rights of individuals." This concept was first announced in the 1958 case of *Van Gend en Loos* that dealt with duties on imports from Germany into the Netherlands that interfered with free movement of goods. The case involved not only the validity of the customs taxes, but also the recourse of individuals who felt that the guarantees of the treaties were being ignored by a national government. The Court of Justice announced that the European Community constituted a "new legal order,"

It consists of the foreign ministers of the member states, who are at times represented by other ministers when specific problem areas are under discussion—energy, transport, health, agriculture, and so on. The council meets several times a month; every six months the presidency passes in rotation among the member nations. It discusses measures proposed by the commissioners and votes either to accept or reject them.

The voting system whereby decisions are made is a "weighted" one. The larger states have more votes. (In 1990 Britain, France, West Germany, and Italy had ten votes each; Spain eight; Belgium, Greece, the Netherlands, and Portugal five; Denmark and Ireland three; Luxembourg two.

Proposals are considered passed if they obtain 54 votes.) If, however, a state feels that its vital national interests are at stake, it has the right to block a decision by vetoing it, even if every other government votes in favor.

The existence of the power of veto remains controversial. In 1984, French President Mitterand pointed out the absurdity of running as complex an organization as the EU "by the rules of the Diet of the old kingdom of Poland, where every member could block the decisions." By the 1990s, there was strong support for a reform to eliminate it, but members failed to reach overall agreement—the countries in favor of retaining the veto were Britain, Denmark, and Greece.

that signatories to the treaties had limited their sovereign rights, and that the treaties conferred legal rights, as well as obligations, on individual citizens.

The treaties of the Community include no "bill of rights," although certain economic rights are specifically mentioned. The Court of Justice has, nonetheless, moved far in the creation of a set of rights, both economic and social. The Treaty of Rome, for example, specifically dictates comparable pay for men and women, inclusive of indirect compensation.

The European Court of Justice has also been active in removing trade barriers among nations that interfered with the Community's stated goal of a common market. The landmark *Cassis de Dijon* decision in 1979 emerged when Germany tried to halt the sale of a French beverage in Germany because it had an insufficient alcoholic content. The court concluded, as it would again later when Italy refused the sale of German pasta, that "if it's good enough for a Frenchman, it is good enough for a German." The equation is the same for any two or more nationalities within the Community. That single legal principle was able to sweep away thousands of restrictions that had been erected to halt imports among the member states. Imports from sister countries could, thereafter, be barred only on grounds of public health or safety.

Proponents of greater economic and political integration in Europe have applauded the bold initiatives of the European Court of Justice. The judges in Luxembourg have been hailed for assuring integration of the markets of Western Europe and for "democratizing" the Community through their handling of human rights. The court has, in fact, been in the forefront of integration.

Some commentators on both sides of the Atlantic have criticized the court's extreme activism or its willingness to exceed the legal tradition's norms of simply applying the law objectively and impartially. These critics note the court's tendency to create law that comports with the judges' personal notions of how things *ought* to be and accuse the court of usurping legislative powers. They argue that when judges exceed their mandate of interpreting law and make forays into lawmaking, the legitimacy and efficacy of the judiciary may be jeopardized. This line of argument says less about the outcomes of specific court decisions or their policy implications and more directly focuses on the traditional role of courts and judges in Western democracies. Another criticism addresses the policies that the court has pursued. That analysis targets the political agenda of the judges, who, as the argument goes, have allowed their enthusiasm for the European experiment, not the treaties or other relevant laws, to guide their decisions. The European Court of Justice, like other Western courts, is undoubtedly politicized, but whether that should be viewed as positive or negative is likely dependent on the political persuasion of the observer.

The European Community entered a new era with the passage of the Single European Act with its goals for the end of 1992. Before that deadline arrived, the leaders of the member states had already made a commitment to amend the founding treaties to achieve monetary union and to explore closer political union. A reconsideration of the division of powers of the Parliament also received implicit agreement. These developments may well transform the role of the European Court, as may the sheer size of the Community, as the number of countries seems likely to swell beyond 15 to 18 or even more. What will not change, however, is the significant contribution that the European Court made in defining sovereignty and forging unity in the first 35 years of community history.

THE EU INSTITUTIONS

The notion of a European Parliament was established by the Treaty of Rome. Enlarged along with the EU, and elected by popular vote since 1979, its powers are limited. It cannot legislate and has no right to control or replace the executive organs. It oversees and expresses opinions on the commission's proposals and has control over part of the EU budget; the greater part of the funds—71 percent—is under the supervision of the Council of Ministers.

The members of the European Parliament are directly elected in their home countries, by the electoral system in force in each. In 1989, there were 81 members from each of the four largest nations, 60 from Spain, 25 from the Netherlands, 24 each from Belgium, Greece, and Portugal, 16 from Denmark, 15 from Ireland, and 6 from Luxembourg. They take their seats in the assembly not as national delegations, but according to their party—Christian Democrats, Liberals, Socialists, Communists, and so on. A Rainbow Group brings together Greens and other ecologists, as well as several smaller parties—one of which is the Danish anti-EU party, the People's Movement against the community.

The Parliament originally met in both Strasbourg and Luxembourg, and Eurocrats spent considerable time and energy transporting files and records back and forth each

British shoppers buying German beer in a French supermarket for cross-Channel shoppers near the Calais ferry docks. Mid-1990s. With the disappearance of many European tariff and customs barriers in January 1993, products circulated freely within the EU. By 2002, customers could use the same currency to buy them—the Euro—in 12 of the member states.

month. In 1981, it voted to hold all of its sessions in Strasbourg, where it meets about eight times a year for one-week sessions.

The EU's legal arm is the European Court of Justice, composed of 13 members, which meets in Luxembourg. It oversees compliance with the Treaty of Rome and makes sure that all executive decisions are in accordance with the treaty's provisions. It hears cases at all levels, from member nations to individual persons.

More broadly, the European Court sought to develop a body of "community law," dealing with economic, trade, and social issues. Community law applies throughout the member states and supersedes national law. It thus represents the principal instance to date of the surrendering of national sovereignty to a supranational institution.

Both the Parliament and court were created by the Treaty of Rome. A new institution, the European Council, came into being in 1974. Made up of the heads and foreign ministers of the member governments, it generally meets three times per year at highly publicized "European Summits," which are held in appropriately picturesque settings. The Council is the only EU body that has some jurisdiction in all fields. Because its meetings permit direct confrontation of government leaders, they are often stormy. At the same time, they sometimes manage to resolve thorny problems by hard bargaining.

The Parliament building for the EU Parliament, known as the Council of Europe. 1990s. Although the administrative headquarters are in Brussels, Belgium, the European Parliament meets in this location in Strasbourg, France. The city is a river port with access to two major European rivers, the Rhine and the Rhône. Flags of the member states fly outside the main Council Hall.

THE FUTURE OF THE EUROPEAN UNION

Throughout the 1970s and 1980s, public opinion in Europe varied widely on whether membership of the EU was a good thing. In a poll taken in 1985, 72 percent of Italians polled were in favor of EU membership, and only 4 percent against. At the other extreme, only 29 percent of Danes, and 37 percent of Britons favored the organization, and 31 and 30 percent respectively were against it.

THE SINGLE EUROPEAN ACT

Meanwhile in 1986, the EU moved another stage forward with the passage of the Single European Act. The most immediate new goal the act set out was the completion by the end of 1992 of a unified European internal market. By that date there were to be no more trade barriers among members. All frontier and border formalities would disappear for European Community citizens. Labor and capital could circulate freely. There would be further progress toward economic and monetary union. More generally, members would work together to improve the environment and to establish a common plan of social legislation. These last two aims met with less than unanimous approval; some states, most vocally Britain, felt that the ecological and social plans were unrealizable and represented interference in domestic affairs.

The late 1980s were marked by bursts of frantic activity as the various nations began to prepare themselves for the end of 1992. With no forms of restriction in effect, each individual firm and company would be in direct competition with the whole of Europe. This had increasingly been the case for manufacturers and traders since the EU's early days. After 1992, however, it applied to a host of service industries, such as banking and insurance, which in many cases had been protected by government regulations. Portuguese or Irish investors looking for the best interest rates could send their money to Germany. Car owners in Italy, where insurance rates are high, could insure their vehicles with French or Belgian companies. Many insurance and other service firms began to open branches in countries other than their own. American and Japanese firms, hitherto discouraged by protectionist legislation in individual European countries, also began to eye the vast new market with interest.

On the other hand, for all the difficulties it presented, European economic unity could create a bloc strong enough and independent enough to stand up to the United States and Japan. Already by 1987, in fact, Western Europe was the world's largest trading power, although not, of course, a unified power in the political sense; it handled 37 percent of global trade, more than that of the United States and the Soviet Union combined. The Western European nations also held one-third of the world's monetary reserves and contributed 36 percent of the world's development aid—all this with only 6 percent of the world's population.

Poster illustrating the replacement of national currencies by a single one, the Euro. Mid-1990s. The old national bills are fanned out behind the coin representing one Euro. The transition to a single currency in 12 of the member states (Britain, Denmark, and Sweden have not joined the "Euro area") took place from January 1, 1999, to January 1, 2002, and proved surprisingly smooth.

NEW MEMBERS FOR THE EUROPEAN UNION

As the EU prepared to face 1992, it had to grapple with a new problem: whether to admit new members. Switzerland, a member of EFTA, signed an agreement in 1977 to abolish tariffs on industrial products for EU partners. Its neutral status, and its unwillingness to allow free movement of labor, meant that it would not seek membership in the foreseeable future.

Austria and Finland, however, presented different issues. Neutral since the end of World War II, they theoretically served as bridges between East and West. Even so, by 1987 around half of Austria's exports went to EU countries, principally West Germany, and only about 12 percent to the Soviet Union and Eastern Europe. Finland's position was similar. With the collapse of the Soviet bloc's communist regimes in 1989, and the imminent end of the Cold War, the status of these two countries inevitably changed. The interests of European economic unity, as well as their own interests, led both Austria and Finland to become full members in 1995. Sweden also joined in the same year, while Norway rejected membership in a popular referendum.

The application of Turkey presented more formidable problems. Although only a small part of Turkey lies on the European continent, the Turkish government contended that the country's economy was basically linked with that of Mediterranean Europe. Morocco, in informal approaches to the EU, made a similar argument. In addition, as a leading partner in NATO, Turkey plays an important role in European defense.

Several factors combined to make it unlikely that the Turkish application would be accepted in the near future. In the first place, government rule in Turkey did not correspond to the broadly based democratic systems and traditions that operated in most of the EU member countries most of the time. Second, political instability in Turkey would make negotiations difficult. Third, years of implacable animosity between Greece and Turkey—intensified by the Turkish invasion and annexation of northern Cyprus in 1974—made a Greek veto likely. Finally, the admission of Turkey would create a precedent with far-reaching consequences. The European Community began as an association of partners sharing a common history and culture; divergence from that principle could prejudice the chances of a later political union. When Turkey renewed its application in 1997, members' reactions continued to be negative. On the other hand, Cyprus—providing that it achieved unification—was encouraged to apply.

THE EU AND EASTERN EUROPE

The idea of a shared history and culture, however, made the liberalization of Eastern Europe a potential milestone in the EU's history. Countries such as Czechoslovakia, Hungary, and Poland had played a key role in European history and produced some of the leading figures in European intellectual life, literature, and music. Furthermore, access to the EU's rich markets would help them rebuild economies worn down by years of Stalinism. As a final touch of enlightened self-interest, if the EU members helped reconstruct the Eastern European economies, they would be creating a future market for their own products.

One Eastern bloc country—East Germany—was assured entry by the unification of East and West Germany. Most of the others began negotiations as soon as new governments had been installed. After the spring elections of 1990, Hungary and Czechoslovakia made their initial approaches. Czechoslovakia signed an agreement of economic cooperation with the EU and began the process of adaptation that membership would require. Hungary, whose economy was in a healthier state, looked to join the EU at an earlier date. Poland seemed another future applicant, and Bulgaria also signed a treaty of economic cooperation in 1990. At the 1997 meeting that rejected Turkey's renewed application, the slow process of admitting Hungary, Poland, and the Czech Republic (the richer half of the now-divided former Czechoslovakia) began. All of these nations should become full members by 2004.

Putting the Path Toward European Integration in Perspective

By the early 1990s, the cause of European economic unity had done much to heal the scars of half a century earlier. The countries of Western Europe weathered the economic slumps and political uncertainties of the 1970s to emerge as a leading world economic force. By committing themselves to the 1992 deadline, they hastened the further process of unification. Few claimed that 1992 would be less than traumatic; it was clear that the pressures of competition would strain each country's resources and run the risk of adversely affecting the lives of countless ordinary citizens. Yet the process was by now irreversible.

Many factors remained vague. Monetary union, the next stage if any form of political union was to be achieved, fiercely divided the EU membership, with Britain resisting anything that could be construed as a loss of national sovereignty. By the spring of 1998, it was decided that most of the members would proceed toward monetary union beginning January 1, 1999. The economies of Greece and Portugal were judged too weak to participate, and Britain and Denmark chose not to join the single European currency, the Euro. The plan was for participating members to phase out their national currencies over three years, leaving only the Euro in circulation by 2002.

The landscape of European history seemed permanently changed. As a tumultuous and often cataclysmic century drew toward its close, the Old Continent, whose economic strength and moral standing had been shattered in 1945, once again began to emerge as a leading world power.

Questions for Further Study

1. How successfully does the political and administrative structure of the European Union compensate for national differences among the various members?
2. Which are the most likely candidates for new members by the early 21st century? What effect would their joining have on the EU?
3. What are the arguments for and against monetary union?

Suggestions for Further Reading

Bjorn, Claus, Alexander Grant, and Keith J. Stringer. *Nations, Nationalism and Patriotism in the European Past.* Copenhagen, 1994.

Daltrop, A. *Politics and the European Community.* New York, 1987.

Egan, Michelle P. *Constructing a European Market: Standards, Regulation, and Governance.* New York, 2001.

European Commission. *Eurobarometer, Public Opinion in the European Union, Trends 1974–1994.* Luxembourg, 1994.

Kotlowski, Dean J., ed. *The European Union: From Jean Monnet to the Euro.* Athens, OH, 2000.

Padoa-Schioppa, T. *Efficiency, Stability and Equity: A Strategy for the Evolution of the Economic System of the European Community.* Oxford, 1988.

Smith, Anthony D. *National Identity.* Harmondsworth, 1991.

Wiarda, Howard J., ed. *European Politics in the Age of Globalization.* Fort Worth, TX, 2001.

Woolf, Stuart. *Nationalism in Europe, 1815 to the Present. A Reader.* New York, 1996.

Zeff, Elenor E., and Ellen B. Pirro, eds. *The European Union and the Member States: Cooperation, Coordination, and Compromise.* Boulder, CO, 2001.

InfoTrac College Edition

Enter the search term *single European market* using the Subject Guide.

EPILOGUE: FACING THE 21ST CENTURY

By the end of the 20th century, with the prospect of economic union in sight, Europe had regained an independent position in world political and economic affairs. As Soviet control in Eastern Europe ended, and the tensions of the Cold War began to relax, European nations began to look toward a status that did not lock them into an unconditional alliance with either the United States or the Soviet Union.

The generation of political leaders of the late 1980s saw a series of European figures attain international standing. The conservatives Thatcher and Kohl, and the socialists Mitterand and Gonzalez, all represented approximately a decade of continuity in their respective countries—Britain, West Germany, France, and Spain. In Italy the Socialists, under the leadership of Bettino Craxi, became key members of the ruling government coalition. The Greek Socialist leader Andreas Papandreou finally lost power in 1989, when a series of scandals brought down his government.

In Eastern Europe, the Czech Václav Havel became one of the most articulate spokesmen of the "new politics." Above all, the rise of Mikhail Gorbachev in the Soviet Union produced a thaw in East-West relations and made possible the abrupt dismantlement of the Soviet-supported regimes in Eastern Europe.

Several new problems began to excite public attention. The oil crisis of the 1970s had led many countries to explore the alternative of nuclear energy. The Three Mile Island accident in the United States of 1979, followed by the much more serious accident at Chernobyl in the Soviet Union in 1986, raised widespread doubts about dependence on nuclear power. General concern about damage to the environment became focused in the growing strength of the "Green" movement.

The mood of political stability continued to be overshadowed by terrorist activities on both right and left. In some cases, such as Northern Ireland and Spain, terrorism was related to specific local issues, often nationalist in origin. In West Germany and Italy, terrorists tried to bring down political and social systems on ideological grounds. A third category of terrorist attacks was related to issues outside Europe, most notably the Palestinian problem. The attack on September 11, 2001, on New York and Washington, D.C., by planes hijacked and piloted by members of the Al-qaeda terrorist organization focused world attention on the continuing threat posed worldwide by terrorists.

BETWEEN EAST AND WEST: THE SEARCH FOR EUROPEAN INDEPENDENCE

The two world wars brought to an end centuries of European dominance in international affairs and left most European countries unable to rebuild their economies without aid from one of the two superpowers: the United States and the Soviet Union. In the case of Western Europe, U.S. assistance was offered and accepted; in Eastern Europe, the Soviet Union imposed Stalinism. The result in both cases was to create alliances that left Europe divided and locked into virtually unconditional support for their respective patrons.

EUROPE AND NUCLEAR WEAPONS

After 1945, a few strong European leaders asserted their right to independence, including Tito in Yugoslavia and de Gaulle in France. For the most part, however, Western Europe welcomed the "Atlantic Alliance," seeing the American military presence as essential to European security. European leaders, most notably West German Social Democratic leader Helmut Schmidt, supported the installation of medium-range American nuclear missiles on NATO bases in West Germany, Britain, Italy, Belgium, and the Netherlands. The "Two-Track Decision"—to continue arming and negotiating at the same time—was taken late in 1979; it provoked widespread demonstrations and protests in the countries involved.

The missiles were installed in response to the Soviet deployment of nuclear weapons on Eastern European soil, in particular in East Germany. Thus by the mid-1980s each superpower possessed the ability to wage nuclear war in Europe without using weapons located in its own territory.

In 1985 the growing economic crisis in the Soviet Union, and the arrival on the scene of Mikhail Gorbachev, led to the renewal of détente. As Gorbachev sought ways to reduce the burden on the Soviet economy of defense spending, he proved increasingly willing to negotiate significant arms reductions. The American position under Ronald Reagan—that negotiation required a further arms buildup—became moderated. In 1987 the two superpowers signed a treaty to reduce medium-range nuclear weapons. Thus at the end of the 1980s both sides began to dismantle their European armaments.

Although the medium-range arms were under American control, they formed part of the NATO forces. Two countries, Britain and France, maintained their own independent nuclear forces. The French continued a program of nuclear testing in the Pacific. In 1985, when the Greenpeace environmental movement threatened to send its boat, *Rainbow Warrior,* to interfere in the tests, the French Defense Ministry had the vessel sunk; one person was killed. Public protests in France forced the resignation of the defense minister and the head of foreign intelligence operations. Nonetheless, France continued to maintain its nuclear capacity, and in 1987 embarked on an expensive and ambitious five-year rearmament plan. In 1996, to a barrage of international protest, the French carried out a series of underground nuclear tests in the Pacific. Similar outrage greeted the nuclear tests of three non-European powers—those of China in 1996 and of India and Pakistan in 1998.

Britain's aging nuclear force became the focus of fierce public debate in the late 1980s. The Thatcher government announced its intention of replacing the old Polaris submarines with updated craft, capable of firing American-made Trident missiles. Thatcher's opponents argued that, in addition to the vast expense of the change, the easing of tension between East and West made an independent British nuclear deterrent increasingly irrelevant.

The process of détente continued through the end of the 1980s and was rapidly accelerated by the liberalization in Eastern Europe of 1989. As politicians and generals alike began to rethink the future role of NATO and the Warsaw

A demonstration in favor of nuclear disarmament, England. 1981. As the umbrellas show, the participants are not deterred by the weather. In the center are two skulls, their hats decorated with the flags of the Soviet Union (hammer and sickle) and the United States (stars and stripes). The symbol of the Campaign for Nuclear Disarmament (CND) is on the banners at the rear. This symbol, which was first designed in 1958, is known more broadly in the rest of the world as the peace symbol.

Earl Young/Archive Photos

Pact alliance, it seemed possible that by the 21st century European security would be in predominantly European hands. The role of the independent British and French nuclear forces in a European defense plan would depend on government decisions and on public reactions. In 1983 an opinion poll in Britain showed eight out of ten people in favor of an independent British deterrent, but this broad support began to shrink.

By the end of the 20th century, NATO approved applications from several former Soviet allies, including the Czech Republic, Poland, and Hungary, and its leaders signed an agreement with the Soviet Union: the "Partnership for Peace." The occasion signaled reluctant Soviet acceptance of the enlargement eastward of NATO.

POLITICAL LEADERSHIP IN THE LATE 20TH CENTURY

Although the progress in disarmament of the 1980s was principally because of the improved relations between the United States and the Soviet Union, European nations and their leaders continued to play a part on the international scene. French and Italian troops joined the U.S. Marines in an unsuccessful attempt to stabilize conditions in Lebanon between 1982 and 1984. In 1987, with Iraq and Iran locked in violent conflict, British and American ships swept the waters of the Persian Gulf to protect neutral ships from underwater missiles.

NEW LEADERS IN BRITAIN AND WEST GERMANY

The chief political leaders of the 1980s remained in power for most of the decade, although by 1990 several seemed to be losing popular support (see Topic 90). In Britain and West Germany, conservative parties governed. The British prime minister for the entire decade was Margaret Thatcher—Britain's first woman premier—who was elected in 1979. A firm advocate of transatlantic cooperation, she helped U.S. forces to make an air attack on Libya in 1986 by providing the use of British landing and refueling facilities.

By 1990, with Britain's fundamental economic problems still unsolved, there was a growing feeling that a new leader should take the Conservatives into the next election. In the routine leadership election of December 1990, Thatcher failed to win the necessary percentage of votes on the first ballot and withdrew. John Major subsequently was elected Conservative leader and became prime minister. After narrowly winning the general election of 1992, the Conservatives were finally swept from power by a Labour landslide in 1997. In the intervening years, Labour's popular new leader, Tony Blair (born 1954), succeeded in replacing his party's old working-class image with one of efficient modernity. New Labour's position as the party of government was reinforced by a further overwhelming victory in the general election of 2001, which saw the

Conservative party once again routed. A ballot to choose a new Conservative leader in the fall of 2001 polarized the party on the issue of whether Britain should join the vast majority of European Community members in replacing their national currency with the Euro.

Helmut Kohl became chancellor of West Germany in 1982. Like Thatcher's, his chief support came from the prosperous middle classes. Less divisive than his British equivalent, he used his exuberance and glowing optimism to promote party unity and present the most favorable image possible of West Germany's international standing. He strengthened ties with Eastern Europe and the Soviet Union, while remaining a strong ally of the United States. By the end of the decade, the American–West German relationship seemed about to supersede the American–British one as the cornerstone of the United States' ties to Western Europe.

Domestic problems—unemployment, immigration, pollution—were beginning to erode the Christian Democrats' popularity, when German politics were suddenly shaken up by the fall of East Germany's communist regime. From the very start, Kohl led the drive for a reunited Germany. In the East German elections he campaigned widely and visibly for the East German Christian Democratic party, promising that West Germany would guarantee the value of the East German mark as equal with that of the West German currency. The West German mark was, in fact, worth around 10 times the value of its East German equivalent. His promise, which cost West Germany an enormous amount of money and led to inflation and unemployment there, was implemented a few months later with certain provisos.

Kohl's wholehearted support helped the East German Christian Democrats win the election and become the country's leading political force. Back in West Germany, however, the economic strain of reunification began to create doubts about the wisdom of Kohl's speed. The Social Democrats, while endorsing the goal of eventual German unity, advocated a slower pace. In regional elections in May 1990, the Social Democrats made significant gains, and the Christian Democrats lost control of one of the houses of Parliament. As both parties prepared for national elections in December 1990, it seemed that West Germans were as concerned with their pocketbooks as with the notion of a reunited Germany, yet the speed of events was irresistible: on October 3, 1990, Germany became reunited. With the approaching end of the century, optimism at the end of 45 years of division became tempered, however, with preoccupation at the financial price of reunification. Voters' worries about the German economy—in particular the replacement of the German mark with the proposed standard European currency, the Euro—threatened Kohl's bid for reelection in 1998. In the end, the Socialists, led by Helmut Schroeder, defeated Kohl and the Christian Democrats, but not because of economic fears: A scandal concerning fundraising for his party left Kohl accused of corruption. The hitherto unassailable Chancellor was forced to resign, and his party became thoroughly discredited.

SOCIALIST LEADERS IN FRANCE AND SPAIN

The socialist leaders of France and Spain, François Mitterand and Felipe Gonzalez, came to power in 1981 and 1982, respectively. By 1990, both were undergoing a fall in popularity, in part because of their jettisoning of socialist principles in an attempt to solve economic problems.

By the early 1990s, with the political parties preparing for the presidential elections of 1995, the Socialists began to divide up in support of various potential candidates. In consequence, Mitterand's legendary skill at political maneuvering was tested to its limits. Nonetheless, Mitterand's own standing as a senior European statesman allowed him, together with Kohl, to coordinate a European response to the issue of German reunification. His lofty dignity and air of sibylline wisdom also served to resolve differences at fractious European summits. The 1995 election saw the victory of Mitterand's old rival Jacques Chirac, with a strong showing by the socialist candidate, Lionel Jospin. Two years later, in May 1997, Jospin led his socialists to victory in a surprise general election, thus inaugurating five years of "cohabitation" with a right-wing president, and Jospin and Chirac prepared to do battle for the presidency in 2002. Chirac emerged victorious, largely because strong support for Jean Marie LePen, leader of the far-right National Front, knocked out Jospin in the first round of voting.

For most of the 1980s, the moderate and pragmatic Gonzalez presided over Europe's most popular socialist government. Before his election in 1982, he opposed Spanish membership in NATO. By 1986, the year in which Spain entered the EU, he had changed his mind; he was sufficiently convinced of the importance of continued membership to call a popular referendum. To the general surprise, he won victory by a wide margin. An avowed internationalist, Gonzalez did much to facilitate Spain's return to European affairs after the Franco years of isolation.

Like his colleagues elsewhere in Europe, Gonzalez proved less successful in solving domestic economic problems. His mildly conservative policies of wage restraint and monetary caution failed to halt rising inflation, while angering the unions and his left-wing support. Widespread demonstrations led to a decline in Socialist power. By 1990 the Socialists were still in control and Gonzalez was a popular figure, but neither party nor party leader could afford to ignore their supporters; the honeymoon had been a long one, but it was over. In the spring of 1996, a conservative government came to power, although only with the support of smaller regional parties. The same coalition was reelected in 2001.

GOVERNMENT CRISES IN ITALY AND GREECE

In Italy the usual creation and collapse of coalition governments dominated by the Christian Democrats was briefly interrupted in 1981–1982, when the Republican leader Giovanni Spadolini (1925–1994) formed two center-left governments of short duration. The Socialists provided a more consistent interlude, when Bettino Craxi led a left-center government that lasted from 1983 to 1986—three and a half years, a record in postwar Italian politics.

Craxi's rise to prominence in Italian political life began with his election as Socialist leader in 1976. Over the following decade, the Socialists slowly increased their share of the votes, rising from 9.6 percent in 1976 to 16.8 percent in the regional elections of 1990. (The same period saw the Italian Communist party in precipitous decline, falling from 34.4 to 24.4 percent.) Craxi's own combative and aggressive personality proved a mixed blessing. There was a general feeling that his government was efficient and "got things done." On the other hand, his histrionic oratory and tough political style, coupled with an unfortunate resemblance to Mussolini—both leaders bald and portly—led to doubts. In cartoons and television satirical programs, Craxi became regularly portrayed as Italy's late and unlamented *Duce*.

The fall of the Craxi government was followed by another protracted period of instability, during which the country's economy continued to boom. Carlo de Benedetti, a leading industrialist, was heard to remark that, with all the confusion in Rome, he and his colleagues could get on with running Italian business successfully and uninterruptedly. By 1988, however, government was firmly back in the hands of the Christian Democrats, under the leadership of Giuliano Andreotti (born 1919). The coalition's chief partners, Christian Democrats and Socialists, continued to bicker as Craxi alternately threatened and cajoled. As Italy entered the 1990s, its eccentric political system seemed likely to continue relatively unchanged.

Yet in the spring of 1993, a series of investigations began to unfold that implicated a high proportion of Italy's ruling class in massive bribery and corruption. The scandal came to be known as *Mani Pulite,* or "Clean Hands." The base of operations was Milan, and one of the chief investigating magistrates, Antonio di Pietro, rapidly became a popular hero. In a matter of months, many of Italy's leading politicians, most notably Craxi, were driven from office. After a period of caretaker governments, and seven months during which Silvio Berlusconi, one of the leading businessmen in Italy, served as prime minister, elections in April 1996 brought a center-left alliance, the Olive Branch, to power for the first time in Italian history. The largest single party, the Democratic Party of the Left (PDS), consisted of the majority of the former Italian Communist party, but the alliance also included former Christian Democrats: Its leader, Romano Prodi, had served as a state bureaucrat under Christian Democratic rule. The alliance became the first party in modern Italian history to remain in power for the full term of five years, but over time it became weakened by internal squabbles among its various components. In 2001, a right-wing coalition, led once again by Silvio Berlusconi, achieved a clear majority and looked set to govern for the next five years.

Greece spent the 1980s under socialist government. In 1981 the Panhellenic Socialist Movement (PASOK) won an electoral victory whose size was unparalleled anywhere else in Europe. Their leader, the charismatic if controversial Andreas Papandreou (born 1919), instituted a wide-ranging program of reform. His government liberalized the divorce laws, restructured agriculture, and began to move from a pro-Western position in foreign affairs to an independent nationalism: Among the recurrent causes of tension between Greece and the United States was the presence of American forces on Greek territory.

The Greek economy remained in bad shape. The Socialists did little to modernize industry or introduce new technologies, and the country remained dependent on foreign aid. In 1988, a personal scandal involving Papandreou—he announced plans to divorce his wife and marry his mistress—shook his party. Subsequent revelations of widespread corruption in government circles, which also involved Papandreou directly, led to his fall from power. A period of inconclusive elections finally ended in May 1990, when a conservative government was returned to office with the narrowest of margins—one seat. By the late 1990s, with the Socialists once again in power, the economic problems facing Greece's new rulers were formidable: rampant inflation, growing unemployment, and increasing foreign debt.

THE DISSOLUTION OF THE SOVIET UNION

The two years from 1989 to 1991 dramatically transformed the entire situation in Eastern Europe as well as the nature of global politics. The revolution of 1989 (see Topic 91) had brought an end to Soviet hegemony over the nations behind what was once called the "Iron Curtain." Then, in 1990 to 1991, the Soviet Union collapsed under the stress of the fundamental changes that had been wrought by Gorbachev.

NEW LEADERSHIP IN EASTERN EUROPE

With the revolutions of 1989, virtually all countries in Eastern Europe underwent a change of leadership. In some cases this was more apparent than real. The new regime in Romania, under the leadership of Ion Iliescu (born 1930), retained a suspicious number of those politicians who had served under Ceausescu. Bulgaria, too, moved slowly in replacing the old guard. Hungary, East Germany, and Czechoslovakia, however, all elected new noncommunist leaders, who in turn nominated new heads of state.

One of these, the Czech Václav Havel (born 1936), began to emerge as one of the leading representatives of the new order in Eastern Europe. A playwright and intellectual, Havel became president of Czechoslovakia in 1990. Traveling widely in Eastern and Western Europe, and to the United States, he spoke eloquently and emotionally of the needs of the new democratic nations and of the urgency of reconciling old hatreds. Even his influence, however, could not prevent the country from splitting into two independent nations: the Czech Republic and Slovakia.

In Poland, the beginning of 1990 saw the beginnings of a split in the hitherto united Solidarity leadership. As Polish Prime Minister Tadeusz Mazowiecki (born 1927) introduced unpopular economic reforms along generally liberal lines, Lech Wałesa, Solidarity's most prominent leader,

began to press for more conservative policies. Wałesa had been prepared earlier to hand over the business of government to his colleagues and occupy a symbolic leadership position, but there were signs of coming conflict. Wałesa and Mazowiecki both ran for election as Poland's president. Wałesa won. By the time of Poland's next presidential election in 1995, however, disillusioned voters rejected Wałesa and turned to a former Communist politician.

THE END OF SOVIET HISTORY

By 1990, the greatest of all changes in post–world war history had been wrought by the leader whose own position seemed least secure: Mikhail Gorbachev (see Topic 91). Almost as striking as the actual achievements themselves was the change in the character of Soviet leadership, symbolized by the prominent role played in Soviet public life visits abroad by Gorbachev's wife, Raisa.

Among the qualities brought by Mikhail Gorbachev to his position was an awareness of the importance of "image" in a world of global communications. His predecessors had done nothing to relieve the monolithic uniformity of Soviet leadership or its secrecy. Gorbachev took part in much-publicized "walk-arounds," on which he met people in the street. Outside the Soviet Union these mainly consisted of opportunities for passersby to shake hands with the famous man; the public relations sessions blocked traffic in most of the cities Gorbachev visited. On home ground, the walk-arounds often led to lively debate, with Gorbachev listening to complaints and arguing back. Early in 1990, when the possibility of Lithuania breaking away from the Soviet Union seemed increasingly likely, Gorbachev made an unsuccessful attempt to prevent the move by going there and presenting his case against independence.

Soviet leaders after Stalin severely discouraged the "cult of personality." Little was known about their private lives or families—Yuri Andropov's wife made her first public appearance at her late husband's funeral in 1984. Furthermore, although women were officially equal to men in Soviet society, very few played any part in public life.

From his first visits abroad, Gorbachev was accompanied by his wife Raisa (1932–2000). Like an American president's wife, the Soviet first lady played an important role in humanizing the lofty affairs of state. Raisa's role seemed modeled on the American system. While her husband held meetings with President Reagan on his visit to the United States in 1987, she visited the White House; however, a less than friendly encounter there with Nancy Reagan led to a distinctly cool relationship between the two wives.

Gorbachev's power clearly remained dependent on the success of his economic reforms and not on his public image. In the winter of 1990–1991, as food supplies grew increasingly short in the Soviet Union's principal cities, Boris Yeltsin, elected president of the Russian Republic in 1989, stepped up his hostile criticism of Gorbachev's program. The issue of whether individual republics could break away from the Soviet Union became the cause of widespread demonstrations and protests.

ACROSS CULTURES

MARTHA GELLHORN IN CUBA

With growing instability in the Soviet Union, Moscow was no longer able to maintain the same level of support for its Communist allies. Its breakup in 1991 was accompanied by similar collapses in Communist regimes throughout Eastern Europe. One Communist government, however, that of Castro's Cuba, continued to rule, despite the end of Soviet financial aid and an American boycott on trade and travel.

An interesting picture of life there in the years immediately preceding the collapse of the Soviet Union emerges from a visit to Cuba in the 1980s by the writer and journalist Martha Gellhorn ("Cuba Revisited," in *The Best of Granta Travel*, London, 1991). Gellhorn had lived in Cuba with the writer Ernest Hemingway, to whom she was formerly married, between 1939 and 1944. Her account tries to give a balanced picture of the weaknesses—and achievement—of Castro's regime.

Announcing that she is "a foreign journalist," she visits a secondary school, where

> I was shown the school bulletin board with its smiling photographs of the "martyrs"—handsome girls and boys, not much older than the children here, killed by Batista's police for their clandestine work in the Revolucion. The school was unpainted cement inside and out, built on the cheap in 1979.

> The English teacher was nervous and nice and desperately eager for his class to perform well. Each child read aloud a sentence from their textbook, dealing with Millie's birthday party. Offhand, I couldn't think of a deadlier subject. "Toothbrush" and "toothpaste" (Millie's birthday presents!) are very hard for them to say; also "room." His own accent was odd; the kids were choked with stage fright, rivaling mine.

> Afterward, refreshments were served.

> Snacks had been laid out in the principal's office. I looked at these poorly dressed men and women and grieved to think of them chipping in for this party. They were so excited about me because the school had never received a visitor before, no Cuban personage, let alone a foreigner. They spoke of their students with pride; it must feel good to teach such lively and willing children.

Gellhorn makes clear that "The undeniable shame of the Cuban government is political prisoners," and describes how released prisoners "have reported atrocious prison conditions, brutality from jailers, denial of family visits and mail, appalling malnutrition, periods of solitary confinement and barbarous medical neglect." On the other hand, she says:

> You can name in minutes the few governments which hold no political prisoners. This ugly fact does not condone Cuba but puts it into perspective. My sources did not suggest that political arrests were a continuing frequent process in Cuba. But a small country existing under a relentless state of siege, persecuted by the strongest nation on earth, is not in the best shape for flourishing freedom.

Toward the end of her trip, she returned to the house where she and Hemingway had lived almost half a century earlier, now turned into the Museo Hemingway, where the staff took her on a tour.

> I recognized all the furniture I had ordered from the local carpenter, and lapsed into giggles over the later addition of stuffed animal heads and horns on every wall. In the master's bedroom, the biggest buffalo head I had ever seen, including hundreds on the hoof, glowered over the desk. . . . "He did not write here," said one of the staff. "He wrote *For Whom the Bell Tolls* at this desk, but that was pre-buffalo."

Early in 1991, Soviet troops used tanks to block demonstrators in Lithuania who were threatening to take over a radio station. Worldwide disapproval of the bloodshed focused on the timing of the move, which came as the crisis in the Persian Gulf turned into open war, and many feared that events in the Middle East would distract international attention from the Baltic, as the Suez crisis of 1956 had from Hungary (see Topic 91). Gorbachev condemned the use of force and claimed that he had not been consulted in advance. In any event, the political future of the Soviet Union remained shrouded in uncertainty. A referendum held in the spring of 1991—which was boycotted by some republics—gave Gorbachev a majority in favor of maintaining Soviet unity. Nevertheless, although the central government in Moscow continued to direct defense, foreign policy, and currency matters, the individual republics assumed considerable power over internal regional affairs. Gorbachev then stunned party followers by dropping Marxism-Leninism as the nation's official doctrine. Other changes followed rapidly. By 1991, Moscow had begun to abandon the state-directed economy in favor of a market-driven system. Russian voters also backed Yeltsin's proposal of popular election for the Soviet president.

Yeltsin's standing became further enhanced when he led the opposition to an abortive coup by a group of conservative hardliners in the fall of 1991. As huge crowds filled Moscow's streets in protest against the coup, Yeltsin's public defiance made him the hero of the moment. In the ensuing confusion, a discredited Gorbachev stepped down and Yeltsin was elected president. Despite recurrent bouts of ill health, he ran for reelection in 1997 and won. It was thus under his leadership that the Soviet Union dissolved into Russia and a series of independent republics, and the complex process of negotiating the terms of new relationships began. The new loosely linked confederation became known as the Commonwealth of Independent States. Yeltsin's grip on power became increasingly undermined by continuing economic gloom and by a disastrous conflict in the Asian Republic of Chechnya. As Russian soldiers tried to gain control there, with heavy loss of life on both sides, bomb explosions—purportedly set off by Chechen terrorists—ripped through Moscow. After naming and discarding a series of prime ministers, on New Year's Eve 1999, in a surprise move, Yeltsin resigned, naming his then current prime minister, Vladimir Putin, his successor. The following year, Putin won election in his own right as president.

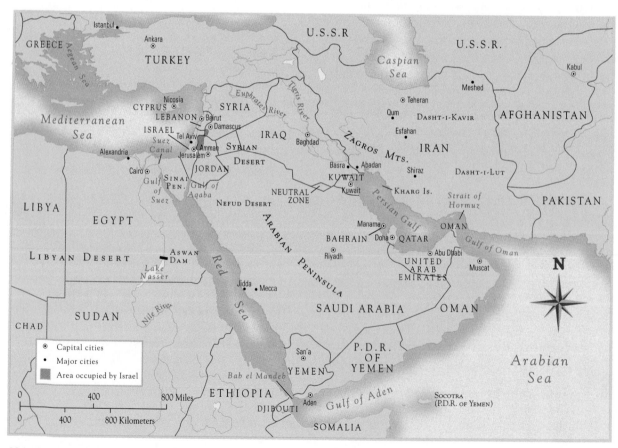

Map 95.1 The Middle East, Mid-1980s. The Middle East has continued to be a center for world tensions throughout the end of the 20th century and the beginning of the 21st. The Israeli-Palestinian conflict has dominated the headlines, but the Gulf War of 1991, and renewed hostilities there in 2003, the Allies' successful campaign to remove the Taliban government in Afghanistan after the terrorist attacks of September 11, 2001, and the U.S.-British invasion of Iraq in 2003 are only the most obvious events to occur there.

THE GULF WAR

Events in the Middle East clearly demonstrated the collapse of Soviet power. On August 2, 1990, Iraqi troops invaded the neighboring oil-rich state of Kuwait. Over the following weeks, a consensus gradually emerged at the United Nations to impose economic sanctions on Iraq, while 29 nations began to send troops and supplies to the Persian Gulf to form an alliance under UN auspices. By far the largest contingent—almost half a million participants—came from the United States, but other members of the alliance included Britain, France, and Italy. Egypt and Syria were among the Arab states to participate.

As the months passed, with no sign of concessions from Iraq's increasingly belligerent dictator, Saddam Hussein (born 1937), at the urging of the United States, the United Nations issued an ultimatum: If Iraq failed to withdraw from Kuwait by January 15, 1991, the coalition forces would take military action. The Soviet Union sent no forces to the Persian Gulf and launched several independent peace initiatives, but in the end supported UN action.

The deadlock was broken when the allied forces duly began massive aerial bombardments of Baghdad and other Iraqi cities and military installations. Among Iraq's responses was the shelling of Israel, which is not a member of the UN coalition, in the hope of provoking Israeli forces into action, and thereby detaching from the coalition states such as Syria, which are traditionally hostile to Israel. For the first time in its history, Israel did not respond to provocation, and the allied forces remained intact (see Topic 89).

After a month of bombing had crushed Iraqi powers of resistance and morale, allied victory in the ground campaign took only a few days. Iraq and the allies signed a cease-fire agreement that restored Kuwait's sovereignty. Iraqi forces withdrew, leaving Kuwait devastated, with many of its oil wells in flames. Iraq plunged into civil war, with the remaining forces of Saddam Hussein battling with Kurdish and Shiite rebels.

Among the terms of the cease-fire was a proviso that Iraq would dismantle and destroy its stockpile of chemical weapons, and UN inspectors were given the task of overseeing the process. Seven years later, in the winter of 1997–1998, tensions again flared when the Iraqis refused to open certain "Presidential Palace Compounds" to inspection, and the situation dragged on with no apparent resolution.

With the escalation of terrorism marked by the attacks on New York and Washington of September 11, 2001, Iraq's disarmament became once again the focus of international attention. The Iraqi authorities refused to allow the return of weapons inspectors until, in September 2002, under the threat of military action, they finally agreed to comply with United Nations orders. The UN Security Council passed a resolution the following November, giving Iraq "one last chance," and the United States began a massive troop build-up in the Gulf.

Over the next few months, the weapons inspectors proceeded to conduct their mission, and their heads reported at regular intervals to the Security Council. The general impression was that the Iraqis were grudgingly but increasingly cooperating. The nature and speed of that collaboration, however, began to split world opinion, in particular that of the chief Western allies.

The United States, under the leadership of President George W. Bush, urged the need for military action. Of the five permanent members of the Security Council, only Britain offered unqualified support. China and Russia favored allowing the inspectors more time to complete their work, while France led increasingly strong opposition to war on the part of many of the European powers, strongly backed up by Germany: Gerhard Schroeder, the German Social Democratic leader had won a narrow election victory in the fall of 2002 by vowing that Germany would play no part in any forthcoming Gulf War.

The deadlock continued throughout the spring of 2003, marked by unprecedented public demonstrations throughout Europe and much of the rest of the world against war. Nevertheless, in March 2003, the United States, Britian, and Australia invaded Iraq, toppling the regime of Sadam Hussein in a matter of weeks. In the wake of this war, the future of Iraq, and indeed of the entire Middle East, is far from clear.

THE ENERGY CRISIS AND THE NUCLEAR DILEMMA

Europe's industrial rebirth after World War II was heavily dependent on imported oil supplies. Unlike the United States, there are only scanty oil deposits on European territory. In 1960, the Organization of Petroleum Exporting Countries (OPEC) was founded by the world's main oil producers: Iran, Iraq, Kuwait, Libya, Saudi Arabia, and Venezuela. Membership subsequently extended to Qatar, Indonesia, United Arab Emirates, Algeria, Nigeria, Ecuador, and Gabon. As the industries of many countries came to rely on oil supplies, the power of OPEC increased dramatically.

In 1973, OPEC quadrupled world oil prices, and in the years between 1974 and 1980 the price of oil tripled again. In the 1980s, OPEC's ability to control the market began to decline, as its members failed to agree on production limits, and non-OPEC members started to produce oil and natural gas. Nevertheless, the industrial world had received a severe shock. The booming years of the 1960s gave way to a period of economic crisis, as energy costs began to absorb production profits.

NUCLEAR ENERGY

One solution to steeply rising energy costs was to introduce conservation measures. A more attractive, and less stringent, answer seemed to lie in the development of nuclear energy programs. The heat generated by the process of nuclear fission within a reactor can be used to produce electricity. The disposal of radioactive waste from the process presented problems, however; at first, it was stored in concrete vaults lined with stainless steel.

For many European countries, lacking their own natural energy supplies, the production of artificial energy seemed an ideal solution to the problem of outside suppliers and their demands. In France, government sponsorship encouraged the construction of a network of nuclear plants that was to provide more than 60 percent of the country's energy needs. By 1985, West Germany was producing one-third of its energy by nuclear processes.

The potential dangers of this new energy source were the difficulty of storing increasing quantities of waste and the possibility of a major accident at a nuclear energy plant. The cost of such a disaster, it was clear, would be immense in both human and financial terms. As early as 1957, the U.S. Congress passed the Price-Anderson Act, limiting insurance company liability for nuclear disasters to a small fraction of any projected claims. Yet the construction of nuclear plants continued throughout the industrialized world, as businesses sought to cut their dependence on imported energy and governments saw an easy way to meet their needs.

The first serious nuclear failure occurred in 1979, at the Three Mile Island site, near Middletown, Pennsylvania. As a result of a failure of the reactor's cooling system, it began to emit "puffs" of radiation. Hasty action prevented the meltdown of the reactor's core and the explosion of a hydrogen bubble that had formed inside.

Far more disastrous was the accident at Chernobyl, near Kiev, in the Soviet Union. On April 26, 1986, one of the reactors there exploded, scattering radioactive debris over thousands of miles. Approximately 135,000 people living in the region were evacuated, and food products throughout Europe were contaminated—from Welsh lamb to Parmesan cheese. The burning reactor was eventually buried in concrete.

THE ENVIRONMENTAL MOVEMENT

The dangers of nuclear pollution would be added to the list of causes that environmental movements were waging throughout Western Europe and the United States. The effects of nuclear fallout had, of course, been all too clear at the end of World War II, with the bombing of Hiroshima and Nagasaki. During the 1950s public preoccupation about human interference with nature continued to mount. In 1962, an American biologist, Rachel Carson (1907–1964), published *Silent Spring*, a dramatic account of the dangers of other forms of pollution, in particular pesticides.

By the late 1960s, environmental groups—the "Greens"—were drawing attention to crisis situations in many parts of Europe. In the heart of the continent, industrial plants in Austria, Switzerland, West Germany, France, and Holland were discharging ever-greater quantities of industrial waste into the river Rhine. The Mediterranean was so polluted in places that swimming in it was dangerous. In many cities exhaust fumes and traffic vibrations were damaging historic buildings and monuments; they included the Gothic cathedrals of northern Europe and the Parthenon in Athens. Industrial cities, both in Europe and in North America, were plagued with smog, a form of air pollution produced by factory and automobile fumes.

The Greens roused considerable public support. Britain set up a Department of the Environment in 1970, and France followed a year later. In 1972 a conference meeting in Stockholm established a United Nations Environment Program to deal with issues on an international basis.

THE ENVIRONMENTALISTS AND NUCLEAR ENERGY

In West Germany, the Greens developed into a significant political force. Part of their success was a result of the grave

The atomic power station at Calder Hall, England. 1970s. Campaigns against nuclear weapons merged in the 1970s with worries about the growing pollution of the environment. The "Green" lobby, which became an active political force in many European countries, created a significant movement to defend nature. By the beginning of the 21st century, a new fight had developed against genetically modified food (GMF).

Demonstration by members of the Green Party in West Germany. 1980s. Yet another cause taken up by the German Green Party in the 1980s was opposition to the deployment of the German army (*Bundeswehr*) outside Germany. The signs read (*left to right*): Greens don't wear olive green (i.e., military uniform); German soldiers and weapons worldwide? NO; German troops in the whole world? Say NO. The first significant participation of German forces outside Germany took place in the NATO campaign in Kosovo in Spring 1999.

problem presented by the condition of the country's forests: between one-third and half of them were at risk of dying of pollution, much of it caused by acid rain (the result of air moisture combining with chemicals emitted by factories and automobiles). The Chernobyl disaster galvanized the Greens into action and increased their public support. In the election of 1987 they won 8.3 percent of the votes, a notable improvement over their 5.6 percent in 1983.

The protests led by the Greens forced the West German government to cut back its nuclear energy program. The building of plants and waste disposal facilities was halted, often blocked by angry crowds of demonstrators. As a result, West Germany was forced to import increasing quantities from abroad. In 1988 it was the highest per capita importer of energy of any major industrialized country.

In Italy, also, public protests led to the suspension of a nuclear energy program. As a country particularly poor in natural energy resources, Italy had welcomed the chance to produce its own nuclear resources. Three plants were constructed, and plans were made to increase the number. With growing concern, however, fueled by the Chernobyl disaster, the Socialists and other parties sponsored a referendum that allowed the public to express its opinion: no more nuclear energy. Work at the existing plants was phased out and new construction suspended. The Italians turned for energy supplies to natural gas, to be supplied by two pipelines, one from the Soviet Union and one from Algeria and Libya. Both projects were inaugurated in 1982, and work was stepped up in the late 1980s.

France was too dependent on nuclear energy to be able to eliminate it. Although Mitterand's Socialist government briefly suspended new plant construction in the early 1980s, by 1986 two-thirds of the country's electricity was generated by nuclear plants. Britain's coal supplies, together with natural gas from under the North Sea, made the provision of nuclear energy less vital. Nonetheless, by the 1990s nuclear power provided 13 percent of electricity there.

The European country most dependent on nuclear energy was Sweden, despite strenuous efforts on the part of environmentalists to block the building of new plants. In 1980, a referendum produced a compromise. The govern-

ment would complete 12 plants, to be functioning by 1985, but all of them would be shut down by 2010. No Swedish political party opposed a nuclear phase-out, although it presented huge problems, and the future of the country's energy supplies remained in doubt.

IN SEARCH OF SAFE NUCLEAR POWER

The dilemma presented by the dangers of nuclear energy dominated the planning of individual governments but also crossed national boundaries. As Chernobyl showed, radioactive fallout could spread over thousands of miles. One solution was the construction of safer reactors. In the late 1980s, the Swedes started to pioneer the latest nuclear technology in their Process Inherent Ultimately Safe Reactor (PIUSR).

The invention of a process to manufacture energy by nuclear fusion, rather than by fission, offered the hope of a more long-term solution. Fusion would require only small amounts of fuel, and none of the byproducts would be radioactive. Research into methods of generating energy by fusion led to the construction of particle accelerators in Western Europe and the United States. In 1988, the U.S. Energy Department announced the building of a "Supercollider" near Dallas, at a cost of $6 billion, a project that was never completed.

By the last decade of the 20th century, efforts were stepped up to find an alternative solution to the problem that faced countries in all parts of the world: The advantages of nuclear energy—clean, capable of being produced in quantity—were overshadowed by its dangers.

TERRORISM AND THE POLITICS OF VIOLENCE

One of the problems that continued to plague the world in the latter part of the 20th century was terrorism. In a reaction to the general political stability of the major Western democracies, groups supporting a variety of causes used violence—or the threat of violence—for political ends.

TERRORISM AND NATIONALISM

In several Western European countries, nationalist groups or regions claimed the right to home rule. The Basques, a people of unknown origins, inhabit the Pyrenees area of southwestern France and northern Spain; there are around 100,000 in France and 600,000 in Spain. In the Spanish Civil War, many Basques fought against Franco's Falangists, and the region was subsequently subdued. In 1952, a Basque nationalist movement was formed, which soon split into a militant and a moderate wing. The moderates stood for election; the militants turned to the gun. Both wings demanded local autonomy.

The 1970s and 1980s were marked by a string of assassinations, for which ETA (the militant Basque organization) claimed credit. The moderates, condemning the use of violence, became an increasing force in local politics. In the 1986 regional elections, Basque nationalist parties won two-thirds of the seats. The government made concessions, giving the Basques the right to raise their own taxes and to replace the national police and the Civil Guard with an all-Basque police force. The moves reduced support for the terrorists, and cooperation between French and Spanish antiterrorist forces produced a higher level of arrests. Nonetheless, the assassinations continued sporadically and discouraged foreign investors in the region, one of Spain's most industrialized areas.

Similar separatist violence scarred Corsica and the German-speaking region of northern Italy. Europe's most bitter terrorist campaign, however, was that waged by the Irish Republican Army (IRA) for control of Northern Ireland. In 1922, the island had been divided, with the lower 26 counties forming the independent, predominantly Catholic Republic of Ireland. The northern, mainly Protestant part rejected "Home Rule" (independence), and remained part of Britain, although with its own parliament, Stormont.

Relations between Protestants and the Catholic minority in Northern Ireland were soured by centuries of mutual mistrust and hate. In 1969, peaceful street demonstrations led to open violence. By 1972, the British government felt obliged to disband Stormont and govern the region directly, seeking to satisfy the Protestant majority while protecting Catholic interests. Over the following decades the IRA battled against a string of illegal paramilitary Protestant groups in their campaign to drive out the British and assume control. Between 1969 and 1998, some 3,000 people were killed in bombings and street fighting.

The British tried a series of ways to reduce the bloodletting and restore local government. After the death of 10 IRA hunger strikers in prison in 1981, a new Northern Ireland Assembly was elected in 1982, but dissolved four years later. In 1983 a law was passed granting pardon (or at least lenience) to "informers" in either the Protestant organizations or the IRA; it led to a dramatic increase in the number of arrests. Yet at the end of the same year, IRA terrorists exploded a bomb outside London's Harrod's depart-

British soldiers guarding 1,000 pounds of homemade fertilizer explosives. 1997. The explosives were found in an abandoned van on the grounds of Belfast Castle at a time when negotiations were about to resume between Protestants and Catholics in Northern Ireland; the election of a Labour government, not tied to the positions of its Conservative predecessors, had created a new mood of guarded optimism.

ment store in the middle of Christmas shopping crowds, and in 1984 blew up a hotel in Brighton at which a Conservative party conference was taking place. Further IRA and paramilitary Protestant bombings continued throughout the late 1980s, some of them aimed at British troops outside Northern Ireland, on bases in England and West Germany. An IRA cease-fire, announced in 1994, lasted only a little more than a year. With the exclusion from all-party talks of the Sinn Fein movement, widely seen as the political wing of the IRA, there seemed little hope of progress, although the arrival in power of Tony Blair's "New Labour" party offered the possibility of a fresh start to negotiations. They resumed in the winter of 1997–1998, with both Sinn Fein and the leading Protestant groups represented at the conference table. Discussions were overshadowed by a series of acts of violence by extremists on both sides. Nonetheless, agreement was reached in April 1998, and its terms were approved by a large majority a month later in a referendum held in both Northern Ireland and the Republic of Ireland. As preparations began for the selection of a Cross-border Council later that year, the mood seemed cautiously optimistic.

INTERNATIONAL TERRORISM

Terrorist activities elsewhere in Europe were inspired by ideological rather than nationalistic issues. In West Germany and Italy, extreme left-wing groups tried to destabilize the established social and economic order, as a prelude to political revolution (see Topic 90). Italy was further plagued by extreme right-wing violence. The worst single incident was the bomb explosion in Bologna's railway station in August 1980, at the height of the holiday season; more than 80 people were killed. Although those responsible were never caught, they seem to have been part of a far-right terrorist group.

As investigators throughout Europe and the Middle East began pooling information and working more closely in collaboration, a picture began to emerge of links between the various terrorist groups. The IRA, the Italian Red Brigade, and the West German Red Army Fraction all used similar weapons, often Soviet made. Libya provided training camps for would-be terrorists. There were even connections between groups in Europe and Japanese terrorists.

The threat of terrorism was intensified by the activities of groups from outside Europe. The Palestine Liberation Organization (PLO) and its various splinter factions were all active throughout the 1970s and 1980s; their operations provoked Israeli reprisals and counterattacks (see Topic 89). Iran, Iraq, and Syria were accused of harboring, if not encouraging, terrorists. A string of airplane hijackings and bombings culminated in the explosion over Lockerbie, Scotland, of a crowded Pan American flight bound for the United States a few days before Christmas 1988. Suspicion fell on Iran or Syria as the base from which the bomb planting was organized; experts later discovered that the plastic explosive responsible was manufactured in Czechoslovakia,

a claim subsequently confirmed by Václav Havel, Czechoslovakia's new president.

By the 1990s most governments were resigned to the fact that only a drastic and unacceptable curtailment of their citizens' liberties could lead to a serious curtailment of terrorist activities. They turned instead to increased security measures, international police collaboration, and diplomatic pressure to limit the damage. No country, however, seemed immune. On September 11, 2001, a group of 19 terrorists forming part of the Al-qaeda organization, 15 of them Saudi Arabian citizens, hijacked four commercial jets. They flew two of them into New York's World Trade Center and a third into the Pentagon in Washington. The fourth plane crashed in Pennsylvania, perhaps because of the intervention of some of the passengers. The victims were numbered in the thousands. The Al-qaeda terrorist group, together with their leader, Osama bin Laden, had been protected by the fundamentalist Taliban regime, which maintained a tenuous hold over the government of Afghanistan. In October 2001 an alliance led by the United States launched an offensive against the Taliban. Within weeks, the extreme Muslim regime was driven from power, and many of the Al-qaeda terrorists were captured. Yet the leadership remained at large, and the threat posed by terrorism seemed even more difficult to eradicate.

A number of terrorist attacks occurred in the following months, and police throughout Europe and the United States tried to identify and arrest members of actual or potential terrorist cells, although it remained unclear how many of these had direct links with Al-qaeda. The most devastating was a bomb blast on the Indonesian island of Bali—which took around two hundred lives—although others occurred in Yemen and Kuwait. On the eve of a potential Gulf War, authorities were preparing for the threat of further atrocities.

The aftermath of a terrorist car bomb explosion in the center of Paris. 1980s. Various ambulances can be seen approaching the wreck: The one in the foreground has been sent by the Paris fire brigade. The most recent terrorist incident in Paris occurred on July 14, 2002, when a lone gunman failed in his attempt to assassinate French President Jacques Chirac as he rode in the traditional Bastille Day parade.

Gaillarde-Maous-Sola/Gamma

PERSPECTIVES FROM THE PAST

ANALYZING TERRORISM

Two of the leading terrorist organizations operating in Europe after World War II were the Irish Republican Army (IRA) in Northern Ireland and the Red Army Fraction (RAF) in Germany, both of which accompanied their campaigns of violence with barrages of propaganda. The first selection below consists of an objective description of the RAF and an example of their propaganda. Then follow a statement of intentions of the IRA and a counterstatement from an opposing Protestant extremist group. Perhaps the most notorious terrorist operating in the last 20 years has been Abu Nidal, whose career is described in a "portrait" first published in the *Washington Post*. Finally, Walter Laqueur, one of the world's leading authorities on terrorism, places the phenomenon in perspective.

Terrorism in Germany: The RAF

The description of the RAF reprinted below comes from a longer article by Hans Josef Horchem on terrorism in Europe.

The RAF is the oldest and most dangerous German terrorist organization. In June 1980 the RAF took over the remaining cadre of the second German terrorist group, the "Movement of 2nd of June."

The RAF retained its structure and its system of organization after the unification with the "Movement of 2nd of June." Hierarchical order does not exist and decisions are made collectively. In an attack every member has to fight unto death.

The commando unit includes only 20 people. The attack against Hanns Martin Schleyer was made with only 20 members of the RAF, in spite of the fact that extensive logistic preparations were necessary.

The commando unit is living underground and depends on the "legal environment," which includes approximately 200 people. In the seventies the legal units were organized in "Anti-Fascist Groups" or in "Committees against Isolation-Torture." These names don't exist anymore. But the supporters of these groups compose a reservoir for illegal activities in the future.

Enough money is available. The "war booty" of the "Movement of 2nd of June" after the kidnaping of the Austrian industrialist Palmers in November 1977 is now in the hands of the RAF. Of the original 4 million Deutschmark the RAF has spent about 2 million Deutschmark.

The RAF propagates only one thing, that is armed conflict, and tries to win comrades-in-arms for this. "The armed campaign is the highest form of class struggle." The leading force and the avant-garde of the class-struggle is not the working class but the "revolutionary intelligence."

Already in 1971 the RAF said in its publication "Close the Loop-holes of the Revolutionary Theory—Build up the Red Army": "It is not the organizations of the industrial working class, but the revolutionary sections of the student bodies that are today the bearers of the contemporary conscience." The industrial proletarians inside the developed capitalist countries have changed into an "aristocracy of workers." Therefore a true revolutionary cannot rely on them anymore.

The long-range strategy of the RAF was then and is today aimed at "U.S. imperialism" and its chief ally in Europe, the Federal Republic of Germany.

From Horchem, H. J. "European Terrorism: A German Perspective." *Terrorism: An International Journal*, Vol. 6, no.1. Copyright © 1982.

The IRA and Their Protestant Extremist Opponents

Both the IRA and the extremist Protestant groups in Northern Ireland who oppose them have used propaganda as well as violence in their campaign for public support. For all the extreme divergences in their positions, they perceive a common enemy in the British government, as the following two excerpts from their declarations make clear.

The effect of the IRA bombing campaign can be gauged in many different ways. Firstly, they have struck at the very root of enemy morale, confining and tying down large numbers of troops and armored vehicles in center city areas, thus relieving much of the pressure on the much-oppressed nationalist areas. In terms of direct financial loss (structural damage, goods, machinery), also in the crippling of industrial output and perhaps worst of all in the scaring-off of foreign capital investments, IRA bombs have hit Britain where she feels it most—in her pocket.

England always found unfortunate soldiers quite dispensable and to a certain extent replaceable, but she always counted in terms of cost to the Treasury. Any peace through the granting of freedom emanating to rebellious colonies from London came by means of calculation—the cost of occupation. Since 1969 a bill of warfare running to at least a conservative 500,000,000 pounds has not gone unnoticed back home in Britain where recent opinion polls showed that over 54% of the ordinary people wanted the troops withdrawn forthwith.

Already some 1,500 troops have left Northern Ireland never to return. In many cases death certificates have been issued as for fatal road accident victims to the unsuspecting next-of-kin of soldiers killed in action in a heartless attempt at cooking records and hiding telling manpower losses. Suddenly Northern Ireland has become England's Vietnam. In the knowledge that the will to overcome of a risen people can never be defeated by brute force or even overwhelming odds more enlightened politicians have seen the light and are themselves thinking along Tone's famous dictum: "Break the connection!"

Great Britain too, of course, has suffered losses other than bomb damage and loss of personnel. Her prestige and credibility in terms of world opinion and world finance have been se-verely shaken; her duplicity and selective sense of justice have been seriously exposed; her puerile hankering after "holding the last vestige of the Empire" has marked her as a recidivist nation, psychologically vulnerable, unstable, and mentally immature.

From *Freedom Struggle* by the Provisional IRA.

We are not good at propaganda and not good at extolling our Virtues or admitting our faults. We just stick to our points of view, bow our heads, and pray for it all to die down for another fifty years or so.

Gradually, however, we have come to realize that this time other factors have come into the age-old conflict of the Scots-Irish versus the Irish-Irish, or if you prefer it that way, the Protestants versus the Catholics in Ireland.

Traditionally the English politicians let us down—betrayal we call it. The Catholics try to overwhelm us so we are caught in between two lines of fire. Second-class Englishmen, half-caste Irishmen, this we can live with, and even defeat, but how can we be expected to beat the world revolutionary movement which supplies arms and training, not to mention most sophisticated advice on publicity, promotion, and expertise to the IRA?

The British army in Ulster has good soldiers who are being set up like dummy targets. The orders of the politicians are tying both hands behind their backs. The British public says: "Send the soldiers home." We say: "Send the politicians and the officers home and leave us the men and the weapons—or, why not send the soldiers home and leave us the weapons and we will send you the IRA wrapped up in little boxes and little tins like cans of baked beans."

The politicians who rule our lives from England do not understand us. They stop the army from defending us properly and stop us from defending ourselves. We do not like these flabby-faced men with pop eyes and fancy accents. . . .

From statement of Protestant Extremist Group, Dublin *Sunday World*, June 9, 1973.

Continued

Abu Nidal: A Portrait

One of the features of terrorism over the past 20 years has been the link between terrorist campaigns in various parts of the world. The Palestinian Abu Nidal, who operated in Europe and throughout the Middle East, was a powerful and frightening symbol of international terrorism. He died in Baghdad in 2002, under mysterious circumstances.

Abu Nidal left a calling card last fall in an interview with the German magazine Der Spiegel. "I can assure you of one thing," he said. "If we have the chance to inflict the slightest harm to Americans, we will not hesitate to do it. In the months and years to come, the Americans will think of us."

Americans may indeed be thinking of Abu Nidal following recent events. His real name is Sabri Khalil al-Banna, and he is one of those on whom Libyan leader Muammar Khadafy will most likely depend to carry out his campaign to attack American interests. It is clear that the Libyans are supporting Abu Nidal, and he is linked to last December's bloody attacks at the Rome and Vienna airports, only the most recent example of the mayhem that he has made his life's work.

Here is a snapshot of the man who describes himself as America's enemy: His politics are those of revenge and revolution on a grand scale. He seeks through terror a retributive and perfect justice that can never be achieved. He moves through a shadowy inter-connected world of international and Arab terrorist networks that have given him a mystique larger than life. And yet through all of this there is something very ordinary, small and marginal about him—something that seems to reinforce the fact that terror, no matter how brutal, is only a symptom of a failed cause and of the frustrations of a desperate man.

Perhaps even more frightening than the man himself is his relationship to those Arab regimes willing to tolerate his excesses. In a world where assassinations and violence have become legitimate tools of political struggle, Abu Nidal and those like him provide important services in the never-ending fight for influence and power. He is not simply a product of the Arab-Israeli conflict but of an intra-Arab struggle in which ideology is subordinated to regime survival and personal vendetta. How else can we explain that a man who in 1976 tried to kill the Syrian foreign minister could be operating out of Damascus seven years later?

Who is this elusive figure and what is the nature of the environment in which he operates? Is he simply the hired gun of state-sponsored terrorism, or is he the genuine revolutionary he claims to be?

One of the most frustrating aspects of dealing with Abu Nidal is that so little is known about him. Even in the murky subterranean world of international terrorism, he is a mystery. Despite two recent interviews, rumors still abound that he is dead or incapacitated and that his operations are run by committee. In a recent interview, Abu Nidal claimed that he had undergone plastic surgery. His interviewers usually ask him for some proof of his identity and wonder themselves whether he is who he claims to be. During one interview, Abu Nidal reportedly ripped open his shirt to show an inquisitive journalist scars from a much rumored heart operation.

His method of operation only enhances his reputation as a secretive shadowy force likely to appear anywhere at any time. The entire Abu Nidal organization is tightly compartmentalized and may not number more than a few hundred. The structure of the organization further obscures the links between operations and the master command. Capitalizing on the shadowy terrorist network in Europe and the Middle East, Abu Nidal further covers his tracks. Thus, in the Rome and Vienna operations, the terrorists could have been trained in Lebanon, acquired Libyan confiscated Tunisian passports, and obtained weapons in Europe. . . .

The lessons drawn from studying Abu Nidal and his world are not heartening ones. Indeed the consistency and effectiveness of his operations lead to the conclusion that his brand of terrorism is likely to remain a permanent feature of the Middle East's political landscape. Even more sobering is the recognition that Abu Nidal's terror has become very much a permanent fixture of shifting rivalries between Arab regimes. He remains effective because he is willing and able to provide services for a variety of patrons.

Nonetheless, in the end there are limits to what Abu Nidal can hope to achieve. He represents no constituency with any real power, he can never achieve anything positive for Palestinians. He can only destroy and intimidate until he himself is destroyed. More like him may follow, but their legacy will not be any more enduring.

From Miller, Aaron. "Portrait of Abu Nidal," *Washington Post,* March 30, 1986. Reprinted with permission of Aaron Miller.

Reflections on Terrorism

The following extracts come from an article by Walter Laqueur, chairman of the International Research Council of the Center for Strategic and International Studies in Washington, DC, one of the leading experts on terrorism in all its forms.

Fifty years hence, puzzled historians will try to make sense of the behavior of Western governments and media in the 1980s vis-a-vis terrorism. Presidents and other leaders have frequently referred to terrorism as one of the greatest dangers facing mankind. For days and weeks on end, television networks devoted most of their prime-time news to terrorist operations. Publicists referred to terrorism as the cancer of the modern world, growing inexorably until it poisoned and engulfed the society on which it fed, dragging it down to destruction.

Naturally, our future historian will expect that a danger of such magnitude must have figured very highly on the agenda of our period—equal, say, to the danger of war, starvation, overpopulation, deadly diseases, debts, and so on. He will assume that determined action was taken and major resources allocated to the fight against this threat. And he will be no little surprised to learn that, when the Swedish Prime Minister was killed in 1986, the Swedish government promised a reward for information leading to the apprehension of his killer that amounted to less than 10% of the annual income of an investment banker or a popular entertainer—not necessarily of the front rank; that the French government offered even less

for its terrorists; that West Germany was willing to pay only up to $50,000 "for the most dangerous." The United States, always a great believer in the effectiveness of money, offered up to $500,000, again not an overwhelming sum considering the frequency of the speeches about terrorism and the intensity of the rhetoric. . . .

On the basis of these and other facts, our historian will lean towards revisionism. He may well reach the conclusion that there was no terrorism, only a case of mass delusion—or that hysteria was deliberately fanned by certain vested interests, such as producers of anti-terrorist equipment perhaps or the television networks which had established a symbiotic relationship with the terrorists, providing them with free (or almost free) entertainment for long periods.

These are, of course, the wrong conclusions. The impact of terrorism is measured not only in the number of victims. Terrorism is an attempt to destabilize democratic societies and to show that their governments are impotent. And if this can be achieved with a minimum effort, if so much publicity can be achieved on the basis of a few attacks, there is no need to make greater exertions. It is also true that there have been ominous new developments such as the emergence of narco-terrorism and of state-sponsored terrorism on a broader level than before. If terrorism was never a serious threat as far as America was concerned, let alone other major powers such as Russia, China or Japan, it is also true that in certain Latin American countries, but also in places like Turkey and Italy, it was for a while a real danger.

In short, there has been (and is) a terrorist menace in our time. But the historian of the future will still be right in pointing to the wide discrepancy between the strong speeches and the weak actions of those who felt threatened. And he must be forgiven if he should draw the conclusion that the "age of terrorism" perhaps never understood the exact nature of the threat. . . .

How to eradicate terrorism? Moralists believe that terrorism is the natural response to injustice, oppression, and persecution. Hence the seemingly obvious conclusion: Remove the underlying causes which cause terrorism and it

Continued

will wither away! This sounds plausible enough, for happy and content people are unlikely to commit savage acts of violence. But while this may be true as an abstract general proposition, it seldom applies to the real world, which is never quite free of conflicts. The historical record shows that while, in the nineteenth century, terrorism frequently developed in response to repression, the correlation between grievance and terrorism in our day and age is far less obvious. The historical record shows that the more severe the repression, the less terrorism tends to occur. This is an uncomfortable, shocking fact, and has, therefore, encountered much resistance. But it is still true that terrorism in Spain only gathered speed af-

World Trade Center, New York, following a terrorist attack on September 11, 2001.

FROM THE ATLANTIC TO THE URALS: EUROPE'S "COMMON HOUSE"

As national governments and international bodies wrestled with the day-to-day problems of environmental pollution and political violence, more visionary leaders began to look to a distant time when the geographic unit of Europe would achieve some form of union. Mikhail Gorbachev wrote of a "common house," in which members of the family might live at peace, all in their own ways.

Gorbachev's image implied a continuing political and social diversity, but economic developments and the communications revolution increased the speed with which conformity spread. The revolutions of 1989, furthermore,

ter Franco died, that the terrorist upsurge in West Germany, France, and Turkey took place under social democratic or left-of-center governments, that the same is true with regard to Peru and Colombia, and that more such examples could easily be adduced.

Terrorism has never had a chance in an effective dictatorship, but hardly a major democ-

ratic country has escaped it. There is a limit to the perfection of political institutions, and however just and humane the social order, there will always be a few people deeply convinced that it ought to be radically changed and that it can be changed only through violent action. . . .

From Laqueur, Walter. "Reflections on Terrorism," *Foreign Affairs,* October 1986.

were waged by people anxious to share in the benefits— as they perceived them—of capitalism. Hungarians, Czechs, and Poles of the last decade of the 20th century tried to build societies modeled on those of Western European nations.

Perhaps in reaction against the tendency toward broad supranational groupings, nationalism continued to create friction in both East and West. In Western Europe, the various separatist movements continued to agitate. Attempts to establish order in the new Eastern European democracies were challenged by ethnic divisions going back to the Hapsburg and Ottoman empires. The country most dramatically affected was the region of the former Yugoslavia known as Bosnia, where conflict raged between Serb, Croat, and Muslim groups. An international peace-keeping force, led by U.S. troops, tried to impose the settlement terms negotiated in the "Dayton Accord," a peace plan negotiated in 1995. The peacekeepers were originally scheduled to withdraw by the summer of 1998, but by the beginning of that year it became clear that they would need to remain in place to prevent further conflict. Further violence in the region occurred in 1999, when the Serbs drove thousands of ethnic Albanians out of the province of Kosovo. The scenes of mass deportations, recalling the horrors of World War II, galvanized public opinion, and a NATO bombing campaign finally produced a Serbian retreat and surrender by June of that year— although not without great loss of life among both the Albanians and the Serbian military and civilian population. In February 2002, President Milosevic of Serbia went on trial at the International Court of Justice at The Hague,

Photograph of the earth taken from space. The bulk of the image is taken up by the continent of Africa, where human life probably began. Europe, above, is partially concealed by clouds, and the Arabian peninsula is in the top right-hand corner.

European Space Agency/Science Photo Library/Photo Researchers

Holland, for war crimes; he was the first national leader to be prosecuted for "crimes against humanity" since the Nuremberg trials after World War II. International peace-keepers remained in place in both Bosnia and Kosovo.

Toward New Perspectives

Europe faced the 21st century with new hopes and old fears. The burying of old national rivalries, the end of the Cold War, the search for increased cooperation and eventual union—all these held out possibilities of peace and an improvement in the material conditions of millions.

Yet many problems remained unsolved and are probably incapable of solution. The consequences of a transition to a postindustrial society in the West and the breakup of the Soviet Empire in the East were unpredictable. The nuclear energy issue demonstrated all too clearly that technological progress was a dual-edged sword. Most important, the ability of the European family members to live peaceably with one another in their respective parts of the "common house" was going to be sorely tested.

Questions for Further Study

1. How have events since 1989 changed the global political landscape? What are their consequences likely to be for the early 21st century?
2. On the basis of the experience of the past half-century, how successful is terrorism as a means of producing radical change?
3. What are the major environmental issues of our times, and how great is their threat? Is uncontrolled population growth more or less dangerous to the quality of human life?

Suggestions for Further Reading

Bello, Walden F., ed. *The Future in the Balance: Essays on Globalization and Resistance*. Oakland, CA, 2001.

Bush, George, and Brent Scowcroft. *A World Transformed*. New York, 1998.

Gashi, Alush. *The Denial of Human and National Rights of Albanians in Kosovo*. New York, 1992.

Gilbert, Martin. *A History of the 20th Century: 1952–1999, Challenge to Civilization*. London, 1999.

Gorbachev, Mikhail. *Memoirs*. London, 1996.

Gurr, Nadine. *The New Face of Terrorism: Threats from Weapons of Mass Destruction*. New York, 2000.

Kaplan, Robert. *Balkan Ghosts: A Journey Through History*. New York, 1994.

Lear, Linda. *Rachel Carson: Witness for Nature*. New York, 1997.

Lovenduski, J. *Women and European Politics: Contemporary Feminism and Public Policy*. Amherst, MA, 1986.

Malcolm, Noel. *Kosovo: A Short History*. London, 1998.

Nye, Joseph S. *The Paradox of American Power: Why the World's Only Superpower Can't Go It Alone*. New York, 2002.

Schlesinger, J.R. *America at Century's End*. New York, 1989.

Shull, Tad. *Redefining Red and Green: Ideology and Strategy in European Political Ecology*. New York, 1999.

Talbott, Strobe, and Nayan Chanda, eds. *The Age of Terror: America and the World After September 11*. New York, 2002.

Yeltsin, Boris. *The View from the Kremlin*. London, 1994.

InfoTrac College Edition

Enter the search term *Green parties* using Key Terms.

GLOSSARY

absolutism Form of government in which rule rested in the hands of a king who claimed to rule by divine right and was responsible only to God.

abstract expressionism Painting style of the mid-20th century that made no reference to recognizable subjects—they were abstract—and sought to express interior states of feeling.

Anabaptist Sixteenth-century sect that made concern over the idea of baptism a central aspect of its doctrine. Rejecting the idea of predestination, the Anabaptists based their doctrine on the belief that adults alone, not children, were able to choose to enter a religious faith.

anarchists Those espousing a political theory that advocated the overthrow of all forms of authority, especially governments.

Australopithecus Species of hominid dating to about 4 million years ago. Between four and five feet tall, they had broad thumbs and could use their hands to grip, and also walked upright.

Babylonian Captivity The removal of the papacy for 75 years to Avignon, France, in the last quarter of the 14th century.

Baroque Seventeenth-century artistic style featuring the appearance of new forms and subjects, ranging from still life painting to the design of private townhouses to opera. The expression of strong emotions, an interest in psychological states of mind, and the invention of elaborate technical display were key features of the Baroque style.

Bauhaus The 20th century's most influential school of architecture and design. The innovations of Gropius and his colleagues derived from a new attitude toward the nature and function of a building, based on the possibilities of advanced construction techniques.

benefice In medieval society, a special grant of land to a vassal in return for cavalry service. Vassals could use the benefice to defray the expenses incurred in providing their horses, armor, and weapons.

Black Death A pandemic of plague (pneumonic and bubonic) in 1347–1348, which swept across Europe, wiping out perhaps 35 million people—one-third of the population.

Blitzkrieg Literally, "lightning war." A combination of rapid-moving, heavily armed armored tanks, supported by aircraft and motorized infantry units, applied by the Germans during World War II.

Bolsheviks Radical Marxists, led by Lenin and dedicated to violent revolution; seized power in Russia in 1917 and subsequently were renamed the Communists.

bourgeoisie Originally medieval merchant-artisans, city dwellers who represented a new culture opposed to the ideals and values of the feudal system and became influential allies of the kings in their struggles to resist the power of the traditional lords. The middle classes.

caliph A term meaning "deputy of the Prophet," used for the supreme head of all Muslims in the medieval world.

chansons de geste Vernacular literature in the Middle Ages, heroic epics in the tradition of minstrels' recounting heroic deeds.

Chartists Group of mid-19th-century radical reformers in Britain who called for wholesale parliamentary reform; among the provisions were universal adult male suffrage, a secret ballot, and the abolition of property qualifications for members of Parliament.

chivalry Late medieval code of behavior whereby knights were bound by the ideals of loyalty, honor, and pride.

collectivization Stalinist program in the Soviet Union that required all peasants to turn their land and livestock over to the state, keeping only their houses and personal property. Every collective received production quotas. Peasants shared the work as well as the profits or losses the cooperative earned.

communes Self-governing centers in late medieval Europe, particularly in northern and central Italy, founded by townspeople who either rebelled against their overlords or purchased charters from them. The communes developed distinctive forms of self-government that stimulated patriotism and civic pride and controlled all aspects of economic activity.

conceptual artists Artists of the 1970s who aimed to create "objects" or experiences that were not intended to be bought or sold, or put in a museum. Their works, often consisting of unlikely materials such as cornflakes or ice, were installed and then dismantled.

consuls The two chief magistrates of the Roman Senate, who were elected annually. Each consul had his own army, to prevent the other one from seizing power.

cottage industry System in which families worked in the home to produce textiles and some finished goods.

Cubism Artistic style of the 20th century whose adherents abandoned traditional perspective, and in a series of experimental canvases, tried to find new ways of seeing their subjects geometrically.

cuneiform The earliest known form of writing, invented by the Sumerians around 3000 B.C., from two Latin words, *cuneus* ("wedge") and *forma* ("shape"). The wedge-shaped symbols were drawn or impressed on soft clay tablets.

Dadaist movement Artistic movement of the early 20th century that was born out of anger, frustration, and despair. Its response was to reject the past and all its works, and to create meaningless nonsense.

demesne Part of the arable land of a medieval manor, reserved for the lord's use and farmed for him by the peasants.

diaspora The gradual spread of Jews throughout many parts of the ancient world. The term is sometimes still used for Jews living outside Israel. Today used to describe the dispersal of peoples around the globe.

dictator In the Roman republic, leader who would, in time of national crisis, serve as supreme commander for a maximum term of six months.

Enlightenment The 18th-century intellectual movement, fusing several currents of thought from the late 17th century, in which philosophers applied the same attitudes of the scientific revolution to broader questions of human behavior.

Epicureanism Greek philosophy, popular in Roman times, based on the teachings and writings of Epicurus (341–271 B.C.), whose aim was to free humans from the threat of divine retribution or the fear of the unknown. It held that we are free to live our lives according to principles of moderation and prudence in the pursuit of pleasure.

Expressionists Artists of the early 20th century, mainly German, who used their art to express strong emotions.

Fascism Political program, originating in Italy, that combined left-wing and right-wing elements and took advantage of the postwar atmosphere of nationalist frustration and fear of Bolshevik revolution that pervaded Italian political life. Benito Mussolini created the Fascist regime in Italy in 1922.

feudalism A set of contractual arrangements between free men in the Middle Ages; it was, however, restricted to noble landowners. Feudal relationships involved two elements: vassalage, a personal bond established between two men based on military service, and a relationship between the king and powerful magnates.

Futurists Artists of the early 20th century, mainly Italian, who boldly rejected all traditional forms of culture and turned instead to the cult of the machine and the technological future.

Gothic Medieval architectural style that took Romanesque barrel vaults and stone supporting ribs and combined them to form high, pointed rib vaults. The results were lofty, light, and airy structures, with the spaces between the vaults cut away and filled with stained-glass windows. To ensure that the buildings were stable, architects added outside supports called "flying buttresses" that shored up the walls.

Great Schism The existence of two popes in the late medieval church (one in Rome and one in Avignon). *See also* Babylonian Captivity.

guilds Cooperative associations in medieval Europe, which maintained a monopoly of crafts and trade in a region, settled disputes, insisted on quality control, and established fair weights and measures.

Hellenistic Term used to refer to the history and culture of the peoples "Hellenized"—that is, brought under Greek influence—by Alexander's conquests.

helots Serfs acquired from Spartan conquests, not bought and sold as slaves of individual Spartiates, but belonging to the state, who mostly worked the land.

heresy Holding of religious beliefs different from the church's official doctrines.

hominids The forerunners of modern humans.

Homo erectus Hominid species that appeared around a million years ago and is far closer to our own species than previous hominid varieties.

Homo neanderthalis Another variant of *Homo sapiens*, the earliest found in Europe in the Neander Valley of the river Rhine. Neanderthal people flourished from about 40,000 to 80,000 years ago.

Homo sapiens Hominid species from which our own subspecies, *Homo sapiens sapiens*, developed.

Homo sapiens sapiens Modern humans; sometimes called Cro-Magnon.

Huguenots French Calvinists (Protestants).

humanism A late medieval spirit conditioned by a rebirth of interest in Classical culture and its values, and a new emphasis on human beings as the center of the world.

iconoclastic controversy Byzantine movement of the 8th century, condemning the use of icons (images of sacred figures).

imperialism *See* New Imperialism.

Impressionists Artists of the 19th century who sought to give a literal impression of light and color. Avoiding any kind of organized form, and hoping to paint without interpreting their subject, they tried to reproduce the overall visual impact of what they saw.

Inquisition A traveling tribunal during the 16th century that conducted inquiries into heresy in various locations. Those who refused to confess were tried, often with the use of torture to extract confessions—and without confession, there could be no conviction. Because heresy was considered a civil as well as a religious crime, those found guilty were punished by the local rulers rather than by the church. The most active tribunal was that in Spain.

jihad In Islam, a holy war to convert unbelievers, in which those who die fighting for the cause win salvation.

laissez faire Literally translated as "let it be," the 18th-century belief, espoused by Adam Smith, that the natural laws of economics require only noninterference to be successful.

latifundia Large landed estates in early Roman times, most of which were in southern Italy and Sicily.

lay investiture The medieval practice in which laymen began investing bishops not only with symbols of their fiefs but with spiritual symbols as well.

liberalism Ideology that held that people should be free. Political liberalism held that a representative system was the wisest form of government because it allowed for stability, the participation of the middle classes, and the protection of basic freedoms such as equality before the law and freedom of speech. Liberal economic theory, which argued that prosperity would result from economic forces that were allowed to operate freely without government intervention, lay at the core of political liberalism.

Mannerism Sixteenth-century artistic style in which the figures were deliberately distorted and exaggerated, replacing the calm, Classical balance of Renaissance art with sophisticated elegance and intricate fantasy.

manors Estates owned by a lord and worked by peasants in exchange for protection.

Marxism The theories of Karl Marx, including the belief that historical change depends not only on economic factors, but also on an inherent and inevitable class struggle, ending in a "dictatorship of the proletariat," which would abolish existing political systems, make all production public, and bring about a classless society in which the state would "wither away."

mercantilism Eighteenth-century economic theory and policies designed to increase national revenue (based on the supply of gold and silver) and economic power at the expense of other states, as well as to enhance private business and international trade.

Mesopotamia The land between the rivers Tigris and Euphrates, where urban life first developed; a flat region of the Middle East stretching from eastern Asia Minor to the Persian Gulf.

Modernism Revolutionary new artistic and literary styles that emerged in the years before 1914.

monasticism The general concept of monasticism is common to many religions, in which the followers of many faiths have sought to withdraw from the ordinary world and the corruption of society in order to devote themselves completely to worship and prayer.

mystery religions Greco-Roman religions that offered secret initiation ceremonies, individual salvation, and intense emotions. They emphasized that the lives of their members had an essential meaning and purpose.

nationalism An awareness of cultural and territorial identity— the identity of people who share a common language, history, and traditions in a given region.

Nazism Nazi ideology, especially the policies of state-controlled economy, racist nationalism, and national expansion. Also called "National Socialism," after the National Socialist German Workers' Party, founded in Germany in 1919 and brought into power in 1933 under Adolf Hitler.

Neoclassicism An 18th-century European revival of the art of ancient Greece and Rome.

Neolithic (New Stone) Age Period between 7000 and 4000 B.C. when settled and stable human communities were cultivating crops and domesticating animals, but had not discovered metals and still used stone tools and weapons.

Neoplatonist Adherent to a philosophy that flourished from the 3rd to the 6th century A.D., deriving from the teachings of the 4th-century B.C. Greek philosopher Plato and describing the universe as consisting of a systematized order, containing all levels and states of existence. Renaissance Neoplatonists revived the idea of seeking to escape from the bonds of earthly existence in order to rise upward toward union with God.

New Imperialism An increasingly frenzied drive on the part of many European powers during the latter half of the 19th century for territorial conquest beyond Europe. This surge of aggression resulted in the domination of virtually all of Asia and Africa by a handful of Western powers.

nominalists Adherents to a medieval school of thought based on method and solid fact, which claimed that knowledge should rest on direct experience and not on abstract reason.

Old Regime The transition in European history that led up to the French Revolution of 1789.

Paleolithic (Old Stone) Age Period some 10 thousand years ago, from the first use of stone implements around 2.5 million years ago to the introduction of farming around 8000 B.C. The latter stages are sometimes called the Mesolithic, or Middle, Stone Age.

patricians The kings and ruling class of early Rome, who formed a kind of self-perpetuating aristocracy based on a closed group of families who intermarried among themselves.

perioikoi Spartan "dwellers around," consisting of conquered neighboring peoples who vastly outnumbered the Spartiates and had no political rights.

phalanx A new infantry formation of the Greek Archaic era, consisting of rows of eight men, each heavily armed.

philosophes Literally translated from the French, "philosophers." The 18th-century *philosophes* were not so much original thinkers as popularizers and propagandizers who circulated the ideas of others in the form of pamphlets, plays, novels, or works of history.

plebeians The majority of early Romans, who were without privileges of birth or rank.

plainsong Medieval form of music, consisting of a single or "monophonic" musical line to which one voice (either a solo or a group in unison) chants the words of a religious text, generally without any form of accompaniment.

polis A Greek word generally translated as "city-state," the chief form of social and political organization from the beginnings of Greek culture.

Puritans English religious group that spearheaded a reform movement that sought to "purify" the Church of England of all remnants of Catholicism.

Ramapithecus The earliest species of hominid, dating to about 8 to 4 million years ago.

Reformation A movement of spiritual and institutional reform in the early 16th century that became a genuinely revolutionary wave breaking the thousand-year religious unity of western and central Europe by creating a series of new Protestant churches that rejected the authority of Rome.

Renaissance The period between 1300 and 1550 that saw a flowering of artistic and literary genius, beginning in Italy. It was accompanied by the rise of a new world view that placed a concern for the human condition at the center of intellectual life.

revolutionary syndicalism A unique current of radical thought in the 1870s, which evolved when elements of the anarchist tradition merged with an aspect of trade union strategy. Its principal theorist, Fernand Pelloutier, propounded the view that the seed of the future stateless society lay in the concept of the union. Syndicalists proposed direct action by the working class to bring about the revolution, with the general strike as their principal weapon.

rococo Artistic style of the mid-18th-century that was intended as a contrast to the Baroque. Rarely weighty or serious, it aimed for charm and lightness, and replaced Baroque drama with grace and harmony.

Romanesque Medieval architectural style whose characteristics are partly the result of the need for large buildings capable of containing crowds of people. Heavy stone walls could support Roman-style stone arches and barrel-vaulted stone roofs, providing a structure that, unlike the early Christian basilicas, was fireproof.

Romanticism Artistic style of the late 18th and early 19th centuries. Romantic artists, writers, and composers explored the irrational, probing the world of emotion. Two aspects of life had a special appeal: nature, with its mysterious unpredictability, and the exotic, in the form of remote times and faraway places.

salon Cultural institution of the 18th century, involving gatherings in private homes for intellectual discussion.

scholasticism The medieval attempt to reconcile the sacred teachings of the church with the knowledge acquired by human reason and experience. Its practitioners sought to apply Greek philosophical ideas—principally those of Aristotle—to Christian doctrine. They believed that reason, although always subordinate to faith, served to increase the faithfuls' understanding of their beliefs.

scientific method The method of testing theoretical ideas by means of practical experiments.

scientific revolution Seventeenth-century movement away from the medieval world view to a more rational, scientific perspective.

serfs Peasants attached by heredity to the land, who could not leave the manor without the lord's permission. Serfs owed certain services and dues to the lord, such as obligatory labor on the demesne for two or three days each week and the payment of a yearly tax known as the *taille*.

Social Darwinism Social Darwinists asserted, based on Charles Darwin's idea of survival of the fittest, that those in society who were emerging at the top were evidently the fittest and thus qualified to "survive." The bitter strife of competitive industry, they claimed, would lead slowly but inevitably to the upward movement of civilization.

socialism Ideology that called for a community in which the products of common labor are divided among all, according to their needs; for economic equality that should be accompanied by similar political and social reform.

Sophists Itinerant teachers in ancient Greece, who debated the skills of rhetoric and the qualities needed for success in political life.

Stoicism Philosophy founded by Zeno (335–263 B.C.), who taught that the force governing the world was Reason. Through the power of Reason it was possible to learn virtue, which was the supreme good. Those who lived virtuously were under the protection of Divine Providence, which would never allow them to suffer evil.

subinfeudation Feudal system whereby the same individual could be both a lord to one man and a vassal to another. Moreover, a noble could become the vassal to more than one lord.

Surrealism Artistic movement of the early 20th century that set out to discover the deeper meanings that lie beneath the surface of the conscious mind.

Symbolists Writers of the 19th century who aimed to use poetry as a means of escaping from reality.

syndicalism *See* revolutionary syndicalism.

totalitarianism Political theory in which governments are dominated by one political party and the most basic civil liberties are suspended. Such governments normally control the educational systems, economic policy, and mass media, and create an array of social institutions to indoctrinate and mobilize the population.

tyrant The popular leaders of ancient Greece who rode to power on the wave of revolt, rather than rising to power in a constitutional way.

utopians The earliest socialist thinkers, whose ideas were derided by their more militant successors as being naive and impractical.

vassal A soldier who served a man of greater authority during the Middle Ages.

Part 4. 337: By courtesy of the Trustees of the National Gallery, London **341 left:** © Cliché Bibliothéque National de France, Paris **341 right:** © Giraudon/Art Resource, NY **342:** © Giraudon/Art Resource, NY **343 right:** By courtesy of the National Portrait Gallery, London **343 left:** Hulton Getty Collection **346:** Kunsthistorisches Museum, Wien oder KHM, Wien **350 bottom:** © Scala/Art Resource, NY **350 top:** © Christie's Images Incorporated (2003) **353 left:** © Erich Lessing/Art Resource, NY **353 right:** INDEX/Tosi **355:** © Scala/Art Resource, NY **358:** Summerfield Press, Ltd. **359:** © Canali **361 top:** INDEX/Tosi **361 bottom:** Summerfield Press Ltd. **362:** © Scala/Art Resource, NY **363:** © Erich Lessing/Art Resource, NY **364:** © Erich Lessing/Art Resource, NY **365:** © Erich Lessing/Art Resource, NY **370 top:** © Scala/Art Resource, NY **370 bottom:** Canali Photobank, Italy **374:** Rare Books Division, The New York Public Library, Astor, Lenox and Tilden Foundations **375:** 375, The Metropolitan Museum of Art, Fletcher Fund, 1919 (19.73.120) **376:** Copyright Réunion des Musées Nationaux/Art Resource, NY **377:** By courtesy of the Trustees of the National Gallery, London **378:** Derechos Reservaados © Museo Nacional del Prado, Madrid **379:** Photograph © 2003 Museum of Fine Arts, Boston. Albrecht Dürer, German, 1471–1528. *The Fall of Man (Adam and Eve)*, 1504 Engraving. Catalogue Raisonné: BARTSCH (Intaglio). 001:Meder, 1, II, a. Platemark: 25 x 19.4 cm (9 15/16 x 7 5/8 in.). Museum of Fine Arts, Boston. Centennial gift of Landon T. Clay: 68.187 **385:** Ara Güler, Istanbul **386:** © National Maritime Museum, London **390:** © Novosti **393:** Bibliotheque Nationale, Paris, France/Bridgeman Art Library **397:** © Newberry Library, Chicago/SuperStock **400:** The Metropolitan Museum of Art, Gift of J. Pierpont Morgan , 1900. (00.18.2) Photograph © 1979 The Metropolitan Museum of Art **401:** The Granger Collection, New York **403:** The Ancient Art & Architecture Collection Ltd. **407:** The Toledo Museum of Art, Toledo, Ohio (Purchased with funds from the Libbey Endowment, Gift of Edward Drummond Libbey) **409:** © Mary Evans Picture Library **410:** © Snark/Art Resource, NY **411:** The Ancient Art & Architecture Collection Ltd. **416:** Musees Royaux des Beaux-Arts de Belgique/A.C.L. **417:** National Gallery, London **418:** Collection Furstlich Waldburg-Zeil'sches Gesamtarchiv Leutkirch/Artothek **420:** Collection The Right Honorable Earl Spencer, Althorp House **421:** AKG London **424:** Palazzo Medici-Riccardi, Florence, Italy/Bridgeman Art Library

Part 5. 427: Rijksmuseum, Amsterdam **430:** © Fotoburg Marburg/Art Resource, NY **431:** AKG London **432:** Institut Amatller d'Art Hispánic–Arxiu Mas. **436:** © Foto Marburg/Art Resource, NY **439:** © Mary Evans Picture Library **442:** © Erich Lessing/Art Resource, NY **443:** © CORBIS/Bettmann **447:** By courtesy of the National Portrait Gallery, London **449:** © Alinari/Art Resource, NY **450:** © Mary Evans Picture Library **452:** Mansell/TimeLife Pictures/Getty Images **457:** AKG London **458 left:** © Réunion des Musées Nationaux/Art Resource, NY **458 right:** © Superstock **459:** The National Gallery, London **461:** © CORBIS/Bettmann **466:** The Granger Collection, New York **468:** The Metropolitan Museum of Art, Fletcher Fund, 1927. (27.59) Photograph © 1983 The Metropolitan Museum of Art **469:** British Museum,

London, UK/Bridgeman Art Library **473:** Rijksmuseum, Amsterdam **474:** © Giraudon/Art Resource, NY **478:** By permission of the British Library. 145. C.4 Folio 122 **479:** Herzog Anton Ulrich Museums Braunschweig Kunstmuseum des Landes Niedersachsen **482:** Rijksmuseum, Amsterdam **483:** © Victoria & Albert Museum, London/Art Resource, NY **487:** © Scala/Art Resource, NY **488:** Canali Photobank, Italy **489:** © Alinari/Art Resource, NY **490:** Copyright Réunion des Musées Nationaux/Art Resource, NY **491:** Copyright Réunion des Musées Nationaux/Art Resource, NY **492:** Staatliche Museen Kassel, Gemäldegalerie Alte Meister **493 left:** Johann Sebastian Bach, "Klavierbuchlein fur Anna Magdalena Bach," 1725. Courtesy of Riemenschneider Bach Institute, Baldwin-Wallace College, Berea, OH. **493 right:** AKG London **494:** Courtesy of William Duiker **496:** Rare Books Division, The New York Public Library, Astor, Lenox and Tilden Foundations

Part 6. 499: © Frick Collection, New York **503:** © Scala/ Art Resource, NY **505:** National Library of Medicine, Bethesda, MD **506:** Frans Hals, René Cartes (1596–1650), Statens Museum for Kunst, Copenhagen. Photography by Hans Peterson **507:** By courtesy of the National Portrait Gallery, London **511:** © Scala/Art Resource, NY **512:** Derechos Reservaados © Museo Nacional del Prado, Madrid **513:** © CORBIS/Bettmann **518:** © Réunion des Musées Nationaux/Art Resource, NY **519:** © Art Resource, NY **520:** The Metropolitan Museum of Art, Gift of the Wildenstein Foundation, Inc. 1951. (51.34) Photograph © 1979 The Metropolitan Museum of Art **521:** Chateau de Versailles, France/Peter Willi/Bridgeman Art Library **524:** © Giraudon/Art Resource, NY **529:** By courtesy of the National Portrait Gallery, London **531:** © CORBIS/Bettmann **535:** By courtesy of the National Portrait Gallery, London **536:** By courtesy of the National Portrait Gallery, London **542:** AKG London **544:** AKG London **545:** Foto Marburg/Art Resource, NY **548:** The Granger Collection, New York **549:** The Granger Collection, New York **550:** © bpk, Berlin, Kulturbesitz, Berlin **551:** AKG London **552:** Courtesy of William Duiker **559:** The Granger Collection, New York **560 right:** Picture Library, National Portrait Gallery, London **560 left:** Picture Library, National Portrait Gallery, London **562 bottom:** © Scala/Art Resource, NY **562 top:** © Frick Collection, New York **563 top:** Anthony Kersting **563 bottom:** © Internationale Stiftung Mozarteum (ISM) **569:** The Granger Collection, New York **572 top:** © National Maritime Museum, London **572 bottom:** The Granger Collection, New York **573:** Museum Boymans van Beuningen, Rotterdam **574:** Copyright Guildhall Library Corporation of London **578:** © CORBIS/Bettmann **580:** © Victoria & Albert Museum, London/Art Resource, NY **581:** The Granger Collection, New York **582:** © CORBIS/Bettmann **589:** Reproduction of *The Village School* by Jan Steen. Courtesy of the National Gallery of Ireland **590:** Copyright Réunion des Musées Nationaux/Art Resource, NY **591:** The National Gallery, London **592:** © Giraudon/Art Resource, NY **593:** The Metropolitan Museum of Art, Harris Brisbane Dick Fund, 1932 [32.35 (124)] **595 left:** © Giraudon/Art Resource, NY **595 right:** © Chateau de Versailles, France/Giraudon/ Superstock **598:** The Granger Collection, New York **599:** © CORBIS/Bettmann **600:** © Giraudon/Art Resource, NY

Part 7. 608: © National Gallery of Art, Washington, D.C./Superstock **612:** © Giraudon/Art Resource, NY **613:** © Giraudon/Art Resource, NY **615:** © Novosti **620:** The Granger Collection, New York **626:** The Granger Collection, New York **627:** © Mary Evans Picture Library **628:** Mansell/TimeLife Pictures/Getty Images **629:** Mansell/TimeLife Pictures/Getty Images **634:** The Granger Collection, New York

636: © Réunion des Musées Nationaux/Art Resource, NY 641 top: © CORBIS/Bettmann 641 bottom: © Réunion des Musées Nationaux/Art Resource, NY 644: © CORBIS/Bettmann 649: © Archivo Iconografico, S. A./CORBIS 651: © CORBIS/Bettmann 652: Derechos Reservaados © Museo Nacional del Prado, Madrid 655: Hulton Getty Collection 659: The Granger Collection, New York 661: © CORBIS/Bettmann 664: © Giraudon/Art Resource, NY 665: Hulton Getty Collection 672 bottom: © Cliché Bibliothéque National de France, Paris 672 top: Hulton Getty Collection 673: Andrew Haslam/National Trust Photographic Library 676: © Giraudon/Art Resource, NY 683: Copyright Réunion des Musées Nationaux/Art Resource, NY 684: AKG London 685: By permission of the Houghton Library, Harvard University 686: Staatliche Museen zu Berlin 687 top: Copyright Réunion des Musées Nationaux/Art Resource, NY 687 bottom: © Giraudon/Art Resource, NY 688 left: The Granger Collection, New York 688 right: The Granger Collection, New York 689: Copyright Réunion des Musées Nationaux/Art Resource, NY 695: © Mary Evans Picture Library 696: © CORBIS/Bettmann 698: © CORBIS/Bettmann 704: © Mary Evans Picture Library 705: Hulton Getty Collection 706: Hulton Getty Collection 707: Hulton Getty Collection 714: David King Collection, London 715: The Granger Collection, New York 716: © Sovfoto 717: © CORBIS/Bettmann 722: © Mary Evans Picture Library 723 top: © Culver Pictures 723 bottom: Hulton Getty Collection 728: The Granger Collection, New York 729: The Granger Collection, New York 731: Brown Brothers 735: © Culver Pictures 736: Mansell/TimeLife Pictures/Getty Images 738: Deutsches Museum, Munich 739: Courtesy of the Fogg Art Museum, Harvard University Art Museums, Bequest from the Collection of Maurice Wertheim, Class of 1906 740: Hulton Getty Collection 745 top: The Granger Collection, New York 745 bottom: Keystone-Mast Collection, UCR/California Museum of Photography, University of California, Riverside 748: James Helme/Royal Photographic Society 750: © Mary Evans Picture Library 751: © Culver Pictures 758: © Culver Pictures 759: Print Collection, Miriam and Ira D. Wallach Division of Art, Prints and Photographs, The New York Public Library, Astor, Lenox and Tilden Foundations 760: The Metropolitan Museum of Art, H. O. Havemeyer, 1929 (29.100.129). Photograph © 1992 The Metropolitan Museum of Art 761: Gemaldegaleria, Dresden, Germany/Bridgeman Art Library 762: Thomas Eakins *Swimming*, 1885, oil on canvas. Purchased by The Friends of Art, Fort Worth Art Association, 1925; acquired by the Amon Carter Museum, 1990, from the Modern Art Museum of Fort Worth through grants and donations from the Amon G. Carter Foundation, the Sid W. Richardson Foundation, the Anne Burnett and Charles Tandy Foundation, Capital Cities/ABC Foundation, Fort Worth Star-Telegram, the R.D. and Joan Dale Hubbard Foundation, and the people of Fort Worth. Amon Carter Museum, Fort Worth, Texas 767: The Granger Collection, New York 768 left: The Granger Collection, New York 768 right: The Granger Collection, New York 770: © Mary Evans Picture Library 772: Hulton Getty Collection 778: © Erich Lessing/Art Resource, NY 780: © CORBIS/Bettmann 781: © Sovfoto 784: © Mary Evans Picture Library 786: The Granger Collection, New York 789: The Granger Collection, New York 790: © CORBIS/Bettmann 793: Collection, Brandywine River Museum (acquisition made possible by Beverly and Ray Sacks) 795: Brown Brothers 802: By permission of the British Library. Photo 430/30 [8] 803: By permission of the British Library. Photo 430/80 [9] 806: © Mary Evans Picture Library 807: © National Gallery of Art, Washington D.C./Superstock 808: Courtesy of William Duiker 811: Hulton Getty Collection 812: © CORBIS/Bettmann 816: © Sovfoto 817: © Culver Pictures 818: Hulton Getty Collection 820 left: INDEX/Pizzi 820 right: © Culver Pictures 822: © Culver Pictures 828: Hulton Getty Collection 830: © CORBIS/Bettmann 831: The Granger Collection, New York 832: Thomas Gilcrease Institute of American History and Art, Tulsa, OK 836: Richard Wagner Museum, Triebschen-Luzern, Switzerland 840 bottom: Cincinnati Art Museum, John J. Emery Fund 840 top: © Archivo Iconografico, S. A./CORBIS 840: Digital Image © The Museum of Modern Art/Licensed by SCALA/Art Resource, NY 842 left: Copyright © 2003 The Munch Museum/The Munch-Ellingsen Group/ARS, NY

842 right: © 2003 Artists Rights Society (ARS), New York/ADAGP, Paris. Photo by David Heald/© The Solomon R. Guggenheim Foundation, New York (PN 54.1412)

Part 8. 848: © 2003 Estate of Pablo Picasso/Artists Rights Society (ARS), New York 854 top: Robert Hunt Library 854 bottom: Robert Hunt Library 860 bottom: © CORBIS/Bettmann 860 top: © DIZ SV-Bilderdienst 863: © Syndicated Features Limited/The Image Works 867: © CORBIS/Bettmann 876 left: Hulton Archive by Getty Images 876 right: Hulton Archive by Getty Images 877: © CORBIS/Bettmann 879: © CORBIS/Bettmann 883: Robert Hunt Library 885: Hulton Archive by Getty Images 889: © CORBIS/Bettmann 892 left: Hulton Archive by Getty Images 892 right: Hulton Archive by Getty Images 893: Robert Hunt Library 894: Roger-Viollet/Getty Images 901 bottom: © AP/Wide World Photos 901 top: R. Bettini/Grazia Neri 902: Hulton Archive by Getty Images 903: Hulton Archive by Getty Images 904: © CORBIS/Bettmann 908: © Sovfoto 912: © AP/Wide World Photos 913: Hulton Archive by Getty Images 914: AKG London 915: © CORBIS/Bettmann 918 right: © CORBIS/Bettmann 918 left: Hulton Archive by Getty Images 923 top: Avery Architectural and Fine Arts Library, Columbia University in the City of New York 923 bottom: Hulton Archive by Getty Images 924: Hulton Archive by Getty Images 925: The Granger Collection, New York 927: Hulton Archive by Getty Images 930: © 2003 Estate of Pablo Picasso/Artists Rights Society (ARS), New York. Copyright CNAC/MNAM/Dist. Réunion des Musées Nationaux/Art Resource, NY 932 left: Courtesy of Nigel Nicolson 932 right: Courtesy of Nigel Nicolson 933: © 2003 Artists Rights Society (ARS), New York/ADAGP, Paris/Succession Marchel Duchamp 934 top: Digital Image © The Museum of Modern Art/ Licensed by SCALA/Art Resource, NY. © 2003 Salvador Dali, Gala-Salvador Dali Foundation/ARS, New York 934 bottom: © 2003 Estate of Pablo Picasso/Artists Rights Society (ARS), New York 935: Ezra Stoller © Esto 936: © CORBIS 941: © AP/Wide World Photos 942: © AP/Wide World Photos 943: © CORBIS/Bettmann 945: Robert Capa © 2001 by Cornell Capa/Magnum Photos 946: © 2003 Estate of Pablo Picasso/Artists Rights Society (ARS), New York 948: © AP/Wide World Photos 955: Hulton Archive by Getty Images 956: © CORBIS 958: © CORBIS/Bettmann 959: AKG London 964: The Granger Collection, New York 966: © Sovfoto 968: Hulton Archive by Getty Images 972: © CORBIS/Bettmann 975 left: © CORBIS/Bettmann 975 right: Hulton Getty Collection 977: © AP/Wide World Photos 979 top: Robert Hunt Library 979 bottom: © AP/Wide World Photos 981: © CORBIS/Bettmann 985: © AP/Wide World Photos 987: AKG London 988: AKG London 992: Robert Hunt Library 993: © AP/Wide World Photos 997: Copyright OGPI 1997 999: © CORBIS/Bettmann 1002: AKG London 1003: Robert Hunt Library 1004: Markel/Liaison/ Getty Images 1005: Reuters/Stinger/Archive Photos/Getty Images 1010 left: Robert Hunt Library 1010 right: Robert Hunt Library 1012: © CORBIS/Bettmann 1013 top left: © AP/Wide World Photos 1013 top right: Michael Peto/Hulton Getty Collection 1013 center: Archive Photos/Getty Images 1013 bottom left: Keystone/Hulton Getty Collection 1013 bottom right: © AP/Wide World Photos 1014: Courtesy of Guerrilla Girls 1017: Benisch and Partner 1020: © DIZ SV-Bilderdienst 1021: Digital Image © The Museum of Modern Art/Licensed by SCALA/Art Resource, NY 1022 top: Copyright © 1998 The Andy Warhol Foundation for the Visual Arts/Artists Rights Society (ARS), New York. Copyright The Andy Warhol Foundation, Inc./Art Resource, NY. © 2003 Andy Warhol Foundation for the Visual Arts, ARS, New York 1022 bottom: © Christo1972, photo Harry Shunk, artists Christo and Jeanne-Claude 1024: Patrick Ingrad/Getty Images 1025: Robert Hunt Library 1029: Photo News/Gamma 1034 bottom: © DIZ SV-Bilderdienst 1034 top: © AP/Wide World Photos 1035: © DIZ SV-Bilderdienst 1039: Earl Young/Archive Photos/Getty Images 1046: Keystone/Hulton Getty Collection 1047: © DIZ SV-Bilderdienst 1048: © Syndicated Features Limited/The Image Works 1049: Gaillarde-Maous-Sola/Gamma 1054: © Robert Essel NYC/CORBIS 1055: © SPL/Photo Researchers

INDEX

Note: Page references in *italics* indicate map or figure.